MTV

Roadtrips
U.S.A.

1st Edition

WILEY
2007
BICENTENNIAL

Wiley Publishing, Inc.

John Vorwald

A former editor at Frommer's Travel Guides, **John Vorwald** (lead writer; Las Vegas to Baja) gave up his sexy cubicle for the wealth and security of the freelancer's life. When not driving from Vegas to Mexico, he can be found writing and editing restaurant and nightlife reviews for *BlackBook* magazine, where he is managing editor of the BlackBook Guides. Favorite roadtrip song: *The Road Goes on Forever*, The Highwaymen.

Dara Bramson

Dara (Festival Season) is seeking professional help for her festival/roadtrip addiction. She's honored to be a member of this intrepid roadtrip crew. In addition to her Northeast festivals journey during summer 2006, she lived in London, New York City and visited Paris for a full 12 hours. A Miami native, Dara will graduate from Florida International University with degrees in journalism and history. She teaches hip-hop dance and has an absurd collection of vintage clothing that's often mistaken for her grandmother's. Favorite roadtrip song: *Sky Is Falling*, Blackalicious.

Kelsy Chauvin

Born in southern Louisiana and educated in Seattle, **Kelsy Chauvin** (American Highways) now lives in Brooklyn, New York. She is a writer and photographer of varied interests, with an emphasis in exploration. (www.kelsychauvin.com) Favorite roadtrip song: *Title and Registration*, Death Cab for Cutie.

Nick Honachefsky

Nick Honachefsky (Down the Shore) has wrestled a 300-pound mako shark, been shot at in the Greek Islands, surfed Playa Hermosa in Costa Rica and loves dogs, especially puppies. Shunning the suit and tie dragdown, he's become a full time outdoor adventure freelancer, columnist, screenwriter and book author who's traveled the worldwide circuit. A Villanova graduate, Nick regularly contributes to

ESPN, *Saltwater Sportsman, Sport Fishing, Gannett USA* newspapers, and is currently late for Happy Hour. Favorite roadtrip song: *Atomic Dog*, George Clinton and Parliament Funkadelic.

Maya Kroth

Since eating her way through the south (Southern Barbecue Roadtrip) and drinking at rock dives from SoCal to Seattle (Rocking the West Coast), **Maya Kroth** has been spending a lot of time at her local gym in San Diego, where she spends her days writing and editing *WHERE* magazine, sipping dirty martinis and obsessing about Padres baseball. She favors ribs over brisket and has a weakness for scruffy guys in indie rock bands. Favorite roadtrip song: *Out of Gas*, Modest Mouse.

Ashley Marinaccio

Ashley (Paranormal Northeast) is honored to be a part of the MTV Roadtrips U.S.A. crew. She's a theatre and anthropology major at Pace University in Manhattan and is actively involved in many clubs and organizations both on and off campus. She's traveled to Lebanon, Jordan, South Africa, Syria and hopes to do much more traveling in the future. For now, you'd most likely find Ashley in the theater as she's a director, actor and playwright whose focus is on creating theatre around political and social justice issues. Favorite roadtrip song: *Imagine*, John Lennon.

Heather McNiel & Dan Yim

Heather McNiel's first attempt at travel writing was at the age of 12, when her family moved to Europe. Sadly, the young writer found that there was no market for her *Travel Tips for Twelve Year Olds*. Heather currently lives and works in Minneapolis, with her partner, Dan Yim. They wrote the Urban Heartland roadtrip. As a native Southern Californian, **Dan Yim** was skeptical about life in the Midwest, but was won over by the prospect of ice-fishing and an end to his long commutes on the 405. He now lives in Minneapolis, where he works as a teacher and regularly complains about how slow Minnesotans drive. Favorite roadtrip song: *Ooh, Las Vegas*, Cowboy Junkies.

Valerie Willis

Valerie Willis (Retro Roadtrip) was born and raised in small-town Oklahoma and has a bachelors degree in Professional Writing from the University of Oklahoma. Her three passions are travel (of course), art, and chocolate and she hopes to never grow up. Favorite roadtrip song: *Out On The Open Road* from *A Goofy Movie*.

Ethan Wolff

Ethan Wolff's (First Americans) first post-college address was Albuquerque, NM, but Manhattan's low cost of living eventually drew him back east. His Frommer's guide *NYC Free & Dirt Cheap* has all the details. Ethan's favorite roadtrip author is Oakley Hall, his favorite roadtrip film is *Two-Lane Blacktop*, and favorite roadtrip song is Bob Dylan's *One More Cup of Coffee*.

Kathleen Warnock

Kathleen Warnock (editor) has been going on road-trips and editing books for some time now. Her favorite trips include seeing Joan Jett & the Blackhearts in Denmark and Australia. Her roadtrip reports and reviews have appeared in *ROCKRGRL, Bust, Metal Maidens, Gargoyle* and other publications. Her roadtrip play, "Rock the Line," (United Stages) won the Robert Chesley Playwriting Award. Favorite roadtrip song: *Light of Day*, Joan Jett & the Blackhearts.

Published by:

Wiley Publishing, Inc.

111 River St.

Hoboken, NJ 07030-5774

ISBN: 978-0-7645-8776-4

Editor: Kathleen Warnock

Production Editor: Ian Skinnari

Cartographer: Andrew Murphy

Cover & Interior Design: Eric Frommelt

Production by Wiley Indianapolis Composition Services

For information on our other products and services or to obtain technical support, please contact our Customer Care Department within the U.S. at 800/762-2974, outside the U.S. at 317/572-3993 or fax 317/572-4002.

Wiley also publishes its books in a variety of electronic formats. Some content that appears in print may not be available in electronic formats.

Manufactured in the United States of America

5 4 3 2 1

Table of Contents

TABLE OF CONTENTS

Acknowledgments

John Vorwald: Thanks especially to Ron Raposa at the Rosarito Convention & Visitors Bureau; to Spencer Villasenor at the Hard Rock Hotel & Casino; and, to Nicolette and Rochelle Vorwald for aiding in my research.

Dara Bramson would like to thank: her parents for sending her all over the world; Lyn for being her number one fan! Harris for being a knight in shining armor; Ashley for boundless entertainment; Ian for naming her Adventure Girl; and everyone else who housed her, fed her and made her traveling experiences so remarkable. She'd like to dedicate the festivals chapter to the adventurers who forfeit a few days of sleep and showering for their love of music, peace and festival life.

Kelsy Chauvin's Acknowledgments: My tremendous thanks to representatives of the visitor's bureaus, chambers of commerce, and other hosts in each city I visited on this cross-country trip, and also to Fort Greene's Pillow Café. I am especially grateful to Kim Musler for her companionship and contributions on the road and elsewhere.

Maya Kroth's Thank-Yous/Acknowledgments: These chapters would not have been possible without the hospitality of my unofficial tour guides in Atlanta (Joe B., Court B., Richard, and Rebecca), Charlotte (Claire, Vicki and Adam), Portland (Britt D.) and Seattle (John R.), as well as the many who sent me in the right direction with recommendations, including Alicia at Doug Fir, Jen at the Triple Door, Julianne Andersen, Kristin Zero, Joan at Sub Pop, Aaron Axelson at Live 105, Adam Gnade, Jolene Pellant, Juli Cotta at the Troubadour, Spencer Sloane, Jennifer Maerz, Chris Nilsson, Geoff Sherr and Andras Jones. I would also like to thank Scott Roberts, Scott McClard, Patrick Neely, Bill at Fat Matt's and Granny for opening their kitchens and sharing their stories; Kathleen Warnock and John Vorwald for not firing me after the 9,575th annoying email; Lou and the fam for putting up with me; Scott Richison for the pancake; talk radio for getting me through some long and lonely stretches of highway; and Blanche, for being the best rented minivan a broke writer's salary can buy.

Ashley Marinaccio: Big thanks to Dara Bramson and Jessica Marinaccio for making this writing journey both entertaining and fun. She dedicates her chapter to Roger Salerno, Aseel Sawalha, Meghana Nayak and Ruis "Doc" Woertendyke who are incredible mentors and who'll be sorely missed after May 2007 . . . but most of all, who for better or for worse, will enjoy the hell out of the places in this chapter.

Dan Yim & Heather McNiel: Thanks to Kate Molitor at First Avenue in Minneapolis for getting us into an awesome show, and to Matt Jenson for the inside scoop on Kansas City. A special shout out goes to the long-suffering bartenders of Salt Lake City, who spent lots of time explaining the liquor laws to us. Thanks.

Valerie Willis: Thank you to my sister Elena Willis for being a fantastic navigator, an amazing travel partner, and for putting up with me for an entire month in a car that smelled of fish guts and rotten peaches.

Ethan Wolff thanks: The rangers and staff at Chaco Canyon for being sympathetic, to Mike Finney and Les Graff for sharing their love of Arizona, and to Jenny Bauer for being so much fun to travel with.

The editor wishes to thank Ian Skinnari, production editor extraordinare; Andrew "Dice" Murphy for the fabulous map icons; Frommer's classic authors Harry Basch & Shirley Slater for blazing the trail (in an RV); and Lollion Chong at MTV. For the extra set of eyes: Libby Campbell, Patti Binger, Lauren Varga, Patrick Gabridge, Mary K. Tilghman, Alexia Meyers, Jennifer Reilly, Cate Latting, Melinda Quintero, and Christine Ryan.

An Invitation to the Reader

In researching this book, we discovered many wonderful places—hotels, restaurants, shops, and more. We're sure you'll find others. Please tell us about them, so we can share the information with your fellow travelers in upcoming editions. If you were disappointed with a recommendation, we'd love to know that, too. Please write to:

MTV Roadtrips U.S.A., 1st Edition
Wiley Publishing, Inc.
111 River St.
Hoboken, NJ 07030-5774

An Additional Note

Please be advised that travel information is subject to change at any time—and this is especially true of prices. We therefore suggest that you write or call ahead for confirmation when making your travel plans. The authors, editors, and publisher cannot be held responsible for the experiences of readers while traveling. Your safety is important to us, however, so we encourage you to stay alert and be aware of your surroundings. Keep a close eye on cameras, purses, and wallets, all favorite targets of thieves and pickpockets.

Star Ratings, Icons & Abbreviations

Every hotel, restaurant, and attraction listed in this guide has been ranked for quality, value, service, amenities, and special features using a star-rating system. Hotels and restaurants are rated on a scale of zero (recommended) to three stars (exceptional). Attractions, shopping, and nightlife are rated according to the following scale: zero stars (recommended), one star (highly recommended), two stars (very highly recommended), and three stars (must-see). In addition to the star-rating system, we also use four feature icons that point you to great deals, in-the-know advice, and unique experiences. Throughout the book, look for:

 The most happening restaurants, hotels, and things to do—don't leave town without checking these places out.

 When cash flow is at a trickle, head for these spots: no-cost museums, free concerts, bars with complimentary food, and more.

 Savvy advice and practical recommendations for learning opportunities, whether you're a current student, or a student in the school of Life.

 This denotes a fact or warning you need to know about (such as legal, cultural and personal advice) gained from hard-won experience. Not knowing these things could delay your trip, or add a *lot* to your budget!

Introduction: Why You Should Hit the Road, Jack!

There's nothing quite as freeing as watching all that's familiar disappear into the rearview mirror. As the confines of the world grow ever closer and its content more homogenous, sometimes you need to step out of the routine and demands of everyday life, whether for a weekend or a season, to see what's different in other places, to spend some time with yourself, or to blow off all that energy that's been building up.

It's time for a roadtrip.

Welcome to the first edition of *MTV Roadtrips U.S.A.* The United States is a pretty big place, and we've only got 864 pages. How do you even begin to cover what there is to see and do on a good portion of the continent? (And we're not even talking about Canada and, except for a sliver of it, Mexico!) In this case, I found some writers with wanderlust, people from different parts of the country, and asked them: "What's the roadtrip you've always wanted to take? Where do you want to go that is your idea of a great journey?" And they told me.

Californian Maya Kroth wanted to follow bands up the West Coast . . . and look for the best barbecue from Austin to the Carolinas. Valerie Willis, from landlocked Oklahoma, wanted to do a classic beach trip from Miami to the Outer Banks. Ashley Marinaccio wanted to look for ghosts in the Northeast. Heather McNiel and Dan Yim, newly arrived in Minneapolis, wanted to find what's cool in the Midwest. Dara Bramson wanted to go to festivals and fairs; Nick Honachefsky wanted to introduce people to the Jersey Shore experience, and continue down to Maryland. New Yorker

Ethan Wolff wanted to go West to explore the settlements of the first Americans. John Vorwald wanted to drive from the desert to the beach, from the bling and glitz of Las Vegas to the Pacific waves washing up against the shore of Baja California. And Kelsy Chauvin wanted to drive from border to border, along American highways.

So they did. They took along cameras and notebooks and ate at roadside diners and gourmet restaurants, stayed at campgrounds, hostels, old-fashioned motor courts and famous hotels; visited unique museums and parks, and climbed mountains and rode waves, and partied some and explored a lot. Then they came home and wrote about it.

The results are between these covers: 10 trips that cover the U.S. from shore to shore, each with a different focus, theme, and style. That, and a chapter on planning your own trip: because these trips aren't meant to be replicated, stop-by-stop. They are meant to inspire, to motivate, and to instruct. Whether you want to visit every ballpark in the American League, or every National Park in the Pacific Northwest, your roadtrip is your own journey. And we want you to take it.

Editor's Playlist: Music to Edit Roadtrips By

→ *Welcome to My Life,* **Melissa Ferrick,** "Valentine Heartache," 2001

→ *I Love New York City,* **Andrew W.K.,** "I Get Wet," 2002

→ *The Road,* **Chapter in Verse,** EP, 2000

→ *Foot On the Gas,* **Sexpod,** "Goddess Blues," 1995

→ *Wildwood Days,* **Bobby Rydell,** "Best of Bobby Rydell," 1995

→ *Good Morning Baltimore,* **Hairspray,** "Original Broadway Cast," 2002

→ *Carolina Girls (Are the Best in the World),* **General Johnson & the Chairmen of the Board,** "The Beach Music Anthology," 1992

→ *Roadrunner,* **Jonathan Richman & the Modern Lovers,** "Modern Lovers," 1976

→ *Graceland,* **Paul Simon,** "Graceland," 1986

→ *Love is All Around,* **Joan Jett & the Blackhearts,** 1996

→ *Kansas City/Hey, Hey, Hey, Hey,* **The Beatles,** "Beatles for Sale," 1964

→ *Rocky Mountain High,* **John Denver,** "Rocky Mountain High," 1973

→ *Paint Me Back Home in Wyoming,* **Chris LeDoux,** "Paint Me Back Home in Wyoming," 1978

→ *All My Exes Live in Texas,* **George Strait,** "Ocean Front Property," 1987

→ *Flyer,* **Nanci Griffith,** "Flyer," 1994

→ *Wicked Little Town,* **Hedwig & the Angry Inch,** Original Cast recording, 1998

→ *Everywhere I Go,* **The Muffs,** "The Muffs," 1993

→ *Rock Star,* **Hole,** "Live Through This," 1994

→ *What a Wonderful World,* **Joey Ramone,** "Don't Worry About Me," 2002

We hope you'll use this book as a springboard, that as you read, ideas for your own trip are percolating in your head, and pretty soon, you'll be on your way. If you've got some time stretching out before you—whether it's a 3-day weekend or a break between schools, jobs, homes—you need to get moving.

Go for what you need: a joyful spree to blow off some steam, or a focused pilgrimage to explore who you really are, or what you really love—you'll be changed at the end of the journey. And you'll bring what you learned on the trip home with you.

Go on . . . get out there! And tell us about it after. We need some ideas for the next edition.

We'll see you when you get back (if we aren't off on our own trip).

Drive safely, stop to look at things, and be careful of speed traps. Home safe!

—*The Editor*

The Basics: Planning Your Roadtrip

By Maya Kroth

The lure of the road is hard to resist. The classic American roadtrip promises mystique and adventure, and it takes courage, rebellion even, to leave behind the comforts of home to answer the call. The romance of it is enough to make you want to jump in the car *right now* and hit the highway, wind in your hair, and go as far as your gas tank allows. That adventuresome spirit is key to a successful roadtrip. But so is planning—and a little bit goes a long way. Overplanning can be a serious buzzkill; but not having enough time/money/antifreeze can be even worse. Try to keep your foot off the gas just long enough to consider a few of the following key trip-planning factors.

Stuff to Figure Out Before You Go

How Much Time Do I Need?

The length of your roadtrip will have almost as much to do with defining your experience as the area of the country you're exploring. Most of the trips listed in this book are expandable, meaning you can probably do some version of the trip in as short as a few days, or stretch it out for several weeks or—if you're really into it—months.

Think about how much ground you want to cover, and where you'll start and end. Are you moving cross-country, or just doing a quick loop around the state? Do you have time to do a round-trip drive, or would you rather rent a car, drive as far as possible in one direction, and fly home when you're done? (Or, the other way around...) Either way, give yourself enough time—an afternoon, a full day, a couple of days—to explore the spots you really want to hit, then add in a little extra time for emergencies or just wandering aimlessly. Often it's those unplanned detours that become the most memorable parts of the trip.

The trips in this book include mileage and approximate travel times between

(photo: Kelsy Chauvin)

stops, so consult our **Trip in a Box** section as you plan your own trip. If you're customizing your own trip, spend some time with Google or Yahoo maps, or Mapquest, to figure out about how long it'll take to get from point A to point B.

And decide how much time you want to spend driving every day—some drivers can go for 10 hours or more a day; others need to stop every few hours. Give yourself time to actually step into the scenery you're seeing from the car window. Regardless, plan regular pit stops to gas up, stretch, grab coffee, or just chat up a cute local.

LONG WEEKENDS

If you've got work, school, or family obligations, it can be tough to get away for longer than a couple of days, but don't let that stymie your wanderlust. If your time is limited, pick a compact area like New England, which has lots of attractions clustered close together so you won't spend all of your precious time racing from place to place. Consider limiting your daily mileage to a reasonable figure—say, 100 or 200 miles—so you're not pulling long, boring, and potentially dangerous shifts behind the wheel. Being on the road is a crucial part of the trip, for sure, but you want to have some time to enjoy your destination, too.

A couple of our chapters are planned just that way: You can have a great time and fulfilling experience in 3 or 4 days. We also break down the longer trips into sections that are doable in less time, while still providing the essence of the trip.

A COUPLE WEEKS

If you can spare it, 2 or 3 weeks is a great span of time for a roadtrip: long enough to get used to the rhythm of the road and see a variety of different places, but not so long that you want to throttle your traveling companions with their seatbelts ('cause let's face it, even the most charming passenger gets tiresome after you've been stuck in an enclosed space for days on end).

Two weeks is enough time to cross the country once at a somewhat leisurely pace, or thoroughly explore a region like the West Coast or the Southwest. Try to avoid scheduling too many 8- and 10-hour drive days, and break up the monotony with shorter jaunts.

THE WHOLE DAMN SEASON

If you have the time, a summer- or winter-long roadtrip promises to be one of the most unforgettable experiences of a lifetime. Three months allows plenty of time to get well acquainted with the entire country. Ever wanted to visit all 30 major league ballparks in a single baseball season? A summer trip will give you plenty of time to do so without rushing.

When to Go

Really the question of "when" will depend heavily on whether you're building your trip around an event or set of events. If you're a big fan of the Bard, for example, it makes sense to plan your trip to Ashland, OR, while the town's annual Shakespeare festival is going on. If you couldn't care less about iambic pentameter, but always wanted to explore Southern Oregon, then go in winter, when tourists are scarce and cheap hotel rooms abundant. All of the themed roadtrips in this book include a calendar of events to help your planning, along with arguments for which season lends itself best to that particular trip.

THE CASE FOR SPRING

Spring, like fall, has the benefit of being on the shoulder of the main tourist season in the U.S. (summer). When you're roadtripping, reduced traffic is a key factor. Depending on what part of the country you're visiting, you'll also be able to enjoy decent weather and scenic spring blooms. If you're a student, that post-midterms week off could be the perfect excuse to get out of town.

THE CASE FOR SUMMER

By far the most popular season for road-tripping, summer has it all: great weather, plenty of festivals and other fun activities to check out in every destination, and *lots* of other people on the road. Of course, gas prices tend to soar in the summer (as they did in 2006), which could drive up the cost of your trip. Also, if your trip will be taking you through the South or the desert, expect some stultifying temps between June and September.

THE CASE FOR FALL

There's no better time to be somewhere like New England, for example, than when the leaves are turning and all that other quaint stuff that caused Emily Dickenson and Robert Frost to write volumes of poetry. But fall has its own downside. Temperatures cool considerably, and you're more likely to encounter rain. And foliage season is actually high season in the most picturesque parts of New England. On the other hand, it's a great time to tour the South (and Southwest) as the blast-furnace temperatures give way to temperate autumn.

THE CASE FOR WINTER

Maybe you're a snow bunny. Maybe you need an excuse to take the long way home for the holidays. Maybe you just can't get off work any other time of year except the dead week between Christmas and New Year's. These are all good reasons to take a road trip in winter. The downside? Well, there's the weather (duh), plus the increased risk of crossing paths on the road with someone who had too many hot toddies at a holiday party. If you choose to travel in winter, make sure you're prepared—that your car is outfitted appropriately for whatever weather conditions you may come across. And, of course, winter is high season in places like Miami, so expect to pay higher prices in the resort areas that are in warm climates.

What Kind of Roadtripper Are You?

Figuring out your traveling style is key to any roadtrip. Do you have what it takes to fly solo? If you do, be extra vigilant. If you take companions, figure out how they fit into the personality profiles below, then be sure you've got a good balance of each.

THE SOLO FLYER

○ I can't wait till I can afford to ditch my roommates.

○ I get cranky if I don't get enough "me time."

○ I like to shop and go to the movies alone.

○ Jack Kerouac is my favorite writer ever.

For some, roadtripping solo has a huge romantic allure—just you, the tunes blasting, and miles of open road. Nobody around to change the station, whine "are we there yet?" or hassle you about your driving. *Aaahh,* the bliss of solitude: Where you can hear yourself think, and ponder the mysteries of the universe (and your own life).

Of course, it can get lonely and a little boring out there all alone. Plus, it's almost always safer to travel with another person, especially considering how many potential hazards can crop up on a roadtrip.

THE NAVIGATOR

○ Mapquest is my homepage.

○ I don't need a compass to tell you where north is.

○ I never get stuck in traffic because I know every back-alley shortcut in town.

○ I never have problems refolding the map.

Good navigators do their homework, planning routes and exits ahead of time. They also know how to think on their feet and find their way back to the freeway when they go astray, and they're not too proud to pull over and ask for directions when they're really lost. This person might be the one doing most of the trip planning and will probably spend most of the trip planted in the passenger seat.

THE DRIVER

○ I don't like giving up control.

○ I always know who's in my blind spot.

○ I think Jeff Gordon has the Best. Job. Ever.

○ I can go zero to 60 in 3.4 seconds. In a Prius.

Drivers take their job seriously, and the good ones are alert, aware of what's going on around them, but not easily distracted by roadside attractions. They pay attention to signs, don't get ruffled by whatever's going on in the back seat, and let their passengers do the less critical stuff, like changing the music, passing the chips, and calling for directions to the hotel. The driver should have a good relationship with the navigator—you'll be spending a lot of time together.

THE KNOW-IT-ALL

○ I do the crossword puzzle every day in pen, and kick ass at *Jeopardy!*

○ I'm sure there's a better/faster/more efficient way to get there.

○ I'll tell you all about that painting/sculpture/landmark; after all, I double-majored in Pre-Columbian Art History and Victorian-Era Feminist Philosophy.

○ I already read about that place in the *Times* and it's totally overrated.

There's one of these in every group. The know-it-all can be annoying at times, reciting obscure facts about, well, *everything.* But don't throw him or her out of the moving car just yet—with the equivalent of a tour guide riding with you, you might learn something new about the places you're exploring.

THE BASICS

THE EXPLORER

o Disney World? Statue of Liberty? Space Needle? *Puh-lease*... where the crowds are, I am not!

o I like to have a plan—then throw it out the window at 75 mph.

o I'd rather eat at the diner recommended by the gas station attendant than the fancy joint listed in the Zagat guide.

o There's nothing more fun than getting lost.

If it's off the map and not in the guidebook, the explorer's got to check it out. Uber-planners should let their explorers take over once in a while, even if it means straying from the plan, since that's often when the roadtrip takes its most memorable, surprising, and serendipitous turns. But sometimes the explorer needs to be reined in and reminded that you can't stop at every lake for an impromptu skinny dip if there's any hope of making it to Kansas City by midnight.

THE ZEN OPTIMIST

o The phrase "go with the flow" is my mantra.

o I believe everything happens for a reason.

o It's okay; we'll just catch the next subway/train/ferry/flight.

o So what if we have a flat and the next gas station's 70 miles away? We need to walk off those Cheetos anyway.

They can be annoying, but it's good to have the optimist around to get you through a roadtrip's inevitable rough patches. Plus, the optimist's free-spirited nature can help get the overplanner to ease off the agenda and start enjoying those serendipitous discoveries that can become the best part of the trip.

Vital Documents

Car Insurance

Drivers in the United States are required to carry proof of insurance at all times—minimum coverage levels vary, but you should definitely have liability, which covers the other person's damages if you hit them. It's recommended that drivers also invest in uninsured motorist insurance (in case somebody hits you and can't pay the damages) and collision, which covers you in the event of a wreck that's your fault.

If you're renting a car, check with your own insurance company first to see if your rental is covered. If not, or if coverage is minimal, consider purchasing the additional damage waiver from the rental car company. Also check to see if the credit card you use for the rental covers the cost of insurance; some do, and it can save you some bucks with the car-rental company.

MEXICAN CAR INSURANCE

Drivers can go up to 22km into Mexico without a vehicle permit, but if you're headed farther than that you'll need one.

They cost about $22 and are available at the border, but you'll need to make sure you have the following documents: your driver's license, registration, and title; a passport or birth certificate or other proof of citizenship; and a tourist card (if required).

Mexican car insurance, while not required, is *highly* recommended, because if you find yourself involved in an accident the fuzz can throw you in jail until it's determined which driver is responsible for the damages. You can purchase it on a per-day basis at various insurance dealers along the border. It runs between $10 and $12 per day. As you approach the U.S.–Mexico border, look out for signs that advertise

"Mexican Car Insurance" off the highway. The signs will lead you to small Fotomat-style drive-throughs, where you can buy enough insurance to cover your time in Mexico. If you're renting a car, note that many companies don't allow their cars to leave the country, so be sure to ask about that policy before making a reservation.

ID, Please . . .

Never travel without ID—preferably two forms of it, including at least one that has your picture on it. The most common form of identification is a driver's license, which all drivers need to have. Passports have you covered for photo ID. If you don't have a drivers' license issued in the United States, you may want to apply for an **International Driving Permit,** which has to be issued in the same country as your drivers' license. Keep these two documents together at all times. Get information about who needs/how to acquire an International Driving Permit at **http://ntl. bts.gov/faq/intdl.html**.

To ensure hassle-free entry and exit at the Canadian and Mexican borders, carry a passport or proof of U.S. citizenship plus photo ID with you when you cross any international borders. For more international documentation requirements, check **http://travel.state.gov**.

Travel Insurance

Because travel insurance covers things like costs incurred by travel delays and cancellations, it's most beneficial for travelers with a lot of prepaid or non-refundable expenses like airfare and advance hotel fees. But it can still come in handy for roadtrippers because it also covers emergency medical expenses and lost or stolen baggage.

The cost of travel insurance varies widely, depending on the cost and length of your trip, your age and health, and the type of trip you're taking, but expect to pay between 5% and 8% of the vacation itself. You can get estimates from various providers through **InsureMyTrip.com**. Enter your trip cost and dates, your age, and other information, for prices from more than a dozen companies.

On-the-Road Assistance Services

We highly recommend having some form of on-the-road help line, whether it's OnStar, AAA, a roadside assistance program through your car's manufacturer, or through your cellphone provider.

If you need a jump, a tow, or just directions to the nearest pizza joint, onboard assistance services like OnStar can help, while AAA provides not only roadside assistance if you're broken down, but also free maps and trip-planning services, which can be a huge help even before you set out. (Not to mention the bail bond you get when you join.) AAA memberships run about $50 per person per year; deluxe memberships, called AAA Plus, are also available for about $75 to $90 per year, with amenities including more miles of free towing—a perk that can come in handy when you're broken down in the middle of nowhere. Also, many cellphone providers now offer roadside assistance service for only $2 to $3 a month. Check with your cell company for information.

Enroll in one of these programs before you leave and carry any relevant ID cards and phone numbers with you on your trip. See "On the Road Maintenance" under the "Car Safety" section below for more info.

THE BASICS

The Money Part

How Much Will It Cost?

The cost of your roadtrip is entirely up to you—do you *need* to eat in the best restaurants and stay in four-star hotels, or are you okay with being more grass roots for a while? This book gives you options for both, though most of the emphasis is on more affordable options, especially when it comes to hotels and food, which seem to be the biggest cash-suckers.

Speaking of cash, when you're away from home you want to make sure you're never completely without greenbacks—it's the one form of payment that nobody will turn down if you get into a bind on the road. On the other hand, you don't want to have your entire life savings in a sweat sock on your passenger seat either. Credit and debit cards are a good way to go, in combination with cash, which you might want to stash somewhere secure, like in an obscure place in your car, rather than the glove box, or in a hotel safe if you're staying in a hotel that offers one. A good rule of thumb is not to keep all your cash/cards in one place.

FOOD & LODGING

Throughout the book we divide the hostels/hotels and restaurants by price range, from "Cheap" to "Doable" to "Splurge." You know what your budget is, and what's important for you to experience on your trip, so you can plan accordingly.

Here's a general guideline for lodging/food pricing in this book:

For **Sleeping,** we figure the average nightly rate for a double room will be:

- ◌ **Cheap:** $75 per night to much less
- ◌ **Doable:** $75–$125
- ◌ **Splurge:** $125 and (way, way) up.

For **Eating,** the average price of a main dish, without alcoholic beverages, is about:

- ◌ **Cheap:** $10 or less
- ◌ **Doable:** $10–$20
- ◌ **Splurge:** $20 or more

And even if most of your nights will be spent in hostels or budget hotels, and your meals consist of pizza and drive-through, think about budgeting for, and treating yourself to, something deluxe you *know* you will enjoy. A constant stream of crappy motels and convenience-store grub can bum you out and keep you from fully enjoying your time on the road. Whether it's a meal at a world-class restaurant, or a night in a killer hotel, this is still a vacation. Pamper your road-weary self with a little luxury when you need and deserve it.

FUEL & CAR COSTS

At the rate gas prices have been fluctuating the past few years, this is one of the hardest costs to predict. But you can get a rough idea by doing a few simple calculations.

If You're Planning on a Lot of Parking . . .

. . . that is, visiting National Parks and Federal Recreational Lands on your roadtrip, then consider whether the Annual "America the Beautiful" pass makes sense for you to purchase. An $80 pass gives you access to all Federal recreation sites that charge an entrance fee for one year from the date of sale. (Which means you can also use it for any N.P.s in your area when you get home). It also includes admission for everyone else in the car (up to four adults). The pass can be obtained in person at the park, by calling ☎ 888/ASK USGS, Ext. 1, or at **http://store.usgs.gov/pass**.

First, calculate the total mileage of your trip (this book provides city-to-city mileage estimates, or you can look it up with a simple search on the Net). Next, figure the average miles per gallon you're getting out of your gas tank; this can be tricky, and MPG rates can vary wildly based on how old the vehicle is, what type of engine it has, if it's being properly maintained, if you're driving it in the city or on the highway, and about a zillion other variables. A general guideline for new vehicles is about 30 MPG highway for compact cars, and less (sometimes a *lot* less) for trucks and SUVs. (If you're renting a car, the agent should be able to provide you with fuel economy info on your rental; the website **http://fuel economy.gov** also has online trackers and fuel economy information by make and model.) Finally, figure out what the going rate is per gallon of gas in the area you're headed; you can find up-to-the-minute rates by zip code at **www.gas buddy.com**. Note that gas prices in the U.S. averaged from $2.30 to $3 per gallon in 2006, with the lowest prices generally found in the South and Midwest and highest on the West Coast and in urban centers. If you're renting your ride, remember these regional rates when the rental agent gives you the option to prepay for fuel at a specified price: Sometimes you can catch a huge break if they offer you Kansas prices for fuel for a car you'd otherwise be filling up in San Diego—going the other direction, you could get screwed.

So: total mileage ÷ miles per gallon fuel economy = number of gallons of gas you'll need. That number × average price per gallon in the area you're traveling = total approximate cost of gas for your roadtrip. For example, for a 1,500-mile roadtrip in a midsize car getting 30 MPG in an area where gas is about $2.50 per gallon, expect to pay around $125 for gas.

TIPPING

We don't need to tell you how important tips are to service industry workers, so be good to those hard-working folks. If you stay in hotels that actually have bellhops, tip **bellhops** at least $1 per bag ($2–$3 if you have a lot of luggage) and always tip housekeeping $1 to $2 per day (more if you've left a disaster area behind). Tip the **doorman** or **concierge** at higher-end hotels only if he or she has provided you with some specific service (for example, calling a cab for you or hooking up hard-to-get theater tickets). Tip the **valet** $1 every time you get your car. Tip **cabbies** 10% to 15%, and kick in at least 15% to 20% (after tax, before any discounts) to restaurant **servers** and **bartenders**.

TAXES

The United States has no value-added tax (VAT) or other indirect tax at the national level. Every state, county, and city may levy its own local tax on all purchases, including hotel and restaurant checks and airline tickets. These taxes will not appear on price tags. We do include the local tax rates, including room taxes, in the "Nuts & Bolts" sections in each chapter.

How to Pay

CREDIT & DEBIT CARDS

If at all possible, travel with at least one major credit card. You need one to rent a car, and hotels and airlines usually require one for reservations and security deposits. Credit cards, specifically Visa and MasterCard, are the most widely used form of payment in the country. A lot of places also take **American Express, Diners Club,** and **Discover**—but then again, some don't.

You can get cash advances from your credit cards at banks or ATMs, provided you know your personal identification number (PIN). Debit cards draw money directly from your checking account, and if they have a Visa or MasterCard logo on the front, they're accepted everywhere credit cards are.

TRAVELER'S CHECKS

Back before international ATMs and global bank networks, and when Pan Am was still in business, there were these quaint things called traveler's checks. (Ask your grand-parents about 'em.) When you had an upcoming trip, you'd go to your bank or American Express office and buy these checks in set denominations (of $20 or $50, usually), and then bring them with you on vacation. You could use them to pay for things like hotel bills, or you could trade them in for cash at the local bank or Amex office in your destination. Because the traveler's checks were numbered and pro-tected, even if you lost them or they were stolen, your money would be protected.

Well, guess what? Good ol' traveler's checks are still out there! Nowadays, they're less widely accepted at hotels and other businesses, but the fundamental idea behind traveler's checks is still a good one:

You can cash them as you go along, and your money is protected in case of loss or theft of the checks. And given the fees you'll pay for ATM use at banks other than your own, this old-fashioned method of carrying money on the road isn't such a crazy idea.

You can get traveler's checks at almost any bank. **American Express** offers denominations of $20, $50, $100, $500, and (for cardholders only) $1,000. You'll pay a service charge ranging from 1% to 4%. You can also order American Express trav-eler's checks over the phone by calling ☎ **800/221-7282.**

Visa offers traveler's checks at Citibank locations nationwide, as well as at several other banks. The service charge ranges between 1.5% and 2%; checks come in denom-inations of $20, $50, $100, $500, and $1,000. Call ☎ **800/732-1322** for information. **AAA** members can obtain Visa checks for a $9.95 fee (for checks up to $1,500) at most AAA offices or by calling ☎ **866/339-3378.** **MasterCard** also offers traveler's checks. Call ☎ **800/223-9920** for a location near you.

Eating Well: Roadfood

One of the great joys of the roadtrip is getting the chance to sample real, authentic regional grub. We definitely recommend avoiding corporate chains in favor of the little mom-and-pop joint whose hushpuppies you can't find any-where else. Seek out those one-of-a-kind experiences while on your trip—ask your cabbie/cop/cashier what their favorite diner is, then go there and order the special. And instead of stocking up on chips and soda from the generic Gas 'N' Sip on your way out of town, buy fresh produce from the local farmer's market.

Keeping a healthy diet on the road is hard, but not impossible. Almost any place you go has something resembling a health food store, so eat veggies whenever possible. Keep a cooler in the car stocked with healthy munchies—carrot sticks, celery, yogurt, string cheese—rather than chips, candy bars, and other calorie-loaded snack foods. Always carry bottled water—hydration is key to keeping your body in top shape while traveling.

If you want to do some more advanced scouting online, check **www.road food.com**, which has postings and recommendations from thousands of traveling foodies.

Good advice, not just in Maine! (photo: Ashley Marinaccio)

GOOD OL' CASH

You shouldn't have a hard time finding an ATM in your travels through the U.S.; the **Cirrus** (☎ 800/424-7787; www.master card.com) and **PLUS** (☎ 800/843-7587; www.visa.com) networks span the country; you can find them even in remote regions.

Look at the back of your bankcard to see which network you're on, then call or check online for ATM locations at your destination. Be sure you know your PIN and daily withdrawal limit before you depart. *Note:* Remember that many banks impose a fee every time you use a card at another bank's

Saving Cash on the Road

→ **Buy local produce.** Shopping at roadside fruit stands or farmers', markets will usually net the freshest and the cheapest local produce and give you a chance to chat with the locals.

→ **Cash or charge?** Some gas stations charge more when you use a credit card than when you pay cash. Keep your eye out for stations that list the same price for credit or cash. If there's no sign that says so, ask before filling the tank.

→ **Pump wisely.** Gas prices are often much higher at stations right off the freeway, but if you venture into town a bit, you're likely to save several cents on the gallon.

→ **Clip and save.** Look for coupon books and other discounts or promotions aimed at travelers, often available at state welcome centers, hotel lobbies or convenience stores.

→ **Take advantage of hotel freebies.** In-room coffee, a breakfast buffet, travel-size toiletries, even Wi-Fi—if your hotel offers it to you gratis, take it.

ATM, and that fee can be higher for international transactions (up to $5 or more) than for domestic ones (where they're rarely more than $2). In addition, the bank from which you withdraw cash may charge its own fee.

Don't forget the handy **"cash-back"** feature available at many grocery and convenience stores, and at U.S. Post Offices; sometimes all you need to do is buy a stick of gum and they'll give you anywhere from $10 to $100 cash back from your account.

Finally, if you find yourself completely tapped out, stop short of selling your plasma and remember you can always have someone back home wire you some dough on the road via **Western Union.** Call ☎ **800/325-6000** or visit westernunion.com for locations and information.

Getting Around

Navigating

Get well acquainted with the area you're headed before you go. Study maps (the ones in this book are a great place to start), familiarize yourself with the names of major cities, and get a general feel for the geography of the area. This book provides an outline of overall routes and highways you might be taking, but you might consider printing out door-to-door directions from home, or at least have a general idea of where you're headed every day.

Cars equipped with an on-board navigation system are a boon for roadtrippers, as are the new handheld navigation devices, sometimes called GPS-pods or travel companions, which come equipped not only with global positioning but also dining information and IM, photo, and mp3 capability. Many rental-car companies also offer portable GPS systems for an added charge.

Take a few minutes before crashing out each night to think about where you're going tomorrow, how long it'll take to get there, when's the best time to leave, and so on. And look ahead at your itinerary to get your bearings with the layout of your next stop before you get there.

By Car

Taking your own car is the simplest way to go and can also be a safe choice, considering you're already well acquainted with the car's quirks. But the most important quality to look for in a car is reliability. If you're borrowing your folks' car, drive it around a bit before you leave so you can get comfortable with it, then make sure your insurance, or your folks' insurance, covers you to drive it. Whatever car you use, definitely take it to a mechanic for a routine checkup before you go. If one of your tires is going bald, or if your brakes need new pads, better to get that fixed before you take off.

If you're picking up a rental car for the trip, take the time before you leave the lot to familiarize yourself with its dashboard, signals, seat adjusters, stereo controls, any kind of GPS equipment, and all the stuff you're not going to have time to focus on at 75 mph on the interstate, or when looking for an unmarked destination in a small town.

ONE-WAY TRIPS

If time is scarce, a one-way trip can feed your wanderlust without cutting into your work/school/family time. The downside to a one-way trip is that it's likely to be more expensive, since you've got the added costs of car rental (most likely) and air travel to or from your trip's start or end point (or both). If you're flying somewhere and renting a car, know that most rental agencies will allow you to return their cars to a different drop-off location, but it may cost you—sometimes a lot—so check with your car-rental agency before renting.

Similarly, if you're flying in to one city, driving a while, and flying home from a different city, an airline may charge you more for such an "open-jaw" itinerary. Or, you can just buy two one-way tickets if that turns out to be cheaper than an open-jaw ticket.

SIZE MATTERS

To maximize comfort while maintaining a decent fuel economy, we like midsize cars for roadtrips, when given a choice. While compact cars generally get the best gas mileage, the extra few bucks might be worth it for a driver who's 6'4" and about to drive 1,000 miles. Midsize cars also offer a bit more power and security in case your trip takes you through steep grades and/or unpredictable weather. Heavier cars with bigger engines, like trucks and SUVs, will handle environmental factors even better, but is it worth it if you're only getting 12 miles to the gallon? You'll have to decide which size makes the most sense for your trip. Think about the terrain, the grade of any climbs (will you be going through the mountains?), and the weather (do you expect heavy winds? thunderstorms?), then choose a car that will make you feel comfortable and secure as you navigate through your trip.

CAR RENTAL

For booking rental cars online, the best deals are usually found at rental-car company websites, although all the major online travel agencies also offer rental-car reservations services. Priceline and Hotwire work well for rental cars, too; the only "mystery" is which major rental company you get, and for most travelers the difference between Hertz, Avis, and Budget is negligible. Expect to pay about $20 to $40 per day for car rental (depending on where you're picking it up; it can be a *lot* more in major urban areas), plus potential added fees for gas, insurance, and returning the car to a different city than where you rented it.

What If I'm under 25?

Contrary to popular belief, it is possible to rent a car if you're under the age of 25. Many companies will rent to drivers age 21 and older (sometimes even as young as 18),

THE BASICS

provided they have a decent driving record—and are willing to pay the extra fee, which varies by state and by company, from as little as $10 to $20/day to almost $75/day in some places.

AUTO TRANSPORT

Want to get paid to drive instead of shelling out to a rental company? Hook up with a car transport service, which matches wannabe drivers with car owners who need to move their vehicles from point A to point B. Some companies will pay expenses and cover insurance costs; **Auto Driveaway**, for example, has an online form for interested drivers age 23 and up; find out more at **www.autodriveaway.com**.

CAMPERS & RVS

If your trip involves camping in national parks and other remote locations, and if you have an RV at your disposal, this could be a great roadtrip option. Many metro areas have nearby RV parks where sites run about $20 per night, plus you could save a ton of cash by sleeping and cooking in the vehicle rather than shelling out for hotels and pricey restaurants in each city. But if your trip hits a lot of urban areas, the RV might not be the best bet, as navigating city streets and freeways can be anxiety-producing, and being cloistered in your self-contained vehicle could keep you from soaking up the unique culture and character of the places you're visiting. But for visiting national parks and driving in some of the wide-open spaces in the Midwest, Southwest, and Far West, an RV can be the way to go.

A book you might wish to pick up if you're heading out in an RV is Frommer's *Exploring America by RV*, by Harry Basch & Shirley Slater. The editor of this book has edited the last three editions of the book, which is an excellent resource both on specific info about RVs, and on fun places to go with them.

No Car? No Problem!

If you don't have a car, or don't trust your vehicle to do a lap around the continent, and can't shell out the bucks for a rental, don't despair. Some of the trips in this book are quite doable with public transit, both local and between major cities. The Northeast is pretty much designed to be easily accessible by train and bus, and if you're heading to a major urban area, some of our authors will advise you to park your car and get around on foot, by bus, light rail, taxi, or whatever mode of transport is most efficient.

MOTORCYCLES

Devoted bikers will tell you there's no other way to travel—you get better parking, access to the carpool lane, and the automatic cool associated with riding a Hog (though Harley owners will tell you that *only* their bikes can be called Hogs). But motorcyclists have to be extra vigilant on the road, since bikes are much easier to miss a blind spot than other vehicles. And don't forget to always wear a helmet and pack the appropriate safety gear (even if a state doesn't have a helmet law, do you *really* want to risk driving without one?). Also, riding a bike for long distances is really for more experienced riders, or small groups, since you have to take into consideration things like inclement weather completely changing your travel plans, where to carry your belongings, and safe places to park your bike.

Driving Tips

Even the most passionate driver can get bored staring at endless expanses of long, flat highway. If you find yourself jonesing for a way to make the time go by quicker, try **books on tape/CD**—they make 'em out of tons of great titles these days, and friends of ours (traveling musicians) swear by 'em for entertainment on long hauls.

Traveling with **good music** is key, too—you'll see we've sprinkled some trip-themed **playlists** throughout the book, so if your car's got a CD player, burn some mixes before you leave. iPods are invaluable on the road, but only if you've got the right adapter and/or speakers, because it's *really* stupid to drive with earbuds in. Satellite radio provides hundreds of options, too (ask your rental car company about Sirius- or XM-equipped rides), but don't forget to tune into terrestrial radio on a regular basis to get a flavor of the region you're passing through, or just catch up with the syndicated talk show hosts you're addicted to back home. If traveling with friends, road games like "I Spy," "Twenty Questions," and others you used to play as a kid can prove to be fun retro distractions.

What to Bring

Now that you know who you're bringing, how long you're going, and what you're driving, you can think about what to pack. If it's just you and your guitar in mom's mini-van, you've got no worries; but if you're squeezing your entire sorority into a Ford Focus, you're gonna have to be selective.

Luggage

When you're essentially living out of your car, organization is key; so when it comes to luggage, keep it simple: pick one bag that makes it easy to get into, find what you need, and get out. Or, pack one big bag with everything you'll need for the whole trip, then one smaller bag that you can use to carry only what you need for that night's hotel or campground stay—PJs, toiletries, a change of clothes. A backpack, large purse, or shoulderbag is useful, too, especially if you'll be doing a lot of walking during the day.

Clothing & Toiletries

Don't like to recycle outfits? You'll never last on the road. As long as you've got a good combo of comfy driving gear, nicer going-out clothes, and stuff to sleep in, you'll be covered. Remember that many hotels have laundry service and almost every town has a laundromat (which we list in the Nuts & Bolts sections), so you can have clean clothes again whenever you need 'em. If you're staying in hotels, you probably don't need to pack shampoo, lotion, or soap, but a toothbrush, toothpaste, deodorant, contact lens solution, razors, and personal care items like condoms and tampons are a must. Most chain hotels/motels either have hair dryers in the rooms, or you can ask for one at the desk. If you don't want to bring your own, all of this stuff is readily available at convenience stores and pharmacies. Don't forget sunscreen!

Sporting Equipment

If you have an affinity for outdoor stuff, don't forget to pack related apparel—hiking boots and socks; skis, snowboards, boots, poles, and other snow gear (plus snow chains for the car); skateboard, bicycle, or inline skates; a bathing suit; whatever your outdoor exploration might require.

If you're camping, make sure you've got a tent (and all related stakes and poles), air mattress or pad, sleeping bag, pillow, compass, and so on. Here's another hint from our traveling musician friend: Make sure you set up the tent at least once before you go. After dark in a strange campground is not the place to learn how to do it.

Extras

In addition to all your paperwork and documents (travel itinerary, maps, money, credit cards, ID, insurance, AAA card, out-of-country visas or permits, and so on), don't forget your **iPod** (and car adapter, charger, and earbuds); digital **camera** (and backup batteries, charger, cables, and software if you want to upload on the road); a **cooler** to carry drinks and snacks in the car; and **reading matter,** including books on tape.

Safety & Health

Anytime you're away from home, it's important to be on top of your game. Stay healthy on the road by taking good care of yourself before you leave—take vitamins, try not to party *too* much, get plenty of sleep, and if you have any specific health concerns, see your doctor before you go. While on the road, remember that different parts of the country have different local bacteria and other environmental factors that may increase your chances of getting sick if your body's not used to dealing with them. Make sure to get a lot of sleep so you're alert and aware on the road—anything can happen out there, so it's important not to panic if unforeseen hazards or crises arise.

Defensive Driving

Don't get too comfortable in those bucket seats. While roadtripping, always keep an eye on those blind spots, don't speed, use signals . . . basically just get back in touch with your 16-year-old self the week you took your driving test. While driving, keep your headlights on, as more states are requiring them in the daytime. You may also want to avoid driving at night—get an early start and slide into your destination by mid-afternoon. Above all, stay alert (or pull over if need be for a quick power nap).

Weather

Make sure you're prepared for any weather conditions you might encounter. If you're headed to the Rockies in December, for example, carry snow chains. Thunderstorms can come out of nowhere in certain parts of the country—remember that roads are most slippery during the first few minutes of rain, especially if it's the first storm after several days of dry weather, when roads get slick as the moisture mixes with oils in the pavement. In cold-weather areas, black ice and snow can make for treacherous driving conditions. Check that you have full tread on your tires, and if you're feeling unsteady, pull over until the weather passes.

Tickets

While maximum speed limits on freeways may vary wildly—from 65 mph on most regular interstates to 80 mph in west Texas—one thing is constant: If you're caught speeding, you're gonna get fined. Speeding can also be extremely inconvenient for residents of California, Alaska, Hawaii, Montana, Oregon, Michigan, and Wisconsin—states that are not signatories to the Non-Resident Violators Compact. What that means is drivers with license plates from these seven states are subject to having their driver's license confiscated

 Things to Watch Out For

Throughout this book, you'll find boxes marked "Uh Oh!" to let you know to be on the lookout for something that can screw you up, get you lost, or cost you unnecessary money. For example, almost *every* author in this book got at least one speeding or parking ticket. So when they say to slow down or feed the meter . . . believe them!

Uh oh! Remember to feed the meter! (photo: Ashley Marinaccio)

and being required to go to the nearest office of a judge, sheriff, or justice of the peace to appear before an officer, post bond, and/or pay a fine. If said officer is not available, the individual may be jailed until a court appearance can be arranged, which may be several hours later.

If you're cited for speeding in another state, it can still affect your insurance and driving record in your home state. Other ticketable offenses can include not wearing a seatbelt, talking on a cellphone while driving, and, in certain areas of Delaware, changing clothes in the car (though we're not sure how strictly they enforce that one).

Drugs & Alcohol

The legal age for purchase and consumption of alcoholic beverages in the U.S. is 21; proof of age is required and often requested at bars, nightclubs, and restaurants, so always bring ID when you go out. Do not carry open containers of alcohol in your car or any public area that isn't zoned for alcohol consumption. The police can fine you on the spot. And nothing will ruin your trip faster than getting a citation for DUI ("driving under the influence"), so don't even think about driving while intoxicated.

And unless you've got a prescription for medical marijuana, which is sort of legal in some parts of California, and often even if you *do* have a scrip, pot, acid, mushrooms, and all the other powders are still illegal in the United States. If you're caught with any substances, expect to face the consequences—anything from a fine to extensive jail time, depending on the state.

Personal Safety

Watch your back on the road as you would on any other trip. Don't leave your stuff unattended, and don't leave valuables in the car overnight—take 'em in the hotel with you. Rooms often come equipped with a safe; if not, the hotel usually has one. If you're taking your computer with you, make sure to back up your hard drive before you leave in case of theft. A sturdy laptop security cable is also a good idea, as is installing tracing software like **zTrace** (www.ztrace.com), **Computrace** (www. absolute.com), or, for Macs, **Undercover** (www.orbicule.com).

Have a good security system on your car, and carry a padlock if you have valuables to lock up. Be on the lookout for scammers, and know where your wallet and important papers are at all times. At night, and when exploring uncharted territories during detours, stay in populated areas.

Pre-Trip Health

If you suffer from a chronic illness, consult your doctor before your departure. For conditions like epilepsy, diabetes, or heart problems, wear a **MedicAlert identification tag** (☎ 888/633-4298; www. medicalert.org), which will alert doctors to your condition and give them access to your records through MedicAlert's 24-hour hot line. Pack **prescription medications** and carry copies of your prescriptions in case you lose your pills or run out. Know the generic name of prescription medicines, just in case a local pharmacist is unfamiliar with the brand name. It's also a good idea to pack an extra pair or two of **contact lenses** or **prescription glasses.**

HEALTH INSURANCE

Most health insurance policies cover you if you get sick away from home—but verify that you're covered before you depart, particularly if you're insured by an HMO. Contact the **International Association for Medical Assistance to Travelers (IAMAT)** (☎ 716/754-4883; www.iamat.org) for tips on travel and health concerns in the areas you're visiting, and for lists of local doctors.

The United States **Centers for Disease Control and Prevention** (☎ 800/ 311-3435; www.cdc.gov) provides up-to-date information on health hazards by region or country and offers tips on food safety.

Allergens & Diseases

Different parts of the country have different plants, bugs, pollens, and bacteria that can irritate allergies and cause other discomfort. Research your destination before you go if you tend to be sensitive to environmental hazards. Diseases common in the U.S. include the flu, hantavirus (a rodent-borne disease found mostly in the

Your Portable Medicine Cabinet

The following is a list of medications and health aids you might want to have on hand when traveling in the United States:

→ **Sunblock** (as well as sunglasses and a wide-brimmed hat) during summer months; if you're headed for a mostly outdoors vacation in fall or winter, bring along the sunscreen as well.

→ Enough **prescription medication** to last your entire trip and a copy of your prescription(s)

→ **Antidiarrheal** medication

→ **Stomach-calming** medication like Pepto-Bismol or Gaviscon

→ **Insect repellent** containing DEET during the summer

→ A **pain reliever** like aspirin, acetaminophen, or ibuprofen

→ **Antifungal** or **antibacterial** cream or ointment

→ An **antihistamine** if you're traveling during allergy season, or know you might have an allergic reaction to something.

→ A **first-aid kit** for the car. They really don't take up much space, and it's a smart idea to have bandages, antiseptic, and other supplies in case of injury.

All of the above are readily available at most supermarkets and pharmacies, but do you really want to be in the position of having to track down some Imodium AD when you're in the middle of a 400-mile haul? Pack a small medicine kit with some basics, and you'll always be prepared.

THE BASICS

western United States), and Lyme disease (especially in the northeast and Midwest). West Nile virus, mad cow disease, E. coli, salmonella, and bird flu have recently been making headlines; other hazards include poisonous snakes and plants like poison ivy and poison oak.

Playing Safely

If you strike up a friendship, say, a very *close* friendship with a traveling companion or someone you meet on the road, remember that STDs are *not* a souvenir you want to bring home with you. And that the Mr. or Ms. Right (or Right Now) you met at the swim-up bar in Jersey or Las Vegas might be a walking gonorrhea case. *Always* use, or insist your partner use, a latex condom (or polyurethane if you're allergic)

when you're doing . . . whatever it is you'll be doing.

Condoms that are not latex are less effective against disease transmission and pregnancy and should be avoided.

Obviously, you can get condoms at almost any pharmacy or convenience store, but you might want to keep some with you in case you're having a moment, and you're miles from any retail establishment, or really don't want to go find one.

And of course, you should always avoid shared needles for tattoos, piercings, or injections of any kind (it's illegal for needles to be reused in reputable tattoo and piercing shops in most places). Always make sure that you watch the establishment open a fresh needle—again, it's not worth the risk.

Car Safety

Get to know the ins and outs of your ride and make safety and maintenance a top priority.

TRIP PREP

Make an appointment with your mechanic for an oil change and a tune-up; make sure to have all your belts, brakes, and tires and systems (especially the cooling and A/C) checked. Tell your mechanic that you're planning a long trip and have him look into any specific problem areas. Make sure you've got all the necessary tools and any special equipment like snow chains, and check to be sure your spare tire is inflated. Double-check that you've got all the right paperwork, too: driver's license, insurance card, registration, and AAA or other roadside assistance information.

ON-THE-ROAD MAINTENANCE

Tire Care

In your tool kit, make sure you have the tools to repair a flat tire: car jack, lug wrench, a fully inflated spare, and an air-pressure gauge (tire pressure is measured in pounds per square inch; recommended pressure level varies but is usually printed on the side of the tire). Aerosol tire-seal products like Fix-A-Flat can help get you from a potentially dangerous breakdown location to a safer location. If you're running low on air, most gas stations have an air hose equipped with a built-in pressure gauge.

Fluids, Hoses, Belts & Filters

Know how to check and maintain your car's fluid levels. Oil, coolant, and window washer fluids are the easiest to check and most likely to require refilling, though you should also know how to monitor fluid levels in your transmission, power steering, brakes, and battery (ask your mechanic or consult your owner's manual if you don't know how or where to check these levels).

Have your mechanic recharge your A/C with Freon before your trip. Check your radiator hose for leaks and your car's various belts (fan, drive, timing) for cracks. Oil, fuel, and air filters should also be checked and, if necessary, replaced prior to your trip.

WHAT TO DO IF . . .

Your Car Overheats

While driving long stretches, especially in hot weather, keep an eye on the temperature gauge and make sure you have plenty of antifreeze/coolant in your trunk. If your engine starts running hot, turn on the heater to let some engine heat escape (this will help if the fan or fan belt is broken). Pull over and *carefully* pop the hood to check your coolant levels (and know where your coolant reservoir is located). Never open your radiator cap while the car is overheating unless you want a hot geyser of boiling antifreeze in the face—engines usually cool in about 20 minutes. Add coolant to the reservoir's fill line and then look for green liquid dripping out from under the car, which could be the sign of a coolant leak. If the problem continues, take the car to a mechanic.

Your Battery Dies

If you leave your lights on overnight or sit listening to the stereo too long with the engine off, you might run down your battery. Carry jumper cables in the trunk and if you feel uncomfortable asking someone for help, call AAA, which can either give you a jump or in some cases even deliver and install a new battery. Connect the cables in the following order: positive cable (usually red) to positive node of dead battery; positive cable to positive node of live battery; negative cable (usually black) to negative node on the live battery. Then connect the remaining negative cable to a non-painted metal surface of the dead car (connecting directly to the battery can cause explosions, in rare cases). Start the live car and let it run for a minute or so, then start the dead car. Remove cables in backwards order from the way they were connected.

Let the revived car run for a few minutes, then shut it off and see if it starts again on its own. If not, the problem may lie with corroded battery posts, bad jumper cables, or other malfunctioning parts like the starter or alternator. A mechanic should be able to diagnose the problem fairly quickly.

You Get a Flat

If you get a flat, pull over safely on level ground as far from traffic as possible. Apply the emergency brake and park the car in gear. Turn off your engine, turn on your hazards, and put a large rock behind the diagonally opposing tire to prevent the car from rolling. Remove the hubcap and use the lug wrench to loosen (but don't remove) the lugnuts (turn 'em counter-clockwise or just remember the rhyme "Righty Tighty, Lefty Loosey"). Jack up the car until the tire is completely off the ground, then remove the lugnuts and remove the tire. Put the new tire on, screw the lugnuts back on, then lower the wheel, tighten the lugnuts completely, and check the tire pressure. If you're riding on a smaller-than-usual tire (a "donut"), make sure to obey the speed limit for the tire, usually displayed on a bright-yellow sticker on the rim. Donuts shouldn't be taken very fast, so stay in that slow lane if you have to take the freeway. Get a new tire as soon as you can.

You Lock Your Keys in Your Car

Hey, don't be embarrassed; it happens to the best of us. To prepare for a lockout, make spare copies of your key and put one somewhere you might actually be able to get to if you're locked out (hint: *not* in the glove box). Some people are wary about those magnetic key holders that attach under a bumper or behind the wheel well as they give would-be thieves great access

to your stuff, but in a pinch they can get you out of a jam. You can also carry a plastic cardkey (available free to AAA members) in your wallet; it's the size of a credit card and can get you into your car (but it won't start the ignition). If you have manual door locks and are handy with a coat hanger, try the old coat hanger trick: Slip the hanger through an open window or slide it between the window and the door to unhook the lock from the inside. If that fails, find someone with a slim jim—cops often carry one, as do many mechanics—or call a locksmith; even that costs less than replacing the window you'd have to smash to get in. And some of the road assistance services (like OnStar, at least according to their heartrending commercials where small infants are accidentally locked into cars by their absent-minded parents) can automatically unlock your car doors if you call them and give them your personal code.

You Start Skidding

If you find yourself fishtailing, remember what your driving instructor taught you: "Turn into the skid," which means ease off the gas and brakes while quickly turning the wheel in the direction you want the front of the car to go (down the road). Make sure to correct your steering once you've straightened your skid; otherwise, you could start to skid in the other direction.

You Have a Blowout

If you get a flat on the freeway, don't panic and don't slam on your brakes. Instead, grip the steering wheel firmly and let the car slow itself down slowly by easing off the gas. Gently steer toward the shoulder or to the next exit, if possible. Brake lightly until you come to a stop. If you have to stop and change your flat on the freeway, do it safely and make sure have some indicator to passing police cars that you need help (flares, reflectors, raised hood, and so on).

THE BASICS

You Hit an Animal

Keep your eyes out for deer, rabbits, dogs, and other animals that somehow find their way to freeways or rural roads. While it's never pleasant to have to hit one, if you know you don't have time to avoid a collision, remember that hitting the poor guy might be the lesser of two evils if the alternative is swerving into a potentially injurious wreck. In areas with "watch for wildlife" signs, slow down, and if you see an animal you may be able to avoid, steer straight and brake sharply but not so hard as to lock up your brakes. However, if you know you're going to hit the animal no matter what, and if it's a sizable creature, experts advise actually *speeding up* to prevent the struck animal from crashing through your windshield and into your lap.

You're Surrounded by Semis

You know who spends lots of time on the road? Truckers. And on some routes you'll be surrounded by 'em—big, giant 18-wheelers—whose drivers may well be tired. Keep your distance when driving behind these guys—rocks and other cargo could come flying at your windshield, causing a costly crack—and never cut a truck off on the freeway; with all those axles, they have a much longer braking time than you do.

The Going Gets Tough . . .

Go slow around dangerous curves, especially in snowy conditions. And don't get intimidated or competitive if you notice other drivers going at speeds you're not comfortable with. They might be locals who know the twists and turns better than you, or they might just be lousy drivers. If you're going up a steep hill, downshift into the right gear and, if necessary, turn off your A/C to ensure you have enough power. When going downhill, go slow and pump your brakes so they don't lock up. Never go downhill in neutral or when the car is not running; you'll have almost no control or ability to stop.

Downshifting into a lower gear and applying the emergency brake can also slow you down if your brakes fail.

You Get in an Accident

The National Safety Council says one in eight drivers will be involved in a car wreck each year. If it happens to you, make sure, first off, that everyone involved is physically okay. Always report the accident to the local cops and/or highway patrol, and call emergency services, if need be, and get the names of all people involved in the crash as well as any witnesses. Get insurance information and drivers' license numbers for the drivers involved, and make notes of date, time, place, weather, and any other specifics associated with the crash.

You are almost always required to report accidents to the police by local law, and you'll also want to do so for insurance purposes. Insurance companies will want to know the accident report number, and other information you will need from the police.

And not contacting the police after an accident constitutes "leaving the scene" in most jurisdictions, so you could be liable for a ticket or worse. (A friend of ours found this out when she skidded into a stop sign and drove to a nearby police station to report it . . . and was cited for "leaving the scene.")

You Need Help

In an emergency, **dial** ☎ **911** for immediate police assistance. For more minor situations we highly recommend automobile-association membership to would-be roadtrippers. **AAA, the American Automobile Association (**☎ **800/222-4357; http://travel.aaa.com)**, is the country's largest auto club and supplies its members with maps, insurance, and, most important, emergency road service. *Note:* Foreign driver's licenses are usually recognized in the U.S., but you should get an international one if your home license is not in English (p. 9).

Many new cars also come equipped with programs like **OnStar,** which connects you with operators who can provide information and directions as well as emergency assistance. If renting a car, ask the rental agent if there are any OnStar-equipped vehicles available.

Keeping in Touch

Communicating with the folks back home is important for basic safety reasons, but don't forget that one of the best parts of any roadtrip is the escape from the everyday. We're so addicted to our laptops/CrackBerrys/cellphones that sometimes it's necessary to completely disconnect and decompress.

Sure, it can be fun to blog your roadtrip for your friends back home, post photos from the road, and so on, but to soak in the total road experience, try not to get consumed with communications.

By Snail Mail

What a quaint concept! Letter writing might seem old-fashioned, time-consuming, and even expensive in the digital age, but never underestimate the sentimental value of snail mail. E-mails get deleted, but postcards from the Grand Canyon, scenic Sheboygan, and ol' San Antone can live on refrigerator doors for years.

SENDING

At press time, domestic postage rates were 26¢ for a postcard and 41¢ for a letter. Always include zip codes when mailing items in the U.S. If you don't know the zip code, visit www.usps.com/zip4. For more information go to **www.usps.com** and click on "Calculate Postage."

RECEIVING

If you aren't sure what your address will be in a U.S. town, mail can be sent to you, in your name, c/o **General Delivery** at the main post office of the city or region where you expect to be. (Call ☎ **800/275-8777** for information on the nearest post office.)

The addressee must pick up mail in person and must produce proof of identity (driver's license, passport, and so on). Most post offices will hold your mail for up to 1 month, and are open Monday to Friday from 8am to 6pm, and Saturday from 9am to 3pm.

OVERSEAS

For international mail, a first-class letter of up to 1 ounce costs 84¢ (63¢ to Canada and Mexico); a first-class postcard costs 75¢ (55¢ to Canada and Mexico); and a preprinted postal aerogramme costs 75¢. For more information go to **www.usps.com** and click on "Calculate Postage."

By Phone

DOMESTIC & INTERNATIONAL CALLS

Pay phones are becoming more and more scarce, but you can still find 'em in most towns. Local direct-dial calls in most areas cost 25¢ to 50¢; for long-distance and international calls, you may want to purchase a pre-paid phone card, which provides a certain number of minutes of talk-time that varies depending on when and what country you're calling; phone cards are available at almost every convenience store, pharmacy, and gas station. If you're calling out of the country, be sure to know the correct country and city codes of the location you're calling (visit **www.timeanddate.com** to find a breakdown of international dialing codes).

TIME DIFFERENCES

The United States has six time zones: the standard four (Pacific, Mountain, Central,

THE BASICS

and Eastern) plus one each for Hawaii and Alaska. In the lower 48, each zone is 1 hour ahead of the last.

Many major highways have signs indicating when you're leaving one time zone and entering the next, and most cellphone clocks automatically update (if yours doesn't, just power it off and then turn it back on again). Keep time differences in mind when making that phone call to friends or family back home—especially after a long night out.

CELLPHONES

Just because your cell works at home doesn't mean it'll work everywhere in the U.S. (thanks to our nation's fragmented system). It's a good bet that your phone will work in major cities, but take a look at your wireless company's coverage map on its website before heading out; T-Mobile, Sprint, and Nextel are particularly weak in rural areas. And even if your phone works, you may actually be unwittingly roaming on another company's network—and paying through the nose for it. Contact your wireless company before you leave and while on the road to ensure you're not getting overcharged.

If you need to stay in touch at a destination where you know your phone won't work, **rent** a phone that does from **InTouch USA** (☎ **800/872-7626**; www.intouch global.com) or a rental-car location, but beware that you'll pay $1 a minute or more for airtime. If you're venturing deep into national parks, you may want to consider renting a **satellite phone ("satphones")**. A satellite phone is different from a cellphone in that it connects to satellites rather than ground-based towers. Unfortunately, you'll pay at least $2 per minute to use the phone, and it only works where you can see the horizon (that is, usually not indoors). In North America, you can rent Iridium satellite phones from **RoadPost** (www.roadpost.com; ☎ **888/290-1606** or 905/272-5665). InTouch USA (see above) offers a wider range of satphones but at higher rates.

If you're not from the U.S., you'll be appalled at the poor reach of our **GSM (Global System for Mobiles) wireless network,** which is used by much of the rest of the world. Your phone will probably work in most major U.S. cities; it definitely won't work in many rural areas. (To see where GSM phones work in the U.S., check

Insider Tip: Free 411

Say you forgot which exit you're supposed to take to get to the hotel, or you need to know what time the box office closes at that theater downtown, but you forgot to write down the phone number. The only option is to call 411 on your cell, right? Wrong! With cellphone companies charging up to $2 per call for directory assistance, it pays to have a few money-saving tricks up your sleeve, including these two free alternatives to 411. First, try **Google SMS,** a service that at press time was only in beta, meaning it's not official yet, even though it's been around for years. Here's how it works: You text a message with the name of the business and the city and state or zip code (for example, "Jimmy's Pizza Baltimore MD") to 46645 (or GOOGL), and within a few seconds Google texts you back with the number. It's not perfect, but it's saved me a bundle on 411 fees (regular text messaging fees apply). Then there's **1-800-FREE-411,** which uses voice recognition to provide automated business, residential, and government listings—all free, provided you're willing to listen to a short advertisement.

Photo Tips for the Road

....

→ **Take along a spare camera—or two.** Even if you've been anointed the "official" photographer of your travel group, encourage others in your party to carry their own cameras and provide fresh perspectives—and backup. Your photographic "second unit" may include you in a few shots so you're not the invisible person of the trip. (And sometimes cameras fall into the ocean . . . just ask Retro Roadtrip author Valerie Willis!)

→ **Stock up on digital camera memory cards.** At home, it's easy to copy pictures from your memory cards to your computer as they fill up. During your travels, cards seem to fill up more quickly. Take along enough digital film for your entire trip or, at a minimum, enough for at least a few days' of shooting. At intervals, you can copy images to CDs. Many camera stores and souvenir shops offer this service, and a growing number of mass merchandisers have walk-up kiosks you can use to make prints or create CDs while you travel.

→ **Share and share alike.** No need to wait until you get home to share your photos. You can upload a gallery's worth to an online photo sharing service. Just find an Internet cafe where the computers have card readers, or connect your camera to the computer with a cable. You can find online photo sharing services that cost little or nothing at **www.clickherefree. com.** You can also use America Online's **Your Pictures** service, or commercial enterprises that give you free or low-cost photo sharing: Kodak's **EasyShare gallery** (www.kodak.com), **Yahoo! Photos** (www.photos. yahoo.com), **Snapfish** (www.snapfish.com), or **Shutterfly** (www. shutterfly.com).

out www.t-mobile.com/coverage.) And you may or may not be able to send SMS (text messaging) home.

Texting

For short notes ("Arrived safely!" or "Have my stuff shipped—I'm never coming home!"), SMS, or text messaging, can be a great way to keep in touch with folks back home as well as traveling companions you've been temporarily separated from. Just make sure you know how many texts, if any, are included in your wireless plan. And seriously, never text while driving, no matter how good you think you are at multi-tasking.

By E-mail

Web-based programs like Yahoo!, Gmail, and Hotmail are helpful when you're using different public computers to access your

e-mail. Set one up before you leave if you don't already have one. If you have friends or family that want to get e-mail updates from your trip, set up a distribution list in advance that includes all their addresses. To find cybercafes in your destination, check **www.cybercaptive.com** and **www.cybercafe.com**. Aside from formal Internet cafes, most **public libraries** offer Internet access, and most business-class hotels offer dataports for laptop modems. Wherever you go, bring a **connection kit** of the right power and phone adapters, a spare phone cord, and a spare Ethernet network cable—or find out whether your hotel supplies them to guests.

WI-FI

If you're traveling with your own wireless-card-equipped laptop, you'll find plenty of hotels, cafes, and retailers—even whole neighborhoods and cities—are signing on as Wi-Fi hotspots. Some providers charge a fee, but it's becoming increasingly easier to log on for free, thanks to city-subsidized connectivity, and restaurants and cafes that offer Wi-Fi free with purchase. **T-Mobile Hotspot** (www.t-mobile.com/hotspot) serves up wireless connections at more than 1,000 Starbucks coffee shops nationwide. **Boingo** (www.boingo.com) and **Wayport** (www.wayport.com) have set up networks in airports and high-class hotel lobbies.

BLOGGING

Posting your travelogue to a website is a fantastic way to let everybody know how you're doing without wasting hours in an Internet cafe e-mailing all your friends one by one. Many services are free and super easy to use even if you're totally not tech-savvy. **Blogspot.com** offers free, easy-to-use blog software, and social networking sites like **Myspace** and **Friendster** each have built-in blog capability. Bonus: Your friends can comment on your posts to let you know how jealous they are of all the fun you're having.

The downside of blogs is that anyone can theoretically read what you're posting; if security is an issue, you may want to set up password protection on your postings.

Tips on Accommodations

Depending on how much of a planner you are, you may or may not want to reserve your lodging in advance. If you're getting in to a city late, or you're headed somewhere during tourist season when vacancy could be scarce, definitely reserve ahead. But there's something to be said for rolling into town and stumbling upon a great little find.

Booking Online

If you are booking in advance, shopping online is a good way to go. You can book through the hotel's own website or through an independent booking agency (or a fare-service agency like Priceline. com). These Internet hotel agencies have multiplied in mind-boggling numbers, competing for the business of millions of consumers surfing for accommodations around the world. This competitiveness can be a boon for those who have the patience and time to shop and compare the online sites for good deals—but shop they must, for prices can vary considerably. And keep in mind that hotels at the top of a

site's listing may be there for no other reason than that they paid money to get the placement.

Of the "big three" sites, **Expedia.com** offers a long list of special deals and "virtual tours" or photos of available rooms so you can see what you're paying for (a feature that helps counter the claims that the best rooms are often held back from bargain booking websites). **Travelocity** posts unvarnished customer reviews and ranks its properties according to the AAA rating system. **Trip Advisor** (www.tripadvisor. com) is another excellent source of unbiased user reviews of hotels. While even the finest hotels can inspire a misleadingly poor review from picky or crabby travelers, the body of user opinions, when taken as a whole, is usually a reliable indicator.

Other reliable online booking agencies include **Hotels.com** and **Quikbook.com**. An excellent free program, **TravelAxe** (www.travelaxe.net), can help you search multiple hotel sites at once, even ones you may never have heard of—and conveniently lists the total price of the room, including

Saving Cash on Your Room

The **rack rate** is the maximum rate that a hotel charges for a room. Hardly any-body pays this price, however, except in high season or on holidays. To lower the cost of your room:

→ **Ask about special rates or other discounts.** You may qualify for corpo-rate, student, military, senior, frequent flier, trade union, or other discounts. There's almost always a AAA discount.

→ **Dial direct.** When booking a room in a chain hotel, you'll often get a better deal by calling the individual hotel's reservation desk rather than the chain's main number.

→ **Book online.** Many hotels offer Internet-only discounts, or supply rooms to Priceline, Hotwire, or Expedia at rates much lower than the ones you can get through the hotel itself.

→ **Remember the law of supply and demand.** Resort hotels are most crowded and therefore most expensive on weekends, so discounts are usually avail-able for midweek stays. Business hotels in downtown locations are busiest during the week, so you can expect big discounts over the weekend. Many hotels have high-season and low-season prices, and booking even one day after high season ends can mean big discounts.

→ **Look into longer-stay discounts.** If you decide you want to stick around one place for a while (say at least 3 or 4 days), you should ask manage-ment to lower your per-night cost.

→ **Avoid excess charges and hidden costs.** When you book a room, ask whether the hotel charges for parking. Use your own cellphone, pay phones, or prepaid phone cards instead of dialing direct from hotel phones, which often have exorbitant rates. And don't be tempted by the room's minibar offerings: Most hotels charge and arm and a leg for water, soda, and snacks. Finally, ask about local taxes and service charges, which can increase the cost of a room by 15% or more.

→ **Consider enrolling in hotel "frequent-stay" programs,** which are upping the ante lately to win the loyalty of repeat customers. Frequent guests can now accumulate points or credits to earn free hotel nights, airline miles, in-room amenities, merchandise, tickets to concerts and events, discounts on sporting facilities—and even credit toward stock in the participating hotel, in the case of the Jameson Inn hotel group. Perks are awarded not only by many chain hotels and motels (Hilton HHonors, Marriott Rewards, Wyndham ByRequest, to name a few), but individual inns and B&Bs. Many chain hotels partner with other hotel chains, car-rental firms, airlines, and credit card companies to give consumers additional incentive to do repeat business.

the taxes and service charges. Another booking site, **Travelweb** (www.travelweb. com), is partly owned by the hotels it rep-resents (including the Hilton, Hyatt, and Starwood chains) and is plugged directly into the hotels' reservations systems—unlike independent online agencies, which have to fax or e-mail reservation requests to the hotel, a good portion of which get misplaced in the shuffle. More than once,

In Praise of the Hostel Experience

When I first hit Europe by myself at 20 with a Eurailpass and a backpack, staying at hostels was not just the cheapest way to go; it was where I met other people (some of whom became traveling companions), found out where to go and what to do, often got a free breakfast or cheap dinner, and generally learned how to not just get from one place to the other, but to enjoy the ride in every way possible. (Paris, Dublin, Berlin, I'm talking to *you* . . .). Whether it was an official Hostelling International hostel, or a private "backpacker," I almost always had a blast.

I was gratified to discover that there are *lots* of hostels (80 HI hostels, and hundreds of unofficial "backpackers") in the U.S. . . . and most Americans don't use them. As mentioned in the section below, some people can't deal with bathroom-down-the-hall; others think they're just for students, or you must be a member; others just don't know they're there. But they are: in many major cities, in parks, and far-flung destinations (some are seasonal). When you're at a hostel, you can stay in old brownstones, a lighthouse, a tepee. Sometimes you are in a large room filled with bunk beds, or a smaller suite with just a few, and an attached bathroom. In Boston, my significant other and I stayed in a private room . . . that had bunk beds.

My American hostel experience has included stays in Las Vegas (where I played nickel slots and went to see the band); Virginia Beach (on the beach, and then I went to see the band); Washington, D.C. (practically within spitting distance of the Capitol, then we went to see the band); Los Angeles (perched high on a Hollywood Hill, then I went to see the band); and Seattle (where I woke to an amazing view of the harbor . . . then I went . . . you get the picture).

For information on how to join Hostelling International USA (which also gives you membership in all international HI hostels), visit **www.hiusa.org**. Membership is free if you're under 18, $28 annually for people 18 to 54. As a member, you can make pre-paid reservations at HI hostels, and are eligible for a lot of discounts, from long-distance calling to bus travel to organized tours.

—*The Editor*

travelers have arrived at the hotel, only to be told that they have no reservation. To be fair, many of the major sites are improving in service and ease of use, and Expedia.com will soon be able to plug directly into the reservations systems of many hotel chains—none of which can be bad news for consumers. In the meantime, you should definitely get a confirmation number and bring along a printout of any online booking transaction.

Hotels & Motels

When it comes to cost and cleanliness hotels can run the gamut—if consistency is

a concern, generic chains are a safe bet, but you'll get a better sense of the town you're in if you stay at a one-of-a-kind place. To get into serious roadtrip mode, stay at motels; the word is short for "motor hotel" and the concept arose in the mid-20th century as car culture grew in popularity. Motels are usually located on or near the interstate and tend to be pretty affordable; with their wacky, attention-getting signage, they can also be a kitsch-lover's paradise.

Hostels

Hostels are a cheap option for those who don't mind sharing a bathroom and crashing

Good Sources of (Free) Info

Always stop at the tourist information offices or welcome centers when you enter a new state on an interstate highway. You can pick up everything from maps to campground booklets to info on visitor discounts—all of it free.

out in a bunk bed. Okay, okay, some of 'em have private rooms you can get for an extra fee, but the hostel experience is still miles away from your average chain hotel—which can be a good or bad thing depending on your perspective.

On the plus side, you'll meet tons of people from all walks of life, and amenities like bike rental and self-catering kitchens make for a more homey atmosphere (cooking your own meals also saves cash). The drawbacks? Some hostels have curfews, which can be a drag, and the dormitory situation—travelers are sometimes packed 30 to a same-sex dorm—may not be for everyone. Since hostels are geared toward travelers and not just cash-strapped locals, some require lodgers to show proof that they're actually traveling, in which case it's smart to carry a passport.

A good resource if you're new to hostelling is **www.hostels.com**, which has info on many U.S. and international hostels, as well as a booking engine. You might also consider joining a membership organization like **Hostelling International** (www.hihostels.com), which has locations in many major U.S. cities; members often have access to cheaper rates and special privileges, like advance booking (see box on p. 30).

Camping

Is the Great Outdoors calling your name? Try a campground. Even the most bustling metropolitan areas usually have a campground within city limits or a short drive outside of town, and this low-cost lodging can save you a ton. In addition to traditional tent sites, many locations also offer RV parking and hookups. And even if you didn't pack a tent, don't rule out a campground: Many locations (including most KOA campgrounds) have **stand-alone cabins** that offer a little more protection from the elements at a slightly higher rate (check ahead, though—you sometimes must bring your own bedding). The following directories can help you book your site:

○ **Bureau of Land Management,** 270 million acres of public land. Ask for free camping information from BLM, Department of Interior, Room LS406 (Public Affairs), 1849 C St. NW, Room 5600, Washington, DC 20240 (☎ **202/452-5125;** www.blm.gov).

It's Fun to Stay at the . . .

If you're on a budget, consider that many cities have **YMCAs** with cheap rooms for rent—especially in urban centers (New York has four, as well as a YMHA which offers rooms to travelers; we've also stayed at YMCAs in San Diego and New Haven). Rooms tend to be modest and you might have to walk down the hall to use the bathroom, but the low rates can make even the most spartan surroundings seem nice. In New York City, the rates range from $72 to $89 with shared bath; $105 to $140 with private bath (which is reasonable . . . for New York City). To find out whether the Y offers accommodations where you're heading, search "YMCA of [insert destination]" on the Net.

A Recommended Series from Frommer's

If you're planning on doing a lot of camping on your trip, check out *Frommer's Best RV and Tent Campgrounds in the U.S.A.* (Wiley Publishing, Inc.), a guide that gives individually written, detailed profiles and overall quality ratings of nearly 5,000 of the best campgrounds in the country in every state except Hawaii, and also lists their rates, hookups, facilities, and amenities. There's a national guide with ratings and rankings of almost 10,000 campgrounds in the United States. The guide is available at your favorite bookstore, or can be ordered online directly at Frommers.com.

○ **KOA,** 460 campgrounds in the United States, Canada, and Mexico. You can receive a guide free, or send $5 for an annual guide from Kampgrounds of America Executive Offices, P.O. Box 30558, Billings, MT 59114-0558 (☎ **406/248-7444;** www.koa.com).

○ **National Association of RV Park and Campgrounds** has a directory with listings of more than 3,000 RV parks and campgrounds. National ARVC, 113 Park Ave., Falls Church, VA 22046 (☎ **703/241-8801;** www.gocampingamerica.com).

○ **National Forest Service,** 4,000 campgrounds. For a free guide, write to U.S. Department of Agriculture Forest Service, Public Affairs Office, 1400 Independence Ave., Washington, DC 20250-0003 (www.fs.fed.us).

○ **National Wildlife Refuges,** 488 refuges. For free publications, write to U.S. Fish and Wildlife Services, Public Affairs Office, 1849 C St. NW, MS-5600/MIB, Washington, DC, 20240 (☎ **202/452-5125;** http://refuges.fws.gov).

○ **Trailer Life Campground, RV Park and Services Directory** covers 12,500 campgrounds in the United States, Canada, and Mexico. Available for $25 at bookstores and camping stores, or write to the following address: 2575 Vista del Mar Dr., Ventura, CA 93001 (☎ **800/234-3450;** www.tldirectory.com).

Making Campsite Reservations by Phone

You can call ☎ **877/444-6777** for campsite reservations in **national forests** and **U.S. Army Corps of Engineers Campgrounds—** although the line is usually busy and applicants wait on hold for a long time. The line is operative daily from 7am to midnight Eastern Standard Time. Registered members can make reservations via their website at **www.reserveusa.com**.

○ **U.S. Army Corps of Engineers,** 53,000 campsites near oceans, rivers, and lakes. For free publications, write to U.S. Army Corps of Engineers, OCE Publications Depot, 2803 52nd Ave., Hyattsville, MD 20781-1102 (☎ **301/394-0081;** www.usace.army.mil).

○ **Wheelers RV Resort & Campground Directory.** The cost is $15 from Print Media Services, 1310 Jarvis Ave., Elk Grove Village, IL 60007.

○ **Woodall's Campground Directory.** Purchase one for $22 by writing to 2575 Vista del Mar Dr., Ventura, CA 93001 (www.woodalls.com).

○ **Yogi Bear's Jellystone Park Campground Directory** is free from

Leisure Systems, Inc., 6201 Kellogg Ave., Cincinnati, OH 45230 (☎ **800/ 558-2954;** www.campjellystone.com).

Sleeping in the Car

While more than half the states permit some overnight parking in highway rest areas, except where posted, there are some safety risks associated with sleeping in the car: carjacking, robbery, and so on. In that case, it may be worth spending a few extra dollars on a cheap hotel or campground fees if it buys you security and peace of mind.

Various Roadtrip Resources

The following books, movies, and tunes are guaranteed to get you amped about your upcoming roadtrip.

Required Reading

○ *On the Road* (Penguin, 1999) by Jack Kerouac: the roadtripper's Bible.

○ *Travels with Charley* (Penguin, 2002) by John Steinbeck: One of America's most celebrated writers takes his dog on the road.

○ *Killing Yourself to Live: 85% of a True Story* (Scribner, 2006) by Chuck Klosterman: A former *Spin* columnist drive cross-country visiting rock-'n'-roll death sites.

○ *Zen and the Art of Motorcycle Maintenance: An Inquiry into Values* (HarperTorch, 2006) by Robert Pirsig: A father-son cross-country motorcycle trip evolves into a meditation on Western philosophy.

Required Watching

○ *Road Trip* (2000): Breckin Meyer and Amy Smart star in this college road-movie caper.

○ *The Straight Story* (1999): Only David Lynch could make compelling entertainment out of the story of a guy traveling hundreds of miles to visit his brother—on a riding tractor.

○ *Easy Rider* (1969): Dennis Hopper and Peter Fonda are two idealistic longhairs experiencing 1960s America from the leather seat of a Harley.

○ *Y Tu Mama Tambien* (2001): This Spanish-language stunner tracks Diego Luna and Gael Garcia Bernal through some steamy scenes in the Mexican countryside.

○ *Thelma & Louise* (1991): Geena Davis and Susan Sarandon are two women you don't want to mess with.

○ *National Lampoon's Vacation* (1983): Chevy Chase and Beverly D'Angelo pack up the rest of the Griswold clan for a family roadtrip to WallyWorld.

○ *The Simple Life 2: Road Trip* (2004): They're no Fonda and Hopper, but Paris Hilton, Nicole Richie, and their pink truck still provide endless, mindless entertainment.

Required Listening

You can't do a roadtrip without some great roadtrippin' tunes. Period.

We don't go anywhere without our iPods. If you're anything like us, you'll dig the playlists we put throughout these chapters with songs designed to fit the trips you're taking: a little Elvis in Memphis, some Mudhoney in Seattle, and a bunch of just generally awesome driving tunes.

On the Web

The Web is a treasure-trove of information for would-be roadtrippers; there's a website for everything, it seems, and a quick Google search could lead you to your new favorite spot, whether via an online newspaper story or some dude in Arkansas' "What I Did On My Summer Vacation" blog.

THE BASICS

Travelers' bulletin boards are a particularly useful tool. Travelers from all walks of life form online communities and offer their two cents on anything from the best pancake breakfast in Boise to an opinion on whether or not that new hotel in Atlanta is overpriced.

Got a question? Just post it to the right board/site/group in the ether and, most likely, you'll get at least a few responses, often within just a few hours.

Virtual Tourist (www.virtualtourist.com) has more than 700,000 members posting threads about anything from the best cafes in Brooklyn to cheap lodging in Crimea. For foodies, **Chowhound** (www.chowhound.com) is an invaluable resource for all things food-related. With so many people posting so many notes on so many topics, these forums can seem overwhelming at first, but once you get used to 'em (hint: use the search box), they become a traveler's best friend.

Here are a few of our favorite online trip-planning resources:

- **Speed Traps** (www.speedtrap.org)
- **Gas Prices** (www.gasbuddy.com, www.gaspricewatch.com)
- **Maps** (www.mapquest.com, www.google.com/maps)
- **Subway Navigator** (www.subwaynavigator.com)
- **Time and Date** (www.timeanddate.com)
- **Travel Warnings** (http://travel.state.gov)
- **Visa ATM Locator** (www.visa.com)
- **Weather** (www.intellicast.com, www.weather.com)

Travel blogs are also great for advance scouting of cities, hotels, restaurants, and so on. Some of our favorites include:

- www.gridskipper.com
- www.salon.com/wanderlust
- www.travelblog.com
- www.travelblog.org
- www.worldhum.com
- www.writtenroad.com

For Travelers with Special Interests or Needs

Student Travelers

A valid student ID will often qualify students for discounts on airfare, accommodations, entry to museums, cultural events, movies, and more. Students planning to hit the road might want to check in with **STA Travel** (☎ **800/781-4040** in North America; www.sta.com or www.statravel.com), the biggest student travel agency in the world.

Single Travelers

Solo travelers can have a grand old time on the road. Don't feel weird about hitting the town on your own—it'll give you an exhilarating sense of freedom, and you might stumble into adventures that never would have happened if you'd just stayed at the hotel reading a book.

Remember that most natives are friendly and curious about travelers coming through their town, and they're often even more likely to strike up a conversation with you if you're by yourself. One exceedingly common pitfall of traveling for too long on your own, however, is that when you do finally interact with people, you're so relieved for the human contact that you tend to talk too much. Don't let this happen to you—you'll come off as a crazy person, even if you're not!

TravelChums (☎ **212/787-2621**; www.travelchums.com) is an Internet-only travel-companion matching service with elements of an online personals-type site, hosted by the respected New York–based Shaw Guides travel service. The Single Gourmet Club (www.singlegourmet.com/chapters.php) is an international social, dining, and travel club for singles of all ages, with club chapters in 21 cities in the U.S. and Canada. Annual membership fees vary from city to city.

Many reputable tour companies like Singles Travel International (☎ 877/765-6874; www.singlestravelintl.com) and Backroads (☎ 800/462-2848; www.backroads.com) offer singles-only trips. For more information, check out Eleanor Berman's latest edition of *Traveling Solo: Advice and Ideas for More Than 250 Great Vacations* (Globe Pequot), a guide with advice on traveling alone, either solo or as part of a group tour.

Travelers with Disabilities

Many travel agencies offer customized tours and itineraries for travelers with disabilities. Flying Wheels Travel (☎ 507/451-5005; www.flyingwheelstravel.com) offers escorted tours and cruises that emphasize sports and private tours in minivans with lifts. Access-Able Travel Source (☎ 303/232-2979; www.access-able.com) offers extensive access information and advice for traveling around the world with disabilities. Accessible Journeys (☎ 800/846-4537 or 610/521-0339; www.disabilitytravel.com) caters specifically to slow walkers and wheelchair travelers and their families and friends.

Avis has an "Avis Access" program that offers such services as a dedicated 24-hour toll-free number (☎ 888/879-4273) for customers with special travel needs; special car features such as swivel seats, spinner knobs, and hand controls; and accessible bus service.

Organizations that offer assistance to disabled travelers include MossRehab (www.mossresourcenet.org), which provides a library of accessible-travel resources online; the American Foundation for the Blind (AFB) (☎ 800/232-5463; www.afb.org), a referral resource for the blind or visually impaired that includes information on traveling with Seeing Eye dogs; and SATH (Society for Accessible Travel & Hospitality) (☎ 212/447-7284; www.sath.org; annual membership fees: $45 adults, $30 seniors and students), which offers a wealth of travel resources for all types of disabilities and recommendations on destinations, access guides, travel agents, tour operators, vehicle rentals, and companion services.

For more information specifically targeted to travelers with disabilities, the community website iCan (www.icanonline.net/channels/travel) has destination guides and several regular columns on accessible travel. Also check out the quarterly magazine *Emerging Horizons* (www.emerging horizons.com; $14.95 per year, $19.95 outside the U.S.); and *Open World* magazine, published by SATH (see above; subscription: $13 per year, $21 outside the U.S.).

Gay & Lesbian Travelers

In the U.S., metropolitan areas seem to have more gay bars and clubs than more remote or suburban areas—we've recommended a few spots to hit in most of the roadtrips listed in this book. The International Gay and Lesbian Travel Association (IGLTA) (☎ 800/448-8550 or 954/776-2626; www.iglta.org) is the trade association for the gay and lesbian travel industry, and offers an online directory of gay- and lesbian-friendly travel businesses; go to their website and click on "Members."

Gay.com Travel (☎ 800/929-2268 or 415/644-8044; www.gay.com/travel or www.outandabout.com) is an excellent online successor to the popular *Out & About* print magazine. It provides regularly updated information about gay-owned, gay-oriented, and gay-friendly lodging, dining, sightseeing, nightlife, and shopping establishments in every important destination worldwide. It also offers trip-planning information for gay and lesbian travelers for more than 50 destinations, along various themes, ranging from Sex & Travel to Vacations for Couples.

The following travel guides are available at many bookstores, or you can order them from any online bookseller: *Spartacus International Gay Guide* (Bruno Gmünder Verlag; www.spartacusworld.com/gayguide) and *Odysseus: The International Gay Travel Planner* (Odysseus Enterprises Ltd.), both good, annual, English-language guidebooks focused on gay men; and the *Damron* guides (www.damron.com), with separate, annual books for gay men and lesbians.

Minority Travelers

Minority travelers in the U.S. shouldn't expect to encounter any problems—this is the 21st century, after all. And yet . . . it's always a good idea to check what the buzz is on various travel message boards and Internet groups.

On the Net, there are a number of helpful travel sites for African-American travelers in particular: **Black Travel Online** (www.blacktravelonline.com) posts news on upcoming events and includes links to articles and travel-booking sites.

Then there are the following collections and guides: *Go Girl: The Black Woman's Guide to Travel & Adventure* (Eighth Mountain Press), a compilation of travel essays by writers including Jill Nelson and Audrey Lorde, with some practical information and trip-planning advice; *Travel and Enjoy Magazine* (☎ 866/266-6211; www.travelandenjoy.com; subscription: $38 per year), which focuses on discounts and destination reviews; and the more narrative *Pathfinders Magazine* (☎ 877/977-PATH; www.pathfinderstravel.com; subscription: $15 per year), which includes articles on everything from Rio de Janeiro to Ghana as well as information on upcoming ski, diving, golf, and tennis trips.

Eco-Tourists

The **International Ecotourism Society** (TIES) defines eco-tourism as "responsible travel to natural areas that conserves the environment and improves the well-being

---

Frommers.com: The Complete Travel Resource

For an excellent travel-planning resource, we highly recommend **Frommers.com** (www.frommers.com), voted Best Travel Site by *PC Magazine*. We're a little biased, of course, but we guarantee that you'll find the travel tips, reviews, monthly vacation giveaways, bookstore, and online-booking capabilities thoroughly indispensable. Among the special features are our popular Destinations section, where you'll get expert travel tips, hotel and dining recommendations, and advice on the sights to see for more than 3,500 destinations around the globe; the Frommers.com Newsletter, with the latest deals, travel trends, and money-saving secrets; our Community area featuring Message Boards, where Frommer's readers post queries and share advice (sometimes even our authors show up to answer questions); and our Photo Center, where you can post and share vacation tips. When your research is finished, the Online Reservations System (www.frommers.com/book_a_trip) takes you to Frommer's preferred online partners for booking your vacation at affordable prices.

of local people." You can find eco-friendly travel tips, statistics, and touring companies and associations—listed by destination under "Travel Choice"—at the TIES website, **www.ecotourism.org**. If you're leaning more on the green side of things, pay a visit to **www.responsibletravel. com** (whose motto is "holidays that give the world a break"), a UK-based site that books travel all over the world. **Ecotravel. com** is part online magazine and part eco-directory that lets you search for touring companies in several categories (water-based, land-based, spiritually oriented, and so on). Also check out **Conservation International** (www.conservation.org)— which, with *National Geographic Traveler*, annually presents World Legacy Awards (www.wlaward.org) to those travel tour operators, businesses, organizations, and places that have made a significant contribution to sustainable tourism.

Before You Leave: The Checklist!

Here are a few things you might want to do before you walk out the door to ensure to the most efficient and drama-free roadtrip.

→ Do need to buy anything special, like theater tickets, in advance?

→ How's the weather? Is it 100°F in Houston? Is it sleeting in Boston? Pack accordingly.

→ Did you check to make sure all of your favorite hot spots and tourist destinations are open on the days that you'll be in town? Does that excellent little BBQ shack 300 miles outside of Kansas City only serve brisket on Tuesdays from 1 to 1:15 p.m.? Is Old Faithful erupting as faithfully as ever? You never know!

→ Did you find out your daily ATM withdrawal limit? Do you have your credit card PIN numbers? If you have a five- or six-digit PIN, did you obtain a four-digit number from your bank?

→ Do you have the credit card you used to reserve your hotel room/car rental, and so on? (Along with your printed confirmation, you often need to show them the credit card you used to make the reservation).

→ If you bought traveler's checks, have you recorded the check numbers, and stored the documentation separately from the checks?

→ Did you pack your camera, an extra set of batteries, and enough film/ memory?

→ Did you remember to pack battery chargers for your cellphone/laptop/iPod?

→ Did you bring your ID and any other cards that could entitle you to discounts (AAA, frequent flier, student ID cards)?

→ Did you bring emergency drug prescriptions and extra glasses and/or contact lenses? (See "Your Portable Medicine Cabinet," p. 21.)

→ Did you leave a copy of your itinerary with someone at home?

→ If you're bringing a cellphone, did you check with your wireless provider to make sure it can make/receive calls in the areas of the country you're traveling too? Will there be any extra fees? What about text messaging?

As You Head out the Door . . .

The Most Important Planning You'll Do:

○ Plan to spend at least part of your trip doing stuff that's not on your plan.

○ Plan to meet locals. One of the easiest ways to learn about a place is to spend time with its people.

○ Plan to take pictures, but not too many. Live in the moment and enjoy your present as much as possible.

○ Plan to eat something weird.

○ Plan to hit the road again!

We'll see you out there. Home safe!

Festival Season in the Northeast and Mid-Atlantic

Text & Photos by Dara Bramson

Give the credit to King Louis I of Bavaria. He and the missus put together a horse race to celebrate their marriage in October of 1810. The event went so well it became an annual event called Oktoberfest and inspired countless beer-fueled food and drink festivals around the world. Here in the U.S., festivals have grown, mushroomed, blossomed, and . . . sand castled? From music to wine to Gay Pride, give us a theme and we'll show you how to party.

Come summertime the Northeast and Mid-Atlantic regions turn into a festival hot spot. When the weather warms up, most folks in the chillier regions can't wait to get out of hibernation. Obvious destinations like New York City will draw any hipster within a reasonable drive, but plenty of little-known festivals are equally enjoyable—even if you won't see as many skinny jeans, Mohawks, or tattoos.

Case in point: I was ready to ditch the Vintage Virginia Wine Festival after an hour-long trek on the Metro from DC, plus a wait at the station, plus a 20-minute ride on a big yellow school bus. That is, until the bus pulled into a stunning mountain clearing where thousands of people lounged on blankets or danced with abandon, while sampling tasty, free-with-the-price-of-admission wine. In short, just because it's not in *Spin,* doesn't mean it's not a kickass event.

Festivals are a boon to those of us who love to roadtrip, but lack time, money, or both. When you absolutely *have* to bug out, and you do not have 2 weeks or access to a car, there's still a way to blow off some steam: head to a place where there will be thousands of others like you for a long weekend: whether you're standing shoulder-to-shoulder and screaming, or donning your best drag (or both!).

Though festival activities can be the bulk of your journey, in most of these cream-of-the-crop cities and regions a little sightseeing (and side partying) is always at hand, and if you know where to look, also won't blow your budget. If you've been thinking about a visit to a big city, a roadtrip to a festival or event is a good way to explore the place in a reasonable chunk, not to mention that you'll probably run into other kindred spirits far from home (both locals and other sojourners) and have people to hang out with.

With reasonable and reliable public transportation, the Northeast and Mid-Atlantic are parts of the country you can successfully navigate without a car (in fact, if you are arriving by car, it's frequently best to park it as soon as you arrive). Trains and buses can be a great alternative to appointing DDs or paying through the nose for gasoline. Whether you only have a weekend, or you have time to string a couple of festivals together over a week or two, grab some friends, a camera, and go!

For the sake of logic, we're starting at the northernmost point of the journey (New York City) and heading south (to some cool fests in Baltimore, DC, and Virginia) then hanging a right into West Virginia and Tennessee for some serious partying and music at the All Good Music Festival and Bonnaroo.

You could very well hit every one of these festivals (and a long, strange trip it would be . . .) but this section of the book, more than all the others, is designed to be sectional, as it were, with segments you can plug-and-play completely on their own.

And we hope you will!

Let's get this party started . . .

Festival Season Roadtrip

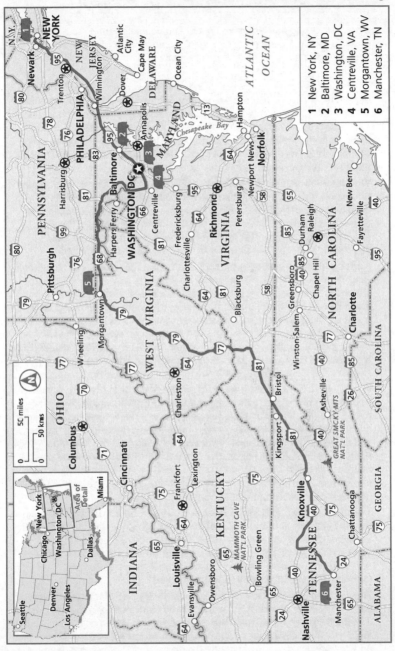

1 New York, NY
2 Baltimore, MD
3 Washington, DC
4 Centreville, VA
5 Morgantown, WV
6 Manchester, TN

Some Famous Festivals, Past & Present

Once the festival bug has bitten, you might find yourself wanting to travel ever farther afield for bigger and more outrageous gatherings. While the Dead is . . . well, dead, there are still some world-class festivals on this continent and others to satisfy your wanderlust.

➡ The largest performing arts festival in the world (with some 150,000 attendees in recent years) is the **Glastonbury Festival,** held on a 900-acre farm in England's enchanted Vale of Avalon. The festival has been around since 1970, when attendance was 1,500 and the £1 price of admission included free milk from the farm. Recent performers have included the White Stripes, Coldplay, and The Killers. The next one is set for June 22 to 24, 2007; **www. glastonburyfestivals.co.uk.**

➡ **Woodstock** was held at a 600-acre dairy farm in New York in 1969, during the "hippie era." Over 500,000 people showed up for performances by legends like Crosby, Stills, Nash & Young, Jimi Hendrix, Janis Joplin, The Grateful Dead, Jefferson Airplane, Santana, and The Who. On the site today is the brand-new **Bethel Woods Center for the Arts** (☎ 866/ 781-2922), a concert venue with rock, pop, and jazz performances.

➡ **Burning Man** is a weeklong art and community-based festival in the Black Rock Desert of Nevada. It's known for an eccentric array of attractions (topless mass bike rides, effigy burning, bars on wheels), elaborate art setups, and a slew of fascinating people. The attendance tops 35,000 and pretty much anything goes except for cash transactions (most everything here— from drinks to dance halls—is included in the entry fee). And, oh yeah, there's a giant burning man. Entry fees run from $195 to $280, though it's also possible to volunteer to work in exchange for attending. It'll be held August 27 to September 3, 2007; **www.burningman.com.**

➡ Head Down Under to South Australia, where Adelaide is home to Australia's largest performing arts festival, the **Adelaide Festival,** which takes place over 3 weeks in March in even-numbered years. The festival includes literary and visual arts as well as dance, opera, classical music, jazz, cabaret, and comedy. The festival includes a Writers' Week and the **Adelaide Fringe Festival.** In February or March, the 3-day **WOMADelaide Festival** of world music takes place. Crowds of 60,000 or more turn up to watch Australian and international artists. For more information, visit **www.adelaidefestival. org.au** and **www.womadelaide.com.au.**

➡ The **Great American Beer Festival** is the largest beer festival in the country, held annually in Denver, CO (we pass through Denver in the "Cool in the Midwest" roadtrip starting on p. 424). Over 41,000 people attended in 2006. In 2005, over 1,500 beers were on tap—the world record for most beers tapped at once. The next one is October 11 to 13, 2007 at the Colorado Convention Center; **www.beertown.org.**

➡ The first official **Mardi Gras** was held in 1838. It's one of the most rowdy community-wide parties in the world and has survived even the ravages of Katrina (and you'd be spending your roadtrip dollars to help rebuild the city!). Mardi Gras (that's French for Fat Tuesday) falls on the day before Ash Wednesday, so people can get their partying in before Lent. **www. mardigrasneworleans.com.**

Superlatives: The Highs & Lows

➡ **Best place not to shower for 4 consecutive days: Bonnaroo Music & Arts Festival** in Manchester, TN. Nearly 100,000 music-obsessed hippies aren't showering for the half-week fest, so why should you? See p. 103.

➡ **Best place to see wine-happy people stumble off a bus:** The **Vintage Virginia Wine Festival** in Centreville offers round-trip transportation from the nearest Metro stop. Waiting for the bus itself is entertainment enough. *Note:* Beware of flying wine bottles. See p. 87.

➡ **Worst place to get pulled over: Manchester, TN,** and **Masontown, WV,** host two of the biggest hippie fests around. Even if you don't have drugs on you, the cop will assume that you want drugs, or are on drugs. (Honestly, Mom, we don't! We aren't!) See p. 103 and 99.

➡ **Best city to get in a (verbal!) bar fight:** Happy Hour is huge among political professionals in Washington, DC, but everyone looks the same so it's impossible to tell who the person next to you voted for. See p. 96.

➡ **Best city to re-create** *Super Size Me:* The city beside the home of the **All Good Music Festival,** Masontown, WV, is one of the smallest cities in the country, yet it boats over 15 different fast-food chain restaurants. See p. 99.

➡ **Worst hotel for a family vacation: The Gershwin Hotel** in New York City is smack between an S&M club and the Sex Museum. Not that there's anything wrong with that. Just not with the 'rents. Eww. See p. 62.

➡ **Best place to dress up as a denizen of the deep on Memorial Day:** The **Mermaid Parade,** on Coney Island in New York City, is a costumed tribute to the long-forgotten Mardi Gras celebrations that were held there in the early 1900s. See p. 50.

➡ **Best place to groove to the (incessant) beat: Starscape** in Baltimore, MD, is among the top electronic music festivals in the United States. There's no shortage of thumping beats at the 6pm to 6am event. See p. 72.

➡ **Best Place to see undraped female parts:** It's a toss up between Bonnaroo Music & Arts Festival in Manchester, TN, and the Mermaid Parade in Coney Island, NY. There's no shortage of boobies at either, though you have to be alert for cleverly camouflaged chests. See p. 103 and 50.

➡ **Best giveaways that would typically be uncomfortable to receive on a street corner:** At the **Capital Pride Street Festival** in Washington, DC, volunteers hand out flavored condoms and dental dams (and candy!), among other sex-friendly paraphernalia. See p. 85.

➡ **Worst festival to attend if you have an allergy to Aqua Net: HonFest** in Baltimore, MD, attracts over 20,000 people, a scary percentage of whom are dressed as self-described "Hons": "Sixties-era women with beehive hairdos, blue-eye-shadow, spandex pants, and something, anything leopard print." See p. 73.

➡ **Best place to learn drug jargon (not that we ever used any of it, Mom!):** The **All Good Music Festival** in Masontown, WV, played host to nearly 10,000 hippies in 2006. Heaven for law enforcement—if they had access. See p. 99.

Just the Facts

Trip in a Box

....

Note that in this chapter you'll also find "Festival in a Box" with the essential information on each gathering in each section.

States   New York; Maryland; Washington, DC; Virginia; West Virginia; Tennessee.

Trip Time   Certain festivals last as long as 1 week, while others may only be a day-long event.

Hitting the Highlights   While some festival dates overlapped during 2006 (it's inevitable once the good weather hits and the different towns and industries schedule their annual events), season, dates, and locations are always subject to change. Dates are posted as far as a year in advance on event websites, so you can start planning your weekends and conjoined festivals months in advance. Generally, it shouldn't be too hard to hit multiple events.

When to Go   As mentioned above, most of the festival fun takes place in summer, though fall festivals extend the tourist season in some destinations. Not coincidentally, the timing is especially good for students and people with, you know, day jobs.

The Money Part

A handful of the festivals are fairly inexpensive, including some that are free. Several events require pre-purchased tickets, though I think the paycheck sacrifice is worth it. Many festivals offer discount rates for groups, pre-registration, or members of affiliated organizations. Gas, that perennial nemesis, will be a major cost factor in any roadtrip. The Northeast has efficient, economical city-to-city transportation, however, so a carless (as opposed to careless) roadtrip for Northeast festivals is not impossible (see "Transportation," below)— plus you'll save a ton on parking. Most stops are in or near big cities, so prices will be a little inflated. That said, major urban centers also offer the most economic diversity— usually there's a budget alternative for just about any need.

ACCOMMODATIONS

The longer, pricier festivals typically include accommodations (even if it's just a tent

space), and that's usually the most cost-effective way to sleep. A couple of hundred dollars extra on a festival ticket is much less than you'd spend on a weekend of big city hotels. Festivals like Bonnaroo and All Good Music don't require additional cash for sleeping, though I recommend investing in a sturdy, waterproof tent and a comfy sleeping bag and pillow. If you've got a crew to split expenses with, renting an RV may be the way to go; many people do this at the music festivals. (For information on renting RVs, and driving them, we recommend the spiritual granddaddy of this book: Frommer's *Exploring America by RV*, by Harry Basch & Shirley Slater, which is filled with good information and suggestions for trips.)

More formal lodging arrangements in the cities run from quite spartan to super swanky. Fortunately, most cities have hostels near the events. Even in upscale places like New York and DC, you can find a hostel room for less than $50 a night. If you're on the road with friends, consider going in together on a quad, suite or adjoining rooms.

TRANSPORTATION

Try to use public transportation whenever possible. The Northeast is not Wyoming, so we're not talking 12 Greyhound transfers over 4 days here (the exceptions are the music festivals in Tennessee and West Virginia). We'll go into more detail about getting there in their specific sections.

By Bus

Several companies operate daily, affordable service between the large and small cities in the Northeast. I booked several last-minute tickets between New York, Baltimore, and DC easily and fairly cheaply.

A New York to DC bus ride takes about 4 hours (catch an express, not a local!) and can cost in the range of $55 to $75 round-trip on a Greyhound or Peter Pan bus depending on whether you use any discounts or promotional fares. Boston, Philadelphia, and surrounding areas also have good coverage to and from each other.

Washington Deluxe (☎ **866/287-6932;** www.washny.com) runs between New York, Brooklyn, and DC. Pick-up and drop-off spots are usually at landmarks near major subway stops, such as Penn Station in New York or Union Station in DC. The various Chinatowns offer a lot of service at the lowest prices (sometimes as low as $35 for a round-trip between New York and DC), though friends of ours who have used the services have had complaints about the comfort of the ride, and the condition of the buses. Visit www.staticleap.com/chinatownbus for a complete list of "Chinatown buses."

Here are the toll-free numbers and websites of the major lines

○ **Greyhound** (☎ 800/231-2222; www.greyhound.com)

○ **Trailways** (☎ 703/691-3052; www.trailways.com)

○ **Peter Pan** (☎ 800/343-9999; www.peterpanbus.com)

By Train

Amtrak (☎ **800/USA-RAIL;** www.amtrak.com) is another, more luxurious, city-to-city option. Trains are more like a plane plus legroom and minus seatbelts than they are like Greyhound buses. They also offer food and (non-disgusting) bathrooms.

On the East Coast, service runs from Miami all the way up to Boston, hitting just about every point in between. You can take regular commuter service (least expensive); Metroliner (more expensive, reserved seating); or Acela service (very fast, *very* expensive). Students are eligible for discounts, as are groups of three to six. A one-way regular fare from DC to New York runs about $60 before discounts (keep an eye out for seasonal sales and offers for companion tickets).

Getting Around in the Cities

Within Northeast cities, public transit is wide-ranging and cheap. For example, Washington, DC's Metro runs between $1.35 and $3.90 per ride, depending on the distance you're traveling. New York City's subway is $2.00 per ride to go anywhere (or you can buy various passes for more extensive travel). Specifics on public transit are in each city section.

For getting to and from the airport (if you're flying in or out of wherever you're headed for), **Super Shuttle** (☎ **800/ BLUEVAN;** www.supershuttle.com) operates in most major US cities. One-way fares between New York airports and Manhattan can run as low as $13, compared to the $45 flat taxi rate (or you can take the AirTrain from Manhattan to Newark, which is a great deal and convenient, or the AirTrain from Manhattan to JFK, which is not a

Go Ask Alice . . .

As you attend many of these festivals (particularly the music ones), you might notice that there are people taking drugs. Since that's been going on pretty much since music festivals were invented, it shouldn't come as any great surprise. We are not going to go all parental on your ass and tell you to eschew all mind-altering substances (for all we know, you might not partake in anything anyway). That's your decision. What we *strongly* suggest is that you make an informed decision and be responsible for your behavior: Check out the laws regarding possession and sale of controlled substances, carrying open containers of alcohol, and the penalties in each jurisdiction. Then ask yourself: Is it worth it? Whether it's a desk-appearance ticket that'll cost you a few hundred bucks or a lengthy, expensive trial that will screw your future career, use your damn head. Each year, people get it really, really wrong at festivals and end up assaulted, injured, hospitalized, or dead (or doing significant or fatal damage to someone else) because they seem to think that nothing can go wrong when they're at a party. So know what you're eating and drinking, who you're doing it with, who's got your back, and who's driving home. We've never thought puking, passing out, or requiring IV fluids was an essential part of having a good time at a show (we need our wits and reflexes about us to avoid the pit and the showoff crowd surfers and to protect our spots at the stage).

—The Editor

great deal or convenient). By regular public transit (bus, subway, light rail, or Metro, which you can do in New York, Baltimore, and Washington), the trips run $2 to $7.

FOOD

Most of these stops are in or near major cities, so everything from dirt-cheap to über-posh is on hand. It should be easy to track down a decent, non-fast food meal for under $10 (except in self-contained or remote festivals/fairs). Consider light grocery shopping if you'll be somewhere for a while. Food at the festivals is frequently rather pricy for its captive audience, but you won't go hungry. For day-long festivals, consider bringing your own snacks. Stuffing a sandwich, fruit, and chips in your bag beats dropping $5 on a limp hot dog.

OTHER TRIP-SPECIFIC EXPENSES

Not every festival is all-inclusive: Some charge extra for specific events within their confines. The JVC Jazz Festival in New York, for example, offers events with admission prices from free entry to $100 (and up!).

Another expense to consider if you're headed to an outdoor fest is a blanket (and a lounge chair if they're permitted). Either buy an inexpensive one at the local big box store, or bring a decrepit one from home that you can trash at the end of the trip. As mentioned above, if you're planning on camping out, a sturdy (and waterproof!) tent, and a decent sleeping bag (rather than a ratty old Girl Scout one or one with cartoon characters) is a great investment.

We'll also note that since most of the destinations on this trip are major cities, you can and should buy a city or state-specific guide if you're planning on spending more than a day or so on the ground. We're giving you the quick tour through most of these places on this trip, and you would do yourself a favor to do more in-depth research for a longer stay.

FESTIVAL SEASON

I mean really . . . cover all New York has to offer in 30 pages? It's hard enough in 300! Frommer's just happens to publish a whole lot of *great* guides to New York City, Maryland/Delaware, Virginia, and Washington, DC, among others, so, word to the wise . . . y'know.

Music & Mermaids in New York City

We're prejudiced, but we think New York City is a great place to visit any time, for just about any reason. We also know that if you're not from around here, it's a pretty big apple to bite into without a plan. One of the following festivals can be your entry point, and while you're here you can enjoy some of the . . . everything else that the city is famous for: food, partying, attitude, museums, landmarks, sports, you get the idea.

We'll give you the details about a famous festival in Manhattan and a couple over in Brooklyn, the sprawling, diverse borough that's two islands away from the mainland, and give you some favorites and advice on where to stay, eat, and party (and even take in a little culture). So grab your Metrocard, your tickets to the show, and your appetite for the hustle and bustle of the Naked City. (Eight million stories . . . more like 10 million now!)

We'll also advise you that if you're going to hang around for a few days, pick up a New York City–specific guidebook that goes into great detail on the neighborhoods, famous attractions, and other stuff we won't have time to cover here if we're going to make it all the way to the Deep South in one chapter.

One book we highly recommend (its author took another of the roadtrips in this book, "On the Trail of the First Americans") is *New York City, Free & Dirt Cheap,* by Ethan Wolff. (Say "thank you," Ethan!)

New York City Nuts & Bolts

Area Codes 212 and 646 are Manhattan area codes. 718 and 347 are assigned to the outer boroughs. The 917 area code is primarily assigned to cellphones. All calls between these area codes are local calls.

Business Hours In general, stores are open at least 10am to 6pm, with many places keeping later hours, and lots of things available 24/7. Banks are usually open Monday through Friday 9am to 5pm, with additional hours on Saturday mornings.

Doctors For non-emergencies, head to walk-in medical centers. DOCS at New York Healthcare (55 E. 34th St. between Park and Madison aves.; ☎ 212/252-6001) is open Monday through Thursday 8am to 8pm, Friday 8am to 7pm, Saturday 9am to 3pm, and Sunday 9am to 2pm. The NYU Downtown Hospital offers physician referrals (☎ **888/698-3362**).

Emergencies Dial ☎ **911** for fire, police, and ambulance. The Poison Control Center can be reached at ☎ 800/222-1222.

Internet The Times Square Visitors Center (☎ 212/768-1560) has computer terminals available daily from 8am to 8pm at 1560 Broadway, between 46th and 47th streets. In the heart of Times Square, at 234 W. 42nd St. between Seventh and Eighth avenues, you'll find the huge, first-outside-of-Europe **easyInternetcafé** (☎ 212/398-0775), which is equipped with 15-inch flatscreen monitors and a speedy T-3 connection. One buck will get you access; the amount of available time depends on how busy they are.

Libraries New York libraries include The New York Public Library on Fifth Avenue at 42nd Street (☎ 212/930-0830) and the mid-Manhattan branch at 455 Fifth Ave. at 40th Street (☎ 212/340-0833). Check the website for other branches, in just about every New York neighborhood: www.nypl.org. You can access the Internet for free, and even make a reservation to use a computer at a specific branch.

Liquor Laws The legal drinking age in New York is 21. Liquor and wine are sold only in licensed stores, which can be open 7 days a week. Wine and beer can be purchased in grocery stores and delis 24 hours a day, except Sunday before noon. Last call at most bars is 4am, although many close earlier.

Newspapers & Magazines There are three major daily newspapers: the *New York Times*, the *Daily News,* and the *New York Post*. Free weeklies available in newsboxes all over town and in lots of stores and bars include the venerable *Village Voice* (sponsor of the Siren Festival, p. 52) and *NYPress*. The glossy *Timeout New York* (not free, it costs $2.99) is a valuable resource not just for what's on, but for informed recommendations as to what's worth your time. For GLBT news and events, look for free publications *Gay City News, The Blade,* and bar magazines *GONYC* (lesbian) and *HX* (gay men).

Pharmacies Duane Reade (www.duanereade.com) has 24-hour pharmacies in midtown at 224 W. 57th Street, at Broadway (☎ 212/541-9708); on the Upper West Side at 2465 Broadway, at 91st Street (☎ 212/799-3172); and on the Upper East Side at 1279 Third Ave., at 74th Street (☎ 212/744-2668).

Police Dial ☎ 911 in an emergency; otherwise, call the NYPD headquarters at ☎ 646/610-5000 or 718/610-5000.

Taxes Sales tax is 8.625% on meals, most goods, and some services, excluding clothing and footwear items under $110. Hotel tax is 13.25% plus $2 per room per night (including sales tax). Parking garage tax is 18.25%.

Time For the local time, call ☎ 212/976-1616. New York City is on Eastern Standard Time (EST).

Weather Look in the upper-right corner of the front page of the *New York Times* or call ☎ 212/976-1212 for the current temperature and the next day's forecast. You can also check www.cnn.com/weather or www.weather.com.

All that Jazz: The JVC Festival

In 1984, JVC began sponsoring a string of jazz festivals that soon became among the most successful in the world. This is a Big Daddy, world-class festival that draws attendees from all over.

At venues throughout Manhattan, from small clubs to Carnegie Hall, artists like Ray Charles, B.B. King, Herbie Hancock, Earth, Wind & Fire, and Sting are just a few of the many musicians who have been a part of JVC over the years.

JVC Festival in a Box

Contact www.festivalproductions.net.

Dates June 18 to 30, 2007.

Hours Check the 2007 schedule website for times and dates of shows.

Location The JVC Jazz Festival holds its events in various venues throughout the city, from large concert halls to clubs, parks, schools, and galleries, which are generally easily accessible by public transit, if not bus or taxi.

Schedule There are over 60 events scattered throughout the city at about a dozen venues. In 2006, the lineup included various symphonies and orchestras, Hank Jones, Herbie Hancock, Chris Botti, Lizz Wright, and Etta James.

Tickets Some events were free, while those with charges ran from $15 into the hundreds. Five events were completely free, and six were $15 and under.

MORE NEW YORK JAZZ

Below are a just a few of the places you can soothe your jones for jazz in New York year-round; there are many more venues and jazz "nights" at some clubs, along with events everywhere from museums to churches (St. Peter's Church at 54th and Lexington celebrates a jazz Mass!). An excellent guide to who's where when in New York is the **New York City Jazz Club Bible** at http://bigapplejazz.com.

→ **Lenox Lounge** This beautifully renovated classic is a symbol of Harlem's current renaissance. The intimate, Art Deco–cool back room—complete with zebra stripes on the walls and built-in banquettes—hosts top-flight live jazz vocalists, trios, and quartets for a crowd that comes to listen and be wowed. Blues and R&B are the province of Thursday. The cover never goes higher than $15, which makes Lenox Lounge a good value to boot. There's a warm, cozy, and immensely popular bar up front. Good soul food is served. Well worth the trip uptown for those who want a genuine Harlem jazz experience. *288 Malcolm X Blvd. (Lenox Ave.; between 124th and 125th sts.). ☎ 212/427-0253. www.lenoxlounge.com. Subway: 2, 3 to 125th St.*

→ **St. Nick's Pub** ★ As unpretentious a club as you'll find, St. Nick's in Harlem's Sugar Hill district is the real deal, with live entertainment every night and never a cover. On Tuesday it's Oldies but Goodies provided by Sexy Charles and Poetry on the Hill, hosted by Chance & Lilah; all the other nights are devoted to jazz, straight up and rarely with a chaser. *773 St. Nicholas Ave. (at 149th St.). ☎ 212/283-9728. Subway: A, C, D, B to 145th St.*

→ **Smoke** ★★ A superstar in the New York jazz scene and the best place to hear it on the Upper West Side, Smoke is a welcome throwback to the informal, intimate clubs of the past—the kind of place that on most nights you can just walk in and experience solid jazz. And though it seats only 65, for no more than a $25 cover, Smoke still manages to attract big names like the Steve Turre Quartet, Ron Carter, Eddie Henderson, and John Hicks. Sunday through Thursday there is no cover and each night has a theme, including funk on Wednesday with the Hot Pants Funk Sextet, Latin jazz on Sunday, and my favorite, Hammond organ grooves on Tuesday with Mike LeDonne on the organ and the incomparable Eric Alexander on sax. There are three sets

JVC Playlist 2006

→ *A Sunday Kind of Love,* **Etta James,** "At Last," 1999

→ *Big Lie, Small World,* **Sting,** "Brand New Day," 1999

→ *Cruisin',* **Smokey Robinson,** "Motown Legends," 1995

→ *Go Underground,* **B.B. King,** "Indianola Mississippi Seeds," 1989

→ *Harlequin Tears,* **Toshiko Akiyoshi,** "Desert Lady/Fantasy," 1994

→ *When Love Comes To Town,* **Herbie Hancock feat. Jonny Lang and Joss Stone,** "Possibilities," 2005

→ *Georgia On My Mind,* **Ray Charles,** "Standards," 1998

nightly and a very popular Happy Hour. *2751 Broadway (between 105th & 106th sts.).* ☎ *212/864-6662. www.smokejazz.com. Subway: 1 to 103rd St.*

→ **The Village Vanguard** ★★ What CBGB is (or was . . .) to rock, The Village Vanguard is to jazz. One look at the photos on the walls will show you who's been through since 1935, from Coltrane, Miles, and Monk to recent appearances by Bill Charlap and Roy Hargrove. Expect a mix of established names and high-quality local talent, including the Vanguard's own jazz orchestra on Monday nights. The sound is great, but sightlines aren't, so come early for a front table. If you are looking for serious jazz, this is the place. *178 Seventh Ave. South (just below 11th St.).* ☎ *212/255-4037. www. villagevanguard.net. Subway: 1, 2, 3, 9 to 14th St.*

And with that snapshot of one corner of the New York Scene, we'll head across the East River to our next festival.

The Mermaid Parade at Coney Island (Brooklyn)

From 1903 to 1954, Coney Island celebrated Mardi Gras. The Mermaid Parade pays homage to this forgotten celebration, as well as "the sand, the sea, the salt air and the beginning of summer, as well as the history and mythology of Coney Island, Coney Island pride, and artistic self-expression," at least according to the Mermaid Parade website. There's no shortage of artistic self-expression here—including plenty of bold folks expressing themselves with nudity.

Mermaid Festival in a Box

Contact   Call ☎ 718/372-5159 or visit www.mermaidparade.com.

Dates   Saturday, June 23, 2007 (the 25th anniversary!)

Directions   Take the D, Q, N, or F subway train to Stillwell Avenue (last stop).

Schedule   The event features a parade with dozens of eccentric floats, characters, and music starting Saturday morning, and segueing into other gatherings and events until into early the next day.

Who Can Participate   Crowds tend to be participatory, dressing for the event. Anyone can march, and many do.

Tickets   Free to watch or march in the parade! (The Mermaid Ball has an admission fee; see below.)

Weather   Rain or shine.

Playlist: Mermaid Parade 2006

→ *Allo Allo (Hello I Love You)*, **Les Sans Culottes,** "Fixation Orale," 2004

→ *Suavemente*, **Elvis Crespo,** "Suavemente," 1998

→ *Bop To The Top*, **The Gemz,** "Blue Is For Girls," 2006

→ *Mardi Gras Mambo*, **Zachary Richard,** "Mardi Gras Mambo," 1989

→ *Sky*, **Sonique,** "Hear My Cry," 2000

The Mermaid Parade and its surrounding events typically run from 10am until . . .

Each year, a different celebrity King Neptune and Queen Mermaid is invited to preside, riding in the Parade and "assisting in the opening of the Ocean for the summer swimming season by marching down the Beach from the Boardwalk, cutting through ribbons representing the seasons, and tossing fruit into the Atlantic to appease the Sea Gods." In the past, Talking Head David Byrne, Queen Latifah, Guardian Angel Curtis Sliwa, Moby, and David "Buster Poindexter" Johansen have ruled (and did they ever!).

The King and Queen lead off the parade in an ornate float. Who's in the parade? Why everyone! People from New York and beyond dress up in costumes (frequently with a nautical theme) and join the march.

The Parade is followed by the **Mermaid Parade Ball** (www.mermaidparadeball. com), a post-parade gathering (which does have an admission fee, ranging from $10 general admission to $50 VIP), featuring live music, raffles and performances by burlesque and sideshow acts.

ᴹᵀᵛ🙂 Step Right Up & Learn About Coney!

Climbing the staircase to the second floor of the historic building at 1208 Surf Avenue (near W. 12th Street) brings you to a small but fascinating museum of Coney Island memorabilia. The view from the windows overlooks landmark rides like the **Cyclone Rollercoaster,** the **Wonder Wheel,** and the **Parachute Jump.** The museum itself is full of antiques and fun relics of old rides. A visit is *certainly* worth the modest admission price of 99¢.

The Coney Island Museum is the only museum in the world dedicated to interpreting and preserving the history of Coney Island. Our collection is continually growing and a walk around the gallery will give you a sense of the importance of this place to the nation and the world.

Currently on display you can see: The Steeplechase Horse! The Boardwalk Rolling Chair! Funhouse Distortion Mirrors! Cases of great antique souvenirs! If you or your out of town friends are new to Brooklyn and/or amusement park history why not come and look at vintage bumping cars instead of just read about them? In summer, there are regular "Ask the Experts" lectures on Coney Island on Sunday afternoons.

For more information, call ☎ **718/372-5159**; or visit **www.coneyisland.com/ museum.shtml** The museum is open on Saturdays and Sundays, year round, from noon to 5pm. Visiting hours may be expanded during the summer season.

— The Coney Island Museum (www.coneyisland.com)

FESTIVAL SEASON

(You can also volunteer to work before/ during the event for free admission to the ball.)

Another Coney Island Event: The Siren Music Festival

This festival, sponsored by *The Village Voice,* and after six years now a summer tradition, offers a strange sight: the uniting of thousands of New York hipsters with Coney Island carnies. Over 150,000 people made their way to this leading indie rock event in 2006; the number seems to go up every year. From noon to 9pm, a seemingly endless parade of groups graces the stage. It's all-day, all-ages, and it's free, making it a must-go for any broke hipster.

The 2006 lineup included the Scissor Sisters, Art Brut, The Stills, Deadboy And The Elephantmen, and The MisShapes DJs among others. The trendy crowd, who likely are the first in line at MisShapes bashes, still deserve credit for roughing it through a hot NYC summer in honor of some of indie rock's latest idols.

Playlist: Siren Songs
2006
....

→ *Laura,* **Scissor Sisters,** "Scissor Sisters," 2004

→ *I Don't Want To Fall In Love,* **She Wants Revenge,** "She Wants Revenge," 2006

→ *Halo The Harpoon,* **The Stills,** "Without Feathers," 2006

→ *Monument,* **Dirty On Purpose,** "Hallelujah Sirens," 2006

→ *Time Will Cut You Down,* **Priestess,** "Hello Master," 2006

Siren Music Festival in a Box
....

Contact   www.villagevoice.com/siren.

Date   Saturday, July 21, 2007.

Hours   The event runs from noon to 9pm.

Location   Coney Island, NY.

Schedule   In 2006, the lineup included the Scissor Sisters, She Wants Revenge, Stars, Art Brut, The Stills, and DJs The MisShapes.

Tickets   Free!

Transportation   By subway, take the D, F, Q, or N train to Coney Island/Stillwell Avenue; or the F or Q train to W. 8th Street/NY Aquarium.

Weather   Rain or shine.

Another Part of the Borough: Brooklyn Hip-Hop Festival

In only its third year, this festival has attracted thousands of fans. Big names like Lupe Fiasco (recently featured with Kanye West on his new album) have signed on. And any festival that can hold a crowd for 8 hours in the rain (as it did in 2006) must be worthwhile.

The all-day outdoor event celebrates all aspects of the hip-hop music movement with various performers on a single outdoor

FESTIVAL SEASON

The Cyclone roller coaster overlooks Brooklyn's Siren Music Festival.

If You Want to Stick Around Coney Island

Along with the festivals (and museum) detailed above, there's a lot to do and see. Coney is better visited in the summer, so if you're heading out to the Siren Festival or the Mermaid Parade, take in some of these other activities. For more information, check the website, **www.coneyisland.com**.

→ **Burlesque on the Beach** runs every summer Friday at 10pm. The event resuscitates the good ol' "girly revues" of Coney Island's past. The event combines "old style burlesque, sideshow freaks, strange women, new vaudeville and toe tappin' music," as the website puts it. Check the website for the themes of upcoming shows.

→ Head to the **Coney Island Circus Sideshow** to see one of the last remaining genuine sideshows in the country. Freaks, wonders, and human curiosities are all part of the performance—just hope they don't choose you as a volunteer. Summer shows typically run Fridays from 2 to 8pm and Saturdays and Sundays from 1pm to 11pm. Tickets are $6.

→ The **Brooklyn Cyclones** (named for the famous wooden roller coaster at nearby Astroland), the New York Mets' A-level farm team, have their very own waterfront stadium at Coney Island. KeySpan Park sits right off the legendary boardwalk. What's more, with bargain-basement ticket prices (which topped out at $14 in 2006), this is a great, cheap way to see a game. The season runs June through September. For information, call ☎ 718/449-8497 or visit **www.brooklyncyclones.com**.

FESTIVAL SEASON

stage. Wes Jackson, president of a festival sponsor said the festival's mission is to "shine the light on the positive aspects of hip-hop culture." Though the day might wind up hot or rainy, fans so far have not let it compromise their festival experience.

Raingear, snacks and water are good things to stuff in your bag, but keep in mind that space is cramped and your foremost priority will be bouncing to the beats.

Brooklyn Hip-Hop Festival in a Box

Contact   www.brooklynbodega.com/aboutthebhf.htm.

Date   June 23, 2007.

Location   Tobacco Warehouse in DUMBO, Brooklyn.

Events   Music guests at the 2006 festival included Big Daddy Kane, Lupe Fiasco, Rhymefest, and Sleepy Brown.

Tickets   The festival is free, but you'll have to register ahead of time on the website for your tickets.

Transportation   The best way to get to the event is by subway. Take the A/C to High Street. Exit to Cadman Plaza West (CPW). Walk west, toward the BQE, down the hill; CPW turns into Old Fulton Street. Walk down the hill, take a right at Front Street. First left is Dock Street; entrance to Empire Fulton Ferry Park and the Tobacco Warehouse, is one block ahead on Water Street OR take the 2/3 to Clark Street . Exit to Clark/Henry Street. Walk west on Henry; take a right on Middagh Street and then a left on Cadman Plaza West/Old Fulton. (See above). OR take the F to York Street . Walk down York or Washington Street until you get to the waterfront.

Weather   Rain or shine.

Getting Around

Okay, now that we've sent you all over town, we're going to tell you how to do just that. Here's a hint: Use public transportation. The **Metropolitan Transit Authority** (**www.mta.nyc.ny.us**) is responsible for the majority of New York's public transportation. Their website has a comprehensive listing of schedules, fares, and routes.

BY CAR

My advice? Don't. Really. Don't. New York City drivers have a knack for ignoring federal, state, and local driving regulations. Being a pedestrian is already life-threatening; driving is worse. There are dozens of parking garages around the city and they all charge an arm and a leg for daily

Playlist: Brooklyn Beats 2006

→ *I'll Take You There,* **Big Daddy Kane,** "The Very Best of Big Daddy Kane," 2001

→ *Chicago-Rillas,* **Rhymefest,** "Blue Collar," 2006

→ *Too Much,* **Maya Azucena,** "Too Much," 2004

→ *The Storm,* **The Procussions,** "5 Sparrows for 2 Cents," 2006

→ *Good Times,* **Strange Fruit Project,** "The Healing," 2006

→ *Touch the Sky,* **Kanye West feat. Lupe Fiasco,** "Late Registration," 2005

DUMBO Is Not an Elephant

DUMBO stands for Down Under the Manhattan Bridge Overpass, another of the NYC acronyms along the lines of SoHo (South of Houston), Nolita (North of Little Italy), and Tribeca (Triangle Below Canal). Williamsburg (Brooklyn) is sometimes called Billburg, but not by anyone who actually lives there, unless they are a hipster using it ironically.

parking. You'll quickly discover, however, that paying that lump sum is preferable to sticking money in meters all day or—worst of all—paying to get your car back when it's towed. Garages start around $25 and go up to $45 (that's for a single *day*). If you must drive into town, check with your hotel to see if they have free or discounted parking.

BY BUS

Yellow curbs and blue and white signs with bus emblems will direct you to NYC bus stops. Some cities lure public bus customers by lowering prices, but NYC fares are the same as the subway. $2/ride. The only upside is that you can transfer to another bus or subway for free, within 2 hours, if you use your MetroCard. Bus stops are every couple of blocks near the right-side corner, in the direction of the traffic flow. Stops have schedules (which are really just rough approximations), or you can check the MTA website (www.mta. nyc.ny.us).

BY SUBWAY

Millions take the subway every day and it's usually the fastest way to travel around the city. You can get to almost every venue listed above by subway or bus. The subway (don't ever call it the Metro) runs 24 hours a day, every day, and the only drawback is having to stand during rush hour. Each ride is $2, but consider getting a pass (aka a MetroCard) if you plan on staying for a while. For $10, get six rides (buy 5, get 1 free). Like the bus, you can use your MetroCard to transfer from the subway to a bus for free, within 2 hours. You can also get unlimited ride cards for different time spans; 1 day unlimited is $7; 1 week unlimited is $24.

Most subway stations have automated machines to purchase cards by cash, debit, or credit cards. There are also plenty of

Word Up: New York Vocabulary

→ **chawklit** *noun*. A food, beverage, or candy flavor made out of cacao. *What flavor do you prefer; vanilla or chawklit?*

→ **daw** *noun*, *plural* **daws**. A moveable barrier that seals an entranceway. *Most people make sure to lock their daws at night.*

→ **hawba** *noun*. A body of water with a dock or port. *Last week we went to the hawba to look at the boats.*

→ **nyawk** *noun*. A state in the Northeast United States. *Albany is the capital of Nyawk.*

→ **peezapaula** *noun*. An Italian-style restaurant where they serve pizza. *It started raining before they got to the peezapaula.*

→ **yuma** *noun*. A comic amusement. *Comedians have to have a great sense of yuma. (See also: Trump, Donald, "yuuuge!")*

subways in short

A trusty subway map will be your friend in New York City, but here's a quick crash course in deciphering subway symbology:

4, 5, 6 trains run up and down the east side, and to the Bronx and Brooklyn. The **7** train runs from Times Square to Flushing, Queens.

1, 2, 3, A, C, E, F, B, D trains run up and down the west side and to the Bronx and Brooklyn. (The F, N/W, and D run to Coney Island.)

N, R, Q, W trains run diagonally cross town from east to west and under Seventh Avenue, and then out to Queens and Brooklyn.

S trains run between Times Square and Grand Central.

L trains run cross town on 14th St. between Eighth Avenue and Brooklyn.

This is just a fast and rough rundown, without details of express trains, which skip stops along the way.

personnel at stations who will answer questions, grudgingly, if needed. If they're not in the booths, look for the men and women in the red vests.

For more info, call ☎ **800/METRO-CARD** or 212/METROCARD Monday through Friday 7am to 11pm, Saturday and Sunday 9am to 5pm, or visit www.mta.nyc.ny.us/metrocard. Log on to www.mta.info for the latest schedule details. Pick up a free subway map from the **Times Square Visitors Center** (1560 Broadway, between 46th and 47th sts.), or ask for one at a station.

How Do You Get to Carnegie Hall?

These are the subway stops closest to these top attractions/neighborhoods:

→ American Museum of Natural History **B, C** to 81st Street
→ Brooklyn Bridge **4, 5, 6** to Brooklyn Bridge–City Hall
→ Carnegie Hall **N, R, W** to 57th Street.
→ Chinatown **6, J, M, Z, N, R, W** to Canal Street
→ Chrysler Building **4, 5, 6, 7, S** to Grand Central–42nd Street
→ Ellis Island **4, 5** to Bowling Green or **N, R** to Whitehall Street
→ Empire State Building **B, D, F, V, N, R, Q, W** to 34th Street–Herald Square
→ Grand Central Terminal **4, 5, 6, 7, S** to Grand Central–42nd Street
→ Greenwich Village **A, C, E, B, D, F, V** to West 4th Street
→ Guggenheim Museum **4, 5, 6** to 86th Street
→ Metropolitan Museum of Art **4, 5, 6** to 86th Street
→ Museum of Modern Art **E, V** to Fifth Avenue
→ Rockefeller Center **B, D, F, V** to 47–50th streets–Rockefeller Center
→ Staten Island Ferry **1** to South Ferry (first five cars)
→ The Cloisters **A** to 190th Street
→ Times Square **1, 2, 3, 7, N, R, W, S** to 42nd Street–Times Square
→ Wall Street **4, 5** to Wall Street or **N, R** to Rector Street
→ Yankee Stadium **4, B, D** to 161st River Avenue–Yankee Stadium

FESTIVAL SEASON

Manhattan Festivals

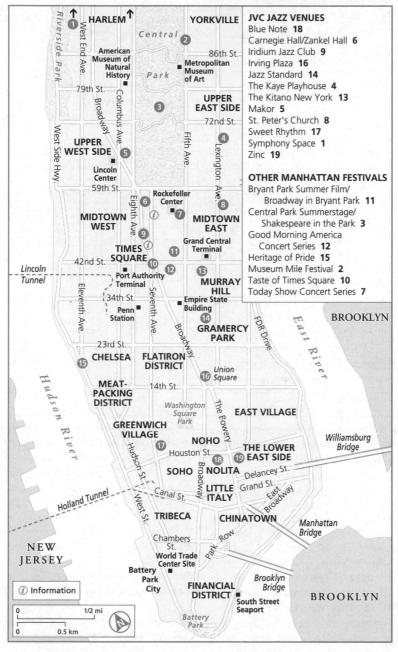

HARLEM

YORKVILLE

Riverside Park
West End Ave.

Central

American Museum of Natural History

Park

86th St.

Metropolitan Museum of Art

79th St.

Broadway

Columbus Ave.

UPPER EAST SIDE

72nd St.

UPPER WEST SIDE

West Side Hwy.

Lincoln Center

59th St.

Fifth Ave.

Lexington Ave.

Rockefeller Center

MIDTOWN WEST

Eighth Ave.

MIDTOWN EAST

Grand Central Terminal

TIMES SQUARE

42nd St.

Lincoln Tunnel

Port Authority Terminal

34th St.

Penn Station

Eleventh Ave.

Seventh Ave.

Broadway

MURRAY HILL

Empire State Building

GRAMERCY PARK

23rd St.

FDR Drive

BROOKLYN

East River

CHELSEA

FLATIRON DISTRICT

Union Square

MEAT-PACKING DISTRICT

14th St.

Washington Square Park

EAST VILLAGE

Hudson River

GREENWICH VILLAGE

NOHO

Houston St.

The Bowery

Williamsburg Bridge

SOHO

NOLITA

Delancey St.

THE LOWER EAST SIDE

Broadway

Hudson St.

West St.

Canal St.

LITTLE ITALY

Grand St.

East Broadway

Holland Tunnel

TRIBECA

CHINATOWN

Manhattan Bridge

Chambers St.

Park Row

NEW JERSEY

World Trade Center Site

Battery Park City

Brooklyn Bridge

BROOKLYN

FINANCIAL DISTRICT

South Street Seaport

Battery Park

ⓘ **Information**

0 — 1/2 mi
0 — 0.5 km

N

JVC JAZZ VENUES
Blue Note **18**
Carnegie Hall/Zankel Hall **6**
Iridium Jazz Club **9**
Irving Plaza **16**
Jazz Standard **14**
The Kaye Playhouse **4**
The Kitano New York **13**
Makor **5**
St. Peter's Church **8**
Sweet Rhythm **17**
Symphony Space **1**
Zinc **19**

OTHER MANHATTAN FESTIVALS
Bryant Park Summer Film/
  Broadway in Bryant Park **11**
Central Park Summerstage/
  Shakespeare in the Park **3**
Good Morning America
  Concert Series **12**
Heritage of Pride **15**
Museum Mile Festival **2**
Taste of Times Square **10**
Today Show Concert Series **7**

Harlem Festivals/Jazz

HARLEM JVC FESTIVAL VENUES
Schomburg Center for
  Research in Black Culture **5**
Smoke **2**
Studio Museum in Harlem **3**
Symphony Space **1**
OTHER JAZZ VENUES
Lenox Lounge **4**
St. Nick's Pub **6**

🚇 Subway stop

BY TAXI

At the end of a long night, even if you're only a couple blocks from home, taxis are good alternatives to walking in heels. The base fare is $2.50, plus 40¢ every ¹/₅ mile and 40¢ for every 2 minutes stopped in traffic. (At press time, the drivers had successfully lobbied for an increase in the fare for "waiting time.") Bridge and tunnel tolls are not included. There's also a $1 surcharge between 4 and 8pm and a 50¢ surcharge after 8pm and before 6am.

There's a 24-hour taxi hot line (☎ 212/ NYC-TAXI) for complaints and further information.

Remember the "Cross Street"

As I learned the hard way, addresses can be very tricky in New York. If you're going to 75 Third Ave., for example, you need to tell the driver you're going to Third Avenue and 11th St.; "11th St." aka "the cross street" means everything. There is some arcane methodology—a formula that can be applied to work out the cross street on your own—but it's rather complex to keep in your head. (Actually, it's also printed in the front of the phone book, but who wants to walk around with a phone book?)

So look at your destination on a map or call the place where you're going. They are used to people asking "what's the cross

Brooklyn Festivals

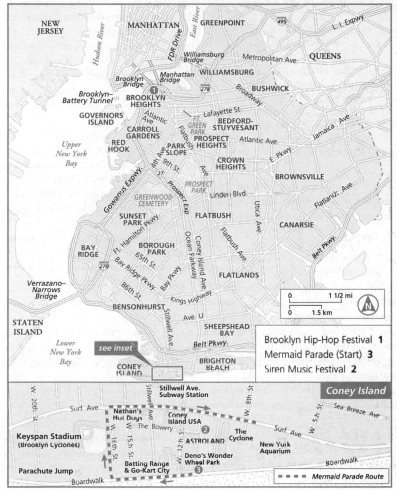

Brooklyn Hip-Hop Festival **1**
Mermaid Parade (Start) **3**
Siren Music Festival **2**

street?" When you get in the cab, tell the driver your cross streets ("43rd Street between 8th and 9th Avenues" for example), not the address (311 W. 43rd St.).

ON FOOT

Most people come home from New York having lost a couple of pounds. What's their secret? Walking. New York is a city of power walkers. Bring your sneakers and a

sense of direction. Map or no map, it's fairly easy to navigate the city if you know where you're going (especially above 14th St. in Manhattan, as the city is laid out in an easy-to-follow grid).

If you need directions, ask. New Yorkers are generally friendly and helpful if you stop them on the street. I'd even go so far as to say New Yorkers *love* to give directions,

A Free Bus in NYC?

FREE Use the free **Downtown Connection** to hop around various Financial District destinations, like Battery Park City, the World Financial Center, and the South Street Seaport. The buses run daily from 10am to 8pm. For schedules, call the **Downtown Alliance** at ☎ **212/566-6700,** or visit www. downtownny.com.

and you can often get into a detailed conversation with several strangers over the best route to any one place.

Sleeping

With all that festivity, you must be tired! So, where are you staying? And let's be realistic: People here pay thousands of dollars a month to live in closet-size apartments with four roommates. New York City is not the most broke-person-vacation-friendly city. But note that there are alternatives for those willing to make some sacrifices. If your budget limits you to under $100/night, you'll probably have to share a bathroom or shower. If you've never slept in the city before, plan to keep an open mind when it comes to what you think "small" is. Unless your rich parents are putting you up at the Waldorf-Astoria, don't bother to bring your jump rope along—even the hallways will be too narrow. A night on the sidewalks? Don't even think about it. Summer's a busy time in New York, and you have to look sharp for bargains, but they are there if you know where to find them.

HOSTELS

➔ **Hostelling International** You can't go wrong staying near Central Park. There's a subway near this hostel, the place is clean, and the staff is nice. Tons of restaurants and nightlife are within walking distance, too. You don't have to be a member of Hostelling International to stay here, but you get a slight discount if you are. *891 Amsterdam Ave. at West 103rd. Subway: 1 to 103rd St. ☎ 212/932-2300. www.hinewyork.org. Shared rooms start at $29/night. Amenities: Open 24 hr.; TV room; use of kitchen; sheets and towels included; cafe/bar; luggage storage; lockers.*

There are a few more private hostels (also known as "backpackers") in Manhattan, including the very centrally located **Big Apple Hostel** (☎ 212/302-2603; www.big applehostel.com) at 119 West 45th Street in the Theater District, with rates from $30 to $80 nightly.

Visit **www.hostels.com/en/us.ny.ny. html** for a fairly thorough listing of hostel-style accommodations and other super-cheap lodgings (complete with ratings and reviews).

CHEAP

Though rates vary widely, the various national chain hotels that have branches in the city can run as low as $89/night for a double if you get a good special. Some times of year (the winter holiday season especially), it's pretty hard to come by a deal at all. But in the summer, especially if you do your homework, and scout around for the best deals, you can manage a decent room (with its own bathroom!) for under $100. The rooms themselves are pretty standard, small and clean; there's often a free continental breakfast, or at least a 24-hour coffee/tea area. If you're just planning on using the room to rest, shower, and change, and don't feel the need to stay at a historic or quirky hostelry, there's nothing wrong with hitting Priceline or one of the other booking sites.

Some chains that offer low rates include **Best Western** (☎ 800/780-7234; www.

Taxi-Hailing

Here's how to grab a cab, if you're a cab-grabbing newbie: It's best to stand on the far corner when you're hailing a taxi so you can also signal drivers turning from the cross street when the light changes. Keep an eye out for the medallion lights on top of the taxis, which are lit in the middle when available (if they're lit on the edges, the cab is off-duty), and dark when in use. You can't take more than three passengers in a regular-size taxi (you can fit more in the minivan style), and the driver is required to take you to your destination in the five boroughs, including the airport.

bestwestern.com), with two Midtown locations and one at the South Street Seaport; **Howard Johnson** (☎ **800/446-4656;** www.hojo.com) on the Lower East Side; **Apple Core Hotels** (www.applecore hotels.com), which include the **Comfort Inn Midtown,** the **Ramada Inn Eastside,** a Red Roof, the **Super 8 Hotel Times Square,** and a La Quinta Inn (7 W. 32nd St.; ☎ **212/736-1600).** Other cheap choices to attempt are the **Days Hotel Midtown** (790 Eighth Ave. at 48th St.; ☎ **800/321-7460** or 212/581-7000; www. daysinn.com), or **Choice Hotels** (☎ **877/ 424-6423;** www.hotelchoice.com), which supervises **Comfort Inn, Quality Hotel,** and **Clarion Hotel** chains.

B&BS/APARTMENT RENTALS

There are also some B&B and private apartment rentals in the city, which may require a stay of more than 1 night. But if you're going to be in town for several days, and/or with a few friends, a furnished apartment might be the best value for you.

Several agencies can help you find rooms for as low as $90/night. Try **As You**

Like It (☎ **800/277-0413** or 212/695-3404; www.furnapts.com); **Abode Apartment Rentals** (☎ **800/835-8880** or 212/ 472-2000; www.abodenyc.com); **City Sonnet** (☎ **212/614-3034;** www.citysonnet. com); **Manhattan Lodgings** (☎ **212/ 677-7616;** www.manhattanlodgings.com); and **New York Habitat** (☎ **212/255-8018;** www.nyhabitat.com).

B&B and apartment rentals in the doable range, starting at $105, can be located through **Manhattan Getaways** (☎ **212/956-2010;** www.manhattanget aways.com). They'll require a 3-night minimum stay. Units through **A Hospitality Company** (☎ **800/987-1235** or 212/ 813-2244; www.hospitalityco.com) start at $139/night and $850/week.

Below are a few more non-chain hotel recommendations in various neighborhoods in Manhattan, from Downtown to Uptown in the "Doable" range if you want to stay in a place with a bit more personality or tradition.

Greenwich Village

➔**Larchmont Hotel** ★★ With extras like comfy cotton bathrobes, slippers, and ceiling fans, it's hard to complain about a shared bathroom—especially with rates this low. The hotel is clean and new. Make sure you book well in advance, however; 6 to 7 weeks to be safe. *27 W. 11th St. between 5th and 6th aves.* ☎ *212/989 9333. www. larchmonthotel.com. Single $70–$95; double $90–$125. Rates include continental breakfast. Subway: A, B, C, D, E, F, V to W. 4th St. (use 8th St. exit); F to 14th St. Amenities: Tour desk; limited room service; shared kitchen. In room: A/C, TV, hair dryer, safe, ceiling fan.*

Chelsea

➔**Chelsea Lodge** ★ You'll have to compromise on size in exchange for having your own bathroom and shower, but this place is well-kept, newly renovated, and in a great location. Plus you won't be subjected to

More NYC Fests! A Calendar of Events

There are so many summer events and festivals (both one-offs and annual affairs), as well as all-over-the-city street fairs every weekend, that you can pick and choose from celebrations of every kind and in every borough all summer long. Here are just a few of the most popular:

→ **New York City Summer Restaurant Week** ran from July 10 to July 14 and July 17 to July 21 in 2006. During these weeks (once in winter and once in summer each year), the top restaurants in New York City offer fixed-price, three-course meals. Lunch is $24.07 and dinner is $35. ☎ 212/484-1222. www.nycvisit.com.

→ The **Museum Mile Festival** will cram your full dose of cultural New York into just 1 day. In 2006, the event was held on June 13th from 6 to 9pm. "New York's biggest block party" goes down on Fifth Avenue between 82nd and 105th streets, a stretch that's home to the Museum of the City of New York, the Guggenheim Museum, and The Metropolitan Museum of Art, among others. All museum admissions are free for the day. **www. museummilefestival.org**.

→ **Heritage of Pride** is New York City's GLBT Pride celebration. A rally, marches, and festival are among the events in this weeklong celebration (though there are events throughout the month of June) culminating in a massive parade down Fifth Avenue on Sunday of Pride Week (Dyke March happens the day before). June 17 to June 24 is the date for Pride Week in 2007. Many events are free and there are tons of fun activities that run throughout the week. **www.hopinc.org**.

→ **Central Park Summer Stage** is an annual summer series featuring musicians and authors. In 2006, performers included Fiona Apple, Damien Rice, Sonya Kitchell, Damien Marley, Umphrey's McGee, Galactic, Ben Harper, Ani Difranco, Seu Jorge, and Bonnie Raitt. Many events are free, although more and more (and usually the star-studded

seeing your neighbors in towels. *318 W. 20th St. between 8th and 9th aves.* ☎ *800/373-1116 or 212/243-4499. www.chelsealodge.com. Single $95; double $110. Subway: A/C/E to 23rd St. Amenities: A/C; TV; wireless Internet; ceiling fan.*

→ **Colonial House Inn** ★★ If summer heat isn't your thing, consider this cozy inn, where the roof deck has a clothing-optional area. While the clientele is largely gay and lesbian (the building was the first home of the Gay Men's Heath Crisis), all are welcome. The charming four-story, 20-room walkup in the heart of Chelsea is an intimate find in a city where 30 floors is

puny. *318 W. 22nd St. between 8th and 9th aves.* ☎ *800/689-3779 or 212/243-9669. www. colonialhouseinn.com. Shared bathroom $80–$125; private bathroom $125–$140. Subway: A/C/E to 23rd St. Amenities: Free breakfast.*

Midtown

📺 **Best 🌑** → **Gershwin Hotel** ★★★ In a city of bland high-rises, you'll be drawn in by the shining horns that jut from the entrance of this funky hotel in the Flatiron District. It's clean and has great service, especially for the moderate price range. Plus the Museum of Sex and an S&M club are nearby. *7 E. 27th St. between 5th and* ones) are benefits concerts and require ticket purchases. **www.summer stage.org**.

→ The **HBO Bryant Park Summer Film Festival** is held Mondays on the lawn in Bryant Park, which is directly behind the main branch of the New York Public Library. Films (usually classics or New York–centric flicks) begin at dusk (between 8 and 9pm), and blankets and snacks are recommended. **www.bryantpark.org**.

→ **Celebrate Brooklyn** is nearing its 30th year. Dozens of musicians perform annually in a beautiful bandshell inside Prospect Park. There is a suggested donation of $3, although a handful of "benefit concerts" carry higher ticket costs. **www.celebratebrooklyn.org**.

→ **A Taste of Times Square** features both food and theatrical performance each June. Admission is free. There are stages for live music, and over 50 restaurants in the area participate. ☎ **212/768-1560;** www.timessquarenyc.org.

→ **Broadway in Bryant Park** is a free event held on select summer Thursdays at 12:30pm. The performances feature on- and off-Broadway stars singing the biggest hits from their shows. Several musicals are often combined. July 20, 2006, featured *Shout! The Mod Musical, The Phantom of the Opera, The Color Purple,* and *Wicked.* **www.bryantpark.org**.

→ The **Good Morning America Concert Series** is held Fridays at 7am throughout the summer. In 2006 the lineup included the Dixie Chicks, Prince, Mary J. Blige, The Pussycat Dolls, The Beach Boys, Pharrell, Kanye West, Christina Aguilera, and Lionel Richie. The free event is held in Bryant Park at 42nd Street and Sixth Avenue. **The Today Show** also boasts a free summer concert series on Fridays at 7am at Rockefeller Center (between 49th and 50th St. near 5th Ave.) but a 6am arrival is late if you want to see anything. Performers in recent summers have included Prince, Mary J. Blige, Pink, Nick Lachey, Pharrell and Jimmy Buffett.

Madison. ☎ *212/545-8000. www.gershwinhotel. com. Double $99–$189 (usually under $150); family room $189–$219. Extra person $10. Subway: N/R, 6 to 28th St. Amenities: A/C; TV; dataport; hair dryer; iron; bar; tour desk; Internet access.* **Note:** *Check website for discounts, 3rd-night-free specials, and other packages. Also ask about (much cheaper) dorm-style rooms.*

→**Thirty Thirty** ★ The space was once the home of the illustrious Danceteria night-club, Madonna's hangout in her early years in town. Now it's a reasonably priced, trendy hotel on the East Side in Midtown that's clean and a bit more spacious than the average New York closet with a bed.

There's no room service, but the city that never sleeps is not limited in the delivery department. *30 E. 30th St. between Madison and Park.* ☎ *800/497-6028 or 212/689-1900. www.thirtythirty-nyc.com. Double $115–$145; double with kitchenette $145–$195; quad $185– $245. Subway: 6 to 28th St. Amenities: A/C; TV; dataport; hair dryer; dry cleaning/laundry service.* **Note:** *Last minute deals and promos can run as low as $99; call or check the website.*

Harlem
→**The Bed and Breakfast Mont Morris** ★ If you want to experience authentic New York, spend a couple nights in Harlem.

Finding Event Info: Recommended Websites

Here are some reliable websites with opinionated recommendations of the best stuff in NYC in any given week.

➤ **www.freenyc.net.** If you're a fan of free fun, this site is a must. They call themselves "NYC's premier guide to quality free and cheap events." Check out nightlife, open bars, art, film, and community and fringe events.

➤ **www.nonsensenyc.com.** This website lists "independent art, weird events, strange happenings, unique parties, and senseless culture in New York City." You have to sign up for the e-mail list, but you'll be pleasantly surprised when you find tons to do in your e-mail box.

➤ **www.villagevoice.com.** This website has it all: The most trendy selections in music, film, arts, restaurants, clubs, bars . . . and all the content from the weekly paper *The Village Voice* (as well as online-only content).

➤ **www.nyctourist.com.** For hotel and general tourist information, log on to this website. You can buy tickets here for everything from Broadway shows to museums and sporting events.

Book well in advance, because there are only 2 (sharable) units. The area is safe and within walking distance of the lively 125th Street area, which itself is a quick ride on the A train (express) to Midtown. Sharable studios include a private bathroom, and the larger one has a kitchen. *56 W. 120th St. at Lenox Ave. ☎ 917/617-4354. www.mont morris.com. $99–$109 per night for 2 people $20 extra for additional guest. Subway: 2/3 to 116th St. Amenities: phone (with voicemail); wireless internet; A/C; hair-dryer; iron; ironing board; microwave; mini-fridge in smaller studio; full kitchen in larger studio. Continental breakfast at Settepani Bakery down the block.*

Eating

There are approximately 80 kajillion restaurants in New York City, and some of the world's finest (and most expensive) dining, as well as cheap cuisine, including ethnic styles found only in New York (and in their countries of origin). We are barely scratching the surface below, but these are all reliable recommendations. If you smell something heavenly wafting down the street, most places post a menu in the front

Surfing for the Best Rate

Before you start Googling "New York City hotels," look into these reservation services for some of the best rates: **Quikbook** (☎ 800/789-9887 or 212/779-7666; www.quikbook. com), **Hotel ConXions** (☎ 800/ 522-9991 or 212/840-8686; www. hotelconxions.com), and **Hotel Reservations Network** (☎ 800/ 715-7666; www.hoteldiscount.com). They aren't guaranteed to come up with rock bottom rates every time, but as you troll the net, if you spot a great rate, grab it!

window, so you can see if it's something you can afford. If not, there will be something just as interesting around the next corner.

SUPPLIES

There's a **Trader Joe's** (☎ 212/529-4612; www.traderjoes.com) at 142 East 14th St., near Union Square, open from 9am to

A Memorable B&B in Brooklyn

📺 Best ♥ **Akwaaba Mansion** ★★ is a marvelously refurbished 1860s mansion in Bedford-Stuyvesant which has an Afrocentric flavor (*akwaaba* means welcome in a language in Ghana). The price approaches "Splurge" but it's an affordable one (especially in New York!) for the experience. The decor combines clean, fresh colors and unique antiques. The four units all have private bathrooms (some with Jacuzzi), and a hearty Southern breakfast, along with afternoon tea is provided. *347 MacDonough St.* ☎ *718/455-5958. ww.akwaaba.com. Double occupancy $150–$165. Subway: A to Utica Avenue. Walk to near corner (Stuyvesant Ave.) and make a left. Four blocks to MacDonough Street and make a left to 347 MacDonough. Amenities: Garden, sun porch, TV and game room. In room: A/C, CD player.*

10pm daily. Down the street on 14th St. is a **Whole Foods Market** (www.wholefoods.com), open 8am to 10pm daily.

In the heart of Union Square on 14th and Broadway is the city's most famous **Greenmarket,** which operates every Monday, Wednesday, Friday, and Saturday. It operates year-round between 8am and 6pm, offering the season's freshest produce, meat, cheese, baked goods, and lots of other good stuff. There are many other greenmarkets that operate seasonally around town; for a comprehensive list, visit **www.nycvisit. com/content/index.cfm?pagePkey=658**.

The city's myriad delis and storefront markets are also a place to pick up fresh food, fresh sandwiches, drinks, and picnic supplies.

TAKEOUT TREATS
West Village
→ **Gray's Papaya** HOT DOGS If you want to do NYC bohemian (or penniless student) style, scrounge up 95¢ and buy yourself a hearty hot dog or three. If you have some extra money, wash it down with their mysterious papaya concoction. Mmmm. *402 Sixth Ave. at 8th St.* ☎ *212/ 260-3532. Hot dog 95¢. Cash only. Subway: A/C/E to W. 4th ST. Daily 24 hr.*

📺 Best ♥ → **Magnolia Bakery** ★★ BAKERY This is a tiny place, which explains why the line often creeps out the door—besides the fact that they've got the best baked goods in town. Known for their scrumptious cupcakes, but most everything else is delectable, too. *401 Bleecker St. at 11th St.* ☎ *212/462-2572. Cupcakes start at $2.50. Cash only. Subway: A/C/E to 14th St. Mon noon–11:30pm; Tues–Thurs 9:30am–11:30pm; Fri 9am–12:30pm; Sat 10am–12:30pm; Sun 10am–11:30pm.*

Union Square
→ **Max Brenner** ★★ FRENCH/BAKERY "Chocolate by the Bald Man" is a strange slogan, but once you catch a whiff of the chocolate fountain you won't care who's responsible. Waffles, crepes, and sandwiches, as well as (obviously) chocolate are on the menu. Don't miss the chocolate pizza! *841 Broadway between 13th and 14th sts.* ☎ *212/388-0030. www.maxbrenner.com. Subway: N/R/W; 4/5/6 to Union Sq. Menu items start at $5.50; individual items vary. Mon– Wed 8am–midnight; Thurs–Sat 8am–1am; Sun 9am–11pm.*

EATING OUT

All the restaurants below fall into the "Cheap/Doable" range; we list them by

Sources for Serious Foodies

We're assuming you're not here to break the bank at the higher-end places (and we're talking $500 a person at a place like Masa), so we're focusing on food that's interesting, tasty, and covers a range of cuisines. If you do want to splurge, or to venture out a bit in search of a specific cuisine or style or restaurant here are some places where you can start:

Your best online sources are **Citysearch (www.citysearch.com)**, which runs a restaurant page that's updated weekly as part of its comprehensive offerings; **New York Metro (www.newyorkmag.com)**; **New York Today (www.nytoday. com)**, the *New York Times*'s arts and lifestyle site, where you can access a database of the paper's stellar restaurant reviews; and *The Village Voice* (**www. villagevoice.com**), especially for the cheap-eats reviews by Robert Sietsema.

The best online source for the serious foodie is **www.chowhound.com**, a national website with message boards in local areas, including New York, where you can make an inquiry about a certain restaurant, type of food, location, and so on, and within a few hours, you might have five or more informative responses.

If you do want a reference book on hand while you're in the city, I suggest the colorful, reviewer-written *Time Out New York: Eating & Drinking* guide. If you don't feel the need for a big ol' book, stop at any newsstand for a copy of *Time Out New York,* whose "Eat Out" section always includes listings for *TONY*'s 100 Favorite Restaurants in every issue, as well as coverage of new openings and dining trends. Weekly *New York* magazine also maintains extensive restaurant listings in its listings section at the back of the magazine.

—*Brian Silverman (author, Frommer's New York City 2007)*

neighborhood, Downtown to Uptown, with a box on Brooklyn.

Chinatown

→ **Big Wong King** CHINESE This place has been open for over 30 years and is a no-fail food feast. There are scads of places in Chinatown, both good and bad, but this one is highly recommended. *67 Mott St. between Canal and Bayard.* ☎ *212/ 964-0540. Appetizers $1.50–$5; soups $3–$5; noodles $5.25–$11. Cash only. Daily 8:30am– 9pm. Subway N/R, 6 to Canal St.*

→ **New York Noodletown** ★ CHINESE Some say this place looks like a school cafeteria, but don't let the fluorescent atmosphere fool you. The food is sophisticated, and it's served in big portions. Plus it's cheap and stays open late. What else could you ask for at 3am? *28½ Bowery at*

Bayard St. ☎ *212/349-0923. Main courses $4–$13. Cash only. Daily 9am–3:30am. Subway: N/R, 6 to Canal St.*

East Village/Lower East Side

→ **Around the Clock** ★★ DINER Just like the name says, open round-the-clock, plus you can order just about anything. I've tried banana pancakes, hummus and pita, and the omelet—all good, all reasonable. *8 Stuyvesant St. between 3rd Ave. and 9th St.* ☎ *212/598-0402. Appetizers $2.95– $5.95; salads $3.25–$6.95; entrees $5.95–$12. Around the clock! Subway: L to 3rd Ave.*

MTV **Best** ⚫ → **Chickpea** ★★★ MIDDLE EASTERN Not only is the food here fresh and homemade, it's kosher! Plus, the place is clean and cheap, and the employees aren't grimy. I vote Chickpea the best falafel in New York City. For only $4 get a yummy falafel pita with all the tahini you care to drown it in. The charming back room lounge of the St. Marks location is a nice place to cool your jets. *23 Third Ave. between 9th and St. Marks and 210 East 14th St. between 2nd and 3rd aves.* ☎ *212/254-9400. www.chickpearestaurant.com. Sandwiches $3.70–$6.50; combo plates $6.70–$14; sides start at $2.50. Daily 10am–midnight. Subway: L to 3rd Ave.*

➜ **Katz's Delicatessen** ★★ DELI In New York Jewish deli spirit, you won't go hungry while you wait for your pastrami or corned beef here—complimentary dill pickles are provided for your noshing pleasure. Katz's has become a major tourist favorite, which is maybe not such a surprise given the place has been around since 1888. Remember to tip your carver when he gives you a taste of the delectable meat he's making your sandwich with. *205 E. Houston St. at Ludlow St.* ☎ *212/254-2246. Sandwiches $2.15–$10; other dishes $5–$18. Sun–Tues 8am–10pm; Wed–Thurs 8am–11pm; Fri–Sat 8am–3am. Subway: D/F to 2nd Ave.*

➜ **Pommes Frites** ★★ BELGIAN You'll have less trouble choosing what you want to eat than what you want to dip it in. This place makes the best Belgian fries, served with a selection of dozens of sauces, like roasted garlic mayo, pesto mayo, curry ketchup, Parmesan peppercorn, peanut satay, cheddar cheese, and smoked eggplant mayo. *123 2nd Ave. between 7th and 8th sts.* ☎ *212/674-1234. www.pommesfrites.ws. Regular $4; large $6.25; double $7.50; sauces 75¢ each or 3 for $1.75. Cash only. Sun–Thurs 11:30am–1am; Fri–Sat 11:30am–3:30am. Subway: D/F to 2nd Ave.*

➜ **S'Mac** ★ MAC & CHEESE The bright orange room will get you in the mood for something cheesy. Macaroni and cheese is the specialty, with many variations including exotic possibilities like cheeseburger, Gruyère, Cajun, and brie. *345 E. 12th St.*

between 1st and 2nd aves. ☎ *212/358-7912. www.smacnyc.com. Sizes: Nosh $4.25–$6.75; major munch $6.50–$9; mongo $11–$16. Tues noon–10pm; Wed–Sun noon–11pm. Subway: L to 1st Ave.*

Greenwich Village

➜ **Peanut Butter & Co.** SANDWICHES Every variation on PBJ that you've considered but not made because it was too unhealthy or weird can be found here. Try "The Elvis" with peanut butter, bananas, honey, and bacon; the "White Chocolate Wonderful" with white chocolate peanut butter and orange marmalade; or the simple "Fluffernutter" with peanut butter and marshmallow fluff. *240 Sullivan St. between Bleecker and W. 3rd sts.* ☎ *866/ILOVEPB. www.ilovepeanutbutter.com. Sandwiches $4–$7. Sun–Thurs 11am–9pm; Fri–Sat 11am–10pm. Subway: A/C/E to W. 4th St.*

Chelsea

➜ **La Nacional** ★ SPANISH If you're into historical New York, this is another gem from the late 1800s. It's not that well-known, partially because it's not easy to find. For excellent tapas, the search is well worth it. Ask about flamenco performances and dance lessons on the second level. And if you're a seafood fan, don't pass up the paella. *239 W. 14th St. between 7th and 8th aves.* ☎ *212/243-9308. Tapas $4–$9; main courses $15–$18. Cash only. Daily noon–11pm. Subway: A/C/E to 14th St.*

Midtown

➜ **Burgers & Cupcakes** ★ BURGERS/ CUPCAKES Their motto: "I love burgers. I love cupcakes. That's it." The menu is limited, though dessert is extensive. It's also great hangover food—take advantage of free delivery and order cupcakes in bed. *458 9th Ave. between 35th and 36th sts.* ☎ *212/643-1200. www.burgers andcupcakes.us. Burgers $5.95; cupcakes $2. Daily 11am–8pm. Subway: A/C/E to 34th St.*

Cheap & Doable Eats in Brooklyn

➔ Making focaccia in the Cobble Hill neighborhood since 1904, it's safe to say **Ferdinando's Focacceria** ★ has it down pat. The house specialty is the *panelle:* a deep-fried pancake made of chickpea flour and served in all manner of variations. *151 Union St.* ☎ *718/855-1545. Panelle $3; main courses $10–$13. Cash only. Mon–Thurs 10:30am–6pm; Fri–Sat 10:30am–9pm. Subway: F to Carroll St.*

➔ **Rice** ★ is true to its name: you'll find rice, rice, and more rice at the DUMBO outpost of this minichain. But there are other choices on the Asian Fusion menu: curries, salads, and beans . . . all served with rice. *81 Washington St.* ☎ *718/222-9880. www.riceny.com. Rices $1–$3.50; entrees $4–$10. Cash only. Daily noon–midnight. Brunch Sat–Sun 10am. Subway: F to York St.; A/C to High St./Brooklyn Bridge.*

➔ **Seawilliamsburg** ★★ is notable for its eye-catching, exotic space. At the Williamsburg outpost of the "Spice" group of restaurants, The Thai food is all good, and though portions look small, you'll leave satisfied. Lunch specials are especially economical; the $6 pad Thai and salad with peanut sauce is my personal favorite. *114 N. 6th St.* ☎ *718/384-8850. www. spicenyc.net. Lunch $6–$7; appetizers $3–$6; dinner $6–$16. Sun–Thurs 11:30am–1am; Fri–Sat 11:30am–2am. Subway: L to Bedford Ave.*

Upper East Side

➔ **Serendipity 3** ★★ AMERICAN/ DESSERTS The food's okay, but the crowds are here for the desserts. Frozen Hot Chocolate is the signature dish, but you won't be disappointed with celestial carrot cake, lemon icebox pie, and anything with fudge. There are generally huge lines on the weekends, and they don't take dessert reservations, but weeknights shouldn't keep you waiting too long. *225 E. 60th St. between 2nd and 3rd aves.* ☎ *212/838-3531. www.serendipity3.com. Main courses $7–$18; deserts $5–$17. Sun–Thurs 11:30am–midnight; Fri 11:30am–1am; Sat 11:30am–2am. Subway: N/R/W; 4/5/6 to 59th St.*

Upper West Side

➔ **Celeste** ★ ITALIAN This all-around good Italian spot has unique menu items like fresh egg noodles with cabbage, shrimp, and sheep's cheese. They don't take reservations and they're usually busy, so try not to show up during rush hour if you're short on time. *502 Amsterdam Ave. between 84th and 85th sts.* ☎ *212/874-4559. Pizza $10–$12; antipasto $7–$10; pasta $10; main courses $14–$16. Cash only. Mon–Sat 5–11pm; Sun noon–3:30pm. Subway: 1 to 86th St.*

Partying

Shecky's New York Bar, Club & Lounge Guide (☎ 212/777-BARS; www.sheckys. com) is printed annually and offers up-to-the-minute nightlife news on the website. A couple more websites offering advice on everything from crowds to the best Happy Hours, include **www.drinkdeal.com**, which allows you to sort by neighborhood and type of drink (and day of the week); and **www.murphguide.com**, which is a particularly good source if you are seeking out an Irish pub, of which there are many in New York. Here's a small sampling of places you can start (or end) a pub crawl:

BARS
East Village/Union Square

➜**Beauty Bar** ★ Don't feel bad about hanging out in the bar too long and blowing off your manicure appointment: "Martini & Manicure" Happy Hours here are just $10. *231 E. 14th St. between 2nd and 3rd aves. ☎ 212/539-1389. Mon–Thurs 5:30pm–4am; Fri–Sun 7pm–4am. Subway, L to 3rd Ave.*

➜**Cosmic Cantina** ★ This late-night fave attracts locals seeking a stiff drink—and maybe a burrito. The food is organic, which may sound a bit bland, but at 5am at least you'll know it's safe. They have great drink and Happy Hour specials. Sit in the back room for a true cosmic experience. *105 3rd Ave. at 13th St. ☎ 212/420-0975. Burritos $5–$12; drinks start at $4. Cash only. Daily 11am–5am. Subway: L to 3rd Ave.*

➜**Union Bar** This college hang may be on the cliché side, but it gets points for being clean and architecturally striking. There's an extensive drink menu and a sizeable seating area. This is also a nice place to go out if you don't want to get too dressed up. *204 Park Ave. South between 17th and 18th sts. ☎ 212/674-2105. www.unionbar.com. No cover. Mon–Fri 5pm–4am; Sat 8pm–4am. Subway: 4/5/6, L, N/R/Q/W to Union Square.*

Meatpacking District

➜**Plunge at Hotel Gansevoort** ★★ LOUNGE/BAR Expect to dress the part and come with a small group or a large roll of bills if you're going to glide past the doorman here. Although other neighborhood spots are more cutthroat, this is definitely a glamour crowd hang. You'll find one of the best views in the city, but don't expect cheap drinks—once a place is featured on *Sex and the City,* the price of cosmopolitans goes through the roof. (Yes, even after the show finished its original run.) *18 9th Ave. 15th Floor at 14th St. ☎ 212/660-6736. No cover if the doorman likes you.*

Cocktails $15. Daily 11am–3am. Subway: A/C/E to 14th St.

Midtown

➜**Local West** ★★ LOUNGE/BAR Right across from Penn Station and around the corner from Madison Square Garden you'll find this popular Happy Hour hangout. The inside and rooftop bars are always hopping, with good DJs, solid bar grub, and black-clad waitresses who keep your drinks coming all night. *1 Penn Plaza at 33rd St. and 8th Ave. ☎ 212/629-7070. www.localcafenyc.com. Reasonable drinks; food $6–$15. Daily 11am–4am. A/C/E or 1/2/3 to 34th St./Penn Station.*

CLUBS
Meatpacking District

➜**One** ★★ DANCE Maybe they call it One because it's one of the only clubs in the area that you can get into without knowing the owner or promoter. There's still a chance you'll see a famous face in the closed-off VIP area, though it's usually just investment bankers flashing AmEx Blacks. There's ample room to dance, and unless the DJ goes techno crazy, the music is usually good. The place also serves meals and snacks, drinks in the $9 range, small plates in the $12 range. *One Little W. 12th St. ☎ 212/255-9717. www.onelw12.com. Daily 4pm–4am. Usually no cover for girls; possible cover for guys.*

Flatiron District

➜**Porky's** DIVE In the back left corner of this place, as part of the decor, a chair shoved through a window says "This place sucks." It actually doesn't suck completely, though it can get as hot as a non-air-conditioned subway on a summer day. (To their credit, they do have fun dance music.) Check their website for drink specials; sometimes they'll have all-you-can-drink events, which only last an hour or so (10–11pm when I went), and you'll have to get there early to better push your way to the bar. There's food, too, and you can "buy" VIP treatment including cutting the line, hors d'oeuvres, and an open bar for you and a guest for between $40 and $60 depending on the package you want. *55 W. 21st St. between 5th and 6th aves. ☎ 212/ 675-8007. www.porkysnyc.com. Cover varies, usually $5–$10 or free; check website for nightly specials. Subway: N/R/Q to 23rd St.*

Brooklyn

→ **Tainted Lady Lounge** ★ LOUNGE This Williamsburg shrine to the sauciest ladies around features wall-to-wall painted pinups. A banging jukebox and fun DJs make this place a hipster magnet. *318 Grand St. between Havemeyer St. and Marcy Ave. ☎ 718/302-5514; www.taintedlady.com. Daily 5–9pm. $2 Miller High Life and Pabst Blue Ribbon, $3 margaritas, everything else $1 off. Mon–Fri 5pm–4am; Sat–Sun 11am–4am. Subway: L to Lorimer St.*

→ **Triple Crown** LOUNGE For new and original DJs, this is the place to go. Located in Williamsburg, there's no shortage of hipsters, though the place caters more toward the true hip-hop crowd. It's recommended by Brooklyn Hip-Hop Festival staff. *108 Bedford Ave. at 11th St. ☎ 718/ 388-8883. www.triplecrownpage.com. No cover. Happy Hour through 9pm daily. Daily 6pm– 4am. Subway: L to Bedford Ave.*

LIVE MUSIC

East Village/Lower East Side

→ **Irving Plaza** CONCERTS This all-ages venue may get packed with youngsters with fake ID, but the programming is excellent, and ticket prices ($10–$25) are under control. The space is pretty intimate, so if an act you love is coming through town, your money will be well spent. It's spacious but not too large, and if you're not

into getting shoved around by a crowd, you can watch from an upstairs balcony. *17 Irving Place. ☎ 212/777-6800. www.irving plaza.com. Tickets starting at $10. Check website for schedule. Subway: N/R/W/Q, 4/5/6, L to Union Square.*

→ **Pianos** ★★ VARIETY/PIANO BAR This hot spot hosts an abundance of events: live music nightly at 7pm, DJs nightly at 10pm, and comedy nights on Sunday at 8pm. Pianos won "Best Cheap Night" in *New York Magazine's Bar Guide* so expect to see a good amount of cheap hipsters. *158 Ludlow St. between Stanton and Rivington. ☎ 212/505-3733. Live music $8 cover. Daily noon–4am. Subway: D/F to 2nd Ave.*

→ **Tonic** ★★ VARIETY Experimental music rules here. You can hear live jazz, rock, and electronic sounds, plus DJs on Thursdays through Saturdays from 9pm until closing. The lounge space is good for chilling, too. *107 Norfolk St. between Rivington and Delancey sts. ☎ 212/358-7501. Cover $5– 15. Subway: D/F to 2nd Ave.*

Risque Business: The Museum of Sex

MTV Best ● At the **Museum of Sex** ★★★ you can learn all *kinds* of things your parents never told you! The 2006 exhibitions included "Mapping Sex in America," "Stags, Smokers and Blue Movies: The Origins of American Pornographic Film," and "The Presidential Bust of Hillary Rodham Clinton." *233 Fifth Ave. at 27th St. ☎ 212/689-6337. www. museumofsex.com. Students $14; adults $15. Check the website for coupons. Sun–Fri 11am–6:30pm; Sat 11am–8pm. You must be 18 or older to enter.*

Some Other Stuff to See & Do

Just to let you know . . . this is *hardly* a comprehensive listing, but you know if you want to hit a museum (like the Met!) or a baseball game to SEE a Met (or a Yankee!) or visit the Statue of Liberty, or some other "Only in New York" experience, pick up *Frommer's New York City 2007*, which is full of useful information and includes a fold-out sheetmap (and which the editor of this book also edited).

What follows is a highly personal list of some of my favorite spots in NYC:

Head to the **South Street Seaport** ★★ (Pier 17 at Fulton and South sts.; ☎ 212/ SEA-PORT; www.southstreetseaport.com) on Lower Manhattan's historic waterfront for dozens of tasty restaurants, lively street performers, or just a beautiful view. The mall here is open Monday through Saturday 10am to 9pm and Sunday 11am to 8pm, with some restaurants staying open later. **Bodies . . . The Exhibition** ★★ (11 Fulton St., across from South Street Seaport; ☎ 888/9BODIES or 646/ 837-0300; www.bodiestheexhibition.com) presents an incredible display of the ins and outs of the human body . . . literally. It's *not* for the squeamish! (It's also a bit pricey: $26.50 admission on weekdays, $27.50 on weekends).

PLAYING OUTSIDE
Visiting Central Park

Central Park ★★★ (between Fifth Ave. and Central Park West and 59th and 110th sts.; **www.centralparknyc.org**) is visited by 25 million people each year. You'll still have plenty of room; the park spans 843 acres, or 6% of Manhattan. As long as the weather is nice, it's a beautiful place to lounge around, play sports, or exercise. Visit the website for information on guided tours and events.

A Grand (Free) Tour of Grand Central

FREE My favorite indoor/outdoor tour is the **"Grand Tour"** ★★★ (tour of the neighborhood in and around Grand Central Terminal, 42nd St. at Park Ave.) by Justin Ferate. Ferate is entertaining and engaging, and you'll be blown away by how little you know about one of New York's most important landmarks. The tour is given on Fridays at 12:30pm. For more information on the tour (and the neighborhood) visit www. grandcentralpartnership.org.

A TV TOUR

➜**Sex and the City Tour** ★ If you're a fan, you'll love visiting the sites from the series on this 3-hour tour. You'll see the Jimmy Choo boutique, Carrie's apartment stoop, the SoHo gallery where Charlotte worked, and other key locations. *Near 5th Ave. and 58th St. (exact location provided upon purchase).* ☎ *212/209-3370. www.scene ontv.com. $36/ticket. Daily 11am and 3pm; Sat–Sun 10am, 11am, and 3pm.*

In addition to *Sex and the City,* other On Location Tours include *The Sopranos, Step Mom, Ghostbusters,* and *Home Alone II.*

For other tour itineraries, visit www. nycvisit.com or **www.nyctourist.com**.

Back to the Mainland

We hope you've enjoyed your quick tour of the city and that you'll be back to visit (or even live here) one of these days. We haven't even talked about the stuff there is to do in the winter.

But it's time to board the bus, or get on the train, or pick up the car from the garage, and head south to our next set of festivals.

FESTIVAL SEASON

Hello, Hon! Let's Rave in Baltimore, MD

Ah, Baltimore, one of the most satisfyingly weird towns around. Where Frank Zappa was born, Edgar Allan Poe died (and the NFL team is named after one of his poems), and John Waters still lives, where they have a museum for visionary art and one for Babe Ruth. It's a big city and a laid-back Southern town, home of television's *Homicide* and *The Wire*, film's *Diner* and *Hairspray*. Called both Charm City and Mobtown, Baltimore is also in the festival business, and we'll profile two of the events, as well as direct you to some of the more interesting attractions, restaurants, and other doings. Oh, and bring your mallet,

because if you like crabs, you've found your bliss.

First up, the festivals.

Starscape Music Festival

For the past 9 years, an empty parking lot, a couple of tents, and 1,500 people are the ingredients for the largest dance party in Maryland. While the sun is going down on the eve of the event, the small groups scattered around make it look more like a middle-school dance than a legendary rave. But once the sun sets and the music starts, the party gets going and continues for 12 hours straight.

Baltimore Nuts & Bolts

Area Code The area code in Baltimore is 410. (You must dial it even if you are calling within the area code.)

Emergencies Dial ☎ 911 for fire, police, or ambulance.

Liquor Laws Restaurants, bars, hotels, and other places serving alcohol may stay open 6am to 2am. On Sunday and election days, some opt to close. The legal age to buy or consume alcohol is 21.

Newspapers & Magazines The major daily newspaper is *The Baltimore Sun*. *The City Paper* is the city's weekly alternative. It's published Wednesdays and has excellent listings. The *Washington Post* is also widely available.

Pharmacies Rite Aid is at 17 W. Baltimore St. (☎ 410/539-0838). Walgreens is at 19 E. Fayette St. (☎ 410/625-1179).

Police Dial ☎ 911 for emergencies, ☎ 311 for non-emergencies requiring police attention.

Post Office The main post office is at 900 E. Fayette St. (☎ 410/347-4202). It's open Monday to Saturday 7:30am to 10pm. Other area post offices are at 111 N. Calvert (☎ 410/347-4202) and 130 N. Greene St. (☎ 410/539-8575). Both are open weekdays, 8:30am to 5pm.

Taxes The state sales tax is 5%. The hotel tax is an additional 7.5%.

FESTIVAL SEASON

Transit Information Contact the Mass Transit Administration (MTA) at ☎ 866/
RIDE-MTA or 410/539-5000 (www.mtamaryland.com) for bus, Light Rail, and Metro
info.

Visitor Information The Visitor Center (☎ 877/BALTIMORE) is located at the
Inner Harbor, by Harborplace. You can stop at the Downtown Partnership's offices
at 217 N. Charles St. for directions, maps, and other information. Or ask one of the
Public Safety Guides wearing the purple caps.

Weather Call ☎ 410/936-1212.

Starscape Festival in a Box

Contact www.starscape2006.com.

Dates Saturday, June 9, 2007.

Food Bring along water and snacks to the festival. Food vendors are set up alongside the perimeter of the event, with everything from hot dogs to falafel. But don't
trust that anything is actually edible.

Hours 6am–6pm

Location Fort Armistead Park, 3984 Fort Armistead Rd., Baltimore, MD 21226. Fort
Armistead Park is actually outside of Baltimore proper, in an area called Curtis Bay,
about 25 minutes south of downtown. It can be reached by car from the Baltimore
Beltway (I-695) taking the Hawkins Ave. exit. For complete directions, visit the website.

Parking If you arrive early, parking will be available close to the gate. Otherwise,
expect a bit of a trek from up or down Fort Armistead Road.

Tickets $45 in advance, $50 at the gate.

Weather Rain or shine. In 2006, the event went on amid a rainstorm and many
Starscapers were unhappy. The Starscape staff has promised that all electronic areas
will be tented in 2007.

Also in Baltimore: HonFest

Close your eyes and imagine what the person who says "HEY HON!" looks like.
HonFest says that the ingredients for
Baltimore's best Hon are "'60s-era women
with beehive hairdos, blue-eye-shadow,
spandex pants and something, anything

leopard print." Now imagine thousands of
them. If you don't have an interest in con-
verting yourself into a Hon, you can still join
over 20,000 people for music, dancing, and
wild events—and if you change your mind,
you can always go to the Hon Boutique and
get Hon-i-fied!

Playlist: Starscape 2006

- *Jamilia,* **The Disco Biscuits,** "Uncivilized Area," 2000
- *Photek - No. 1 Sound,* **DJ Craze,** "Miami Heat," 2005
- *By My Side,* **Soldiers of Jah Army,** "Get Wiser," 2006
- *End Of The World Party,* **Medeski Martin & Wood,** "End of the World Party (Just in Case)," 2004
- *Do Do Wop Mix,* **Paul Johnson mixed by DJ Feelgood,** "Djmixed.com," 2001
- *Wish I Didn't Miss You,* **Angie Stone mixed by DJ Dave Nada**
- *Freedom Time,* **Soldiers of Jah Army,** "SOJA EP," 2000

Word Up: Raver Lingo

- **dehydration** the number-one cause of death among ravers
- **glow stick** a colorful raver tool that can be mesmerizing when spun around
- **hella** a slang term meaning "very," popularized by Cartman in South Park
- **trails** the visual remnants that appear when spinning glow sticks
- **tribal** a genre of house music that tends to make ravers appear to be from ancient civilizations
- **word** a slang term meaning "I agree"

Popular events at recent fests have been both cultural and athletic, including:

- Spam bowling!
- A Pat Benatar lip-synch contest
- A "Hon Run" pitting runners in beehives, carrying trays in a footrace to see who can maintain her "elegance and grace."

The first "hon" contest took place in Baltimore in 1994 but the history of hon-hood dates much further back. If you've seen films like *Diner* and (of course) *Hairspray,* then you're familiar with a certain Baltimore style: friendly, fun-loving, and larger-than-life (with a unique accent).

The formerly working-class, row-housed neighborhoods have gentrified, with restaurants, boutiques, clubs and galleries wedging themselves into the old neighborhoods.

Honfest is a chance to see Baltimore, both old and new, and enjoy some local delicacies ranging from crab cakes to the

HonFest Playlist 2006

- *Dancing Queen,* **Abba,** "Greatest Hits," 1993
- *Dream Lover,* **Dion,** "Runaround Sue," 1961
- *Hit Me With Your Best Shot,* **Pat Benatar,** "Crimes of Passion," 1980
- *I Hate Myself for Loving You,* **Joan Jett & the Blackhearts,** "Up Your Alley," 1988
- *Backyards,* **Bee Hives,** "Broken Social Scene," 2004
- *Summer in the City,* **Lovin' Spoonful,** "Summer in the City," 1967
- *It's My Party,* **Lesley Gore,** "The Golden Hits of Lesley Gore," 1965

(not-so-premium) National Bohemian (aka "Natty Boh") beer.

Baltimore Festivals

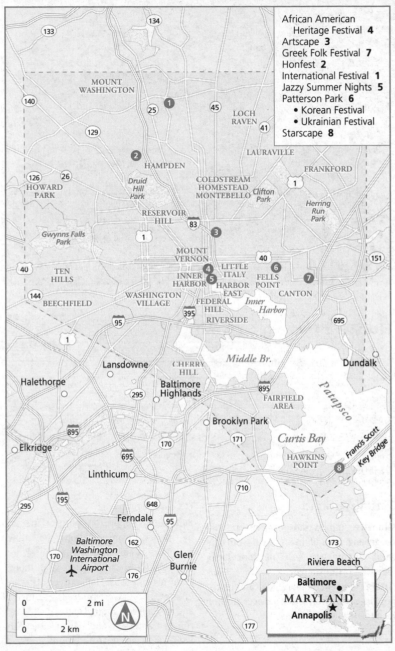

African American
   Heritage Festival **4**
Artscape **3**
Greek Folk Festival **7**
Honfest **2**
International Festival **1**
Jazzy Summer Nights **5**
Patterson Park **6**
   • Korean Festival
   • Ukrainian Festival
Starscape **8**

How ya doin', Hon?

HonFest Festival in a Box

Contact ☎ 410/243-6800 or www.honfest.net.

Dates June 9 (11am–10pm) and 10 (noon–6pm), 2007.

Hours 11am–8pm.

Location In Hampden (an old-school Baltimore neighborhood, northwest of the Inner Harbor) on 36th Street.

Admission Free!

Weather Rain or shine.

Getting Around

Baltimore's public transportation is great for getting around town, so if you can avoid driving, do so. The **Maryland Transit Administration** (☎ 866/RIDEMTA; www.mtamaryland.com) operates bus, subway, and train services around the city.

BY CAR

Baltimore is simple to explore on foot and by public transportation. Downtown Baltimore is easy to navigate by car, too. The streets run on a simple grid, though many are one-way. Major streets: Howard, Charles, and Calvert run north; Cathedral and St. Paul run south; Lombard and Pratt run east and west; and Martin Luther King Boulevard runs north and south.

Word Up: Baltimore Vocabulary

➤ **accent** *noun.* Something that is not done purposefully. *I got on the wrong train by accent so I was late for my appointment.*

➤ **Ballmer** *noun.* The name of a city in Maryland. *HonFest and Starscape take place in Ballmer.*

➤ **hon** *noun.* An endearing term, referring to someone sweet. *How you doin', hon?*

➤ **Merlin** *noun.* The name of a state on the Northeast coast of the United States. *Virginia, Washington, DC, and Merlin are all very close.*

➤ **share** *noun.* To bathe. *I'm going to take a share before we go out.*

➤ **tawlet** *noun.* A bathroom fixture with a hollow, water-filled bowl. *The tawlet is overflowing onto the floor.*

➤ **wooder** *noun.* An odorless, colorless liquid. *When people are thirsty, they may be dehydrated and need wooder.*

Parking

There are 13 municipal garages and 21 lots throughout Baltimore. A list can be found at **www.ci.baltimore.md.us/government/parking/operations.html**. Rates generally range from $8 for lots to $1.00 hourly for meters.

BY BUS

MTA buses run all over the city. The fare is $1.60 and exact change is required upon boarding. Check the website for stations, routes, and maps.

BY SUBWAY

Though it's not as extensive as DC's or New York's, Baltimore's **Metro** subway covers 15½ miles with 14 stations. Parking is available at all stations, so consider leaving the car and taking the Metro to your destination. One-way fares are $1.60. Stations are open Monday through Friday 5am to midnight, Saturday and Sunday 6am to midnight.

BY LIGHT RAIL

The **Light Rail** is what remains of Baltimore's old streetcar system. It runs 27 miles above ground and travels north–south from northern Timonium to southern Glen Burnie, including Penn Station and Camden Station. If you're traveling within the downtown Baltimore region, including Camden Yards, the performing arts district, the Inner Harbor, or Mount Washington, it's a great way to get around. One-way tickets are $1.60. Trains run every 15 to 30 minutes Monday through Friday 6am to 11pm, Saturday 7am to 11pm, and Sunday 11am to 7pm.

BY TAXI

Baltimore taxis start with $1.80 on the meter and charge 20¢ per ⅛ mile. Try **Yellow Checker Cab** (☎ 410/841-5573) or **Arrow Cab** (☎ 410/261-0000).

BY WATER & SEAPORT TAXIS

The Inner Harbor, Harborplace, Fells Point, Little Italy, Canton, and Fort McHenry are all serviced by **Ed Kane's Water Taxi & Trolley** (☎ 800/658-8947 or 410/563-3901). Unlimited day tickets are $6 and include discount coupons for local restaurants, shops, and museums. There are 13 water taxis that run about every 15 to 20 minutes in summer. Weekdays they go from 10am to 11pm, extended to midnight on the weekends.

FESTIVAL SEASON

MTA Day Passes

....

If you're planning on making your rounds via public transportation, the MTA's unlimited day pass allows trips on all MTA services for $3.50.

ON FOOT

If you follow the major streets (see "By Car," above) it's hard to get lost. The Inner Harbor is charming and particularly easy to navigate because there are so many landmarks in the area: the American Visionary Arts Museum, the Maryland Science Center, Harborplace, the National Aquarium, the Constellation, and the Maritime Museum can all be found here, in addition to a profusion of shops and restaurants.

Sleeping

CHEAP/DOABLE

➜ **Days Inn Inner Harbor** If you're willing to give up proximity to the harbor (by 2 or 3 blocks), you can get a great deal at this modern nine-story hotel, between the 1st Mariner Arena and the convention center, 3 blocks from Camden Yards. It's got a good setup, including "work zone" rooms with large desks, kitchenettes, and plenty of space; good if you're traveling with a companion or two. *100 Hopkins Place (between Lombard and Pratt sts.), Baltimore, MD 21202.* ☎ *800/DAYS-INN or 410/576-1000. www.days innerharbor.com. 250 units. $99–$189 double. Parking $15. Amenities: Restaurant; outdoor pool; health club;. In room: A/C, TV w/Nintendo 64, Wi-Fi, coffeemaker, hair dryer, iron.*

➜ **Radisson Plaza Lord Baltimore** If you love grand old hotels with modern conveniences, this one's for you. The 23-story French Renaissance–style hotel, which opened in 1928, still retains its old-fashioned charm. The grand lobby boasts soaring columns and a glittering chandelier. Those who need extra space should consider a one-bedroom parlor suite or a corner room, which comes with king-size bed and sleeper sofa. The hotel is convenient to Mount Vernon attractions; the Inner Harbor is only 5 blocks away. *20 W. Baltimore St. (between Charles and Hanover sts.), Baltimore, MD 21202.* ☎ *800/333-3333 or 410/539-8400. Fax 410/625-1060. www.radisson. com/lordbaltimore. 439 units. $99–$279 double. Valet parking $25. Amenities: Restaurant; bar; coffee shop; health club; Jacuzzi; sauna. In room: A/C, TV, Wi-Fi, fridge or microwave upon request, coffeemaker, hair dryer, iron, 2-line phone.*

An alternative to staying downtown and worrying about parking—especially if you plan to see only the Inner Harbor attractions—is a hotel near Baltimore/Washington International Thurgood Marshall Airport that offers free shuttle service to the North Linthicum Light Rail station. You can often score great deals on the BWI hotels on Priceline. About 15 airport hotels have such shuttles. From North Linthicum, it's a 15-minute ride to the Camden Yards station, which is just 6 blocks from the Inner Harbor.

Closest to the airport are the **BWI Airport Marriott,** 1743 W. Nursery Rd. (☎ **800/228-9290** or 410/859-8300; www. marriott.com), which has an indoor pool; **Country Inn & Suites by Carlson BWI Airport,** 1717 W. Nursery Rd. (☎ **800/ 456-4000** or 443/577-1036; www.country inns.com/bwiairport), which has an indoor pool; and **Four Points by Sheraton BWI Airport,** 7032 Elm Rd. (☎ **888/625-5144** or 410/859-3300; www.starwoodhotels. com).

SPLURGE

➜ **Hyatt Regency Baltimore** ★★★ The eye-catching all-glass Hyatt was the Inner Harbor's first hotel 20 years ago, and it's

Charm City Calendar of (Other) Events

→ **Jazzy Summer Nights (www.vmginc.net)** is a free jazz music series that runs from June through September. Performers include both local and national jazz and soul artists.

→ The **Showcase of Nations Ethnic Festivals** features dozens of events throughout the summer. Free events in 2006 included the **Greek Folk Festival, African American Heritage Festival, International Festival, Ukrainian Festival,** and **Korean American Festival,** to name a few. All festivals feature native dancing, costumes, and cuisine. **www.bop.org.**

→ **Artscape** is a free annual event held in late July with musical performances, visual arts exhibitions, film, theater, and an art market. The 2007 event will be held July 20 to 22 with four outdoor stages featuring musical performers. According to the website, Artscape is also America's largest, municipally produced arts festival. **www.bop.org.**

still one of the best. Sure, Baltimore has more luxury hotels now, but the Hyatt still has the best location. It's a short walk across a skywalk to the Inner Harbor, another skywalk to the convention center, and a few blocks to the stadiums. Accommodations are your standard hotel-chain style, but they have breathtaking harbor views. It's often busy, but not too noisy, and the staff here couldn't be nicer. *300 Light St., Baltimore, MD 21202.* ☎ *800/233-1234 or 410/528-1234. Fax 410/685-3362. www.baltimore.hyatt.com. 486 units. $125–$300 double. Ask about packages and discounts. Self-parking $19, valet parking $25. Amenities: Rooftop restaurant; bar; outdoor pool; recreation deck w/jogging track, putting green, 2 tennis courts, basketball court; health club; executive-level rooms; Wi-Fi in lobby. In room: A/C, TV, high-speed Internet access, minibar, hair dryer, iron, safe.*

Eating

SUPPLIES

The **Baltimore Farmers Market** (Holliday and Saratoga Sts. underneath the Jones Falls Expwy.; ☎ **410/752-8632**) is a great place to pick up fresh snacks or

supplies. The market is held on Sundays from May through December, from 8am to sellout, which is usually around noon.

There's also a **Whole Foods Market** (1001 Fleet St.; ☎ **410/528-1640;** www.wholefoods.com) near Eastern Avenue.

TAKEOUT TREATS

Little Italy/Fells Point

→ **Bonaparte Breads** ★★ FRENCH/BAKERY You can't beat a place with great breakfast and lunch specials, on top of scrumptious pastries and a charming view. Between sandwiches, quiches, fruit, and baked goods, you'll find plenty to choose from. *903 S. Ann St.* ☎ *410/342-4000. Breakfast $7; lunch $11. MC, V. Daily 8am–9pm; lunch served until 3pm.*

→ **Vacarro's** ★ DESSERT Excellent coffee and cappuccino and hefty servings of gelato are just some of the reasons to stop by. The wait is usually long, but it's worth it—especially if it's your birthday, when you can choose a free desert off the birthday menu. *222 Albemarle St.* ☎ *410/685-4905. Desserts $2.95–$7.50. Mon–Wed 7:30am–10pm; Wed–Thurs and Sun 7:30am–11pm; Fri–Sat 7:30am–1am.*

Surf Baltimore: Recommended Websites

→ **www.bop.org.** The home of the Baltimore Office of Promotion & The Arts will keep you informed on the latest events and attractions in the city.

→ **www.baltimore.org.** The website of the Baltimore Area Convention and Visitors Association has a calendar of events, trip planner, and deals and discounts around town.

→ **www.marylandnightlife.com** lists the best bars, restaurants and festivals in the Baltimore area. Read descriptions; get locations and phone numbers as well as information on cover charges and specials.

EATING OUT
Cheap

→ **Amicci's** ★ *LITTLE ITALY* ITALIAN Baltimore is known for its seafood and Amicci's doesn't tarnish the reputation. The place is casual, with big, tasty dishes. Don't run away if there's a bit of a line; the service is great and you'll be seated quickly. *231 High St. ☎ 410/528-1096. Dishes $7.90–$14. Sun–Thurs 11:30am–10pm; Fri–Sat 11:30am–11pm.*

→ **Café Hon** ★★ *HAMPDEN* AMERICAN If you're going to HonFest, a meal here is required eating. The cafe is a home-cooked heaven, with comfort food faves like spaghetti, mashed potatoes, and grilled cheese. Just don't tell your mom about their "Much Better Than Mom's" meatloaf. *1002 36th St. ☎ 410/243-1230. www.cafehon.com. Lunch $3.95–$9.95; main courses $8.95–$14. Mon–Thurs 7am–9pm; Fri 7am–10pm; Sat 9am–10pm; Sun 9am–8pm.*

→ **Grill Art** *HAMPDEN* AMERICAN Salads and sandwiches keep it simple, although there are also more out-there choices like jalapeno-cheddar bread and eggplant flan. There's a hearty brunch on Saturdays and Sundays, though weekends tend to get busy and reservations are recommended. To save a couple of bucks, try this one for lunch. *1011 W. 36th St. ☎ 410/366-2005. Lunch $4.95–$11. Tues–Thurs 11am–3pm and 5–9:30pm; Fri 11am–3pm and 5–10:30pm; Sat 8:30am–3pm and 5–10:30pm; Sun 8:30am–3pm.*

→ **PaperMoon Diner** ★ *HAMPDEN* DINER This offbeat spot is a collegiate favorite, probably because you can wake up at 2pm and order breakfast. Sandwiches and burgers are also on the menu, which has a sizeable health food selection. *227 W. 29th St. ☎ 410/889-4444. Main courses $7–$14. Daily 24 hr., reservations required for 5+.*

→ **Tapas Teatro** ★★ *MOUNT VERNON* INTERNATIONAL This is Baltimore's specialty spot for tapas, and one of the best spots in town. Paella is an excellent choice if you're hungry. They also have great sangria and a huge wine and beer selection. *1711 N. Charles St. ☎ 410/332-0110. Menu items $2.95–$15. Tues–Fri 5pm–2am (food served until 11pm); Sat–Sun 4pm–2am (food served until midnight).*

Doable

→ **Kali's Court** ★★ *FELLS POINT* GREEK/SEAFOOD Baltimore seafood and Greek traditions unite at this town fave, worshiped for their enormous, delicious crab cakes. Reservations are highly recommended, though you'll probably still wait for your table. Add this to the lunch-is-much-less list, and you won't have to wait as long. *1606 Thames St. ☎ 410/276-4700. www.kaliscourt.net. Lunch $8–$11; main courses $17–$23. Mon–Sat 11:30am–2:30pm and 5–10pm.*

➔ **Sabatino's** ★ LITTLE ITALY/ITALIAN
It's a near-certainty that you'll take home leftovers if you order individually, so consider going family-style if you're with two or more. Sabatino's is open later than most formal Baltimore restaurants, which makes it a great last stop. *901 Fawn St.* ☎ *410/727-9414. www.sabatinos.com. Lunch $8–$15; main courses $10–$22. Daily noon–3am.*

➔ **Tio Pepe** ★★ MOUNT VERNON
SPANISH Hit this town favorite at lunchtime for a low key, reasonably priced meal, and little or no wait. At dinner, move it to the "Splurge" category. It's known for its great sangria and desserts that are too tempting to refuse. Chocolate soufflé anyone? *10 E. Franklin St.* ☎ *410/539-4675. Lunch $11–$20. Mon–Fri 11:30am–2:30pm; Mon–Thurs 5–10pm; Fri 5–11pm; Sat 5–11:30pm; Sun 4–10pm.*

Splurge

➔ **Black Olive** ★★ FELLS POINT GREEK
Their fixed-price lunch is $17, but it's worth it. You get to choose from the catch of the day, other fresh seafood, and Greek favorites. Reservations are strongly recommended. *814 S. Bond St.* ☎ *410/276-7141. www.theblackolive.com. Fixed-price lunch $17; main courses $20–$30. Daily noon–2:30pm and 5–10pm.*

➔ **Charleston** ★★ HARBOR EAST
AMERICAN/SEAFOOD Another unrivaled seafood joint that caters to the rich and beautiful. A full, five-course dinner runs between $70 and $80, but you can find a few menu items that won't displace a night at a hotel. Unique soups, vegetables, cheeses, and wines make good sharing options. *1000 Lancaster St.* ☎ *410/332-7373. www.charlestonrestaurant.com. Main courses $26–$34. Mon–Thurs 5:30–10pm; Fri–Sat 5:30–11pm.*

MTV🆄 B'more: Crabtown and College Town!

If you're into the college partying scene, **www.baltimorecollege town.com** will be your top choice for prospects. With 15 colleges in the Baltimore area, there's no shortage of frat fun anywhere in the city. The site also features several other searchable listings categories of interest to students, from discount tickets to events listings in sports, arts, and various attractions.

➔ **Obrycki's** ★★ FELLS POINT SEAFOOD
This is a true crab house, with crab soup, crab cocktail, crab balls, crab cakes . . . need I continue? Other menu options include a creative seafood salad and sandwiches. *1727 E. Pratt St.* ☎ *410/732-6399. Lunch $6.95–$14; main courses $15–$29. Mon–Fri 11:30am–10pm; Sat 11:30am–11pm; Sun 11:30am–9:30pm.*

Partying

Power Plant Live (intersection of Market Place and Water St.; **www.power plantlive.com**; see listing below) is a sectioned-off area a few blocks off the Inner Harbor with bars and clubs galore. **Fells Point** (www.fellspoint.us) is another nighttime hot spot for bars and restaurants; it's a waterfront neighborhood filled with drinking establishments that was once a haunt for sailors, and on occasion, a Fell's Point pubcrawler still manages to fall in the water.

At an average Baltimore bar or club, expect to pay around from $1.75 pints to $5 mixed drinks outside of Happy Hour or special promotions. (The fancier places, of course, charge more.)

FESTIVAL SEASON

BARS
Harbor East
➔ **James Joyce Irish Pub and Restaurant** ★ IRISH PUB Furnishings were shipped over from Ireland to add the authentic feel here. This local hangout offers a worthy beer selection as well as an extensive menu. It was voted Baltimore's best bar food in *Baltimore* magazine. *616 S. President St. ☎ 410/727-5107. www.thejames joycepub.com. Drinks starting at $3.25. Mon–Sun 11am–2am.*

Fells Point
🅼 Best ♦ ➔ **Horse You Came In On Saloon** ★★ SALOON When 2-for-1 and all-you-can-drink Happy Hours start at opening and last until 9pm, the crowds can't be hard to find. Happy Hours run every day of the week, and there's live music on weekends at 5 and 10pm. *1626 Thames St. ☎ 410/327-8111. www.horse saloon.com. No cover, drink specials vary. Check website for current specials. $5 buy-1-get-1-free specials; $10 all-you-can-drink specials. Mon–Sun 2pm–2am.*

🅼 Best ♦ ➔ **Max's Taphouse** ★★ PUB How can you go wrong with the largest beer selection in Baltimore? Plus, they have daily Happy Hour specials and pub grub. *737 S. Broadway. ☎ 888/675-6297 or 410/675-MAXS. www.maxs.com. Daily 10:30am–2am.*

➔ **The Wharf Rat** BREWPUB Not to be confused with the support group "Wharf Rats," a group of drug- and alcohol-free concertgoers. In fact, the dozens of ales and draughts on tap would make this pub the worst place for that group. *801 S. Ann St. in Fells Point and 206 W. Pratt St. in Camden Yards. ☎ 410/244-8900. www.thewharfrat. com. No cover. Drinks start at $4. Mon–Sat 11:30am–1am.*

Hampden
➔ **HonBar** ★ Right next door to its sister, Café Hon. Drinks, food, and live music are available. This place won "Third Coldest Beer" in Baltimore. At least they weren't fourth, right? *1002 36th St. ☎ 410/243-1230. www.cafehon.com. No cover. Mon–Thurs 7am–10pm; Fri 7am–10pm; Sat 9am–10pm; Sun 9am–8pm.*

CLUBS
Power Plant Live
➔ **Cancun Cantina** DANCE If you're in the mood to wear your cowboy boots, head over to this rowdy bar. Don't be

Take a Tour, Hon!

Themed, guided walking tours are given by various companies in the Baltimore area. Prices start around $5 and a full list of the tours can be found on the BAVCA website, **www.baltimore.org**.

You can go on a self-guided Architectural History Tour in the old dock neighborhood of Fells Point (812 South Ann St.) through The Preservation Society (☎ **410/675-6750;** www.preservationsociety.com). Reservations are not necessary and the tour is free.

The Preservation Society also runs an interesting tour on immigration to Baltimore, which was second only to Ellis Island in terms of American immigration ports. Hear the stories of "exodus and assimilation into a new culture and country" on the tour, which goes from Fells Point to Locust Point. Reservations are required for the tour, which runs for 1½ to 2 hours the third Saturday of every month at 12:30pm for $10, $5 for students. Call the society at the phone number above, or visit their website.

Bizarre Baltimore (Kind of Redundant)

→ The **American Visionary Art Museum** features work by "self-taught, psychotic or often time compulsive" artists. An interesting piece: A replica of the *Lusitania* made out of 194,000 toothpicks. 800 Key Hwy. ☎ **410/244-1900.** www.avam.org.

→ **Atomic Books** is a colorful, offbeat bookstore that carries everything deemed too-taboo at your local Borders or chain bookstore. They also host live music nights and readings. Upcoming events include "I Hate the 80s Night" and "Atomic Knit Night." 1100 W. 36th St. ☎ **410/662-4444.** www.atomicbooks.com.

→ The **American Dime Museum** pays homage to anything and everything weird. Fiji mermaids, shrunken heads, and two-headed babies are only the beginning. Don't miss the rubber band ball and the sideshow paraphernalia. 1808 Maryland Ave. ☎ **410/230-0263.** By appointment only. www.dimemuseum.net.

→ The **Edgar Allan Poe House & Museum** was Poe's home from 1833 to 1835. Baltimore claims the legendary writer as one of its most famous citizens, although he only lived a small portion of his life there. Poe was buried in 1849 in the Westminster Graveyard in downtown Baltimore. It's said that he still haunts the city. 203 North Amity St. ☎ **410/396-7932.**

surprised when you see a hip-hop-clad group at the bar; the other side of the deck caters to techo/hip-hop heads with a DJ and dance floor. *7501 Old Telegraph Rd. ☎ 410/761 6188. Typically no cover. Tues and Thurs 4pm–midnight; Wed and Fri 4pm–2am; Sat 6pm–2am; Sun 7pm–2am.*

→**Iguana Cantina** DANCE Hip-hop and Latin dance beats have kept the crowds flocking back here since 2004. Or maybe it's the phenomenal drink specials. Either way, the 21+ crowd can't wait to get on the dance floor. *124 Market Place. ☎ 410/244-0200. www.iguanabaltimore.com. Cover varies by night; Thurs $12 open bar; Fri ladies $5 open bar, guys $5 before 10pm and $10 after 10pm; Sat $12 open bar before 10pm, $18 after 10pm; Sun ladies $5, guys $10, buckets of Corona $10. Thurs–Fri and Sun 9pm; Sat 8pm.*

LIVE MUSIC

The **Pier Six Pavillion** ★★ (731 Eastern Ave.; www.piersixpavillion.com) is one of the main concert venues in Baltimore,

hosting major national tours. Check the schedule online for upcoming acts.

For local live music, hit up the **Claddagh Pub Restaurant** ★ (2918 O'Donnell St.; ☎ 410/522-4220) in the Canton neighborhood. Live entertainment, including local bands and DJs, can be found 5 nights a week. For a "rock-'n'-roll dueling piano show," head to **Howl at the Moon** (22 Market Place; ☎ 410/783-5111). The **Lodge Bar** ★ (10 Market Place; ☎ 443/524-2011; www.thelodgebarbaltimore.com) is a rustic, mountain cabin-style bar with live band and DJ sets every Thursday through Sunday until 2am.

More Stuff to See & Do

A COUPLE OF COOL MOVIE HOUSES

→**The Charles Theatre** ★★ Unlike typical movie theaters, this Baltimore staple shows specialty films, foreign films, and classics. The 108-year-old building boasts 1,150 seats in a 23,000 square foot space.

Check the website for a current film schedule. *1711 North Charles St.* ☎ *410/727-FILM.* *www. thecharles.com. Matinees $6; evenings $8. Check website for schedule.*

→ **The Senator Theatre** ★★★ This single-screen Art Deco theater was built in 1939 and hosts many movie premieres (including some by Baltimore auteur John Waters). It's a much-loved (and attended) local icon in the northern part of Baltimore. Check the website for a current film schedule. *5904 York Rd.* ☎ *410/435-8338. www. senator.com. All tickets $8, cash only. Free parking. Check website for schedule.*

HALL OF FAMER'S HOME

The **Babe Ruth Birthplace** (216 Emory St.; ☎ 410/727-1539; www.baberuthmuseum. com) is a must-see for sports fans. The baseball legend was a Baltimorean and the museum features rare artifacts, photos, and videos. Yankee fans are welcome, too. Sigh.

Bye, Bye, Baltimore!

See you later, hon! It's time to head about 40 miles south to a different city, and a whole different state of mind: Washington, DC.

Pride & Wine: A Couple of DC & VA Fests

It's great to be in DC when you know more people have come to dress in drag than to visit the White House. Capital Pride features a week of events, parties, and workshops, culminating with a fabulous parade on Saturday and a free, full-day street festival on Sunday. Although there are more than enough Pride-related events to keep you busy for the entire week, DC has no shortage of attractions—even without a White House visit.

Washington, DC Nuts & Bolts

Area Codes   Within the District of Columbia, it's 202.

Drugstores   **CVS,** Washington's major drugstore chain, has two 24-hour locations: in the West End, 2200 M Street NW (☎ 202/296-9877) and Dupont Circle, 7 Dupont Circle NW at 20th and P streets (☎ 202/785-1466). Both stores have round-the-clock pharmacies.

Emergencies   In any emergency, call ☎ 911.

Internet Access   Try Cyberstop Café (1513 17th St. NW; ☎ 202/234-2470; www. cyberstopcafe.com), where you can get a bite to eat while you surf one of 11 computers. The cafe is open from 7am to midnight Monday through Friday, opening at 8am on the weekends. Computer rental is $6.99 per half-hour or $8.99 per hour.

Maps   Free city maps are often available at hotels and throughout town at tourist attractions. You can also contact the Washington, DC Convention and Tourism Corporation (901 7th St. NW, 4th floor, Washington, DC 20001; ☎ 202/789-7000; www.washington.org).

Police   In an emergency, dial ☎ 911. For a non-emergency, call ☎ 202/727-1010.

Weather   Call ☎ 202/936-1212 or visit www.weather.com.

Washington, DC Area Festivals

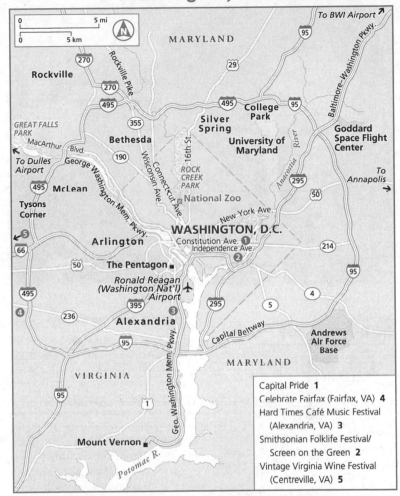

Capital Pride **1**
Celebrate Fairfax (Fairfax, VA) **4**
Hard Times Café Music Festival
    (Alexandria, VA) **3**
Smithsonian Folklife Festival/
    Screen on the Green **2**
Vintage Virginia Wine Festival
    (Centreville, VA) **5**

Capital Pride Festival in a Box

Contact   Call ☎202/797-3510 or visit www.capitalpride.org.

Dates   In 2006, Capital Pride ran from June 2 through June 11. Check the website for 2007 dates.

Tickets   The parade and street festival are free. Evening dance parties or bar events may have a cover. In 2006, the opening night dance party was $12. Some events offer discount advance tickets. Many of the featured workshops and events are free.

Having a fabulous time at DC Pride.

DC Ditties: Pride Playlist

→ *Don't Leave Me This Way,* **Thelma Houston,** "Best of Thelma Houston," 2004

→ *Wrong,* **Kimberly Locke,** "One Love," 2004

→ *Be My Lover,* **La Bouche,** "Sweet Dreams," 1996

→ *Free,* **DJ Paulo,** "Fireball: Volume 3," 2003

→ *Dance The Night Away,* **The Gemz,** "Blue Is For Girls," 2006

→ *This Is Your Night,* **Amber,** "This Is Your Night," 1992

→ *We're In The Money/Pennies From Heaven,* **Bernadette Peters,** "Sondheim, Etc., Etc.," 2005

→ *Finally,* **CeCe Peniston,** "Finally," 1992

PRIDE OF THE DISTRICT

The best part of Capital Pride has to be the wrap up street festival on the closing day. While the nightly parties, events, and lectures are entertaining and fun, the final fest brings the whole group together in a setting that's family-friendly while still keeping the essence of what Pride is all about: fun, individuality, unity. You'll see biker dudes dressed in full leather, plenty of tattoos, and couples strolling with their kids. The handouts were, hands down, the best part (among them: condoms, dental dams, candy, even clothing) but besides leaving with bags full of goodies, the food was great and the whole atmosphere was energizing and friendly.

Events hit a wide range of styles and cultures at DC Pride: 2006 saw an opening night dance party as well as the Mr. Capital Pride Leather Meet & Greet; a Town Hall Meeting: Building Bridges Without Destroying Identities hosted by the Human Rights Campaign; Annual LGBT Pride Week

Vintage, VA Playlist

- → *Chill, Relax. Now,* **Scott Miller & The Commonwealth,** "Upside Downside," 2003
- → *Dance,* **Old School Freight Train,** "Run," 2006
- → *Cannonball,* **Hackensaw Boys,** "Love What You Do," 2005
- → *Ridin' That Midnight Train,* **Ricky Skaggs,** "Bluegrass Rules!," 1997
- → *Fastball,* **Yonder Mountain String Band,** "Yonder Mountain String Band," 2006
- → *Good 'Ol Girls,* **John McCutcheon,** "Mightier Than The Sword," 2006
- → *Rain Please Go Away,* **Alison Kraus,** "Lonely Runs Both Ways," 2004
- → *Tango Chutney,* **Old School Freight Train,** "Run," 2006

Interfaith Service: "Many Faiths, All Proud!" with a featured choir; Mr. and Miss Capital Pride Pageant; a Bachelor Auction of desirable DC bachelors and their "special gift packages"; Liquid Ladies—the Official Ladies Dance of Capital Pride; and of course, the Capital Pride Parade; and the 31st Annual Pride Street Festival.

Across the River: Vintage Virginia Wine Festival

If they're scheduled close enough to each other, you can base yourself in DC to attend this Virginia festival. Virginia has been making wine since 1608. This event, the state's oldest and largest wine festival, attracts hundreds of wineries. You'll have more than enough time to stroll and sample wine, but there's also lively entertainment and plenty of space to dance. Admission includes unlimited tasting, so expect to stumble off the bus a little tipsy at the end of the day. (It's not too far from DC, so you can take the Metro and not have to worry about getting behind the wheel once.)

Vintage Virginia Festival in a Box

Contact Call ☎ 540/745-FEST or visit www.vintagevirginia.com

Dates In 2006, the festival was held on June 3 and 4.

Food Food is available for purchase, but it's mostly fast food-type grub: hamburgers, hot dogs, fries. Outside food is allowed in.

Hours Gates are open from 10am to 8pm both days of the festival.

Location Bull Run Regional Park is at 14925 Compton Road, in Centreville, VA.

Restrictions No pets, outside alcohol, illegal substances.

Schedule In addition to the wineries present, there are over 70 vendors, artists, and exhibitors. There were also performances throughout the day, including country-tinged shows by Scott Miller & the Commonwealth, John McCutcheon, Hackensaw Boys, Old School Freight Train, Blue Mule, and Smooth Kentucky.

Tickets In 2006, tickets were $20 in advance and $25 the day of the event. Tickets included a commemorative wine glass, musical entertainment, and unlimited wine tasting. (Yes, they will check your ID.) Designated Driver tickets were available for $12. Group rates were offered.

FESTIVAL SEASON

Transportation   For $10 you can buy a "No Worries Single Day Shuttle Pass" that covers round-trip transportation to the Vienna, VA, Metro Station. The Vienna Metro Station is the last, most western stop on the Metro orange line, which is 30 minutes from central DC. On weekends, a one-way fare to the Vienna Metro Station from Metro Center is $2.35. Parking at the Vienna Metro Station is $3.75 for a full day. If you get there early enough you shouldn't have a problem: there are 5,849 all-day spots. Shuttle service runs from 10am to 6pm.

Weather   The event goes rain or shine. June in Virginia can be hot and humid, so dress accordingly.

Getting Around

I say I'd like to raise my kids in DC because the street layout will help them learn their letters and numbers. DC's streets are numbered (running north and south) and lettered (running east and west), which is almost a foolproof system, even for tourists. There are four quadrants (Northeast, Northwest, Southwest, and Southeast), although visitors often spend most of their time in Northwest. Between some of the streets are named avenues like Independence and Constitution. Yes, even the streets are politically inclined. Public transportation is highly recommended, especially because it's easy to take the Metro from the suburbs to the heart of the city.

BY CAR

The streets of DC are quite congested during the week and driving in the city may be tricky if you haven't done it before. My advice: Avoid it if you can. All the one-way streets complicate navigation. Paying for parking (if you find a spot) on main streets is not cheap: $1/hour with a two-hour max.

Word Up: Wine Lingo

Here's a helpful glossary of a few terms that will let you sound like . . . well, not a wine expert, but you can throw 'em out as you're tippling.

→   **balance:** a wine that has no dominating element

→   **body:** the consistency of a wine. Some wines have a watery texture, others are creamy

→   **big:** high alcohol content

→   **crisp:** a wine with a tasteful, fruity acidity

→   **fat:** a full-bodied wine

→   **fermentation:** the process in which grape sugar becomes ethyl alcohol and carbon dioxide through heat release

→   **finish:** the aftertaste of a wine

→   **nose:** the smell of a wine

→   **oaky:** wines that are fermented or aged in oak barrels often pick up some of that flavor

→   **tannin:** chemicals found in grape skins, seeds, stems, and even wood barrels that may give younger wines a bitter taste

→   **vintage:** the year that a wine's grapes were harvested

Transfer Tip

If you're going to continue a Metro journey by bus, grab a transfer in the mezzanine of your originating underground Metro station. You'll get a discounted rate of 85¢ each way for the bus fare after you ride the Metrorail. (Sorry, bus-to-subway transfers are not permitted.)

There are also blackout times during rush hours (7–9:30am and 4–6:30pm on weekdays). *Beware:* If your car gets towed after 7pm on Friday or throughout the weekend, you won't get it back until 9am on Monday at the earliest. Local parking garages are generally open weekdays from 6am to 11pm. Rates start at about $8/hour and go up from there. To find a parking garage, contact **Parking Management, Inc.** (☎ 202/785-9191; www.pmi-parking. net) for maps, hours, and prices.

Suburban Metro stations have parking, starting at $3.50/day during the week, with weekends free. Contact the **Washington Metropolitan Area Transit Authority** (☎ 202/962-1234; www.wmata.com) for a comprehensive listing. If you do end up driving and you plan on staying for the entire week, try to book a hotel that includes cheap or free parking.

BY METRO

DC's **Metro** (☎ 202/637-7000; www. wmata.com) is one of the most efficient and clean systems in the world. Five color-coded zones comprise the system, stretching into Virginia and Maryland, and stopping at museums, theaters, landmarks, colleges, and even Ronald Reagan Washington National Airport. Grab a "Pocket Guide" at any Metro station; the map will give you the lowdown on the entire system. Fares range from $1.35 to $3.90, depending on the distance you're traveling. Service hours are Monday through Thursday 5am to midnight; Friday 5am to 3am; Saturday 7am to 3am; and Sunday 7am to midnight.

BY BUS

Patriotic red, white, and blue signs will direct you to **Metrobus** (☎ 202/ 637-7000; www.wmata.com) stops. Unfortunately, these signs fail to inform you where you're headed. What's even worse is that the posted schedules at the stops are usually outdated. Call for routing information, or check the online schedule. You can also request a free map, bus schedule, and information about lots, hours, locations, and so on. Within DC, the base fare is $1.25 and transfers are free and valid for 2 hours from the time of boarding. Travel outside of the city may increase the price. A 1-week pass is $11, available online and at Metro Center stations around town. When possible, the underground Metro is the way to go. The plus side of the buses is that they run almost 24/7.

A Fair Fare

If you're planning on using the Metro a lot over the course of a day, consider buying a **1 Day Pass** for $6.50, which will give you unlimited Metro rides from 9:30am until closing. If you think you'll only use the Metro once or twice in a day, it's best to put a lump sum on a card and use it as you go. All stations have fare machines, but use small bills, as change is limited. Machines do accept debit and credit cards. Regular fares apply during the most hectic travel times: 5 to 9:30am and 3 to 7pm weekdays, and 2 to 3am Friday and Saturday nights. Fares are reduced at all other times.

DC "Do"s: A Calendar of More Events

Oh, do they have festivals in DC! As one of our nation's visitor magnets, you can find a dizzying array of events showing off the best in area music, food, and booze, all summer long.

→ **Washington, DC Summer Restaurant Week** is a January and midsummer favorite. Similar to New York and Miami, DC's version features the best of the best for less—much less. Fixed-price, three-course lunches will be $20.07, with dinners going for $30.07. Log on to **www.washington.org/ restaurantwk** for participating venues.

→ *"Great Food. Good People. Cheap Prices."*—a slogan no one will complain about—is the motto of the Hard Times Café in Alexandria, VA. If you like a good ol' fiesta, sans unruly crowds, check out their **Hard Times Café Music Festival (www.hardtimes.com)**. This free annual event, usually held the first week of June, features local country stars, plus ample food and drink—don't miss the cafe's killer signature chili. Wash it down with a cold Bud, served from oversized trucks lining a closed-off street in the heart of quaint Old Town Alexandria. The event is a short walk from the King Street Metro station, which is easily reached from DC's yellow or blue Metro lines. Even if you're not a huge country music fan, you'll still enjoy the easygoing crowd, which includes everyone from frat boys to grandmas.

→ **The Smithsonian Folklife Festival (www.folklife.si.edu)** will celebrate its 41st year in 2007. The annual event, held on the National Mall, prides itself in being an "international family reunion" that brings people together through activities as diverse as song, dance, storytelling, art, and even cooking. It's a great way to get a taste of a different culture without having to break out the passport. The 2007 festival will be held from June 27 to July 1 and July 4 to July 8. Daytime events run from 11am to 5:30pm, with evening programming starting at 6pm.

→ Northern Virginia's largest annual party is **Celebrate Fairfax (www. celebratefairfax.org)**. In 2006, artists Collective Soul, Sister Hazel, and Sugar Ray performed. The event, held about 20 miles from DC in Fairfax, VA, takes place in early June. Games, food, and entertainment attract thousands of visitors. Tickets are $10 at the gate.

→ **Screen on the Green** is a favorite local summertime movie ritual. Free movies at the National Mall are shown June through August. Bring your blankets and some snacks, Monday nights at dusk. ☎ **877/262-5866.**

BY TAXI

Taxis are a DC no-no. Unlike the Big Apple, short trips here don't always translate into low fares: DC's taxicab system is split into a zone system that can seem incomprehensible. You'll pay $6.50 for a single zone and up to $19 for an eight-zone ride. An innocent 3-minute ride can cross three zones, setting you back $11. From 7 to 9:30am and 4 to 6:30pm on weekdays there's a rush-hour surcharge of $1. If you have more than one bag, they'll add on 50¢ per piece, plus $2 for larger pieces. There's also a $1.50 charge for every person over the age of one. Yeah, it sucks.

Oh, and before you start dialing, try hailing one first, as fares for phoned-in taxis are $1 extra. If you must: **Diamond Cab Company**

(☎ 202/387-6200) or **Yellow Cab** (☎ 202/
544-1212; www.dctaxi.dc.gov).

ON FOOT

DC is 67 square miles, but it's a pedestrian-
friendly place, with a map on what seems
like every street corner. The Metro system
services the major neighborhoods, so you
won't have to endure a full-body workout
when you get off at the nearest stop. The
Capitol building is the center of DC, the
meeting point of the four quadrants. The
numbered and lettered streets take off
from there, with SW, SE, NE, or NW tagged
to the end of addresses. For lettered
streets, forget about J, X, Y, or Z—they
don't exist. As you get further away from
the Capitol, you'll notice the streets take
on two-syllable names, and then three-
syllable names. These names roughly follow alphabetical order, so you can tell
which direction you're going (the alphabet
goes up as you travel north). Diagonal
streets are named after U.S. states.

Sleeping

Plenty of low-cost accommodations can
be found within the city or a short Metro
ride away. DC's neighborhoods range from
the swanky Georgetown to the colorful
Dupont Circle to the funky Adams-Morgan.
Fortunately, the convenience of the Metro
won't limit you to only one of these areas
just because your temporary bed is there.

HOSTEL/CAMPING
In DC

➜ **Hostelling International** ★★ This hostel is in a safe neighborhood less than a
mile from the White House (and walking
distance from the bus and train stations).
The colorful paintjob inside will distract
you from the lackluster rooms, though the
place is admirably clean and livable.
Private rooms are available, as well as
rooms with 6+ beds. Towels and bedding
are provided, but don't take a shower
expecting a waiting towel—ask for one
upon arrival. The staff is friendly, and
offers good advice about what to see and
do, as well as organized tours. *1009 11th
Street NW.* ☎ *202/737-2333. www.hiwashington
dc.org. Single $79; double $89; quad $33; dorm
$29. All non-members pay a $3 per person per
night temporary membership fee. Amenities:
Free wireless Internet; paid computers; laundry facilities; storage lockers; all bathrooms
shared.*

FESTIVAL SEASON

Surf DC: Recommended Websites

➜ **www.washington.org**. If you're being touristy, this website is a must. The
DC Convention and Tourism Corporation's website will guide you through
the capital whether you're looking for a hotel, restaurant, mall, or just basic
facts about the city. The website also features a database of major annual
events that can be searched by date and category.

➜ **www.dc.gov**. This is the official site of the DC government. Locals whine
about the site because they only visit it to pay parking tickets, but there are
tons of useful event and activity listings for travelers.

➜ **www.culturaltourismdc.org**. This grassroots organization collaborates
with local companies to promote some of the cooler, little-known events in
the area. Find itineraries, calendars, tours, and interesting facts you won't
find on other websites.

➜ **www.washingtonian.com**. Check out the "What's Happening" section for
updated information on activities, festivals, and events in the area.

Outside DC

→**Aquia Pines Camp Resort** If you want to rough it in the wilderness, head to this resort in Stafford, VA, about 45 minutes outside of DC. Opt for a cozy cabin to ensure a bug-free sleep, or pitch your tent if you're really hardcore. The reservation-only campsite also welcomes RVs. Cabins come in two varieties, rustic or luxury (at a rate that's still a lot less than a luxury hotel). *3071 Jefferson Davis Hwy. ☎ 800/726-1710 or 540/659-3447. www.aquiapines. com. 3-night minimum stay; rates based on double occupancy. Campsite $39; Group rate $8.50 for 6+; Rustic cabin $52; Luxury cabin $115. Amenities: Free wireless Internet; water; telephone. Check website for add-on costs.*

→**Cherry Hill Park** ★ More like a mini-Disneyworld than a campground, this park offers free nightly movies, a cafe, and a heated pool and sauna. It's also the closest park to DC, with both Gray Line and Metro buses providing connection to downtown attractions. Bring your own tent or RV, or rent a cabin or air-conditioned trailer—with fully equipped kitchens and cable, of course. *9800 Cherry Hill Road, College Park, MD ☎ 800/801-6449 or 301/937-7116. www. cherryhillpark.com. Tents $38; RVs $50; Cabins $70; Trailers $95. Rates include 2 people, additional people are $5 each. Amenities: Water; sewer and electric hookups; restrooms; hot showers; laundry room.*

→**Bull Run Regional Park Campground** This campground is within walking distance of the Vintage Virginia Wine Festival—so close, in fact, it shares the park site's name. (And the rates stay the same during the festival! But book ahead if you're planning on camping at Vintage Virginia.) Group rates are available. *7700 Bull Run Dr. ☎ 703/631-0550. www.nvrpa.org. Non-electric site $20; electric site $26; check website for other rates.*

CHEAP

There's a **Days Inn** (4400 Connecticut Ave. NW.; ☎ 800/DAYSINN or 202/244-5600; www.daysinn.com) that offers rooms from $58 a night and is walking distance to Metro stations. On the other side of town, about 5 miles southeast, is a **Howard Johnson Express Inn** (600 New York Ave. NE.; ☎ 800/446-5656 or 202/546-9200; www.hojo.com) that runs from $76 per night in the summer.

→**Kalorama Guest House** ★ Known for airy, spacious rooms, this clean, good-value spot is a perfect alternative for travelers who don't want to rough it in a true hostel but are still budget conscious. This place is an antiques-lover's dream. Vintage finds inside match the classic Victorian exterior. *1854 Mintwood Place. NW between 19th St. and Columbia Rd. in Adams Morgan. Metro: Dupont Circle. ☎ 202/667-6369. www. kaloramaguesthouse.com. Double with shared bathroom $65–$75; double with private bathroom $90–$100; suite or apt $120–$135. Extra person $5 in doubles, $10 in suites. Amenities: Continental breakfast; A/C; $7 parking (limited); free local calls; access to laundry; ironing; kitchen facilities.*

DOABLE

In 2006, the **Crowne Plaza at Washington National Airport** (1480 Crystal Dr.; ☎ 800/2CROWNE or 703/416-1600; www. cpnationalairport.com) and the **Holiday Inn National Airport at Crystal City** (2650 Jefferson Davis Hwy.; ☎ 800/HOLIDAY or 703/684-7200; www.hinational airport.com) offered special rates for Capital Pride attendees starting as low as $129.

→**Jurys Normandy Inn** ★ This boutique inn, a part of the Irish-owned Jurys chain of nice business-class hotels, is in the heart of DC. While you may not have tons of space, the staff is nice and the rooms are charming. *2118 Wyoming Ave. NW.* ☎ *800/424-3729 or 202/483-1350. www.jurysdoyle.com. Singles start at $89. Amenities: Exercise room, pool, and restaurant at its sister hotel around the corner.*

SPLURGE

If you're going to splurge, do it right. And the predictable Ritz-Carlton or Hyatt are not the places to do it—especially since you can splurge in DC without busting the budget. DC's selection of Kimpton Hotels (**www.kimptonhotels.com**) is extensive and their colorful, individualized auras totally justify a little extra money. The Kimpton Hotels in DC include: Hotel George, Hotel Helix (see below), Hotel Madera (see listing below), Hotel Monaco, Hotel Palomar, Hotel Rouge, and Topaz Hotel.

Regular rates are reasonable, though you'll pay a hefty premium for one of the legendary "specialty rooms." Some of your choices: **Nosh Room** with a kitchenette and grocery shopping service; **Screening Room** with an additional TV, DVD player, and library of DVDs; and **Zone Room,** with plasma screen TV, high-tech stereo system, lava lamp, and lounge chair.

MTV **Best** ✪ → **Hotel Helix** ★★ You won't check in with humans; illuminated "pods" with flatscreen computers do the job instead—after you walk past the giant blue lawn chairs and automatic curtains, that is. While the rooms are über colorful, Kimpton somehow manages to make bright orange bathroom vanities and lime-green armoires seem modest and subtle. Twenty-two-inch flatscreen TVs are another distraction, if you need one. *1430 Rhode Island Ave. NW between 14th and 15th sts. Metro: McPherson Sq.* ☎ *866/508-0658 or 202/462-9001. www.hotelhelix.com. Double $139–$309; add $50 to double rate for specialty rooms; add $100 to double rate for suites; extra person $20. Best rates usually Sun–Mon. Amenities: A/C; TV w/pay movies; 2-line phones w/dataports;*

minibar; hair dryer; iron; Nintendo; CD player; Web TV access (for a fee); free wireless Internet access.

MTV **Best** ✪ → **Hotel Madera** ★★ Eccentric animal print fabrics, satiny pillows, and sleek, black granite bathroom vanities are as exciting as the spacious rooms. It's in a lively neighborhood in Dupont and has a great restaurant, **Firefly.** Housed in a 1940s-era building, the hotel still gleams with a super sleek modern aura. *1310 New Hampshire Ave. NW between N and O sts. at Dupont Circle. Metro: Dupont Circle.* ☎ *800/368-5691 or 202/296-7600. www.hotelmadera.com. Double $139–$339; extra person $20. AE, DC, DISC, MC, V. Amenities: Evening wine hour; $26 parking; free wireless Internet; onsite hybrid car available for rental; CD and DVD library; day pass to nearby gym.*

Eating

As an international city, DC has some amazing global eats. Though it's easy to drop a load of cash, you can also find quick, cheap bites that aren't going to leave you penniless or clog your arteries.

Keep your eyes open for Happy Hour specials during the week. Tons of restaurants do dinner and drink specials during the 5pm to 8pm time frame, when many DC employees are decompressing from running the nation with a little liquid "attitude adjustment." If you want to search for something specific, visit **www.washingtonian.com/dining** to search by food type, price, and neighborhood.

SUPPLIES

There are at least seven **Safeway** (1701 Corcoran St. NW, 514 Rhode Island Ave. NE, or 1800 20th St. NW; ☎ **877/SAFEWAY; www.safeway.com**) grocery stores in central DC. Typically, this chain is clean and budget-conscious, making it a great place to stock up on water, snacks, beer, and other festival supplies. Generally, they're open until midnight.

There are also three **Whole Foods Markets** (2323 Wisconsin Ave. NW, 1440 P St. NW, 4530 40th St. NW; **www.whole foodsmarket.com**) around DC. These super health food stores stay open 8am to 10pm daily.

TAKEOUT TREATS

For something a little different, try one of the three Asian Fusion–themed **Teaism** ★★ (800 Connecticut Ave. NW, 2009 R St. NW, 400 8th St. NW; ☎ **888/8TEAISM;** www.teaism.com) teashops and restaurants in DC. Beyond tea you'll find yummy Japanese, Thai, and baked goods, all available for take-out. Stop by Thursday or Friday between 5:30 and 7:30pm for Happy Hour—free hors d'oeuvres with the purchase of a drink. In Georgetown, head to **Dolcezza** ★★ (1560 Wisconsin Ave.; ☎ **202/333-4646**) for the-real-thing gelato: Their secret is lots of cream. It's not cheap ($4/scoop), but if you want the real McCoy, this is where it's at.

Dessert all day long is the motto of **CakeLove** ★★ (1506 U St. NW; ☎ **866/ 708-7100** or 202/588-7100). They have every imaginable flavor of cake, pastry, and baked good—all made from scratch. Right next door is its sister, **Love Café** (1501 U St. NW; ☎ **202/265-9800**), serving breakfast, sandwiches, salads, and soups, starting at $3. On a more carnivorous note, stop by **Morton's Steakhouse** (1050 Connecticut Ave.; ☎ **202/955-5997;** www.mortons.com; also 3251 Prospect St. NW; ☎ **202/342-6258**) during weeknight Happy Hour (5–7pm) to sample free steak sandwiches.

EATING OUT

If you're on the go and don't feel like eating pure lard, healthy chains can be found all over DC. **Baja Fresh** (1333 New Hampshire Ave. and 1990 K St. NW; **www.bajafresh. com**) serves fresh, Mexican-style food.

The menu includes hefty burritos and salads for way under $10. **Così** (10th St. and E St. NW; 12th St. and G St. NW; and 15th St. and K St. NW; **www.getcosi.com**) is also a chain fave, with everything from sandwiches and soups to pizzas and salads. There are more than 10 in central DC. You can find similar fare at the 15 area **Au Bon Pain** (**www.aubonpain.com**) cafes, known for their reasonable prices and clean atmospheres.

Cheap

📺 Best ◐ → **Amsterdam Falafelshop**
★★ *ADAMS-MORGAN* MIDDLE EASTERN If you're not in the mood for pizza but still want something with a little grease, head to 2425 Achttiende Straat NW (that's Dutch for 18th St.), in Adams-Morgan. Don't fret if you're feeling indecisive—there are only three menu items (falafels, fries, and brownies), and you can't go wrong with any of them. *2425 18th St. NW. Metro: Woodley Park-Zoo/Adams Morgan ☎ 202/234-1969. www.falafelshop.com. Falafel $3.85–$5.50. Cash only. Sun–Mon 11am–midnight; Tues–Wed 11am–2:30am; Thurs 11am–3am; Fri–Sat 11am–4am.*

→ **Ben's Chili Bowl** ★ *U STREET* AMERICAN You don't have to settle for street meat when you leave the club. At Ben's, you can grab a chili dog, turkey sub, or cheese fries and not regret it a few minutes later. *1213 U St. NW. ☎ 202/667-0909. Main courses $2.50–$6.05. Cash only. Mon–Thurs 6am–2am; Fri–Sat 6am–4am; Sun noon–8pm.*

→ **Booeymonger** *GEORGETOWN* DELI The name of this place alone should make you look twice. Choose from dozens of sandwiches or create your own. The Scheherazade is a favorite, combining turkey, Swiss cheese, mango chutney, and mayo on a baguette. *3265 Prospect St. NW. ☎ 202/333-4810. Sandwiches $4.75–$6.50. Daily 8am–noon.*

→**The Diner** *ADAMS-MORGAN* AMERI-CAN Still dancing on tables at 4am and your stomach's grumbling? Not a problem: You can still grab some grub in Adams-Morgan at this all-night joint. If you're in the mood for plain (or feeling queasy), stick with eggs, coffee, or grilled cheese. Otherwise, sample more offbeat fare like grilled fresh salmon club sandwiches. *2453 18th St. NW. Metro: Woodley Park-Zoo/Adams Morgan* ☎ *202/232-8800. Sandwiches from $2.99; burgers, full breakfasts start at $6.99. Daily 24 hr.*

→**Haad Thai** ★ *DOWNTOWN* THAI This Thai joint is one of the few downtown so lunchtime on weekdays can be busy. You'll always be safe with standard fare like pad Thai and chicken satay, but most everything on the menu is tasty and won't kill you with spiciness. *1100 New York Ave. NW. Metro: Metro Center.* ☎ *202/682-1111. Lunch main courses $5–$9; dinner reservations recommended, main courses $8–$17. AE, DC, MC, V. Mon–Fri 11:30am–2:30pm and 5–10:30pm; Sat noon 10:30pm; Sun 5–10:30pm.*

→**Le Bon Café** ★ *CAPITOL HILL* AMERICAN Simple sandwiches, salads, and homemade baked goods are the draw at this tiny, popular cafe on Capitol Hill. Big bad chains may rule the majority of the street, but this gem is worth seeking out; it's tasty and cheap. *2120 2nd St. SE. Metro: Capitol South.* ☎ *202/547-7200. Breakfast items $1.25–$4.25; lunch fare $3.85–$8.25. Mon–Fri 7:30am–4pm; Sat–Sun 8:30am–3:30pm.*

Doable

→**Kaz Sushi Bistro** ★★ *FOGGY BOTTOM* JAPANESE One of the best sushi restaurants in the DC area, Kaz caters mostly to businessmen and hard-core sushi aficionados. Grab a seat at the bar to watch the master in action: Chef/owner Kaz is one of only a few chefs who can handle blowfish, which is poisonous if not cut correctly.

Don't worry—it's only served in winter. *1915 I St. NW. Metro: Farragut West.* ☎ *202/530-5500. www.kazsushi.com. Sushi a la carte $3.50–$7; lunch main courses $10–$18; dinner main courses $13–$25. Mon–Fri 11:30am–2pm and 6–10pm; Sat 6–10pm.*

→**Kramerbooks & Afterwords Café & Grill** ★★ *DUPONT CIRCLE* AMERICAN You may find yourself at this joint more than once; It's a bookstore, live music venue, and restaurant serving breakfast, lunch, dinner, and after-hours meals on the weekends. When you've partied all night and that Red Bull won't let you sleep, stop by this Dupont Circle for a bite and a book all night Friday or Saturday. The menu covers quesadillas to French toast to fries. *1517 Connecticut Ave. NW. Metro: Dupont Circle.* ☎ *202/387-1400. Breakfast $1.25–$8.25; lunch $4.50–$13; dinner $10–$18. Mon–Thurs 7:30am–1am; Fri–Sat 24 hr.*

→**Pizzeria Paradiso** ★ *DUPONT CIRCLE* ITALIAN One of the, if not *the*, best pizzas in DC. Choose from 29 toppings, cooked up in an oak-burning oven. There's also create-your-own panini and tempting desserts. *2029 P St. NW. Metro: Dupont Circle.* ☎ *202/223-1245. Sandwiches and salads $4.50–$7.95; pizzas $9.50–$17. Mon–Sat 11:30am–11pm; Sun noon–10pm.*

→**Tony Cheng's Seafood Restaurant** ★ *DOWNTOWN* CHINESE If you're in the mood for authentic Chinese that doesn't look like it was cooked on a sidewalk, Tony Cheng's is the place to go. It's been in business for almost 30 years and is famous for its Cantonese roast duck. Head up to the second floor, above Tony Cheng's Mongolian Restaurant. *619 H St. NW. Metro: Gallery Place/Chinatown.* ☎ *202/371-8669. Lunch main courses $5–$13; dinner main courses $7–$29. Daily 11am–11pm.*

MTV **Best** ● →**Zaytinya** ★★★ *DOWNTOWN* MEDITERRANEAN Not many 4-year-old restaurants serve a thousand

FESTIVAL SEASON

heads per night on weekends. This one does. (The popularity is a testament to the kitchen's skill.) You're better off sharing lots of little dishes, even though you probably won't understand what you're ordering. Let the waiters guide you through the menu while you're nibbling on free pita bread. *701 9th St. NW. Metro: Gallery Place/Chinatown.* ☎ *202/638-0800. Mezze items $3.75–$9.75; lunch main courses $7.25–$8.95; dinner main courses $18–$23. Sun–Mon 11:30am–10pm; Tues–Thurs 11:30am–11:30pm; Fri–Sat 11:30am–midnight.*

[MTV] (Best ❂) →Zed's ★★★ *GEORGETOWN* ETHIOPIAN   If it's good enough for Hillary Clinton and Clint Eastwood, it's good enough for you. Try something different in this charming, authentic Ethiopian spot, known for its tasty lamb and chicken dishes. They also have superb pastries, and a full bar. *1201 28th St. NW.* ☎ *202/333-4710. www.zeds.net. Main courses $9–$18. AE, DC, MC, V. Daily 11am–11pm.*

Splurge

→Kinkead's ★★ *FOGGY BOTTOM* AMERICAN/SEAFOOD   It might be a little over the top for poor college students, but if you're a seafood fan looking for a decent sit-down meal, this is a must-go. The award-winning chef specializes in the fruits of the sea, but there's also solid beef and poultry. Great for a light lunch, but evenings are lively with a pianist or band almost nightly. *2000 Pennsylvania Ave. NW. Metro: Foggy Bottom.* ☎ *202/296-7700. www. kinkead.com. Lunch and dinner main courses $22–$37; light fare $6–$25. Mon–Sat 11:30am–2:30pm; nightly 5:30–9:30pm; light fare served weekdays 2:30–5:30pm. Reservations recommended.*

Partying

DC may be chock-full o' serious-looking government suits and policy wonks during the day, but things get significantly looser

come nightfall. And, of course, there are *lots* of colleges in the area, whose students always keep things young and hopping.

BARS

Downtown/East End

→Lima Restaurant ★★ LOUNGE/DANCE   This multifaceted restaurant/bar/club/ lounge is over the top when it comes to dinner prices, but their drink specials and dancing can't be beat. Bop to house and dance music in the lounge starting at 10pm. The colorful, dimly lit space radiates style. *1401 K St. NW. Metro: McPherson Sq.* ☎ *202/789-2800. www.limarestaurant.com. Beer $4; wine $5. Happy Hour Mon–Fri 5–7pm; Lounge Tues–Sun 9pm–late night.*

Dupont Circle

→Café Citron ★★ LATIN   For salsa lessons and great drinks, hit up this colorful spot. Brush up on your flamenco on Monday nights, listen to Latin jazz on Tuesdays, and take a free salsa lesson Wednesday. They say their music will make you move, even if you don't dance. *1343 Connecticut Ave. NW. Metro: Dupont Circle.* ☎ *202/530-8844. Drinks start at $2.75; pitchers start at $19. Usually no cover. Mon–Thurs 11:30am–2am; Fri–Sat noon–3am. Happy Hour Mon–Fri 5–7pm.*

Foggy Bottom

→Froggy Bottom Pub PUB   Look up college pub in the phonebook and you'll find this place. It's collegiate through and through, right down to the neon pizza sign in the window, pool tables, and hoards of GW students clad in Greek-life shirts. The pub slows down during the summer, but it's still a good Happy Hour option. *2142 Pennsylvania Ave. NW.* ☎ *202-338-3000. No cover. Mon–Wed and Sun 11am–1am; Thurs–Sat 11am–3am. Happy Hour daily 4–6pm.*

Georgetown

→Bistrot Lepic ★ BISTRO/WINE BAR   This Georgetown favorite is highlighted by a Tuesday night ritual: complimentary wine tasting at the Wine Bar. *1736 Wisconson Ave. NW.* ☎ *202/303-1111. Wine tasting complimentary, Tues 6–8pm.*

CLUBS
Dupont Circle
→ **The Eighteenth Street Lounge** ⋆ DANCE/LOUNGE   Dress to impress or you won't get in. From new club music to classic jazz, you can dance or just chill at this hip hideaway—if you get past the velvet ropes. *1212 18th St. NW. Metro: Dupont Circle or Farragut North.* ☎ *202/466-3922. Cover varies, usually $10, free before 10pm if the bouncer is in a good mood. Mon–Wed 10pm–3am; Thurs–Sat 5:30pm–3am.*

→ **MCCXXIII** DANCE   If theme nights "Spank Me!" and "Lust" don't alarm you, you've been to one too many frat parties. It's called 12-23 (like its address), and even a small dance floor won't stop anyone from shakin' it, though the drinks can be expensive. *1223 Connecticut Ave. NW. Metro: Dupont Circle or Farragut North.* ☎ *202/ 822-1800. www.1223dc.com. $10 cover after 10pm, visit website for free pass Tues 9pm–2am; Wed–Thurs 6pm–2am; Fri 5pm–3am; Sat 9pm–3am; Sun 8pm–2am.*

Foggy Bottom
→ **McFadden's Restaurant and Saloon** ⋆ DANCE   "St. Patrick's Day every day" is the motto of this cliché-ridden college hang. DJs spin live after 9pm Tuesdays through Saturdays. You can eat and drink, too, with Happy Hour specials plentiful on weeknights. *2401 Pennsylvania Ave. NW. Metro: Foggy Bottom.* ☎ *202-223-2338. Cover usually $5. Mon 5:30pm–midnight; Tues and Thurs–Sat 11:30am–2am; Wed and Sun 11:30am–midnight.*

Northeast
→ **Love** ⋆⋆ DANCE   It's the "it" club in DC. Red carpet lines the walls of a sleek, dimly lit space that parties 'til dawn 3

More Live Music (Free!)

⟶ **FREE**   **Jazz in the Garden** (**www.nga.gov**) is a free concert series held Fridays throughout the summer at the National Gallery's sculpture garden.

⟶ **FREE**   **Sunset Serenades** (**www.nationalzoo.si.edu**) feature all types of live music performances on Lion/Tiger Hill at the National Zoo. These concerts are held on summer Thursdays from 6:30 to 8pm.

nights a week. Usher, Christina Milan, and Fat Joe all threw parties here during the summer of 2006, on top of TI, Kelis, and Lil' Wayne concerts. *1350 Okie St. NE. Metro: Rhode Island Ave.* ☎ *202/636-9030. www. welcometodream.com. Cover starts at $10 but website promotions often offer free passes. Thurs and Sun 9pm–3am; Fri–Sat 9pm–3am.*

LIVE MUSIC
Ⓜ **Best** ❶ → **9:30 Club** ⋆⋆ CONCERTS   Any serious music fan in DC (and probably in the Mid-Atlantic) has been to this place. It's only open on show nights, which is pretty much every night. More like a concert venue than a club, you'll see a ticket charge instead of a cover. Everyone who's anyone has played the 9:30 at some point; R.E.M., Beastie Boys, Radiohead, Nirvana, the Smashing Pumpkins, and James Brown are only the beginning. For cheaper prices, and to make sure you don't get sold out, get your tickets in advance. *815 V St. NW. Metro: U Street-Cardozo.* ☎ *202/265-0930. www.930.com. Tickets $10–$50. Check website for schedule.*

→ **Smithsonian Jazz Café** ⋆ JAZZ   Head back to tourist central for a worthwhile serving of the best local jazz pros.

FESTIVAL SEASON

Tip Top DC Tours

The combination of serious heat and a large expanse of ground to cover for the monuments can make daytime tours tedious. There's no shortage of bland, educational tours in DC, but with a little careful hunting even college students with short attention spans can find walks that are guaranteed to entertain.

→ The **Spies of Washington Tour** (☎ **703/569-1875;** www.spiesofwashington tour.com) is led by former Air Force intelligence officer Carol Bessette. Get the lowdown on espionage-related sites in the DC area, specifically in and around the White House. Tours cost $12/person.

→ The **I've Got A Secret** walking tour will debunk your foolish DC myths and give you equally preposterous truths instead. The website will whet your appetite: "a tree house on the Mall, a ghost in a castle, a brothel, 19th-century redwood trees, a canal and the severed leg of a Civil War general." Find out more for yourself for $10. Check **www.washingtonwalks.com** for the updated schedule.

→ **Monuments by Moonlight** (☎ **202/832-9800**) will give you something to look forward to during steamy DC days. Get some magnificent views of the memorials, including the FDR, the Lincoln, the Vietnam Veteran's, the Korean War Veteran's, and Iwo Jima on the Virginia side. But wait, there's more. You'll also get to see the Capitol Building, the White House, the Jefferson Memorial, and the Washington Monument. The tour takes about 2½ hours and costs around $28.

Cover includes the show and a cocktail—the cost will be close to what you'd drop on drinks at a club anyway. Make this your first stop, before abandoning all sense of taste in the wee hours of the night. *10th St. NW and Constitution Ave. NW in the National Museum of Natural History. Metro: Federal Triangle or Smithsonian.* ☎ *202/357-2700. Cover and a cocktail $10. Fri 6–10pm.*

A MARKET AND A COFFEEHOUSE

The **Eastern Market** ★★ (Metro: Eastern Market; www.easternmarket.net) was built in 1873 and still hosts food, collectible, and crafts stalls. You'll find tons of cheap, fun jewelry, furniture, and vintage clothing at the Sunday flea market. There's fresh food daily, and a farmers market on the weekends.

If you're a poetry buff, stop by the Grace Church in Georgetown the third Tuesday of every month for **Poetry Coffeehouse** (1401 Wisconsin Ave. NW. ☎ **202/ 333-7100;** www.gracedc.org). Listen to or share some poetry while grabbing free Starbucks and dessert.

A QUICK OVERVIEW OF TOP ATTRACTIONS

DC is obviously a goldmine of popular attractions. Some of the more interesting (and free) sites include the fairly new **National World War II Memorial** (17th and Constitution Ave. NW; Metro: Farragut West; ☎ **800/639-4WW2** or 202/426-6841; www.wwiimemorial.com), with gorgeous fountains and spacious lawns; the enormous **Lincoln Memorial** (23rd St. NW between Constitution and Independence; Metro: Foggy Bottom; ☎ **202/426-6842;** www.nps.gov/linc); and the **National Museum of American History** (Constitution Ave. NW between 12th and 14th sts.; Metro:

The Exorcist Steps . . . and other Spooky Sites

⟶ **The Exorcist Steps** are a super-steep, 97-step staircase at 36th and Prospect Street NW in Georgetown. Prominently featured in the movie *The Exorcist*, this spooky site is still a tourist attraction for horror enthusiasts. If you've heard the tales about the nine deaths associated with the production and a mysterious fire that destroyed a set, you'll know why the stairs keep passersby uneasy.

⟶ The **Woodrow Wilson House** is said to be haunted by mysterious sounds and unexplained events. 2340 S St. NW ☎ **202/387-4062.** www.woodrowwilsonhouse.org.

⟶ The **Old Stone House** is the oldest haunted building in DC, dating back to the 18th century. There's reputedly a cruel spirit in residence, George, who's been known to attack women. 3051 M St. NW. ☎ **202/426-6851.** www.nps.gov.

⟶ The **Stephen Decatur House** is the site of many ghost sightings. Decatur, an American naval officer, died in the early 1800s. Many claim to feel a somber presence in the first floor room where he died. 748 Jackson Place NW. ☎ **202/842-0920.** www.decaturhouse.org.

Smithsonian or Federal Triangle; ☎ 202/633-1000; www.americanhistory.si.edu) which recently mounted exhibits on polio and first ladies.

PLAYING OUTSIDE

On Fridays, the *Washington Post*'s weekend section lists cycling trips around DC. You can rent a bike through **Big Wheel Bikes** (1034 33rd St. NW; ☎ 202/337-0254; www.bigwheelbikes.com), **Thompson's Boat Center** (2900 Virginia Ave. at Rock Creek Parkway NW; Metro: Foggy Bottom; ☎ 202/333-4861 or 202/333-9543; www.thompsonboatcenter.com), and **Fletcher's Boat House** (Reservoir and Canal roads; ☎ 202/244-0461; www.fletchersboathouse.com). Throughout the summer you can rent paddleboats for use on the various canals and rivers at the Tidal Basin, off Independence Avenue (☎ 202/479-2426). Four-seaters are $16/hour and two-seaters are $8/hour, daily from 10am to 6pm.

FESTIVAL SEASON

All Good Music Festival (Masontown, WV)

For nearly 20,000 happy fans, All Good caters to the most hard-core remnant of the hippie scene each summer. This festival is similar to Bonnaroo (p. 103) in the way the camping experience completes the scene, but as far as crowds go, this is a whole different ballgame. These folks above all else here to groove—not to gather photographic evidence that they did something cool.

Don't be surprised to see people wandering aimlessly at all hours of the day. Do expect to pity those who are hung over while the blistering sun is at its peak and there's no air-conditioned refuge. Anticipate lots of blatant drug offers. My biggest mistake: no flashlight. At night especially, the well-lit fields look blissful compared to the shadowy corners of your campsite.

Unless you're planning on several pairs of earplugs and sleeping in your car, expect to get little sleep: The thumping beats from the nearby stages will echo at all hours of the day.

But ultimately, you won't miss your sleep. You'll be too afraid you'll miss something.

Masontown Nuts & Bolts

Area Codes The area code in Masontown is 304.

Drugstores There's a Rite Aid at 415 E. Main St. (☎ 304/329-2212).

Emergencies In any emergency, call ☎ 911.

Hospitals West Virginia University Hospital (☎ 304/598-4400) is located in nearby Morgantown.

Police For a non-emergency, call ☎ 304/864-6741.

Weather For current weather in Masontown, check www.weather.com.

All Good Festival in a Box

Contact www.allgoodfestival.com.

Dates July 13 to 15, 2007

Hours Gates open Friday at 9am and remain open 24 hours until Monday at noon. Early arrival allowed starting at 5pm Thursday for $10 in advance, or $15 at the gate (per person).

Location All Good is held on the 665-acre Marvin's Mountaintop in Masontown, WV, overlooking the Alleghany Mountains.

Restrictions The norm: No violence, weapons, illegal substances, animals, fires, etc.

Schedule **Activities:** In addition to the music, you can find Drum Magic (a seminar and performance by a music healer); Kirtan, the art of Devotional Chanting; All Good yoga; Rhythmic Alchemy (a music workshop involving South African gum boot dance, Brazilian cup rhythm, stomp rhythms, African songs, and rhythmic improv activities); and Helpful Herbs for Campers (a seminar in herbal studies and creations). **Music:** Based on 2006, here's the kind of thing you can expect: on Thursday evening, there were six sets from 7:15pm to 2am. Most people don't arrive until Friday morning, as the headlining acts are Friday through Sunday. In 2006, sets ran from 2pm to 4am Friday, 11:30am to 3am Saturday, and 11:30am to 7pm Sunday. There were no overlapping sets, which is a plus for getting to see all the artists, though it's frustrating when you know you'll have to fight for a good spot at the bigger shows. In 2006, the lineup included Ween, The Black Crowes, Les Claypool, John Medeski & The Itch, Trey Anastasio, Mike Gordon, Disco Biscuits, Soldiers of Jah Army, Hot Buttered Run, and Mofro and The Wailers.

Tickets   In 2006, limited early-bird tickets were $89 and $104. When those sold out, which they did quickly, advance 3-day, 3-night tickets were $119. One-day passes are not available. Tickets can be purchased through www.ticketmaster.com, or www.walther-productions.com (both of which add an additional service charge). Check the All Good website for other ticket outlets in Maryland, Virginia, Pennsylvania, Delaware, West Virginia, New Jersey, and Massachusetts.

Weather   The average All Good weekend temperatures for the past 5 years are 84°F as a high and 61°F as a low.

Getting There

Flying or driving are the best modes for getting here. Once you arrive in Morgantown, if you need a cab, call the 24-hour **Yellow Cab Company** at ☎ **304/ 292-7441** or 304/292-3336.

In terms of distance-from-other-places, Morgantown is about 91 miles, about a 1¹⁄₂- hour drive, from Pittsburgh; 219 miles, about a 3¹⁄₂-hour drive, from Baltimore; and 319 miles, about a 5-hour drive from Cincinnati.

BY CAR

Like Bonnaroo, you'll be happy you have your car at your disposal if you need to a place to keep your stuff, or just want the freedom to leave when you want. On the website they say vehicles and cars will be separated, but they didn't enforce it whatsoever in 2006. RVs and buses are allowed for $30 (advance) or $40 (at the gate). Visit the website, **www.allgoodfestival.com** for specific directions.

All Good tents at the All Good Music Festival.

FESTIVAL SEASON

Playlist: All Good Grooves 2006

- → *Voodoo Lady,* **Ween,** "Chocolate and Cheese," 1994
- → *I Shot the Sheriff,* **Bob Marley & The Wailers,** "Burnin'," 2001
- → *Lust Stings,* **Les Claypool,** "Of Whales and Woe," 2006
- → *Remedy,* **The Black Crowes,** "Greatest Hits 1990-1999: Tribute Work in Progress," 2000
- → *Alive Again,* **Trey Anastasio,** "Trey Anastasio," 2002
- → *Long Way To Go,* **Railroad Earth,** "Elko," 2006
- → *Let Down,* **Easy Star All-Stars feat. Toots & The Maytals,** "Radiodread," 2006
- → *Morning Sun,* **Tea Leaf Green,** "Taught To Be Proud," 2005
- → *Pineapple,* **John Medeski & David Fiuczynski,** "Lunar Crush," 1994
- → *Natural Mystic,* **Steel Train,** "1969," 2003

BY AIR

The nearest airport is **Pittsburgh (PA) International Airport** (☎ 412/472-3525; www.pitairport.com). Some low fares to Pittsburgh in summer last year included: $133 round-trip from Washington, DC; $203 from Los Angeles; and $123 from Miami.

From the airport to the All Good site is 93 miles, so you'll either need to rent a car or organize some other transportation. Contact **Enterprise Rent-A-Car** (☎ 800/ 736-8222 or 304/366-3600; www. enterprise.com), **Budget Car Rental** (☎ 800/621-2844; www.budget.com), **Hertz Rent-a-Car** (☎ 800/654-3131; www.hertz.com), or Avis Car Rental (☎ 800/331-7272; www.avis.com).

Getting Around

You'll be on foot once you're at the festival. The site isn't quite as complicated as Bonnaroo's. I was lucky and ended up on the mountain, overlooking the main stages. We were far enough away to have some peace and quiet, but we could still see what was going on and hear the music. A map isn't necessary with All Good, but if you're way up in the mountains, don't forget your flashlight!

Sleeping

CAMPGROUNDS

You can most certainly camp at the festival. In fact, it's part of the whole experience. For details on what to bring/how to set up, see the Bonnaroo section (p. 108).

CHEAP

In nearby Morgantown, there's a **Radisson Hotel Waterfront Place** (2 Waterfront Place; www.radisson.com) with rates from $89/night, and a **Ramada Inn** (www.ramada.com) with rates starting at $73/night. About 30 minutes away in Fairmont there's a **Comfort Inn and Suites** (1185 Airport Rd.; www.comfortinn.com) starting at $66/night and a **Super 8 Motel** (2208 Pleasant Valley Rd.; www.super8.com) with rates from $50/night.

More About West Virginia on the Web

- → **www.wv.gov.** This is the official website of the state of West Virginia. Check the website for a complete listing of statewide events, festivals, and activities.
- → **www.westvirginianetwork. com.** For more information on arts, entertainment, shopping, travel, and tourism, this website has it all.

Rope a What?

In a faraway corner of the All Good festivities is the **Ropeadope Stage,** a small spot hidden away on the mountaintop. There's an awesome lineup, music seminars, and dancing. I didn't discover Ropeadope until the day before we left, but if they have it in 2007, I really recommend you check it out. DJs and MCs spin funk, hip-hop, soul, and groove. Music seminars included DJ Logic, John Medeski, Stanton Moore, and Karl Denson.

Detour: Moundsville Penitentiary

On your way in our out of town (if you're headed west), you might pass through Moundsville, which is about 84 miles/2 hours west of Masontown. There you'll see the 10-acre, Gothic-style, **Moundsville Penitentiary,** closed in 1995. See a formerly working electric chair and solitary confinement cells, or go on a ghost hunt. If you can't make it to the site, visit the flashy website—it'll bring you back to childhood visions of haunted houses. **www.wvpentours. com.**

Once you know you're headed to the festival, make a reservation, as rooms can be hard to come by that weekend.

Eating

There are food vendors at the festival who are open all weekend. There's nothing gourmet, but it's stuff you can totally survive on. I still suggest picking up some supplies on the way in to save some money; fruits and non-refrigerated snacks are your best bet.

SUPPLIES

Before you head into the festival, stop at Morgantown's **Kmart** (6540 Mall Rd.; ☎ **304/983-6070;** www.kmart.com) to stock up on supplies. For other snacks and supplies, there's also a **7-Eleven** (2942 University Ave.; ☎ **304/599-4460**) nearby.

TAKEOUT/EATING OUT
Cheap

Morgantown is about 20 minutes outside of Masontown (you'll probably drive through

it on your way to the festival) and you will discover that this is another city where fast-food fanatics will never suffer. You name it, they've got it. In Morgantown, there's an **Applebee's** (1065 Van Voorhis Rd.); **Arby's** (331 Patteson Dr. and 9411 Mall Rd.); **Blimpie Subs and Salads** (1899 Earl L Core Rd.); **Burger King** (340 Patteson Dr.); **Chick-Fil-A** (9415 Mall Rd.); **KFC** (1608 Sabraton Ave.); **Little Ceasers Pizza** (204 Venture Dr.); **Long John Silvers** (Monongahela Blvd.); **McDonald's** (1820 Sturgiss Ave.); **Panera Bread** (357 Patteson Dr.); **Papa John's Pizza** (229 Beechurst Ave.); **Pizza Hut** (374 Patteson Dr.); **Ruby Tuesday** (512 Venture Dr.); **Sbarro** (WVU Mountain Lair Bldg.); **Subway** (Ashebrooke Sq.); and **Taco Bell** (427 Patteson Dr. and 7 Commerce Dr.).

FESTIVAL SEASON

Bonnaroo Music & Arts Festival (Manchester, TN)

One weekend every year, a small town in Tennessee increases its population by some 1,350%. Little Manchester explodes from 8,000 to 108,000 people. The annual festival there could be called the modern equivalent of Woodstock. Though the farm site that hosts the event may be on the selling block, Bonnaroo itself seems strong enough to survive anywhere.

Some of the biggest names in rock join jazz, hip-hop, and electronica stars every year. Though most of your time will probably involve music in some capacity (talking about music, listening to music, or hearing music as you fall asleep and wake up), the complete experience itself is mind-blowing—to say the least.

Manchester **Nuts & Bolts**

Area Code   The area code in Manchester is 931.

Doctor   Medical tents are set up around the Bonnaroo site and are equipped to deal with minor medical emergencies. In 2006, more than a few people suffered from dehydration. The Bonnaroo staff is also prepared for more severe (perhaps drug-related) issues.

Drugstores   There's a Wal-Mart at 2518 Hillsboro Blvd. (☎ 931/728-6000; www.walmart.com) with a 24-hour pharmacy. There's also a Walgreens at 806 McArthur St. (☎ 931/728-0653).

Emergencies   Find a staff person, or go to the nearest security station or medical tent. Otherwise, dial ☎ **911.**

Hospitals   Manchester's local hospital is the Medical Center of Manchester (2345 Murfreesboro Hwy.; ☎ 931/728-6354).

Libraries   Coffee County Manchester Public Library is at 1005 Hillsboro Blvd. (☎ **931/723-5143**), and is open Monday through Saturday from 9am to 5pm.

Liquor Laws   The drinking age in Tennessee is 21 and it's illegal to have an open container in the car. Tennessee also has a weird liquor law that doesn't allow you to sell beer and liquor in the same store.

Police   The number for the Coffee County Sheriff's Dept. is ☎ 931/728-3591. Contact the Manchester Police Dept. at ☎ 931/728-2099.

Post Office   The city's post office (☎ 800/ASK-USPS) is located at 1601 Hillsboro Blvd., and is open Monday through Friday 8am to 5pm and Saturday 8am to noon.

Time Zone   Manchester's time zone is Eastern Standard Time.

Useful Telephone Numbers   For roadside assistance, call AAA (☎ 800/222-4357). For a tow truck call Hullett's Service Center (☎ 931/728-0158). Call Farrell's Lock and Key for a locksmith (☎ 931/581-0989). Because pets are not allowed on-site, call the nearby Animal Heath Clinic (☎ 931/728-6633) or the Coffee Veterinary Hospital (☎ 931/728-1430) if you need somewhere to leave your pet.

Weather   For local weather conditions in Manchester, visit http://manchester.tn. local-weather.ws.

Bonnaroo Festival in a Box

Contact www.bonnaroo.com.

Dates June 14 to 17, 2007.

Hours In 2006, the parking lot and campground opened at 7am on Thursday and closed at 3pm on Monday. Within the festival, activities run 24 hours a day.

Lost & Found If you've lost a person or an item, check the nearest information tent. Staff can radio other tents if need be.

Radio WFTZ, 101.5 FM, was Radio Bonnaroo the weekend of the event. Tune in on your way there for music and traffic announcements and other news.

Restrictions The usual prohibitions apply: weapons, fireworks, illegal substances, pets, glass containers, and so on. Check the website for a complete list, including "no referring to yourself in the third person." *Note:* Illegal substances will be abundant, but unless you have glass in an extremely covert place, they will find it and take it.

Schedule **Activities:** There's no shortage of stuff to do at this festival. My personal favorite was the Silent Disco, dubbed "the world's weirdest wireless dance party." They'll hand you a set of headphones when you enter the space, which is filled with hundreds of hippies bopping silently. Another cool option in 2006 was the Sonic Forest, a 1,000-sq. ft. sound- and motion-sensored set. You could "play" the forest by passing between 16 8-inch tall cylinders containing speakers, lights, and photoelectric cells that trigger the effects. Yoga classes were offered every morning, on top of dozens of art exhibits, silent auctions, funky interactive tents, puppet shows, break- and belly dancing performances, and a 24-hour movie theatre—and that's all on top of the music lineup. **Music:** The big news for the 2007 lineup: The Police will be headlining Bonnaroo on their reunion tour. Other headliners include The White Stripes, Tool, and Widespread Panic, along with Damien Rice, Decemberists, Spoon, Lily Allen, the Hold Steady, Feist, Tortoise, Cold War Kids, Annuals, Wilco, the Flaming Lips, DJ Shadow, Sasha & Digweed, and Hot Chip.

Tickets Ticket prices in 2006 ranged from $170 to $105. Tickets include camping and parking. (See "Getting Around," if you're planning on coming in an RV.) There was a $15 service charge per ticket. A 10–tickets-per-order limit was enforced, and ticket shipping ran between $9.50 and $11.50. Tickets can be purchased via the website. Day passes are not typically sold. Check the website for VIP packages.

FESTIVAL SEASON

Getting There

BY CAR

Most festivalgoers drive to the event. I definitely recommend it. Not only will you have a place to stash your valuables (including booze), you'll have some retreat if it rains—which is likely. The Bonnaroo website provides directions. If you're taking an RV, keep in mind that you won't be allowed to park among the cars. RV parking passes run about $40 per RV.

This might be the only shower you'll get the whole festival!

If you are driving, here are some distances to ponder. Manchester is:

- ⟳ 650 miles, about 10½ hours from DC
- ⟳ 185 miles, about 3 hours from Atlanta
- ⟳ 2,068 miles, about 30 hours from Los Angeles (people do it!)

The nearest large town to Manchester is Nashville, which is about 65 miles away. Chattanooga is about 70 miles away.

Why They Like Bonnaroo

"I wish there was one of these when I was growing up. It's a perfect opportunity for the fans to see so many different types of bands, that all appeal to people that love music, and people that are willing to seek out music. For the bands, it's a chance to play for people that never heard you before, so that's a win-win situation."
—*Warren Haynes, guitarist for Gov't Mule, on Bonnaroo*

If you'd like the convenience of staying in an RV at Bonnaroo, but don't feel comfortable piloting one across the country, consider a local rental. Get in touch with **Cruiseamerica,** a nationwide network for RV rental, which includes **B & C Rentals** (201 Donelson Pike; ☎ **800/671-7839;** www.cruiseamerica.com/koa) in Nashville, offering both campers and RVs.

BY AIR

The two closest airports to the Bonnaroo site are **Nashville International Airport** (One Terminal Dr.; ☎ **615/275-1675;** www.nashintl.com), about 60 miles away, and **Chattanooga Metropolitan Airport** (1001 Airport Rd.; ☎ **423/855-2202;** www.chattairport.com), about 70 miles away. Shuttle service runs from the Nashville airport to Bonnaroo on Thursday and Friday of the festival, and back to the airport starting Monday morning. Round-trip tickets are about $55; one-way tickets are $30. Tickets can be purchased via the Bonnaroo website.

BY TRAIN & BUS

Amtrak (☎ **800/USA-RAIL;** www.amtrak.com) and **Greyhound** (☎ **800/231-2222;** www.greyhound.com) both service the Manchester area. I don't recommend either. The cheapest Amtrak tickets from New York in 2006 were in the $200 to $300 range. Greyhound? My friend took it in 2006 and then had to walk a mile to the festival site. The closest Greyhound stations are at 617 Woodbury Hwy. (☎ **931/728-6348**), which is 1 mile away, and another in Murfreesboro at 2029 South Church St. (☎ **615/893-5531**).

BY TAXI

If you need a taxi from an airport, Amtrak, or Greyhound station, call **ADC Cab** at

Playlist: Bonnaroo 2006

→ *Karma Police,* **Radiohead,** "OK Computer," 1997

→ *Bowl of Oranges,* **Bright Eyes,** "Lifted or The Story Is in the Soil, Keep Your Ear to the Ground," 2002

→ *Sky is Falling,* **Blackalicious,** "Blazing Arrow," 2002

→ *Crosstown Traffic,* **Soulive,** "Breakout," 2005

→ *Monroe Dancin',* **Ricky Skaggs & Kentucky Thunder,** "Brand New Strings," 2004

→ *Don't Do Me Like That,* **Tom Petty & the Heartbreakers,** "Damn the Torpedoes," 1979

→ *Martyr,* **Rusted Root,** "When I Woke," 1994

→ *Indestructible,* **Matisyahu,** "Youth," 2006

→ *Djarabi,* **Toubab Krewe,** "Toubab Krewe," 2005

→ *Welcome to Jamrock,* **Damien "Jr. Gong" Marley,** "Welcome to Jamrock," 2005

→ *Love Me Like You,* **The Magic Numbers,** "Magic Numbers," 2005

FESTIVAL SEASON

☎ 931/723-0232 or **A Absolute Brown's Taxi Cab** at ☎ 931/728-7392.

Getting Around

Unless you bring those sneakers with skates that pop out of the bottom, walking will be your mode of transportation once you're at the festival site. If you ignore all other advice, don't ignore this: KEEP YOUR MAP. You'll get one when you arrive and you can pick one up almost anywhere on-site. Bonnaroo is massive—700 acres. Getting lost was a daily occurrence for me. Centeroo is the core of the festival, where both the stages and activities are. You'll also find food vendors and souvenir-type booths. Even if you've learned your way around the first day, don't expect to maintain your sense of direction at night, especially if you're camped far away. Even with lights, once night falls all the campsites look identical.

Most importantly, you'll need a map just to know which stage you're going to. No, I wasn't referring to Which Stage. The 2006 performing areas included: Which Stage, What Stage, This Tent, That Tent, and The Other Tent. Fortunately, figuring all that

 Smokey's on the Road

On empty, open roads I know it's tempting to test out how fast your car really goes. DON'T. Bonnaroo is no secret to local police. We got pulled over on the way there and we were only doing 10 mph over the speed limit.

out is probably the most thinking you'll have to do all weekend.

Sleeping

Unless you have a luxurious RV or think that staying in a local hotel qualifies as coming to Bonnaroo, plan on roughing it in a tent. Do take into consideration that you'll have a long trip back home the last day. Consider staying in a hotel the night before you leave, even if it's just long enough for a shower (would *you* want to sit next to you on a plane after 4 unwashed days?).

CAMPGROUNDS

The Bonnaroo map plots out each campsite. While you may not know where you're entering when you get to the site, try to camp close to Centeroo, away from port-o-potties but close enough that you

Red & Blue Make . . . Beautiful Music

"This festival here is in Tennessee, this is basically the heart of red state America. And people come for the music, the community of the music. And this is one place where the bitterness that you see in the partisan divide in America, both sides come together here and move it up and enjoy themselves thoroughly. This is one place that actually . . . the healing of this country is actually taking place, now as we speak."
—*Bob Weir on politics in music*

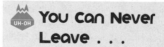 **You Can Never Leave . . .**

Once your car is in, it's *in.* If you're caravanning with friends in more than one car, wait to drive in and park when you're all together. Staff will direct you to a campsite—if you tell them you're with the car (or cars) behind you, they'll make sure you're parked side by side.

Word Up: Manchester Vocabulary

→ **ah** *noun*, plural **ahs.** The organ you see with. *Human beings have two ahs.*

→ **bawl** *verb* (used without object). To change water from a liquid state to a gaseous state by heating. *To make spaghetti, you must bawl the water.*

→ **flare** *noun*, plural **flares.** The colorful blossom of a plant. *The garden was full of beautiful flares.*

→ **kumpny** *noun.* A group of people. *We expect the kumpny to arrive soon.*

→ **munt** *noun*, plural **munts.** A time period spanning approximately 4 weeks in a year. *During Christmas time, schoolchildren have a one munt break from school.*

→ **ranch** *noun*, plural **ranches.** A commonly used metal tool. *Hand me the socket ranch so I can tighten the bolt.*

→ **warsh** *verb* (used with object). To apply water for the purpose of cleansing. *Before you eat dinner, make sure to warsh your hands.*

can sprint there in the middle of the night without a map if you need to. (Don't worry, by the second day you'll be squatting on the grass anyway.)

OFF-SITE

I highly recommend booking a cheap hotel in Manchester for the last night. Six of us crammed into a rundown motel; two on the bed, four in sleeping bags on the floor. It might sound hellish, but after not showering for 4 days, anything with a shower is delightful. Book in advance; Manchester hotel owners know people will take anything that's available, so prices get jacked *way* up at the last minute.

There's a **Day's Inn** (2259 Hillsboro Blvd. ☎ 931/728-9530; www.daysinn.com) that has rooms for $79/night. Nearby is a **Ramada** (2314 Hillsboro Blvd.; ☎ 931/728-0800; www.ramada.com) with accommodations starting at $49/night.

Detour: Nashville's CMA Music Festival

Nashville is only about an hour or so outside of Manchester. Why not detour to the country capital of the world? The **Country Music Association Music Festival (www.cmafest.com)** is held about a week before Bonnaroo (June 7–10 in 2007). Tickets range from $125 to $155 for 4-day passes. The 2006 lineup included The Charlie Daniels Band, Lynyrd Skynyrd, Trisha Yearwood, Carrie Underwood, SHeDaisy, and LeAnn Rimes. According to our roadtrip buddy Patti, (who introduced us to the music of Blake Shelton): "It was once noted for being the place to meet all the country celebrities. Not anymore. The convention hall has become a place for businesses to showcase their products and new (never-have-beens and probably never-wont's) artists to meet people and try to gather some interest. To meet your favorite country singer, you almost always have to be a member of their fan club and go to their fan club party." For more on the Music City, turn to the "American Highways" roadtrip, where it is the starting point of the cross-country chapter.

FESTIVAL SEASON

Surfing Bonnaroo: Recommended Websites

➜ **www.manchestertn.com**. This website has the lowdown on local attractions and businesses in Manchester.

➜ **www.manchestertimes.com**. The hometown newspaper will keep you up to date on news, weather, and events.

Eating

You aren't coming to Manchester for top-of-the-line dining, so don't have high expectations. There are plenty of fast-food joints, but most of your time will be spent on-site. Before you start your carefree

Don't Be Without These at Bonnaroo

You will thank me for demanding that you take Bonnaroo preparation seriously. I was lucky; I camped out with a group of veteran Bonnarooers, who brought a mosquito tent, lamps, a grill, plenty of water, and some sense of direction. If you're coming in a car, you'll have plenty of space for surplus supplies. Overpack just to be safe. The Bonnaroo website, www.bonnaroo.com, has a complete list of recommendations, but I've included some of my own:

➜ **Camping Gear.** When you're at your campsite, you won't want to sit in your 2-foot wide tent/sauna, and with bugs and heat you'll be needing some form of shade/shelter. Try to take both a sturdy, waterproof tent for sleeping, and an additional netted, shaded tent. You'll be even happier if that second tent is big enough to stand in. (A tarp will work if you don't opt for a second tent.)

➜ **Food.** Before you enter the festival grounds, stock up on nonperishable food; chips, fruits, and vegetables are always safe bets, too. If you have a cooler, bring what you can fit and what you'll use, but nothing that will rot or attract bugs if you forget about it.

➜ **Raingear.** This list includes a waterproof tent, rain boots, towels, flip-flops, and extra shoes. Last year we were lucky, but in 2005 there were horror stories about seriously flooded tents. Keep your fingers crossed for next year, and come prepared just in case.

➜ **Other Supplies.** Let me be philosophical; nothing is certain. There are port-o-potties (which are completely intolerable by Day 2), but that's not a guarantee there will be toilet paper. The Bonnaroo website claims it provides drinking water and wash stations, but don't be fooled. The drinking water is safe, but treated with overpowering sulfur, and a wash station means a trailer with sinks, not showers. Buying water on-site for $1 adds up quickly. So don't forget: Bring lots of bottled water, ice, bug spray, blanket for seating, sunscreen, hat, sunglasses, extra toilet paper, trash bags, flashlight, extra batteries, backpack, bag or CamelBak, camera, and baby wipes as shower alternatives (remember that unless you want to pay $10 or more, you won't have a proper shower all weekend). Also, if you find an outrageous-looking balloon or similar large decoration—get it. That will serve as your landmark to follow home.

FESTIVAL SEASON

Advice from a Bonnaroo Vet

When we asked our roadtripping buddy Patti (aka JettheadPB) what she would tell newbies about Bonnaroo, here's her response: "I don't think you can stress how HOT it is. Seriously. *HOT HOT HOT.* . . . kill you kind of hot. The water was the hardest commodity to come by. We rented an RV and we never were able to hook up to the facilities they were supposed to have. It really was a no-hassle place, though, as far as partying. The staff didn't seem to care at all. Our RV area turned into a big-ol block party." Thanks, Patti!

weekend, prepare well and stock up on grub. Although the festival has tons of food vendors, things like fresh fruit are hard to come by. Vendor items range from $1 to $10. I recommend the $1 grilled cheeses and falafel, but stay away from the Chinese food. Most plates of food run about $5 to $8.

SUPPLIES

There's a **Wal-Mart** (2518 Hillsboro Blvd.; ☎ 931/728-6000; www.walmart.com) near the Bonnaroo site. You can stock up on water and snacks just before you reach the site. It's open 24 hours and has a pharmacy. There's also a **Walgreens** (806 McArthur St.; ☎ 931/728-0653; www. walgreens.com) nearby.

TAKEOUT TREATS/ALCOHOL

There's a **Russell Stover Candies** (2244 Hillsboro Blvd.; ☎ 931/723-2488) in Manchester if you have a sweet tooth. You can buy beer at most local stores, but you'll have to look a little harder to find hard liquor. Nearby locations include **Bill's Liquor Store** (801 McArthur St.; ☎ 931/728-3346), **Oak Liquor Store** (1002

Interstate Dr.; ☎ 931/728-2260), and **Interstate Liquors** (20 Expressway Dr.; ☎ 931/728-7366).

EATING OUT

Manchester is a staunch representative of the Fast Food nation. Nearby there's an **Arby's** (2194 Hillsboro Blvd.; ☎ 931/728-6626); **Burger King** (56 Expressway Dr.; ☎ 931/728-5768); **KFC** (2189 Hillsboro Blvd.; ☎ 931/728-3845); **McDonalds** (2211 Hillsboro Blvd.; ☎ 931/728-0726); **Pizza Hut** (1308 Hillsboro Blvd.; ☎ 931/728-4599); and **Cracker Barrel** (103 Paradise St.; ☎ 931/723-1358). All are within a few miles of the Bonnaroo site.

If you want to be daring and try some native grub, stop by **Bubba's Barbeque** (905 Hillsboro Blvd.; ☎ 931/723-4691); **Captain D's Seafood Restaurant** (2166 Hillsboro Blvd.; ☎ 931/728-1130); **Gasthaus German Restaurant** (1401 Hillsboro Blvd.; ☎ 931/723-1500); or **Golden Dragon Chinese Restaurant** (1402 Hillsboro Blvd.; ☎ 931/728-0407).

BARS

If you somehow have the stamina to party on after Bonnaroo, there are a couple local bars and pubs in Manchester you can hit: **Bottoms Up Sports Bar** at 1922 McArthur St. (☎ 931/728-6188) and **Dewey's and Eva's Pub** at 1703 Hillsboro Blvd. (☎ 931/728-9304).

 They Were Serious about No Glass . . .

Two bottles of absinthe were going to be the highlight of my friends' Bonnaroo . . . until they were confiscated on the way in because they were glass. Remember: Alcohol is allowed on-site, but glass bottles are not. Hang onto your water bottles, or buy some plastic containers.

Shakedown Street

Bonnaroo does not openly endorse illegal substances, but in the area known as "Shakedown Street" the drugs are all over. If you pass through you'll get asked multiple times if you want to buy anything from acid to ecstasy to coke, so don't take it personally. Shakedown also has all sorts of fun jewelry and souvenirs, and there's no shortage of anti-Bush bumper stickers.

What Else to See & Do

➔ **Manchester Arts Center** ★ This theater has weekly performances, including Sundays and matinees. The 2006–2007 season will feature *Into the Woods, Charlotte's Web*, and *West Side Story*, among other plays. *909 Hillsboro Blvd.* ☎ *931/728-3434. www.manchesterartscenter.com. Most tickets start at $10.*

➔ **Tennessee Skydiving Center** ★ If Bonnaroo wasn't exciting enough, take a leap from 13,000 feet. It's not cheap, but you probably should do it once in your life. What better time than to cap off Bonnaroo? ☎ *931/455-4574. www.tennskydive.com. Skydive with training and equipment costs $195; with video $270.*

➔ **Rollerscape** Take it back to the old school at mid-Tennessee's best skating facility. The rink, in Tullahoma, about 20 minutes out of Manchester, offers both speed and inline skates. *Do note:* The first Monday of every month is Christian Music Night. ☎ *931/454-1268. 200 Ledford Mill Rd.*

www.rollerscape.com. Cover starts at $3 depending on the day and time; regular skates $1; speed skates $2; inline skates $2.50. Mon and Thurs 6–9pm; Fri 7–11pm; Sat 10am–11pm; Sun 1:30–4:30pm.

What a Long, Strange Trip It's Been . . .

Some of the best times in my life were spent with the people I met at festivals, people I didn't know before who were there for one reason: to have a great time. To rough it in the country might be uncomfortable for a few days, but I highly recommend it. Even if you decide you never want to do *that* again, you'll have the photos to prove you did it once!

Detour: Jack Daniel's Distillery

FREE The Jack Daniel's distillery is about 40 minutes outside of Manchester in Lynchburg, TN. (They do call it "Tennessee whiskey," after all.) Ironically, it's in a "dry" county (where the sale of liquor is illegal). The distillery is a beautiful and enormous tour-worthy site. Tours are given every 15 minutes from 9am to 4:30pm, except on holidays. Tours last about an hour and a half. You can also check out a comprehensive, self-guided online tour. The website points out that there is one advantage to the actual tour: You can sample the product all along the way. ☎ **877/SPIRITS.** www.jackdaniels.com.

The Paranormal Northeast

Text & Photos by Ashley Marinaccio

The truth is out there, to quote Fox Mulder. It just depends which truth you're looking for. Is it history that's not in textbooks (like the local stories of haunted bridges, large-headed people, and lost pirate treasure)? Is it science that's not provable in labs (like ghosts, hauntings, and other paranormal experiences)? Is it a nonmainstream religious practice, like Wicca? Is it in the continued fascination with a heinous crime from long ago that still haunts a small town?

Well, we certainly aren't going to answer all those questions in one roadtrip, but you can explore some of them in this journey from Pennsylvania through New England, where we'll stop to look at places out of the ordinary.

The Northeast is packed with spooky spots. In 1600s Salem, Massachusetts, women and men accused of witchcraft faced bloody executions. Almost 200 years later, another town in Massachusetts became a legend when Lizzie Borden allegedly took an axe to her parents. (She was acquitted because at the time it was thought that a woman could never execute such a plot.) On a less sinister level, Rhode Island and New Hampshire once served as pirate havens—there are rumors of buried treasure hidden away in pirate caves just off the coast.

So put on your skeptic's (or believer's) cap, and get ready to drive to the outskirts of . . . whatever.

The end of the road, so to speak . . .

Superlatives: The Highs & Lows

➔**Most Well-Rounded State for Legend and Folklore Buffs: Massachusetts.** It's not just ghosts here, folks. There are also pirates, murders, and witch trials. Yikes! See p. 148.

➔**Scariest B & B: The Lizzie Borden Bed & Breakfast** in Fall River, MA. Do you have what it takes to stay overnight in a room haunted by the ghost of a murdered woman? See p. 146.

➔**Site Most Likely to Make You Believe in Ghosts: Crybaby Bridge** in New Hope, Pennsylvania. There are tons of stories about hauntings and strange images near the spot where a mother and her two children died. There is something out there, but you'll have to see it for yourself. See p. 123.

➔**Most Awesome Abandoned Theme Park: Holy Land, USA,** in Waterbury, Connecticut. Why Connecticut was chosen as the site of the new Holy Land is an enigma to me, and to the thousands of visitors this overgrown theme park attracts each year. The Holy Land isn't actually a working theme park anymore. It has been abandoned for quite a number of decades and in death attracts more people than it did in life. See p. 137.

➔**Coolest Occupation:** Mollie Stewart, parapsychologist and ghost hunter. She owns Spellbound's Ghostly Parlour and leads a nightly walking tour in Salem, Massachusetts. See p. 167.

➔**Most Caring State:** Maine is a state that certainly cares about its residents. One of the first signs to greet me upon my arrival was "Snack Wisely! Remember snacks are not meal replacements." Thanks, Maine—now point me in the direction of the nearest lobster shack! See p. 174.

The Paranormal Northeast

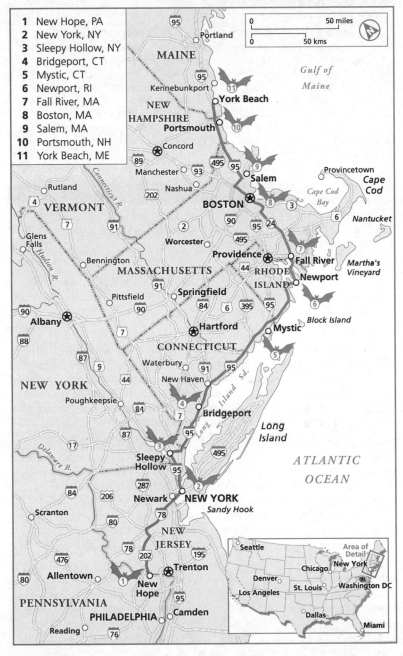

1 New Hope, PA
2 New York, NY
3 Sleepy Hollow, NY
4 Bridgeport, CT
5 Mystic, CT
6 Newport, RI
7 Fall River, MA
8 Boston, MA
9 Salem, MA
10 Portsmouth, NH
11 York Beach, ME

Who Ya Gonna Call?

Do you believe in ghosts? Plenty of theories explore what's allegedly behind the dead who don't realize that they are, well, *dead*. Some believe that ghosts are really "residual energy left behind by an emotionally strong person or event." Other theories suggest ghosts are "telepathic images that sensitive people pick up in specific cases." Others believe spirits come from time/space slips. Sigmund Freud believed that ghosts are actually the visions of people who are afraid of death—in other words, they don't exist. There are plenty other skeptical approaches like that of Arthur C. Clarke, host of "Mysterious World," who believes that it is our mind playing tricks on us. (Information from **www. ghosts.org**.)

Just the Facts

Trip in a Box

Total Miles   418 miles.

Route   Most of your trip will be spent on I-95, though you will also spend quality time on I-278 (from New Hope to New York), I-87 to Sleepy Hollow, and I-287 merging into I-95 for Bridgeport. I-95 North will mostly be your route for the rest of the way.

States   Pennsylvania, New York, Connecticut, Rhode Island, Massachusetts, New Hampshire, and Maine.

Trip Time   You could spend the rest of your life—and even some of your afterlife— exploring these places. Realistically (and assuming that you aren't leaving home to become a professional ghost hunter, cryptozoologist, or historian), if you want to collect some exciting tales without feeling rushed or overwhelmed, the trip could last about 5 to 7 days (plus the few extra days you might want to spend in the big cities).

Hitting the Highlights   There are several ways to break this trip up if you are short of time. The New Hope, New York, and the Connecticut stops can easily be done in 3 days or less. If you want to spend the weekend in Massachusetts, you can check out Boston, Salem, and Fall River (Lizzie Borden country) in 3 days, on top of an optional excursion to Rhode Island for some whale-watching. You can also take the extreme northern route and hit the highlights of Massachusetts, New Hampshire, and Maine in a few days' time.

When to Go   Early June through the end of October is the height of the tourist season for most of these places. There are plenty of advantages to spending your summer vacation on the road in the Northeast—on top of having access to all of the hotspots, you can hit the beautiful beaches and make the most out of the maritime attractions. October is another fantastic time. Not only will you be spending the Halloween season in areas where practically every day is Halloween, you'll get New

England's famous fall foliage at the beginning of its prime. You should probably skip winter. Most of the attractions close up and although snow-covered New England is very beautiful, it's also uncomfortably cold and can make driving difficult if there's inclement weather (which there usually is because it's the Northeast . . . and winter).

The Money Part

I spent the majority of this trip awestruck that my own backyard (my own extended backyard) has so many offbeat places to visit at (relatively) inexpensive prices. Having grown up in New Jersey, I know all too well about New York–area prices, so it was a pleasant surprise to see how cheap things got as I headed north. (Boston is an exception, and watch out in the cities and suburban areas during high tourism summer and Halloween seasons.) Make sure you bring money for shopping, as these places have some unique shops and markets.

ACCOMMODATIONS

Lodging is expensive, especially if you're planning on "splurging," or finding refuge in some of the Northeast's poshest vacation destinations. The budget-conscious aren't totally out of luck, however. I recommend using hostels/chain motels whenever you can, and splurging on the unique overnight accommodations at least once, staying at a place like the Lizzie Borden Bed & Breakfast in Fall River, Massachusetts, or Emily's Room at the Logan Inn in New Hope, Pennsylvania.

In general, on this trip I think bed-and-breakfasts are good places to stay. There are, of course, very high-end ones, but there are also some that are less expensive than rooms in hotel chains, plus you'll get a bit of personal attention and a good breakfast.

TRANSPORTATION
By Car

Gas prices may determine the money you do (or don't) spend on fun during your trip through the northeast. Try to avoid buying gas on major highways/at rest stops, as those stations almost always cost more than if you get off the highway. If you take a detour into town, you may be able to get gas for a few cents cheaper. Although it doesn't seem like a lot, trust me, it will add up. Allot $45 to $50 for gas money (more if you're driving a gas guzzler). At the time I was traveling in Summer 2006, gas prices fluctuated from $2.69 per gallon (in rural and some suburban areas) to $3.15 (at the rest stops on the highway).

By Public Transportation

Since the major towns in the Northeast are very well connected by all kinds of public transit, you could actually do a great deal of this trip without a car. The farther reaches of it (New Hope, PA and northern New England) are a bit harder to get to without your own set of wheels, but New York City and its suburbs are easily accessible, and there is plenty of cheap transportation between NYC and Boston.

For more specifics on getting around the East Coast without a car, turn to p. 45 in the "Festivals" chapter.

FOOD

There are cheap eats throughout the Northeast, and you don't have to eat at the national fast food chains (unless you want to). Delis, diners, and food stands abound. Sometimes the best way to save (especially if you'll be on the road for a while) is to go buy the fixings for some meals (breakfast and lunch) and keep them in a cooler in the car, or in the mini-fridge at your motel. This chapter will have plenty of options whether you're dining in or out. If you're planning on eating out every meal, put aside at least $15 to $30 for food per day.

So, You Wanna Go Ghost Hunting?

There are several "must haves" for ghost hunters. Most of these objects are easy to get at your local hardware or electronics store. I recommend visiting **www.castleofspirits.com/Australianghosthunters/ghequip.html** for a list of necessary objects and the functions they serve. You may also want to check out sites like www.ghoststore.net for purchasing authentic ghost hunting equipment online. The following items are considered essentials by the ghost hunters' website above:

→ **Notebooks** containing both plain and graph paper. You also may want to have a tiny scrap paper pad handy.

→ **Pens/pencils** for taking notes.

→ **Recording device**—you can buy a cheap one at your local electronics shop.

→ **Camera**—a 35mm is ideal for picking up orbs when the film is developed.

→ Thin and thick nylon **twine.**

→ A ball of black **wool** and white wool.

→ White material **tape** and transparent adhesive tape

→ Green gardening **twine.**

→ **Fuse wire.**

→ **Baby powder.**

OTHER EXPENSES

This trip will take you to plenty of museums and on walking tours. Although many offer student discounts, the full price usually doesn't go above $15 per person. Most of the museums average $8 per entrance/ guided tour. There are almost always bargains or discounts available if you purchase your tickets online, and some museums have days or evenings with free admission. If you're a student, be sure to bring your ID for any available discounts.

Starting Out: New Hope, PA

New Hope is a small town just over an hour's drive from New York City and is a must-see for anyone with an interest in ghosts, the paranormal, or strange phenomena.

Almost every shopkeeper has a ghost story, from the County Fair Chocolatier to the folks at the Logan Inn. Take a few minutes to chat with the locals. Plenty of people flock to New Hope looking for the same things you are. The residents are not only used to the questions, they take pride in their town's legends and enjoy sharing them with others.

New Hope Nuts & Bolts

Area Code   The telephone area codes in New Hope, PA are 215, 267, and 445.

Business Hours   The shops and restaurants are generally independently owned, with the average business hours of the town being from 10am to 5 or 6pm.

Drugstores Eckerd Drug Store at 6542 H Logan Square (☎ 215/ 862-9228).

Emergencies Call ☎ **911** if you need immediate police, fire, or emergency assistance.

Hospitals Warminster Hospital, 225 Newtown Rd., Warminster, PA 18974 (☎ 215/ 441–6600, main number; 215/441-6775, emergency room); Frankford Bucks Hospital, 380 North Oxford Valley Rd., Langhorne, PA 19047 (☎ 215/949-5000, main number; ☎ 215/949-5260, emergency room); Doylestown Hospital, 595 West State St., Doylestown, PA 18901 (☎ 215/345-2200).

Libraries The Free Library of New Hope is located at 93 W. Ferry St. (☎ 215/ 862-2330; www.newhopeartsinc.org).

Liquor Laws The drinking age is 21, though in some clubs it's "18 to party"; you must be 21 to drink.

Newspapers & Magazines The *New Hope Gazette* (www.newhopegazette.com) is New Hope's main newspaper. Bucks County has a few other publications including the *Doylestown Patriot* (www.doylestownpatriot.com), *The Advance* in Newton (www.advanceofbucks.com), and the *Bristol Pilot* (www.bristolpilot.com).

Police The New Hope Police Department is located at 41 N. Main St. (☎ 215/ 862-3033; www.newhopeborough.org). In case of an emergency, dial ☎ **911.**

Post Office The nearest U.S. Postal Office in New Hope is at 325 W. Bridge St. (☎ 215/862-2445).

Weather If you want to know how to pack before you arrive, point your browser to **www.cnn.com/weather** or **www.weather.com**.

Getting Around

ON FOOT

Since New Hope is relatively small and very walkable, your best bet is to keep your car parked at your hotel or inn and enjoy New Hope by foot. Driving can be a hassle. Make sure that if you decide to park your car at a meter, you return to keep it fed. If you run out of time, you'll probably get a ticket ($20) and that's not an expense you should have to spend your hard-earned money on!

Haunted New Hope Recommended Reading

→ *Haunted New Hope: The Delaware Valley's Most Haunted Town* (Black Cat Press, 2006), by Lynda Lee Macken. Lynda Lee Macken (www.lyndaleemacken.com) has a series of books on haunted places throughout the U.S. This book sheds light on hotels, shops, restaurants, and streets that are frequented by the spirit world.

→ *Bucks County Ghost Stories,* by Charles J. Adams (Exeter House Books, 1999). This is an older, thoroughly written guide that includes all areas of Buck County. I recommend this book for anyone looking to explore outside the New Hope area. Both this book and Lynda Lee Macken's book are available in many stores on Main Street in New Hope.

PARANORMAL NORTHEAST

"The Majik Horse"—One of the most haunted buildings in New Hope.

Parking

Should you decide to park your car for the day, you have two options. You can park in a lot and pay a fee for the day, or deal with the parking meters on the street. There's a parking lot behind the Starbucks on Main Street, which charges $10 per day, and in my opinion is better than having to deal

More than Ghosts: New Hope Events

New Hope is certainly one "crafty" place. Here's a guide to some of New Hope's annual cultural, music, and arts happenings:

→ The **Annual Outdoor Arts & Crafts Festival** (**www.newhopechamber. com**), one of New Hope's most popular events, is held the first weekend in October. Here, visitors have the opportunity to enjoy a variety of art mediums and new artistic endeavors. A must-see for art buffs.

→ Each year in May, the New Hope LGBT community and supporters come together to celebrate their pride and show support for a weekend at the annual **Somewhere Over the Rainbow Festival,** 6175 Old York Rd., New Hope (☎ 215/862–8819; **www.newhopecelebrates.com**).

→ The **Winter Festival** (**www.winterfestival.net/bydate.htm**) in New Hope and Lambertville is an annual festival celebrating the beauty of winter.

→ 1929 was the start of the **Phillip's Mill Art Exhibition,** which is now held annually either at the end of September or beginning of October; it features artists from around the area living within a 25-mile radius of New Hope. Check out **www.phillipsmill.org/index.html** for more information.

New Hope Highlights

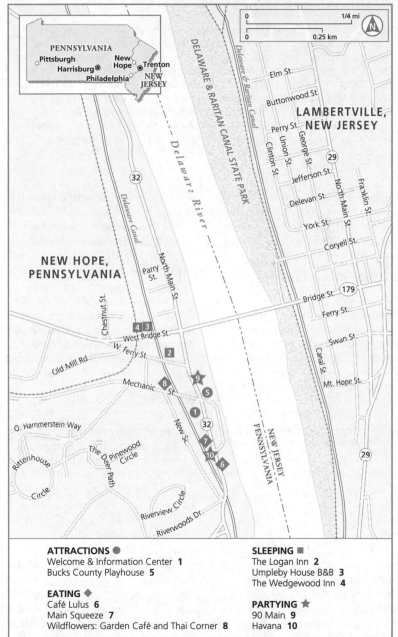

ATTRACTIONS ●
Welcome & Information Center **1**
Bucks County Playhouse **5**

EATING ◆
Café Lulus **6**
Main Squeeze **7**
Wildflowers: Garden Café and Thai Corner **8**

SLEEPING ■
The Logan Inn **2**
Umpleby House B&B **3**
The Wedgewood Inn **4**

PARTYING ★
90 Main **9**
Havana **10**

A Tour of Spooky New Hope

Can you see dead people? Candlelit walks through New Hope's fable-ridden streets are a highlight for many visitors, and a must-see for anyone who wants a good scare. You'll hear about the ghost of disgraced Vice President Aaron Burr, who is said to appear in the window of the Logan Inn. You'll also visit the Esca Restaurant, which is said to have many spirits of former slaves fleeing along the Underground Railroad. **Ghost Tours** ★★★ are given once a week from June through November, rain or shine. They are offered twice a week in October, including Halloween night. All tours begin at 8pm and are $10 per person. No reservations are required. Private tours are also offered year-round for $11 per person in groups of six or more. For more information, visit **www.GhostToursofNewHope.com**.

with refilling the pesky meters every few hours (and getting a ticket if you run out of time). If you're staying for a few days, you'll be able to keep your car parked (for free) at your B&B or hotel.

Witches of New Hope

New Age spirituality and Wicca practices are popular in New Hope. Many shops on Main Street and throughout town are owned and operated by witches. The shopkeepers are friendly and an excellent source of information about the practice; you should pose any questions in a respectful way.

A great shop that will help answer your questions about Wicca is **Gypsy Heaven** (115G South Main St.; ☎ 215/862–5251). There are several free pamphlets and brochures inside the store, as well as a bookstore/library. The owner, Tammi Jesberger, a Wicca practitioner for over 15 years, leads groups and hosts classes and book signings on Wicca.

Her brochure "Witches Today" contains a good quote for orienting yourself: "Witches are not Satan Worshippers. They are not the wicked witch of the East, nor are they the three women in the *Witches of Eastwick.* Witches do not fly on brooms or turn people into toads. Witches are not evil. They do not cast spells on people and they certainly

never gain power through the suffering of others."

Mystickal Tymes (127 South Main St.; ☎ 215/862–5629; www.mystickaltymes. com) is another shop worth seeing, with herbs, incense, stones, and items pertaining to Wicca. The owners are friendly and eager to speak to tourists, and they have an excellent book section with titles on Eastern thought, Buddhism, Hinduism, and New Age philosophy. A beautiful white cat named Morgana stands guard inside the store.

Sleeping

There are many bed-and-breakfasts, inns, and hotels in New Hope and the neighboring towns. Plenty of spirits can be found scattered around hallways and dining rooms, and some ghosts even have their own favorite rooms (which they aren't always happy to share). Ask at the front desk for information and tales surrounding your particular inn.

Staying overnight in one of the bed and breakfasts below can be a highlight of your journey, especially if you happen to come face-to-face with strange happenings. The downside of overnighting in New Hope is that places can get expensive, especially at the height of the tourist season, from June through October. For those who want to start their trip off with a scare, spending a night at the Logan Inn is highly recommended.

There is only one chain hotel in the area. **Best Western New Hope Inn** (☎ 215/862–5221; www.bwnewhope.com) at 6426 Lower York Road isn't exactly cheap, with rooms starting at $133 per night.

DOABLE

→ **Inn at Stoney Hill** Enjoy a cute, country atmosphere in one of the eight guest rooms that come complete with large, comfy beds and a bouquet of flowers. If you're craving a Jacuzzi, they're available in specific rooms. Of course, after a good night's sleep you're invited downstairs to enjoy a hearty breakfast. *105 Stoney Hill Rd., New Hope, PA 18938.* ☎ *215/862-5769. www. innatstoneyhill.com. 8 units. $99–$149 midweek; $159–$259 weekends/high season. Amenities: A/C; high-speed Internet; Jacuzzi in some rooms.*

→ **Maplewood Farm Bed & Breakfast** Surrounded by thick woods and pastures of grazing sheep, cows, and goats, you'll find the Maplewood Farm Bed & Breakfast. While staying overnight at Maplewood Farm, you'll enjoy quaint guestrooms and a sumptuous full breakfast with fresh eggs that come directly from beneath the chickens that you'll meet surrounding the inn as you enter. In addition to the guest amenities, if you come in the summer you can enjoy a beautiful swimming pool surrounded by gardens and forest. *P.O. Box 86, New Hope, PA 18938.* ☎ *215/766-047. www. maplewoodfarm-bb.com. 5 units. Rates from $115–$175 (lower midweek). Amenities: A/C; all rooms have private bathrooms.*

→ **New Hope Motel in the Woods** ★★ Close to Main Street, but far enough off the main drag to provide a woodsy, intimate atmosphere, the New Hope Motel in the Woods is an ideal spot to stay, spreading over 5 acres of land. All rooms come with a refrigerator, cable TV, stereo, and telephones, and the motel has a heated pool during the summer. Dogs are also welcome (there's a $25 fee if you bring along Fluffy). *400 West Bridge St., New Hope, PA 18938.* ☎ *215/862-2800. www.newhopemotel inthewoods.com. 28 units. Double: Weekend rates start $129 for two people; $20 for extra person. Amenities: A/C; fridge in room.*

→ **The Pineapple Hill Bed and Breakfast** This inn is another one of New Hope's estates, which dates back to the late 1700s. There are rumors that a few of the original owners still come around from time to time. If you're looking for a place to stay that encompasses all of the charm of New Hope, see if you can book a room here. They certainly do have the best breakfasts. Enjoy your fair share of

Van Sant Bridge, aka Crybaby Bridge

MTV **Best ♦** Crybaby Bridge is an old covered bridge just outside New Hope. Legend has it that a turn-of-the-20th-century mom killed her two children by throwing them off the bridge, before following them into the water. Tons of sworn testimony attests that if you go out to the bridge at night you will hear the babies crying from below. One story has it that you have to first drive across the bridge and park your car. When you turn around to come back you will encounter an entity that prevents you from crossing. Stories about the Van Sant Bridge have been circulating for over a century. It remains a popular place for local kids to play "chicken" and "truth or dare."

pastries, breads, jams, cereals, and whatever hot entree is served for the day. This place also has high-speed Internet access. If you're planning on staying here, know there is a 2-day minimum stay. *1324 River Rd., New Hope.* ☎ *215/862-1790. www.pineapple hill.com. 9 units. Rates $104–$189 (off season); $139–$249 high season. Ask about packages. Amenities: All rooms have fireplace; private bathroom.*

➔**The Umpleby House Bed and Breakfast Inn** ★★★ This haunted hot spot is said to be visited by the ghosts of Colonel Buckley and Mr. Black, two mill runners for the original owners. Guests have reported seeing the old Colonel walking the halls, or the light from his lantern bobbing through the hallways. If you're not one for ghost sightings and would prefer just a classic, upscale place to stay with a great morning breakfast and beautiful seasonal gardens, this is certainly the spot. *111 West Bridge St.* ☎ *215/862-3936. http://1833umplebyhouse.com. 8 units. Rooms $90–$159 midweek; Suites $159–$225 midweek; Rooms $125–$199 weekends/holidays; suites $189–$289 weekends/holidays. Amenities: Private bathrooms; A/C; high-speed internet; some rooms have Jacuzzis, fireplaces.*

➔**The Wedgwood Inn** Another beautiful Victorian hideaway prone to spirit sightings. The Wedgwood is next to the Umpleby House and is supposedly visited by the spirit of a 12-year-old girl who was separated from her family while escaping on the Underground Railroad. The inn is located on the site of the stop. If you have a craving for some delicious afternoon tea and all-day goodies, this is the spot to be. Garden enthusiasts should also consider this location because of its ideal location near Bowman's Hill Wildflower Preserve (www.bhwp.org), which holds the annual Tohickon Flower Show each September. Pennsylvania's Longwood Gardens,

an other prime location for wildlife enthusiasts, is also close by. *111 W. Bridge St., New Hope, PA.* ☎ *215/862-2570. www.wedgwood inn.com. Doubles/Suites from $125–$245. Amenities: Private bathrooms; A/C; Some rooms have fireplaces, Jacuzzis.*

SPLURGE

Ⓜ Best☻ **The Logan Inn** ★★★ Founded in 1727, this is Bucks County's oldest inn. Room no. 6 is supposedly haunted by the ghost of Emily, the mother of a former owner. Many people have reported feeling extreme temperature drops, mysterious rearrangements of belongings, banging from the closet and drawers, and the sound of mysterious laughter. Emily is a friendly ghost, however, who apparently just wants her presence to be felt in the room. If you can't get into Room no. 6, you may come into contact with other sprits— the place is reported to be crawling with them. For additional creepiness, note that among the inn's previous incarnations was a stint as a makeshift morgue. All rooms are nonsmoking. *10 West Ferry St., New Hope, PA.* ☎ *215/862-3931. www.loganinn.com. 16 units. Feb–Apr $100–$145 standard room; May–Oct 31 $135–$170. Specials are available on Sun and Tues. Amenities: Private bathrooms; A/C; high-speed Internet access.*

➔**The Lexington House** This place is close enough to town to get there easily, but far away enough to make you feel as though you're part of a period film set in the 18th century. The Lexington House is a renovated house from 1749, complete with an additional carriage house and ruins of an old stone barn from the era. Each room comes with its own bathroom, fresh flowers, and a robe. Of course, in the morning there is a homemade, scrumptious breakfast in the dining room. *6171 Upper York Rd., New Hope, PA.* ☎ *215/749-0811. www.lexington house.com. 6 units. Rates $130–$195.*

Amenities: Private bathrooms; outdoor pool (summer only); innkeepers' reception every Sat afternoon.

→ **The Inn at Bowman's Hill** ★★ Here's my choice for a romantic getaway if you're on a roadtrip with your special someone. The Inn is 3 miles from New Hope's downtown, but the distance is part of the attraction. You can enjoy fine Italian dining in addition to heated Jacuzzis and gorgeous fireplaces. There is certainly a reason why the Inn at Bowman's Hill was noted in 2006 as one of the "Top 10 Romantic Inns" in the nation by American Historic Inns. You have the choice to stay in one of the five unique rooms, each with a king size featherbed, travertine bathroom, and spectacular view. If you're splurging, I recommend booking the Orchard Retreat room which includes a spectacular view of the pond, forest, and—you guessed it—orchard. There is also a private veranda attached to this room. Another recommendation would be to stay in the Tower Suite room, which is the master bedroom, and the ideal spot for all hopeless romantics with its custom finishings, ridiculously large marble bathroom, high ceilings, and private sitting room. You can enjoy fine Italian dining in addition to heated Jacuzzis and gorgeous fireplaces. There is a seasonal swimming pool and, of course, gourmet breakfast in the morning. *518 Lurgan Rd., New Hope, PA.* ☎ *215/862-8090. www.theinnatbowmanshill. com. 5 units. $295–$535. Amenities: Swimming pool/hot tub (seasonal); complimentary snacks and bottled water; high-speed Internet; gas fireplace; DVD player.*

Eating

New Hope boasts a variety of independently owned restaurants and eateries. Many places are moderately priced and definitely "doable" on a budget. However, since this is a hot tourist area, the bars, clubs, and hangouts, especially on Main

PARKING TICKETS

Although there are parking lots in New Hope where you can pay a daily fee, a cheaper option is to find a space and feed the meter. However, be aware that the New Hope police are constantly on the search for timed-out meters, so you have to be extra careful. I received a $15 parking ticket for being 5 minutes late; $15 isn't all that bad, but you can park in a lot for the day for $10, and not worry about having to feed the meter.

Street, can become quite expensive during high season (June–Oct). The restaurants are worth checking out, though. There is some destination dining here, and while it might cost a lot, you can have some really great meals if you feel like a splurge.

Cheap

→ **Café Lulu's** ★ MEDITERRANEAN/ AMERICAN If you arrive early in the morning and want to grab a quick bite, this is the place to go. Lulu's pancakes are some of the best in town. Breakfast stops at noon, but lunch is just as great. The wide-ranging menu takes in falafel, hummus, grape leaves, as well as all-American BBQ chicken sandwiches, quesadillas, Caesar salads, and corn dogs. I recommend the Mediterranean chicken sandwich, which comes with spicy fries and pita bread for $8.50. Credit cards are accepted for an additional charge of $1.50. You may want to take advantage of the "bring your own liquor" policy (there's no corkage or pouring fee). *110 South Main St.* ☎ *215/862-3222. Daily 10am–9pm.*

→ **Main Squeeze** ★★★ JUICE BAR/ VEGETARIAN CAFE "It's worth looking for!" is the slogan, because this place is a little tricky to track down (it's up some steps, next to Havana's on Main St.). With a laid-back atmosphere and a variety of juices, smoothies, wraps, frozen drinks, and breakfast specials, this is a great option for a small snack or inexpensive lunch. *95 S. Main St. ☎ 215/862-6330. Sandwiches, salads, and wraps under $10; snacks $1.50–$6.50. Daily 9:30am–8pm, open later on weekends.*

Doable

➔**The Landing Restaurant** AMERICAN The beautiful atmosphere of The Landing Restaurant puts visitors beneath the woods and at the bank of the river in the heart of New Hope. They have a great all-day menu that has a variety of tasty entrees including everything from paninis to lobster ravioli. They also have an array of exciting side dishes including calamari and sweet potato fries (I recommend them both). *22 N. Main St. ☎ 215/862-5711. www.landingrestaurant.com. Entrees $7.95–$28. Daily 11am–5pm.*

MTV (Best ❂) ➔**Wildflowers: Garden Café and Thai Corner** ★★★ THAI The lovely atmosphere of Wildflowers alone is enough to warrant a visit to this little hide-away. Although the food is pricier than the norm for the budget diner, anyone who enjoys Thai food will find it's worth it. (Non-Thai eaters may want to pay a visit for desserts alone.) *8 West Mechanic St. ☎ 215/862-2241. www.wildflowersnewhope.com. Appetizers $6–$10; Soups $3–$4; Sandwiches $4–$9; lunch specials $9–$12; dinner entrees, $8–$18. Open daily for lunch and dinner.*

Splurge

➔**Marsha Brown Refined Creole Kitchen & Lounge** ★★★ CREOLE This cool spot is inside a 125-year-old stone church on New Hope's Main Street and it's where you can get some good old Southern comfort food in the middle of Pennsylvania. Not only will you eat some delicious food but you'll have the chance to learn about Southern dining, including the differences between Creole and Cajun (this is a Creole spot). Some of the Creole favorites include Eggplant Ophelia and Granmere's Comfort Custard. This is one of those places where you could make an entire meal based on starters. Be sure to try Basin Street Mussels, Crawfish Springrolls, and Lollipop Lamb Chops. There's also a Raw Bar for fresh shellfish. After this dining experience, you may just want to take your next roadtrip down south. *15 S. Main St., New Hope. ☎ 215/862-7044. www.marshabrownrestaurant.com. Entrees $18–$35. Mon–Thurs 5–10pm; Fri 5–11pm; Sat 2–11pm; Sun 2–9pm.*

Partying

The size of New Hope may limit the amount of places for you to party, but there are a couple of fun nightspots. When the town closes down, which is relatively early, these are the places to head to.

➔**Havana** LATIN/NIGHTCLUB/LIVE MUSIC One of New Hope's oldest nightclubs provides live music every night of the week, along with cocktails, drinks, and a variety of Latin food. This is a favorite local hang-out, with great food and an even better atmosphere. It's very popular among the adult crowd in New Hope. Check the website for the latest schedule of performers. *105 S. Main St. ☎ 215/862-9897. www.havananewhope.com. $10–$16 entrees. Daily noon–2am.*

➔**90 Main** LOUNGE/BAR "Bringing the city vibe to New Hope" is how this joint advertises itself, and it does feel like something straight out of Manhattan. If you're looking for New Hope's college-age crowd, they're probably here. There is a chic lounge on the ground level and an upstairs VIP room for private parties. Dinner and drinks are served from 5pm to 2am during the summer months. Weekend hours extend to 3pm to 2am. Dinner and drinks are served from 5pm to 2am during the summer months. Don't be fooled . . . not only is this a classy lounge, but it's a pretty darn good restaurant, too. The menu includes an eclectic variety of what 90 Main calls "World Fusion," including everything from sushi and salads to chicken wings, burgers and crab cake sandwiches. Valet parking is available on Thursday, Friday, and Saturday beginning at 5pm. Weekend hours extend to 3pm to 2am. *90 Main St.* ☎ *215/ 862-3030. www.90mainlounge.com. $13–$18 entrees.*

What Else to See & Do

There are a few other non-ghostly things to do in New Hope. Most people are attracted to New Hope for its downtown area where there are tons of small shops and fascinating, independently owned boutiques. If you have already had your fill of the downtown area, then check out some of New Hope's other attractions below.

Playing Outside

TOURS BY FERRY & TRAIN

➔ **Wells Ferry Boat Rides** If you have an urge to learn a little more about the history of New Hope, Bucks County, and the surrounding area, there is no better way to go then aboard the Wells Ferry. These Ferry rides date back to 1718 when King George gave John Wells, founder of New Hope, permission to operate the first ferry. The contemporary tours still follow the same route as they did 200 years ago. Wells Ferry Boat Rides is located on the original site at the end of Ferry Street in the heart of New Hope. This narrated tour on the Delaware River will give you a little history and a glimpse of New Hope's varied architecture. Wells Ferry departs every hour on the hour from noon to 7pm, May through October, weather permitting. *14 East Ferry St.* ☎ *215/862-5965. www.wellsferry boatrides.com.*

➔ **New Hope & Ivyland Railroad** Here's your opportunity to climb aboard history and take a glimpse into the past. The Ivyland Railroad is a restored, vintage train complete with coaches, bar cars, and, of course, a steam locomotive. Tours leave every day and the theme of the tour depends on the season you're visiting. There are dinner trains, murder mystery nights, holiday rides, and, of course, during New Hope's favorite Halloween season, there are nightly themed train tours that delve into some of the area's transit mysteries, including the "Big Wreck" in October 1922. If you aren't exactly in the mood to be spooked, you can check out

---

QUICK Shop

Main Street is lined with funky vintage shops, costume collections, medieval shops, and music stores. For a useful map of the shopping district, stop by the **New Hope Visitors Center** at 1 West Mechanic St. (☎ **215/862-5030**). To track down the hottest underground music, records, CDs, not to mention novelty bumper stickers, T-shirts, and hookahs, you cannot miss **Spinsters Records & Toxic Waste Dump** (110 S. Main St.; ☎ **215/862-2700**). **Against the Grain** (88 S. Main St.; ☎ **215/862-4900;** www.medievalgallery.com) is a medieval weaponry gallery that carries fantasy, custom-made, and collectible swords. There are also several sections of costumes, jewelry, and furniture along the same theme. Even if you don't plan on purchasing anything, this is a great spot just to browse and read up on the origins of the weaponry.

some of Pennsylvania's beautiful fall colors on the "foliage" tour. Tours depart hourly from noon to 3pm on weekends during the off season, and more often/daily during the summer. The fare is $13 for adults, and there are special seasonal tours, including a Christmas "Polar Express." *32 W. Bridge St.* ☎ *215/862-2332. www.newhoperailroad.com.*

A WILDLIFE PRESERVE

➔ The Bowman's Hill Wildlife Preserve

Get in touch with nature at the Bowman's Hill Wildlife Preserve, open year-round. Admission for visitors is $5 for adults and includes a guided tour offered at 2pm. Admission fees are waived on Community Open House Days and on the days of the annual Fall and Spring plant sales. They have dozens of wildlife trails where you can hike and explore the Pennsylvania outdoors. There are also a number of educational programs, which include garden shows, wildlife tours, and bird-watching. This is the perfect spot to indulge your inner nature buff or to just work off all the great food you've been eating. You can see over 1,000 species of plants, animals, and birds. Guided tours are also available *1635 River Rd., New Hope.* ☎ *215/862-2924. www. bhwp.org.*

On the Road to New York City & the Hudson Valley

New Hope, PA to New York City, NY 69 miles

On the Road Nuts & Bolts

Where to Fill Up   There are plenty of gas stations along the road and throughout New York City. Your best bet is to fill up in New Jersey, as gas in NYC is *very* expensive. New Jersey has some of the cheapest gas on the East Coast.

The Tolls   You will pay $6 to enter the Holland Tunnel and cross into New York.

The Fastest Way   Take I-287 North and merge onto I-78 East via Exit 21 toward New York City. There are plenty of signs that point you toward New York City.

The Long Way Around   You can take a ride through Northern New Jersey and spend some time enjoying the sites. At any rate, you will have to pass through New Jersey, why not take your time and see what Jersey is about?

Rules of the Road   65 mph is the speed limit for the highways. There is a strictly enforced "no right turn on red" policy once you enter NYC. If you forget that little detail, it will cost you—$100 or more if you're caught by the NYPD. Driving through NYC is tough enough; don't put yourself through more stress by adding additional expense.

Passing through NYC

You think I'm kidding? This is going to be the quickest trip through the Big Apple you'll ever take, unless you're changing planes.

If you'd like to hang around for a few days (or a few years), you certainly have my blessing, and we do spend a few days in the city in the Festivals chapter (p. 47). For the purposes of this trip, however, we're going to focus on the ghosts of Manhattan, and a few of their more remarkable haunts.

Detour: Northern New Jersey

I-287 North will take you through Northern New Jersey (on your way to New York). You may want to stop into some of the towns. I recommend checking out **Montclair** (Exit 80), a quaint little Jersey town which is often used as a filming spot for many TV shows and films. You may recognize some of the surrounding area as being prime real estate on television shows like *Ed, The Sopranos,* and *Law & Order* (the whole franchise). There are also many restaurants, theaters, and coffeehouses that may appeal if you want to take a break and have a meal before you hit New York.

For nature buffs, also along the way in Northern New Jersey is the **Great Swamp Wildlife Refuge** in Basking Ridge, NJ. For legend buffs, this is supposedly one of the homes of the Jersey Devil. It is said that if you're out at night, alone on the roads near the Great Swamp, you may come into contact with the creature. Check out the Great Swamp on the Web at **www.friendsofgreatswamp.org.** The wildlife preserve is open 7 days a week but there are also guided tours given on particular days with varying themes. Be sure to check out the website for the most up-to-date information. For more about the legend of the Jersey Devil, see the box on p. 217.

GHOSTLY TOURS

➔ **Ghosts of New York Tours** ★ Is New York City the most haunted city in America? In five different tours around various parts of the city, the folks at New York Talks & Walks guide you to where famous folk once resided (and still may linger). Do the tales of Poe still give you a tingle? Consider the **Edgar Allan Poe and His Ghostly Friends of the East Village** tour. The **Ghosts of Times Square** tour has a theatrical bent, and there's even a tour designed for children. Tours last around 90 minutes, and the total walking distance is less than a mile. Group and individual tours can be arranged. For a list of upcoming tours, see the schedule posted on the website. *Tickets: $15. Ghosts of New York.* ☎ *718/591-4741. www.ghostsofny.com.*

GHOSTLY APARTMENT HOUSE

➔ **The Dakota** Looming over Central Park at 72nd Street, this is one of NYC's poshest apartment buildings. It was built between 1880–84. It's also got a legendary history. Celebrity residents have included Judy Garland, William Inge, Paul Simon, and Lauren Bacall. It's reported that ghosts of young children in early 20th-century clothing have been spotted, and of course, this is also the site where John Lennon was killed. It's said that his spirit sometimes haunts the gate near where he was murdered. The Dakota has been the setting for several films, including the ultra-creepy *Rosemary's Baby.* Although you can't go inside (that's limited to residents), The Dakota's rich history, architecture, legend, and lore make it worthy of a look. It's also across the street from the "Strawberry Fields" memorial in Central Park, where

Let's Not Repeat Ourselves . . .

For **"New York City Nuts & Bolts"** and **"Getting Around,"** turn to those sections in the chapter, "Festival Season: On the Road in the Northeast and Mid-Atlantic," starting on p. 39, which also starts off in NYC (and heads in a completely different direction . . .)

Recommended Reading: Haunted NYC

→ *Ghostly Gotham: New York City's Haunted History,* by Lynda Lee Macken (Black Cat Press, 2002). Macken (who's also written books on haunted New Hope and New Jersey) packs a lot of information into the 112-page book.

→ *Ghosts of New York,* by Susan Blackhall (Thunder Bay Press, 2005). The author visits the White Horse Tavern, where Welsh poet Dylan Thomas died after drinking 18 straight whiskies but still likes to hover around his favorite table, among other NYC haunts.

And a recommended website:
http://gonyc.about.com/od/halloween/a/haunted_newyork.htm.

each year, thousands gather to celebrate John Lennon's birthday. *1 West 72nd St. (at Central Park).*

A HAUNTED RESTAURANT & BAR

→**Ear Inn** Ear Inn is arguably the oldest bar in Manhattan (there are several other places who claim the distinction)—it's definitely located in one of the city's oldest surviving buildings, built in 1817. In fact, the recent discovery of charred timber in the attic has led some NY historians to believe that the building was constructed with remains of wood that survived the great fire of 1776, which wiped out nearly a third of the buildings in the city. A spirit named Mickey, a sailor struck and killed by a car in front of the bar, supposedly haunts the place. Live music runs 3 nights a week,

and at 3pm on Saturdays you'll find open mic poetry. (It's sometimes ghastly, but not really ghostly.) Happy Hour is Monday–Friday 4 to 7pm. *362 Spring St. (between Greenwich and Washington sts.).* ☎ *212/226-9060. Daily 11:30am–4am.*

→**One if by Land, Two if by Sea Restaurant** ★ AMERICAN Staff and employees have frequently seen the ghost of Aaron Burr here. (The restaurant, which is one of the city's most expensive, is in a carriage house that was purchased by the Burr family at the end of the 1700s.) Guests have reported seeing plates and silverware freakishly tossed from tables and counters. A colonial atmosphere still reigns inside. *17 Barrow St. (in Greenwich Village).* ☎ *212/255-8649. www.oneifbyland.*

The Most Fabulous Ghosts in the World!

Ghosties and ghoulies and lots of dead celebrities parade the streets of Greenwich Village every October 31st. Tens of thousands of costumed revelers fill Sixth Avenue in one of New York's greatest traditions. The event was begun in 1973 by a puppeteer, who paraded from house to house for the people in the community. Eventually, the Theatre for the New City became involved and started producing a larger scale version for their "City in the Streets" program. The parade is now covered by worldwide media and has been called "The greatest event of its kind for October 31st." A word of warning: Make sure to keep valuables such as cameras and wallets securely with you at all times. **www.halloween-nyc.com.**

Manhattan Myth: The Legend of George Frederick Cooke

The **Saint Paul's Chapel Burial Ground** at Broadway and Fulton Street is home to the body of George Frederick Cooke, a prominent actor in the early 1800s. Cooke died in 1811 and was buried headless, after donating his head to science to pay off his medical bills. His skull was used thereafter in many productions of *Hamlet*. It has been reported that George Cooke's ghost roams around the graveyard, searching for his missing head.

com. *Prix-fixe menu starts from $75–$95 for dinner. Daily 5:15pm–11pm. Bar opens daily at 4pm.*

NOT HAUNTED, BUT SPOOKY

→ **Albion Club** This is the largest Goth club in New York. Guests must show up in appropriate dark or period clothing. Drinks start at $5 and up. There is a $15 cover fee but there is a $10 reduced rate if you contact synthpunk@synthetek.net to be placed on the guest list. *251 W. 30th St. between 7th and 8th aves.* ☎ *718/260-0092. www.albionclub.com. Sat 10pm–4:30am.*

A HAUNTED HOSPITAL

→ **Sea View Hospital** ★★ Get on the Staten Island Ferry for a visit to this little-known and reputedly haunted ruin. Are you up for exploring an abandoned asylum? Okay, so it's not completely abandoned, but behind the area still in use as a nursing home lies the ruins of the Farm Colony. In the 1890s, the colony was used as a tuberculosis infirmary and to house the mentally ill. With its huge, abandoned, gothic towers (which house quite a few cat colonies) and overall creepy vibe, this is a

ghost hunter's dream. (It's also a location scout's dream—many films and music videos have been shot on the grounds.) A director of the Staten Island Shakespearean Theatre (which used to have a building on the grounds) reported hearing strange footsteps and seeing what appeared to be an old man in turn-of-the-20th-century clothing walking around the hallway.

When the director turned to ask the old man what he was doing in the building, the man was nowhere to be found. He later asked the security guards outside if there was anyone still left on the grounds and they said "no." Stories like this are common legends among Staten Islanders. If you want to experience this place for yourself, get an official tour through the museum. You'll see ancient medical equipment used by turn-of-the-20th-century TB doctors and you'll get a sense of a day in the life of the patients and doctors that used to reside here. The hospital is reachable by the Ferry and Staten Island bus service, but your best bet is to drive because the bus schedule can be unreliable and the grounds can be hard to maneuver on foot. *Sea View, 460 Brielle Ave., Staten Island.* ☎ *877/ 5SEAVIEW.*

On the Road to the Hudson Valley

After checking in on the ghostly sights of New York City, you'll be heading north to the Hudson Valley, where you'll pass through a bit of Washington Irving country.

THE HISTORIC HUDSON

I recommend just passing through for the day before moving on to Connecticut. This part of the Hudson Valley is approximately 30 to 40 miles north of New York City, and a very easy day trip or stopover. If you choose to stay the night, I have several hotel suggestions listed below (p. 132.)

Your first stop along the historic Hudson should be at the **Historical Society**

The Legend of Sleepy Hollow

Washington Irving, one of America's first internationally known authors, is most famous for writing "The Legend of Sleepy Hollow," as well as the oversleeping Rip Van Winkle. On your visit to the Hudson Valley, stop by Irving's estate and learn about the inspiration behind his legendary thriller. Where the inspiration for his characters came from and why he chose Sleepy Hollow are just two of the many details you'll learn. Guided house tours of the Irving estate are given daily from April through December and on weekends in March. Each October, the Washington Irving Manor opens its doors to the public for **Legend Weekend**. Weekend events include reenactments of the Legend of Sleepy Hollow and other Halloween favorites. Check out the Historic Hudson Valley's Visitor Center for details (www.hudsonvalley.org). Regular admission for adults is $10. The estate is located at West Sunnyside Lane in Tarrytown, New York, about 28 miles north of New York City.

(1 Grove St., Tarrytown; ☎ 914/631-8374). You can grab information on the latest happenings in town. You can also pick up background information on Tarrytown and the Legend of Sleepy Hollow, and see exhibits at the Historical Society building.

If you need more information, stop by the **Historic Hudson Valley's Visitor Center** (150 White Plains Rd., Tarrytown; **www.hudsonvalley.org**). This is another site where you can pick up information and brochures on the latest happenings in the Hudson Valley. There is also a cute museum shop where you can purchase books, souvenirs, and handicrafts by local artists.

A Colonial Mansion

FREE →**The Philipsburg Manor** The Philipsburg Manor was established during the late colonial period by the Philipses, a northern slave-owning family. Costumed guides provide visitors a glimpse into the daily life of the time. *Rte. 9, Sleepy Hollow.* ☎ *914/631-3992; www.hudsonvalley.org/ philipsburg. Admission is free but guided tours cost $10 per adult. Open Wed–Mon Apr–Dec and weekends in Mar.*

Sing Sing Artifacts

About 6 miles north of Sleepy Hollow, Ossining, NY, is home to the infamous **Sing Sing Prison,** which has played host to (and

Recommended Reading: Hudson Valley

The Legend of Sleepy Hollow, by Washington Irving. Ichabod Crane, the Headless Horseman, and Abraham Van Brunt are the legendary characters in Washington Irving's classic short story about the terrifying happenings in the New York City suburb of Tarrytown.

been the site of the deaths of) many a murderous criminal. **The Ossining Heritage Center** (95 Broadway, Ossining; ☎ **914/ 941-3189**) has relics from the prison, including actual-size jail cells and a primitive electric chair. Check the schedule for daily walking tour information and prices.

Sleeping

There are several chains in the area. The **Doubletree Inn at Tarrytown** (☎ **800/ 553-8118**; www.doubletree.hilton.com) has recently reopened after renovation.

If you want something a little more authentic (and pricey!), check out **Tarrytown House Estate & Conference**

Flaming Pumpkins on the Hudson!

The Great Jack O' Lantern Blaze ★★ at Van Cortlandt Manor is one of Westchester County's newest rituals. The Blaze is held for three weekends in October and gives visitors the chance to see more than 3,000 carved pumpkins on display. The Van Cortland Manor is in Croton-on-Hudson, about 6 miles north of Ossining. Tickets for the event ($10) can be purchased online at **www.hudsonvalley.org**. The manor itself is open every day but Tuesday, April through October, and weekends only November and December. www.hudsonvalley.org/vancortlandt.

Center, 49 East Sunnyside Lane ★ (☎ **800/553-8118;** www.tarrytownhouseestate.com) where the occasional special might knock the room rate down to around $150 a night, or **The Castle on the Hudson** ★★, 400 Benedict Ave. in Tarrytown (☎ **800/616-4487** or 914/631-1980; www.castleonthehudson.com), which is also definitely a splurge (from $300 on up . . .), though some of their packages include meals at Equus restaurant (see below).

Eating

Cheap

➔ **The Horseman Diner** ★★ AMERICAN/PIZZA Sleepy Hollow is proud of their horseman, and this restaurant proves it with movie posters, mosaics, and statues of the legend. Aside from the Hollow vibe, this is the place to go if you want a hearty and delicious meal. There's a fantastic variety of salads, served in a tortilla shell, and an array of sandwiches for under $10. Specialty pizzas are $8 to 15. If you want a Sleepy Hollow souvenir T-shirt, for $12 you can pick one up here with a picture of—you guessed it—the Headless Horseman on the front. *276 N. Broadway, Sleepy Hollow.* ☎ *914/631-7491. Meals $8–$15. Daily: 6am–11pm.*

Doable

➔ **Horsefeathers** AMERICAN This is a Tarrytown favorite. Pick from your choice of American favorites, including everything from sandwiches to prime rib. This place also has a fine array of appetizers, soups, salads, and desserts. It's the perfect spot to relax after spending the day exploring the historic Hudson's surrounding areas. *94 N. Broadway, Tarrytown, NY.* ☎ *914/631-6606. www.horsefeatherstarrytown.com. Lunch and dinner Mon–Wed 11:30am–10pm; Thurs–Sat 11:30am–11pm; Sun 11:30am–9pm. Weekend brunch 11:30am–4pm.*

Splurge

➔ **Equus at the Castle on the Hudson** ★★★ AMERICAN One of the most famous restaurants in Westchester is **Equus,** in the heart of the Castle on the Hudson, an absolutely beautiful guesthouse and restaurant that looks like something from out of medieval Europe. The Castle on the Hudson is worth a visit, even if you do not plan on eating here (though I highly recommend the food). Like all good castles it has daily high tea in addition to a variety of dishes fit for royalty. The menu changes according to season, but you can guarantee that whatever the seasonal choices are, you'll be impressed. There's a prix-fixe dinner for $74, which includes appetizers, entrees, and dessert. The Sunday brunch costs $54 per person. During the summer season, there is a huge swimming pool surrounded by fantastic gardens. If you can afford it, you can spend the night in one of the beautifully renovated guest rooms. *400 Benedict Ave., Tarrytown, NY.* ☎ *914/631-3646. www.castleonthehudson.com. Breakfast 7–10:30am; lunch noon–2:00pm; dinner 6–9pm; Sat 5:30–10pm; Sunday Champagne Brunch 11:30am–2:30. Castle High Tea daily 2:30–5pm.*

On the Road to Connecticut

Tarrytown/Sleepy Hollow NY to Bridgeport, CT 43 miles

On the Road Nuts & Bolts

Where to Fill Up   Anywhere in the Hudson Valley. Make sure you fill up in the smaller towns before heading back up the highway where gas is more expensive.

The Tolls   There are no tolls.

The Fastest Way   Take I-287 E to exit 8 White Plains/Rye. Merge onto I-95N and cross into Connecticut and take the Wordin Avenue exit (Exit 26).

Rules of the Road   65 mph is the speed limit. Pay attention to exit signs because they creep up on you, and sometimes it's a huge pain to have to turn around at the next exit and backtrack.

Welcome to Bridgeport

This is more of a detour than a true stop, but I did want to visit the circus . . . or the museum that memorializes one of the greatest showmen ever. (You can also explore Barnum's legacy in New York City as well, with the ghost tours described in the NYC section.)

In 1871, Phineas Taylor Barnum founded his famous circus, but before that, he served as Mayor of Bridgeport and in the Connecticut legislature. During his lifetime, he was one of the most well-known people in the United States, a true entrepreneur.

Because of his strong ties to Bridgeport, the city is still crazy about him. There is an entire museum and festival named for him (below).

Barnum's Bridgeport

MTV Best ◗ **The Barnum Museum** ★★★ (820 Main St., Bridgeport; ☎ **203/ 331–9881;** www.barnum-museum.org) is definitely worth a stop. He was a politician, entrepreneur, civic leader, and all-around showman. Those are a few of the words that can be used to describe P.T. Barnum, creator of the "Greatest Show on Earth." In today's society, the idea of exhibiting people with physical deformities or afflictions is definitely not cool. In Barnum's day, "freaks" were put on display, and many made their livings (and made lots of money for Barnum) by working in his shows and exhibitions. In this museum, most of the exhibits are a celebration of Barnum's life and contributions to society, but there are also a few that will get you thinking about how times have changed (and if, in fact, they have). You'll see exhibits of many of the acts he promoted including Tom Thumb, Jumbo the Elephant, Egyptian mummies, and the "Siamese Twins Chang and Eng." *Adults $5, students and seniors $4, children under 17 $3, free for children under 4. Tues–Sat 10am–4:30pm; Sun noon–4:30pm.*

Another Barnum event in Bridgeport is the annual **Barnum Festival,** held from April through September at various venues. Festival activities occur throughout the city and consist of comedy shows, costume parades, concerts, and parties. For a schedule of events visit **www.barnumfestival. com** or ☎ **866/867-8495.**

Welcome to Mystic

Bridgeport to Mystic 74 miles

As you travel up the Northeast coast, you will not be able to miss the stories and myths surrounding lost ships at sea and pirates. Mystic, Connecticut, is a great place to start your journey into the land of maritime myths. Since Mystic has one of the most renowned seaports in the world, Victorian architecture, and museums, you will certainly be able to gather a good amount of background knowledge of Northeast myths that will serve you well as you continue on your roadtrip.

On the Road **Nuts & Bolts**

Where to Fill Up   Anywhere along the way.

The Fastest Way   Merge onto I-95 toward New Haven. Take the Allyn Street exit 89 toward Mystic. Turn right onto Allyn Street and left onto New London Road.

Rules of the Road   65 mph is the limit. Do not get caught talking on your cellphone while driving. Connecticut has a strict "no cellphones on the road" rule. The fine can be up to $100. Drivers 18 or older are allowed to use a hands-free device to take phone calls; however, drivers age 16 and 17 are not permitted to use any type of cellular device while on the road.

MYSTIC SEAPORT ★★

The **Mystic Seaport** is one of America's best maritime museums. The seaport includes museums featuring vessels, nautical folk art, paintings, ship models, plans, historic buildings, and countless other artifacts dealing with maritime history. There are also boat rides, shopping villages, ship preservation yards, and plenty of other exhibits. So what's so weird about Mystic, you ask? During the Halloween season throughout October, Mystic has a fantastic haunted production called **Nautical Nightmares** that will not only scare the pants off of you, but introduce you to the dark side of Mystic: the ghost tales, legends, and unsolved mysteries. Yes, every town has them. This is a seasonal program, so you must check the website for the schedule. *75 Greenmanville Ave., Mystic, CT.* ☎ *888/9Seaport. www.visit mysticseaport.com. Admission $17.50 adult/ $12 children. Daily 9am–5pm Apr–Oct; 10am– 4pm Nov–Mar.*

SLEEPING
Cheap

There are plenty of ho-hum but adequate area motels that can soak up the traffic at all but peak periods, meaning weekends from late spring to early fall plus weekdays in July and August, when it is necessary to have reservations. Good planning and research can get you a room at a major chain for around $100 a night, though if you're willing to stay in nearby Groton, the prices drop off quite a bit. Pick of the litter may be the **Best Western Sovereign,** north of Exit 90 (☎ **800/528-1234** or 860/536-4281), with a pool and restaurant. Nearby competitors are the **Comfort Inn** (☎ **800/228-5150** or 860/572-8531), **Days Inn** (☎ **800/325-2525** or 860/572-0574), and **Residence Inn** (☎ **800/331-3131** or 860/536-5150).

EATING
Cheap

➔**Kitchen Little** ★ AMERICAN Not much more than a shack by the water, this

Connecticut's Melonheads: Be on the Lookout!

Every state has a legend . . . or two . . . or three. The legend of the Melonheads (tiny humans with deformed bodies and huge heads who've been exiled by society) has been flying around for decades now. It is said that the Melonheads came from Ohio, from one of the experiments of a man named Dr. Crow, who in the 1940s was hired to take care of children with hydrocephalism (a condition that causes water on the brain), but instead performed evil experiments on them, torturing them with all kinds of nasty injections and experimenting with radiation, causing their heads to swell even more and their bodies to become disfigured. Legend has it that the surviving kids escaped one day, killed Dr. Crow, ate his body, and headed straight out into the woods, never to be heard of again until they reproduced in the woods and created a colony of Melonheads.

Melonhead tribes have been typically thought to live in Ohio but there have been Melonhead sightings in Connecticut. There are several theories as to where they came from. Some say they migrated from Ohio and created a colony in the Connecticut woods and others believe that they are the descendants of a family that was shunned during the Puritan days because of rumors of inbreeding.

Wherever they came from, there are plenty of stories and accounts from people warning outsiders to stay off the backwood Connecticut roads at night, as Melonheads have been known to attack local animals, and even in some cases come after people. Wherever they are, be on the lookout so that you don't end up like Dr. Crow! (For more info, check out **www.WeirdUS.com**.)

is the sort of place dismissed and passed every day by hundreds of tourists hurrying on to the Seaport. They're missing not only 45 distinct breakfast choices, including at least a dozen three-egg omelets, but also some of the coast's tastiest clam and scallop dishes. At lunch, you must have the definitive clear broth clam chowder, maybe the whole belly clam rolls, and absolutely the fried scallop sandwich. Or the lobster roll, with no fillers, only tail and claw flesh. Expect a wait in summer and tight quarters inside. They serve only breakfast on weekends. Try to snare a table out back, in view of the tall ships. Rte. 27, 1 mile south of I-95. ☎ 860/536-2122. *Reservations not accepted. Main dishes $3.45–$13. Mon–Fri 6:30am–2pm; Sat–Sun 6:30am–1pm.*

Detour: Old Homes in New London

Two of the oldest houses in New England, **The Hempstead Houses** are a few minutes from the downtown Mystic area in New London, CT. These houses have been some of the most documented in literature and art from the 17th century, and were built by Joshua Hempstead, a farmer and shipbuilder. This is also the only Underground Railway stop open to the public in Connecticut's African American Freedom Trail. There are tours of this site from May to October, but during the Halloween season there are storytellers who give tours of the grounds that include ghost stories and haunted legends. *11 Hempstead St., New London.* ☎ **860/247-8996** *or 860/443-7949;www.hartnet.org. May–Oct Mon–Fri 9am–5pm.*

The Haunted Inns of Mystic

→ **The House of 1833** This mansion was also known as "The White House" during the 19th and early 20th centuries. Back in the late 1800s, a woman named Elizabeth died in the house and to this day, people have reported feeling her presence watching them on the lower levels of the house. *72 N. Stonington Rd., Mystic.* ☎ *800/FOR-1833 or 860/536-6325; www.houseof 1833.com. Rates: $139–$250 Jan–Apr; $149–$250 Nov–Dec; $179–$350 May–Oct.*

→ **The Red Brook Inn** Here, you have the option of staying in the Haley Tavern or Crary Homestead, both built during the late 1700s, and which have not been restored since then. Guests have reported seeing a mysterious old woman who haunts the North room of the Crary Homestead. It is said that she is the wife of the original owner who is angry about her husband remarrying another woman after she died. *P.O. Box 237, Old Mystic,* ☎ *860/572-0349; www.redbrookinn.com. Rates: $130–$149.*

→ **Mystic Pizza** ★ PIZZA Yes, it's famous. You've probably seen the movie and maybe have bought the frozen pizzas at your local grocery store. If you want the real experience, you have to come to the restaurant. Apparently, the writer came up with the concept for the movie from her visit to Mystic. "Slice of Heaven" T-shirts like the one worn by Julia Roberts in the movie are on sale for $14.95. *56 W. Main St.* ☎ *860/536-3700. Daily til closing.*

Doable

→ **GoFish** ★★ SEAFOOD This is the place to go for fantastic seafood and a wide array of sushi. With its busy atmosphere and fun location near many hot shopping spots, GoFish is the place to go for some of that famous New England seafood you're always hearing about. *Olde Mistick Village, at Exit 90 off I-95.* ☎ *860/ 536-2662. Reservations not accepted. Main courses $16–$24. Sun–Thurs 11:30am–9:30pm; Fri–Sat 11:30am–10:30pm.*

Detour: Abandoned Amusement Park

Who knew Connecticut was once so . . . Holy. Connecticut is home to 〔MTV〕〔Best♦〕 **Holy Land USA** ★★★, well, what used to be the Holy Land. The theme park was born in the early 1950s and was at one point a theme park dedicated to bringing to life the stories of the Bible. There was a miniature Bethlehem, Garden of Eden, statues, pillars, underground catacombs, and tons of church history including facts about every single pope. To the people of Waterbury, it is still an important city landmark. Over the years, people have tried to restore it, including a group of nuns and a couple of Boy Scout troops Holy Land USA is about 90 minutes east of Mystic CT and is one of those places you should explore at your own risk, since the park has been closed for over 2 decades. It overlooks I-84 and the Brass Mill Center on Slocum Road. To get there, head east on I-84 and exit on S. Main Street; stay straight on McMahon Street, then turn right on Baldwin Street, then left on Pleasant Street, which turns left on Emerald, then go right on Ayers Street to end.

On the Road to Rhode Island

Mystic CT to Newport, RI 49 Miles

On the Road **Nuts & Bolts**

The Tolls   Have $3 for bridge tolls.

The Fastest Way   Merge onto I-95 from Mystic toward Providence, RI. Cross into Rhode Island. Merge onto RI-102 toward North Kingstown and turn left onto Victory Highway. Continue to follow Victory Highway until you merge onto RI-4 toward Narragansett. Turn right onto US-1 and merge onto RI-138 toward Jamestown/Newport. Take RI-138E toward Scenic Newport.

The Long Way Round   There is a scenic route that will take you up the Rhode Island coast and past many of its famous beaches. If you follow US-1 north you will have the opportunity to find access to Charlestown Beach, Snug Harbor, Narragansett Pier, and Plum Beach. Each of these places has a great history along with some legendary haunted lighthouses. It could be well worth your time to check into spending a few days exploring these places.

Pirates, Aliens & Ghosts . . . Oh, My!

THE LEGEND OF CAPTAIN KIDD

According to maps, legends, and nautical guides, there are several caves where pirates hid out with their booty along the coast of Rhode Island. Jamestown, RI, and Newport are two pirate-hunting hot spots. In fact, some people have even gone as far as searching for these caves and found the actual locations of where the pirates buried their treasure.

Although no recent treasure has been uncovered, if you do the research you can find the spots and see the 15- to 20-foot underwater hideaways. For more information on Rhode Island's pirate hunters and some accounts of people's hunts for pirate artifacts, check out **http://strangene.com/legends/legends.htm**.

Welcome to Newport

VISITOR INFORMATION

For advance information available 24 hours, call **visitor information** (☎ **800/976-5122** outside R.I., 800/556-2484 in R.I; www.goNewport.com). In town, stop by the excellent **Newport Gateway Visitor Center,** 23 America's Cup Ave. (☎ **800/326-6030** or 401/849-8048). Open daily from 9am to 5pm (until 6pm Fri–Sat), it has attendants on duty, brochures, a lodging-availability service, a cafe, a souvenir stand, restrooms, and panoramic photos showing the locations of mansions, parks, and other landmarks. The building is shared with the bus station.

GETTING AROUND

Most of Newport's attractions, except for the mansions, can be reached on foot, so leaving your car at your hotel or inn is wise. Parking lots aren't cheap, especially at the waterfront, and many streets are narrow. The metered parking along Thames Street is closely monitored by police, and fines are steep (although in the off season, the meters are hooded and parking is free for up to 3 hr.). Renting or bringing a bicycle is an attractive option.

Newport, RI Highlights

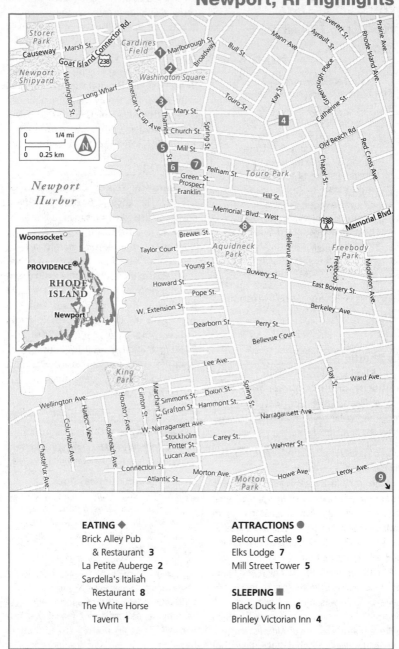

EATING ◆

Brick Alley Pub
   & Restaurant **3**
La Petite Auberge **2**
Sardella's Italian
   Restaurant **8**
The White Horse
   Tavern **1**

ATTRACTIONS ●

Belcourt Castle **9**
Elks Lodge **7**
Mill Street Tower **5**

SLEEPING ■

Black Duck Inn **6**
Brinley Victorian Inn **4**

Recommended Reading for Rhode Island

→ **Haunted Newport,** by Eleyne Austen Sharp (Austen Sharp, 1999). This book details Newport's haunted history and folklore. After reading this, you'll want to stay in Rhode Island a few extra days to unearth some of the state's mysteries.

→ **Ghosttraveller: Rhode Island Haunts website: www. ghosttraveller.com/rhode_ island.htm#theaters**. This is a fantastic site that details many of Rhode Island's most haunted attractions. There's also a link that will connect you with some ghost hunting tips from the pros.

By Shuttle Bus

The **Rhode Island Public Transit Authority,** or **RIPTA** (☎ 401/781-9400), has a free shuttle bus that follows a roughly circular route through town, making stops at major sights.

OLD STONE MILL: NEWPORT'S MYSTERY TOWER

The old stone fortress known as Newport's Tower has become one of Newport's finest legends. Over the centuries, it has been called many names including "Round Tower," "Touro Tower," "Newport Tower" and "Old Stone Mill."

The tower itself is 28 feet high and made of stone arches 3 feet thick. Some people believe that it was built by Norsemen long before Columbus came to America, others believe that is was one of America's primitive lighthouses and a handful believe that

it was used as an ancient beacon to make contact with life on other planets.

Historians have discovered that maps of Rhode Island dating back to the 1600s show evidence of the stone structure. Currently, the most accepted explanation for its existence is that it was used as a mill in the 1700s. This theory comes from the discovery of a similar structure, the Chesterton Mill in England. The tower is located in Touro Park in Newport.

Sleeping

The **Gateway Visitor Center** (☎ 800/ 976-5122 or 401/849-8040; www.gonew port.com) lists vacancies in motels, hotels, and inns.

Many of the better motels are in Middletown, about 2 miles north of downtown. Possibilities include the **Courtyard by Marriott,** 9 Commerce Dr. (☎ 401/ 849-8000); **Newport Ramada Inn,** 936 W. Main Rd. (☎ 401/846-7600); **Newport Gateway Hotel,** 31 W. Main Rd. (☎ 401/ 847-2735); and **Howard Johnson,** 351 W. Main Rd. (☎ 401/849-2000). Newport itself has a **Marriott,** 25 America's Cup Ave. (☎ 401/849-1000).

A Tour of Haunted Newport

The **Haunted Gateway Tour,** starting at 23 America's Cup Ave. in Newport, includes regional folklore, local legends, and graveyard haunts. It's given by Haunted New England Cemetery Ghost Walks. Admission: $10. For tickets and scheduling information call ☎ 401/ 364-6621. Weekends Apr–Oct. Tickets must be purchased at the Gateway Visitor Center. No walk-ups allowed.

Newport's Haunted Castles

For such a small state, there are plenty of great haunts and legends surrounding Rhode Island, and in Newport particularly for legend and ghost enthusiasts. Below are a couple more in Newport:

→ **Belcourt Castle**   This castle (one of Newport's famous "cottages") was built in the late 1800s for Oliver Hazard Perry Belmont, who had inherited a fortune from his father, a banker. Today, descendants of the original Belcourt family still live there. There is a chapel in the mansion that has a sculpture of a monk. It is said that the same monk from the sculpture often appears by the staircase. The Belcourt Castle is open for tours, including ghost tours, a Halloween Ball (during Oct), and Candlelight tours. *657 Bellevue Ave. (at Lakeview Ave.).* ☎ *401/846-0669. Admission $10 adults, $8 seniors and college students. Feb–May Sat–Sun and holidays 10am–3pm; Memorial Day to mid-Oct daily 9:30am–4:30pm; mid-Oct to Nov daily 10am–4pm; Dec (special tours) 10am–3pm. Closed Jan.*

→ **Elks Lodge**   A child's apparition has been seen and heard walking the halls, and reports of lights flickering on and off. *141 Pelham St., Newport.* ☎ *401/846–0815.*

HAUNTED BED & BREAKFASTS

Newport has three well-known haunted inns. **The Black Duck Inn** (29 Pelham St.; ☎ 800/206-5212; www.blackduckinn.com), built in 1898, has a ghost that enjoys playing with the lights, flicking them on and off, and locking doors. Guests have also reported hearing heavy footsteps coming from rooms that have nobody in them on numerous occasions. There are 8 guest rooms, 6 with private bathrooms. Rates run from $115 to $210.

The Agincourt Inn (formerly The Inn at Shadow Lawn) was built in 1856. It is the home to several spirits and numerous stories involving Native American ghosts and spirits of people who escaped via the Underground Railroad. There have been psychic interventions at the house to get some better understanding of the energies inside. It's at 120 Miantonomi Ave. (☎ 800/352-3750 or 401/847-0902; www. agincourtinn.com). Rates are $79 to $250, with higher prices on holidays/weekends.

Finally, the **Brinley Victorian Inn** was built in 1850. In 1870, the owners renovated it and added a second building. Now the two are connected by a courtyard, porch and parlor. Both the Brinley and its surrounding area still look as if it is something out of the 1800s, with its Victorian decor and surrounding cobblestone

A Spooktacular Event

Each year Newport celebrates October with a spooktacular **Haunted Newport Festival.** The program features events like the Sea Witch Costume Ball, Newport Pirate Walk, Old Town Ghost Walk, and Halloween Horror Film Festival, which screens up-and-coming indie horror films. Submissions are accepted for the film festival from around the country, and prizes are given to the winners with the best films during the festival. **www. hauntednewport.net/haunted newport.htm.**

streets. There are plenty of paranormal phenomena reported; most notorious is the ghost that steals mints off of the guests' pillows and throws them into cracks in the wall. Other ghosts throw clothes and belongings of guests all over the floors of the room. Don't believe it? Check out the Brinley for yourself. Rates start at $139 per room on the weekdays from May through October and $199 on weekends. The winter season rates are relatively cheaper, starting at $99 on weekdays and $129 on weekend. ☎ **800/999-8523** or 401/849-7645. It's at 23 Brinley Street, Newport RI. www.brinleyvoctorian. com.

Eating

EATING OUT

For pure bargain dining in pricey Newport, the bountiful pastas of **Salas**, 343 Thames St. (☎ **401/845-8772**), are a perfect choice for hungry travelers.

Cheap

➜ **Flo's Clam Shack** ★ SEAFOOD Located just past Easton's Beach over the Newport/Middletown line, this old-timer is more than a lopsided strand-side shanty—but not *much* more. Step up to the order window, choose from the handwritten menu, and receive a stone with a number painted on it. What you'll get, if you're wise, are clams, on a plate or on a roll. Cooked swiftly to order, they're as tender as any to which you might have set your teeth. This is the place, also, to sample "chowda" and that Rhode Island specialty, stuffies. Upstairs are a raw bar and deck. Sundays feature live music from 2 to 6pm. *4 Wave Ave., Middletown, RI. ☎ 401/847-8141. Main courses $7.25–$12. Cash only. Apr–Dec 11am–9pm. Closed Jan–Mar.*

➜ **Jack & Josie** NEW AMERICAN Fun is on the menu at this quirky corner spot, a sort of poolroom-luncheonette-sports-bar-Internet-cafe. Within the airy, well-lit space are five computer terminals ($10 per hour), three pool tables, plasma TVs, and a free-form sofa defining the eating area, with several brushed aluminum tables. Food? Mostly soups, salads, and sandwiches, along with contemporary twists, as in the warm pear and goat cheese salad and "The Jack," thin slices of sirloin with carmelized onions, fig compote, and arugula saga blue cheese. But the dishy owner—who is neither Jack nor Josie, which are actually the names of her dogs—has added several entrees, including a quiche of the day, roasted pork tenderloin, meat loaf, and a roasted salmon filet wrapped in prosciutto. BYOB. Herbal teas, smoothies, and specialty coffee drinks are options. *111 Broadway. ☎ 401/851-6900. Main courses $6.95–$10. Daily 10am–11pm (extended hours in summer). Closed 1 week in Mar.*

Doable

➜ **Brick Alley Pub and Restaurant** AMERICAN/SEAOOD This is one of Newport's most popular restaurants for locals and tourists. With its cool setting near the water in downtown Newport, it's the place to go for anything from a burger to seafood. There is also a variety of steaks, pastas, and seasonal specials. *140 Thames St. ☎ 401/849-6334. Reservations recommended for dinner. Main courses $15–$22. Mon–Fri 11:30am–10pm (Fri until 11pm); Sat 11am–11pm; Sun 11am–10pm.*

➜ **Sardella's Italian Restaurant** ITALIAN In the mood for fine Italian dining? Sardella's is the place to go for great pastas, salad, and Italian bread. The beautiful atmosphere and location in Newport almost rivals that of Italy . . . almost. There is a bar and three dining rooms, including an outside garden patio where lunch and dinner are served daily. Choose from a variety of Italian favorites including pasta, fish and every kind of parmigiana that you can imagine. *30 Memorial Blvd. West, Newport, RI.* ☎ *401/849-6312. www.sardellas. com. Appetizers/Salads $5–$12; pasta $6–$17; entrees $14–$30. Mon-Thurs, 5–10pm; Fri–Sat, 5–11pm; Sun, 4–10:30pm.*

MTV (Best ●) → **Sea Shai Hibachi Garden** ★★★ JAPANESE/KOREAN I think this is one of the most entertaining restaurants in Rhode Island. You will enjoy watching your food prepared right in front of you by some of the Northeast's most talented Hibachi chefs. Take your pick of seafood, vegetables, chicken, and beef, among other appetizing entrees. Be sure to save some room for dessert. Sea Shai is known for its delicious ice-cream assortments, including fried vanilla ice cream and flavors like green tea, ginger, and red bean. *14 Long Wharf Mall. Newport.* ☎ *401/ 841-0051. www.seashai.com. Lunch: $6–$10; Dinner: $10–$24. Daily 11:30am–2:30pm; 5–10pm.*

MTV (Best ●) → **The White Horse Tavern** ★★★ AMERICAN One of America's oldest taverns, The White Horse was built in the early 1670s. The original owner of the tavern was the father of an infamous pirate who struck major riches pirating the Red Sea and eventually took over the tavern. This building, still with many of its original walls, stairways, and beams, has many legends surrounding it. There have been many sightings of an old man who appears in shabby clothing by the right side of the fireplace. It is said that he was one of the owners of the house who died tragically. The menu features an array of steaks, poultry, and seafood. Prices are significantly lower on the Tavern menu, available from 5pm Sunday through Thursday. Sunday Brunch is also available and features some New England breakfast and lunch favorites. *25 Marlborough St. (at Farewell).* ☎ *401/849-3600. Reservations recommended, essential for dinner. Jackets*

required for men at dinner. Main courses $13–$25. Mon–Fri 6–9pm; Sat–Sun noon–2:30pm and 6–9pm.

A Haunted Restaurant?

→ **La Petite Auberge** FRENCH Built in 1714, La Petite Auberge was once the home of an American Naval hero. It is said that he still roams the dining room around closing time. Restaurant staff has reported feeling a presence and seeing the image of an old man in ragged clothes roaming around. Many locals say the French cuisine is the best in town. *19 Charles St., Newport, RI.* ☎ *401/849-6669. Entrees $20–$40. Mon–Sat 6–11pm; Sun, 5–10pm.*

What Else to See & Do

SEEING NEWPORT'S FAMOUS "COTTAGES"

That's what wealthy summer people called the almost unimaginably sumptuous mansions they built in Newport in the last decades before the 16th Amendment to the Constitution permitted an income tax.

Say this for the wealthy of the Gilded Age: They knew a good place to put down roots when they saw it.

When driving or biking through the cottage district (walking its length is impractical for most people), consider the fact that most of these astonishing residences are still privately owned. That's almost as remarkable as the grounds and interiors of the nine that are open to the public.

Also, resolve to visit only one or two estates per day: The sheer opulence of the mansions can soon become numbing. Each residence requires 45 minutes to an hour for its guided tour. If at all possible, go during the week to avoid crowds and traffic.

Six of the mansions are maintained by the **Preservation Society of Newport County,** 424 Bellevue Ave. (☎ **401/847-1000;** www.newportmansions.org), which also operates the 1748 Hunter House, the

1860 Italianate Chepstow villa, the 1883 Isaac Bell House, and the Green Animals Topiary Gardens in Portsmouth. The Society sells a **combination ticket,** good for a year, to five of its properties; the cost is $31 for adults, $10 for children 6 to 17. Individual tickets for The Breakers are $15 for adults, $10 for children, while individual tickets for Kingscote, the Elms, Chateau-sur-mer, Marble House, Hunter House, and Rosecliff are $10 for adults, $4 for children. They can be purchased at any of the properties. Credit cards are accepted at most, but not all, of the cottages. Special events, such as the festive Thanksgiving and Christmas celebrations, cost extra. The Society conducts an hour-long walking tour past the mansions, and the price includes a ticket to The Breakers and a second mansion of your choice. Tours are priced at $25 for adults and $9 for ages 6 to 17. Parking is free at all the Society properties.

The mansions that aren't operated by the Preservation Society but are open to the public are Belcourt Castle (see "Haunted Castles" box above), Beechwood, and Rough Point.

During the winter, the mansions of the Society take turns each year staying open through the period, with an additional one or two openings on weekends.

ORGANIZED TOURS & CRUISES

Several organizations conduct tours of the mansions and the downtown historic district. Between May 15 and October 15, the **Newport Historical Society,** 82 Touro St. (☎ 401/846-0813), offers two itineraries. Tours of Historic Hill leave on Thursday and Friday at 10am and tours of the Point on Saturday at 10am; each takes about 1½ hours. Tours of Cliff Walk leave on Saturday at 10am and take about 2

hours. Tickets cost $7 and can be purchased at the Society or at the Gateway Visitor Center (see "Visitor Information," earlier in this section).

Newport on Foot (☎ 401/846-5391) leaves the Gateway Visitor Center twice daily on 90-minute tours. Call for details and times. Tickets are $7 per person, free for children under 12.

Viking Tours, based at the Gateway Visitor Center, 23 America's Cup Ave. (☎ 401/847-6921), has narrated bus tours of the mansions and harbor cruises on the excursion boat *Viking Queen.* Bus tours—daily in summer, Saturdays from November to March—are 1½ to 4 hours and cost $20 to $42 for adults, $12 to $19 for children 5 to 11. Boat tours, from late May to early October, are 1 hour in length and cost $10 for adults. In July and August, the cruise can be extended to include a stop and tour of Fort Adams; $14 for adults.

Hanging Out: The Beach & Beyond

Fort Adams State Park, Harrison Avenue (☎ 401/841-0707; www.fortadams.org), is on the thumb of land that partially encloses Newport Harbor. It can be seen from the downtown docks and reached by driving or biking south on Thames Street and west on Wellington Avenue (a section of Ocean Dr., which becomes Harrison Ave.). The sprawling 1820s fort for which the park is named is under restoration, work that can be viewed by guided tour. Admission is $6 for adults. Boating, ocean swimming, fishing, and sailing are all possible in the park's 105 acres. Open from Memorial Day to Labor Day.

BEACHES

The longest and most popular beach in the area is **Easton's Beach** ★, along Route

138A, the extension of Memorial Boulevard, east of town. There are plenty of facilities, including a bathhouse, eating places, picnic areas, lifeguards, a carousel, and the **Newport Aquarium** (☎ **401/849-8430**).

On Ocean Drive, less than 2 miles from the south end of Bellevue Avenue, is **Gooseberry Beach** ★, which is privately owned but open to the public. Parking costs $8 Monday through Friday, $12 Saturday and Sunday.

A BEAUTIFUL WALK

Cliff Walk ★★ skirts the edge of the southern section of town where most of the cottages were built, and provides better views of many of them than can be seen from the street. Traversing its length, high above the crashing surf, is more than a stroll but less than an arduous hike. For the full 3½-mile length, start at the access point near the intersection of Memorial Boulevard and Eustis Avenue. For a shorter walk, start at the Forty Steps, at the end of Narragansett Avenue, off Bellevue. Leave the walk at Ledge Road and return via Bellevue Avenue. Figure 2 to 3 hours for the round-trip, and be warned that there are some mildly rugged sections to negotiate, no facilities, and no phones. The walk is open from 9am to 9pm.

BIKING

Biking is one of the best ways to get around town, especially out to the mansions and along **Ocean Drive** ★★. Among several rental shops are **Firehouse Bicycle,** 25 Mill St. (☎ **401/847-5700**); **Ten Speed Spokes,** 18 Elm St. (☎ **401/847-5609**); and **Scooters,** 411 Thames St. (☎ **401/619-0573**).

Adventure Sports Rentals, at the Inn on Long Wharf, 142 Long Wharf (☎ **401/849-4820**), rents not only bikes and mopeds, but also outboard boats, kayaks, and sailboats; parasailing outings can be arranged.

On the Road to Fall River, MA

Newport, RI to Fall River, MA 21 miles

On the Road Nuts & Bolts

The Tolls   There are no tolls.

The Fastest Way   Start on Broadway in Newport, headed north. This turns into West Main Road (RI-114). Merge onto RI-24N toward I-195-N and cross into Massachusetts. Merge onto MA-138 toward North Tiverton, RI and take the I-195E exit toward New Bedford/Cape Cod.

The Long Way Round   Instead of getting onto I-195N, you can stay straight on W. Main Road and turn left onto Bristol Ferry Road (RI-114). Continue to follow RI-114 north and make a right onto Metacom Street and another right onto Child Street (RI-103). Cross into Massachusetts. Turn right onto Grand Army Highway and follow to US-6E which will become Davol Street. Turn sharp left to the I-195 ramp toward New Bedford/Cape Cod. The total traveling time should be about an hour.

PARANORMAL NORTHEAST

Lizzie Borden welcomes you to Fall River!

Welcome to Fall River

LIZZIE BORDEN IN FALL RIVER

Fall River loves Lizzie Borden, and for good reason. The accused axe murderess's home brings in thousands of tourists a year, all who hope to get an inside glimpse of the true story behind Lizzie Borden. **The Lizzie Borden Bed & Breakfast Museum** 🅼 Best⦾ ★★★ (92 Second St., Fall River; ☎ 508/675–7333; www.lizzie-borden.com) is the actual site where the infamous murders occurred. In 1996 the house, which was built in 1845, was renovated into a B&B. For overnight guests, a full breakfast of bananas, johnnycakes, sugar cookies, and coffee is served (similar to the one that the Bordens had on the day of the murders).

If you're only passing by, visitor tours are given every hour between 11am and

The Legend of Lizzie Borden

"Lizzie Borden took an axe and gave her mother forty whacks . . . when she saw what she had done she gave her father forty one."

Nobody really knows who wrote the nursery rhyme, but the Borden murders remain one of the greatest unsolved mysteries of the 19th century. Was Lizzie Borden really capable of killing her father and stepmother? Critics in the early 19th century did not believe that any Christian woman could commit such a crime. You can take a tour of the place, read the books, and come to your own conclusions. You can also stay overnight in one of the family members' bedrooms, and yes, you can even stay in the room where Abby Borden was murdered. Rooms start at $150 per night from November through April and $175 May through October. On my tour of the Lizzie Borden house, I learned that the nursery rhyme isn't quite factual: Lizzie's father was killed before his wife and it was her stepmother who was murdered next. Lizzie's mother had died when she was a baby, and she reportedly did not get along with her father's second wife. Abby Borden received 19 blows to the head with a hatchet and Andrew Borden received 10 blows to the head. The Lizzie Borden case has been the subject of many books and even a film during the 1970s.

Recommended Reading/Viewing

Lizzie Borden in Popular Culture

The nursery rhyme was just the first manifestation of the hold the Borden murders have on the popular imagination. There have been both nonfiction books and novels, plays, films, an opera, and even a ballet *(Fall River Legend)* about the suspected murderess.

→ *The Legend of Lizzie Borden* (1975). This TV movie isn't available on tape or DVD, but catch it if you can when it's broadcast. Elizabeth Montgomery gives a chilling portrayal of Lizzie, and one version of how she might have committed the crimes.

→ *The Lizzie Borden Sourcebook,* edited by David Kent (Branden Books, 1992). A compilation of first-hand reports from the time of the crime through Lizzie's death, including a complete transcript of Lizzie's testimony at the inquest.

→ *Lizzie Didn't Do It!,* by William Masterson (Branden Books, 2000). An investigation into the mystery that vindicates Lizzie.

3pm for $10. There are three floors full of terrifying history. Guests have the option of staying in Lizzie Borden's own room, in the room where Abby Borden was killed, or for the squeamish there are six other less symbolic rooms.

Don't relax too much, though, because strange things have been reported throughout the entire house. On my visit to the B&B, I asked the museum staff if they'd seen anything strange. None of them said they believed in ghosts per se, but a few said strange things happen in the house. A psychic comes in and does weekly séances with the guests of the B&B. Have the spirits of Abby and Andrew Borden been contacted? You will have to make your own visit to find out. For more information on staying over, call or visit the website.

More Lizzie at the Fall River Historic Society

→ **The Fall River Historic Society** ★★
Another must-see stop for those wanting an extra glimpse into the Borden tragedy. On display at the Lizzie Borden Exhibit is her prison lunch pail, police photographs of the crime scene, the hatchet blade used

in the crimes, among other things. The Historic Society also has a large collection of Victorian costumes and art. *451 Rock St., Fall River, MA.* ☎ *508/679-1071. Admission $5 adults, $3 children 6–14, children under 6 admitted free. Tues–Sun 9am–4:30pm.*

What Else to See & Do

BATTLESHIP COVE

Located about 10 minutes from the Lizzie Borden House, you can visit the Battleship USS *Massachusetts,* which fought in 35 battles during World War II, is still considered one of America's all-time most powerful vessels and it is one of the ships at **Battleship Cove,** the world's largest collection of historic Naval ships. You will have the chance to board a few real battleships and even an attack submarine. *5 Water St., Fall River.* ☎ *508/678-1100. www.battleshipcove.com. Admission $14 adults, $12 seniors, AAA/veterans. Print out web coupon for $1 discount. Daily 9:30am–5:30pm July 4–Sept 4; 9am–5pm Sept 5–Oct 28; 9am–4:30pm Oct 29–Mar 10; 11am–5pm Mar 11–July 3. Closed Thanksgiving, Dec 25, Jan. 1.*

PARANORMAL NORTHEAST

FALL RIVER CAROUSEL

Battleship Cove also features a vintage **carousel** ★, which was moved there after serving the customers of the Lincoln Amusement Park in in North Dartmouth for over 70 years. A Victorian pavilion was constructed to house the attraction after its move, and also houses a cafe. The pavilion now perches over Heritage State Park, offering panoramic views of the ships. The carousel is open seasonally and you can go on it for $1 a ride ($5 for 7 rides)

On the Road to Boston, MA

Fall River, MA to Boston, MA 55 miles

On the Road **Nuts & Bolts**

Where to Fill Up   There are rest stops located about every 30 miles along the interstate where you can fill up, though the prices are a bit higher than if you get off and go a few blocks. It's a calculated choice of which one to use: The rest stop stations are a bit more expensive, but looking for a gas station in an unfamiliar town can get you lost.

The Tolls   About $5. There will be one $1 toll and another $2 toll, depending on which side you enter and if you need to use the bridge crossings.

The Fastest Way   Start out going east on I-195 and merge onto MA-24N via exit 8B toward Boston. Make a left on exit 8B. Merge onto I-93N via Exit 21 toward Boston.

The Long Way Round   There are plenty of smaller back roads you can take to get to Boston. As long as you're good with directions and keep going north, you will most probably see signs for Boston, unless of course you get really off track and begin heading west.

Rules of the Road   65 mph is the speed limit. There are no handheld cellular devices permitted while driving on the highway (though many people use them anyway). Having a headset will make life much easier. When traffic permits, drivers may turn right at a red light after stopping, unless a sign is posted saying otherwise. Seat belts are mandatory for adults and children. Be aware of two state laws, if only because drivers break them so frequently it'll take your breath away: Pedestrians in the crosswalk have the right of way (most suburbs actually enforce this one), and vehicles already in a rotary (traffic circle or roundabout) have the right of way.

Welcome to Boston

We're passing through Boston pretty quickly on this trip, but it's a large, exciting city where you could certainly hang out and do lots of things that have exactly nothing to do with ghosts and the paranormal.

It also is a good place to base yourself for a couple days to explore both Beantown's haunted history as well as Salem's (it's an easy excursion from Boston to Salem, either in your own car or by public transit).

Boston Nuts & Bolts

Area Codes Eastern Massachusetts has eight area codes: Boston proper, 617 and 857; immediate suburbs, 781 and 339; northern and western suburbs, 978 and 351; southern suburbs, 508 and 774. *Note:* To make a local call, you must dial 1 + the 3-digit area code + the 7-digit number.

Drugstores Downtown Boston has no 24-hour pharmacy. The pharmacy at the **CVS** at 155–157 Charles St. in Boston (☎ 617/523-1028), next to the Charles T stop, is open until midnight on weeknights, 10pm on weekends. The pharmacy at the **CVS** in the Porter Square Shopping Center, off Massachusetts Avenue in Cambridge (☎ 617/876-5519), is open 24 hours, 7 days a week.

Emergencies Call ☎ **911** for fire, ambulance, or the Boston, Brookline, or Cambridge police. This is a free call from pay phones. For the state police, call ☎ 617/523-1212, or ☎ ***77** from a cellphone.

Internet Access For a tech-happy area, Boston has few cybercafes. Your hotel might have a terminal for guests' use, and many hotels offer on-premises wireless access (often for a daily fee). **Tech Superpowers,** 252 Newbury St., 3rd floor (☎ 617/267-9716; www.newburyopen.net), also offers access by the hour ($5/hr.; $3 minimum).

Liquor Laws The legal drinking age in Massachusetts is 21. In many bars, particularly near college campuses, you might be asked to show identification if you appear to be under 30 or so. Some bars and clubs "card" (check the ID of) everyone who enters. Liquor stores and a few supermarkets and convenience stores sell alcohol. Liquor stores and the liquor sections of other stores are open Monday though Saturday and open at noon on Sunday in communities where that's legal. Last call typically is 30 minutes before closing time (1am in bars, 2am in clubs).

Post Office The main post office, at 25 Dorchester Ave. (☎ 617/654-5302), behind South Station, is currently open daily 24 hours, but has been known to reduce hours when the budget is tight.

Radio FM stations include 89.7 (WGBH: public radio, classical, jazz), 90.9 (WBUR: public radio, classical), 92.9 (WBOS: album rock), 93.7 (WQSX: dance hits), 94.5 (WJMN: dance, rap, hip-hop), 96.9 (WTKK: talk), 98.5 (WBMX: adult contemporary), 99.5 (WKLB: country), 100.7 (WZLX: classic rock), 101.7 (WFNX: progressive rock), 102.5 (WCRB: classical), 103.3 (WODS: oldies), 104.1 (WBCN: rock, Patriots games), 105.7 (WROR: '60s and '70s), and 106.7 (WMJX: pop, adult contemporary).

Smoking Massachusetts is an anti-tobacco stronghold. State law bans smoking in all workplaces, including restaurants, bars, and clubs.

Taxes The 5% state sales tax in Massachusetts does not apply to groceries, prescription drugs, newspapers, or clothing that costs less than $175. The tax on meals and takeout food is 5%. The lodging tax is 12.45% in Boston and Cambridge.

PARANORMAL NORTHEAST

Transit Info Call ☎ 617/222-3200 for the MBTA (subways, local buses, commuter rail) and ☎ 800/23-LOGAN for the Massachusetts Port Authority (airport transportation).

Weather Call ☎ 617/936-1234.

Getting Around

BY CAR

Park the car (in Harvard Yard if you must). Don't try to get around by driving in Boston. The traffic, the aggressive drivers, the lack of parking add up to an experience you don't want to have. Park the car and get around on foot, by T (the subway), and by bus.

Parking

It's practically impossible to find parking in some areas. Most spaces on the street are metered (and patrolled until at least 6pm Mon–Sat) and are open to nonresidents for 2 hours or less between 8am and 6pm. The penalty is a $40 ticket—even the most expensive garage is cheaper. Read the sign or meter carefully. In some areas parking is allowed only at certain hours. Rates vary in different sections of the city (usually $1/hr. downtown); bring plenty of quarters. Time limits range from 15 minutes to 2 hours.

It's best to leave the car in a garage or lot and walk. A full day at most garages costs around $25, but some downtown facilities charge as much as $35, and hourly rates can be exorbitant. Many lots charge a lower flat rate if you enter and exit before certain times or if you park in the evening.

The city-run garage under **Boston Common** (☎ 617/954-2096) accepts vehicles less than 6 feet, 3 inches tall. Enter from Charles Street between Boylston and Beacon streets. Many businesses in Faneuil Hall Marketplace validate parking at the **75 State St. Garage** (☎ 617/742-7275).

Good-size garages downtown are at **Government Center** off Congress Street (☎ 617/227-0385), **Sudbury Street** off Congress Street (☎ 617/973-6954), the **New England Aquarium** (☎ 617/723-1731), and **Zero Post Office Square** in the Financial District (☎ 617/423-1430).

ON FOOT

You can best appreciate Boston at street level, and walking the narrow, picturesque streets takes you past many gridlocked cars.

Even more than in a typical large city, be alert. Look both ways before crossing, even on one-way streets, where many bicyclists and some drivers blithely go against the flow. The "walk" cycle of many downtown traffic signals lasts only 7 seconds, and a small but significant part of the driving population considers red lights optional anyway.

BY THE "T"

The **Massachusetts Bay Transportation Authority,** or MBTA (☎ 800/392-6100 or 617/222-3200; www.mbta.com), is known as the T, and its logo is the letter in a circle. It runs subways, trolleys, buses, and ferries in Boston and many suburbs, as well as the commuter rail, which extends as far as Providence, Rhode Island. **Fares will increase in 2007**. Expect to pay at least $1.50 for the subway and $1 for the bus. The recent introduction of an automated fare-collection system raised the possibility of zoned fares, but that's not official, either. You can check the website or quiz the phone representatives for details before your trip.

For information on all the forms of public transit in Boston, call or visit the website of the **MBTA** (Massachusetts Bay Transportation Authority; ☎ **617/222-3200;** www.mbta.com).

BY BUS

The MBTA runs buses and "trackless trolleys" (buses with electric antennae) around town and to and around the suburbs. The **Silver Line** (which looks like a branch of the subway on some maps but is a bus line) runs on two routes: from Temple Place, near Downtown Crossing, to the South End and Roxbury, and from South Station to the airport via the South Boston waterfront, including the convention center and the World Trade Center.

BY TAXI

Taxis are expensive and not always easy to find—seek out a cabstand or call a dispatcher. Cabstands are usually near hotels. There are also busy ones at Faneuil Hall Marketplace (on North St. and in front of 60 State St.), South Station, and Back Bay Station, and on either side of Mass. Ave. in Harvard Square, near the Harvard Coop bookstore and Au Bon Pain.

To call ahead for a cab, try the **Independent Taxi Operators Association,** or ITOA (☎ 617/426-8700); **Boston Cab** (☎ 617/536-5010 or 617/262-2227); **Town Taxi** (☎ 617/536-5000); or **Metro Cab** (☎ 617/242-8000). In Cambridge, call **Ambassador Brattle** (☎ 617/492-1100) or **Yellow Cab** (☎ 617/547-3000).

Haunted Boston

GHOST TOURS

➜**Ghosts & Gravestones** This 90-minute tour departs from Old Town Trolley stop #1, at the end of the Marriott Long Wharf Hotel on Atlantic Avenue (by the corner of Atlantic Ave and State St.). Hear about Boston's most sinister characters, from the

Angel of Death to the Boston Strangler, in addition to visiting local burial grounds and other shiver-inducing areas in a trolley and on foot, with a guide dressed as a 17th-century gravedigger. *Reservations required.* ☎ *617/269-3626. www.ghostsandgravestones.com. $30 adults (discount if booked on website). Weekends only in May; Daily Jun–Oct.*

➜**Haunted Boston Ghost Tours** ★ The 90-minute walking tour meets in Boston Common at the Central Burial Ground Cemetery at the corner of Boylston Street and Tremont Street and takes visitors to some of Boston's most historical sites where there have been rumors of ghost sightings. ☎ *617/605-3635. Reservations required. www.hauntedboston.com. Adults $18. Daily at 8pm May–Nov.*

CEMETERIES & OTHER PLACES PEOPLE DIED

FREE ➜**Boston Massacre Site** A ring of cobblestones on a traffic island marks the location of the skirmish that helped consolidate the spirit of rebellion in the colonies. On March 5, 1770, angered at the presence of royal troops in Boston,

PARANORMAL NORTHEAST

colonists threw snowballs, garbage, rocks, and other debris at a group of redcoats. The soldiers panicked and fired into the crowd, killing five men. Their graves, including that of Crispus Attucks, the first black man to die in the Revolution, are in the Old Granary Burying Ground (see below). *State St. at Devonshire St. T: Blue or Orange Line to State.*

FREE → **Copp's Hill Burying Ground**
★ The second-oldest cemetery (1659) in the city is the burial place of Cotton Mather and his family, Robert Newman, and Prince Hall. Hall, a prominent member of the free black community that occupied the north slope of the hill in colonial times, fought at Bunker Hill and established the first black Masonic lodge. The highest point in the North End, Copp's Hill was the site of a windmill and of the British batteries that destroyed the village of Charlestown during the Battle of Bunker Hill on June 17, 1775. Charlestown is clearly visible (look for the masts of USS *Constitution*) across the Inner Harbor. No gravestone rubbing is allowed. *Off Hull St. near Snowhill St. Daily 9am–5pm (until 3pm in winter). T: Green or Orange Line to North Station.*

→ **King's Chapel and Burying Ground**
Architect Peter Harrison sent the plans for this Georgian-style building from Newport, RI, in 1749. Rather than replacing the existing wooden chapel, the granite edifice was constructed around it. Completed in 1754, it was the first Anglican church in Boston. George III sent gifts, as did Queen Anne and William and Mary, who presented the communion table and chancel tablets (still in use today) before the church was even built. The Puritan colonists had little use for the royal religion; after the Revolution, this became the first Unitarian church in the new nation. Today, the church conducts Unitarian

Universalist services using the Anglican Book of Common Prayer.

The **burying ground** ★★, on Tremont Street, is the oldest in the city; it dates to 1630. Among the scary colonial headstones (winged skulls are a popular decoration) are the graves of **John Winthrop,** the first governor of the Massachusetts Bay Colony; **William Dawes,** who rode with Paul Revere; **Elizabeth Pain,** the model for Hester Prynne in Nathaniel Hawthorne's novel *The Scarlet Letter;* and **Mary Chilton,** the first female colonist to step ashore on Plymouth Rock. *58 Tremont St. ☎ 617/227-2155. www.kings-chapel.org. Chapel: Year-round Sat 10am–4pm; summer Mon and Thurs–Fri 10am–4pm, Tues–Wed 1–4pm. Check website for up-to-date hours. $2 donation suggested. Services Wed 12:15pm, Sun 11am. Burying ground: Daily 8am–5:30pm (until 3pm in winter). T: Green or Blue Line to Government Center.*

FREE → **Mount Auburn Cemetery** ★
This is the final resting place of many well-known people and is also famous simply for existing. Dedicated in 1831, it was the first of America's rural, or garden, cemeteries. The establishment of burying places removed from city centers reflected practical and philosophical concerns. Development was encroaching on urban graveyards, and the ideas associated with Transcendentalism and the Greek revival (the word *cemetery* derives from the Greek for "sleeping place") dictated that communing with nature take precedence over organized religion. Since the day it opened, Mount Auburn has been a popular place to retreat and reflect. Visitors to this National Historic Landmark find history and horticulture coexisting with celebrity. The graves of Henry Wadsworth Longfellow, Oliver Wendell Holmes, Julia Ward Howe, and Mary Baker Eddy are here, as are those of Charles Bulfinch,

James Russell Lowell, Winslow Homer, Transcendentalist leader Margaret Fuller, and abolitionist Charles Sumner. In season you'll see gorgeous flowering trees and shrubs (the Massachusetts Horticultural Society had a hand in the design). Stop at the office or front gate to pick up brochures and a map. You can rent an audiotape tour ($7; a $15 deposit is required) and listen in your car or on a portable tape player; there's a 60-minute driving tour and two 75-minute walking tours. The Friends of Mount Auburn Cemetery conduct workshops and lectures and coordinate walking tours; through June 2007, keep an eye out for events related to the cemetery's 175th anniversary. Call the main number for topics, schedules, and fees. The cemetery is open daily from 8am to 5pm October through April, 8am to 7pm May through September; admission is free. Animals and recreational activities such as jogging, biking, and picnicking are not allowed. *Mount Auburn St. ☎ 617/547-7105. www.mount auburn.org. MBTA bus nos. 71 and 73 start at Harvard station and stop near the cemetery gates; they run frequently on weekdays and less often on weekends. By car (5 min.) or on foot (30 min.), take Mount Auburn St. or Brattle St. west from Harvard Square; just after the streets intersect, the gate is on the left.*

(FREE) ➔ **Old Granary Burying Ground**
★ This cemetery, established in 1660, was once part of Boston Common. You'll see the graves of patriots **Samuel Adams, Paul Revere, John Hancock,** and **James Otis;** merchant **Peter Faneuil** (spelled "Funal"); and Benjamin Franklin's parents. Also buried here are the victims of the **Boston Massacre** (see above) and the wife of Isaac Vergoose, who is believed to be **"Mother Goose"** of nursery rhyme fame. Note that gravestone rubbing, however tempting, is illegal in Boston's historic

cemeteries. *Park and Tremont streets, Daily 9am–5pm.*

Sleeping

In both Boston and Cambridge there are a multitude of hotels and hostels to choose from. **The Massachusetts Office of Travel and Tourism's** website can be reached at **http://web.massvacation. com/jsp/home.jsp**.

HOSTEL

➔ **Hostelling International–Boston**
This hostel near the Berklee College of Music and Symphony Hall caters to students, youth groups, and other travelers in search of comfortable, no-frills lodging.

Accommodations are dorm-style, with six beds per room. There are also a couple of private rooms that sleep one or two. The air-conditioned hostel has two full dine-in kitchens, 29 bathrooms (men and women have separate facilities), a large common room, and meeting and workshop space. It provides linens, or you can bring your own; sleeping bags are not permitted.

The enthusiastic staff organizes free and inexpensive cultural, educational, and recreational programs on the premises and throughout the Boston area. Hostelling International also operates a summer-only hostel just outside Kenmore Square. *12 Hemenway St., Boston, MA 02115. ☎ 888/999-4678 or 617/536-9455. Fax 617/ 424-6558. www.bostonhostel.org. 205 beds. Members of Hostelling International– American Youth Hostels $28–$45 per bed; non-members $31–$48 per bed. Members $70–$100 per private unit; nonmembers $73–$106 per private unit. Children 3–12 half-price; free for children under 3. Rates include continental breakfast. T: Green Line B, C, or D to Hynes/ICA. Amenities: Access to nearby health club ($6); shuttle; coin-op laundry; Internet access (free). 1st-floor units and bathrooms are wheelchair* accessible; wheelchair lift at building entrance. In room: A/C, lockers, no phone.

CHEAP

➔ **Anthony's Town House** The Anthony family has operated this four-story brownstone guesthouse since 1944, and a stay here is very much like spending the night at Grandma's. Many patrons are Europeans accustomed to guesthouse accommodations with shared bathrooms, and budget-minded Americans won't be disappointed. Each floor has three high-ceilinged rooms furnished in rather ornate Queen Anne or Victorian style and one bathroom with an enclosed shower. Smaller rooms (one per floor) have twin beds; the large front rooms have bay windows. Guests have the use of two refrigerators, and the staff will supply a VCR, DVD player, hair dryer, or iron on request. The guesthouse is 1 mile from Boston's Kenmore Square, about 15 minutes from downtown by T, and 2 blocks from a busy commercial strip. The late-19th-century building is on the National Register of Historic Places, and there's no smoking on the premises. 1085 Beacon St., Brookline, MA 02446. ☎ 617/566-3972. Fax 617/ 232-1085. www.anthonystownhouse.com. 10 units, none with private bathroom. $68–$98 double. Extra person $10. Weekly rates and winter discounts available. No credit cards. Limited free parking. T: Green Line C to Hawes St. In room: A/C, TV, high-speed Internet access, no phone.

➔ **YWCA Boston, Berkeley Residence** This pleasant, convenient hotel and residence offers a dining room, patio garden, piano, and library. Formerly for women only, it now accommodates men, too. The dorm-style guest rooms are basic, containing little more than beds, but they're well maintained and comfortable. The well-kept public areas include a TV lounge. 40 Berkeley St., Boston, MA 02116. ☎ 617/375-2524. Fax 617/375-2525. www.ywcaboston.org.

200 units, none with bathroom. $60 single; $90 double; $105 triple. Rates include full breakfast. T: Orange Line to Back Bay or Green Line to Arlington. Amenities: Cafeteria; computer w/Internet access; coin-op laundry.

DOABLE

➔ **Harborside Inn** ★★ This renovated 1858 warehouse is across the street from Faneuil Hall Marketplace and the harbor, and a short walk from the Financial District. The nicely appointed guest rooms have queen-size beds, hardwood floors, Oriental rugs, and Victorian-style furniture, creating the feel of an apartment rather than a hotel. The rooms surround a sky-lit atrium; those with city views are more expensive but can be noisier. Still, they're preferable to the interior rooms, whose windows open only to the atrium. Rooms on the top floors have lower ceilings but better views. 185 State St. (between Atlantic Ave. and the Custom House Tower), Boston, MA 02109. ☎ 888/723-7565 or 617/ 723-7500. www.harborsideinnboston.com. $120–$210 double; $235–$310 suite. Extra person $15. Off-site parking $20; reservation required. T: Blue Line to Aquarium, or Blue or Orange Line to State. Amenities: Restaurant; access to nearby health club ($15); concierge; room service until 10pm; laundry service; dry cleaning; In room: A/C, TV, wireless Internet access ($10/day), hair dryer, iron.

SPLURGE

➔ **Omni Parker House** ★★ The Parker House has operated continuously longer than any other hotel in America (since 1855!), but it's hardly stuck in the 19th century. There's wireless Internet access in the guest rooms and public spaces, and regular renovation keeps the property in excellent shape. Guest rooms, a patchwork of more than 50 configurations, aren't huge, but they are thoughtfully laid out and nicely appointed. Many overlook Old City Hall or Government Center. The hotel is popular with sightseers, who can economize by taking advantage of a weekend deal, especially in the winter, or by booking an "economy petite single." The pattern on the bedspreads, so gaudy that it's elegant, is a reproduction of the original, and the lobby of the 14-story hotel boasts its original American oak paneling. *60 School St., Boston, MA 02108. ☎ 800/THE-OMNI or 617/227-8600. www.omnihotels.com. $159–$189 economy room; $189–$289 double; $249–$399 suite. Valet parking $36. T: Green or Blue Line to Government Center, or Red or Green Line to Park St. Amenities: 2 restaurants, bar; 24-hr. exercise room; access to nearby health club ($20); concierge; tour desk; 24-hr. room service; laundry service; In room: A/C, TV w/pay movies and Nintendo, wireless Internet access, minibar, coffeemaker, hair dryer, iron, robes.*

Eating

TAKEOUT TREATS

If you're walking the Freedom Trail, pick up food at **Faneuil Hall Marketplace** and cross Atlantic Avenue or buy a tasty sandwich in the North End at **Il Panino Express,** 266 Hanover St. (☎ **617/720-5720**), and stroll down Richmond Street toward the harbor. From either direction, walk past the Marriott to the end of Long Wharf and eat on the plaza as you watch the boats and planes, or stay to the left of the hotel and eat in Christopher Columbus Waterfront Park, overlooking the marina.

In the **Back Bay,** stop at **Trader Joe's,** 899 Boylston St. (☎ **617/262-6505**), for prepared food. At the foot of **Beacon Hill,** pick up all you need for a do-it-yourself feast at **Savenor's Market,** 160 Charles St. (☎ **617/723-6328**).

EATING OUT

Cheap

→ **Buddha's Delight** ★ VEGETARIAN/ VIETNAMESE Fresh and healthy intersect with cheap and filling at this busy restaurant. The menu lists "chicken,"

The Scoop on Ice Cream

No less an expert than Ben Cohen of Ben & Jerry's has described Boston as "a great place for ice cream." (That goes for Cambridge, too!) In Cambridge, Try **Christina's,** 1255 Cambridge St., Inman Square (☎ **617/492-7021**); **Herrell's,** 15 Dunster St., Harvard Square (☎ **617/497-2179**); or **Toscanini's,** 1310 Mass. Ave., Harvard Square (☎ **617/354-9350**), and 899 Main St., Central Square (☎ **617/491-5877**). Favorite Boston destinations include **Ben & Jerry's,** 174 Newbury St. (☎ **617/536-5456**) and 20 Park Plaza (☎ **617/426-0890**); **JP Licks,** 352 Newbury St. (☎ **617/236-1666**); and **Steve's,** Quincy Market, Faneuil Hall Marketplace (☎ **617/367-0569**).

"shrimp," "pork," and even "lobster"—in quotes because the kitchen doesn't use meat, poultry, fish, or dairy (some beverages have condensed milk). The chefs fry and barbecue tofu and gluten into more-than-reasonable facsimiles using techniques owner Cuong Van Tran learned from Buddhist monks in a temple outside Los Angeles. Between trying to figure out how they do it and savoring Vietnamese cuisine's strong, clear flavors, you might not miss your usual protein. To start, try fried "pork" dumplings or a delectable salad. Move on to "shrimp" with rice noodles, any of the house specialties, or excellent *chow fun. 3 Beach St., 2nd floor. ☎ 617/451-2395. Main courses $5.50–$13; lunch specials $6.50. Sun–Thurs 11am–9:30pm; Fri–Sat 11am–10:30pm. T: Orange Line to Chinatown.*

→ **Café Jaffa** MIDDLE EASTERN/ MEDITERRANEAN A long, narrow brick room with a glass front, Café Jaffa looks more like a snazzy pizza place than the excellent Middle Eastern restaurant it is. The reasonable prices, high quality, and large portions draw hordes of students and other thrifty diners for traditional Middle Eastern offerings such as falafel, baba ghanouj, and hummus, as well as burgers and steak tips. Lamb, beef, and chicken kabobs come with Greek salad, rice pilaf, and pita bread. For dessert, try the baklava if it's fresh (give it a pass if not). There is a short list of beer and wine, and many fancy coffee offerings. *48 Gloucester St.* ☎ *617/536-0230. Main courses $5–$16. Mon–Thurs 11am–10:30pm; Fri–Sat 11am–11pm; Sun noon–10pm. T: Green Line B, C, or D to Hynes/ICA.*

➔ **S&S Restaurant** ★★ DELI *Es* is Yiddish for "eat," and this Cambridge classic is as straightforward as its name ("eat and eat"). Founded in 1919 by the great-grandmother of the current owners, the wildly popular brunch spot draws what seems to be half of Cambridge at busy times on weekends. It's northeast of Harvard Square, west of MIT, and worth a visit during the week, too. With huge windows and lots of light wood and plants, it looks contemporary, but the brunch offerings are traditional dishes such as pancakes, waffles, fruit salad, and fantastic omelets and cinnamon rolls. The bagels are among the best in the area; you'll also find traditional deli items (corned beef, pastrami, tongue, potato pancakes, and blintzes), and breakfast anytime. Be early for brunch, or plan to spend a good chunk of your Saturday or Sunday standing around people-watching and getting hungry. Or dine on a weekday and soak up the neighborhood atmosphere. *1334 Cambridge St., Inman Sq.* ☎ *617/354-0777. www.sands restaurant.com. Main courses $4–$15. Mon–Wed 7am–11pm; Thurs–Fri 7am–midnight; Sat 8am–midnight; Sun 8am–10pm; brunch Sat–Sun until 4pm. Free parking; get token from cashier on weekends. T: Red Line to Harvard, then no. 69 (Harvard-Lechmere) bus to Inman Sq.; or Red Line to Central, then a 10-min. walk on Prospect St.*

Doable

➔ **Bangkok Blue Thai Restaurant** ★★★ THAI The location of this restaurant, near the heart of Copley Square, is perfect for warm evenings where you can sit outside and watch the action in the park. If you have never had Thai food before, feel free to ask one of the helpful waitstaff who will help you decide which dish to choose. Whatever you do, don't leave without trying one of the signature spring rolls. *651 Boylston St.* ☎ *617/266-1010. bkkblueboston. com. Main courses $13–18. Mon–Fri 11:30am–3pm and 5–10pm; Sat–Sun noon–10pm.*

➔ **Brasserie Jo** ★ REGIONAL FRENCH One of the most discriminating diners I know lit up like a marquee upon hearing that Boston has a branch of this Chicago favorite. The food is classic—house-made pâtés, fresh baguettes, superb shellfish, salad Niçoise, Alsatian onion tart, *choucroute*, coq au vin—but never boring. The house beer, an Alsace-style draft, is a good accompaniment. The casual, all-day French brasserie and bar fits well in this neighborhood, where shoppers can always use a break but might not want a full meal. It's also a good bet before or after a Symphony or Pops performance, and it's popular for business lunches. The noise level can be high when the spacious room is full—have your tête-à-tête at a table near the bar. *In the Colonnade Hotel, 120 Huntington Ave.* ☎ *617/425-3240. www. brasseriejoboston.com. Reservations recommended at dinner. Main courses $6–$15 at lunch, $15–$27 at dinner; plats du jour $18–$32. Mon–Fri 6:30am–11pm; Sat 7am–11pm; Sun 7am–10pm; late-night menu daily until 1am. Valet and garage parking available. T: Green Line E to Prudential.*

Splurge

MTV Best ● →**The Helmand** ★★★
AFGHAN   This is the place to go for exciting cuisine. There is a grandiose variety of both meat and vegetable dishes. This is an especially great choice for vegetarians, since Afghan food relies heavily on vegetables. Try the kabobs, baked rice, yogurt dishes, and Afghan meatballs. Make sure to also save room for dessert. Never eaten Afghan food before? No problem at all. Ask one of the helpful waiters or waitresses who will be glad to assist you with ordering and describing ingredients in some of the dishes. *143 First St.* ☎ *617/492-4646. Reservations recommended. Main courses $12–$20. Sun–Thurs 5–10pm; Fri–Sat 5–11pm. T: Green Line to Lechmere.*

→**Ye Olde Union Oyster House** ★ NEW ENGLAND/SEAFOOD   America's oldest restaurant in continuous service, the Union Oyster House opened in 1826, and the booths and oyster bar haven't moved since. The food is tasty, traditional New England fare, popular with visitors walking on the adjacent Freedom Trail and savvy locals. They're not looking for anything fancy, and you shouldn't, either—the best bets are simple, classic preparations. At the crescent-shaped bar on the lower level of the cramped, low-ceilinged building (a National Historic Landmark "where Daniel Webster drank many a toddy in his day"), try oyster stew or the cold seafood sampler of oysters, clams, and shrimp to start. Follow with a broiled or grilled dish such as scrod or salmon, or perhaps fried seafood or grilled pork loin. A "shore dinner" of chowder, steamers or mussels, lobster, corn, potatoes, and dessert is an excellent introduction to local favorites. For dessert, try gingerbread with whipped cream. *Tip:* A plaque marks John F. Kennedy's favorite booth (no. 18), where he often sat to read the Sunday papers. *41 Union St. (between North and Hanover sts.).*

☎ *617/227-2750. www.unionoysterhouse.com. Reservations recommended. Main courses $8–$22 at lunch, $17–$29 at dinner; lobster market price. Sun–Thurs 11am–9:30pm (lunch menu until 5pm); Fri–Sat 11am–10pm (lunch until 6pm). Union Bar daily 11am–midnight (lunch until 3pm, late supper until 11pm). Validated and valet parking available. T: Green or Orange Line to Haymarket.*

Partying

BARS & LOUNGES

→**Casablanca** ★★ Students and professors jam this legendary Harvard Square watering hole, especially on weekends. You'll find excellent food, an excellent jukebox, and excellent eavesdropping. *40 Brattle St., Cambridge.* ☎ *617/876-0999. T: Red Line to Harvard.*

→**The Hong Kong** ★ This fun hangout is a retro Chinese restaurant on the first floor, a bar on the second floor, and a small dance club on the third floor. It's also the home of the scorpion bowl, a rum-based concoction that has contributed to the destruction of countless Ivy League brain cells. Nevertheless, you might see Harvard football players here. Never mind how I know. *1236 Mass. Ave., Cambridge.* ☎ *617/864-5311. www.hongkongharvardsq.com. T: Red Line to Harvard.*

→**Pho Republique** The atmosphere seems to get cooler as the numbers on Washington Street get higher. The lounge is the place to be at this trendy Vietnamese restaurant, which serves creative cocktails and pan-Asian nibbles to a chic after-work crowd. *1415 Washington St.* ☎ *617/262-0005. www.phorepublique.net. T: Silver Line bus from Downtown Crossing.*

LIVE MUSIC

MTV Best ● →**Abbey Lounge** ★★★ "Cheap Booze and Rock 'n' Roll." The Abbey has received Boston's honor of being the best dive bar in town, according to its regulars. There is live music 5 nights a week (Wed–Sat), and some of Boston's best underground rock 'n' roll and grittiest garage bands get the chance to play at this spot. There are two stages, one for main acts and a smaller one for acoustic and solo performers. This place promises to be a wild night of fun. *3 Beacon St. ☎ 617/441-9631. www.abbeylounge.com. Mon–Sat 10am–1am; Sun noon–2am. Cover $5–$7. Nearest T: Central Sq. Station.*

→ **Bill's Bar** "Boston's dirtiest rock club" is Bill's motto. This club is nostalgic of Boston's grittiest rock-'n'-roll glory days. Both mainstream and indie metal bands come here to play 7 nights a week. There is plenty of booze and loud music at this underground grind. You can check the band schedule on Bill's website. *Open nightly from 9pm to 2am. 5½ Lansdowne St. ☎ 617/421-9678. www.billsbar.com. Cover $5–$15, usually $10 or less. T: Green Line B, C, or D to Kenmore.*

→ **The Middle East: Restaurant and Nightclub** ★★ Not only is this a fabulous restaurant, but at nighttime this place comes to life with local bands, open mics, and acoustic acts. Of course, if you're looking for something with a Middle Eastern flare, you should also check out the Belly Dancing shows and Continental Drift/ African Diaspora music nights. Check the website for the schedule. There is live music and entertainment 7 nights a week. Food is a bit on the pricier side but worth it, especially if you're looking to try something new. There is a great variety of both meat and vegetarian dishes. *472 Massachusetts Ave., Cambridge, MA. ☎ 617/864-EAST. www.mideastclub.com. 11am–midnight Sun–Wed; 11am–1am Thurs–Sat. Weekend brunch Sat and Sun 1pm–3pm.*

GLBT NIGHTLIFE

→ **209 at Club Café** ★★ This fun South End spot draws a chic crowd of men and women for conversation (the noise level is reasonable), dining, live music in the front room, and video entertainment in the back room. Thursday is the busiest night. Open daily until 2am; the kitchen serves lunch weekdays, Sunday brunch, and dinner nightly. *209 Columbus Ave. ☎ 617/536-0966. www.clubcafe.com. T: Green Line to Arlington or Orange Line to Back Bay.*

→ **Jacques** ★ The only drag venue in town, Jacques draws a friendly crowd of gay and straight patrons who mix with the "girls" and sometimes engage in a shocking activity—that's right, disco dancing. The eclectic entertainment includes live music (on weekends), performance artists, and, of course, drag shows. *79 Broadway, Bay Village. ☎ 617/426-8902. www.jacques cabaret.com. Daily noon–midnight. Cover $6–$8. T: Green Line to Arlington.*

→ **Paradise** Not to be confused with the Boston rock club (well, you can, but it won't be quite the same experience), the Paradise attracts an all-ages male crowd. There's a stripper every evening. Thursday is college night. *180 Mass. Ave., Cambridge. ☎ 617/494-0700. www.paradisecambridge. com. Sun–Wed until 1am; Thurs–Sat until 2am. T: Red Line to Central, then a 10-min. walk.*

What Else to See & Do

A BUNCH OF GREAT MUSEUMS

→ **Harvard Museum of Natural History and Peabody Museum of Archaeology & Ethnology** ★ These fascinating museums house the university's collections of items and artifacts related to the natural world. The world-famous academic resource offers interdisciplinary programs and exhibitions that tie in elements of all the associated fields. You'll certainly find something interesting here, be it a dinosaur skeleton, a hunk of meteorite, a Native American artifact, or the Glass Flowers.

The **Peabody Museum of Archaeology & Ethnology** ★ boasts the **Hall of the North American Indian,** where 500 artifacts representing 10 cultures are on display, and is home to the only surviving artifacts positively attributed to the Lewis and Clark expedition. Photographs, textiles, pottery, and art and crafts of all descriptions fill the galleries. *Harvard Museum of Natural History: 26 Oxford St.* ☎ *617/495-3045. www.hmnh. harvard.edu. Peabody Museum: 11 Divinity Ave.* ☎ *617/496-1027. www.peabody.harvard. edu. Admission to both $7.50 adults, $6.50 seniors and students, free to all until noon Sun year-round and Wed 3–5pm Sept–May. Harvard Hot Ticket $10 adults, $8 seniors and students. Daily 9am–5pm. T: Red Line to Harvard, cross Harvard Yard, keeping John Harvard statue on right, and turn right at Science Center, first left is Oxford St.*

FREE ➔**Museum of Afro-American History** ★★ The final stop on the **Black Heritage Trail,** this museum offers a comprehensive look at the history and contributions of blacks in Boston and Massachusetts. It occupies the **Abiel Smith School** (1834), the first American public grammar school for African-American children, and the **African Meeting House,** 8 Smith Court. Changing and permanent exhibits use art, artifacts, documents, historical photographs, and other objects—including many family heirlooms—to explore an important era that often takes a back seat in Revolutionary War–obsessed New England. Children enjoy the interactive touch-screen displays and multimedia presentations, and the patient, enthusiastic staff helps them put the exhibits in context. The oldest standing black church in the United States, the meetinghouse opened in 1806. William Lloyd Garrison founded the New England

Anti-Slavery Society in this building, where Frederick Douglass made some of his great abolitionist speeches. Once known as the "Black Faneuil Hall," it also schedules lectures, concerts, and church meetings. *46 Joy St.* ☎ *617/725-0022. www. afroammuseum.org. Free admission; donations encouraged. Mon–Sat 10am–4pm. Closed Jan 1, Thanksgiving, and Dec 25. MBTA: Red or Green Line to Park Street, or Red Line to Charles/MGH.*

➔**Museum of Fine Arts** ★★★ One of the world's great art museums, the MFA works nonstop to become even more accessible and interesting. Every installation reflects a curatorial attitude that makes even those who go in with a feeling of obligation leave with a sense of discovery and wonder. That includes children, who can launch a scavenger hunt, admire the mummies, or participate in family-friendly programs scheduled year-round (and extra offerings during school vacations).

Among the numerous highlights of the magnificent collections are the **Impressionist** ★★★ paintings (including one of the largest collections of Monets outside of Paris), Asian and Old Kingdom Egyptian collections, classical art, Buddhist temple, and medieval sculpture and tapestries.

None of this comes cheap: The MFA's adult admission fee (which covers two visits within 10 days) is among the highest in the country.

To begin, pick up a floor plan at the information desk or take a free guided tour (weekdays except Mon holidays 10:30am–3pm, Wed at 6:15pm, and Sat–Sun 11am–3pm). The I. M. Pei–designed West Wing (1981) contains the main entrance, an auditorium, and an atrium with a tree-lined "sidewalk" cafe. There are also a restaurant and a cafeteria. The excellent Museum

Shop carries abundant souvenirs and a huge book selection. *465 Huntington Ave.* ☎ *617/267-9300. www.mfa.org. Admission $15 adults, $13 students and seniors when entire museum is open; or $13 and $11, respectively, when only West Wing is open. Admission good for 2 visits within 10 days. Voluntary contribution ($15 suggested) Wed 4–9:45pm. Entire museum Sat–Tues 10am–4:45pm, Wed 10am–9:45pm, Thurs–Fri 10am–5pm; West Wing only, Thurs–Fri 5–9:45pm. Closed Jan 1, Patriots Day, July 4, Thanksgiving, and Dec 25. T: Green Line E to Museum or Orange Line to Ruggles.*

➔ **Museum of Science** ★★★ For the ultimate pain-free educational experience, head to the Museum of Science. The demonstrations, experiments, and interactive displays introduce facts and concepts so effortlessly that everyone winds up learning something. Take a couple of hours or a whole day to explore the permanent and temporary exhibits, most of them hands-on and all of them great fun.

Among the 500-plus exhibits, you might meet a dinosaur or a live butterfly, find out how much you'd weigh on the moon, battle urban traffic (in a computer model), or climb into a space module. Activity centers and exhibits focus on fields of interest—natural history (with live animals), computers, the human body—while others take an interdisciplinary approach. The separate-admission **theaters** are worth planning for. Even if you're skipping the exhibits, try to see a show. If you're making a day of it, buy all your tickets at once—shows sometimes sell out. Tickets are for sale in person and, subject to a service charge, over the phone and on the Web.

The **Mugar Omni Theater** ★★★, which shows IMAX movies, is an intense experience, bombarding you with images on a five-story domed screen and digital sound. The engulfing sensations and steep pitch of the seating area will have you hanging on for dear life, whether the film is about Bengal tigers; the Nile; or volcanoes, earthquakes, and tornados. Features change every 4 to 6 months. The **Charles Hayden Planetarium** ★★ takes visitors into space with daily star shows and shows on special topics that change several times a year. On weekends, rock-music laser shows take over. At the entrance is a hands-on astronomy exhibit called **Welcome to the Universe.** *Science Park, off O'Brien Hwy. on bridge between Boston and Cambridge. ☎ 617/723-2500. www.mos. org. Admission to exhibit halls $15 adults,. Admission to Mugar Omni Theater, Hayden Planetarium, or laser shows $9 adults, July 5 to Labor Day Sat–Thurs 9am–7pm, Fri 9am–9pm; day after Labor Day to July 4 Sat–Thurs 9am–5pm, Fri 9am–9pm. Closed Thanksgiving and Dec 25. T: Green Line to Science Park.*

On the Road to Salem, MA

Boston/Cambridge to Salem, MA 16 miles

Salem is the heartland for Northeast ghost stories and is open year-round; you will have just as much fun in this town in June as you would at the end of October (Halloween is a particularly festive time around here!). It's close enough to Boston (45 min.) that you can make it a day trip by car or use mass transit that runs daily from Boston to Salem.

With all the legends and lore that surround this town, it's certainly going to be one of the highlights of your fringe roadtrip.

On the Road **Nuts & Bolts**

The Fastest Way From Boston it's a 30-minute drive. Take I-93N to Ext 37-A to Route 128N and follow the signs toward Lynn/Salem. Make sure you do not follow signs to Salem, New Hampshire.

The Long Way Round From Boston to Salem it's a ride on I-95 toward "Peabody/Gloucester." Once you merge onto exit 45 via Gloucester, you'll see signs that say "Toward Salem/Marblehead." Follow those signs. Massachusetts does a great job of labeling roads and exits.

Rules of the Road Once you get into the country and the downtown Salem areas, the speed limit drops a lot and fast, from 45mph to 25mph. Watch out for speed traps.

Getting There & Getting Around

BY CAR

From Boston, take Route 1A north to Salem, being careful in Lynn, where the road turns left and immediately right. You can also take I-93 or Route 1 to Route 128 and then Route 114 into downtown Salem.

Parking

There is a parking garage across the street from the Peabody Museum and Salem Welcome Center. For $12 per day, it's your best bet, especially if you're taking a day trip.

Hotels and B&Bs may have their own parking. Be sure to check with the hotel first. There are also meters on the street. If you're only planning on staying a few hours, finding metered parking is your best bet.

BY TRAIN /BUS

From Boston, the **MBTA** (☎ **617/222-3200;** www.mbta.com) operates trains from North Station and bus no. 450 from Haymarket (Orange or Green Line). The train is more comfortable but runs less frequently. It takes 30 to 35 minutes; the round-trip fare is $7.50. The station is about 5 blocks from the downtown area.

The one-way fare for the 35- to 55-minute bus trip is $3.45.

BY FERRY

There is round-trip service by water available on the Salem Ferry, which leaves Boston from the New England Aquarium. The trip takes about 45 minutes. It costs $11.95 one way, $21.95 round-trip before 4pm; $9.95/$19.95 after 4. There are 5 or 6 departures each day, starting around 7am, and running every couple hours. The Ferry is in operation from late May through November 1. For info on tickets and schedule call ☎ **978/741-0220** or visit www.salemferry.com.

GETTING AROUND ON FOOT

Salem is arguably the easiest place to maneuver in Massachusetts. Once you park (or get off the train), just follow the red line on the sidewalk that leads you through town. You've heard of following the yellow brick road . . . well, in this case to see the witches you follow the red tape and it leads you to all of Salem's legendary sites.

BY SALEM TROLLEY

Tours on Salem's trolleys are available for $12. This is a fun way to get around the city plus take in some of Salem's history and

Recommended Reading for Salem

→ *Our Silent Neighbors: A Study of Gravestones in the Salem Area,* by Betty J. Bouchard (Peabody Essex Museum, 1991). This is a guide to everything you will need to know about Salem's gravestones and symbolism in grave carving. The second edition of this book also includes a guide to the area's graveyards.

→ *Narratives of the New England Witchcraft Cases,* edited by George Lincoln Burr (Dover Publishing, 2002). A guide to everything you need to know about the Salem Witch Trials from direct quotes by the people involved.

→ *A Guide to the Salem Witch Hysteria of 1692,* by David C. Brown (David Brown Book Company, 1984). A must-have for those interested in the trials. This book gives a unique insight into the mind frame of the people involved in the witch hysteria.

→ *Hunting for Witches: A Guide to the Salem Witch Trials,* by Frances Hill (Commonwealth Editions, 2002). This book describes over 50 sites you can visit today and their relation to the Salem Witch Trials.

folklore. Tickets are available on board the trolley or can be purchased at Salem's Visitor's Center (☎ **978/744–5469;** www. salemtrolley.com). Allow 2 hours for the trolley tour.

Sleeping

CAMPING

Cape Ann Campsite is in West Gloucester, close to Salem. Each campsite comes with a fireplace and picnic table

Recommended Website

Haunted Happenings of Salem: For the latest updates on all of Salem's haunts, check out **http://hauntedhappeningssalem.com.** This will give you the latest in tours, events, parades, parties, festivals, art shows, and attractions. Throughout the month of October, there is a free Haunted Happenings Guide that is distributed throughout Salem.

and if you are the outdoor person who can't part with your laptop, this site now has Wi-Fi. *Atlantic Street, West Gloucester MA.* ☎ *978/283–8683. www.camp-ann.com/campsite. Campsites: $25–$30 for 2 people, additional $2–$8 per extra person. Open May–Oct.*

You can get a free **guide to Massachusetts camping** at the State Welcome Center off of I-95. You can see the guide online at **www.campmass.com**.

CHEAP/DOABLE

There's a **Comfort Inn** (☎ 978/777-1700) at 50 Dayton St. in Salem, where doubles go for about $70 per night. A **Days Inn** (☎ 978/777–1030; www.daysinndanvers. com) is at 152 Endicott St., in nearby Danvers, offering doubles from $69 to $119.

→ **The Inn on Washington Square** This beautiful Greek revival home built in 1850 is another one of Salem's restored houses turned bed-and-breakfast. With its gorgeous Victorian exterior, including gardens and beautiful architecture, in addition to the furnished living rooms, sitting rooms, and guest rooms, this is a

Salem Highlights

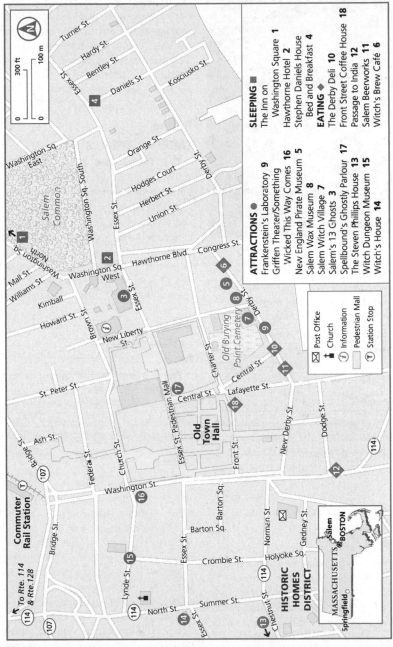

SLEEPING ■
The Inn on
   Washington Square **1**
Hawthorne Hotel **2**
Stephen Daniels House
   Bed and Breakfast **4**

EATING ◆
The Derby Deli **10**
Front Street Coffee House **18**
Passage to India **12**
Salem Beerworks **11**
Witch's Brew Café **6**

ATTRACTIONS ●
Frankenstein's Laboratory **9**
Griffen Theater/Something
   Wicked This Way Comes **16**
New England Pirate Museum **5**
Salem Wax Museum **8**
Salem Witch Village **7**
Salem's 13 Ghosts **3**
Spellbound's Ghostly Parlour **17**
The Steven Phillips House **13**
Witch Dungeon Museum **15**
Witch's House **14**

☒ Post Office
✝ Church
ⓘ Information
   Pedestrian Mall
Ⓣ Station Stop

One of Salem's witchy museums.

fantastic option for an overnight stay in Salem. *53 Washington Sq. North.* ☎ *978/741-4997.* *www.washingtonsquareinn.com.* *$100–$250.*

➔ **Stephen Daniels House Bed and Breakfast** This is a renovated 300-year-old captain's house and one of the few three-story houses in Massachusetts from its time that is still intact. And the most popular room is the Great Room, which features a woodburning fireplace, 18th-century canopy bed, large, colorful Oriental rugs, wing chair, and desk, There's a private garden, filled with seasonal flowers. Pets are welcomed here also! Along with breakfast, guests are invited to partake of afternoon tea. *1 Daniels St.* ☎ *978/744-5709. Rates: $120–$135.*

SPLURGE

➔ **Hawthorne Hotel** ★★★ Can you guess who this hotel is named after? The Hawthorne Hotel is probably as famous in Salem as the author himself. Located in an ideal spot in the center of town, each of the rooms in the hotel is complete with 18th-century-style furnishings. Of course,

you also have your modern-day amenities like telephone, Internet, and cable television in every room. There are two award-winning restaurants in the hotel, where breakfast, lunch, and dinner are served daily and there's a jazz brunch on Sundays. *18 Washington Sq. West, Salem, MA.* ☎ *978/744-4080.* *www.hawthornehotel.com.* *$104–$309 depending upon season.*

Eating

TAKEOUT TREATS

➔ **The Derby Deli** DELI/SANDWICHES You have your choice of every typical deli sandwich plus some funky grilled plates such as lamb and beef kabobs, steak tips, and beef skewers. There is surf and turf plus some great vegetarian options and salads. Since all orders are available for takeout, this is a great place to buy food and go across the street to the port and enjoy the beauty of Salem's old waterways. *245 Derby St.* ☎ *978/741-2442. $4.75–$11. Mon–Sat 10:30am–10pm; Sun noon–8pm.*

EATING OUT

Cheap

➔ **Front Street Coffeehouse** COFFEE/DESSERT/SANDWICHES This is the hangout for many of Salem's locals. Meet and greet some of Salem's younger crowd while enjoying a sandwich, snack, or drink. *20 Front St.* ☎ *978/740-6697. $1.75–$6. Daily 11am–6:30pm.*

➔ **Witch's Brew Cafe** ★ AMERICAN This cute little place, hidden away from the bustle of the downtown area, is a great spot to relax and grab a drink at the bar. Although the regulars aren't the young crowd, the food is good and it's the quieter alternative if you've had a busy day sightseeing. This is also a good place to grab a quick lunch. I highly recommend the New England clam chowder; because I became a chowder aficionado on the road, I often think back to the Witch's Brew Cafe with

The Witches Way

It's hard not to walk around Salem and wonder how such an event like the Witch Trials of 1692 could have ever occurred. Where did the paranoia come from and can something like it ever happen again? I tracked down a few people whose work in Salem is to help visitors answer these questions and talk to them about their own perceptions of today's witches. Among them is Tom, a staff member at the **Salem Witch Village** (282 Derby St.; ☎ **978/740-9229;** www.salemwitchvillage.net). I asked him what questions he's asked the most about today's witches.

"Among the most popular is the relationship between witchcraft and Satanism and the origins of the broom," he says. "There is absolutely no relationship between witchcraft and Satanism. In fact, they are on two completely different sides of the spectrum. Our religion stems from European Tribal and pagan roots that date back long before Christianity." And as for the broom? "It stems from an ancient fertility ritual which never involved broomsticks until witchcraft became taboo and we needed to perform the rituals in secrecy." To find out more about the stereotypes and myths that have become associated with today's witches, visit Tom and the gang at the Salem Witch Village.

fond memories. *156 Derby St.* ☎ *978/745-8717. $5.75–$14. Daily 11:30am–10pm.*

Doable

➜**Passage to India** ★★ INDIAN If you enjoy Indian food or if you are in the mood to try something new, Passage to India is certainly a good place to check out. The intimate and quiet environment makes for nice relaxing at the end of a long day. There is a good variety of dishes to choose from plus all dishes are made using no preservatives and no MSG. *157 Washington St.* ☎ *978/832-2200. www.passageindia.com. Appetizers $1.50–$8; entrees $8–$14. Cash only. Sun–Wed 11:30am–10:30pm; Thurs–Sat 11:30am–11pm.*

➜**Salem Beer Works** ★★ AMERICAN Can you guess what Beer Works is noted for? Aside from good beer they also have a fantastic array of sandwiches, pizza, and appetizers. Make sure to try something off of the Beer Works "Favorite" list like the Sesame Ginger Stirfry or BBQ'd Baby Back Ribs. If you miss Salem's Beer Works, you can also check out one of its two other locations in Boston. *278 Derby St.* ☎ *978/745-BEER. www.beerworks.net. Main courses $6–$17. Sun–Thurs 11:30am–midnight; Fri–Sat 11:30am–1am.*

Witch Way in Salem

MUSEUMS & HISTORIC HOMES

➜**Salem Witch Museum** ★★ The main draw of the museum (a former church) is a three-dimensional audiovisual presentation with life-size figures. The show takes place in a huge room lined with displays that are lighted in sequence. The 30-minute narration tells the tale of the witchcraft trials and the accompanying hysteria. The well-researched presentation recounts the story accurately, if somewhat overdramatically. One of the victims was crushed to death by rocks piled on a board on his chest. There's also a small exhibit that traces the history of witches, witchcraft, and witch hunts. *19½ Washington Sq., on Rte. 1A.* ☎ *978/744-1692. www.salemwitchmuseum.com. Admission $7.50 adults. Daily July–Aug 10am–7pm;*

PARANORMAL NORTHEAST

On Trial for Witchcraft

MTV **Best ❖** *Cry Innocent: The People Versus Bridget Bishop* ★★★: If you want to put yourself in the place of the Puritans and those on trial for witchcraft, you must experience *Cry Innocent,* a live reenactment produced by Gordon College Students and History Alive. The presentation begins in the center of Salem's Essex Street, where you watch Bridget Bishop get arrested and follow her to Old Town Hall to watch her trial. The witnesses present evidence to you, the jury, and at the end, you vote on whether Bishop will stand a formal trial and hear the punishment for her actions. *Tickets can be purchased at the box office at Old Town Hall. $8 adults,.* ☎ *978/867-4747. www.cryinnocent.com.The show is presented daily from June 26–Aug 27 throughout the day; in Sept on Sat only, at 11:30am, 1:30 and 3pm. Oct 7–31 daily at 11am and 1pm.*

Sept–June 10am–5pm; Closed Jan 1, Thanksgiving, and Dec 25.

MTV **Best ❖** → **Salem Witch Village** ★★★ What exactly is a witch? Do people still hold the same ideas today about witches as they did in 1692? The Salem Witch Village is the place to ask those questions. A tour designed in collaboration with Salem's current Witch Community is given daily by a few of Salem's practicing witches. On this tour you will learn everything there is to know about contemporary witchcraft, where symbols such as the broomstick and black cat came from, how today's witches view themselves, and even find more of an understanding on how the world views today's witches. Visitors on the tour even have the opportunity to witness a real live spell casting performed by practicing witches. The guides are available to answer any questions you may have about the myths and realities associated with witches. Open daily year-round with extended hours during the summer months and in October. *282 Derby St.* ☎ *978/740-9229. www.salemwitchvillage.net. $5.50 adults. Daily Apr–June, 10am–6pm;*

Visiting the Ghostly Parlour

MTV **Best ❖** **Spellbound's Ghostly Parlour** ★★★ is at 190 Essex St. (☎ **978/745-0138**), in one of the most fascinating museums in Salem. Mollie Stewart has assembled a rare collection of artifacts ranging from Old Oujia Boards, Ghost and Orb pictures, a Vampire Killing Kit, and Voodoo tools used everywhere from Africa to New Orleans. You can also read about real ghost-hunting experiences and look at photographs of expeditions done around the country. In addition, learn about the origins and legends surrounding vampires and other worldly mythical beasts. *$10 adults/$7 students and seniors/$5 children.*

If this doesn't give you the chills, stick around until 8pm for the **Spellbound Walking Tour,** which meets in front of the Visitor's Center Building at #2 Liberty St. Mollie Stewart leads the group to some of Salem's most haunted areas in search of spirits (see box below). *$13 adults/$10 students and seniors/$7 children. www.spellboundtours.com.*

July–Aug. 10am–9pm; Sept 10am–6 pm; Oct: Extended hours; Nov–Dec, 10am–5pm; Jan–Mar 11am–4pm. Closed Thanksgiving, Dec 25, Jan 1.

➔**Witch Dungeon Museum** What was it like to be one of the accused thrown in jail for witchcraft in 1692? You can share the experience that those women and men had at the Witch Dungeon Museum. You will see cells the actual size of the ones where the accused waited before standing trial and even the Gallows Hill, where many were hanged. A live reenactment of the trial of Sarah Good is also performed, taken from the original court transcripts. 16 Lynde St. 978/741-3570. www.witchdungeon. com. Admission $7, or by combination ticket ($16). Daily 10am–5pm Apr–Nov.

MTV **Best ✪** ➔**Witch History Museum** ★★★ If you're in need of some background on Salem's Witch hysteria of 1692, then this is the place to see first. The Witch History Museum is one of Salem's most popular museums. Learn not only about Salem's witch trials, but about the hysteria that occurred throughout New England. The Witch History Museum, Witch Dungeon Museum, and Pirate History Museum are under the same management, and you can buy a combination ticket to get into all three for $16 (a savings of $5 over individual admissions). 197-201 Essex St. ☎ 978/741-7770. www.witchhistorymuseum.com. Admission $7 adults. Daily 10am–5pm Apr–Nov.

➔**Witch House** Salem's legendary **Witch House** is the only authentic house with direct ties to the 1692 Witch Trials still standing. On the tour of the house, you'll learn all about Puritan daily rituals and lifestyle. You'll also gain a deeper insight into the house's owner, Judge Jonathan Corwin, and the role he played during the Salem Witch trials. Was he a good man or bad man? What were his responsibilities to the accused and to his community? This time you will be the judge. 310 Essex St. ☎ 978/744-8815. www.salemweb.com/witch house. Admission w/guided tour $10 adults; self-guided tour $8. Open daily May 2 to early Nov 10am–5pm, by appointment off season.

WITCH THEATRICS

Salem has quite a few reenactments of Puritan days and theatrical presentations. There are some talented actors, including many theater students from the nearby Boston area. *Cry Innocent: The People Versus Bridget Bishop* is a reenactment of the witchcraft examination of Bridget Bishop in 1692. (See box above for performance information.)

Something Wicked This Way Comes at the Griffen Theatre investigates the testimony of John Westgate, the Witch of Gloucester, and other tales of Salem ghosts in a 30-minute performance. General admission is $8 for adults, and the show runs from June through September

Mollie Stewart: A Real Life Ghost Hunter

Mollie Stewart, proprietor of **Spellbound's Ghostly Parlour** (131 Essex St.; ☎ **978/745-0138**; www.spellboundtours.com), is a licensed Ghost Hunter with the International Ghost Hunters Society and a certified parapsychologist. Mollie has been around in the ghost world. She's been featured on numerous television and cable programs discussing hauntings around the country. I asked her if she ever gets spooked doing the work that she does, and she said that the only time she ever felt uneasy was when she was ghost hunting at the prison site of Alcatraz.

Arrr! A Pirate Museum

The **New England Pirate Museum** ★ ★ ★ 📺 Ⓑest🌟 (274 Derby St., near the waterfront; ☎ 978/741-2800; www.piratemuseum.com) is a great place to avast, ye mateys and talk like a pirate. After visiting this museum I found that the Hollywood pirates are a lot less interesting than the real ones who controlled the northeast waterways during the 1700s. The guided tour through the museum will introduce you to some of New England's most popular pirates and even show you some artifacts that have been recovered from shipwrecks off the Massachusetts coast. *Admission $7, or combination ticket with Witch Dungeon Museum, Witch History Museum and the New England Pirate Museum for $16. Daily 10am–5pm May–Oct; weekends in Nov.*

throughout the day from 10am–5pm. *Griffen Theatre, 7 Lynde St. ☎ 978/825-0222. www.griffentheatre.com.*

WALKING TOURS

Salem is a haven for walking tours. Practically everywhere you go, you'll find signs reading "Best Walking Tours in Town." Each one of the tours has its advantages, depending on what kind of experience you're looking for.

➔ **Cemetery 101: Grave Matters** The Salem Cemetery is one of the oldest in the country and home to some legendary spirits. You can explore the site on your own or with a guided tour. On the guided tour, you will be introduced to some of the old

Puritan burial rituals in addition to learning the history behind the carvings and engravings on the stones. This is certainly some valuable information that you can take with you for other cemetery tours. ☎ *978/745-0666. www.salemhistoricaltours.com. Adults $10, students/seniors/military $8. Daily at 1pm (lasts 1 hr.).*

📺 Ⓑest🌟 ➔ **Candlelit Ghostly Tours** ★ ★ ★ This fabulous walking tour is sponsored by the Salem Wax Museum (below). On this tour, you'll go through Salem's most famous graveyard by candlelight. You'll be introduced to some of the lore and legends behind the people buried there. *Reservations and tickets available at*

Detour: Whale-Watching

Right outside of Salem, in nearby Gloucester, is the opportunity to see ocean giants up close. Take a break from ghost and pirate hunting and see the mammals that have been the subject of many marine legends and folklore. **Cape Ann Whale Watch** departs from Rose's Wharf on Route 128, exit 10 in Gloucester. For directions and online reservations, visit **www.SeeTheWhales. com**. *Adults $41/children 4–15 $35. Whale sightings are guaranteed. Boats leave daily. Trips available in the morning and afternoon. Check website for updated seasonal schedule.*

Another firm that offers whale-watching excursions is the **7 Seas Whale Watch and Charters** (☎ **888/283-776**), which also leaves from Gloucester and is a quick 30-minute ride from Salem by hopping on MA-128 and getting off the first exit at Washington Street. *$40 adults/children under 16 $26. Daily boat tours. www.7seaswhalewatch.com for schedule and directions.*

Salem's Shopping Scene

Salem is a shopper's haven for offbeat and eccentric goodies. You can find many interesting (and schlocky) gifts and souvenirs.

→ **Wicked Goodz** (6 Central St.; ☎ 978/745-3119). Everything Salem is at this shop. Boast about your experience with "Salem" hoodies and T-shirts and buy souvenirs for everyone. There are also key chains, glasses, books, dolls, pens, and every other "Wicked" accessory you can think of for reasonable prices.

→ **Samantha's Costumes** (177 Essex St.; ☎ 978/745-0444; www.sam costumes.com). This is the best costume shop I have ever seen (and I'm a bona-fide costume freak). Who cares if Halloween isn't for another 8 months? Get your shopping done ahead of time and wow your friends and family in an authentic costume from America's "Halloween Capital." Take a look at the variety of masks, wigs, makeup, and accessories.

→ **Penelope's Pet Boutique** (99 Washington St.; ☎ 978/745-0566). Don't leave Salem without picking out a gift for your best animal friend. Penelope's Pet Boutique has everything your dog or cat will ever need (and then some). Is your dog secretly wishing she was a biker? Indulge your pet's fantasies by buying it clothes and accessories. Watch out though, because those doggie rain slickers can get rather expensive.

→ **Salem's Vintage Photography** (☎ 978/745-6462; www.salemsvintage photography.com). Leave Salem with a souvenir of you and your friends as part of history. You can be photographed as your favorite legend in Salem or look as if you stepped out of a picture from anywhere between the 1920s through the 1940s. Inside the Museum Place Mall right in the center of Downtown Salem (www.museumplacemall.com).

→ **Laurie Cabot: The Cat, The Crow and The Crown Inc.** (63R Wharf St.; ☎ 978744-6274; www.lauriecabot.com). Laurie Cabot is Salem's most famous witch and she owns this shop in Salem that draws in many tourists. The witch shop sells stones, clothing, books, jewelry, and many other odds and ends pertaining to witches and the craft.

the Salem Witch Village. 282 Derby St. ☎ 978/740-9229. www.salemwaxmuseum. com. Nightly 7:30 and 8:30pm.

→ **Haunted Footsteps Ghost Tour** Salem is certainly a haven for haunted ghost tours. On this one, you'll hear stories of mysterious murders, encounters with spirits, and the paranormal. Tours are given nightly April 1 through October 5 at 8pm; October 6 through October 31 at 7 and 8pm. All tours meet at 8 Central St. www. salemhistoricaltours.com. Adults $14/students and active military $10/children $8.

More Haunted Attractions

Aside from the "real" haunts, Salem also has a collection of haunted attractions and theme park–style haunted houses. As cheesy as this may sound, some of them can be pretty scary, especially for younger audiences. At 131 Essex St. is a 3-D attraction called **Salem's 13 Ghosts** (☎ 978/744-0013; www.salems13ghosts.com), where visitors can literally become one with the ghouls. Don't forget your 3-D glasses, given to you in the lobby before entering. It's open daily, May through November, admission $9.50 adults.

Frankenstein's Laboratory (288 Derby St.; ☎ **978/740-2929;** www.salem waxmuseum.com) is another experience where you can walk through a maze of mishaps in the dungeon of Salem's Wax Museum while monsters jump out at you. It's open daily April to June, 10am to 6pm; July to August, 10am to 10pm; September 10am to 6pm; October extended hours; November to March, 11am to 4pm. Closed Thanksgiving, Deccember 25, and January 1. Admission is $6.

More Stuff to See & Do

SALEM'S MARITIME HISTORY

Salem's location on the Northeast coast in addition to its 200 years of rich history make it a prime location for maritime legends. Pirates, haunted lighthouses, ghost ships, mysterious disappearances . . . Salem has seen it all and is eager to share these extraordinary tales with visitors.

➔ *Fame* No, I'm not talking about the movie. I'm talking about the 1812 privateer ship *Fame,* where you can sail on the same waters as the merchants, traders, pilgrims, and pirates sailed 400 years ago. Cruises leave from the Pickering Wharf Marina

and last one hour and 45 minutes. There are also sunset cruises available. ☎ *978/ 729–2600. $25 adults/$15 children. Cruises are given daily. Check online for schedules at www.schoonerfame.com.*

➔ **Salem Wax Museum** Enjoy the combination of Seafarers and Witches, two of Salem's most famous legends at the **Salem Wax Museum.** The museum is a walk through Salem's rich haunted history told by some beautifully sculpted Wax figures. These sculptures are so real looking you'll have to walk by again to be sure that they're just wax. *288 Derby St. ☎ 800/298-2929. www.salemwaxmuseum.com. $6 adult. Discounts available online. Daily Apr–June 10am–6pm; July–Aug 10am–10pm; Sept 10am–6 pm; Oct: Extended hours; Nov–Mar 11am–4pm. Closed Thanksgiving, Dec 25, Jan 1.*

FREE ➔ **The Steven Phillips House** A free museum for anyone interested in the details of early 20th-century living. The Steven Phillips House gives a detailed look into how the maritime Phillips family and domestic staff lived during the 1900s. One of the few free sites in all of Salem. *34 Chestnut St. ☎ 978/744-0440. www.phillips museum.org. Free Admission. Open the Sat before Memorial Day through Oct Mon–Sat 10am–4pm.*

On the Road to Portsmouth, NH

From Salem, MA to Portsmouth, NH 46 miles

On the Road Nuts & Bolts

The Tolls There is a 70¢ toll at the New Hampshire crossing.

The Fastest Way Get onto I-95 and take it straight up into New Hampshire. Take Exit 7 toward Portsmouth/Downtown.

The Long Way Round You can stop in Gloucester for an extra day. There are plenty of museums worth checking out. I recommend just heading straight up to Portsmouth and enjoying some of the sites that New Hampshire has to offer.

Welcome to Portsmouth

New Hampshire is a small state; when you're driving on I-95, you seem to be in and out of it in just a few minutes. But there are definitely a few things worth stopping for, so pull off the interstate, and take some time to explore Portsmouth.

VISITOR INFORMATION

The **Greater Portsmouth Chamber of Commerce,** 500 Market St. (☎ 603/436-1118; www.portcity.org), has an information center between Exit 7 and downtown. From Memorial Day to Columbus Day, it's open Monday through Wednesday, 8:30am to 5pm; Thursday and Friday, 8:30am to 7pm; and Saturday and Sunday, 10am to 5pm. The rest of the year, hours are Monday through Friday, 8:30am to 5pm. In summer, a second booth is at Market Square in the middle of the historic district. A good website with extensive information on the region may be found at **www.seacoastnh.com.**

GETTING AROUND

On Foot/By Trolley

Most of Portsmouth can be easily reconnoitered on foot, so you need park only once. Parking can be tight in and around the historic district in summer. The municipal parking garage nearly always has space and costs just 50¢ per hour; it's located on Hanover Street between Market and Fleet streets. Strawbery Banke Museum (see below) also offers limited parking for visitors.

There's also now a free "**trolley**" (☎ 603/743-5777) circulating central Portsmouth in a one-way loop from July to early September. It hits all the key historical points. Catch it at Market Square, Prescott Park, or Strawbery Banke.

HAUNTED PORTSMOUTH

A Walking Tour

📺 Best ● → **Haunted Pubs of Portsmouth Tour** ★★★ Portsmouth has one of America's oldest brewing histories. On the Haunted Pubs of Portsmouth Tour, you'll learn all about the rich history surrounding these old maritime hot spots. What better way to honor history then by taking a tour of the local legends and folklore surrounding many of these pubs and then stopping in for a drink? Unfortunately the Haunted Pubs of Portsmouth Tours do not run daily, so you have to schedule early in advance and make your reservations. ☎ 207/439-8905. www.newenglandcuriosities. com/pubs.htm. Admission $25.

A Haunted Prison

→ **The Castle–Abandoned U.S. Naval Prison** Trespassing on this property is seriously off limits, so if you do so, you're doing it at your own risk. Since these coastal states have such a maritime history, I couldn't write this chapter without including a nod to The Rock, a U.S. Naval Prison in the Portsmouth Naval Shipyard that has been closed since the early 1970s. The prison's population climbed from 601 in September 1943 to nearly 2,000 by the year's end. By August of 1945 its population reached 3,088. The Navy closed and abandoned this prison in 1974. The structure is now being sought out by major corporations for renovation and commercial use. As you can imagine, the legends that surround this bad boy are endless.

Sleeping

HOTELS/MOTELS

There are plenty of chain hotels in Portsmouth, NH. A **Best Western** is at 508 U.S. Highway 1 Bypass, Interstate Traffic

Portsmouth, NH Highlights

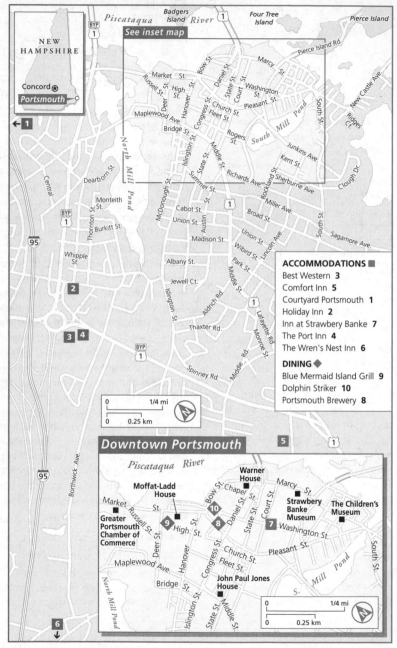

ACCOMMODATIONS ■
Best Western **3**
Comfort Inn **5**
Courtyard Portsmouth **1**
Holiday Inn **2**
Inn at Strawbery Banke **7**
The Port Inn **4**
The Wren's Nest Inn **6**

DINING ◆
Blue Mermaid Island Grill **9**
Dolphin Striker **10**
Portsmouth Brewery **8**

Downtown Portsmouth

Circle in Portsmouth (☎ **603/436-7600**; www.bestwestern.com). The **Comfort Inn** is at 1190 Lafayette Rd. in Portsmouth (☎ **603/433-3338**; www.comfortinn.com). The **Holiday Inn** of Portsmouth is at 300 Woodbury Ave., www.holidayinn.com, and the **Portsmouth Courtyard Marriot** is at 1000 Market St. (☎ **603/436-2121**; www.courtyard.com). Rates vary, so see what you can come up with on their websites or Priceline.com. You should be able to score a room for under $100.

BED & BREAKFASTS

The Wren's Nest Village Inn, a few miles south of downtown Portsmouth at 3548 Lafayette Rd., Rte. 1 (☎ **888/755-9013**), has guest rooms starting at $69. **The Port Inn** also has rates starting at under $100 and is on the Route 1 Bypass at the Traffic Circle in Portsmouth. Room rates are seasonal and more expensive during the peak summer months (☎ **800/282-PORT**).

→**Inn at Strawbery Banke** ★ This historic inn, in an 1814 home, is ideally located for exploring Portsmouth: The historic site of Strawbery Banke is a block away, and Market Square (the center of the action) is 2 blocks away. The friendly innkeepers have done a nice job of taking a cozy antique home and making it comfortable. Rooms are tiny but bright and feature stenciling, wooden shutters, and beautiful pine floors; one has a bathroom down the hall. *314 Court St., Portsmouth, NH 03801. ☎ 800/428-3933 or 603/436-7242. www.innatstrawberybanke.com. 7 units. Spring, summer, and early fall $145–$150 double; off season $100–$115 double. Rates include breakfast. 2-night minimum stay Aug and Oct weekends. In room: A/C, no phone.*

Eating

CAFE SCENE

Portsmouth has perhaps the best cafe scene in northern New England; my favorites are **Breaking New Grounds** (☎ **603/436-9555**), off Market Square, with outstanding espresso shakes and good tables for chatting; **Caffe Kilim** (☎ **603/436-7330**) at 79 Daniel St., across from the post office; and **Me and Ollie's** (☎ **603/436-7777**) at 10 Pleasant St., well known locally for its bread and homemade granola.

EATING OUT
Cheap

→**Blue Mermaid Island Grill** ★ CARIBBEAN A taste of the Caribbean in the heart of Portsmouth, NH. Try some tasty Caribbean favorites like Cajun seafood cake, calamari, and grilled scallops on wontons. There's live entertainment, including open mic nights. *The Hill (at Hanover and High sts., facing the municipal parking garage). ☎ 603/427-2583. www.bluemermaid.com. Main courses: lunch $5.95–$14, dinner $13–$21 (most around $15–$17). Sun–Thurs 11:30am–9pm; Fri–Sat 11:30am–10pm.*

→**Portsmouth Brewery** BAR FOOD/AMERICAN New England beer, anyone? The Portsmouth Brewery has some of the best beer in New Hampshire. If you are a beer connoisseur, then this is a must-see for you. The food is what you would expect at any pub, traditional bar foods like hamburgers, wings, and, of course, some New England seafood. Check the website for the current On Tap beers. Past favorites have included India Pale Ale, Wild Rice Ale, Altbier, Black Cat Stout, and Farnum Hill Cider. *56 Market St. ☎ 603/431-1115. www.portsmouthbrewery.com. Main courses: lunch $5.25–$8.95, dinner $11–$22. Daily 11:30am–12:30am.*

Doable

→**Dolphin Striker** NEW ENGLAND/SEAFOOD If you are in the mood for some traditional New England cuisine, then make a visit to the Dolphin Striker. The restaurant's setting is in a historic

Detour: America's Stonehenge?

Maybe it's the name "Salem" that attracts strange things . . . Up in the New Hampshire countryside, about 40 miles southwest of Portsmouth, in the town of North Salem, are 30 acres of human-made rock dwellings that were left behind by a group of unknown people. For 2 centuries "America's Stonehenge" has baffled historians and archaeologists alike. Artifacts that have been found at the site date back to close to 1000 B.C. and some charcoal found at the site dates back over 4,000 years. It is clear that whoever the people were who built these massive structures had a keen idea of architecture and astronomy. You can see for yourself; it's open 9am to 5pm daily, except for Christmas and Thanksgiving. Admission is $9 (there's a discount coupon on the website). *105 Haverhill Road Salem, NH, ☎ 603/893-8300; www.stonehengeusa.com.*

brick warehouse (that has obviously been restored) in the heart of the town of Portsmouth. On the menu are plenty of traditional New England specialties like lobster, seasonal fish, and crabs, along with some land favorites. You have your choice of sitting in the main dining room or relaxing a bit in the downstairs pub. *15 Bow St. ☎ 603/431-5222. www.dolphinstriker.com. Lunch $6.95–$11; dinner $17–$28. Tues–Sun 11:30am–2pm and 5–10pm.*

On the Road to York Beach, ME

Portsmouth, NH to York Beach, ME 14 miles

The last stop on our roadtrip takes you all the way up to the northernmost state in the Northeast. Maine is crawling with a rich, fantastic, and somewhat spooky history. The south is a haven for lighthouses.

In Portland, a little further up the road, there is also the museum of cryptozoology. (If you have no idea what cryptozoology is, you will soon find out.)

On the Road Nuts & Bolts

Where to Fill Up   Fill up in one of the quaint gas stations in Portsmouth, NH, before heading up the coast to Maine.

The Tolls   There is a $2 bridge toll at the border of New Hampshire and Maine.

The Fastest Way   Get back onto I-95 and head north.

The Long Way Round   There are certainly plenty of "long roads" you can take to get to Maine. If you're traveling during the fall season, I recommend traveling up through Northern New Hampshire and checking out the foliage. New Hampshire residents love to brag about how their foliage is some of the most sought after in the world. People come from all over the country and internationally to see the autumn beauty. I highly recommend grabbing some pumpkins, pie, and apple cider and experiencing nature's beauty. If you're not traveling during the fall, then take the more coastal route and enjoy some of the northeast's beautiful beaches.

Recommended Reading for Maine

Check out the following books featuring some of Maine's most infamous legends, haunts, and mythic creatures:

➢ *Maine Ghosts and Legends: 26 Encounters with the Supernatural,* by Thomas A. Verde (Down East Books, 1989). Tom Verde became interested in Maine ghosts and legends when he was researching a series for public radio. He discovered that Maine has a rich history of supernatural phenomena.

➢ *Ghosts on the Coast of Maine,* by Carol Oliveri Schulte (Down East Books, 1996). Schulte presents 25 stories—allegedly true—of ghosts in Coastal Maine.

➢ *Cryptozoology A to Z: The Encyclopedia of Loch Monsters, Sasquatch, Chupacabras and Other Authentic Mysteries of Nature,* by Loren Coleman and Jerome Clark (Fireside, 1999). Coleman, a forty-year veteran of crypto-zoological field expeditions and research, has written several books on nature's mysterious creatures. He is a professor at the University of Southern Maine and lives in Portland.

➢ *Anything by Stephen King.* How could we *not* mention Maine native "Master of Horror" Stephen King? King wrote his first horror story at the age of twenty and at one time had five books on the *New York Times* bestseller's list. Some of his most acclaimed work includes popular favorites (some of them set in Maine) such as *Salem's Lot*, *Pet Sematary*, *The Tommyknockers*, *Carrie*, and *Cujo*. King still lives in Bangor, ME, and if you pass through there, you can ask for directions to his house. It's not open to the public, but you can see it from the street.

Welcome to the Yorks, ME

"The Yorks," are three shore towns, just across the border from New Hampshire that share a name but little else.

York Village is full of early (17th-century) American history and architecture, and has a good library. **York Harbor** reached its zenith during America's late Victorian era, when wealthy urbanites constructed cottages at the ocean's edge.

But it's **York Beach** I like the best: a beach town with amusements, taffy shops, a small zoo, gabled summer homes set in crowded enclaves, a great lighthouse, and two good beaches—a long one perfect for walking or tanning, plus a shorter one within a minute's walk of restaurants, souvenir shops, candy shops, an arcade, and even a palm reader.

York Beach is a good base for excursions around the lower Casco Bay, and up into Portland. In summer, it's packed with visitors, and you'll have a harder time finding reasonably priced hotels and meals; still that's most likely the time you'll be traveling, as the attractions, hotels, and restaurants this far north tend to shut down for the season by the end of September.

If you can make your trip very early or late in the season, you might find fewer crowds and more bargains.

VISITOR INFORMATION

The **York Chamber of Commerce** (☎ **207/363-4422**) operates an information center at 571 Rte. 1, a short way from the turnpike exit. It's open in summer daily from 9am to 5pm (until 6pm Fri), limited days and hours the rest of the year.

PARANORMAL NORTHEAST

Snacking wisely on a Maine lobster.

Sleeping

York Beach has a number of motels facing Long Sands Beach. Among those with simple accommodations on or near the beach are the **Anchorage Inn** (☎ 207/363-5112) and the **Long Beach Motor Inn** (☎ 207/363-5481).

CAMPING

There are many opportunities to camp in Maine, especially during the summer months. **Dixon's Coastal Maine Campground** (☎ 207/363–3626; www.dixons campground.com) is at 1740 US Rte. 1 in Cape Neddick, convenient to York Beach and Ogunquit. It welcomes both tents and RVs, and has restroom and shower facilities, as well as an in-ground pool. It's open from May 15 until Columbus Day. Nightly rates range from $26 to $38, depending on how many are in your party and whether you want water/electric.

You can also pick up a free copy of Maine's camping sites at the state Welcome Center off of I-95.

HAUNTED INNS OF OGUNQUIT

About 15 minutes north of York Beach is Ogunquit, which houses three of southern Maine's notoriously haunted inns.

The Puffin Inn at 433 Main St. (☎ 207/646-5496; http://puffininn.com) has quite a number of tales surrounding it. The house was built in the early 1800s by a sea captain named Walter Perkins, who decided to move the house once he'd built it. It's now uphill from its original location, where it was pulled by a horse. Past owners of the Inn have reported seeing apparitions in the basement and attic. There are also reports of hearing footsteps and rustling coming from unoccupied rooms and, of course, the feeling of another presence in the room. Room nos. 8 and 9 are considered the most haunted. All 11 rooms have private bathrooms or showers. Off-season rates range from $69 to $129, in summer from $139 to $189.

Room no. 2 at **The Old Village Inn** at 250 Main St. (☎ 207/646–7088; www.theold villageinn.net) is another one of Ogunquit's most notoriously haunted spots. For years now there have been stories circulating about the spirits, strange temperature drops, and lights that refuse to turn off in the room. Several rooms boast a view of the Ogunquit River and ocean. All have private bathrooms as well as A/C, refrigerators, and WiFi Hot Spots. Rates are from $60 to $75 off season and $110 to $150 in summer.

The **Nellie Littlefield House** (☎ 207/646-1692; www.nellielittlefieldhouse.com) has a ghost named Rory, thought to be a previous owner of the house who refuses to leave. Both the owner and guests have reported having strange phenomena go on in the house, including electronics going wild, witnessing apparitions, and feeling presences in the room. All the bedrooms are individually decorated, some with antiques and period furniture. All have private bathroom and A/C. Four rooms have private decks and ocean views. Early and late season rates range from $99–$175; high season and holiday rates range from $180 to $230.

DOABLE

→**Candleshop Inn: Bed & Breakfast and Holistic Retreat Center** Not only does this B&B offer a fabulous ocean view of Maine, but it is also a holistic retreat center offering daily yoga, massages, and a home-cooked vegetarian breakfast. There are two rooms with complete bathroom and ocean views; and several with shared bathroom. Some rooms have hand-painted murals; others have soothing rocking chairs. *44 Freeman St., York* ☎ *888/363-4087 and 207/363-4087. www.candleshopinn. com. $75–$120 off season; $90–$170 summer, holidays.*

SPLURGE

→**Stage Neck Inn** ★★ A hotel in one form or another has housed guests on this windswept bluff between the harbor and the open ocean since about 1870. The most recent incarnation, constructed in 1972, is furnished with an understated, country club–like elegance. The hotel is modern, yet offers an old-fashioned sense of intimacy lacking in other modern resorts.

Take a break from ghostbusting to walk along the coast at York Beach.

PARANORMAL NORTHEAST

Visiting Old York Village

York, ME is one of New England's oldest and most well-preserved towns. Many of the buildings date back to the 17th and 18th centuries. If you want to learn a little more about York's history, visit the **Old York Historical Society** ★★ at 207 York St. (☎ **207/363-4974**). The museum has several walking tours through old houses, buildings, and sites left behind by some of Maine's earliest colonists. John Hancock is famous for his oversize signature on the Declaration of Independence and the insurance company named after him. What's not so well known is his checkered past as a businessman. Hancock was the proprietor of Hancock Wharf, a failed enterprise that's but one of the intriguing historic sites in York Village, a fine destination for those curious about early American history. Settled in 1624, York Village has several early buildings open to the public. A good place to start is **Jefferds Tavern,** across from the handsome old **burying ground.** Changing exhibits document various facets of early life. Next door is the **School House,** furnished as it might have been in the 19th century. A 10-minute walk on Lindsay Road brings you to **Hancock Wharf,** next door to the **George Marshall Store.** Also nearby is the **Elizabeth Perkins House,** with its well-preserved Colonial Revival interior. The one don't-miss structure is the intriguing **Old Gaol,** built in 1719 with musty dungeons for criminals. (The jail is the oldest surviving public building in the U.S.) Just down the knoll is the **Emerson-Wilcox House,** built in the mid-1700s. Added to periodically over the years, it's a virtual catalog of architectural styles and early decorative arts. *5 Lindsay Rd., York.* ☎ *207/363-4974. Admission $7 adults, $3 children 4–16, free for children under 4. Tues–Sat 10am–5pm; Sun 1–5pm (last tour at 4pm). Closed mid-Oct to mid-June.*

Almost every unit has a view of the water. Pretty York Harbor Beach is a few steps away, where you can sun or swim, and the two clay oceanside tennis courts—reserved for guests—are quite popular as well. *Stage Neck (P.O. Box 70), York Harbor, ME 03911.* ☎ *800/340-1130 or 207/363-3850. www. stageneck.com. 58 units. May to Labor Day $235–$345 double; early fall $185–$255 double; winter $135–$185 double; spring $165–$210 double. Amenities: 2 dining rooms indoor pool; outdoor pool; tennis courts; fitness room; Jacuzzi; sauna; room service; in-room massage. In room: A/C, TV/VCR, dataport, fridge, coffeemaker, hair dryer.*

Eating

Restaurants in Maine boast some of the most delicious seafood in the country, and because there is so much of it, it's comparatively cheap, well, compared to other places around the U.S.

TAKEOUT

➜ **Anthony's Food Shop** DELI/PIZZA In addition to a variety of fresh pizzas, burgers, and subs, Anthony's also offers a great breakfast menu complete with their signature Green Mountain coffee. Be sure to check out Papa Tony's specialty pizzas like the Roman Holiday (with eggplant, tomato, olives, and artichoke hearts) or the Double Cheeseburger (double hamburger with extra cheese). *679 Rte. 1., York* ☎ *207/363-2322. www.anthonysfoodshop. com. Sandwiches $4–$6; pizzas $11–$18. Daily, 6am–closing.*

EATING OUT
Cheap/Doable

➔**Bob's Clam Hut** ★ FRIED SEAFOOD
In business since 1956 (takeout only until 1989), Bob's has an old-fashioned flavor—despite being surrounded by slick factory outlet malls—while serving up heaps of fried clams and other diet-busting entice-ments with great efficiency. Order at the front window, get a soda from a vending machine, then stake out a table inside or on the deck with a Route 1 view, waiting for your number to be called. The fare is sur-prisingly light, cooked in cholesterol-free vegetable oil; onion rings are especially good. *Rte. 1, Kittery.* ☎ *207/439-4233. Reservations not accepted. Sandwiches $1.50–$4.95; dinners $5.25–$19. Daily Memorial Day to Labor Day 11am–7pm (Sat–Sun till 8pm). Open year-round, hours vary in off season.*

➔**Chauncey Creek Lobster Pier** ★★
LOBSTER POUND Okay, lobster's not exactly "cheap," but it's cheaper here at a roadside lobster pound than it is almost anywhere else. Chauncey's is one of the best lobster pounds in the state, not least because the Spinney family, which has been selling lobsters here since the 1950s, takes such pride in the place. You reach the pound by walking down a wooden ramp to a broad deck on a tidal inlet, where some 42 festively painted picnic tables await. Lobster is the specialty, of course, but steamed mussels (in wine and garlic) and clams are also available. BYOB. Feel free to bring along your own cooler full of beer, wine, soda, chips, watermelon, and what-have-you. *Chauncey Creek Rd. (between Kittery Point and York off Rte. 103; watch for signs), Kittery Point.* ☎ *207/439-1030. Reservations not accepted. Market-priced lob-sters; other items $1.50–$13. Daily 11am–8pm (until 7pm during shoulder seasons); closed Mon after Labor Day. Closed Columbus Day to Mother's Day.*

➔**Goldenrod Restaurant** ★ AMERICAN
This beach-town classic is the place for local color—it's been a summer institution in York Beach since 1896. It's easy to find: Look for visitors gathering at the plate-glass windows watching ancient taffy machines churn out saltwater taffy in volumes large enough (9 million candies a year) to keep busloads of dentists wealthy. The restau-rant, behind the taffy and fudge operation, is short on gourmet fare, long on atmos-phere. Diners sit around a stone fireplace or at an antique soda fountain. Meals are basic and filling: waffles, griddle cakes, club sandwiches, egg and bacon sandwiches. *Railroad Rd. and Ocean Ave., York Beach.* ☎ *207/363-2621. www.thegoldenrod.com. Main courses: breakfast $2.75–$5.50, lunch and dinner $2.95–$8. Memorial Day to Labor Day daily 8am–10pm (until 9pm in June); Labor Day to Columbus Day Wed–Sun 8am–3pm. Closed Columbus Day to Memorial Day.*

Shopping
ANTIQUING

Coastal Maine is paradise for antiques collectors and those looking to find inter-esting alternatives to mainstream depart-ment stores. Take a ride down **Route 1** in York Beach, ME, and you'll be inundated by antiques shops on every side of the street. A map with the exact location of antiques shops can be obtained for free at the **Maine Welcome Center** along I-95.

FLEA MARKETS

If the antiques shops don't suit your fancy, be sure to check out southern Maine's largest flea market, the **Cascade Flea Market** located at the corner of Route 1 and 98 in Saco (☎ **207/282-8875**). The market is open from May through October, weather permitting, and it's a great place to find both new and used clothing and merchandise.

M T V 🛈 Museum of Cryptozoology ★★★

Crypto . . . what? We couldn't end this weird excursion without dipping our fingers briefly into one more taboo subject . . . cryptozoology. Yes, that would be "the study of hidden animals," a field that combines archaeology, zoology, and anthropology, and goes on the hunt for mythic creatures like Bigfoot, the Dover Demon, feejee mermaid, Nessie, the Mothman, and plenty of others. Basically, they study these creatures and try to prove (or disprove) their existence. Even if Cryptozoology 101 wasn't an accredited major at your school, you can still dig your hands into it by visiting the "unofficial" **Museum of Cryptozoology** (**www.lorencoleman.com**) in Portland.

The museum also happens to be the home of the internationally acclaimed cryptozoologist Loren Coleman. There is no charge to enter the museum but finding it could prove to be a little tough, since it's in his home and there is no sign outside. Make sure you check out the website and contact him before you visit. His website will also provide you with a lot more information of cryptozoology in addition to articles and books on the field.

OTHER SHOPS OF INTEREST

Among the coastal boutiques, you'll be sure to find some treasures. York's downtown shopping area has stores that will perk interest in everyone ranging from the avid surfers to antiques collectors, treasure hunters, artists, and trendy fashionistas. Among the ones I loved to browse along Route 1 are:

Gravestone Artwear (250 York St.; York Beach; ☎ 207/351-1434; www.gravestoneartwear.com) is a store with items to die for. Here is the place where you can buy gravestone rubbing supplies, medieval pendants, jewelry, ghost stories and other reference books, velvet cloaks, and more. You'll wish you found this spot earlier in the trip.

Visit the **Lighthouse Depot** (US Rte. 1 N., Wells, ME; ☎ 207/646-0608; www.LighthouseDepot.com) for some lighthouse memorabilia. Aside from learning about the rich history and legends surrounding lighthouses, you can pick up collectibles, books, arts, handcrafts, furnishings, and clothing, yes, all dedicated to the magnificent lighthouse.

For the funkiest handmade home furnishings, be sure to stop by **Painted Treasures** (264 Rte. 1; ☎ 207/363-5460; www.paintedtreasuresbyphyllis.com). Each of the pieces is hand-painted by New England artists. Painted Treasures is the place to go for the best pillow accents, tablecloths, ceramics, ceramic jewelry sets, and furniture pieces. I can guarantee that you've never seen anything quite like this anywhere else.

Playing Outside

BEACHES

York Beach consists of two beaches—**Long Sands Beach** ★ and **Short Sands Beach**—separated by a rocky headland and a small island capped by scenic **Nubble Light.** When tide is out, both offer plenty of room for sunning and throwing Frisbees. When tide is in, they're both cramped. Short Sands fronts the town of York Beach and is better for families with kids, with its candlepin bowling and video arcades.

Long Sands runs along Route 1A, across from a profusion of motels, summer homes, and convenience stores. Changing rooms, public restrooms, and metered parking (50¢ per hour) are available at both beaches; local restaurants and vendors provide other services, including snacks.

What a Long, Strange Trip It's Been . . .

And we hope you enjoyed yourself on this meander up the creepy East Coast. Maybe you'll keep an eye out for the paranormal close to home now. Maybe you'll just pull out a filling chomping on saltwater taffy.

But as you now know, even if the truth *isn't* out there, a good time is just waiting down the road.

Down the Shore: Wet & Wild on the East Coast

Text & Photos by Nick Honachefsky

S hake the sand out of your bedsheets, whip out the string bikinis (or Speedos!), and get ready to plant your feet in the sands of the greatest summertime Happy Hour known to man. Everybody's got a "shore story": night swimming in the Atlantic, grinding against your partner in oceanside bars barely clothed, and pouring margaritas down the hatch as the sunset or sunrise creases the horizon. We've spent considerable time over the summer(s) mastering the art of Going Down the Shore, and are happy to pass along our accumulated wisdom (or what we can remember).

Now you have to understand, I'm from Jersey. That means "the Shore" (or "Down the Ocean" as they say in Maryland) is comprised of beach towns from the North Jersey Coast down to Ocean City, MD; summertime destinations for over a century, coming into their own post-WWII and despite some downspins here and there, never really out of style. If you grew up in the mid-Atlantic, chances are your family brought you to one of these beach towns as a kid for 2 weeks every summer; you might have had your first kiss on a boardwalk here; spent a few summers in high school or college dishing fries at Thrashers or lifting kids onto rides; sharing a house or apartment with a bunch of buddies; and eventually, you'll be the Mom or Dad bringing your kids here. It's the circle of life, man.

So in this journey, we're starting at the top and heading south on a ride that might earn you a trip to jail (but we really hope not!) or setting you up with that oh-so-romantic fantastic Mr. or Ms. Right (or Right Now). The Jersey Coast is a legendary

When the sun goes down, there's still plenty of action Down the Shore.

scene of wet and wild all-out partying: MTV put its infamous Beach House here for 2 years. Starting from the flashy, tacky boardwalks at Point Pleasant, Seaside Heights, and Ocean City (NJ), we'll head south for Wildwood's blinking lights and Atlantic City's casinos, to the Cape May's end-of-land serenity in a Victorian town. From Cape May you'll drive onto a boat (the Cape May-Lewes Ferry), which will take you across the Delaware Bay over to the laid-back Delaware Coast's surreal scenic backdrops with fantastic fare and low key, yet happening, bistros and bars, all the way down to Ocean City (MD's) boisterous 156 oceanside avenues of boardwalk bling and seductive bayside bars.

The Shore nightlife scene is not only a birthright for East coasties, it's a mandatory test to see if you've got what it takes to call yourself a Party Animal. In addition to the mayhem and madness of $1 shots and wet T-shirt contests, we'll guide you to the secluded nooks and crannies to kick back and take it slow and low in the natural beauty and silence of untouched pockets of protected, undeveloped stretches like Island Beach State Park (NJ), Delaware Seashore, and Assateague State Park (MD).

You'll find some world-class surf breaks at Manasquan Inlet (NJ), launch a pumpkin out of a cannon in Delaware, and check out some wild ponies (we're talking about little *horses!*) in Maryland. Sometimes life's a bitch. But Down the Shore, life's a beach.

Superlatives: The Highs & Lows

→ **Worst Drink Known to Man: GutBuster,** Macky's Bayside Bar & Grill. To prove that humans will drink anything as long as it gets you drunk faster, Macky's Bar in Ocean City, MD, offers the

GutBuster, a 24-ounce can of Keystone beer topped with a shot of 151 on top, all for the low, low price of $2. See p. 247.

→ **Best Chance at Hooking Up: Seacrets.** A total of 17 bars on the bayside of Ocean

City, MD, offer not only convenient hiding and hanging out spots, but they even offer tube rafts on the water in the bay to shag. See p. 249.

→ **Coolest Blues Bar: Ragin' Cajun,** Belmar, NJ. Eat alligator sausage while getting blanketed by Billy Hector and Stringbean and the Stalkers grinding blues riffs in a 20×20 dining room. See p. 193.

→ **Most Eclectic Scene: Seaside Heights, NJ.** It's a mix of surfers, punks, Gucci hoochies, stray children and dogs, as everyone competes at (or watches) tons of mindless boardwalk games to launch huge rubber frogs with mallets and win a life-sized stuffed Barney. See p. 196.

→ **Creepiest Overheard Remark: Broadway Bar and Grill,** Point Pleasant Beach, NJ. Salty commercial fisherman with a tattoo of a giant squid on his back: "Yeah, we've dragged up some weird stuff out there.

Airplanes, missles, a few dead guys. One had a nice Rolex on. Still works." See p. 206.

→ **Surfer's Paradise: Manasquan Inlet NJ.** World-class East Coast break pumps with 4- to 8-foot waves on the north jetty for some glassy, tasty tubes. See p. 196.

→ **Most Silent Stretch: Lewes DE to Fenwick Island.** The quietest leg of the trip by far, except for the stopovers in Rehoboth Beach and Dewey. It's not a long trip, but it is a good time to hit a nearby section of Delaware Seashore State Park to regroup or relish in coastline beauty. See p. 238.

→ **Best Use of $35 on a boat: Captain Mike Bogan of the *Gambler* fishing charter boat:** "The cost of getting on a trip? We'll take you out there for free. You just gotta pay $35 for us to bring you back." See p. 208.

Just the Facts

Trip in a Box

Total Miles From Sandy Hook, NJ, to Ocean City, MD, approximately 350 miles.

Route Route 36 to Route 35 along the Jersey Coast, the Garden State Parkway (GSP) exits for Long Beach Island, Ocean City, NJ, and Sea Isle City locales, Cape May Ferry to Lewes DE, Route 1 South to Delaware Beaches and Ocean City, MD.

States New Jersey, Delaware, Maryland

Trip Time Six days to hit it all from Sandy Hook, NJ, to Ocean City, MD, though you could make the drive in 2 to 3 days.

The Short Version This trip can be done in about 4 days, but the 350 miles covered are so tightly packed with stuff to see and do, you can spend 3 days in one locale and not see half of what's there.

The Long Version You could definitely spend at least 10 days on this trip if you really want to see it all. It's mostly a straight shot down the Eastern Seaboard, sometimes with 25 mph zones and stop lights every block slowing the pace down.

Down the Shore Roadtrip

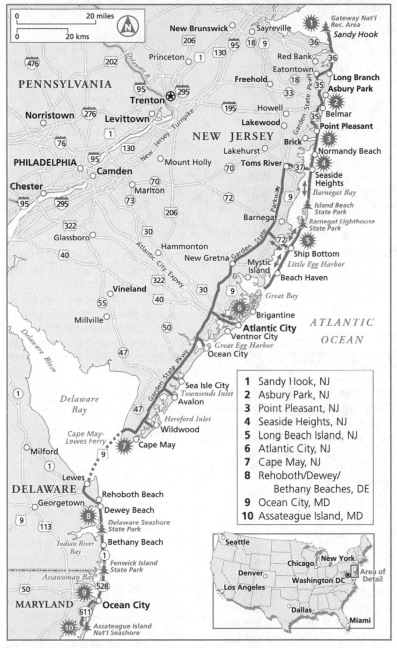

1	Sandy Hook, NJ
2	Asbury Park, NJ
3	Point Pleasant, NJ
4	Seaside Heights, NJ
5	Long Beach Island, NJ
6	Atlantic City, NJ
7	Cape May, NJ
8	Rehoboth/Dewey/ Bethany Beaches, DE
9	Ocean City, MD
10	Assateague Island, MD

Hitting the Highlights The good news is that most highlights in any locale are all within a few miles of each other, so you won't waste any time traveling so much. Break it up to hit the North and Central Jersey (80 miles), Long Beach Island (70 miles), South Jersey (90 miles), Rehoboth and Dewey (40 miles), to Ocean City, MD (20 miles).

When to Go Flat out summertime from Memorial Day to Labor Day. It's the shore, man! Sun, bikinis, Jacuzzis, suntan lotion, mindless noontime drinking, and the Atlantic Ocean work best in the heat of the summer. Get on it! But . . . if you can't get away (or can't afford the high prices) during the summer, the "season" (particularly the farther south you go) has been expanding into early May and well into the fall over the last few years. You can find lodging bargains at the hotels/B&Bs that have opened already or not yet closed for the winter; it's possible to eat at uncrowded restaurants, and stroll along nearly deserted beaches and boardwalks (and still party with the locals). You won't be swimming and tanning, but there's still plenty to see and do, and it is a good time to chill out, particularly with a good friend or sweetie.

The Money Part

Make sure the ATM card is ready to be abused, and fatten up that wallet. Constant cover charges, booze runs, rides and games, taxis, and outrageous hotel rates will up your budget considerably, but you'll have fun spending it. A day and night out can run from $50 to $100 bucks if you go out to party. If you throw one where you're staying, it'll be cheaper but you'll be missing out on the nightlife scene. Summertime prices go way up in the shore towns, but Happy Hour specials, cheap pizza and sandwiches, and affordable buffet-style meals can help stem the flow of cash from your wallet.

ACCOMMODATIONS

Hotels run the gamut from cheapo $49 nights in places of dubious location and amenities, to $350 a night (and up!) if you have to have an ocean view and a fluffy bathrobe.

The seasonal swing in prices is dramatic. From Memorial Day through Labor Day, the price range at the cheap end for decent places runs from about $79 to $149 for a double with something like a kitchenette

or at least a fridge, a hotel pool, and Jacuzzi privileges, with some discount coupons for local establishments thrown in.

Off-season rates can run from $49 for perfectly acceptable digs to less than $200 for some really fine lodgings in the spring and fall. If you plan on spending weekends at the shore in-season, note that many hotels require a minimum 2 to 3 day stay, and will not book single night stays, so plan accordingly. There is a noticeable lack of campgrounds along this route, as most of the land along the coast has been developed (or overdeveloped) though some state parks do offer campground accommodations. Note that New Jersey has a state "Room Occupancy" tax of 5%.

TRANSPORTATION

You won't be spending a ton of money on gas this trip, and depending on whether you have a gas guzzler or subcompact, you can expect to spend from $35 to $50, depending on whether there's another huge price hike come summer. You may also spend a few dollars on tolls when you are traveling on the Garden State Parkway (GSP), a limited-access highway that runs most of the length of the Jersey Coast. The standard car toll is 35¢ on the main road at two-way toll plazas and 70¢ at one-way toll plazas. Some individual exits require a toll of either 70¢, 35¢, or 25¢. Both the Turnpike and the Parkway now allow for payment with the E-Zpass.

You will be spending more money on cab rides that can run from $10 to $40 depending on how far you go and how many people you can split the bill with. *Note*: Taxi rates are usually the same throughout the year, but cabdrivers will usually inflate rates on their own during summer season; if you get a rate from the dispatcher over the phone, hold the driver to it!

Public transportation, with several towns offering convenient buses and trolleys, generally runs a reasonable $2 to $5 to get you around town. Most hotels offer free parking, and almost every town has parking meters (which take quarters, and generally charge 25¢ an hour).

If you're driving all the way down, you'll have to pay for **The Cape May-Lewes Ferry** from Cape May, NJ, to Lewes, DE, across the Delaware Bay. It costs $54 round-trip, and $29 one-way with your car during the high season, from April through October. Fares are $23 one-way and $38 round-trip from November to March.

FOOD

Just how badly do you want that lobster and shrimp dinner? Shore food can be extremely affordable, as innumerable shoreside shacks offer NY and NJ style pizza slices, Philly cheesesteaks, fries, and fountain Cokes that can make a meal for under $5; but if you want to splurge, you can always find an ultra-fresh seafood dinner to consume while you're watching the sun set over the bay or ocean, especially in Point Pleasant, NJ, or Ocean City, MD, for as low as $15 to $30. All-you-can-eat buffet deals of $6.95 to $13 are offered everywhere from breakfast through dinner, and classic joints such as the **Chicken or the Egg** (p. 215) in Long Beach Island, NJ, and the **Ocean Bay Diner** (p. 203) in Point Pleasant Beach, NJ, are open 24/7.

Be smart about your budget; if you want quality food at least once a day, eat the boardwalk food for breakfast and lunch, and go nuts at dinner. Or if you've got a room with a kitchenette or minifridge, bring along breakfast food and sandwich fixings and other snacks for a meal or two a day.

OTHER EXPENSES

New Jersey beaches charge for use of the sands, and daily **beach badges** will run you from $3 to $7, weekly badges will hit you for around $20, and you can buy a season pass for $40 if you plan on coming back. (A beach badge is just that: a plastic pass that you must display on your bag or swimsuit when you go on the beach.)

Plan on spending $25 to $40 for charter boat fishing trips, which includes rod and reel rental and bait.

You can't pass up hitting the serenity and wonder of the **National Parks** of **Sandy Hook** and **Island Beach** State Parks in NJ, the **Delaware Seashore National Park,** and the **Assateague National Park** in MD. Daily usage fees run from $5 to $10. If you're planning on staying over at a campground, fees will cost you $16 to $20 a night.

If you want to let the air out of the tires and do a little **beach-buggying,** a 3-day permit runs $50. For the entire season, it's $195 at Island Beach State Park. And if you get too close to one of the wild ponies of Assateague, then budget for a visit to the emergency room and the painkillers and some dressings for the hoofmarks on your chest.

Starting Out: Sandy Hook to Manasquan, NJ

DOWN THE SHORE

North Jersey Shore Nuts & Bolts

Area Code The telephone area code in North Jersey is 732.

Dentist 2640 Hwy. 70, Bldg. 8, Suite 101A Manasquan (☎ 732/528-2205).

Emergencies Call ☎ 911 if you need the police, the fire department, or an ambulance.

Hospitals If you need healthcare services in the northern part of the state, you should go to Monmouth Medical Center, 300 Second Ave. Long Branch (☎ 732/222-5200).

Laundry To clean up try Manasquan Dry Cleaners, 83 Main St., Manasquan (☎ 732-223-0711).

Libraries Manasquan Library 55 Broad St. ,Manasquan (☎ 732/223-1503); Sea Bright Library, 1097 Ocean Ave., Sea Bright (☎ 732/758-9554).

Newspapers & Magazines The daily *Asbury Park Press* (www.app.com) covers all local and national angles; *The Islander* is the summertime periodical to dial you in to seasonal happenings.

Pharmacies Diamond's Pharmacy is at 444 Ocean Blvd., Long Branch (☎ 732/222-1299).

Police The Long Branch Police Department is at 344 Broadway, Long Branch (☎ 732/222-1000).

Post Office Brielle Post Office, 412 Higgins Ave., Brielle (☎ 732/528-6112).

Taxes Taxes are 7% statewide.

Getting Around

This part of the trip is basically a straight shot down the northern coast down New Jersey Route 36 (which begins just off the GSP at Tinton Falls) and Route 35 that parallels the coastline. In Belmar, you can jump on Route 71 to take you into the heart of Belmar

The Route 36 corridor is a straight shot down the northern part of the coast buffeted by large 15-foot seawalls on the ocean side and million dollar mansions on the river side, with most restaurants and watering holes a simple turn off the road. **Third Avenue** in Belmar and **Manasquan** town hold the collegiate raucous and rowdy club scene, as the riverside bars and restaurants dotted along the **Manasquan River** host some more laid-back venues with breathtaking views and breezy ambience.

BY CAR

You won't find many public parking spaces from Sandy Hook to Long Branch, except in parking lots for restaurants and bars. Along the Route 36 Sea Bright to Bradley Beach stretch, you'll find parking meters that cost 25¢ per 15 minutes.

BY TRAIN

The **Jersey Coast Line** of **NJ Transit** trains run from Penn Station NYC to Bay Head and hits most towns in this part of

It's all right to hit another car here, but not on the Garden State Parkway!

the Jersey Coast, stopping every 5 minutes or so. Long Branch, Asbury Park, Sea Bright, and Manasquan stations are on this line, and you can pop on and off the train with town-to-town tickets running $3 to $14 round-trip. For schedules and rates,

GPS? No, GSP!

Not to be confused with "The Turnpike" (aka "The New Jersey Turnpike"), the other major toll-road in New Jersey is the **Garden State Parkway (GSP),** a road that runs along the coast from Paramus in North Jersey down to Cape May (Exit 0) at the very tip of the South Jersey coast. From start to finish, it'll cost about $3.85 in tolls, but the annoying thing is that the cost is broken up with tollbooths every few miles where you'll be nickel-and-dimed (or 35¢) to death, depending on which direction you're traveling. Have small bills, pocket change, or an E-ZPass in the window.

visit **www.njtransit.com**. This is actually a relatively fun, convenient way to get around here without worrying about driving.

Starting Out: Sandy Hook, NJ

The North Jersey shore officially begins right here, at **Sandy Hook** at the **Gateway National Recreation Area** ★★. Here you'll find 7 miles of beaches, evening beach concerts, hiking trails, salt marshes, and over 300 species of birds to watch.

Ranger tours are available year-round through the sands and sedges. **Sandy Hook Visitor's Center** at Spermaceti Cove is an 1894 U.S. Life-Saving Station that features exhibits on the peninsula's natural environment. It's open daily 10am to 5pm.

The beacon of the Hook is the historic **Sandy Hook Lighthouse.** Built at the request of New York City merchants wanting to protect their ships entering the harbor, it was lighted for the first time on June 11, 1764. The octagonal tower was the fifth lighthouse in the colonies and remains the oldest operating lighthouse in the U.S. today.

North Jersey Coast Events

There's always something cooking in season or off season down the shore, usually revolving around sandy sports and the beach way of life. Here are a few ideas to drop in on:

→ If you're in the mood to see some balls get hit around, be sure to stop by the Belmar beaches during the first week in July where the **AVP (American Volleyball Professional) Tour** ★★ kicks it on their nationwide circuit. See top pros like Karch Kiraly serve, dig, and spike around and kick up some sand. ☎ **877/AVP-TIXX.**

→ Since 1974 a very green **Belmar St. Patrick's Day Parade** ★ shakes down Main Street in Belmar, the first or second weekend in March. Entertained by 5,500 marchers, 40 bands, 20 floats, and a lot of fire engines, this gathering is an all-out wintertime hootenanny, attended by a mass of over 200,000 spectators swilling umpteen thousands of gallons of green beer in 2006. Even if you've never kissed the Blarney Stone, you're guaranteed to end up kissing someone. ☎ **732/681-6262.**

→ Ho, ho, ho . . . or something. Barbizon **models** liven up downtown Red Bank around Thanksgiving weekend, posing in the shop windows as live mannequins. It draws a crowd. 1 Broad St., Red Bank. ☎ **732/842-4244.** www.redbankrivercenter.org.

Occupied by British soldiers during the American Revolution, it was bombarded by cannons and overtaken by Patriot troops. Open to climb on Saturdays and Sundays from April through mid-December. Be sure to also visit the **Fort Hancock Historic District** overlooking Sandy Hook Bay, housing Revolutionary War gun batteries and over 100 historic buildings (Route 36, Highlands ☎ 732/872-5970).

The first of the Jersey Shore towns proper is Asbury Park, which is finally emerging from a decades-long decline to become a shore destination once more. That rebirth has endangered what was until recently the town's most famous venue, the awesome and historic **Stone Pony,** ★★★ which is still kicking along at the shore (surrounded by new development). The vibe is electric and rich in tradition here and the venue offers top-line performers such as Johnny Winter, Method Man, Buckethead, and if you hit it right, you may be graced by random cameo appearances by none other than Jersey's rock godfathers Bruce Springsteen or Jon Bon Jovi. Shows run year-round; check the most recent venues at www.stonepony online.com. It's at 913 Ocean Ave. (directly across the street from the boardwalk and beach), Asbury Park (☎ 732/502-0600).

Sleeping

With multimillion-dollar McMansions chockablock along the coast, there is a noticeable lack of inexpensive hotels and motels along this stretch. You won't find many old-school beachside family-owned establishments here; though, if you have a bit of dough to spend, you can get a high-class setup for the night. To save a few bucks, you'll be staying farther off the beachfront and heading inland. In fact, I'd say it's better to move down to the Central Jersey Coast to stay for the night, where cheapo motels run rampant and cab rides to the nighttime spots aren't too expensive.

That said, here are a few places to spend the night on the North Jersey coast.

CHEAP

➔ **Travelodge Wall Spring Lake Belmar** Get wet in the largest outdoor swimming pool in the area, (36x30). The motel's 52 rooms encircle a grassy courtyard picnic/barbeque/fun area where you can play Frisbee golf and cook up some burgers and steaks. It's not that far from the beach (about a half-mile). *1916 State Highway 35, Wall.* ☎ *732/974-8400. www.travelodge.com. 52 units. $69–$109 single to double. Amenities: Iron; hair dryer; coffeemaker.*

DOABLE/SPLURGE

➔ **Bradley Beach Inn** ★ Eight oceanview rooms furnished in a traditional beach house style with oceanview porches and wood-shingled exterior are on offer here. Each has air-conditioning, which is only occasionally needed at the shore, but nice to have during a hot spell, and you also get a complimentary breakfast on the extended front porch. It's mere steps to beach, and quite popular, so book ahead of time. *900 19th Bradley Beach Ocean Ave.* ☎ *732/774-0414. Midweek specials Sun–Thurs starting at $60 per night, breakfast included. Weekend rates from $105–$165 single or double. Amenities: Cable TV.*

➔ **Breakers Hotel** ★★ Basically, this is a huge mansion on the Spring Lake beachfront, a throwback to early Jersey Shore days when people stayed at boardinghouses at the shore. Rooms here are decorated with a beachy motif (what a surprise!), in sea-glassy colors of sky blue, alabaster white, and light pink. Watching the sun rise from the oceanfront view windows is a soul-satisfying experience. *1506 Ocean Ave., Spring Lake.* ☎ *732/449-7700. www.thebradleybeachinn.com. $100–$290 single queen-size bed; $220–$435 in season for oceanfront. Amenities: Private bathroom; TV; telephone; A/C; minifridge; pool; private beach.*

➔ **Evergreen Inn Bed and Breakfast** ★★★ This 130-year-old beach villa offers themed rooms: The White Pine room has a whitewashy nautical vibe; the Juniper room a rustic, cozy, log cabin feel; and spread throughout the inn are quaint antique clocks and maritime *objets,* such as colorful hurricane polished glass. Double whirlpools, in-wall electric fireplaces, and private balconies in rooms are enhanced by an eye-opening, award-winning breakfast. Go ahead, treat yourself. *206 Hwy. 71 Spring Lake.* ☎ *732/449-9019. www.evergreeninn.net. 10 units. $229–$279 per night queen-size beds. Amenities: Cable TV.*

ᴹᵀᵛ🔵 **Big Time Brawling (and Where to Learn It!)**
....

Pro wrestling, the **WWE (World Wrestling Entertainment),** and **ECW (Extreme Championship Wrestling)** owe some serious props to Jersey for churning out some of the brawlingest backstreet bad dudes and vise-grip heavyweight contenders known in the squared circle. Hardcore pro wrestling fans know that former world heavyweight champ **Diamond Dallas Page,** as well as **Bam Bam Bigelow,** and **Kanyon** hail from the Jersey Shore, and that big time bullies **Balls Mahoney,** the **Sandman,** and **Raven** regularly enter the rings in Asbury Park to dole out damage in backbreaking matches at Ocean County Community College. Ever want to learn the Cobra Clutch or the recently outlawed Jackknife Powerbomb? Give a shout out to **Iron Mike Sharp's Wrestling School** in Asbury Park (☎ **908/750-1665**).

VCR, microwave, coffeemaker, award-winning Evergreen Breakfast

➔ **Ocean Place Resort & Spa** ★★ With its high-end, decadent ambience, you might feel a little awed walking into the stately Greek column lobby adorned with tropical Madagascar Dragon plants and ground palms. There's an outdoor whirlpool, open-air heated pool, and comprehensive fitness center. Rooms are complete with crisp linens and plush comfy pillows, a writing desk and work area in each room for business, and a large lounge sofa to catch a noontime nap. Spa treatments include massages and Reiki, full facials, exfoliation, hydrotherapy, and microdermabrasion. The Pier Village shopping district is directly adjacent to the resort as well as a relaxing promenade to soak in the inspiring surroundings. *1 Ocean Blvd., Long Branch.* ☎ *800/411-7321 or 732/571-4000. www.oceanplaceresort.com. 252 units. Off season single/double $99–$200; in season $300–$500. Amenities: Coffeemaker; ironing board; indoor pool.*

Eating

Fill up on snacks at places like **Windmill Hotdogs** (below), because there's no real meal deal in town. There are, however, waterfront bistros like **The Sandbar** and **Union Landing** on the Manasquan River where scrumptious seafood awaits. For a basic lunch, pick up a sandwich or salad at a convenience store, and head south for some solid maritime eats.

SUPPLIES & TAKE OUT TREATS

Stay on Ocean Avenue in Asbury Park and Ocean Grove, and you'll find many grocery stores where you can pick up grilling meat and vegetables, paper plates, and condiments for your own barbecue. Try **Wegman's** on Route 35 on Ocean Avenue in Ocean Grove.

There are also a few franchise sandwich shops like **Subway.** (But really, don't eat a cheesesteak from there when you're in Jersey at the shore! There are far more authentic places just around the bend.) We can, however, recommend **Bagels International,** 48 Main St., Bradley Beach (☎ **732/775-7447**), for a bag of bagels to munch on all day long. Be sure to grab a few "Everything" bagels; they're the best!

When it comes to North Jersey, there are a *lot* of pizza joints. Try **Federicos Pizza** at 705 Main St., Belmar (☎ **732/681-7066**) for some high-quality dough (after all, the dough makes the pizza).

Ice-cream treats can be found at the **Beach Plum Ice Cream Parlor,** 420 Main St., Bradley Beach (☎ **732/776-9122**), where the homemade ice-cream delights include Cookies & Cream and Strawberry Cheesecake flavors. Hours are 11am to midnight daily.

EATING OUT
Cheap

➔ **Pete and Eldas** ★ ITALIAN Specializing in platter-style thin-crust pizza, this place has billed itself as "The Original" for 50 years, with recipes straight from Sicily. Belly up to any of the 36 bar stools and crunch through the tangy tomato basil pies as you watch the big game on one of the eight plasma TVs. This is the definition of a great beer and pizza place. Get motivated and win a free P&E T-shirt if you can eat, *by yourself,* one extra, extra large pie. (And by then, you'll probably need an XXL T-shirt.) *96 Woodland Ave., Hwy. 35, Neptune City.* ☎ *732/774-6010. www.peteandeldas.com. Average entree $7–$12. Daily 11:30am–1:15am.*

➔ **Vic's Italian Restaurant** ★ ITALIAN/AMERICAN They've been serving Italian cuisine since 1947, for four generations, in the Guinco family, and at Vic's you'll find homestyle, crispy thin-crust pizza pies or sumptuous Shrimp a la Marinara dishes on the patio, complemented with a decent wine list. Try Bolla Valpolicella Classico to make your meal the complete Italian experience. *Corner of Evergreen Ave. and 60 Main St., Bradley Beach.* ☎ *732/774-8225. www.vics pizza.com. Tues–Thurs 11:30am–11pm; Fri–Sat 11:30am–midnight; Sun Noon–11:00pm.*

→ **Windmill** AMERICAN The ultimate Jersey dog: 4 ounces of crisp and crackly Sabrett hot dog on the sizzlin' griddle, burst open, hot juices rupturing the natural casing, ready for you to wolf down. A side of the ol' Krinkly Kut fries completes the equation for a fast, filling meal. *North Long Branch, 200 Ocean Ave.* ☎ *800/HOTDOG1. www.windmillhotdogs.com. $5–$10. Mon 11am–8pm; Tues 11am–8pm; Wed 11am–8pm; Thurs 11am–8pm; Fri 11am–9pm; Sat 11am–9pm; Sun 11am–8pm.*

Doable

→ **Bahr's Landing** ★ AMERICAN/SEAFOOD Steeped in maritime history, this dockside restaurant was established in 1917 by schooner captain John Bahrs, and the famous Jack's clam chowder is a must-eat, followed by fresh-off-the-dock lobster. If you're handy with a fishing rod, bring your catch in to be cooked, grilled, fried, or blackened for just $10. *2 Bay Ave., Highlands.* ☎ *732/872-1245. www.bahrs.com. Entrees $12–$23. Daily 11:30am–10:30pm summertime; Daily 11:30am–10pm off season.*

→ **Ragin Cajun'** ★★★ SEAFOOD/CAJUN This place is a deceptively humble, Mississippi-born, honey of a spot, set back in the shadows of Shark River. Once you're there, order a tastebud-popping Spicy Alligator Sausage and some Blackened Chicken Bites. The downhome ambience is electrified by live blues from String Bean and the Stalkers and Billy Hector's Blues Band. Simple and stylishly gritty, you may come in empty but you'll leave with a little

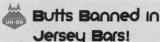

Butts Banned in Jersey Bars!

New Jersey put the cigarettes out all across the state and passed a law to prohibit smoking inside all restaurants and bars a couple years back, an excellent move considering you don't have to wake up smelling like you just sat downstairs in some college basement party. Most bars will allow you to loiter outside to light one up, making a sophomoric scene much like the old smoking halls in high school in the '80s.

bit of soul. *1102 River Rd., Belmar.* ☎ *732/ 280-6828. Soups and appetizers $5–$8; spicy entrees $10–$22. BYOB. Tues–Sun 5–10pm.*

→ **Sandbar** ★ AMERICAN/SEAFOOD Take a barstool on the outside balcony 20 feet above the Manasquan River and watch sportfishermen haul out mako sharks and yellowfin tuna onto the docks while you feast on fresh-off-the-boat shrimp and scallop dishes, and grilled ahi steaks that were on the same dock a few hours ago. Treat yourself with the Chilean sea bass Oregenatta for $23. *Brielle Yacht Club Marina, 201 Union Ave., Brielle.* ☎ *732/ 528-7750. www.sandbarrestaurant.com. Pizzas $8; entrees $10–$24. Daily; 11am–closing.*

Splurge

→ **Mahogany Grill** ★★★ SEAFOOD/AMERICAN/ASIAN Executive chef Jon Bugsy King's culinary artistic expertise presents high-class fare like Asian duck, and spring rolls rolled with sesame seeds, cucumber salad, and you'll find a Thai chili mango sauce on his signature dishes of braised short rib ravioli covered in a cauliflower cream sauce with cippolini onions and a side of English peas. Put away the sandals and T-shirts (there's a dress code).

But the food is worth dressing up for. *142 Main St., Manasquan.* ☎ *732/292-1300. www. themahoganygrille.com. Appetizers $8–$17; signature dishes $22–$34. Open for dinner 5–10pm, bar open at 4pm.*

Partying

Aside from a few oceanside clubs in **Sea Bright**, there's not much to the stretch from Sandy Hook to Long Branch in the way of lettin' loose, but once you hit the Belmar area down into Manasquan, the taps start flowing. Dockside bars like the ones on the **Manasquan River** offer light, breezy ambience, while off-beach clubs on **Main Street in Belmar** get tightly jammed with twenty-something roustabouts.

BARS, PUBS & CLUBS

➜ **Bar Anticipation** ★★ CLUB The premier club on the stretch, the just-21 scene packs the multileveled club for beat-the-clock drink specials from 4 to 7pm, and afterwards, woozy patrons attempt volleyball games on the sand court, bouncing between two outside bars and fueled by high-octane cover bands. The place can get ultra-packed, but there's plenty of room; still, you don't want to start up with someone: The 15 earpiece-wearing bouncers will have you on your face fast (trust me). Fun! *703-5 16th Ave., Lake Como.* ☎ *732/ 681-7422. www.bar-a.com. Cover $10 weekends.*

➜ **Boathouse Bar and Grill** ★ BAR Not just a high-end sports bar with 32 TV sets to watch the Yankees or whoever (Yankees rule here!), the place gets a fun crowd on Thursdays with $3 bottle specials to put down while playing pool, darts, Megatouch video games, Golden Tee Golf, and spontaneous games of Rock, Paper, Scissors. This is a Belmar favorite away from the crowds of the other clubs. *1309 Main St., Belmar.* ☎ *732/681-5221. www.boat housebarandgrill.com. $5 cover most summer weeknights.*

➜ **Donovan's Reef** ★ BAR/CLUB This hot spot is named after the John Wayne film and bills itself as the "only shore bar with its own private lifeguarded beach," where you can relax in summertime glory and lounge sipping margaritas underneath real palm trees, swim, play volleyball, eat, and listen to live cover bands pumping out tunes. There are plenty of laughs to be had with Bud specials every Saturday and $1 drafts the rest of week. *Route 36 Sea Bright.* ☎ *732/842-6789. www.donovansreefseabright. com. 11am–closing.*

➜ **Leggett's** ★ BAR/CLUB Jam packed with a crowd that waits to hear the results of the nightly spin-the-wheel drink specials every hour, random couples stumble hand in hand to the local rental houses afterwards to continue the block party or roll around on the beach. This spot is the hub of the Manasquan party scene; $5 Buckets of Miller Lites on Wednesdays start the afternoon off right. *217 First Ave., Manasquan.* ☎ *732/223-3951. www.leggetts. us. Cover on weekends $5.*

➜ **Parker House** ★ BAR Happy Hour Central for the more affluent summer beachgoer; you'll see lines of khaki-wearing polo shirted guys and girls in sundresses extending around the block, get packed in the downstairs bar, or filter out on the patio to suck down $1 Bud bottle Fridays. The rule of thumb is Guidos upstairs with the DJ, preppies downstairs. *1 Beacon Blvd.* ☎ *732/449-0442. www.theparker houseonline.com. Things start jumpin' after*

Word Up: Guido

Gui-do: (n.) Slick haired, muscle-bound, tight T-shirt North Jersey guy who loves techno dance music; takes his shirt off on the dance floor to flex. Yo-Yo-YO!

The Water Taxi Booze Cruise

The **party barge** on the Manasquan River sails between Union Landing, Sandbar, Jack Baker's Wharfside, and Clark's Landing, offering passage on sunset cruises to those who want to experience four waterfront bars in one night safely. For $20, you can ride the night train, well night *boat*, and even buy bottled beers for $4 on board if you can't wait 'til the boat docks. The whole circuit is about an hour long. Miss a stop? Who cares! Crack another one and catch the next ride. For info, call ☎ **732/528-9248**. Board at the Brielle Yacht Club docks by Union Landing.

5pm Fri–Sun, though open for business 11am–2am. Live band and DJ Fri–Sun and holidays. Reggae jams groove from 3–7pm Sat–Sun. Cover $5–$10 weekends.

➔ **Union Landing** ★★ PATIO BAR The drawing card of UL is an open-air dockside patio bar that whips up a mellow twenty- and thirty-something crowd into a summer breeze frenzy. Barefoot sportfishermen straight off the boat spin tales of the day's catch during late afternoon and early evening while the place fills up with a boisterous but contained younger crowd until last call, which lasts longer than you think. 622 Green Ave., Brielle. ☎ 732/528-6665. www. unionlanding.com. No cover.

What Else to See & Do

SHARK RIVER: FOSSILS, SKATING AND GOLF

Live that childhood dream of becoming a paleontologist, and hunt down some **fossil shark teeth** ★ at **Shark River Inlet.** Currents from the Shark River wash out thousands of shark teeth and other Cretaceous Era fossils from the fertile inland sediment out into the inlet and ocean. Your best bet for a good find is to hit the North Jetty at low tide and get close to the sand to sift through and find some pointy specimens.

Shark River is part of the Monmouth County Park System (☎ **732/842-4000**; www.mounmouthcountyparks.com) and

one of 33 beautifully preserved open spaces in the county. Another gorgeous park in the area is **Seven Presidents Park** ★ in Long Branch, where you'll find 38 acres of space, including an activity center, a boat launch, fishing, a playground, swimming area, sand volleyball courts, a pavilion with snack bar, and restrooms.

Admission and parking fees are charged from Memorial Day weekend through Labor Day weekend. In-season beach badges are $40 for ages 12 to 16; $50 for adults 17 to 64; and $20 for adults 65 and older, and are available for purchase 9am to 4pm daily at the park's pavilion on Ocean Avenue in Long Branch. Season parking passes are $50. Admission is free during the rest of the year. The park is open every day from 8am to dusk.

Inside Seven Presidents is one of the state's finest skate parks. **Skateplex** ★ is at the North end of the park, and features a short paved trail, landscaped open play areas, restrooms, drink machines, a picnic area with tables, parking, and two areas exclusively for skaters. There is a 75x150-foot rink for in-line skating, hockey, and lessons; and a skatepark for both skateboarders and in-line skaters with a bowl and a series of quarter pipes, wedges, and fun boxes. Open year-round.

Feelin' a little Caddyshack? Designed by Scottish golf pro Joseph "Scotty" I'Anson in the early 1900s, **Shark River Golf Course** features tight, narrow fairways; deep-faced bunkers; and the challenge of small, well-protected greens. The holes vary from a short, drivable par 4 to a long, risky par 5, with some strong par 3 holes mixed in. Avoid the gophers to receive "full and total consciousness" (Thanks, Bill Murray!). It's at 320 Old Corlies Rd. in Neptune (☎ 732/922-4141). Greens fees for 18 holes run from $23 to $27 week-day/weekends. Tee times are available through the tee time reservation system after the purchase of a Monmouth County Resident ID card or a Non-Resident Reservation ID Card. Reserve a tee time at www.monmouthcountygolf.org, or call ☎ 732/758-8383.

MORE PLAYING OUTSIDE

Fishing/Kayaking/Surfing

The way to kick back and feel like the Old Man of the Sea is to rent a 16-foot boat with an 8-horsepower engine for $60 a day from **Fisherman's Den** in Belmar (☎ 732/681-5005) at the Belmar Marine Basin. You can cast off on the Shark River, drop a line baited with a bloodworm or clam to fish for fluke, bluefish, and porgies all day long in the saltwater river or set out traps and crablines off the gunwale to pull a bushel of blueclaws into the boat for an evening crab bake. You'll be the hit of the barbecue, and known as King of Crabs (and that's a good thing).

A half-mile inside the Manasquan River lies an island locally known as **Treasure Island.** Originally it was called Osborn Island. Robert Louis Stevenson, vacationing in the area, called it "Treasure Island" in 1888, 5 years after his novel of the same name was published. Its official name is now Nienstedt Island, in honor of the family who donated the land to the borough. It is home to indigenous marine waterfowl such as merganser ducks, cormorants, osprey, and is surrounded by marine life like clams, oysters, weakfish, and bluefish. Rent a kayak at **Manasquan Kayak Rentals,** 537 Main St., Manasquan (☎ 732/292-1987), and tour it for yourself.

A world-class **surf break** is at the Manasquan Inlet's north jetty. If you don't have your own, you can pick up a surfboard from **Inlet Outlet** surf shop, 146 Main St., Manasquan (☎ 732/224-5842; www.inletoutlet.com). Enter the lineup and ride a right-oriented wave that peels off the north Manasquan Jetty rocks, which are protected from the wind, and hang on as the wave glasses over the break, making for mind-bending rides and occasional tubes during hurricane groundswells.

Respect the lineup and wait your turn, as locals will not give out any breaks (and won't appreciate it if you cut the line). You can find other breaks just north of the inlet in Spring Lake off the jetties that break not as clean and perfect, but definitely less crowded.

On the Road: Point Pleasant to Seaside Heights

Sandy Hook, NJ to Point Pleasant, NJ 44 miles

The thing to remember on this trip is that the whole thing is one long destination packed with eclectically different venues all along this part of the coast. So when you're driving . . . you're there. This stretch hits the Barnegat Barrier Island and is stuffed with joints where you can get the freshest seafood, a 14-mile beach state park, picturesque beachfront mansions, two active inlets, and the most famous boardwalk on the coast.

New Jersey Coast: Point Pleasant to Bay Head

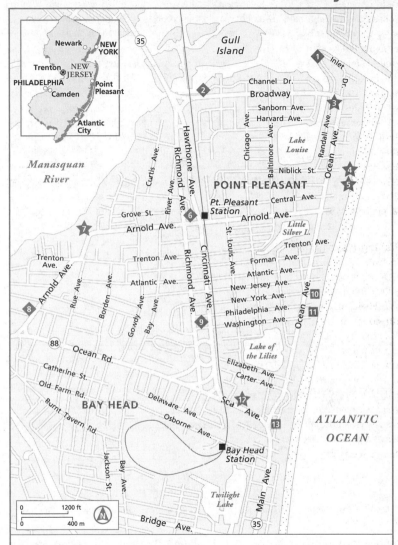

SLEEPING ■

Point Pleasant Manor **13**
Sand Pebble
  Motor Lodge **11**
White Sands Oceanfront Spa
  and Resort **10**

EATING ◆

Captain Ed's **8**
Frankie's Bar and Grill **6**
Red's Lobster Pot **1**
Spike's Fishmarket **2**
Surf Taco **9**

PARTYING ★

The Ark **12**
Broadway Bar and Grill **3**
Clark's Landing Bar and Grill **7**
Jenkinson's **4**
Martell's Tiki Bar **5**

On the Road Nuts & Bolts

Where to Fill Up   The town of Manasquan has plenty of Exxons and Valeros to gas up at. Self-service? What's that? In New Jersey, the station attendant pumps your gas (it's the law!).

The Tolls   None, unless you do the Garden State Parkway (GSP) shortcut then you'll pay 35¢ at exit 105 then 25¢ at exit 98.

Major Highways   Route 36 to Route 35.

The Back Roads   You can skip going through Asbury Park and Bradley Beach and hop on the Garden State Parkway, making a right off of Route 36 to Joline Avenue west, get on at exit 105 down to exit 98 to get to Manasquan. Stay on Route 34 south to Route 35 south. From Manasquan, hop on over to the Route 35 drawbridge, and Point Pleasant greets you on the other side.

Central Jersey Shore Nuts & Bolts

Area Code   The telephone area code in Central Jersey is 732.

Emergencies   Call ☎ 911 if you need the police, the fire department, or an ambulance.

Hospitals   For healthcare services in the central part of the shore go to Ocean Medical Center, 425 Jack Martin Blvd., Brick, ☎ 732/840-2200.

Laundry   To clean up try Bright & Kleen, Richmond Ave., Point Pleasant Beach, ☎ 732-892-5007.

Libraries   Grab a book to read at 710 McLean Ave., Point Pleasant, ☎ 732-892-4575. You can also access the Internet here.

Newspapers & Magazines   The daily *Asbury Park Press* (www.app.com) covers all local and national angles; the *Islander* is the summertime periodical to dial you in to seasonal happenings.

Pharmacies   Try the Eckerd, 1702 Grand Central Ave., Lavallette, ☎ 732/793-1910.

Police   Point Pleasant Boro Police at 2233 Bridge Ave., Point Pleasant, ☎ 732/892-0060; Seaside Heights Police, 116 Sherman Ave., Seaside Heights, ☎ 732/793-1800.

Post Office   Point Pleasant Post Office, 410 Arnold Ave., Point Pleasant.

Getting Around

Crossing over the Route 35 drawbridge into Point Pleasant, you officially land on the Barnegat Barrier Island, and enter the realm of pure shore Jerseyana. The state's two most popular boardwalks, **Jenkinson's** in Point Pleasant and **Casino Pier** in **Seaside Heights,** are lit up with crazily blinking multicolored lights, attracting hordes of visitors to miniature golf, games of chance (which may or may not be rigged), carnival rides, and tons of artery-clogging eats.

Playlist: Getting Some . . . Jersey Flavor

When driving in New Jersey, you are required by law to play at least one Bruce Springsteen or Bon Jovi song. No, not really. But it's a good idea to get into the Jersey state of mind.

→ *You Give Love a Bad Name*, **Bon Jovi**, "Slippery When Wet," 1986

→ *Jersey Girl*, **Bruce Springsteen**, "Live 1975–1985"

→ *Wanted Dead or Alive*, **Bon Jovi**, "Slippery When Wet," 1986

→ *Cold Beverage*, **G-Love and Special Sauce**, "G-Love and Special Sauce," 1994 (well, Philly!)

→ *Bad Medicine*, **Bon Jovi**, "New Jersey," 1988

→ *Thunder Road*, **Bruce Springsteen**, "Born To Run," 1975

→ *Red Dragon Tattoo*, **Fountains of Wayne**, "Utopia Parkway," 1999

BY CAR

On-street parking with meters is available along the stretch of Route 35 north or south in Long Branch and Sea Bright, except for Point Pleasant and Seaside Heights. Pre-pay public parking lots can be found at Jenkinson's and Seaside Heights, costing 25¢ for 15 minutes, and random open lots are always around, with hustlers charging anywhere from $8 to $15 for the day.

BY TAXI

If you plan on getting sloshed, be smart; take a cab, or most likely a van when you call up **Briggs Taxi Point Pleasant,** ☎ 732/892-1313 (ask for fast-talking Ted!), or **Aaaaa Nora Taxi & Limo Seaside Heights** (Gotta love being first in the phone book!), ☎ 732/830-6672. The vans are busy all night, picking up and dropping off people in the summertime swing. Beware a common scam: Some drivers tell you it'll be $15 for the ride out to wherever you're going, then charge $40 for the same ride back. Your best bet is to negotiate the entire fee beforehand, and get the taxi driver's name when you're quoted a price, and hold them to it when you arrange a pickup time.

BY TRAIN

NJ Transit trains run from Penn Station in Manhattan to Bay Head and hit most towns of the Jersey Coastline, with a stop every 5 to 10 minutes. Point Pleasant and Bayhead stations are the final stops on the line and lie in this section of coast. For schedules and rates, check **www.nj transit.com**.

Round-trip from Penn Station to Bay Head is $19.50. Shorter legs of the trip range from $2 to $15.

Sleeping

Keep in mind when you're booking any shore hotel, motel, or B&B on this trip that from Memorial Day to Labor Day you will be paying top prices, especially on weekends. There's no such thing as a discount during high season.

Many establishments will only book a minimum of a 2- or 3-day block over a weekend, meaning you're out of luck for 1-night stays. You can play the waiting game if you want, as some places will let the room go if they haven't booked it for a block by about 9pm, but it's a risky plan. Fall, winter, and spring rates are noticeably less expensive, except in the towns

Detour: Trot on Over to Freehold

Got the itch to bet on some ponies? **Freehold Raceway** is the cure. Established in 1853, the horse park features live standardbred harness races for trotters and pacers 10 months of the year, from August through May. The racetrack is open 7 days and nights a week for year-round thoroughbred and harness racing simulcasts from tracks throughout North America. Bet on the exacta, trifecta, or box it all up . . . Run, horsie, run! Located at the traffic intersection of Route 9 and Route 33 in Freehold, NJ, directly across the street from the Freehold Raceway Mall. 130 Park Ave., Freehold; ☎ **732/462-3800;** www. freeholdraceway.com. It's about 20 minutes' drive inland; visit the website for exact directions.

where they've extended their seasons with late fall/holiday events.

CHEAP

➜**Sand Pebble Motor Lodge** ★ At the north end of Ocean Avenue, easy walking distance to the Point Pleasant boardwalk, this place is across the street from the beach, offering clean, comfortable rooms, as well as Victorian-style suites, which cost a bit more. *905 Ocean Ave., Point Pleasant Beach.* ☎ *732/899-7712. www.sand pebblenj.com. 35 units. Off-season to summer rates $69–$169 single, $89–$219 double; $149–$349 Victorian suites. No pets. Free passes to Bradshaw's Beach 3 blocks south. Amenities: Outdoor pool; sun deck; cable TV.*

➜**Tradewinds Motor Lodge** The rooms here surround a glistening outdoor pool in a horseshoe shape. The newly renovated rooms sport air-conditioning and tile floor bathrooms for a pleasant beach stay. The heated pool and sun deck are a sweet way to spend the day, and it's only steps to the white sand beaches. *2000 Grand Central Ave., Lavallette.* ☎ *732/793-2100. www.tradewinds nj.com. 45 units. $65–$155 double. Amenities: Cable TV; fridge; beach badges; heated outdoor pool; free parking.*

Seaside Heights

A majority of the motels in Seaside Heights are sketchy, providing sometimes just a

bed and a lamp, with some pretty nasty rooms. You can find a mess of cheap motels here from a block to 3 blocks from the beach, and if that's all you can afford/all that's available, these are the best of the lot: **Thunderbird Motel,** 132 Kearney Ave., Seaside Heights (☎ **732/ 793-8500**), with rates from $49 to $119, and the **Mark III,** 207 Carteret Ave., Seaside Heights (☎ **732/793-4000**), which offers A/C, pool, hot tub, free pizza by the pool, and is pet-friendly at $55 to $109. Stick with these unless you have a strong stomach and the ability to ignore discomfort.

DOABLE

➜**Point Pleasant Manor** ★ Designed as a sort of secluded cove to block out the boisterous summertime noise, this place is just a block from the beach and steps from the Ark and Marlin bars and restaurants, and minutes away from downtown shopping in Point Pleasant's Arnold Avenue section. Here you'll find clean, beachy rooms with ample space containing inviting beach decor, loveseat, and coffee tables. *310 Sea Ave., Point Pleasant Beach.* ☎ *732/899-7300. www.pleasantmanor.com. $89–$209 single; $89–$319 double. Amenities: Dataport; outdoor pool.*

➜**Starlight Motel** Just out of reach of Seaside's loud nighttime rants and

Events on the Central Jersey Shore

→ A can't-miss jam is the **Festival of the Sea** ★ in Point Pleasant on Arnold Avenue, which is usually held in mid-September. There are vendors hawking fresh seafood dishes, and maritime artwork and trinkets line the street. The fest began in 1975 as an end-of-summer gathering, with local bands livening up the event. Stop in at the Point Pleasant Elks club on Arnold Avenue to grab some $2 drafts to wash down all that seafood. Contact the Point Pleasant Chamber of Commerce at ☎ **732/295-8850** or visit www. pointpleasantbeach.com.

→ If you happen to have a set of *cojones* that doesn't mind shrinkage, join the ranks of liquored-up locals for the **Polar Bear Plunge** in Seaside Heights, as certified nuts dive into the Atlantic Ocean every year in late February when the water runs a bone-chilling 35°F. It's for a good cause: The New Jersey Special Olympics. Folks sporting rubber ducks, goofy hats, and wearing nothing but swim trunks dive into the icy waters early in the morning. Log on to **www.njpolarplunge.org** to learn more.

→ The surf dudes from **Volcom** run a wave-pumpin' surf tourney every year through Seaside Heights on their nationwide **Volcom Surf Tour** ★★ during mid-October. Churny 6- to 8-foot swells in 2006 were ridden for big time bucks and tons of surf-related promo giveaways littered the crowd of hundreds. Check **www.transworldsurf.com** for the upcoming schedules.

→ Every year over 1,000 surf fishermen gather on the beaches of Island Beach State Park the first weekend in October to sling clams and lures into the surf in aspiration to claim the coveted **Governor's Cup** trophy. And it's a pretty big deal; the Governor of New Jersey attends to present the cup to the winner of the tourney. The whole day is about beach buggies, barbecues, and brother (and sister) hood. **www.state.nj.us/dep/fgw**.

→ Get country real quick at the **Albert Music Hall,** 131 Wells Mills Rd., Rt. 532, Waretown (☎ **609/971-1593;** www.alberthall.org) as some fiddlin' and twiddlin' goes on at the bluegrass, country, and traditional music festival in early November. Word has it the Jersey Devil himself is lured in by the bluegrass music and always makes an appearance.

→ Celebrate Barnegat Bay at the **Barnegat Bay Festival,** Van Sant Avenue, Island Heights (☎ **732/255-0472**); sponsored by the Barnegat Bay Estuary program, the gala affair has plenty of swashbuckling activities including scavenger hunts, pontoon boat tours, face painting, and fish printing, with vendors peddling nautical jewelry and wares. Held the first week in June.

→ During mid-June, be on the lookout for sharks! The Point Pleasant Charter Boat association hosts its annual **Mako Mania** fishing tournament (☎ **732/ 892-3666;** www.makomanianj.com), where evening outdoor parties are held at Clark's Landing Marina, as spectators watch the weigh-ins on the Manasquan River. Big sharks hit the scales from 150 to 700 pounds, bringing some *ooh's* and *ahh's* from the crowd.

debauchery, it's a 4-minute taxi ride to the festivities. Clean, uncrowded beaches and easy daywalking adventures and shopping in nearby Lavallette are all within a half-mile. The cozy, clean kitchenette and homestyle feel invite you to grab some shrimp, pasta, and clams to cook up a seafaring meal. *1963 Rt. 35 North, Ortley Beach.* ☎ *732/793-4321. www.starlightmotel.com. $125–$160 single; $135–$170 double; $150–$200 suite. Amenities: A/C; free parking.*

→ **Surfside Motel** Featured on the second season of "The Apprentice," this seaside motel received a genuine Donald Trump face-lift with revamped and refaced rooms with new carpet, paint, and bathrooms. Now, it's one of the more comfortable Seaside places. It's across from the public beaches and nonstop blinking amusements and rides of Casino Pier. The rooms are of average size, but they have a homey feel, and hey, they've been on reality TV. *201 Ocean Terrace.* ☎ *732/793-1400. www. surfsidemotelseaside.com. 57 units. $49–$189 single and double. Amenities: Daily maid service; free parking.*

SPLURGE

→ **White Sands Oceanfront Spa and Resort** ★★★ The crown jewel of this stretch has a posh, classy look with stately columnar architecture and tropical plants adorning the open space. The amenities include a well-kept gym, indoor pool, Jacuzzi, oceanside pool, steam room, sauna, free private beach, and indoor bar. Rooms have private balconies to soak up the sunshine. The service-oriented staff always has something happening for you and yours with location-sponsored Carnival days, sandcastle building days, and scheduled events throughout the week. *1205 Ocean Ave., Point Pleasant.* ☎ *732/899-3370. www.thewhitesands.com. $90–$525 double.*

Amenities: Free continental breakfast, private deck, gift shop.

Eating

Walk the planks of the boardwalks and prepare to be assaulted and tempted by the enticing (well, sometimes) smells of deep-fried Oreo cookies (really!), stuffed cheesesteaks, cotton candy, Italian sausage and pepper sandwiches, and Greek gyros at every turn. Oh, it's so bad, and it tastes so good. Off the boards, some classy and stunning oceanside restaurants dish out seafood specialties that would be fit for King Neptune himself. Poke around a bit and you'll find a bit of everything from straight-off-the-boat catches of the day, awesome Italian sopressata, to fresh Garden State produce (tomatoes! corn-on-the-cob!) on the the menus of the restaurants, and eventually in your satisfied tummy.

SUPPLIES

For the over-21 crowd, your first stop before the party should be at **A & P Liquors** (1201 Richmond Ave., Point Pleasant Beach, ☎ **732/892-9353**) to load up on the 30 packs of what's on sale, and discounted bottles of Captain Morgan and wine. **Cornerstone Wine and Liquors** (1401 Grand Central Ave., Lavallette; ☎ **732/793-7545**) is the filling station for the southern part of the stretch.

You can pick up groceries for BBQ and kitchenette stuff at the **24-hour A&P** at 5 Ortley Plaza off Route 35, Seaside Heights. For Jersey Fresh produce, load up on all the nectarines, tomatoes, bananas, and peppers you can bag at **Big Ed's** produce stand at the corner of Route 35 north and Ortley Avenue in Lavallette.

TAKEOUT TREATS

For tasty gourmet sandwiches and wraps, hit the **Normandy Beach Market** ★★

Best Breakfasts at the Shore

To quell that early morning hankerin', **Sunny Hunny Pancake House,** 1907 Route 35, Ortley Beach (☎ **732/793-3717**), flips out fluffy, soft blueberry pancakes topped with fresh blueberries, homemade whipped cream, and maple syrup. Hash browns and Spanish omelets will have you anchored for an afternoon at the beach, and don't forget to wish the life-size Elmo and Winnie the Pooh characters who welcome you a Good Morning. It's open 7am–3pm daily. The **Bayside Café,** 607 Bay Blvd., Lavallette (☎ **732/830-8804**), sits bayside (obviously) on Barnegat Bay where you can enjoy the sunrise on the outdoor veranda and let the omelets melt in your mouth. Open from very early until 3pm, you can also get some quality lunches of grilled bacon and cheese sandwiches, or a fried shrimp sandwich from $6 to $12. The endless cup of coffee keeps flowing here. Start your morning at 7am for breakfast or end it at 4am for munchies, at the open 24/7 **Ocean Bay Diner,** 1507 Hwy. 88 and Route 35, Point Pleasant (☎ **732/295-1070**), a classic Greek diner with an eight-page menu stacked with grilled Reuben sandwiches, lamb gyros, meatballs and spaghetti, and everything in between to stave off those hunger pangs.

(534 Route 35, North Normandy Beach; ☎ 732/793-8788). You'll find the Jersey-style pork roll, egg, and cheese is $3.95 and sucks up a hangover like a vacuum. There's a range of hearty sandwiches, like The Cubano sandwich of succulent ham slices, pickles, Swiss cheese on a Kaiser roll, and grilled chicken with pesto mayo sauce, Jersey tomatoes, and mozzarella cheese that will set you back anywhere from $6 to $10.

The 24-hour **WAWA** ★ is the omnipresent gastronomical goldmine of the New Jersey/Pennsylvania area. We particularly love the one in Normandy Beach. At any Wawa, you can find made-to-order cold cut and chicken salad sandwiches, orange and energy juices and drinks, all variations of chips, coffee, ice cream, Tastykakes, smokes, newspapers, and a public bathroom. Everything you need for a roadtrip is relatively cheap and ready to go in 5 minutes. Tell Crazy Cashier Rob and Manager Betty I sent ya for a solid laugh and a free chicken salad sandwich! It's at 3485 Route 35 North, Normandy Beach (☎ 732/830-2760).

Pick up the state's finest homemade cheesecakes at **Charlie's Farm Market,** Route 35, Normandy Beach (☎ **732/793-3300**), for creamy delights topped with fresh strawberries, blueberries, and kiwi fruit. At the outdoor cafe under a canopy, you can enjoy made-to-order tasty tuna sandwiches and light Italian panini sandwiches.

EATING OUT
Cheap
→ **Coppo's** ★ ITALIAN This Mom & Pop joint is quiet and homey. It serves simple pizza pies and light-flaky deli-style sandwiches for a quick bite before you go back to the beach, and then amps up the Italian flare with a motherland lobster Fra Diablo and devilishly spicy scungilli with marinara sauce. *1506 Grand Central Ave., Lavallette.* ☎ *732/830-1888. Salads, appetizers $5–$7; dinners $10–$20. Wed–Mon 5–10pm, closed Tues.*

→ **Spike's Fishmarket** ★ SEAFOOD Fresh from the trawlers that unload their catch off the back dock, the clams, shrimp, and fish dishes were still in the water when you got up this morning. Pick the dish you

DOWN THE SHORE

Diamond Dallas Recommends . . .

Not only does **Vesuvio's Pizza** at 1305 Beaver Dam Rd., Point Pleasant (☎ **732/899-4495**) have some tasty pizza and the most genuine cheesesteaks this side of Philly, but local native pro wrestler and former heavyweight title holder **Diamond Dallas Page** (whose finishing move is "the Diamond Cutter") considers Vesuvio's cheesesteaks the best in Jersey, as he told an interviewer on an episode of *WWE Raw*. Bang!

want out of the shaved-iced spread at the display counter. A heaping portion of Seafood Jambalaya mixed with flaked whiting, fiery bell and red peppers, white rice, clams, and scallops could set a five-alarm fire on your tastebuds, and a four-some serving of stuffed and baked clams oreganato will leave you happy. *415 Broadway, Point Pleasant Beach, NJ.* ☎ *732/295-9400. Finger appetizers, bowls $4–$9; entrees $7–$13. 11:30am–9:30pm weekdays; 11:30am–10:30pm weekends.*

➜ **Surf Taco** ★★ MEXICAN The "Locals-Only" vibe of the joint isn't a reason to stay away: Just take a look at the wide-smiled high school girls working the register, surf videos on three TV screens, and games like Connect Four that can be played while you wait for your order. The namesake Surf Taco is made with battered codfish, diced tomatoes, shredded lettuce, and a creamy cilantro sauce. Platters come equipped with a hearty side of black beans and rice. Bring your favorite six-pack and finish the legendary Tsunami burrito in under 15 minutes and you're on the wall of fame. *1300 Richmond Ave., Point Pleasant, NJ.* ☎ *732/701-9000. www.surftaco.com. Bowls,*

combos, and tacos $3–$12. Daily 11am–9:30pm.

Doable

➜ **Bum Rogers** ★ SEAFOOD The name gives away the ambience. Salt-encrusted surf fishermen coming from Island Beach State Park a block away fill the paper-tabled saloon to gobble up too-good-to-be-true crab specials. Order 'em by the two dozen garlic-style, or chock up a bowl of thick and meaty crab bisque. *2207 Central Ave. South Seaside Park.* ☎ *732/830-2770. www.bumrogers.com. 11:30am–9pm weekdays; 11:30am–10pm weekends.*

➜ **Frankies Bar and Grill** ★★ AMERICAN The place is always bustling with locals or tourists, daytime or nighttime. The huge square brass-railed bar is the centerpiece of the dining rooms that surround it. You won't be able to finish the lightly fried calamari appetizer by yourself, but split 'em with someone, and maybe order the buffalo chicken tenders, covered with an unbelievably tasty sauce. Full-on porter-house steaks and Jersey Burgers topped with the area's Pork Roll are a beer-buzzed patron's delight. *414 Route 35 South, Point Pleasant Beach, NJ.* ☎ *732/892-6000. www.rodstavern.com. Sandwiches and salads $6–$12; entrees $10–$20 Open daily 11:30am–2am. Food served until 1am.*

➜ **Pop's Garage** ★★ MEXICALI At this coastal surf-inspired Mexican joint, steps from the beach, fill up on a mid-afternoon mole' enchilada laden with shrimp, fish

Word Up: Pork Roll

"Pork Roll," aka Taylor Ham, is a Jersey-created treat that is in essence a thin slice of circular pork. You put about four slices on a Kaiser roll with salt, pepper, ketchup and that's good eatin'.

tacos, or a Karma burrito overstuffed with chicken, broccoli, carrots, and cauliflower. A 1967 26-foot "Silver Bullet" Airstream Winnebago converted into a walk-in surf art gallery and Juice bar completes the most excellent experience. *Corner of 6th and Route 35 North, Normandy Beach.* ☎ *732/830-5770. Appetizers and lunch $5.95–$11; dinner $8.95–$18. BYOB. 8am–10pm. Daily*

➜ **Twin Fin Cafe** ★ AMERICAN A beach bistro inside Used To Be's Bar, I can recommend that you jump on Tara's Tuna Bites rolled in coconut and served with sweet and sour sesame sauce, or belly up for Pappardelle and Shrimp Lavanco tossed with pancetta and asparagus tips in a delicate sage cream sauce. It's legit fine fare. *287 Route 35, South Mantoloking.* ☎ *732/892-5900. Starters and sandwiches $6–$13; entrees $12–$20. Noon–10pm.*

Splurge

➜ **Captain Ed's** ★★★ AMERICAN/ SEAFOOD Home of the "Steak on a Stone" where your porterhouse, filet mignon, prime rib, or rib-eye comes smoking on a sizzling Hot Rock, draped and drizzled with portobello mushrooms, browned onions, hot peppers, and cracked black peppercorns blanketed by melted, aged, and shaved provolone cheese. Don't overlook the shellfish and fresh fish dishes, which are blackened, scampied, or Cajun-cooked with crabmeat stuffing. *1001 Arnold Ave., Point Pleasant.* ☎ *732/892-4121. www.captain edsplace.com. BYOB. Crab fritters to sashimi $7–$10; steak and seafood specialties $13–$24. Daily 4:30pm to "whenever."*

➜ **Labrador Lounge** ★★ AMERICAN/ SEAFOOD Owners Marilyn Schlossbach and Scott Szegeski infuse a sandal-wearing, surfer-style with the classiness of the high-end cuisine served a bit north of here in Manhattan. Marilyn used to breed champion Labradors and with the profits, she opened up her restaurant. She and

Scott currently have two resident Labs, Sake and Harry, that sniff and peruse the grounds. There's an outdoor sand-pebbled veranda kissed with clean ocean breezes, as well as a posh indoor setting. Must-haves are the Chuchee coconut-based Thai stir-fry of seasoned chicken and Asian vegetables and lip-smackin', slow-cooked baby back ribs drenched in tangy home-made BBQ sauce. A vibrant aquarium of Technicolored fishies crafted like a movie screen inside the wall completes the wonderful experience. *3581 Hwy. 35 North.* ☎ *732/830-5770. www.Kitschens.com. BYOB. Appetizers and salads $7–$15; gourmet entrees $14–$29. Daily 11:30am–10pm.*

➜ **Red's Lobster Pot** ★★ SEAFOOD Tony Soprano (that is, the actor who portrays him, James Gandolfini) frequents this dockside establishment just off the Manasquan inlet and across from the commercial fishing fleet. Nothing compares to the seafaring Clams Posillipo or Lobster Broiled and Stuffed. *Inlet Dr., Point Pleasant Beach, directly across street from Coast Guard Station.* ☎ *732/295-6622 www.redslobster pot.com. No reservations. BYOB. Appetizers, bisques, and salads $6–$11; succulent entrees $12–$25. Daily noon–9pm.*

Partying

From Manasquan Inlet to Barnegat Inlet, this stretch is bolstered by the boisterous and flashy Boardwalk clubs of **Jenkinsons, Tiki Bar, Surf Club,** and **Bamboo Club** in Point Pleasant and Seaside Heights to "off-the boards" watering holes touting daily specials such as **Used To Be's** and **Captain Hooks.** Grab a copy of the free *Islander* or *Jetty Magazine,* which detail the wheres and whens of cover bands, and drink specials of the local scenes each week.

This area is a cross-section of the circus of humanity with a wide array of partygoers from Guido "Seaside Tony and Tina" clubbers twirling glow sticks while wearing tight muscle shirts and gravity defying skirts, to black-clad Manhattan metrosexuals sipping apple martinis, to long-haired, coconut-scented surfers playing Jackass.

Bring the camera; you're sure to see something unusual go down with such a mix.

BARS, PUBS & CLUBS
Point Pleasant Beach

➜ **The Ark** BAR Pub-style and dimly lit, the shadowy booths are carved with the names of drunk locals and you'll hear lots of lively banter. Live weekly entertainment includes the likes of the Zenmen's funky riffs on Thursdays and almost-famous crooners at karaoke night on Wednesdays. Get the Arkburger platter, $5.95 for a perfect piece of ballast to anchor you for a night's festivities. *401 Route 35, Point Pleasant Beach, NJ.* ☎ *732/295-1122. www.the arkpubandeatery. Daily 11:30am–1:00am. Kitchen closes at midnight.*

➜ **Broadway Bar and Grill** BAR Captain Quint from "Jaws" has nothing on the local patronage here. Hands down, this is the saltiest fisherman's bar on the East Coast, where tiger shark jaws jut out from the walls, and absolutely true stories of steadying through the Perfect Storm permeate the place. At Happy Hour, you can get $1 domestics from 7 to 10am, you read it right; then again from 4 to 7pm; $3 domestic pints last all night long. *106 Randall Ave., Point Pleasant Beach.* ☎ *732/899-3272. Daily till 2am.*

➜ **Clark's Landing Bar and Grill** BAR Grab a cold one on the outside deck Tiki bar, kick back, and watch the spectacular sunset on the Manasquan River. The older thirty- to forty-something crowd is semi-upscale with khakis and sandals. Clark's is known as *the* place for an early get-your-drink-on. No rowdiness here, just a lot of good laughs and smiles. *847 Arnold Ave.,*

Point Pleasant. ☎ *732/899-1111. 4pm–7pm Happy Hour $2.50 domestics. Bar open until 10pm weekdays; 1am weekends.*

➜ **Jenkinsons** ★★ CLUB The hub of the Jersey cover band scene, Jenkinsons is where you'll find The Benjamins, The Nerds, and Dog Voices cranking out party hits on weekends spiced with the ultimate presence of sporadic old school metal acts like Warrant (YEAH!) and Quiet Riot showing up to play. Drinks hit you up for $4 domestic cans to $5 well drinks, with covers from $5 to $10 on weekends. Step outside to the boardwalk for a breather and play some spin-the-wheel games to win a stuffed Spongebob Squarepants for your date. You'll find moderate lines on weekends. *Boardwalk, 300 Ocean Ave. Point Pleasant Beach, NJ.* ☎ *732/295-4334. www.jenksclub.com. Daily til closing.*

➜ **Martell's Tiki Bar** ★ BAR Tropical drink specialties such as the Coastal Kiss of Amaretto Di Sonnaro, Southern Comfort and Pineapple Juice, and the Lava Lamp Margarita of Cuervo Gold Tequila, Triple Sec, and Chambord launch you into the islands for around $6 a pop. The Tiki bar is a boardwalk pier that juts 100 yards out over the Atlantic, but the spot also offers a Beach Club and Bar at $5/$6 weekday/weekend for a badge to use the private beach. For snacks, a raw bar also offers up scrumptious seafaring delights of oysters and clams. On Sunday afternoons, Dr. Cheeko's reggae sounds attract hundreds for a last call before Monday's workday *Boardwalk, Point Pleasant Beach.* ☎ *732/892-0131. $5–$10 cover weekends.*

Normandy Beach/Lavallette

➜ **Crab's Claw** BAR Owner Sam Hammer, Sr.'s passion for his alma mater West Virginia's Mountaineers is apparent from the completely yellow and blue-painted bar upstairs draped in WV regalia. The main bar downstairs is usually surrounded two to three deep with Yankee fans, local drunks, and daytrippers looking to be a part of history and join the ranks of the "100 beer club." Professional surfer Sam Hammer, Jr., stops in to have a drink when not on tour. *601 Grand Central Ave., Route 35 North Lavallette* ☎ *732/793-4447. www.thecrabsclaw.com. Daily. Lunch—closing. No cover.*

➔ **Used to Be's** ★★ BAR   The clientele is comprised of local salty landscapers with dusty pickup trucks and surfers in wet boardshorts, spliced with wandering visitors during the daytime. Happy Hour runs from noon to 6pm with $2 Miller Lites. The place gets a different vibe after dark when barely-legal twenty-somethings take over, especially on Thirsty Thursday Surf Nites that pull everybody in a 20-mile radius for $1 domestics and $3 well drinks. Rich Meyer's traveling band (among others) plays summertime Saturdays to bring in a dance-on-the-bar vibe and tons of hotties. *287 Route 35, Mantoloking.* ☎ *732/892-3770. www.usedtobes.com. Daily until closing. $3—$5 cover Thurs—Sat.*

Seaside Heights

➔ **Bamboo Bar** ★★★ CLUB   Girls Gone Wild! It's absolute mayhem here, with knucklefisted bass beats pumping at every corner; it's always ass to elbow in the place after 11pm and the scene is everything your mom doesn't want you to be doing. Wet T-shirt contests explode unplanned on stage and in the crowd, shower shots of straight vodka come out of hoses, and sleazy pickup lines erupt at any given point under pink neon–lit palm trees. Voted #1 Singles Bar in NJ, the club is open till 3am, organizes Bachelorette and Divorce parties, and off-season specials after Labor Day. Everyone still talks about that time a few years back when NFL quarterback Drew Bledsoe got kicked out of here. *201 Boulevard, Seaside Heights.* ☎ *732/830-3660.*

www.bamboobar.com. Cover $10 most weekend nights. Weekends til 3am during the season.

➔ **Captain Hook's** BAR/PUB ★ Got a bet to settle? Want to make a new bet? Hook's offers every available option with Ping-Pong, darts, pool, arcade games, air hockey, basketball shooting: every out-and-out trash-talking pseudo-sporting game you need to exhibit your prowess, fueled by endless drafts and mixed drinks. Fridays rule here, and the wintertime weekends are just as fun as the summer. *1320 Boulevard, Seaside Heights.* ☎ *732/830-0006. Daily til closing. $5 cover on weekends.*

➔ **Joey Harrison's Surf Club** ★★ CLUB   The combination of an inviting beachfront walkout bar, north Jersey "Gucci Hoochies," Bob Marley's Legendary Wailers, muscle-bound hardbodies, hard-charging surfers, and tons of booze makes for one hell of a schizophrenic ride any day of the week. Groove bands like G-Love and Special Sauce and the Wailers, combine with techno-tripped DJs headline summer shows, and the Sunday afternoon reggae "fun in the sun" party is a worldwide blast. Bring your drink on the beach and jump in the ocean. *1900 Ocean Ave., Ortley Beach.* ☎ *732/793-6625 (surf line), 732/830-8000 (office). www.joeyharrisonssurfclub.com. Open until 3am summertime. Cover $5—$10 most weekends.*

What Else to See & Do
AN AQUARIUM

Finding Nemo has never been easier. **Jenkinsons Aquarium** ★★ (www.jenkinsons.com) on the boardwalk is so inherently cool, adults head on over to gawk at the fishies. Five saltwater tanks exhibit local Atlantic fish such as fluke, bluefish, striped bass, sand tiger sharks, smooth dogfish, and porcupine pufferfish flowing behind the glass. Hear the barking of the

Visit the MTV Beach House

Undeniably strange and poppin' enough for MTV to put a Beach House here for 2 years (1999 and 2002), the Seaside Heights playhouse now lies silent without TV cameras and tanned beauties and hunks, but the aura stays alive. The house sits on the very north end of the boardwalk. You've seen the bleached blondes on TV and wet and wild beach ball parties, but you wanna know what really hits the summertime in Seaside? For a good laugh, you've got to check out **www.njguido.com**, all about the summer lifestyle at the Jersey shore from a bunch of self-proclaimed (and proud of it) Guidos. Enjoy.

resident seals and hang around for shark feeding time. Disgusting . . . yet cool, as the toothy guys devour their dinners of rotten fish. Check out the penguins Hollywood style on the Penguin Cam. Here are the feeding schedules. **Penguins:** noon and 7:30pm daily; **Seals:** 10am, 3, and 8pm daily; **Atlantic Sharks:** 9pm Monday, Wednesday, and Saturday; **Pacific Sharks:** 4pm Tuesday, Thursday, and Sunday; **American Alligators:** 9pm Tuesday, Friday, and Sunday. A-w-e-s-o-m-e!

MINOR LEAGUE BASEBALL

Take me out to the ballgame already! The **Lakewood Blueclaws** are the Class A affiliate of the Philadelphia Phillies. You can wash back $4.50 beers while cheering on the antics of mascot Pinchy the Crab. If you hit it lucky, you can even see MLB players getting ready to come off the disabled list and playing their way back into shape (Derek Jeter made an appearance off the DL a couple summers ago). And the major leaguers tend to park home run balls like they're in Little League. The Blueclaws play at 2 Stadium Way, Lakewood, NJ (☎ 732/901-7000; www.blueclaws.com).

PLAYING OUTSIDE

Activities at Island Beach State Park

Need some peace and quiet? Pay the $4 entry fee and enter Island Beach State Park ★★ (☎ 732/793-0506; www.state.nj.us/dep/parksandforests), a pristine and

serene 10-mile oasis at the southernmost point of the Barnegat barrier island. You can take a hike through beachplummed sand dunes and marsh trails to search for stinkpot turtles and spy one of the state's largest osprey colonies. Keep your eyes open for the wily red foxes that call the island home.

If you've got a beach-buggy ready vehicle, buy a 3-day permit for $50, let the air out of the tires to 18PSI (pounds per square inch), and hop on the sands to chase the fish. Check out the **New Jersey Beach Buggy Association** at **www.njbba.org** for complete details on beach buggying.

Surf fishing is the finest along the Eastern Seaboard, with striped bass, bluefish, weakfish, and fluke. Gear up with fresh clams from **Betty and Nicks Bait and Tackle** in Seaside Heights (☎ 732/793-2708, www.bettyandnicks.com).

Charter Fishing Boats

Want to get into some real fishy business? Stop in at the Manasquan Inlet on the Point Pleasant side and hop on a party boat to battle with summer flounder, hard-fighting bluefish, barrel-chested striped bass, and tasty black sea bass. Fees generally run from $28 to $42 for a half-day trip from 8am to 12:30pm or 2 to 6:30pm.

The Gambler (☎ 732/295-7569) offers three or four daytrips that go from 7:30am to 3:30pm. Another recommended boat is the *Dauntless* (☎ 732/892-4298; www.dauntlessfishing.com). Both party boats

New Jersey Coast: Ocean Beach to Seaside Heights

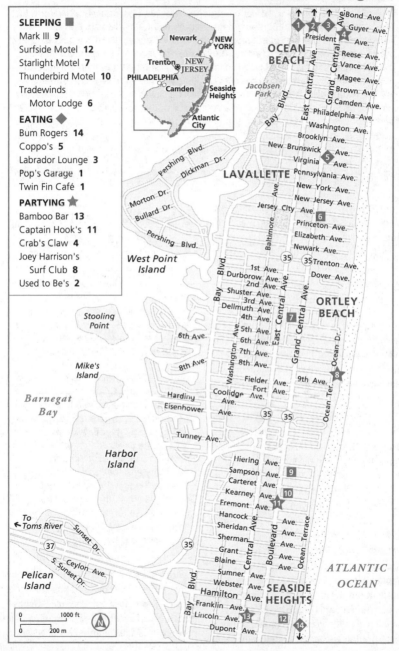

SLEEPING ■
Mark III **9**
Surfside Motel **12**
Starlight Motel **7**
Thunderbird Motel **10**
Tradewinds
  Motor Lodge **6**

EATING ◆
Bum Rogers **14**
Coppo's **5**
Labrador Lounge **3**
Pop's Garage **1**
Twin Fin Café **1**

PARTYING ★
Bamboo Bar **13**
Captain Hook's **11**
Crab's Claw **4**
Joey Harrison's
  Surf Club **8**
Used to Be's **2**

DOWN THE SHORE

Detour: Six Flags Great Adventure

Before you exit the Point Pleasant section of the trip, hop on Route 34 North to Route 195 West to exit 16, then 1 mile west on Route 537 for **Six Flags Great Adventure.** It's like the Boardwalks of the Jersey Shore with bigger and badder toys, prizes, and spinning wheels. The sickest ride around is Kingda Ka ✮, which the park claims is the world's tallest (456 ft.) and fastest (128 mph in 3.3 seconds) roller coaster on Earth. You'll have a ball jiving around with life-size Looney Tunes Tweetybirds, Bugs Bunnys, and Yosemite Sams running rampant, enough cotton candy and ice cream to juice you up for decades, and rides; you can bet somebody in your crew is going to hurl their lunch. General admission is $60 but there's an online special for $50, and Coca Cola runs a summertime special in Jersey on their products which usually offers quality discounts on park entry fees. Yes, you show up with an empty Coke can and you get in for cheaper. We're not too proud to do that. Jackson, NJ. ☎ **732/928-1821.** www.sixflags.com.

run 7 days a week for striped bass, bluefish, black sea bass, summer flounder, blackfish, ling, and tuna, depending on the season.

Night bluefish trips on the *Cock Robin* (☎ **732/892-5083**) run from 7:30pm to 12:30am. Boats rent rods and reels for you for around $3, and supply all bait and limited tackle, but you can always pick up anything you need at **Reel Life Bait and Tackle,** 2421 Bridge Ave., Point Pleasant (☎ **732/899-3506**), since it's open 24 hours a day, 7 days a week from Memorial Day through Labor Day.

Surfing

Surf's up at **Brave New World,** 1206 Richmond Ave., Point Pleasant (☎ **732/899-8220**); pick up boards, trunks, wax, some aloha, and hit the local beach breaks. Mid-August Midnight Madness starting on a certain August midnight, ending midnight next day, gives you a chance to load up on bargains with 50% to 80% off most clothes in the store, and the line is always at least an hour long at any given time.

Brave runs a surf Pro-Am during mid-September where local pros and amateurs battle it out for local bragging rights. Also check out **Ocean Hut,** 3111 Rte. 35 North, Lavallette (☎ **732/793-3400**), during mid-July for appearances and autograph

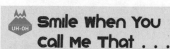

Smile When You call Me That . . .

Just so you know, when you hear someone referring to you as **Benny, Shoobie,** or **Touron,** it might get ugly. Coastal locals have pet names for tourists, split up by the regions. North and Central Jersey shore locals call them "Bennys," a term meaning you're either from Bayonne, Elizabeth, Newark, or New York. On Long Beach Island and south to Cape May, you'll be called a "Shoobie," a reference to old-time Philadelphia city folk who rode the train to the beach carrying their meals in a shoebox. Delaware and Maryland locals use the term "Touron," quite simply, a tourist/moron. Word to the wise: If you hear one of those terms thrown your way, and the thrower isn't smiling, you may want to move along quickly.

sessions with world-class surfers like Kelly Slater, Darrick Doerner, and Rob Machado.

Late September marks the **Grudge Match,** a surf event of down-and-dirty proportions to claim the title Best in NJ. Local

The author and a friend. And another guy.

pro Sam Hammer owns it, and everyone is looking to beat him down. The Grudge Match is a bragging rights tourney in NJ, where amateurs and pros from across the state compete to rub it in each other's faces.

It promises zero WQS (World Qualifying Series) points and $3,000 to first place only. There is no scaffolding, no three-day party, and no posers. It's about pride and respect, a valuable commodity in New Jersey.

On the Road to Long Beach Island

Central Coast to Long Beach Island 55 miles

Heading off the Barnegat Barrier Island, you hop on Route 37 through Toms River, (aka "Little League World Champions Highway," as Toms River won the LL World Series in 1999) and proceed the 7 miles through Toms River until you get to the Garden State Parkway. This 7-mile stretch is a neon gauntlet with every imaginable fast-food chain, gas station, coffee shop, and oddity store you can assemble. It's not pretty to look at, but you'll find anything you need here to fill up with.

The northern half of Long Beach Island (LBI) is dominated by beachfront mansions, while the southern half is loaded with the rest of society. A point to note is that on summertime weekends, the traffic on the 7-mile Route 72 causeway can back up for several miles, ouch! The best advice I can give you is to get there on a Thursday to miss all the bumper-to-bumper hassle that's a guarantee on Fridays.

On the Road **Nuts & Bolts**

....

Where to Fill Up   Most gas stations are on the north sides of Route 35 roughly 6 miles or so apart. The Route 37 corridor has plenty of gas stations to fill up; the WAWA going west has the cheapest gas.

The Tolls   Before LBI you'll hit one toll on the GSP costing 35¢.

Major Highways   Route 35 to Route 37 west, 7 miles to GSP south, to exit 63 Long Beach Island. Then Route 72 (Causeway) over the bridge onto LBI, onto Long Beach Boulevard.

The Back Roads   You can take Route 37 to Route 9 south, which parallels the GSP, but there are tons of stoplights and even more backed up traffic, so it's not recommended.

Long Beach Island Nuts & Bolts

Area Code   The telephone area code in Long beach Island is **609.**

Emergencies   Call ☎ **911** if you need the police, the fire department, or an ambulance.

Hospitals   Healthcare services are found at Southern Ocean Center, 1361 Route 72 West, Manahawkin (☎ **609/978-0600**).

Information Center   On the island between 8th and 9th streets at 265 West 9th St., Ship Bottom(☎ **609/494-7211**; www.discoversouthernocean.com).

Libraries   Grab a book to read at 217 South Central Ave., Surf City (☎ **609/494-2480**).

Newspapers & Magazines   The daily *Asbury Park Press* (www.app.com) covers all local and national angles; the *Beachcomber* is the summertime periodical to dial you in to seasonal happenings.

Pharmacies   Try Kapler's Pharmacy, Bay Avenue and Centre Street, Beach Haven (☎ **609-492-9221**).

Police   Engleside Avenue, Beach Haven (☎ **609/492-0505**).

Post Office   1601 Long Beach Blvd., Ship Bottom (☎ 609/494-7234).

Welcome to Long Beach Island

LBI is an 18-mile-long barrier island just off the coast of New Jersey. There are both ocean and bay beaches. You arrive on the island from the **Causeway** (Rte. 72) at the community of Ship Bottom. North of Ship Bottom is a stream of hugely expensive McMansions and the private beaches of Loveladies, Brant Beach, and Harvey Cedars, though Barnegat Light beach is accessible and user-friendly.

South of Ship Bottom are the towns of Spray Beach, Surf City, and Beach Haven, where most everything interesting is happening, offering a twisted blend of family-friendly atmosphere from the Philadelphia suits and ties to the rowdy out-of-college and out-of-a-job twenty- and thirty-something crowds.

GETTING AROUND
By Car

Long Beach Island is simply one long, straight stretch north to south. Long Beach Island Boulevard is the main drag, and is riddled with traffic lights every 3 blocks or so, making summertime traveling an exercise in patience. If you plan to hit LBI on a

Playlist: A Jersey Boardwalk Soundtrack

- ⇥ 10 Automatic, **The Black Keys,** "Rubber Factory," 2004
- ⇥ We like to Party!, **Venga Boys,** "The Platinum Album," 2000
- ⇥ Scenario, **A Tribe called Quest,** "The Low End Theory," 1991
- ⇥ Gasoline, **Audioslave,** "Audioslave," 2001
- ⇥ No Sleep till Brooklyn, **Beastie Boys,** "Licensed to Ill," 1986
- ⇥ Teenage Dirtbag, **Wheatus,** Single for movie "Loser," 2000
- ⇥ Pour Some Sugar on Me, **Def Leppard,** "Hysteria," 1987
- ⇥ Hand on the Pump, **Cypress Hill,** "Cypress Hill," 1991

weekend in summertime, there's always a huge backup on the Route 72 causeway of at least 1 to 3 hours every Friday and Saturday. Tune in to 101.5 FM for traffic updates every 15 minutes.

By Taxi
You can always use a taxi to get around late night. Call **Express Taxi, Limo & Van Service,** LBI area (☎ 609/492-1616).

Sleeping

LBI caters more to a high-end vacationer, hosting mostly families and older people, with most party people chipping in to rent houses for the summer. Thus, there's a lack of cheaper motels. In-season rates virtually double, but the more "doable" spots have limited view rooms at discounted rates. We list both off-season and peak rates to give you an idea of the yearly swings.

CHEAP

"Cheap" is a fuzzy concept on LBI. About the closest thing to inexpensive is the

Islander Motel (1202 Central Ave., Ship Bottom; ☎ 609/494-6964; www.islander motel.net), 1 block from the beach, where the amenities include a small playground, grill, ice machine, microwaves in the rooms, and kids stay free. It's clean and airy, and rates run from $49 to $159 for a double, on up to $180 a night on holiday weekends. Like we said "cheap" is as cheap does.

DOABLE

➔**Coral Seas Oceanfront Motel** ★★
Basking in the views of the Atlantic, this can be the perfect romantic getaway or just a place to crash for the night. Each oceanfront room boasts a private balcony with ocean views; all the rooms overlook the oversize heated swimming pool for an excellent opportunity to scope out potential night-time friends. 21 Coral St. ☎ 609/492-1141. www.coralseasmotel.com. 50 units. Doubles $89–$209. Amenities: TV; bathroom with tub and shower; fridge; coffeemaker; telephone.

➔**Drifting Sands Oceanfront Motel** ★
At one of the island's year-round proper-ties, you can enjoy the ocean at the height of summer, the calmer fall, or on a cozy win-ter break. There are a number of lodging configurations, including oceanfront rooms with private balconies, efficiency apart-ments, and suites. 119 East 9th St., Ship Bottom. ☎ 609/494-1123. www.dslbi.com. Low season: $85–$175; Summer: $108–$320. Amenities: A/C; cable TV; and Internet access.

Hey . . . I'm Not Sneezing!

A quirky fact of Long Beach Island is that because of its distance from the mainland, pollen generally doesn't make it across the bay, so those who suffer from hay fever report finding relief on the stretch of barrier island.

Fishing & Chowder: Events on LBI

→ The last Saturday in September, crowds fill the streets of Beach Haven for **Chowderfest** (☎ 800/ 292-6372; www.chowderfest. com/Chowderfest/chowder fest.asp), Taylor Avenue ball field, Ninth Street and Taylor Avenue, from 10am to 4pm, in a bustling carnival where local chowder gurus try to one-up each other for the esteemed title of "Best Tasting Chowder."

→ Surf fishing is a rite of passage off of LBI, and good thing the **Long Beach Island Surf Fishing Tournament** (☎ 609/494-7211; www.lbift.com) is there to renew the rite. Every year from mid-October to mid-November, surf fishermen compete to bag the biggest striped bass, bluefish, and weakfish to push the scales down for a payout that can reach thousands of dollars.

→ **Jolly Roger** ★★ A motel with a bed-and-breakfast feel, views off private balconies on the upper level give you a sense of B&B seclusion, with daily maid service, beach badges, and a quaint "Secret Treasures Gift Shoppe" all adding to the breezy and comfortable vibe. *150 steps from the beach at 5416 South Bay Blvd., Beach Haven Inlet.* ☎ *609/492-6931. www.lbinet. net/jolly. $85–$185 per night during season.*

SPLURGE

→ **Sandcastle** ★★★ When you're not on the beach, relax with the contents of the Sandcastle's book, video, and DVD library, or work out in the exercise room. There's also Internet access, a rooftop deck, outdoor Jacuzzi, poolside cabana, and complimen-

tary bikes, beach badges, beach chairs, and sumptuous full breakfast. This is definitely the prize accommodation of the LBI shore. *710 Bayview Ave., Barnegat Light.* ☎ *609/ 494-6555. www.SandcastleLBI.com. $170–$410.*

→ **Surf City Hotel** ★ This place is newly renovated, with a loaded venue of a restaurant, pub, Shucks Clam Bar, and Beach Club lounge open all summer. Pine-planked paneling gives a genuinely classic feel to each room, classy and refined for an old-school beach vibe. The Club lounge offers a variety of musical entertainment including a summer-long "American Idol" competition complete with a grand prize of a recording contract from music execs; that's sure to get you cheering wildly or cringing in fear. *8th St. and Long Beach Blvd., Surf City.* ☎ *609/494-7281. www.surfcityhotel. com. $105–$375. Amenities: AC; cable TV; hairdryer; fridge.*

Eating

Strangely enough, LBI doesn't have anywhere near the amount of restaurants you'd think an 18-mile-long island would, but the (many) folks with their own houses probably eat in a lot. Most eateries are geared toward breakfast, afternoon snacks, and late-night munchies, though you can find enough quality eateries to enjoy a splurge.

SUPPLIES

All along Long Beach Boulevard from Ship Bottom southward you will encounter shopping centers, but to load up on food, hands down, the large and in charge **Acme** shopping center (9601 Long Beach Blvd., Beach Haven Park, ☎ **609/492-9718**) is the place to go.

To pick up anything and everything that isn't food, from razors to flip-flops to beach chairs and lipstick, try either of the **Hand's Department Stores** on Long Beach Boulevard in Surf City and Beach Haven.

TAKEOUT TREATS

LBI has a dynamic ability to cater to both families and the party-hearty bunch, and one thing they all need is a good breakfast. There are some darn good breakfast bistros to chow down after the sun rises.

Honey Bubbles on 114th St. and Long Beach Boulevard, Haven Beach (☎ **609/ 492-5735**), emits a smooth, pleasant aura for a breakfast bistro, perfect to eat fluffy pancakes under puffy cloud morning LBI sky. If you've got to get to the beach fast, hit up **Bagels & Beyond,** 41st St. and Long Beach Boulevard, Brant Beach (☎ **609/ 494-4400**), to load up on bags of bagels to bring back to the bunch. Eveningtime can't be mellow enough if you don't have ice cream. **Baskin–Robbins** at 74th St. and Long Beach Boulevard, Beach Haven Crest (☎ **609/494-6867**), is the place to grab that hot fudge sundae you've been craving all day long while baking yourself on the beach.

You can get your jolt of caffeine while checking your e-mail or the latest box score at the **How you Brewin?** coffee shop and Internet cafe at 2020 Long Beach Blvd. (☎ **609/494-2003;** www.howyou brewin.com).

EATING OUT

Cheap

➜**Chicken or the Egg** ★★ AMERICAN Flat-out *the* place to get late night goodies that are both tasty and filling, with chicken this and chicken that, that are so good you'll forget about your hangover in the morning. The best part? It's open 24 hours 7 days a week, though from 1:00am on, lines are longer than you may want to wait, but totally well worth it. *207 North Bay Ave. at Centre St., Beach Haven.* ☎ *609/ 492-3695. www.492fowl.com. Sandwiches $6– $10; sides $3–$6. Open 24/7.*

➜**Lex Mex** ★ MEXICAN Forget Taco Bell. For genuine Mexican sit down or takeout, owner and surfer Greg Luker brings a blend of Central American surf culture sure to get your hot sauces sizzlin'. Bring your own tequila and mix it with the in-house margarita machine. *7th St., Ship Bottom, directly ahead once you land on the island from the Causeway.* ☎ *609/361-LEXX. Burritos, taco platters, chimichangas $7–$15. Daily in season. Closed in winter.*

Doable

➜**Black Whale Bar and Fish House** ★ SEAFOOD/AMERICAN Get hypnotized by the backlit slidebox on the north wall showcasing surfers lining up rights, pictures of striped bass in the surf, ethereal sunsets, and other shore scenes. Grab a pint of the house Black Whale Ale and it becomes even more surreal. Freshly caught fish of the day mixed with dirty rice and beans, jambalaya, and crab cakes send the tastebuds to Happyland. *Centre St. and Pennsylvania Ave., Beach Haven.* ☎ *609/ 492-0025. Entrees $12–$26. Daily til closing.*

➜**Kubel's Too** AMERICAN The sister location to Kubel's in Barnegat Light, the darkly lit pub vibe gives way to hunger-satisfying sandwiches and Happy Hour half-price appetizer specials from 4 to 7pm that pack in the locals for crab dip for $4 to spicy mussels at $3.75. Don't forget the straight up filling and tasty sandwiches. *8200 Long Beach Blvd. and 82nd St.* ☎ *609/ 494-4731. Sandwiches, bar food $6–$13. Daily til closing.*

➜**Mud City Crab House** ★ SEAFOOD Off the island, though with a view of the sodbanks, which are like little creeks cutting through marsh banks with reeds, and other grasses, making for a beautiful setting and rustic ambience and seclusion; treat yourself to delicious Ipswich clams, rare peppercorn tuna appetizer, and Crab Imperial with whomping jumbo lumps, the best seafood before you hit the island, though islanders will leave LBI to come here for dinner. *1185 East Bay Ave., Manahawkin.* ☎ *609/978-3660. Closed Wed. Open 11am–10pm. BYOB. Most major credit cards accepted. Average price of dinner for 2, $30–$40. Handicapped accessible. Closes for the season late Oct.*

Splurge

→ **Engleside Inn** ★★ ASIAN/SEAFOOD/AMERICAN It doesn't have a Japanese name, but you can bet the freshest sushi on the island is here. Order up a dry martini while sampling a succulent spicy tuna roll or yellowtail sashimi. Here's a hint: It's kind of a higher-end clientele, so don't wear your *Dukes of Hazzard* T-shirt. There are three different dining options at the Engleside. Along with the sushi bar, you can have a nice sitdown at the fine dining Leeward Room, and more casual eating poolside at the Sand Bar. *Engleside Ave. and ocean front.* ☎ *800/762-2214. www.engleside. com. Sushi rolls $6–$12; dishes $12–$25. Daily til closing.*

→ **Octopus's Garden** ★★ SEAFOOD The comfortably close, casual atmosphere, and BYO mentality makes for relaxed dining on just-caught pan-seared sea bass or tender scallops blended with artichoke hearts. Lobster spring rolls just add the icing on the cake. Homemade decadent desserts top it all off. *5th St. and Long Beach Blvd., Surf City.* ☎ *609/494-1200. Entrees $12–$25. Daily til closing.*

Partying

On LBI, most of the nightlife trickles down to the bottom of the island to the town of Beach Haven. The farther south you go, the younger, yet still legal, it gets. There are a few clubs and bars in Ship Bottom and virtually none north of the Causeway. Pick up a copy of the free *Beachcomber,* which details the week's happenings. Most bars in Beach Haven are within some sort of walking distance to each other, but you *must* be careful, because the police in LBI

enforce **zero-tolerance zones,** meaning no warnings or second chances for horseplay and jackassery; so on-street antics need to be more sedate, unless you want to finish the night in the local jail.

→ **Bakers Porthole** PUB Order up a "World Famous Roast Beef" sandwich at a true dive bar crackling out Toby Keith and '80s pop hits on the rusted jukebox. Since it opened in 1936, this kickin' dinosaur survived the 1944 Hurricane and the 1962 Great March Storm and still dishes out enough attitude to keep non-wanted travelers out, even though the bartender is a dead ringer for Winona Ryder (FYI: Don't be the next in line to tell her that). *1620 Long Beach Blvd., Ship Bottom.* ☎ *609/ 494-4242 Cash only. Daily til closing.*

→ **Buckalews** BAR Built in 1874 on the marshes of Mud Hen Creek, this is the sort of spot where high-octane cover bands may or may not allow you to snatch the microphone and sing the latest hits (try it!). Be prepared for some frenzied fun at the most respectable dive bar on the island. *101 North Bay Ave. at Center St. Beach Haven.* ☎ *609/492-1065. www.buckalews.com. Music 7 nights a week. 11:30am to 1am.*

→ **Daddy O's** ★★ BOUTIQUE/BAR Opening its doors in summer of 2006, this swanky boutique is a major draw for hipsters and locals as a wide, comfortable stainless steel bar, fiber-optic lighting, and a sit-back and chill vibe put this spot on the map for class acts. Order up a dry martini and don't worry about feeling too swank. It's definitely the New Styler in town with potential not yet realized. There's also an acclaimed restaurant and posh lodging attached. *44th St. and Long Beach Blvd., Brant Beach.* ☎ *609/494-7051. Daily til closing.*

→ **Hudson House Bar** PUB/BAR The "Hud" is like a stray dog: You love it because it's so homely, and come to appreciate its

Detour: Beware the Jersey Devil!

"Let this one be a devil!" An embittered woman named Mother Leeds was about to give birth to her thirteenth child inside Shourd's House, a cedar-planked shack in the Jersey pine marshes of Leeds Point. The year was 1735. Mother Leeds's words were spoken from exasperation and damnation of her irresponsible husband's lack of commitment and care for her 12 other children. Her words carried on the howling winds deep into the depths of the shadowy Jersey Pine Barrens. As midwives gathered around, Mother Leeds pushed and pushed, and a baby boy was finally delivered and placed into her outstretched arms. Then, the stories say, something happened. In an instant, the boy shook convulsively and began to writhe in pain. The baby transformed to the onlookers' disbelief, sprouting leathery wings out of its back, horns piercing out of the top of his head, talons poking through his hands, and morphing into a horrible horse-demon's face. The thirteenth child let out a suffering shriek, attacking and killing almost everybody in the room, including his own mother, flew up the chimney, and took flight into the darkness outside. The Jersey Devil was born, so the story goes. Wanna see where he was born? Take exit 48 off the GSP and head down Route 9 to route 561. Take a left onto Mott's Creek Road and hold on tight. Somewhere in those woods is the foundation of the reputed birth-house. But beware! Signs with skulls and crossbones, and Keep Out or be Shot are tacked all over the trees, and the "Piney" locals, well, they mean business.

inner beauty. Why does everybody keep coming back? Maybe because it's the only bar on the island with a Grandfather clause that allows it to be open 1 day a year for 24 hours, which is usually New Year's Eve. This speakeasy-style joint always offers a good time. *19 E. 13th St., N. Beach Haven.* ☎ *609/492-9616. Daily til closing.*

➜ **Joe Pop's Shore Bar** ★ CLUB Though you're packed in like sardines, it's not so bad considering most everybody is good-looking and scantily clad. With a constantly rotating lineup of entertainment, circuit cover bands like Big Orange Cone and the Benjamins crank out those tunes you hear on Greatest Party Hits albums; it's a bit overdone, but tons of fun. *2002 Long Beach Blvd.,* ☎ *609/494-0558. www.joepops.com. In summer, daily til closing.*

➜ **The Ketch** ★★ CLUB/BAR This is as kind-of-clubby as it gets in LBI, with several stages of bands, blacklighted DJs, and outside patio mish-mosh. *People* magazine

players hang here when in town; MTV's *Real World* filmed a clip here; and some Denver Broncos wide receivers were here the last time I checked in. The outside deck is fun for sunsets, but the upstairs balcony is where you can get a bird's-eye view of the whole scene unfolding. *529 Dock Rd. Beach Haven.* ☎ *609/492-3000. Daily til closing.*

➜ **Kubel's** BAR Salty? How 'bout that; this was one of the final three sites chosen for the bar scene in the Hollywood block-buster, *The Perfect Storm.* You can feel Blackbeard's presence over the long oak bar, and the patronage is definitely a representation of the ocean's children with swashbuckling tales running rampant. Order up a buffalo chicken sandwich before you head to Barnegat Bay or Barnegat Inlet to catch some weakfish and bluefish. *Bayview Ave., Barnegat Light.* ☎ *609/494-8592. Daily til closing.*

➜ **Marlins** ★ BAR Pump up the volume. Watch out for crazy covers, but also be on the lookout for the quality and quantity of good times as two rectangular bars flank the stage. Fridays are the white-hot time to check in. Two bars, one up a level, overlook the action and ensure a good vantage point of potential hotties on the dance floor. And it's easy stumbling distance to Chicken and the Egg for late night munchies. *2 South Bay Ave. Beach Haven.* ☎ *609/492-7700 Cover $5–$10. Seasonal, daily til 2am.*

→ **The Sea Shell** ★ BAR Poolside hanging, indoor and outdoor patio cover bands, and tons of high-octane energy drive this place, and you'll enjoy the amount of hot action that moves through this hybrid hotel hangout. The outside pool by the Tiki bar is open for swimming during the afternoon hours, but push your friends into the pool at night and expect to be kicked out. *On the ocean at Centre and Atlantic Ave., Beach Haven.* ☎ *609/492-4611. www.seashell-lbi.com. $5 cover some weekends. Tues–Sat, 3pm–closing.*

What to See & Do

Standing as a beacon of hope and guidance for 19th- and 20th-century ships, the Barnegat Lighthouse, fondly called "Ol' Barney," has shone stalwart and strong on the north end of Long Beach Island for over 150 years. The 172-foot tower, marking

the entrance to Barnegat Inlet, was built in 1858, and the red-and-white painted structure is still in operation today. **Barnegat Lighthouse State Park** ★, Broadway and the Bay, Barnegat Light (☎ **609/494-2016;** www.state.nj.us/dep/parksandforests), the area offers true swashbuckling lore as the vicinity was once a hideout of Captain Kidd and his pirates, but now the protected sands offer a panoramic beach with fishing, swimming, picnicking, and nature trails to saunter through. Laminated nature guides on the trails explain the history of the lighthouse, along with identifying the flora and fauna you will encounter. It's truly spectacular.

A stop-by at **Historic Viking Village,** Barnegat Light, where the commercial fishing fleet docks, is a further exploration of the area's maritime heritage. You can browse the shops for antiques, jewelry, and local art, watch trawlers unload their catches, or take a free 1-hour guided Dock Tour (Fri at 10am) to see how the commercial fishing industry operates. It's at 19th and Bayview Avenue, Barnegat Light (☎ **609/ 361-7008;** www.vikingvillage.net).

THEATER & MOVIES

If you're feeling a little bit Broadway, stop by the **Surflight Theatre** (☎ **609/ 492-9477;** www.surflight.org) and get

Detour: Tuckerton Seaport

A worthwhile detour to experience "the way it used to be" along the Jersey Shore is to turn off the GSP at exit 58, take 539 east to Route 9 south (Green St.). The **Tuckerton Seaport** ★★ is on the left across from the lake. It's dedicated to preserving, presenting, and interpreting the maritime history, artistry, heritage, and environment of the Jersey Shore and the contributions of its baymen. Duck decoy carving demonstrations, sailing schools, kayak tours of the back bay, and historic tours of the bayman's life are daily attractions. For some real fun, hit it during the first week of August when the Greenhead Fly Festival and Kayak Race takes place to celebrate the all-too-familiar regional nuisance, the vicious Greenhead Fly. *120 W. Main, Tuckerton.* ☎ *609/296-8868. www.tuckertonseaport.org. It's open 7 days a week 10am–5pm May–Sept. $8 admission.*

in touch with your inner showgirl at this professional theater that runs plays and musicals from May through December. An island fixture since 1950, there are also shows for children. Tickets generally run from $17 to $25.

Don't let the rains and winds get you down; like everybody does when the weather turns sour, it's time to see the latest blockbusters, and no better place to see the flicks than at **Franks Theatre Beach Haven Park.** Five jumbo screens will have the movie of the month playing for sure, and this is a great option for those stormy days. It's at 4 Long Beach Blvd., Beach Haven Park (☎ **609/492-6906**).

PLAYING OUTSIDE
Parasailing
Can't say I've done it, but if you want to drift 500 feet above the bay on a parachute dragged by a 35-foot boat, then parasailing's your huckleberry. At **Beach Haven Watersports and Parasailing** (Bay Haven Marina, 2702 Long Beach Blvd., Beach Haven Gardens; ☎ **609/492-0375**; www.bhpara sail.com), you can fulfill that dream and get a bird's-eye breathtaking view of the LBI beaches, the inlet and lighthouse, and the entire island. The operation will let you descend gently back into the water for a small dip, then shoot you back skyward for a real rush.

Strange Rides
For more ground- and water-based transit, check out **Mental Rental** at 202 W. 27th St., Ship Bottom (☎ **609/361-0080**), with some unique stuff to ride such as a party bike that has seven people sitting in a circle pedaling while one person steers. There's also the Pumgo, a skateboard that operates without pushing, as well as the Wheelman, a throwback to the ol' school Penny-Farthing bike; you know, the really, really old-school one with the big wheel up front and small one in back. All of these are rentable for $8 to $12 per half-hour. The shop also offers for sale some crazy towables like the Halfpipe Thrash and Big Bertha, which are glorified tow tubes, as well as specialized inflatable lounge chairs and bars for the pool.

Surfing
To get the latest surf forecast or get pointed in the right direction to a local surf break, stop in to **Farias' Sales & Rentals,** 5th St. and Long Beach Blvd., Surf City (☎ **609/494-8616**), known as the surf specialists of the island.

Surf Fishing
Surf fishing is one fun pastime to kick back and pull in some fishy fare for dinnertime; and to get set up with the right stuff, stop in at **Fisherman's Headquarters,** 280 W. 9th St., Ship Bottom (☎ **609/494-5739**) as soon as you get on the island, just over the causeway. Pick up bait, rods and reels, and some local knowledge to tie you into a striped bass, bluefish, or kingfish from the suds. By the way, no fishing license is required to fish Jersey beaches.

On the Road **Nuts & Bolts**

Where to Fill Up Any rest stop on the GSP; the cost is generally about the same as in the local towns, so there's no need to exit the parkway.

The Tolls A 70¢ toll on GSP then a 25¢ toll on Atlantic City Expressway (ACE).

Major Highways Route 72 to GSP south, to exit 38 Atlantic City Expressway.

The Back Roads No back roads here, unless you take exit 40 through Absecon to get to AC.

On the Road to the South Jersey Shore

Long Beach Island to Cape May, 71 miles

Finally we come to the East Coast's Sin City. Atlantic City is "Always Turned On" (AC's slogan) and the 24/7 experience at the **casinos** is where dreams are supposed to come true and empires can be built around a few quarters pushed into slot machines while big-busted chicks serve free drinks all night long. It's a sure bet you'll have the chance to let it all ride and go home a bum or a hero (usually in that order). The brand new **Borgata** is flanked by landmark favorites **Trump Plaza** and **Taj Mahal;** they all have their respective merits, from free parking to excellent no-charge buffets.

Once you head farther south of the AC, you'll find the OC, New Jersey's Ocean City, that is. The **Ocean City boardwalk** boasts a family-friendly atmosphere with Ferris wheels, roller coasters, and tons of oh-so-chewy indigenous saltwater taffy. Cape May's got **Victorian charm** and cruising around the avenues lined with B&Bs (it almost feels like you're surrounded by giant dollhouses); but you can sleep and enjoy sumptuous breakfasts in them.

South Jersey Shore Nuts & Bolts

Area Code The telephone area code in south Jersey is 609 or 856.

Beach Badges Almost all the beaches in South Jersey require you to display a "beach badge" during the summer. We list which hotels include use of a beach badge in the "Amenities" section. Otherwise, expect to pay $5–$10 per day.

Emergencies Call ☎ **911** if you need the police, the fire department, or an ambulance.

Hospitals Healthcare services are available at **Shore Memorial Hospital,** 914 Haven Ave., Ocean City (☎ 609/391-8105).

Laundry To clean up try **Scrub a Dub Laundromat,** 418 Atlantic Ave., Ocean City (☎ 609/399-8123).

Libraries 30 Mechanic St., Cape May Court House (☎ 609/463-6350); **Wildwood Crest,** 6301 Ocean Ave., Wildwood Crest (☎ 609/522-0564).

Newspapers & Magazines The daily *Atlantic City Press* has local information and news (www.atlanticcitypres.com), as well as the *Courier Post* (www.courier postonline.com).

Pharmacies 1601 Haven Ave., Ocean City (☎ 609/391-0103).

Police **Ocean City Police Department,** 835 Central Ave., Ocean City (☎ 609/399-9111); Atlantic City Police Department (☎ 609/347-5780; acpolice.org).

Post Office **Ocean City:** 859 Ocean Ave., Ocean City (☎ 609/399-0475); **Cape May:** 700 Washington St., Cape May (☎ 609/884-3578).

Taxes Taxes are 7% statewide.

Welcome Center Atlantic City Welcome Center is on the AC Expressway Rest Stop at Bass River exit 55.

Down to Exit 0 Playlist: Cruising the GSP

- → *Que Onda Quero,* **Beck,** "Guero," 2005
- → *Super Bon Bon,* **Soul Coughing,** "Irresistible Bliss," 1996
- → *Flowin' on the D-Line,* **Digital Underground,** "Sons of the P," 1993
- → *Eurotrash Girl,* **Cracker,** "Garage D'Or," 2000
- → *Flashlight,* **Parliament,** "Funked Up: The Best of Parliament," 2002
- → *Banditos,* **The Refreshments,** "Fizzy, Fuzzy, Big and Buzzy," 1996
- → *Only,* **Nine Inch Nails,** "With Teeth," 2005

Sleeping

There's definitely more affordable lodging along this stretch of coast, and if you can score a room free of charge in **Atlantic City** through casino comps, you're ahead of the game. The shores of **Ocean City** and **Wildwood** have the least expensive options, as they cater more toward the early 20s crowd, but if you want to live with incredible creature comforts, book a B&B or oceanfront hotel in **Cape May.**

CAMPGROUNDS

If you plan on roughing it a bit, stop in to **Seashore Campsites** to pitch a tent. Much more than just pine trees and a fire pit, you'll find picnic tables, a heated swimming pool, lakeside beach, full hookups, a rec hall, laundromat, firewood, ice, and even minigolf. And it's only 5 minutes from the beach; why not sleep under the stars? *720 Seashore Rd. Cape May.* ☎ *609/884-4010.*

www.seashore campsites.com. AAA approved. Rate from $20 (low season) to $48 (June-Sept). See website for complete breakdown.

CHEAP

The deal with Atlantic City casino hotels is simple. Gamble a ton and you stay for free. Whenever you throw down some ducats, always ask or sign up for a comp card that tracks how much you gamble during a session. If you spend a good amount of time throwing away, or maybe even winning money, casinos will want you to stay and offer either discounted or comp rooms. If not, you can expect to pay daily rates from $49 to $249 at Borgata, Bally's, Caesars, and Trump Plaza; but it's tough securing a room on a weekend unless you reserve a few days in advance. The casinos are also a good place to park. Parking is only about $2 to $5 for the night in the casino high-rise lots. For rates and availability, call ☎ **866/345-7773** or check out www.atlanticcity.com.

→**Florentine Family Motel** Kind of cool, cheesy ambience is the hallmark of this Wildwood favorite, as inflatable palm trees overlook the outdoor pool and at night the pool gets lit up with a virtual Technicolored light show, the place is a real trip, an example of the architecture that Wildwood calls "doo wop." Conveniently located on the boardwalk and beach block, you've got two gas barbecues to cook out on, and the hotel offers casino packages to entice you. Enjoy the relaxed atmosphere and all the fun and games of Wildwood within a stone's throw. *19th and Surf Ave., North Wildwood.* ☎ *609/ 522-4075. www.florentinemotel.com. $63–$129. Amenities: WI-FI; wake-up service; elevator; dataport.*

→**Impala Island Inn** Though this is a standard "shore motel" in Ocean City, with adequate rooms, and close to the beach, its extra sleeper sofa and king-size beds in

Events & Festivals on the South Jersey coast

→ Mix and mingle with all the high rollers who enter the **Mid-Atlantic $500,000 Offshore Fishing Tournament** ★★ every year at South Jersey Marina and the Canyon Club (☎ **609/884-2400;** www.ma500.com). Participants compete to catch the largest tuna, marlin, dolphin, and wahoo for a piece of a, sit down for this, $1.5-million pie. Watch the boats come in to weigh in their catches at the Canyon Club all week long during the third week of August, and see who's going to be in the money, as many times the standings change with photo finishes, keeping everyone on their toes.

→ Think you've got game? Put your skills to the test, Magic, and hit up the largest holiday basketball tournament in the state at the **Basketball Classic,** held at the Wildwood Convention Center the week after Christmas. Teams from all over the USA compete for ultimate bragging rights on the court. 4501 Boardwalk, Wildwood. ☎ **609/729-9000.** www.bbclassic.net.

most rooms allow for the comfort of having a few extra sleepers to crash for the night. The centerpiece pool also has plenty of lounge chairs to chill out on poolside while enjoying the midday sun. *1001 Ocean Ave., Ocean City.* ☎ *609/399-7500. $70–$189 king/double. Amenities: Cable TV; outdoor pool; fridge; telephone w/voicemail.*

→ **Pavilion Motor Lodge** An easy stay in Ocean City, the Pavilion is an old-school square box right on the beach; there are no streets to cross to the beautiful, relaxing Atlantic Ocean. Take a refreshing swim, stroll the sands, or ride a bicycle on Ocean City's 5-mile boardwalk. *801 Atlantic Ave., Beach Block of 8th St., Ocean City.* ☎ *609/ 399-2600. www.pavilionmotorlodge.com. $65 fountain view to $180 pool view. 3-day minimum stay in July–Aug. Amenities: Cable TV; fridge; A/C/heat; direct dial phone; daily maid service; free parking; laundry.*

DOABLE

→ **Anchor Inn** ★ Absolutely traveler-friendly, this clean Ocean City lodge, 1½ blocks from the beach and boardwalk offers spacious rooms to fit up to five people, classic homestyle decor with front porch and wicker rocking chairs under a striped canopy to lounge about during the

after-beach hours. *1018 Wesley Ave., Ocean City.* ☎ *609/399-8662. www.anchorinnocnj. com. $85–$135, add $20 extra for 1-night stay. Amenities: Private bathroom; fridge; AC; TV; beach badge.*

→ **Avalon Inn** ★ Located steps from the quieter Avalon beaches, this is the perfect place for travelers looking for a little more peace and quiet, though easily within reach of good times at the boardwalk. Rooms are equipped with two double beds or a king-size bed, and the appeal is not so much of a grand hotel experience, but more like a haven in a secluded area of beach. *7929 Dune Dr., Avalon.* ☎ *609/368-1543. www.avalon-inn.com. $79–$239. Amenities: Kitchenette; fridge; microwave.*

→ **Montreal Inn** ★★★ Directly across the street from the beach in Cape May, many of the Montreal's rooms have full terraces that hold a couple of chairs for an up close and personal view of the waves breaking. Purpose-built as a motel in 1967, this spotless place is a welcoming, family-owned operation with a loyal clientele that books next summer's rooms when they are checking out this summer. There's a restaurant, bar, and attached liquor store, and a combination of rooms that range from simple

Atlantic City: America's Favorite Playground

This is Atlantic City. Here's a complete listing of the sin bins and where they are for lodging and gambling:

→ **Atlantic City Hilton,** Boston Avenue and Boardwalk (☎ **609/347-7111;** www.hiltonac.com)

→ **Bally's Atlantic City,** Park Place and Boardwalk (☎ **609/340-2000;** www.ballys.com)

→ **Borgata,** Renaissance Pointe (☎ **609/317-1000;** www.theborgata.com)

→ **Caesars,** Arkansas Avenue and Boardwalk (☎ **609/348-4411;** www.caesars.com)

→ **Harrah's,** 777 Harrah's Boulevard at Brigantine Bay (☎ **609/441-5000;** www.harrahs.com)

→ **Resorts,** North Carolina Avenue and Boardwalk (☎ **609/344-6000;** www.resortsac.com)

→ **Showboat,** 801 Boardwalk at Delaware Avenue (☎ **609/343-4000;** www.showboatatlanticcity.com)

→ **Tropicana Casino and Resort,** Iowa Avenue and Boardwalk (☎ **609/340-4000;** www.tropicana.net)

→ **Trump Marina,** Huron Avenue and Brigantine Boulevard (☎ **609/441-2000;** www.trumpmarina.com)

→ **Trump Plaza,** Mississippi Avenue at the Boardwalk (☎ **609/441-6000;** www.trumpplaza.com)

→ **Trump Taj Mahal,** 1000 Boardwalk (☎ **609/449-1000;** www.trumptaj.com)

---

doubles to family accommodations with full kitchens. There's at least a minifridge and microwave in each of the rooms. There are some excellent spring and late fall specials, which drop the prices unbelievably, especially during midweek. *Beach at Madison Ave.* ☎ *800/525-7011. www.montreal-inn.com. $52–$275, add $20–$30 more for weekends. Amenities: Pool; on-site laundry; In-room: Cable TV, microwave, full kitchens in some rooms, stove, self-controlled AC/heat, fridge.*

SPLURGE

Cape May is world-famous for its Victorian B&Bs, which add a colorful, stately touch to the downtown area (all of which is a National Historic landmark). The prices usually reflect a night's stay, weekend stay, or at least a 2- to 3-night block, but it's well worth staying at one for the decadent experience of a lifetime. You can check out a full line of the B&Bs at **www.capemaytimes.com,** but here are a couple of my favorites:

→ **The Queen Victoria** ★★★ One of America's most renowned B&Bs, the service is impeccable with a cater-to-you philosophy; just ask. Sit before brick fireplaces in the cooler weather, and in summer, sit in a rocking chair on the porch and get pampered. Afternoon tea, sweets, and other treats are served in true British fashion each day. The Victorian elegance and charm take it to the utmost level of posh comfort. *102 Ocean St., Cape May.* ☎ *609/884-8702. www.queenvictoria.com. $155–$455. Amenities: Full buffet breakfast; afternoon tea; private bathrooms; whirlpool tubs; TV; fireplaces; complimentary use of bicycles; beach towels; chairs.*

Real Monopoly: The Thimble, The Dog, or "The Club"?

No matter what little green or red houses you own on Baltic Avenue in Monopoly, the reality is that the opulence of AC is stuck inside a seedy place. The city has thrown millions of dollars into the restructuring and renewal of the area to make it more user-friendly, but it's always best to be mindful of your surroundings if you venture outside the casino area. When parking, even in the gated casino lots, lock up the cars, jam on that Club, and turn on the alarms, as crime will find you even there. (I'm a slow learner . . . you'd think I'd figure this out after the first car stereo got stolen, but it took the next broken window and stereo to get smart.) Outside, Boardwalk bums are gregarious and mostly shady: Keep the small talk to a minimum, unless you're looking to pull a Chance card that may say "Go Directly to Jail" or "Bankrupt."

→ **Windward House Inn** ★★★ This is a gracious Edwardian seaside inn, family-hosted for 30 years. The inn is decked out with museum-quality antiques against backdrops of stained glass and gleaming oak and chestnut paneling. For the chill of winter, fireplaces warm you right up, and in summertime spend the day on the front porch sipping tea. *24 Jackson St., Cape May.* ☎ *609/884-3368. www.windwardhouseinn. com. 6 units. $100–$250 Amenities: Private bathrooms; ceiling fans; A/C; fridge; hair dryer; TV/VCR; gourmet breakfast; tea served each afternoon.*

Eating

SUPPLIES

Anywhere along the grid pattern beach streets you will inevitably find a **WAWA**, as the convenience store chain has taken over southern Jersey. You can buy anything from lighter fluid to aluminum foil to a turkey club sandwich. Look for the flying Canadian goose on the sign, pull in, and load up.

TAKE OUT TREATS

Probably one of the strangest, yet lip-smackin' tasty treats along the Atlantic City to Cape May stretches is the chewy goodness called **Salt Water Taffy** ★. This

sticky and sweet concoction was born right here in Atlantic City. Legend has it that Salt Water Taffy received its name by accident when a high tide surf sprayed sea foam over a candy merchant's boardwalk establishment and dampened his stock of candy. The next morning, with his candy wet and salty he responded to a girl's request for taffy with a sarcastic but witty, "You mean Salt Water Taffy." At the same time Joseph Fralinger, a former glass-blower and fish merchant, opened a retail store on the Boardwalk and within a year, Fralinger had added a taffy concession and spent the winter perfecting the Salt Water Taffy formula, first using molasses, then chocolate and vanilla, eventually reaching 25 flavors. Fralinger packed 1-pound oyster boxes with Salt Water Taffy, and the 1-pound box remains the most popular Atlantic City souvenir almost 125 years later. Taffy comes in blueberry, mango tangerine, bay breeze, among 22 other flavors. Fralinger's has eight locations from Atlantic City to Cape May, but the original location is in Atlantic City at New York Avenue (☎ **609/ 344-1519**). There's another AC location at Tennessee Avenue (☎ **609/344-0758**). For general information, or if you've got a craving for the good stuff and are nowhere

Got Any Spare Change?

....

Alright, what are you gonna do with all those single dollar bills left over in your front pocket? Well, you know. **Bare Exposures,** a gentlemen's club (ahem, a "strip club,") lies just outside the casinos, south of Caesar's Palace on the main drag: Look for the neon lights, and if it's your game, you can waste those dollar bills faster than at the blackjack tables. They fit right into the girls' costumes! It's at 2303 Pacific Ave, ☎ **609/449-0999.**

near Atlantic City, call ☎ **800/93-TAFFY,** or visit www.seashoretaffy.com.

EATING OUT

Cheap

→ **Anchorage** ★★ PUB/AMERICAN The everyman's bar and grill with a menu stacked with well-done classic bar food. Hot-wing style buffalo chicken sandwich and plank fries satisfy thoroughly, and while you wait, feel free to shoot some stick at the three pool tables or take aim at one of the two dartboards. *823 Bay Ave., Somers Point.* ☎ *609/926-1791. Sandwiches and dishes $8–$14. Carryout available 11am–2am.*

→ **Mack and Mancos** ITALIAN This is the best pizza on the boards. It's a puffy, solid pie of genuine pepperoni, sausage, peppers, the real Italian deal. You can order up strombolis and calzones to mix it up. It's also great for people-watching, as you can follow their boardwalk cams at 7th and 9th streets as you eat your yummy slice. *8th, 9th, and 12th sts., Ocean City Boardwalk.* ☎ *609/399-2548. www.mackandmancos.com. Slices $2; pies $14 with the works.*

Doable

→ **Bubba Mac Shack** ★ SEAFOOD/AMERICAN/CAJUN Down-home Cajun style baby back ribs and bumpin' blues bands soak the joint with spice. Intense sunsets overlooking Ships Channel enhance anyone's experience, but the taste of a MacDaddy Black Angus burger or Bubbas Tucks Racks of Ribs will truly put you in the sunshine. The original location on Bay Avenue in Somers Point has closed, but now they're down on the boardwalk in Ocean City. *Boardwalk between 9th & 10th sts., Ocean City.* ☎ *609/398-1635. www.bubbamac.com. Shrimp appetizers $3–$7; ribs and seafood $10–$21. Daily til closing.*

→ **Obidiah's** ★ SEAFOOD Legend speaks of 18th-century Captain Obidiah Pilkington stopping on shore to spin his seafaring stories while sucking down garlic crabs. Why not name the place after him? The rich mahogany flamed birchwood bar looks just great with a plate of Imperial stuffed shrimp cured with crispy bacon, and a bowl of creamy crab bisque on top of it. *½ mile over Ocean City 34th St. bridge, Roosevelt Blvd. Marmora.* ☎ *609/390-3574. $6–$14 soups and appetizers; $18–$33 seafood specials. 5pm–close.*

→ **Warren's Lobster House** ★★ SEAFOOD/AMERICAN Nestled inside Fisherman's Wharf, the House has spent 50 years as a fish market, coffee shop, and seasonal outside raw bar in the commercial fishing community. Snacks and cocktails are served aboard a docked schooner, and the larger-than-life menu features Crab Imperial, whole lobsters cooked to order, crabs, mussels, and oysters, strip steak, and chicken Française. This place is a Cape May must. *Fisherman's Wharf, Cape May Harbor.* ☎ *609/884-3064. www.lobsterhouse.com. Lobster and seafood plates $13–$29. Sun–Thurs 11:30am–8:30pm; Fri–Sat til 9pm.*

Splurge

→ **Sails** ★★★ AMERICAN/SEAFOOD Ultra chic and trendy, the place is a little out of

Ocean City: A Dry Town at the Beach

Though Ocean City gets a regular crowd of visitors to its boardwalk and beaches, don't look to do any partying here, because it's a dry town: There's no booze for sale and no bars. You can always run to the neighboring town of Somers Point to grab some alcoholic beverages, or head to points south in Avalon or Sea Isle City for the nightlife, but you won't find any Jesus Juice on sale in OC.

its time in Somers Point, but somehow the vibe of the "City" restaurant with customers in suits, ties, and silk, perched along the banks of the Somers Point backwaters, makes a kind of sense. The outside dock Tiki bar serves up tropical concoctions, while inside, the spotless dining room serves up starters like Old Bay steamed and peeled Gulf Shrimp, and crab and lobster au gratin, which run $10 to $20. Entrees include the likes of an applewood smoked bacon-boarded 10-ounce filet mignon, with a side of 1-pound lobster. Entrees run $20 to $45. *998 Bay Ave., Somers Point.* ☎ *609/926-9611. www.njsails.com. Daily, lunch 11am–5pm; dinner 5–11pm; bar open til 2am*

Partying

You can rage all hours of the night at the 24/7 casinos in AC that offer a full-on scene whether it's 5pm or 5am, but more civilized and less hedonistic scenes lay in the towns of Somers Point, Sea Isle, and Cape May, where a large influx of Philadelphians combine polo shirts with board shorts to take over the towns come summertime.

➜ **BBar** ★★★ BAR Steps away from the craps and blackjack tables inside the Borgata, beautiful people dropping tons of Benjamins step aside to regroup or celebrate here. The best part? Sit down at the video poker games at the bar, shove some dollar bills in, and you drink for free. *Borgata Casino.* ☎ *609/317-1000. Daily til closing.*

➜ **C-View** PUB A classic corner dive bar with dingy, musty countertops and tons of crusty character. It's cash only at this old man bar, where you can fill up with cheap, watery drafts in preparation to head out for a day's fishing, or to simply take the edge off. *Corner of Washington St. and Texas Ave., Cape May.* ☎ *609/884-4712. Daily til closing.*

➜ **Cabanas** ★ BAR Though it attracts a slightly more upscale crowd, don't be lulled into thinking this place has a great deal of maturity. Pool tables, Megatouch games, Digital Jukebox, and wall-mounted TVs keep the college image alive and kickin'. Sunset Happy Hours are daily from 4 to 7pm with half-price well drinks, beer, and wine. *Beach and Decatur aves., Cape May.* ☎ *609/884-4800. Live music Wed–Sat. Daily til closing.*

➜ **Carney's** ★ BAR What starts out as a mildly good time usually ends up with grind dancing and tons of hootin' and hollerin'. Weekends are a total meat market, with a winner-take-all mentality where rich guys compete with local surfers for the attention of the ladies. The place goes off the hook during the Mid-Atlantic Offshore Fishing Tournament mid-August for a week of revelry. Sunday's special is $5 buckets of Rolling Rock. *401 W. Beach Dr., Cape May.* ☎ *609/884-4424. Daily til closing.*

➜ **House of Blues** ★★★ BAR The AC member of the HOB chain offers dusty, lowdown blues beats with good times and prime time acts. From Angels in Airwaves to A Tribe Called Quest to Buddy Guy, the house is rockin' with famous acts. Keep an eye out for surprise appearances: native Jerseyans Bruce Willis and Jack Nicholson have been known to show up and bust out a harmonica. *801 Boardwalk at Showboat.* ☎ *609/236-BLUE. www.hob.com. Daily. Ticket prices vary, usually $15 and up.*

→ **Irish Pub** ★ PUB You can always remember coming here from the casinos, but you might not remember leaving. Thick Guinness pints are on tap with a frothy head. This place is a semi-seedy locale that's the kickoff point for a 24-hour gambling binge. About as Irish as it gets. *St. James Place at the Boardwalk.* ☎ *609/344-9063. www.theirishpub.com. Free parking. Open 24 hr. with full menu served anytime.*

→ **Tun Tavern** ★★ BAR Won some money at AC? Across the street from the Convention Center, where high rollers and lucky winners buy the bar drinks around the house, it's always bouncing and bustling with pretty people. You'll find a match for the night if you've got the dough to last it out and make it happen. *Two Miss America Way, across from Convention Center.* ☎ *609/347-7800. Sun–Tues 11:30am–midnight; Wed–Sat 11:30am–2am. Thurs is Ladies night.*

→ **Ugly Mug** ★ PUB Decorated with mugs hanging from the ceiling, reminiscent of old barber shop days, the ones that face the ocean belong in respect and remembrance to dearly departed drinkers who still have a place at the bar. After 10pm, the place gets rowdy and boisterous, with music, live or DJ, where a young crowd rubs shoulders and starts football chants spontaneously, women included. On Thursdays, there's live music and $2 Coors Lights. *426 Washington St., Cape May.* ☎ *609/884-3459. Daily til closing.*

What Else to See & Do

CAPE MAY'S CONCRETE SHIP

On Sunset Beach (at the end of Sunset Blvd.), the sign reads: "Remains of experimental concrete ship. One of 12 built during World War I. Proven impractical after several trans-Atlantic trips because of weight. Broke loose during storm (June 1926) went aground. Attempts to free her were futile." This is the *Atlantus.* Located at **Cape May Point on "Sunset Beach,"** the remains of the ship are a strange sight. The half-sunken wreck, lodged and immobile in the thick sands just outside the surf, is beautiful to see at sunrise and sunset, and commands respect and surf fishermen from all reaches to ply its waters. Sunset Beach is also the home of the "Cape May Diamonds," small crystals that wash out of the Delaware River and down into the Bay. Collectors polish the rocks, which in fact do shine like diamonds.

MARGATE'S LUCY THE ELEPHANT

You've never seen a 65-foot tall wooden elephant on a beach before! **Lucy the Elephant** is an eccentric, endearing landmark built by entrepreneur James Vincent de Paul Lafferty, Jr., in 1881, that stands proud along the beachfront in Margate, capturing the attention of visitors. Her enormous gray and goofy presence marks the site of a historic hotel, the "Lucy the Elephant Hotel," (duh), long since closed, but Lucy is a landmark you can tour to see how this 90-ton mammoth pachyderm was constructed. Find out how many pieces of timber, tons of bars and bolts, and kegs of nails were used to put her together and learn the sometimes comical history of ship captains sighting her and reporting a wild elephant on the Jersey beaches. *Exit 36 off GSP to Rte. 563, eastbound, over Margate Bridge, right Ventnor Ave., 1 block. Lucy on your right. Open Apr–Dec. Hours vary depending on season. Call ahead for information. Admission $5 adults/$3 children.* ☎ *609/823-6473. www.lucytheelephant. org.*

Playing Outside

WHALE-WATCHING

One of the most fascinating sojourns along the Jersey Shore is to see humpback, minke, and pilot whales and dolphin breaching water and spouting out streams of foam, with even a few sea turtles thrown in the mix. Wanna see 'em? The 110-foot **Cape May Whale Watcher** ★ sails out of the Miss Chris Marina, fully stocked with a snack bar, table seating, and 350 feet of railside space to see all of the majestic creatures that frequent the shore off Cape May from March through December. If you don't see any sea-spawned mammals on a trip, well, the next trip's on them. Fares run $35 for a 3-hour tour (hello Gilligan's Island!) (☎ **800/786-5445** or 609/884-5445; www.capemay whalewatcher.com).

CAPE MAY POINT STATE PARK

The **Cape May Lighthouse,** in Cape May Point State Park (Cape May Point State Park ☎ **609/884-2159;** www.state.nj.us/dep/parksandforests; Lighthouse Tours ☎ **609/884-5404**), is the centerpiece of the 190-acre beachfront park. The park sits at the southernmost point of New Jersey and features over 2 miles of nature trails (one half-mile section on raised boardwalk), a World War II bunker, and two gun mounts that were built to protect the Delaware Bay. The historic lighthouse was built in 1859 and maintained by the Mid-Atlantic Center for the Arts, and contains a kid-friendly, homemade museum with displays about erosion, seashore life, the Lenni-Lenape Indians, freshwater wetlands, and a salt-water aquarium. You can climb the lighthouse to its top, and it will definitely induce vertigo, believe me, as you wind up the stairs to the top. The park is open from 8am to 4:30pm weekdays, with longer hours during the summer months.

Hiking

There are three marked trails at the park you can follow to see the varied terrain and wildlife. The **Red Trail** is .5 miles and is wheelchair-accessible. This trail offers hikers access to both the lighthouse pond west and east. Each pond has a blind or platform at the water's edge to view wading birds, ducks, swans, as well as the occasional osprey, which come to rely on these freshwater ponds for food and habitat for breeding.

The **Yellow Trail** is 1.5 miles long. This trail offers hikers the opportunity to see different habitats, including wetland marsh, coastal dune, and the beach.

The **Blue Trail** is 2 miles long. Like the yellow trail, this trail offers hikers myriad habitats in which to view flora and fauna found here at the park. The blue trail offers a longer hike along the beach and coastal dune. Both the yellow and blue trails allow hikers the opportunity to view shore birds, as well as view other wildlife along the shore.

Fishing

Weakfish, bluefish, flounder, tautog, and striped bass reward surf fishing enthusiasts.

Birding/Migration

The tip of Cape May is one of the most popular sites in North America for viewing the fall bird migration. Many species of birds can be seen in the natural areas throughout the year.

Cape May Point is known as a major migratory route. Many sea/shore birds and songbirds migrate through this area in the spring. At the end of the summer, dragonflies and monarch butterflies migrate through the area, stopping briefly to gain their strength before continuing their journey across the Delaware Bay. Cape May also hosts the annual migration of the Horseshoe Crab along the Delaware Bay, where they come ashore to lay their eggs. These protein rich eggs are an important food source for Ruddy Turnstones, and Red Knots.

Cape May is viewed by many as the premier hawk migration route for North America. In the fall thousands of hawks are counted as they pass the narrow corridor of land along the Cape May peninsula heading south. This offers bird-watchers of all ages the opportunity to see these beautiful birds in flight as they soar across the fields and meadows, on their southward trek across the Delaware Bay. You might also ascend the platform with your binoculars to see bald eagles, turkey vultures, and many other raptors.

The **Cape May Bird Observatory,** 600 Route 47, North Cape May (☎ **609/ 861-0700**), is host to bird-watching and tracking seminars that follow the peak migrations in spring and fall, but year-round field trips and nature hikes to observe local hawks, songbirds, herons, and owls keep it very lively.

On the Road to the Delaware Beaches

Cape May to Delaware Beaches, 43 miles

On the Road Nuts & Bolts

Where to Fill Up Plenty of gas stations are on the grid streets of Ocean City, Sea Isle, and Atlantic City, but there is also an Exxon gas station on the median of the AC Expressway, a mile or two outside of AC.

The Tolls There's a 35¢ toll on GSP, and a $29 one-way fare for Cape May–Lewes Ferry for a car and driver (Apr–Oct). It's $23 the rest of the year.

Major Highways GSP south to exit 0 (Cape May). Route 109 west to Cape May Ferry. Once you get off the ferry, take Route 1 South to Delaware beaches.

Tip Definitely reserve your trip on the Cape May–Lewes Ferry. Otherwise, you may be in for a wait until there's a space.

Rehoboth and Dewey beaches are definitely the sleepiest and mildest of the road trip, but you can certainly kick it back and relax with a few spots that tear it up during the nighttime.

Rehoboth is where most of the action is, while the smaller towns Dewey Beach and Fenwick Island are south of Rehoboth and get even quieter, though the Route 1 bars and restaurants are known to stir it up. Both Rehoboth and Dewey are popular destinations for GLBT travelers from Philly to DC, with a number of gay-owned venues.

Delaware Beaches Nuts & Bolts

Area Code The telephone area code in Delaware is 302.

Chamber of Commerce, Rehoboth–Dewey Beach 501 Rehoboth Ave. (☎ 800/441-1329 or 302/227-2233), open year-round 9am to 5pm, Saturday 9am to 1pm.

Chamber of Commerce, Bethany–Fenwick 36913 Coastal Highway (Route 1) adjacent to Fenwick Island State Park (☎ 800/962-SURF or 302/539-2100).

Emergencies Call ☎ **911** if you need the police, the fire department, or an ambulance.

Hospitals Beebe Hospital, 424 Savannah Rd., Rehoboth Beach (☎ 302/645-3289, emergency; 302/645-330, non-emergency.

Laundry Clothes 2 You, 36 Midway Shopping Center, Rehoboth Beach (☎ 302/645-6660).

Libraries Rehoboth Beach Public Library, 226 Rehoboth Ave., Rehoboth Beach (☎ 302/227-8044).

Pharmacies Happy Harry's Discount Drug Store, 4396 Hwy. 1, Rehoboth Beach (☎ **302/226-0220**).

Police Rehoboth Beach police (non-emergency ☎ 302/227-2577).

Post Office Rehoboth Beach Post Office (☎ 302/227-8406).

Taxes Delaware is Duty Free! No Retail taxes. Woo-hoo!

Getting Around

BY CAR

The main areas of these beach towns are quite walkable, so you might want to leave your car at the hotel when you're exploring town, though it's useful to have one to head a little inland to the outlets or for other shopping (though the traffic on Route 1 can get quite congested during high season, and weekends during shoulder seasons).

Drive on the ferry at Cape May, drive off in Delaware!

Delaware Beaches

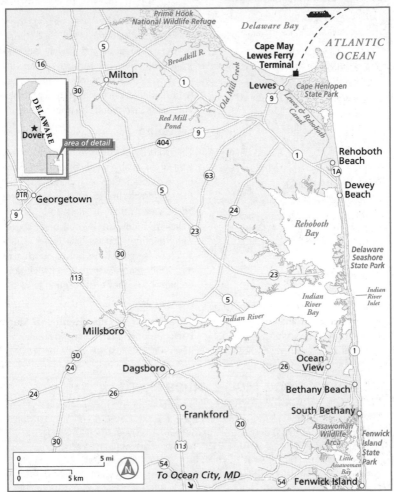

Parking

Parking in Rehoboth Beach can be difficult. Muni-meter parking is in effect from Memorial Day to mid-September, daily from 10am to midnight. Change machines are in the first and third blocks of Rehoboth Avenue.

To park in a non-metered area, you need a **parking permit.** Permits for daily, weekly, or seasonal parking are available from the Parking Meter Division, 30½ Lake Dr. (behind City Hall), or from real-estate offices and downtown merchants. They cost $30 for a week, $10 for a weekend day, and $5 for a weekday. The police will explain the rules and help you get change. Call ☎ **302/227-6181** for information. Once you've parked, leave your car and walk. Almost everything is within a few blocks of the boardwalk and the main street, Rehoboth Avenue.

Playlist: Chillin on the Easy Stretch

→ *Badfish,* **Sublime, "**40 Oz. to Freedom," 1992

→ *Gone Daddy Gone,* **Violent Femmes,** "Violent Femmes," 1982

→ *Don't Follow,* **Alice N Chains,** "Jar of Flies," 1994

→ *The Zephyr Song,* **Red Hot Chili Peppers,** "By the Way," 2002

→ *Beverly Hills,* **Weezer,** "Make Believe," 2005

→ *You've Got Her in Your Pocket,* **The White Stripes,** "Elephant," 2003

BY BUS/TROLLEY

Public transportation is the **DART,** a beach bus that operates a daily shuttle along Route 1 to Rehoboth and to the border of Ocean City. A daily pass is $2.10 per person or $7 per carload when parking at the park-and-ride lot off Delaware Route 1 (☎ 800/553-DART).

The **Jolly Trolley** (☎ 302/227-1197; www.jollytrolley.com) runs a shuttle between Rehoboth and Dewey beaches from Memorial Day through Labor Day daily every half-hour from 8am to 2pm, with limited service May and September. The fare is $2 for adults ($3 after midnight).

Sleeping

The majority of hotels and motels in this area are actually south of the Delaware line in Ocean City (Maryland) (p. 242), though you can find some nicely furnished beach-view rates in Rehoboth Beach. Delaware hotels are a good place to get some quality sleep, as bars close at 1am and noise levels are less boisterous than in the other shore towns. (Fenwick and Bethany boast they are the "quiet towns.")

CAMPING

Campgrounds at **Cape Henlopen State Park** are open March 1 to November 30. Reservations must be made at least 24

Sail Away! Cape May-Lewes Ferry

The coolest part of this road trip doesn't even involve the car (except for driving it onto the boat). At exit 0 of the GSP, take Route 109 West for 1½ miles to the Cape May–Lewes Ferry (☎ 800/64-FERRY; www.capemaylewesferry.com). Reserve in advance for a sweet 17-mile, 80-minute ride from Cape May, NJ, across the Delaware Bay to Lewes, DE, to continue the trip. Sandwiches, bottled water, snacks, and a bar are on the vessel, and four decks of outdoor tables, arcades, benches, and chairs allow for sunbathing, hanging out, or just sipping cold drinks while you leisurely glide across the bay waters.

Reservations are recommended (*essential* in high season), and even if you have one, remember to arrive at least 30 minutes prior to departure to ensure a spot, and at the peak of summer, get there at least 1 hour before departure to get in line for a spot with your car; otherwise, if it's full, you may have to wait for the next voyage.

When you get there, check in, and you'll be given a plastic tag for your rearview mirror, which indicates you've paid. You line up in several rows on a parking area that leads to the lower level of the ferry, which pulls in and discharges the cars from Delaware. Then staff directs you to pull onboard. If you're first on, you'll be first off in Lewes.

hours in advance. Call ☎ **877/987-2757.** There are 139 sites with water and 17 without. Nonresidents pay $29 per night for water sites and $27 for sites without. Two sites are accessible, and 12 are set aside for tent camping only.

CHEAP

→ **Atlantic View Hotel** This oceanfront lodge is steps away from the white sands and rolling surf, with an outside front wooden walkaround deck that wraps around the oceanfront side for lounging on sleeper chairs. Wake up in your plush overstuffed bed and open the balcony sliding doors and smell the morning Atlantic air. It's a very classy, affordable stay. Minimum length stays in season. *2 Clayton St., Dewey Beach.* ☎ *800/777-4162 or 302/227-3878. www.atlanticview.com. $135–$214 holidays; $44–$209 off season. No pets. Closed Nov–Feb. Amenities: Coffeemaker; maid service; wake-up calls; pool; hair dryer; breakfast; beach badges.*

→ **Fenwick Islander** ★ Straddling the Delaware/Ocean City state line, this three-story motel features a clean, flowery atmosphere, with quiet, peaceful surroundings. Balconies on the second and third stories overlook a sleepy dockside

canal. The rooms are standard efficiency, but cozy and warm. *Ocean Hwy. and South Carolina Ave., Fenwick Island.* ☎ *302/539-2333 or* ☎ *800/346-4520. www.fenwickislander.com. 63 units. $45–$159. Closed Nov–Mar. Amenities: Kitchenette; A/C; microwave; fridge.*

DOABLE

→ **Beach View Motel** A mere 50 yards from the surf, enjoy private balconies to breathe in fresh ocean air; very roomy double beds have classic pine headboards, making this a fine spot to put the bags down for a night of revelry or relaxation. *6 Wilmington Ave., Rehoboth Beach.* ☎ *800/288-5962 or 302/227-2999. www.beachview motel.com. $44–$194. Closed Nov–Mar. Amenities: Pool; hair dryer; free parking; microwave; continental breakfast.*

→ **Comfort Inn Rehoboth** Near the busy Rehoboth outlets and only 2 miles from the beach, the spacious rooms here are enough to stretch your legs without paying the prime time rates of the oceanfront hotels. There's an adjacent restaurant and lounge for all-inclusive hanging out. A DART bus stop is right outside to take you to the beach. *4439 Rehoboth Beach.* ☎ *800/590-5451 or 302/226-1515. $59–$250. Amenities: Wi-Fi; A/C; hair dryer; iron*

GLBT Rehoboth: A Gay Old Time in DE

Rehoboth is a gay destination of choice for GLBT travelers from the Mid-Atlantic, especially Philly, Baltimore, DC, and as far south as Richmond. If you've been to Provincetown or Fire Ireland, you'll find Rehoboth a bit less pretentious, a bit less expensive, and less *completely* gay than those other destinations. The crowds mix freely at the various bars, and many gay-owned businesses depend on a straight clientele as well. And everyone can enjoy a good drag act!

For a helpful round up of GLBT eating, sleeping, and partying, check out the FunMaps available around town, or visit them online at **www.funmaps.com/ rehoboth.htm**, and definitely swing by **Lambda Rising** bookstore at 39 Delaware Ave. (☎ **302/227-6969**; www.lambdarising.com), where you can also pick up the local GLBT publications that list the happenings in the entire region.

Events Along the Delaware Beaches

→ The first week in June's always a-hoppin' with the annual **Blues at the Beach** shindig, highlighting local blues and jazz bands that groove out sit-back soulful riffs. In October, the Annual Rehoboth Beach Autumn Jazz Festival warms up the crisp fall air; be sure to hit both venues (☎ 800/29-MUSIC; rehobothjazz.com). Combine the blues bash with the **Taste of Coastal Delaware Festival,** downstate's largest food event, with wine dinners, the Bethany Craft Festival, and the all-inclusive coastal Delaware food festival finale to end the weekend. Contact Bethany-Fenwick Area Chamber of Commerce (☎ 302-539-2100).

→ October signals the dinner bell for surf fish throughout Delaware waters, and the **Annual Fall Surf Fishing Tournament** is a major draw for fish and fishermen alike as they fish north of the Indian River inlet through Fenwick. This tourney is twice the fun as it lasts 2 days. Visit **www.brtackle.com** or **www.oldinlet.com** for more info.

→ One cool event to poke your head into is the **Independent Rehoboth Beach Film Festival** (☎ 302/645-9095; www.rehobothfilm.com), held the first weekend in November. Check out some talented and some downright weird entries from indie filmmakers whose work might grade the screen of your multiplex one day . . . or not!

→ **Oceanus Motel** ★ With stunning wide windows and beach views from the higher level rooms, this L-shaped three-story motel lies only 2 blocks from the beach and is a guaranteed pick by AAA and Best Value. There are over 100 shops within walking distance. *6 Second St., Rehoboth Beach.* ☎ *302/227-8200 or 800/852.5011. www. oceanusmotel.com. $65–$199 double. Closed Nov–Mar. Amenities: Fridge; microwave; breakfast; Wi-Fi; free parking.*

SPLURGE

→ **Bellmoor Inn** ★★ Once a family-owned standard shore resort, new ownership kept some of the smaller, less-expensive accommodations (which are cozy, well-appointed, and some of which look out on the pool), and added a new set of rooms and suites designed to give the feel of a small luxury hotel (along with a spa). As the only destination spa in town, it's done well with the choosy vacationers from DC, Baltimore, and Virginia. The top of the line accommodations in an English-country style decor,

fireplace, and lavish furnishings look like the stage from the board game Clue. There's a library, a game room (with board games!), an enclosed garden, and two pools (one adults only). There's a full breakfast served in the morning, and tea in the afternoon. *6 Christian St., Rehoboth Beach.* ☎ *302/227-5800. www.thebellmoor.com. $165–$625. Amenities: Wi-Fi; high-speed Internet; coffeemaker.*

Eating

The farther south you get, the more Southern the people get (remember, the Delaware beaches are well below the Mason-Dixon line). People are more polite, and the service, although slower, is more friendly, and that's comin' from a Jersey boy so believe me, it's a nice change.

Along Route 1 coming out of Lewes toward Rehoboth, you'll find a seemingly endless strip of every commercial business known to man. Fast-food joints, grocery stores, and convenience stores/gas stations are packed in one congested stretch.

Pick up supplies here before you head farther south. The spotless and friendly restaurants on Rehoboth Avenue are the centerpiece here.

TAKEOUT TREATS

[MTV] **Best ◉** ➜ **Thrashers Fries** AMERICAN A hometown favorite, chipped and browned fries, sizzled in 100% peanut oil are local sustenance. Their fans swear they're the best fries you'll eat, especially doused in malt vinegar. Small to large buckets run $4 to $7 and are the perfect snack to fuel up or to just get something in your stomach after a day on the beach. You can also find Thrashers down in Ocean City (MD), and there's even an outpost in Baltimore. *Wilmington Ave., Rehoboth Beach.* ☎ *302/227-7366. Takeout only. Daily 10:30am–11:30pm. May–Oct.*

EATING OUT

Cheap

➜ **Go Fish Fish-n-Chips** BRITISH Bringing Limey style from across the Big Pond with an alleyway feel from Picadilly Lane, you can order the namesake battered fish, but also consider the Big Ben half-pound Angus Burger, which is grilled to your liking with a bunch of chips ("fries" to Yankees). Wash it all down with a bottle of Theakston's Old Peculiar. *24 Rehoboth Ave., Rehoboth Beach.* ☎ *302/226-1044. www. gofishdelaware.com. Crab dip and softshell crab $8–$10; steak and trout dishes $15–$24. Daily May–Sept; Fri–Sun Oct–May.*

➜ **Hooters** AMERICAN If you're a straight guy (or a lesbian who likes to look) . . . well, c'mon it's Hooters! You go there for the scantily clad, well-endowed women serving hot wings and buffalo tenders. The gazebo-style establishment overlooks Rehoboth Avenue with views of the ocean, as well as views of well, hooters. You won't get any local culture here, just Americana at its finest. Tasty stuff. *70 Rehoboth Ave., Rehoboth Beach.* ☎ *302/226-7588. Daily til closing.*

Doable

➜ **Dogfish Head** ★★★ AMERICAN/ SEAFOOD Touting the admirable slogan of "Beer and Benevolence," this woodsy bar and restaurant, brewpub, and distillery offers craft-brewed ales including the smooth, satisfying Shelter Pale Ale and the Chateau Tahu, a recipe extracted from a 9,000-year-old tomb in ancient China. Wash down the wonderful hoppy brews for $3 to $5, with Drunken PEI Mussels served with braised fennel, garlic, and a strong pale ale to start, and end up with a chicory Stout Rib-eye woodgrilled and accompanied by whipped potatoes and green beans. Grab a T-shirt while you're there. The place also regularly features live music, brewing demonstrations, and classes. *320 Rehoboth Ave., Rehoboth Beach.* ☎ *302/226-BREW. www.dogfish.com. Leafy, green things and Cajun egg rolls $5–$10; filling entrees $12–$22. Daily for lunch and dinner.*

➜ **Harpoon Hannahs** ★ SEAFOOD/ AMERICAN Though known as a fantastic local nightlife hotspot, the place prides itself for its homemade warm breads, including a sweet raisin and savory rye, with blueberry and coconut muffins. Add a basket of any bread to the tropical mandarin orange and shrimp salads, and you've got a healthy, hearty meal at hand. Don't overlook the 50¢ rib specials. *142nd St. (at Rte. 54), Fenwick Island.* ☎ *800/ 227-0525 or 302/539-3095. www.harpoon hannas.oceancity.com. Reservations not accepted. Main courses $4.95–$11 lunch, $8.95–$25 dinner. Daily 11am–9pm (Sun brunch 10am–3pm), with extended hours in summer.*

➜ **Rusty Rudder** ★ AMERICAN/SEAFOOD Five-way Flounder Thursdays include your choice of almandine, piccata, fried, broiled, or stuffed; and you should also check out The Land and Sea Buffet on Fridays. Both specials are served year-round, each for $14 and well worth the price. Every table has a water view of the Rehoboth Bay,

Detour: Beware of Airborne Pumpkins!

Have you ever imagined launching liquid nitrogen-filled pumpkins out of homemade cannons and catapults, just to see how far they can go? Me, too! The bartender at Dogfish Head in Rehoboth Beach enlightened me to an annual happening every November in Millsboro, DE: **Punkin' Chunkin'** ★★, a happy hoe-down featuring live bands, many tasty beverages, and accompanying buffoonery. The 2007 version will be held Nov. 2 to 4. The cannons fire pumpkins nearly a mile with centrifugal machines using huge John Deere Tractor engines, "the World's Most Dangerous Slingshot," and *trebuchets* (that's classical catapults to you and me). Read all about it (and prepare to duck). **www.punkinchunkin.com**.

perfect ambience to dine and sip on a treat from the martini bar. *113 Dickinson St. (on the bay), Dewey Beach.* ☎ *302/227-3888. www.deweybeachlife.com. Main courses $5.95–$15 lunch, $12–$49 dinner. Summer daily 11:30am–10pm (Sun brunch 10am–2pm); Oct–Apr Thurs–Sun 11:30am–9pm.*

Splurge

➜ **Claws Crab House** ★★ SEAFOOD Brand spankin' new on the scene in 2006, a classy crab house with paper layouts on pine wood tables offers clawed crustaceans ready to be feasted upon. No reservations are accepted, but you can call ahead to reserve crabs. The all-you-can-eat special for $29.95 includes corn on the cob and cornbread. *167 Rehoboth Ave., Rehoboth Beach.* ☎ *877/302-CLAW or 302/227-CLAW. Price per dozen crabs: $30 small, $40 medium, $55 large. Mon–Thurs 4–10pm; Fri 4–11pm; Sat noon–11pm; Sun noon–10pm.*

Partying

A little more laid back than the shores of Jersey, The First State's beaches offer a more conversation-minded attitude in the bars, especially in the pleasantly perfect streets surrounding Rehoboth Avenue, which is where all the venues are. A few nights can get rowdy in the town of Dewey Beach. This scene is a good place to take a night out, but an easy one.

➜ **Bottle and Cork** ★★ CLUB Kickin' it since 1936, from May through October, the joint with 100-plus acts ranging from the likes of Dave Matthews, Joan Jett & the Blackhearts, Buddy Guy, and the Allmans, I go along with their self-proclaimed moniker: "Greatest Rock and Roll Bar in the World." At least in Delaware, it certainly is. *1807 Rte. 1 and Dagsworthy St., Dewey Beach.* ☎ *302/227-7272; www.deweybeachlife.com/ ent_bc.html Tickets range from $7–$40, depending on the act. 21+ to enter.*

➜ **Irish Eyes Pub** ★ PUB You can expect a well-pulled pint of Guinness and Smithwick's to go down well as you sit among college students, young professionals, and other transients looking to get green. The reverend Bob Levi from the Howard Stern Show does regular comedy appearances here, sure to offend everybody. Drink specials are round-the-clock. *52 Rehoboth Ave., Rehoboth Beach.* ☎ *302/ 227-5258. Daily 11am–1am.*

➜ **Purple Parrot Grill** GAY BAR Palm trees and tropical flare envelop the fun in the sun atmosphere with fruity island drinks and a light atmosphere. Gay and lesbian friendly, the place welcomes anyone who likes to hang out and enjoy the ambience. The menu is eclectic and not too expensive. There are live shows (including drag shows) and karaoke. *247 Rehoboth Ave., Rehoboth Beach.* ☎ *302/226-1139. Sun–Thu 5–9pm; Fri 5–9:30pm; Sat 10:30am–10pm.*

→Rams Head Beach House ★★
BAR/PUB Another excellent Rehoboth
brewpub (and adjunct to the original in
Annapolis, MD), this is a joint where beer
geeks can go wild with rating and comparing
the many, many brews, but any amateur can
enter and attempt to consume the 100
World Famous Beers and earn a silver-
plated Rams Horn goblet to drink $2.50
drafts out of—just don't do it in one sitting!
A half block from the beach, the credo of the
brewpub says: "Where Great Minds Meet."
Don't prove 'em wrong. *15 Wilmington Ave.,
Rehoboth Beach.* ☎ *302/227-0807. www.rams
headtavern.com/Rehoboth. Mon–Sat 11am–
1am; Sun 10am–1am. Sun brunch 10am–2pm.*

→The Starboard Restaurant & Bar BAR
Another self-proclaimed, World Greatest
bar, it's also the home of the World's
Greatest Bloody Mary Smorgasbord. Get
this: The house is set up like a lab with 700
available ingredients and a choice of 18
brands of vodkas to craft the perfect morning, afternoon, or evening Bloody Mary. It's
an ultra-friendly atmosphere; the mantra
states "Never A Cover . . . Because We Care!"
2009 Rte. 1, Dewey Beach. ☎ *302/227-4600.
www.thestarboard.com. Closed Jan–Mar. Daily
til closing in season.*

What to See & Do
Brewery Tour!
Once you put the rubber back on the road
off the ferry, make a beeline straight to the
Dogfish Head Craft Brewery ★★,
3 miles west of Lewes, off Route 16 in
Milton (☎ **888/8DOGFISH;** www.
dogfish.com; p. 235). With oodles of tasty,
quirky brews, you can see the method
behind the madness of how that thirst-
quenching brew is crafted and packaged.
Make sure you take the 1-hour walk and
drink-through tour Monday, Wednesday,
and Friday at 3pm.

SHIPWRECK MUSEUM
FREE Avast, ye scurvy lads! The
DiscoverSea Shipwreck Museum at
Route 1 and Bayard Street, Fenwick Island
(☎ **302/539-9366**), is one piratey place as
artifacts such as coins, chains, jewelry, and
weapons recovered from the many shipwrecks of the 17th through 20th century
are on display upstairs. (The museum is
open 10am–3pm.) Downstairs, **Sea Shell
City** offers anything and everything shells
from magnets to necklaces as well as a
shell display, which helps you identify the
ones you found walking the Delaware
beaches. Buy your very own hermit crabs
to take with you from $2 for a little guy to
$40 for a monster. Hours Memorial Day
through Labor Day are 11am to 8pm,
September through May 11am to 4pm.

FINDING AN OUTLET (LOTS OF THEM!)
Shoppers take note that in three locations
on either side of Route 1 on the way to
Rehoboth Beach you'll find the incredibly
popular (and huge) **Tanger Outlets**
(www.tangeroutlet.com), home of 130-plus
clothing, accessory, shoe, and cookware
outlets including Gap, Old Navy, Liz
Claiborne, Nike, J. Crew, and many more.

Tour buses pull into the huge parking
lots, and folks come from all over to take
advantage of "No Sales Tax" Delaware. The
malls are crowded all year, but particularly
around holiday time, and on rainy days in
the summer. (Hotels around the outlets
usually stay open year-round, as opposed
to the beachfront hotels, which are mostly
seasonal).

Last time we were down there, we got
some great bargains on jeans at L.L.Bean,
some slammin' bras at Maidenform, and a
gorgeous red Coach bag (can you tell this
sentence is being written by the editor of
this book, and not the Jersey guy?). Open
Monday through Saturday 9am to 9pm and
Sunday 11am to 7pm (☎ **302/226-9223**).

PLAYING OUTSIDE
A Fun Park

C'mon! Let's go to **Jungle Jim's Adventure Land**! It's about 1½ miles north of Rehoboth Beach, Route 1 and Country Club Road (☎ 302/227-8444; www.funatjunglejims. com). How can you beat go-carts, minigolf, bumper boats, rock-climbing walls, outdoor rides, and a water park snaked out with slides and slippery rides? Open May through September from 10am to 10pm. An All-Day Pass, if you're over 42 inches tall (and you are, aren't you?) is $28. After 4 pm, over 42 inches tall is $20.

Biking

Bike among open air breezes and shade tree cover; Rehoboth is the ideal spot for pedaling around. Try out **Bob's Bicycle** rentals, 30 Maryland Ave. (☎ 302/227-7966), which rents one-speed mountain bikes, tandems, and cruisers. Rates for rental are $5 to $7 per hour, $10 to $30 per day. There are marked biking trails in all the state and local parks.

The **Delaware Bicycle Council** (☎ 302/760-BIKE; www.deldot.gov/static/bike) produces *Delaware Maps for Bicycle Users.* All roads are marked and color-coded according to their suitability for cyclists, so there's no guesswork involved in planning your route. Maps can be obtained online.

Bicycling on your own near the beaches is a breeze thanks to the level terrain and the wide back roads. Even a trip up Route 1 from Bethany to the Indian River Inlet is easy.

Boating

Kick it back and relax with a paddle through the still waters of the Assawoman Bay via kayak. The salt marshes and sodbanks are dotted with egrets, herons, and a wide variety of bayshore wildlife. Call **Coastal Kayak** (☎ 877/44-KAYAK or 302/539-7999; www.coastalkayak.com), which is on the bay side across from the

entrance to Fenwick Island State Park (see below). Group tours run $40 and last about 2 hours. Individual rental of kayaks ranges from $15–$20 an hour, depending on whether it's a single or a double, up to $45/$55 for the day. You can also rent sailing catamarans and windsurfing gear, for prices ranging from $45 to $65 an hour.

For even more fun, **Quest Kayak** (☎ 302/644-7020; www.questfitness kayak.com) is set up to tour the Broadkill River with a pint of Dogfish Head waiting for you at the end of the paddle.

In addition, you can rent kayaks, pedal boats, sailboats, Hobie catamarans, and jet skis at **Bay Sports**, 111 Dickinson St., Dewey Beach (☎ 302/227-7590). Kayaks or pedal boats run $15 to $25 an hour, cats are $50 to $65 depending on size.

Delaware Seashore/Fenwick Island State Parks

As you head down Route 1, you will pass entrances for both the **Delaware Seashore State Park** (☎ 302/227-2800) and **Fenwick Island State Park** (☎ 302/539-9060), both of which offer bird and wildlife watching, surf fishing, and hiking trails to appease your inner-Davy Crockett.

You actually travel all the way through the Delaware Seashore State Park as you head south on Route 1, as well as passing over and through Fenwick Island State Park, so essentially, you can't miss it. From Fenwick and Rehoboth, only about a 20-minute drive to get to a part of the park.

Fenwick Island offers 3 miles of pristine beaches, and the chance to see the sun rise over the Atlantic, and set over Assawoman Bay, while Delaware Seashore offers 6 miles of secluded beaches, including 500 sites for RVs and campers, along with a boat ramp. Admission is $4 for Delaware residents, $8 for out-of-staters. For more information, visit **www.destateparks.com**.

On the Road to Ocean City, MD

Delaware Beaches to Ocean City, 19 miles

on the Road Nuts & Bolts

Where to Fill Up   There are plenty of gas stations all along Route 1 south and north outside of Lewes.

The Tolls   None.

Major Highways   Route 1 south into Ocean City.

The Back Roads   No back roads here. It's a straight shot from Delaware.

Welcome to Ocean City

A completely different shore than you've seen so far, the Ocean City stretch offers lots of high-rise hotels and a wide barrier beach island that takes advantage of both bayside and beachside options, where the city revolves around sunrise and sunset shenanigans. Always entertaining, over 150 streets of good times await, with tons of fun within walking distance from anywhere.

Ocean City Nuts & Bolts

Area Code   The telephone area code in Ocean City is 410 and 443. Remember to dial the area code, even when you're making a local call.

Beach Wheelchairs   Free beach-accessible chairs are available from the Ocean City beach patrol. Reserve a chair at the Convention Center or police department by calling ☎ 410/723-6610.

Chamber of Commerce   Heading into town, you can stop in at the information booth for information. ☎ 888-OCMD-FUN or 410/213-0552, www.oceancity.org. Open 9am to 5pm daily, Route 707 and 50 1½ miles from Ocean City.

Convention and Visitors Bureau   The **Ocean City Convention and Visitors Bureau** operates a visitor center in the Roland E. Powell Convention Center, 4001 Coastal Hwy., at 40th Street, bayside (☎ 800/OC-OCEAN or 410/289-8181; www. ococean.com). Open daily from 9am to 5pm.

Emergencies   Call ☎ 911 if you need the police, the fire department, or an ambulance.

Hospitals   75th Street Medical Center, 7408 Coastal Hwy. (☎ 410/524-0075). The Atlantic General Hospital, 9733 Healthway Dr., Berlin (☎ 410/641-1100).

Libraries   The Ocean City branch of the Worcester County Library at 14th street and Philadelphia Ave. (☎ 410/289-7297).

Newspapers & Magazines   *Ocean City Today* is the weekly newspaper.

Pharmacies   Bailey's at 8th Street and Philadelphia Avenue (☎ 410/289-8191); or CVS at 120th Street and Coastal Highway (☎ 410/524-7223).

Police The non-emergency number for the Ocean City Police is ☎ 410/723-6610; beach patrol is ☎ 410/289-7556.

Post Office Main post office is at 71st Street and Coastal Highway, Bayside (☎ 410/524-7611).

Radio On the FM dial, 106.9 the X for alternative edgy choices.

Taxes State sales tax is 5%.

Transit Information Dial ☎ 410/723-2173.

Weather Check the weather at ☎ 800/OC-OCEAN or 410/213-0552.

Getting Around

BY CAR/PARKING

Parking is difficult, particularly at the height of the season. Most public facilities, such as shopping centers and restaurants, offer free parking for patrons. There are also eight public lots, mostly around the southern end of Ocean City. The meters must be fed $1.25 an hour, but there are change machines at several lots: Worcester Street; Somerset Street and Baltimore Avenue; Dorchester Street and Baltimore Avenue; North Division Street and Baltimore Avenue; and Fourth Street and Baltimore Avenue. These, as well as on-street meters, must be fed 24 hours a day between April 15 and October 15. The first 30 minutes here are free; then the rate is $1 an hour, $1.50 on weekends.

BY BUS

"The Bus," as it's affectionately and simply called, is public transportation running 24 hours a day, arriving about every 15 minutes, along the entire stretch of OC up into Fenwick Island, DE. Don't always count on it being on time, or to stop, but standard operating procedure is to find a stop with a lot of people and you've got a ride; $2 exact change will get you a ticket for a 24-hour period. For information call ☎ 410/723-1607 (www.ococean.com/busflyer.html).

BY BOARDWALK TRAM

The Tram travels 2½ miles from the inlet north to 27th street running every 10 minutes from 7am to midnight. Hail the tram down for a ride and raise your hand high to be let off. Fare is $2.50 one-way. It's a great way to see the boardwalk in all its glory. For information call ☎ 410/723-1607 (www.ococean.com/busflyer.html).

BY TAXI

Taxis are the perfect ride for those who have partied beyond repair, but will cost you more than the bus, $5 to $15, for a ride to most streets. Try **All About Town Taxi**

Playlist: How We Do It in the OC

→ *Ice Cream Man*, **Van Halen**, "1984," 1984

→ *Straight Outta Compton*, **NWA**, "Straight Outta Compton," 1989

→ *Stick 'em Up*, **Quarashi**, "Jinx," 2002

→ *Killing in the Name*, **Rage Against the Machine**, "Rage Against the Machine," 1992

→ *Wasting Time*, **Kid Rock**, "Devil Without a Cause," 1998

→ *Fire Water Burn*, **Bloodhound Gang**, "One Fierce Beer Coaster," 1996

North Ocean City, MD

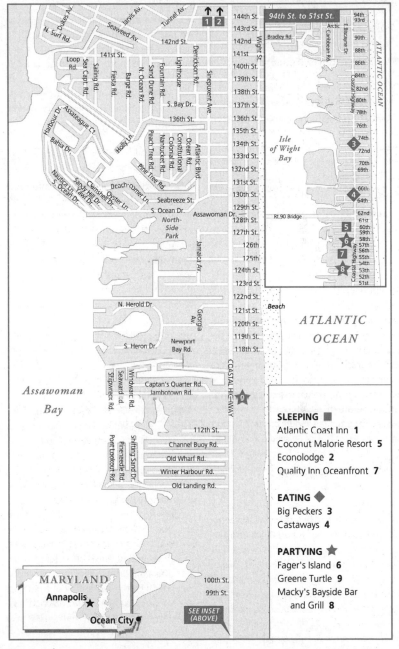

144th St.
143rd St.
142nd St.
141st St.
140th St.
139th St.
138th St.
137th St.
136th St.
135th St.
134th St.
133rd St.
132nd St.
131st St.
130th St.
129th St.
128th St.
127th St.
126th
125th
124th St.
123rd St.
122nd St.
121st St.
120th St.
119th St.
118th St.

94th St. to 51st St.

94th
93rd
90th
88th
86th
84th
82nd
80th
78th
76th
74th
72nd
70th
69th
66th
64th
62nd
61st
60th
59th
58th
57th
56th
55th
54th
53rd
52nd
51st

Isle
of Wight
Bay

Rt.90 Bridge

Beach

ATLANTIC
OCEAN

Assawoman
Bay

MARYLAND

Annapolis ★

Ocean City ●

SEE INSET
(ABOVE)

112th St.
Channel Buoy Rd.
Old Wharf Rd.
Winter Harbour Rd.
Old Landing Rd.

100th St.
99th St.

SLEEPING ■
Atlantic Coast Inn **1**
Coconut Malorie Resort **5**
Econolodge **2**
Quality Inn Oceanfront **7**

EATING ◆
Big Peckers **3**
Castaways **4**

PARTYING ★
Fager's Island **6**
Greene Turtle **9**
Macky's Bayside Bar
and Grill **8**

DOWN THE SHORE

(☎ 410/209-9909) or **Eastern Shore Taxi** (☎ 443/744-4497).

Sleeping

It can be an all-out scramble for a place to bed down, even in the off season, if you don't make a reservation beforehand. Ocean City hotels fill up fast, and the longer you wait to reserve, the more expensive it'll get. Try to base yourself between 50th and 60th streets for easy access to some of the hottest nightclubs and Happy Hour hot spots, or from 10th to 20th streets to be close to the boardwalk.

CHEAP

→ **Econolodge** If you call a few days ahead, you'll probably be able to score a room, with simple yet endearing accommodations, easy livin', and a short ride by bus to all Ocean City attractions. *145th St. and Philadelphia Ave., Ocean City.* ☎ *410/250-1155. $60–$200.*

→ **Thunderbird Beach Motel** For what may be considered cheap for resort high-season rates, plenty of hotels and motels exist to crash for the night, but this is a recommendable option. It's a solid option for roadtrippers because it's so cheap, yet still retains a bit of dignity and cleanliness. Also, it's right in the middle of a hot section of town. *32nd St. and Baltimore Ave., Ocean City.* ☎ *800/638-3244 or 410/289-8136. www.ocmotels.com. $35–$120 1–2 persons, $12 each additional person.*

DOABLE

→ **Atlantic Coast Inn** This place is actually in Delaware, but it's a 1 block stroll to the beach, and near the OC Bus, which will take you to the bustling heart of Ocean City. Rooms are standard shore material, but the kidney-shaped pool outside adds a bit of style. *37558 Lighthouse Rd., Fenwick Island, DE, at 146th St.* ☎ *800/432-8038. www. atlanticbudgetinn.com. $49–$229. Amenities:*

Coin-op laundry; microwave; free parking; coffeemaker; telephone.

→ **Commandeer Motel** Smack dab on the boardwalk, efficiency to classy suites are available. The Promenade suites lead to the second-story deck and pool, while the Captain's suites are more spacious with window views of the boardwalk and beach. *1401 Atlantic Ave., Ocean City.* ☎ *888/289-6166 or 410/289-6166. www.commandeerhotel.com. $61–$243. Amenities: Indoor and outdoor pools; A/C; coffeemaker; fridge; microwave; hair dryer; safe.*

→ **Grand Hotel** ★ A big and comfortably open hotel, it's more of a family-friendly place than party central, with premiere oceanfront views, direct boardwalk and beach access, and lots of room. The 12th-floor high rise deck has whirlpools with ocean views if you want to stay far above it all. *2100 Baltimore Ave., Ocean City, MD 21842.* ☎ *800/447-6779 or 410/289-6191. www.grandhoteloceancity.com. 251 units. $29–$299 double. Free parking. Amenities: Restaurant; lounge; pool bar; indoor and outdoor pools w/sun deck; sauna; salon; game room. In room: A/C, TV, dataport, fridge, microwave, coffeemaker, hair dryer, safe.*

→ **Quality Inn Oceanfront** ★★ This place is an excellent value, with an indoor pool, Jacuzzi, tennis court, game room, and exercise room. You'll also have a chance to meet a scarlet macaw named Chief and a white cockatiel named Macky, who stand upon their cages and strike up a conversation with you. The Atrium bar offers domestic canned beer for $3 a pop, and Casey the bartender can keep you lively and dialed into the nightlife scene, just ask him. Atrium rooms are comfortable but you can hear the commotion of the bar and pool from outside. Ocean view rooms give you great sunrise views. *54th St. and Oceanfront.* ☎ *800/837-3586. $59–$159. Amenities: Microwave; cable; fridge; oven.*

Lower Ocean City, MD

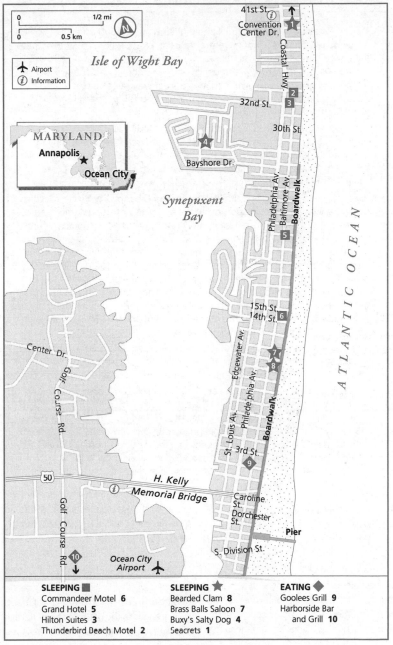

0   1/2 mi

0   0.5 km

✈ Airport
ⓘ Information

Isle of Wight Bay

MARYLAND

Annapolis ★

Ocean City ●

41st St.
Convention
Center Dr.

Coastal Hwy.

32nd St.

30th St.

Bayshore Dr.

*Synepuxent
Bay*

Philadelphia Av.
Baltimore Av.
Boardwalk

ATLANTIC OCEAN

Center Dr.

Golf Course Rd.

15th St.
14th St.

Edgewater Av.
Philadelphia Av.

St. Louis Av.

Boardwalk

3rd St.

H. Kelly
Memorial Bridge

Caroline
St.
Dorchester
St.

Pier

S. Division St.

Golf Course Rd.

Ocean City
Airport ✈

SLEEPING ■
Commandeer Motel **6**
Grand Hotel **5**
Hilton Suites **3**
Thunderbird Beach Motel **2**

SLEEPING ★
Bearded Clam **8**
Brass Balls Saloon **7**
Buxy's Salty Dog **4**
Seacrets **1**

EATING ◆
Goolees Grill **9**
Harborside Bar
and Grill **10**

Bikes, Fish & Hotrods: Events in OC

→ "Loud Pipes Save Lives": You'll see that slogan tattooed on every grizzled guy and girl's helmet during **Delmarva Bike Week** held all over the Ocean City area during the second week of September. It's a good time to see some 100,000 motorcycle enthusiasts riding Fatboys and "Easy Rider" Choppers rolling hard down the Coastal Highway stretch. Good time to hit up the hotels for deals, as you can often find Biker Specials. ☎ **410-629-1560.** www.delmarvabikeweek.com.

→ You're no Tony Hawk, but you've always wanted to learn how to skateboard. Right? Hit up the **Ocean Bowl Skateboard Camp** that runs in June and August, teaching you moves from simple tic-tacs to 720 frontside fakie airs. Ocean Bowl Skate Park, 3rd Street and St. Louis Avenue. ☎ **410-289-2695** or 410-250-0125. www.oceanbowl.com.

→ Catch a buzz and the fish of a lifetime at **The Ocean City White Marlin** open (**www.whitemarlinopen.com**) the first week of August, billed as "The richest marlin tournament in the world" and rightfully so as payout in 2006 doled out $2.3 million for the largest fish. The biggest white marlin alone netted $1.4 million! Stop by the docks at the Harbor Island Marina to spot the boats hauling in the catch and hoisting them to be weighed. It's a full-on party. It's not for white marlin only, though they have the largest payout. You can also fish for tuna, mahimahi, wahoo, shark, blue marlin. Buy-in depends if you enter all the "calcuttas" or sanctioned sidebetting, where you make the real money. Can range from $950 straight tournament entry fee to $10,000 plus with all the calcuttas.

→ On the **Fourth of July** over 300,000 people crowd OC to see things that go boom. The festival with a family-style picnic held at the Northside Park starts at 8pm and fireworks go bang at 9:30pm over the Assawoman Bay.

→ You know the hot rod ZZ Top drives, right? Well how 'bout seeing over 3,000 of those crazy cars all at one show. **Cruisin' Ocean City** takes place the third week of May at the Convention Center, 40th Street and Bay (☎ **410-798-6304;** www.specialeventpro.com), and not only will you get to see some old-school muscle rides, but there's plenty of vendors to pick up that Chevy hat or Ford beats Chevy bumper sticker you've wanted for so long.

SPLURGE

→ **Coconut Malorie Resort** ★★ It's snappy with tropical flair: Palm trees, waterfalls, and white marble floors greet the traveler entering the lobby, and suites overlooking the Isle of Wight bay are impeccable. Caribbean-style suites include Haitian art, luxurious bathrooms with whirlpool tubs, and plenty of space. All the rooms are non-smoking and they mean it: a $500 charge will be added to your bill if you do. A footbridge connects to nightlife hot spot Fager's Island. *200 59th St., Ocean City.* ☎ *800/438-6493 or 800/767-6060. www.coconutmalorie.com. 85 deluxe suites. $85–$278. Amenities: Jacuzzi tubs; free parking; coffeemaker; all nonsmoking rooms.*

→ **Hilton Suites** ★★★ If you've got money to spare, this is the place to spend it. High-end and all lit up, two elevated outdoor

Surf's up big time the second week of June as **Surfrider Weekend** at Castle in the Sand (37th St. and Ocean) hits the sands. Old-school and new school stylers alike compete in the Longboard Team Challenge, with an evening "legends" party, beach party, and kids area through the weekend, and an open surfing event to show your skills on Sunday. **www. surfrider.org**.

Get in touch with your inner Monet, as the third weekend of June exhibits the **Art's Alive Festival,** Northside Park, 127th Street (☎ **800-OC-OCEAN;** www.ococean.com). Over 100 local, regional, and nationally acclaimed artists showcase oil, watercolor, and acrylic paintings, sure to bring out some of that culture you've got deep within you. Saturday 9am to 6pm, Sunday 9am to 5pm.

It's the **Funk Master Flex Celebrity Car & Truck Show,** held at the Convention Center, 40th Street and Bay (☎ **302-436-0183;** www.occar show.com), during the first week of August. The slammingest hoopdies featured in magazines and television showcase their bling, with top-name celebrities making their appearance. Saturday 10am to 10pm, Sunday 10am to 6pm.

Welcome to **Sunfest.** Billed as "Ocean City's biggest festival," shop around for fine art, distinctive crafts, and gourmet delights. There's stuff to do for kids or even your childish self, including pumpkin decorating and scarecrow making. Held the third week of September. Pick up tickets from Ticketmaster (☎ **800-551-7328**) or from the Ocean City Convention Center.

So you've always wanted to polka; now's your shot! The second weekend in October beckons travelers to come to **Oktoberfest** at the Convention Center, 40th Street and Bay (☎ **410-524-7020;** www.oceanpromotions.info). It's 3 continuous days pumping with Polka and Bavarian bands, eat, drink, and be merry scarfing down schnitzels, wursts, and barrels of dark, hoppy beers.

pools, and landscaped lush tropical plants overlook the ocean, and a sweet water park with water slides, a lazy river tube pool, and swim-up bar, make this a fun stay. Two flat-panel 32-inch LCD screens are in every room to watch the game, so you can forget about watching Paris (Hilton that is). *3200 Baltimore Ave., Ocean City.* ☎ *866/729-3200 or 410/289-6444. www.oceancityhilton.com. $99–$439. Amenities: Coffeemaker; room service; high-speed Internet; fitness center.*

Eating
SUPPLIES

You can grab everything from bottled water to fresh bananas, oranges, lettuce and tomatoes at the **Minit Market** 3107 N Coastal Ave., Ocean City (☎ **410/2 89-9137**) as well as load up on paper plates, paper towels, and other such sundries.

A stop by **Seaside Deli Beer & Wine,** 7207 Coastal Hwy., Ocean City (☎ **410/ 524-7207**), can get you set up with all the

To cool down that hunger, see the big guy at Dippin' Dots in O.C.

cold cuts and sandwich materials needed to pack your lunch for the beach.

TAKEOUT TREATS

To soothe that sweet tooth, stop by **Dippin' Dots** ice-cream parlor at 205 Atlantic Ave., Ocean City (☎ **410/289-8877**), for a menagerie of fruity, melt-in-your-mouth flavors. **Dough Roller** pizza on 6909 Coastal Hwy., Ocean City (☎ **410/524-7981**), will take care of that hankerin' for a quick bite to eat. You cannot pass up the chance to have a frothy, thick milkshake, so hit up the **Atlantic Stand,** 424 S Atlantic Ave., Ocean City (☎ **410/289-7203**), to satisfy that chocolate or vanilla craving.

Hanging Out with Pam & Macky Stansell of Macky's Bayside Bar & Grill

Possibly the two most fun-loving people you'll encounter in Ocean City are Pam and Macky Stansell of **Macky's Bayside Bar & Grill** (see below). Celebrating their 13th year of operation in 2006, Pam remarked, "Yeah, all I get out of the anniversary is a Roast Beef Sandwich named after me. Macky gets a steak! What's that all about?" Macky, a friendly man with a Cheshire cat grin and a penchant for ordering shots for the house says, "I love the camaraderie of the people who come here. We've got great ambience, and everybody wants to relish in it, especially the Tiki beach bar out back. That's a fun spot." The Stansells don't discriminate—against dogs, that is. They run a "Yappy Hour" where they encourage canine owners to bring in their pups for doggie treats. And the family-style atmosphere is apparent, as it was raining when I attended a Happy Hour and Pam, seeing me soaking wet, promptly ran upstairs and gave me a brand-new umbrella so I wouldn't look like a wet dog going home.

EATING OUT

Cheap

➔ **Big Pecker's** AMERICAN I got kicked out of grade school one day for wearing a Big Pecker's T-shirt, but that doesn't mean you can't enjoy the fun of the double-entendre spot that's Home of the Bodacious Burger. Hearty chicken sandwiches and a serious sports fan vibe (as long as you root for Baltimore) make this the ultimate sports bar away from home. *73rd St. and Coastal Hwy.* ☎ *410/723-0690. www.big-peckers.com. Open 9am–2am Mon–Fri. Happy Hour 3–6pm Sun–Fri. $1 domestics. $2.50 Guinness. 25¢ wings.*

➔ **Goolees Grill** AMERICANA At this fantastic breakfast joint, you can scarf down Mamma's Breakfast special of two buttermilk pancakes, two eggs, and your choice of two sausages, ham, bacon, or scrapple (if you don't know what scrapple is, you don't want to know), enjoying it on the outside deck or air conditioned inside. Any and all breakfasts of any egg, pancake, bacon, ham, or even (ugh!) scrapple can be found here, made-to-order. And hey, if you want, grab a bottled beer out of the store fridge; why not, it's past noon, right? *203 North Baltimore Ave.* ☎ *410/289-6020. Daily 7:30am–3pm.*

Doable

➔ **Harborside Bar and Grill** ★ AMERICAN/SEAFOOD Two words—Orange Crush. It's the signature drink of the establishment, with freshly squeezed orange juice and some quality liquors to get you loopy. Then add in some spicy Caribbean jerk chicken, chili fries, and chicken Chesapeake lopped with crab imperial chunks. The Harborside Guarantee? "If you're not served within 5 minutes, you'll be served within 10 or 15." Fair enough. *12841 S. Harbor Rd., West End, Ocean City.* ☎ *410/213-1846. Daily 11am–2am; kitchen until 1:30am.*

➔ **Macky's Bayside Bar & Grill** ★★★ SEAFOOD Fantastic maritime fare here; check out the dreamy, creamy crab Alfredo, and fresh from the ocean rockfish sandwiches. Don't overlook Happy Hour snack feasts that include pizza for 75¢ a slice, 99¢ for 2 buffalo tenders and sliders, as well as $2.25 cans of beer, and $2 drafts. The entrees are in the $12 to $26 range. Renowned vocalist Kate Smith serenades patrons (via recording!) as she sings "God Bless America" nightly as the sun sets over the glassy Assawoman Bay. *54th St. (on the bay).* ☎ *410/723-5565. www.mackys.com. Reservations not accepted. Main courses $4.25–$11 lunch, $14–$26 dinner. Daily 11am (dinner served until 10pm; light fare until 1am). Closed mid-Oct to Mar.*

Splurge

→ **Castaways** ★ SEAFOOD/JAMAICAN Though this place turns into a reggae hot spot after dark, you can chill out on the deck and take pleasure in slurping Lobster Ravioli in a light *beurre blanc* sauce or Ahi tuna ceviche in a tangy citrus. Add a house Caesar salad to any entree for $5. *64th St., Bayfront, Ocean City.* ☎ *410/524-9090. Kitchen open till 10pm. Soups and appetizers $6.65–$9.90; entrees $19–$36.*

Partying

With 150-plus avenues, there's always something going down. Concentrate on the boardwalk scene from 3rd to 12th street, between 50th and 60th streets and in the 100 streets for the most centralized action. The ride on the Bus will make traversing the entire stretch in 1 night a very reasonable possibility, but it's best to plan to spend a few days, and take each section on over the course of your visit.

→ **Bearded Clam** PUB/BAR This is both a bar and full-on liquor store, biker and NASCAR central, with some burly characters popping in and out. Freshly squeezed screwdrivers are available, and the Clam boasts the coldest beers and surliest patrons (at times), when it seems like a good idea to step out for a brisk stroll on the boardwalk to get a breather. *15 Wicomico St., Ocean City.* ☎ *410/289-4498. www.thebeardedclam.com. Daily noon–2am May–Sept. Hours change in winter.*

→ **Brass Balls Saloon** ★ PUB Right on the boardwalk, sportfishermen from local tournaments, bikini-clad betties, and college frat boys put 'em back here on the cafe patio deck with the ocean lapping yards away. The Happiest Hour runs from 4 to 6pm Sunday through Friday with $1 Miller Lite drafts and 25¢ hot wings. *Between 11th and 12th sts. on the Boardwalk.* ☎ *410/289-0069. Daily til closing.*

→ **Buxy's Salty Dog** ★ PUB Known as "The Safe Place to Hide Your Bone," this place is a total Pittsburgh Steelers hangout, tattooed with Steeler paraphernalia and 24 TVs to watch the Steelers if they're on. It's a totally pitchers of beer (many pitchers of beer) type of place. Go Steelers! Get used to saying that. DJ Brad is there on Fridays, spinning the latest hits, and Wednesdays are $9.95 all you can eat ribs. *28th St., Bayside.* ☎ *410/289-0973. www.buxys saltydog.com. 11am–2am, kitchen open til 1am.*

→ **Fager's Island** ★★ CLUB/BAR Don't be fooled by the semi-chic atmosphere; there's an arcade room of old-school classics Ms. Pac Man and Galaga steps from the bar. Monday deck parties bring out the noise, and an interesting sight to behold is on Wednesday as Euro-night brings out all the Europeans in town (lots of them come to town every summer as temporary workers) to gyrate to *Discotechque* rave faves. You're gonna be surprised how many citizens of the EU are in Ocean City. *56th St. on the Bay, Ocean City.* ☎ *410/524-5400. www. fagers.com. Daily 11am–2am.*

→ **Greene Turtle** ★ PUB This place is just one big tailgate party to watch whatever Baltimore sports contest is on tap. This is your musty, dark, and downright classic sports bar complete with shouting, arguing, and posturing. Suck down $2 drafts and listen to barflies make ludicrous bets on each and every play. *116th St. and Coastal Hwy., Ocean City.* ☎ *410/723-2120. www. greeneturtle.com.*

➔ **Seacrets** ★★★ CLUB/BAR This is the promised land, as everything and anything a nightlifer could want is found here. Seventeen, count 'em, SEVENTEEN! bars are rolled into one, with all venues and tastes covered from DJs to reggae to rave; if you don't like one spot, bounce to the next bar over sand floors only steps, but worlds, away. Swank chaise longue chairs are offered on the bayside beach to soak up rays or lay out on a floating raft while the staff serves you drinks. Try our favorite frozen cocktail, the Pain in de Ass, which is comprised of multiple layers of frozen rum runner and pina colada, the house specialty. This is the ultimate after dark hookup and funtime spot. *49th St. and the Bay.* ☎ *410/524-4900. www.seacrets.com. Live camera at www.seacretslive.com. Cover varies, usually $3 or more. Daily til closing in season.*

What Else to See & Do

CHECKING OUT THE WILD PONIES

Like some surreal western sketch, wild ponies run along the 37 miles of shoreline and marshes of **Assateague Island State Park and National Seashore** ★★ (☎ **410/ 641-3030**), which is about a 15-minute drive south of Ocean City. By most accounts, these wild ponies descended from a stock of horses that swam to shore from a ship-wrecked 17th-century schooner. The wild horses are a main attraction in the park, and make their silent presence known as you can find piles of horse doo-doo on the roads, trails, and beach; with a keen eye and some luck you can get within a few yards of the equines, though it is prohibited to feed or touch them. It's also dangerous to try, as people have been bitten and kicked when they've gotten too close. Although the ponies are pretty, Assateague Island offers some pristine dunes, beach, marsh, and forest trails straight out of a fairy tale.

The wild horses of Assateague are beautiful to look at . . . but definitely don't touch (they do bite, and kick!).

Heading for the Annual Pony Roundup

The annual **Pony Penning and Auction** ★, a unique exercise in population control, is held on Chincoteague Island, a barrier island adjoining Assateague, on the last Wednesday and Thursday of July each year. The Chincoteague "cowboys" round up the Virginia herd on Wednesday, and thousands of spectators watch as the horses swim from Assateague to Chincoteague, where the foals are auctioned off the next day. Campsites and hotel rooms (only available on Chincoteague and the mainland) fill up fast, so reserve well in advance. If you're staying in Ocean City, get up before dawn and drive the 60 miles to Chincoteague. You'll make it in time for the pony swim and be back in OC for dinner. Although it's exciting to see the ponies swim across the channel, you'll have plenty of company, as in thousands of other people. You may only see the ponies as tiny dots as you wait along the shore shoulder-to-shoulder with hundreds of new friends. Traffic on the small island is almost too much to handle.

Crabbing, surf fishing, and RVing is standard operation here, and you can camp out at the park from April 1 through October 31 at a cost of $30 to $40 per night. Entrance into the state park per day is $3 for residents, $4 for nonresidents; fees for entrance into the National Seashore run $10 per car and are good for a week.

AMUSEMENT PARKS
Frontier Town
Saddle up, Pardner! Time to round up the doggies and hit **Frontier Town,** on Route 611, 4 miles south of Route 50, Ocean City (☎ **410/289-7877;** www.frontiertown. com). Someone with an affinity for Wild West themes created this rootin', tootin' six-shootin' festival in the middle of nowhere, with pony rides, train rides, staged bank holdups, and gunslinging fights. Straight outta the Old West, you'll swear Jesse James is gonna show up. There's also an adjacent water park to cool down from all your rustlin' around. Open April to October, admission for both parks is $18, and they are open 10am to 6pm in season.

Jolly Roger's Speedworld
Live out your NASCAR fantasies and hit up **Jolly Roger's Speedworld,** 30th and Coastal Highway (☎ **410/289-3477;** www. jollyrogerpark.com). The largest go-cart racing complex of its kind in the U.S., the windy speedways will have you and your friends zooming around the track, drafting, and pushing each other around to vie for the pole position. Open Memorial Day to Labor Day, 2pm till midnight; fees that include the minigolf and water park are $25 to $100. A 2-hour unlimited pass to the Speedworld tracks ranges from $28–$35.

FISHING
If you want to get a little further out on the ocean, take a deep sea fishing charter out of two of Ocean City's main marinas: the **Ocean City Fishing Center,** West Ocean City (☎ **800/322-3065** or 410/213-1121; www.ocfishing.com) or the **Bahia Marina,** on the bay at 22nd Street ☎ (☎ **410/ 289-7438;** www.bahiamarina.com). You can run out on half-day party boat trips running approximately 4 hours to put a catch of croakers, bluefish, and sea bass together, or book a charter at the docks to go offshore for sharks, tuna, and marlin. The price range usually runs about $30 to $40 for a 4- to 8-hour trip, rod and reel rental for an extra $3, bait included. You can also

purchase hooks and tackle on boat for $1 to $5, depending on what you need, for example, hooks, sinkers, line. And always tip the mates! They work hard for you: $5 is normal, tip higher if you get exceptional service.

MINIGOLF GALORE!

You can't miss a minigolf course in Ocean City, as the neon-plastic grass greens are omnipresent. Two of the best are **Old Pro Undersea Adventure Golf,** 68th Street and Coastal Highway (☎ 410/524-2645; www.oldprogolf.com), with seven courses spanning OC, where you can play through a submarine and a hanging plastic Shamu. The $12 fee is all worth the effort to beat your friends and talk a little smack on the green. The fee lets you play every Old Pro course in OC, unlimited until 5pm.

Professor Hakker's Lost Treasure Golf, at 139th Street and Coastal Highway (☎ 410/250-5678), has an airplane on the roof. Enough said. The Gold and Diamond courses nail down water traps, caves, and bridges to put you on your own expedition to sink that putt. Open from April through November.

You're no Tony Hawk, but you've always wanted to learn how to skateboard. Hit up the **Ocean Bowl Skateboard Camp** that runs camps in June and August, teaching you from simple tic-tacs to 720 frontside fakie airs. Ocean Bowl Skate Park, 3rd Street and St. Louis Avenue (☎ **410/289-2695** or 410/250-0125; www.oceanbowl.com).

Life's a Beach . . .

And then you have to go home. Eventually! Ocean City gives way to Assateague/Chincoteague, and on down to Virginia Beach, which is practically the only spot we've left uncovered in the Mid-Atlantic in this book (maybe next edition!). Next stop after that is the Outer Banks of North Carolina, which is the end of the Retro Roadtrip (starting in Miami) which is our next chapter. Just in case you haven't spent enough time at the beach.

Retro Roadtrip: Miami to the Outer Banks

Text by Valerie Willis, Photos by Elena Willis

What do superheroes, big sunglasses, and popped collars all have in common? After hibernating in lameness for a couple of decades, they are all making a comeback in the current Retro Revolution. If you are under 25, these things may be new to you. But you instinctively realize they are cool. Things of old are more fashionable today than ever before, but the list doesn't stop with mutant humans, accessories, and shirts with alligators on them. The Southeastern coast has some of the richest history in the country and brings the new-school cool with uber-trendy hot spots.

Along this Retro Roadtrip you will experience the past through drive-ins, vintage shopping, and historic sites that go from the first arrival of humans to the Space Age. And along with the pop culture, old and new, we'll stop, a *lot,* for food, drink, and at swanky clubs, New Age restaurants, and sun-drenched beaches.

From Miami's South Beach to the Outer Banks of North Carolina, we'll follow the sun! So put on your flip-flops, slather on the sunscreen, and head south, retro-chic style.

Superlatives: The Highs & Lows

→ **The Pictures Got Small:** The **Hwy 21 Drive In** in Beaufort, SC, is a serious retro blast. They show current movies in an old-school setting . . . just wait until dark. See p. 297.

→ **Going through the Hoops:** A croquet match at the **Jekyll Island Club Hotel** will take you back to the days of hoity-toity ladies and gentlemen's sports. I'll warn you, though; you'll throw all that gentility out the

Retro Roadtrip: Miami to the Outer Banks

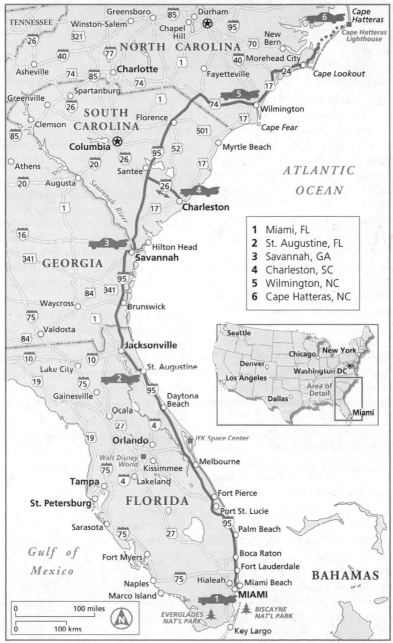

1 Miami, FL
2 St. Augustine, FL
3 Savannah, GA
4 Charleston, SC
5 Wilmington, NC
6 Cape Hatteras, NC

window when your friends get competitive. See p. 283.

➜ **Most Entirely "Retro" Town: St. Augustine, FL,** is the oldest city in the country, so naturally it has a lot to offer in the way of historical sites and old-town charm. See p. 273.

➜ **Best Non-Retro Adventure:** You must take a **Deep Sea Fishing** excursion at some point on this trip. It's intense, and way different from lake or pond fishing. You'll catch huge monster fish like barracudas or sharks. (Mine was a 10-ft. nurse shark!) You can catch and release or they'll let you keep the barracudas, but I don't recommend road-tripping with a dead, smelly fish.

➜ **Most Memorable Night:** No matter how much you drink, no amount of alcohol will make you forget **Club One** in Savannah, GA. It's a gay club with nightly drag shows that draw appreciative crowds for the gender-bending entertainment, including appearances by Lady Chablis, the memorable real-life character from John Berendt's *Midnight in the Garden of Good and Evil.* See p. 295.

➜ **Best Tour(s):** The **San Sebastian Winery** in St. Augustine, FL, gives free tours with free wine tasting (p. 282), but if you don't mind forking over 14 bucks, take the **Haunted Pub Crawl** in Savannah, GA. You'll hit some of the coolest bars in the area, and the more you drink, the better the tour gets (p. 296).

➜ **Scariest Sight:** I'm pretty much scarred for life after experiencing the all-nude **Haulover Beach** in Miami. See p. 268.

➜ **Most Interesting Gastronomic Experience:** In Charleston I ate Carolina Fried Alligator at **Poogan's Porch.** If you haven't had gator before, I'll save you the cost and tell you it just tastes like fishy beef. Go for actual fish. See p. 303.

➜ **Best Beach: Cape Hatteras National Seashore** is a gorgeous 70-mile stretch of beach, and you can spend the whole day beach-hopping from one beautiful sand plot to another. See p. 317.

➜ **Worst Sunburn:** My pale white skin turned a bright crimson at **Cocoa Beach, FL.** Don't forget to reapply sunscreen after playing in the ocean!

➜ **Coolest Vintage Store:** There are two great vintage stores in Miami: **Fly Boutique** has awesome decade dress and **Recycled Blues** has cool retro T-shirts. See p. 258.

➜ **Best Damn-the-Calories Indulgence:** This was tough because sugar is the base of my food pyramid, but the best cupcakes I've ever had were at **Cupcake** in Charleston. I went there every day I was in town (see p. 303). A close second is the chocolate-peanut butter fondue at **The Little Dipper** in Wilmington, NC. See p. 313.

➜ **Most Embarrassing Experience to Have Documented on Camera:** Bikini Bullriding at **City Limits Saloon** in Wilmington, NC. You need to ride a mechanical bull sometime in your life, but make sure there aren't any cameras around to remind you of your alcohol-impaired decision later. (The picture is *not* in this book!) See p. 313.

➜ **Worst Place to Be Stranded:** The parking lot of the **Fountain of Youth** in St. Augustine, FL. My trolley dumped me there and I had to walk forever back to my hotel in the historic district. Maybe worse, the **Cedar Island Ferry Dock** on the way to the Outer Banks is a terrible place to wait 3 hours after the ferry shoves off without you.

➜ **Grossest Car Smell:** Georgia peaches are yummy, but not when they're rotting underneath the passenger seat of your car. That, mixed with the smell of clothes covered in deep-sea fish guts, is vile.

Grab a stool at the counter of Miami's 11th Street Diner.

Just the Facts

Trip in a Box

Total Miles From Miami to Cape Hatteras, 1,040 miles.

Route I-95 to US Route 17 in South Carolina then to state Route 12 at the Outer Banks of North Carolina.

States Florida, Georgia, South Carolina, and North Carolina.

Trip Time 14 days for the whole thing, longer if you would like to linger in the big cities.

Hitting the Highlights Hitting only the bigger towns, you can do it in around a week, or you can do individual legs that last from 4 to 7 days each: Miami to St. Augustine (300 miles), Savannah to Wilmington (300 miles), or Charleston to the Outer Banks (500 miles).

When to Go Winter, spring, or summer would be the best times to go since fall is hurricane season (though if you're willing to gamble that there won't be a hurricane, the fall rates are generally much lower than high season). It's really hot during the summer, which is high season in the Carolinas. Prices drop in the northern parts of this trip during the winter, but they remain high in winter in southern Florida, especially during the holidays. Whenever you're traveling to a beach destination in high season, there may also be a minimum-night stay required.

The Money Part

ACCOMMODATIONS

Your biggest chunk of change will be spent for lodging in Miami. *Everything* costs more in Miami, especially hotels, so in the general price ranges Miami is usually at the top. In locations that have low and high seasons, the cost of accommodations usually rises about $40 per night in the high season, and there are sometimes minimum stays. To cut the cost, there are great campgrounds in most cities that charge $10 to $30 per night. Hostels in some cities cost about $20 per night and cheap hotels range from $50 to $80. Splurge hotels can be $200 a night, and *way* up, during peak seasons.

TRANSPORTATION

You'll be driving about 1,000 miles, so get ready to spend about $100 for gas. Most cities on this trip offer cheap and sometimes free parking, although Miami is an exception. There you'll spend around $30 per night for valet at hotels and the Pay-to-Park

prices are obscene. All of the towns on this trip are pedestrian friendly, and you can usually walk from the major hotels to the nightlife spots so you won't need to worry about cab fares.

FOOD

To eat out at every meal you can expect to spend $20 to $30 a day on cheap/doable restaurants (add more for alcoholic beverages). To cut the cost, there are grocery stores and farmers markets in each location and there are kitchens in some hostels and hotel suites where you can prepare your own meals (not to mention the continental breakfasts that are usually included when you're staying at a chain hotel).

OTHER EXPENSES

Most beaches along the trip don't charge for a beach pass but the ones that do usually only cost around $5 to get in. Club and bar cover charges usually run from $5 to $20. Attractions and historical sites go from $0 to $20 but many offer student discounts.

Starting Out: Miami, FL

Sunny Miami is a city that seems to live each day only for the festivities of each night. With enough attractions and activities to fill up a 24-hour day, make sure you schedule a little time to sleep. Miami is the perfect place to start your retro journey into the past. With vibrant reminders of

the 1950s when the city first became a bustling hub of music, art, and culture, Miami embraces its retro roots but shines with the hottest trends of today.

So don your shades; you'll need them for the sunny days and the neon nights here in Miami Beach.

Miami Nuts & Bolts

Area Code   The area codes in Miami are 305 and 786.

Business Hours   Banks in Miami are generally open Monday to Friday from 9am to 3pm or later, although most banks have 24-hour ATMs. Stores are open from 10am to 6pm Monday to Saturday, but mall shops stay open to about 8 or 9pm. Bars in Miami close around 5am daily.

Doctors   Miami has a **Physician Referral Service** that you can contact at ☎ 305/324-8717.

Drugstores   There are **Walgreens** all over town and many are open 24 hours. Call the Walgreens hot line at ☎ 800/925-4733 for the pharmacy nearest you.

Emergencies   For the police, fire department, or ambulance, dial ☎ **911** from any phone.

Hospitals   There is a 24-hour emergency room at the **Health South Doctors Hospital,** 5000 University Dr., Coral Gables (☎ 305/324-8717).

Internet   Most of the South Beach hotels have wireless Internet in the lobby, but for Internet cafes, check out **South Beach Internet Café,** 1106 Collins Ave. (☎ 305/532-4331) or **Cyber Café,** 1574 Washington Ave. (☎ 305/534-0057).

Laundry/Dry Cleaners   The best 24-hour laundry facility in the South Beach area is **Clean Machine Laundry,** 226 12th St. (☎ 305/534-9429).

Libraries   Miami's main library is at 101 W. Flagler St. (☎ 305/375-2665). The library on South Beach is located at 7501 Collins Ave. (☎ 305/864-5392).

Liquor Laws   You must be 21 or older to purchase or consume alcohol in Florida. It is illegal to have open containers in your car or in a public area not zoned for alcohol consumption and cops won't hesitate to fine you. Make sure you bring your ID with you everywhere because bars and clubs almost always check them.

Lost Property   To report lost or stolen property, call the police department at ☎ **305/595-6263.**

Newspapers & Magazines   The *Miami Herald* is the daily newspaper and has a decent weekend guide. There are a handful of free society magazines that can give you up-to-date info on the hottest clubs and entertainment listings that you can pick up at South Beach boutique stores and restaurants. Among these are the *Lincoln Road Magazine* and *Ocean Drive.*

Police   For an emergency, call ☎ **911.** For other matters, call the police department at ☎ 305/595-6263.

Radio   For rock, tune to WBGG (105.9) or WZTA (94.9); for top-40 tracks, WHYI (100.3); and for hip-hop, MEGA 103 (103.5). If you want serious Miami club music, turn to Party 93.1 (93.1) and for Latin, WDNA (88.9)

Taxes   Florida has a 6% sales tax on everything purchased, including food, and the hotel tax in Miami is 11.5%.

Time Zone   Miami is on Eastern Standard Time.

Transit Information   For information regarding Miami transit, contact the **Metro Dade Transit Agency** at ☎ 305/770-3131 or check the website, www.co.miami-dade.fl.us/transit.

Useful Telephone Numbers   To hear current time and temperature, call ☎ 305/324-8811.

Weather   Miami's hurricane season runs from August to November. You can hear up-to-date weather information by calling ☎ 305/229-4522. The latest hurricane advisories are available at www.nhc.noaa.gov and weather and tide info can be accessed at www.srh.noaa.gov/mfl.

RETRO ROADTRIP

Getting Around

Miami has a transportation network that involves trains, buses, and taxis, but it is easier to drive your own car rather than rely on the slow-circulating bus system that doesn't have a lot of stops. To explore the city of Miami, you'll definitely need a car; but for South Beach, everything is pretty close together and it is easy to get around on foot.

I-95 runs into Downtown Miami and there are a few causeways that will get you to South Beach. These are the 79th Street, Julia Tuttle, Venetian, and MacArthur causeways, and you'll usually have to pay a $1 to $2 toll. In South Beach, Ocean Drive is the street nearest the ocean; Collins and Washington avenues are parallel to Ocean Drive and have a lot of hotels, restaurants, and shops on them; and Lincoln Road runs perpendicular to those and is between 16th and 17th streets.

BY CAR

Remember to allow extra time when driving over causeways because the drawbridges frequently open up and stop traffic for a few minutes. Also, avoid driving down Ocean Drive at night because it is *always* congested. As for parking, there are Pay-to-Park meters on every street that charge around $1 per hour, or if you don't want the hassle of repaying every few hours, there are parking garages everywhere and many restaurants offer valet. Just be ready to fork out anywhere from $5 to $25 for valet and garages during nightly special events.

BY BUS

If you're smart, you won't attempt to get around town by bus. The bus system is

Rockin' the Retro in Miami

There are a ton of happenin' places around Miami, but the classics haven't gone out of style. Here are the ultimate retro stops for your vintage venture:

→ For an authentically retro dining experience, head to the **11th Street Diner,** an eatery from the 1950s located next to a gay club on South Beach. The boomerang Formica, glittery vinyl booths, and '50s decor will take you back to Nick at Nite reruns (although I don't think drag queens made frequent cameos on old-school sitcoms). See p. 263.

→ Opened in 1926, the **Biltmore Hotel** is a landmark in the history of Miami. You can tour it for free and hear fireside tales about its past. See p. 267.

→ Stock up on your vintage garb at one of Miami's many vintage stores. At **Fly Boutique** (650 Lincoln Rd.; ☎ 305/604-8508) you'll find a nice selection of quality vintage clothing, or try **Recycled Blues** (1507 Washington Ave.; ☎ 305/538-0656) for a huge selection of used Levis and old-school T-shirts.

→ For a night of debauchery, check out **Tobacco Road** (626 Miami Ave.; ☎ 305/374-1198). It has been around for over 80 years and it's still a hoppin' nighttime joint. This was where Al Capone and his mobsters hung for smooth jazz and long drags on their stogies. If you want a younger and trendier crowd, but are keen to stick to the theme, hit up the party at **PawnShop.** This is one of Miami's hottest clubs, located in a 1930s pawn shop, complete with vintage furniture and retro adornments. See p. 258.

Miami Highlights

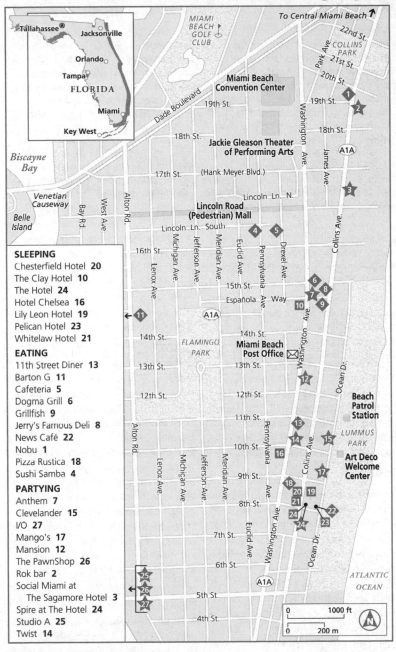

To Central Miami Beach ↑

MIAMI BEACH GOLF CLUB

Miami Beach Convention Center

Jackie Gleason Theater of Performing Arts

(Hank Meyer Blvd.)

Lincoln Road (Pedestrian) Mall

Biscayne Bay

Venetian Causeway

Belle Island

FLAMINGO PARK

Miami Beach Post Office ✉

Beach Patrol Station

LUMMUS PARK

Art Deco Welcome Center

ATLANTIC OCEAN

FLORIDA — Tallahassee ®, Jacksonville, Orlando, Tampa, Miami, Key West

SLEEPING
Chesterfield Hotel **20**
The Clay Hotel **10**
The Hotel **24**
Hotel Chelsea **16**
Lily Leon Hotel **19**
Pelican Hotel **23**
Whitelaw Hotel **21**

EATING
11th Street Diner **13**
Barton G **11**
Cafeteria **5**
Dogma Grill **6**
Grillfish **9**
Jerry's Famous Deli **8**
News Café **22**
Nobu **1**
Pizza Rustica **18**
Sushi Samba **4**

PARTYING
Anthem **7**
Clevelander **15**
I/O **27**
Mango's **17**
Mansion **12**
The PawnShop **26**
Rok bar **2**
Social Miami at
    The Sagamore Hotel **3**
Spire at The Hotel **24**
Studio A **25**
Twist **14**

0 — 1000 ft
0 — 200 m

A History of Miami, MTV Style

Miami's history begins long before Columbus days. The Tequesta Indians were the first residents of the tip of the peninsula. Europeans arrived in the 1600s. Fast forward a few hundred years to 1896. A man named Henry Flagler was in charge of the railroad that ran down the east coast, and he decided to extend the tracks to Miami and grace the area with its first hotel. This made Miami a prime target for ambitious land settlers, city developers, and the first wave of sun-seeking visitors. Fast forward again to the post-Depression era and Miami's second economic boom when the Art Deco style of architecture took hold, much of which still exists today all over South Beach. The third boom struck in the '50s when the beach became a cultural hotbed for visitors, and celebrities like the Rat Pack. Cultural diversity bloomed during the next few decades and after an influx of refugees arrived after Castro's revolution in Cuba, Miami became what it is today: a bilingual, neon, leopard-print-wearing, party-loving, crayon box-of-colors, crock-pot-of-culture.

slow moving and you will probably spend most of your time waiting at bus stops. But if you want to try it, the fare is $1.25 and bus maps are available at the Greater Miami Convention and Visitor's Bureau (701 Brickell Ave., Suite 700; ☎ **800/933-8448**), or you can call ☎ **305/770-3131** for more public-transit info.

ON FOOT

South Beach is very pedestrian friendly, but don't expect to be able to walk from the most southern tip to Lincoln Road. Your best bet is to park somewhere central and walk from there rather than try to hike from South to North and back again.

Sleeping

Finding super cheap *anything* in Miami is almost impossible, and that includes hotels. Most hotel rates are moderate to insanely expensive, and camping is inadvisable because of the crime rate and the Scary Larrys who lurk on the beach at night. However, many of the South Beach hotels are fun, trendy, and attract a lot of young travelers so you're guaranteed a great time. Many of the SoBe hotels offer significant rate discounts if you book directly from their websites, so start your

search for the lowest rates online. The places near Ocean Drive are closest to the beach and the nighttime action, but if you're a light sleeper beware: The nightly party on South Beach doesn't cool down until dawn, so unless you're a part of the commotion, you'll hear it all night.

CHEAP

→ **The Clay Hotel** If you're interested in mingling with Europeans and international backpackers, there's no better place than this rustic hotel and hostel. Situated on bustling Washington Avenue and Espanola Way, there are attractions, shops, restaurants, and beaches within walking distance to keep you and your new international friends busy during your stay. *1438 Washington Ave.* ☎ *305/534-2988. www.clayhotel.com. Winter $27 dorm beds (4-, 6-, 8-person), $53–$68 double; off season $27 dorm beds. $48–$56 double. Parking $10. Amenities: Cafe; access to health club; bike rental; concierge; kitchen; coin laundry; lockers; Internet access.*

DOABLE

→ **Hotel Chelsea** This hotel is popular with young twenty-somethings because of its interactive atmosphere provided by

Veering off Retro Road: Miami Festivals

There's always some sort of festival going on in Miami. Whether it's for food, music, sports, or art, celebrations here happen year-round. This is just a tiny taste of the festival smorgasbord:

→ The **South Beach Wine & Food Festival** in February is 3 days of stomach-stuffing goodness. World-renowned chefs (you'll recognize many as Food Network personalities) and professional winos come together to share their skills and their culinary creations with onlookers. You can sample all the tasty treats and get cooking advice from great chefs. **www.SoBeWineandFoodFest.com.**

→ Also in February is the **Volleypalooza Model Volleyball Tournament.** 350 top fashion models (yeah, I said models) in teams sponsored by their respective agencies spike, dive, and primp their way to the final championship. The victors get a trophy and cash to donate to a charity. Spectator sports never looked so good. **www.volleypalooza.com.**

→ The **Winter Party Festival** in November is a whole week of parties, music, and dancing all for the good cause of HIV/AIDS awareness. Each year has a theme for nightly parties, and creativity is encouraged in participants' costumes as long as their outfits are completely white. This is a favorite LGBT event, but anyone is welcome. **www.winterparty.com.**

→ August is **Miami Spice Restaurant Month** where dozens of local restaurants offer special lunch and dinner menus at reduced rates. Three-course meals are dished up all month to any interested taker. Good deals don't last long in Miami so scarf it while it's hot. **www.miamirestaurantmonth.com.**

RETRO ROADTRIP

daily Happy Hours, communal breakfasts, and a cozy outdoor seating area at the entrance of the building. The decor is half-hearted feng shui and the slate tiled bathrooms have full-length mirrors that are sure to have an effect on your personal Zen. *944 Washington Ave. ☎ 305/543-4069. www.thehotelchelsea.com. 42 units. Winter $155–$225; off season $85–$155 double. Continental breakfast and complimentary cocktails included. Valet parking $30. Amenities: Bar; concierge; Internet access; gym passes; VIP passes to all South Beach clubs; free airport shuttle. In room: CD player, minibar, safe.*

→**Chesterfield Hotel** ★ Ever seen a concierge double as a club DJ? Meet the Chesterfield. At night the tribal/safari decorated lobby transforms into a mini VIP club for guests of this and a few other SoBe Hotels. The rooms are small and the showers are "open" (meaning door or curtain-less) but you won't be spending too much time away from the party in the lobby. *855 Collins Ave. ☎ 305/531-5831. www.thechesterfieldhotel.com. 50 units. Winter $125–$235 double; off season $75–$95 double. Continental breakfast and complimentary cocktails included. Valet parking $30. Amenities: Free airport shuttle. Concierge; Internet access; In room: Dataport, minibar, safe, CD player.*

→**Lily Leon Hotel** ★★ Formerly two separate hotels, the Lily and the Leon combined and are now the perfect solution for group traveling. The double rooms are spacious and have pullout sofas for extra travelers, or better yet, reserve a junior suite that comes with two queen-size beds, a pullout sofa, and a minikitchen. *835–841 Collins Ave. ☎ 305/673-3767. www.lilyleon*

hotel.com. 36 units. Winter $145–$245 suite; off season $100–$195 suite. Complimentary cocktails included. Amenities: Concierge; lobby bar and restaurant; room service; laundry service; free airport shuttle. In room: Fridge, CD player.

SPLURGE

→ **The Hotel** ★★★ Unlike many of Miami's upscale hotels, The Hotel is warm and welcoming from the minute you set foot inside the porthole-windowed lobby. A whimsical color scheme is woven throughout and is a refreshing change from the stark whiteness that is all too common among South Beach hotels. The rooms are simple but happy and have colorful mosaic tiled bathrooms. The first floor contains a funky bar, the Asian-inspired restaurant **Wish,** and an outdoor courtyard lounge that is situated beneath umbrellas and palm trees. Head up to the top floor and soak up some rays and incredible ocean views at the rooftop pool and Spire bar. 801 Collins Ave. ☎ 877/843-4683. www.thehotelofsouthbeach.com. 53 units. Winter $165–$325 double; off season $150–$225 double. Self parking $10 per day, valet parking $25 per day. Amenities: Bar; lounge; rooftop pool; restaurant; Fitness studio; concierge; Internet access; complimentary beach chairs and umbrella. In room: dataport, Minibar, CD player.

→ **Pelican Hotel** ★★ Created by the funky hipsters who came up with Diesel Jeans, this arty hotel captures the essence of the diverse culture of Miami. Each of the rooms and suites is decorated in a unique (and usually bizarre) theme with names like "Halfway to Hollywood" or the most popular "Best Whorehouse" room that has red velvet walls and brothel-style lamps. 826 Ocean Dr. ☎ 800/7-PELICAN or 305/673-3373. www.pelicanhotel.com. 30 units. Winter $180–$250 double; off season $135–$155 double. Valet parking $22. Amenities: Restaurant; bar;

Internet access; room service; laundry service; complimentary beach towels and chairs. In room: Dataport, fridge, safe, CD player.

→ **Whitelaw Hotel** ★ At first glance this hotel seems like just another South Beach hotel with its sheer draperies and industrial metal accents, but make your way into any of the rooms and you will find a surprising coziness in the all white space. Continental breakfast is included, but for a small fee you can upgrade the standard coffee and muffin to an omelet filled with absolutely anything you want. The lobby bar buzzes every evening from 7 to 8pm when the complimentary drinks and conversation flow freely. 808 Collins Ave. ☎ 305/398-7000. www.whitelawhotel.com. 49 units. Winter $165–$190 double; off season $125–$145 double. Breakfast and complimentary drinks included. Valet parking $30. Amenities: Internet access; laundry service; free airport shuttle; complimentary VIP nightclub access; complimentary beach club access. In room: Dataport, minibar, safe, CD player.

Eating

SUPPLIES

There are a few minigrocery stores on South Beach, but your best bet for finding everything you need for a picnic is the **Publix** supermarket (1920 Dade Blvd.; ☎ **305/534-4621**).

TAKE-OUT TREATS

→ **Dogma Grill** HOT DOGS This isn't your run-of-the-mill boiled mystery-wiener hot dog stand. Oh no, at Dogma there are 22 specialty topping combinations atop all natural beef or veggie franks. Choose from imaginative options like the Tropicale with mozzarella, bacon, and pineapple; or the Burrito Dog wrapped inside a flour tortilla with chili, bacon, mustard, and cheddar. If you don't want to leave your cozy towel and umbrella, they'll deliver your dog right to the beach. *1500 Washington Ave.* ☎ *305/ 695-8259. www.dogmagrill.com. Hot dogs $3–$6. Sun–Thurs 11am–midnight; Fri–Sat 11am–4am.*

EATING OUT

Cheap

➜**11th Street Diner** AMERICAN This stainless-steel greasy spoon is South Beach's only authentic retro diner (the building dates back to the 1940s) and it is the perfect setting to recap the night's events over breakfast or gravy-smothered fried things. A diverse customer clientele flows in all night from the nearby clubs and gay bars, so you're sure to have a memorable experience. *1065 Washington Ave.* ☎ *305/534-6373. Entrees $5–$15. Daily 24 hr.*

➜**Jerry's Famous Deli** ✶ DELI The only thing bigger than the plates at Jerry's is the menu (there are over 700 items). With sandwiches, pasta, pizza, burgers, breakfast all day, and traditional Jewish deli favorites, they make sure nobody leaves without needing to loosen their pants. Service is slow, but you'll need a lot of time to make a dent in your dinner anyway. *1450 Collins Ave.* ☎ *305/532-8030. www.jerrysfamousdeli.com. Breakfast $6–$12; lunch and dinner $8–$20. Daily 24 hr. Valet parking $10.*

➜**Pizza Rustica** ✶ PIZZA Perhaps it's that pizza always tastes better in the middle of the night, but you will undoubtedly encounter a line of Rustica addicts whatever the hour. The gigantic slices come in traditional varieties or house specialties like arugula salad pizza, chicken Parmesan pizza, or chocolate hazelnut pizza. Whether you go for lunch, dinner, or a late night bite, just remember the pizza is definitely worth the wait. *863 Washington Ave.* ☎ *305/674-8244. www.pizza-rustica.com. Slice $3.75. Credit cards not accepted. Daily 11am–6am.*

Doable

➜**Cafeteria** ✶✶ AMERICAN If you don't mind the haughty service, there's no better place to go for gourmet comfort food. You won't find mac & cheese this good outside of grandma's kitchen, and the tomato basil soup with grilled cheese croutons is to die for. If you've got a sweet tooth, go for the lip-smacking waffle banana split or the nummy peanut butter cup with peanut butter ice cream. If your full stomach gives you a second wind, head to the room behind the dining area and dance off the calories at the restaurant's "back stage" club. *546 Lincoln Rd.* ☎ *305/672-3448. Main courses $6–$16. Daily 24 hr.*

➜**Grillfish** ✶✶ SEAFOOD The elegant bar and faded frescolike wall mural make this restaurant seem much pricier than it is. The wide variety of the freshest seafood is plainly grilled (why drown it in sauce when the fish is this good?) and when they have them, the lobster rolls melt in your mouth. *1444 Collins Ave. (on the corner of Collins and Española Way).* ☎ *305/538-9908. www.grillfish.com. Lunch $10–$23; dinner $13–$20. Daily 11:30am–4pm and 5:30pm–midnight.*

➜**News Café** ✶ AMERICAN If your *US Weekly* is out of date, head here to peruse newspapers from all over the world during mealtime. This 24-hour outdoor cafe is the best place to watch the Ocean Drive hubbub at night or to fill your stomach during a day at the beach. The service is a bit aloof, but the varied menu and all-day breakfast ensure tasty treats for all. *800 Ocean Dr.* ☎ *305/538-6397. www.newscafe.com. Breakfast $4–$14; lunch and dinner $9–$22. Daily 24 hr.*

➜**Sushi Samba** ✶✶ SUSHI It isn't Nobu, but it's pretty darn close. The location on Lincoln Road makes this mod yet colorful sushi bar a bumpin' dinner scene.

If you're here for the sushi, try any of the creative raw combination rolls like Green Envy (tuna, salmon, asparagus, and a wasabi pea crust with Key lime mayo) or the Pacific (king crab, avocado, and Asian pear). The ceviches and tartares are tasty too, but if you prefer well-done to raw, there are many succulent land and sea entree options to choose from as well. *600 Lincoln Rd.* ☎ *305/673-5337. www.sushi samba.com. Dinner reservations suggested. Lunch $8–$20; dinner $12–$27. Sun–Thurs noon–midnight; Fri–Sat noon–2am.*

Splurge

🅜 Best ♨ → **Barton G** ★★★ AMERICAN People don't go to Barton G just for a meal; they go for the *experience*. It's a one-of-a-kind carnival for the eyes and taste buds with imaginative entrees and elaborate

Word Up

Disco Nap: The afternoon sleepy time you'll need to dance 'til daybreak at Miami's rockin' clubs.

presentations. Lobster and Gruyre "Pop-Tarts" are brought to your table in an actual toaster, popcorn shrimp is served over (duh) popcorn in a movie theater popcorn bucket, and the calamari salad bucket hangs on a 2-foot fisherman statue. Now for dessert, try the cotton candy that comes on a circus cotton candy cart with giant popcorn balls covered in chocolate, white chocolate, and caramel, and as if the whole restaurant won't be looking at your table anyway, the waiter lights sparklers

The flaming cotton candy cart at Barton G.

on the cart to draw even more attention. *1427 West Ave.* ☎ *305/672-8881. www.bartong. com. Reservations suggested. Main courses $8–$30. Daily 6pm–midnight. Valet parking $10.*

→**Nobu** ★★★ SUSHI There's a high probability that you'll spot celebrities here since stars flock to the scene, but chances are you won't be able to remove your attention from the incredible sushi long enough to snap a pic. The raw slivers of sea creatures and elaborate rolls are some of the best bites in the world, but the bite out of your budget is less appetizing. Scoring a table can be miserable, so come before 7:30 or after 10:30 to reduce the wait. *1901 Collins Ave. (at the Shore Club Hotel).* ☎ *305/ 695-3232. Main courses $10–$30. Sun 7–11pm; Mon–Thurs 7pm–midnight; Fri–Sat 7pm–1am. Reservations recommended.*

Partying

Miami really comes to life after about 11pm. Bars, lounges, and clubs don't wind down until 5 or 6am, so you'll need to alternate taking shots of liquor with shots of espresso to last until dawn. Most clubs will make you stand in an ego-humbling line before they let you past the velvet rope, but you can avoid this by having your hotel concierge put you on the VIP list ahead of time. A tip on velvet ropes: To get past them, dress to impress. Girls, this means cleavage and leg, and guys, this means stand next to cleavage and leg. On weeknights, the hottest places to see and be seen are at the upscale hotel bars, and the "in" places to be during the weekend change like the tide, so check with your concierge to make sure you're in the know.

BARS & LOUNGES

→**Clevelander** Perhaps one of the most touristy night spots on Ocean Drive, this bar attracts the fratty college crowd. The pink neon lights are mesmerizing at night, but during the day it's a great spot to grab a fruity beverage while baking on the beach. *1020 Ocean Dr.* ☎ *800/815-6829. www.clevelander.com. No cover. Drinks $4–$5. Sun–Thurs 5pm–3am; Fri–Sat 5pm–5am.*

→**Social Miami at The Sagamore Hotel** ★ Sip in style as you peruse the art at this gallery-like hotel lounge. The vibe is classy and chic and so are the people, but watch your tab; the drinks are crazy expensive. *1617 Collins Ave.* ☎ *786/594-3344. No cover. Drinks $12–$16. Daily 7pm–2am.*

→**Spire at The Hotel** ★ Located on the roof of The Hotel, the squishy sofas on this colorful patio provide an ideal Atlantic view spot. The "Electric Cocktails" double as glowsticks (they have lighted neon ice cubes) so you won't have trouble finding your drink in case of a power outage. The theme continues with the cool, blue neon Tiffany sign. *801 Collins Ave.* ☎ *305/531-2222. No cover. Drinks $8–$15. Thurs–Sat 6pm–1am.*

CLUBS

→**I/O** This laid-back dance club is a sanctuary for all of you indie kids. The three part club consists of an anime bar, a dance floor, and an outdoor bar to drink under the stars (or the neon light–polluted Miami sky). *30 NE 14th St. (downtown Miami).* ☎ *305/ 358-8007. www.iolounge.com. Cover charge $5– $10. Drinks $5–$9. Thurs–Sat 10pm–5am.*

→**Mango's** With enough tequila, you'll be booty dancing better than Shakira at this Ocean Drive Latin club. Leopard print bikini clad girls dance on tables to blaring music and there's no hesitation to break it down with the nearest stranger. *900 Ocean Dr.* ☎ *305/673-4422. www.mangostropicalcafe. com. Cover charge $5–$15. Drinks $5–$8. Daily 11am–5am.*

→**Mansion** ★ With a central stage and six bars on two stories, this nightclub is huge so hang on to your buddies or you'll lose them in the action. There's loud music, great dancing, and with bars in every corner, you won't get thirsty. *1235 Washington Ave.* ☎ *305/531-5535. Cover charge $20–$30. Drinks $8–$14. Thurs–Sat 11pm–5am. Valet parking $20–$30.*

→ **Rok bar** Getting in can be a pain, but once you're there feel free to mosh and headbang the night away to the screaming rock tunes. Come on Tuesday night for "Dead Rockstar Party" or even better, "Wasteland" on Thursdays to jam to '80s music. *1905 Collins Ave.* ☎ *305/538-7171. www.rokbarmiami.com. Cover charge $15–$20. Drinks $8–$12. Thurs–Sat 10pm–5am.*

→ **Studio A** ★★ Whether your flavor is indie, bang-swooping emo, hip-hop, or '80s electronic, you'll find music and dancing to suit your style. There are weekly themed parties and live music every week that draw in diverse crowds (it's also a favorite venue for gays and lesbians). Check the website for live shows and buy tickets ahead of time so you won't run the risk of getting shut out at the door. *60 NE 11th St. (downtown Miami).* ☎ *305/358-ROCK. www.studioA.com. Cover charge $15–$20. Drinks $8–$12. Thurs–Sat 10pm–5am (check website for other weekly shows and concerts).*

→ **The PawnShop** ★★ With its varied soundtrack, upbeat dancing, lounge for relaxing, and vintage vibe (it was a pawn shop in 1930 and all the colorful furniture is secondhand), this is definitely one of the best clubs in Miami. Hit it up on Thursdays for an old-school house party, Fridays for indie rock, or Saturdays for hip-hop and R&B. *1222 NE 2nd Ave. (across from the Miami Performing Arts Center).* ☎ *305/373-3511. www.thepawnshoplounge.com. Cover charge $15–$20. Drinks $8–$10. Thurs–Sat 10pm–5am.*

THE GAY & LESBIAN SCENE

→ **Anthem** Every Sunday, the club Crobar transforms into this gay hot spot. The best place to bump and grind is the first floor,

whereas the second level is best for mellowing and mingling. *1445 Washington Ave.* ☎ *877/CRO-SOBE. Cover $20. Drinks $7–$10. Sun 10pm–4am.*

→ **Twist** The plethora of hot fellas, 2-for-1 drinks every day until 9pm, and lack of a cover charge make Twist the queen of Miami's gay scene. You'll stay entertained by the backyard Cabana Bar, game room, and legendary drag queens, but if you get bored just sit back and enjoy the hunky eye candy. *1057 Washington Ave.* ☎ *305/538-9478. www.twistsobe.com. No cover. Drinks $7–$10. Daily 1pm–5am.*

What Else to See & Do

A MEMORIAL & A MUSEUM

FREE → **Holocaust Memorial** ★★ From the street you'll be beckoned by the *Sculpture of Love & Anguish*, which shows concentration camp victims climbing up a huge hand reaching for the sky. This in itself is an attraction, and even if you don't go in the museum (But why not? It's free!), you should at least stop to marvel at the beautiful statue. The museum is an amazing tribute to the millions of Jews who lost their lives in the Holocaust. *1933 Meridian Ave. (at Dade Blvd.).* ☎ *305/538-1663. www.holocaustmmb.org. Free admission. Daily 9am–9pm.*

A Notorious Scene

Versace Mansion (Amsterdam Palace): You can't actually go inside the old Versace Mansion, but you can creep outside the gates on Ocean Drive and see where the late designer was murdered on the steps of his own home. Some say you can still see where his blood stained the concrete, but deciphering blood stains from spilled drinks, gum, dirt, and trash may be tricky. *Ocean Drive and 11th Street.*

Un Día en Little Havana

Little Havana is Miami's miniature version of Cuba. There are Cuban restaurants, coffeeshops, record stores, furniture stores, cigar factories, and nightclubs. The main drag is "Calle Ocho," SW 8th Street, and you could spend an entire afternoon hanging out and walking the streets here. Oh, and many of the people *hablan español* only, so bring your pocket dictionary or brush up on that semester of Spanish before you come.

➜ For authentic Cuban food check out **El Cristo Restaurante** ✦ (1543 SW 8th St; ☎ **305/261-2947**). You won't find a better Cuban sandwich in Miami and the sweet plantains are incredible. **Versailles** ✦✦ (3555 SW 8th St.; ☎ **305/444-0240**) is a little more upscale and popular with the Little Havana upper echelon. They have helpings *muy grandes,* as well as delicious pastries and a mean café con leche. They're open late, too, so you can hit 'em up for black beans and rice after a night of salsa dancing.

➜ You must visit a cigar factory while in Little Havana. At **La Gloria Cubana Cigar** (1106 SW 8th St.; ☎ **305/858-4162**), they'll show you around the factory and you'll see about 40 veteran Cuban rollers who methodically layer, wrap, and roll leaves of tobacco into the popular stogies.

➜ Visit **Maximo Gomez Park** (801 SW 15th Ave.) to watch the old men duel with dominos and chess from morning to sunset every day. Watch out, though; if you manage to face-off with one of them, you *will* get beat.

➜ If you stay until nightfall, head to **Casa Panza** ✦ (1629 SW 8th St.; **305/594-3717;** cover $0–$10). Enjoy a Spanish meal and load up on sangria before you salsa the night away. Come on Tuesday, Thursday, or Saturday for the House of Flamenco, with shows at 8 and 11pm.

RETRO ROADTRIP

➜**Miami Art Museum at the Miami–Dade Cultural Center** ✦✦ The MAM features an eclectic mix of modern and contemporary works by such artists as Eric Fischl, Max Beckmann, Jim Dine, and Stuart Davis. There are also fantastic themed exhibits such as the Andy Warhol exhibit, which featured all-night films by the artist, make-your-own pop art, cocktail hours, and parties with local DJs. JAM at MAM is the museum's popular Happy Hour, which takes place on the third Thursday of the month and is tied in to a particular exhibit. *101 W. Flagler. ☎ 305/375-3000. www.miamiartmuseum.org. Admission $5 adults, $2.50 students and seniors, free for children under 12. Tues–Fri 10am–5pm; 3rd Thurs of each month 10am–9pm; Sat–Sun noon–5pm.*

ORGANIZED TOURS

FREE ➜**Biltmore Hotel Tour** ✦ Take advantage of these free Sunday walking tours and enjoy the hotel's beautiful grounds. The Biltmore is full of history, mystery, and a few ghosts. There are also weekly fireside sessions about the hotel's early days led by local storytellers and accompanied by a glass of champagne. Call ahead to confirm. *1200 Anastasia Ave., Coral Gables. ☎ 305/445-1926. www.biltmorehotel. com. Free admission. Tours depart on Sun at 1:30, 2:20, and 3:30pm. Storytelling sessions are every Thurs at 7:30pm.*

➜**Miami Duck Tours** If you're not easily embarrassed, you'll probably get a kick out of this "quacky" tour. You'll tour Miami and South Beach's highly populated hot spots in a bizarre looking vehicle (a transportation mutant combining a bus and a boat) before splashing into Biscayne Bay to see mansions of the rich and famous from the water. *Departure location 1665 Washington Ave.* ☎ *786/276/8300. www.ducktoursmiami. com. Tickets $26 adults, $22 seniors, $18 children.*

PLAYING OUTSIDE
Beaches
You don't need a beach tag or to pay an admission fee to use the Miami beaches, which are part of the county park system. You may need to pay a parking fee. For information on the beaches, their facilities and amentities, visit **www.miamidade. gov/parks/beaches.asp**.

➔ **Haulover Beach** If you want to avoid tan lines, this is the place to do it. There's a quarter-mile-long "clothing optional" section of the beach for those who prefer their birthday suit to a swimming suit, but if you'd rather keep yourself covered, head to the "clothing required" south end. *10800 Collins Ave.* ☎ *305/947-3525. $4 parking fee. Restrooms, lifeguard, showers, and concessions available.*

➔ **Lummus Park Beach** ★★ This is the beach that runs along Ocean Drive on South Beach. You can sunbake topless (it's legal on Lummus) and then skip on over to Ocean Drive for a refreshment if you get too hot. But please, don't forget to put your top back on. *Ocean Dr. between 6th and 14th sts. Restrooms and changing facilities available.*

➔ **Matheson Hammock Park Beach** ★★ This beach is not as bustling as Lummus, but it is beautiful, there's less of a crowd, and the waves are calm. *9610 Old Cutler Rd. (in South Miami).* ☎ *305/665-5475. Restrooms and changing facilities available.*

Biking
➔ **Miami Beach Bicycle Center** You can rent a bike by the hour or for the entire day to cruise through the Art Deco District and

pedal your way around famous movie locations, hotels, and celeb homes. You can bike up and down the beach paths along Ocean Drive or ask the guys in the store if you are craving more technical trails. You can also research your own bike trails at **www.trails.com**. *601 5th St.* ☎ *305/674-0150. $8 per hour or $20 for up to 24 hr. Mon–Sat 10am–7pm; Sun 10am–5pm.*

Jet-Skiing
➔ **American Watersports** Straddle one of these WaveRunners and speed into the horizon. They rent by the half-hour and the hour, and the company also offers guided tours through some of the islands. The jet skis fit three people, so you can split the cost of one with your friends. *300 Alton Rd. (at the Miami Beach Marina on South Beach).* ☎ *305/538-7549. www.jetskiz. com. $65 per half-hour, $120 per hour. Daily 10am–7pm.*

Kiteboarding
➔ **Miami Kiteboarding** This sport requires you to stand on a tiny surfboard and attach yourself to a large kite. As a beginner, you are at the mercy of the wind, being thrashed about upon the ocean, but the more experienced are able to steer the wind-vessel and even attempt flips and tricks. Take advantage of the ocean winds and become, if not an expert, then someone who can say you've actually kiteboarded. The instructors will customize lessons to fit your skills with classes ranging from 1 to 15 hours. If you already are an expert kiteboarder, they'll rent you one lesson-free. *Call ahead as meeting locations differ depending on the wind.* ☎ *305/345-9974. www. miamikiteboarding.com. Lessons $100 for 1 hr.; rentals $100 half-day, $150 full day. Open hours and days depend on wind levels.*

Scuba Diving & Snorkeling
➔ **South Beach Dive and Surf Center** See Miami from under the sea, with professional divers who will show you the best

underwater wreckage and reefs for the best viewing. Or, if you're certified, you can rent the gear and go out on your own dive or snorkel excursion. *850 Washington Ave.* ☎ *305/531-6110. www.southbeachdivers. com. $65 for a 1-day snorkel trip; $75 for a two-tank dive; snorkel rentals $15; scuba rentals $40. Mon–Sat 9am–7pm; Sun 9am–3pm.*

Zoo/Aquarium

➔**Miami Metrozoo** ★ This zoo really feels more like a safari because there are no cages, just moats of water separating the animals from you and each other. The grounds are huge so you'll need a couple of hours or more to see everything. *12300 SW 152nd St. (South Miami).* ☎ *305/251-0400. www.miamimetrozoo.com. Admission $12 adults, $11 seniors, $7 children (ages 3–12).*

Daily 9:30am–5:30pm. Ticket booths close at 4pm.

➔**Miami Seaquarium** It isn't SeaWorld, but you can still watch choreographed shows of flippy dolphins and splashing whales. If you have a load of cash to drop, sign up for the Water and Dolphin Exploration Program ($140 per participant and $32 per observer) and you'll get to swim with the dolphins in the Flipper Lagoon. The program is offered at noon and 3:30pm daily. For reservations call ☎ **305/365-2501.** *4400 Rickenbacker Causeway (South Side).* ☎ *305/361-5705. www. miamiseaquarium.com. Admission $25 adults, $20 children (ages 3–9). Daily 9:30am–6pm. Ticket booths close at 4pm.*

On the Road to Cocoa Beach, FL

Miami to Cocoa Beach, FL 200 miles

There are two route options from Miami to Cocoa Beach. You can either take I-95 N past Melbourne to Florida Route 520 E until you intersect with Route A1A, or take US 1 all the way from Miami. Cocoa Beach is at the intersection of A1A and FL 520.

If you take I-95, don't expect any amazing ocean views out of the passenger window. You'll see some palm trees and billboards and that's about it, but the drive is much, *much* shorter than taking the US 1 scenic route. US 1 takes you through some little coastal towns where the speed limit can drop to 35 mph and the, *ahem*, somewhat-older-than-you drivers can sometimes slow you to the speed of oozing molasses.

Welcome to Cocoa Beach

Cocoa Beach is a small coastal community just south of the Kennedy Space Center and has little to offer someone looking for a lot to do other than just lay on the beach. However, the sleepy mood of the town is

Detour: Greyhound Races

FREE If you're not in a rush to get to Cocoa Beach, or you just get bored on the road, stop in Melbourne, FL, just north of Palm Bay and catch the racing excitement. At **Melbourne Greyhound Park** (1100 N Wickham Rd. at the corner of Wickham and Sarno; ☎ **321/259-9800;** www.melbourne greyhoundpark.com), you can get a taste of the age old sport of horse racing on a smaller dog-size scale. Place bets on your favorite pooch and you just might score a few extra bucks for gas to get you the rest of the way to Cocoa. The pups race every day at 12:45pm year-round, and there's no admission fee. There's also simulcasts of harness and thoroughbred racing and jai alai, and live poker if you are in the mood for some Texas Hold 'Em.

RETRO ROADTRIP

Beachy Beats: Playlist for the Road to Cocoa

→ *Shake Your Coconuts*, **Junior Senior**, "D-D-Don't Don"t Stop The Beat," 2003

→ *Mainline Florida*, **Eric Clapton**, "461 Ocean Blvd.," 2004

→ *Another Sunny Day*, **Belle & Sebastian**, "The Life Pursuit," 2006

→ *Ocean*, **The Velvet Underground**, "VU," 1987

→ *Florida Heat*, **Alex Kash**, "Florida Heat," 2005

→ *7/4 (Shoreline)*, **Broken Social Scene**, "Broken Social Scene," 2005

→ *I Dream of Jeannie*, **Big Kahuna & The Copa Cat Pack**, "Shake Those Hula Hips," 2001

→ *Swimming Suit*, **Tahiti 80**, "Puzzle," 2000

→ *Road*, **Nick Drake**, "Pink Moon," 2003

→ *Catcha Wave*, **The Beach Boys**, "Surfer Girl/Shut Down, Vol. 2," 2001

perfect for a leisurely afternoon of sun-soaking and wave splashing. You'll only need an afternoon here unless you plan on seeing the Kennedy Space Center, in which case you should plan on spending an entire day. Note that rooms can be hard to find when there's a rocket launch scheduled.

Getting Around

Getting around is easiest by car. It's pretty spread out so you won't want to walk everywhere. There are parking places all over and metered parking is offered in lots all the way up the beach on A1A.

Sleeping

The newest chain motels in this area are the **Hampton Inn Cocoa Beach** (3425 Atlantic Blvd.; ☎ 877/492-3224) and **Courtyard by Marriott** (3435 Atlantic Blvd.; ☎ 800/321-2211). They stand side by side and access the beach via a pathway through a condo complex. In general, you can get a double for around $110 to $170 during high season.

CHEAP

→ **Wakulla Suites** ★★ From the outside, this bright orange and teal motel reeks of gaudiness with its enormous plastic totem poles and fake bamboo, but for the price it is the best deal on the beach. The "rooms" are actually spacious suites with fully equipped kitchens, breakfast nooks, and living rooms, and the beach is just a short walk away. This is a great place to stay if you're traveling with a group or on a budget, because you can prepare your own meals and not feel too cramped with your travel buddies. You'll be so blinded by the bargain that you won't even mind the obnoxious Tiki motif. Oh, and you must be 21 to stay so bring an ID; they check them meticulously. *3550 N. Atlantic Ave. ☎ 321/ 992-5852. www.wakullasuites.com. $89–$175 for a 2-bedroom suite, highest prices during launch dates. Amenities: Cafe; pool; Internet access; concierge; game room. In room: Fully equipped kitchen, breakfast nook.*

DOABLE

→ **Doubletree Hotel Cocoa Beach Oceanfront** ★ Right on the beach, this full-service hotel has spacious rooms, each with its own balcony. The **3 Wishes** bar and lounge is connected to the lobby, so you can pop in from the beach or pool for a frozen fruity beverage before stuffing your face with the complimentary chocolate chip cookies. *2080 N. Atlantic Ave. ☎ 800/ 552-3224. www.cocoabeachdoubletree.com.*

Cocoa Beach, FL.

$125–$179 double. Amenities: Restaurant; lounge; pool; fitness center; room service; laundry service; concierge; ATM. In room: Dataport, fridge, microwave, wireless Internet.

SPLURGE

➔ **The Inn at Cocoa Beach** ★★ If Miami didn't suck your pockets completely dry, this pink hotel on the beach is definitely worth the splurge. They serve complimentary wine and cheese every afternoon and there is an honor bar in the lobby where you can mix your own drinks. The best part is the hearty breakfast free to guests, which offers an assortment of fresh breads, muffins, fruits, and eggs that you can enjoy in the dining room or on the outdoor patio. Make sure you introduce yourself to the inn parrots Tango and Tangi before heading to the beach just outside the back gate. *4300 Ocean Blvd.* ☎ *800/343-5307 or 321/799-3460. www.theinnat cocoabeach.com. 50 units. $135–$295 double. Rates include breakfast and afternoon tea. Amenities: Bar; heated outdoor pool; sauna; massage; laundry service; Internet access. In room: Dataport, minibar.*

Eating

EATING OUT

➔ **Coconuts on the Beach** FLORIDIAN The food here is isn't much to write home about (though it isn't bad), but the real reason to come is for the ambience. They have a huge outdoor patio and bar overlooking the ocean where you can replenish your energy during or just after a day at the beach with a cocktail or a bite to eat. The dress is so casual here that even the waiters are sometimes seen wearing their swimsuits. *2 Minutemen Causeway.* ☎ *321/784-1422. www.coconutsonthebeach.com. Main courses $7–$20. Daily 11am–2am. Happy Hour Mon–Fri 4–7pm.*

Home of Sitcom & Comic

Cocoa Beach was the setting for the sitcom *I Dream of Jeannie* and it is also the birthplace of Carrot Top.

A History of Cocoa Beach, MTV Style

Okay, so it's not quite as historically significant as some of the other places you'll visit on this trip, but that's only because it wasn't even on the map until NASA set up camp next door. An attorney named Gus Edwards founded the village in 1925, but it didn't see much action until the '60s when people flocked to Cape Canaveral and used Cocoa as a home base. In 1969, thousands of people flocked to the area to witness the launch that turned out to be "one small step for man and one giant leap for mankind." Cocoa Beach felt a giant leap in their tourist levels and still host those hoping to experience one of the frequent launches from this site.

→ **Fischer's Seafood Bar & Grill** ★ SEAFOOD This locally popular seafood joint has all sorts of astronaut autographs and photographs covering the walls to commemorate launches and landings at the Kennedy Space Center. The food at this publike lounge is great as are the prices, and if you time your visit during a launch from the cape, you'll receive a free drink. 2 S. Atlantic Ave. ☎ 321/783-2401. Main courses $9–$16. Mon–Fri 11am–10pm; Sat 11am–11pm. Closed Christmas.

Partying

Your best bet for fun after dark is on the **Cocoa Beach Pier** (401 Meade Ave.; ☎ **321/783-7549**). There's a tin-roofed **Boardwalk Tiki Bar** ★ where live reggae music plays most nights and it's a prime place to watch the sunset over a round of daiquiris.

What Else to See & Do

→ **John F. Kennedy Space Center** ★★★ Whether you were a space camp kid or not, you'll appreciate the sheer grandeur and technological achievements at NASA's primary space-launch facility. You'll start your visit at the Kennedy Space Center Visitor Complex where there are exhibits of NASA rockets and the Mercury Mission Control Room from the 1960s. You could certainly spend your whole day at the visitor complex, but you must take a KSC tour to see the actual space center, where rockets and shuttles are prepared and launched. On launch days, the center is closed at least part of the day. These aren't good days to see the center, but they're great days to observe history in the making. For $38 per adult and $28 per child (ages 3–11), you get a combined ticket that entitles you to admission to the center for the shortened operating hours, plus at least a 2-hour excursion to NASA Parkway to see the liftoff. You must pick up the tickets, available 5 days before the launch, on-site. For an out-of-this-world experience, have lunch with an astronaut ★, a once-in-a-lifetime opportunity available every day ($20 adults, $10 kids 3–11). Call ☎ **321/449-4400** to make a reservation. There are several different tours offered: The basic one is included in the price of admission, and leaves every 15 minutes; the

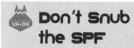

Don't Snub the SPF

According to the National Cancer Institute, the number one cause of cancer in females ages 20 to 29 is melanoma caused by sun damage. So, you should always wear sunscreen at the beach and don't forget to reapply after playing in the ocean.

NASA Up Close tour is an additional $24 and requires a reservation. (The website cautions that the tours usually sell out, so if you've got your heart set on this tour, call ahead or reserve online!) *NASA Pkwy. (6 miles east of Titusville, a half-mile mile west of Fla. 3). ☎ 321/449-4444. www.kennedys pacecenter.com. Admission $30 adults, $20 children (ages 3–11). Audio tours $5 per person. Daily 9am–5:30pm. Shuttle-bus tours daily 9:45am–2:15pm. Closed Christmas and some launch days.*

PLAYING OUTSIDE

FREE → **Lori Wilson Park** This stretch of sand is backed by a forest of live oaks, and houses a small but interesting nature center if you get bored laying out. *Atlantic Ave. at Antigua Dr. ☎ 321/868-1123. Open daily from sunrise to sunset. Restrooms available.*

FREE → **Cocoa Beach Pier** ★ This rustic pier was built in 1962 and has 842 feet of fishing, shopping, and dining overlooking the wide sandy beach. It's the most popular beach around, and when you get thirsty you can pop on up to the Tiki bar on the pier. *Meade Ave. (½ mile north of 520, off A1A). ☎ 321/783-7549. Open daily from sunrise to sunset.*

On the Road to St. Augustine, FL

Cocoa Beach to St. Augustine, FL 130 miles

Route options here are the same as your last drive: I-95 or US 1. For the fast way, take I-95 N and merge onto US 1 at exit 298 and drive about 15 miles to Carrera Street and turn right to get to the historic district. For the scenic version, take A1A N to US 1 N toward Titusville and continue on US 1 until you hit St. Augustine. Turn right on Carrera Street to reach the historic district. *Warning:* Between New Smyrna Beach and Daytona the traffic is pretty slow going. Be prepared for frequent stops and low speed limits.

If you're not in a hurry to get to St. Augustine, I'd recommend taking US 1 instead of I-95. It is certainly slower (the highest speed limit is 65 mph) but the drive is much more entertaining. You'll pass by the **Kennedy Space Center** and some boat marinas.

Along the way you can stop in New Smyrna Beach at **Banana Split Republic** (1044 Dixie Freeway; ☎ **386/427-1994**), a cute little house with rocking chairs and picnic tables in front that serves gelato, smoothies, and hot dogs. Next door is **Perrine's Produce,** a farmers market with local produce where you can stock up on fruits and veggies for the road.

Welcome to St. Augustine

When exploring places-of-old in the Southeast, St. Augustine is essential because it actually *is* the oldest-of-places in the entire US. St. Augustine has existed since 1565 when it was settled by the Spanish, and still has vestiges of the quaint European charm that residents and visitors have enjoyed for centuries.

Because tourism is St. Augustine's major industry, there are tons of restaurants, attractions, shops, and nightlife opportunities. You'll need at least 2 full days here to see the sights, but you could easily stay entertained for 4 in this adorable pedestrian-friendly town.

RETRO ROADTRIP

St. Augustine Nuts & Bolts

Area Code   The area code in St. Augustine is 904.

Business Hours   Banks are usually open Monday to Friday from 9am to 5pm. Bars in the historic district are generally open to about midnight on the weekdays and 1am on weekends.

Drugstores   There are a bunch of pharmacies outside the historic area, but in the historic district there is a **CVS** at 150 San Marco Ave. (☎ 904/824-2838).

Emergencies   For any emergency dial ☎ 911.

Hospitals   St. Augustine's hospital is Flagler Hospital West at 400 Health Park Blvd. (☎ 904/819-5155).

Internet   Internet is available at most hotels and B&Bs, but other than that the best place is **All Stars Bar & Grill,** 72 Spanish St. or at **St. John's County Public Library** (see "Libraries," below).

Laundry/Dry Cleaners   To do your laundry in the historic district, check out **Mariotti's Laundry & Dry Cleaners** at 314 Ponce De Leon Blvd. (☎ 904/829-9784).

Libraries   The county library is **St. John's County Library** and is located at 1960 N. Ponce De Leon Blvd. (☎ 904/827-6940).

Liquor Laws   You must be 21 to purchase or consume alcohol in Florida, and beer and wine are sold in grocery stores. Alcohol is not permitted on St. Augustine beaches.

Lost Property   To find your lost stuff or report a stolen item, call the police at ☎ 904/741-3600.

Newspapers & Magazines   The daily newspaper here is called *The St. Augustine Record.*

Police   For an emergency, call ☎ 911 and for all other matters dial ☎ 904/471-3600.

Radio   For top-40 tracks tune to WSOS (94.1), for Christian WAYL (91.1), for college radio WFCF (88.5), and for smooth jazz WSJF (105.5). On the AM dial, talk radio is WFOY (1240), oldies is WSOS (1170), and country is WAOC (1420).

Taxes   Florida has a 6% sales tax and the hotel tax in St. Augustine is 9%.

Weather   For emergency weather info, call ☎ 904/209-1200.

Getting Around

If you aren't staying in the historic district, the easiest way to get around is to park at the **St. Augustine Visitor Information Center** at 10 Castillo Dr., at San Marco Avenue (☎ **904/825-1000**). It costs anywhere from $0 to $3 depending on the season. From there, you can walk all over the historic district or take one of the many trolleys to the tourist attractions. The trolleys run from 8:30am to 5pm daily and you can get on and off as you please. Three-day Trolley tickets are available at the visitor center and are $20 for adults and $7 for children.

St. Augustine Highlights

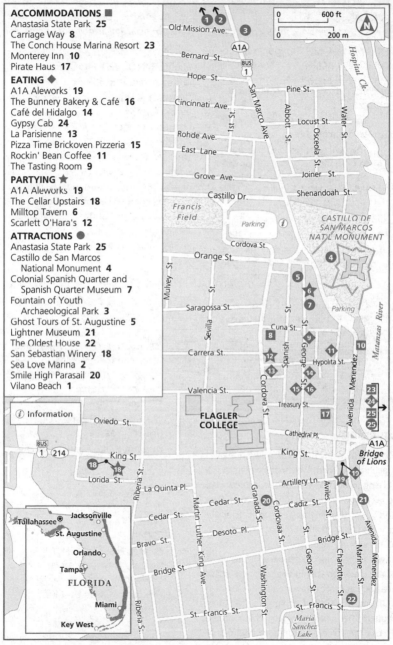

ACCOMMODATIONS ■
Anastasia State Park **25**
Carriage Way **8**
The Conch House Marina Resort **23**
Monterey Inn **10**
Pirate Haus **17**

EATING ◆
A1A Aleworks **19**
The Bunnery Bakery & Café **16**
Café del Hidalgo **14**
Gypsy Cab **24**
La Parisienne **13**
Pizza Time Brickoven Pizzeria **15**
Rockin' Bean Coffee **11**
The Tasting Room **9**

PARTYING ★
A1A Aleworks **19**
The Cellar Upstairs **18**
Milltop Tavern **6**
Scarlett O'Hara's **12**

ATTRACTIONS ●
Anastasia State Park **25**
Castillo de San Marcos
   National Monument **4**
Colonial Spanish Quarter and
   Spanish Quarter Museum **7**
Fountain of Youth
   Archaeological Park **3**
Ghost Tours of St. Augustine **5**
Lightner Museum **21**
The Oldest House **22**
San Sebastian Winery **18**
Sea Love Marina **2**
Smile High Parasail **20**
Vilano Beach **1**

ⓘ **Information**

Shotgun! (Know the Rules . . .)

I know how those Shotgun rules can get a little hazy, so here are the official rules of passenger seat riding according to **www.shotgunguide.com**:

→ The first person to yell "Shotgun" gets the front seat.

→ The yell must be loud enough to be heard by at least one witness, but in the case of a tie, the driver has the last call.

→ All occupants of the vehicle must be outside of the building and on the way to the vehicle.

→ The driver has the right to suspend or remove all Shotgun privileges from one or more persons.

→ Carsick passengers who are likely to hork are automatically given Shotgun.

→ The driver may institute the "Survival of the Fittest" law, where whoever can take the passenger seat by force gets Shotgun.

Sleeping

Most of the goings-on in St. Augustine take place in the downtown historic district, so staying in or near the area will allow you to leave the car parked for a couple of days and walk all over this pedestrian-friendly city. The only problem is that because it is a preserved historic area, big hotels haven't been able to set up shop, so most of the places to stay in the historic district are bed–and–breakfasts.

If you don't mind driving to the sites, though, there are some big chain hotels across the river on Anastasia Island. Try the **Best Western Ocean Inn** (3955 A1A S.; ☎ 904/471-8010) or the **Hampton Inn St. Augustine Beach** (430 A1A Beach Blvd.; ☎ 904/471-4000). Both range from $60 to $90 per night for a double.

CAMPGROUND/HOSTEL

→ **Anastasia State Park** ★ This is one of the most beautiful campgrounds I have ever seen. The tent sites are covered by a beautiful canopy of moss-covered trees, and the best beaches in the area are just a short walk away. *1340-A A1A S. (1½ miles north of S.R.312 on A1A).* ☎ *904/461-2000 or 904/461-2033. www.floridastateparks.org. $25. Amenities: Campfires permitted; food/beverage service; full hookups; hot showers; ice; laundry; pay phones; pets on leash; picnic shelter; tables; tenters welcome; water access.*

Playlist: Jives for the Drive to St. Aug

→ *The Bronze Beached Boys (Come On Let's Go)*, **Pas/Cal,** "The Handbag Memoirs," 2003

→ *I Dreamed I Saw St. Augustine*, **Bob Dylan,** "John Wesley Harding," 1967

→ *The Iron Sea*, **Keane,** "Under the Iron Sea," 2006

→ *Another White Dash*, **Butterfly Boucher**, "Flutterby," 2004

→ *All At Sea*, **Jamie Cullum,** "Twentysomething," 2004

→ *The Sea & The Rhythm*, **Iron & Wine,** "The Sea & The Rhythm," 2003

→ *Orange Blossom Special*, **Johnny Cash,** "Orange Blossom Special," 1965

→ *Roadside*, **Chris Pureka,** "Driving North," 2004

→ *Vintage People*, **Eisley,** "Telescope Eyes," 2005

Stranded!

Keep an eye on the time when you're riding the trolleys. Most of them stop running around 5pm and drop you off at the Old Jail (across the street from the Fountain of Youth). They don't give you any warning that the last stop is the farthest from the historical district, so get off before they start heading into the horizon or you'll be stranded at the Fountain of Youth like I was.

➔ **Pirate Haus** ★ Walk up the stairs to this top-floor hostel and you'll find yourself aboard a pirate's Jolly Roger. The dorm-style or private rooms are cloaked with Caribbean murals complete with lockers to hide your booty. The owner/pirate captain will ensure you have a good time with his bounty of helpful information and all-you-can-eat pancake breakfast. Eat up, me hearties, yo ho! *32 Treasury St.* ☎ *904/808-1999. www.piratehaus.com. $17 6- or 8-person dorm beds; $50–$65 private rooms. Pirate pancake breakfast included. Amenities: Fully equipped kitchen; rooftop patio with BBQ; Internet access; common room; laundry facilities; bicycle and boogie board rental. In room: Fridge, lockers in dorm rooms.*

CHEAP

➔ **Monterey Inn** For the price, you can't find a better choice than this modest, wrought-iron-trimmed motel overlooking the Matanzas Bay and close to the attractions and nightlife of the Old City. Three generations of the Six family have run this

RETRO ROADTRIP

Getting to Know St. Augustine, Old School

St. Augustine is the oldest city in the country, so naturally, there are tons of ways to blast back to the past:

➔ The best way to relive St. Augustine's history is to experience the **Colonial Spanish Quarter.** It's a living museum where costumed reenactors inhabit the restored 1740 colonial village. They can answer any questions you have about what life was like in the old days and they'll demonstrate their crafts for any interested audience. See p. 281.

➔ For a spookier rendition of St. Aug's past, sign up for a **Ghost Tour of St. Augustine** and learn about all the creepy crawlies of the area. You might even have your own encounter with an ancient spirit . . . but don't bet on it. See p. 282.

➔ MTV Best ♪ It's not exactly retro, but if you're interested in a different kind of "vintage," the **San Sebastian Winery** will give you a free tour (and free wine tasting). If you like what you taste, the local winery will ship bottles home for you (depending on what state you live in) so you won't have to use up that precious space in your suitcase or car trunk. See p. 282.

➔ There's a delightful vintage store that has great quality clothes and accessories from decades past. **The Way We Were** (86 Charlotte St.; ☎ 904/825-0114 or 904/824-1617) is on a side street 1 block west of the Matanzas River, but it's well worth the time you'll spend trying to find it.

➔ If you're in the market for antiques, San Marco Avenue between Mulberry and Old Mission streets is a smorgasbord of antiques stores. Most of the stores are well organized and stuffed with so much old paraphernalia you're sure to find what you're looking for.

A History of St. Augustine, MTV Style

The Spanish explorer Juan Ponce de Leon (who I imagine wore a huge hat with a big feather) set out in 1513 in search of a place called Bimini, an island rumored to contain the Fountain of Youth. He must have been steering his ship under the influence of a different kind of fountain because he instead ran aground on the eastern shore of Florida. Being a proud Spaniard, Ponce thrust his feather in the sand and claimed Florida for his mother country.

The area was semi-neglected by Spain for the next 50 years until some Frenchmen set up camp where Jacksonville is today. This annoyed the Spanish, so they sent Don Pedro Menendez de Aviles to St. Augustine to give the French the boot.

Poor St. Aug hadn't seen the end of fighting. The town was repeatedly pillaged by bands of pirates, and then when England claimed Georgia, fights between the Spanish and the Brits broke out. During the next few centuries, Florida remained a hot property, contested by different crowns, finally ending up as American territory, and admitted as a U.S. State (the 27th) in 1845.

Fast forward to 1886. A fella called Henry Flagler who ran around with John D. Rockefeller came to town. He was filthy rich and decided to bring a railroad through St. Augustine that connected it to other East Coast cities. He built some hotels and gave people around here so much land and money that they worshipped him for his contributions and named pretty much everything around here after him. A hundred or so years and a few restorations later, here we are enjoying living history in what was once just a feather in the sand.

simple two-story motel, and they keep the 1960s building and grounds clean and functional. Rooms are not especially spacious, but they're good enough to sleep in after a day at the beach. *16 Avenida Menendez (between Cuna and Hypolita sts.).* ☎ *904/824-4482. www.themontereyinn.com. 59 units. $59–$159 double. Amenities: Heated outdoor pool. In room: Dataport.*

DOABLE

→**The Conch House Marina Resort** ★★ This waterfront tropical hideaway is just 1 mile from the historic district, but looks like it belongs miles away in the remote Caribbean. The standard rooms are spacious, but if you're traveling in a group, the suites can't be beat. They have a bedroom, living room with a pullout sofa, and a full kitchen where you can prepare your own meals. The resort also houses a Caribbean restaurant with an outdoor

patio and private "dining huts" that are suspended over the water; the resort bar is on a dock in the marina. Make sure to be here Sunday evenings for the famous reggae boat party where you can dance and drink without ever getting your feet wet. *57 Comares Ave. (¾ miles south of the Bridge of Lions, turn left after Bank of America).* ☎ *800/940-6256 or 904/829-8646. www. conch-house.com. 17 units. $95–$125 double; $150–$175 suite. Closed Christmas. Amenities: Concierge; marina; pool; restaurant; bar; laundry. In room: Full kitchen.*

SPLURGE

→**Carriage Way** ★★ In the historic district, this Victorian-era inn is a haven of relaxation. The cozy rooms are decorated in period motif, but if you're traveling with a group, your best bet is to rent out the Carriage Way cottage a few doors down. It has two bedrooms and a living area and

St. Aug Festivals: Music, Lights & Happy Birthday!

→ **FREE** The **Nights of Lights** held from November through January sparkles every night of the holiday season. It gives new meaning to stapling twinkle lights on your house, because this celebration traces its roots back to the Spanish tradition of displaying a lit candle during Christmas. The whole city lights up in a Griswold brilliance at 6:30pm. **www.nightsoflights.com.**

→ **FREE** **Music by the Sea** is a concert series that takes place every Wednesday from May to September. It features a different musician each week and dinner is provided by a local restaurant. Bring your own chair or blanket, and enjoy the music and ocean breezes. **www. staugbchcivicassoc.com.**

→ **FREE** The **St. Augustine Birthday Celebration** is the perfect way to experience the Old City's history. Complete with reenactments, cake, and a free concert, it's well worth the price (okay, so it's free, but it's still a great time). **www.staugustinegovernment.com.**

can sleep six people (more if you squish). The fresh baked cookies, breezy porches, and incomparable hospitality make this house a home away from home. *70 Cuna St.* ☎ *904/829-2467 or 800/908-9832. www. carriageway.com. 11 units. $99–$149 double. Breakfast and complimentary beverages included. Amenities: Free use of bikes; wireless Internet. In room: Dataport.*

Eating

TAKEOUT TREATS/CHEAP

→ **The Bunnery Bakery & Café** ★ BAKERY Stacks of giant warm cookies and globs of frosting dripping off the enormous cakes will leave you drooling on the display case in this bakery and cafe. Order dessert first or you'll fill up on the chicken salad and pineapple stuffed croissant sandwich. On second thought, get both; you'll walk off the calories on the all-pedestrian St. George Street. *121 St. George St. (between Treasury and Hypolita sts.).* ☎ *904/829-6166. Breakfast $3–$7; lunch $4–$8. Cash only. Daily 8am–3pm. Closed Jan 1, Easter, Thanksgiving, Dec 24 & 25.*

→ **Café del Hidalgo** SALADS/DELI/GELATO This popular lunch cafe invites you to test your culinary skills. Create your own salad from the menu of fresh toss-ins. The "small" portion is more than enough for one, but save room and order the coconut gelato to go. You'll spend the rest of your stroll through the historic district licking the creamy drippings from your fingers. *35 Hypolita St.* ☎ *904/823-1196 Main courses $3–$9. Sun–Thurs 9:30am–9pm; Fri–Sat 9:30am–10pm.*

→ **Pizza Time Brickoven Pizzeria** PIZZA According to the locals, this St. George Street pizzeria tosses the best pies in town. You can look through the window for a peek at the enormous slices, but be warned; if you do, you won't be able to pass up the cheesy goodness. Design your own thin crust pizza or choose from the specialty options including my favorites, eggplant, tomato, and Romano, or ham, artichokes, mushrooms, and olives. *124 St. George St.* ☎ *904/819-0133. Slices $3–$4; whole pizzas $14–$24. Sun–Thurs 10:30am–10:30pm; Fri–Sat 10:30am–11pm.*

→**Rockin' Bean Coffee** CAFE Get your morning (or afternoon or nighttime) caffeine fix at this cool coffee cafe. The wall art portraying rock-'n'-roll musicians adds color and life to the simple decor. If you like what you're sipping, you can take home the beans in bulk as a souvenir. *48 Charlotte St.* ☎ *904/824-5198. Coffee drinks $1–$3; pastries $1–$5. Daily 8:30am–10:30pm.*

DOABLE

→**A1A Aleworks** ★★ SEAFOOD Beer lover, meet A1A. This Victorian-style restaurant owns its own microbrewery and serves its homemade brews on tap. The food is a mixture of Caribbean, Cuban, and Floridian and the best item on the menu is the won-ton-wrapped ahi tuna stick appetizer. If you just want the beer *sans* food, the downstairs bar is energetic and loud and, of course, proudly pours the house brews. *1 King St.* ☎ *904/829-2977. Main courses $7–$28. Sun–Thurs 11am–10:30pm; Fri–Sat 11am–11pm. Happy Hour Mon–Fri 4–7pm. Late night menu served at the downstairs bar.*

→**Gypsy Cab** ★★ TEX-MEX The so-called "urban cuisine" of this local favorite is really more of an eclectic take on Tex-Mex. The portions are huge and the menu changes daily, but the black bean soup is a scrumptious regular staple. Head here for lunch and take home your leftovers for dinner. *828 Anastasia Blvd. (east of the Bridge of Lions).* ☎ *904/824-8244. www.gypsy cab.com. Lunch $6–$12; dinner $12–$21. Mon–Thurs 4:30–10pm; Fri 4:30–11pm; Sat 11am–11pm; Sun 10:30am–10pm.*

MTV Best ◐ →**The Tasting Room** ★★★ TAPAS This contemporary take on the Spanish tapas bar offers exquisite service, excellent food, and an extensive wine list. The chef melds flavors like mango, passionfruit, and goat cheese, or lobster, coconut, and plantains for tastes that are unforgettable. The portions are a bit skimpy, but it's all for the better because

you'll want to try a little of everything. Leave room for dessert; the chocolate espresso truffle cake with raspberry coulis is a warm, gooey Spanish fiesta in your mouth. *25 Cuna St.* ☎ *904/810-2400. Tapas $4–$11; entrees $9–$13. Tues–Sat 5–11pm.*

SPLURGE

→**La Parisienne** ★★ CONTEMPORARY FRENCH La Parisienne is a welcome change from the local Americana that's the mainstay of the local cuisine scene. The seasonal menu features fresh seafood, and if they're offered, start with pan-seared sea scallops in a citrus sauce. The weekend brunch menu features beignets, eggs Benedict, and scrambled eggs with smoked salmon. *60 Hypolita St. (between Spanish and Cordova sts.).* ☎ *904/829-0055. www. laparisienne.net. Reservations recommended. Main courses $19–$28. Tues–Fri 5–9pm; Sat–Sun 11am–3pm and 5–9pm.*

Partying

St Augustine is a great place to party because you can walk *everywhere*. Also, there are no cover charges, so you can hop from bar to bar; but get an early start, because the bars close at 1am.

BARS

→**A1A Aleworks** ★ This microbrewery is the best place to come for great beer and boisterous young crowds. There is live music Thursday through Saturday at the downstairs bar and you can order food from the upstairs restaurant late. *1 King St.* ☎ *904/829-2977. Drinks $3–$6. Sun–Thurs 11am–11:30; Fri–Sat 11am–1am.*

→**The Cellar Upstairs** ★★ On the roof of the San Sebastian Winery, this open air bar features the best live jazz in town. They serve their own house wines, as well as a selection of beer, and the atmosphere is so chill you could spend all night here soaking up the music (and the alcohol). *157 King St.* ☎ *904/826-1594. www.sansebastianwinery.*

com. Drinks $3–$6. Fri 4:30–11pm (or later); Sat–Sun noon–11pm (or later). Live music Fri–Sat 7–11pm.

➜ **Milltop Tavern** You won't miss the gigantic wooden water wheel jutting out from the side of this upstairs tavern. The outdoor patio built atop a sprawling oak tree is an ideal place for listening to the live music that plays from 1pm until close every day. The food is so-so, but it's a fun place to hang out. *19½ St. George St. ☎ 904/829-2329. www.milltop.com. Drinks $3–$5. Daily 1pm–1am. Happy Hour Mon–Fri 5–7:30pm.*

➜ **Scarlett O'Hara's** An old wood house contains a maze of cozy rooms with working fireplaces to host a restaurant and upstairs bar. Rumor has it that the man who built it drowned in the upstairs bathtub (where the "Ghost Bar" is now) and late at night his ghost can be heard moaning and splashing around upstairs. But before you hightail it from the spirits, make sure the sounds aren't coming from the person next to you. *70 Hypolita St. (at Cordova St.). ☎ 904/824-6536. www.scarlettoharas.net. Drinks $3–$8. Daily 11am–1am. Happy Hour Mon–Fri 4–7.*

What Else to See & Do

The best way to see all of the major sites is on an **Old Town Trolley Tour** (167 San Marco Ave; ☎ **904/829-3800;** www.trolleytours.com). Your $20 ticket is good for 3 days of hopping on and off the orange and green narrated tram that goes all over the city.

THE TOP ATTRACTIONS

➜ **Castillo de San Marcos National Monument** ★ America's oldest and best-preserved masonry fortification took 23 years to build and has survived centuries of attacks. Today, the old bombproof storerooms surrounding the central plaza house exhibits documenting the history of

the fort, a national monument since 1924. Popular torchlight tours of the fort are offered in winter (call for schedule). *1 E. Castillo Dr. ☎ 904/829-6506. www.nps.gov. casa. Admission $6 adults for a 7-day pass, $2 children 6–16. Fort daily 8:45am–4:45pm; grounds daily 5:30am–midnight.*

➜ **Colonial Spanish Quarter and Spanish Quarter Museum** ★ This is like the Colonial Williamsburg of St. Augustine. It's a miniature town that is a reproduction of what the area was like in the 1700s and has actors portraying workers in the town (try to get them to break character; it's almost impossible). Also, if you're there after hours, check out the minitown's tavern where an authentic 1700s bartender will serve you homemade sangria (don't worry, the sangria isn't from the olden days). *33 St. George St. (between Cuna and Orange Sts.). ☎ 904/825-6930. www.historicstaugustine.com. Admission $7 adults, $5.50 students, $6 seniors. Daily 9am–5:30pm (last entry 4:30pm). Tavern open Thurs–Sat 2–9:30pm, Sun noon–7pm.*

➜ **Fountain of Youth Archaeological Park** There's no actual evidence that this spot was visited by Ponce de Leon on his quest for pre-plastic surgery Botox. There is, in fact, a fountain, but you wouldn't want to drink this water even if it gave you super-awesome powers because it tastes *vile.* So without any true historical significance, and water that will trigger your gag reflex, you can safely pass this place by. *11 Magnolia Ave. ☎ 800/356-8222. Admission $6 adults, $5 seniors, $3 children 6–12. Daily 9am–5pm.*

➜ **Lightner Museum** ★★ This ornate museum is a hodgepodge of fabulous collectibles. From stuffed birds to mummies to steam engine models, you're sure to find something here that piques your interest. Make sure you are here at 11am or 2pm when a room of automated musical

A Ghostly Tour!

We highly recommend you go on a **Ghost Tours of St. Augustine** ★★★. This fun and interesting series of ghost tours includes a bus tour, a walking tour, and a boat tour, all guided by entertaining storytellers who make even the lamest of ghost stories amusing. All of the tours are after dark so it's the perfect activity between dinner and bar hopping. *Information and ticket sales in the City Gate Plaza.* ☎ **904/461-1009** *or 888/461-1009. www.ghosttours ofstaugustine.com. Tickets: $12 walking tour, $22 riding tour, $35 boat tour (discount coupons available online). Call for tour times.*

instruments pipes up into a spooky period music concert. Also check out the cafe in what used to be a gigantic aboveground swimming pool. *75 King St.* ☎ *904/824-2874. www.lightnermuseum.org. Admission $8 adults, $2 students with ID and children 12–18, free for children 11 and under. Daily 9am–5pm (last tour at 4pm).*

➜**The Oldest House** This is supposedly St. Augustine's earliest original colonial dwelling, and is generally packed with visitors. Hit it up if you're dying to see how colonists lived in the 17th century, but you can also just check it out as you walk by, and save the admission fee for something else. *14 St. Francis St. (at Charlotte St.).* ☎ *904/ 824-2872. www.staugustinehistoricalsociety. org Admission $6 adults, $4 students, $5.50 seniors. Daily 9am–5pm.*

FREE ➜**San Sebastian Winery** ★★★ Two words: *free wine.* It's true; you'll tour St. Augustine's own winery and see the process of making different wines, sherries, and sparkling wines, and at the end of the tour you'll taste each of the house varieties. The whole tour takes about 45 minutes. *157*

King St. ☎ *904/826-1594 or 888/FLA-WINE. www.sansebastianwinery.com. Free admission. Mon–Sat 10am–6pm; Sun 11am–6pm.*

PLAYING OUTSIDE

Beaches

➜**Anastasia State Park** ★★ This is by far the best and most beautiful beach in the area. The 4 miles of beach are backed by white sandy dunes and face a lagoon where you can watch wildlife while soaking up the sun. *1340-A A1A S. (On Anastasia Blvd. [Fla. A1A] across the Bridge of Lions and just past the Alligator Farm).* ☎ *904/461-2033 or 904/461-2000. www.floridastateparks.org. $5 per vehicle, $1 per pedestrian. Daily 8am–8:30pm. Restrooms; picnic area; grills; chairs, beach umbrellas, and surfboards available for rent.*

➜**Vilano Beach** If you'd like a beach away from the hordes of other sun-worshippers, this is the place to go. It isn't crowded, but because of erosion, the sand is rocky and a bit irritating to tender tootsies. *Vilano Rd. (A1A N to May St., right on A1A past the North River). $3 summer admission fee, free in the winter. Free parking. Restaurant and convenience store near the pier.*

Deep-Sea Fishing

➜**Sea Love Marina** ★ Cap'n Frank Timmons, Jr., will take you out to sea for a full-day or half-day trip to catch snapper, grouper, and porgie. The fee includes all the rods, bait, and tackle you'll need to reel in your catch, and you can even take your fish home with you (but *do not* leave it in your car). We caught a shark! *250 Vilano Rd. (at Sea Love marina).* ☎ *904/ 824-3328. www.sealovefishing.com. Half day $50 adults, $40 children, $45 seniors; full day $70 adults, $60 children, $60 seniors.*

Hiking

➜**Anastasia State Park** If you're too restless to just sit on this beach, there are some beautiful nature walks around the area. Pick up a map at the ranger booth on your way in. *(On Anastasia Blvd. [Fla. A1A] across the Bridge of Lions and just past the Alligator Farm).* ☎ *904/461-2033 or 904/461-2000. www.floridastateparks.org. $5 per vehicle, $1 per pedestrian. Daily 8am–8:30pm. Restrooms; picnic area; grills; chairs, beach umbrellas, and surfboards available for rent.*

Parasailing

➔ **Smile High Parasail** If you're not afraid of heights, this is a great way to get an aerial view of the city. You (and two others if you don't want to go alone) will soar into the air under a giant smiley face parasail. The boat driver will dip you into the water for a refreshing soak, or you can opt to stay dry if you wish. *111 Avenida Menendez #C (in the St. Augustine Municipal Marina).* ☎ *904/819-0980. www.smilehigh parasail.com. 700 ft. flight $65 per person, 1000 ft. $75, 1400 ft. $90.*

On the Road to Jekyll Island, GA

St. Augustine, FL to Jekyll Island, GA 115 miles

The best way to get to Jekyll Island is on I-95. From Ponce de Leon Boulevard in St. Augustine, take State Road 16 west to I-95 north. Follow the interstate through Jacksonville and on into Georgia and exit at US 17 N (exit 29). Follow US 17 until it forks and take Georgia State road 520 onto the island. You'll have to pay the $3 fee after crossing the Jekyll Island Causeway.

If you get hungry along the way, check out the **Florida Citrus Center** (right off I-95 at exit 373). It's a farmers market that sells Florida oranges and grapefruits and Georgia peaches, so you can stock up on road snacks. You can't miss the bright neon signs for it that tell you exactly when to turn off.

Welcome to Jekyll Island

There's not a whole lot to do on this tiny island, so you'll only need an afternoon if you even decide to stop at all (you can exclude this stop to shorten the trip). On the other hand, if you just want to chill out a bit and relax, it's an excellent place to stop.

The number of cheap hotels is slim to none, so consider driving the rest of the way to Savannah after you've gotten your fill of the lifestyles of the rich and fabulous. On the other hand, if you have some extra cash to blow, spend the night at the **Jekyll Island Club Hotel** ★★★ (371 Riverview Dr.; ☎ 800/535-9547; www.jekyllclub.com). The resort is beautiful and the grandiose accommodations will make you feel like a millionaire. Off-season rates start at $129 a night for a single; in high

Jams for the Journey to Jekyll Island

➔ *Rich,* **Yeah Yeah Yeahs,** "Fever To Tell," 2003

➔ *$100 Dollar Bill, Ya'll,* **Ice Cube,** "Ice Cube Greatest Hits," 2000

➔ *The Great Filling Station Hold Up,* **Jimmy Buffett,** "A White Sport Coat and A Pink Crustacean," 1987

➔ *Bling,* **Euricka,** "The Golden Child," 2003

➔ *Island In The Sun,* **Weezer,** "Weezer (Green Album)," 2001

➔ *Oceans,* **The Format,** "Dog Problems," 2006

➔ *Good Times Roll Pt. 2,* **RJD2,** "Deadringer," 2002

➔ *Lookin' Through The Windows,* **Jackson 5,** "Jackson 5: The Ultimate Collection," 1996

➔ *Island,* **The Rockfords,** "The Rockfords," 2000

Jekyll Island Club Hotel, Jekyll Island, GA.

season, you'll pay $399 a night for the Presidential Suite.

You can take the $18 tour of this historic district from the **Museum Orientation Center** (Stable Rd.; ☎ **912/635-4036**) that departs daily on the hour from 10am to 3pm, but I'd recommend touring the area on foot yourself (you'll save 18 bucks!). Maps of the historic area are available in the Museum Orientation Center or at the tollbooth at the entrance to the island.

For a marvelous retro diversion, have afternoon tea in the **Jekyll Island Club Dining Room** (in the Club House; ☎ **912/635-2400**) served daily from 4 to 5:30pm. The cheapest food at the resort is at **Café Solterra** (in the Club House) but if you want to splurge, go to **Courtyard at Crane** (in Crane Cottage; ☎ **912/635-2600**) and try the shrimp bisque and cottage calamari.

The best retro activity on Jekyll Island (and one that's just plain fun anyway) is a well-contested game of croquet. Sign up for a time on the Jekyll Island Club croquet

A Brief History of Jekyll Island

Although this teeny island is just a speck on the map, it has some "rich" historical significance. It was once the exclusive, private winter hangout for some of the wealthiest people in the country. From 1886 to 1942, bigwigs like the Rockefellers, Pulitzers, Goulds, Morgans, and Cranes bought the island and set up the Jekyll Island Club and each built a "cottage" (that is, a really fancy house) surrounding the central club. Then in 1942, the government asked the owners not to use the island during WWII due to "concerns in the resident's security," a sketchy circumstance if you ask me, so the bigwigs moved out and moved on to swankier resorts in Europe. Today the island is an exquisite yet sleepy historic district for even us common folk to visit.

court and challenge your companions to a game of Sticky Wicket. Sign up in the Club House.

There are three beaches around the island, but by far the best is the **St.**

Andrews Picnic Area (on Riverview Dr. beyond the Summer Waves water park). There aren't any bathrooms or lifeguards, but there is a picnic area nearby. Soak up the sun and then move on to Savannah!

On the Road to Savannah, GA

Jekyll Island to Savannah, GA 90 miles

From Jekyll Island, take the Jekyll Island Causeway off the island to GA 520, then veer west on US 17 to I-95 N. Stay on I-95 for about 70 miles and then merge onto I-16 E toward Savannah. I-16 will lead you straight into the heart of downtown Savannah.

Welcome to Savannah

This good-size city has the feel of a quaint Old South town with its restored homes, antebellum mansions, horse-drawn carriages, and sprawling oaks dripping with Spanish moss. Savannah is the largest urban National Historic Landmark District in the country.

Savannah Nuts & Bolts

Area Code   Savannah's area code is 912.

Business Hours   Banks are open Monday to Friday from 9am to 5pm and a few have 24-hour ATMs. Stores are usually open Monday to Saturday from 10am to 6pm and sometimes on Sunday afternoons. The bars here are open to midnight on weekdays and 2 or 3am on Friday and Saturday.

Dentist   For dental care, go to **Abercorn South Side Dental** at 11139 Abercorn St. (☎ 912/925-9190).

Doctor   Call the hospital for doctor referrals. (See "Hospitals," below.)

Drugstores   There are a few drugstores throughout town, and a **CVS** at 12012 Abercorn St. (☎ 912/925-5568).

Emergencies   Dial ☎ **911** for fire, police, or ambulance.

Hospitals   The two hospitals in Savannah are **Candler General Hospital** at 5353 Reynolds St. (☎ 912/819-6000) and **Memorial Medical Center** at 4700 Waters Ave. (☎ 912/350-8390). Both have 24-hour emergency units.

Internet   The best places to find wireless Internet is at **Gallery Espresso** at 234 Bull St. (☎ 912/236-7133).

Laundry/Dry Cleaners   If you're needing to do laundry (and chances are, by now you will), go to **Whiteway Laundry & Dry Cleaners** at 348 Whitaker St. (☎ 912/238-3690) or **The Best Cleaners and Laundry** at 1002 Waters Ave. (☎ 912/232-1171).

Libraries   The Savannah library is the **Chatham County Public Library** at 537 E. Henry St. (☎ 912/652-3600).

Liquor Laws   You must be 21 to purchase or consume alcohol in Georgia. Also, alcohol is permitted on Tybee Beach, but glass bottles are not.

Lost Property   To find or report a lost or stolen item, contact the police department at ☎ 912/651-6675.

Newspapers & Magazines   The main daily newspaper in Savannah is the *Savannah Morning News.*

Police   To contact the police for non-emergency matters, call ☎ 912/651-6675.

Radio   For hip-hop, turn to WQET (94.1), rock is WIXU (95.5), country is WAEV (97.3), Christian is WLXP (88.1), and public radio is WSVH (91.1). On the AM dial, talk radio is WGMQ (630) and news radio is WTKS (1290).

Taxes   Georgia has a 6% sales tax and the accommodations tax on your hotel room will be 6%.

Time Zone   Savannah is on Eastern Standard time.

Transit   For transit information, contact **Chatham Area Transit** at ☎ 912/233-5767.

Weather   For up-to-date weather, call ☎ 912/964-1700.

Getting Around

The beautiful grassy squares throughout the city are one of the reasons it's so satisfying to explore Savannah on foot. It's easy to get from the Forsyth Park end of the historic district to the river in 30 minutes or less.

If you need to drive, parking is plentiful. There are meters on every street, but be careful at night; you can get a hefty ticket for parking in a "sweep" zone. Purchase a **Visitor Day Parking Pass** for $8 at the Visitor Center, which saves you from having to carry around handfuls of quarters and having to visit the car to top up the meter every couple hours.

There are also garages that offer free parking nights and weekends at the corner of York and Montgomery streets and at the corner of State and Abercorn streets. There is a municipal bus line, but it isn't ideal for seeing the city. For route and schedule information, call **Chatham Area Transit** at ☎ 912/233-5767.

If you need to call a cab, **Adam Cab Co.** (☎ **912/927-7466**) runs 24 hours.

Retro-Savvy Savannah

Savannah's rich history makes for a whole slew of retro beats. Here are just a few of the vintage opportunities:

○ The greasy spoon **Clary's Cafe** has been around Savannah since 1903 and was even mentioned in *Midnight in the Garden of Good and Evil*. Locals have been eating eggs and bacon here for generations. See p. 292.

○ **The Pirates' House** restaurant and bar has been welcoming travelers since 1793. From pirate days when rum was the grog of choice, to today where you'll binge on down-home Southern cooking, it holds a rich history involving pirate buccaneers and their ghosts. See p. 293.

○ There are a handful of **historic homes** that beg to be toured in Savannah, and if you love the historic homes, then go to it; we have to confess we're *not* the home tour type. We preferred watching them go by (slowly) from a bus or trolley seat. See p. 295 for bus tour listings.

○ One of the most retro ways to see the city is by a horse-drawn **Carriage Tour.**

Savannah Highlights

EATING ♦
Bistro Savannah **11**
Café at City Market **7**
Clary's Café **25**
Gallery Espresso **22**
Gryphon Tea Room **23**
The Lady & Sons **10**
Mrs. Wilkes' Dining Room **24**
The Pirates' House **13**
Soho South Café **21**
Vinnie Van GoGo's Pizzeria **8**

PARTYING ★
45 Bistro Bar **15**
Club One **2**
Jen's and Friends **14**
Molly MacPherson's
   Scottish Pub **9**
Moon River Brewing Company **4**
Savannah Smiles **1**
Wet Willie's **5**

SLEEPING ■
Bed and Breakfast Inn **27**
Catherine Ward House Inn **29**
Courtyard by Marriott **20**
Fairfield Inn by Marriott **31**
Inn at Ellis Square **3**
Masters Inn Suites **30**
The Mulberry **12**
Park Avenue Manor **28**
Thunderbird Inn **17**

ATTRACTIONS ●
Fort Pulaski **32**
Mercer House
   Williams Museum **26**
Murder Afloat **6**
Old Town Trolley Tours **18**
Savannah History Museum **19**
Telfair Mansion and
   Art Museum **16**
Tybee Island **33**

Savannah Savvy Songlist

....

- → *On The Road Again,* **Willie Nelson,** "On The Road Again," 2001
- → *Peaches,* **The Presidents Of The United States Of America,** "The Presidents Of The United States Of America," 2004
- → *O' Sailor,* **Fiona Apple,** "Extraordinary Machine," 2005
- → *Savannah Mama,* **Blind Willie McTell,** "Pig 'N Whistle Red," 2003
- → *Georgia,* **Elton John,** "A Single Man (UK Version)," 2001
- → *Walking With A Ghost,* **Tegan & Sara,** "So Jealous," 2004
- → *Cold Beverage,* **G. Love & Special Sauce,** "G. Love & Special Sauce," 1994
- → *Savannah Woman,* **Tommy Bolin,** "Snapshot," 2006
- → *Savannah Smiles,* **Jodi Shaw,** "Snow On Saturn," 2005
- → *Why Georgia,* **John Mayer,** "Room For Squares," 2006

An authentic antique carriage takes you over cobblestone streets for a bumpy rendition of Savannah's history. Call ☎ **912/236-6756** for reservations.

○ Savannahians come to the **Abercorn Antique Village** (201 E. 37th St.; ☎ **912/233-0064;** www.abercornantiques.com) to shop in a self-described setting of "shabby-chic." Vendors featuring some 50 dealers and designers are set up in a historic house, a cottage, and an adjacent carriage house. The store is well organized and the antiques are high quality.

○ The **Clipper Trading Company** (201 W. Broughton St.; ☎ **912/238-3660;** www.clippertrading.com) has all sorts of imported Southeast Asian antiques. The decorative accents and furniture are separated according to country of origin to make it easy on you if you're looking for something in particular.

Sleeping

The majority of places to stay *in* the historic district are B&Bs that charge a pretty penny for a room in their historic homes, and those are certainly nice for a splurge. But there are also plenty of big hotels (both high-end and more modest chains) by the river that are mostly within walking distance of major attractions, restaurants, and nightlife.

CHEAP

→ **Fairfield Inn by Marriott** This reliable budget hotel offers standard but comfortable appointed guest rooms with large, well-lighted desks and well-kept bathrooms. Health club privileges are available nearby, as are several good, moderately priced restaurants. *2 Lee Blvd. (at Abercorn Rd.).* ☎ *800/228-2800 or 912/353-7100. www. mariott.com. $59–$109 double. Continental breakfast included. Amenities: Breakfast room; lounge; pool. In room: Dataport.*

→ **Masters Inn Suites** It isn't exactly in a convenient location (the Historic District and River St. are 8 miles away), but if you don't mind driving to town, the price is worth it. The large suites have a kitchen and dining area, a sofa, and one or two beds. *7110 Hodgson Memorial Dr.* ☎ *800/344-4378 or 912/354-8560. www.mastersinn-savannah.com. $69–$99 suite. Continental breakfast included. Amenities: Pool; sauna; fitness center; Concierge; Internet access. In room: Microwave, fridge, dining area.*

DOABLE

→ **Bed and Breakfast Inn** ★★ If you're craving the cozy feel of Mom's house without the interrogation of why you were out

Gracious tree-lined squares fill Savannah.

so late, this little inn is the perfect solution. You'll get a room reminiscent of your granny's, a full breakfast, and complimentary wine and cheese in the afternoon. Unlike some places, the hosts welcome younger travelers (like me and my sister) and you'll get a more authentic Savannah experience away from the impersonal chain hotels on Bay Street. *117 W. Gordon St. (at Chatham Sq.).* ☎ *888/238-0518 or 912/ 238-0518. www.savannahbnb.com. 18 units. $89–$169 double. Full breakfast and wine included. Amenities: Breakfast room; lounge; Internet access. In room: Fireplaces in some.*

→ **Courtyard by Marriott** Like the others in this chain, built around a landscaped courtyard, this place is one of the more recommendable motels bordering the Historic District. Many Savannah motels, though cheap, are quite tacky, but this one has renovated suites with separate seating areas, oversize desks, and private patios. *6703 Abercorn St.* ☎ *800/321-2211 or 912/ 354-7878. www.marriott.com. $99–$102 double. Continental breakfast included. Amenities:*

Breakfast room; bar; lounge; pool; fitness center; laundry service. In room: Dataport.

→ **Inn at Ellis Square** ★ This Historic Bay Street hotel is right near City Market and the hubbub on River Street. The motif is elegantly Victorian and the first floor lounge with leather sofas, a fireplace, and bar is a great place to mingle with other travelers. The rooms are capacious and inviting, but the concierge will suggest so many activities out and about that you won't be spending too much time in your room. *201 W. Bay St.* ☎ *912/236-4440. www. innatellissquare.com. $99–$129. Continental breakfast included. Parking $9 per day. Amenities: Breakfast room; lounge; bar; pool; Concierge. In room: Dataport, fridge.*

→ **Park Avenue Manor** ★★ Historic and cozy, this is Savannah's premier gay-friendly (straight welcoming) guesthouse. The small-scale inn has a well-rehearsed management style and an emphasis on irreverently offbeat Savannah. The place is noted not only for its comfort and warm welcome, but for one of the best Southern

A Quick History of Savannah, MTV Style

In February of 1733, James Edward Oglethorpe was sent to Savannah from England to help settle the thirteenth colony. Oglethorpe named the colony after good King George II and began to plan the first Georgian city. When Oglethorpe arrived, the area was already populated by a Native American tribe, and the friendly chief Tomo-chi-chi made friends with the foreigner and helped him found Savannah.

Fast forward to the peaceful era after the Revolutionary War. The cotton business was booming in the South and the results of the economic high times can still be seen today in the lavish homes and churches that remain. Huge fires destroyed half the city in 1796 and again in 1820. (People, don't leave open flames unattended around bales of cotton. Bad idea!) And as if Savannahians hadn't had enough bad luck, right after that second fire, a Yellow Fever epidemic broke out and killed 1 in 10 of Savannah's residents. It didn't take long for them to bounce back and rebuild before the Civil War. Savannah was the final destination when General Sherman began his march to the sea. After putting almost all the cities and towns on his way to the torch, Sherman chose to spare Savannah from the flame, and presented it to President Lincoln as a Christmas gift. It remained a somewhat sleepy Southern town until early in the 20th century. But after WWI, the boll weevil decimated the cotton industry, and the South's economy was thrown into havoc even before the Great Depression. Post-WWII, there was a move to modernize and industrialize the city but local women's groups began to organize to preserve the historic districts, and their movement kept much of the town intact (and gave birth to the booming tourism industry).

breakfasts in town. *107–109 W. Park Ave.* ☎ *912/233-0352. parkavenuemanor@ bellsouth.net. 4 units. $130 double. Full breakfast included. Amenities: Breakfast room; lounge. In room: No phone.*

→**Thunderbird Inn** From the outside, this two-story motel might give you the heebie-jeebies, but try to look past the teal and orange exterior and revel in the retro. The rooms are basic but clean and the price won't break your budget. *611 W. Oglethorpe Ave.* ☎ *912/232-2661 or 866/324-2661. www. thethunderbirdinn.com. $99–$129 double ($85 for 3 or more nights). Continental breakfast included. Amenities: Concierge; Internet access. In room: Fridge.*

SPLURGE

→**Catherine Ward House Inn** ★ The contemporary decor of the Catherine Ward House is a refreshing change from the grandma-ish Victorian motif seen in some of the other historic homes of Savannah. The breakfasts are scrumptiously fattening with entrees like strawberry and cream cheese–stuffed croissant French toast. Leslie Larson, the innkeeper, is an excellent source of things to do in Savannah, or a friendly companion to converse with when you're in the house. There's also a carriage house available for rental if you're traveling with a group. *118 E. Waldburg St.* ☎ *912/234-8564. www.catherine wardhouseinn.com. 10 units. Full breakfast included. $149–$189 double; $269–$299 carriage house. Amenities: Breakfast room; lounge; laundry service; Internet access. In room: Dataport, fridge, fireplaces.*

→**The Mulberry** ★★ Registered as Historic Hotel of America, this Holiday

Essential (Not Just Recommended!) Reading

Read John Berendt's *Midnight in the Garden of Good and Evil* (or watch Clint Eastwood's movie version. But really, the book is better). Locally known as "The Book," this publication put Savannah on the tourist map, and many of the sites and people in the book exist in real life, like the drag queen Lady Chablis. You can, in fact, take "Midnight" tours to visit many of the sights Berendt wrote about. One van tour, offered by **Savannah Tours** (☎ 888/653-6045; www.savannah tours.us), departs daily at 10am, and runs for 3 hours. The $44.95 fee ($39.95 if you order online) includes pickup at your lodgings.

Inn—owned gem is a step above the other chain properties on Bay Street. The building is situated around a serene central courtyard, with many of the rooms and open corridors overlooking the patio cafe. Even if you aren't staying here, you might want to take a jaunt through the first floor to observe the perfectly preserved historic decor. *601 E. Bay St.* ☎ *877/468-1200. www. savannahhotel.com. $140–$210 double. Amenities: Cafe; bar; pool; fitness center; Concierge; Internet access; complimentary afternoon tea and entertainment. In room: Microwave, fridge.*

Eating

Along River Street, there are a few touristy restaurants and some national chains, but if you know where to look, you can find good seafood around those parts. Try **River House Seafood** (125 W. River St.; ☎ 912/234-1900) or **River Street Oyster Bar** (411 E. River St.; ☎ 912/232-1565).

City Market (219 W. Bryan St., ☎ 912/232-4903, www.savannahcitymarket.com), which is made up of historic market buildings converted into art studios/galleries, shops, and restaurants, hosts many great restaurants and the area is so lively you can eat, then hang out around the area all night long. Mom-and-pop—style eateries

RETRO ROADTRIP

Savannah Festivals: St. Patty's Day Is Very Big

There is almost always something going on in this city, but here are a few of the highlights:

→ Savannah has the second largest **St. Patrick's Day Celebration** in the country after New York City. The weekend party brings in more than 250,000 visitors every year and everything from cocktails to grits are dyed green for the occasion. **www.savannahsaintpatricksday.com**.

→ In May, the river comes alive with the **Savannah Seafood Festival on the River.** It's not all fish, though; there are also arts and crafts, live entertainment, and a daily beach party. **www.savriverstreet.com**.

→ Also in May is a celebration of Savannah's rich Scottish heritage. The **Scottish Games Festival** holds clan competitions, bagpipe music, and traditional Scottish food and drinks. Call ☎ 912/232-3945 for more info.

→ **Oktoberfest** in Savannah is weekend-long German bash. There is bratwurst tasting, beer drinking, entertainment, and even wiener dog races to ensure a hearty party. **www.savriverstreet.com**.

Boo! America's Most Haunted?

Savannah claims to be America's most haunted city. Many locals and visitors alike report seeing ghosts and spirits around town, so be on the lookout for hazy lurking bodies. **Savannah Tours (☎ 888/653-6045;** www.savannahtours.us) offers a nightly "Ghosts of Savannah" walking tour for $18.95 ($15.95 if you purchase online).

are scattered all over town, so you'll never be too far away from a good meal.

SUPPLIES

To stock up on picnicking supplies before hitting the beach, there's a **Kroger Sav-On** supermarket (311 E. Gwinnett St.; ☎ **912/231-2260**) in the Historic District that will have almost everything you'll need. It's 3 blocks east of Forsyth Park.

EATING OUT

CHEAP

➔**Café at City Market** ★ EUROPEAN Set in the lively City Market, this dineresque cafe is perfectly described as retro chic. Big Band music plays overhead as you munch on gourmet sandwiches and hand-tossed pizzas. Don't be fooled by the white tablecloths; the prices will fit your budget. *224 W. Saint Julian St. (in City Market). ☎ 912/236-7133. cafesav@aol.com. Main courses $7–$13. Daily lunch 11:30am–3:30pm; dinner 6–10pm.*

➔**Clary's Cafe** ★ AMERICAN This greasy spoon has been a Savannah staple since 1903. They serve traditional breakfast favorites as well as elaborate concoctions like Crabcakes Benedict or the hearty Hoppel Poppel with scrambled eggs, chunks of salami, potatoes, onions, and peppers served with grits and biscuits. They also do

lunch, but if you want Clary's at its best, order breakfast any time of the day. *404 Abercorn St. (at Jones St.). ☎ 912/233-0402. Breakfast $4–$8; main courses $6–$8. Daily 8am–4pm.*

➔**Gallery Espresso** DELI/CAFE Other than brewing a great cup of joe, this coffee shop also serves soups, salads, and sandwiches for a decent price. If you just want an afternoon snack, get the Cheese Board, a loaf of French bread with three types of cheeses, and wash it down with a bottle of wine. You'll surely be inspired by the Savannah art and artists that frequent the cafe and make it a cool place to hang out while you check your e-mail. *234 Bull St. (at the corner of Bull and Perry sts.). ☎ 912/233-5348. www.galleryespresso.com. Main courses $5–$10. Daily 8am–midnight.*

➔**Vinnie Van GoGo's Pizzeria** ★ PIZZA This is *the* best pizza in all of Savannah. Locals and tourists love this place so much there's always a wait, but the atmosphere is rowdy and fun, and you can spend your wait time thinking about how to customize your pie. *317 W. Bryan St. (in City Market). ☎ 912/233-6394. www.vinnievangogo.com. Medium and large pizzas $9–$15. Cash only. Mon–Thurs 4–11:30pm; Fri 4pm–1am; Sat noon–1am; Sun noon–11:30pm.*

DOABLE

➔**Gryphon Tea Room** ★ TEA/DELI This modernized tea room is the perfect place for an afternoon pick-me-up. With funky orange accents on an otherwise bland interior, it attracts the nearby Savannah College of Art & Design (SCAD) students and faculty to daily breakfast, lunch, and high tea. The tiny petit fours, scones, and cucumber sandwiches served with tea are delightful, but if you're seeking a full stomach, opt for an entree instead. *337 Bull St. (on the corner of Bull and Charlton sts.). ☎ 912/525-5880. Full tea service $7–$15; main courses $6–$15. Mon–Fri*

8:30am–9:30pm; Sat 10am–9:30pm; high tea Mon–Sat 4–6pm.

→ **The Lady & Sons** ★★ SOUTHERN When I asked a local what made Paula Deen's restaurant so good, she said, "Well it's because there's one stick of butter on every plate and one pound of sugar in every pitcher of tea." Deen's show on Food Network has made the popularity of her Southern home cookin' skyrocket so that it is almost impossible to score a table here (people line up around the block each morning). To skip the line, get the buffet to go and picnic in one of the many oak-shaded squares around the area. *120 W. Congress St.* ☎ *912/233-2600. www.ladyand sons.com. Reservations recommended for dinner. Main courses $6–$13 lunch, $18–$24 dinner. All-you-care-to-eat-buffet $13 lunch, $17 dinner. Sun buffet $15. Mon–Sat 11am–3pm; Mon–Thurs 5–9pm; Fri–Sat 5–10pm; Sun 11am–5pm (buffet only).*

→ **Mrs. Wilkes' Dining Room** ★ SOUTHERN Missing Grandma's home cooking? Stand in line for a seat at one of the long tables in the basement dining room of the late Mrs. Wilkes's house and prepare yourself for a belly-busting lunch. The daily menu selection of meals like fried or barbecued chicken, rice and sausage, black-eyed peas, corn on the cob, okra, and corn bread are served family-style on gigantic plates in the middle of the table. A meal here is a genuine Savannah institution. *107 W. Jones St. (west of Bull St.).* ☎ *912/232-5997. www.mrswilkes.com. Lunch $13. No credit cards. Mon–Fri 11:30am–2pm.*

→ **The Pirates' House** ★★ SOUTHERN They say this place is haunted by pirate ghosts of the past, and along with that delightful prospect, this looming wooden shack offers not only delicious southern cooking, but also the chance to dine in the very location that Robert Louis Stevenson received his *Treasure Island* inspiration.

(That Stevenson was actually referencing The Pirates' House in his book is doubtful, since there is no record that he even visited the city, but who are we to crush the legend?) Stuff your belly at the "fried chicken with all the fixins" buffet or order from the menu, but make sure you load up on your pirate garb at the gift shop. *20 E. Broad St.* ☎ *912/233-5757. www.thepirates house.com. Main courses $8–$13 lunch, $16–$25 dinner. Lunch buffet $14. Lunch Mon–Sat 11:30am–3:30pm; dinner nightly 5:30–10:30pm.*

📺 Best● → **Soho South Café** ★★★ INTERNATIONAL This eclectic and arty cafe is a little taste of New York's SoHo. Local art lines the colorful walls and fills the waiting room that doubles as a gallery. The funky decorative accents like a Christmas tree, outdoor umbrellas, and a vintage mannequin floating overhead create a delightful carnival for your eyes. Try the Shrimp-N-Grits with Cajun cream sauce or the tasty jumbo lump crab cake sandwich. *12 W. Liberty St.* ☎ *912/233 1633. www.sohosouthcafe.com. Main courses $7–$11 lunch, $15–$25 dinner. Mon–Sat 11am–4pm; Tues–Sat 5:30–9:30pm; Sun 11am–4pm.*

SPLURGE

→ **Bistro Savannah** ★★★ SOUTHERN FUSION The eclectic art decorating the inside of this upscale bistro reflects the creative culinary masterpieces of the chef. This arty eatery serves incredible seafood with entrees like barbecued grouper over grits, as well as interesting and enticing flavor combinations like crispy pecan chicken with blackberry bourbon sauce. If you like shellfish, try my favorite, the scrumptious mussels in spicy Thai sauce. The mood is elegant without being too pretentious and the staff is knowledgeable and friendly. *309 W. Congress St.* ☎ *912/ 233-6266. Reservations recommended. Main courses $15–$24. Sun–Thurs 5:30–10:30pm; Fri–Sat 5:30–11pm.*

Partying

I've never experienced a better town for bar-hopping than Savannah. The two main areas for bar-hopping are City Market and along River Street. Here, the bars are all within walking distance from each other so you can spend all night going from pub to pub. And the best thing, you'll never be without a drink in your hand because town rules allow bars to mix your cocktail in a to-go cup so you can take it with you.

BARS & PUBS

→ **45 Bistro Bar** This hotel bar might seem a little uptight at first, but it's actually a laid-back place to chill in a leather-clad library lounge. You'll feel cozy enough in the scholarly cave to sip the potent cocktails all night. The mingling of strangers doesn't really happen (until, of course, everyone's downed enough booze) so it's more fun to come with a group. *123 E. Broughton St. (in the Marshall House Hotel).* ☎ *912/234-3111. Drinks $4–$8. Sun–Thurs 6–10pm; Fri–Sat 6pm–1am.*

→ **Jen's and Friends** ★ If you're fed up with standard dry martinis and sick of cosmos, you're sure to find a martini to suit your palate at Jen's. They have over 100 different martinis, from the caramel apple martini to the Twix bar martini. It's a tiny place, but there's outdoor seating if you'd rather sip your 'tini away from the bar's bustle. *7 E. Congress St.* ☎ *912/238-5367. jensandfriends@yahoo.com. Drinks $4–$9. Mon–Thurs 11am–midnight; Fri 11am–2am; Sat 3pm–2am.*

→ **Molly MacPherson's Scottish Pub** ★ As the only Scottish pub in Savannah, Molly MacPherson's proudly represents the old country. Scottish flags, coats of arms, kilt wearing bartenders, and a nightly bagpipe player all make this pub a Great British experience. You can also get Scottish pub fare like Bangers and Mash and Shepherd's Pie. The only thing that isn't Scottish is Charlie, the ghost who allegedly haunts the bar. *311 W. Congress St.* ☎ *912/239-9600. www.macphersonspub.com. Drinks $4–$7. Mon–Thurs 11am–11pm; Fri–Sat 11am–2am; Sun noon–11pm.*

→ **Moon River Brewing Company** If you love a good microbrew, then head for Moon River. This is Savannah's only brewery and you can see the award-winning beers being brewed through windows next to the bar. The mood is cool and jazzy thanks to live music, and although the beer is the star of the show, the food is pretty good, too. *21 W. Bay St.* ☎ *912/447-0943. www. moonriverbrewing.com. Drinks $4–$7. Sun–Thurs 11am–11pm; Fri–Sat 11am–2am.*

MTV Best● → **Savannah Smiles** ★★ A memorable night is guaranteed as you watch and sing along with ivory-tickling comedians at this dueling piano bar. Tucked away in an ominous alley, it may seem sketchy from outside but once in, you'll be invited to request songs and laugh along with the pianists' crude humor. Insider trick: Buy the piano players a drink and you'll be more likely to hear your requested song. *314 Williamson St. (off Bay St. behind Quality Inn).* ☎ *912/52-SMILE. Cover charge $5. Drinks $4–$8. Wed–Sat 7pm–3am. Dueling piano show starts at 9pm. Happy Hour 6:30–8pm.*

→ **Wet Willie's** If you're in the mood for a frat party, like dancing to Vanilla Ice, or just want to get plastered fast, Wet Willie's is the place for you. They serve Jell-O shots and over a dozen kinds of daiquiris made with 190-grain alcohol that have names like "Attitude Adjustment" and "Call a Cab." Come late after the restaurant crowd leaves for the ideal party experience. *101 E. River St.* ☎ *912/233-5650. www.wetwillies. com. Drinks $5–$8. Mon–Thurs 11am–1am; Fri–Sat 11am–2am; Sun 12:30pm–1am.*

THE GAY & LESBIAN SCENE

📺 (Best ♪) ➜ **Club One** ★ This is the premier gay bar in town and also welcomes the gay-friendly straight crowd. The basement level is a video bar with pool tables and a relaxed atmosphere, the street-level segment has a techno glowstick vibe, and the third floor hosts the nightly drag shows where performers lip sync to Melissa Etheridge, Tina Turner, and anything else that's worthy of chest or booty shaking. Famed local drag queen Lady Chablis also stops by to perform here; check the website for her schedule. *1 Jefferson St. ☎ 912/232-0200. www.clubone online.com. Cover after 9:30pm $10 for those 18–20, $5 for those 21 and up. Drinks $4–$8. Mon–Sat 5pm–3am; Sun 5pm–2am. Shows nightly at 10:30pm and 12:30am.*

What Else to See & Do

While you've probably noticed that I think Savannah is a *great* party town, it's also a beautiful, refined city, with a fascinating history. So with or without your to-go cup, do make the time to take a tour (see "Tours," below) or spend some time soaking up some culcha as well as liquid refreshment.

THE TOP ATTRACTIONS

➜ **Fort Pulaski** This Union fort was completed in 1847 with walls 7½ feet thick and was taken by Georgia forces at the beginning of the war. The pentagonal fort has galleries and drawbridges crossing the moat. You can still find shells from 1862 embedded in the walls. There are exhibits of the fort's history in the visitor center. *15 miles east of Savannah off U.S. 80 on Cockspur and McQueen islands at the very mouth of the Savannah River. ☎ 912/786-5787. www.nps. gov/fopu. Admission $3 adults, free for those 16 and under. Daily 9am–7pm. Closed Christmas and Thanksgiving.*

➜ **Mercer House Williams Museum** Featured in "The Book," this house has been restored and is now open to the public. Although many of its most elegant contents were auctioned off at Sotheby's in October 2000 for $1 million—including the Anatolian carpet upon which the hapless Danny Hansford is reputed to have fallen after being shot—furniture and art from the private collection of Jim Williams are on display. *429 Bull St. ☎ 877/430-6352. www.mercerhouse.com. Admission $13. Mon–Tues and Thurs–Sat 10:30am–3:40pm; Sun 12:30–4pm; closed Wed and off season.*

➜ **Savannah History Museum** Housed in the restored train shed of the old Central Georgia Railway station, this museum is a good introduction to the city. In the theater, *The Siege of Savannah* is replayed and an exhibition hall displays memorabilia from every era of Savannah's history. *303 Martin Luther King, Jr. Blvd. ☎ 912/238-1779. www.chsgeorgia.org/shm. Admission $4 adults, $3.50 students and seniors, $3 children 6–11. Mon–Fri 8:30–5pm; Sat–Sun 9am–5pm.*

➜ **Telfair Mansion and Art Museum** ★ The oldest public art museum in the South houses a collection of American and European paintings. The house was built for Alexander Telfair, son of Edward Telfair, the governor of Georgia. The period rooms have been restored, and the Octagon Room and Dining Room are particularly outstanding. The Telfair is also the home of the famous statue "The Bird Girl" (featured on the cover of The Book). *121 Bernard St. ☎ 912/232-9743. www.telfair. org. Admission $8 adults, $2 students, $1 children 6–12. Mon noon–5pm; Tues–Sat 10am–5pm; Sun 1–5pm.*

TOURS

➜ **Architectural Tours of Savannah** ★ These small tours are led by Jonathan

Another Savannah Murder Mystery

. . . Only this one isn't of the "true crime" variety. In **Murder Afloat** ★★ you'll witness and try to solve a murder mystery aboard a riverboat cruise. Actors depict the heinous crime; the audience helps uncover clues and solve the mystery. Bring your pipe and magnifying glass, and play Sherlock for a night. Dinner is not available, but there is a cash bar onboard. *9 E. River St. (behind City Hall).* ☎ *912/232-6404. www.murder afloat.com. Tickets $27 adults, $19 children under 12. Thurs nights only 9–11pm. Reservations suggested.*

Stalcup, a SCAD graduate with a Master of Architecture who knows everything there is to know about Savannah architecture from past to present. The walking tours offered range from the beginning of colonial history to current times and are very entertaining. ☎ *912/604-6354. www. architecturalsavannah.com. Tickets $20 adults, $10 students, $5 children ages 6–12. Reservations required, times and tours may vary.*

➔ **Old Town Trolley Tours** ★ This is the best and easiest way to see Savannah's top attractions. It's a hop-on/hop-off narrated bus tour so you can browse the sites at your own leisure. The operators also offer a "Ghosts and Gravestones" tour which takes you to the haunted places in town and even inside the spooky Colonial Park Cemetery. *234 Martin Luther King, Jr. Blvd.* ☎ *912/233-0083. www.historictours.com. Tickets $23–$25. Daily. Reservations required for Ghosts and Gravestones.*

MTV **Best** ➔ **Savannah Spirits Haunted Pub Crawl** ★ You'll get the best of Savannah's "spirits" on one of these nightly bar tours. You'll hop from pub to pub all night learning about the ghosts that haunt bars in the most haunted city in the country. The guides dress in period costume to enhance the experience and their corny jokes get funnier as the tour pours on. *506 E. Oglethorpe Ave.* ☎ *912/604-3007. www.ghostsavannah.com. Tickets $14 adults, $12 seniors. Tours nightly at 8pm.*

PLAYING OUTSIDE
Beaches

FREE ➔ **Tybee Island** ★★ This 5-mile stretch of sand is the closest beach to Savannah. It takes about 30 minutes to get there but the salt marshes and sand dunes create the perfect setting for a relaxing day at the beach. There are also great restaurants in the area and hotels if you don't want to make the trek back to home base, Savannah. Also, Bonaventure Cemetery (prominently featured in The Book) is an easy detour on the way to Tybee Island. It's beautiful, with lots of old oaks dripping with moss, and it's set on the river. Johnny Mercer is buried here. (For more information and directions, visit **www.bon aventurehistorical.org**.) *From Savannah take US 80 until you reach the ocean.* ☎ *800/868-BEACH. Open sunrise to sunset. Free admission and parking. Picnicking and restrooms available.*

Fishing

➔ **Amicks Deep Sea Fishing** This daily charter features a 41-foot custom-built boat, and the rod, reel, and tackle are provided. You'll have to bring your own lunch, but beer and soda are sold on board. *6902 Sand Nettles Dr.* ☎ *912/897-6759. $95 per person. All-day trip 7am–6pm. Reservations recommended.*

Running

The president of the Savannah Striders Club calls this quaint town "the most beautiful city to jog in." The historic avenues

Fun for Free in Savannah

→ (FREE) Take a box of chocolates to a bench in **Chippewa Square** and reenact the famous *Forest Gump* scene at the place it was filmed. (The actual bench is no longer there, as it was a prop for the film!)

→ (FREE) Check out the **Kessler Hat Collection** at the fabulous Mansion on Forsyth Park (700 Drayton St.; ☎ 912/238-5158). The collection contains 100 hats dating all the way back to 1860.

→ (FREE) For a free night activity, head to City Market at the corner of Jefferson and W. Saint Julian streets. Live bands play in the central courtyard a few nights a week and every weekend. You can just relax in the cool night air to the sound of local musicians. For current events call ☎ 912/525-CITY or go to **www.savannahcitymarket.com**.

provide an exceptional setting for your run. The Visitor Center can provide you with jogging route maps.

For a brisk jaunt, there is a jogging trail around the one-mile perimeter of Forsyth Park, but if you'd rather go for a longer run, try the Old Savannah-Tybee Trail that starts at Highway 80 at Bull River. It's a 6.5-mile scenic hiking trail. Check out **www.savystrider.com** for more info on routes and weekly group runs.

Hanging Out

There are 20 grassy squares all over town shaded by mossy live oaks. These are great places to relax, think, and rest your feet. **Forsyth Park** ★★ is the best park to chill out at with its marble fountain and enormous grassy area for Frisbee throwing, football playing, jogging, or just lounging. The park is at Gaston Street between Whitaker and Drayton and it is open 24 hours a day.

On the Road to Charleston, SC

Savannah, GA to Charleston, SC 120 miles

From Savannah, take GA 21 north and merge onto I-95 north crossing into South Carolina. Take the SC-63 exit to Walterboro and follow SC-64 (Charleston Hwy.) to US 17 (Savannah Hwy.) and continue east on

MTV Best ♀ → *Detour:* Nights at the Drive-In

If you're making the drive in the evening, consider stopping off in Beaufort, SC. The **HWY 21 Drive In** (55 Parker Dr.; ☎ 843/846-4500; www.hwy21drivein.com) shows current films in an old-fashioned setting, complete with car speakers if you opt not to tune in on your radio. There is a concession stand with burgers, hot dogs, pretzels, and popcorn if you want to combine dinner with your movie, and the tickets are only $4! If you're not ready to head to Charleston after the movie, stay for a double feature. To get to Beaufort from Savannah, take US 17 north to SC 170 north, then take US 21 north and the drive-in will be on your left at Parker Drive. The gates open at 6:30 every night and close after the last screening, usually around midnight and it is open year-round.

Charleston Chanties: Carolina Playlist

→ *Here It Goes Again,* **OK Go,** "Oh No," 2005

→ *What Happened To The Sands,* **Pas/Cal,** "Oh Honey, We're Ridiculous," 2004

→ *Charleston Alley,* **Hendricks, Lambert & Ross,** The Hottest New Group In Jazz," 1996

→ *Southern Anthem,* **Iron & Wine,** "The Sea & The Rhythm," 2003

→ *Just A Little Bit South Of North Carolina,* **Anita O' Day & Gene Krupa,** "Let Me Off Uptown!," 1999

→ *Me & The Minibar,* **The Dresden Dolls,** "Yes, Virginia," 2006

→ *Charleston Rag,* **Eubie Blake,** "Memories Of You," 2003

→ *Happy Frappy,* **Guster,** Parachute, 2004

→ *Oh My Sweet Carolina,* **Ryan Adams,** Heartbreaker, 2000

that for about 30 miles. You'll run right into Charleston.

The drive is pretty, but traffic can really slow down after you exit from the interstate. Watch out for cops between Walterboro and Charleston, which is lined with small-town speed traps.

Welcome to Charleston

At first glance, Charleston seems like an old Southern town that hasn't changed since the days of Rhett Butler (and the city certainly encourages that idea). Somewhere above the cobblestone streets and behind the historic plantation homes, however, you'll see that Charleston is actually a trendy urban metropolis.

There are a lot of sights to see, but Charleston is also a great place to relax, shop, and experience the Low Country. To see the top sights you'll need at least 2 days, but add more if you want to get a real feel for the city. Try to hit Charleston on a weekend, because the nightlife here is one of a kind!

Charleston Nuts & Bolts

Area Code Charleston's area code is 843.

Business Hours Banks are generally open Monday to Friday from 9am to 5pm and sometimes on Saturday. Bars are open to 2am daily.

Drugstores There are drugstores all over the place in town, but if you're near the highway, there's a **CVS** at 1603 Highway 17 (☎ 843/971-0764).

Emergencies For an emergency, call ☎ **911.**

Hospitals The **Charleston Memorial Hospital** at 326 Calhoun St. (☎ 842/792-2300) offers 24-hour emergency care.

Internet Most of the hotels around town have Internet available, but outside of your room, the best bets are **Kool Beanz Koffee & Kreme** at 433 King St. (☎ 843/

722-9915), **Port City Java** at 261 Calhoun St. (☎ 843/937-9352), or **Moe's Southwest Grill** at 381 King St. (☎ 843/577-7727).

Laundry/Dry Cleaners   For laundry and dry cleaning service, hit up **Arrow Dry Cleaners & Laundry** at 80 Calhoun St. (☎ 843/723-3087) or **East Bay Cleaners** at 480 East Bay St. (☎ 843/577-4430).

Libraries   The **Charleston County Library** is located at 68 Calhoun St. and can be reached at ☎ 843/805-6802.

Liquor Laws   In South Carolina you must be 21 or older to purchase or consume alcohol. Beer and wine are sold in grocery stores 7 days a week, but liquor stores are closed on Sundays.

Lost Property   To report a lost or stolen item, call the police at ☎ 843/577-7077.

Newspapers & Magazines   The daily news source for the area is *The Charleston Post & Courier* (www.charleston.net). It has a great weekend section.

Police   For non-emergency matters, the police department can be reached at ☎ 843/577-7707.

Post Office   For all of your mailing needs, there is a post office at 83 Broad St. (☎ 843/577-0688).

Radio   On the FM dial, turn to WSSX (95.1) for top-40, WSCI (89.3) for public radio, WALC (100.5) for current tracks, WEZL (103.5) for country, and WFCH (88.5) for religious. On the AM dial, turn to WTMA (1250) for news talk and WQSC (1340) for sports radio.

Taxes   South Carolina has a 6% sales tax. Charleston has a 6% accommodations tax for your hotel room and a 7% tax for restaurant food.

Time Zone   Charleston is on Eastern Standard Time.

Transit Information   For information on buses and other transit operations, contact **Charleston Area Convention Visitor Reception & Transportation Center** at 375 Meeting St. (☎ 843/853-8000).

Weather   For current weather, call ☎ 843/744-3207.

Getting Around

Charleston is very spread out, so if you're not staying in the heart of the city, a car is essential. I recommend parking somewhere central and walking from there to avoid the hassle of finding a new parking spot. There are parking facilities sprinkled throughout the city, but the most convenient are at King Street between Queen and Broad streets and on George Street between King and Meeting streets.

Two central garages are at Wentworth (☎ **843/724-7383**) and at Concord and Cumberland (☎ **843/724-7387**) and both charge $8 for the whole day.

There is also the **Downtown Area Shuttle** (☎ **843/724-7420**), which is a quick, reliable bus system around the main downtown area. The fare is $1.25, or you can buy a day pass for $4.

Retro-Charged Charleston

Charleston has some awesome retro romps, but make sure you save time for the cool current Charleston, too!

Festivals in Charleston: Grits & Arts

From the world famous to the down home, you can get your festival on here:

→　For some knee slappin,' side stitching, and laughing-so-hard-Coke-comes-out-your-nose, head here in January for the **Charleston Comedy Festival.** With improv, sketch acts, and stand-up comedy, you're sure to get in a few good laughs. **www.charlestoncomedyfestival.com.**

→　Also in January is the popular **Low Country Oyster Festival.** If you're a shellfish fan, it doesn't get any better than this. There are oyster-shucking contests and oyster-eating contests and for those just there for the food, oysters are sold by the bucket. **www.charlestonrestaurantassociation. com/oyster_festival.php.**

→　The one and only **World Grits Festival** is held each April in St. George, only a few minutes away from Charleston. The celebration consists of a parade, live music, clogging, and, of course, grits. **www.worldgritsfestival.com.**

→　When the founders of the famous Spoleto, Italy, arts festival were looking for an American counterpart to host a sister festival, their gaze settled on Charleston. Founded by composer Gian Carlo Menotti in 1977, Charleston's **Spoleto** (box office ☎ **843/579-3100;** www.spoletousa.org) is one of the major arts festivals in North America. Held annually in May and June, it also spawned an offshoot called **Piccolo Spoleto,** a more home-grown and youth-oriented celebration that runs around the same time as the international festival.

○ You must see a plantation while in Charleston. **Middleton Place** is one of the best, with beautiful gardens, a bona fide plantation home, and stable yards. There is even a restaurant with old-fashioned Southern plantation food. See p. 305.

○ **Charles Towne Landing** is the Colonial Williamsburg of Charleston. A living museum with workers in period costume and animals roaming the countryside, this is a replica of what the first South Carolina settlement was like in 1670. See p. 305.

○ Just a block from the Visitor Center, the **King Street Antique Mall** (495 King St.; ☎ 843/723-2211; www.kingstantique mall.com) has thousands of interesting antiques. Furniture, rugs, estate jewelry, chandeliers, and even European taxidermy line the tables and display cases, and the prices aren't too expensive.

○ With a proclamation of "Charleston's best dive since 1955," any retro roadtripper must check out **Big John's Tavern.** Around for decades, Big John's is still going strong and attracts a young, fun crowd every night. See p. 304.

Sleeping

There are a lot of great hotels in the historic district, but they tend to be pricey. The super cheap stays are either in North Charleston (which is not the safest neighborhood) or way south of town, but there are definitely some affordable finds downtown. Avoid big chain hotels here if you can, because the local places are the real stars of the Charleston hotel selection.

HOSTEL/CHEAP

→**Charleston's Not So Hostel** ★ For travelers on a budget, this is a great find. Located downtown in an 1850s historic home, you'll meet and mingle with other

Charleston Highlights

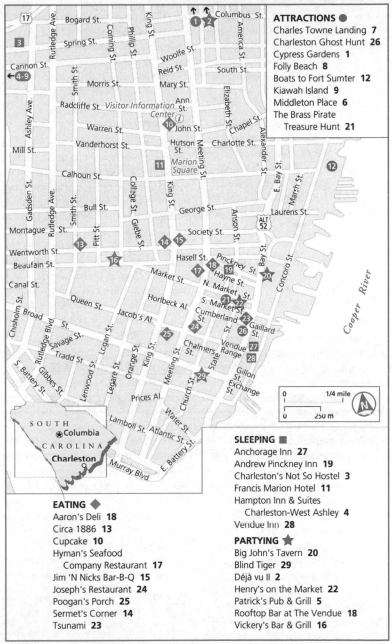

ATTRACTIONS ●

Charles Towne Landing **7**
Charleston Ghost Hunt **26**
Cypress Gardens **1**
Folly Beach **8**
Boats to Fort Sumter **12**
Kiawah Island **9**
Middleton Place **6**
The Brass Pirate
   Treasure Hunt **21**

EATING ◆

Aaron's Deli **18**
Circa 1886 **13**
Cupcake **10**
Hyman's Seafood
   Company Restaurant **17**
Jim 'N Nicks Bar-B-Q **15**
Joseph's Restaurant **24**
Poogan's Porch **25**
Sermet's Corner **14**
Tsunami **23**

SLEEPING ■

Anchorage Inn **27**
Andrew Pinckney Inn **19**
Charleston's Not So Hostel **3**
Francis Marion Hotel **11**
Hampton Inn & Suites
   Charleston-West Ashley **4**
Vendue Inn **28**

PARTYING ★

Big John's Tavern **20**
Blind Tiger **29**
Déjà vu II **2**
Henry's on the Market **22**
Patrick's Pub & Grill **5**
Rooftop Bar at The Vendue **18**
Vickery's Bar & Grill **16**

travelers on the porches or over an all-you-can-eat waffle breakfast. There are both dorm-style rooms and private rooms for those who don't want roommates they've never met before. *156 Spring St.* ☎ *843/722-8383. www.notsohostel.com. $19 dorm beds; $55 private rooms. Amenities: Coin laundry; bike rentals; Internet access. In room: Lockers.*

➜ **Hampton Inn & Suites Charleston-West Ashley** Airy and strangely tropical, this Hampton Inn is a few minutes away from downtown but the prices are *much* cheaper than its sister hotels in the historic district. The suites have separate living areas and kitchenettes and the open lobby has a cozy fireplace. *678 Citadel Haven Dr. (I–526 and Hwy. 17).* ☎ *843/573-1200. www.charleston-hotels.net. $79–$99 double. Breakfast included. Amenities: Concierge; fitness center; pool; laundry service; Internet access. In room: Kitchenette, living area.*

DOABLE

➜ **Anchorage Inn** ★ This small hotel is quiet and dark. Most of the rooms are windowless but this makes it much easier to sleep in without that pesky sun shining in your eyes. This is a great place for some R&R and the location is stellar, but if you're looking to mingle and party with other travelers, hit up one of the bigger hotels. *26 Vendue Range.* ☎ *800/421-2952 or 843/723-8300. www.anchoragencharleston.com. 19 units. $89–$189 double. Continental breakfast and afternoon tea included. Parking $10. Amenities: Breakfast room; laundry service; Internet access. In room: Dataport.*

➜ **Andrew Pinckney Inn** ★ This West Indies–style boutique inn is in the heart of the historic district and overlooks the harbor. The historic value rooms are a bit cramped, but the price can't be beat and the two-story, town-house suites are perfect for group travel. The beautiful rooftop garden terrace is a great place to hang out

and enjoy beautiful views over breakfast or a drink. *40 Pinckney St. (at the corner of Church and Pinckney sts.).* ☎ *843/937-8800. www.andrewpinckneyinn.com. 41 units. $89–$199 double. Continental breakfast included. Parking $12 per day. Amenities: Rooftop garden terrace; laundry service; concierge; tour pick up in lobby; Internet access. In room: Dataport.*

SPLURGE

➜ **Francis Marion Hotel** ★★ This European-style historic hotel is on King Street, just a short walk to almost everything. The rooms are elaborate and large and service is impeccable. The hotel's restaurant serves great Southern fare at breakfast, lunch, and dinner, and jazz piano music is often played in the lounge. *387 King St.* ☎ *877/756-2121 or 843/722-0600. www.francismarioncharleston.com. $88–$230 double. Parking $10–$15. Amenities: Restaurant; bar; fitness center; room service; laundry service; concierge; wireless Internet. In room: Dataport, minibar.*

➜ **Vendue Inn** ★★ The location of this boutique hotel is just one of the many reasons to stay here. It's close to the harbor, the historic district, great restaurants, and hoppin' nightlife. The rooms are elegant and warm, and the interior accessories that clutter the halls and lobby add interesting dimension to the hotel. Don't miss the **Rooftop Terrace** bar on the roof for awesome views and nightly parties. *19 Vendue Range.* ☎ *800/845-7900 or 843/577-7900. www.vendueinn.com. 65 units. $169–$189 double. Full Southern breakfast included. Valet parking $14. Amenities: 2 restaurants; bar; room service; laundry service; Concierge; complimentary bicycles. In room: Dataport.*

Eating

There are two things that Charleston restaurants do especially well: seafood and Southern. While you're here, try the

Charleston delicacy she-crab soup and anything fishy. You won't be disappointed.

TAKE-OUT TREATS

MTV Best● → **Cupcake** ★★★ CUP-CAKES Do not leave Charleston without a visit to Cupcake. The towers of gooey frosting atop warm, fluffy cupcakes put even NYC's Magnolia Bakery to shame. With almost 30 different flavors such as chocolate butterscotch chip, lemon blueberry, and black bottom with cheesecake filling, there is a cake and frosting combo to suit any cupcake connoisseur. *433 King St. ☎ 843/853-8181. Cupcakes $2.75 each, $30 per dozen. Mon–Sat 10am–7pm.*

EATING OUT

Cheap

→ **Aaron's Deli** DELI This deli serves up hearty New York–style sandwiches. From burgers and kosher corned beef, to turkey and Swiss, these big sandwiches will fill up your stomach without emptying your pockets. *213 Meeting St. ☎ 843/723-6000. www.hymanseafood.com. Sandwiches $5–$12. Daily 11am–1am. Closed Jewish holidays, Thanksgiving, and Christmas.*

→ **Joseph's Restaurant** ★★ BREAK-FAST/SANDWICHES This quaint eatery serves incredible breakfasts with choices like filet eggs Benedict (poached eggs over a grilled beef filet with roasted peppers all on a biscuit), huge piles of pancakes, and customized gourmet omelets. Lunch is recommendable as well with meaty sandwiches, pasta, and salads. You can enjoy your food inside or out on the breezy patio. *129 Meeting St. ☎ 843/958-8500. www.josephsofcharleston.com. Main courses $6–$10. Mon–Sat 8am–3pm; Sun 9am–2pm.*

Doable

→ **Hyman's Seafood Company Restaurant** ★★ SEAFOOD There may be a wait here for dinner, but it's worth every minute for the best seafood in town. This

place is huge and has multiple dining rooms devoted to different specialties like shellfish or deli sandwiches. Not only is the fish amazing, but the value is great, too. *213–217 Meeting St. ☎ 843/723-6000. www.hymanseafood.com. Main courses $9–$23. Daily 11am–1am. Closed Jewish holidays, Thanksgiving, and Christmas.*

→ **Jim 'N Nicks Bar-B-Q** BBQ If you've had more seafood than you can handle, head to this barbecue joint for land animals only. Try the Bar-B-Q nachos or Bar-B-Q quesadillas, or if you're really hungry, don't miss the baby back ribs. They're succulent and smothered with warm barbecue sauce. *288 King St. ☎ 84/577-0406. www.jimnnicks.com. Main courses $7–$20. Sun–Thurs 10:30am–9pm; Fri–Sat 10:30am–10pm.*

→ **Poogan's Porch** ★ LOW COUNTRY In this charming historic home right off King Street, you'll enjoy delicious low country cuisine, friendly service, and a touching tale of the canine who started it all. "Poogan," a beloved neighborhood pet, enjoyed sunning himself on the front steps of the wooden porch and is now interred in the front lawn. Whether you visit the cafe to mourn the loss of Poogan or to savor flaky honey-butter biscuits, Carolina alligator, and fried green tomatoes, this delightful eatery guarantees a memorable Southern experience. *72 Queen St. ☎ 843/557-2337. www.poogansporch.com. Main courses $14–$25. Mon–Fri 11:30am–3pm and 5–9:30pm; Sat–Sun 9am–3pm and 5–9:30pm.*

→ **Sermet's Corner** ★ MEDITERRANEAN The arty inside, casual dining, and social atmosphere attract a trendy crowd to this King Street cafe. The food is fresh and healthful with great salads, soups, and a market fish du jour. The atmosphere is a bit more formal at dinner, but it is a great place to stop for lunch during a day of King Street shopping. *276 King St. ☎ 843/853-7775.*

Main courses $8–$15 lunch, $11–$17 dinner. Daily 11am–10pm.

➔ **Tsunami** SUSHI/STEAKS The sushi is great, but what makes Tsunami a good find is the atmosphere. It's loud and lively, and the location among trendy nightspots on Bay Street attracts the fun college crowd. Accompany your sushi roll with the signature Tsunami Flirtini or just sip your sake at the bar. *215 E. Bay St. ☎ 843/965-5281. Main courses $8–$16; sushi rolls $4–$9. Mon–Fri 5pm–midnight; Sat–Sun 4:30pm–midnight.*

Splurge

➔ **Circa 1886** ★★★ CONTEMPORARY In the carriage house of the fabulous Wentworth Mansion, Circa 1886 provides an exquisite dining experience. Chef Marc Collins experiments with flavors to create one delicious culinary masterpiece after another, like salmon crusted in lime and coconut and juniper spiced antelope loin. The food is pretty pricey but some of the best in Charleston. *149 Wentworth St. ☎ 843/853-7828. www.circa1886.com. Main courses $20–$30. Mon–Sat 5:30–9:30pm.*

Partying

Charleston's young crowd and casual atmosphere makes for a great nightlife. Most places don't have a cover charge and the bars usually close around 2am. Dress is fairly casual for a night on the town. Jeans are acceptable almost everywhere as long as you dress them up with a nice shirt. Check out **www.charlestonhappyhour. com** for the best drink specials and live music listings for every bar in town.

BARS

➔ **Big John's Tavern** ★ This no-frills bar calls itself "Charleston's best dive since 1955," and I must concur. The atmosphere is rowdy and young, and you never know what will happen on any given night here. At this seedy spot, anything goes. You can

write profanity on the walls, carve names into the tables, dance on the bar and the waitstaff will only cheer you on. (Just look at the lingerie hanging from the walls and ceiling.) Tuesday is karaoke night but every night is a guaranteed good time. *251 East Bay St. ☎ 843/723-DIVE. www.bigjohns tavern.com. Drinks $3–$6. Daily 4pm–2am.*

➔ **Blind Tiger** There's been a bar at this spot since 1803 and it even remained open during prohibition. It was a local secret then, and it remains a local haven from the more touristy bars around town. The turnout is older, but there is a great deck out back that makes for a relaxed hangout. *36–38 Broad St. ☎ 843/577-0088. Drinks $3–$7. Mon–Fri 4pm–2am; Sat 1:30pm–2am; Sun 2pm–2am.*

➔ **Henry's on the Market** Being on Market Street makes this cozy pub a convenient tourist hangout. The crowd tends to be older, but there is often live music to pick up the pace. For a rowdier time, show up after 12:30am when the noise level rises and the intoxicated tourists freely pick up tabs. *54 N. Market St. ☎ 843/723-4363. Drinks $4–$7. Mon–Fri 4pm–2am; Sat–Sun noon–2am.*

➔ **Rooftop Bar at The Vendue** ★★ If you like views with your booze, climb to the rooftop of The Vendue for 360–degree landscapes of the city. With three levels of rooftop to hang out on, it's no wonder this is one of the hottest local spots. Collegiate crowds relax and drink all night with only music and stars for company. *19 Vendue Range (take the elevator to the roof). ☎ 843/ 577-7970. Drinks $4–$6. Daily 11:30am–11:30pm.*

➔ **Vickery's Bar & Grill** ★ This is one of the most popular gathering places in Charleston for the younger crowd, especially students. It's also a good dining choice, with an international menu that includes jerk chicken and gazpacho. But the real secrets of the place's success are its 16-ounce frosted mug of beer for $2.50 and the lively atmosphere. *15 Beaufain.* ☎ *843/577-5300. Drinks $2.50–$6. Daily 11:30am–1am.*

THE GAY & LESBIAN SCENE

➔ **Déjà vu II** Some say this is the coziest "ladies bar" in the Southeast. The clientele is almost exclusively gay and mostly lesbian, and the club hosts weekend entertainment by all-girl bands. This late-night hot spot is charming and unassuming. *4634 Prulley Ave. (North Charleston).* ☎ *843/554-5959. www.dejavuii.com. Cover varies. Drinks $4–$7. Hours vary, call ahead.*

➔ **Patrick's Pub & Grill** This fun gay bar doesn't have an official dress code, but unless you're wearing leather or skintight jeans, you'll look like an outsider. I recommend the latter, as leather makes a hot guy a super-sweaty guy. *1377 Ashley River Rd. (Hwy. 61).* ☎ *843/853-8270. Drinks $3–$6. Daily noon–2am.*

What Else to See & Do

To see Charleston's top sights fast, take a bus tour (see "Tours," below). You'll want the extra time to play in this fun town. If you're tired of sightseeing, Charleston is a great city for shopping. You could spend an entire day perusing and purchasing at the boutiques and national chains on King Street, and there are a few shops on East Bay as well.

THE TOP ATTRACTIONS

➔ **Charles Towne Landing** ★★ Much like the Spanish Quarter in St. Augustine, this is a huge living museum built to re-create the first 1670 settlement. They have bikes available for rent for $3 an hour, and you can use one to get around the expansive grounds. Your experience here will be authentic, with buildings, lagoons, and a forest re-created just like they were way back when. *1500 Old Towne Rd. (SC 171 between US 17 and I-126).* ☎ *843/852-4200.*

www.discoversouthcarolina.com. Admission $5 adults, $3 children, $3.75 seniors. Daily 8:30am–5pm. Closed Christmas Eve and Christmas Day.

➔ **Cypress Gardens** ★★ This freshwater swamp a couple dozen miles north of Charleston proper is a habitat for alligators, woodpeckers, ducks, otters, owls, and other animals and you can take boat rides among the foliage. There are garden walking trails through beautiful flora and there is a reptile center, aquarium, and butterfly house on site. *US 52, Moncks Corner (take US 52 24 miles north of Charleston).* ☎ *843/553-0515. www.cypressgardens.com. $9 adults, $3 children, $8 seniors. Daily 9am–5pm. Closed major holidays.*

➔ **Fort Sumter National Monument** ★ It was here that the first shot of the Civil War was fired on April 12, 1861. Park rangers are on hand to answer your questions, and you can explore the small museum filled with artifacts related to the first siege. A complete tour of the fort, conducted daily from 9am to 5pm, takes about 2 hours. To get to the fort, take a tour offered by **Fort Sumter Tours** (360 Concord St., Suite 201; ☎ **843/722-1691;** www.fortsumtertours.com). *www.nps.gov/fosu. Admission to the fort free; the boat trip costs $14 adults, $8 children, $12.50 seniors. Daily 9am–5pm.*

➔ **Middleton Place** ★★★ This was the home of Henry Middleton, president of the First Continental Congress, whose son, Arthur, was a signer of the Declaration of Independence. Today, this National Historic Landmark includes America's oldest landscaped gardens, the Middleton Place House, and the Plantation Stable yards. A plantation lunch is served at the **Middleton Place Restaurant** (☎ **843/556-6020**), with specialties like she-crab soup, hoppin' John and ham biscuits, okra gumbo, and corn pudding. Dinner is also served nightly. *Ashley River Rd. (take US 17 to SC 61 14 miles northwest of Charleston).* ☎ *843/556-6020. www.middletonplace.org. Admission to gardens $20 adults, free for children. Tour of house additional $10 adults, $6 children. Gardens and stable yards daily 9am–5pm; house Mon noon–4:30, Tues–Sun 10am–4:30pm.*

TOURS

→The Brass Pirate Treasure Hunt ★

This is the most fun way to see the historic district. You get a clue sheet and have to follow the clues that lead you through the historic sites downtown while weaving in pirate mysteries all along. You have to figure out the riddles to find the clues at historical pirate sites and you learn the scurvy truth behind Charleston's history. The whole hunt takes about 2 hours, not counting the Happy Hour break you'll need to refresh your mind in between solving riddles. *40 N. Market St. #12 (in the Rainbow Market).* ☎ *843/425-5850. www.the brasspirate.com. $30 clue sheet for 4 people. Daily 9am–5pm.*

→Charleston Ghost Hunt

You'll hear stories of murder, suicide, curses, and hauntings on this candlelight walking tour. Many claim to have seen actual ghosts on this spooky tour, but with some of the sketchy street-roamers in the city, it's hard to say if that's true or not. You might bring a garlic necklace to ward off the spirits just in case. *Meet in front of the United States Custom House. 200 East Bay St.* ☎ *843/ 813-5055. www.charlestonghosthunt.com. $16 adults. Reservations required. Nightly tours at 7 and 9pm; Fri–Sat 10:45pm; seasonal midnight tours.*

→Doin' the Charleston Tours ★

Entertaining and educational, you'll learn Charleston history and see the sites from the comfort of your air-conditioned bus seat. On board, video screens show historic

images while you drive by the places they have become, so history becomes reality. Tours last about 90 minutes. *Meet at the Visitor Center, 375 Meeting St. for pick-up.* ☎ *843/763-1233 or 800/647-4487. www. dointhecharlestontours.com. $18 adults. Daily tours at 9:30am, noon, 2:30pm, 4:30pm.*

PLAYING OUTSIDE

Beaches

FREE →**Folly Beach** ★ This is Charleston's most popular beach in the area, even though it isn't the most beautiful. It's in the West Islands and has bathrooms, parking, and shelter at the western end. *Take US 17 East to SC 171 South to Folly Beach. Bathrooms, picnic area, shelter available.*

FREE →**Kiawah Island** ★★ This is the area's most beautiful beach, and it's only 30 minutes from Charleston. The best beachfront is at Beachwalker County Park on the southern end of the island. *Take US 17 East to SC 171 South, turn right onto SC 700 Southwest to Bohicket Rd. That turns into Betsy Kerrigan Pkwy. and dead-ends at Kiawah Pkwy. where you'll turn left and go straight to the island. Canoe rentals, bathrooms, showers, changing facilities area available.*

Biking

→**Bike the Bridge Rentals** Charleston is a great city to tour by bike because it is relatively flat. This bike rental store will send you out with a snazzy ride and recommendations of what to do in the area. I recommend the ride to Folly Beach. It's scenic and it's about 30 miles round-trip. Take Murray Boulevard in downtown east to State Route 30 and follow that south to Folly Road. This will dead-end at the beach so you can recuperate as you soak up the sun and sea water. *40 Market St.* ☎ *843/853-BIKE. www.bikethebridgerentals.com. $15 3-hour rental; $25 all-day rental. Daily 9am–6pm.*

Kayak Tour

→**Paddlefish Kayaking** ★ These guided nature tours will lead you through creeks and marshes to see dolphin, ospreys, otters, and lots of other local wildlife. The trip is leisurely and interesting and takes about 2 hours. *Bristol Marina at Lockwood Blvd.* ☎ *843/330-9777. www.paddlefishkayaking. com. $40 adults, $30 children. Daily tours at 8am, 10:30am, 1pm, 3:30pm, 6pm Mar–Sept.*

On the Road to Wilmington, NC

Charleston, SC to Wilmington, NC 170 miles

To get to Wilmington from Charleston, take US 17 North the whole way. That's it. You can give your map-reader a rest this time.

This is probably the most grueling drive of the entire trip. It's long, and driving through Myrtle Beach, SC, takes forever. *A word to the wise:* Put blinders on and resist the urge to stop in this Vegas of the East Coast. There are tons of neon lights, inflatable, motorized mascots, and larger-than-life buildings that try to seduce naïve drivers to pull over; but I'm telling you, if you do, you'll never get out!

Instead, fill up your tank and your stomach in Georgetown, just south of Myrtle Beach, and drive straight through to Wilmington. Great detours other than Georgetown's historic downtown include **Pawley's Island** and **Huntington Beach State Park**, both just north of Georgetown right on US 17 and perfect for laying on the beach without the crowds of Myrtle Beach.

Welcome to Wilmington

Although Wilmington is a historic Southern town, it is hoppin' today because of one of its main industries: filmmaking. This little town is known as "Hollywood East" (at least around these parts) because of the volume of film production that's done here. Once you see it, you'll understand that it's a great setting for film and TV. It was the location for *Divine Secrets of the Ya-Ya Sisterhood, I Know What You Did Last Summer,* and *Sleeping with the Enemy* among others. It is also the setting for the WB drama *One Tree Hill* and was where *Dawson's Creek* was shot.

Don't Lose Your Head Getting Here!

In the days before roadtrippers traveled in cars, the main mode of transportation was by train. One rainy night in 1867, conductor Joe Baldwin was in the rear coach as his train approached Wilmington when he realized that the car had come unhooked from the rest of the train. It was losing speed and Joe knew he had to do something fast since another train was behind him. He stood at the back of the car and swung his lantern to get the other conductor's attention, but the night was so foggy that the fellow in the other train couldn't see the signal. So with a screaming smash, the two locomotives collided and poor Joe Baldwin's head was severed from his body. Now, on rainy nights just outside Wilmington, they say a swinging light can sometimes be seen, carried by Joe's body, looking for its head.

More Beach Tunes: Wilmington Playlist

→ *North Carolina Bound,* **Lil Ed Williams,** "Keep On Walkin," 2005
→ *Beyond The Sea,* **Bobby Darin,** "The Legendary Bobby Darin," 2004
→ *Long Line Of Cars,* **Cake,** "Comfort Eagle," 2002
→ *Another Town,* **Regina Spektor,** "Begin To Hope," 2006
→ *You Sank My Battleship!,* **This Is My Fist,** "A History Of Rats," 2006
→ *I Don't Wanna Be (One Tree Hill Theme Song),* **Gavin DeGraw,** "Chariot," 2003
→ *The Road,* **Keegan Smith,** "Out Of Darkness," 2005
→ *Girls On The Beach,* **The Beach Boys,** "Little Deuce Coupe/All Summer Long," 2001
→ *Bend In The Road,* **Donavon Frankenreiter,** "Donavon Frankenreiter," 2004

Wilmington Nuts & Bolts

Area Code   The area code in Wilmington is 910.

Business Hours   Banks are open from 9am to 5pm Monday to Friday and the bars stay open to 2am or later every day.

Drugstores   The most convenient drugstore in the historic district is **Tom's Drug Co.** at 1 N. Front St. (☎ 910/762-3391). There is also a pharmacy in the **Safeway** at 3316 Wilshire Blvd. (☎ 910/343-8921).

Emergencies   For an emergency, dial ☎ **911.**

Hospitals   The main hospital is the **Cape Fear Hospital** at 5301 Wrightsville Ave. (☎ 910/452-8100) and there is an emergency branch at **Cape Fear Hospital Emergency Medical Services** located at 218 N. 2nd St. (☎ 910/343-4800).

Internet   The best place for Internet in the area is at **Port City Java** at 21 N. Front St. (☎ 910/762-5282).

Laundry/Dry Cleaners   The best (and coolest) place to do your laundry is at **Soapbox Laundro Lounge** at 255 Front St. (☎ 910/251-8500).

Libraries   Wilmington's library is the **New Hanover County Library** at 201 Chestnut St. (☎ 910/798-6300).

Liquor Laws   You must be 21 or older to purchase or consume alcohol. Beer and wine are sold in grocery stores.

Lost Property   To report a missing item, contact the police department at ☎ 910/343-3610.

Newspapers & Magazines   The *Wilmington Star News* covers Wilmington daily news as well as news for all of southeastern North Carolina.

Police   To contact the police for non-emergency matters, dial ☎ 910/343-3610.

RETRO ROADTRIP

Post Office   If you need to mail a letter, bring it to 152 N. Front St.

Radio   On FM, WMNX (97.3) is urban contemporary, WRQR (104.5) is rock, WWQQ (101.3) is country, WDVV (89.7) is religious, and WHQR (91.3) is public radio.

Taxes   North Carolina has a 7.5% sales tax and Wilmington has a 6% hotel tax.

Time Zone   Wilmington is on Eastern Standard Time.

Transit Information   For public transportation information, contact the **Wilmington Transit Authority** at ☎ 910/343-0106.

Getting Around

Wilmington is a very pedestrian-friendly town. If you're staying in the historic district, you can walk everywhere you need to go, including restaurants and bars. If you're not staying around here, there are parking meters on the streets that charge $1 for 2 hours, and empty spots are easy to come by.

There are also parking lots at Water and Grace streets, Market and 2nd streets, and at 2nd Street between Chestnut and Grace. The lots charge $1 per hour after the first, but no more than $5 per day.

VISITOR CENTER

The **Visitor Center** (☎ 910/341-4030; www.cape-fear.nc.us/visitors/visitors_services.asp) is at 24 N. 3rd Street (at the corner of Third and Princess sts.) It's open Monday to Friday 8:30am to 5:00pm, Saturday 9:00am to 4:00pm and Sunday 1:00 to 4:00pm, Closed Thanksgiving and Christmas Day. There's another (seasonal) booth at the foot of Market Street at Water Street which operates April to May 9:00am to 4:30pm, June to August 9:30am to 5:00pm, September to October 9:00am to 4:30pm.

Old-World Wilmington

This little village has been around since 1739 and has a lot of that antique charm. Check out these retro opportunities to make the most of old-world Wilmington:

○ You'll get a whiff of what life was like aboard a WWII battleship at the **USS**

North Carolina Battleship. This is the original 1941 war cruiser and you can tour it daily, and on occasion, they will even have reenactments of historic battle action inside the ship. See p. 314.

○ You'll find the biggest antiques selection on Castle Street between 6th and 3rd streets. There are about five different stores in the area that specialize in furniture, accessories, art, and toys. My favorite is **Acorn Attic** (507 Castle St.; ☎ **910/620-7959**). It has unique antiques finds that differ from the standard selection.

A History of Wilmington, MTV style

The village of Wilmington was established in 1739 and was named for the Earl of Wilmington. The town's significance was in the port, which was a hub of shipping trade. Not much happened here other than the occasional tide change until the Civil War when the river and Fort Fisher became major strongholds for the South. After that, things calmed significantly. The battleship *North Carolina* brought some visitors in after World War II, and the town's profile is probably higher now than it has ever been because of its growing reputation as a television/film production town.

Wilmington Festivals: Cars, Boats & Scarecrows (Boo!)

Wilmington loves festivals. Even if the turnout's not huge for all of them, you'll get a better feel for the culture of this lovely town by hitting up any of the events. Check out what's going on during your trip at **www.cape-fear.nc.us/home/events.asp**.

➔ **Rims on the River** in April features a parade and show of vintage cars, all made before 1970, and it takes place right on River Street. **www.dbawilmington.com/rims_on_river.htm**.

➔ The **Arts and Antiques Show** in September is one of the biggest art festivals here. It features local artists, photographers, and sculptors as well as a huge selection of antiques. **www.dbawilmington.com**.

➔ October is an interesting time to visit because during the **Scarecrow Festival,** over 60 creatively decorated scarecrows adorn the streets of downtown. Local restaurants and stores sponsor decorative scarecrows as a festive fall accent.

➔ The **NC Holiday Flotilla** is a lighted boat parade through the Intracoastal Waterway. Yachts of all shapes and sizes light up in holiday colors after dark and a fireworks show marks the finale. **www.ncholidayflotilla.org**.

○ **Barbary Coast** is Wilmington's oldest bar. It has stayed in business far longer than the other bars around town and offers a nightly $1 beer special. The building isn't the only old thing this bar has though; the clientele is seasoned as well, but it's a lot of fun. See p. 313.

○ **Flashbax Vintage Boutique** (30 N. Front St.; ☎ **910/762-9828;** www.flashbax.net) has clothing and accessories dating from the seventies all the way back to the early 1900s. It is organized well and there is a huge selection of retro garb lining the walls and racks.

Sleeping

The options for places to stay in the historic downtown are limited, especially if you're on a tight budget. If you don't mind driving to the outskirts, consider staying in one of the many chain hotels outside the historic district.

CAMPGROUND

➔ **Camelot Campground** This KOA is the best campground around and is halfway between the beach and historic downtown. Tent sites are available as well as newly renovated cabins with grills and picnic tables. *7415 Market St.* ☎ *888/562-5699. www.wilmingtonkoa.com. $20–$30 tent sites; $45–$95 cabins. Amenities: Pool; laundromat; Internet access.*

CHEAP

➔ **Coast Line Inn** This Best Western inn was designed to complement the restored historic rail depot that it's named for. The inn's rooms all have good views of the Cape Fear River, and the location couldn't be better. The staff is friendly and they even deliver breakfast to your door each morning. *503 Nutt St.* ☎ *800/617-7732 or 910/763-2800. www.coastlineinn.com. 53 units. $89–$129 double. Continental breakfast included. Amenities: Restaurant; fitness center; room service. In room: Dataport.*

RETRO ROADTRIP

Wilmington, NC Highlights

SLEEPING ■
Camelot Campground **22**
Coast Line Inn **2**
Front Street Inn **19**
Riverview Suites **5**
The Wilmingtonian **15**

EATING ◆
Café Phoenix **11**
Circa 1922 **7**
Dock Street Oyster Bar **17**
Slice of Life **8**
The Little Dipper Fondue **21**
Trolly Stop **4**
YoSaké **14**

PARTYING ★
Barbary Coast **20**
City Limits Saloon **9**
Liquid Room **10**
Reel Café **18**
The Whiskey **12**

ATTRACTIONS ●
Airlie Gardens **1**
EUE/Screen Gems Studios **3**
Henrietta III **16**
Twice Baked Pottery
   Painting Studio **13**
USS *North Carolina*
   Battleship Memorial **6**
Wrightsville Beach **23**

DOABLE

➜ **Riverview Suites** ★ These spacious suites are perfect for traveling with a group. Each has a balcony, kitchenette, and pullout sofa so you can easily fit four people. The location is convenient too, just a short walk to downtown restaurants, shops, and sites. *106 N. Water St.* ☎ *910/772-9988. www.wilmingtonhilton.com/riview suites.htm. $89–$139 suite. Amenities: Restaurant; lounge; fitness center; pool; discounted tickets to attractions; beach pass. In room: Kitchenette, washer and dryer, iron.*

SPLURGE

MTV Best ● ➜ **Front Street Inn** ★★★
This quirky boutique hotel is a delightful alternative to the big, impersonal hotels around town. Each room is uniquely decorated with an individual personality and you see pictures of them online when you're making your selection to choose the room that most suits you. Breakfast is the perfect time to get tips from other travelers, or ask the friendly staff for recommendations. *215 S. Front St.* ☎ *910/762-6442. www.frontstreetinn.com. 12 units. $128–$148 double. Breakfast included. Amenities: Balconies; bar; fitness area; game room; bikes; Internet access. In room: Minibar, VCR/DVD player.*

➜ **The Wilmingtonian** ★★ This is Wilmington's premier inn and all the rooms are actually luxurious suites that can sleep up to four people. The second and third floor rooms have balconies and all suites have kitchenettes. The hotel pub offers beer and wine Wednesday to Saturday from 5:30 to 1am, so you won't have to walk far to your bed after your nightcap. *101 S. 2nd St.* ☎ *800/525-0909 or 910/343-1800. www.thewilmingtonian.com. 40 units. $130–$159 suite for 2; $219–$239 suite for 4. Continental breakfast included. Amenities: Restaurant; bar; room service; laundry service; Internet access. In room: Dataport.*

Eating

SUPPLIES

The **Water Street Farmers Market** on Saturdays is the best place to get fresh produce, honey, meat, and other locally grown items. The street market runs between Princess and Market streets and is open 8am to noon from April to October, and 9am to 1pm during November and December.

TAKE-OUT TREATS

→**Trolly Stop** HOT DOGS Whatever your diet or food preferences, this hot dog joint has a frank for you. Choose from all-meat, all-beef, no-carb turkey dogs, and veggie dogs, and then spice up your wiener with a dozen condiments before taking it to go. *212 N. Front St.* ☎ *910/343-2999. Hot dogs $3–$5. Mon–Sat 11am–4:40pm.*

EATING OUT

Cheap

→**Slice of Life** PIZZA This dark little pub is where you'll find the best pizza and late-night food in town. It's a no-frills kind of place with simple topping selections and a random smattering of Tex-Mex on the menu. They're open until 3am so you can have pizza and beer way after the other restaurants close. *122 Market St.* ☎ *910/251-9444. www.grabslice.com. Slices $2.50; whole pizzas $12–$14. Daily 11:30am–3am.*

Doable

→**Café Phoenix** ★ MEDITERRANEAN This spacious and airy bistro is in an old dry-goods store. It has an upscale feel without upscale prices or attitude. Lunch is casual, serving soups, panini, and focaccia. Dinner is a bit more elaborate, with specialties like Chianti tuna and seafood paella. *9 Front St.* ☎ *910/343-1395. Main courses $6–$10 lunch, $10–$25 dinner. Mon–Sat 11:30am–10:30pm; Sun 11am–10pm.*

→**Circa 1922** ★★ INTERNATIONAL Occupying a 1920s bank building, this classy restaurant still has that old elegant feel of the roaring decade. The menu has a delightful mix of Spanish tapas, seafood, sushi, and sashimi, so order a few items to sample a bit of everything. The food is delicious, the service friendly, and the value is terrific. There's usually a wait on weekends but hanging out at the bar makes the time fly. *8 N. Front St.* ☎ *910/762-1922. www. circa1922.com. Tapas $7–$14; main courses $10–$12. Sun–Thurs 5–10pm; Fri–Sat 5–11pm. Bar daily 5pm–midnight (later on weekends).*

→**Dock Street Oyster Bar** SEAFOOD This hole-in-the-wall place is one of Wilmington's best-kept secrets. The oysters are brought in fresh daily and served in buckets to any interested patron. There are fish entrees, but your best bet is to pick one of the steamed shellfish options, or better yet, the Steamer Platter with oysters, snow crab, shrimp, mussels, clams, and crawfish. *12 Dock St.* ☎ *910/762-2827. www.dockstreetoysterbar.com. Main courses $8–$15. Sun–Thurs 11:30am–10pm; Fri–Sat 11:30am–11pm.*

→**YoSaké** ★ ASIAN/SUSHI This is quite possibly the best sushi in historic downtown. They have traditional rolls, but try some of the signature house varieties like the "ginormous roll" filled with a bunch of fish and veggies to make a huge multibite roll. For the non-sushi eater, they have terrific cooked entrees like miso drunken noodles and shanghai firecracker shrimp tempura. *33 S. Front St.* ☎ *910/763-3172. Sushi rolls $4–$14; main courses $12–$24. Daily 5pm–2am. Half-price appetizer and sushi menu daily 5–7pm.*

SPLURGE

MTV **Best●** → **The Little Dipper Fondue** ★★ FONDUE Whether for dinner or just for dessert, this quirky Swiss bistro has delicious food and a delightful ambience. You'll get a choice of meat and an array of veggies to cook at your table, but make sure you save room for the deliciously drippy chocolate fondue. You can opt to dip your fruit, mallows, and cheesecake in milk chocolate, white chocolate, liquor-spiked chocolate, or my favorite, half peanut butter and half chocolate. *138 S. Front St.* ☎ *910/251-0433. Main courses and fondue $15–$23. Tues–Sun 5–11pm.*

Partying

Don't expect Wilmington to have a huge party scene. It is, after all, a smaller town with a relaxed atmosphere. There are some great bars here, and you can find live music any night of the week.

BARS & CLUBS

→ **Barbary Coast** This grungy grafittied pub is Wilmington's oldest bar (ca. 1946). They have a huge beer selection and there is a daily $1 beer special. The clientele here consists of regular locals and a few lost tourists, but for the most part, it's just a fun place to get a cheap beer. *116 S. Front St.* ☎ *910/762-8996. www.barbaryc.com. Drinks $1–$5. Daily noon–3am.*

→ **City Limits Saloon** ★ Dig out your Wranglers and don your cowboy boots for Wilmington's only country bar. The night will be memorable (well, *you* might not remember, but your friends sure will) with frequent bar dancing and mechanical bull riding. Thursday is college night and draws a crowd for the ever-so-classy bikini bull-riding. *28 N. Front St.* ☎ *910/763-2336. www. hellyeahwilmington.com. Drinks $3–$7. Thurs–Sat 9pm–2am.*

→ **Liquid Room** As Wilmington's best dance club, the Liquid Room attracts the

---

Waterfront & Film Tours of Wilmington

→ The *Henrietta III* ★ is a riverboat that will take you on a 45-minute narrated cruise around the Wilmington waterfront, passing sites like the Cotton Exchange, the Riverfront Park, and the battleship USS *North Carolina*. The season runs from May 1 to mid-December. The boat also offers murder-mystery cruises, evening party cruises, and nature cruises. *Boards at corner of S. Water and Dock sts.* ☎ *800/676-0162 or 910/343-1611. www. cfrboats.com. $8 adults, $4 children. Tours depart daily at 11am and 3pm. Reservations not required.*

→ *One Tree Hill* fans, grab your cameras for this guided tour of **EUE/Screen Gems Studios** ★. You can't visit the sets while they're doing the actual filming, but guides will show you props and you'll get to see set pieces from *Dawson's Creek* and *Matlock*. The walking tours are offered most weekends, but if you can't make it, hit up the Visitor Center for a map of self-guided *OTH* town tours. *1223 N. 23rd St.* ☎ *910/343-3433. www. screengemstudios.com. Cost and tour times vary, call ahead.*

ᴍᴛᴠ🛉 PotterinG Around

No, not Joey Potter . . . *Dawson's Creek* is canceled, silly! Rather, swing by **Twice Baked Pottery Painting Studio** if you need redeeming after that high school pottery class gone bad; tuck into Twice Baked for a second stab at the art. Just pick your pre-made mug, piggy bank, or coaster and paint away. You won't be graded this time. *6 Market St.* ☎ *910/343-9886. Mon–Fri 10am–6pm, Sat 11am–8pm, Sun noon–8pm.*

young partiers. You'll hear an array of techno mixed music, and they have great nightly drink specials. *23 Market St.* ☎ *910/ 362-0809. Cover charge $2–$5 (free for women over 21). Thurs–Sat 9pm–2am.*

➔**Reel Café** There is a little something for everyone at the Reel. The two levels of nightlife are situated above the first floor Reel Café so you can pop downstairs if you get the munchies. The second floor club has a large dance floor which hosts middle-age tourists until midnight when the young crowd puts their dancing shoes on, and the third floor rooftop bar is a relaxed, chic place to chill all night. *100 Front St.* ☎ *910/251-1832. Cover charge $5–$10. Drinks $4–$6. Daily 9pm–2am.*

➔**The Whiskey** ★ This rock-'n'-roll saloon is a local favorite for music, mingling, and mixers. The Whiskey has live music at least 5 nights a week and is a strong supporter of regional musicians. The vibe is laid-back and not too crowded and the cover is free until 11pm. *1 S. Front St.* ☎ *910/763-3088. Cover charge $0–$5. Drinks $3–$6. Sun–Thurs 9pm–2am; Fri–Sat 7pm–2am.*

What Else to See & Do

There's not a whole heck of a lot to do in downtown Wilmington as far as historic attractions go, but there are dozens of great boutiques around town, and on Saturday mornings, the Water Street farmers market provides a great excursion. If you just need a great place to chill out outside, go to the Riverwalk near the visitor info booth. There are benches and the occasional live guitarist, and it's right on the water.

THE TOP ATTRACTIONS

➔**Airlie Gardens** Once the plantation home of a wealthy rice planter, these gardens are surrounded by huge lawns and serene lakes. The blooms are at their height in the early spring, but even when they're faded it's a great place for a beautiful walk. During the spring and summer, weekly outdoor concerts are held here. *US 76. (Take US 76 toward the beach and look for signposts).* ☎ *910/798-7700. www.airlie gardens.org. Admission $8 adults, $1 children under 12. Tues–Thurs and Sat 9am–5pm; Fri 9am–7pm.*

➔**USS North Carolina Battleship Memorial** The USS *North Carolina* was commissioned in 1941 and is permanently berthed here as a memorial to the state's World War II dead. You can tour most of the ship and the Exhibit Hall houses a "through their eyes" exhibit focusing on recollections of the battleship's former crew. A visitor center offers a large gift shop and snack bar. *Eagle Island (on Cape Fear River across from the historic district at the junction of Hwy. 17/74/76/421).* ☎ *910/251-5797. www.battleshipnc.com. Admission $9 adults, $8 seniors, $4.50 children. May 16–Sept 15 daily 8am–8pm; off season daily 8am–5pm.*

PLAYING OUTSIDE
BEACHES

→ **Wrightsville Beach** ★ A whole mile of soft sand set against a beautiful ocean makes this the best beach in the area. It's 6 miles south of Wilmington and is really popular, so don't expect to be alone much.

The south end is really windy and great for kiteboarding and surfing, but not ideal for swimming. *6 miles east of Wilmington on US 74/76. Lifeguards between the Johnnie Mercer Pier and the Crystal Pier. Metered parking available for $1 per hour. Open daily from dawn to dusk.*

On the Road to Hatteras Island, NC

Wilmington to Hatteras Island, NC 170miles

Getting to the Outer Banks is a little bit tricky. You'll drive a bit and then hop on a couple of ferries to get to the islands, so plan enough time to catch the boats. The drive isn't very scenic on US 17, but once you start driving on the state roads, you'll pass through some rural towns that make for good eye candy.

On the Road Nuts & Bolts

Where to Fill Up   Make sure to fill up before you get on the ferries because gas prices are heinous on the Outer Banks. There are lots of gas stations on US 17 until Jacksonville, and after that your best bet on State Road 24 will be in Morehead City.

The Tolls   There aren't any tolls for the roads, but be prepared to pay $10–$15 for the Cedar Island ferry to Ocracoke.

The Fastest Way   Take US 17 North to State Road 24 East right before Jacksonville. This highway will take you to Morehead City where it turns into US 70 East. Merge onto SR 12 North toward Cedar Island. At Cedar Island hop onto the Cedar Island Ferry to Ocracoke which takes about 2¼ hours. At Ocracoke, drive across the island to the north tip and jump on the free ferry to Hatteras.

The Long Way Round   You don't want to know, trust me. The fast way is long enough!

Rules of the Road   The speed usually runs about 55 mph on the highways and even slower through the rural parts, so watch out for cops where the speed drops.

Helpful Ferry Info   The first ferry you'll take is the Cedar Island ferry to Ocracoke, NC. This will cost you $10 to $15 and it takes a little over 2 hours, so pack a snack and enjoy the view. The departure times vary depending on the season, so check the website at **www.ncferry.org** to find the best time for your schedule and make *sure* you make a reservation (☎ **800/856-0343**) to avoid waiting 3 hours for the next boat. The free ferry from Ocracoke to Hatteras is a much shorter ride (only 40 min.) and departs every hour to half-hour from 5am to midnight so you don't need to make a reservation.

RETRO ROADTRIP

Ferry Inconvenient

Sometimes the ferries fill up as soon as boarding begins, so to avoid an *extremely* inconvenient wait at the ferry dock, plan on getting there at least 30 minutes before the boat shoves off, and when it's possible to make a reservation, make one! For the ferry schedule call ☎ **800/BY-FERRY** or visit www.outer-banks.com/ferry.

Welcome to Hatteras Island

This is the last stop on our trip, but you'll end with a relaxing beach town where you can lay on the sand all day with nothing to worry about other than making sure you're getting an even tan. So take in the sun and the short history of the island and enjoy your last hurrah at this beautiful seashore.

The main drag, and often the *only* drag, is Route 12. It runs along the skinny strip of island and all of the restaurants and motels are clearly visible from the road. There are a bunch of clean, but cheap, motels in the area and I recommend getting one with a kitchenette because the restaurants here are limited. Check out the **Outer Banks Comfort Inn** (Route 12, Buxton; ☎ **800/432-1441**), **Hatteras Marlin** (Route 12, Hatteras; ☎ **252/986-2141**), or **Breakwater Inn** (on the harbor, Hatteras; ☎ **252/986-2565**). All have rates under $100 per night and they offer suites with kitchenettes.

As for restaurants, your best bet is at the southern tip of the island at **Austin Creek Grill and Bakery** (Hatteras Landing beside the Ferry Docks; ☎ **252/986-1511**) or in Buxton at **Buoy's Restaurant** (Route 12, Buxton; ☎ **252/995-6575**). They both serve great seafood, and the delicacies at the Austin Creek Bakery are lip-smacking sweet. There are grocery stores every few miles on Route 12, so if you are self-catering or picnicking, you'll always be able to find food and supplies.

For nightlife, head to the **Sandbar** (Route 12, Buxton; ☎ **252/995-3413**). It isn't the most happening place we've been to, but you're not really here for the sparkling nightlife. They're open late and offer karaoke every Friday night for entertainment.

Playlist: Rockin' on the Road (and Ocean) to the Outer Banks

→ *Windsurfing Nation*, **Broken Social Scene**, "Broken Social Scene," 2005

→ *Sea King*, **Eisley**, "Marvelous Things EP," 2003

→ *The Ocean*, **Barefoot**, "Changes In The Weather," 2005

→ *Islands*, **Cat Power**, "The Greatest," 2006

→ *The Road*, **Tenacious D**, "Tenacious D," 2001

→ *The Frozen Island*, **Of Montreal**, "Coquelicot Asleep In The Poppies," 2004

→ *The Island*, **Le Tigre**, "This Island," 2004

→ *Lighthouse*, **The Hush Sound**, "Like Vines," 2006

→ *A Pirate Looks At Forty*, **Jimmy Buffett**, "Boats, Beaches, Bars & Ballads," 1992

→ *Sail On, Sailor*, **The Beach Boys**, "The Beach Boys Classics," 2002

The candy-striped Cape Hatteras lighthouse.

What Else to See & Do

The **Cape Hatteras Lighthouse** ★ (www. nps.gov/caha) is the biggest attraction here, other than the beach. You can climb the 248 steps for $6 and get the best view of the coast at the top, or if you're not up for the climb, peruse the museum and visitor center on the lighthouse lawn. Climbing hours are daily from 9am to 5pm.

PLAYING OUTDOORS

Beaches

Beaches are all around you; This entire stretch of island is the **Cape Hatteras National Seashore,** one of the best you'll ever visit, and there's plenty of places to walk, sun, and enjoy. Just walk east or west for 5 minutes and you'll find yourself on sand with ocean in front of you. Glorious! There are places to pull off all along Route 12, so you can spend all day beach hopping, or park at the **Hatteras Lighthouse** and chill at the beach there.

Hang Gliding

For those inspired by the legacy of Orville and Wilbur, try your hand at hang gliding with **Kitty Hawk Kites** (☎ 877/FLY-THIS; www.kittyhawk.com). An instructor

A History of the Outer Banks, MTV Style

A long time ago, in the late 1500s, two groups of settlers attempted to found a town on the north tip of the Outer Banks. This seemed like a great idea because they were guaranteed ocean views and pristine beaches right on their back patios (patios? Did they have decks in the 1500s?). However, both groups mysteriously disappeared without a trace. Naturally, people weren't too eager to take up residence here after that, so in the early 1700s the Outer Banks became a pirate hideout, home to the infamous Blackbeard. Things calmed down, and stayed pretty calm (except for the wind) for a long time after that, but in 1903, that wind drew a couple of brothers from Ohio to the Outer Banks, and they were Wright about manned flight.

will lead you on an airborne adventure over sand dunes just like the Wright Brothers.

Horseback Riding

If you'd rather stay on land, try a horseback ride on the beach offered by **Equine Adventures** (Frisco; ☎ 252/995-4897). The tours are scenic and are offered in the morning or afternoon.

Watersports

Whatever watersport you're into, they have it here. Fishing charters go out daily on the *Miss Hatteras* (☎ 252/986-2365) and cost $40 for a half day and $100 for a

full day. They also offer dolphin cruises in the evening.

The marshes around the island make kayaking an interesting activity. **Kitty Hawk Kayaks** (MP13 Nags Head across from Jockey's Ridge; ☎ 800/948-0759) offers a selection of kayak tours from alligator and dolphin tours to sunrise, sunset, and moonlight tours.

For snorkelers and scuba divers, **Outer Banks Diving** (Route 12, Hatteras; ☎ 252/986-1056) will outfit you with gear, guides, and tips on the best wrecks to watch.

Be Pampered at Pamlico

For one last splurge, stay at the 📺 Best❂ **Inn on Pamlico Sound** ★★★ (Route 12, Buxton; ☎ 252/995-7030; www.innonpamlicosound.com). This is the coolest place to stay in the Outer Banks, hands down. You'll have so much fun at this little inn, you'll have to rouse yourself to go outside and explore the island. It won't be hard . . . you're right on the beach and have docks, kayaks, a pool that overlooks the water, and a 14-person home theater with reclining chairs and a serious sound system. The private restaurant serves the best food on the island and it is only for inn guests. Dinners are delectable, with seafood so fresh that it was swimming in the ocean the morning of, and breakfasts are three-courses and absolutely scrumptious. Innkeepers Steve and Laura Nelson will bend over backwards to make sure your time in Hatteras is enjoyable, but I guarantee if you stay here, it will be.

Free Frolics on Hatteras Island

→ **FREE** **Go Crabbing.** All you'll need for this simple activity is a long cord and some bait (chicken necks, fish heads, other dead gross things that you can get from the butcher at any of the island groceries) tied to the end. Stand on the beach and toss the baited end of the cord into the water. Wait a few minutes and then pull in your line to see if you can cancel those dinner reservations and have crab instead. If you really want to eat your catch, put them live into a pot of boiling water until the shells turn red (6–10 min.) and voila! your very own crabby cuisine. Crabs are best caught on the Sound (inland) side of the island rather than the ocean side and the best time to go crabbing is summer, although they'll bite in spring and fall also. You don't need a permit for crabbing, but you're going to need a lot of patience.

→ **FREE** **See the Famous Blue Marlin.** This gigantic fish was caught in 1962 and weighs 810 lbs. It is housed at the Hatteras village library and helped the island gain the title "Blue Marlin Capital of the World." You can see this rare site anytime, as it is encased in class on the front of the building. Hwy 12, Hatteras Village.

On the Road Back to the Mainland

Don't worry, I wouldn't leave you on Hatteras Island all by yourself! There's a bridge connecting Hatteras to the rest of North Carolina at the top of the island, so you won't have to backtrack or mess with any of those pesky ferry rides. Just follow NC 12 and veer west at Whalebone Junction. Follow the US 64 bypass to US 64 to mainland North Carolina. By following US 64, you can reach US 17 and also I-40 and I-95. Happy traveling!

Tracks for the Drive Back

→ *Heading Home,* **Donavon Frankenreiter,** "Donavon Frankenreiter," 2004

→ *Promised Land,* **Elvis Presley,** "Elvis: 2nd To None," 2003

→ *I Miss You,* **Bjork,** "Post Live," 2004

→ *Stickshifts & Safety Belts,* **Cake,** "Fashion Nuggett," 1996

→ *Back Home,* **Eric Clapton,** "Back Home," 2005

→ *The Long Way Home,* **Norah Jones,** "Feels Like Home," 2004

→ *Homeward Bound,* **Simon & Garfunkel,** "The Essential Simon & Garfunkel," 1966

→ *Reunion,* **Stars,** "Set Yourself On Fire," 2005

→ *Hello, Goodbye,* **The Beatles,** "1," 1967

→ *Send Me On My Way,* **Rusted Root,** "When I Woke," 1994

RETRO ROADTRIP

A Southern BBQ Roadtrip

Text & Photos by Maya Kroth

I f you think barbecue is about hot dogs and burgers cooked over charcoal on your backyard hibachi, think again. Real barbecue, like they do it in the South, involves smoking various cuts of meat for hours, sometimes *days,* over indirect heat until it's so tender it almost falls apart. Talk to Southerners about what makes good barbecue and you'll get a wildly varied array of answers: Some insist, "The secret's in the sauce," while others say sauce just hides poor-quality meat. Some make sauce from tomatoes, others from mustard, molasses, vinegar, or even mayonnaise. Some load their smokers with hickory, others use mesquite, oak, cherry, or pecan; still others don't even use wood smokers. Texans cook everything from turkey and sausage to beef and mutton, while a Charlottean might contend that barbecue strictly consists of pork shoulder and pork ribs. The one thing everyone agrees is that no one agrees on who makes the best barbecue. Texans will assure you theirs is the best, but you'll just hear the same thing in Memphis, Alabama, and the Carolinas. Everyone has an opinion in barbecue country.

From ribs and brisket slow-smoked on the Salt Lick's open pit on a quiet farm-to-market road near Austin to chopped-pork-and-barbecue-slaw sandwiches prepared in the electric cookers at Jimmy's Barbecue just off the interstate in Lexington, North Carolina, and lots of urban and roadside joints in between, you'll discover the regional differences in barbecue across the south (and while my trip doesn't hit Kansas City, dedicated 'cue-seekers will want to take a trip to this northern outpost sometime, too).

In addition to giving you a guide to where to get the best barbecue across the south, and what to do before and after, we'll take a few detours to places like Elvis's birthplace (in Tupelo, Mississippi) and the largest urban bat colony in North America (beneath the Congress Avenue Bridge in downtown Austin, Texas).

So grab your iPod, gas up the station wagon (or hybrid!), and prepare to ditch your South Beach discipline for a steady diet of pork ribs, beef brisket, beans, pork shoulder, coleslaw, potato salad, pork sausage, and, oh yeah, did I mention pork? Don't stress: You're still young; your arteries can take it (maybe).

Superlatives: The Highs & Lows

➜ **Worst place to get a speeding ticket:** Sulphur Springs, TX, where "It's not like the state of California, where you can just sign off on a ticket. In the state of Texas you have to appear before a judge," my polite-yet-stern police officer informed me. (I end up getting off with a mail-in payment option when no judges could be located—an apparent rash of crime in Sulphur Springs, pop. 14,551?). See p. 344.

➜ **Best Ribs:** It's a tough call, since all the joints I tried were uniformly tasty, but the falling-off-the-bone dry slabs at **Neely's**

Bar-B-Que in Memphis won my eternal devotion. See p. 354.

➜ **Best everything else: The Salt Lick** outside of Austin, which smokes an incredibly good turkey dish, plus unbelievable ribs, brisket, sausage, cobbler, and spicy *habanero* sauce. See p. 330.

➜ **Best dive:** With $1.50 drafts and a smart-ass bartender who stings regulars with good-natured barbs like, "We know *your* family tree don't branch," **Adult Day Care Hideaway** in Hot Springs, AR, wins, hands-down. See p. 347.

The secret's in the sauce.

SOUTHERN BBQ ROADTRIP

➔Most expensive Brazilian wax: The Spa at the Arlington Hotel in Hot Springs, AR, charges a whopping $100 for the treatment. Ouch. See p. 346.

➔Best job title: Vibemaster, the person behind the Glenn Hotel's comfortable, luxuriously hip vibe in Atlanta. See p. 374.

➔Best place to buy stuff to take home to Mom: Abbott Farms off I-85 in South Carolina, where they'll put peaches in everything from cobbler to ice cream to hot sauce. See p. 380.

➔Most satisfying way to carb load: The maple-iced homemade cinnamon rolls at Vicki's Coffee Corner in Hot Springs, AR. Get one slightly warmed and wash it down with an apple-ginger lemonade. Don't worry; you'll get plenty of protein on the rest of the trip. See p. 346.

➔Most aggressive roadside advertising: The six—count 'em—giant billboards on I-85 near Lavonia, GA, for Café Risqué: "Open 24 Hours! Great food! Pool tables! Pancakes! Exit 173!" Who would've thought a strip club off the interstate would have that kind of marketing budget? See p. 380.

➔Feistiest Granny: Smokee Hollow's Ellen Norris, who is well-connected with law enforcement in Alabama's Fayette County and tougher than she looks—you should hear about what happened to the guy that tried to run off with her meat smoker. See p. 365.

➔Best use of $50 (if you really, really hate Peter Cetera): Getting the piano player at Silky O'Sullivan's in Memphis to stop playing "You're the Inspiration" *right freaking now.* See p. 359.

➔Most "awww"-inducing shop: House of Mews in Memphis, which is home to dozens of homeless cats. The agency tries to find homes for each of them. See p. 360.

➔Most surprising cameo by a convenience-store snack: The unexpected Fritos piled in layer three of six of the hot tamale spread at McClard's Barbecue in Hot Springs, AR. The other five layers consist of: tamales, beans, beef, onions, and cheese. See p. 344.

Just the Facts

Trip in a Box

....

Total Miles   From Austin, TX, to Lexington, NC, 1,700 miles.

Route   I-35 from Austin to Dallas; I-30 to Little Rock; I-40 to Memphis; I-78 to Birmingham; I-20 to Atlanta; and I-85 to Lexington.

States   (West to East) Texas, Arkansas, Tennessee, Mississippi, Alabama, Georgia, South Carolina, North Carolina.

Trip Time   6 days or more for the whole thing, from Austin to Lexington.

The Short Version   This trip is designed to hit the most different-style barbecue centers in the shortest amount of time, so routes are mostly straight lines between Austin, Memphis, Atlanta, and Charlotte. If you speed through, you can see it all in about 5 or 6 days, but you could end up driving up to 10 hours per day.

The Long Version   You can easily stretch this trip out for weeks; indulge yourself with a few extra days in Texas touring the Barbecue Trail; have a leisurely time

Southern BBQ Roadtrip

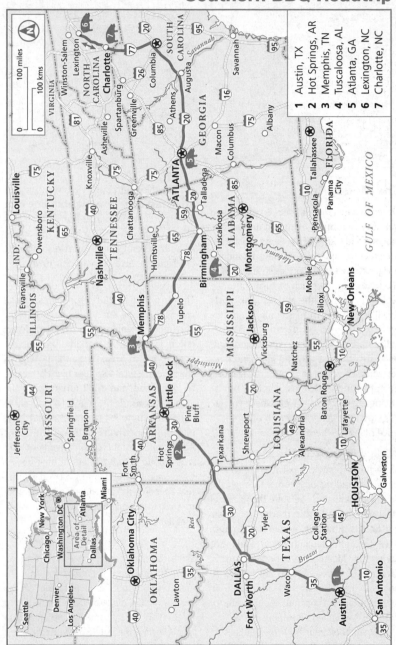

1 Austin, TX
2 Hot Springs, AR
3 Memphis, TN
4 Tuscaloosa, AL
5 Atlanta, GA
6 Lexington, NC
7 Charlotte, NC

among the spas and bathhouses in the resort town of Hot Springs, soak up music in Memphis, and big-city nightlife in Atlanta, or get sporty with professional teams in Charlotte.

Hitting the Highlights If you're a weekend warrior who's gotta get back to the office or school right away, you can break this trip up into less-hurried legs that last from 3 to 7 days: Austin to Memphis (650 miles), Memphis to Atlanta (450 miles), or Atlanta to Lexington (300 miles).

When to Go There's really no bad time to eat barbecue, but summertime in the South is *hot*, and humid, so this trip is best taken in the milder seasons: spring if you want to time it with Memphis in May's big barbecue cooking contest, or fall, when Lexington hosts its annual Barbecue Festival.

The Money Part

Never having visited the South, I had fantasies about it being an untouched wonderland full of pristine Victorian architecture, grannies sipping lemonade on front porches, and prices straight out of the 1850s. Not so much, it turns out. The reality is the South—at least the parts you'll see on this trip—isn't all that different from the rest of the country. There's still a Starbucks on every corner, and frappuccinos still cost way too much, no matter whether you're in London, Singapore, or Hot Springs, Arkansas. You may not be paying Big City prices everywhere you go, but stuff isn't generally much different in price than elsewhere in the country.

ACCOMMODATIONS

Since this trip sticks mostly to metropolitan areas and major arteries through the South, lodging won't be quite the financial steal you might find in more rural areas. For budget travelers, Austin and Atlanta have fun, affordable hostels, while Hot Springs and Memphis have none; in Austin, camping is a great, cheap alternative to hotels, while in Hot Springs $28 separates a KOA cabin from a spacious room at a fancy hotel on downtown's Bathhouse Row.

You can book yourself into chains using online travel sites for an average of about $50 to $75 per night, or you can book quaint, only-in-the-south B&Bs via **www.bedand breakfast.com** or **www.bbonline.com** for around $100 per night or more. If you allow yourself one splurge, do it at Atlanta's Glenn Hotel—an awesome, chic crash pad for an awesome, chic town.

TRANSPORTATION

This trip runs about 1,700 miles, which means you'll be spending about $140 for gas (more if you're side-tripping). Many hotels provide free parking, but upscale ones in metro areas like Atlanta tend to charge extra (up to $20 per night or more), so call ahead, and don't forget to tip the valet. If you drink, consider a cabbie budget of $10 to $15 per night of partying, plus tip, in metro areas, though cities like Austin and Memphis offer convenient (and free) public transit trolleys in their downtown neighborhoods. Oh, and don't forget that speeding tickets will add considerably to that transportation budget, so watch that lead foot.

FOOD

Since this is a foodie roadtrip, you may want to budget a bit more for food to ensure that you take advantage of all the gastronomical pleasures the South has to offer. Plan to eat one or two barbecue meals a day; budget as little as $3 when you're just grabbing a pulled pork sandwich, or $10 to $15 (plus tax and tip) if you're going all out with ribs, sides, and dessert. The good news? Servings in the South—especially Texas—are generous, to say the least. A to-go box from the Salt Lick can feed you for days (just make sure that cooler's stocked with ice, and never travel with any potato salad, slaw, or anything else made with mayonnaise). And if you've got any room in that belly for non-barbecue-related eats, tack on a few more dollars in your budget for breakfast: about $5 (for coffee and muffins) to $15 (for sit-down eggs or pancakes) per person per day.

Starting Out: Austin, TX & the Barbecue Trail

Austin, Texas: quite possibly the coolest city in the country (and for sure the best in Texas). And not just for barbecue; it's a hotbed for all genres of music (the city calls itself "The Live Music Capital of the World"), as well as nightlife, scenery, and general eccentricity. Not your typical southern town, Austin's more akin to San Francisco or Seattle than, say, Houston. You'll find "Keep Austin Weird" bumper stickers affixed to various things, so try to partake in a bit of that quirkiness during your stay.

Austin Nuts & Bolts

Area Code   The telephone area code in Austin is 512.

Business Hours   Banks and offices are generally open Monday to Friday 8 or 9am to 5pm. Some banks offer drive-through service on Saturday 9am to noon or 1pm. Bars and clubs tend to stay open until midnight during the week, 2am on weekends.

Doctor   The Medical Exchange (☎ 512/458-1121) and Seton Hospital (☎ 512/324-4450) both have physician referral services.

Drugstores   You'll find many Walgreens, Eckerd, and Randalls drugstores around the city; most HEB grocery stores also have pharmacies. Several Walgreens are open 24 hours. Have your zip code ready and call ☎ 800/925-4733 to find the Walgreens branch nearest you.

Emergencies   Call ☎ 911 if you need the police, the fire department, or an ambulance.

Hospitals   Brackenridge, 601 E. 15th St. (☎ 512/324-7000); St. David's, 919 E. 32nd St. at I-35 (☎ 512/397-4240); and Seton Medical Center, 1201 W. 38th St. (☎ 512/324-1000), have good and convenient emergency-care facilities.

Internet   Downtown Austin's free wireless network covers the area between Town Lake on the south, 7th Street on the north, Lamar Boulevard on the west, and I-35 on the east. The Austin Visitor Center offers free Internet access; all branches of the Austin Public Library provide free access to the Internet (just your library card or photo ID), and all of Austin's city parks are Wi-Fi friendly. Most branches of Schlotzsky's Deli, a chain that originated in Austin, offer free Internet access via computer stations, and several also offer free Wi-Fi. Try the delis at 106 E. Sixth St., downtown (☎ 512/473-2867), and at 1915 Guadalupe (☎ 512/457-1129), near the University of Texas.

Laundry   The only laundromat anywhere near downtown is Kwik Wash, 1000 W. Lynn (☎ 512/473-3725). It's not within walking distance of any city hotels, but it's a short drive away from some of them.

Libraries   Downtown's Faulk Central Library, 800 Guadalupe St. (☎ 512/974-7400), and adjoining Austin History Center, 810 Guadalupe St. (☎ 512/974-7480), are excellent resources. To find the closest local branch, visit www.ci.austin.tx.us/library. As mentioned above, all Austin libraries offer free Internet access.

Liquor Laws   You have to be 21 to drink in Texas, it's illegal to have an open container in your car, and liquor cannot be served before noon on Sunday except at brunches (if it's billed as complimentary).

Lost Property   You can check with the police to find out whether something you've lost has been turned in by calling ☎ 512/974-5000.

Newspapers & Magazines   The daily *Austin American-Statesman* (www.austin360.com) is the only large-circulation, mainstream newspaper in town. The *Austin Chronicle* (www.auschron.com), a free alternative weekly, focuses on the arts, entertainment, and politics. Monday through Friday, the University of Texas publishes the *Daily Texan* (www.dailytexanonline.com), covering everything from on-campus news to international events.

Police   The non-emergency number for the Austin Police Department is ☎ 512/974-5000.

Post Office   The city's main post office is at 8225 Cross Park Dr. (☎ 512/342-1252); more convenient to tourist sights are the Capitol Station, 111 E. 17th St., in the LBJ Building, and the Downtown Station, 510 Guadalupe St. For information on other locations, phone ☎ 800/275-8777.

Radio   On the FM dial, turn to public-radio KUT (90.5) for NPR, KASE (100.7) for country, KUTZ (98.9) for modern rock, and KGSR (107.1) for folk, reggae, rock, blues, and jazz. AM stations include KVET (1300) for sports, and KJCE (1300) for soul and Motown oldies.

Taxes   The tax on hotel rooms is 15%. Sales tax, added to restaurant bills as well as to other purchases, is 8.25%.

Television   You'll find CBS (KEYE) on Channel 5, ABC (KVUE) on Channel 3, NBC (KXAN) on Channel 4, Fox (KTBC) on Channel 2, and PBS (KLRU) on Channel 9. Austin cable channels include Channel 8, with nonstop local news, and Channel 15, the city-run Austin Music Network, emphasizing Austin and Texas artists.

Time Zone   Austin is on Central Standard Time and observes daylight saving time.

Transit Information   Call Capital Metro Transit (☎ **800/474-1201** or 512/474-1200 from local pay phones; TTY 512/385-5872).

Weather   Check the weather at ☎ **512/451-2424** or www.news8austin.com/content/weather.

Austin Highlights

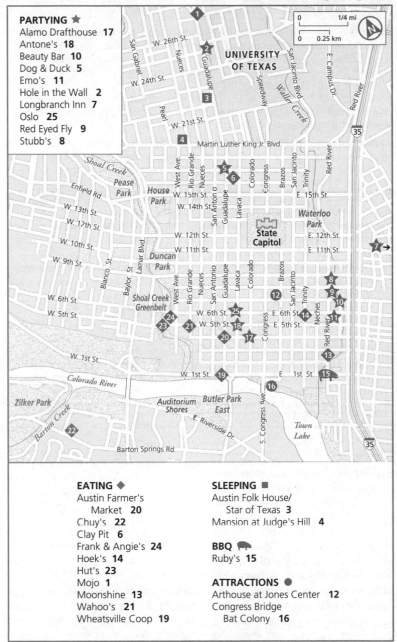

PARTYING ★
Alamo Drafthouse **17**
Antone's **18**
Beauty Bar **10**
Dog & Duck **5**
Emo's **11**
Hole in the Wall **2**
Longbranch Inn **7**
Oslo **25**
Red Eyed Fly **9**
Stubb's **8**

EATING ◆
Austin Farmer's
    Market **20**
Chuy's **22**
Clay Pit **6**
Frank & Angie's **24**
Hoek's **14**
Hut's **23**
Mojo **1**
Moonshine **13**
Wahoo's **21**
Wheatsville Coop **19**

SLEEPING ■
Austin Folk House/
    Star of Texas **3**
Mansion at Judge's Hill **4**

BBQ 🐷
Ruby's **15**

ATTRACTIONS ●
Arthouse at Jones Center **12**
Congress Bridge
    Bat Colony **16**

Surf Austin! (On the 'net)

Austin is one of the country's most wired cities, and I'm not talking caffeine. You can get a very good idea of where to stay, where to eat, what's on, and all kinds of useful info while you're planning your trip from some handy websites we list below. If you're not e-oriented, call the **Austin Visitor Center,** 209 E. Sixth St., Austin, TX 78701 (☎ 866/GO-AUSTIN), to receive a general information packet in the snail mail; otherwise, log on to **www.austintexas.org**. Austin is such a plugged-in city that it's tough to select just a few websites. However, some do stand out for their depth and breadth:

➔ **www.austin360.com** Movie times, traffic reports, restaurant picks, homes, jobs, cars . . . this site, sponsored in part by the *Austin-American Statesman,* the city's daily newspaper, is a one-stop clicking center for a variety of essentials. It's easy to navigate, too.

➔ **www.austinchronicle.com** The online version of Austin's excellent alternative tabloid, the *Austin Chronicle*, has everything you would expect: muckraking stories; hard-hitting book, movie, and restaurant reviews; personal ads; and above all, attitude. And it looks a lot better online than it does on paper.

➔ **www.ci.austin.tx.us** Talk about big government: **Austin City Connection** is proof positive that practically everything in Austin falls under the aegis of its municipal system, from air quality to bus schedules and parks and recreation. A surprising number of museums (including the one devoted to O. Henry) are covered on this site, too.

➔ **www.utexas.edu** After the city government, the University of Texas might have the largest network of influence in town. In addition to providing info about the many on-campus museums, entertainment venues, and sports teams, this website links to an array of visitor-oriented sites, including the *Austin Chronicle Restaurant Guide,* the City of Austin Hike and Bike Trails, and the Austin Ice Bats hockey team. Wouldn't want the students—or their visiting parents—to get hungry or bored, right?

Getting Around

Downtown Austin is bounded on the south by Town Lake (a reservoir on the Colorado River) and on the north by Martin Luther King Jr. Boulevard, with I-35 to the east and Lamar to the West; in this patch you'll find the State Capitol, the nightlife meccas of **Sixth Street,** the **Red River District,** and the **Warehouse District.** Just across the Congress Avenue Bridge, South Austin's **SoCo** (or South Congress) nabe is another one worth checking out for its art galleries, hipster boutiques, cafes, and clubs. **The Drag,** a stretch of Guadalupe west of UT,

is packed with pubs, restaurants, shops, while gentrifying **East Austin** has lots of historic local character by day and some shady local characters by night.

BY CAR

Driving in Austin is, uh, a *challenge.* There are so many poorly marked one-way streets downtown that even the most sober driver can get confused, make a wrong turn, and have some 'splainin to do. At night you practically need X-ray vision to read the poorly lit street indicators. Highways are just as frustrating; I-35 is congested and mined with tricky on-and-off ramps and a confusing complex of upper and lower levels; it's easy to miss your exit or find yourself exiting when you don't want to, so stay on your toes.

BY TROLLEY

The 'Dillo is a free trolley ★ with seven routes serving downtown, UT, South Congress, and East Austin. The Orange and Silver 'Dillos are particularly geared toward sightseeing, while the Starlight and Moonlight rides, available Thursday through Saturday from 6pm to 3am, shuttle you around downtown's hottest nightspot and restaurant areas.

ON FOOT

As long as you've got good shoes and aren't in a huge hurry, the best way to see downtown Austin is on foot. It's pretty easy to get oriented in the gridlike downtown: Congress divides the east and west street designations, and street addresses correlate to numbered streets, so if you're looking for, say, Buffalo Billiards, 201 E. 6th St., you know it's 2 blocks east of Congress, while Stubb's Barbecue, 801 Red River, is near the intersection of Red River and 8th St. Places designated with South addresses (S. Lamar, S. First, S. Congress) are on the other side of the river. Go anywhere outside the central areas, though, and you're better off hopping in the car or in a cab.

BY TAXI

If you need a ride, try **Austin Cab** (☎ 512/478-2222), **Roy's Taxi** (☎ 512/482-0000), and **American Yellow Checker Cab** (☎ 512/452-9999). Rides cost from $1.50 to $1.75 at the flag drop, plus $1.75 for each additional mile.

Brisket Country: Where to Get the Best Barbecue in Austin

Texas considers itself the barbecue capital of the world. (But then again so do Memphis, Kansas City, and just about every town in North and South Carolina—even Santa Maria, CA, makes that claim).

In Texas you'll find mostly pork ribs, brisket, and sausage—sometimes called the "holy trinity" of meats—and, in some places, chicken, turkey, even barbecued mutton (pork shoulder becomes more frequent as you head east). In Texas, meat is generally smoked over mesquite or live oak, while hickory is more common farther east. If you're interested in exploring Austin as a city, stay in town and you'll find some damn fine 'cue at places like The Iron Works or Sam's, when you just gotta have a brisket sandwich at 2am. But for a more authentic barbecue experience, head out to Driftwood, Lockhart, and the towns along the Barbecue Trail, a 30-mile ring of barbecue-loving communities surrounding Austin (see "Farther Outta Town: Along the Barbecue Trail," on p. 331), whose family-owned joints are worth the 30- to 45-minute drive.

IN TOWN

➔ **The Iron Works** ★★★ Until 1977, this building housed the ironworks of the Weigl family, who came over from Germany in 1913. Cattle brands created for Jack Benny, Lucille Ball, and Bob Hope are displayed in front; beef ribs are popular, with the brisket running a close second. Lean turkey breast and juicy chicken are also smoked to perfection. *Red River and E. 1st sts.* ☎ *800/669-3602 or 512/478-4855. www.ironworksbbq.com. Sandwiches $2–$4.25; plates $6–$12. Mon–Sat 11am–9pm. Closed Sun.*

➔ **Ruby's** ★★ On the UT campus, Ruby's serves up brisket and chopped beef sandwiches alongside Greek salad, gumbo, and vegetarian jambalaya, which isn't something you'll find at your everyday barbecue joint. *512 W. 29th St.* ☎ *512/477-1651. Sandwiches $3–$5; plates $6–$15. Daily 11am–midnight.*

SOUTHERN BBQ ROADTRIP

➔**Sam's** ★★ It don't look like much from the outside, but Sam's cooks up brisket and ribs so fierce Stevie Ray Vaughan had 'em shipped all the way to New York. The late-night hours and popular brisket make it *the* after-bar snack stop in East Austin. Try the barbecued mutton. *2000 & 12th St.* ☎ *512/478-0378. Sandwiches $3.10–$4.20; plates $7.50–$8.25. Sun–Thurs 10am–2am; Fri–Sat 10am–3am (hours may vary; call ahead).*

OUTTA TOWN

📺 Best ❢ ➔**The Salt Lick** ★★★ If it weren't for the unmistakable barbecue-smoke smell (their T-shirts read, "You can smell our pits from miles away"), it'd be easy to miss this joint, which is so famous for its pork ribs, brisket, and secret-recipe sauce that it draws celebs like Sandra Bullock, Matthew McConaughey, and U2; they do brisk mail-order business, too. If you've got an appetite, the best bet here is the all-you-can-eat family-style platter—beef, sausage, and pork ribs, plus sides and bread ($16/person)—and the fresh-baked peach cobbler (get it a la mode—it's *soooo* worth it). Boozehounds should note that the Lick is BYOB, a holdover from a time when Hays County was dry; pick up some brews at the gas station up the street. *18300 FM 1826, Driftwood.* ☎ *512/858-4959. www.saltlickbbq.com. Sandwiches $7–$8; plates $7–$15. Cash only. Daily 11am–10pm.*

Five Minutes with the Salt Lick's Scott Roberts

Scott Roberts' dad started the Salt Lick in 1969; when he quit the bridge-building business, he and Scott's mom jotted down a list of 100 things they could do to make money and vowed to try each one until something stuck. The Salt Lick was #13.

The Lick's pride is its sauce, whose recipe is a closely guarded family secret. It tastes sweet, but unlike most barbecue sauces contains no tomatoes at all—just mustard, vinegar, and 40-odd other ingredients, including Texas-specific ones like cayenne and chili powder. Scott says the mix of ingredients helps differentiate his 'cue from other varieties across the South. The Lick makes its classic sauce as well as a habanero-spiked version, which somehow manages to pack a spicy punch without setting your mouth on fire.

Sauce covered everything on the family-style platter we ordered, which arrived with pork ribs, beef brisket, and sausage. We also tried some surprisingly moist chicken and the most amazing smoked turkey I've ever tasted, plus bread, potato salad, coleslaw, beans, onions and pickles, and a giant pitcher of iced tea. "My dad always served everything family style," Scott recalls, "because he wanted to make sure everyone had enough to eat."

Uh, yeah. There'd be no shortage of food at this meal; if anything, I wondered whether all these to-go boxes would fit in my minivan, especially when our waiter brought out the peach and blackberry cobbler. The recipe, Scott claims, is a sore spot for Mrs. Eccles and Mrs. Halls, two local women in their eighties who both claim responsibility for the cobbler's tastiness. "That's ridiculous," Scott says of the theft claim, "I stole it from both of them."

But who really cares whether he's begging, borrowing, or stealing—whatever it is, it's working. At this rate the world may never know about those 87 other ideas Scott's dad had up his sleeve; but with food this good, I, for one, can deal with that.

These are the sentiments at the Salt Lick.

FARTHER OUTTA TOWN: ALONG THE BARBECUE TRAIL

If you want to spend a few extra days exploring Texas-style barbecue, smoke your way along the **Central Texas Barbecue Trail,** which runs through the towns of Elgin, Lockhart, Luling, Round Rock, and Taylor. In Elgin, try **Southside Market & BBQ** ★★ (1212 Hwy. 290; ☎ 512/281-4650); **Luling Bar-B-Q** ★★ (709 E. Davis St.; ☎ 830/875-3848) in Luling; **Cooper's** ★★ (403 N. Mays St.; ☎ 512/255-5638) in Round Rock and **Mikeska's** (300 W. 2nd St.; ☎ 512/365-3722) in Taylor. For more info check out www.texasbbqtrail.com.

The town of **Lockhart** fancies itself home to the world's best barbecue—a claim you should get used to, because you'll hear it from every place you'll stop on this trip. Run by the same family since 1932, **Black's Barbecue** ★★ (215 N. Main St.; ☎ 512/398-2712) is open 8 days a week, according to its sign, while **Chisolm**

Trail ★★ (1323 S. Colorado St.; ☎ 512/398-6027) offers killer hot sausage and fried catfish. **Kreuz Market** ★★★ (19 N. Colorado St.; ☎ 512/398-2361) and its sister **Smitty's Market** ★★ (208 S. Commerce St.; ☎ 512/398-9344) are known for their no-nonsense "no plate, no sauce, no silverware" policy (so prepare to get dirty).

Sleeping

Being a city of festivals, the Texas state capital, and just a cool place all around, Austin tends to be pretty crowded, so it's best to make lodging plans *well* ahead of time, especially if you want to stay close to the action downtown (or if you're heading for South by Southwest). If you crave cheap rates and easy freeway access, take your pick of generic chains off I-35 (see below); but for a little bit more you can stay somewhere with more authentic Austin character. With the construction of new downtown hotels and restoration of

Texas Festivals: More BBQ!

While any chance you get to chow down on Texas barbecue should be cause for celebration, there are a few formal festivals worth checking out if you're in the neighborhood:

→ **Texas Barbecue Festival** Started in 2005 in a farmers market, this Austin festival attracted so many fans it wouldn't be a surprise to see it held in a larger venue next time. Expect sauce samples, panel discussions, and, of course, a lot of meat at the 1-day event, held annually in October; **www.texasbarbecuefestival.com.**

→ **Texas Hill Country Wine & Food Festival** Not solely a barbecue festival, this annual event—going on for over 2 decades—covers menus and topics ranging from "Chocolate and Chiles" to "Film Noir and Pinot Noir." Barbecue junkies won't want to miss the Sunday Fair, an all-day outdoor party with recipes and grilling demos from top local chefs, plus live music and family activities. The 4-day event happens in April; **www.texaswine andfood.org.**

→ **Chisholm Trail Roundup** Held the second week of June in Lockhart, the Chisholm Trail Roundup is a combination barbecue/music festival and rodeo. There are contests for best chili and black-eyed peas, but the barbecue cook-off is the main attraction; **www.chisholmtrailroundup.com.**

old ones in recent years, you shouldn't have too much trouble finding a place that fits your budget.

CAMPGROUNDS/HOSTELS

→**Austin Motel** ★★ A convenient (but not quiet) SoCo location and reasonable rates help draw repeat guests to this funky motel, whose marquee reads, "So Close Yet So Far Out!" Other assets are a classic kidney-shaped pool, a great neon sign, free HBO, free coffee in the lobby, and **El Sol y La Luna,** a solid Latin restaurant that's popular with Town Lake athletes on weekend mornings. *1220 S. Congress St. (south of Nelly, about ½ mile south of Riverside).* ☎ *512/441-1157. www.austinmotel.com. 41 units. $60–$90 single; $80–$122 double; $143–$153 suite. Free parking. Limited number of rooms for pets; one-time $10 fee. Amenities: Outdoor pool.*

→**Hostelling International–Austin** On the hike-and-bike trail with views of Town Lake that others pay through the nose for,

this hostel has the standard amenities (laundry, kitchen) plus fancy stuff like Wi-Fi. *2200 S. Lakeshore Blvd. (east of I-35, on the southern shore of Town Lake).* ☎ *800/725-2331 or 512/444-2294. www.hiaustin.org. 39 beds in 4 dorms. $17 for AYH members, $3 additional for nonmembers. Free parking. Amenities: Kayak/bike rentals; Internet kiosk; Wi-Fi; co-op laundry; kitchen. In room: No phone.*

→**McKinney Falls State Park** Even if you don't have a tent, you can camp out close to downtown at McKinney Falls, where facilities include screened shelters with hot-water sinks, ceiling fans, grill and fire ring, electricity, and bunk beds (no mattresses or bedding provided), plus standard campsites with water and electricity. *5808 McKinney Falls Pkwy. (US-183 S to McKinney Falls Pkwy.).* ☎ *512/243-1643. www. tpwd.state.tx.us/spdest/findadest/parks/mc kinney_falls. 8 walk-in tent campsites ($12/ night, not reservable), 81 campsites ($16/ night), 6 screened shelters ($35/night + 6%*

More Austin Events: Food, Music & Kites!

Sure, Austin's home to great barbecue, but they don't call it the live music capital of the world for nothing. Here's an intro to some of the city's music festivals and other noteworthy annual events:

→ The **SXSW Festival,** held in March all over downtown, is *the* place to be for anyone in the music industry who wants to be the next big thing (or those who want to hear the next big thing). The music/film/interactive festival celebrated its 20th birthday in 2006 with tons of international movies, panels on blogging and podcasting, and showcases from more than 1,300 bands from all over the world (**www.sxsw.com**).

→ An outgrowth of the TV show of the same name, the **Austin City Limits** music festival started in 2002 and now sprawls throughout the massive Zilker Park for 2 days every September with sets by more than 100 rock, reggae, hip-hop, and Americana bands. Past performers have included Ryan Adams, Wilco, Ben Harper, Modest Mouse, and about a trillion others (**www.aclfestival.com**).

→ One of the largest literary events in the Southwest, the 2-day **Texas Book Festival** draws the literati from all over the U.S. in late October, though Texas authors rule the roost (☎ 512/477-4055; www.texasbookfestival.org).

→ Held the last Sunday in August in Waterloo Park, the annual **Hot Sauce Festival,** sponsored by the *Austin Chronicle,* is the largest hot-sauce contest in the world, featuring more than 300 salsa entries, judged by celebrity chefs and food editors. The bands that play this super party are *muy caliente,* too (☎ 512/454-5766; www.austinchronicle.com).

→ *Rushmore*'s Max Fischer would love Austin's annual **Kite Festival,** one of the oldest events of its kind in the country, held the first Sunday in March in Zilker Park (☎ 512/647-7488; www.zilkerkitefestival.com).

occupancy tax). Rates do not include $4 daily entrance fee.

CHEAP

There are plenty of chain hotels a few exits down I-35 from downtown Austin. Off the Oltorf Exit you'll find a **Best Value Inn** (2525 S Interstate 35; ☎ 800/444-6835; www.bestvalueinn.com), which runs about $45 per night for a double, including free hot breakfast, a fitness center, and a pool. A little farther north on the frontage road is a **La Quinta Inn** (1603 E Oltorf St.; ☎ 800/346-8357; www.lqcom), which also has a pool and rates around $79/night.

Next door is **The Woodward Hotel & Conference Center** (3401 I-35 S; ☎ 800/444-6835; www.woodwardaustin.com),

which has doubles from around $69 to $79 and suites from $89 to $99 (AAA and other discounts available).

DOABLE

→ **Austin Folk House and Star of Texas Inn** ★★ The Austin Folk House and its slightly more traditional sister property are two UT-adjacent B&Bs converted from late 19th-century homes with all the modern conveniences. A block away from each other, both feature bike rentals, Wi-Fi, free breakfast, and a video library to go with the in-room VCRs. Ask about discounts. *Austin Folk House: 506 W. 22nd St. (between San Antonio and Nueces). ☎ 866/472-6700 or 512/472-6700. www.austinfolkhouse.com. 9 units. $109–$225 single or double. Star of*

Texas Inn: 611 W. 22nd St. (at Rio Grande).
☎ *866/472-6700 or 512/472-6700. www.starof texasinn.com. 9 units. $80 single; $109–$155 double.*

➜ **Hotel San José** ★★★ Just down the street from the Austin Motel and adjacent to Jo's Coffee, this revamped 1930s motor court is the epitome of SoCo cool. Right across the street from the famed Continental Club, the hotel sees its share of touring musicians, so while you'll get more amenities for your money elsewhere, you won't get a hipper scene. Don't miss the open-air markets, film nights, and other events held in the parking lot behind Jo's. *1316 S. Congress Ave.* ☎ *800/574-8897 or 512/444-7322. www.sanjosehotel.com. 40 units. $80 (for 3 rooms with shared bathroom); $140–$170 double; $190–$250 suite. Discounts available; lower rates during the week. Free parking. Dogs accepted for $10 per day (each animal). Amenities: Bar/lounge; coffee shop; outdoor pool; bike rentals; breakfast-only room service; dry cleaning. In room: Dataport, high-speed Internet, CD player.*

SPLURGE

➜ **Mansion at Judges Hill** ★★ Most hip hotels tend to be cold and angular, but this opulent, turn-of-the-20th-century mansion (with an added wing built in 1983) manages to be both posh and cool. Rooms in the mansion wing are most interesting since they're furnished with real antiques, but the modern accents and free Wi-Fi make this place feel more fun than fusty. *1900 Rio Grande (at 19th St.).* ☎ *800/311-1619 or 512/495-1800. www.mansionatjudgeshill. com. 48 units. North Wing rooms $139–$199 single or double; Mansion rooms $139–$299 single or double; suites $139–$389. Free parking. Pets accepted (North Wing only) with $150 refundable deposit. Amenities: Restaurant; bar. In room: Dataport, high-speed Internet, CD player.*

Eating

If you stick to an all-meat-all-the-time diet, you may not make it to the end of this roadtrip. Sneak in veggies as often as possible, and if you've got any room in that belly for non-barbecue-style grub, take advantage of Austin's fine Tex-Mex and other regional cuisines.

SUPPLIES

With live music, cooking demos, and more, the most notable of this city's many farmers markets is the **Austin Farmers' Market** ★, held downtown at Republic Square Park, Fourth Street at Guadalupe, every Saturday from 9am to 1pm March through November (☎ **512/236-0074;** www.austinfarmersmarket.org).

South Congress Organic Farmers' Market, held Saturday from 8am to 1pm year-round in the parking lot of El Gallo Restaurant, 2910 S. Congress Ave. (☎ **512/ 281-4712**), is smaller, but you've got the guarantee that all the goods are locally grown without chemicals.

In addition to the farmers' markets, here are a couple of places open more frequently to stock up on food for your cooler, motel fridge, or that spur-of-the-moment picnic.

➜ **Central Market** ★★ Aah, foodie heaven! Not only can you buy every imaginable edible item at these gourmet megamarkets—fresh or frozen, local or imported—but you also can enjoy the cooking of a top-notch chef in the restaurant section, which features cowboy, bistro, Italian, vegetarian—you name it— cuisines. Moreover, prices are surprisingly reasonable. A monthly newsletter announces what's fresh in the produce department, which jazz musicians are entertaining on the weekend, and which gourmet chef is holding forth at the market's cooking school. The newer Westgate

No underage boozing at Chuy's!

Shopping Center branch, 4477 S. Lamar (☎ 512/899-4300), in South Austin, is as impressive as its history-making sibling north of UT. *4001 N. Lamar. ☎ 512/206-1000. www.centralmarket.com. Open daily, 8am–9pm.*

✦Wheatsville Food Co-Op DELI This member-run, vegan-friendly grocery is famous for its Tempeh Chili Frito Pie, but we've got it on good authority that the southern-fried tofu on focaccia with dill mayonnaise and barbecue sauce is just to die for. You don't need to be a member of the co-op to shop here. *101 Guadalupe. ☎ 512/478-2667. www.wheatsville.coop. Deli open 9am–9pm daily.*

✦Whole Foods Market ★★ The first link in what is now the world's largest organic and natural foods supermarket chain celebrated its 25th birthday by opening an 80,000-square-foot store near its original downtown location (as well as an adjacent office tower to serve as corporate headquarters). From chemical-free cosmetics to frozen tofu burgers, Whole Foods has long covered the entire (organic) enchilada, and now it's looking to compete with Central Market (see above) in the food-entertainment arena by creating a 600-seat amphitheater, a playscape, gardens, on-site massages, a cooking school, and more. The northwest store in Gateway Market, 9607 Research Blvd. (☎ 512/345-5003), will not be subject to this extreme makeover. *525 N. Lamar Blvd. ☎ 512/476-1206. www.wholefoods.com. Open daily, 8am–10pm.*

TAKE-OUT TREATS

For morning-after caffeination, hit up **Mojo,** near UT (2714 Guadalupe; ☎ 512/477-6656), which serves up java, pastries, and attitude 24/7. Musicians turn up for the creative sandwiches and dark-roasted java drinks at **Jo's** ★★★ (1300 S. Congress;

ᴍᴛᴠ🇺 Can't Believe I Ate the Whole Foods...

If all the yummy food you're eating in Austin gives you the "do-it-yourself" urge, head on over to **Whole Foods Market Culinary Center,** at the 525 N. Lamar Blvd. branch. You can spend a morning, an afternoon, or an evening in a hands-on workshop, learning how to make culinary magic . . . then eating it! Recent workshops have included "I'll Take Steak!", "Cutting Edge Knife Skills" and "Big Game Party," in which you learn to prepare a feast *for* the Big Game (football, that is!) . . . not from the big game. Classes range from 2 hours to all day, with related classes (during events like "Cheese Week") running over several days. Tuition ranges from $15 to $200 (for the week-long events). See what's on offer at **www.wholefoodsmarket.com/stores/calendars/LCC.html**; to register, call ☎ **512/542-2340** or email austincookingschool@wholefoods.com.

☎ **512/444-3800**), a hip outdoor hangout across the road from the Continental Club.

Feed your sweet tooth at Austin's homegrown ice-creamery, **Amy's** ★★, which has nine locations, including one on the west side of downtown, 1012 W. Sixth St. at Lamar Boulevard (☎ **512/480-0673**); one in SoCo, 1301 S. Congress Ave. (☎ **512/440-7488**); and even one the airport.

And while late-night pizza's not hard to come by after last call on Sixth Street, sometimes you just need your slice to be served under a black light against a deafening backdrop of metal. That's the time for **Hoek's** ★, aka Death Metal Pizza (320 E 6th St.; ☎ **512/708-8484**).

EATING OUT

Cheap

➜ **Chuy's** MEXICAN Wacky decor (Elvis tchotchkes everywhere, hubcaps on the ceiling) and "big as yo' face" burritos keep people coming back to Chuy's, which has been a local landmark ever since First Daughter Jenna Bush got busted here for underage drinking. *1728 Barton Springs Rd.* ☎ *512/474-4452. www.chuys.com. Main courses $6–$9. Sun–Thurs 11am–10pm; Fri–Sat 11am–11pm.*

➜ **Frank & Angie's** ITALIAN/PIZZA This corrugated tin-roof building fronted by a neon sign and backed by a creek-view patio is as casual as it gets, and you'll roll your eyes when you peruse the menu; it's chock-full of such groaners as "Corleone Calzones" and "Angiepasto." But the prices are reasonable and the pies hit the spot. *508 West Ave.* ☎ *512/472-3535. Sandwiches and calzones $5–$6.75; 18-in. pizzas $14–$17. Mon–Sat 11am–10pm; Sun 4–10pm.*

➜ **Hut's Hamburgers** ★ AMERICAN This burger shack is classic Texas. Opened in 1939 as Sammie's Drive-In, Hut's now serves 19 types of burgers—many of them named after '50s and '60s rockers—plus blue-plate specials of meatloaf, chicken-fried steak, and catfish. Still, it wouldn't be Austin without a 100% fat-free veggie burger on the menu. *807 W. 6th St.* ☎ *512/472-0693. Sandwiches and burgers $3.50–$6; plates $6–$7. Daily 11am–10pm.*

➜ **Magnolia Cafe** ★★ AMERICAN Even with two locations, Magnolia's has always got a line of people out the door, all waiting to tuck into the buttery Love *migas* (eggs with tomatoes, onions, and peppers scrambled in a spicy garlic butter) and gingerbread pancakes at breakfast. Beat the crowd by showing up in the middle of the night; these joints are open 24/7. *2304 Lake Austin Blvd.* ☎ *512/478-8645 and 1920 South*

Congress. ☎ *512/445-0000. www.cafemagnolia. com. Breakfast $2.25–$7.50; entrees $5.75–$9.95. Open 24 hr.*

→ **Mother's Cafe & Garden** VEGETAR-IAN   The crunchy granola crowd that frequents this Hyde Park cafe enjoys an international array of veggie dishes, with heavy south-of-the-border representation. You'll find classic chiles rellenos, burritos, and nachos, along with more unusual spicy tempeh enchiladas. The tropical shack–style back garden is appealing, and the young staff is friendly, but not nauseatingly so. There's a good, inexpensive selection of local beers and wines. *4215 Duval St.* ☎ *512/451-3994. www. motherscafeaustin.com. Sandwiches and salads $4–$8; entrees $7–$9. Mon–Fri 11:15am–10pm; Sat–Sun 10am–10pm (brunch until 3pm).*

→ **Threadgill's** AMERICAN   Janis Joplin was a regular at Threadgill's Wednesday-night hootenannies in the '60s. In 1980 the club added on a diner, which is now almost as famous as the original honky-tonk, thanks to its huge chicken-fried steaks, fried okra, broccoli-rice casserole, and garlic-cheese grits. *6416 N. Lamar Blvd.* ☎ *512/451-5440. www.threadgills.com. Reservations not accepted. Sandwiches and burgers $5.95–$7.95; main courses $6.25–$15. Mon–Sat 11am–10pm; Sun 11am–9pm. Also at 301 West Riverside Drive,* ☎ *512/472-9304, south of downtown, just off South Congress.*

→ **Wahoo's Fish Tacos** ★★ MEXICAN   An import from Southern California (which explains the skateboard company decals stuck to every available surface), Wahoo's is a health-conscious newcomer to Austin's west side. Try the blackened fish taco/enchilada combo platter with spicy Cajun white beans and sticky rice, all drenched in a creamy (and addictive) green salsa. *509-A Rio Grande St.* ☎ *512/476-3474. www.wahoos.com. Bowls and combos*

$4–$10. Sun–Mon 11am–9pm; Tues–Wed 11am–10pm; Thurs–Sat 11am–3am.

Doable

→ **Clay Pit** ★ INDIAN   Housed in a historic building and lit with soft lamps and votive candles, the Clay Pit is all about vibe and creative curries prepared by a New Delhi–trained chef. Try the coriander calamari with cilantro aioli followed by *khuroos-e-tursh* (chicken stuffed with nuts and mushrooms in a cashew-almond cream sauce) or any of the many veggie-friendly dishes. Swing by at lunch for the bargain buffet. *1601 Guadalupe St.* ☎ *512/322-5131. www.claypit.com. Reservations recommended. $6.95 lunch buffet; main courses $9–$16. Mon–Thurs 11am–2pm and 5–10pm; Fri 11am–2pm and 5–11pm; Sat–Sun 5–11pm.*

→ **Moonshine** ★ AMERICAN   Dig into comfort food on Moonshine's shady patio across from the Convention Center, where you'll find dishes like "corn dog" fried shrimp, horseradish-crusted salmon, corn-flake-fried chicken salad, and, for dessert, peanut butter pie. Or just come to get sauced on the joint's signature Moonshine Jug of "white lightening" with peach and spice. *303 Red River St.* ☎ *512/236-9599. www.moonshinegrill.com. Reservations recommended. Salads and sandwiches $6–$9; main courses $11–$20. Mon–Thurs 11am–10pm; Fri 11am–11pm; Sat 5–11pm.*

Splurge

→ **Uchi** ASIAN/JAPANES   In a converted '30s-era bungalow and decorated by Austin's "it" designers Joel Mozersky and Michael Hsu, this trendy sushi spot is all about super-fresh fish and innovative preparations, like *Uchiviche* (citrus-cured whitefish and salmon mixed with tomato, peppers, cilantro, and Thai peppers) and tempura pumpkin. *801 S Lamar Blvd.* ☎ *512/916-4808. www.uchiaustin.com. Limited number of reservations accepted until 7pm, then*

open seating. Sashimi $10–$30; rolls $4–$12.
Sun–Thurs 5:30–10pm; Fri-Sat 5:30–11pm.

Partying

There's no shortage of places to get your drink on in Austin; you just have to choose your neighborhood. **Sixth Street** is all about bar after club after bar after club, often filled with drunk UT students, while the clientele gets a little more sophisticated as you head west toward **the Warehouse District. East Austin, Red River,** and **SoCo** are hipster-friendly, while **The Drag,** near UT, has more laidback options.

BARS, PUBS & CLUBS
Downtown/Red River/
Warehouse Districts

➜**Oslo** ★★ CLUB This series of narrow rooms, done in black and white with retro minimalist furnishings, is *the* place to see and be seen in Austin for those who've long eschewed Sixth Street. Creative drinks and appetizers are served until 10pm, when things start kicking inside (with art exhibitions, DJs, and live performers) while the line begins to stack up outside. *301 W. 6th St.* ☎ *512/480-9433. www. oslo-austin.com. No cover most nights.*

📺 Best❢➜**Alamo Drafthouse** ★★★ MOVIE THEATER Chinese food and Chinese beer accompany kung fu films at this Warehouse District spot, which screens all kinds of alt and cult movies, and features lectures by celebs as varied as James Ellroy and Pauly Shore. *409 Colorado St.* ☎ *512/476-1320. www.drafthouse. com.*

➜**Beauty Bar** ★★ BAR New York, San Francisco, Vegas, and LA all have one; now Austin's got a haven of its own where haircut hipsters can hang out and sip Stella Artois against a kitschy beauty-parlor decor. *617 E 7th St.* ☎ *512/236-8010.*

www.myspace.com/beautybaraustin. Sun–Wed 9pm–2am; Thurs–Sat 6pm–2am. Cover varies from free to $5+.

East Side

➜**Longbranch Inn** BAR A regulars' bar on the East Side, the LBI is no-frills and no-nonsense: no cover, no booze (just beer and wine), dim lighting, one pool table, and bands. Behind the massive wooden bar sits co-owner/bartender Kevin "Kumbala" Crutchfield, who won *Austin Chronicle's* Best Bartender in 2004. *1133 E. 11th St.* ☎ *512/472-5477. www.longbranchinn.com. Mon–Sat 4pm–2am; Sun 6pm–2am.*

UT Campus

➜**Hole in the Wall** BAR Locals suffered a scare when this landmark venue lost its lease after nearly 3 decades of hosting musicians like Stevie Ray Vaughn, Doug Sahm, and Reverend Horton Heat; 5 years later it's still going strong. *2538 Guadalupe.* ☎ *512/477-4747. www.holeinthewallaustin. com. Mon–Fri 1pm–2am; Sat–Sun noon–2am. No cover.*

➜**Dog & Duck Pub** PUB This comfy British pub has darts, Irish jams, bagpipes, and hearty brews. The bangers and mash taste authentic, too—not that that's necessarily a good thing. *406 W. 17th St.* ☎ *512/ 479-0598. www.doganduckpub.com. Mon– Sat 11am–2am; Sun noon–2am. No cover.*

LIVE MUSIC
Rock/Folk

➜**Emo's** ★ Austin's last word in alternative music, Emo's has hosted acts of all sizes and flavors, from the late, great Johnny Cash to Green Day. The front room holds the bar, pool tables, and pinball machines. You'll have to cross the outside patio to reach the backroom where the bands play. *603 Red River St.* ☎ *512/477- EMOS. www.emosaustin.com. Daily 7pm–2am. Cover $8–$15. Shows are all ages unless otherwise noted.*

➔ **The Red Eyed Fly** ★ A good representative of the Red River music scene, the Fly showcases Texas's top rock, pop, and punk acts—as well as national touring bands—at its great outdoor stage. *715 Red River St.* ☎ *512/474-1084. www.redeyedfly.com. Daily 8pm–2am. Cover $5–$12. All shows 18+ (no cover for those 21+ in the lounge).*

➔ **Stubb's Bar-B-Q** ★★ Great barbecue + awesome music = Stubb's. Hear everything from singer-songwriters to hip-hop battles to all-out country jams inside, while the Waller Amphitheater out back hosts bigger acts, like Matisyahu, whose first release was a live album recorded here. *801 Red River St.* ☎ *512/480-8341. www.stubbsaustin. com. Tues–Wed 11am–10pm (bar open till 2am); Thurs–Sat 11am–11pm (bar open till 2am); Sun 11am–9pm. Cover $6–$25.*

Jazz/Blues/Country

➔ **Antone's** ★★ Willie Nelson, Stevie Ray Vaughan, Buddy Guy, Etta James, and Edgar Winter are no strangers to Antone's. This all-ages joint is still the place to be despite relocating to the Warehouse District; sadly, owner C. J. Antone passed away in May 2006. *213 W. 5th St.* ☎ *512/320-8424. www.antones.net. Daily 8.30pm–2am. Cover $8–$35. All ages.*

➔ **Continental Club** ★★ Alt-country, singer/songwriter, and rockabilly rule the roost at this Austin classic, but the Continental Club still does it up trad-country-style with its Hank Williams and Elvis birthday parties. They have a killer happy hour, too. *1315 S. Congress Ave.* ☎ *512/441-2444. www.continentalclub.com. Mon–Fri 4pm–2am; Sat 2pm–2am; Sun 9pm–2am. Cover $5–$20. All ages.*

What Else to See & Do

There's so much to do in Austin you might be tempted to cancel the rest of the trip and stick around town. For the sake of the barbecue hunt, try not to get too distracted, but do take advantage of the many outdoor recreation options this city has to offer—trust me, after eating ribs for a week, you'll be grateful for the exercise.

MOVIES, BATS &ART

Thursday nights the Hotel San Jose and Jo's Coffee host **Rock 'n' Reel,** where they invite a band to play live in the parking lot behind Jo's; then later they'll screen a movie chosen by the band, anything from *Goodfellas* to *The Wedding Singer.* Plus Jo's sells refreshments—including beers for just two bucks—during the show. It's at

---

ᴹᵀⱽ🖐 50,000 **Longhorns Can't Be Wrong!**

Nearly 50,000 students occupy 120 buildings at the **University of Texas at Austin,** founded in 1883. The Texas Union Information Center, at 24th and Guadalupe (☎ **512/475-6636**), is the best place to get information about the campus; it's open Monday through Friday from 7am to 3am (really), Saturday from 10am to 3am, and Sunday from noon to 3am. The ground floor of the Main building/UT Tower (near 24th and Whitis) is the point of departure for free campus tours, which are designed for prospective students, but open to all. It's a lot tougher to get on the free **Moonlight Prowl Tours,** packed with amusing anecdotes of student life and campus lore, because they're held only a few evenings a month and they fill up quickly, but if you want to give it a try, log on to **www.utexas.edu/tours/prowl** and fill out the registration form. UT is at Guadalupe and I-35, Martin Luther King Jr. Boulevard, and 26th Street. (☎ **512/ 471-3434;** www.utexas.edu).

ᴍ ᴛ ᴠ 🖐 Hook 'em Horns!

The **UT Longhorns and Lady Longhorns** shoot hoops (Nov–Mar) at the Erwin Center (see above), UT's **baseball** team plays February through May at Disch-Falk Field (just east of I-35, at the corner of Martin Luther King Jr. Blvd. and Comal), while the school's nationally ranked **football** team (Football? In Texas? Who would've thought . . .) often fills the huge Darrell K. Royal/Texas Memorial Stadium (just west of I-35 between 23rd and 21st sts., E. Campus Dr., and San Jacinto Blvd.) during home games, played August through November. **UT Soccer** is played August through December on Friday or Sunday at the Mike A. Myers Stadium and Soccer Field, just northeast of the UT football stadium at Robert Dedman Drive and Mike Myers Drive.

The most comprehensive source of information on the various teams is **www. texassports.com**, but you can call the **UT Athletics Ticket Office** (☎ 512/471-3333) to find out about schedules and **UTTM Charge-A-Ticket** (☎ 512/477-6060) to order tickets.

1316 S. Congress Ave. (☎ **800/574-8897** or 512/444-7322; www.joscoffee.com; admission is free).

Try not to freak out when you see **1.5 million bats** ★ emerging from under the Congress Avenue Bridge on summer evenings. Austin has the largest urban bat population in North America, thanks to a deck reconstruction on the bridge in 1980 that made it the perfect baby-hatching environment for about 750,000 pregnant females migrating from central Mexico to various places in the Southwest each March. The mommies each give birth to a single pup, each of which goes bug-hunting at dusk in the summer. Get more info on the winged mammals at the kiosk on the north bank of the river, just east of the bridge, or call **Bat Conservation International** (☎ 512/327-9721; www.batcon.org). To find out when the bats are going to emerge from the bridge, call the *Austin American-Statesman* **Bat Hot Line** (☎ 512/416-5700, category 3636).

An early-21st-century addition to downtown's art scene, the **Arthouse at Jones Center** is home to, and the exhibition venue for, Arthouse (long known as Texas

Fine Arts Association), which has promoted visual art in Texas since 1911. Its venerable history notwithstanding, this place is completely cutting edge. Genres range from representational to performance art, and artists of all ethnicities are represented. Arthouse is at 700 Congress Ave. (☎ 512/453-5312; www.arthousetexas. org). Admission is free and it's open Tuesday, Wednesday, and Friday 11am to 7pm; Thursday 11am to 9pm; Saturday 10am to 5pm; Sunday 1 to 5pm.

HANGING OUT

FREE ➔ **Zilker Park** ★ Named after the German immigrant who donated the first 40 acres of the 347-acre space, Zilker Park is Austin's favorite public playground. Its centerpiece is Barton Springs Pool, but visitors and locals also flock to the Zilker Botanical Garden, the Austin Nature Preserves, and the Umlauf Sculpture Garden and Museum. In addition to its athletic fields (nine for soccer, one for rugby, and two multiuse), the park's got a 9-hole Frisbee golf course and a beach volleyball court. *2201 Barton Springs Rd.* ☎ *512/476-9044. www.ci.austin.tx.us/zilker. Free admission. Daily 5am–10pm.*

PLAYING OUTSIDE
Canoeing

Canoeing on Town Lake is a great way to spend an afternoon; rent canoes at Zilker Park for $10 an hour or $30 all day (☎ 512/478-3852; www.fastair.com/zilker; Sat, Sun, and holidays only, Oct–Mar). **Capital Cruises,** Hyatt Regency boat dock (☎ 512/480-9264; www.capitalcruises.com), also offers hourly rentals on Town Lake.

Swimming

The best known of Austin's natural swimming holes is **Barton Springs Pool** in Zilker Park, but you can also take the plunge at **Deep Eddy Pool** (401 Deep Eddy Ave., at Lake Austin Blvd.; ☎ 512/472-8546), and **Hippie Hollow** on Lake Travis, 2¹/₂ miles off FM 620 (www.co.travis.tx.us/tnr/parks/hippie_hollow.asp), where you can let it all hang out in a series of clothing-optional coves. Admission to Barton Springs and Deep Eddy pools is $3 for adults. Day permits to Hippie Hollow are $10 per vehicle per day, $5 per day for pedestrians and bicyclists.

SPECTATOR SPORTS
Horse Racing

Pick your ponies at **Manor Downs,** 8 miles east of I-35 on U.S. 290 East (☎ 512/272-5581; www.manordowns.com), Texas's oldest parimutuel horse racetrack. The track is open for live racing on Saturday and Sunday mid-February through May (general admission $2; main grandstand general seating $3; box seats or entrance to Turf Club restaurant/bar $5).

Other Pro Sports

There are no major league teams in Austin, but you can see the minor-league **Round Rock Express** baseball team at the Dell Diamond (3400 E. Palm Valley Rd. in Round Rock; ☎ 512/255-BALL or 244-4209; www.roundrockexpress.com), the **Austin Ice Bats** hockey team (☎ 512/927-PUCK; www.icebats.com) at Travis County Exposition Center (7311 Decker Lane, about 15 min. east of UT), and the **Austin Wranglers** arena football team (☎ 512/491-6600; www.austinwranglers.com) at the Erwin Center (just west of I-35 on Red River between Martin Luther King Jr. Blvd. and 15th St.).

On the Road to Hot Springs, AR

Austin, TX to Hot Springs, AR 489 miles

I'm not gonna lie: The first leg of this road-trip is *long*. And flat, dry East Texas leaves something to be desired in terms of scenery. If you're trying to get out of the state as fast as possible, just don't go too fast, because getting a speeding ticket in a place like Sulphur Springs could derail your whole schedule (p. 344). Make sure you've got a good sound system, and enjoy these tunes from some of Austin's finest during your drive. (*Note:* The band Boss Hogg is actually from New York, not Austin, but with a lyric like "I'm in Texas/I'm in pain," they just had to be included. Trust me, you'll relate after 6 hours on the road.)

East Texas Highlights

Interstate 35 takes you north past Waco and a random Czech enclave in the town of West (stop for a kolache; see below). Heading east from Dallas toward the Arkansas State Line, you'll drive through Fate, Texas (about 8 miles northeast of Dallas off I-30)—which makes a good photo-op if you're not into that whole free-will thing.

If you're not averse to taking your time, check out the **Puddin' Hill Store** in Greenville (about 23 miles northeast of Fate), where you can pick up Pecan Fruit

Austin to Hot Springs Playlist

→ *Lines in the Suit*, **Spoon**, "Girls Can Tell," 2001

→ *Speeding Motorcycle*, **Daniel Johnston**, "Yip/Jump Music," 1983

→ *Mamas Don't Let Your Babies Grow up to Be Cowboys*, **Willie Nelson**, "Waylon & Willie," 1978

→ *Your Eyes Are Liars*, **Sound Team**, "Movie Monster," 2006

→ *Mark David Chapman*, **. . . And You Will Know Us by the Trail of Dead**, "Madonna," 1999

→ *Magnificent Seventies*, **American Analog Set**, "From Our Living Room to Yours," 1997

→ *The Way*, **Fastball**, "All the Pain Money Can Buy," 1998

→ *My Favorite Record*, **Asylum Street Spankers**, "My Favorite Record," 2002

→ *Black Grease*, **Black Angels**, "Passover," 2006

→ *Texas*, **Boss Hog**, "Boss Hog," 1995

→ *Caliente*, **Supersuckers**, "The Smoke of Hell," 1992

→ *A Real Country Song*, **Dale Watson**, "Blessed or Damned," 1996

Cake from a recipe Mary and Sam Lauderdale crafted almost a half-century ago, or take a tour of the bakery and candy kitchen the in the fall. Hours are Monday through Saturday 10am to 5pm, and Sunday from 1 to 5pm. The store is located at 201 E. Interstate 30 at Exit 95/Division St. (☎ 800/545-8889; www.puddinhill.com).

In the border town of **Texarkana** (about 130 miles east of Greenville) you can check out the **Ace of Clubs House,** a 22-sided house built in the shape of a playing-card club. Legend has it James Draughon built the 1885 structure as an homage to the card that won him a huge pot in poker game. It's at 420 Pine St. (☎ 903/793-4831; www.texarkana museums.org/ace_of_clubs_house.htm).

The house is open Tuesday through Saturday for guided tours, from 10am to 4pm (the last tour starts at 3pm). Admission is $5 adults, $3.50 students.

With its vast lawns and clean bathrooms, the **Arkansas State Welcome Center** (2222 Interstate 30, Texarkana; ☎ 870/772-4301; open daily 8am–5pm, and until 6pm in the summer) is also a convenient place to stop and pick up some tourist pamphlets (during business hours) or just watch the sun go down, and eat some of your leftover Salt Lick barbecue. You'll also pass through Hope, AR (where Bill Clinton was born), before getting off the interstate and heading down Arkansas State Route 7 toward our next stop: Hot Springs.

On the Road Nuts & Bolts

Where to Fill Up   Anywhere in Texas, but I like the combination Chevron/Czech bakery just north of Waco (p. 343). Just make sure you've got a full tank before getting off the 30 in Arkansas: You've got about 20 miles of nothing but dark road ahead.

The Fastest Way I-35 to Dallas, I-20 to I-30 over the Arkansas state line to Arkadelphia, then AR-7 for about 20 miles into Hot Springs. This should take about 8 hours, depending on traffic.

The Long Way Round It'll take a lot longer, but if you take I-79 E out of Austin, you can check out **New Zion Missionary Baptist Church** in Huntsville and Davy Crockett National Forest; if you stay on the 79, you'll pass through Palestine and Jefferson and hook up with the 30 again around Texarkana. Austin to Huntsville is about 4 hours; Huntsville to Hot Springs is another 9 hours or so.

Rules of the Road Watch your speed through Hopkins County in Texas, where speeding tickets require an appearance before a judge!

Have a Seat According to www.dumblaws.com, it's illegal in Texas to have more than three sips of beer while standing up.

Picnic Point Arkansas State Welcome Center is a nice place for a rest/bathroom break; it's just across the Arkansas State Line off Interstate 30.

Welcome to Hot Springs

About an hour southwest of Little Rock, Hot Springs isn't exactly what leaps to mind when Yankees think of Arkansas. It's posh, quaint, picturesque—as far from backwoods as you can get. The resort town, which dates back to 1804, was built around the 47 natural hot springs of **Hot Springs National Park,** whose healing waters flow at several spas on downtown's Bathhouse Row. The town motto is "We Bathe the World." (Is it just me, or does that conjure a semi-creepy mental image?) Now a destination for outdoorsy types from the four-state area (that's Texas, Louisiana, Tennessee, and Arkansas), Spa City is also famous for being the childhood home of a sax player named Bill Clinton.

Getting Around

Hot Springs Village is a park-and-stroll kind of downtown, with restaurants, cafes, and shops lining the main drag, Central Avenue. Ditch the van at the free public lot on Exchange Street at Bath Street, 1 block

SOUTHERN BBQ ROADTRIP

Detour: Crazy for Kolaches

The heart of Texas seems like the unlikeliest place for a pocket of Eastern Europeans, but the town of West, just north of Waco (about 120 miles north of Austin on I-35), is home to some of the most authentic Czech cooking in the country. Skip the traditional roadtrip grub of chips and beef jerky and try a *kolache* instead at **Kaska's Czech Bakery** (215 S. George Kacir Dr. off Exit 351; ☎ **254/826-5908**). Kaska's looks like a regular gas station mini-mart on the outside (and does, in fact, sell gas) but inside the place stocks smoked sausage and kolaches, which are kind of like danishes. In Europe they traditionally come with a fruit or poppyseed filling, but in Texas they wrap pastry dough around anything from sausage and cheese to jalapeño peppers and call it a kolache (pronounced, in Texas anyway, like "ko-*LATCH*-ee"). You'll also find cottage cheese pies, pound cakes, and various things iced (oddly) with pineapple cream cheese. Does this mean Prague is the new Maui?

License & Registration, Ma'am

Don't get caught doing 87 mph in a 70 mph zone like I was through Sulphur Springs, Texas, where the polite but stern state trooper that pulled me over gave a hard look at my out-of-state driver's license and informed me that "Hopkins County's not like the state of California, where you can just sign off on a ticket. In Hopkins County you have to appear before a judge, and you will appear before a judge tonight." Yikes. When no judges were available to take my "case" that evening, the officer let me go with a citation and instructions to call the judge first thing in the morning, warning that if I didn't, the good state of Texas would suspend my driver's license. I might be $160 poorer now, but at least I got out of Texas.

west of Central. You will, however, need to drive to McClard's, the famed barbecue joint beloved by the likes of Bill Clinton and Aerosmith.

If It's Good Enough for Bill . . . Barbecue in Hot Springs

In Bill Clinton's home state, barbecue styles may vary from place to place, but you're still likely to see tomato-based sauces and beef brisket as you would in Texas, though sausage, turkey, and chicken are rarer finds in the pits. In fact, at McClard's, you won't even find a barbecue pit. You should definitely make a stop there, though!

➔ **McClard's Barbecue** ★★★ This is the main reason for a stop in Hot Springs. You won't find a pit—their pork shoulders, briskets, and ribs are smoking in a sweltering smokehouse out back, which the family finally had to rebuild from steel after it burned down for the third time. And while it's the traditional 'cue that earned McClard's a high profile nationally, locally their biggest seller is something called a **Hot Tamale Spread** ($8.50), a mountain made from two spicy beef tamales topped with Fritos, then a layer of beans, more beef, a sprinkling of onions, and a blanket of bright orange shredded cheese. With crackers on top. Sounds gnarly—is actually *really* good. Yeah, better pop a TUMS now. *505 Albert Pike Rd., Hot Springs, AR.* ☎ *501/624-9586. www.mcclards.com. Sandwiches $3–$6; plates $7–$9. Tues–Sat 11am–8pm. Cash only.*

Restaurants vs. Joints

There's a difference between a barbecue restaurant and a joint, Scott McClard (owner of McClard's Barbeque) explained. "A barbecue restaurant is tablecloths, hostess, all about the atmosphere," he says. "A barbecue joint you will almost drive by and not notice, except for the cars outside. It could be an old gas station, an old grocery store, or, in our case, a 60-year-old stucco building held up by 100 layers of paint. This is where the real food hangs out! Real cooks who care about serving real barbecue. It's food-driven, not atmosphere-driven."

It's the difference between a dive bar and a martini lounge; or the difference between your corner coffee shop and the multinational chain purveying high-priced coffee drinks.

Hot Springs Highlights

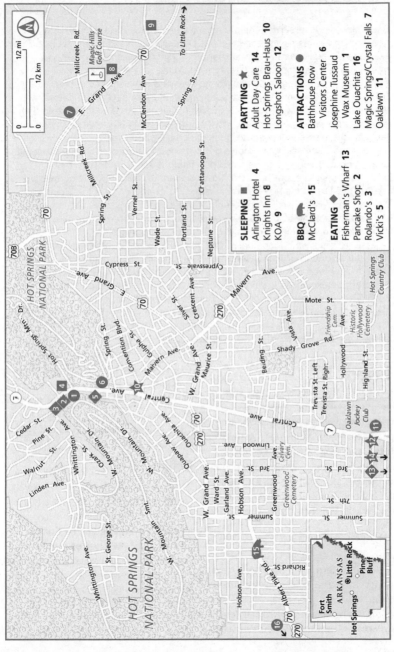

SLEEPING ■
Arlington Hotel **4**
Knights Inn **8**
KOA **9**

BBQ ■
McClard's **15**

EATING ◆
Fisherman's Wharf **13**
Pancake Shop **2**
Rolando's **3**
Vicki's **5**

PARTYING ★
Adult Day Care **14**
Hot Springs Brau-Haus **10**
Longshot Saloon **12**

ATTRACTIONS ●
Bathhouse Row
Visitors Center **6**
Josephine Tussaud
Wax Museum **1**
Lake Ouachita **16**
Magic Springs/Crystal Falls **7**
Oaklawn **11**

Five Minutes with Scott McClard

Scott McClard is a fourth-generation barbecue master and married father of two who knows his new music (he loves Bedouin Soundclash) and looks a little like Tony Hawk. He runs his great-grandpa's joint with his two uncles and various other family members that got roped into the family biz.

McClard's sauce recipe comes from a wayward traveler unable to pay the $10 tab for his 2-month-long stay at the Westside Tourist Court, a diner/hotel owned by the elder McClard in the 1920s. In lieu of cash, the drifter offered this sauce recipe, which is still in use today, and, according to the label on the bottle, stored in a safety deposit box in downtown Hot Springs.

When the Depression hit, Scott's great-granddad started making barbecued goat—about the only meat he could get during those hard times. They don't serve goat anymore, but McClard's does sell about 3,000 pounds of meat per week. They fire up the hickory smokers every day at 3am, and the beans and slaw are made by hand every morning. The tamales used in the hot tamale spread are hand-rolled by a dedicated woman in her 60s, who guesses she's rolled close to a million of 'em in her 35 years at McClard's.

McClard's is a well-documented favorite of President Clinton (who once sat down for an interview with Dan Rather inside the tiny joint), and Scott says he's filled up Air Force One with barbecue more times than he can count. But it was almost more exciting boarding Aerosmith's tour bus when the band had McClard's cater a recent show. "Joe Perry's really into barbecue," Scott says. "He's got his own sauce and a few smokers. But they were just drinking soda in the bus," he says with a hint of disappointment. "There weren't any girls or anything. They just wanted to talk about barbecue."

Sleeping

Since Hot Springs is a resort town, much of the lodging you'll find in the village consists of fancy hotels with a bathhouse or spa attached; the historic **Arlington Hotel and Spa** ★★ (239 Central Ave.; ☎ 800/643-1502; www.arlingtonhotel.com; singles $78, doubles $94), with its natural hot pool, backyard trail access to the park, and luxe rooms, is well worth the price.

Cheaper accommodations are available just outside of the historic downtown at the **Knight's Inn** off the 70 near Magic Springs (1871 East Grand Ave.; ☎ 501/624-4436; www.knightsinn.com; rooms from $53). If you're camping, pitch your tent at **Hot Springs National Park** for $10 a day.

There's also a **KOA** 2 miles from downtown with tent sites and cabins (838 McClendon Rd.; ☎ 800/562-5903 or 501/624-5912; www.hotspringskoa.com; tent sites $26 per night double occupancy; cabins $50 per night double occupancy).

Eating

Who knew soy milk was big in Arkansas? For better-than-Starbucks java and possibly the best cinnamon roll in the south, try 📺 Best❤ **Vicki's Coffee Corner** (406 Central Ave.; ☎ 501/624-2939; Sun–Thurs 9am–6pm, Fri–Sat 9am–9:30pm).

The limited menu at the **Pancake Shop** ★★ (216 Central Ave.; ☎ 501/624-5720; www.pancakeshop.com; $2–$6; daily until 12:45pm) doesn't keep people from forming lines out the door for a taste of its legendary hams, sausage, and flapjacks. For a non-pork related dinner, try the *chivo* (that's goat) quesadillas or the Popeye (spinach) burrito at **Rolando's Nuevo Latino Restaurante** (210 Central Ave.; ☎ **501/318-6054;** www.rolandos restaurante.com; entrees $12–$18; daily 11am–close) or the lakeside steak/seafood spot **Fisherman's Wharf** (5101 Central Ave.; ☎ **501/525-7437;** Sun–Thurs 11am–9pm, Fri–Sat 11am–10pm).

Partying

There's not a lot going on here, but you can definitely find a good time in Hot Springs. I liked the [MTV Best] **Adult Day Care Hideaway** ★★ (State Rte. 7 about 5 miles south of downtown Hot Springs), and not just for the bar's priceless name. You expect it to be one of those places where the jukebox screeches silent when you walk in and a gruff-looking guy at the end of the bar says, "We don't take kindly to strangers 'round here." But it's just a chill dive with cheap beer, a pool table, and a static-y karaoke machine that's occasionally fired up by a boozed-up regular.

The bartender at Adult Day Care tipped me off to **Longshot Saloon** (2720 Central Ave.; ☎ **501/624-4344;** www.longshot saloon.net; daily 8am–5am), a biker bar across the street from the racetrack that opens at 8am for karaoke, dancing, and rib-eye steaks and the fun doesn't stop almost till the sun comes up. If you stop there, you gotta sign your name on the ceiling—it's tradition.

If you like a little goulash with your Grolsch, check out **Hot Springs Brau-Haus** (801 Central Ave.; ☎ **501/624-7866**), which has claims to have the biggest selection of German beers in Arkansas, plus Czech, Dutch, and Belgian brews.

What Else to See & Do

Hot Springs is a great place to get some much-needed exercise after all that time in the car. Take a hike, rent a jet ski for a day on the lake (see below), or treat yourself to a mineral bath and massage at one of the town's famous bathhouses.

Try a private 20-minute soak in a 100°F thermal mineral bath at one of several spas on **Bathhouse Row.** The bath is generally followed by hot-pack application and massage, plus a facial or any other services you care to order—at least one place even offers Brazilian waxes (in Arkansas!). Big hotels like the Arlington and Majestic also offer bath services. Visit **www.hotsprings.org** for info.

WAXING HISTORICAL

→ **Josephine Tussaud Wax Museum** This downtown attraction (which is not connected to the London or New York Madame Tussauds, who apparently did not have an Arkansas cousin) features "wax" celebrities, politicians—even a re-creation of "The Last Supper," plus tributes to 9/11 firefighters and Princess Di. *250 Central Ave.* ☎ *501/623-5836. www.rideaduck.com/wax museum/index2.html. Admission $9. Summer hours: Sun–Thurs 9am–8pm; Fri–Sat 9am–9pm. Winter hours: Sun–Thurs 9:30am–5pm; Fri–Sat 9:30am–8pm.*

PLAYING OUTSIDE

Take a hike along the 26 miles of trails in **Hot Springs National Park** ★★★ to get scenic views of the Ouachita Mountains. You can also drive through the park—but, let's be honest, you could use the cardio, barbecue fiend. No mountain bikes are allowed in the park. Stop by the Visitors' Center (open 9am–5pm daily) at 369 Central Ave. or call ☎ **501/624-2701** for more information.

SOUTHERN BBQ ROADTRIP

Running of the Tubs (and Other Events)

→ Named after the late local businessman who thought it'd be funny to put bathtubs on wheels and race them down the village's main drag, the **Stueart Pennington Running of the Tubs** takes place in May, with awards for funniest and most original tub (☎ 501/321-2277).

→ Hailed by the *New York Times* and *USA Today*, the **Hot Springs Music Festival** is a 14-day celebration of all things classical held every June (**www.hotmusic.org**).

→ The 2-day **Hot Springs Blues Festival** features local and out-of-town talent and an annual club crawl every September (**www.spacityblues.com**).

→ **Hot Springs Documentary Film Festival** is held for 10 days in October, showcasing dozens of short and feature-length docs (☎ 501/321-4747; www.hsdfi.org).

→ **Spa-Rib Cook-Off:** Held in downtown Hot Springs in July, this cook-off features barbecue competitions in two categories: meat and sauce. Tickets cost $5, and ticket holders get to taste the competition ribs after the judging's been completed (☎ 501/525-2261).

→ In 2005 the **Hot Springs Jazz Festival** (**www.hotspringsjazzfest.org**) debuted its Exotic Barbecue competition, featuring anything you can imagine that's not pork, beef, and chicken: gator, goat, venison, squirrel, emu, eggplant—you name it. Admission is free; pulled pork sandwiches are not.

The EPA says **Lake Ouachita** is one of the cleanest lakes in the U.S. Less than an hour west of Hot Springs in the protected, undeveloped hills of the Ouachita National Forest, the lake has more than 1,000 miles of shoreline and hundreds of islands to explore. Divers will find tons of sea life like jellyfish and sponges, and the fishing's good here, too. Rent a WaveRunner at **Tiny's Water Toys** at Mountain Harbor Resort on the south side of the lake (10 miles east off the town of Mount Ida on Hwy. 270; ☎ 870/867-1296). Jet skis rent for $120–$150/hour and inner tubes are $35/day. (Pricey!)

The Lake Ouachita State Park Visitors Center is on the north side of the lake; to get there, take 270 west for 13 miles, then 227 north for 12 miles to arrive at 5451 Mountain Pine Rd. in Mountain Pine. Call ☎ 501/767-9366 for info. There's no fee to enter the park, and it's $10 a night for camping.

Open daily in the summer and on weekends during shoulder season, **Magic Springs Amusement Park** (1701 E. Grand Ave.; ☎ 501/318-5370; www.magicsprings. com) has dozens of rides like the Arkansas Twister, while sister property **Crystal Falls Water Park** is home to a wave pool and water slides. The admission fee in 2006 was $36 for adults, and $6 for parking.

People have been betting the ponies at **Oaklawn Racetrack** (2705 Central Ave.; ☎ 800/OAKLAWN; www.oaklawn.com) for more than 100 years; you can, too, during racing season, which runs from January to April. Admission is free during "simulcast" season (when races from other parts of the country are broadcast); and $2 for general admission during the live racing season.

On the Road to Memphis, TN

Hot Springs, AR to Memphis, TN 188 miles

This next leg is quick and easy; leaving Hot Springs on I-70 heading east, you'll see the roller coasters of Magic Springs; after about 7 miles you get on I-30 East, which takes you through Little Rock, where you'll see a lot of signs for Bill Clinton this and Bill Clinton that. If you're still hungry, you might stop at Little Rock's **Whole Hog Café** (2516 Cantrell Rd. off I-30 Exit 141A; ☏ **501/664-5025**), which has won a bundle of contest trophies. You'll cross the Arkansas River, but otherwise there's not a tremendous amount of scenery. Unless you count the waffle houses that spring up every 5 feet and the giant XXX Superstore along I-40 E outside of Little Rock.

Continue on I-40 East for about 125 miles. Memphis sits right on the border of three states, so it's a little unclear when you're actually crossing into Tennessee. Complicating matters is West Memphis, which is actually its own city in Arkansas. Soon after passing West Memphis, you'll see the stately skyline of the *actual* Memphis while crossing a bridge over the Mississippi River, which is how you'll know you've arrived in M-Town (exit Riverside Dr. to get to the heart of downtown).

Welcome to Memphis, TN

Ah, Memphis: birthplace of the blues, home of rock 'n' roll, pork capital of the world. Situated on the east bank of the Mississippi River, just north of the Mississippi state line, Memphis is rich in civil rights and music history. This is a city you'll want to spend at least a little extra time in, especially if you like live blues. There are sights to see and ribs to eat, so what are you waiting for?

Memphis Playlist: Birthplace of the Blues

→ *3 O'Clock Blues*, **BB King**, "Singin' the Blues," 1991

→ *Heartbreak Hotel*, **Elvis Presley**, "Elvis Presley," 1956

→ *Memphis in June*, **Hoagy Carmichael**, "Hoagy Sings Carmichael," 1956

→ *(Sittin' on) The Dock of the Bay*, **Otis Redding**, "The Dock of the Bay," 1968

→ *In the Street*, **Big Star**, "#1 Record/Radio City," 1972

→ *It's Your Thing*, **Booker T and the MGs**, "The Booker T. Set," 1969

→ *Ninety Miles Away*, **Arthur Lee and Love**, "Once More Again," 1996

→ *Eight Days on the Road*, **Aretha Franklin**, "Let Me in Your Life," 1974

→ *It's Hard Out Here for a Pimp*, **Three Six Mafia**, "Hustle & Flow Soundtrack," 2005

→ *Señorita*, **Justin Timberlake**, "Justified," 2002

SOUTHERN BBQ ROADTRIP

Memphis **Nuts & Bolts**

Area Code The telephone area code in Memphis is 901.

Business Hours Banks are generally open Monday to Thursday 8:30am to 4pm, with later hours on Friday. In general, stores downtown are open Monday to Saturday 10am to 5:30pm. Bars are allowed to stay open until 3am, but may close between 1 and 3am.

Doctors If you should find yourself in need of a doctor, call the referral service at **Baptist Memorial Hospital** (☎ 901/227-8428) or **Methodist/LeBonheur Healthcare** (☎ 901/726-8686).

Emergencies For police, fire, or medical emergencies, phone ☎ **911.**

Hospitals The **Baptist Memorial Hospital Medical Center** is at 899 Madison Ave. (☎ 901/227-2727), with another location in East Memphis at 6019 Walnut Grove Rd. (☎ 901/226-5000).

Libraries An impressive new main branch of the **Memphis/Shelby County Public Library** is at 3030 Poplar Ave. Midtown and East Memphis. Elsewhere around town, there are more than 20 other branches (☎ 901/415-2700).

Liquor Laws The legal drinking age in Tennessee is 21. Bars are allowed to stay open until 3am every day. Beer can be purchased at a convenience, grocery, or package store, but wine and liquor are sold through package stores only.

Newspapers & Magazines The *Commercial Appeal* is Memphis's daily and Sunday newspaper. The arts-and-entertainment weekly is the *Memphis Flyer,* and the monthly city magazine is *Memphis Magazine.*

Pharmacies (late-night) There are about 60 **Walgreens Pharmacies** in the Memphis area (☎ 800/925-4733 for the Walgreens nearest you). Several have 24-hour prescription service, including the one at 1863 Union Ave. (☎ 901/272-1141 or 901/272-2006).

Police For police emergencies, phone ☎ **911.**

Post Office The main post office is at 555 S. Third St., and there's a branch in East Memphis at 5821 Park Ave. in the White Station area (☎ 800/275-8777).

Radio Memphis has more than 30 radio stations broadcasting country, gospel, rhythm and blues, and jazz. WEVL at 89.9 FM plays everything from alt-rock to Cajun; NPR talk can be heard on 88.9 FM, and NPR classical on 91.1 FM.

Taxes The state sales tax is 9.25%. An additional room tax of 6.7% on top of the state sales tax brings the total hotel-room tax to a whopping 15.95%.

Time Zone Tennessee is on Central Standard Time (CST) or Central Daylight Time, depending on the time of year—making it 2 hours ahead of the West Coast and 1 hour behind the East Coast.

Transit Info Call ☎ 901/274-MATA for the MATA bus system route and schedule information. Call ☎ 901/577-2640 for information on the Main Street Trolley.

Weather For weather information, phone ☎ 901/522-8888.

Memphis Highlights

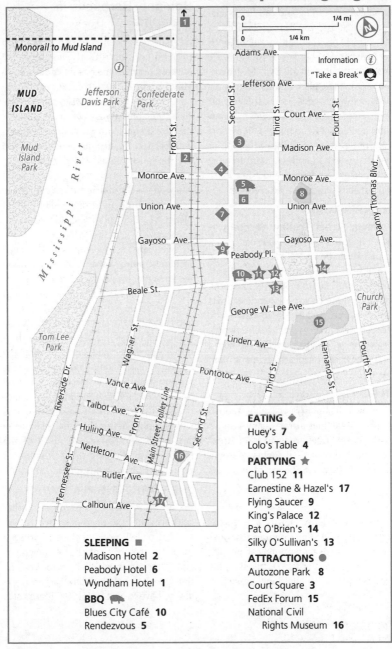

Monorail to Mud Island

MUD ISLAND

Jefferson Davis Park

Confederate Park

Mud Island Park

Mississippi River

Tom Lee Park

Adams Ave.

Jefferson Ave.

Court Ave.

Madison Ave.

Monroe Ave.

Union Ave.

Gayoso Ave.

Peabody Pl.

Beale St.

George W. Lee Ave.

Church Park

Linden Ave

Puntotoc Ave.

Vance Ave.

Talbot Ave.

Huling Ave.

Nettleton Ave.

Butler Ave.

Calhoun Ave.

Front St.

Second St.

Third St.

Fourth St.

Danny Thomas Blvd.

Hernando St.

Fourth St.

Riverside Dr.

Wagner St.

Front St.

Main Street Trolley Line

Second St.

Third St.

Tennessee St.

0   1/4 mi
0   1/4 km

Information ⓘ
"Take a Break" ☕

EATING ◆
Huey's **7**
Lolo's Table **4**

PARTYING ★
Club 152 **11**
Earnestine & Hazel's **17**
Flying Saucer **9**
King's Palace **12**
Pat O'Brien's **14**
Silky O'Sullivan's **13**

ATTRACTIONS ●
Autozone Park **8**
Court Square **3**
FedEx Forum **15**
National Civil
    Rights Museum **16**

SLEEPING ■
Madison Hotel **2**
Peabody Hotel **6**
Wyndham Hotel **1**

BBQ 🐖
Blues City Café **10**
Rendezvous **5**

Getting Around

Memphis is sprawling and can be confusing to navigate, so you'll probably be doing a lot of driving. The main neighborhoods are **Downtown,** home to historic Beale Street entertainment district, **Midtown,** whose Overton Square and Cooper-Young nabes are pretty cool, and East Memphis, which straddles the I-240 and has new malls and lots of shopping. For a short stay, your best bet is to find a hotel in or near the neighborhood you want to hang out it and get ready to spend a few extra bucks cabbing around in the evenings.

BY STREETCAR

The **Main Street Trolley** (☎ 901/577-2640) operates 1920s trolley cars on a circular route down Main Street from the Pyramid to the National Civil Rights Museum and Central Station, past the Tennessee State Visitors Center. The fare is $1 each way, with a lunch-hour rate of 60¢ between 11am and 1:30pm. An all-day pass is $3.50; exact change is required. Board the trolley at any of 20 stations along Main Street.

ON FOOT

Downtown Memphis is walkable, though the only areas that attract many visitors are the Beale Street area and Main Street from the National Civil Rights Museum north to the Pyramid. The rest of the city is not walkable.

BY TAXI

Try **Checker/Yellow Cab** (☎ 901/577-7777) or **City Wide Cab Company** (☎ 901/324-4202), or have your hotel call one for you. The first mile is $2.30; after that, it's $1.60 per mile. Each additional passenger is 50¢ extra.

Dry vs. Wet, Nachos vs. Bologna: Barbecue in Memphis

Memphis has been considered *the* go-to town for pork, particularly ribs and pulled pork shoulder, ever since the **Memphis In May** (p. 354) cooking contest put the city on the map, barbecue-wise, back in the '70s. Memphis-style 'cue differentiates itself by serving both wet ribs (meat basted with barbecue sauce during cooking) and dry-rub (meat rubbed with dry seasonings during or just after cooking), and while you won't see as much chicken or sausage here as you do in Texas, you'll still get plenty of beans, potato salad, and sweet coleslaw.

There are more than 100 barbecue restaurants in town, and competition between them is fierce. The bar is set *very* high and Memphians are discerning about their barbecue, so the food can't just be good, it's got to be creative, too. That's why you'll find things like barbecue pizza, barbecue spaghetti, and barbecue bologna on some local menus, while the barbecue nachos from Neely's purportedly outsell hot dogs at the FedEx Forum. At the end of the day, the worst barbecue in Memphis is still probably better than the best barbecue you'll have anywhere north of the Mason-Dixon. Prepare those arteries; it's gonna be a tasty, cholesterol-laden ride.

TOP BARBECUE IN MEMPHIS

➜ **Corky's** ★ The enticing aroma of barbecue permeates the air at this place, known for its pulled pork shoulder barbecue topped with tangy coleslaw. Photographs and letters from satisfied customers line the rough-paneled lobby, where you always have to wait for a table. There's also a drive-up window for immediate barbecue gratification. The downtown location is right around the corner from Beale Street. *175 Peabody Place* ☎ *901/529-9191. www.corkys bbq.com. Main courses $3–$20. Sun–Thurs 10:45am–9:30pm; Fri–Sat 10:45am–10pm.*

➜ **Cozy Corner** ★★ This Midtown 'cue shop is just what it sounds like. From the counter you can see the kitchen at work, while photos of celebrity patrons like Robert Duvall line the wall in the rear dining room. Ribs and fried bologna are the specialty, but you can also get stuff like Cornish game hen and barbecue spaghetti. *745 N. Parkway.* ☎ *901/527-9158. Sandwiches $5; plates $6–$10. Tues–Sat 10:30am–5pm.*

Five Minutes with Patrick Neely

....

I'd heard about **Neely's Bar-B-Que** (see above) from several states away, so at dinnertime I was a little surprised to drive up to a building that looked from the outside like a Denny's; the inside wasn't much to write home about either: '70s-style decor, Naugahyde booths, wood paneling, and lighting reminiscent of a pizza parlor. Plus, there was hardly anyone there. *This* is supposedly one of the best barbecue places in the country?

Talking to Patrick, the owner, I quickly learned that, in Memphis anyway, lunch is prime barbecue time, which explained the relative emptiness of the place. And after sampling one of Neely's ultra-tender dry ribs—probably the best I had on this trip—I was sold. It might employ a hostess and it might not be housed in a dilapidated, 100-year-old building, but Neely's, in spirit, is a *joint*—a place where food rules.

A spinoff of his uncle Jim's Interstate BBQ across town, Neely's started out of then-23-year-old Patrick's desire to support his mother after his dad died. With some money borrowed from grandma and a steadfast belief in barbecue, Neely's was born. Eighteen years later, it's still here, with devotees both local and from out of town (Al Roker, Jay Leno, and Dennis Quaid are all fans).

In custom-designed smokers in back, pork shoulders cook quietly all night long at 250°F. The kitchen whips up wet and dry ribs, brisket, turkey, pulled pork, and the traditional sides (potato salad, rolls, pork and beans, and sweet slaw) plus an excellent sweet tea. But, to stay ahead in the competitive Memphis 'cue scene, Neely's innovates with dishes like barbecue nachos (chips topped with pork shoulder, barbecue sauce, and cheese), barbecue spaghetti (pasta with barbecue sauce instead of tomato paste and pork shoulder in lieu of meatballs), and spuds (a baked potato piled high with pulled pork, cheese, and the usual baked potato fixins). Patrick, who opened a Neely's outpost in the FedEx Forum, claims the barbecue nachos outsell hot dogs at sporting events.

Before I leave, Patrick (who's also a judge in the Memphis in May cooking contest) demonstrates pork-rib perfection with a slab that rests on a nearby counter. Grabbing a single bone from the middle of the slab, he barely gives it the slightest twist and the bone pulls free with not a shred of meat attached. "Now *that's* a done rib," he says.

Amen!

SOUTHERN BBQ ROADTRIP

MTV **Best ♦** ➜ **Neely's Bar-B-Que ★★★**
In addition to the regular barbecue fare, Neely's (a spin-off of Jim Neely's Interstate Barbecue across town) also serves barbecued spaghetti, barbecue nachos, and barbecued bologna. There's also a barbecue salad for figure-conscious diners. (See "Five Minutes with Patrick Neely," above, for more on Neely's.) *670 Jefferson Ave. in Downtown.* ☎ *901/521-9798. www.neelysbbq. com. Sandwiches $3–$6; platters $8–$17. Mon–Thurs 10:30am–8pm; Fri–Sat 10:30am–10pm; Sun 11–7pm. Also at 5700 Mt. Moriah Rd. in East Memphis;* ☎ *901/795-4177.*

➜ **The Rendezvous Restaurant ★★** A downtown institution since 1948, the Rendezvous is probably the most famous place in town. Known for its ribs, this huge, cozy cellar across from the Peabody Hotel is decorated with strange objects and has a large bar upstairs. Be sure to ask if they still have any of the red beans and rice that are served nightly until the pot is empty. *52 S. Second St.* ☎ *901/523-2746. www.hogsfly. com. Main plates $6.50–$17. Tues–Thurs 4:30–10:30pm; Fri 11:30am–11pm; Sat noon–11pm.*

Also Recommended . . .

Other joints to try if you're near Memphis's main attractions include **Blues City Café** (138 Beale St.; ☎ **901/526-3637**), which makes a mean tamale and claims to serve Beale Street's best ribs. There are a bunch of joints near Graceland, which is in one of the city's poorer neighborhoods: Try **Interstate Barbecue Restaurant** (2265 S. Third St.; ☎ **901/775-2304**); and **A&R Bar-B-Q** (1802 Elvis Presley Blvd.; ☎ **901/774-7444**), which is popular for its barbecued pizza and killer ribs.

Sleeping

Memphis, like any other urban center, has higher lodging costs than a small town off the Interstate, so plan accordingly. Hostels are hard to come by but luxury hotels are

The Super Bowl of Swine: Memphis in May

"It's the Super Bowl of Swine. The College of Pig Knowledge. The Granddaddy of Grills. The Largest Pork Barbecue Cooking Contest on the Planet." But you can call it "Memphis in May." This monthlong event includes the Beale Street Music Festival, International lectures, and classical music, but the biggest attraction, for our purposes anyway, is the **World Championship Barbecue Cooking Contest,** 3 smoky, pork-filled days drawing close to 100,000 people from all over the world to downtown's Tom Lee Park. The barbecue contest is held over a weekend in mid-May (☎ **901/525-4611; memphisinmay.org**).

not; check below for a few in-between options.

CAMPGROUNDS

Memphis has no centrally located campgrounds, but you can camp at the **Memphis-Graceland RV Park and Campground.** Within walking distance of Graceland, the park has free Wi-Fi and a pool, and it welcomes pets as long as you keep 'em on a leash. It's at 3691 Elvis Presley Blvd. (☎ **866/571-9236** or 901/396-7125; memphisgracelandrvpark.com). Tent sites run from $21 to $95 (double occupancy); and there are cabins available for $40 a night (double occupancy).

CHEAP

Chain motels in Memphis include the **Hampton Inn Medical Center/Midtown,** 1180 Union Ave. (☎ **901/276-1175**), charging around $89 for a double; **Red Roof Inn,** 42 S. Camilla St. (☎ **901/526-1050**), charging about $49 for a double; and **Motel 6,** 210 S. Pauline St. (☎ **901/528-0650**), which charges around $54 for a double with Wi-Fi in the lobby and on the second floor.

DOABLE

➔ **French Quarter Suites Hotel** ★ Its perch in the heart of Overton Square used to be a big plus, but just as this fledgling Midtown entertainment district has been upstaged by a newly revitalized Downtown, so have the few hotels here. Though this building looks charming enough with its French Quarter–style courtyards and balconies, the guest rooms and public areas suggest that the hotel has not been as well maintained as others in town. On the plus side, all bathtubs have Jacuzzis. *2144 Madison Ave.* ☎ *800/843-0353 or 901/ 728-4000. www.memphisfrenchquarter.com. $109–$119 double. Amenities: Outdoor pool; exercise room; limited room service; laundry service; complimentary airport shuttle. In room: Dataport, wet bar.*

➔ **Wyndham Gardens Hotel** This property offers a lush garden setting and interior touches including plantation shutters and marble floors; plus, the lobby is wireless. The Wyndham's popular with conventioneers thanks to its location near the convention center, and because it's a bit far from the action of Beale Street, this isn't your best bet. *300 N. Second St.* ☎ *901/ 525-1800. www.wyndham.com. $99–$129 single or double. Self-parking $5. Amenities: Restaurant; outdoor pool; exercise room; limited room service; dry cleaning. In room: Fax, dataport w/high-speed Internet access.*

SPLURGE

➔ **Madison Hotel** ★★ Built on the site of a former bank building, the Madison's historical outside is met with bold, modern furnishings inside. From the elegant lobby, with its grand piano and musical instrument motif, to the rich, solid colors in the guest rooms, the Madison is a contrast between classic and modern. Whirlpool baths or jet tubs are available in lots of the rooms. Nightly turndown and twice-daily housekeeping service keep guests feeling pampered. Take the elevator to the outdoor rooftop for breathtaking views of the Mississippi River and surrounding downtown. Every Thursday evening from April through mid-October, the hotel hosts sunset parties here, featuring live jazz. *79 Madison Ave.* ☎ *866/44-MEMPHIS or 901/333-1200. www.madisonhotel memphis.com. $220–$260 double; $330 and up for suite. Valet parking $15 (unlimited access). Amenities: Restaurant/lounge; indoor pool; fitness center; concierge; 24-hr. room service; lobby library. In room: Dataport w/high-speed Internet access, minibar, safe, CD player.*

➔ **The Peabody Memphis** ★★ For years, The Peabody enjoyed a reputation as one of the finest hotels in the South—a reputation it maintains since being totally renovated in 2004. Marble columns, gilded mezzanine railings, hand-carved and burnished woodwork, and ornate gilded plasterwork on the ceiling give the lobby the air of a palace. Its dominant feature is its Romanesque marble fountain, where the famous Peabody ducks hang out. The hotel's French-inspired bistro, **Chez Philippe,** has long been the best restaurant in Memphis, and its lobby-level Italian restaurant Capriccio is also well regarded. The entire hotel offers Wi-Fi. *149 Union Ave.* ☎ *800/PEABODY or 901/529-4000. www.peabodymemphis.com. $210–$345 double; $380 and up for suite. Valet parking $17; self-parking $12. Amenities: 2 restaurants; 2 lounges; gym; pool; steam room; sauna; concierge; 24-hr. room service; massage; valet/laundry service; shoe-shine stand. In room: Wi-Fi.*

QUACK! QUACK! Here Come the Peabody Ducks

It isn't often that you find live ducks in the lobby of a luxury hotel. However, ducks are a fixture at the elegant Peabody Memphis. Each morning at 11am, the ducks, led by a duck-master, take the elevator down from their penthouse home, waddle across a red carpet, and hop into the hotel's Romanesque travertine-marble fountain. Each evening at 5pm they waddle back down the red carpet and take the elevator back up to the penthouse. During their entry and exit, the ducks waddle to John Philip Sousa tunes and attract large crowds of curious onlookers.

The Peabody ducks took up residence in the lobby in the 1930s when Frank Schutt, the hotel's manager, and friend Chip Barwick, after one too many swigs of Tennessee sippin' whiskey, put some of his live duck decoys in the hotel's fountain as a joke (such live decoys were legal at the time). Guests thought the ducks were a delightfully offbeat touch and they have become a beloved fixture at the hotel.

Eating

TAKE-OUT TREATS

At the edge of the Cooper-Young neighborhood, you can quaff a cup o' joe and listen to live music or poetry at hippie haven **Otherlands** ★★, 641 S. Cooper St. (☎ 901/278-4994). A few blocks away is another little dive called **Java Cabana,** 2170 Young Ave. (☎ 901/272-7210).

For yummy stuff like meat-and-cheese sandwiches on grilled focaccia, head for **Fratelli's in the Garden,** 750 Cherry Rd. (☎ 901/685-1566, ext. 118). Relocated from Downtown to the Memphis Botanic Garden, the market and deli offers tiramisu for dessert, and take-home gourmet pastas, olive oils, cheeses, and imported beers.

RESTAURANTS

Cheap

➜ **Huey's** ★ AMERICAN Ask Memphians where to get the best burger in town, and you'll invariably be directed to Huey's. This funky tavern is open late and also has one of the best beer selections in town. The original Huey's, 1927 Madison Ave.

(☎ 901/726-4372), in Overton Square, is still in business as well. 77 S. Second St. ☎ 901/527-2700. www.hueys.cc. Reservations not accepted. Main courses $5–$10. Daily 11am–2am.

➜ **On Teur** CAJUN This funky little restaurant on a seedy block near Overton Square serves Cajun home cooking as satisfying as it is affordable. Try the Big Easy "samich" made with homemade New Orleans chaurice sausage, onions, and spicy voodoo mustard on a hoagie, or the spicy shrimp N'awlins in a Cajun sauce. You can bring your own wine or liquor for a small corkage fee, but you can't buy it here. The room can be pretty smoky, so take note if you're not down with the secondhand smoke action. 2015 Madison Ave. ☎ 901/725-6059. Main courses $9–$15. Tues–Sun 11am–2pm; Tues–Sat 5–10:30pm.

➜ **Patrick's** ★ SOUTHERN Patrick's is the reincarnation of the old Buntyn, a local favorite since the 1930s. Everyone comes for the good, old-fashioned home-cookin': corn muffins and homemade, Southern-style biscuits appear on your table as soon as you sit down, while entrees include calves' liver smothered in onions, fried chicken, meatloaf, catfish steak, or maybe chicken and dumplings—and the portions are Southern-style, too. Don't be shy about asking for that doggie bag. *Park Ave. at Mt. Moriah.* ☎ *901/682-2852. Main courses $4–$13. Daily 11am–10pm.*

Doable

➔**Beauty Shop** ★★ NEW AMERICAN The Beauty Bar chain of hipster hangouts purportedly threatened to sue this Cooper-Young bar/eatery, which maintains that it developed its retro beauty shop gimmick independently. Housed in an actual 1960s-era beauty shop and brought to you by the same folks behind Memphis hotspots Automatic Slim's and Cielo, this place seats you for dinner at refurbished hair-dryer chairs and serves innovative global cuisine (try the Thai cobb or the sugarcane tuna with grits). *966 S. Cooper St.* ☎ *901/272-7111. Reservations recommended. Main courses $14–$24. Mon–Fri 11am–3pm; brunch Sat 10am–2pm, Sun 10am–3pm; dinner Mon–Thurs 5–10pm; Fri–Sat 5–11pm.*

➔**Lo Lo's Table** ★ CONTINENTAL Don't be intimidated by this trendy downtown restaurant's focus on "Low Country

Elvis Week & More: Events in Memphis

Here's an intro to some of the city's music festivals and other noteworthy annual events:

→ Held annually around January 8, **Elvis Birthday Week** is an international gathering of Presley fans who come to Graceland to celebrate the birth of "The King." And in the second week in August there's **Elvis Tribute Week,** held at Graceland and citywide (☎ 800/238-2000).

→ The 2-day **Beale St. Zydeco Festival** features more than 20 acts performing downtown in mid-February (☎ 901/529-0999).

→ **International Film Festival** hits Midtown Memphis the second week in April (☎ 901/273-0014).

→ **Carnival Memphis,** held in June, is a citywide celebration drawing almost half a million people with exhibits, music, crafts, and events (☎ 901/278-0243).

→ **Cooper Young Festival** has arts, crafts, food, and other fun stuff in mid-September (☎ 901/276-7222).

→ Held in Midtown each September, the **Southern Heritage Classic** pits college football rivals against each other at Liberty Bowl Stadium (☎ 901/398-6655).

→ If county fairs are your thing, the **Mid-South Fair,** held at the end of September, is 10 days of rides, food, games, shows, a midway, and a rodeo (☎ 901/274-8800).

→ In November the **International Blues Competition** brings musicians from around the country for performances at various venues, the W. C. Handy Awards, and post-show jam. For more information, call the Blues Foundation at ☎ 901/527-BLUE.

SOUTHERN BBQ ROADTRIP

European cuisine." You can get a juicy cheeseburger and Bud Light here along with more esoteric specialties like Moroccan barbecued salmon or the classic French coq au vin. Try the chocolate torte or tiramisu for dessert. *128 Monroe Ave.* ☎ *901/522-9449. Main courses $15–$22. Mon–Fri 11am–2:30pm; Mon–Thurs 5:30–10pm; Fri–Sat 5:30–11pm.*

Splurge

➔ **Tsunami** ★★ PACIFIC RIM/SEAFOOD Consistently ranked one of the best restaurants in Memphis, Tsunami's Pacific Rim cuisine includes apps like pot sticker dumplings with chile-soy dipping sauce and entrees like wasabi-crusted tuna, duck breast with miso-shiitake risotto, or roasted sea bass with black Thai rice and soy *beurre blanc.* Crème brûlée fans should not miss Smith's sublime Tahitian-vanilla version of this classic. *928 S. Cooper St.* ☎ *901/274-2556. www.tsunamimemphis. com. Reservations recommended. Main courses $18–$28. Mon–Sat 5:30–10pm.*

Partying

For the full-on Memphis tourist experience, you gotta go down to **Beale Street,** where you can walk up to any bar, buy a drink, and carry it right down the street to the next bar, often even into the next bar. Someone will probably try to sell you a $12 wristband that gets you access to 12 clubs *sans* cover—it's probably not worth it unless you're really planning on hitting all 12 clubs, since many Beale St. joints like Coyote Ugly don't accept the wristband, so you'll have to pay an additional cover. If tourism's not your scene, cruise up to **Overton Square** or **Cooper-Young,** where the locals and hipsters hang, while the college crowd kicks it on Highland.

BARS, PUBS & CLUBS

➔ **Boscos Squared** Live jazz jams on Sundays at this Overton Square pub,

known for its Famous Flaming Stone Beer and great wood-fired-oven pizzas. If you're a cheap date (or you just like saving money), you'll appreciate that parking is free and much more hassle-free than at the downtown and Beale Street brewpubs. Plus, the food is better. *2120 Madison Ave.* ☎ *901/432-2222. www.boscosbeer.com. Daily 11am–3am. No cover.*

➔ **Club 152** ★ Beale Street's best dance club is three floors of hot DJs action open nightly until 5am. Expect the mixmasters to spin techno, house, and alternative until the wee hours. *152 Beale St.* ☎ *901/544-7011. www.club152memphis.com. Daily 5pm–5am. Cover varies.*

➔ **Flying Saucer Draught Emporium** When Beale Street becomes too crowded, the locals make tracks to this nearby haven for beer lovers. Live music Thursday through Saturday, a lively pub atmosphere, and enough variety of brews to keep the blues away keep patrons satisfied—and coming back for more. *130 Peabody Place.* ☎ *901/523-8536. www.beerknurd.com. Mon–Wed 11am–1am; Thurs–Sat 11am–2am; Sun noon–midnight. Cover $3 on live-music nights.*

➔ **Pat O'Brien's** ★★ Hoist a Hurricane at this replica of the New Orleans nightspot that opened on Beale a few years ago. A hit with the Mardi Gras set, this big brick compound contains a big, boozy beer hall, a posh piano bar, and a multilevel outdoor patio, complete with a fountain—and decent views of the Memphis skyline hovering a few blocks away. *310 Beale St.* ☎ *901/529-0900. www.patobriens.com/memphis.html. Sun noon–10pm; Mon–Thurs 4–10pm; Fri–Sat noon–3am. Cover varies.*

LIVE MUSIC

Rock

➔ **Young Avenue Deli** ★★ Not so much a delicatessen as it is a cool hangout for young adults who like to eat and drink, this hot spot is also where you're likely to hear some of the best concerts by up-and-coming indie, alt-rock, and experimental artists. Live music is featured most nights. *2119 Young Ave.* ☎ *901/278-0034. www.young avenuedeli.com. Daily 11am–3am. Cover $5–$20.*

Jazz/Blues

→**Blues City Café** ★ This club across the street from B.B. King Blues Club takes up two old storefronts, with live blues wailing in one room (called the Band Box) and a restaurant serving steaks, tamales, and barbecue in the other. Local rock band FreeWorld plays here regularly. *138–140 Beale St.* ☎ *901/526-3637. www.bluescitycafe. com. Sun–Thurs 11am–3am; Fri–Sat 11am–5am. Cover $4–$5.*

→**King's Palace Café** ★ With its battered wood floor, this bar has the most authentic, old-time feel of any club on Beale Street. Though this is primarily a restaurant serving good Cajun food, including a knockout gumbo, there's live jazz and blues nightly. *162 Beale St.* ☎ *901/ 521-1851. www.kingspalacecafe.com. Sun–Thurs 11am–10:30pm; Fri–Sat 11am–close. No cover.*

Piano Bars

📺 Best ● →**Silky O'Sullvan's** ★★
This Beale Street piano bar is one helluva good time, especially if you have a soft spot in your heart for buckets full of booze and Elton John tunes. Wednesday through Sunday, dueling piano players take turns playing your requests: $20 buys any song you want; $10 more if you want your song played next. And if you really gotta hear "Tiny Dancer," like, *now*, for $50, they'll stop whatever they're currently playing mid-song and cut to your request. Boozehounds should try the $18 "Diver," a

Walking in Memphis . . . on Beale Street

Beale Street, where the blues gained widespread recognition, is the epicenter of Memphis's nightclub scene. The sidewalks and parks of Beale Street (not to mention its clubs) are alive with music nearly every day of the week and almost any hour of the day or night.

Known as one of the best blues clubs in the world, **B.B. King Blues Club** (147 Beale St.; ☎ **800/443-0972** or 901/524-5464) has a killer house band and occasionally attracts famous musicians who have been known to get up and jam with whomever is on stage that night. And yes, the "King of the Blues" does play here occasionally, though not on a regular basis. Across the street, **Blues City Café** (138–140 Beale St.; ☎ **901/526-3637**) takes up two old storefronts, with live blues wailing in one room (called the Band Box) and a restaurant serving steaks, tamales, and barbecue in the other. Although relatively new on the Beale Street scene, **The Black Diamond** (153 Beale St.; ☎ **901/521-0800**) has caught on in a big way and has attracted the likes of the Memphis Horns, Matt "Guitar" Murphy, Isaac Hayes, and The Nighthawks to get up on the stage here. And **Rum Boogie Cafe & Mr. Handy's Blues Hall** (182 Beale St.; ☎ **901/528-0150**) features live music nightly and dozens of autographed guitars, including ones signed by Carl Perkins, Stevie Ray Vaughan, Billie Gibbons of ZZ Top, Joe Walsh, George Thorogood, and other rock and blues guitar wizards.

For links to various clubs and other businesses along Beale, click on **www. bealestreet.com**.

yellow bucket full of a gallon's worth of heavily spiked fruit punch. If you see a white-haired dude with a kick-ass moustache sipping champagne in a throne-on-wheels out front, stop and say hello to Mr. O'Sullivan himself. *183 Beale St.* ☎ *901/ 522-9596. www.silkyosullivans.com. Mon 4pm–close; Tues–Sat 11am–close; Sun noon–close.*

➔ **Earnestine & Hazel's** ★ Although it's actually 4 blocks south of Beale Street, this downtown dive, which was once a sundry store that fronted for an upstairs brothel, has become one of Memphis's hottest nightspots. In 2004 it was the greasy backdrop for the Jack White/Loretta Lynn video *Portland, Oregon.* On Friday and Saturday nights, there's a piano bar early; and then later in the night, the best jukebox in Memphis keeps things hot. Things don't really get cookin' here until after midnight. *531 S. Main St.* ☎ *901/523-9754. Mon–Thurs 5pm–2am; Fri–Sat 5pm–3am; Sun 7pm–2am. No cover.*

What Else to See & Do

Memphis has tons of history for music lovers. And we're not talking dusty textbook kinda history—this is dirty nightclub, scandalous, rock-'n'-roll history. You might learn more in just 1 day of sightseeing in Memphis than you did all last semester.

THE TOP ATTRACTIONS

➔ **Graceland** ★★ Second only to the White House, Elvis's mansion is the most visited home in America. Graceland, which looks kind of like a small theme park or shopping mall, is now Memphis's biggest attraction, containing the King's two jets, his racquetball building, the Elvis Presley Automobile Museum (complete with the famed pink Cadillac), his grave, and the Sincerely Elvis collection of Elvis's personal belongings, right down to his

sneakers. Do the guided tour to get the full experience. The anniversary of Elvis's birth (Jan 8, 1935) is celebrated each year with several days of festivities, and mid-August's Elvis Week, commemorating his death on August 16, 1977, is celebrated both here and throughout Memphis. Each year from Thanksgiving until January 8, Graceland is decorated with Elvis's original Christmas lights and lawn decorations. *3734 Elvis Presley Blvd.* ☎ *800/238-2000 or 901/332-3322. www.elvis.com. Graceland Mansion Tour $22 adults, $20 students. Mar–Oct Mon–Sat 9am–5pm, Sun 10am–4pm; Nov–Feb 10am–4pm daily. (Dec–Feb mansion tour does not operate Tues). Closed Thanksgiving, Dec 25, and Jan 1. Take Bellevue South (which turns into Elvis Presley Blvd.) south a few miles of downtown, past Winchester Ave. Graceland is on the left.*

🅜 Best➊ ➔ **House of Mews** ★★ Okay, so it's not really a "top" attraction, but pet lovers have to check out this cat rescue agency housed in a small storefront in Cooper-Young. Home to dozens of homeless cats, House of Mews is operated by an all-volunteer staff out of the goodness of their hearts. So cute! *944 S. Cooper.* ☎ *901/ 272-3777. www.houseofmews.com. Wed–Fri 1–5pm; Sat–Sun noon–4pm.*

➔ **National Civil Rights Museum** ★★★ Once the Lorraine Motel, it was here that Dr. Martin Luther King, Jr., was assassinated on April 4, 1968. The motel has been converted into a museum documenting the struggle for civil rights. Multimedia presentations and life-size, walk-through displays include historical exhibits: a Montgomery, Alabama, public bus like the one Rosa Parks rode; a Greensboro, North Carolina, lunch counter; and the burned shell of a freedom-ride Greyhound bus. *450 Mulberry St. (at Huling Ave.).* ☎ *901/521-9699. www.civilrightsmuseum.org. Admission $12* *adults, $10 students. Mon and Wed–Sat 9am–5pm; Sun 1–5pm. (May–Aug open until 6pm.)*

→ **Soulsville USA: Stax Museum of American Soul Music** ★★★ Opened in spring 2003, the museum sits near the long-gone site of the original Stax recording studio, which during the 1960s and 1970s cranked out world-famous hits by Otis Redding, Booker T, Al Green, Aretha, and others. Don't miss Isaac Hayes's gold-plated, shag-carpeted *Superfly* Cadillac. And if the spirit moves, you can also get your groove on at the museum's psychedelic dance floor. *926 E. McLemore Ave. ☎ 901/946-2535. www.soulsvilleusa.com. Admission $9. Mar–Oct Mon–Sat 9am–4pm, Sun 1–4pm; Nov–Feb Mon–Sat 10am–4pm, Sun 1–4pm. Closed major holidays. Take Danny Thomas Blvd. south to Mississippi Blvd. Turn left onto Mississippi Blvd., then left on E. McLemore Ave.*

Best 🌑 → **Sun Studio** ★★ Everyone from Elvis and Johnny Cash to U2 and Liz Phair has recorded at this still-active recording studio. Serious music buffs will probably dig being able to touch the King's mic, but others might be baffled by why a small, nondescript brick building on a crappy corner in Memphis is such a big deal. You people can wait next door at the Sun Studio cafe, a 1950s-style former diner and a musicians' hangout. *706 Union Ave. (at Marshall Ave.). ☎ 800/441-6249 or 901/521-0664. www.sunstudio.com. Admission $9.50. Daily 10am–6pm (studio tours conducted on the hour, 10:30am–5:30pm). Closed some holidays.*

PLAYING OUTSIDE

In downtown Memphis, between Main Street and Second Avenue and between Madison and Jefferson avenues, you'll find **Court Square,** the oldest park in Memphis. With its classically designed central fountain and stately old shade trees, this park was long a favored gathering spot of Memphians. Numerous historic plaques around the park relate the many important events that have taken place in Court Square.

Pro sports abound in downtown Memphis. The NBA's **Memphis Grizzlies** (☎ **901/205-1234;** www.nba.com/grizzlies) are the city's NBA team. Since 2004, they have played at their new downtown arena, the FedEx Forum. The **Memphis Redbirds** Baseball Club (☎ **901/721-6000** or 901/523-7870; www.memphisredbirds.com), an AAA affiliate of the St. Louis Cardinals, play at AutoZone Park, 2 blocks east of The Peabody Memphis hotel on Union Avenue. **Boxing on Beale** is held the first Tuesday of the month at the New Daisy Theatre (☎ **901/634-6175;** $12–$15).

On the Road to Tuscaloosa, AL

Memphis, TN to Tuscaloosa, AL 234 miles

The drive out of Memphis is flat and easy, barring any freak weather phenomena (I got caught in a torrential, wipers-on-high downpour entering Mississippi that turned into partly cloudy conditions just a few minutes later.) Take Highway 240 south, then switch to US-78 east via I-55; once you get out of the city, there's not a whole lot of traffic, which makes this one of the more pleasant drives of the trip.

Just Outside Memphis

Pretty much as soon as you leave Memphis city limits, you'll start seeing billboards advertising **Elvis's Birthplace and Museum** in Tupelo, Mississippi (see

Detour: Elvis's Birthplace & Museum

You'll see billboards for **Elvis's Birthplace** ★★ all the way from Memphis to Tupelo, Mississippi. When visiting this tiny town just a few miles off the interstate (take the Veterans Blvd. exit off I-78 and follow the signs), you get the feeling Tupelo's economy survives on tourism dollars from fans of the King, who was born in a two-room house that's been preserved, complete with original furniture and decorations and sweet little old ladies reciting the story of Elvis and his family, who lived here for about 4 years during the Depression before Elvis's dad missed some payments and lost the house. For $2.50 you can tour the house; $6 gets you access to a separate museum full of photos, recording equipment, and furniture from Graceland, all from the personal collection of a Presley family friend (admission to both the museum and the house is $7; discounts are available for kids). Access to the Elvis chapel—seriously—is free, though, as is a ride on the Presley family porch swing. *306 Elvis Presley Dr., Tupelo, MS 38801.* ☎ *662/841-1245. www.elvispresleybirthplace.com. Mon–Sat 9am–5:30pm (May–Sept); Mon–Sat 9am–5pm (Oct–Apr); Sun 1–5pm year-round. Closed Thanksgiving and Christmas.*

"*Detour:* Elvis's Birthplace & Museum," above), a worthwhile (if obvious) tourist trap for fans of the pelvis-thrusting one. About 90 miles past Tupelo is the turnoff for Alabama Route 13 toward Tuscaloosa, which takes you through rural Fayette County, past some tiny towns, and **Granny's Smokee Hollow** barbecue (p. 364) before entering the maze of highways around Tuscaloosa.

On the Road Nuts & Bolts

Where to Fill Up Anywhere in Memphis or along AL-13 through Alabama.

The Fastest Way I-78 east out of Memphis to AL-13 south (just before Jasper) to Tuscaloosa. AL-13 will turn into US-43: just continue going straight. Follow signs for I-20 once in Tuscaloosa to go to Dreamland. This will take you about 4 or 5 hours, depending on how heavy your foot is and how many stops you make.

The Long Way Round To see more of Mississippi, travel south on 55 out of Memphis to Jackson (about 3 hr.), then catch the 20 east to cut back toward Tuscaloosa (another 3 hr.). Or skip Tuscaloosa and get your 'cue in Decatur by taking the 240 east out of Memphis to TN-385 east to US-72 toward Decatur (about 4¹⁄₂ hours' drive).

Rules of the Road In case you were wondering, it's illegal in the state of Alabama to be blindfolded while operating a motor vehicle. It is also apparently legal to drive the wrong way down a one-way street if you have a lantern attached to the front of your automobile. Also, about two in three Alabama counties are "dry" and don't sell alcohol.

SOUTHERN BBQ ROADTRIP

Welcome to Tuscaloosa

About an hour east of Birmingham, Tuscaloosa is a *huuuuuuuuge* college sports town that's also home to the original location of a legendary, now-franchised barbecue joint named Dreamland. Unless you're a hard-core football fan, that's essentially the only reason to stop in Tuscaloosa; you might also consider taking your barbecue quest into Decatur, about an hour north of Birmingham, for a taste of Big Bob Gibson's award-winning white sauce.

Getting Around

Tuscaloosa is a knot of convoluted highways, and nobody seems to know their way around. To make matters worse, there are *two* Dreamlands here—the original on the hill at 15th Avenue and Jug Factory Road, and a second one in the nearby town of Northport. There's a complicated bypass system and plenty of ways to get lost or turned around, so be vigilant with road signs and don't hesitate to stop and ask for directions. It'll save you time in the long run.

The Laws of Slaw: Alabama 'Cue

Remember *Fried Green Tomatoes?* ("The secret's in the sauce!") That was one example of Alabama barbecue—in fact, if you're, like, a serious Mary Stuart Masterson fan, you can visit the place that movie was based on during this roadtrip (see "On the Road to Atlanta," p. 365). Alabamians, like Memphians, love their pork, so you'll find

Mapquestionable?

Don't count on those directions you got online; these country roads have 10 different names and directionals. When in doubt, ask for directions. Alabamians are a friendly folk.

a lot of pulled pork sandwiches and ribs here, often smoked over hickory. Sauce is still generally tomato-based, and a little zingier than in other parts of the South—maybe something rubbed off from those spice-loving Cajuns down in Louisiana.

➜ **Big Bob Gibson's** ★★ Another of the state's best-known joints, whose pork and chicken has won awards at tons of cookouts, including several at Memphis in May. Their mayo-and-vinegar-based white sauce has one friend of mine raving about it from 2,000 miles away, and when they debuted a red sauce in 1997 it was promptly named "Best Barbecue Sauce in the World" at a Kansas City sauce contest. Gibson's started as a backyard venture in 1925 and has been in the family for four generations with two locations in Decatur. *1715 6th Ave. SE.* ☎ *256/350-6969 and 2520 Danville Rd. SW.* ☎ *256/350-0404. www.big bobgibsonbbq.com. Sandwiches $3; plates $5–$20. Daily 9:30am–8:15pm.*

➜ **Dreamland** ★ This famous, if somewhat overrated, barbecue joint is now franchised across Alabama and Georgia, but the original location is here in Tuscaloosa. According to legend, John "Big Daddy"

SOUTHERN BBQ ROADTRIP

Mmmmm . . . Christmas Cook-Off

Christmas on the River Cook-Off: This weeklong event, held just after Thanksgiving, has been going on for 35 years in Demopolis, Alabama, about 60 miles south of Tuscaloosa. Floats and activities attract about 40,000 people, but it's the Alabama State Championship BBQ Cook-off that's the real draw (☎ **334/ 289-0270;** www.demopolischamber.com).

Granny's infamous smoker.

Bishop opened his hilltop joint in 1958 after having a dream about a place that served nothing but ribs, sauce, and white bread—and though Bishop has since sold this location, the menu remains much the same today, though you can also get rib sandwiches, potato chips, iced tea, and banana pudding for dessert. Cluttered with sports memorabilia and autographed headshots, the interior of Dreamland is dark and a little gloomy, but that doesn't stop people from packing the place out for a taste of their hickory-smoked ribs. Hey, if it's good enough for Joe Namath and Toby Keith . . . *5535 15th Ave. East (from McFarland Blvd., turn left onto Jug Factory Rd., go to the top of the hill and turn right at the Dreamland sign), Tuscaloosa, AL 35405. ☎ 205/758-8135. www.dreamlandbbq.com. Sandwich $5.95; slab $18. Sun–Thurs 10am–9pm; Fri–Sat 10am–10pm.*

→ **Smokee Hollow B-B-Q** ★★ Alabama's got *so* many 'cue joints that it's worth exploring not just these famous places but also the random mom-and-pop joints on the side of the road. While driving south on Alabama Route 13, I discovered a beat-up old sign on the side of the road that simply read "Granny's Back." Figuring I had to find out who Granny was, where she'd gone, and what brought her back, I walked past the joint's sign (boasting "Best B-B-Q in the South!") and wandered in for a pulled-pork sandwich and a chat, which taught me that Granny's return was the result of the last owner defaulting on her payments, forcing the five-foot-nothing gray-haired Granny to repo her restaurant. There's a funny story involving the shiny stainless-steel smoker out back (see "Five Minutes with Granny," below) and probably plenty more tales to tell, but I'll let you find those out on your own. *14664 Hwy. 13 N, Eldridge, AL 35554. ☎ 205/487-3556. Sandwich $3–$5; plates $6–$8. Sun–Thurs 10am–9pm; Fri–Sat 10am–10pm.*

Five Minutes with Granny

Ellen Norris is the feisty proprietor of **Smokee Hollow** (see above), a dusty, old barbecue joint off the 13 in rural Fayette County, Alabama. Somewhere in her 60s, she's got white hair, a round belly, and bifocals that magnify her blue-eyes to twice their actual size. She's also got a no-bull attitude and a brand new stainless steel smoker gleaming proudly out back, next to the rickety wooden stage where the local gospel choir sings the first Friday of the month.

The smoker, like everything in these parts, it seems, has a story. When Granny recently had to repossess Smokee Hollow from a deadbeat owner, she discovered the original barbecue pit had fallen into disrepair; on the advice of her daughter, she ordered a new rotisserie smoker from a big-shot dealer in the city, who took $5,000 from Granny and gave her a loaner to use while hers was being built, which he said would only take a week.

A week passed, then two, and Granny started to get worried—where was the new smoker? Where was her five grand? The plot thickened when the dealer came 'round to pick up the loaner, which he'd sold to another customer. "You're not leaving here with my smoker until you give me my $5,000 back," Granny said, but that didn't stop the guy from hitching it up to the back of his pickup.

Little did he know Granny's ex-husband, Hubert, was the sheriff (both before going to jail on felony charges and after, when the county re-elected him). "You won't get out of Fayette County!" Granny yelled as the guy drove off. Sure enough, he didn't, and Granny got to keep her smoker, which to this day smokes gloriously greasy ribs under the Alabama sun (although, interestingly, Granny now stocks Smokee Hollow with rival "Yerby for Sheriff" bumper stickers).

On the Road to Atlanta, GA

Tuscaloosa, AL to Atlanta, GA 200 miles

There's a word I only ever used when trying to finish the crossword puzzle: *kudzu*. I always wondered what it meant, and while driving from Alabama into Georgia, I found out. Kudzu's that green, climbing ivy-ish thing that grows on all the trees in Georgia, and it's *everywhere*. Apparently it's next to impossible to kill, and you'll get an eyeful of it on this drive. (For a window-box full of more info on the green stuff, see p. 716.)

On I-20 east out of Birmingham, you'll pass through Irondale, AL, home to the **Irondale Café** (1906 First Ave. N; ☎ 205/956-5258; www.irondalecafe.com; closed Sat and Mon), famous for being the setting for *Fried Green Tomatoes*, the movie

based on the book by Fannie Flagg. If you're craving some chicken-fried steak and cornbread muffins, get off I-20 at Exit 133 (Kilgore Memorial Dr./20th St.), turn left, and proceed for 8 blocks until you see the cafe on your left.

Around Exit 162 you'll pass **Logan Martin Lake** (www.loganmartin.info), which has hike, bike, and horseback riding trails, plus good fishing, swimming, and boating. You'll also drive through the city of Talladega, home to the **Talladega National Forest** (☎ 256/362-2909; www.fs.fed.us/r8/alabama), which contains the southern edge of the Appalachian Mountains as well as waterfalls, streams, and wildlife.

Atlanta Playlist: College-Rock Craving

Here are a few tunes from some of the bands to come out of Northeast Georgia, a longtime hotbed for great alternative and indie rock and hip-hop, plus some other unforgettable Georgia songs:

➧ *Roam*, **B-52s**, "Cosmic Thing," 1989
➧ *Wraith Pinned to the Mist (And Other Games)*, **Of Montreal**, "Sunlandic Twins," 2005
➧ *Southern Hospitality*, **Ludacris**, "Back for the First Time," 2000
➧ *Atlanta*, **Stone Temple Pilots**, "No. 4," 1999
➧ *Atlanta Blues*, **Louis Armstrong**, "Louis Armstrong Plays W.C. Handy," 1954
➧ *Georgia*, **Elliott Smith**, "From a Basement on the Hill" (unreleased)
➧ *Georgia Boy*, **Al Green**, "The Belle Album," 1977
➧ *Georgia On My Mind*, **Ray Charles**, "The Genius Hits the Road," 1960
➧ *Hey Ya!*, **Outkast**, "Speakerboxxx/The Love Below," 2003
➧ *Yeah*, **Usher**, "Confessions," 2004

Fans of auto racing and Will Ferrell will be stoked to stumble upon the **Talladega Superspeedway** (3366 Speedway Blvd; ☎ 877/GO-2-DEGA; www.talladegasuperspeedway.com), which hosts the NASCAR NEXTEL Cup series and was the backdrop for the 2006 movie *Talladega Nights*. Other races are held at the speedway as well, but if nothing's going on you can still take a behind-the-scenes tour during business hours. Tours cost $5; admission to the Motor Sports Hall of Fame, which houses a variety of racing memorabilia, is an additional $10 fee.

Finally you'll cross into the Eastern time zone and soon after you'll come upon the giant metropolis that is Atlanta.

Atlanta Nuts & Bolts

Area Codes In metro Atlanta, you must dial the area code (404, 770, or 678) and the seven-digit telephone number, even if you are calling a number within the same area code. It is not necessary to dial "1" before the area code when calling between communities within the Atlanta local calling area, even if they have different area codes.

Emergencies To report a fire, summon the police, or procure an ambulance, simply dial ☎ 911.

Hospitals/Emergency Rooms **Piedmont Hospital,** 1968 Peachtree Rd., just above Collier Road (☎ 404/605-3297), offers 24-hour full emergency-room service, as does **Grady Health Systems,** 35 Butler St., downtown (☎ 404/616-6200). For life-threatening medical emergencies, dial ☎ 911.

Liquor Laws No alcohol is served at bars, restaurants, or nightclubs between 4am and 12:30pm on Sunday. In addition, alcoholic beverages are not sold on Sunday in liquor stores, convenience stores, or grocery stores. The drinking age is 21.

Newspapers & Magazines   The major newspaper in town is the *Atlanta Journal-Constitution* (www.ajc.com). Its "Weekend Preview" section, published every Friday, includes dining and entertainment happenings; also pick up *Atlanta* and *Jezebel* magazines as well as *Creative Loafing* (www.cln.com), a cool (and free) local alt pub.

Pharmacies   The **Kroger** supermarket chain (☎ 800/576-4377) operates several pharmacies that are open 24 hours. Call the above number for the nearest location.

Police   Call ☎ **911** in an emergency. Call ☎ 404/853-3434 for non-emergencies.

Post Office   Open 24 hours a day, Atlanta's main post office is located not in the downtown area, but close to Hartsfield-Jackson Atlanta International Airport at 3900 Crown Rd., Atlanta, GA 30304 (☎ 800/ASK-USPS).

Taxes   Sales tax in Atlanta is 7%. Hotel and motel guests within the city of Atlanta and Fulton County pay a total of 14%. Of that tax, 7% is sales tax and 7% is room tax.

Taxis   Call **Yellow Cabs** (☎ 404/521-0200), **Checker Cabs** (☎ 404/351-1111), **Atlanta Lenox Taxi** (☎ 404/872-2600), or **Buckhead Safety Cab** (☎ 404/233-1152) in Buckhead.

Time   Call ☎ 770/455-7141. Atlanta is on Eastern Standard Time (EST).

Transit Info   To find out how to get from point A to point B via MARTA (bus and rail), dial ☎ 404/848-4711.

Weather   Call ☎ 770/455-7141.

Welcome to Atlanta

Hotlanta, the ATL, whatever you call it, Atlanta might be the most expensive city you'll encounter on this trip, so save your pennies, 'cause you'll need 'em here. On the other hand, it's also a really freakin' fun place to hang out, so you won't regret dropping a little extra coin for a memorable time in the capital of the Peach State. From its pro sports teams and picture-postcard architecture to its bumpin' nightlife and ultra-fun people (not to mention tasty barbecue), Atlanta definitely doesn't suck.

Getting Around

BY CAR

I got stuck in traffic hell driving into **downtown** Atlanta during a hip-hop show at Centennial Park. Congestion in that area can get insane, but Atlanta's developing downtown—something of an after-dark ghost town just a few years ago—is worth checking out despite traffic hassles. Nearby **Midtown** is full of bars, restaurants, and cute shops, as is upscale **Buckhead;** other neighborhoods worth a trip include hipster haven **Little Five Points,** or L5P, and nearby Inman Park, as well as the yuppified Virginia-Highlands. I'd recommend exploring Atlanta by car, but here are a few public transit and cab options, just for fun.

BY MARTA & BATMA

Atlanta's subway (commonly referred to as **MARTA** because it's operated by the Metropolitan Atlanta Rapid Transit Authority) moves more than half a million people every day via **two lines:** South–north trains **(orange line)** travel between the airport and Doraville and North Springs; east–west trains **(blue line)** travel between Indian Creek (east of Decatur) and Hamilton E. Holmes. They

The "Peachtree" Problem

I asked a particularly well-traveled cabbie in Memphis if he knew where to get good barbecue in Atlanta, and he said, "All I know about Atlanta is you don't want to be on Peachtree." I didn't get his joke until I arrived in the ATL and noticed that practically every other street is named Peachtree: Peachtree Way, Peachtree Road, Peachtree Memorial Drive, Peachtree Battle Avenue, Peachtree Circle, Peachtree Walk; then there's Peachtree Street Northeast and West Peachtree Street Northwest . . . damn, I know Georgians are serious about their peaches, but this is ridiculous.

There are almost 50 streets named Peachtree in Atlanta, but the one most people refer to is Peachtree Street, the bar-and-restaurant-filled main drag that runs more or less parallel to Piedmont Avenue from downtown through Midtown and into Buckhead. It can be confusing, but as long as you keep a map in the car, you'll be, well, just peachy.

intersect at **Five Points Station** in downtown Atlanta, where you can transfer to another train for free. Fare is **$1.75** for any ride. MARTA trains generally arrive and depart every 8 to 10 minutes, daily from 5am to 1am. Schedule and route info: ☎ **404/848-4711;** www.itsmarta.com.

The **Buckhead Area Transportation Management Association (BATMA)** operates **"the buc,"** free shuttle buses that run every 8 to 15 minutes between the two MARTA rail stations in the area—Lenox and Buckhead—and the hotels, malls, and other businesses along Piedmont and Peachtree roads. The buses operate weekdays from 7am to 10pm. For more information, inquire at your hotel or visit www.batma.org.

BY TAXI

Atlanta is not New York. It's not possible to step outside and hail a cab at all times, though there are always cabs waiting outside major hotels and most MARTA stations, except the downtown ones. Cab rides within the Downtown Zone and in Buckhead cost $5 flat for one passenger, $1 for each additional rider—just keep in mind that the flat fee applies if you cross the zone or just go 1 block. Elsewhere the

rate is $1.50 minimum and 20¢ for every ¹⁄₆ mile after the first.

If you need a ride call **Atlanta Lenox Taxi** (☎ 404/872-2600), **Yellow Cabs** (☎ 404/521-0200), **Checker Cabs** (☎ 404/351-1111), or **Buckhead Safety Cab** (☎ 404/233-1152).

A Mishmash of Style: Barbecue in *Hot*lanta

It can be argued that Georgia doesn't really have its own style of barbecue, so you won't notice a marked difference in the meat offered here compared to, say, Alabama, though different parts of the state take their cues, so to speak, from different styles. (You might find more vinegar-based sauces in the part of the state which is closer to the Carolinas, for example.) Beyond the fact that most Georgia barbecue is based on pork (ribs and shoulder), it's hard to generalize, so just eat it and see what you think. In Georgia you'll find a dish called Brunswick Stew, a tomato-based concoction thick with beans, corn, veggies, and meat (sometimes beef or pork, sometimes rabbit or—yikes—squirrel). Just don't bring up the stew if you ever happen to be in a room with residents of Brunswick, Georgia, and

Brunswick County, Virginia, who both lay claim to the original recipe—you just might cause a brawl. I also started noticing more sweet potato pie in Georgia, so if you saved any room after the ribs, try a slice.

ATLANTA'S TOP BARBECUE

➔ **Daddy D'z** ★ Near Turner Field, this place is known for its ribs and 'Que wraps, which are little pieces of pork fried in dough. Live blues accompanies the grub on weekends. *264 Memorial Dr. SE.* ☎*404/222-0206. www.daddydz.com. Sandwiches $3–$8; plates $11–$15. Mon–Thurs 11am–10pm; Fri–Sat 11am–12:30am; Sun noon–9:30pm.*

➔ **Dean's** ★ This family-run joint, which dates back to 1947, smokes its pork for 15 hours, so you can imagine how good the chopped pork sandwiches are, especially when served with some tangy house barbecue sauce. Set on ribs? Sorry, you won't find any here—owner Roger Dean doesn't like 'em. *9480 S. Main St., Jonesboro, GA 30236.* ☎ *770/471-0138. Sandwiches $3.25;*

plates $7.50. Open for lunch and dinner Tues–Sat. Closed Sun–Mon. Cash only.

➔ **Fat Matt's Rib Shack** ★★ This blues and barbecue shack is a favorite among locals who like their ribs as smoky as their music. This joint truly is a shack, where patrons order up at the counter (often after waiting in a line snaking out the door into the parking lot), then sit elbow-to-elbow at plastic tables while chowing down on pork ribs, barbecued chicken, and pulled pork sandwiches washed down with ice-cold local beer. Live blues packs 'em in nightly around 8pm. The OG Fat Matt's serves sides of coleslaw, baked beans, and Brunswick stew, but rumor has it the sides are better (and the lines often shorter) at the **Chicken Shack** next door, which dishes up glazed carrots and collard greens along with ribs and (duh) chicken. Vegetarians beware, though: There's a good chance those greens have been cooked with pork. "Well, *yeah.* Of course!" says Chicken Shack's manager/cook Bill, who assures me, "I don't put pork in everything. I don't

Lines out the door at Fat Matt's.

Atlanta Highlights

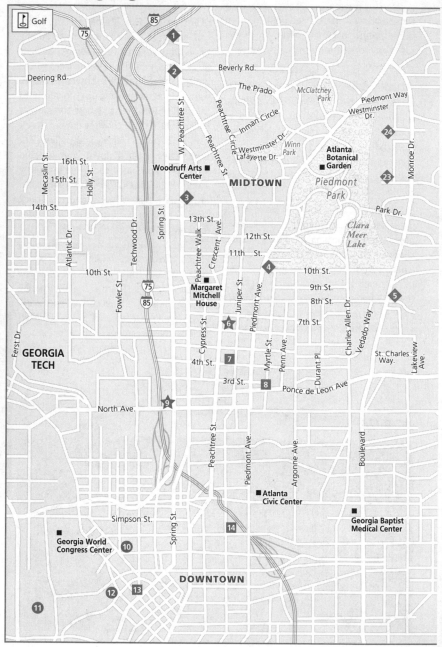

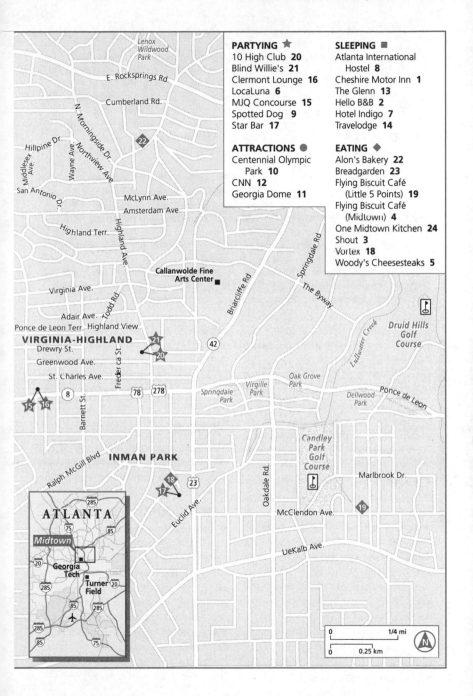

PARTYING ⭐
10 High Club **20**
Blind Willie's **21**
Clermont Lounge **16**
LocaLuna **6**
MJQ Concourse **15**
Spotted Dog **9**
Star Bar **17**

ATTRACTIONS ●
Centennial Olympic
  Park **10**
CNN **12**
Georgia Dome **11**

SLEEPING ■
Atlanta International
  Hostel **8**
Cheshire Motor Inn **1**
The Glenn **13**
Hello B&B **2**
Hotel Indigo **7**
Travelodge **14**

EATING ◆
Alon's Bakery **22**
Breadgarden **23**
Flying Biscuit Café
  (Little 5 Points) **19**
Flying Biscuit Café
  (Midtown) **4**
One Midtown Kitchen **24**
Shout **3**
Vortex **18**
Woody's Cheesesteaks **5**

Five Minutes with Bill Sirmon (on Fat Matt)

Fat Matt himself wasn't around the day I stopped in for ribs, but I did get a chance to sit down with Bill Sirmon, who runs the Chicken Shack next door. Bill told me that Matt Harper opened Fat Matt's 15 years ago on the site of an old Dunkin' Donuts. Like Dreamland's John Bishop, Harper had a simple idea: Cook nothing but ribs and chicken, and do it better than anybody else.

Fat Matt's first roasts its ribs, then browns them over a hickory fire before glazing 'em in sauce, putting 'em back in the smoke cooker to render off more fat and tenderize the meat even more. Then they finish the ribs on the hickory fire again and douse 'em with more sauce.

The sauce, naturally, comes from a secret recipe crafted by Matt and a woman named Sylvia, whose sister Rosie has been in charge of mixing it fresh daily for the last 12 years or so. There's not a lot of vinegar or mustard in the sauce, because, according to Bill, "barbecue is *supposed* to be *red,* especially if you're in Georgia."

"It's an art," he continues. "A masterpiece can be made with a few strokes of the brush, and it's the same way with barbecue."

Fat Matt's artful cooking draws all kinds of celebrities—the day I was there I ran into the Atlanta Hawks' Travis Best; Fat Matt, meanwhile, was on his way to the airport, personally delivering six slabs of ribs to Will Ferrell.

put pork in the potato soufflé, and I don't put pork in the creamed corn." *1811 and 1821 Piedmont Rd. (a few blocks south of Cheshire Bridge Rd.).* ☎ *404/607-1622. www.fatmatts ribshack.com. Ribs and chicken $3.75–$18; chopped pork sandwiches $3.95. Cash only. Rib shack open Mon–Thurs 11:30am–11:30pm; Fri–Sat 11:30am–12:30am; Sun 2–11:30pm. Chicken Shack open Wed–Thurs 11am–5pm; Fri–Sun 11am–6pm; closed Mon–Tues.*

➔ **Harold's** ★ Near the Federal clink where Al Capone was once incarcerated, Harold's dates back to the 1940s. Known for its chopped barbecue sandwich and "cracklin'" cornbread (with pork baked right in!), Harold's also serves a traditional Brunswick stew but, sadly, no booze. *171 McDonough Blvd.* ☎ *404/627-9268. Sandwiches $3.75; plates $7.75. Mon–Fri 10:30am–8pm; Sat 10:30am–7:45pm. Cash only.*

➔ **Rolling Bones** ★ Offering Texas-style 'cue from a converted 1940s garage, Rolling Bones serves ribs, brisket, and chicken along with beans, mustard greens,

and slaw. There's also a drive-through for dine-and-dashers. *377 Edgewood Ave. SE.* ☎ *404/222-2324. www.rollingbonesbbq.com. Sandwiches $6–$8; plates $8–$12. Mon–Thurs 11am–9pm; Fri—Sat 11am–10pm; Sun 12:30–8pm.*

Sleeping

Atlanta is expensive across the board, especially for lodging. Still, with a variety of options from campgrounds to B&Bs, it's not impossible to stay on budget.

CAMPGROUNDS/HOSTELS

➔ **Atlanta International Hostel** With an excellent location in the heart of Midtown, this is the first full hostel in Atlanta. The family-run place has more than 100 beds, along with a family cat, family dog, family goldfish, and family pet birds. There's also a pool table, laundry, cable, free lockers, free donuts and coffee, free maps, plus all standard hostel features, including kitchen. *223 Ponce de Leon Ave. NE.* ☎ *404/875-9449. www. atlantahostel.com. Bunk bed $22..*

'cue calendar

➜ **BBQ, Blues and Bluegrass Festival** Held in August at Harmony Park in the Oakhurst neighborhood of Decatur, this event features live music, 'cue, refreshments, and more, and costs just $5 (☎ **404/377-0494;** www.decaturga.com).

➜ **Barnesville Barbecue and Blues Festival** About an hour south of Atlanta in Barnesville, this annual event takes place in April and features cooking contests for ribs, pulled pork, chicken, and brisket as well as kabobs, wings, and chili (☎ **770/358-5884;** www. barnesville.org).

➜**Stone Mountain Park Campground** This large campground in the woods has many sites overlooking the lake, especially in the tent section. All sites have barbecue grills, and public facilities include a dining pavilion, swimming pool, laundries, and showers. The park's beach is close by; leashed pets are allowed. This is a popular place, so call first; reservations must be made at least 1 week in advance, but you can book your spot up to 90 days ahead. *P.O. Box 778, Stone Mountain, GA 30086.* ☎ *800/385-9807 or 770/498-5710. www.stone mountainpark.com. $23–$45 per night.*

CHEAP

➜**Cheshire Motor Inn** Homey hospitality and personal touches define this budget hotel, located next to the famous Colonnade restaurant. The rooms and bathrooms are clean and basic (and most have minibars), and the grounds are nicely landscaped. Don't be put off by the inn's location; Cheshire Bridge Road is an odd mix of sleazy bars and secondhand furniture and antiques shops, but the restaurant

and motel are completely respectable. *1865 Cheshire Bridge Rd. NE (near the intersection of Piedmont Rd.), Atlanta, GA 30324.* ☎ *800/ 827-9628 or 404/872-9628. 58 units. $65 double. Extra person $5. Free parking. In room: Minibars in most rooms.*

There's also a **TraveLodge** downtown at 311 Courtland St. NE (between Baker St. and Ralph McGill Blvd.). It's got a pool, business center, dry cleaning, and laundry (☎ **800/578-7878** or 404/659-4545; www. travelodge.com; $59–$109 double).

DOABLE

➜**Hello B&B** This small B&B is tucked into the Morningside neighborhood between Midtown and Virginia Highlands, walking distance from a variety of shops, restaurants, and clubs. With a garden and a porch overlooking a stream, this is the picture postcard of Southern living. Bonus: There's a hot tub! *1865 Windemere Dr. NE (I-85 to Exit 88, left on Windemere).* ☎ *404/892-8111. members.aol.com/hellobnb. Free parking in off-street lot. Four units. $105–$150. Amenities. Laundry; bike rental; luggage storage; Wi-Fi; gym; Web access in lobby.*

➜**Hotel Indigo** ★★ This is what happens when a big corporate chain tries its hand at boutique hotel style. Opened in 2004, the Indigo (across the street from the Historic Fox Theatre) has rooms with hardwood floors and beds with oversize pillows in funky color combinations and spa-style showers, which are the perfect treat after a long day out on the town. *683 Peachtree St. (between Third St. and Ponce de Leon Ave.).* ☎ *404/874-9200. www.hotelindigo. com. 139 units. $119 double. Self-parking $7. Amenities: Business center; coin-op laundry. In room: High-speed Internet access.*

SPLURGE

MTV **Best** ➜**The Glenn** ★★★ This is exactly what you should think of when you hear the phrase "hip boutique property." From the zillion-thread-count linens to the

SOUTHERN BBQ ROADTRIP

Hot Events in Hotlanta

→ **Atlanta Dogwood Festival** This huge 3-day Piedmont Park festival takes place in April with live music, food, kite-flying contests, a hot-air balloon display, and the National Disc-Dog Championship (a Frisbee tourney for the pups). Call ☎ 404/329-0501 or visit www.dogwood.org for info.

→ **Music Midtown** This musical extravaganza usually takes place in Midtown at the beginning of May. Events include concerts (past performers range from Bob Dylan to Ashlee Simpson), an artists' market, and food booths. Music Midtown was canceled in 2006; no word yet on whether it'll happen again in the future. Call ☎ 770-MIDTOWN for more information.

→ **Atlanta Pride Festival** Piedmont Park celebrates LGBT life with 3 days of events in June, including a women's march, parade, concerts, arts, and more. Admission is free; call ☎404/929-0071 or visit www.atlantapride.org.

→ **Virginia-Highlands Summerfest** Held one weekend early in June, this neighborhood arts and music festival includes a juried arts-and-crafts show, an artists market, food booths, and lots of free entertainment in John Howell Park. All events are free. For more information, call ☎ 404/222-8244, ext. 9 or visit www.vahi.org.

→ **Atlanta Film Festival** For 9 days in mid-June, the IMAGE Film & Video Center at 535 Means St. screens hundreds of films by top independent media artists. Admission averages $6 per movie, and films are shown at several venues around the city, including some newly added outdoor venues. Call ☎ 404/352-4225 for details or visit www.imagefv.org.

→ **Atlanta Jazz Festival** The week before Memorial Day this festival has hosted stars like Wynton Marsalis, Nancy Wilson, and Shirley Horn, to name a few. Admission is charged to most events, but concerts in Piedmont Park on Memorial Day Weekend are free. For details call the **Performing Arts Hotline** at ☎ 404/817-6851, visit www.atlantafestivals. com, or call the city's **Bureau of Cultural Affairs** at ☎ 404/817-6815.

→ **Montreaux Atlanta Music Festival** Also over Labor Day weekend, this event features jazz, blues, gospel, reggae, and zydeco performed in different venues around the city, including Centennial Olympic Park and Piedmont Park. You have to pay to get into most events, but concerts in Piedmont Park on Labor Day weekend are free. For details call the **Performing Arts Hotline** at ☎ 404/817-6851, visit www.atlantafestivals. com, or call the city's **Bureau of Cultural Affairs** at ☎ 404/817-6815.

→ **Peach Bowl** Held between Christmas and New Years at the Georgia Dome, this football game always sells out, so get tickets in advance. Call ☎ 404/586-8499 for information.

rain showerheads to the gourmet minibar (where Oreos share space with imported chocolate and bubbly), The Glenn is all sleek, hip, urban, and modern, despite being housed in a building that dates back to 1923. Rooms feature leather furniture, flatscreen TVs, free Wi-Fi, and Aeron desk chairs, along with a welcome note from some guy whose official title is 📺 Best● "Vibemaster." If you're gonna get spendy at any point on this trip, this is the place to do it. *110 Marietta St. NW.* ☎ *866/40-GLENN or 404/521-2250.*

www.glennhotel.com. 93 rooms; 16 suites.
Standard rooms $159–$239; suites $279–$339.
Valet parking $21/day. Amenities: Restaurant/
bar. In room: CD player with MP3 hookup, Wi-Fi,
minibar.

Eating

SUPPLIES & TAKE-OUT TREATS

➔ **Alon's Bakery** ★ BAKERY This bakery
has loads of delectable baked goods for a
snack (some of the best pastries in town),
and a variety of made-to-order sandwiches at reasonable prices. Try the garlic-
roasted lamb or the Tuscany (goat cheese,
arugula, roasted eggplant). 1394 N. Highland
Ave. NE. ☎ 404/872-6000. www.alons.com.
Sandwiches $6–$9. Mon–Fri 7am–8pm; Sat
8am–8pm; Sun 9am–4pm.

➔ **Ann's Snack Bar** ★ SANDWICHES
The rules at Ann's are as simple as the
decor: "Do not curse" is one; find out for
yourself what the other seven are while
noshing on a Ghetto burger (piled with
bacon, onions, chili, and cheese), a pair of
deep-fried chili dogs, or a coleslaw–
topped Hood burger. 1615 Memorial Dr.
☎ 404/687-9207. Burgers $4–$5. Mon–Sat
11am–9pm. Cash only.

➔ **The Breadgarden** ★ SANDWICHES
Tucked away on a little dead-end street,
this sandwich stop is worth seeking out,
especially if you want to picnic in nearby
Piedmont Park. You can design your own
sandwich, but it's hard to come up with
anything better than the Mediterranean
vegetarian—goat cheese, roasted red peppers, tomatoes, Kalamata olives, eggplant,
and olive spread on whole grain bread.
549–5 Amsterdam Ave. ☎ 404/875-1166.
Sandwiches $5–$7. Mon–Wed 9am–4pm;
Thurs–Sat 9am–6pm.

➔ **Woody's Famous Philadelphia
Cheesesteaks** SANDWICHES/SUBS
Gourmet it ain't, but this casual little lunch
spot near Piedmont Park, barely bigger

than a hot dog stand, serves up excellent
Philly cheesesteaks, Italian subs, Polish
sausages, and hot dogs. The ordering line
snakes out the door, so arrive at off-peak
hours or be prepared to wait. Stay cool
with an orange freeze or one of Woody's
extra-thick, old-fashioned milkshakes. 981
Monroe Dr. NE (at Tenth St.). ☎ 404/876-1939.
Hot dogs and sandwiches $2–$5. No credit
cards. Tues–Sat 11am–5pm.

RESTAURANTS
Cheap

➔ **Flying Biscuit Café** ★★ NEW AMERI-
CAN This neighborhood hangout has
great biscuits and sage sausage that keep
folks waiting up to an hour and a half for a
table at both the L5P and Midtown locations. The Biscuit serves breakfast all day,
with highlights including orange-scented
French toast with raspberry sauce and
honey crème anglaise, plus Love Cakes, a
mix of black bean and cornmeal, sautéed
and topped with tomatillo salsa, sour
cream, feta, and raw onion spears. Budget-
conscious Rachael Ray shot her "$40 a
Day" show here, so you know it won't
break the bank either. Midtown: 1001
Piedmont Ave. ☎ 404/874-8887. L5P: 1655
McLendon Ave. (at Clifton Rd.). ☎ 404/687-
8888. Breakfast $5.95–$8.95; main courses
$6.95–$14. Sun–Thurs 7am–10pm; Fri–Sat
7am–10:30pm.

➔ **The Vortex** ★ BURGERS Hard to miss
that giant skull on the corner of Moreland
and Euclid in L5P. Inside that gaping jaw is a
burger bar designed by what must have
been a skeleton-loving interior decorator;
you'll find menu items like the Coronary
Bypass (a patty topped with a fried egg,
cheese, bacon, and mayo), plus standard
sandwich fare and a meatless burger for
the veggies. 438 Moreland Ave. NE. ☎ 404/
688-1828. www.thevortexbarandgrill.com.
Starters $3.75 $7.50; burgers $6.25 $7.95.
Sun–Thurs 11am–midnight; Fri–Sat 11am–3am.

Doable

➔ **One Midtown Kitchen** ★ NEW AMERI-CAN This sophisticated, New York–style place serves food that's delicious but not too pricy (someone finally figured it out!). The atmosphere is high energy—maybe the high spirits are left over from the restaurant's previous life as a swinging club. This place is a local favorite, especially with a younger crowd working their way up the ladder to six figures. The late-night hours on weekends make this a great place for dining after clubbing. *559 Dutch Valley Rd. NE.* ☎ *404/892-4111. Reservations recommended. Starters $5–$11; entrees $14–$19. Mon–Thurs 5:30pm–midnight; Fri–Sat 5:30pm–1am; Sun 5:30–10pm. Valet parking.*

➔ **Shout** ★★ SUSHI Shout, the sister restaurant to another popular joint, called Twist (get it?), is all kinds of chic and the go-to spot for singles—the huge space houses a sushi lounge and several bars, not to mention a rooftop deal with more of those trendy cabanas everyone's so nuts over. The menu is tapas, pizza, sushi, and eclectic stuff like Thai beef salad with vermicelli. *1197 Peachtree St NE.* ☎ *404/846-2000. www.heretoserverestaurants.com. Appetizers $5–$12; entrees $12–$28. Mon 11:30am–10pm; Tues–Thurs 11:30am–11pm; Fri–Sat 11:30am–midnight; Sun 3–10pm.*

Splurge

➔ **Jöel** ★★★ FRENCH/FUSION Joel Atunes, the award-winning, French-trained chef behind The Dining Room at Ritz-Carlton Buckhead, has opened his own place, which blends East and West in dishes like butternut-curry gnocchi or langoustines with bok choy. The restaurant boasts a 62-foot stainless steel stove (the longest in the country), employs a dozen chefs, and has a 300-bottle-long wine list. *3290 Northside Pkwy. (Piazza at Paces).* ☎ *404/233-3500. www.joelrestaurant.com. Reservations recommended. Appetizers*

$9–$14; entrees $26–$38. Lunch Tues–Fri 11:30am–2pm; dinner Mon–Thurs 5:30–10pm, Fri–Sat 5:30–10:30pm.

Partying

Nightlife turns up all over Atlanta, but the biggest concentration of clubs and bars is in **Buckhead** (near the intersection of Peachtree Rd. and E. Paces Ferry Rd.); in **Virginia-Highland** (at the intersection of Virginia and N. Highland aves., and on N. Highland just north of Ponce de Leon Ave.); in **Little Five Points** (near the intersection of Moreland and Euclid aves.); and downtown near Peachtree Center.

Buckhead is like a huge, unruly frat party, with lots of people and cars cruising the streets. It gets rowdier, sometimes even violent, as the night goes on. Virginia-Highland is full of upper-20- and 30-somethings and professionals. Little Five Points is an eclectic mix of hipsters and local eccentrics, while outta-towners and conventioneers often hang out Downtown.

BARS & PUBS

➔ **Bed** ★★ Everyone knows the only reason to go out is to get lucky, so why not cut to the chase and furnish your club with actual beds? That's the sexy concept behind this upscale bar/restaurant mini-chain (you might remember when they shot that episode of *Sex and the City* at the one in New York, or you heard about Paris and Nicky partying at the one in Miami). Bed serves as The Glenn Hotel's house restaurant and dark, swanky lobby bar, which serves yummy cocktails made with fresh muddled fruit; the rooftop bar is very South Beach—cabanas with bottle service and DJs spinning for scantily clad people who make you remember why they nick-named this place Hotlanta. *110 Marietta St. (inside the Glenn Hotel).* ☎ *404/222-7992. atl.bedrestaurants.com. Starters $7–$12; entrees $18–$30. Restaurant open Mon–Thurs*

6am–11pm; Fri 6am–midnight; Sat 11am–3pm and 5pm–midnight; Sun 11am–3pm and 5–11pm. Rooftop bar opens at 5pm.

➔ **LocaLuna** ★ With a semi-lame tropical island vibe, LocaLuna mixes up Brazilian tapas and lively Samba music. Wash down your tilapia and shrimp seviche or lula frita (fried calamari) with a top-shelf tequila or flavored rum. *836 Juniper St. NE* ☎ *404/875-4494. www.loca-luna.com. Tapas $3–$6 per plate. Lunch Tues–Fri 11:30am–2:30pm. Dinner Tues–Thurs 5–11pm; Fri–Sat 5pm–12:30am; Sun 5–10pm. Bar open later (until 3am Fri–Sat).*

➔ **The Spotted Dog** ★★ This is a newish British-style pub that was converted from an old firehouse, but rumor has it this was almost the site of the *Real World Atlanta* house. With its laid-back vibe, the building probably sees a lot less drama as a pub than it would have if it hosted MTV's signature seven strangers. With velvet upholstery on the furniture inside and a patio with picnic tables outside, the pub is cozy and comfortable—especially after a few of their signature mint julep iced teas. Try the gooey, stinky blue cheese chips. *30 North Ave. NW.* ☎ *404/347-7337. www.dereklawford pubs.com. Mon–Thurs 11am–1am; Fri–Sat 11am–3am; Sun 11am–midnight.*

CLUBS

➔ **Clermont Lounge** ★ A dive bar/strip joint in the basement of the Clermont Hotel, where both the furniture and the dancers at this place are showing their age. Featured on Dave Attell's "Insomniac," the lounge found fans in the likes of Kid Rock and Marilyn Manson. *789 Ponce De Leon Ave. NE.* ☎ *404/874-4783. www.clermontlounge. com. Daily 1pm–3am. Cover on Sat.*

➔ **Johnny's Hideaway** ★ A hit with the over-40 crowd for more than 20 years, this joint's been rediscovered by hipsters of late. Host Johnny Esposito is a well-known

Atlanta character at this Buckhead bar, which features music ranging from big-band jazz to '80s, and don't be surprised to see the occasional celeb (George Clooney and Robert Duvall have been known to drop in). Check out the Frank Sinatra Room, filled with over 100 pieces of memorabilia. *3771 Roswell Rd. (2 blocks north of Piedmont Rd.).* ☎ *404/233-8026. www.johnnys hideaway.com. No cover; 2-drink minimum after 8pm.*

➔ **The Star Bar** ★★ Housed in a former bank, this funky and cavernous Little Five Points club features the "GraceVault"—a small shrine filled with Elvis posters, an all-Elvis jukebox, Elvis clocks, and other memorabilia. Live music Wednesday through Saturday nights runs the gamut from rockabilly to rock and R&B. *437 Moreland Ave. NE (between Euclid and Mansfield aves.).* ☎ *404/681-9018. Cover $5–$10. Closed Sun.*

LIVE MUSIC
Rock

➔ **Lenny's** ★ Bands like This Bike is a Pipe Bomb and Whiskey Sh*t Vomit play the small stage at Lenny's, which calls itself the CBGB of Atlanta. The crowd at this Cabbagetown dive consists of regulars during the day and hipsters after dark for weekly dance nights, karaoke, and live acts. *307 Memorial Dr. SE.* ☎ *404/577-7721. www.lennysbar.com. Mon–Fri 11am–4am; Sat 11am–3am. Cover around $5.*

➔ **MJQ Concourse** ★★ A nightlife mecca hidden in the basement of an old parking garage on Ponce de Leon; inside you'll find multiple bars, loungey areas, and dance floors that set the backdrop for DJs spinning house, hip-hop, downtempo, drum 'n' bass, and more, while an associated venue called the 〔MTV〕〔Best⬤〕 **Drunken Unicorn** hosts up-and-coming indie bands. *736 Ponce de Leon Ave. NE* ☎ *404/870-0575.*

Mon–Wed 10pm–4am; Thurs–Fri 11pm–4am; Sat 11pm–3am. Cover $5–$8. Drunken Unicorn shows 18+ unless otherwise noted.

➜ **10 High Club** This Virginia-Highland nightspot lives underneath the Dark Horse Tavern and is decorated with Elvis Costello record sleeves. A neon purple bar meets the hooch needs of local boozers, who pile in to see music ranging from singer/songwriter to rockabilly. *816 N Highland Ave. NE.* ☎ *404/873-3607. www.tenhighclub.com. Tues 9pm–1am; Wed 10pm–3am; Thurs 9pm–2am; Fri–Sat 9pm–3am. Cover $5–$8. All Ten High shows are 21+.*

Blues

➜ **Blind Willie's** ★ This well-known club features live blues from around the country, but local bands are part of the scene, too. The bar usually opens about 8pm, and there's a limited bar menu, but the big attraction is the music, which starts around 10pm. *828 W. Highland Ave.* ☎ *404/873-2583. www.blindwilliesblues.com. Sun–Thurs 8pm–1am; Fri–Sat 8pm–2am. Cover $3–$10. All shows 21+.*

What Else to See & Do

With so many great bars and restaurants, cute neighborhoods, and giant array of different stuff to do, Atlanta's worth an extra day (or more) just to explore. From going behind-the-scenes at the nerve center of media to doing the tomahawk chop at Turner Field, the ATL will keep you entertained.

THE TOP ATTRACTIONS

➜ **Atlanta Motor Speedway** Some 30 miles south of the city in Hampton, GA, this track hosts two NASCAR NEXTEL Cup races a year—one near the beginning of the season and one nearly dead last, as well as Busch Grand National, IMSA, and ARCA events. Race tickets are usually available right up until the start of the race, and some are pretty reasonable. Smart fans get

there early and camp out. Track tours run daily every half-hour when races are not going on. The $5 admission includes information on the track's history and tours of the the Petty Garden (a tribute to racing legend Richard Petty), garages and Victory Lane, not to mention a couple of laps around the track in the Speedway van. Call ☎ 770/707-7970 for tour info. *1500 N Hwy. 41 (about 30 miles south of Atlanta on US 75; exit 218 and go west on Hwy. 20 for 10 miles).* ☎ *770/946-4211 or* ☎ *404/249-6400. www. atlantamotorspeedway.com.*

FREE ➜ **Centennial Olympic Park** ★★★ Built for the 1996 Olympics (then redesigned and reopened in 1998), Centennial Park is full of rolling lawns, public art, rock gardens, pools, and fountains; it's a living monument to the city's memories—both good and bad—of that seminal event. Conceived as a town square, it's where everyone flocked to celebrate the games, and after the bombing in the park that claimed two lives, it was where people gathered to try to revive the Olympic spirit. These days the park hosts a number of free events each month—festivals, artists' markets, and concerts. Take a run through the Olympic rings-shaped fountain, or just chill and enjoy a fountain "concert"—water and light displays set to music. Don't miss the Quilt Plazas and the *Quilt of Remembrance,* which pays respect to the bombing victims. Find more park info at the visitor center on International Boulevard, in the southwest corner of the park, across from the CNN Center. *285 International Blvd. NW (at Techwood Dr.).* ☎ *404/222-PARK (7275). Free admission. Daily 7am–11pm.*

➜ **CNN Studio Tour** ★★★ The world's largest newsgathering organization is based in Atlanta and gives 40-minute guided walking tours that allow a behind-the-scenes look at the high-tech world of

24-hour TV network news in action. Make a videotape of yourself reading the news from behind a CNN anchor desk before heading up a eight-story escalator to discover the magic of the Blue Chromakey system (it's what's used to broadcast that big map behind the weather folks), see how on-air graphics are made, and learn the secrets of the TelePrompTer. From a glass-walled observation station on another level, you'll get a bird's-eye view of the main newsroom, from writers composing news scripts to newscasters at work. *CNN Center, Marietta St. (at Techwood Dr.).* ☎ *404/827-2300 or 877/4CNN-TOUR. www.cnn.com/studiotour. Admission $8. Reservations are recommended, but some tickets are available on a first-come, first-served basis on the day of the tour and go on sale at 8:30am. Tours given daily every 20 min. 9am–5pm. Arrive early; most tours sell out. Closed Easter, Thanksgiving, and Christmas Day.*

PLAYING OUTSIDE

MTV Best ♥ FREE → **Piedmont Park**
★ ★ ★ This the city's most popular and centrally located recreation area (with its main entrance on Piedmont Ave. at Fourteenth St.); it was once a farm and a Civil War encampment. Today it hosts concerts and music festivals and contains softball fields, soccer fields, public tennis courts, a public pool, and paths for jogging, skating, and cycling. Stop by the visitors center at the Piedmont and Twelfth St. entrance for more info or to take a walking tour (departing Sat at noon Apr–Oct). Parking is tough, though; you're better off taking MARTA to the Arts Center station and walking the few blocks down Fourteenth Street. Don't miss the Atlanta Botanical next door. *Piedmont Ave. at 14th St.* ☎ *404/875-7275. www.piedmontpark.org. Daily 6am–11pm. Parking very limited.*

Spectator Sports

Atlanta has four professional major league teams: the Braves, the Hawks, the Falcons, and the (NHL) Thrashers. Good tickets can be extremely hard to come by during a winning season, so plan in advance.

Baseball fans, it's time to learn the tomahawk chop, the **Atlanta Braves'** ★ ★ ★ signature rally gesture. The Braves play at Turner Field during baseball season (Apr–Oct). Tickets are $5 to $48 in advance, or try your luck with $1 bleacher seats or $5 standing-room-only tickets, both of which go on sale on game day only. Tours of the stadium are offered year-round, on the hour during business hours except on days when the Braves have afternoon home games. Tours last about an hour and include a visit to a luxury suite, the press box, the clubhouse, the dugout, the Braves Museum and Hall of Fame and more. Tickets are $10; call ☎ 404/614-2311 for tour info. Turner Field is at 755 Hank Aaron Dr. SE; ☎ **404/522-7630;** www. atlantabraves.com; the box office is open Mon–Fri 8:30am–6pm, Sat 9am–5pm, Sun 1–5pm.

The **Atlanta Hawks** play NBA basketball in Philips Arena from November to April, while the NHL's **Atlanta Thrashers,** named after Georgia's state bird, take to the ice there from October to May. (Philips Arena: 1 Philips Dr.; box office open Mon–Fri 9:30am–5pm; closed on weekends except on event days open at noon. Hawks tickets: ☎ **404/827-3865;** www.nba.com/hawks; $10–$65. Thrashers tickets: **404/584-PUCK;** www.atlantathrashers.com; $10–$200.)

The **Atlanta Falcons** are the city's NFL franchise, playing eight games (plus exhibitions) each season in the Georgia Dome. Watching a game in the Dome is an interesting, noisy experience. Pre-season games start in August; post-season games end as

SOUTHERN BBQ ROADTRIP

late as January, depending on how well the team plays. (Georgia Dome: 1 Georgia Dome Dr.; ☎ **404/249-6400;** www.atlanta falcons.com; Mon–Fri 9am–5pm and event days through end of event; tickets are $40–$104.)

On the Road to Lexington & Charlotte, NC

Atlanta, GA to Lexington, NC 298 miles

Saying "goodbye" to Atlanta, hop on Peachtree Street heading north until you see signs for Interstate 85, which will take you toward our next stop, Lexington, North Carolina. Get used to even more kudzu as you leave Atlanta on the flat, wide, well-maintained I-85 freeway heading north.

On the Road Nuts & Bolts

Where to Fill Up   Anywhere; there are gas stations at least every few miles off the 85.

The Fastest Way   I-85 all the way to Lexington. With limited stops, this drive takes about 5¹/₂ to 6 hours.

The Long Way Round   You'll see more of rural Georgia—and squeeze in an extra 'cue stop—if you detour to **Hot Thomas** just outside Watkinsville (see "Hot Thomas Barbecue near Watkinsville," below). It'll take about an hour or so to get to Hot Thomas, depending on traffic, and another 5 or 6 hours to Lexington. If you want to see more of the south and have some more time, you might want to take the 20 east out of Atlanta to hit Augusta and Columbia, South Carolina, before catching the 77 north to Charlotte.

Rules of the Road   Speed limits remain the same on I-85 through Georgia and into the Carolinas (70 mph on interstate highways in rural areas, 65 in urban areas in NC, 60 in urban areas in SC). But it *is* against the law to rollerblade on a state highway in North Carolina.

Crossing into the Carolinas

Georgia leaves its final mark on the departing traveler at the state-line town of Lavonia, known for its quaint, historic downtown and several enormous billboards advertising **Café Risque**—a roadside topless bar off Exit 173 of I-85 that not only has naked girls but also, apparently, great pancakes.

Across the South Carolina state line near the town of Cowpens, 📺 Best☻ **Abbott** **Farms** ★★ (I-85 N exits 78 and 83; ☎ **800/764-0076;** www.abbottfarms online.com; Mon–Sat 7am–8pm) is worth a stop—especially if you still haven't bought anything to bring home to jealous friends and family members. This roadside produce and canned-goods joint makes you rethink Georgia's Peach State title—aside from bags overflowing with fresh ripe peaches, Abbott's stocks hundreds of jars of peach-related stuff: peach pie, peach ice cream, peach syrup, salsa, hot sauce,

Detour: Hot Thomas Barbecue near Watkinsville

While asking around for barbecue recommendations in Georgia, I got a tip about **Hot Thomas** (☎ 706/769-6550; 3753 Greensboro Hwy., about 5 miles south of a suburb of Athens called Watkinsville). "I would drive to the Bahamas for it," said Atlantan Spencer Sloan, who blogs at www.goldenfiddle.com and knows, like, everything there is to know about everything cool. The place serves a limited menu of pork plates and sandwiches, plus coleslaw and Brunswick stew. Only problem is it's only open Tuesday through Friday from 11am to 6pm, but—if you believe Spencer anyway—it's worth the drive, and then some. To get there, get off the 85 at GA-316/University Parkway and go about 40 miles. Turn right on Oconee Conn (which becomes Mars Hill Rd then Experiment Station Rd.) for about 5 miles, then turn right on North Main, bear left on Greensboro Highway, and continue for 5 miles. To get back on the interstate, go north on Greensboro Highway for 5 miles, then right on Main for 1½ miles, and right at Oconee Veterans Parkway for about 3 miles. Take US 129 North around Athens to US 441; go north for about 20 miles until you see the exit for I-85 North.

cobbler, salad dressing, you name it. They give free samples, too!

In addition to having peach mania, they also sell local barbecue sauce, honey, pickled okra, moonshine jelly (made with real bathtub booze), and something called chow-chow, a spicy cabbage-and-peppers concoction. Don't miss the Southern Peach Pecan Preserves and the Sweet Potato Butter. Get a loaf of cinnamon pecan bread for your aunt and grab yourself a bag of boiled Cajun peanuts—sounds weird, tastes awesome.

Welcome to the Piedmont

The Carolinas have a long history of barbecue, and that's the only real reason to stop in **Lexington, NC,** in particular. Lexington hosts a barbecue festival every year that draws nearly 100,000 people to the tiny town, which otherwise has, well, *nothing* going on. Put it this way: When I asked my waitress at Jimmy's Bar-B-Q what there was to do, she said, "We got really excited when we got an Applebee's, 'cause they have alcohol!"

Like we said, it's a *small* town, so for your lodging and partying you'll probably want to head south to nearby Charlotte.

Chopped Pork and Vinegar: Carolina 'Cue

In the Carolinas, you'll notice a marked difference from typical Western-style barbecue. It's strictly about pork, and sauce (sometimes called "dip") is thinner and more vinegary than states to the west. You might find chopped pork on the menu rather than pulled; that just means they take a cleaver to it after it's been pulled off the bone. You may also be able to order your pork course-chopped (chunkier) or fine-chopped.

Carolinians use oak or hickory wood smokers or electric heat to cook the pork, and they throw in their two cents when it comes to side dishes, too: slaw, for example, may come in white (with mayo), yellow (with mustard) or red (with barbecue sauce). Other yummy sides include collard greens and hushpuppies (bite-size chunks

Mmmm . . . South Carolina peaches!

of delicious deep-fried cornmeal batter). There's variation within the state, too; in the east, they use the whole hog, and you'll see more mustard, vinegar, and hot peppers in the sauce, while the Lexington (or Piedmont) style uses mostly pork shoulder.

In Lexington, which boasts a barbecue joint for around every 1,000 residents, **Jimmy's** ★ (1703 Cotton Grove Rd.; ☎ 336/357-2311) serves awesome hushpuppies along with its chopped pork, plus super sweet chess pie (that's pecan pie without the pecan topping). **John Wayne's** (601 W. 5th St.; ☎ 910/249-1658) is a little harder to find, but once you get there you can try notable 'cue, authentic sides, and spicy sauce. **Lexington #1** (Business Loop I-85; ☎ 910/249-9814), also known as Honey Monk's for its owner, Wayne Monk, is one of the more renowned local joints, along with **Speedy's** (1317 Winston Rd.; ☎ 910/248-2410) and **Stamey's** (4524 S. NC 150 Hwy.; ☎ 910/853-6426).

Welcome to Charlotte

Since one of our other roadtrips ("American Highways") starts in Charlotte, there's a lot of information on the city in that chapter, as well, starting on p. 699, so we'll do more of a quick roundup of the sleeping/eating/partying/hanging as we hit the end of *this* roadtrip. But don't worry. We're still all about the barbecue!

SLEEPING

Pitch your tent at the **Charlotte KOA** just over the South Carolina border (940 Gold Hill Rd., Fort Mill, SC 29708; ☎ 888/562-4430; tent sites $30–$35; cabins $35–$60).

The Blake is a stylish boutique hotel in Uptown Charlotte (555 S. MacDowell; ☎ 704/372-4100; $129 and up), while the historic, Euro-style **Dunhill** is more old-school, with live piano music in the lobby and four-poster beds in the cozy rooms upstairs (237 N. Tryon St.; ☎ 800/354-4141, $149–$199 double). If you've got cash left at this point in the trip, splurge on the four-star **Park Hotel,** a tasteful and stylish six-story hotel in Southpark's commercial center (2200 Rexford Rd.; ☎ **800/334-0331** or 704/364-8220; $99–$220 double; $225–$895 suite).

EATING

Get the Cajun meatloaf at **Dish** in Plaza Midwood (1220 Thomas Ave.; ☎ **704/344-0343**), and don't crinkle your nose when they serve you fried pickles with ranch dressing along with your late-night barbecue at **Penguin** (1921 Commonwealth Ave.; ☎ **704/375-6959**). Or check out **Bonterra Dining & Wine Room** (1829 Cleveland Ave.; ☎ **704/333-9465;** www.bonterra dining.com), which is situated in an 1895 church in Charlotte's historic Southend District.

PARTYING

Get your booze on at **Cans** (no, not a nudie bar), which until recently only served beer out of a can, but now you can find the regular array of liquor here, too (500 W 5th St.; ☎ **704/940-0200**). If you're Uptown, check out the DJs, open mics, and draft pints at **RiRa Irish Pub** (208 N. Tryon St.; ☎ **704/333-5554**).

Find live music at the historic **Double Door Inn** (218 E. Independence Blvd.; ☎ **704/376-1446**), where Buddy Guy and Stevie Ray Vaughn played. Or party with the LGBT crowd at **Scorpio** (2301 Freedom Dr.; ☎ **704/373-9124**).

WHAT TO SEE & DO

Every October the NASCAR NEXTEL Cup Series packs 'em in at the 167,000-capacity **Lowe's Motor Speedway** (5555 Concord Pkwy. S. Concord, NC 28027; ☎ **704/455-3200**), while the **Coca-Cola 600** draws crowds in late May. The 1.5-mile long track

Festival of 'Cue!

The Barbecue Festival has been held for almost a quarter-century in historic uptown Lexington, draws around 100,000 people to the little town, and was named one of the Top 10 food festivals in the country by *Travel + Leisure*. Held one Saturday in October, the festival features music on five stages and free admission. Call ☎ **356/956-1880** or visit **www.barbecuefestival.com** for info.

also hosts NASCAR Busch Series races and Craftsman Truck Series events, and has seen its share of Hollywood suits when movies like *Days of Thunder* were filmed there.

If you want to get outside, try hiking at the nearly 1,000-acre **McDowell Park and Nature Preserve** (about 12 miles south of the city center on NC 49; ☎ **704/588-5224**) or paddle-boating and fishing at Lake Wylie at the heart of the park. Get cultured at the **Mint Museum of Art** (2730 Randolph Rd.; ☎ **704/337-2000;** www. mintmuseum.org; closed Mon), which has tons of European and American art, as well as gold coins originally minted at the facility back when it was a branch of the U.S. Mint from 1837 to 1913.

If you're in town and want to catch an NFL game, a limited number of single-game tickets are available. For tickets to see the **Carolina Panthers,** visit the Bank of America Stadium Ticket Office (☎ **704/358-7800;** 800 S. Mint St., southeast side of the stadium; Mon–Fri 8:30am–5:30pm); or order through Ticketmaster (☎ **704/522-6500;** www.cpanthers.com or www. ticketmaster.com). The city also has a pro basketball team, the **Charlotte Bobcats** (☎ 704/262-2287; www.nba.com/bobcats), who got a new, $265-million uptown arena in 2005.

Well, if you're still itching to get behind the wheel for a few (thousand) more miles, just turn to the last chapter in this book, and take off on the "American Highways" roadtrip, which takes you from Charlotte to El Paso.

But if you're full of barbecue and memories, and missing your own comfy bed, then it's time to turn your eyes homeword, and with a belch and an antacid, go back to the rest of your life/the real world.

Or, you could always open up a barbecue restaurant!

Cool in the Midwest

Text & Photos by Heather McNiel & Dan Yim

I f someone asks you about the coolest cities in the U.S., if you're on one of the coasts, then New York City and Los Angeles probably come to mind, and maybe Washington, DC, or San Francisco. In some quarters, there's an attitude that pretty much everything between the coasts is a backwater. Have you heard the term "flyover state"? But we beg to differ.

On this roadtrip through the cities of the Heartland, we started in Minneapolis, which has cool cred dating back to when Mary Tyler Moore threw her hat in the air (and is the home of the Mall of America, which is ironically cool); we also wanted to see if any real jazz and blues joints still exist in Kansas City; and whether there is any connection between Denver's mile-high altitude and its reputation as one of the most partying cities in the nation (Denver is the home base of the 18th cycle of *The Real World*. Coincidence?). We also had a burning desire to find out if Salt Lake City is really as weird as everyone says.

As we pulled away from home at the start of our 1,573-mile trip, we weren't sure what we'd find. As we made our way through the cornfields, rolling prairies, mountains, and deserts of the interior, we became more and more drawn in. We splurged once in while, but we mostly saved our money for partying with the locals we met at pubs and bars who, by the way, were very cool and incredibly friendly.

Ready to rock at the famous First Avenue in Minneapolis.

Did we come bearing stereotypes? Hell, ja! And they were blown away in some cases and totally reinforced in others; but after making this trip, we have a whole new appreciation for life in the Urban Heartland.

Superlatives: The Highs & Lows

→ **Worst place to be the designated driver: Denver, Colorado.** In a city filled with microbreweries and inveterate partiers, the last thing you want is to be stuck with car keys. Walk or get a cab instead.

→ **Best place to sample Midwestern culture: Nye's Polonaise Room** in Minneapolis, Minnesota, where polka bands play oompah music for an awesome mix of hip young singles and old-school, buttoned-up Midwestern types. See p. 403.

→ **Best brunch served by drag queens:** Unambiguously good brunch fare is delivered by ambiguously gendered servers at the outrageous **Petticoat Bruncheon,** every weekend at Denver's **Bump and Grind Café.** See p. 432.

→ **Worst (and best) place for shopaholics:** At the ginormous **Mall of America,** in Bloomington, Minnesota, if you only spent 10 minutes in each store it would still take you 86 hours to hit every shop. See p. 404.

→ **Best place to fill up: Oklahoma Joe's** in Kansas City, Kansas, offers the winning combination of gas station and barbecue joint, allowing you to fill your gas tank and your belly at the same time. See p. 417.

→ **Best   I-can't-believe-it's-vegan moment:** Biting into a sinfully delicious fudge brownie at the vegan bakery and restaurant **WaterCourse   Foods** in Denver, Colorado. See p. 433.

→ **Worst place to be stuck looking for a liquor store:** Finding a needle in a haystack is child's play compared to finding the carefully hidden state-run liquor outlets in Mormon-friendly **Salt Lake City, Utah.** See p. 452.

→ **Best site for a horror flick:** The dilapidated **Wyoming Frontier Prison** is where many a Wild West outlaw met his final, grisly end. See p. 443.

→ **Weirdest example of Americana:** The **Garden of Eden,** in Lucas, Kansas, is a half-acre of outlandish concrete sculptures, built by a Civil War veteran who insisted he be buried on-site in a glass-topped coffin. See p. 425.

→ **Best organized religion icon: Temple Square** in Salt Lake City, UT, the religious hub of the Church of Jesus Christ of the Latter-Day Saints, has its own unconventional beauty. See p. 457.

→ **Worst place to get a ticket: Colby, Kansas,** not far from the Colorado border, where police officers are just itching to catch anyone speeding along I-70. So keep your eye on the road (and the speedometer) and your hands upon the wheel. See p. 425.

Trip in a Box

Total Miles 1,573 miles from Minneapolis to Salt Lake City.

Route I-35W and I-35 from Minneapolis to Kansas City; I-70 from Kansas City to Denver; I-25 and I-80 from Denver to Salt Lake City.

States Minnesota, Iowa, Missouri, Kansas, Wyoming, Colorado, Utah

Trip Time At least 7 days for the whole trip.

The short version The route from Minneapolis to Salt Lake City will take 7 days if you spend one full day in each city and one day driving, but that's pushing it. If you have less than a week, you could probably cut the trip to two stops and about 4 to 5 days.

The long version Although you can make the entire trip in 7 days, you'll only have one full day to explore each city, which is a bummer. Ideally, you should try to spend 1 to 2 days in each location, which would make the trip about 9 days. If you've got more time, you can always extend your adventure by taking some side trips.

Hitting the Highlights If you're really short on time, try a two-city combo trip: Minneapolis to Kansas City (4 days) or Kansas City to Denver (4–5 days). Dead-set on visiting Mormon country? Go for the Denver(Salt Lake City trip (4–5 days).

When to Go Since this trip will take you through areas that may experience heavy snowfall in the winter and extremely hot temperatures in the summer, early summer (before it gets too hot), or fall are probably the best time. If you do decide to travel in July or August, make sure you have good air conditioning in your car!

The Money Part

Although you may be driving through rural areas, your destinations are definitely urban. Unless you live in a small town, you'll find that most things cost about what they would at home. Besides budgeting for food, gas, and accommodations, you should also take into account how much you want to spend on entertainment. Most cities on this trip have a plethora of night life, and a few drinks, a concert ticket, and a cab back to your hotel will add up faster than you think.

Accommodations

Accommodations in urban areas can be pricey; most chain hotels will run from $60 to $80 per night, although there are budget alternatives. Minneapolis, Denver, and Salt Lake City all have affordable hostel options. You can find good independent budget hotels in Salt Lake City and Denver, and for the adventurous there's always camping. Whatever your budget, plan ahead so you're not left stranded on the roadside; during the summer tourist season these cities attract lots of visitors, and budget accommodations may be snapped up quickly by vacationing families.

Transportation

This trip runs a little over 1,500 miles, so gas should cost you around $200, more if you plan to do side trips. Additional car-related expenses may include parking fees at downtown hotels and attractions, and tips for the valet service. Plus, if you speed through Kansas, you might as well budget for a $150 to $200 ticket; it's practically guaranteed they'll catch you.

Once you get to a city, save some cash and a lot of hassle by leaving the car in your hotel lot and visiting the downtown areas on foot; lot parking can run up to $7, and sometimes meters are scarce. Public transportation options will run from $1.50 to $2.50 for a one-way ticket (you can usually get a 1-day pass for $6 or less.)

Food

While you'll find some splurge-worthy restaurants on this trip, there are also great ethnic and American eateries where you can fill up for $10 or less. If you grab breakfast on the cheap at diner-style joints, or do the muffin-and-coffee routine, you could potentially spend as little as $25 to $28 a day on food and still eat pretty well. A couple of microbrews with your burger will send your budget up into the $35 range, making Happy Hours an attractive option. Some Happy Hour food specials are just a bunch of wimpy fried mozzarella sticks or a few pitiful stuffed potato skins, but places like Rudolph's BBQ in Minneapolis offer cheap and tasty pulled pork sandwiches and riblets, in portions that almost make dinner unnecessary.

Starting Out: Minneapolis, MN

Minnesota's Twin Cities of Minneapolis and St. Paul lie on either side of the Mississippi River. Minneapolis is about 10 miles west of downtown St. Paul. In Minneapolis you'll find most of the skyscrapers, clubs, attractions, and nightlife. The state capital of St. Paul offers a slower pace and a more European sensibility.

You'll probably want to spend most of your time in Minneapolis, making occasional trips about 10 miles east on I-94 to see a museum or other attraction in St. Paul. Minneapolis has a thriving art and music scene (home of The Replacements, anyone?) and sells more theater tickets per capita than anywhere else in the country except New York City.

Urban Heartland Roadtrip

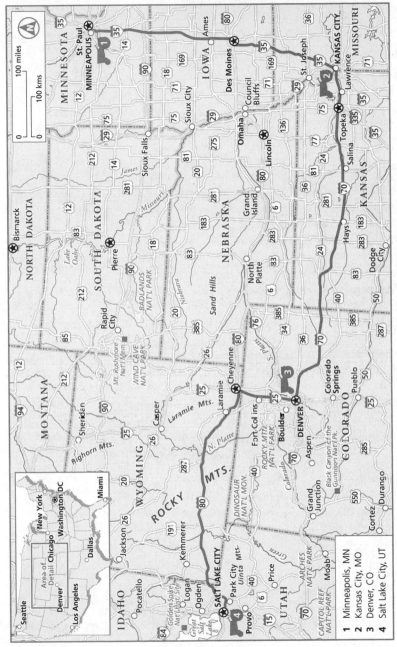

1 Minneapolis, MN
2 Kansas City, MO
3 Denver, CO
4 Salt Lake City, UT

Minneapolis **Nuts & Bolts**

Area Code   The area code in Minneapolis is 612; in St. Paul it's 651. To place a local call between these area codes, just dial the ten-digit area code and number; no need to include the "1."

Business Hours   Banks and offices are generally open Monday to Friday 9am to 5pm; some banks also have hours on Saturday. Most department stores are open until 9pm every day except Sunday, when many close at 7 or 8pm. Supermarkets are generally open until 9pm, although there are some in the area open 24 hours. Bars are generally open daily until 2am.

Drugstores   Several Walgreens pharmacies in the Twin Cities are open 24 hours. Depending on your location, try the store at 2426 Hennepin Ave. S. (☎ 612/377-2733), or the Northeast Minneapolis store at 2643 Central NE (☎ 612/789-6205).

Emergencies   Call ☎ 911 if you need the police, fire department, or an ambulance.

Hospitals   **Fairview University Medical Center,** 420 Delaware St. SE, Minneapolis (☎ 612/273-3000) has a 24-hour emergency room, as does **St. Joseph's Hospital,** 69 W. Exchange St. in St. Paul (☎ 651/232-3000).

Internet   The brand-new downtown Minneapolis central library at 300 Nicollet Mall (☎ 612/630-6000) offers free Wi-Fi access, as do many of the local coffee shops.

Laundry   Get your clothes all clean at the coin-operated **Rainbow Laundromat** (☎ 612/377-3365), located at 2540 Hennepin Avenue S. The staff will do your laundry for $1 a pound. The catch is you have to have a 10-pound minimum.

Liquor Laws   As in other states, the legal drinking age in Minnesota is 21. Only 3.2% beer is sold in grocery and convenience stores, and liquor stores are closed on Sundays. The legal blood alcohol limit is 0.08.

Newspapers & Magazines   The major daily in Minneapolis is the **Star Tribune** (www.startribune.com), which competes with the St. Paul-based **Pioneer Press** (www.twincities.com). **The Rake** (www.rakemag.com) is a free monthly magazine covering Twin Cities' culture, entertainment, and art (its motto: "Fight Commonism!"), while the free weekly newspaper **City Pages** (www.citypages.com) offers extensive weekly event info.

Police   For non-emergencies, contact the Minneapolis Police Department (☎ 612/370-4777).

Radio   Tune your FM radio to KNOW (91.1) for Minnesota Public Radio broadcasting. KCMP "The Current," their sister station (89.3), offers the best in new and original music. Check out KXXR (93.7) for rock, WGVX (105.1) for alternative, and KTTB (96.3) for hip-hop and R&B. For news and sports, tune in to AM KSTP (1100).

Taxes   Minnesota is unusual in not having a sales tax on clothes. Maybe they compensate by having high restaurant and alcohol taxes: Restaurant tax is 10%, and the alcohol tax is 9% in general, and 12.5% in downtown Minneapolis. The general sales tax is 7% in Minneapolis and 6.5% in the rest of the state. Hotel tax is 13%.

Television   You'll find PBS (KTCA) on channel 2, CBS (WCCO) on channel 4, ABC (KSTP) on channel 5, Fox (KMSP) on channel 9, and NBC (KARE) on channel 11.

Time Zone   The Twin Cities are within the Central Time Zone.

Transit Information   Call the Metropolitan Transit Commission (☎ 612/373-3333) for info, or check out their website at www.metrotransit.com.

Useful Numbers   For road conditions in Minnesota, call ☎ 511.

Visitors' Center   The Minneapolis Convention and Visitors Bureau is at 250 Marquette Ave. S, Suite 1300 (☎ 888/676-MPLS; www.minneapolis.org). GLTB travelers should check out the bureau's gay travel website (www.gltbminneapolis.org). Stop by the Visitors Bureau, open Monday through Friday from 8am to 5pm, for free maps of the Twin Cities area and guides to local restaurants and attractions. Alternately, you can download and print free maps anytime (PDF format) at their website.

Weather   Call ☎ 763/512-1111 to get the time and latest weather info; or go online to weather.wcco.com.

Getting Around

Minneapolis streets are laid out along a north-south grid pattern, except in downtown, where streets run northwest-southeast along the Mississippi River. The downtown area includes the pedestrian-friendly **Nicollet Mall,** which has lots of shops, restaurants, and pubs; the historic **Riverfront;** and the **Warehouse district,** where much of the city's nightlife is located. Across the river is the **Northeast** neighborhood of Minneapolis, a somewhat gritty part of town that has housed generations of immigrants, and is now becoming a popular destination for artists and indie types. Running south out of downtown is **Nicollet Ave.,** known as "Eat Street" for its wealth of affordable ethnic restaurants. Just to the southwest, near the intersection of Lake St. and Hennepin Ave., you'll find the popular **Uptown** neighborhood, which has lots of boutiques and restaurants.

BY CAR

It's fairly easy to get around the Twin Cities area by car. Local drivers were recently voted "most courteous" in the nation, and traffic isn't really that bad, especially if you're used to huge metro areas like New York and Los Angeles. Major highways include the twin branches of I-35 (I-35W runs through Minneapolis and I-35E through St. Paul); I-94, which runs east-west through both cities; and the I-494 and I-694 beltways.

As in many downtown areas, parking and one-way streets can be problematic. It may be more convenient to take public transit and then see things on foot. For areas outside downtown, you will probably want to drive, although the bus or light rail can provide easy access to some attractions.

BY BUS/LIGHT RAIL

The Metropolitan Transit Commission and other regional bus services operate more

COOL IN THE MIDWEST

than 130 city and suburban **bus** lines, providing access to many of the popular destinations. Metro Transit also operates the **Hiawatha Line,** a light rail route which runs south from the Warehouse district in downtown Minneapolis to the Minneapolis airport and the Mall of America.

Within the downtown Minneapolis and St. Paul areas, the fare for the bus and light rail is always 50¢. If you travel outside the downtown zones, the fare is $2 (rush hour) or $1.50 (non-rush hour).

Bus fare is paid upon boarding, but light rail tickets must be pre-purchased at vending machines, which are available at all light rail stops. Free transfers, good for 2½ hours, are available from the bus to the light rail or other bus lines.

If you plan on riding public transportation more than a couple of times, get the $6 day pass, which will give you unlimited rides on the bus and light rail in all zones. Day passes are available at the Metro Transit Store in downtown Minneapolis (719 Marquette Ave.) or from any of the light rail vending machines. For more public transit info, visit www.metrotransit.org.

ON FOOT

Residents of the Twin Cities are big fans of the outdoors. They also have a definite ecological mindset, so you may see more people walking and biking here than in the other places you'll visit. It's very easy to get around downtown on foot, whether you're at street level, or using the skyway system (made up of 62 second-story bridges between buildings—a real godsend during the frigid winters).

If you take public transportation or drive out of downtown, you'll find many great neighborhoods to explore on foot. We can't leave out the miles of beautiful trails that make up the **Grand Rounds,** especially the **Chain of Lakes,** which connects the Lake of the Isles, Lake Harriet, and Lake Calhoun, and is really worth checking out.

BY TAXI

If you need to get a cab in downtown Minneapolis, head to one of the designated taxi stands; otherwise call **Rainbow Taxi** (☎ 612/332-1615) or **Yellow Taxi** (☎ 612/824-4444). Cab fare is $2.50 at the flag drop and $1.90 for each additional mile.

Sleeping

While Minneapolis does have a hostel, other cheap accommodations in good areas are hard to come by. Our advice is to try one of the options listed here, or a chain hotel in one of the surrounding suburbs to the south or east. The Twin Cities area is one of the safest in the nation, but we don't recommend staying in north Minneapolis, as the area has become increasingly crime-ridden in the last few years.

CAMPGROUNDS/HOSTELS

➔ **Minneapolis International Hostel** A few minutes from downtown, this hostel has tons of character and historic charm. A brick Victorian mansion built in the early 1900s, the spot retains much of the elegance its time while providing budget travelers with a safe and convenient lodging option. Room rates vary depending on whether you're staying in a dormitory or a private room (single and double private rooms are available). Be sure to check out the Minneapolis Institute of Arts (across the street!), with free daily admission. *2400 Stevens Avenue S.* ☎ *612/522-5000. www. minneapolishostel.com. 10 units; 6 small dorm-style rooms; 2 single private rooms; 2 double private rooms. Dorms $24–$29 per night. Private rooms $34–$60 per night. Amenities: Kitchen; free on-street parking; free local calls; free Wi-Fi; Internet kiosk.*

Minneapolis Highlights

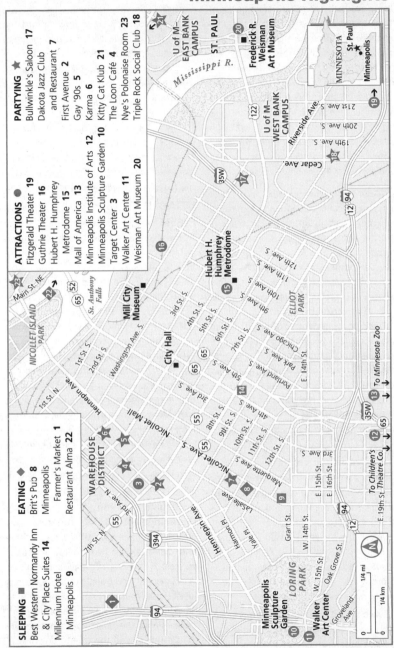

SLEEPING ■

Best Western Normandy Inn & City Place Suites **14**
Millennium Hotel Minneapolis **9**

EATING ◆

Brit's Pub **8**
Minneapolis Farmer's Market **1**
Restaurant Alma **22**

ATTRACTIONS ●

Fitzgerald Theater **19**
Guthrie Theater **16**
Hubert H. Humphrey Metrodome **15**
Mall of America **13**
Minneapolis Institute of Arts **12**
Minneapolis Sculpture Garden **10**
Target Center **3**
Walker Art Center **11**
Weisman Art Museum **20**

PARTYING ★

Bullwinkle's Saloon **17**
Dakota Jazz Club and Restaurant **7**
First Avenue **2**
Gay '90s **5**
Karma **6**
Kitty Cat Klub **21**
The Loon Café **4**
Nye's Polonaise Room **23**
Triple Rock Social Club **18**

➔**Minneapolis Northwest KOA Campground** Fifteen miles northwest of Minneapolis, this well-maintained campground is open from April through October and offers tent and RV sites as well as cabins. The wooded grounds are beautiful in the summer and fall. While there aren't a ton of extra amenities, the campground does offer free Wi-Fi. *10410 Brockton Lane, Maple Grove, MN.* ☎ *763/420-2255. 150 RV sites $28–$38/night; 15 tent sites $26–$28/night; 2 cabins $42–$44/night. Amenities: Pool; coin-op laundry; free Wi-Fi; snack bar; mini golf.*

CHEAP

For cheap accommodations, you can check the rates of chain hotels in Minneapolis and the surrounding 'burbs. Possibilities include the no-frills **Motel 6** (7640 Cedar Ave. S., Richfield, MN; ☎ **612/861-4491**) with rates from $49 per night. A little farther south is the **La Quinta Inn**, near the Mall of America (7815 Nicollet Ave. S., Bloomington, MN; ☎ **952/881-7311**), which runs about $59 per night and offers free breakfast and an indoor pool, sauna, and free Wi-Fi. **Days Inn** in Minneapolis (2407 University Ave. SE; ☎ **612/623-3999**) has rates from $69 per night and includes continental breakfast and Wi-Fi.

➔**AmericInn Richfield** Just south of the city proper and minutes from downtown is the first ring suburb of Richfield and the AmericInn. While you won't get luxury accommodations, you can expect a comfortable room, free Wi-Fi, and a continental breakfast included. For budget travelers, this is a good option. *1200 E. 78th St., Richfield, MN.* ☎ *612/869-8600. 56 units. $78–$89 single or double, includes continental breakfast. Free parking. Amenities: Indoor pool. In room: Cable TV, coffeemaker.*

➔**Evelo's Bed and Breakfast** ★ A beautifully restored 1897 Victorian home, this bed-and-breakfast is conveniently close to downtown, the trendy Uptown neighborhood, and the gorgeous Lake of the Isles. It also offers surprisingly affordable rates. The four guest rooms are done up in Victorian style, and each comes with a coffeemaker, small fridge, telephone, and TV. The only downside is you'll have to share bathrooms with other guests. Location, price, and fabulous breakfasts included in the tariff far outweigh this inconvenience, at least in our opinion. *2301 Bryant Ave. S.* ☎ *612/374-9656. 4 units. $65 single; $85 double, including breakfast. Free on-street parking. In room: TV, coffeemaker, fridge, telephone.*

DOABLE

➔**Best Western Normandy Inn & City Place Suites** ★ Most of the downtown hotels are expensive, but this chain manages to offer nice rooms and amenities at a decent price. The rate is especially good given the location: three blocks from the light rail system and within easy walking distance of almost every downtown attraction. A free continental breakfast, Wi-Fi, and other amenities are available; the only downside is the $6.95 per day parking fee, although you do have unlimited access to your vehicle with no valet fees. All in all, it's a pretty good deal. *405 S 8th St.* ☎ *612/370-1400. 199 units. $94–$124 single or double occupancy. Amenities: Indoor pool; sauna; hot tub; fitness center; free evening cookies and milk. In room: Cable TV, free Wi-Fi, coffeemaker, free local calls.*

➔**Fairfield Inn Minneapolis Bloomington/Mall of America** This affordable chain hotel offers comfortable and clean rooms (with pillow-top mattresses), a continental breakfast, and free Wi-Fi access. Additionally, this location is just across from the Mall of America (you have to go inside at least once for the spectacle). From the mall, you can take the light rail north all the way to downtown, eliminating the need to pay for (and find) parking downtown. *2401 American Blvd. E. Bloomington, MN. ☎ 952/858-8475. 134 units, including 15 suites. $119–$129 single or double. Free parking. Amenities: Indoor pool; hot tub. In room: Cable TV, free Wi-Fi, coffeemaker, free local calls.*

SPLURGE

➜ **Millennium Hotel Minneapolis** ★★ Right in downtown Minneapolis, this slick, modern hotel offers rooms with skyline views and skyway access to many downtown locations. It's also close to the Warehouse district and the best nightlife in town. An indoor pool, sauna, and fitness center are on-site, and the hotel's martini bar is a popular hot spot for pre-dinner drinks. Rooms are spacious and comfortable; but unfortunately there's no free Wi-Fi, and parking will cost you $14 daily (with unlimited access). The hotel often offers package deals, especially in conjunction with downtown events, so definitely check the website or call to see if anything is available. *1313 Nicollet Ave. ☎ 612/332-6000. www.millenniumhotels.com. 322 units. $153 $178 single or double occupancy. Parking $14 daily, unlimited access. Amenities: Indoor pool; sauna; fitness center; on-site restaurant and bar. In room: Cable TV, coffeemaker, Internet access ($9.95 per day).*

Eating
SUPPLIES

Open daily from April through December, the outdoor **Minneapolis Farmers' Market** (312 E. Lyndale N.; ☎ **612/333-1718;** www.mplsfarmersmarket.com) is the premier destination for all kinds of local food products, from veggies to fresh fish. The biggest market crowds are on summer weekends, but vendors are out selling their wares every day from 6am to 1pm. A secondary location on Nicollet Mall in downtown, open every Thursday from May through October, makes it easy for locals to pick up fresh food on the way home.

For other supplies, check out the **Wedge Community Co-op** (2105 Lyndale Ave. S.; ☎ **612/871-3993;** www.wedge.coop). You don't need a membership to shop here, and you'll find great organic products, snacks, and baked goods.

TAKEOUT TREATS

➜ **Crema Café** ★ The gelato-style ice cream at Crema Café almost convinced us we were in some warm, Mediterranean resort town, and not in a cute Italianate courtyard on busy Lyndale Avenue. Inside the stucco building you'll find local ice-cream addicts deciding between flavors like vanilla rum, grapefruit Campari sorbet, and chocolate-covered strawberry. *3403 Lyndale Ave. S. ☎ 612/824-3868. Summer: daily 8am–10:30pm. Winter: Fri–Sat 6:30–11:30pm; Sun 3–8pm. Bus line: 4.*

➜ **Dunn Bros** Grab a cup of caffeinated delight at this coffee shop on Nicollet Mall, where all the beans are roasted on the premises under the watchful eyes of the barista/roasters. A local franchise, Dunn Bros is a favorite destination for Twin Cities coffee drinkers. Most of the clientele prefers their brew dark, strong, and straight up, but you can still get a yummy mocha here, too. *925 Nicollet Mall. ☎ 612/332-7545. www.dunnbros.com. Free Wi-Fi. Mon–Thurs 6am–6pm; Fri 6am–7pm; Sat 7am–7pm; Sun 8am–5pm. Bus line: 18, 10, 11, 17, or 25*

➜ **French Meadow Bakery** Freshly prepared muffins, bagels, sandwiches, and salads and can be found at this popular eatery on Lyndale. Pop in to pick up some to-go items, or have a seat in the cafe (open daily from 6:30am) for some their delish pancakes or egg dishes. *2610 Lyndale Ave. S.*

☎ 612/870-7855. www.frenchmeadow.com. Sun–Thurs 6:30am–9pm; Fri–Sat 6:30am–11pm. Bus line: 4.

→ **Isles Bun and Coffee Company** ★★ Got a sweet tooth? Head to this outpost for the most heavenly cinnamon rolls you've ever tasted. The huge rolls, dripping with nuts, caramel, and cinnamon, are about the only thing served here besides strong cups of coffee. Nobody's complaining, 'cause who could ask for anything more? 1422 W. 28th St. ☎ 612/870-4466. Mon–Sat 6:30am–4pm; Sun 7am–3pm. Bus line: 6, 12, or 17.

→ **Spyhouse Espresso Bar and Gallery** Hang out with local art students, ex-hippies, and the next Great American Writer (well, maybe not) at the Spyhouse Espresso Bar and Gallery, on Nicollet near the Minnesota College of Art and Design. Besides serving damn good coffee, this place shows decent art (hence the "gallery"), and plays interesting music. 2451 Nicollet Ave. ☎ 612/871-3177. Mon–Fri 7am–midnight; Sat–Sun 8am–midnight. Bus line: 18.

EATING OUT
Cheap

→ **Bad Waitress Coffee Shop & Diner** AMERICAN On the corner of 26th Street and Eat Street, this self-consciously ironic retro-diner serves updated American fare. Customers write down their own orders, then take them up to the front to pay—hence the "bad waitress" reference. A server will eventually bring your grub, after you've had time to check out the "class-B" superhero pictures (the ones who never got their own movie) and use the free Wi-Fi. The crowd is mostly young, with some aging hipsters thrown in. Try the pumpkin pancakes for breakfast. 2 E 26th St. ☎ 612/872-7575. Breakfast and lunch $3–$9. Daily 7am–midnight; kitchen closes at 11pm. Bus line: 18.

→ **Baja Sol Tortilla Grill** MEXICAN Near the trendy Uptown area, this Mexican mini-chain delivers healthy, tasty food at an affordable price. Classics like tacos, burritos, and quesadillas are served on their homemade tortillas. What really makes the place is the chips-n-salsa bar, with salsa choices ranging from Minnesota-bland to a five-alarm salsa roja. One of our favorites was the one made with tomatillo, mango, grilled corn, and fire-roasted peppers. 2300 Hennepin Ave. S. ☎ 612/374.9900. Entrees: $4–$7. Daily 11am–9pm. Bus line: 26, 12, or 17.

→ **Birchwood Café** ★ AMERICAN/VEGETARIAN Tucked away in the Seward neighborhood, this cute cafe has a serene vibe that makes you feel like you're already more in tune with nature, and a menu that changes weekly. Vegetarians will find much to enjoy, including the veggie pizza and the Veggie Lucy sandwich, a mozzarella-stuffed black-bean patty with cilantro. Birchwood has options for both vegans and carnivores, making this a versatile destination. Breakfasts and Sunday brunches are yummy; try one of the quiches or veggie strata. 3311 E 25th St. ☎ 612/722-4474. Breakfast and Brunch $3–$9. Lunch $7–$10. Mon–Fri 7am–10pm (9pm in winter); Sat 8am–10pm; Sun 9am–2pm Bus line: 24.

→ **Broder's Cucina Italiana** ★ ITALIAN In southwest Minneapolis, this classy little deli is somewhat off the beaten path, but it's worth a visit if you're looking for really good Italian food at friendly prices. From pizza to pasta dishes to Italian dessert delicacies, everything here says homemade; we especially liked the lasagna and the cannoli. Most of the clientele are neighborhood residents and some walk from their homes (probably a good idea, as there's very limited street-side parking). There are tables if you decide to dine in, or you can grab your food and run. *Note:* Don't confuse this place with its more upscale sister restaurant, Broder's Pasta Bar, across the street. *2308 W. 50th St.* ☎ *612/925-3113. Salads, pasta, and panini: $3–$8. Dessert: $2–$5. Mon–Thurs 11am–9pm; Fri 11am–10pm; Sat 9am–10pm; Sun 10am–9pm. Bus line: 46.*

📺 Best ⬤ → **Holy Land Bakery, Grocery & Deli** ★★ MIDDLE EASTERN Fantastic Middle Eastern food can be found at this combination grocery and restaurant in the Northeast neighborhood of Minneapolis. You'll see representatives from all ethnicities and economic classes scarfing down dolma, falafel, lamb kabobs, and schwerma plates. To sample lots of options, try the lunch buffet from 11am to 3pm Monday through Thursday; and 11am to 9pm Friday through Sunday. The place is so popular with locals that many Holy Land products (including the amazing hummus) are now sold at more upscale groceries throughout the city. *2513 Central Ave. NE.* ☎ *612/781-2627. Entrees: $5–$10. Weekday buffet: $7.80. Weekend buffet: $8.80. Daily 9am–10pm. Bus line: 10.*

→ **Pho 79** ASIAN For great cheap Vietnamese food, you have to try this hole-in-the-wall restaurant on Eat Street. Their specialty is a meaty, flavorful soup served with fresh basil, bean sprouts, and rice noodles, known as *Pho* (pronounced "Fuh"). We've sampled great Pho in authentic Vietnamese restaurants, but this little Midwest outpost served up the best version we've ever had. If you're not into the soup, there are plenty of rice dishes; all are tasty and incredibly affordable. *2529 Nicollet Ave.* ☎ *612/871-4602. Entrees: $5–$8. Mon–Sat 10am–9pm; Sun 10am–8pm. Bus line: 18.*

→ **Sunnyside Up Café** SOUTHWEST/ AMERICAN This little cafe offers traditional breakfast and lunch fare, but its real specialty is Southwest and Mexican-style breakfasts, which locals line up for on weekends. This isn't fine dining, but the huevos rancheros, scrambled eggs and chorizo, and the Cowboy Tort (ground pork layered with tortillas, smothered in refried beans, salsa, and cheese, and topped with two eggs) are all winners. We also recommend the Santa Fe French toast; it was the best we'd ever had. *Note:* This restaurant takes cash only. *2704 Lyndale Ave. S.* ☎ *612/870-4817. Breakfast and lunch: $3–$8. Mon–Fri 6:30am–3pm; Sat–Sun 7am–3pm. Bus line: 4, 21.*

DOABLE

→ **Brit's Pub** ★ PUB GRUB This popular downtown British-themed pub attracts big crowds for its weekday Happy Hour (Mon–Fri 4:30–6:30pm), especially in the summer, when Minneapolitans crowd the large sidewalk patio and every table is taken. The traditional pub food is a hearty mix of favorites like fish and chips, bangers and mash, sandwiches, and burgers, plus a fairly large salad selection. Still, reserve some space for the beer, before heading out back to check out the lawn bowling. It's a British thing, and we didn't get the rules, but the crowd is a friendly mix of fans who love to explain and onlookers who love to be confused. *1110 Nicollet Mall.* ☎ *612/332-3908. www.brits pub.com. Burgers and sandwiches: $7–$9. Entrees: $12–$16. Daily 11am–2am. Bus line: 10, 11, 17, 18, 25.*

→ **Pizza Luce** PIZZA Walk into this Seward pizza joint on any given day and there's usually a meeting of Somali immigrants talking business in the bar area, a host of representatives from the multicolored hair and tattooed set at the outside tables, and a few couples or singles with babies in tow. What unites the crowds is $2 draft beer during Happy Hour (4–7pm) and ridiculously good pizza. There's plenty of fun, creative selections, like the Mexican-themed "Pizza Lupe," but you can't go wrong with "The Classic": sausage, pepperoni, green peppers, olives, and extra cheese. *2200 E. Franklin Ave.* ☎ *612/332-2535. www.pizzaluce.com. Additional locations Downtown and Uptown. Pizza: $11–$18. Daily 11:30am–2am. Bus line: 2.*

➜ **Rudolph's** ★★★ AMERICAN/BBQ Traditional dividing lines melt away when good BBQ is on the menu. You'll find an upbeat, diverse crowd in this dim and crowded space, decorated with photos of old-school movie stars (the place is named after silent-film star Rudolph Valentino). In business since 1975, Rudolph's consistently gets rave reviews. Most everything is good, but we favor the rib-tips with sweet, spicy dipping sauce, or the pulled pork sandwich. You can get generous appetizer-sized portions of both on the cheap at the insane Happy Hours (3–7pm and 10pm–closing), when drinks are 2-for-1 and the apps are just $3.75. *1933 Lyndale Avenue S.* ☎ *612/871.8969. www.rudolphs ribs.com. Sandwiches and burgers $8–$11. Entrees $13–$24. Daily 11am–1am. Bus line: 2, 4, or 113.*

➜ **Yummy** ★ ASIAN One of the best Chinese restaurants in the Twin Cities, Yummy has outstanding food and passes the test of attracting a significant Asian clientele. (No offense intended to non-Asian folks, but one of us is Asian-American and refuses to eat at any Chinese restaurant that doesn't have a certain Asian-to-non-Asian ratio). We particularly liked the pea tips with garlic sauce, the Mongolian beef, and the moo shoo pork. Good dim sum is also served in the afternoons. While you can find cheaper alternatives to Yummy, we're pretty sure you won't find better food. *2450 Nicollet Ave. S.* ☎ *612/870-8000. Entrees: $8–$15. Open Sun–Mon 11am–10pm;* Wed–Thurs 11am–10pm; Fri–Sat 11am–midnight. Bus line: 18.

SPLURGE

➜ **Restaurant Alma** ★★ FRENCH/AMERICAN What sets this restaurant apart from many other splurge-worthy choices is an unbending commitment to seasonal, local ingredients. Chef Roberts, a kitchen dweller since age 14, applies his perfectionist tendencies to a menu divided into three sections: starters, grains/pastas, and entrees. Each section has four choices; the idea is to offer a few near-perfect dishes rather than a laundry list of average options. You can choose one course off of each menu section for a $42 three-course meal, which we highly recommend. If that's a little steep, you can just get one of the fabulous entrees. *528 University Ave. SE.* ☎ *612/379-4909. www.restaurantalma.com. Starters $9–$11. Middle courses $13–$14. Entrees $24–$27. Mon–Sat 5pm–close. Bus line: 2.*

Partying

Whether you want to get your groove on, experience the local music scene, or just kick back at a local bar, you'll find the right spot. Downtown and the Warehouse district are full of upscale, flashy clubs and bars; Uptown is a little more laid-back, but still has a definite hipster-vibe. Check out the area surrounding the U of M for a cheap, college-friendly scene, or try the local bars or pubs near where you're staying. Minnesotans are, on the whole, a friendly and accepting bunch, so you'll feel welcome in most places.

BARS, PUBS & CLUBS
Downtown/Warehouse

➜ **Gay '90s** CLUB Drag shows, dancing, karaoke, and general ass-shaking draw big, friendly crowds to this downtown gay bar and club, supposedly the largest in the

Festivals A-Plenty in Minneapolis

- Head to the District del Sol in St. Paul's West Side neighborhood (which is south of downtown St. Paul). on May 5th and 6th for a **Cinco de Mayo** festival that regularly draws crowds of over 100,000. Celebrate Hispanic culture and the Mexican victory over the French in 1862 with flamenco dancing, food, music, crafts, and a salsa tasting. **www.districtdelsol.com**.

- Warm summer nights get even warmer during the annual Twin Cities **Hot Summer Jazz** festival, held in mid-June. With multiple events at different stages throughout the city, plus well-known jazz musicians, the popularity of the event has soared. Crowds usually exceed 70,000 people over the course of the celebration. **www.hotsummerjazz.com**.

- One of the largest Pride festivals in the U.S., the Twin Cities **GLBT Pride Festival** takes place every year in June in the Loring Park neighborhood of Minneapolis. The 2-day event features a popular parade, multiple music events, fireworks, and a large history pavilion. ☎ **612/305-6900; www. tcpride.com**.

- Minneapolitans celebrate all things connected to summer at the **Aquatennial,** a 10-day festival held in mid-July. Events include beach volleyball, a triathlon, sandcastle building, and outrageous competitions in boats made out of empty milk cartons. The festival ends with a terrific fireworks show that rivals anything put on for the 4th of July. **www. aquatennial.com**.

- The Minneapolis **Uptown Art Fair,** held every year in early August, began over 40 years ago as a small event where artists propped up their wares on the sidewalk. Today, the event is a nationally recognized 3-day fine-art fair featuring the work of over 350 artists and attracting some 300,000 people a day. **www.uptownminneapolis.com/art-fair**.

- Each August, Minneapolis welcomes hundreds of writers, actors, directors, and artists for a marathon of edgy theater known as the **Minnesota Fringe Festival.** With 800 performances at over 20 venues scattered throughout the city, this multiday event is the largest non-juried performing arts festival in the U.S. **www.fringefestival.org**.

- For a real slice of Minnesota life, you have to go to the annual **Minnesota State Fair,** which features everything from prize pigs to huge pumpkins. Be sure to check out the Minnesota State Dairy Princess competition, where finalists' faces are carved into 90-pound blocks of butter and put on display in a refrigerated booth. (That would make them . . . like buttah!) The fair runs from late August through Labor Day in St. Paul. **www.mnstatefair.org**.

- Billed as the "oldest and coldest celebration in the nation," the St. Paul **Winter Carnival** in January offers ice-fishing contests, hockey, ice-skating, curling, and other ice-related events, including the Midwest's largest ice-carving competition. Brrr . . . better bring your long johns if you're coming to this. **www.winter-carnival.com**.

COOL IN THE MIDWEST

Midwest. A lot of straight people party here, too, especially on dance nights. With three dance floors, two restaurants, and seven bars, there's more than enough room for everyone to get their groove on. (Although one bar in the back remains exclusively gay and male.) *408 Hennepin Ave.* ☎ *612/333-7755. 18+. Daily until 1am.*

→ **Karma** CLUB Featuring the best hip-hop and R&B DJs, this elaborate downtown club draws a high-fashion crowd who really let loose on the dance floor. Expect a long line outside the door. Once you get inside, the 9-foot chandelier, multiple plasma screens, and purple velvet couches should clue you in: This is an over-the-top kind of experience. *315 1st Ave.* ☎ *612/333-3200. www.karmampls.com. 21+, some nights 18+. Cover $5–$10. Tues–Sun 9pm–2am.*

→ **The Loon Cafe** BAR Back in the 1980s, before the Warehouse district became the nightlife capital of Minneapolis, this sports bar and grill paved the way for revitalization. Today, the bar still offers sports coverage and tasty pub grub, while serving as a great pre-game stop for those on their way to the Target Center. Try the legendary spinach dip; it's delish. *500 1st Ave. N.* ☎ *612/332-8342. Mon–Sat 11am–1am; Sun 11:30am–midnight.*

Uptown

→ **Figlio** ★ BAR This cool, upscale restaurant and bar in Uptown is almost always busy, but it gets especially packed during the two Happy Hours. A crowd spanning college-age to early-30s hits the bar for the $2 tap beer and appetizer menu. Try the local Summit Pale Ale and an order of mini-fries topped with Gorgonzola cheese (yummy). Favorites like Newcastle Brown and Guinness are also on tap, on top of house wine specials. Weekday Happy Hours run 4 to 7pm and 10pm to midnight; Saturday Happy Hour is noon to 7pm, and Sundays are Happy Hour all day. *3001 Hennepin Ave.* ☎ *612/822-1688. www.figlio.com. Sun–Thurs 11:30am–1am; Fri–Sat 11:30am–2am.*

→ **Williams Uptown Pub & Peanut Bar** PUB College kids and young professionals get serious about partying at this multi-level

Pretty Buildings: Twin Cities Architecture

The Minneapolis art scene has been buzzing in the last couple of years, as several museums and theaters have completed building projects and expansions, including the **Walker Art Center,** the **Children's Theater Company,** the **Minneapolis Institute of Arts,** and most recently, the **Guthrie Theater.** The Guthrie's new $125-million building, designed by French architect Jean Nouvel, features a circular form with a cantilevered bridge extending out toward the river. While the dark-blue metallic exterior has been unfavorably compared to that of an Ikea store, at night the metal glows an eerie, beautiful indigo. The Guthrie's not the first stainless steel architectural attraction in the city, however.

The **Weisman Art Museum,** designed by Frank Gehry and completed in 1993, features the architect's trademark jutting curves and angles. It has also garnered its share of humorous descriptions, including an "exploding silver artichoke." Both buildings are worth seeing while you're here; the Guthrie is on the west bank of the Mississippi (818 S. 2nd St.; ☎ **612/225-6000;** www.guthrie theater.org), and the Weisman (333 E. River Rd.; ☎ **612/625-9494;** www. weisman.umn.edu) is less than 2 miles away on the east bank, an easy walk or bike ride if the weather is fine.

You can get your polka on at Nye's.

pub with a ridiculous beer selection: 300 bottled varieties and 70-some on tap. The downstairs bar is more casual, with peanut shells littering the floor. (Besides the peanuts and Buffalo wings, the food's not that great.) Plan to eat elsewhere and then come here to have a beer, play pool, or get an eyeful of the Minnesota college scene. *2911 Hennepin Ave. S.* ☎ *612/823-6271. Mon–Wed 4pm–1am; Thurs–Fri 4pm–2am; Sat noon–2am; Sun noon–1am.*

Nicollet

→ **Azia & Caterpillar Lounge** ★ BAR We got a tip on this über-slick restaurant-lounge from our waiter at **Yummy** (p. 398), who heads to the Caterpillar lounge almost nightly. Gays, straights, and undecideds mingle easily in the upscale lounge, while DJs spin almost nightly by the dance floor. The dress code is supposedly casual, but everyone we saw was all glammed up for a night on the town, so don't come in your grubbies. Happy Hour kicks in at 10pm and lasts till closing at 2am, making this a great spot for late-night drinks. Asian-themed

snacks will keep you from drinking on an empty stomach. *2550 Nicollet Ave.* ☎ *612/813-1200. www.aziarestaurant.com. Mon–Sat 11am–2am; Sun 3pm–2am.*

University Environs

→ **Bullwinkle's Saloon** BAR The one-buck domestic taps served at the daily Happy Hour probably explain why this is the dive bar of choice for U of M students, but we liked the casual atmosphere and tasty, cheap food (try the famous dogs). It can get packed during any televised game, so if you're on your own, try the "Lonely Guy" burger, served with chopped garlic and melted pepper jack cheese—it may help clear you a seat. *1429 Washington Ave. S.* ☎ *612/338-8520. www.bullwinkles.net. Mon–Sat 11am–1am; Sun noon–1am.*

LIVE MUSIC

Rock/Indie/Eclectic

MTV Best ◉ → **First Avenue** ★★ While probably most famous as the place where Prince got his start, this Minneapolis institution has hosted just about every big

Culture Vulture: Twin City Theaters

Minneapolis is an important theater center in the U.S., with major regional theaters and a thriving professional scene. Its stages have nurtured major American playwrights, and continue to produce important new work. In addition to beautiful old houses like the **Orpheum Theatre**, the **State Theatre**, and **Pantages Theatre** in the Historic Theatre District (www.hennepintheatre district.org), which present touring shows, comedy, dance, music, and theater, there's a lively scene for homegrown work and revivals by local companies. Here are some of the companies that make the (theater) scene in Minneapolis:

➜ **The Guthrie Theater** One of the oldest regional theaters in the U.S. (opening in 1963), the Tony-winning Guthrie has recently moved into brand-new digs in the Theatre District that have three performance spaces for their revivals and re-imaginings of classic work and development of new plays. They led off 2007 with a revival of *The Glass Menagerie*. Ticket prices range from about $20 to $40 in the larger space, with $15 rush tickets available 45 minutes before the show, and tickets in the $15 range in the smaller spaces. There are also ongoing classes, and a backstage tour available. *818 South 2nd Street;* ☎ *877/44-STAGE; www.guthrietheater.org.*

➜ **McGuire Theater** The result of the Walker Art Center's recent expansion effort, this brand-new, 385-seat theater offers performances of new and experimental works by companies like The Riot Group. Tickets are generally $20 and are available for purchase at the Walker Art Center box office or online at the museum's website. *www.walkerart.org. 1750 Hennepin Ave.* ☎ *612/375-7600.*

➜ **Mixed Blood Theater** Since 1976, Mixed Blood has presented new work and revivals that utilize a multi-racial company, "using theater as a vehicle for artistry, entertainment, education and social change. Mixed Blood

name in the business. It's also seen tons of smaller local and touring acts, who play in the connected Seventh Street Entry venue. On nights when there isn't a big show, you'll find local DJs spinning for crowds of mostly friendly locals. Affordable prices and a low-key vibe make this a popular alternative to some of the more upscale downtown clubs. *701 1st Ave.* ☎ *612/332-1775. www.first-avenue.com. 21+, some nights 18+. Cover $3–$6 for dance nights.*

➜**Kitty Cat Klub** ★ For its pure, eclectic love of music, this local club deserves mad props. There's everything from folk to reggae to bossa nova (and it's all classified neatly for you by genre on the website). A crowd of indie-intellectual types and Bohemian-luxe decor offer a definite alternative to the downtown club scene. *315 14th Ave. SE.* ☎ *612/331-9800. www.kitty catklub.net. Mon–Sat 9am–1am; Sun noon–1am. Cover $5–$8 most shows.*

➜**Triple Rock Social Club** Local punk acts plus a good dose of rock usually comprise the lineup at this small venue and bar, where clean-cut college kids mingle with more serious punk devotees. If a band isn't playing, check out the jukebox, a weird mix of punk and other genres. Don't miss the food and drink here—we found a good beer selection and a surprisingly vegan-friendly menu. *629 Cedar Ave. S.*

Theatre addresses artificial barriers that keep people from succeeding in American society." With plays ranging from Dael Orlandersmith's *Yellowman* to a revival of *The Pajama Game*, the company offers several productions a season with tickets in the $11–$28 range. *1501 S. Fourth St.; ☎ 612/338-0937; www.mixedblood.com.*

→ **Penumbra Theatre**   Founded in 1976, the Penumbra Theatre company is one of the most influential Black theaters in the nation, offering productions that reflect the diverse experiences and contributions of African Americans. Past productions have included the plays of the late Pulitzer prize winner August Wilson, who debuted at the Penumbra in 1982. Tickets range from $15 to $40, and are available for purchase online at the theater's website. *270 N. Kent St., St. Paul; ☎ 651/224-3180; www.penumbratheatre.org.*

→ **Theatre de la Jeune Lune**   This theater's French name, "Theatre of the New Moon," reflects its commitment to offering new artistic perspectives on a wide variety of traditional works. A recent recipient of the Regional Theatre Tony Award, the Theatre de la Jeune Lune's productions are highly physical and visually stunning. Tickets are $15 to $30, depending on the performance, and may be reserved by calling the box office. *105 N. First St.; ☎ 612/332-3968; www.jeunelune.org.*

→ **The Jungle Theater** located in Uptown, mixes classic and contemporary plays, in its mission to present new work by new artists (which it has done since 1991) in an intimate, 150-seat theater. *2951 Lyndale Ave. S.; ☎ 612/ 822-7063; www.jungletheater.com.*

In addition. The **Brave New Workshop** (2605 Hennepin Ave. S.; ☎ **612/332- 6620;** www.bravenewworkshop.com) spends weekends putting on outrageous live sketch comedy reviews similar to *Saturday Night Live.*

☎ *612/333-7399. www.triplerocksocialclub. com. 21+, some nights 18+. Cover $5–$8, some shows tickets only.*

Jazz/Blues

→ **Dakota Jazz Club and Restaurant** ★ Formerly located in St. Paul, the Dakota moved to the Nicollet Mall in Minneapolis a few years back and St. Paul jazz aficionados have been mourning ever since. The hot new location still offers the same great local and national jazz acts, plus even better food. Check the website for schedules and ticket info, or if you're in the mood for a big splurge, make a dinner reservation and listen to top jazz while dining on

award winning cuisine. *1010 Nicollet Mall. ☎ 612/332-1010. www.dakotacooks.com.*

Piano Bar/Polka

🅼 Best ♥ → **Nye's Polonaise Room** ★★ Get a true taste of the Midwest at this historic piano bar and polka joint, where locals and out-of-towners have been coming for over 50 years. You can bet the glitzy old-school decor is real, not retro. Hearty singalongs and oompah polka music accompany traditional Polish fare and stiff drinks. Stop in for a couple of cocktails and some fun, but don't expect fashionable crowds; people here are keeping it real. *112 E Hennepin Ave. ☎ 612/379-2021. Mon–Sat 11am–2am; Sun 4pm–2am. No cover.*

COOL IN THE MIDWEST

What to See & Do

With twenty major museums, live music opportunities, and all kinds of theater, it's practically a given that your time here will get your creative juices flowing. Besides the area's well-known art and theater scene, there are also plenty of outdoor attractions and nightlife galore. Minneapolis has its own unique blend of art and culture, with the added bonus of unpretentious friendliness.

THE TOP ATTRACTIONS

→ **Fitzgerald Theater** Owned by Minnesota Public Radio, the historic Fitzgerald Theater is famous for hosting Garrison Keillor's *A Prairie Home Companion* radio show. It has recently garnered even more attention for its "starring role" in the Hollywood film written by Keillor and loosely based on the radio program. While the weekly radio show is often broadcast from locations across the U.S., there are still plenty of opportunities to be a part of the live audience at the Fitz.

Lindsay Lohan, however, will probably not be in attendance. In addition to Keillor's show, the theater also presents music, comedy, and spoken word performances. *10 E. Exchange St. St. Paul, MN.* ☎ *651/290-1221. http://fitzgeraldtheater.publicradio.org/. Tickets for Prairie Home Companion $10–$40. Tickets available at the box office or through Ticketmaster.*

→ **Mall of America** It's a madhouse inside this shrine to American consumerism: With 520 specialty stores, several major department stores, restaurants, movie theaters, and a theme park (complete with roller-coaster). Whether you wear out your credit cards, or somehow manage to just window shop, you really should stop by this mother-of-all-malls, if only for a quick peek. We recommend taking the light rail to and from, unless you're actually planning on shopping, in which case you'd better clear out your car trunk. *60 E. Broadway, Bloomington, MN.* ☎ *800/879-3555. www.mallofamerica.com. Mon–Fri 10am–9:30pm; Sat 9:30am–9:30pm; Sun 11am–7pm.*

The Twin Cities Shopping Experience

From incense and smoking paraphernalia to T-shirts and gifts, **Electric Fetus**, established in 1968, has a little bit of everything, plus a whole lotta music. One of the best independent music stores in the country, the Electric Fetus offers tons of genres, on top of plenty of local bands. Most of the staff work on the side as musicians, artists, or DJs (or is it the other way around?), so ask for their top picks. This a must-shop for anyone interested in the Twin Cities music scene. *2000 4th Ave. S.* ☎ *612/870-9300. www.electricfetus.com. Mon–Fri 9am–9pm; Sat 9am–8pm; Sun 11am–6pm.*

Showcasing the work of local clothing, accessory, and jewelry designers, the unique **Design Collective** ★★ is a Minneapolis treasure. Owned and operated by designer Christina Nguyen, the store was created with the dual mission of providing access to affordable couture clothing and giving fledgling artists a chance to show their original designs. Today, the store features the work of over 60 local designers. An ever-changing lineup of stylish options runs from T-shirts and skirts to wristbands and neckties. As an antidote to Mall of America madness, or just as an exercise in artistic appreciation, this is a stop worth making. *1311 26th St W.* ☎ *612/377-1000. www.designcollectivempls.com. Mon 11am–7pm; Wed–Sat 11am–7pm; Sun noon–6pm.*

Minneapolis . . . with a cherry on top.

FREE ➜ **Minneapolis Institute of Arts** ★ With a collection of 100,000 objects of fine and decorative art spanning 5,000 years, the MIA offers visitors a unique look at the history of world art. Exhibits include contemporary photography, European masters, and a 2,000-year-old mummy. You'll also find intriguing architecture and design, including a portion of a house designed in the Prairie School style. *2400 S. 3rd Ave. ☎ 888/MIA-ARTS. www.artsmia.org. Free admission (except select special exhibits). Tues–Wed and Fri–Sat 10am–5pm; Thurs 10am–9pm; Sun 11am–5pm. Bus line: 18 or 11.*

➜ **Walker Art Center/Minneapolis Sculpture Garden** Having completed its 130,000-square-foot expansion project, the Walker Art Center is once again open to the public, with nearly twice its original space. This vanguard contemporary art institution continues to display edgy, groundbreaking exhibitions of painting, sculpture, photography, and multimedia art. They also host performance art, film

viewings, lectures, and spoken-word events. Adjoining the Walker is the **Minneapolis Sculpture Garden** ★, the largest urban sculpture garden in the country. While you're there, don't miss the famous Claes Oldenburg and Coosje van Bruggen sculpture "Spoonbridge and Cherry." (It's just what its name implies, on a startling scale.) *1750 Hennepin Ave. ☎ 612/375-7622. www.walkerart.org. Admission $8 ($5 with student ID); free admission Thurs 5–9pm and first Sat of every month. Free admission to sculpture garden. Museum Tues–Wed and Sat–Sun 11am–5pm; Thurs–Fri 11am–9pm. First Sat 10am–5pm. Sculpture garden daily 6am–midnight. Bus line: 4, 6, 12, or 25.*

MORE THINGS TO SEE & DO

If you think you can handle one more museum, check out the **Science Museum of Minnesota** (120 W. Kellogg Blvd.; ☎ 651/221-9444; www.smm.org). The museum highlights natural history, science, and technology, and features hands-on exhibits. Also housed here is a popular

COOL IN THE MIDWEST

collection of "questionable medical devices," including mechanisms to increase breast size and cure erectile dysfunction.

Indie film fans may be interested in the **Oak Street Cinema** (309 Oak St. SE), and the **Bell Auditorium** (10 Church St. SE), two independent theaters operated by the Minnesota Film Arts society (www.mnfilm arts.org; see website for schedule) that show documentary, independent, and foreign films.

PLAYING OUTSIDE

The Twin Cities have some of the loveliest park systems in the country. With more than 1,000 lakes dotting the landscape, wrapped by 300 miles of parkland trails (visit **www.minneapolisparks.org** for maps and information about the walking/ biking trails), there are plenty of outdoor activities to enjoy within the city limits.

FREE → **Grand Rounds Scenic Byway** ★ This 50-mile greenbelt of lakes, parks, pathways, and bike trails surrounds the city of Minneapolis and offers many scenic, historic, and recreational attractions. With seven different districts, the beltway includes many of the most popular outdoor destinations in the city, including the Chain of Lakes (comprised of the Lake of the Isles, Lake Harriet, and Lake Calhoun) and Minnehaha Falls. Information and maps of the byway are available at the Longfellow House in Minnehaha Park. *4800 Minnehaha Ave. S.* ☎ *612/230-6400. www. minneapolisparks.org/grandrounds. Mon–Fri 8am–4:30pm.*

FREE → **Minnehaha Falls and Park** Immortalized in Hendry Wadsworth Longfellow's famous *Song of Hiawatha* poem, this 53-foot waterfall is a popular destination for visitors regardless of the season. In the summer, Minneapolitans head here to picnic and hike in the 171-acre Minnehaha Park. There are also 15 miles of

jogging and bike trails. In the winter, brave tourists come to check out the sight of a nearly-frozen waterfall. The park is also the site of the first frame house built west of the Mississippi. Who knew? *4801 Minnehaha Ave. S.* ☎ *612/230-6400. Daily 6am–10pm. Light rail stop: Minnehaha Park Station.*

Swimming

There're plenty of lakefront beaches and swimming areas to enjoy in Minneapolis, and every local has their own "secret" spot. Lakes are monitored by the Minneapolis Park and Recreation Board to ensure they're safe to swim in. You can check their reports and get more information about the beaches online at **www.minneapolis parks.org**.

Lake Harriet is one of the most popular lakes, with sandy beaches; try Harriet North beach (Lake Harriet Pkwy., 2 blocks east of Roseway Rd.) or Harriet Southeast beach (4740 E. Harriet Pkwy.). Lake Calhoun also has some good beaches. The Lake Calhoun North beach (2710 W. Lake St.), just west of Uptown, is famous for its gorgeous view of the downtown area.

Canoeing

Whether you're a novice or an expert, the Minneapolis area provides plenty of opportunities for canoeing. One of the best places in the city for paddling is Lake Calhoun, which provides scenic views of downtown.

Head to **Wheel Fun Boat Rentals** (3000 Calhoun Parkway E.; ☎ **612/823-5765**) for canoe, kayak, and paddle-boat rental during the summer season. The season runs from April through September, weather permitting. Expect to pay around $13 for a 1-hour canoe rental, with additional hours available at a discounted rate.

If you're interested in a serious canoeing adventure, the **Minnesota Department of Natural Resources** information center

(500 Lafayette Rd., St. Paul, MN; ☎ 651/ 296-6157) provides maps and information on the state's waterways. You can also go online at www.dnr.state.mn.us/canoeing. The **REI** outfitters store in Bloomington (750 W. American Blvd.; ☎ 952/884-4315) has info and a good selection of gear to rent or purchase.

Biking

Minneapolitans are *big* fans of biking. On weekends you'll see packs of serious cyclists, as well as casual bikers just pedaling to the nearest co-op to get some supplies. Some city residents actually commute nearly year-round by bicycle. We don't think we're up to winter biking, but if you're in Minneapolis in more temperate weather, you can rent a bike at **Calhoun Rental** (1622 Lake St.; ☎ 612/ 827-8231), just 1 block from the Chain of Lakes paved bikeway.

For maps and other information on biking in Minneapolis, pick up the *Bicycle Guide and Commuter Map* at any local bike shop, or check out the city's website, **www.ci.minneapolis.mn.us/bicycles**.

SPECTATOR SPORTS

With five major teams representing basketball, football, baseball, soccer, and hockey, there's always some kind of sport going on in the Twin Cities.

Baseball

The Major League **Minnesota Twins** ☎ 612/33-TWINS; http://minnesota.twins. mlb.com) have won three recent division titles and continue to find loyal support from their home state. Fans complained for years that the Hubert H. Humphrey Metrodome, where the Twins have played home games since 1982, is totally unsuited to baseball. The pleas were finally heard and a new field should be completed by 2010. Tickets start at $7, going up to $108, in

a rather complex system you can go over on the team website. (Certain times of year, and games with certain teams are cheaper than games against top rivals, for example.)

Football

The Metrodome is also home to the NFL's **Minnesota Vikings** (☎ 612/338-4537; www.vikings.com). While baseball fans complain about the Metrodome, football enthusiasts don't seem to mind as much. Some fans even debate whether the dome, with its propensity to trap and amplify sound, actually provides a home-team advantage. The Vikings have sold out 91 consecutive home games (as of the end of 2006), so it's a bit of a challenge to get a ticket to a game; try various online ticket sale sites.

Basketball

Minnesota is home to both NBA and WNBA teams. The **Minnesota Timberwolves** (☎ 612/989-5151; www.nba.com/timber wolves) and the **Minnesota Lynx** (☎ 612/ 673-1600; www.wnba.com/lynx) both play home games at the Target Center in downtown Minneapolis. Tickets range from $9 to $99 for the T-Wolves; and $10 to $110 for the Lynx.

Hockey

The NHL's **Minnesota Wild** (☎ 651/989-5151; www.wild.com) play their home games at the Excel Center in downtown St. Paul. Ticket prices range from $16 to $92.

Soccer

Since 1994, the United Soccer League's **Minnesota Thunder** (☎ 651/917-8326; www.mnthunder.com) has been the state's professional soccer team. In 2005, the Thunder made it to the semifinals in the US Open Cup. The team plays home games at the James Griffin Stadium in St. Paul.

COOL IN THE MIDWEST

On the Road to Kansas City, MO

Minneapolis, MN to Kansas City, MO 432 miles

Ease on down the road by moseying on down to Kansas City, home of live jazz, blues, and barbeque. The shortest leg of the entire trip (approximately 432 miles), the I-35 route takes you almost directly south, through Minnesota and Iowa farmland. This mix of old and new Kansas City tunes should get you ready for good times.

On the Road **Nuts & Bolts**

Where to Fill Up   There are plenty of gas stations on I-35, but if you have time, stop in Madison County, Iowa. You can see the covered bridges and John Wayne's birthplace. The gas station is just across the street from the visitor center, which has area maps (see below).

The Fastest Way   Take I-35W from Minneapolis south to join I-35, which will take you all the way down to Kansas City, Missouri. This should take about 6 hours, depending on traffic.

Check your E-Mail   You may be driving through cornfields, but you can still log on to the Internet (Iowa rest stops along I-35 are equipped with free Wi-Fi. Signs are posted inside the shelters with directions on how to log on.

Detour: Crossing the Bridges of Madison County, IA

Rolling fields of corn eventually lose their charm, so ease your boredom by stopping in **Madison County, Iowa,** to see the covered bridges featured in the popular novel and film, *The Bridges of Madison County.* Take Exit 52 off I-35 and go west 1 mile to St. Charles, where you'll see the **Imes Bridge** and the **St. Charles Welcome Center** (housed in a restored Presbyterian church) on your left (202 E Main St.; ☎ 641/396-2506). Park behind the center, then take the footpath to the bridge. Inside the welcome center you can pick up maps of the area showing the location of the other bridges, but be warned: The staffers are extremely talkative, so it may be hard to get out the door again.

Once you've managed to tear yourself away, continue west, following the signs to the **Holliwell** and the **Cutler-Donahoe** bridges. By this time, you'll be near downtown **Winstead,** featured in the movie, but famous in its own right as the birthplace of Marion Robert Morrison (that's John Wayne to you). Visit the Duke's restored childhood home to see rare photographs and letters, plus the eye patch he wore in the film *True Grit* (216 S. 2nd St.; ☎ 515/462-1044; www.johnwaynebirthplace.org).

By this time, you're bound to be hungry, so stop for lunch at the **Northside Café** (61 W Jefferson St.; ☎ 515/462-1523), the restaurant in the *Bridges* flick where Clint Eastwood stops for coffee. After lunch, visit the **Hogback, Cedar,** and **Roseman** bridges, which are located a few miles outside town, or head back to I-35 and continue on to Kansas City.

Kansas City Playlist: New and old

→ *Kansas City/Hey, Hey, Hey,* **The Beatles,** "Beatles for Sale" 1964
→ *You Almost Had It,* **The Golden Republic,** "The Golden Republic," 2005
→ *Little Wet Head,* **Minus Story,** "No Rest for Ghosts," 2005
→ *Radio,* **Elevator Division,** "Disco," 2004
→ *Kansas City,* **Muddy Waters,** "Muddy 'Mississippi' Waters Live," 2003
→ *Last Headline,* **The Supernauts,** **"Medicine & Love"** 2005
→ *I'll Be Back on Sunday,* **Flee the Scene,** "Doubt Becomes the Addiction," 2006
→ *I'm Tired of That,* **Ida McBeth,** "Special Request," 1999
→ *Parker's Mood,* **Charlie Parker,** "The Genius of Charlie Parker," 2005

Kansas City Nuts & Bolts

Area Code The telephone area code in Kansas City, MO, is 816; in Kansas City, KS, it is 913.

Business Hours Most banks are open on weekdays from 8 or 9am until 5pm. Some banks offer drive-through service during normal business hours and on Saturdays from 8am until noon. Bars and clubs are generally open until 1:30 or 3am, depending on the location's liquor license.

Drugstores **Walgreens** Pharmacy, at 39th Street and Broadway, is open 24 hours (☎ 816/561-6980).

Emergencies Call ☎ **911** if you need the police, fire department, or an ambulance.

Hospitals Saint Luke's Hospital, 4400 Wornall Rd. (☎ 816/932-2000); and Truman Medical Center, 2301 Holmes (☎ 816/556-3000) have emergency care facilities.

Hot lines Suicide Hotline (☎ 816/889-3940); Sexual Assault Hotline (☎ 816/531-0233).

Internet Free Wi-Fi access is available at the Central Library downtown at 10th St. and Baltimore (☎ 816/701-3400); or at the Plaza Branch library, 4801 Main St. (south side of Country Club Plaza) (☎ 816/701-3481).

Laundry/Dry Cleaners If you're out of clean clothes, try Westport Laundry (1409 Westport Rd.; ☎ 816/531-8889), with both self-serve and staff service. And while it's a little far out, you can't beat Fifth Avenue Cleaners (7962 Wornall Rd.; ☎ 816/444-5902) for the price: $1.75 per item. Payment is required in advance, cash only.

Liquor Laws You have to be 21 to drink in Missouri or Kansas, and no alcohol is sold at retail locations on Sunday.

Newspapers & Magazines The *Kansas City Star* is the primary daily newspaper (www.kansascity.com). Other local publications include the *Pitch,* a free alternative monthly covering the art, dining, and music scene (www.pitch.com), and *Kansas City Magazine,* a glossy lifestyle magazine published monthly (www.kcmag.com).

Police For non-emergencies, contact the Kansas City Police Department (☎ 816/234-5000).

Post Office The main post office is located at 300 W. Pershing Rd.; other convenient locations are downtown at 1100 Main St. (City Center Square), or in Westport at 200 Westport Rd. (Westport and Wynadotte St.).

Radio Tune your FM radio to KANU (91.5) or KCUR (89.3) for NPR broadcasting, KMZU (100.7) for country, KRBZ (96.5) for popular alternative music, and KZPL (97.3) for modern rock. For news and sports, check out AM KMBZ (980).

Taxes Kansas City sales tax is 6%; hotel tax is 7.5%.

Television You'll find Fox (WDAF) on channel 4, CBS (KCTV) on channel 5, ABC (KMBC) on channel 9, and NBC (KSHB) on channel 41.

Time Zone Kansas City is on Central Standard Time and observes daylight savings time.

Transit Information Call the Kansas City Area Transportation Authority (☎ **816/221-0660**) for info, or check out their website at www.kcata.org.

Useful Numbers For road conditions in Missouri, call ☎ **800/222-6400;** for Kansas road conditions, call ☎ **800/585-7623.**

Visitors' Center Information for visitors is available by phone at ☎ **800/767-7700,** or visit the Kansas City Visitor Information Centers, located at Union Station (Main and Pershing) and Country Club Plaza (4709 Central). Helpful maps of the city showing the main points of interest and the Metro Area Express (MAX) stops are available at these locations.

Weather Call ☎ **816/561-3694** to get the latest weather info over the phone, or go online to www.thekansascitychannel.com/weather.

Welcome to Kansas City

In its early days, Kansas City was the starting point for wagon trails heading west to Oregon, California, and other westerly destinations. Later, the city became a national center for cattle stockyards and slaughterhouses, which may have something to do with the locals' love for steak and BBQ.

You can always find a good cut of meat in KC, but you may be surprised at what else this town has to offer.

During Prohibition days, Kansas City was *the* party destination for musicians, artists, and boozehounds: Political boss Tom Pendergast allowed alcohol to flow freely and the 18th and Vine district became the epicenter of Kansas City jazz. Today, Kansas City is once again home to cool jazz, a thriving art scene, and a host of young, hip people who have fallen in love with the city's friendly, laid-back vibe.

Getting Around

Kansas City straddles the Missouri and Kansas **state line,** with most of the nightlife, restaurants, and other attractions concentrated on the Missouri side, east of State Line Rd. South of the Missouri river, between I-35 and US Highway 71, lies the **downtown** area, which includes River Market and the up-and-coming Crossroads Arts District.

East of downtown and Highway 71, at the intersection of 18th and Vine, is the historic **jazz district,** which once boasted over 60 jazz clubs. It's now home to several outstanding museums. Restaurants, cafes, bars, and clubs can all be found south of downtown in the **Westport** district, Kansas City's nightlife hub, while the **Country Club Plaza** and **39th Street West** areas also have great dining, shops, and entertainment.

BY CAR

While Kansas City isn't extremely difficult to navigate, one-way streets and construction in the downtown area can be confounding to out-of-towners. We also found that streets names seem to change haphazardly. Except for a few out-of-the-way locations, you can leave your car in the parking lot and get around by public transportation or on foot.

BY BUS

The **MAX,** Kansas City's new Metro Area Express bus line, is a great way to see most of the city's attractions. Operating from 5am until 1am, these modern, climate-controlled buses run along Main Street from River Market to Country Club Plaza, then continue south towards the University of Missouri–Kansas City and its environs. MAX stops have screens featuring real-time arrival information, so you'll always know how long the wait is. Bus fare is $1.25, payable when you board, with transfers available to other bus lines; for $3, you can purchase an all-day pass from the bus driver. Either way, make sure you have the exact amount ready, since you won't get change.

ON FOOT

Although most of Kansas City's districts are too far apart for easy pedestrian access, it's easy to get from one neighborhood to another on the MAX and then jump off to explore the area on foot. Westport, River Market, and Country Club Plaza are especially fun to walk through, with lots of shops and cafes. Good maps that show points of interest and MAX stops are available at most hotels, and at the Kansas City Visitors Centers at Union Station and Country Club Plaza.

BY TAXI

To get a cab, call the **Kansas City Yellow Cab** company (☎ **816/471-5000**), **Checker Cab** (☎ **816/444-4444**), or the **Crown Cab** company (☎ **816/753-9300**). Rates within the city limits are generally $2.20, plus $1.70 per mile traveled.

Sleeping

The Kansas City area has plenty of chain hotels, plus a number of high-end luxury options. Unlike some larger cities on this trip, there are no hostels, so expect to pay between $60 and $80 for a standard room.

CAMPGROUNDS

➔ **Basswood Country Inn and RV Resort** If you're ready to rough it but don't want to *literally* sleep under the stars, try renting a cabin at the Basswood resort, north of Kansas City near the international airport. The cabins house from two to six people and are all equipped with indoor heat and air conditioning; some include kitchens (but no cooking utensils) and cable TV. Beds are provided, but guests must bring their own linens. Laundry facilities, swimming pool, and a general store are on-site. Rates are based on maximum cabin occupancy. Tent areas are also available with water and electricity hook-ups. *15880*

COOL IN THE MIDWEST

Kansas City Highlights

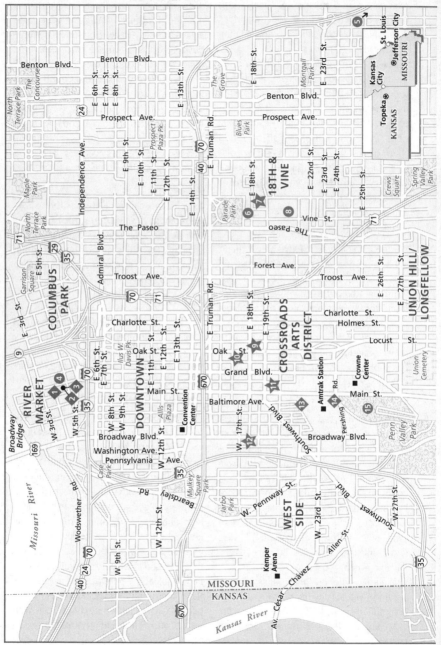

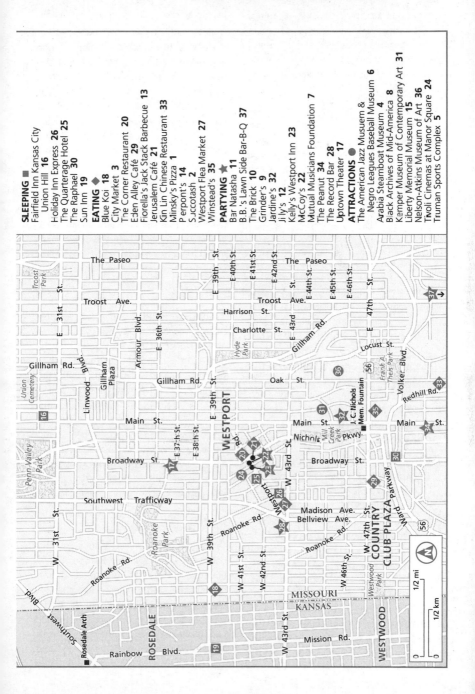

SLEEPING ■
Fairfield Inn Kansas City
Union Hill **16**
Holiday Inn Express **26**
The Quarterage Hotel **25**
The Raphael **30**
Sun Inn **19**

EATING ◆
Blue Koi **18**
City Market **3**
The Corner Restaurant **20**
Eden Alley Café **29**
Fiorella's Jack Stack Barbecue **13**
Jerusalem Café **21**
Kin Lin Chinese Restaurant **33**
Minsky's Pizza **1**
Perpont's **14**
S.Jccotash **2**
Westport Flea Market **27**
Winstead's **35**

PARTYING ★
Bar Natasha **11**
B.B.'s Lawn Side Bar-B-Q **37**
The Brick **10**
Grinder's **9**
Jardine's **32**
Jily's **12**
Kelly's Westport Inn **23**
McCoy's **22**
Mutual Musicians Foundation **7**
The Peanut **34**
The Record Bar **28**
Uptown Theater **17**

ATTRACTIONS ●
The American Jazz Museum &
  Negro Leagues Baseball Museum **6**
Arabia Steamboat Museum **4**
Back Archives of Mid-America **8**
Kemper Museum of Contemporary Art **31**
Liberty Memorial Museum **15**
Nelson-Atkins Museum of Art **36**
Tivoli Cinemas at Manor Square **24**
Truman Sports Complex **5**

Interurban Rd., Platte City, MO. ☎ *816/858-5556. www.basswoodresort.com. 10 cabins, rates range from $55–$119 per night depending on cabin size and amenities. Tent campsites $22 per night, water and electricity included.*

CHEAP

Major chains in the area include the **Best Western Inn** (501 Southwest Blvd., Kansas City, KS; ☎ **913/677-3060**), with single rates from $72 and doubles from $80; the **La Quinta Inn** (1051 N Cambridge St., Kansas City, MO; ☎ **816/483-4120**), with single and double occupancy rates from $74; and the **Comfort Inn** (7300 NE Parvin Rd., Kansas City, MO; ☎ **816/454-3500**), with single and double rates beginning at $65.

➜ **Sun Inn** Affordable prices and a convenient location are the main draws for travelers who stay at the Sun Inn, located just across State Line Rd. in Kansas City, KS. Only a few minutes from the trendy Westport neighborhood (and even closer to West 39th Street's restaurants and shops), this budget hotel offers no-frills, standard rooms and a free continental breakfast. *3930 Rainbow Blvd., Kansas City, KS.* ☎ *913/236-6880. 83 units. $64–$80 single or double occupancy. Free parking. Amenities: Outdoor pool.*

DOABLE

➜ **Fairfield Inn Kansas City Downtown/Union Hill** Friendly staff and a well-maintained property bring repeat guests to this location, situated just south of the Crown Center/Union Station area on Main St. The hotel is quiet and clean, and rooms have free Wi-Fi, cable TV, and an in-room coffee pot. The nearest MAX stop is just a block away, providing convenient access to most of the sights. *3001 Main St. Kansas City, MO.* ☎ *816/931-5700. 116 units. $79–$99 single or double occupancy. AAA discounts available. Free continental breakfast. Free parking. No*

pets accepted. Amenities: Indoor pool; hot tub; fitness center.

➜ **Holiday Inn Express** ★ For location and overall value, it's hard to beat this newly renovated property in the heart of Westport. The rooms are comfortable, with free Wi-Fi access and cable TV, but you won't want to spend much time inside the hotel, since Westport's bars, restaurants, and coffeehouses are all within walking distance. If you do decide to stay in, though, check out the list of local eateries that will deliver to the hotel. *801 Westport Rd. Kansas City, MO.* ☎ *816/931-1000. 109 units. $88–$98 single or double occupancy. AAA discounts available. Free continental breakfast. Free parking. Pets accepted with $25 one time non-refundable fee. Amenities: Fitness center.*

➜ **The Quarterage Hotel** The Quarterage Hotel is in the Westport District, probably the most happening neighborhood of KC. Imagine hitting the bars and sights and then strolling back to your room. Yeah, you pay a little extra, but you avoid the driving and parking hassles. It's a great choice for carefree partying. *560 Westport Rd. Kansas City, MO.* ☎ *816/931-0001. 123 units. $99 and up, single or double occupancy. Free wireless internet. Free hot buffet breakfast. Free parking. No pets accepted. Amenities: Dry sauna; whirlpool; free passes to local gym; cocktail hour in afternoon.*

SPLURGE

➜ **The Raphael** ★★ Overlooking busy Country Club Plaza, this European-style boutique hotel has luxurious rooms, friendly staff, and an old-world ambience. Ask for a room with a view of the Plaza; they're smaller than the rooms facing the back of the building, but the view is worth a little less space. The Plaza's shops and

City Market has been operating in Kansas City since the 1850s.

restaurants are right outside your door, or you can cozy up to the hotel bar for live piano music and drink specials Thursday through Saturday nights. *325 Ward Pkwy., Kansas City, MO.* ☎ *800/821-5343. www.raphaelkc.com. 123 units. $145 double, $170-195 suite. Free valet parking. Amenities: Restaurant; bar. In room: High-speed Internet, Nintendo game console.*

Eating

SUPPLIES

Fruits, veggies, baked goods, and almost anything else food-related can be found at the **City Market** north of downtown at 5th and Main (☎ **816/842-1271;** www.kc-citymarket.com). In operation since the 1850s, the outdoor market is home to Kansas City's farmers' market, plus 37 indoor specialty shops, restaurants, and international groceries. Outdoor market hours are Wednesdays from 9am to 1pm, Saturdays from 6:30am to 3:30pm, and Sundays from 8am to 3pm; the shops have varied hours.

If you've gotta have something organic, gluten-free, free-range, or soy-based, head to **Wild Oats Natural Marketplace** (4301 Main St.; ☎ 816/931-1873), a small natural foods grocery that offers lots of specialty products in addition to healthy everyday basics like granola and trail mix.

TAKEOUT TREATS

➔ **Angie's Italian Ice and Frozen Custard** Order up a traditional shake, malt, ice-cream cone, or fresh frozen custard at the window. Seating is outside only, but that doesn't deter locals, who gather here on summer evenings with their dogs in tow. Try the Turtle (hot fudge, caramel, and pecans over ice cream), or for something a bit different, the fruit gelati, made with layers of Italian ice and frozen custard. Angie's Chicago-style hot dogs are also popular, if you're in the mood for something savory. *1710 W. 39th St.* ☎ *815/405-5815. Daily 10am-10pm. Cash or check only.*

➔ **Broadway Café** ★★ For coffee done right, plus tasty, homemade snacks, you

COOL IN THE MIDWEST

can't beat this cafe, a Kansas City original. In business since 1992, Broadway began roasting its own beans in 1998 and now supplies many other restaurants and coffee joints in the KC area. The original location on Broadway is best for hanging out, with its huge windows, airy brightness, and great people-watching opportunities, but if you just want to grab coffee and run, stop in at Westport Road. *4016 Broadway.* ☎ *816/531-2432 and 301 Westport,* ☎ *816/931-9955. www.broadwaycafeandroastery.com. Mon–Thurs 7am–11pm; Fri 7am–midnight; Sat 8am–midnight; Sun 8am–11pm.*

→ **Chubby's** Open 24 hours a day, this '50s-style diner is a popular destination any time, though it's especially famous for the colorful late-night clientele. Stop by after a night spent in Westport to see and be seen. *3756 Broadway.* ☎ *816/931-2482. Cash only.*

📺 Best ♦ → **Joe's Pizza Buy the Slice** ★★★ In the back of Kelly's Westport Inn, this joint is open until 3am to satisfy your after-hours munchies. From 11am until midnight order a full pie or just a slice; after midnight it's by the slice only. Either way, you can take your pizza back into Kelly's to enjoy with a few beers. And if you're in Westport around lunchtime, try the lunch specials; Tuesdays and Thursdays you can get a slice for $1.25. *4058 Pennsylvania.* ☎ *816/931-2777. www.kellyswestportinn.com. Mon–Sat; 11am–3am; Sun; noon–3am.*

→ **Westport Coffeehouse** Pick up a coffee, smoothie, or made-to-order sandwich at this coffeehouse, tucked away at the intersection of Pennsylvania Ave. and W 40th St. You may decide to stay for a while to use the computers and free Wi-Fi, or come back in the evening for live music upstairs (Thurs–Sun). On weekends, check out standup comedy and small theater productions in the downstairs black box

theater. *4010 Pennsylvania Ave.* ☎ *816/756-3222. Mon–Thurs 7:30am–11pm; Fri 7:30am–1am; Sat 10am–1am; Sun 10am–10pm.*

EATING OUT
Cheap

→ **The Corner Restaurant** AMERICAN What this place lacks in style it makes up for in value. A longtime favorite of Westport locals, this no-frills diner offers an inexpensive but appetizing list of breakfast options all day, every day. Try the Classic Bennie (eggs Benedict) or the breakfast scrambles. A lunch menu is available after 10:30am Monday through Saturday, but Sunday is breakfast only. *4059 Broadway.* ☎ *816/931-6630. Breakfast and lunch $4–$7. Daily 7am–7pm.*

→ **Eden Alley Café** VEGETARIAN In the lower level of the Unity Temple on trendy Country Club Plaza, this feel-good vegetarian restaurant attracts high-end Plaza shoppers, local tattoo artists, and everyone in between. The clientele may not have much in common except their love for Eden Alley's food, but the vibe is warm and relaxed. Try the Betty Bailey Berry salad, served with yummy poppy seed dressing, or the popular vegan burger. *707 W 47th Street (SW corner of 47th and Jefferson).* ☎ *816/561-5415. www.edenalleycafe.com. Starters $3–$5; entrees $6–$9. Mon–Tues 11am–2:30pm; Wed–Sat 11am–9pm.*

→ **Kin Lin Chinese Restaurant** ★ ASIAN UMKC students and locals know this is the place to go for cheap and tasty Chinese food. Portions are generous, and with almost everything on the menu under $8, you won't blow your budget. Between the hours of 11am and 3pm, try the $3.90 daily lunch special, which comes with fried or steamed rice and a spring roll. Our favorite was the Mongolian beef, a chewy, savory, meaty dish with enough green onions to challenge your romantic life for hours. Some vegetarian options are available as well. *314 E. 51st St.* ☎ *816/561-4334. Lunch: $3–$5; Entrees: $5–$8. Mon–Thurs 10:30am–10pm; Fri–Sat 10:30am–10:30pm; Sun noon–10:30pm.*

📺 **Best ☺** → **Oklahoma Joe's BBQ** ★★ AMERICAN A whole lotta gas and BBQ is what you get here. Gasoline, that is. This BBQ joint is operated out of a gas station in urban Kansas City, and there's a constant line of BBQ zealots that makes parking difficult during the lunch rush. But the food makes the hassle and wait worth it. Especially popular is the pulled pork sandwich, rumored to be the best BBQ meat in KC. Another local favorite is the Z-Man sandwich, made with beef brisket, smoked provolone, and onion rings. Owners Jeff and Joy Stehney recommend getting the sandwiches "Carolina style" (with slaw). *3002 W 47th Ave. Kansas City, KS.* ☎ *913/722-3366. www.oklahomajoesbbq.com. BBQ sandwiches $3.95–$5.95; salads $6.25. Mon–Thurs 11am–8:30pm; Fri–Sat 11am–9:30pm.*

→ **Succotash** ★ AMERICAN A hip little eatery that looks out on the City Market, Succotash is a winner for its quirky ambience and amazing food. While open weekdays (except Mondays) for breakfast and lunch, the real action comes weekends, when this becomes a favorite brunch stop for farmers' market shoppers. Try the famous pear-and-pecan pancakes for breakfast, or order the grilled gouda cheese and artichoke heart sandwich for a new twist on an old lunch fave. *15 E. 3rd St.* ☎ *816/421-2807. Breakfast and lunch $4–$8. Tues–Fri 9am–2pm; Sat 8am–3pm; Sun 9am–3pm.*

→ **Westport Flea Market** AMERICAN For a truly eclectic dining experience, visit this working bar and grill that also functions as a flea market on Saturdays and Sundays. The Flea was slated to become a Hooter's restaurant when the owner retired in 2005, but KC locals rallied around the Flea and saved it from orange hotpants. You can still enjoy the best burger in town, surrounded by dingy booths crammed with odds and ends. Ordering is a little tricky: To get a drink, order from the waitress and pay when it arrives; if you want food, order at the counter and wait for your name to be called. *817 Westport Rd.* ☎ *816/931-1986. Cash only, ATM inside. Burgers $5–$8. Sun–Thurs 11am–11pm; Fri–Sat 11am–11:30pm. Shops open Sat–Sun, 10am–5pm.*

→ **Winstead's** AMERICAN For a classic diner meal and garish neon lighting, don't miss the original Winstead's, a Kansas City institution since 1940. The booths are mint-green vinyl monsters that can seat eight people easily. Start your feast with burgers ground daily from steak. For extra calories, down the delicious shakes, or the Winstead "frosty," which predates the Wendy's version by several decades. If you're up early, you can also get a cheap, hot breakfast from 6:30 to 10:30am every morning. *101 Brush Creek (just east of Country Club Plaza).* ☎ *816/753-2244. www.winsteads kc.com. Breakfast $2–$6; burgers $2–$4. Sun–Thurs 6:30am–midnight; Fri–Sat 6:30am–1am.*

Doable

→ **Blue Koi** ASIAN With flavorful dumplings, noodles, and rice dishes, and a hip, colorful interior, this is worlds away from your corner Chinese takeout. To quench your thirst, check out their bubble teas with tapioca. It ain't all kid-friendly *boba*, however: Teas can be customized with a shot of your favorite hard liquor. Try the Blue Koi duck wrap or the crispy tofu for a snack; the Chinese pot roast is delicious if you're ready for a full meal. Vegetarian and vegan items are also available. *1803 W 39th St.* ☎ *816/561-5003. www.kansascitymenus. com/bluekoi. Starters and dumplings $4–$8;*

entrees $9–$11. Mon–Thurs 11am–9:30pm; Fri 11am–10:30pm; Sat noon–10:30pm.

→**Fiorella's Jack Stack Barbecue** AMERICAN With its upscale, sophisticated interior and some of the most popular barbecue in Kansas City, the downtown Fiorella's Jack Stack location proves that you don't have to skimp on style to deliver the goods. Locals swear by their burnt ends, the flavorful finials (yeah, you know you like that word) of a pork or beef brisket. They're smoked a few extra hours for a crusty exterior and fork-tender finish. Tasty sides accompany the 'cue. We asked the employees what their favorite side dish was and almost all of them said the cheesy corn bake. Why? "It's meaty-tasting." They love their meat around here. *101 W. 22nd St.* ☎ *816/472-7427. www.jack stackbbq.com. Lunch and sandwiches $8–$14; entrees $12–$20. Mon–Thurs 11am–10pm; Fri–Sat 11am–10:30pm; Sun 11am–9pm.*

→**Jerusalem Café** MIDDLE EASTERN/ VEGETARIAN If you've had enough of trendy hot spots and pub food, this Westport cafe serves up fresh and healthy Middle Eastern fare in an earthy, laid-back environment. A host of vegetarian and vegan-friendly options are available; try the daily soup or the falafel and hummus sandwich. If you've gotta have your meat, traditional kabobs, gyros, and a delish chicken dill sandwich are on the menu. For an after-dinner smoke, a hookah bar upstairs is open until 3am on weekends and offers a good selection of tobacco. *431 Westport Rd.* ☎ *816/756-2770. www. jerusalembakery.com. Lunch and sandwiches: $5–$9; entrees $11–$13. Mon–Sat 11am–10pm; Sun noon–7pm.*

→**Minsky's Pizza** ITALIAN/PIZZA Three big-screen televisions above the bar, plus multiple other TVs scattered throughout the two-story dining area, make Minsky's Pizza in City Market a true multimedia

experience. Spicy Thai pizza, Philly Cheese steak pizza, or Cheeseburger Pizza (with pickles!) are just a few of their specialties. Vegetarians will like the cheeseless pizza, which is vegan-friendly if ordered on Minsky's original thin crust. Rumor has it that bartenders do shots with the regulars on weekends . . . but you didn't hear that from us. *427 Main St.* ☎ *816/421-1122. www. minskys.com. Calzones and sandwiches $5–$7; medium pizza $13–$14 Sun–Thurs 11am–10pm; Fri–Sat 11am–11pm.*

Splurge

→**Pierpont's** AMERICAN If you're ready to inject a little glamour into your life after a day spent on the road, head to Pierpont's at Union Station for dinner, dessert, or just a drink. The dining rooms are elegant and comfortable, but the large bar area was our favorite. There's a stunning selection of bottles that reaches all the way up to the ceiling, and a library ladder that (if you're lucky) you can watch the barkeep slide down. Dress is anything from jeans and tees to business attire, and the bar serves the full menu. *Reservations recommended. Starters $9–$13; entrees $18–$40.*

Partying

Kansas City's got its share of nightlife, whether you're into live music, kick-back bars, or slick clubs. Westport is great for partying, but expect it to be packed on the weekends, when everyone and his mother heads in from the suburbs. Crossroads has its own artistic, funky vibe and usually isn't as crowded, except on First Fridays, when the local galleries stay open till 9pm and everyone heads out to get a drink afterward.

BARS, PUBS & CLUBS
Downtown/Crossroads

→**Bar Natasha** CLUB Part cabaret and part martini lounge, Bar Natasha's gallery-like interior is punctuated by red velvet couches, local artwork, and a central stage where cabaret entertainers strut their stuff. Performances range from moody to outrageously irreverent, and the clientele is a diverse mix of gay, straight, and everything in between. The bar is also a destination on the first Friday of every month during the Crossroads Art District's free art walk, so don't miss the rotating exhibits. *1911 Main St.* ☎ *816/472-5300. www. barnatasha.com. Mon–Sat 5pm–1:30am.*

➔ **Grinder's** BAR   Owned by local sculptor Jeff "Stretch" Rumaner and situated next to his gallery, Grinder's has an artsy, industrial vibe and quite a selection of unusual beers on tap. Late night and lunchtime eats can also be had; try a homemade pizza with either "fancy pants" or "standard issue" toppings. *417 E. 18th St.* ☎ *816/472-5424. Sun–Thurs 11am–11pm; Fri–Sat 11am–2am.*

➔ **Jilly's** CLUB   Attracting a fun-loving, diverse clientele, this little lounge is hip without trying too hard. Eclecticism rules, with rock bands, DJs, and funk-blues jam nights all part of the regular music lineup; they also have new alternative bands and spoken-word events. Stop by on First Fridays after visiting the Crossroads art galleries. *1744 Broadway.* ☎ *816/221-4977. www.jillyskc.com. Mon–Fri 11am–1:30am; Sat 3pm–1:30am.*

Westport/Midtown

Ⓜ️ Best ● ➔ **Kelly's Westport Inn** ★★★ BAR   Supposedly the oldest building in Kansas City, this historic location has housed everything from a general store to a wrestling club, but since Prohibition ended it's been the bar of choice for Kansas City residents young and old. As spacious as Kelly's is, it fills up fast on weekends, so you may rub shoulders and other parts with fellow happy drinkers before finding a table. All that rubbing can make you hungry. Don't worry—with Joe's

Pizza located in the back (open till 3am), your appetite will be satisfied. *500 Westport Rd.* ☎ *816/561-5800. www.kellyswestportinn. com. Mon–Sat 8:30am–3am; Sun 11am–3am. No cover.*

➔ **McCoy's** PUB   With a large bar area, a cigar room, and an outdoor patio, McCoy's Public House offers something for everyone. Despite the upscale interior, the vibe stays relaxed. In warmer months, the patio offers a prime location for people-watching. The patio is snuggled against the sidewalks of Westport, and many a phone number has been exchanged over the railing. If beer is your thing, try their sampler of microbrews. We predict that you'll love the Hog Pound Brown Ale ★, which was far and away our favorite. *4057 Pennsylvania.* ☎ *816/960-0866. www.mccoyspublichouse. com. Mon–Sat 11am–3am; Sun 11am–midnight. No cover.*

➔ **The Peanut** ★ BAR   Deliciously rundown, the original Peanut has the oldest continuous liquor license in Kansas City. The interior is the mother of all eclectic decorating schemes. The walls and shelves are stuffed with things that slowly accumulated over the years. You feel like you're in some mysterious garage of earthly (or do we mean earthy?) delights. Depending on the night, you might find mellow, boozy locals or raucous college girls dancing on the tables. Either way, it'll be a welcoming environment, and the beer will be cold and cheap. *5000 Main St.* ☎ *816/753-9499. Daily 11am–2am. No cover.*

LIVE MUSIC

Jazz/Blues

➔ **B.B.'s Lawnside Bar-B-Q** B.B.'s Lawnside's winning combination of seriously good barbeque and the blues is well worth a little bit of a drive. Everything is made from scratch, and you can trust blues-loving owners Lindsay (a radio DJ for 22+ years) and Jo Shannon to bring in first-rate musical talent. *1205 E 85th St.* ☎ *816/822-7427. www.bbslawnsidebbq.com. Wed 11am–10pm; Thurs 11am–10:30pm; Fri–Sat 11am–11pm; Sun 4–10:30pm.*

➜ **Jardine's** There's not a bad seat in the house at this cozy, intimate jazz club and restaurant, where musicians mingle with regulars between drinks and do shout-outs to friends from the stage. Try a martini or another cocktail: The attractive bartenders really know how to pour a stiff one. There's usually no cover, though if a "name" is booked, you might have to pay to get in. *4536 Main St.* ☎ *816/561-6480. www.jardines4jazz.com.*

➜ **Mutual Musicians Foundation** The true Kansas City spirit lives on at this historic landmark in the 18th and Vine district, where musicians have been coming since the 1930s for late-night jam sessions on Fridays and Saturdays. Doors don't open till midnight, with music starting around 1:30am. *1823 Highland Ave.* ☎ *816/471-5212. Fri–Sat midnight–4am. No cover.*

Rock/Indie/Eclectic

➜ **The Brick** Showcasing original local talent, as well as some popular larger acts, The Brick is guaranteed to have something fresh and unusual on stage. When a band isn't playing, enjoy karaoke and trivia nights, or relax around the back pool table. If there's a cover, it's usually $5 or less. It is 21+ to get in. *1727 McGee St.* ☎ *816/421-1634. www.thebrickkcmo.com. Mon–Sat 11am–3am.*

➜ **The Record Bar** Don't let the strip mall location fool you: This is the new darling music venue of KC. Hip locals come for national acts like the Octopus Project, We Are Scientists, and Destroyer, plus DJ nights and free B-movie screenings. If you get hungry, create your own antipasto plate from the substantial list of meats, cheeses, and veggies. *1020 Westport Rd.* ☎ *816/753-5207. www.recordbar.com. Sun 2pm–1:30am;*

Mon–Sat 4pm–1:30am. Cover charge is from $5–$12, although some shows are free. Call for more information. All events 21+ unless noted.

➜ **Uptown Theater** Everyone from Sigur Rós to the Strokes has headlined at this 2,500-seat theater. Originally built in 1928, the theater has a gothic rock-opera vibe, with lots of red curtains and ornate details. Besides music and private parties, the venue is also popular for comedy acts. *3700 Broadway.* ☎ *816/753-8665. www.uptowntheater.com. All ages unless noted. Tickets available at www.ticketmaster.com.*

What to See & Do

While it doesn't have the cachet of a city like Denver, Kansas City does have some unique museums and attractions, plus a really fun music and arts scene. The accessibility of most of the main attractions means you can pack a lot into just a few days, and after traveling up and down the MAX a few times, you'll be feeling like a local.

THE TOP ATTRACTIONS

MTV Best ❷ ➜ **The American Jazz Museum** ★★★ and the **Negro Leagues Baseball Museum** ★★ Located under one roof in the historic 18th and Vine district, these museums offer a unique look at American history. At the American Jazz Museum, discover the roots of jazz music and trace its development through interactive exhibits, including listening stations and a mixing room. The film at the visitor center highlights the golden days of Kansas City jazz, when the 18th and Vine district boasted over 60 jazz clubs. The Negro Leagues Baseball Museum tells the story of segregated baseball, from the founding of the Negro National League just a few blocks away in 1920, up until Jackie Robinson (who played for the Kansas City Monarchs) signed with the Brooklyn Dodgers in 1947. *1616 E. 18th St. (18th and*

A couple cool KC shops

With over 6,000 square feet of vintage clothing, **Re-Runs** is *the* destination for vintage hounds, stylists, and Hollywood costumers. Owner Ken Coit manages two locations: a boutique store in Westport and a huge warehouse west of downtown. Ken's careful selection of perfect-condition merchandise, plus an unusually large men's section, makes the Westport store your best bet. If, however, you're set on digging through rack upon rack of classic threads and want thrift-store prices, head to the warehouse. *www.re-runs.com. Store: 4126 Pennsylvania St.* ☎ *816/561-4425. Mon–Fri noon–7pm; Sat 10:30am–7pm; Sun noon–6pm. Warehouse: 1408 W. 12th St.* ☎ *816/221-9002. Sat only, 10am–4pm.*

Looking for a book or CD by a Kansas City artist? Head to **Prospero's Books** for the best selection and (maybe) a chance to hear the artist in person. This indie shop is a second home for Kansas City artists, musicians, and writers. Regular live events include "The Pit," an open-mic poetry night, and "Up Close and Personal," featuring the music of local songwriters. For more local flavor, check out the chapbooks of poetry and other literature published by Prospero's own imprints, Unholy Day and Spartan Press. *1800 W. 39th St.* ☎ *816/531-9673. www.prosperosbookstore.com.*

Vine); American Jazz Museum: ☎ 816/474-8463; www.americanjazzmuseum.com; Baseball Museum: ☎ 816/221-1920; www.nlbm.com. Admission is $6 for either museum, or $8 for both. Both museums Tues–Sat 9am–6pm; Sun noon–6pm.

→**Arabia Steamboat Museum** ★ History buffs and mystery lovers will get a kick out of this unusual museum in Rivermarket, which displays an entire ship's worth of "buried" treasure from the 1850s. The story begins in 1856, when a cargo steamboat filled with merchandise for western settlers suddenly sank in the Missouri River. Preserved in river mud, this virtual time capsule of pre-Civil war life lay untouched and nearly forgotten until excavations began in the 1980s. The wealth of cargo found aboard the *Arabia,* including china, jewelry, hardware, and boots, is on display for visitors, along with a film showing the excavation and preservation of the steamboat. *400 Grand Ave.* ☎ *816/471-4030. www.1856.com. Admission*

$13. Mon–Sat 10am–4pm (last tour); Sun noon–3:30pm. MAX stop: City Market.

FREE →**Nelson-Atkins Museum of Art** Art enthusiasts should not miss the Nelson-Atkins, considered one of the finest general museums in the country. Besides impressive collections of Asian art, 17th- and 18th-century European paintings, and American art, the museum also features a 22-acre outdoor sculpture garden containing over 30 sculptures, including the largest U.S. collection of bronzes by Henry Moore. Unfortunately, much of the contemporary and modern art collection is off view due to the museum's expansion project. Slated to open in summer 2007, the new Bloch Building will house the modern and African art collections, plus gallery space for rotating photography exhibits. *4525 Oak St. (just east of Country Club Plaza).* ☎ *816/931-5722. Free admission (special exhibits may cost extra). Tues–Thurs 10am–4pm; Fri 10am–9pm; Sat 10am–5pm; Sun noon–5pm. MAX stop: Art museums (Main at 45th St.).*

COOL IN THE MIDWEST

→ **Tivoli Cinemas at Manor Square** ★
Hidden among Westport corporate suites
is one of the oldest independent theaters
in Kansas City. With three screening rooms
and an ever-changing repertoire of foreign, indie, and documentary films, you're
bound to find something engaging and
unique. Enter at the Manor Square building
on Pennsylvania Street; the box office is on
the ground floor and opens 30 minutes
before showtime, or you can buy tickets
online at the website. *4050 Pennsylvania St.*
☎ *913/383-7756. www.tivolikc.com. Matinee:*
$6.50; after 6pm: $8.50. MAX stop: 39th St.

MORE STUFF TO SEE & DO

Additional attractions in Kansas City
include the **Kemper Museum of
Contemporary Art** (4420 Warwick Blvd.;
☎ 816/753-5784; www.kemperart.org;
Tues–Thurs 10am–4pm, Fri–Sat 10am–
9pm, Sun 11am–5pm; free admission), where
you'll find outdoor sculptures and a unique
building filled with contemporary artwork.

In Penn Valley Park, check out the
Liberty Memorial Museum (100 W. 26th
St.; ☎ 816/784-1918; www.libertymemorial
museum.org; museum: Tues–Sun 10–5;
tower: Tues–Sun 10–4:15; museum admission $8, memorial tower admission $4, both
$10), which holds a large collection of his-
torical exhibits and materials on World War
I. Take an elevator to the top of the 217-foot
memorial tower for a great view of the city
and nearby Union Station.

On the first Friday of every month, everyone's heading down to the **Crossroads
Arts District** (www.crossroadscommunity
association.org; free admission) to mingle
with artists and creative types. The area's
40+ galleries stay open until 9pm, and many
area restaurant serve special "First Friday"
deals. All of the above attractions are easily
accessible by MAX.

You'll want to drive to the 18th and Vine
district if you want to spend some time at
the **Black Archives of Mid-America**

Shakespeare, Cattle & Jazz: KC Festivals

→ The Bard on the Plains: Since the debut of the **Heart of America
Shakespeare Festival** in 1993, Kansas City residents (and out-of-town visitors) have enjoyed free professional productions of the Bard's plays every
summer at Southmoreland Park, across from the Nelson-Atkins Museum of
Art. **www.kcshakes.org.**

→ The **Plaza Art Fair,** one of the top five fine art fairs in the nation, celebrated
its 75th anniversary in 2006. Held every September at the Country Club
Plaza, the 3-day event features the work of over 200 artists from across the
United States. ☎ **816/753-0100; www.countryclubplaza.com.**

→ Usually scheduled over the Labor Day weekend, the **Kansas City Blues
and Jazz Festival** is a draw for music lovers in Kansas City and beyond.
The 2006 festival featured the legendary Bo Diddley, plus 24 other acts.
www.kansascitymusic.com/festival.

→ Held annually in October or November, the **American Royal** celebration
has been a Kansas City tradition since 1899. Begun as a small cattle show
in the Kansas City stockyards, the event now features livestock shows,
horse competitions, live concerts, a rodeo, and the largest barbecue competition in the world. **www.americanroyal.com.**

Detour: A Trip to Independence, MO

Visit the nearby town of Independence, a 20-minute drive east of Kansas City, for more historic sites, and one oddball attraction. Check out the **Truman Home National Historic Site** (223 N. Main St.; ☎ **816/254-9929;** www.nps. gov/hstr) where U.S. President Harry S Truman lived from 1919 until his death in 1972. The home functioned as the summer White House during Truman's administration, and it's virtually unchanged since his time. You'll also find the **Truman Presidential Museum and Library** (500 W. Hwy 24; ☎ **800/833-1225;** www.trumanlibrary.org) in Independence, where you can see two interactive exhibits on the Truman presidency and check out a replica of the White House Oval Office.

The **National Trails Museum** ★ (318 W. Pacific Ave.; ☎ **816/325-7575;** www. frontiertrails.org) traces the amazing journey of pioneers who traveled toward Oregon and California; check out some of the diaries and stories of what these people went through and you'll be glad you've got a car for your trip west.

For pure weirdness, do not miss **Leila's Hair Museum** (1333 S. Noland Rd.; ☎ **816/833-2955;** www.hairwork.com/leila), a collection of more than 300 wreaths and over 2,000 pieces of jewelry made from (yes, you guessed it!) human hair. If you're interested in staying the night, check out **Ophelia's Inn** (201 N. Main; ☎ **816/461-4525;** www.opheliasind.com), a cute bed-and-breakfast on the main square. Double occupancy rooms are $95 a night.

(2033 Vine St.; ☎ **816/483-1300;** www. blackarchives.org; Mon–Fri 9am–4:30pm; admission $2), one the largest collections of African-American memorabilia, with artifacts, research materials, oral histories, and business records.

PLAYING OUTSIDE

FREE →**Swope Park** At 1,769 acres, Swope Park is the largest park in Kansas City and the second-largest urban park in the nation. Home to the Kansas City Zoo and the Starlight Theater, a popular music venue, the park also offers a swimming pool, two golf courses, a nature center, picnic facilities, horseback riding trails, a Frisbee golf course, and athletic fields for softball, soccer, and rugby. *Meyer Blvd. and Swope Pkwy.* ☎ *816/513-7500. Free admission. Open daily 24 hr.*

SPECTATOR SPORTS

Kansas City is a serious sporting town. Conveniently for fans, the Truman Sports Complex houses both of the Kansas City stadiums east of downtown on I-70. Since the 1970s, Kaufman Stadium has been the home of the **Kansas City Royals** (☎ **800/ 6ROYALS;** www.kcroyals.com); the Royals' regular season lasts from April till September. Tickets begin at $8 and are readily available. Directly across the way is Arrowhead Stadium, where **Kansas City Chiefs** games regularly sell out. Tickets begin at $49, and the packed arena is one of the loudest in the NFL (☎ **816/920-9300;** www.kcchiefs.com).

NASCAR dads and other racing enthusiasts flock to the **Kansas Speedway** for motorsport events, and several racecar driving schools also use the speedway to conduct classes and drive-alongs, if you've always yearned to get in on the action (400 Speedway Blvd., Kansas City, KS; ☎ **913/328-3300;** www.kansasspeedway. com).

COOL IN THE MIDWEST

On the Road to Denver, CO

Kansas City, MO to Denver, CO 604 miles

We'll be honest: Driving through Kansas isn't completely exciting, or even occasionally exciting. It's *very* flat, and after about an hour on I-70 we began to get a strong sense of déjà-vu (haven't we seen that water tower before? What about that tractor?) However, it's a good drive for contemplation, or lacking sufficiently elevated thoughts, rocking out to an excellent playlist.

On the Road Nuts & Bolts

Where to Fill Up Anywhere along the route. Look for the blue signs along the highway to find out which exits have gas stations.

The Tolls $2.25 for a two-axle vehicle on the Kansas Turnpike.

The Fastest Way Take I-70 west out of Kansas City. From Bonner Springs until Topeka, I-70 is part of the Kansas Turnpike, so have your cash and coin ready. From Topeka, continue west on I-70 through the rest of Kansas and into Colorado. It's a little over 600 miles from Kansas City to Denver, so plan on about nine hours of driving, if traffic isn't heavy.

Rules of the Road The speed limit along the I-70 is 70 mph. Highway patrol officers in Kansas are out in full force, especially as you get closer to the Colorado border, so watch the lead foot if you want to avoid a hefty fine.

Where to Stop Take Exit 206 off I-70 to visit the **Kansas Originals Market,** the **Grassroots Art Center,** and the **Garden of Eden,** one of the strangest sculpture gardens you'll ever see.

To break up this long leg of the trip, take a detour on the **Post Rock Scenic** byway, an 18-mile route along the K-232 highway. You can pick up some unique products from Kansas and view some of the most interesting American outsider art in the U.S.

The Post Rock Scenic byway is a little over 200 miles, or a little over 3 hours from Kansas City, MO.

Take Exit 206 off I-70 and head north on K-232. Your first stop will be the **Kansas Originals Market** (233 Hwy. 232; ☎ **785/658-2602;** www.kansasoriginals.

Playlist: Music Heading for the Mile High City

→ *Over My Head (the Cable Car),* **The Fray,** "How to Save a Life," 2005

→ *Firecracker,* **The Hot IQs,** "An Argument Between the Brain & Feet," 2004

→ *The Walls Have Eyes,* **The Photo Atlas,** "No, Not Me, Never," 2006

→ *Queen of the Surface Streets,* **Devotchka,** "Una Volta," 2003

→ *In Spite,* **The Cowboy Curse,** "Nod Up and Down (To the Simulcast Singing)," 2006

→ *Amen Corner,* **Munly & the Lee Lewis Harlots,** "smooch 006," 2004

▲▲ Kansas: One Big Speed Trap
UH-OH

If you're anything like us, you'll probably want to zip through the state of Kansas as fast as possible. That's not a good plan. Kansas state troopers are out and about, looking for people who are just too anxious to leave their fine state. We got our own speeding ticket for a pretty hefty amount just outside of Colby, Kansas; we later found out that one of our friends who traveled the same route got a ticket there, too. As eager as you may be to reach Denver, you're better off keeping to the speed limit (70 mph). We can think of many better uses for the $100 to $200 you'll pay in fines if you get a ticket.

org), where you can find handmade craft items and food products of the "mom would just love this" variety. It's open Monday through Saturday from 9am to 6pm, and on Sunday from 11am until 6pm.

After picking up a few gifts, head north on K-232 towards the town of **Lucas** (pop. 500), where you'll get a dose of off-the-wall originality (aka "outsider art") at the **Garden of Eden** (Kansas and 2nd St.; ☎ **785/525-6395**; www.garden-of-eden-lucas-kansas.com), a bizarre cement sculpture garden and home built in the early 1900s by S.P. Dinsmoor, a Civil War veteran.

Dinsmoor's statues range from the obligatory Adam and Eve figures to elaborate allegorical works. Check out the "Goddess of Liberty," which features Lady Liberty spearing an octopus figure (representing big business) while citizens attack with voting ballots. And don't forget to say hello to Dinsmoor himself: The artist's mummified remains are on view in a glass-topped coffin inside his concrete mausoleum. The Garden is open daily from 10am to 5pm in the summer, and from 1pm until 4pm in the spring. Winter hours are weekends only, from 1 to 4pm. Admission is $6.

For more art of the outsider variety, check out the **Grassroots Art Center** (213 S. Main St.; ☎ **785/525-6118**), a museum chock-full of Kansas "outsider art," including sculptures, carvings, paintings, and mechanized artworks. Summer hours are Monday through Saturday 10am to 5pm and Sunday 1pm until 5pm; winter hours are Monday and Thursday through Saturday from 10am until 4pm (closed for lunch noon–1pm). Admission is $6.

Before you finally head back down to I-70 and on to Denver, stop by the **K-18 Café** (5495 Hwy. K-18; ☎ **785/525-6262**) for a home-cooked meal, served daily from 6:30am until 10pm.

Welcome to Denver

It's no exaggeration that Denver is called the Mile High City. When you climb the State Capitol, you're precisely 5,280 feet above sea level when you hit the 18th step. While the idea of building a city a mile in the air is poetic, Denver's origins are commercial: In 1858, eager prospectors discovered a few flecks of gold where Cherry Creek empties into the South Platte River, and a tent camp sprang up on the site. Although the real gold strike would come later in the surrounding mountains, Denver endured, growing over the years to become the largest city between the West Coast and the Great Plains.

Today, Denver combines a sophisticated urban scene with outdoor adventure, offering visitors a chance to mountain bike, hike, ski, or snowboard, while still having time to make it back for a night of cool music or bar hopping in LoDo.

COOL IN THE MIDWEST

Denver **Nuts & Bolts**

Area Code Area codes in Denver are 303 and 720; local calls require 10-digit dialing.

Business Hours Banks and other local businesses are generally open from 9am to 5pm on weekdays, with some banks open on Saturdays. 24-hour ATMs are located at most banks and at various points in the city. Stores are open 6 days a week, with many also open on Sunday.

Doctors Doctor and dentist referrals are available by calling ☎ 800/DOCTORS.

Drugstores You'll find several national pharmacy chains in the metropolitan area. Walgreens Pharmacy at 2000 E. Colfax Ave. is open 24 hours a day (☎ 303/331-0917). For other Walgreens locations, call ☎ 800/WALGREENS.

Emergencies Call ☎ 911 if you need the police, fire department, or an ambulance.

Hospitals St. Joseph's, 1835 Franklin St. (☎ **303/837-7111**), is just east of downtown and has emergency care facilities.

Internet Free Wi-Fi access is available at the downtown 16th Street Mall and the nearby Skyline Park (www.downtowndenverwifi.com); at the Cherry Creek North shopping district, a 16-block area between University Blvd. and Steele St. (www.cherrycreeknorth.com); and at multiple coffee shops in the metro area. Most Denver public libraries have Wi-Fi access, but there is a charge to use the service.

Laundry/Dry Cleaners Put your dirties in the wash at the cheerful **Clean Green Coin Laundry** (4301 W. 38th Ave.; ☎ 303/480-1861), which is decorated like a mountain lodge with vintage skis and mountain murals. For cheap but reliable dry cleaning, try **Continental Cleaners** (6265 E. Evans Dr.; ☎ 303/504-9855). Payment is required in advance, cash only.

Liquor Laws The legal drinking age in Colorado is 21. Bars can serve alcohol until 2am daily. Outside of bars, alcohol is only available at liquor stores. The lone exception is 3.2% beer, which can be purchased 7 days a week at grocery and convenience stores.

Newspapers & Magazines The *Denver Post* is Colorado's largest daily newspaper (www.denverpost.com). The *Rocky Mountain News* (www.rockymountain news.com) also covers the metropolitan area. By joint agreement, only the *News* prints on Saturday, and only the *Post* appears on Sunday. *Westword,* a free weekly paper, has extensive local entertainment listings. It's also known for its jibes at local politicians and celebrities (www.westword.com).

Police For non-emergencies, contact the Denver Police Department (☎ 720/913-2000).

Post Office The main downtown post office is located at 951 20th St. and is open Monday through Friday from 7am to 10:30pm. For other locations, call the U.S. Postal Service (☎ 800/275-8777; www.usps.com).

Radio Tune your FM radio to KCFR (90.1) for NPR broadcasting, KYGO (98.5) for country, KTCL (93.3) for a mix of modern rock tunes, and KQKS (107.5) for hip-hop and R&B. For news, talk and sports, check out AM KHOW (630).

Taxes State and local sales tax is about 7%; the hotel tax is also around 7%.

Television You'll find CBS (KCNC) on channel 4, ABC (KMGH) on channel 7, NBC (KUSA) on channel 9, and Fox (KDRV) on channel 31. For PBS, try channel 6 (KRMA) or channel 12 (KBDI).

Time Zone Denver is on Mountain Standard Time.

Transit Information Call the Regional Transportation District, aka "The Ride" (☎ 800/366-7433), for route and schedule info. You can also check out their website at www.rtd-denver.com.

Useful Numbers For road conditions in Colorado, call ☎ 303/639-1111.

Visitors Center The downtown visitors center on the 16th Street Mall (918 16th St.; ☎ 303/892-1505) is open weekdays from 8am to 5pm and from 9:30am to 1:30pm on summer Saturdays. Pick up the *Official Visitors Guide* for lots of local information and a good map of the Denver metro area. Other locations to get visitor information are the Colorado State Capitol and the Cherry Creek shopping center.

Weather Call ☎ 303/337-2500 for the latest weather info, or go online to www.9news.com/weather.

Getting Around

It's hard to get lost in Denver as long as you remember that the mountains are to the west; but getting around a city of half a million can still be a challenge. In Denver's downtown area, streets follow an older grid system, which is oriented northeast-southwest, parallel to the South Platte River. Here you'll find the mile-long 16th Street pedestrian mall, and the trendy **LoDo** (Lower Downtown) district, home to popular shops, galleries, and pubs. Surrounding downtown on the south and east are the **Capitol Hill** and **Uptown** neighborhoods, where the newer north-south grid takes over.

BY CAR

Like most large cities, Denver's downtown is congested and full of one-way streets, which can be a hassle for visiting drivers.

Fortunately, the downtown area is fairly compact, with good pedestrian walkways, so cars aren't really necessary. For attractions in downtown and LoDo, save yourself the trouble of driving and enjoy stretching your legs instead. For attractions outside the downtown area, you'll probably need a car.

Parking

If you do decide to park downtown, you should have no problem finding a lot (try **www.downtowndenver.com/findparking.htm**). The maximum daily rate runs from $5 to $12. Most lots are cash only, although a few accept credit cards.

BY BUS /LIGHT RAIL

The Regional Transportation District, or **"The Ride,"** operates bus routes and a light rail line. The local one-way fare is $1.25, with free transfer tickets available.

COOL IN THE MIDWEST

Denver Highlights

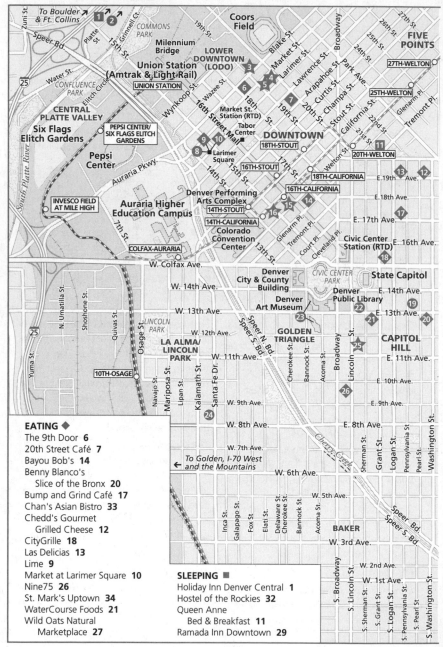

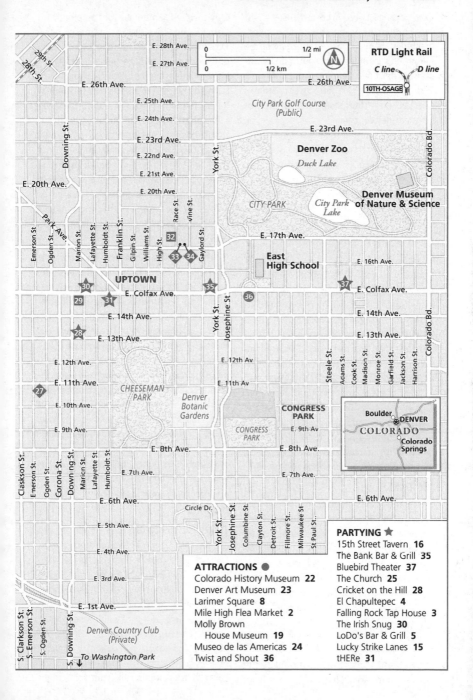

29th St.
28th St.

E. 28th Ave.
E. 27th Ave.

0   1/2 mi
0   1/2 km

RTD Light Rail
C line   D line
10TH-OSAGE

E. 26th Ave.

E. 26th Ave.

E. 25th Ave.

City Park Golf Course (Public)

E. 24th Ave.

Downing St.

E. 23rd Ave.

E. 23rd Ave.

Denver Zoo
Duck Lake

E. 22nd Ave.

York St.

E. 21st Ave.

Colorado Bd.

E. 20th Ave.

E. 20th Ave.

Denver Museum of Nature & Science

Park Ave.

Race St.
Vine St.

CITY PARK

City Park Lake

Emerson St.
Ogden St.
Marion St.
Lafayette St.
Humboldt St.
Franklin St.
Gilpin St.
Williams St.
High St.
Gaylord St.

E. 17th Ave.

32

UPTOWN

33 34

E. Colfax Ave.

East High School

E. 16th Ave.

30
29 31

35

36

57

E. Colfax Ave.

E. 14th Ave.

York St.
Josephine St.

E. 14th Ave.

28

E. 13th Ave.

E. 13th Ave.

Colorado Bd.

E. 12th Ave.

E. 12th Av

Steele St.
Adams St.
Cook St.
Madison St.
Monroe St.
Garfield St.
Jackson St.
Harrison St.

E. 11th Ave.

CHEESEMAN PARK

E. 11th Av

27

Denver Botanic Gardens

E. 10th Ave.

CONGRESS PARK

Boulder ● DENVER
COLORADO
Colorado Springs

E. 9th Ave.

CONGRESS PARK

E. 9th Av

E. 8th Ave.

E. 8th Ave.

Claskson St.
Emerson St.
Ogden St.
Corona St.
Downing St.
Marion St.
Lafayette St.
Humboldt St.

E. 7th Ave.

E. 7th Ave.

E. 6th Ave.

E. 6th Ave.

Circle Dr.

E. 5th Ave.

York St.
Josephine St.
Columbine St.
Clayton St.
Detroit St.
Fillmore St.
Milwaukee St.
St Paul St.

E. 4th Ave.

PARTYING ★
15th Street Tavern **16**
The Bank Bar & Grill **35**
Bluebird Theater **37**
The Church **25**
Cricket on the Hill **28**
El Chapultepec **4**
Falling Rock Tap House **3**
The Irish Snug **30**
LoDo's Bar & Grill **5**
Lucky Strike Lanes **15**
tHERe **31**

E. 3rd Ave.

ATTRACTIONS ●
Colorado History Museum **22**
Denver Art Museum **23**
Larimer Square **8**
Mile High Flea Market **2**
Molly Brown
   House Museum **19**
Museo de las Americas **24**
Twist and Shout **36**

E. 1st Ave.

S. Clarkson St.
S. Emerson St.
S. Ogden St.
S. Downing St.

Denver Country Club (Private)

To Washington Park

Exact change is required for buses. Light rail tickets can be purchased at vending machines beneath the station awnings. Maps and schedules of all routes are available at the Civic Center Station (16th St. and Broadway), Market Street Station (Market and 16th sts.), and online at www.rtd-denver.com.

Don't miss the convenient (and free!) transportation through the heart of downtown and into LoDo. Free buses run up and down the 16th Street Mall between Civic Center and Union Station daily from 6am to 1am, with a bus coming every 75 seconds during peak hours. Expect to wait from 8 to 10 minutes after 9pm.

ON FOOT

Contrary to popular belief, the Mile High City is *near* the mountains, not smack-dab in the middle of them. There's no need to pack your hiking boots unless you're planning to travel west to do some real mountaineering. To see the downtown area, all you need is comfortable shoes. Maps of the area are available at the 16th Street Mall Visitors' Center and the Colorado State Capitol building, or farther south at the Cherry Creek shopping center. The hip and historic LoDo district is perfect for pedestrians. With its many bars and breweries, it's also the best location for a pub crawl.

BY TAXI

The main taxi companies in Denver are Yellow Cab (☎ **303/777-7777**) and Metro Taxi (☎ **303/333-3333**). You can hail a cab on the street, but it's best to telephone ahead or wait for one outside a major hotel. Rates are $2.50 for the first eighth of a mile, plus $2 for each additional mile (25¢ per eighth mile, or fraction of a mile).

Sleeping

CAMPGROUNDS/HOSTELS

➔ **Chatfield State Park** Just outside the Denver metro area, Chatfield is open from May through September for camping, with both RV and tent sites. The state park has a 1,550-acre reservoir for boating, fishing, and swimming, plus 20 miles of trails for biking, hiking, and horseback riding (livery barn and horse rentals on site). The annual Rocky Mountain Hot Air Balloon festival takes place here in late August, drawing in thousands of spectators, so plan well ahead if you're looking for a campsite near that time. *11500 N. Roxborough Park Rd., Littleton, CO.* ☎ *303/791-7275 or 800/678-2267 for state park reservation service. www.parks. state.co.us. 197 sites. $16–$22 per night, plus $5–$6 daily use fee. Advance reservation fee is $8.*

➔ **Hostel of the Rockies** This fairly new (2005) hostel is just north of Colfax Avenue, within walking distance of many attractions and restaurants. Traditional dorm-style accommodations are available (2 to 10 beds per room), with separate bathrooms for each unit. The nearby guesthouse offers private rooms accommodating up to two people. Standard amenities like laundry facilities and a community kitchen are available, as well as outside grills and deck chairs for backyard parties. *1717 Race St.* ☎ *303/861-7777. www.innkeeperrockies. com. 50 beds; $20 per night. 5 private rooms; $38 single occupancy, $5 extra for double. Amenities: Free Internet kiosk; coin-op laundry; kitchen. In room: Coffeemaker.*

CHEAP

There are plenty of chain hotels in and around Denver, but as in most metro areas, even "cheap" chains can get pricy. Two places to check out are the no-frills **Super 8 Motel** on Broadway (5888 Broadway; ☎ **303/296-3100**), which runs from $59 for single and $69 for double occupancy; and the **La Quinta Inn** (3500 Park Ave. W.; ☎ **303/458-1222**), conveniently located off I-25 just north of Coors Field and the LoDo district. Rates run from $71 a night for single or double occupancy and include a complimentary breakfast and free Internet access in all rooms.

→**Cameron Motel** ★★ A small mom-and-pop motel with a cool neon sign and glazed brick walls, the Cameron is only 10 minutes from downtown Denver and is a great alternative to some of the more expensive chains. Built in the 1940s, the property has been completely renovated. There are 60 cable channels, three rooms have kitchenettes, and some also have Internet access. The owners live on-site, and their pride of ownership shows. *4500 E. Evans Ave.* ☎ *303/757-2100. 35 units (14 with shower only). $48–$58 single or double occupancy. Amenities: Free parking. Pets accepted with $5 nightly fee.*

DOABLE

→**Holiday Inn Denver Central** This place is a few minutes drive north of downtown on I-25. The standard rooms are comfortable, and free Wi-Fi is available throughout the property, but the real distinguishing factor here is **Teddy's,** the on-site restaurant and club. With a large dance floor and nightly DJs that play anything from country-western tunes to hip-hop and R&B, the club attracts the young and the young at heart. *4849 Bannock St.* ☎ *303/292-9500. 201 units. $89–$109 single or double occupancy. Amenities: Restaurant/club; laundry facilities; fitness center; outdoor pool; whirlpool; free parking. In room: Coffeemaker, free Wi-Fi.*

→**Ramada Inn Downtown** Centrally located on Colfax, this property attracts vacationing families, business types, and on weekends, more than a few musicians with big-ass tour buses. Hang out in the lobby during the wee hours to spot artists and crews turning in after concerts at the Fillmore, Ogden, or Bluebird theaters. Besides the late-night people-watching, amenities include free Wi-Fi in all rooms

and a fitness center. One extra perk is the Irish Snug pub is just across the street. *1150 E. Colfax Ave.* ☎ *303/831-7700. 150 units. $74–$94 single or double occupancy. Amenities: Restaurant/lounge; laundry facility; fitness center; free parking. In room: Coffeemaker, free Wi-Fi.*

SPLURGE

→**Queen Anne Bed and Breakfast** ★★ History, culture, and comfort are perfectly combined at the Queen Anne, Denver's first urban B&B. Within walking distance of LoDo and downtown, the property's two Victorian mansions overlook a quiet park. Guests get a unique experience of Colorado hospitality, including theme-decorated rooms, fabulous hot breakfasts (try their special blend of dark-roasted coffee), and complimentary glasses of Colorado wine during the pre-dinner hour. Best of all, innkeeper Tom King and his friendly staff make you feel like their only mission in life is to make sure you're enjoying your stay. *2147-51 Tremont Place.* ☎ *800/432-4667. www.queenannbnb.com. 14 units. $85–$185 single and double occupancy; $155–$185 suites. Amenities: Free breakfast; Colorado wine; free parking. In room: Free Wi-Fi.*

Eating

SUPPLIES

The Denver area has a host of small farmers' markets that generally run from June until September or October. On Wednesdays, try the market at **Civic Center Park** in downtown (Broadway and 14th Ave.; www.laughingdogfarms.net). You'll find tons of locally grown organic produce, plus a range of lunch options provided by downtown restaurants.

For Saturday treats, head to Denver's largest farmers' market at the **Cherry Creek Shopping Center** (1st Ave. and University Blvd.; www.coloradofresh

markets.com), where you can pick up veggies, fruit, artisan meats and cheeses, and Colorado wines.

For the basic staples, deli favorites, or even a made-to-order smoothie, the Capitol Hill neighborhood has a **Wild Oats Natural Marketplace** (900 E. 11th Ave.; ☎ **303/832-7701**), open 7 days a week.

TAKEOUT TREATS

→ **Benny Blanco's Slice of the Bronx** For a quick meal or a cheap late-night snack, you can't beat a New York–style pizzeria open until 3am. Stop in to pick up a whole pie, $2 slices, or a "Stan the Man" calzone, deep-fried and stuffed with onions, green peppers, and sausage. You can also call before 2:30am to see if you're in range for free delivery. *616 E. 13th Ave.* ☎ *303/831-1346. www.bennyblancos.com.*

→ **Bonnie Brae Ice Cream** You can't walk here from downtown, but this little shop's rich, creamy flavors, like sinfully cinnamon and deep-dish apple pie, are worth a few minutes' drive any day of the week. Take a seat at the crowded sidewalk patio on a summer evening and enjoy your favorite flavor; ours was cappuccino crunch. *799 S. University Blvd.* ☎ *303/777-0808. Summer Hours: Sun–Thurs 10am–10pm; Fri–Sat 10am–11pm. Winter hours: Sun–Thurs 11am–8pm; Fri–Sat 11am–9pm.*

→ **Market at Larimer Square** Said to be the first espresso bar opened between New York City and Los Angeles, the Market offers European-style coffee drinks and some of the city's most delicious cookies, fruit tarts, éclairs, and cream puffs. If for some odd reason sweets are not your thing, try their upscale—yet still reasonably priced—deli sandwiches and salads. It's all good, but we still prefer the cream puffs. *1445 Larimer St.* ☎ *303/534-5140. Mon–Thurs 6:30am–10pm; Fri–Sun 6:30am–10:30pm.*

MTV Best ◉ → **St. Mark's Uptown** ★★★ There are some coffee places where you should just grab your joe and run, but St. Mark's is definitely not one of them. On a tree-lined street in the Capitol Hill neighborhood, this Euro-bohemian cafe is the perfect place to linger and sip your latte, especially on warm sunny days when the staff opens the huge garage-door-style patio window. Tempting snacks and panini are also on hand if you're in the mood for food. *2019 E. 17th St.* ☎ *303/322-8384. Daily 7am–11pm.*

EATING OUT
Cheap

→ **Bump and Grind Café** ★★★ AMERICAN Not for the strait-laced, this colorful, irreverent cafe gets even more flamboyant on weekend mornings at the famous MTV Best ◉ **Petticoat Bruncheon.** Drag-queen servers strut their stuff in gogo boots and hotpants, while bringing out plates of banana waffles and Mexican eggs Benedict to a hungry, good-humored crowd. Get there early, since the place fills up fast. On weekdays, stop by for tasty sandwiches, panini, and homemade treats. *439 E. 17th Ave.* ☎ *303/861-4841. Breakfast $4–$10; lunch $6–$9. Tues–Fri 7am–3:30pm; Sat–Sun 10am–2pm.*

→ **Chan's Asian Bistro** ASIAN An elegant dining room, affordable prices, and authentic Chinese and Thai specialties make this little bistro a great place to grab an early dinner before hitting LoDo. The pad Thai had lots of flavor and perfectly cooked shrimp, and the sesame beef was just the way we like it: crunchy, chewy, and just a little bit sweet. A small bar area offers bottled beer, wine, sake, and mixed drinks. *2005 E. 17th Ave.* ☎ *303/320-8582. Lunch $6–$8; dinner $7–$10. Mon–Thurs lunch 11am–2:30pm; dinner 4:30–9:30pm. Fri lunch 11am–2:30pm; dinner 4:30–10pm. Sat lunch 11am–2:30pm; dinner 4:30–10pm. Sun 4–9:30pm.*

➔ **Chedd's Gourmet Grilled Cheese** AMERICAN This funky little sandwich shop offers classic grilled cheese on steroids. Order a build-your-own sandwich and then choose from 12 breads, 35 cheeses, and eight meats (that's a total of 3,360 different combinations, for you non-math people) to make your own melted masterpiece. Picnic-style sides like pickles and potato salad are also tasty, or try the tomato-basil soup for a classic pairing. *1906 Pearl St.* ☎ *303/386-3998. Sandwiches $5–$8; soups and sides $2–$4. Daily 11am–8pm.*

➔ **CityGrille** AMERICAN Colorado's political elite head to this popular burger joint right across the street from the capitol building for power lunches. Fortunately, you don't have to be a political fat-cat to enjoy thick sirloin burgers on toasted buns that can stand up to the half-pound patties. Besides burgers, the grill is known for its Colorado green chile, made with pork, jalapeños, and tomatoes; locals drench it over fries. From 10pm until midnight, stop by for one-buck baby burgers, half-priced appetizers, and $2 drinks. *321 E. Colfax* ☎ *303/861-0726. Sandwiches and burgers $7–$9. Mon–Sat 11am–1am; Sun 2pm–1am.*

➔ **Las Delicias** MEXICAN Since 1976, this family-run restaurant has been serving up authentic Mexican food. The friendly staff manages to give good service even during the busy lunch hour, and the menu offers a wealth of flavor-filled options. House specialties include the Carne Adobada (seared marinated pork in two different chile sauces), and the tender Carne Asada plate. Stop by in the morning for a killer breakfast burrito that will get your body moving in all the right ways. *439 E. 19th Ave.* ☎ *303/839-5675. www.lasdelicias. net. Breakfast $3–$7; entrees $6–$10. Mon–Thurs 8am–9pm; Fri–Sat 8am–10pm; Sun 9am–9pm.*

➔ **Pita Jungle** ★ MIDDLE EASTERN For some seriously good Middle Eastern food, visit the Pita Jungle, located near the UC campus. The kitschy outdoor cafe theme may not be your thing, but the decor almost works once you start eating. Days after we left Denver, we were still dreaming about the sampler plate, a selection of stuffed grape leaves, fresh pita bread, tabbouleh, hummus, tzatziki sauce, and other tasty treats. We also loved the beef schwerma plate, piled high with meat, rice, and other goodies. Our absolute favorite was the lentil soup, which is made fresh every day. We've never had soup that good in our lives. Are we exaggerating? Just barely. Seriously, get the lentil soup. *2017 S. University Blvd.* ☎ *720/570-1900. Appetizers and soups $2–$5; sandwiches $4; entrees $7–$13. Mon–Fri 11am–10pm; Sat noon–11pm.*

➔ **20th Street Café** ★ AMERICAN You won't find Wi-Fi or soy milk lattes, but this cozy little breakfast joint in LoDo doesn't seem to need extra perks to draw a crowd. Homemade pancakes, egg dishes, French toast, and biscuits are all served up fresh and hot for under $6, while lunchtime specials like roast beef, chicken-fried steak, and an Asian-inspired pork noodle bowl are only a dollar or so more. Try the Denver omelet for a tasty, filling breakfast that will keep you full till lunchtime. *1120 20th St.* ☎ *303/295-9041. Breakfast $2–$7; lunch $3–$8. Mon–Fri 6am–2:30pm; Sat 7am–1:30pm.*

Best ➔ **WaterCourse Foods** ★★ VEGETARIAN With vegetarian and vegan food so good, even diehard carnivores dine here. Decorated in muted blue-green tones, the interior feels calm and cool even during the packed lunch hour, which attracts everyone from indie types to local business folk. Be sure to try some of the fabulous desserts, like the fudge brownies;

you won't believe they're vegan. *206–214 E. 13th Ave.* ☎ *303/832-7313. www.watercourse foods.com. Breakfast: $5–$9; salads and sandwiches $6–$9; entrees $9.50. Tues–Sun 8am–10pm.*

Doable

→**Bayou Bob's** CAJUN For favorites like gumbo, red beans and rice, blackened catfish, and jambalaya, plus Mardi Gras–style Hurricanes, head to this family-owned restaurant. The atmosphere is casual and friendly, with fishnets, street signs, and Southern-tinged bric-a-brac adorning the walls. The Happy Hour runs from 3 to 7pm, with half-priced appetizers and $2 drinks. Try the spicy fried alligator for something a bit exotic, or keep it classic with fried hushpuppies. *1635 Glenarm St. (in the Paramount Theatre Building).* ☎ *303/ 573-6828. Appetizers $3–$7; entrees $8–$16. Mon–Wed 11am–9pm; Thurs–Sat 11am–10pm.*

→**Lime** ★ MEXICAN Any Mexican restaurant that includes a shot of tequila with their traditional complimentary chips and salsa is all right by us; add the seven types of margaritas mixed at the bar and we're hooked. While the bar is one of the busiest in Denver, the sleek dining room serves up affordable and creative Mexican fare, like zesty green chile and sweet corn tamales. Try the house specialty "Scorpions" for a spicy kick. We could imagine selling our first-born for these flash-fried jalapeno halves stuffed with shrimp and chipotle cheese. *1424 Larimer St.* ☎ *303/893-5463. Entrees $8–$14. Mon–Wed 4–10pm; Thurs–Sat 4–11pm; Sun 11am–close.*

→**The 9th Door** TAPAS Deep red fabrics and shimmery gold tints give this LoDo restaurant and lounge an opulent feel. While the Spanish-style tapas small plates won't fill you up, they're great for grazing and sharing. Popular plates include gambas al ajillo (grilled shrimp in garlic) and pimientos del piquillo rellenos, fire-roasted peppers stuffed with fresh goat cheese, rosemary, and Serrano ham. On Mondays selected wines are half price. *1808 Blake St.* ☎ *303/292-2229. www.the9thdoor.com. Small plates: $6–$12. Mon–Fri 4:30pm–close; Sat 5:30pm–close.*

→**The Saucy Noodle** ITALIAN/PIZZA With its bold red-and-black interior and famous motto "If you don't like garlic, go home," this restaurant more than lives up to its cheeky moniker. Family-owned since 1964, the Noodle offers traditional Italian fare with lots of red sauce and, of course, garlic. The baked pasta dishes are particularly tasty, or change it up with homemade pizzas. A small wine bar with pub tables up front is great if you just want an appetizer and a drink. *727 S. University Blvd.* ☎ *303/ 733-6977. Pizza $13–$15; pasta $11–$15. Mon–Fri 4:30–9:30pm; Sat–Sun 4:30–10pm.*

Splurge

→**Nine75** AMERICAN Serving "comfort food with a rock 'n' roll twist," this urban-chic restaurant has an eclectic mix of entrees and small plates. The menu is long enough to accommodate classic American favorites like buttermilk fried chicken and whimsical dishes like the "Miso (excited about this) black cod." The luxurious bar area in the back has an amazing panoramic view of the Rockies and great signature drinks (try the Tantra), making it a great location to watch a Denver sunset. *975 Lincoln St.* ☎ *303/975-0975. www.nine75-restaurant.com. Small plates: $4–$12; entrees $16–$29. Lunch Mon–Fri 11:30am–2pm. Dinner Mon–Thurs 5–10pm; Fri–Sat 5–11pm.*

Partying

The first permanent structure on the site of modern Denver was supposedly a saloon, and Denver residents have obviously taken this precedent to heart. Whether you're looking for a sports bar, singles bar, gay bar, or a great brewpub,

Denver is sure to have the perfect bar for you. One of the best spots for partying is the historic **LoDo** district, packed with bars, pubs, restaurants, and dance clubs. For more low-key fun, check out some of the bars and clubs along Colfax and in the Capitol Hill neighborhood.

BARS, PUBS & CLUBS
LoDo/Downtown

➜ **Falling Rock Tap House** ✶ PUB The owner's impressive beer bottle collection, and the pub motto, "No crap on tap," should give you a clue about what takes center stage here. With 69 beers on tap, plus various bottled options, this is a true beer lover's paradise. The music is loud and the vibe is friendly, but fewer cheap drink specials mean the crowd is less college-heavy—expect a range of ages and lifestyles. *1919 Blake St.* ☎ *303/293-8338. www.fallingrocktaphouse.com. Daily 11am–2am.*

➜ **LoDo's Bar and Grill** BAR Daily drink specials and a huge rooftop patio with views of Coors Field and the Rocky Mountains make this one of the most popular spots in LoDo, especially on game days. While the large TVs in the bar area scream "sports bar," weekend evenings usher in local DJs spinning records for young, nubile gym-addicts on the prowl. *1946 Market St.* ☎ *303/293-8555. www.lodobarandgrill.com. Daily 11am–2am.*

➜ **Lucky Strike Lanes** BOWLING ALLEY An outpost of the trendy Lucky Strike lanes in Hollywood, this retro-sexy bowling alley and lounge offers 12 lanes, pool tables, a 50-foot bar, and lots of slick video screens and art exhibits. Comfy booths are available for lounging, and the full-service restaurant provides some excellent snacks and burgers. For a sweet and classic dessert, try the root beer float. *500 16th St.*

(3rd level of Denver Pavilions). ☎ *303/629-9090. www.bowlluckystrike.com. Daily 11am–2am.*

Colfax

➜ **The Bank Bar and Grill** BAR Housed in the old Capitol Hill State Bank building, this popular hangout has a lively but understated atmosphere and attracts a fairly diverse clientele, including a lot of intellectual-looking indie types. Two Happy Hours (4:30–6:30pm and 10pm–midnight), decent pub grub (including some vegetarian options), and friendly bartenders mean you can always "bank" on having a great time (yeah, we know that was cheesy). *2239 E. Colfax* ☎ *303/320-9494. www.thebankbarandgrill.com. Daily 10am–2am.*

➜ **The Irish Snug** PUB Owned and operated by brothers and native Dubliners Jim and Frank McCloughlin, this pub gets its name from the tiny, private rooms or "snugs" that offered 19th-century Irish patrons the chance to have a drink without actually being seen at the pub. If you're in the mood for a bit of privacy, two snugs are on the premises. Otherwise, have a seat with the common folk at the bar. Besides beer and Irish whiskey, the Snug also has traditional Irish pub fare and some damn good waffle fries, served either plain, with spicy Buffalo sauce, or Mexican-style with all the nacho trimmings. *1201 E. Colfax Ave.* ☎ *303/839-1394. www.irishsnug.com. Daily 11am–2am.*

➜ **tHERe** ✶ BAR Part cocktail lounge, part coffee bar, part hip hangout, this lesbian-owned and -operated spot has a colorful, warm vibe. Weekly staples for regulars include live bands, Sunday night viewings of *The L Word*, and Saturday night's popular "Dyke Mic" stand-up comedy event. Free Wi-Fi and good coffee make this a good location for relaxing during daylight hours. Plus, where else can you get Pabst Blue Ribbon in cans? *1526 E. Colfax Ave.* ☎ *303/830-8437. www.theredenver. com. Mon–Sat 9am–midnight; Sun 10am– midnight.*

Capitol Hill

➔**The Church** CLUB There's nothing like partying in a former church to add a bit of transgressive glee to your evening. The Gothic-style cathedral houses three dance floors featuring local and international DJs, plus multiple bars (one serves sushi), and a smoking lounge. The acoustics aren't the best, as sound tends to bounce off the walls and arched ceilings, but with packed dance floors and solid reviews from locals, this former house of God must be doing something right. *1160 Lincoln St.* ☎ *303/832-3528. Thurs–Sun 9pm– 2am. Cover $5–$15.*

➔ **Cricket on the Hill** ★ BAR A favorite Capitol Hill destination, this legendary live-music venue delivers stiff drinks, great Happy Hours, and an eclectic crop of new bands just making their way into the local spotlight. Music ranges from straight-ahead rock to alt-country and the blues, all played at top volume, while the diverse crowd includes both live music lovers and fans of cheap booze. *1209 E. 13th St.* ☎ *303/ 830-9020. www.cricketonthehill.com. Daily noon–2am. Cover $3–$6.*

South Denver

➔**BJ's Carousel** BAR This neighborhood-style gay bar decorated with miniature carousel horses has affordable drinks, great meal deals (all-you-can-eat homemade spaghetti, anyone?), and some of the best drag shows and karaoke in town. Though BJ's has a host of regulars, with a reputation for being the "friendliest bar in Denver," visitors will find they receive a warm welcome. *1380 S. Broadway.* ☎ *303/ 777-9880. www.bjsdenver.com. Sat–Mon 10am– 2am; Tues–Fri 4pm–2am.*

LIVE MUSIC
Rock/Indie/Eclectic
➔**Bluebird Theater** ★ Built in 1913 to show silent films, this restored Art Deco theater now rocks almost nightly to intimate, small-scale shows featuring both national and local bands. Carved, vaulted ceilings and red velvet curtains contribute to the artsy feel of this venue, which hosts a range of indie, rockabilly, punk, and alt-country acts. *3317 E. Colfax.* ☎ *303/322-2308. www.gothictheatre.com/venue/detail/ bluebird-theater. Tickets $7–$20.*

➔**15th Street Tavern** Despite the somewhat run-down appearance, this is one of the best places in Denver to score cheap drinks and hear local indie, metal, and punk acts before they get too famous. With past performers including the likes of Bright Eyes, The Shins, and Death Cab for Cutie, this is a real diamond in the rough for music buffs. *623 15th St.* ☎ *303/572-0822. www.15thst tavern.com. Daily noon–2am. Cover varies.*

➔**Gothic Theatre** With acts ranging from bluegrass to jazz, rock, and electronica, it's hard to pin down what genre of music this restored Roaring Twenties theater specializes in. Regardless of what band is playing, the top-quality sound and light system make even small-time acts look big, and the wraparound balcony provides a great vantage point for taking it all in. *3263 South Broadway, Englewood, CO. www.gothictheatre. com. Cover $5–$15.*

Jazz/Country
➔**El Chapultepec** Denver's oldest jazz club, the "Pec" regularly packs an incredibly diverse clientele into its tiny LoDo quarters for nightly jazz. Traditional jazz predominate. Depending on the night, there may be standing room only, but that's a small price to pay for the chance to hear some of the city's best musicians in an intimate, historic venue. *1962 Market St.*

☎ *303/295-9126. Mon–Sun 7am–2am. No cover; 1 drink per set minimum.*

➜**Grizzly Rose** Known to locals as "the Griz" or "the Rose," this 5,000-square-foot dance floor and music venue features live music Tuesdays through Saturdays, drawing national acts like Garth Brooks, Willie Nelson, LeAnn Rimes, and Tanya Tucker, as well as local country and country-western bands. Free dance classes are offered for newbies, and a full-service restaurant and bar is on hand. Beware of Sunday family nights, however, when the place is overrun with kids and tweens. *5450 N. Valley Hwy. (I-25 Exit 215).* ☎ *303/295-1330. www.grizzly rose.com. Tues–Fri 11–2am; Sat–Sun 6pm–2am. Tickets range from $12 to $25, available through Ticketmaster or at the Grizzly Rose. Cover charges for non-concert events are $5, with admission free on Tues–Wed.*

What to See & Do

Trust us, there's no way you can be bored in Denver. Tons of attractions, museums, nightlife, live music, and sports mean there's more than enough to keep you busy for as long as you plan to stay. We recommend you take advantage of at least some of Denver's great outdoor activities.

Even if you're not a big hiker or mountain biker, you can meander through the Denver Botanical Gardens, or take an easy bike ride through parts of the city.

THE TOP ATTRACTIONS

➜**Black American West Museum & Heritage Center** ★ Most people have no idea that nearly one-third of cowboys in the Old West were black. In this museum, filled with artifacts, memorabilia, oral histories, and photographs, their little-known history comes alive, along with that of black doctors, teachers, newspaper reporters, and state legislators. The Victorian mansion that houses the museum belonged to Dr. Justina Ford, the first black woman licensed to

practice in Denver. Known locally as the "Lady Doctor," Ford (1871–1951) delivered more than 7,000 babies, most of them at home, since she was denied hospital privileges. *3091 California St.* ☎ *303/292-2566. Admission $6. June–Sept daily 10am–5pm; Oct–May Wed–Fri 10am–2pm, Sat–Sun 10am–5pm. Light rail: stop #1.*

➜**Denver Art Museum** ★★ Wrapped in a thin, 28-sided wall faced with one million sparkling tiles, this seven-story museum was already unique before its renovation. With the recent completion of an avant-garde addition designed by renowned architect Daniel Liebeskind, however, the museum has hit a whole new level of distinction. The new 146,000-square-foot building, opened in the fall of 2006, is covered in titanium tiles. Its jagged angles and points recall the peaks of the Rockies. Inside, the museum has one of the nation's most impressive collections of Western and regional works, including Fredric Remington's *The Cheyenne*, Charles Russell's *In the Enemy's Country*, and works by Georgia O'Keeffe. The Native American collection is also excellent, with more than 17,000 pieces from 150 North American tribes, spanning almost 2,000 years. *100 W 14th Ave. (at Civic Center Park).* ☎ *720/865-5000. www.denverartmuseum.org. Admission $13 for non-residents ($10 for non-residents with student ID). Tues and Thurs 10am–5pm; Wed and Fri 10am–10pm; Sat–Sun 9am–5pm.*

➜**Denver Botanic Gardens** You'll find 23 acres of outdoor and indoor gardens at this popular attraction, including a traditional Japanese garden, a water garden, a fragrance garden, and a garden inspired by the paintings of Monet (wait, wasn't it supposed to be the other way around?). If you're visiting Denver in the winter, you can still enjoy the dome-shaped Tropical Conservatory, where thousands of tropical

A Great Mile High Music Store

Recently relocated from its digs in an old supermarket, Denver's best independent music store, **Twist & Shout** ★, can now be found in a hip new building on Colfax, next to other indie faves like the Tattered Cover bookstore and the Denver Folklore Center. You can purchase the ingredients for your life's soundtrack here, plus all the accessories you need to go along with it: From posters to buttons, bags, and hats. Check out the section devoted to hip-hop and dance music, as well as the large selection of local Colorado bands. Twist & Shout also hosts a number of in-store appearances and live music events, so check to see if anything is coming up. *www.twistandshout.com. 2508 E. Colfax* ☎ *612/870-9300. Mon–Fri 9am–9pm; Sat 9am–8pm; Sun 11am–6pm.*

and subtropical plants continue to flourish in the damp warmth. It's a nice change from the chilly temperatures outside. *1005 York St.* ☎ *720/865-3500. www.botanicgardens.org. Summer admission: $8.50 ($5 for students with ID). Winter admission: $7.50 ($4 for students with ID). Sep–Apr daily 9am–5pm; May–Sep Sat–Tues 9am–8pm; Wed–Fri 9am–5pm. Bus line: 2, 6, or 10.*

FREE ➜ **Larimer Square** This historic area in downtown Denver has certainly had its ups and downs. In 1858, Larimer Street between 14th and 15th streets was all that existed of Denver. False-fronted wooden stores, hotels, and saloons served gold seekers and other pioneers. By 1870, this was the main street of the city and the site of the first bank, theater, and streetcar line. As the city grew, this area of Larimer declined into a skid row of pawnshops, gin mills, and flophouses. Plans were made to bulldoze the buildings, built in the 1870s and 1880s, but the area was saved when a group of investors purchased the entire block in 1965. The Larimer Square project became Denver's first major historic preservation effort. All of the original buildings were restored, and in 1973 they were added to the National Register of Historic Places. Today, the square hosts many special festivals and events, including an Oktoberfest celebration. During the La

Piazza dell'Arte event each June, over 200 artists create pastel masterpieces on the streets. *1400 block of Larimer St.* ☎ *303/534-2367. www.larimersquare.com. Bus line: 2, 7, 12, 15,16, 28, 28, 31, 32, 38, or 44.*

➜ **Museo de las Americas** ★ The only museum in the Rocky Mountains focusing on the art, culture, and history of Latinos, this museum is definitely worth a visit. Exhibits and collections change regularly; a semi-permanent exhibit tells the story of pre-Columbian Latin America, with a replica of an ornate sunstone and displays on Tenochtitlan, the Aztec metropolis (and site of present-day Mexico City), which was destroyed by invading Spaniards in the 16th century. Be sure to check the website for cultural events, film viewings, and some Spanish-language discussion nights. *861 Santa Fe Dr.* ☎ *303/571-4401. www.museo.org. Admission $4 ($3 with student ID). Tues–Fri 10am–5pm; Sat–Sun noon–5pm. Bus: 9 (10th & Kalamath St.; walk 1 block east, then 1½ blocks south).*

MORE THINGS TO SEE & DO

Need more to see and do in Denver? Check out the home of the "unsinkable" Molly Brown, who survived the *Titanic* disaster and became a national heroine. Now restored to its 1910 appearance, the **Molly Brown House Museum** (1340

Pow Wow Wow! Denver Festivals

→ Get yourself duded up in boots and a cowboy hat for the world's largest livestock show and indoor rodeo, held every January in Denver. The **National Western Stock Show and Rodeo** features livestock auctions, over twenty rodeo performances, Western-themed arts and crafts, and tons of tasty vittles. **www.nationalwestern.com.**

→ More than 1,500 Native Americans representing 85 tribes gather in Denver in March for the **March Powwow,** a 3-day festival of traditional music and dancing. Over 60 different drum groups also participate in the performances, and arts and crafts booths are also open. **www.denvermarch powwow.org.**

→ What began in the 1980s as a small street fair in Denver has grown to become the largest **Cinco de Mayo** festival in the U.S., regularly attracting crowds of over 300,000. The celebration includes live music acts, over 350 different arts, crafts, and food vendors, and a parade. **www.newsed.org/ cinco.htm.**

→ Live music and arts and crafts booths abound at Denver's **A Taste of Colorado** festival, but the real draw is the tasty eats provided by more than 50 Denver restaurants. On Labor Day weekend, bring an appetite to sample the best Colorado's chefs have to offer. **www.atasteofcolorado.com.**

→ Calling all beer lovers! Each October, Denver hosts the **Great American Beer Festival,** the largest and most prestigious beer event in the U.S. The 380 breweries and 1,600 different beers are arranged by geographic area, so you can, in the words of the organizers, take a "walking tour of the nation's beer-blessed landscape." **www.beertown.com.**

Pennsylvania St.; ☎ **303/832-4092;** www. mollybrown.org) offers a view of what life was like in Denver during the first few years of the 20th century. There's a $6.50 admission charge.

The **Colorado Capitol Building** (Lincoln St. and Colfax Ave.; ☎ **303/866-2604**), built of Colorado granite, is worth a visit for the grand interiors, murals, and rotunda. The **Colorado History Museum** (1300 Broadway; ☎ **303/866-3682;** www. coloradohistory.org) illustrates the history of the state through a series of exhibits, including the "Ancient Voices" multimedia exhibit (dedicated to Colorado's Native American tribes) and the "Confluence of Cultures" exhibit (describing the pioneer era.) Admission is $7, $6 for students.

For something a little different, head 10 minutes northeast of downtown to the **Mile High Flea Market** (7007 E. 88th Ave. at I-76, Henderson, CO; ☎ **303/289-4656**), a huge, year-round market with tons of merchandise. The market runs Wednesdays, Saturdays, and Sundays.

PLAYING OUTSIDE
Biking
Voted top city for bicyclists by *Bicycle Magazine,* Denver has more than 130 miles of designated bike paths and lanes, including 85 miles of off-road recreation trails.

The **Denver Bike Map** offers the most comprehensive guide to the metro area's biking paths and trails, available for about $5 at most Denver bike shops, bookstores, or at the City Cashier's office (201 W. Colfax; ☎ **720/865-2780**).

COOL IN THE MIDWEST

A Boat Tour of Downtown Denver

For a cool waterway tour of downtown Denver, check out **Venice on the Creek,** a company specializing in scenic gondola-style rides along Cherry Creek. Tickets are sold "by the bench," with each bench accommodating up to two adults, so it's more cost-effective to bring a buddy along. As your guide describes the history of the city and points out interesting landmarks, you can both relax: Romantic but off-key Italian serenades are not part of the tour. *Ticket kiosk at Creekfront Plaza (Speer Blvd. & Larimer St.) ☎ 303/893-0750. www.veniceonthecreek.com. Tours run from June–Aug. Half-hour tours are $20 per bench; 1-hour tours are $30 per bench.*

Bike rentals, professional repairs, and free bike parking is available at the **Cherry Creek Bike Rack** (171 Detroit St.; ☎ 303/388-1630), or for general information on cycling in Denver, check out **Bike Denver** (☎ 303/417-1544; www.bikedenver.org). If you want to plunk down your cash for a guided tour of the city and local foothills, try **Denver Bike Tours** (☎ 720/641-3166; www.denverbiketours.com), offering 3-hour tours of the city for $80 per person, or half-day mountain tours for $170 per person.

Hiking

With trails to suit every skill level, the Denver area is a great place to begin a hike: Take off for a few hours or a few days, depending on your schedule. Check out Denver's **Mountain Parks** system (**www.denvergov.org**), which includes 31 parks and over 14,000 acres open for free recreational use, including hiking and picnicking.

Just outside Denver's urban sprawl, near Golden, Colorado, is **Mount Falcon Park,** with hiking trails ranging in difficulty from easy to moderate. Bikes are also permitted, and admission is free. The park is open from dawn until dusk; to get there, head west out of Denver on U.S. 285 and go north on Parmalee Gulch Rd.

Finally, for the serious hiking enthusiast, there's always the **Colorado Trail,** stretching 500 miles from Denver to Durango. Information on the route is available from the **Colorado Trail Foundation** (☎ 303/384-3729; www.coloradotrail.org).

Riverboarding

If gliding gently down a shallow creek isn't your idea of a good time, opt for the more adventurous water sport of **riverboarding** ★, which is sort of like body-boarding, only you're wearing a helmet, wetsuit, and flippers, and flying headfirst down Clear Creek on a specially designed "ripboard." The whole experience lasts about 4 hours, including lessons, and costs $45 per person on weekdays, $55 on weekends. *Ripboard ☎ 866/311-2627. www.ripboard.com. Located at Clear Creek Whitewater Park, Golden, CO. Open May–Sept; call ahead for reservations.*

Skiing/Snowboarding

Although most of the serious downhill fun is at resort destinations like Vail and Aspen, there are several ski resort areas closer to Denver worth checking out. **Eldora Mountain Resort** (☎ 303/440-8700; www.eldora.com) is 45 miles west of Denver, with almost 700 acres. The 53 trails there are rated 20% beginner, 50% intermediate, and 30% advanced. West of Denver about 56 miles on I-70 is **Loveland**

Home runs travel a long way at mile-high Coors Field.

Basin and Valley (☎ 800/736-3754; www. skiloveland.com) with 70 trails (17% beginner, 42% intermediate, and 41% advanced) spread out over 1,365 acres. **Winter Park Resort** (☎ 800/729-5813; www.winter parkresort.com) is 73 miles west of Denver, and boasts 2,762 acres and 134 trails, rated 10% beginner, 36% intermediate, and 54% advanced. More information on Colorado skiing is available from Colorado Ski Country USA (☎ 303/837-0793; www. coloradoski.com).

SPECTATOR SPORTS

There's plenty of action for sports fans in Denver, and with most of the stadiums near downtown, it's easy to get to games on foot or by public transportation. Take the light rail C-line directly to Invesco Field at Mile High or the Pepsi Center; from the end of the line at Union Station, Coors Field is just a short walk away.

Baseball

It's estimated that a baseball hit 400 feet at sea-level Yankee Stadium would travel as far as 440 feet at Denver's mile-high Coors Field, home of the National League's **Colorado Rockies** (☎ 800/388-7625; www.coloradorockies.com). The 50,000-seat stadium was designed to have an old-school feel, but it offers all the modern amenities, including an on-site micro-brewery. Tickets are easily come by at the box office, or outside, though it's "buyer beware" if you decide to get your ducats from a scalper. It's $4 for the "Rockpile" in (far) left field, up to $75 for the best seats.

Football

There's rarely an empty seat at Invesco Field at Mile High, where fans of the **Denver Broncos** (☎ 720-258-3333; www. denverbroncos.com) of the NFL often brave chilly weather to cheer on their team.

Games are sold out months in advance, so call early to try to get tickets. Your best bet may be finding someone outside the stadium on game day.

Basketball

Denver's NBA team, the **Denver Nuggets** (☎ 303/405-1111; www.nuggets.com), play home games at the Pepsi Center, located downtown at Speer Boulevard and Auraria Parkway. The regular season runs from October through April. Tickets begin at $10 and are readily available.

Hockey

The Pepsi Center is also home to the NHL's **Colorado Avalanche** (☎ 303/405-1111; www.coloradoavalanche.com), Denver's major league hockey team. The season runs from October through April. Tickets can be hard to come by, not to mention pricey. They start at $21 and go up to $184.

Soccer

Denver and the state of Colorado got their new major league soccer team, the **Colorado Rapids** (☎ 303/405-1111; www.coloradorapids.com), a decade or so ago. The regular season runs from March through October, and the Rapids play their home games at Invesco Field at Mile High. Tickets run from $10 to $25 and are usually available.

On the Road to Salt Lake City, UT

Denver, CO to Salt Lake City, UT 533 miles

This is a pretty long trek through parts of Colorado, Wyoming, and Utah, but you'll find the scenery is quite diverse and engaging. In Wyoming, you'll get high plains and rolling prairies, along with some scenic views of mountain peaks in the distance. As you travel farther west into Utah, you'll see lots of rocky ridges as the road winds through and around a number of canyons and hills. As you admire the scenery, enjoy these Salt Lake City area bands; all selections are found on the *Death By Salt II* compilation CD put together by *SLUG* (Salt Lake Underground), a popular local music 'zine (p. 444).

On the Road Nuts & Bolts

Where to Fill Up   You'll see lots of gas stations on the way to Cheyenne, but once you get on I-80 headed west, they become few and far between. If you don't fill up in Cheyenne, your other option is Laramie; after that, you'll hit a good long stretch of almost empty countryside, with up to 40-mile stretches between gas stations. Don't let the tank get too low, even if you're not the sort of driver who stops just to top up.

The Tolls   There are none.

The Fastest Way   Take I-25 north out of Denver to Cheyenne, Wyoming. From Cheyenne, you'll go west on I-80 through Wyoming, and then into Utah and Salt Lake City. This should take about 7¹/₂ if you don't encounter any traffic.

Where to Stop   Rawlins, Wyoming for a tour of the Wyoming Frontier Prison, and a meal at Rose's Lariat, a popular Mexican restaurant.

Playlist: Samples from Death By Salt II

- *Under Watchful Eyes*, **Vile Blue Shades**
- *Deep Waters*, **Bronco**
- *For the Sake of that Empty Space*, **Red Bennies**
- *Queen of the Surface Streets*, **Devotchka**
- *The Ghost of Porter Rockwell*, **24-oz. Can**
- *Subsequential Space*, **Deadbeats**
- *Eddie's Balloon*, **Mushman**
- *Afterburn*, **Redemption**
- *Message from the Grave*, **Fifi Murmur**

On the Road to Salt Lake: Passing through Wyoming

The history of Wyoming is full of stories involving cattle rustlers, gunslingers, and others on the wrong side of the law. Some the most famous tales involve the legendary outlaws Butch Cassidy and the Sundance Kid, who often laid low near Buffalo, Wyoming, at the famous Hole-in-the-Wall hideout.

By 1890, when Wyoming achieved statehood, the growing population and increasingly vigilant law enforcement meant the outlaws' way of life was nearing a close.

Today, you can tour the 📺 Best♦ **Wyoming Frontier Prison** (500 W. Walnut St.; ☎ 307/324-4422) in Rawlins, Wyoming, where some of the most notorious fugitives from that time period were housed—or in some cases, executed. While it's not for the fainthearted, we found the prison to be fascinating in a sort of twisted, macabre way. Grisly memorials to justice include the gas execution chamber and the specially designed hanging room, which are included on the guided tour.

If touring old prisons isn't your idea of a good time, head to **Rose's Lariat** (410 E. Cedar; ☎ 307/324-5261) for some of the best Mexican food in southern Wyoming. The family-owned establishment is usually crowded with locals, but the wait is worth it. Try the enchiladas smothered in green chile sauce before hitting the road and continuing on to Salt Lake City.

Welcome To Salt Lake City

While it's true that Utah is a state with some pretty strong conservative values, the culture in Salt Lake City is an interesting blend: It's the religious hub for members Church of Jesus Christ of Latter-Day Saints (otherwise known as Mormons), but it's also home to a strong alternative culture, including a distinctive music scene. As the city grows and more non-Mormons make their homes here, SLC is shedding its strait-laced image and becoming more and more well-known for its incredibly diverse outdoor activities The city does have its quirks, particularly the liquor laws (p. 452), but it's a place that always manages to show visitors a good time.

Salt Lake City **Nuts & Bolts**

Area Code   The telephone area code in Salt Lake City and surrounding area is 801.

Business Hours   Banks and offices are generally open Monday to Friday 9am to 5pm; some banks also have hours on Saturday. Most department stores and supermarkets are open daily until 9pm, although there are a few supermarkets open 24 hours. Bars are generally open daily until 1am.

Drugstores   Walgreens Pharmacy (☎ 801/463-4870) at 909 E. 2100 South is open 24 hours.

Emergencies   Call ☎ **911** if you need the police, fire department, or an ambulance.

Hospitals   LDS Hospital, 8th Ave. and C St. (☎ 801/408-1100), and Salt Lake Regional Medical Center, 1050 E. South Temple Holmes (☎ 801/350-4111), have 24-hour emergency rooms.

Internet   Free Wi-Fi access is available at the Main Library at 210 E. 400 South Street (☎ 801/524-8200), along Main Street from South Temple to 400 South, and at the downtown Gallivan Center.

Laundry/Dry Cleaners   Someone in SLC finally got wise and put a bar and a laundromat together, so there's no need to put off doing your laundry. **Stonewash laundro-bar** (☎ 801/521-2534) is located at 247 S. 500 East and is open daily from 7am until midnight. Machines are coin-operated, and the bar is cash only. If for some reason you took dry clean-only clothes on a road trip (hey, it could happen), try City Dry Cleaners (☎ 801/466-2241) at 1068 E. 1300 South.

Liquor Laws   Utah's liquor laws are probably the most complicated in the U.S. (p. 452). Despite the bizarre regulations, it *is* possible to get a drink, as long as you have reached the legal drinking age of 21 or over.

Newspapers & Magazines   The two major dailies in Salt Lake are the *Salt Lake Tribune* (www.sltrib.com) and the *Deseret Morning News* (www.deseretnews.com). The *Salt Lake City Magazine* (www.saltlakemagazine.com) is a slick bi-monthly magazine covering Salt Lake City culture and events, while the free *Salt Lake City Weekly* (www.slweekly.com) offers up-to-the-minute dining reviews, entertainment listings, and local info with an edgy attitude. *SLUG* (Salt Lake Underground; www.slugmag.com) is a popular free music 'zine that has the best reviews and 411 on SLC-area bands.

Police   For non-emergencies, contact the Salt Lake City Police Department (☎ 801/799-3000).

Post Office   The city's main post office is located at 1760 W. 2100 South; the branch closest to downtown is at 230 W. 200 South. For other locations, check the United States Postal Service website (www.usps.com) or call ☎ 800/275-8777.

Radio   Tune your FM radio to KUER (90.1) for NPR broadcasting, KSOP (104.3) for country, KXRK (96.3) for popular alternative music, and KZPL (103.5) for classic rock. For news and sports, check out AM KSL (1160).

Taxes   Salt Lake City sales tax is 6.6%, restaurant tax is 7.6%, and the hotel tax is 11.2%.

Television   You'll find ABC (KTVX) on channel 2, CBS (KUTV) on channel 4, NBC (KSL) on channel 5, PBS (KUED) on channel 7, and Fox (KSTV) on channel 13.

Time Zone   Salt Lake City is on Mountain Time.

Transit Information   Call the Utah Transit Authority (☎ 888/743-3882) for info, or check out their website at www.rideuta.com.

Useful Numbers   For road conditions in Utah, call ☎ 800/492-2400.

Visitors' Center   The Salt Lake City visitors' center is located downtown in the Salt Palace Convention Center, at 90 W. Temple (☎ 800/541-4955; www.visitsaltlake.com). Open daily until 5pm, the center has free copies of the *Salt Lake Visitor's Guide,* which has maps of the downtown area and a guide to local restaurants and attractions.

Weather   Call ☎ 801/575-7669 to get the latest weather info over the phone, or go online to www.kutv.com/weather.

Getting Around

Salt Lake City can be difficult to navigate if you're not comfortable with the grid system, oriented around Temple Square in downtown (see below), but once you get the hang of it you should be fine.

Downtown Salt Lake City, where you'll probably spend a lot of your time, is an interesting blend of religious and commercial activity. LDS church offices, the Family History Library, and other church buildings surround Temple Square, but with all the businesses, hotels, restaurants, and stores around, it doesn't feel much different than any other downtown business district. North of Temple Square is the **Capitol Hill** district, with the Utah State Capitol Building, Council Hall, and some lovely older homes.

 Navigating Salt Lake City

For first-time visitors, Salt Lake City's street system can seem as bizarre as its liquor laws; after all, who ever heard of an address like 230 West 200 South? Fortunately, it's not quite as complicated as it sounds.

Salt Lake City's downtown is laid out on a simple grid system centered on Temple Square, with streets named and numbered based on how far north, south, east, or west they are from that point. The streets surrounding Temple Square are South Temple, West Temple, North Temple, and Main Street (directly to the east). From here, the numbers in the road names increase by 100s in each of the four cardinal directions, with West Temple taking the place of 100 West, 100 North called North Temple, and 100 East known as State Street.

Now back to that address: You would find 230 West 200 South a little over 2 blocks west and 2 blocks south of Temple Square. Got it? If you're still having trouble, get a map and spend some time looking it over. The key is to remember that streets are labeled based on their position relative to Temple Square, not based on their actual direction: For example, "South" streets always run east-west, never north-south.

Finally, if you're asking for directions from a local, be aware that SLC residents regularly refer to streets like 100 South and 900 West as "1st South" and "9th West," so ask for clarification ("100 South?") if you're unsure.

Southeast of downtown you'll find the **Sugarhouse** district. Named after a never-completed sugar mill and easily the hippest neighborhood in SLC, this area has lots of quirky stores, coffeehouses, and bars. Developers have pushed out some small businesses and replaced them with large chain stores, but the area still has a gritty, indie feel.

BY CAR

Once you get the hang of Salt Lake City's street system, you'll find it pretty easy to get around by car. Parts of downtown are easily accessed on foot, but you'll most likely want to drive anywhere outside of the immediate downtown area.

Parking

In general, Salt Lake has lots of parking, although sometimes it may take a while to find a spot downtown. Public lots in the downtown area cost from $1 to $7 per day, although some lots are free with validation from a participating restaurant or shop. Downtown street parking is metered; each half-hour is 25¢, and total time is usually limited to 2 hours (or sometimes 130 min.).

BY BUS/LIGHT RAIL

The Utah Transit Authority (www.rideuta.com) provides **bus service** throughout the Salt Lake City metro area and also operates **Trax,** a light rail line that runs 15 miles from the southern suburb of Sandy to downtown Salt Lake. A second Trax line runs east from downtown towards the University of Utah.

One-way fare for the bus or light rail is $1.50; free transfers from the bus to the Trax line are available. If you're going to be riding public transportation more than a few times, it's best to purchase a **1-day bus and light rail pass** for $4, available at light rail stops from the vending machines.

The best part of Salt Lake City's public transit system is the **downtown free-fare zone,** which roughly runs from 400 South to North Temple, continuing up Main Street to 500 North to include the State Capitol, and between 200 East and West Temple. Within this zone, you can hop on and off the bus and Trax lines as many times as you want and pay absolutely zilch. Maps showing the exact outline of the free fare zone are available on the UTA website, or at the downtown Salt Lake Visitors Center (90 W. Temple).

ON FOOT

Salt Lake City's downtown area is easily accessible on foot, and the UTA's free fare zone makes it easy to hop on or off the bus or light rail if you get tired of walking. If you're walking around on one of those hot-as-heck Utah summer days though, be careful; temperatures well over 100°F can really wipe you out fast.

BY TAXI

For a taxi, call the **City Cab** company (☎ 801/363-5550), **Yellow Cab** (☎ 801/521-2100), or **Ute Cab** (☎ 801/359-7788). Rates are $2 at the flag drop and $1.80 per each additional mile.

Sleeping

You should have no trouble finding affordable accommodations in Salt Lake City, whatever your budget. The 2002 Salt Lake City Olympics resulted in a huge building boom and a surplus of lodging options, so prices are relatively low. Hostel and camping options are also available, but with so many attractive downtown hotels for under $100 a night, Salt Lake City may be the place to splurge a little. After all, you're getting a lot more bang for your buck.

CAMPGROUNDS/HOSTELS

➜ **Camelot Hostel and Guesthouse** Located 1 mile from each other, these two properties offer super comfortable rooms at affordable prices. The brightly painted hostel has small dorm rooms accommodating from two to four people, while the

Salt Lake City Highlights

Salt Lake City

UTAH

To Great
← Salt Lake
(16 mi)

The Gateway/
Union Pacific
Depot

Delta
Center

Salt Palace
(Civic Aud.)

Arrow
Press Sq.

Pioneer
Park

Trolley
Square

Liberty
Park

TO SUGARHOUSE ↘

guesthouse is a renovated four-story Victorian mansion with fully furnished single- and double-occupancy rooms. Both properties have free Wi-Fi access and cable TV in every room, and the guesthouse offers optional in-room minifridges. Best of all, both locations are within the free-fare zone, so you can ride TRAX or the bus into downtown for free. *Camelot Hostel: 165 W. 800 South. 16 units. $14–$25/night. Camelot Guesthouse: 556 S. 500 East. 15 units. $25/night, long-term rates available. Free parking. Amenities: 24-hr. self check-in; bike rentals; kitchen; laundry facilities; free local calls. In room: Wi-Fi, cable TV.*

➔ **Salt Lake KOA/VIP** Just a couple of miles from downtown, this huge, well-maintained campground offers RV and tent campsites, plus cabin rentals and extra luxuries like Wi-Fi access. Two pools are open from May to September, and miles of jogging and biking trails are right behind the campground at SLC's Constitution park. Other amenities include bathhouses, an arcade, coin-operated laundry facilities, and an on-site convenience store. *1400 W. North Temple. ☎ 800/562-9510 www.slckoa.com. 18 tent sites ($23–$30). 200 RV sites ($34–$38); 2 camping cabins ($44–$50). Reservations recommended May–Sept. Pets accepted. Amenities: 2 outdoor pools; hot tub; coin-op washers and dryers; arcade; convenience store; Wi-Fi.*

CHEAP

For an affordable major chain hotel in Salt Lake, try **Days Inn** (315 W. 3300 South; ☎ 800/329-7466), **Econo Lodge** (715 W. North Temple; ☎ 877/233-2666), or **Super 8** (616 S. 200 West; ☎ 800/800-8000). Single and double occupancy rates at these locations are generally under $80, but check around for the best rates.

A good place to check for affordable hotel rooms is **Salt Lake Reservations** (☎ 800/847-5810; www.visitsaltlake.com/reservations), operated by the Salt Lake Convention and Visitors Bureau.

➔ **Carlton Hotel** ★ In the heart of downtown, this affordable hotel combines a historic vibe with up-to-date amenities like free Wi-Fi, a hot tub, and a complimentary hot breakfast. The clean, well-kept rooms are simply decorated, and the friendly staff members are great resources for local info. Still, the best thing about this place is the attractive, old-fashioned building, which gives the feel of a much more expensive luxury hotel. *140 E. South Temple. ☎ 801/355-3418. www.carltonhotel-slc.com. 45 units. $69 single; $74 double; $84+ suites. Free parking. Amenities: Hot tub; sauna; fitness room; free hot breakfast. In room: Cable TV, free local calls, free Wi-Fi.*

➔ **City Creek Inn** Outside, this small, independent motel looks like a vintage '50s-era motor court with a cool neon sign; inside, newly remodeled rooms are clean and comfortable, if a bit spartan (bathrooms are equipped with shower stalls, not bathtubs). Ask for rooms with adjoining second bedrooms if you're traveling with a large group; you'll have all the convenience of a suite without busting your budget. The inn's downtown location and free parking means you can leave your car behind and walk to many of the local attractions and hot spots. *230 W. North Temple. ☎ 801/533-9100. www.citycreekinn.com. 33 units. $48 single; $58 double. Some pets accepted. Free parking. Amenities: Cable TV; free local calls.*

DOABLE

➔ **Metropolitan Inn** ★ This one-time chain motel was gutted in 2003 and is now a first-rate independent, clad in colorful stucco and equipped with stylish guest rooms. Art Deco reproductions and prints of the *Wizard of Oz* hang above the beds (the

Wicked Witch of the West excluded), and rooms feature ultra-comfortable Tempur-Pedic mattresses. The dinky outdoor pool is summer-only; the hot tub is year-round. Free Wi-Fi is available in all rooms, and a computer is available in the lobby if you didn't bring your laptop. *524 S. West Temple.* ☎ *801/531-7100. www.metropolitaninn.com. 57 units. $67–$99 single or double occupancy. Free parking. Amenities: Outdoor pool; hot tub; complimentary breakfast bar. In room: Cable TV, free Wi-Fi, coffeemaker.*

→ **Shilo Inn Suites Hotel** This chain hotel in downtown Salt Lake is conveniently close to all the attractions and includes breakfast vouchers for the on-site restaurant. Stumble downstairs for some scrambled eggs, bacon, and hash browns, then head out to see downtown, just a block or two away. Extra amenities include a large indoor pool and oversize hot tub, plus a fitness center and laundry. *206 S. West Temple.* ☎ *801/521-9500. 200 units. $79–$94 single or double occupancy. Free parking. Amenities: Indoor pool, hot tub, sauna, fitness center; on site restaurant. In room: Internet access, cable TV.*

SPLURGE

→ **Hotel Monaco** ★★ Classy, yet contemporary, this boutique hotel in downtown Salt Lake offers serious luxury with some quirky twists. Lonely? They'll provide a goldfish you can adopt during your visit. Confused? Get an "intuitive reading" of your future during the nightly free wine service. We'll leave the two leopard print robes in the room to your imagination (*rawr!*), but believe us when we say this is a splurge you won't regret. *105 W. 200 South.* ☎ *877/294-9710. www.monaco-saltlakecity. com. 225 units. $109–$209 single or double occupancy. $169–$325 suite. Valet parking: $15. Pets stay free. Amenities: Restaurant; bar; exercise room; sauna; concierge. In room: Cable TV, CD player, coffeemaker, free Wi-Fi.*

Eating

SUPPLIES

Saturday mornings from June through October you can get every kind of locally grown fruit and vegetable at the **Downtown Farmers Market,** held at Pioneer Park (300 South and 300 West) from 8am to 1pm. Vendors are also on hand selling hot coffee, homemade jams, baked goods, meat, artisan cheeses, honey, and fresh flowers.

On weekdays and during the off season, you can find organic produce at the **Wild Oats Marketplace** (6930 S. Highland Dr.; ☎ **801/733-9455**) in the Sugarhouse neighborhood. Fresh baked goods (many from SLC bakeries), snacks, sandwiches, and other organic staples are available.

TAKEOUT TREATS

→ **Beto's Mexican Food** Hard-up college kids and late-night snackers come here for burritos, tacos, and other cheap eats. Open 24/7, Beto's serves fat burritos, carne asada plates, huevos rancheros, and quesadillas for a few bucks each, so indulge in some tasty, greasy goodness. *435 E. 400 South.* ☎ *801/964-8520.*

→ **The Bridge** Vegan sandwiches, pastries, and to-die-for cheesecake can all be found at this hip little cafe not far from downtown. With great prices, friendly staff, organic free-trade coffee, and daily meal specials (Wed is vegan sushi night), this is the kind of place that everyone should feel happy about. *511 W. 200 South.* ☎ *801/359-2278. Mon–Sat 9am–9pm; Sun 10am–9pm.*

→ **Luna's Italian Ice** ★★ Hit up Luna's Sugarhouse for smooth frozen treats that pack a punch of juicy flavor. This small storefront operation serves fruity favorites like lemon, watermelon, mango, and piña colada, as well as chocolate, orange crème,

COOL IN THE MIDWEST

and a Mexican-themed *horchata*. Most flavors are vegan-friendly, ask to be sure. *2126 S. 1100 East.* ☎ *801/485-4050. Mon–Sat noon–10pm.*

➔ **Nostalgia** In downtown SLC, get your caffeine kicks at a sweet little cafe with free Wi-Fi, great food, and a large variety of loose teas. Comfy couches and stuffed chairs are great to lounge on, and the homemade soups are not to be missed. We strongly recommend the tomato Florentine soup, with chunky tomatoes and bits of sweet basil. *248 E. 100 South.* ☎ *801/532-3225. www.nostalgiacoffee.com. Mon–Thurs 6am–10pm; Fri 6am–11pm; Sat 8am–11pm; Sun 8am–10pm.*

➔ **Skool Lunch Deli and Bakery** ★ Although the logo features cafeteria ladies in hair nets, the food here tastes nothing like the tasteless slop from your school days. Instead, this deli serves up fresh sandwiches, homemade soups, and tasty breakfast items to the business crowd at prices even a broke student can afford. Don't miss the homemade cookies. *60 E. South Temple.* ☎ *801/532-5269. www.skoollunch.com. Mon–Fri 7am–3pm.*

➔ **Sugarhouse Coffee** ★ You'll find coffee, snacks, and some good music vibes at this independent coffee shop and hangout, which shares space with **Orion Records.** Late-night hours make this a popular haunt for college kids and other night owls. Get the tattooed barista to make you a mean mocha latte and then kick it at one of the many tables. *2102 S. 1100 East.* ☎ *801/466-7007. www.sugarhousecoffee.com. Mon–Wed 6:30am–1am; Thurs–Fri 6:30am–3am; Sat 7am–3am; Sun 8am–1am.*

CHEAP

➔ **Boondocks Pacific Grill & Café** ★ ASIAN Mainly a lunch destination, this Filipino-fusion restaurant serves up an extensive menu of savory appetizers, noodles, and grilled meats. Try any of the meat satays, served with a special, tangy "Manolo" sauce, as well as the adobo, a national specialty made with dark chicken meat, pork cubes, and coconut milk. The pleasant, multicolored interior is accented with lace-draped tables and high-backed mission chairs. Parking is difficult as street meters are set to only 30 minutes or 2 hours, but it's worth the trouble for this food. *212 E. 500 South.* ☎ *801/363-1759. No alcohol served. Appetizers: $3–$6; entrees $8–$9. Lunch: Mon–Sat 11:30am–2pm; dinner Fri–Sat 6pm–9pm.*

➔ **Café Anh Hong** ASIAN Interior decorating at this location consists of a couple of Chinese lanterns and a fish tank with some fairly despondent looking finned-creatures, but don't let that deter you: The menu offers a solid list of Chinese standards, plus some good, cheap dim sum. We recommend the *har gow,* a savory, meaty shrimp dumpling (but be careful how you pronounce "gow," since it's potentially the foulest of Cantonese vulgarities, depending on the tone you use). For something sweet, try the sesame balls. We'll bet you've never had balls with that texture in your mouth before. *1465 S State Street.* ☎ *801/486-1912. Dim sum: $2–$5; ntrees $5–$13. Daily 11am–10pm.*

➔ **Crown Burgers** AMERICAN Serving up char-broiled burgers, as well as burritos, pastrami sandwiches, and gyros, this Utah mini-chain is a local standby. We're not sure what's up with the European hunting lodging decor (chandeliers and wall sconces in a burger joint?), but we did like the signature Crown Burger, a fat patty topped with pastrami and a secret sauce. Try the fries with fry sauce, Utah's favorite condiment. To us, it tasted like Thousand Island dressing, but aficionados swear there's a big difference. *3190 Highland Dr.* ☎ *801/467-6633. Burgers and sandwiches $2–$7. Mon–Sat 10am–10pm.*

→ **Mo's Neighborhood Grill** AMERICAN Mo's is close to everything downtown, yet truly has a neighborhood feel. Live bands perform most nights from 9pm on, making even a bland weeknight an enjoyable experience. Mo's basic American grub is quite good; pork chops, salads, and a few Mexican basics liven up the mix. The classic starters like Buffalo wings, nachos, and artichoke dip are hard to beat, as are the Friday and Saturday kitchen hours: They serve food till 3am. *358 S. West Temple.* ☎ *801/359-0586. www.mosbarandgrill.com. Starters: $3–$6; sandwiches and burgers $5–$6; entrees $6–$10. Sun–Thurs 11am–midnight; Fri–Sat 11am–3am.*

→ **Ruth's Diner** AMERICAN Opened by a tough-minded former cabaret singer in 1930, Ruth's Diner is the second-oldest restaurant in Utah and a favorite SLC destination for traditional American cooking. While the lunch and dinner menus offer traditional favorites like fat club sandwiches and chicken-fried steak, we recommend ordering off the breakfast menu, served till 4pm daily. Try the fluffy buttermilk pancakes or the Santa Cruz omelet, which comes with one of Ruth's famous mile-high biscuits. *2100 Emigration Canyon.* ☎ *801/582-9380. www.ruthsdiner.com. Breakfast: $4–$8; lunch and dinner $6–$15.*

⟨MTV⟩ ⟨Best ♥⟩ → **Sawadee** ★★★ ASIAN It's not often you come across a restaurant that combines a sophisticated atmosphere with great food and a great price, but this family-run restaurant wins in every category. The recently redecorated interior is sleek and elegant, while the Thai curries, noodles, and meat dishes are affordable, authentic, and incredibly large. You could have fed three people off the one dish of yellow curry we ordered, while the pad Thai noodles would easily have served two. Vegetarian options are also available.

754 E. South Temple St. ☎ *801/328-8424. www.sawadee1.com. Lunch: $6–$8; dinner $7–$10. Lunch: Mon–Sat 11am–3pm; dinner: Mon–Thurs 5–9:30pm; Fri–Sat 5–10pm.*

DOABLE

→ **Café Trio** ITALIAN Named for the three owner-partners, this eatery offers tasty Italian options in a sleek, minimalist interior. Along with flavorful meat and pasta entrees, the restaurant has delicious wood-fired pizzas loaded with fresh herbs and toppings, and large, flavorful salads. For an appetizer, try the popular rosemary flatbread served with creamy goat cheese, roasted peppers, and tomatoes. If the weather's good, dine outside on the large patio. *680 S. 900 East.* ☎ *801/533-8746. Entrees $8–$18. Mon–Thurs 11am–10pm; Fri–Sat 11am 10:30pm.*

→ **The Happy Sumo** ★ SUSHI/ASIAN How much sushi does it take to make a sumo happy? Probably lots and lots! But we couldn't care less, since there's definitely enough on this menu for all us regular people. Besides fresh, traditional sushi and sashimi offerings, Happy Sumo also creates artistic rolls like the Firecracker (tuna, avocado, cucumber, tempura crunchies, and spicy sauce), and the Baja (spicy tuna, avocado, cilantro, and jalapeno peppers). For non-sushi lovers, there are also noodle, cooked seafood, and meat dishes on the menu. *153 S. Rio Grande.* ☎ *801/456-7866. Sushi $4–$6; rolls $8–$14; entrees $7–$18. Mon–Thurs 11:30am–10pm. Fri–Sat 11:30am–10:30pm. Sun noon–9pm.*

→ **Red Iguana** ★ MEXICAN While Salt Lake City has more than its share of Mexican restaurants and taco stands, this colorful family-owned and -operated restaurant has a unique specialty: *Mole,* the spicy, sexy sauce that often contains unsweetened chocolate. At the Red Iguana, you can try several different variations,

COOL IN THE MIDWEST

Liquor Laws in Utah

Sure, you can get a drink in Utah, but some fairly weird temperance laws can make the process a bit difficult. (Mormons are supposed to abstain from tobacco, alcohol, or any beverage with caffeine). There are three kinds of liquor licenses for public houses: a tavern license, a restaurant license, and a private club license.

→ **Tavern licenses** are only granted to establishments we might affectionately call "beer gardens." These are 21+ joints that only serve beer—and 3.2% beer at that. What is 3.2% beer, you ask? It's beer that has 3.2% alcohol by weight, and it's the only kind of beer that is sold at Utah establishments, unless you order an imported bottled beer. Despite what you might be told, 3.2% beer has less alcohol than normal beer: 3.2% alcohol by weight roughly translates to about 4% alcohol by volume, whereas most American beers have 5% alcohol by volume. While you can buy 3.2% beer and those sickly sweet malt liquor beverages at convenience and grocery stores in Utah, anything containing more than 3.2% alcohol is only sold at state-run liquor stores, which are pretty much unmarked and difficult to find.

→ **Restaurant licenses** allow establishments to serve any type of alcoholic beverage, but there's one catch: To order a drink, you also have to order some food. "Food" can be a simple nacho platter or a steak dinner, depending on the restaurant. Another weird quirk about drinking here: Bartenders are not allowed to free-pour. If you order a mixed drink or a shot of something, the bartender has to use a state-approved and -mandated device that measures exactly one ounce of hard liquor, lest the establishment get slapped with some huge fines.

→ **Private club licenses** are issued to the kinds of places that most people would call a bar or a lounge. Like the other types of establishments, they sell 3.2% beer and there is no free-pouring allowed. Unlike restaurants and taverns, however, to get into these places you have to be a "member." Fees for an annual membership run anywhere from $12 to $25, but there are "temporary memberships" that last a few weeks and cost about $4. *Tip:* Pay for one temporary membership, and you can bring in up to seven people for free as your guests.

including the fiery amarillo mole, the classic mole poblano, or the red pipian mole made with peanuts and pumpkin seeds. Traditional Mexican favorites are also available, and beer and wine are served. *736 W. North Temple.* ☎ *801/322-1489. www.rediguana.com. Taco plates $6–$9; Combination and specialty plates $10–$21. Mon–Thurs 11am–10pm; Fri–Sat 10am–11pm; Sun 10am–9pm.*

→ **Sage's Café** VEGETARIAN Fresh, vegetarian, and organic dishes are the basis of the menu at Ian and Kelsey Brandt's health-conscious restaurant, located in a renovated Victorian home. Veggie entrees include tacos stuffed with your choice of tempeh, tofu, or portabello mushrooms, and mushroom stroganoff, made with a creamy blend of the oyster and portabello varieties. On weekends, take in some of the breakfast favorites like blueberry flapjacks, tofu scrambles, or a basil pesto crepe. Some raw-food options are also available. *473 E. 300 South.* ☎ *801/322-3790.*

Breakfast $6–$10; sandwiches: $7–$8; entrees $12–$14. Mon–Thurs 11:30am–2:30pm; 5–9:30pm; Fri 11:30am–2:30pm and 5–10pm; Sat 9am–10pm; Sun 9am–9pm.

SPLURGE

➜ **Faustina** ★★ AMERICAN Sleek and sophisticated design elements meld with warm, earthy colors at this Salt Lake restaurant, creating a vibe that's big city without the attitude. A playful note is added with touches of bright color—an unexpected green wall, and the purple bar—but when it comes to food, Faustina gets serious. Try the pan-roasted Chilean sea bass, or the broiled lamb medallions in a sour cherry reduction. For the ultimate decadent splurge, order the chocolate bento box, which includes chocolate molten lava cake, white chocolate crème brûlée, and two portions of chocolate mousse. *300 S. 454 East.* ☎ *801/746-4441. www.faustinaslc.com. Starters $4–$9; dinner entrees $11–$22; desserts $5–$14. Lunch: Mon–Fri 11am–2:30pm. Dinner: Mon–Thurs 5 9:30pm; Fri–Sat 5–10:30pm.*

Partying

Although Salt Lake City has some odd liquor laws, there are plenty of places to party if you know where to look. Check the listings below to find out what kind of liquor license a place has. In some cases regular old dive bars like X-Wives are listed as "clubs," but refer to the info above and you'll be all set. Make *sure* you have a designated driver or call a cab if you're partying; the Salt Lake City Police has an entire special force devoted to pulling over DUIs.

BARS, PUBS & CLUBS

Downtown area

📺 Best ♦ ➜ **Brewvie's Cinema Pub** ★★★ TAVERN/MOVIE THEATER Want to watch a movie *and* have a beer? Get the best of both worlds at Brewvie's, a combination theater/pub where you can take your booze and food into the movie with you. The two full-screen theaters are equipped with little shelves in front of the seats for your food and drink, and the menu includes excellent onion rings and burgers. Can't find a film to see? Brewvie's also has pool tables and free Wi-Fi, if you just want to kick back in the bar area. Make sure you have your ID. As a tavern, Brewvie's has no membership fee, but is only open to the 21-and-over crowd. *677 S. 200 West.* ☎ *801/355-5500. www.brewvies. com. Daily noon–1am.*

➜ **Club Sound** CLUB With music ranging from local DJs to national touring acts, this place caters to a wide crowd of SLC residents. On Fridays, Gossip!@Club Sound hosts a dance party geared toward gay and lesbian clientele; the crowd is a mix of nubile 18 to 20-somethings ready to party. Although most venues are 18+, there's always one dance floor with a bar reserved for the 21-and-over set. Cover charges at Club Sound fluctuate wildly, ranging from $5 for a night of dancing to $50 for a special event, so call ahead if you're in money-saving mode. *579 W. 200 South.* ☎ *801/328 0255. www.soundslc.com. Thurs–Sat 9:30pm–2am.*

➜ **Port O'Call Social Club** CLUB Occupying about 32,000 square feet over three floors, this is the perfect combination of sports bar and meat market. With sports memorabilia on the walls, a game room with pool tables and pinball machines, and over 40 televisions, Port O'Call has the sports bar part covered; the young clientele take care of the uncovered part. Word has it you can almost put together an entire outfit from what three patrons have on. The club recently expanded to offer a dance floor upstairs, so you can choose between watching the game, busting a move, or just enjoying the eye candy. *78 W. 400 South.* ☎ *801/521-0589. Cover charge Fri–Sat $3–$5, special events $5–$10. www.portocall.com. Daily 11am–2am.*

➔ **Squatter's Pub** ★ RESTAURANT/PUB Given Utah's 3.2% beer law (p. 452), SLC's beer-lovers seem determined to drink more beer to make up for what they perceive to be a silly law. With tap beers served by the half-liter and liter, Salt Lake's original brewpub gives the people what they want. We liked the northwest-style Full Suspension Pale Ale and the Provo Girl Pilsner; both have won several awards. Don't expect a raucous crowd. Most of the clientele are here for a mellow night of good drinks and hearty food ranging from free-range, grass-fed beef burgers to Asian-inspired stir-fry dishes. The menu also includes a variety of vegetarian and vegan options. *147 West Broadway.* ☎ *801/363-2739. www.squatters.com. Burgers $8–$10; entrees $9–$14. Mon–Thurs 11am–midnight; Fri 11am–1am; Sat 10:30am–1am; Sun 10:30am–midnight.*

➔ **X-Wife's Place** ★ CLUB This is definitely a dive bar, but if we lived in SLC, it would be our dive bar of choice. Besides the killer bloody marys (said to be the best in town), this bar has just the right mix of friendly old-timers and college kids. The crowd gets younger as the night wears on, but the vibe is always friendly. The pool tables and jukebox get a lot of use. The outside patio offers a place to talk or smoke, or bring in a pizza from across the street. *465 S 700 East.* ☎ *801/532-1954. Daily 11:30am–1:45am.*

Sugarhouse and Points South

➔ **Piper Down** CLUB While it's billed as an Irish "olde world pub," we were a bit confused on our visit. The clientele consisted of a couple of Harley-Davidson bikers, a full-on cowboy in boots, hat, and spurs, a grandmotherly woman sipping a Guinness, and a smattering of college students arguing about which supermodels have fake boobs. But then, the Irish have always been known for their open-minded hospitality, especially when it comes to the pub. You'll find a friendly welcome any time, although the place really gets hopping on weekends with live music (not necessarily Irish) and big crowds. *1492 S. State.* ☎ *801/468-1492. www.piperdownpub. com. Mon–Sat 4pm–2am; Sun 10am–2am.*

➔ **MoDiggity's** ★★ CLUB Billed as a sports and music bar for women, this unique little bar kicks ass. There's a busy line up of DJs and dancing, live bands, karaoke, poker games, and, of course, sports coverage on large-screen TVs. Attracting a large lesbian crowd, as well as a fair number of straight folk, you'll find MoDiggity's to be a fun, welcoming place regardless of your orientation or background. *3434 S. State St.* ☎ *801/832-9000. www.modiggitys.com. Mon–Thurs 4pm–midnight; Fri–Sat 4pm–2am; Sun 2pm–2am.*

➔ **Fats Pub and Pool** TAVERN With its clean, airy atmosphere and mellow crowd, Fats is definitely not your usual hole-in-the-wall pool joint. Located in the Sugarhouse neighborhood, this relaxed, friendly tavern is the perfect place to play a game of pool, grab some decent brews, and fill up on cheap, tasty fare. Purchase an entree before 6pm and you can rack 'em up for free. *2182 Highland Dr.* ☎ *801/484-9467. Daily 11am–1am.*

LIVE MUSIC

Rock/Indie/Eclectic

➔ **Urban Lounge** Featuring rock, hardcore, and metal acts, as well as some hip-hop and spoken-word, this club is a popular small venue for local and national bands. The venue also hosts "Localized," a monthly showcase of local music put on by

There's a polygamy joke in here somewhere . . .

SLUG magazine. *241 S. 500 East.* ☎ *801/355-4949. www.urbanlounge.net. Cover $5 most nights; check website for more info. All shows 21+ unless otherwise noted.*

→ **Kilby Court** ★ Musicians and locals in the know rave about this SLC gem, an all-ages venue that has been a favored indie and alternative destination since 1999. The location is cramped and there's little to no seating, but this crowd could care less; Kilby Court is all about the music. Check out the cool concert posters designed by Leia Bell, Kilby's in-house artist. *741 S. Kilby Court.* ☎ *801/320-9887. www.kilbycourt.com. Cover $6–$15. All ages.*

→ **The Depot** In Salt Lake's renovated Union Station, this brand-new club has three floors, a three-star restaurant, and a high-energy 1,200-seat venue with a great sound system. Featuring a varied lineup of rock, pop, hip-hop, and other musical genres, the well-designed Depot adds an upscale note to Salt Lake's live music scene. *400 W. South Temple.* ☎ *801/456-2800. www.depotslc.com. All shows 21+ unless otherwise noted. Check website for concert and ticket info.*

Jazz/Blues

→ **Zanzibar** Sometimes strip malls have the best hidden gems, like the one that houses this hip, cozy SLC jazz club. With lots of local bands, plus touring acts, this is a great place to hear live jazz, and sometimes blues, six nights a week. On Sundays, head over for swing dancing from 8pm to midnight; free lessons are provided for newbies. *677 S. 200 West.* ☎ *801/746-0590. Daily 8pm–12:30am. $5 cover Fri–Sat nights.*

What to See & Do

Given Salt Lake City's history as the center of religious life for members of the Church of Jesus Christ of Latter-Day Saints, otherwise known as Mormons, most of the area attractions can be categorized as either "Mormon-related" or

The Mormon Temple anchors SLC's Temple Square.

"non-Morman related." Frankly, if you're not interested in the religious history of Utah, there's not a ton of stuff to see. Still, we think attractions like the residence that housed Brigham Young's multiple wives and their families have their own eccentric charm.

THE TOP MORMON-RELATED ATTRACTIONS

FREE ➜ **Beehive and Lion Houses** ★ Located next to each other, these houses were built in the 1850s as residences for church leader Brigham Young and his large family (27 wives and lots and *lots* of children). The Beehive house, where Young lived, worked, and entertained church and government leaders, has been decorated to resemble its original appearance, giving visitors an idea of what the famous leader's lifestyle must have been like. Only one of his wives lived in the Beehive house at a time; the rest stayed with the children at the Lion house, now a dining and banquet facility. *67 E. South Temple.* ☎ *801/240-2671. www.lds.org/placestovisit. Free admission. Mon–Sat 9am–9pm. Trax stop: Temple Square; walk half a block east.*

FREE → **Family History Library** If you've ever wondered who your ancestors were or where they came from, you're in luck: This is probably the world's largest collection of genealogical records under one roof. LDS church doctrine teaches that families are united forever through marriages and other sacred Temple ordinances, and ordinances like baptism can be administered on behalf of ancestors, which helps explain the Mormons' keen interest in family records. We'll be honest; this is not a quick stop. If you're serious about looking up family info, come prepared with some names, dates, and any other info you have, plus some patience. *35 N. West Temple.* ☎ *800/346-6044. www.familysearch.org. Free admission. Mon 8am–5pm; Tues–Sat 8am–9pm. Closed on major holidays and July 24. Trax stop: Temple Square.*

FREE → **LDS Conference Center** Across from Temple Square on North Temple Street, this huge complex has an equally enormous name: the Conference Center of the Church of Jesus Christ of Latter-Day Saints. The main auditorium for worship services and meetings could easily hold a Boeing 747, while the four-level underground parking lot boasts 1,300 spaces. Still, the real attraction here is the 4-acre **roof garden** ★. Designers have created a wild Utah landscape, complete

with spruce, aspen, and pine trees, plus 21 native meadow grasses and 300 varieties of Utah wildflowers. ☎ *801/240-0075. Mon–Sat 9am–9pm. Free tours of the complex are offered every 15 min. Trax stop: Temple Square.*

FREE → **Museum of Church History and Art** If you're interested in finding out more about the unusual history of the LDS church, check out this collection of historical art and artifacts, including rare Mormon gold coins and the earliest log home in Utah. A variety of multimedia programs and displays give you the history of this religious movement, including info on each of the church presidents. Some of the activities and exhibits are geared toward teaching Mormon history and doctrine to LDS kids (puppet shows?). *45 N. West Temple.* ☎ *801/240-3310. www.lds.org/placestovisit. Free admission. Mon–Fri 9am–9pm; Sat–Sun and most holidays 10am–7pm. Trax stop: Temple Square.*

FREE → **Temple Square** ★★ This 10-acre plot of land in downtown Salt Lake City is sacred ground for LDS church members. While the huge **Temple** is not open to the public, the 6,500-seat **Tabernacle,** home of the famous Mormon Tabernacle Choir, and the Gothic-style **Assembly Hall,** where free concerts are offered on most weekends, are open to visitors. Info about the square is available at the LDS-operated North or South Visitors Centers, located at the northeast and southwest corners of the square.

The best way to see Temple Square is to take one of the 45-minute 🎬 Best● **guided tours** that leave every few minutes from the flagpole in front of the Tabernacle. You'll get a general history of the church and see all the various points of interest. Anyone who's suffered through a show at a venue with horrific acoustics will especially appreciate the tour stop in the

Where to Find SLC's Hot Clothes & Music

As unexpectedly hip little boutique, **Black Chandelier** ★★★ in the Trolley Square Mall features all original ready-to-wear designs by Jared Gold, an Idaho native who got his start crafting clothes and hats for the rave set. After a few years at the Otis College of Art and Design in L.A., Gold landed a deal with Barneys New York and left school. In 2001 he debuted the competitively priced Black Chandelier line. What does all this mean for you non-fashonistas? Get your butt down to this place and pick up some uniquely crafted designer togs for unbelievable prices. Check out the live Madagascar Hissing Roaches sold at the store as pets; they're huge and hand-decorated with Swarovski crystals. (No, it doesn't harm them; but yes, they really are gross.) *Trolley Square Mall 602 S. 500 East.* ☎ *801/359-2426. Mon(Sat 10am(9pm; Sun noon(5pm.*

Independent music stores like **Orion's Music** ★ are unfortunately getting more and more rare; this Salt Lake City shop shares space with Sugarhouse Coffee. The large local section features lots of Salt Lake bands. Ask the knowledgeable staff for their favorite picks, or check the white board hanging from the ceiling for albums that merit special attention. Among these would be *SLUG* magazine's two-disc compilation, *Death by Salt II,* featuring 42 Utah bands. The set is a great purchase for anyone interested in exploring the unique musical culture of Utah, where the religious climate and the outlaw spirit combine to produce a strong independent vibe, reflected in both gritty, hardcore rock sounds and softer, more acoustic tunes. *2110 S. 1100 East.* ☎ *801/531-8181. Mon–Thurs 10am–8pm; Fri–Sat 10am–10pm; Sun noon–6pm.*

Tabernacle; the guide herds you to the back of the 6,500-seat building, while someone up at the front drops three pins—the sound comes through crystal-clear. The tour ends at the North Visitor Center, where a short film on Mormon beliefs is shown. Be aware that you'll be asked to fill out a card with your name and address and indicate whether or not you'd like an LDS missionary to visit you. *15 E. South Temple.* ☎ *800/537-9703. www.visittemplesquare.com. Daily 6am–10pm. Tours: Daily 9am–8pm. Visitors Centers: Daily 9am–9pm. Trax stop: Temple Square.*

THE TOP NON-MORMON-RELATED ATTRACTIONS

→ **Classic Cars International Antique Auto Museum of Utah** We're not big classic car fans, but even we were impressed by the 200 or so antique and classic cars packed into these showrooms. The collection is constantly changing, as most of the cars are for sale, but some of the ones on display included a 1903 Stevens Duryea, a 1912 Ford Model T, a 1936 Packard V-12 two-door convertible, several 1959 big-finned Cadillac convertibles, and a number of 1960s muscle cars. All cars, whether restored or original, are fully operational. *355 W. 700 South.* ☎ *801/322-5509. www.classiccarmuseumsales.com. Admission $6. Mon–Sat 8:30am–4:30pm. Trax stop: 200 W. 825 South. Walk north 1 block to 700 South and about a block and a half west.*

FREE → **Salt Lake Art Center** ★ Featuring contemporary art exhibits by local, regional, and national artists, this gallery and adult art school has a strong civic and social bent, emphasizing art that engages with the issues and the surrounding community. Simultaneous exhibitions often feature works in a variety of different

Film & Belly Dancing: SLC Festivals

⟶ The ever more popular **Sundance Film Festival,** featuring the best in independent films, is held every January in Park City, Utah, a 40-minute drive from Salt Lake City. Some events and screenings inevitably spill over into Salt Lake City and its environs, making the entire area a huge destination for movie buffs. **www.festival.sundance.org.**

⟶ In August, over 600 dancers from around the globe head to Salt Lake for the **Utah Belly Dance Festival,** held every year at Liberty Park. With free admission, dance clinics, and ethnic food vendors, not to mention lithe, undulating bodies, what's not to like? **www.kismetdance.com.**

⟶ You'll find traditional events like horse shows, livestock judging, and arts and crafts competitions, plus some quirky competitions like the rotten sneaker contest at the **Utah State Fair,** held every September in Salt Lake City. **www.utahstatefair.com.**

⟶ Salt Lake City is home to several Greek Orthodox churches and a large number of Americans of Greek descent, and the city's **Greek Festival,** held annually on the weekend after Labor Day, celebrates Greek culture with food, dancing, art displays, cultural events, and a general party-like atmosphere. ☎ **801/328-9681.**

⟶ A spectacular show of holiday decorations draws hundreds of people to the **Temple Square Christmas Lights,** from the Friday after Thanksgiving until January 1. Live music performances, decked-out storefronts, and horse-drawn carriage rides add to the holiday spirit in downtown. ☎ **801/240-1000.**

⟶ While the **First Night New Year's Eve Celebration** in downtown Salt Lake City is primarily family-oriented, with arts and crafts, storytelling, and kid-friendly entertainment, the spectacular midnight fireworks display is fun for anyone. Take a break from the mad partying to ooh and ahh with the kids. **www.firstnightslc.org.**

media, including paintings, photographs, sculptures, and ceramics. Concerts, workshops, and poetry readings are often held at the center, so check the schedule to see if any events are coming up. *20 S. West Temple.* ☎ *801/328-4201. www.slartcenter. com. Free admission; donations welcome. Tues–Thurs and Sat 10am–5pm; Fri 10am–9pm; Sun 1–5pm. Trax stop: Temple Square.*

→ **Utah Museum of Fine Art** With a permanent collection of over 17,000 objects, this is one of the best art museums in the state. Collections include Egyptian, Greek, and Roman artifacts, European paintings, African and Latin American artwork,

Navajo rugs, and 20th-century lithographs. Rotating exhibits highlight shows from other institutions and private collections, and the on-site cafe offers you a place to take a break as you wander the 74,000-square-foot museum. *At the University of Utah, 410 Campus Center Dr.* ☎ *801/581-7332. www.umfa.utah.edu. Admission $4. Tues–Fri 10am–5pm (Wed until 8pm); Sat–Sun noon–5pm. Trax stop: South Campus Dr.*

PLAYING OUTSIDE

There's plenty of outdoor fun to be had in and around Salt Lake City, regardless of the season. Summer activities like hiking, biking, and mountain climbing are popular,

COOL IN THE MIDWEST

and the 2002 Olympics only increased the status of Utah's already well-known winter sports scene. For information on Utah's ski resorts, check out **Ski Utah** (☎ **800/SKI-UTAH;** www.skiutah.com). Another good source for information on the outdoor scene is **www.outdoorutah.com**, where you can order a free copy of the *Outdoor Utah Vacation Guide* and connect to other informative websites.

FREE → **Liberty Park** ★ This popular park just south of downtown covers 100 acres and has trails for walking and jogging, tennis courts, a lake with paddleboat rentals, and picnic facilities. Within the park you'll also find the **Chase Home Museum of Utah Folk Arts** (☎ **801/533-5760;** www.folkartsmuseum.org), which has exhibits of pioneer and Native American art; and the **Tracy Aviary** (☎ **801/596-8500;** www.tracyaviary.org), home to more than 400 birds, including some endangered species. *Located between 500 and 700 East and 900 and 1300 South. Entrances at 900 and 1300 South.* ☎ *801/972-7800. Park: Free admission; open daily 6am–11pm summer, dawn–dusk winter. Call or check websites for museum and aviary information.*

→ **Wasatch-Cache National Forest** ★ With 1.3 million acres scattered across Utah, this preserve offers year-round outdoor fun for residents and visitors. The 216,000-acre Salt Lake Ranger district is only half an hour from downtown. It features wilderness areas for backpacking, designated mountain biking trails, and popular mountain climbing destinations, including the 400-foot granite walls of Little Cottonwood Canyon. With the onset of winter, visitors can also enjoy snowshoeing, back-country skiing, and downhill skiing and snowboarding at the district's four ski resorts. Some of the activities require a permit (and paying a fee) so check the website for specifics. *Administrative office at 125 S. State St.* ☎ *801/236-3400. www.fs.fed.us/r4/wcnf.*

Biking

Salt Lake has a number of bikeways. Some are separate and run parallel to the street, others share the road with motorists, or feature a separate bike lane. Good places to bike include City Creek Canyon, east of Capitol Hill, which is closed to motor vehicles from mid-May through September.

Info on other popular biking spots, as well as bike repair and rentals, can be found downtown at **Guthrie Bicycle** (156 E. 200 South; ☎ **801/363-3727**). Established in 1888, it's quite possibly the nation's oldest operating bike shop.

SPECTATOR SPORTS

The National Basketball Association's **Utah Jazz** (☎ **801/325-2500;** www.utahjazz.com) usually packs the house at the Delta Center in downtown Salt Lake, so plan ahead if you're trying to get tickets.

Other professional sports teams in Salt Lake include the **Utah Grizzlies** (☎ **801/988-8000;** www.utahgrizzlies.com) of the (apparently geographically challenged) East Coast Hockey League (games are held at the E Center in West Valley City); and **Real Salt Lake** (☎ **801/924-8585**), the city's professional soccer team, which plays at the University of Utah's Rice-Eccles Stadium.

Although Utah has no major league baseball team, you can catch a game at Franklin-Covey field with the **Salt Lake Stingers** (☎ **801/325-2273;** www.stingersbaseball.com), a AAA affiliate of the Anaheim Angels.

For college sports, check out the **University of Utah's Runnin' Utes** and **Lady Utes** (☎ **801/581-8849;** www.utautes.com), who compete in 10 women's and 9 men's Division I sports. Tickets for most sports events are available on short notice, but plan ahead for football games.

That's All They Wrote . . .

In the immortal words of Grateful Dead lead-man Jerry Garcia, "What a long strange trip it's been!"

When we started this road trip, we were skeptical about how cool these cities could *really* be. After all, we're coming from Los Angeles, and while Angelinos may not be as cynical as New Yorkers, we are not easily impressed. We expected a low-key, mellow ride with a modest amount of partying thrown in here and there, but we were totally blown away by what these cities had to offer. From high culture, including museums, concerts, book signings, and the performing arts, to partying at clubs, pubs, and local dive bars, every hour of our days and nights was packed with new experiences, good food and drinks, and new friends.

Each city had its own vibe—Minneapolis was artsy and cultured, like a glass of red wine; Kansas City was like a cup of dark coffee, smooth-drinking but with a definite edge; Denver was big, brash, and vibrant, like the beers it produces; and Salt Lake City was a strange cocktail of diverse perspectives—yet all four cities left us craving more. As we think back on this trip, we're eager to do it again. There's a whole lot of stuff going on in the urban heartland, and we're delighted by the fact that we now live right in the thick of it.

On the Trail of the First Americans

Text & photos by Ethan Wolff

Tucked within the spectacular, desolate landscapes of the Southwest lies an American Atlantis. The ruins of the ancients are scattered across the region, many in surprisingly good condition thanks to isolation and a dry climate. When you get into the backcountry, walking miles without seeing water, food, footprints, or anything else that might indicate another human being has ever come this way, these mysterious ruins can be startling. Not only were people able to survive for more than a few days or weeks in these extreme conditions—this was their *home*.

By the best guesses, the Southwest has been inhabited for 13,500 years. The original Stone Age Paleo-Indians lived in pit houses and hunted mastodons, mammoths, and other game. Over the millennia, their settlements became more elaborate. (Some people think the pit houses evolved into *kivas,* underground spiritual chambers you'll find among the ruins.) Starting in about A.D. 850 the people began to construct the stone and mud cities that stand today as memorials to their society. I was floored by the craftsmanship, the way each stone is precisely aligned—all the more intriguing when you consider the masonry would have been hidden by layers of stucco. Wood ceiling beams, which look like they were cut last month and not 800 years ago, are likewise laid with an enviable attention to detail. The people were able farmers of squash, corn, and beans, impressive given they were often working with less than 8 inches of rain a year. (Sophisticated irrigation systems helped them redirect as much as half a million gallons for every inch of summer rain.)

First Americans Roadtrip

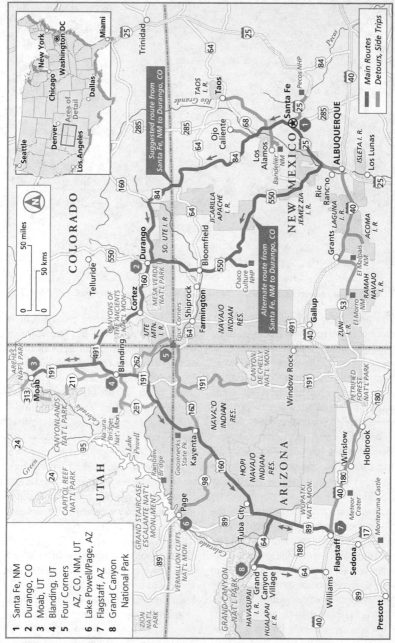

Newspaper rock records over 1,000 years of observations by the First Americans.

The people also left behind incised rock drawings, or **petroglyphs.** These symbols, often of stylized animals, are like an American Lascaux. The longer you look at them, the more enigmatic they become. Recent scholarship has unveiled some amazing things, like the exact year each beam at Pueblo Bonito was cut (scientists can read the tree rings), or the solar and lunar calendars the people made in the rocks. Still, no one can say exactly why the people invested so much time and energy in building up their great cities, only to walk away forever. By the 13th century, the era was over. Maybe it was drought, maybe the pressure of rival tribes, or maybe it was just time to move on. (While they left these homes behind, their presence is still felt in their descendents: tribespeople whose land covers much of the Southwest.)

This is a remote, sparsely populated part of the country, meaning this may not be the best party trip. Partying, however, can

wear a wallet thin pretty quickly. Budgets are easy to stretch in the Four Corners, where much of the land belongs to the public. If you are craving nightlife, Santa Fe, Moab, and Flagstaff won't let you down. You'll find the big skies and ample elbowroom out here make people open and welcoming. You may find yourself getting hooked as well—there's a reason they call New Mexico "The Land of Enchantment." (Although in more cynical moods, the locals refer to it as "The Land of Entrapment.") Hiking, biking, rock-climbing, four-wheeling, and rafting are just some of the ways you can bring yourself closer to the land.

Some 100,000 ruins have been identified in Arizona alone, so you're not going to be able to see everything. I've tried to highlight the best (or at least my favorite) stop-offs below. When you leave, a sense of awe for what the people accomplished may linger with you. You may find yourself inspired, as I was, by the craft that went into the ancients' creations, and by the harmony they seemed to have developed in the rhythm of their lives and their relation to the land.

Superlatives: The Highs & Lows

→ **Best landscape built on a human scale:** The canyon-level trails at **Natural Bridges National Monument** in Utah seem perfectly proportioned, with sheer walls framing wildflowers, trees, and streams. The punctuation of three stunning natural stone bridges is only a bonus. See p. 509.

→ **Best landscape built on an inhuman scale:** It's just about impossible not to be blown away by the **Grand Canyon.** Although rim views are dandy, you really need to descend to get a sense of the scale: a mile deep, 277 miles long, and up to 18 miles wide. Your sense of where you fit in the grand scheme of things can easily be scrambled. See p. 525.

→ **Best place to feel like you've stumbled onto the Wile E. Coyote and Road Runner set: Arches National Park,** just outside Moab, UT. A blend of the surreal and the scenic, Arches is a wonderland of cliffs, buttes, natural arches, and balanced rocks. If an Acme Corporation box fell from the sky, it wouldn't seem out of place. *Meep meep!* See p. 494.

→ **Best dish in the Southwest:** Green chile is New Mexico's staple dish, and I wouldn't recommend trying it unless you don't mind craving it for months after you leave. For an excellent version of the fiery stuff, try **Tomasita's Cafe** in Santa Fe. See p. 482.

→ **Most interesting graffiti:** A good decade and a half before Pilgrims bumped into Plymouth Rock, Don Juan de Oñate was having his name inscribed at **El Morro,** in New Mexico. A fascinating stream of travelers added their tags over

Road Movies: First Americans Plus the Four Corners

- *Fort Apache,* **John Ford,** 1948
- *Warlock,* **Edward Dmytryk,** 1959
- *Easy Rider,* **Dennis Hopper,** 1969
- *Butch Cassidy and the Sundance Kid,* **George Roy Hill,** 1969
- *Little Big Man,* **Arthur Penn,** 1970
- *Two-Lane Blacktop,* **Monte Hellman,** 1971
- *Koyaanisqatsi,* **Godfrey Reggio,** 1982
- *Raising Arizona,* **Ethan and Joel Coen,** 1987
- *Dances with Wolves,* **Kevin Costner,** 1990
- *Thelma & Louise,* **Ridley Scott,** 1991
- *The Last of the Mohicans,* **Michael Mann,** 1992
- *The New World,* **Terrence Malick,** 2005
- *Cars,* **John Lasseter and Joe Ranft,** 2006

the centuries, making this one of the most historical spots in the U.S. See p. 479.

→ **Best Native American artifacts:** Elegant pottery and tools are only the beginning at the **Edge of the Cedars State Park** in Blanding, UT. I found myself sucked in for hours, checking out an ancient loom, turkey-down blankets, and a vivid sash made of macaw feathers that originated thousands of miles away. See p. 508.

→ **Best 3-D history class:** Detailed geography exhibits join dinosaur skeletons to provide insight into the Colorado Plateau's distant past at the **Museum of Northern Arizona.** Katsinas, pottery, and a fragment of a kiva wall mural illuminate more recent eras. See p. 521.

→ **Best taste of Route 66:** Many of the old 66 towns have fallen on hard times, with their historic hotels converted to self-storage units. **Williams, AZ,** however, has an impressive collection of restored/preserved buildings—maybe because it was the last town on 66 to be bypassed by the interstate. See p. 533.

→ **Worst place for car trouble:** Chaco Canyon is *many* miles from the nearest garage or car mechanic. At the end of 16 miles of rough road, the visitors center offers no food service, so waiting for help from Albuquerque (150 miles away) can make for a long day. See p. 488.

Just the Facts

Trip in a Box

Total Miles   From Santa Fe, NM, to Williams, AZ, via Moab, UT, 750 miles.

Route   From Santa Fe, 64/84 to 160 west, to 491 north, to 191 up to Moab, UT. 191 to 160 to 89 from Moab to Flagstaff.

States   New Mexico, Colorado, Utah, and Arizona (if you want, you can spend time in all four at once; see p. 511).

Trip Time   6 days or more for the whole thing, from Santa Fe to the Grand Canyon.

The short version   You can get a lot out of just the highlights, and the mileage isn't out of control (you won't hit much traffic and a person could drive the whole thing in 15 hr. or so), so 5 days could work.

The long version   There is so much to see around here that you could stretch the visit out by a couple of weeks and still feel like you're just scratching the surface. Those into outdoor activities will particularly want to allow extra days for biking, hiking, camping, and boating.

Hitting the Highlights   You could take three separate trips to the three base-camp cities (Santa Fe, Moab, and Flagstaff). The cities are good launching points for regional attractions, and each would make an excellent long-weekend destination.

When to Go   Folks will steer you away from the desert in the height of summer, when temperatures hover in the low 100s(F), but you can always take advantage of mornings, evenings, and night. Spring and fall have great light and color. Winter is the most underrated and least-traveled time to be out here, though you run the risk of uncooperative weather in the form of storms which can make driving hard and roads hazardous or impassable at the higher ranges.

The Money Part

This is one of the best roadtrips for those on a very tight budget because there isn't all that much to spend money on. The terrain can be desolate and four-star restaurants are few and far between. Costs in the southwest generally are lower than the rest of the country, especially in the freeway towns, which most nights have many more hotel rooms than they know what to do with. Many parks are free; most of those with charges fall into the **National Parks Pass** (see box below) category, meaning there's no charge for cardholders. If you're in the market for souvenirs, Native American arts are widely available. The most exquisitely crafted items can get pretty spendy, but basic gifts are in the range of most budgets.

ACCOMMODATIONS

Hotels along the interstates start around $20 a night ($30 and up for the national chains), although at these prices you're going to find yourself on the seedy side of things. In the towns, you'll find prices a little higher ($60 and up), especially in tourist destinations like Moab and Santa Fe. You'll also find big fluctuations in price, with the good weather months carrying significant premiums.

Fortunately, there are cheap hostel and campsite alternatives all over the Southwest. For me, especially in this part of the country, park campgrounds are the way to go. Prices are low (sometimes free, more often $5 or $10 a night), you're right on top of things, and the plots are usually arranged on some seriously scenic land. Note also that the parks are on some of the least light-polluted places left in the country—if you want to really enjoy Western skies, there's nothing better than sleeping under the stars.

TRANSPORTATION

For parking, you'll find spaces are free and plentiful most everywhere you go in the Southwest. The one exception is downtown Santa Fe, which can get congested. There's lots of meter parking, so bring a handful of quarters and you should be fine. If you're flying into the region from another part of the country, you'll find the airports are somewhat spread out. Most flights into Albuquerque and Flagstaff involve a change of planes. Las Vegas offers more direct flights. There are also small regional airports in Moab and Santa

If You're Planning on a Lot of Parking...

...that is, visiting National Parks and Federal Recreational Lands on your roadtrip, then consider whether the Annual "America the Beautiful" pass makes sense for you to purchase. An $80 pass gives you access to all Federal recreation sites that charge an entrance fee for one year from the date of sale. (Which means you can also use it for any N.P.s in your area when you get home.) It also includes admission for everyone else in the car (up to four adults). The pass can be obtained in person at the park, by calling ☎ **888/ASK USGS**, ext. 1, or at **http://store.usgs.gov/pass**.

Indian Casinos: Gaming the System

One of the biggest changes in the Southwestern landscape in recent years has been the arrival of the casinos. Indian reservations, as sovereign nations, have the right to set their own gambling policies. Congress's 1988 Indian Gaming Regulatory Act set the wheels in motion, and by the early '90's casinos were springing up all over the Southwest. On the plus side, some casinos have provided immense economic benefits for impoverished tribes. If you're not anti-gambling, you could also argue that they've provided a recreational outlet. On the downside, most of the casinos don't exactly blend in seamlessly with the natural environment, and there's some question about where all their revenue is really ending up. If you're interested in hitting the slots or the tables, you'll find many opportunities in Colorado, Arizona, and New Mexico. Utah, not surprisingly, is casino-free. If you're thinking of saving money by staying/eating at casinos, generally, hotel prices aren't any cheaper than nearby chains and the food tends to be cafeteria-quality, so that strategy is more of a money-saver in Las Vegas (see "Desert to the Beach: Vegas to Baja" roadtrip for advice on that).

Fe, but they'll cost significantly more to use. This trip runs about 750 miles, which means you'll be spending about $66 for gas (more if you're side-tripping). Oh, and don't forget that destroying a rental car (p. 490) can add considerably to a transportation budget, so drive extra-carefully when you get off paved ground.

FOOD

Once you leave the metro areas, you may find yourself picnicking more often than dining out. Several of the parks lack even snack bars, so it's a good idea to keep some staples in the trunk and a cooler (with plenty of water) in the back seat. Inside the big cities, you'll eat well, especially if you

develop a taste for Southwestern cooking. New Mexican cuisine is its own thing, distinct from Mexican, Tex-Mex, and Cal-Mex, and it's just about impossible to find outside of the region. Green chile (not chili, thank you) is the staple. Once you acclimate to the heat you may get addicted. Burritos and the like can easily be tracked down for under $10. If you're going to splurge on a nice meal, Moab and Flagstaff have some options, but Santa Fe is the best bet. Even the most humble of joints there can be trusted to serve up grub that explodes with favor. (See the box "Feed Me: A Quick Guide to NM Cuisine," on p. 481, for a glossary and more information on New Mexican cuisine.)

Starting Out: Santa Fe & Northern New Mexico

Though the population is only 70,000, Santa Fe has enough culture for a major metropolis. Art galleries clog Canyon Road, and the summer opera season draws fans from around the world. Top museums explore the area's rich historic legacy— Santa Fe was a capital a full decade before

the Pilgrims had set their eyes on Plymouth Rock. Unfortunately, the ramshackle Spanish streets and ancient adobe walls may have made the city a victim of its own charm: Tourist shops and visitors by the busload have locals calling it "Fanta Say." Don't be deterred by the "Adobe

Disneyland" effect, however. Authentic food and nightlife aren't hard to find, and Santa Fe is a great base of operations for trips into the back country. Some of the most interesting Native American sites on the tour are within an hour's drive.

Santa Fe **Nuts & Bolts**

Area Code   The telephone area code in Santa Fe is 505.

Business Hours   Banks and offices are generally open Monday to Friday 8 or 9am to 5pm. Some banks offer drive-through service on Saturday 9am to noon or 1pm. Bars and clubs tend to stay open until 2am every night but Sunday, when they close at midnight (see "Liquor Laws," below).

Drugstores   Walgreens and Sav-On Drug are the major chains, plus local shops like **Fraser Pharmacy,** 501 Old Santa Fe Trail (☎ 505/982-5524). There's a 24-hour pharmacy at the Walgreens on 1096 St. Francis Dr. (☎ 505/982-9811).

Emergencies   Call ☎ **911** if you need the police, the fire department, or an ambulance.

Hospitals   **St. Vincent Hospital,** 455 St. Michaels Dr. (☎ 505/983-3361, or 505/995-3934 for emergency services), is a 248-bed regional healthcenter. Patient services include urgent and emergency-room care and ambulatory surgery.

Internet   Head to the **Santa Fe Public Library** at 145 Washington Ave. (☎ 505/955-6780), or **FedEx Kinko's,** 301 N. Guadalupe (☎ 505/982-6311) and 730 Saint Michaels Dr. #3 (☎ 505/473-7303). Wi-Fi is gradually coming to the city, with coffee shops and hotels on the leading edge. **Starbucks** is usually a safe bet, including the one at 106 W. San Francisco (☎ 505/982-2770).

Laundry   There are a handful of laundromats around town. One of the more centrally located is **Solana Laundromat** at 949½ W. Alameda St. (☎ 505/982-9877).

Libraries   The **Santa Fe Public Library** is half a block from the plaza, at 145 Washington Ave. (☎ 505/955-6780). There are branch libraries at Villa Linda Mall and at 1730 Llano St., just off St. Michaels Drive. **The New Mexico State Library** is at 1209 Camino Carlos Rey (☎ 505/476-9700). Specialty libraries include the **Archives of New Mexico,** 1205 Camino Carlos Rey, and the **New Mexico History Library,** 120 Washington Ave.

Liquor Laws   The legal drinking age is 21 throughout New Mexico. Bars may remain open until 2am Monday to Saturday and until midnight on Sunday. Wine, beer, and spirits are sold at licensed supermarkets and liquor stores, but there are no package sales on election days until after 7pm, and on Sundays before noon. It is illegal to transport liquor through most Native American reservations.

Newspapers & Magazines   The *New Mexican*—Santa Fe's daily paper—is the oldest newspaper in the West. Its offices are at 202 E. Marcy St. (☎ 505/983-3303). For a slightly edgier take on local news you might try the weekly *Santa Fe Reporter,* 132 E. Marcy St. (☎ 505/988-5541), which has good entertainment listings. It's published on Wednesdays and is available free at stands all over town. Regional magazines published locally are *New Mexico* magazine (monthly, statewide interest) and the *Santa Fean* magazine (10 times a year, Southwestern lifestyles).

Police In case of emergency, dial ☎ **911.** For all other inquiries, call the **Santa Fe Police Department,** 2515 Camino Entrada (☎ 505/428-3710). The **Santa Fe County Sheriff,** with jurisdiction outside the city limits, is located at 35 Camino Justicia (☎ 505/986-2400).

Post Office The **main post office** is at 120 S. Federal Place (☎ 505/988-6351), 2 blocks north and 1 block west of the plaza. It's open weekdays from 8am to 5:30pm, and Saturdays from 9am to 4pm. Some of the major hotels have stamp machines and mailboxes with twice-daily pickup. The zip code for central Santa Fe is 87501.

Radio Local radio stations include **BLU** (102.9), which plays contemporary jazz, and **KBAC** (98.1), which plays alternative rock and folk music.

Taxes A tax of 6.43% is added to all purchases, with an additional 5% added to lodging bills.

Television There are five Albuquerque network affiliates: **KOB-TV** (Channel 4, NBC), **KOAT-TV** (Channel 7, ABC), **KQRE-TV** (Channel 13, CBS), **KASA-TV** (Channel 2, FOX), and **KNME-TV** (Channel 5, PBS).

Time Zone New Mexico is on **Mountain Standard Time,** 1 hour ahead of the West Coast and 2 hours behind the East Coast. When it's 10am in Santa Fe, it's noon in New York, 11am in Chicago, and 9am in San Francisco. Daylight saving time is in effect from mid-March to late November.

Weather For weather forecasts, call ☎ 505/988-5151.

Getting Around

Santa Fe is easy to navigate on foot. Distances in the center of the city are small, and you can check out many museums, churches, restaurants, and art galleries, without having to trek too far. The city's heart, as with so many Spanish towns, is its plaza. Roughly, streets are prefixed "east" or "west," depending on which side of the Plaza they are. The Santa Fe River, a tiny tributary of the Rio Grande, runs east to west through the middle of town.

Santa Fe sits at the foot of the Sangre de Cristo mountain range, with towering Santa Fe Baldy (12,600 ft.!) just 12 miles northeast of the Plaza. North is the Espanola Valley and, beyond that, the village of Taos, 60-some miles away. South

are ancient Indian turquoise mines in the Cerrillos Hills; Albuquerque is about an hour's drive to the southwest. To the west, across the Caja del Rio Plateau, is the Rio Grande, and beyond that you'll find the 11,000-foot Jemez Mountains. Native American pueblos, both abandoned and active, dot the entire Rio Grande valley a short drive away.

BY CAR

Santa Fe has grown organically enough that a lot of the roads are a semi-chaotic jumble. A map will come in handy, though distances are so short you probably won't go too far out of your way when you make wrong turns.

One major puzzler is Paseo de Peralta, a beltlike road that circles much of downtown. The road covers both east and west

Santa Fe Highlights

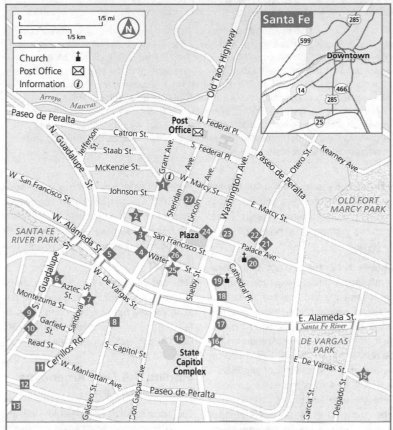

SLEEPING ■
Garrett's Desert Inn **18**
Old Santa Fe Inn **8**
Santa Fe Budget Inn **13**
Santa Fe Motel and Inn **11**
Santa Fe Plaza Travelodge **12**

PARTYING ★
Catamount Bar and Grille **25**
Cowgirl Hall of Fame **6**
The Dragon Room **16**
El Farol **15**
El Paseo Bar and Grill **3**
Evangelo's **2**
Paramount Lounge
 and Night Club **7**
Swig **1**

EATING ◆
Burrito Company Café **21**
Cafe Pasqual's **26**
Coyote Café **4**
Farmers' Market **9**
Los Mayas **5**
Plaza Cafe **24**
The Shed **22**
Tomasita's Cafe **10**

ATTRACTIONS ●
America's oldest house **17**
Loretto Chapel Museum **19**
Mission of San Miguel **14**
New Mexico History Library **27**
Palace of the Governors **23**
St. Francis Cathedral **20**

That's the Ticket: Get a Museum Pass

If you're planning on the complete tour of Santa Fe institutions, you'll want to pick up a **Museum Pass** ★. For $18, you'll have 4 days to visit five institutions (the Museum of Fine Arts, the Museum of Indian Arts & Culture, the Museum of International Folk Art, the Palace of the Governors, and the Museum of Spanish Colonial Art) as often as you like. Note that the museums are closed on Mondays. For broader in-state travel, the **New Mexico Culture Pass** (www.nmoca.org) may be a good option. It's $20, though you're only allowed into each attraction once. In addition to the museums of the Museum Pass above, you also get entrance to institutions in Albuquerque, Las Cruces, and Alamogordo, and six state monuments.

and north and south, so if you don't orient yourself first, it may give you fits. Paseo connects to South Saint Francis Drive, which hits Highway 25 in two places.

BY BUS

Santa Fe Trails (☎ 505/955-2001; www. santafenm.gov/public-works/transit/index. asp) is the city's bus line, but Santa Fe is contained enough that between your feet and your wheels, you shouldn't need to use it. (If there's a big festival going on and you're staying on an outskirt, I recommend shuttling in and out of the Plaza—traffic will be a mess and parking scarce.) There are nine bus routes, with fares of $1 per trip ($2 for a 1-day pass). Monday through Friday, the buses run from 6am until 11pm along the major routes. Saturday hours are 8am to 8pm, and Sunday there's reduced service from 10am until 7:45pm. Most routes start from two logical points: the downtown Transit Center (on Sheridan St., between Marcy St. and Palace Ave., 1 block west of the Plaza), and the Santa Fe Place Mall Transit Center (4250 Cerrillos Rd., which is south of the city, north of 25, and east of the airport).

ON FOOT

The best way to see downtown Santa Fe is on foot. Free walking-tour maps are available at the tourist information center in the Sweeney Center, 201 W. Marcy St. (☎ **800/777-CITY** or 505/984-6760). Remember that you're over a mile high (Santa Fe sits at 7,000 ft. elevation), so you may be huffing and puffing more than you're used to.

BY TAXI

Cabs are difficult to flag from the street, but you can call for one. Expect to pay $2.40 for the initial service and an additional $2.35 or so per mile. **Capital City Cab** (☎ **505/438-0000**) is the main company in Santa Fe.

Finding the First Americans Near Santa Fe

The descendents of Pueblo Indians, Spanish immigrants, and Anglo trailblazers are all part of the mix in northern New Mexico. The Indians were here first—13,500 years ago by most estimates. They count among their heirs the Pueblo, Navajo, and Apache tribespeople whose land covers much of northern New Mexico.

The Spanish first hit the upper Rio Grande in the early 15th century. Santa Fe was made the regional capital in 1610. Spaniards brought sheep and horses, but they also brought exploitation. The Pueblo Indians were more or less enslaved, forced to weave, till, and build churches. By 1680,

Local Etiquette: Tiptoe through the crypto!

Although you'll find Westerners don't much stand on ceremony, there are a couple of things to be aware of out here. Much of America's historic and cultural heritage in the west runs on the honor system. Architectural sites can be damaged easily, so *please* keep off ruins with signs that warn people away. There are plenty of places where you can explore ruins up close without putting them at risk. When you think of it, it's a miracle any of this stuff survived—anything we can do to prolong its existence contributes to the miracle. Avoid touching petroglyphs, getting them wet, or walking on them. If you make it into the backcountry, you may see shards of pottery scattered around unexcavated sites. Robbing from archaeological sites carries heavy penalties, but beyond the legal incentives, you can imagine the larger karmic reasons for not looting our national heritage. Most of the West is hearty enough that you can walk (or bike or drive) freely without worrying about damaging the land. There are some sensitive areas, however, especially around Canyonlands. The crust (sometimes called cryptobiotic soil) is alive with algae, lichens, and bacteria. You'll start recognizing it as a black, puffy growth. If you stay on trails and rock tops, and step carefully when you're around it; you'll help keep the desert alive.

they'd had enough. Their unified rebellion managed to drive the Spaniards out for a dozen years. The Spanish did come back, and New Mexico was their domain until 1821, but the people were never subjugated as brutally again.

The early 1800's saw the arrival of the mountain men, the Anglo hunters, trappers, and traders. They helped lead the way for wagon trains that plied the 800 miles of the Santa Fe Trail (which began in Independence, MO). A century later, in 1912, New Mexico became the 47th state in the union.

All this history ensures that you'll run out of time long before you run out of things to see in the Rio Grande Valley.

In this section of the trip, you can base yourself in Santa Fe (see "Sleeping," "Eating," and "Partying" sections below), but we're grouping the Early Americans attractions together below so you can organize your time both in the city and your daytrips.

TOP ANCIENT SITES

In Santa Fe

➜ **Loretto Chapel Museum** ★★ This place was put on the map with a "Ripley's Believe it or Not!" piece in the 1930s. The spiral staircase in back, leading to the choir loft, makes two 360-degree turns with no visible support. Local lore holds that St. Joseph himself built the "Miraculous Staircase," in the form of a stranger who happened by, put the stairs up without so much as a nail, and then left without charging a fee. More likely, rancher and carpenter Francois-Jean "Frenchy" Rochas did the work, though that doesn't make the staircase look any less miraculous. *207 Old Santa Fe Trail.* ☎ *505/982-0092. www.lorettochapel. com. Admission $2.50. Mon–Sat 9am–5pm, until 6pm in summer; Sun 10:30am–5pm.*

➜ **Museum of Indian Arts & Culture** ★★ An interactive exhibit called "Here, Now and Always" takes visitors through thousands of years of Native American history. The entrance is through a tunnel,

Cowboys & Native Americans

Most of us grew up after the word "Indians" had been dropped from the textbooks, at least as a way of describing the folks who once squared off with cowboys. To me, "Native American" isn't such an improvement—is the first name of a 15th-century Italian mapmaker really that much less offensive? On the East Coast, "Native American" seems to be the descriptor of choice, so I was surprised to hear Westerners (of all stripes) using "Indian" in a casual way. As for the region's ancestor tribes, that's even more complicated. In the '20s, official documents began to refer to the ancient ones as the "Anasazi." This is a Navajo word that roughly translates as "enemy ancestors," so you can imagine why not every tribe embraced it. The phrase "Ancestral Puebloans" showed up next, but it's clunky and also unpopular with the tribes. The most recent signs at sites and museums use "the people" to describe the ancients. Simple and elegant, it's the phrasing I like best.

which symbolizes the *sipapu,* the ancestral Puebloan entrance into the upper worlds. Trickling water, drums, and Native American music provide the soundtrack. The core of the shifting exhibits are gorgeous examples of basketry, pottery, clothing, carpets, and jewelry. *710 Camino Lejo.* ☎ *505/476-1250. www.miaclab.org. Admission $8. Tues–Sun 10am–5pm.*

→ **Museum of Spanish Colonial Art** ★ New Mexico is much better known for its Indian art than its Spanish colonial work, but the latter tradition is pretty amazing. *Santos,* religious figures on wood *(retablos)* or in sculpture *(bultos),* are done in a rustic/naïve way that's much more intriguing than the oppressively pious material of the Old World. The tinwork and straw on display here also demonstrate impressive craftsmanship. *750 Camino Lejo.* ☎ *505/982-2226. www.spanishcolonial.org. Admission $6. Tues–Sun 10am–5pm.*

→ **Palace of the Governors** ★★ This former capital building is the oldest continuously used public structure in America. Exhibits inside detail the building's history (it played a major role in the Pueblo uprising of 1680), and the history of New Mexico. Period rooms, Spanish colonial

animal-hide paintings, and pre-Columbian art are among the highlights. Even if you don't go inside, the Indian jewelry market in front is worth a visit. The craftsmanship is gorgeous, and the sellers are often patient enough to describe to tourists what they do. *North plaza, on W. Palace Ave., between Lincoln Ave. and Old Santa Fe Trail.* ☎ *505/476-5100. www.palaceofthegovernors. org. Admission $8, free Fri 5–8pm. Tues–Sun 10am–5pm, until 8pm Fri.*

FREE → **St. Francis Cathedral** ★ This is the big old church at the east end of the plaza. Archbishop Jean-Baptiste Lamy led the construction (1869–86), which skips adobe for a more traditional European look. If you poke your head inside, make sure to walk up to the north chapel (in front, to your left). The Our Lady of Peace icon there is the oldest representation of the Madonna in the United States, rescued from the old church during the 1680 Pueblo Rebellion. *Cathedral Place at San Francisco St.* ☎ *505/982-5619. Free (donations accepted). Open daily. Mass Mon–Sat 7am and 5:15pm; Sun 8am, 10am, noon, and 5:15pm.*

FREE → **Wheelwright Museum of the American Indian** ★ Traditional Navajo

Markets & Rodeo: Santa Fe Festivals

Santa Fe is well known for its arts festivals, which transform the streets around the plaza into giant, open air art markets/museums.

→ **RODEO! de Santa Fe:** In late June, this 4-day affair features parades and dances, on top of the usual rodeo competitions. Brahma bull and bronco riding, calf roping, steer wrestling, barrel racing, and trick riding are among the events. The rodeo grounds are at 3237 Rodeo Rd., off Cerrillos Rd., 5½ miles south of the plaza. Performances are in the evening Wednesday to Saturday, and on Saturday afternoon; www.rodeodesantafe.org.

→ **Spanish Market:** Spanish-influenced crafts in New Mexico include *santos* (painted and carved saints), textiles, tinwork, furniture, and straw appliqué. Themes in the art often reflect the vibrant local Catholicism. Artwork is for sale, but you don't need to drop money to be intrigued by the craftsmanship. Traditional Hispanic music, dance, foods, and pageantry give the event the feel of a village festival. Around the plaza, last full weekend in July; www.spanishmarket.org.

→ **Indian Market:** The largest all-Native American market in the country, this event brings in some 1,000 artisans. Baskets, blankets, jewelry, pottery, woodcarvings, rugs, sand paintings, and sculptures are among the offerings. Tribal dancing and crafts demonstrations are scheduled in the afternoon. Third weekend in August, book accommodations way in advance if you plan on spending the night; www.swaia.org.

→ **Fiesta de Santa Fe:** Fiesta is the oldest community celebration in the U.S., predating the nation by more than 60 years. Masses, a parade for children and their pets, a historical/hysterical parade, mariachi concerts, dances, food, and arts all fill the city's streets. The highlight is the burning of Zozobra, "Old Man Gloom," a 40-foot-tall effigy, whose Thursday-night destruction kicks off 3 days of partying. Weekend following Labor Day; www.santafefiesta.org.

→ **Canyon Road Farolito Walk:** *Farolitos* are just candles inside brown paper bags, but they give off a haunting glow. During the holiday season they're found all over the state. On Christmas Eve at dusk, musicians and carolers join strollers along Canyon Road, taking in the *farolitos* and small bonfires called *luminarias*.

---

hogans can be seen across the reservations of the Southwest. Look for a roundish structure with a doorway that faces east. The Wheelwright is loosely built on this design, with an interlocking "whirling log" ceiling. The preservation of Navajo ritual practices was the inspiration for this museum. In addition to exhibits on baskets, rugs, and other Navajo creations, check out the arts-and-crafts shop, which can pass for a 20th-century reservation trading post. *704 Camino Lejo.* ☎ *800/607-4636 or 505/982-4636. www.wheelwright.org. Free, donations appreciated. Mon–Sat 10am–5pm; Sun 1–5pm.*

More Stuff to See & Do in Town

For a good photo op, stop by the **Mission of San Miguel** ★★ (401 Old Santa Fe Trail at E. de Vargas St.; ☎ 505/983-3974). The massive adobe walls on this ancient church date back to 1610. This is America's oldest church, and directly across the

At Bandelier National Monument, you can explore remains of houses built in the 1100s.

street to the north you'll find signs alerting you to America's oldest house. Now a boutique, the structure is allegedly haunted, so bring your infrared film.

You can get a great view of the city by taking the path at **Old Fort Marcy Park** ★★ (617 Paseo de Peralta, near Otero St.). Markers delineate Santa Fe history as you climb, culminating in a cross erected in 1920 to commemorate the Franciscan martyrs of the 1680 Pueblo Rebellion.

Many of Santa Fe's art galleries are clustered on **Canyon Road.** Proximity means you can hit a bunch of places conveniently. Contemporary photography, sculpture, and painting are interspersed with Indian art and artifacts. For the latter, I really like the **Morning Star Gallery** (513 Canyon Rd.; ☎ **505/982-8187;** www. morningstargallery.com), which is stocked with museum-quality dolls, jewelry, rugs, and pottery.

OUTTA TOWN

Native American Traces on the Road from Santa Fe

➔ **Bandelier National Monument** ★★★

The ruins of Bandelier are nestled into a lush canyon about an hour north and west of Santa Fe. The canyon, which has a reliable water source, was lived in for thousands of years. You can explore the remains of houses built in the 1100s and used into the mid-1500s. Holes drilled for ancient ceiling beams are still visible in the canyon walls. Pine ladders let you climb up inside. An additional hike through a ponderosa forest takes you to a high cliff with a restored kiva. It's worth the extra walk just to soak up the tranquillity, on quiet days, at least. On summer weekends the park can get hectic, with lines for parking spaces outside the visitors center. *Bandelier: NM 4 (HCR 1, Box 1, Suite 15, Los Alamos, NM 87544-9701). ☎ 505/672-3861, ext*

517. www.nps.gov/band. Admission $12 per vehicle, free with National Parks Pass. Open daily 8am–6pm in summer, closing at 4:30pm in winter, and 9am–5:30pm in spring and fall.

Other Sites to See

There are a couple of other nearby sites worth a visit. The town of **White Rock,** a few miles southeast of Bandelier on NM 4, has stunning river valley views. The **White Rock Overlook** is also a great picnic spot. To reach it from Bandelier along NM 4, take a left on Rover Boulevard, a left on Meadow Lane, and a left on Overlook Road. There'll be signs, too.

On the other side of Bandelier on NM 4 (18 miles from Los Alamos), you'll find the **Valles Caldera National Preserve** (www.vallescaldera.gov). This is one of the world's largest volcanic calderas, created by an eruption some million years ago. The crater valley holds pine forests, making for nice hiking.

Nearby, the little town of **Los Alamos** played a big role in U.S. history. The Manhattan Project, which built the first atomic bombs, was headquartered here. The **Bradbury Science Museum** (15th St. and Central Ave.; ☎ **505/667-4444;** www.lanl.gov/museum; Tues–Sat 10am–5pm; Sun–Mon 1–5pm) provides a good overview of the extreme secrecy the project required. Somewhat creepy displays include an actual 5-ton Little Boy nuclear bomb, similar to the one dropped on Hiroshima.

On an alternative end of the nuclear technology spectrum is **Black Hole** (4015 Arkansas; ☎ **505/662-5053;** Mon–Sat 10am–5pm), a prop shop packed ass to gills with nuclear-age leftovers. The place also works as a kind of museum, with Geiger counters and giant Waring blenders. The owner, Edward Grothus, gives a "critical mass" each Sunday at the next-door "First Church of High Technology."

For more on White Sands and another roadtripper's take on this corner of New Mexico, see the "American Highways" trip, starting on p. 693.

➔ **Pecos National Historical Park** ★★
I-25, the major interstate in the area, bypasses Pecos, which has allowed the town to retain some old-time charm. About 30 minutes' drive south and east of Santa Fe, the area was once home to some 2,000 Pecos Indians. Located along the eastern fringe of the Puebloan realm, their settlement was a major center for trading with Plains Indians. A national park preserves the ruins of their town. More spectacular is an ancient adobe church, once the finest Spanish structure north of Mexico City. Built by the Franciscans around 1620, the original towers, buttresses, and pine beams are startlingly intact. *About 2 miles south of the town of Pecos off NM 63. ☎ 505/757-6414. www.nps.gov/peco. Admission $3 per person, free with National Parks Pass. Open daily 8am–5pm; until 6pm in summer.*

ON THE ROAD TO TAOS

➔ **Taos** ★ There are two ways to get to Taos, 70 miles north and east of Santa Fe. The main highway is pleasant enough, but I recommend the alternative High Road. Take 503 north, and then 76 to 75 to 518. A little convoluted, sure, but you'll pass through stone lowlands, chile farms, and apple and peach orchards. The little towns along the way retain their centuries-old traditions. Chimayo is known for its weaving and Cordova for its woodcarving.

Just outside of Taos there's a great photo opportunity at **San Francisco de Asis church** (60 St. Francis Plaza; ☎ **505/758-2754**). Coming up 518, it's just to your left down 68. The stylized adobe structure has been the subject of many famous paintings and photographs. For a look inside, admission is $3, and it's open Monday through

Saturday 9am to 4pm, plus other times for Mass. Closed to the public first 2 weeks in June, when repairs are done. The best reason to come to Taos, however, is Taos Pueblo.

➔ **Taos Pueblo** ★★★ To get a feel of what Indian villages were like when they were living and breathing entities, check out Taos Pueblo. The Tiwa have been living here continuously for over a thousand years. The pueblo's stacked adobe rooms elegantly match the contours of Taos Mountain in the distance. Guided tours will show you around residents' studios, the ruins of the old church and cemetery, and the well-preserved **San Geronimo Chapel.** Ask permission before taking anyone's photo here; some people will ask for a small payment. If your visit is timed well, you may be able to check out a ceremony. A schedule of dances, processions, and powwows is available online. *From Paseo del Pueblo Norte, travel north 2 miles on Veterans Hwy.* ☎ *505/758-1028. www.taos pueblo.com. Admission $10 per person, $5 camera fee. Daily 8am–4:30pm, closed for 10 weeks in late winter, closed to accommodate some tribal rituals.*

EVEN FARTHER OUTTA TOWN:
Native American Traces South of Santa Fe

If you hook up with the Albuquerque leg of the "American Highways" roadtrip (p. 781), you can catch some intriguing Native American sites.

➔ **Petroglyph National Monument** ★ Albuquerque's western sprawl has brought the city right up to this ancient hunting and gathering area. The dark basalt boulders of an ancient lava flow provided a canvas for some 25,000 petroglyphs, or rock drawings. The Mesa Point Trail is a half-hour jaunt with lots of ancient markings, plus nice city and mountain views. The Rinconada Trail is a longer hike,

following a huge *rincon* (corner) at the base of the lava flow. The petroglyphs themselves have a mysterious quality. Easily recognizable icons like cats, birds, and handprints mix with spirals and enigmatic symbols. Most were made between 1300 and 1650, though some date back thousands of years. Be on the lookout for rattlers—the sleeping one on Mesa Point wasn't very intimidating, but the big fellah who scurried across my path on the Rinconada Trail was pretty scary. *6001 Unser Blvd. NW (3 miles north of I-40 at Unser and Western Trail), Albuquerque, NM.* ☎ *505/ 899-0205. www.nps.gov/petr. Free, parking for the trails $1 per car weekdays, $2 weekends. Visitor Center and Boca Negra area daily 8am–5pm.*

Near Grants, NM, a little over an hour west of Albuquerque, you'll find:

➔ **Acoma Sky City** ★★★ This city has been lived in longer than any other in the U.S., at least since the 11th century. Indian sources date it back another thousand years. The Spanish church, built in 1639, is filled with masterpieces of colonial art. The city is dramatically sited on top of a sheer mesa. Touring is with guides only, via a bus that climbs up the mesa. Despite the vehicles, once you're on top you'll feel like you're in another time. There's no running water or electricity, and the village looks more like something from the Middle Ages than modern strip-mall America. *From Albuquerque, drive west 65 miles to the Acoma–Sky City exit (102), then 15 miles southwest.* ☎ *800/747-0181 or 505/469-1052. www. skycity.com. Admission $10, plus $10 for cameras (film only, no digital). Open daily 8am– 4pm, until 6pm in summer.*

FREE ➔ **El Malpais** ★ Besides the badass name (Spanish for "badlands"), this place boasts cinder cones, lava flows, and ancient ruins and trails. You can hike all over the area, and you can camp out for free if you get a backcountry permit from the visitors center. From NM 53, which exits I-40 just west of Grants, hit the **Zuni–Acoma Trail.** The trail, an ancient Indian trade route, crosses four major lava flows over a 7.5-mile (one-way) hike. **El Calderon,** a forested area 20 miles south of I-40, has a trail that leads past a cinder cone and lava tubes. To see a lava tube sheltering an ancient ice formation, you can visit **Ice Caves Resort** (☎ **888/ICE-CAVE** or 505/783-4303; www.icecaves.com). This is the one part of Malpais that isn't free—private operators charge $9 for access to trails and the cave. Open daily from 8am, closing about 1 hour before sunset. *NM 117 or NM 53. 505/285-4641. www.nps. gov/elma. Visitor center off Route 53 between mile markers 63 and 64. open daily 8:30am–4:30pm.*

📺 Best ● → **El Morro** ★★★ This bluff is secluded enough that most folks have never heard of it, but it lays a claim to being the most historic rock in the U.S. A reliable water source made this a popular stopover, and Zuñi Indians were the first people to mark the rock wall. In 1605 (!), the Spaniard in charge of the New Mexico colonization campaign put his Juan Hancock to the stone, becoming the first European to tag America. A short hike takes you past the dozens of fascinating, historical inscriptions that followed (a free trail guide fills in all the details). If you follow the trail around the mesa top, you'll reach the ruins of Atsinna Pueblo. This beautifully sited Indian settlement has gorgeous views of mesas, a long valley, and El Morro itself. *Off NM 53. 43 miles west of Grants, NM. ☎ 505/783-4226. www.nps.gov/elmo. Admission $3 per person, free with National Parks Pass. Daily 8am–5pm, until 6pm in summer.*

Sleeping

Santa Fe is not the cheapest city to sleep in, but things are kept up well out here, so

you'll feel like you're getting your money's worth. Summer is the high season, with rooms scarce and prices jacked. During Indian Market, the third weekend in August, those prices rise even higher. The peak of winter gets busy, too, as Texans come flooding in (some locals gripe "If God had intended Texans to ski, he would have given them a mountain of their own"). City/state tax (11.5%) is added to every hotel bill.

If your focus is going to be more on the sites outside of town, I'd recommend saving a few bucks by camping or staying in motels on the outskirts. It's not impossible to find affordable stays in the city itself, however.

CAMPGROUNDS/HOSTELS

→**Rancheros de Santa Fe Campground** ★ This RV park also takes folks with tents. Only about 6 miles southeast of Santa Fe, the sites are nestled among 22 acres of piñon and juniper forest. Rustic camping cabins are also available if you're not doing the tent thing. Open March 15 to October 31. *736 Old Las Vegas Hwy. (exit 290 off I-25), Santa Fe, NM 87505. ☎ 800/426-9259 or 505/466-3482. www.rancheros.com. Tent site $17–$20; RV hookup $25–$35; cabins $35–$42. Amenities: Outdoor pool; coin-op laundry; restrooms; showers; grills; cable TV hookups; grocery store; recreation room; tables; fireplaces; nature trails; playground; free nightly movies May–Sept; public telephones; propane.*

Along NM 475 on the road to Ski Santa Fe you'll find two nice, forested sites. Grounds are open May to October and rates per site start around $8 per vehicle per night. **Hyde Memorial State Park** (740 Hyde Park Rd.; ☎ **505/983-7175;** www.nmparks.com), about 8 miles from the city in the Sangre de Cristo Mountains, has good hiking as well as camping.

Near Hyde is the **Santa Fe National Forest** (☎ 505/438-7840; www.fs.fed.us/r3/sfe; reservations ☎ 877/444-6777; www.reserveusa.com), where you can make an advance reservation for one of 44 sites.

Further afield, **Bandelier** (p. 476) has a nice, large campground. On the mesa top, it's open year-round, except in bad winter weather. No reservations are accepted, but with 94 sites, it rarely sells out ($12 a night per site, with flush toilets).

El Morro's (p. 479) campsite is small (only nine sites), but it's in a tranquil little forest area. First-come, first-served (although it's not heavily trafficked), sites are $5 a night, free in winter after the water gets shut off.

CHEAP

➜ **Santa Fe Budget Inn** ★ This two-story, three-building complex is only about a 10-minute walk from the plaza. Rooms are basic and on the small side, but they're in good shape. If you want to avoid street noise, request a room in the back. *725 Cerrillos Rd., Santa Fe, NM 87501.* ☎ *800/288-7600 or 505/982-5952. Fax 505/984-8879. www.santafebudgetinn.com. 160 units. $58–$72 double. Additional person $7. Rates include continental breakfast. Free parking. Pets welcome. Amenities: Outdoor pool. In room: A/C, TV.*

➜ **Santa Fe Plaza Travelodge** ★ This spot on Cerrillos Road is closer to downtown than the Super 8 below. Rooms are clean and nicely lit, and Southwestern-style ceiling borders are a nice touch. *646 Cerrillos Rd., Santa Fe, NM 87501.* ☎ *800/578-7878 or 505/982-3551. Fax 505/983-8624. www.travelodge.com. 48 units. May–Oct $65–$88 double; Nov–Apr $39–$69 double. Free parking. Amenities: Outdoor pool. In room: A/C, TV, fridge, coffeemaker.*

➜ **Super 8 Motel** Super 8s are never going to win any awards for luxury, but this boxy pink stucco job is clean and comfortable. The location, south and west of downtown, is convenient enough. *3358 Cerrillos Rd., Santa Fe, NM 87507.* ☎ *800/800-8000 or 505/471-8811. Fax 505/471-3239. www.super8.com. 96 units. $45–$80 double, depending on the season. Rates include continental breakfast. Free parking. Amenities: Coin-op laundry. In room: A/C, TV, coffeemaker, safe.*

DOABLE

➜ **Garrett's Desert Inn** ★ Built in 1956, a '90s remodel didn't completely obliterate the retro appeal here. There are nice touches like Art Deco tile in the bathrooms, big rooms, and a heated pool. The location, just a couple of blocks from the plaza, can't be beat. *311 Old Santa Fe Trail, Santa Fe, NM 87501.* ☎ *800/888-2145 or 505/982-1851. Fax 505/989-1647. www.garrettsdesertinn.com. 83 units. $79–$149, depending on season and type of room. Amenities: Restaurant; bar; outdoor pool; concierge; room service; in-room massage; laundry service; dry cleaning. In room: A/C, TV, dataport, coffeemaker, hair dryer, iron.*

➜ **Santa Fe Motel and Inn** ★ This small compound is a good pick for keeping within walking distance of the plaza. The main part is two stories, built in 1955. In back are *casitas,* little free-standing houses. For $20 to $60 more than standard rooms, you'll get additional privacy and charm. *510 Cerrillos Rd., Santa Fe, NM 87501.* ☎ *800/930-5002 or 505/982-1039. Fax 505/986-1275. www.santafemotel.com. 23 units. $79–$179, depending on season and room type. Additional person $10. Rates include continental breakfast. Free parking. In room: A/C, TV, hair dryer, iron.*

SPLURGE

➜ **Old Santa Fe Inn** ★ For some real Santa Fe ambience, check out this remodeled 1930s court motel. Handcrafted colonial-style furniture, Mexican-tiled

Feed Me: A Quick Guide to NM Cuisine

For me, half the fun of a trip to the Southwest is getting to eat New Mexican food. I don't even care about the high-end places: A burrito or bowl of green chile from a takeout stand are good enough for me. Even if you're familiar with Mexican and Tex-Mex, you'll find New Mexico cooking is its own thing. Like the state itself, Anglo, Spanish, and Indian influences blend together. The chile pepper (they use the Spanish spelling out here—if you want chili go to Cincinnati) is the key, served red or green, often as a sauce to top enchiladas and burritos. The following glossary refers to New Mexican food, which overlaps with its Four Corner neighbors:

- → **Carne adovada**—Tender pork marinated in red chile sauce and then baked. Tends to be spicy. Insanely good.
- → **Chorizo**—Mexican sausage, often found in breakfast burritos, along with eggs, potatoes, Jack cheese, and red or green chile.
- → **Christmas**—Tortured over which sauce to try, the red or the green chile? Get 'em both, just ask for it "Christmas."
- → **Green chile stew**—Chile soup with meat, potatoes, and sometimes beans. Tends to be hot. The best.
- → **Huevos rancheros**—Fried eggs on tortillas, topped with cheese and chile and/or salsa. Often served with pinto beans.
- → **Masa**—The corn dough used in tortillas and tamales. New Mexican corn comes in six colors, with yellow, white, and blue the most common.
- → **Navajo frybread**—Fried dough. When topped with honey or powdered sugar, similar to fairground faves like funnel cakes, dough boys, and elephant ears.
- → **Navajo tacos**—Frybread topped with beans, beef, and cheese.
- → **Piñon nuts**—Pine nuts, more or less. Available at roadside stands, great smoky flavor.
- → **Posole**—Hominy corn in a soup or stew, sometimes with pork and chile. Very hearty, good cold weather food.
- → **Ristra**—Those strings of chiles you see dangling from porches.
- → **Sopaipilla**—Airy fried dough pocket served with honey, or stuffed with meat and vegetables.

New Mexican food seems like it should travel easily, but like French bread or New York bagels, you just can't find it done right once you get away from the source. I say, eat as much of it as you can while you have the chance.

bathrooms, and gas fireplaces add to the appeal. The location, south of Alameda, is in easy walking distance to downtown attractions. All stays come with a complimentary breakfast burrito. *320 Galisteo St., Santa Fe, NM 87501.* ☎ *800/745-9910 or 505/995-0800. Fax 505/995-0400. www.oldsantafe inn.com. 43 units. Winter $89–$136 double,* *$119–$169 suite; summer $127–$149 double, $199–$249 suite. In room: A/C, TV/VCR, dataport, fridge, coffeemaker, CD player.*

Eating

The culinary offerings in Santa Fe are remarkably sophisticated. Santa Fe excels at New Mexican cooking, from the cheapest tamale stands in the plaza to the world-class restaurants scattered around the perimeter. (You don't have to eat New Mexican; there's also good Asian and Italian, but I personally can never pass up an opportunity for good Southwestern cooking.) Santa Fe's middle-of-the-road spots are especially good—just because you're not dropping big bucks doesn't mean you won't eat well here.

SUPPLIES

The best grocery store in town is the **St. Francis Wild Oats Natural Marketplace** (1090 S. St. Francis Dr.; ☎ **505/983-5333;** www.wildoats.com). Produce is gorgeous and fresh, and the deli department makes great sandwiches. You can also buy Blue Sky, New Mexico's own all-natural soda.

➔**Farmers' Market** ★ Local cheeses, cider, and salsas supplement big selections of fruits and vegetables. Early risers can take advantage of good, strong coffee and fresh pastries. Open April to mid-November, Saturday and Tuesday 7am to noon. *In the Santa Fe Railyard, off S. Guadalupe behind Tomasita's.* ☎ *505/983-4098.*

TAKEOUT TREATS

Close to the plaza, the **Burrito Company Café** (111 Washington Ave., ☎ **505/982-4453)** serves excellent, cheap burritos. Breakfast, lunch, and dinner are all served, with main meals running $3.75 to $8.95 (cash only). There's space to eat inside, or you can picnic in the plaza.

The plaza itself has good street food. My favorite stand is **El Molero,** which sells excellent $4 fajitas, served with fresh guacamole.

Hidden in an industrial park on the outskirts of town, the **Chocolate Maven Bakery and Café** (821 W. San Mateo Rd.; ☎ **505/982-4400;** www.chocolatemaven. com) features addictive gourmet tarts and

pies, in addition to the namesake chocolate. Sandwiches, salads, and burgers are also available, if you're looking for something more substantial. If you stay to eat, the improvised two-story cafe space is eclectic and friendly. Open weekdays for breakfast and lunch, and weekends for brunch from 9am to 3pm.

EATING OUT

Cheap

➔**La Choza** ★★ NEW MEXICAN In an old ranch office, this restaurant has been a local favorite since the '50's. Part of The Shed (p. 483) family, the waits here are under control and the staff is friendly. Blue-corn burritos with *posole,* available meat or vegetarian, are recommended, as are the enchiladas. Portions aren't huge, so you might want to start off with guacamole or nachos. *905 Alarid St.* ☎ *505/982-0909. Lunch or dinner $7–$8.75. Summer Mon–Sat 11am–9pm; winter Mon–Thurs 11am–8pm, Fri–Sat 11am–9pm.*

➔**Plaza Cafe** ★ NEW MEXICAN DINER This greasy spoon right off the plaza is road-trip-friendly, with big maps on the back wall, so you can study where to go next while you eat. Green chile stew, pumpkin *posole,* and piñon hotcakes are among the indigenous exotica on the menu. There are also solid burgers and gyros. For dessert, *tres leches* cake is a local fave, combining three different milks (evaporated, sweetened condensed, and heavy cream). *54 Lincoln Ave. (on the plaza).* ☎ *505/982-1664. No reservations. Main courses $8–$15. Daily 7am–9pm.*

MTV **Best** ● ➔**Tomasita's Cafe** ★★ NEW MEXICAN Cheap prices and good food make for potentially long waits here. Fortunately, the bar serves up a damn fine margarita. The burritos are excellent, as are house special deep-fried chiles rellenos. Locals go nuts for the green chile, often voted the best in town. (The red is no slouch either—ask for Christmas-style if you want to try both at once.) *500 S. Guadalupe St.* ☎ *505/983-5721. Reservations not accepted. Lunch $5.25–$12, dinner $5.75–$13. Mon–Sat 11am–10pm.*

➜ **Tortilla Flats** ✶ NEW MEXICAN Healthy eaters will be attracted to the all-natural ingredients and vegetarian options here, especially fresh vegetarian burritos. The Santa Fe Trail steak is a great option for non-healthy eating: 8 oz. of prime rib-eye smothered in chile and onions. Don't miss the dough pockets called *sopaipillas,* which are made on the spot (you can peek through a window into the kitchen and watch them being made). *3139 Cerrillos Rd.* ☎ *505/471-8685. Breakfast $2–$8; lunch $5–$10; dinner $6–$11. Sun–Thurs 7am–9pm (10pm in summer); Fri–Sat 7am–10pm.*

Doable

➜ **Coyote Café** ✶✶ SOUTHWESTERN This downtown restaurant is famous for its creative *haute* New Mexican cuisine (the chef, Mark Miller, has written 10 cookbooks). Although the swank second-floor main room will put pressure on a roadtrip budget, two other spaces here are very doable. In summer, the **Rooftop Cantina** fills a big terrace with vibrant cooking. Tacos, enchiladas, and rich chicken mole are available. **Cottonwoods,** on the ground floor, has equally good food in a casual space. *132 Water St.* ☎ *505/983-1615. www.coyotecafe.com. Reservations recommended. Main courses $6–$16 (Rooftop Cantina), $19–$36 (Coyote Café), $6–$15 (Cottonwoods). Rooftop Cantina: daily 11:30am–9pm. Dining room: daily 6–9:30pm, 5:30–9pm during opera season. Cottonwoods: daily 11:30am–4pm.*

➜ **Los Mayas** ✶✶ SOUTHWESTERN A festive, South of the Border feel infuses this ramshackle downtown restaurant.

The dining room has an improvised look, with prairie fence walls and old tarps for a roof. The menu is Mexican, rather than New Mexican, and the enchiladas and guacamole are excellent. Margaritas and a stage for Latino performers ensure energy levels are always high. *409 W. Water St.* ☎ *505/986-9930. www. losmayas.com. Reservations accepted. Main courses $17–$22. Daily 5–10pm.*

➜ **The Shed** ✶✶ NEW MEXICAN Truly old school: The hacienda that houses it was built in 1692. It's been a locals' restaurant since the early '50s, especially popular at lunch. Cheese enchiladas and green chile stew are Santa Fe staples. In a nod to the times, you can also find vegetarian and low-fat Mexican items. *113½ E. Palace Ave.* ☎ *505/982-9030. Reservations recommended, but accepted only at dinner. Lunch $5.75–$9.50; dinner $8–$17. Mon–Sat 11am–2:30pm and 5:30–9pm.*

Splurge

➜ **Cafe Pasqual's** ✶✶ SOUTHWESTERN One of Santa Fe's top restaurants, with the crowds to prove it. Breakfast and lunch are highlighted by *huevos motuleños* (two eggs on blue-corn tortillas topped with the trippy combination of sautéed bananas, feta cheese, and green chile). For dinner, start with the Iroquois corn tamale with roasted poblano, zucchini, and asadero cheese, and follow up with spinach, jack cheese, and red onion enchiladas. Dinner is expensive, so consider affordable breakfast or lunch. Try not to come at peak hours, because this place is justifiably popular. *121 Don Gaspar Ave.* ☎ *505/983-9340. Reservations recommended for dinner. Main courses: $5.75–$13 breakfast, $7.75–$15 brunch, $6–$15 lunch, $16–$34 dinner. Mon–Sat 7am–3pm; Sun–Thurs 5:30–9:30pm; Fri–Sat 6–10pm; summer open until 10:30pm daily. Brunch Sun 8am–2pm.*

Partying

When it comes to nightlife venues, Santa Fe will seem more like a small town. There aren't a ton of places or wide varieties of scenes. That said, people are friendly here, and 7,000 feet when you're not acclimated always makes for an interesting night (translation: the liquor hits you harder and quicker). **Canyon Road** and downtown around the **plaza** have some good options if you want to be within stumbling distance of home. Covers are rare for regular old nightspots, although if there's live music, you'll probably have to pay $3 to $7 to get in.

BARS & CLUBS

→ **The Dragon Room** ★ BAR This dragon-themed spot across the alleyway from The Pink Adobe restaurant attracts a nice mix of young and old. Kick back among low-lit, aged elegance, beneath dragons dangling from the ceiling. In addition to solid lunch and bar menus, complimentary popcorn is always close at hand. *406 Old Santa Fe Trail.* ☎ *505/983-7712. Mon–Fri 11:30am–2am; Sat 5pm–2am; Sun 5pm–midnight.*

→ **Swig** ★ NIGHTCLUB This is about as chichi as Santa Fe gets. Swank, high-end decor makes a nice backdrop for a martini-sipping crowd. The lounge serves small Asian plates until 11pm on weekdays and midnight on weekends, making it one of the few Santa Fe spots for late-night food. *135 W. Palace Ave., level 3.* ☎ *505/955-0400. Tues–Sat 5pm–2am.*

LIVE MUSIC

To see national bands, your best bet is to head for Albuquerque. Most tours don't bother detouring an hour or so north, although on occasion a band will skip Albuquerque in favor of Santa Fe. What music is available tends to be homegrown, which is definitely a good thing if you're into Spanish-inflected sounds.

→ **Catamount Bar and Grille** A post-college crowd checks out live rock and blues on weekends here. This is a bit of a sports bar, with billiards upstairs and games on the TVs. *125 E. Water St.* ☎ *505/988-7222. Mon–Sat 11am–2am; Sun noon–midnight. Cover $0–$5.*

→ **Cowgirl Hall of Fame** ★★ RESTAURANT/BAR A festive atmosphere makes for a nice meal, but the hall of fame is worth a visit for just the bar. Music plays just about every night, in an eclectic jumble of blues, folk, and rock. There's also comedy and the always-dubious category of cowboy poetry. In warmer months, the brick back patio is super inviting, lit by strings of mellow white lights. *319 S. Guadalupe St.* ☎ *505/982-2565. www.santafenow.com/rest/cowgirl. Mon–Fri 11am–midnight; Sat 8:30am–midnight; Sun 8am–11pm. Bar: Mon–Sat until 2am; Sun until midnight. No cover for music Sun–Mon and Wed. Tues and Thurs–Sat $3 cover. Special performances $10.*

→ **El Farol** ★★★ RESTAURANT/BAR "The Lantern" is the Canyon Road artists' quarter's original neighborhood bar and one of my favorite spots. The restaurant has cozy low ceilings and hand-smoothed adobe walls that date to 1835. Dinner features a huge selection of tapas, with two outdoor patios going in the summer. Music starts up after 9:30pm, a mix of jazz, swing, and folk. If you're lucky, you might be there for Latin guitar, sometimes accompanied by a lone flamenco dancer, the perfect combination for the old-time Spanish ambience. *808 Canyon Rd.* ☎ *505/983-9912. Reservations recommended. Main courses $8–$15 lunch, $26–$32 dinner. Daily 11:30am–3pm and 5:30–10pm (bar is open until 1am weekdays, 2am Fri–Sat). Usually no cover on weeknights, $7 Fri–Sat.*

→ **El Paseo Bar and Grill** ★ BAR A casual environment here attracts a young crowd. In addition to open-mic Tuesdays, blues to rock to jazz to bluegrass can be heard from local bands. Beer specials run Sundays to Thursdays, $1.50 to $2.50 for the beer of the night. *208 Galisteo St.* ☎ *505/992-2848. www.elpaseobar.com Cover $3–$5 weekends.*

➔ **Evangelo's** ★★ BAR This centrally located hang's tropical decor emphasizes a laid-back, good time vibe. Beers are well represented, with some 60 import bottles available. Live music (jazz, rock, or reggae) plays 3 nights a week, Wednesdays at 7:30pm, and Fridays and Saturdays at 9pm. *200 W. San Francisco St.* ☎ *505/982-9014.*

Mon–Sat noon–1:30am, Sun until midnight. Cover for special performances only.

➔ **Paramount Lounge and Night Club** ★ NIGHTCLUB This and Swig are about as close to big city nightspots as you'll get in Santa Fe. Dance nights here are well attended, especially "Trash Disco" Wednesdays. Besides DJs, there's also live music and the occasional comedy show. In the back of the building you'll find Bar B, a low-key, gay-friendly martini lounge. Live jazz and unplugged singer-songwriters perform in the intimate space. *331 Sandoval St.* ☎ *505/982-8999. Cover $5 for dance nights; call for music performances.*

On the Road to Moab, UT

Santa Fe, NM to Moab, UT 374 miles

The trip to Moab takes up a full day of travel, but there's so much along the way it'd be a shame to rush it. Turn on some regionally relevant bands (such as Calexico and The Shins) and themes, and savor your multistate ride.

On the Road Nuts & Bolts

Where to Fill Up Somehow, the gas stations out here seem perfectly spaced so there's always one when you need one. That said, it's never a good idea to be running on fumes. The parks generally don't have services and their approach roads can be long, so make sure you've got something in the tank before deviating from main roads.

The Tolls It's all free, baby.

The Fastest Way This is the shorter way by mileage, although it takes about as long as the other route. Start up 285/84 north out of Santa Fe, and stay on 84 when the road shifts in Espanola; 84 becomes 64/84, which you take all the way to Pagosa Springs, CO, 153 miles north of Santa Fe. At Pagosa Springs, take 160 west to Cortez, CO, where you'll grab 491 heading north; 491 will dead-end in Monticello, UT. Take a right onto 191, which goes straight to Moab, UT. The trip is 370 miles and will take 7 hours or so, depending on how heavy your foot is.

The Longer Way Round This western route takes you through some beautiful and desolate terrain. Take I-25 south for 30 miles and pick up 550 north. In Durango, CO, take 160, which will take you north and west. In Cortez, Co, grab 491 heading north; 491 will dead-end in Monticello, UT. Take a right onto 191, which goes straight to Moab, UT. The trip is 400 miles and will take 7 hours or so if you go straight through.

Rules of the Road You'll find traffic isn't too heavy along these roads, but don't let your guard down. New Mexico is one of the most dangerous states in the nation when it comes to drunk drivers. Especially in this north area, it's a good idea to drive defensively.

West to the Four Corners Highlights

It's hard to find a road in Northern New Mexico that isn't a scenic route. There aren't a ton of major highways up here, but you do have a choice of routes. I recommend taking US 285 north out of Santa Fe, which will take you straight to:

→ Ojo Caliente Mineral Springs ★★★ Local Indians knew these hot springs well, and considered them a sacred site. The Spaniard Cabeza de Vaca learned of the spot in the 16th century and named it "hot eye." The waters have a rare combination of iron, soda, lithium, sodium, and arsenic.

This is more of a local's place than anything super-posh, which I find more relaxing. The springs are about an hour's drive from Santa Fe. You can camp out here for $12 for two people, plus $5 for each additional guest. Rooms at the historic hotel on-site start at $99/$109, varying by the season. *50 Los Baños Dr., Ojo Caliente, NM.* ☎ *800/222-9162 or 505/583-2233. www. ojocalientespa.com. Entry to mineral pools, steam, sauna, and seasonal mud pool $16 Mon–Thurs, $22 Fri–Sun and holidays. Sunset discounts available after 6pm.*

If you stay on 285, it'll take you through the San Juan Mountains and up to US 64. Taking 64 west to US 84 north will get you

Playlist: Four Corners Themes

→ *Route 66,* **Jason & the Scorchers,** "Still Standing Reissue," 2002

→ *Colorado Bound,* **Townes Van Zandt,** "In the Beginning . . . ," 2003

→ *Another Colorado,* **Jimmie Dale Gilmore,** "Spinning Around the Sun," 1993

→ *The History of Utah,* **Camper Van Beethoven,** "Camper Van Beethoven," 1986

→ *By the Time I Get to Arizona (Whipped Cream Mix),* **Evolution Control Committee,** "Whipped Cream Mixes," 1996

→ *Hotel Arizona,* **Wilco,** "Being There," 1996

→ *Santa Fe,* **Ottmar Liebert,** "Nouveau Flamenco," 1990

→ *Albuquerque,* **Neil Young,** "Tonight's the Night," 1975

→ *Albuquerque,* **Asleep at the Wheel,** "More Songs of Route 66: Roadside Attractions," 2001

→ *Cortez the Killer,* **Built to Spill,** "Live," 2000

→ *Way out West,* **Big Star,** "Radio City," 1974

→ *The Vanishing Race,* **Johnny Cash,** "Bitter Tears," 1964

→ *Cleft in the Sky,* **R. Carlos Nakai,** "Canyon Trilogy, Vol. 5," 1989

→ *Flintstones,* **The Black Lodge Singers,** "Kids' Pow-Wow Songs," 1996

→ *Corona,* **Calexico,** "Convict Pool," 2004

→ *New Slang,* **The Shins,** "Oh, Inverted World," 2001

to the quaint Old West town of Durango (190 miles from Ojo Caliente), which is a good base for a visit to:

ON THE ROAD TO DURANGO/ MESA VERDE NATIONAL PARK

→ **Mesa Verde National Park** ★★ Mesa Verde is the largest archaeological preserve in the U.S. Its 4,000 known sites date from A.D. 600 to 1300, and include the most impressive cliff dwellings in the Southwest. The place is spectacular, a gigantic abandoned city nestled into a dramatic cliff face, which naturally makes it a major tourist magnet. Many of the areas are accessible only by guided Ranger tour, which sounds like a drag, except that limiting the number of people is essential for getting a real feel for the power of this place. If you can get it together, I recommend showing up at dawn and going on an early tour. Rangers tend to be knowledgeable and passionate about their subjects, and the tours are highly engaging. There are also self-guided tour areas on the mesa top, including Spruce Tree House and Step House, although in peak seasons you'll be sharing the sites with lots of other folks. One way to beat the crowds is to make the 12-mile drive to Wetherill Mesa, which is not heavily trafficked. *Park entrance on U.S. 160, 10 miles east of Cortez and 6 miles west of Mancos. ☎ 970/529-4465. www.nps.gov/meve. Entrance $10 per vehicle, free with National Parks Pass. Tours of Cliff Palace, Balcony House, or Long House $3. Open daily, with hours changing seasonally, and several areas closed in winter. Far View Visitor Center open daily mid-Apr through mid-Oct only 8am– 5pm. Chapin Mesa Archaeological Museum open daily 8am–6:30pm mid-Apr through mid-Oct; daily 8am–5pm the rest of the year.*

Sleeping in Durango/Mesa Verde

You can camp right inside the park at the **Morefield Campground** (☎ 800/449- 2288; www.visitmesaverde.com) from May

to early October. With 435 sites, the area rarely sells out. There's good hiking from this canyon, too ($20 per campsite).

Durango is a full-service town, with a bunch of chain hotel options. The **Best Western Mountain Shadows**, 3255 N. Main Ave. (☎ **800/521-5218** or 970/247- 5200), charges $58 to $129 double; the **Comfort Inn**, 2930 N. Main Ave. (☎ **800/ 532-7112** or 970/259-5373), has rates for two from $53 to $129; the **Econo Lodge**, 2002 Main Ave. (☎ **877/883-2666** or 970/ 247-4242), charges $59 to $109 for a double.

Eating in Durango

Durango's dining scene is a nice mix of tourist-friendly and authentically Western. A couple of good brewpubs will let you cover both drinking and eating bases at once.

→ **Carver Brewing Co.** ★ AMERICAN Though still a popular choice for breakfasts and baked goods, Carver has branched out into brewing. Bison bratwurst goes well with beer, as do the steaks. Healthier types can go for the San Juan Salad—mixed greens with grilled portabella, chicken, salmon, or ahi. *1022 Main Ave. ☎ 970/ 259-2545. www.carverbrewing.com. Main courses $5.25–$15. Mon–Sat 6:30am–10pm; Sun 6:30am–1pm.*

→ **Durango Diner** ★ AMERICAN For breakfast and lunch (they're closed by dinner), this local's diner is strong on regional basics. Their green chile, salsa, and enchilada sauce are popular enough that they're available in the nearby supermarkets. Breakfast specials are highlighted by the aforementioned green chile, plus eggs and hot cakes. And yes, the food is much more appetizing than the logo. *957 Main Ave. ☎ 970/247-9889. www.durangodiner.com. Most items $3–$7. No credit cards. Mon–Sat 6am–2pm; Sun 6am–1pm.*

→**Olde Tymer's Café** ★ AMERICAN For an upbeat, noisier scene, this former drugstore is a good pick. The building still has its original tin ceiling and some of its antique bottles. The menu covers bar food, though there are some good salads, including a Cobb. In warm weather, there's a nice patio out back. *1000 Main Ave. (10th St.).* ☎ *970/259-2990. Reservations not accepted. Most items $3.50–$9. Daily 11am–10pm.*

→**Steamworks Brewing Co.** ★ BREW-PUB This brewpub makes the most of its former car dealership digs. The brewing vats stand out in the middle of everything, behind glass. Bar food is hearty, like half-pound burgers, served Southwestern with green chile, pepper jack cheese, and chipotle sauce. Some dozen brewer's beers are usually on tap, including a refreshing bitter pale ale. *801 E. Second Ave. at Eighth St.* ☎ *970/259-9200. www.steamworksbrewing. com. Main courses $6.95–$18; pizza $7.95–$12 (serves 1 or 2). Daily 11am–10pm; bar open until 2am.*

ON THE ROAD TO CHACO CULTURE HISTORIC PARK

The alternative route to Moab takes you through the high desert of western New Mexico. If you follow I-25 to US 550 north, about 160 miles from Santa Fe you'll approach the town of Nageezi, NM. A left turn on C.R. 7900 (about 50 miles west of Cuba, NM, at mile 112.5) takes you down 5 miles of paved road and 16 miles of rough dirt road. (You can call ☎ **505/786-7014** for road conditions; afternoon thunderstorms are common in late summer and the roads often flood when it rains.) Should you decide to chance it over dicey roads (see "Uh Oh! Where's the Nearest Subway Stop?" p. 490), you'll be able to reach:

→**Chaco Culture National Historic Park** ★ This inhospitable canyon improbably supported a large and sophisticated society in the years A.D. 850 to 1250. For sophisticated, just check out the stone masonry, which was built in five distinctive patterns, each showing incredible craftsmanship. Pueblo ruins are spread every few miles along the canyon floor, in sight of a dramatic butte that may have functioned as an observatory. The highlight is Pueblo Bonito, a few miles down a loop road from the visitor center, with over 600 rooms rising up to four stories high. For a nice overhead view, hike up the Pueblo Alto Trail. There are 47 tent sites within the park at Gallo Campground, which charges $10 per night. Although you can get drinking water, there's no food down here, so make sure you're stocked up before trying the drive. *County Rd. 7950, Nageezi, NM 87037.* ☎ *505/786-7014. www.nps. gov/chcu. Admission $8 per vehicle, free with National Parks Pass. Visitor center open daily 8am–5pm; trails open sunrise to sunset.*

Hundreds of miles of engineered roads lead out from Chaco. The people didn't have the horse or the wheel, so the purpose of these highways is a little mysterious. It seems they were more social and ceremonial than pragmatic. Recently, a great road has been discovered that connects Casas Grandes in Chihuahua, Mexico (390 miles away!) with Chaco and then with the Salmon and Aztec ruins, near Farmington, NM. All four settlements are built along the same meridian line. The spacing of the cities has led to theories that the road functioned as a very large-scale history lesson, showing the timeline of the movement of the people.

ON THE ROAD TO SALMON/ AZTEC RUINS

If you're interested in seeing **Salmon,** it's about 35 miles up 550, just before Bloomfield, NM. Aztec, NM, is about 10 miles up from Bloomfield. I recommend these stops only if you're looking for the complete picture, as the ruins at Mesa Verde kind of blow these spots away.

You can get a window to the past at Chaco Canyon.

➜ **Salmon Ruins** Salmon shows the influences of both nearby cultures. The initial walls were built by Chacoan people between 1088 and 1090. (How great is it that we know to the year when a lot of this stuff was built?) Mesa Verde–style masonry was added in the 13th century. A trail guide will lead you through the sites, including stops by a tower kiva and a great kiva. *6131 US 64 (P.O. Box 125), Bloomfield, NM 87413.* ☎ *505/632-2013. Fax 505/632-8633. www.salmonruins.com. Admission $3. Mon–Fri 8am–5pm; Sat Sun 9am–5 pm; in winter opens at noon on Sun.*

➜ **Aztec Ruins National Monument** ★ The name of this park reflects a long-standing prejudice: Early Anglo settlers could not believe that native Americans constructed such impressive works. This pueblo, which shows a strong Chaco influence, was built centuries before the Aztecs were cutting out hearts with obsidian knives and drinking chocolate. The ruin is best known for its sunken Great Kiva, the oldest and largest ever to be reconstructed. When you're in

it, it's hard not to sense some echo of the people who worshipped here. *84 County Rd. 2900, Aztec, NM 87410-0640.* ☎ *505/334-6174, ext. 30. www.nps.gov/azru. Admission $5 per person, free with National Parks Pass. Daily 8am–5pm, until 6pm in summer.*

Sleeping in & Around Salmon

If you decide to linger at Salmon or Aztec, you can camp at the **Bloomfield KOA** (☎ **800/562-8513** or 505/632-8339; www.koa.com), on Blanco Boulevard. Mostly an RV park, they also have space for tents and cabin camping. For two people, tent sites are $24 to $26 per night, and a cabin is $38 to $42.

Camping is also available at **Navajo Lake State Park** (☎ **505/632-2278**; www.nmparks.com), which is 25 miles east of Bloomfield (take 64 to 511). It's $5 per car to get into the park, and tent sites are $8 to $10 per night.

Affordable hotel rooms can be found in nearby **Farmington,** 15 miles due west of Bloomfield. There's a **Motel 6** (1600 Bloomfield Blvd., US 64 at Southside River

Where's the Nearest subway stop?

The wild, wild West is mostly relegated to our national imagination. Those used to the overdeveloped Northeast Corridor, however, may find the infrastructure in the Four Corners a little lacking. This is a sparsely populated region with searing heat and little water, so it's not entirely a surprise that paved roads can seem more luxury than necessity. There are many opportunities to get off solid ground, and unless you're rocking your 4WD vehicle, take it easy on the back roads.

Flash floods are a particular hazard. There may not be a cloud in the sky, but desert drainage carries water immense distances at breakneck speeds. Don't try to cross washes when they're flowing, as you may get swept away, or you may soak your brakes and find yourself unable to stop. Steep ledges with deadly drop-offs offer further incentive to keep your speed down. Another thing you'll want to avoid is bottoming out your rental car on a patch of rough road, like the last little hill on the approach to Chaco Canyon, because you don't want to deal with the car stalling in the middle of the road, and coolant pouring out of your engine, and a couple of park employees graciously trying to pour water into your dinged-up radiator which just drains out into the desert, before the employees laugh politely and shrug when you ask about the nearest taxi or Dodge dealer or tow truck, all of which are many, many miles away, and then being stuck in the canyon for 6 hours without food while waiting for the car rental place in Albuquerque to send a flatbed with a new rental car to replace the one you just ruined, resulting in a bill of $3,275.16, all for hitting one lousy little bump. Trust me on this one.

Rd.; ☎ **505/326-4501;** www.motel6.com) on the edge of town with single rooms for $36 per night.

Back in Aztec, the **Enchantment Lodge** (1800 W. Aztec Blvd., Aztec, NM; ☎ **800/ 847-2194** for reservations only, or 505/ 334-6143; www.enchantmentlodge.com) is popular with passing anglers and comes authentically by its '50s retro feel. Rooms average $50 for two people.

Eating in the Salmon/Aztec Area

Cuisine in the area is anchored by **Blake's Lotaburger,** a New Mexico chain that goes back to the '50s. There are 75 locations scattered around the state, including one in Aztec (224 W. Aztec Blvd.; ☎ **505/ 334-6700;** www.lotaburger.com), and three in Farmington (2220 E. 20th St., ☎**505/ 327-2489;** 1611 W. Main St., ☎ **505/327- 2561;** and 2130 Bloomfield Hwy., ☎ **505/ 327-1141**). Five bucks covers most meals

here, which begin with breakfast burritos ($3) and singed coffee in the morning, and move on to big juicy burgers and crispy onion rings. Drive-up windows maximize convenience.

For a slightly more formal experience, downtown Farmington has a good brew-pub, the **3 Rivers Eatery & Brewhouse** (101 E. Main St.; ☎ **505/324-2187;** www. threeriversbrewery.com). The building once held the town drugstore and newspaper, and the interior is adorned with great finds discovered during the renovation. Food is ambitious for a brewpub, with mandarin orange tilapia and muffuletta sandwiches (main courses are $5–$22 at lunch and dinner). Just about everything seems to wash down well with a pint of Papa Bear's Golden Honey Ale, made with local honey.

Summer in the Desert?

A few of my friends scoffed when I told them I was off to the Southwest in July. Desert summers are indeed extreme, but the Four Corners can be a lot easier to enjoy than, say, Phoenix. My biggest issue turned out to be the cold—while the rest of the west was wilting under 117°F, I was underdressed and shivering through 55°F Santa Fe nights. Elevation is the big factor. Flagstaff, Santa Fe, and the South Rim of the Grand Canyon are all around 7,000 feet, so you can expect reasonable temperatures there. Lower stretches, like Moab, can get hellishly hot, but that doesn't mean they can't be enjoyed. The West has low humidity, so shade is a lot more useful than it is back East, and temperatures often drop significantly overnight. Mornings can also be quite cool, with the hottest part of the day coming in late afternoon and early evening, after the earth has baked all day. If you plan on heavy hiking, try to get as early a start as possible. In the afternoons, lie low in the shadows, hit the pool, or rack up some miles with the car's A.C. cranking. Evenings are also great times to explore. As an added bonus for avoiding midday, you'll catch "magic hour," when the sun's angles shade the rocks and canyons in extraordinary ways. No matter what the temperature, there are a few precautions (see box, "Uh Oh! Weren't *You* Carrying the Extra Water?" on p. 509) you must take in the desert. During lightning storms, avoid being the tallest object around (stay away from lone trees, high ridges, and cliff edges). Sunscreen and sunglasses are necessities, and wide-brimmed hats can be a big help. Hikers should carry at least a gallon of water per person per day. Water alone isn't enough: Backpacks should also be filled with energy bars, fruit, and trail mix. If you drink too much water too fast, you risk water intoxication, which can be fatal. Salty snacks and sports drinks like Gatorade can help keep electrolytes balanced.

If you choose to just drive through, Durango, CO, has more options and more charm (see above).

Welcome to Moab

Moab had a couple of early flirtations with success, as a Colorado River trading post in the early 1800s, as the uranium capital of the world in the 1950s, and as a movie set for westerns into the 1960s. By the late 1980s, however, the town was dusty and forgotten, supporting little more than a few outback outfitters. Recent years have been good to Moab, however, with the film cameras returning (this time shooting SUVs in heroic poses), along with a host of new restaurants, hotels, and bars. The expansion is there to accommodate hordes of bikers, hikers, rafters, and European sightseers, all of whom have discovered the incredible natural playground just beyond Moab's sidewalks.

Moab Nuts & Bolts

Area Code   The telephone area code in Moab is 435.

Business Hours   Banks are generally open Monday to Thursday 9am to 5pm, until 6pm on Friday. Some have Saturday morning hours. Many stores open early (7am or so), especially in summer, to accommodate people headed out early to beat the heat. You can get dinner until about 10pm, and bars are usually open until midnight.

Doctors/Hospitals The full-service **Allen Memorial Hospital,** 719 W. 400 North (☎ 435/259-7191; www.amh-moab.org), offers 24-hour emergency care.

Emergencies For police, fire, or medical emergencies, phone ☎ 911.

Libraries The **Grand County Public Library** is located at 257 East Center St. (☎ 435/259-1111; www.grand.lib.ut.us). The library is open Monday through Wednesday 9am to 8pm, Thursday and Friday 9am to 7pm, Saturday 9am to 5pm, closed Sunday. You can check your e-mail here, with a 15-minute time limit if other people are waiting. Get a login code from the checkout desk.

Liquor Laws The legal drinking age in Utah is 21; 3.2% beer can be purchased at convenience and grocery stores 7 days a week. Stronger beer, wine, and liquor are only sold at state-run liquor stores, which are closed Sundays and state holidays. Bars must stop serving booze by 1am Monday through Saturday and midnight on Sunday.

Newspapers & Magazines The *Times-Independent* is Moab's main paper, published weekly on Thursdays. Alternative newspaper *The Canyon Country Zephyr* comes out every 2 months and *The Moab Happenings* event calendar is published monthly.

Pharmacies There are three drugstores in town: **City Market Food & Pharmacy** (425 South Main St.; ☎ 435/259-5181), **Family Drug** (90 North Main St.; ☎ 435/259-7771), and **Walker Drug & General Store** (290 South Main St.; ☎ 435/259-5959).

Police For police emergencies, phone ☎ 911. The police station is at 115 West 200 South (☎ 435/259-8938). To report vandalism/looting at archaeological sites, call ☎ 800/722-3998.

Post Office The main post office is at 50 E. 100 North (☎ 800/275-8777; www. usps.com).

Radio Moab's public radio station is KUER, at 89.7FM and 106.1FM. Eclectic community radio programming can be heard on KZMU, 90.1FM and 106.7FM.

Taxes Combined city/state tax is 7.75% for retail sales and 8.75% for restaurant food and drink. Overnight accommodations are 12.25% and car rentals are 10.75%.

Time Zone Utah is on Mountain time, making it 1 hour ahead of the West Coast and 2 hours behind the East Coast. The state recognizes daylight saving time.

Transit Info Moab doesn't offer public transit.

Getting Around

Moab's population is only 5,000, although that's enough to make it the biggest town in southeast Utah. The city sprawls a little, with gas stations and fast-food joints stretching out the outskirts, but the central area is easy to navigate. Main Street runs north and south through town (it's the same Route 191 you drove on from Monticello, UT). Center Street is the major cross-intersection, running east and west. Arches National Park is just north of town, and Canyonlands is to the southwest.

Moab Highlights

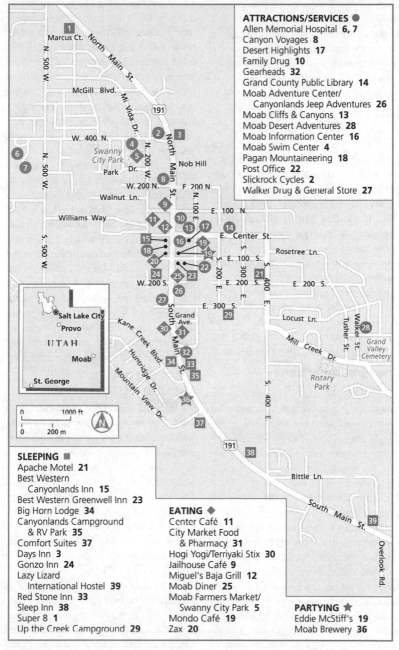

ATTRACTIONS/SERVICES ●
Allen Memorial Hospital **6, 7**
Canyon Voyages **8**
Desert Highlights **17**
Family Drug **10**
Gearheads **32**
Grand County Public Library **14**
Moab Adventure Center/
 Canyonlands Jeep Adventures **26**
Moab Cliffs & Canyons **13**
Moab Desert Adventures **28**
Moab Information Center **16**
Moab Swim Center **4**
Pagan Mountaineering **18**
Post Office **22**
Slickrock Cycles **2**
Walker Drug & General Store **27**

SLEEPING ■
Apache Motel **21**
Best Western
 Canyonlands Inn **15**
Best Western Greenwell Inn **23**
Big Horn Lodge **34**
Canyonlands Campground
 & RV Park **35**
Comfort Suites **37**
Days Inn **3**
Gonzo Inn **24**
Lazy Lizard
 International Hostel **39**
Red Stone Inn **33**
Sleep Inn **38**
Super 8 **1**
Up the Creek Campground **29**

EATING ◆
Center Café **11**
City Market Food
 & Pharmacy **31**
Hogi Yogi/Terriyaki Stix **30**
Jailhouse Café **9**
Miguel's Baja Grill **12**
Moab Diner **25**
Moab Farmers Market/
 Swanny City Park **5**
Mondo Café **19**
Zax **20**

PARTYING ★
Eddie McStiff's **19**
Moab Brewery **36**

ON FOOT

Most of the bars and restaurants are within walking distance of each other, and of several hotels. There's plenty to explore on this central stretch of Main Street. To get to the major parks, you'll need a car (or a shuttle van), however.

BY TAXI

There aren't taxis *per se* in Moab because the distances are so small. Several shuttle companies operate in town, but their bread and butter is transporting people and gear to expedition sites and rafting put-ins. Shuttles offer local taxi service mostly to keep people from getting DUIs. **Black Dog Shuttle & Expedition Support** (☎ 800/241-2591; www.rr-ss. com) charges around $10 per person, with a three-person minimum. Their river trip service, which includes shuttling your car to your put-out spot, starts around $45 per person. **Roadrunner Shuttle** (☎ 435/259-9402; www.roadrunnershuttle.com) offers a similar roster of trips, with a ride from the airport going for $13 per person.

The First Americans in Southeast Utah

New Mexico, Arizona, and Colorado have more famous sites, but the traces of the people are all over Utah as well. Hunter-gatherers were here some 10,000 years ago. The area's quartz was ideal for crafting stone weapons and tools (gouges in rocks and debris piles can still be seen all over the region).

The Ancestral Puebloans (and a second, similar group, the Fremont) began settling down in the area about 2,000 years ago, and they made a home of this harsh environment for an admirable 1,300 years. (Even longer, if you count their current tribal descendents.) On the rock walls of southeast Utah the people left a compelling, mysterious record in the form of

petroglyphs. These graceful etchings are often clan signs, in the form of associated animals. Other markings may be prehistoric maps or billboards, directing travelers to water and game. When you chance upon the markings during a long, hot hike, you may get a sense of the reassurance they may have provided ancient wayfarers. (I always feel slightly less insane knowing somebody else rambled over these badlands, and even had the time to inscribe some commemorative art.)

For a first-timer in this part of the country, it's easy to believe you've accidentally teleported to Mars. Otherworldly red and orange rock walls glow in the low light of dusk and dawn. Eroded buttes, petrified sand dunes, and narrow canyons form scenic conjunctions that rival the great cathedrals. Recreational opportunities here are pretty much unlimited. Accordingly, for this leg of the trip, I recommend letting the ancients take a backseat. Enjoy the historic sites as you come upon them, but don't miss out on the hiking, biking, and rafting that have put this area on the map.

TOP PARK STOPS AROUND MOAB

🎬 Best ✪ → **Arches National Park**
★★★ For me, going to Arches feels like walking onto the set for the Road Runner and Wile E. Coyote cartoons. Over 2,000 arches are scattered across the landscape, plus balanced rocks, spires, and sandstone fins. The park's origins lie with an underground salt bed, deposited by an evaporated sea, which provided the instability for the rocks to heave and collapse. Wind, water, and ice finished the job. You can get a lot out of the park just from behind the wheel of your car. An 18-mile road takes you past the famous sites. Parking and taking short hikes will let you see even more. Near the ruins of the Wolfe ranch, the trail to Delicate Arch has a spur path with a Ute

Southeast Utah Highlights

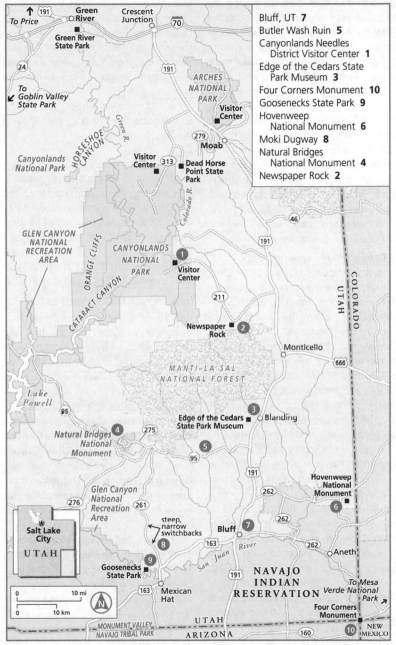

Bluff, UT **7**
Butler Wash Ruin **5**
Canyonlands Needles
    District Visitor Center **1**
Edge of the Cedars State
    Park Museum **3**
Four Corners Monument **10**
Goosenecks State Park **9**
Hovenweep
    National Monument **6**
Moki Dugway **8**
Natural Bridges
    National Monument **4**
Newspaper Rock **2**

petroglyph panel depicting a bighorn sheep hunt. (Horses in the image are a tip-off that it was made after the arrival of the Spanish.) At the park's end, the Devils Garden Trailhead leads to a series of arches, including the 306-ft.-long Landscape Arch. (A partial collapse in 1991 has it looking even more dramatically precarious.) If you want to bone up on the geography, the brand-new visitor center has the scoop in a nicely abbreviated fashion. (You'll also learn that desert pack-rats don't move for generations—some of their nests are 40,000 years old!) *Route 191, 5 miles north of Moab.* ☎ *435/719-2299. www.nps.gov/arch. Admission $10 per vehicle, free with National Parks Pass. Visitor center 8am–4:30pm, with extended hours spring through winter.*

→ **Canyonlands National Park** ★★★
Kind of like the Grand Canyon's "Mini Me," this sprawling park was created by some of the same forces (wind, rain, and the Colorado River). I love this place. It's not as over-the-top spectacular as the Grand Canyon, but the vistas are on a more human (and hence comprehensible) scale, and the remote location makes it easy to feel like you own the entire place. The park breaks up into three sections, Island in the Sky, the Maze, and Needles. Island in the Sky is the most accessible, with stunning views easily reached by paved road and short hikes. Don't miss the unoriginally-but-accurately-named Grand View Point Overlook. Also worth checking out is Upheaval Dome, a mysterious crater formed either by a volcano or a meteorite crash. To see two ancient Indian granaries, both in excellent shape, take the 2-mile roundtrip Aztec Butte trail (it's near Mesa Arch and the Willow Flat campground). The Maze is basically inaccessible unless you're up for some serious backcountry hiking, although distant views of the area are easy to enjoy. Needles deserves a visit of its own (see "On the Road to Flagstaff,

AZ," p. 505). For more ways of exploring the park, see p. 506. *Island in the Sky Visitor Center, 34 miles west of Moab, off Utah 313.* ☎ *435/719-2313. www.nps.gov/cany. Admission $10 per vehicle, or $5 per person, free with National Parks Pass. Visitor center open daily, 8am–4:30pm, extended hours from spring to fall.*

For lots more on outdoor activities in and around the parks, see "Playing Outside," below.

Sleeping

Moab has an excellent tourist infrastructure and it's easy to find a place to bed down here. The region's increasing popularity, however, has had an inflationary effect on hotel rooms. Rates are highest for the peak months of March through October, dropping almost in half for winter. Room tax of 12.25% is added to all bills.

CAMPGROUNDS/HOSTELS

Utah is a very camping-friendly state. So friendly, in fact, that you can pitch your tent for free in several places. (Note, however, that those are primitive sites and they ask you to take everything out, including, er, solid waste.) Contact the **Moab BLM Office** at ☎ **435/259-2100** for more information. Sites include **Highway 313 at Big Mesa** (12 sites) and the **Cowboy Camping Area** (4 sites); **Bride Canyon** along Gemini Bridges Road (6 sites); **Mill Canyon/Cotter Road/Dubinky Road Area** (40 sites); and **Kane Creek Crossing,** where Kane Creek Road crosses the water (28 sites).

If you're in desperate need of a shower, check out the **Moab Swim Center,** 181 W. 400 North (☎ **435/259-8226**). The local campgrounds and some bike shops will also hook you up with streaming water. The cost is about $3 to $5.

More formal camping options include the national parks:

➔ **Arches National Park Devils Garden Campground,** at the north end of the park's scenic drive, is Arches' only developed camping area. The 52 well-spaced sites are nestled among rocks, with plenty of piñon and juniper trees. March through October, the campground accepts reservations for some sites through **National Recreation Reservation Service** (☎ 877/444-6777; www.reserveusa.com), for an extra $9 booking fee. In summer, the campground fills early, often by 9am, with people nabbing the first-come, first-served sites (available starting at 7:30am), so either make reservations or get there early. Sites cost $15 per night. Nearby **Dead Horse Point State Park** has 21 sites, with covered picnic tables and flush toilets. Camping costs $15; reservations are not required, but they're accepted from March through October with a $8 processing fee (☎ 800/322-3770 or 801/322-3770; www.stateparks.utah.gov). If you don't have a reservation, expect the grounds to fill by mid-afternoon in summer.

➔ **Canyonlands** In the Island in the Sky District, **Willow Flat Campground** (elevation 6,200 ft.) has 12 sites, picnic tables, fire grates, and vault toilets; camping is $10. In Needles, **Squaw Flat Campground** has 26 first-come, first-served sites. Bathrooms, fire grates, picnic tables, tent pads, and water are available year-round. Squaw Flat often fills by 10am in peak seasons, late March to June and early September to October. If you get shut-out, you might have better luck on BLM land, 3 miles west of the park, at the **Hamburger Rock Campground** ($6 per site per night, 8 sites). On the road to Needles, you can camp across from **Newspaper Rock** (p. 506). There are eight sites, and although there is no drinking water, you can find vault toilets in the Newspaper Rock parking lot. Note that due to recent flooding,

the BLM is contemplating closing off this area to campers.

There are also several commercial campgrounds, although most are tailored toward RVers. My recommendation is:

➔ **Up the Creek Campground** ★★ This shaded, woody spot with a sweet stream seems more like a country valley than the center of residential Moab. This is good for a quiet night, with no RV generators to disturb the peace in this tent-only campground. You park and walk in to sites (there are carts to help you with gear), and there are some nice amenities (hot showers, flush toilets, and free Wi-Fi). Advance reservations are recommended for weekends and other peak times. *210 East 300 South, Moab, UT 84532.* ☎ *435/260-1888. www. moabupthecreek.com. 19 sites. $15 per site for one person, $10 each additional person up to 4 max. Closed Nov–Feb and July–Aug.*

You might also consider:

➔ **Canyonlands Campground & RV Park** This campground is surprisingly shady and quiet, given its downtown location. Open year-round, it has tent sites as well as RV hookups. Facilities include a self-service laundry, convenience store, playground, and outdoor heated pool. There are also six cabins ($39 for two, bring your own bedding). A City Market grocery store is within walking distance. *555 S. Main St., Moab, UT 84532.* ☎ *800/522-6848 or 435/259-6848. www.canyonlandsrv. com. 144 sites. Tent sites start at $19.*

➔ **Moab Valley RV & Campground** Just 2 miles from Arches National Park, this campground has nice views of the surrounding rock formations. Tenters will appreciate the soft tent surfaces, as well as trees and patches of grass. Facilities include coin-op laundry and convenience store. There are 18 cabins and cottages ($39–$66 for two, $5 per additional guest).

1773 N. U.S. 191, Moab, UT 84532. ☎ 435/259-4469. Fax 435/259-4483. www.moabvalleyrv.com. 134 sites. Tent sites $19 for 2 people, $5 per additional, 4 max. Closed Nov–Feb.

CHEAP

Most people here aren't here for a spa weekend. They came to be rugged, and don't plan on spending much time in the room. For low-frills accommodations, the chains work just fine. The **Super 8**, on the north edge of Moab at 889 N. Main St. (☎ **435/259-8868**; www.super8.com), is the town's largest lodging. **Days Inn**, 426 N. Main St. (☎ **435/259-4468**; www.daysinn.com); **Best Western Canyonlands Inn**, 16 S. Main St. (☎ **435/259-5167**); **Best Western Greenwell Inn**, 105 S. Main St. (☎ **435/259-6151**; www.bestwestern.com); **Comfort Suites**, 800 S. Main St. (☎ **435/259-5252**; www.choicehotels.com); **Motel 6**, 1089 N. Main St. (☎ **435/259-6686**; www.motel6.com); and **Sleep Inn**, 1051 S. Main St. (☎ **435/259-4655**; www.choicehotels.com), are other options. Summer rates for two in standard rooms are generally less than $130 in all of the above; zip code is 84532.

➔**Apache Motel** ★ On a quiet, residential back street, the Apache has a classic retro-motel appeal, complete with a jumbo arrowhead holding up the sign in front. John Wayne stayed here on shoots, and the dark furnishings seem little changed from that mid-1960s era. A bit of a walk to the restaurants and bars, this is a good choice if you're looking for a quiet night. Bikes are permitted in the rooms. *166 South 400 East, Moab, UT 84532. ☎ 800/228-6882 or 435/228-6882. Fax 435/259-5728. www.apachemotel.net. 33 units. Apr–Oct $60; Nov–Mar $42. Amenities: Outdoor heated pool, coffee and tea in lobby. In room: A/C, TV, dataport, fridge.*

➔**Lazy Lizard International Hostel** This hostel is clean, comfortable, and dirt-cheap. The air-conditioned main house has basic dorm rooms plus two private rooms. A separate building contains four private rooms, which look like old-school motel units. The best facilities are the cabins, constructed of real logs, with up to six beds. There's also a camping area. Everyone shares the bathhouses, and there's a phone in the main house. Guests also have use of a fully equipped kitchen; living room with TV, VCR, and movies; gas barbecue grill; and picnic tables. *1213 S. U.S. 191, Moab, UT 84532. ☎ 435/259-6057. Fax 435/259-1122. www.lazylizardhostel.com. 25 dorm beds, 10 private rooms, 8 cabins; total capacity 65 persons. $9 dorm bed; $24 private room double occupancy; from $29 cabin double occupancy; $6 per person camping space. Showers $2 for non-guests. Hostel membership not necessary. Amenities: Outdoor whirlpool tub; coin-op laundry. In room: A/C, no phone.*

DOABLE

➔**Big Horn Lodge** ★ The Big Horn earns its lodge designation with spacious rooms, knotty pine walls, and log furniture. All of the well-maintained units have two queen-size beds and bathrooms with tub/shower combos. The property is within easy walking distance of most downtown restaurants and attractions. Bikes are permitted in the rooms. *550 S. Main St., Moab, UT 84532. ☎ 800/325-6171 or 435/259-6171. Fax 435/259-6144. www.moabbighorn.com. 58 units. Apr–Oct $79–$89 double; Nov–Mar $30–$35 double. Amenities: Restaurant; outdoor heated pool; hot tub; coin-op laundry. In room: A/C, TV, dataport, fridge, coffeemaker, hair dryer, microwave.*

➔**Red Stone Inn** ★ Mountain bikers will feel welcome at this centrally located motel. The exterior has a cabin look, with the theme continuing into the pine-walled rooms. Kitchenettes with microwaves and coffee can be found in every room, which make up for their smaller size with spotless

Music, Cars & Bikes: Events in Moab

If your trip to Moab coincides with one of these events, make sure you arrange your accommodations in advance, as the town's lodgings can fill up quickly.

➜ Vintage hot rods and classic cars take over the streets of Moab for the **April Action Car Show.** Held in late April, the highlight is a Saturday night cruise down Main Street. ☎ **800/635-6622.**

➜ The **Moab Arts Festival** takes place over in Swanny City Park over Memorial Day weekend, with displays that include jewelry, pottery, sculpture, and photography. There's also music, drumming, and other entertainment. ☎ **435/259-2742;** www.moabartsfestival.org.

➜ In early to mid-September, classical, jazz, and bluegrass performers are among the musicians that come to town for the **Moab Music Festival.** A gorgeous red-rock amphitheater hosts the big show, with other venues throughout town. ☎ **435/259-7003;** www.moabmusicfest.org

➜ The **Moab Halloween Bike Fest** succeeded the Fat Tire Festival, which had a 25-year run of biking events. Unfortunately, the tours, climbs, and races didn't go off in '06. Hopefully organization will be better run in '07. Late October. ☎ **435/260-1182;** www.moabbikefest.com.

➜ A ballfield, a rec hall, and a saloon are among the venues that host the **Moab Folk Music Festival** in early November. Both bands and singer-songwriters can be heard. ☎ **435/260-2488;** www.moabfolkfestival.com.

---

maintenance. There's a covered picnic area with tables and gas barbecue grills, and a bike work stand and bike wash station. Bikes are permitted in the rooms. Guests have access to an outdoor heated pool at the sister motel across the street. *535 S. Main St., Moab, UT 84532. ☎ 800/772-1972 or 435/259-3500. Fax 435/259-2717. www. moabredstone.com. 52 units. Summer $60–$75 double; winter $30–$35 double; slightly higher in Sept and during special events. Amenities: Access to heated outdoor pool; coin-op laundry. In room: A/C, TV, dataport.*

SPLURGE

➜**Gonzo Inn** ★ This downtown hotel is funked up, with mix and match furnishings and tweaked colors. There's also a lot of attention to detail, with oversize rooms, and a balcony or patio off of each one. Although slightly more expensive, if you're traveling with a group, this might be a good choice (the one-bedroom suite has a king-size bed

plus a queen-size sleeper sofa, and can accommodate four people). A nice pool area is off to the side. Bikes are not allowed in rooms, although storage is available, as is a wash and repair station in the parking lot. *100 West 200 South, Moab, UT 84532. ☎ 800/791-4044 or 435/259-2515. Fax 435/259-6992. www. gonzoinn.com. $135 double; $179 1-bedroom suite, $299 2-bedroom 2-bath suite. Amenities: Espresso bar; complimentary continental breakfast; heated pool; hot tub; coin-op laundry. In room: Wi-Fi, wet bar, kitchenette, patio or balcony.*

Eating

Moab's dining panorama has been expanding in recent years, and despite the desert location you should have no problem tracking down good, fresh food. Moab's bars double as restaurants, should you want to cover two agendas at once.

SUPPLIES

The best grocery store in town is **City Market,** 425 S. Main St. (☎ **435/259-5181;** www.citymarket.com), open daily from 6am to 10pm. The deli makes tasty sandwiches, there's a big salad bar, and the bakery turns out fresh breads and treats.

Saturdays from mid-May through October, you can get fresh fruits and vegetables and baked goods at the **Moab Farmers Market,** Swanny City Park, 100 West 400 North (☎ **435/259-2326;** www.youthgarden project.org/farmersmarket.htm), open 8am to noon.

TAKEOUT TREATS

Franchise America is well-represented in Moab, with a Burger King, McDonalds, Subway, Pizza Hut, and Domino's Pizza among the selections. **Hogi Yogi/Teriyaki Stix** is a regional chain with a somewhat fresher and healthier take on fast food at 396 South Main St. (☎ **435/259-2656;** www.hogiyogi.com). Focaccia bread sandwiches are $5.50, gourmet salads and teriyaki bowls $5. **Mondo Café** at 59 South Main St. inside McStiff's Plaza (☎ **435/ 259-551;** www.mondocafe.com) is a coffee shop with a good selection of panini ($6.50 each) on fresh focaccia bread.

EATING OUT

Cheap

→ **Moab Diner** ★ AMERICAN/SOUTH-WESTERN The decor leaves no doubt you're in a diner and the food follows suit. Late risers can get breakfast all day here, including eggs, biscuits and gravy, and a spicy breakfast burrito. Hamburgers, sandwiches, and salads are the offerings at lunch. For dinner, there's steak, shrimp, and chicken, plus liver and onions. Dairy rules dessert, with malts, shakes, and sundaes dressing up the ice-cream offerings. The most famous item on the menu is the green chile, which is almost worthy of New Mexico. No alcoholic beverages are served.

189 S. Main St. (2 blocks south of Center St.). ☎ *435/259-4006. Main courses $4.25–$17. Daily 6am–10pm.*

→ **Zax** ★ PIZZA/PASTA Zax tends to be jumping, with carb-craving folks just off the trail taking advantage of all-you-can-eat specials (salad bar, $6.50; pizza with soup and salad, $11). Pizzas are wood-fired and tasty enough, and there's also a bunch of sandwiches, burgers, and pasta. The restaurant has a liquor license, and there's an adjacent bar. *96 S. Main St.* ☎ *435/259-6555. Main courses $8–$12. Daily 11:30am–10:30pm.*

Doable

→ **Jailhouse Café** ★ BREAKFAST This modest little structure was once the town courthouse, and the holding pen there inspired the cafe's name. The large outdoor patio out back is a pleasant spot to fuel up for the day's activity. The menu covers breakfast only, with Southwestern touches like spicy hollandaise on the eggs benedict, or chorizo and tortillas with the three-egg scramble. Don't come around after noon, however—this is strictly an A.M. scene. *101 North Main St.* ☎ *435/259-3900. Main courses $6.35–$7.95. Daily 7am–noon.*

→ **Miguel's Baja Grill** ★★ MEXICAN This narrow Mexican restaurant brings a beach shack vibe to Utah. The seafood-heavy menu seems a little out of place in these parts, but the fish tacos really deliver. There are also burritos, fajitas, and enchiladas, joined by hefty salads, including a charbroiled carne asada version. Mexican beers and strong margaritas keep things festive. *51 North Main St.* ☎ *435/259-6546. www.miguelsbajagrill.com. Main courses $9–$19. Daily 5–10pm.*

Splurge

→ **Center Cafe** CONTEMPORARY AMERICAN Not really a cafe at all, this excellent little restaurant serves innovative seafood and seasonal meat, pasta, and vegetarian dishes. Cedar-planked salmon with applewood-smoked bacon-shallot crust is tasty, as is the grilled venison rack with huckleberry and hazelnut wild rice. A smaller-portion bistro menu offers lighter fare, such as burgers or red beans and rice. The main room has white tablecloths, a wood-paneled ceiling, and a stone fireplace. In back is tranquil courtyard dining. *60 N. 100 West.* ☎ *435/259-4295. www.centercafemoab. com. Dinner reservations recommended. Main courses $14–$28. Daily 5:30pm–closing (time varies). Closed Dec to early Feb.*

Partying

Utah's Mormon population, which doesn't drink, keeps the entire state's partying rep tamped down. Moab does its share of boozing, even if the list of nightlife options is something less than encyclopedic. Bikers, hikers, tour guides, and outfitters mingle inside the Main Street bars. With the sporting lifestyle out here, you can imagine that games are central to the scene. TVs tend to be tuned to sporting events, and you shouldn't have much trouble finding a pool table for showing off your stick skills. Leave the Armani jacket and the heavy eye-shadow in the hotel room, however.

For a good overview of the complex drinking/liquor laws in Utah, see the box "Liquor Laws in Utah" (p. 452) in the "Cool in the Midwest" roadtrip.

BARS AND PUBS

➜ **Eddie McStiff's** ★ This popular brew-pub also boasts a family restaurant and a garden patio. The tavern side has a long bar, low light, and acres of wood. A dozen or so fresh-brewed beers are on tap. Mixed drinks, wine, and beer are sold in the dining room with food only; beer can be purchased with or without food in the tavern. A game room features pool tables, foosball, and shuffleboard. *57 S. Main St. (in*

McStiff's Plaza, just south of the information center). ☎ *435/259-2337. www.eddiemcstiff. com. Main courses $4.75–$18. Mon–Fri 5pm–midnight; Sat–Sun noon–midnight.*

➜ **Moab Brewery** ★ This is another half-family restaurant, half-tavern affair. On the dinner side, popular St. Louis smoked ribs join steaks, sandwiches, and salads. The huge dining room is decorated with sports equipment, including a hang glider on the ceiling. You can sample wheat ale, oatmeal stout, and another four or five brews at the separate bar. There's a gift shop, plus beer-to-go in half-gallon jugs in insulated carriers. Beer is sold in the bar; in the restaurant, diners can purchase beer, wine, or mixed drinks. *686 S. Main St.* ☎ *435/259-6333. www.themoabbrewery. com. Main courses $5.95–$17. Summer daily 11:30am–10pm; winter daily 11:30am–9pm.*

PLAYING OUTSIDE

The local land and tourist agencies come together at the **Moab Information Center,** the town's visitor center (Main and Center sts.; ☎ **800/635-6622;** www. discovermoab.com). This is a good place to get oriented, with videos and brochures like the *Moab Area Mountain Bike Trails* pamphlet. The staff is very knowledgeable and they'll help you find activities best suited to your interests, ability, and equipment. There's also a bulletin board with the latest weather conditions and campsite availability. Open daily in summer, 8am to 9pm, slightly shorter hours in spring and fall, and 9am to 5pm in winter.

BIKING

With apologies to Crested Butte, CO; Moab is the mountain biking capital of the U.S. The scenery is spectacular, the terrain is varied, and the slickrock stretches on for miles. Arches and Canyonlands have four-wheel-drive roads, which rigs and bikes share. Ninety percent of Grand County, where Moab is located, is public land, and

Bureau of Land Management and national forest areas offer tons more to explore.

A good place to start is **Slickrock Cycles,** 427 N. Main St. (☎ **800/825-9791** or 435/259-1134; www.slickrockcycles.com). They can give you loads of information, do repairs, or rent you a bike (starting at $37 for the first day, and $32 for every day after that). You can drive yourself to departure points, or you can get a shuttle service from companies like **Acme Bike Shuttle** (☎ **435/260-2534**), **Coyote Shuttle** (☎ **435/259-8656**; www.coyoteshuttle. com), and **Roadrunner Shuttle** (☎ **435/ 259-9402**; www.roadrunnershuttle.com).

Moab's most famous trail is the **Slickrock Bike Trail** ★★★, a challenging 9²/₃-mile loop that crosses a mesa of eroded apricot-colored Navajo sandstone just a few minutes from downtown Moab. Along the way, you'll have great views of the towering La Sal Mountains, the red-rock formations of Arches, a panorama of Canyonlands, and the Colorado River. The trail is open to both mountain bikes and motorcycles, and it's pretty demanding. Allow 4 to 5 hours, expect to walk your bike in some areas, and don't try it if you're a novice or seriously out of shape. There's a 2¹/₄-mile practice loop if you want to test yourself out first. To access the trailhead from the visitor information center, take Center Street east to 400 East. Turn south (right) and follow 400 East to Mill Creek Drive. Turn east (left) and follow Mill Creek Drive to Sand Flats Road, which you take 2¹/₃ miles east to the BLM's Sand Flats Recreation Area and the trailhead.

A gentler ride is the **Gemini Bridges Trail,** a 14-mile one-way trip past colorful rock formations and the namesake twin natural bridges. This relatively easy trail follows a dirt road mostly downhill, ending at US 191 just under 10 miles from the center of Moab. To save yourself that last 10 miles, this trail lends itself to arranging a shuttle ride. To get to the trailhead from the Moab Information Center, drive north along US 191 to Utah 313, turn west (left), and go about 13 miles. Allow a full day, including getting to and from the trail, and be sure not to miss the stunning Arches view from a hilltop as you approach US 191 near the end of the ride.

FOUR-WHEELING

Another major recreation draw out here is four-wheeling on the back roads. Many of these trails were put in by mining companies in the first half of the 20th century. They tend to be rough and rocky, some with inclines so steep you'll need to put your vehicle in reverse. If you're driving a low-clearance car (see "Uh Oh! Where's the Nearest Subway Stop?" p. 490), you won't get very far. Unless you're rocking an SUV you don't mind putting in peril, the only way to really enjoy four-wheeling out here is on an expedition or with a rental.

Canyonlands Jeep Adventures (inside the Moab Adventure Center, 225 South Main St.; ☎ **866/892-JEEP** or 435/259-4413; canyonlandsjeep.com) will hook you up with a stock Wrangler for $125 a day (souped-up offroad Wranglers are $145). **Cliffhanger Jeep Rental** (inside the Aarchway Inn, 1551 North Hwy. 191; ☎ **435/ 259-0889;** cliffhangerjeeprental.com) has powerful Wolverine 450 ATV 4×4s for $129 per day.

A good, challenging four-wheel-drive trail is **Poison Spider Mesa Trail** ★★, which covers 16 miles of rough road over-looking the Colorado River and Moab Valley. A short-wheelbase, high-clearance vehicle is best. Allow at least 4 hours. To reach the trail from the Moab Information Center, drive north on US 191 for about 6 miles and turn west (left) onto Utah 279. Continue another 6 miles to the dinosaur tracks sign, where the trail leaves the pavement to the right, passing over a cattle guard. From here, simply follow the main trail, which is usually obvious, up switchbacks, through a sandy canyon, and over some steep, rocky stretches. From a slickrock parking area on top, you can take a short walk to Little Arch, which isn't really so little.

An easier trip is the **Gemini Bridges Trail** (see p. 502 for the bike version). Four-by-fours usually drive the route in the opposite direction of the mountain bikers, starting at a dirt road departing from the west side of US 191, about 10 miles north of the Moab Information Center. This involves more uphill driving, which is safer for motor vehicles (and obviously bikes are more fun when they're headed downhill).

ROCK CLIMBING

If you've got your own ropes and clips and all, you'll find oodles of opportunities in the Moab area. The BLM (☎ 435/259-2100; www.blm.gov/utah/moab) is a good place to start for recommendations. The easiest desert tower in the area is **Owl Rock,** inside Arches National Park (p. 494). For crack climbing, **Indian Creek** is the place to go. It's close to Needles (p. 506) in Canyonlands.

If you've never scaled a desert tower or a cracked rock face, you may be interested in some lessons. Local companies offer instruction and guided climbs, with rates starting at $80 per person for groups of three or four. Contact **Desert Highlights,** 50 E. Center St. (P.O. Box 1342), Moab, UT 84532 (☎ 800/747-1342 or 435/259-4433; www.deserthighlights.com), **Moab Desert Adventures,** 801 Oak St., Moab, UT 84532 (☎ 877/ROK-MOAB or 435/260-2404; www.moabdesertadventures. com), or **Moab Cliffs & Canyons,** 63 E. Center St., Moab, UT 84532 (☎ 877/641-5271 or 435/259-3317; www.cliffsand canyons.com). For gear or to rent climbing

shoes, stop at **Pagan Mountaineering,** 52 S. Main St. (☎ 435/259-1117; www.pagan mountaineering.com), or **Gearheads,** 471 S. Main St. (☎ 435/259-4327).

WATERSPORTS: BOATING, CANOEING, RAFTING & MORE

Moab is the only city in Utah on the Colorado River, and it's rapidly becoming a major watersports center. You can travel down the river in a canoe, kayak, large or small rubber raft (with or without motor), or speedy, solid jet boat. Do-it-yourselfers can rent kayaks or canoes for $30 to $35 for a half day and $35 to $45 for a full day, or rafts from $50 to $90 for a half day and $60 to $130 for a full day. There are many outfitters in the area. I recommend **Canyon Voyages** (211 North Main St.; ☎ 800-733-6007 or 435-259-6007, www. canyonvoyages.com), which has reasonable prices and equipment in good condition. They'll also make sure you're outfitted with everything rangers will expect you to have.

If you're looking for a guided version, half-day river trips cost from $32 to $40 per person; full-day trips are usually $40 to $60. Multiday rafting expeditions, which include meals and camping equipment, start at about $175 per person for 2 days. Jet-boat trips, which cover a lot more river in a given amount of time, start at about $60 for a half-day trip, or $95 for a full day.

Public boat-launching ramps are opposite Lion's Park, near the intersection of US 191 and Utah 128; at Take-Out Beach, along Utah 128 about 10 miles east of its intersection with US 191; and at Hittle Bottom, also along Utah 128, about 24 miles east of its intersection with US 191. For recorded information on river flows and reservoir conditions statewide, contact the **Colorado Basin River Forecast Center** (☎ 801/539-1311; www.cbrfc.noaa.gov).

HIKING

Arches and Canyonlands are the first two places to head for great hikes, but they're really only the beginning. In addition to the rock art tours below, I recommend the **Mill Canyon Dinosaur Trail.** Southeast Utah looked very different during the Jurassic days of 150 million years ago. The region's swamps and fern-carpeted forests now reside in the Morrison Formation, in the form of fossilized remains. The Mill Canyon trail includes a sauropod leg bone, vertebrae, ribs, and toe bones. You'll also see the fossil remains of a large tree trunk. To reach the trailhead, drive about 15 miles north of Moab on U.S. 191, then turn left at an intersection just north of highway mile marker 141. Cross the railroad tracks and follow a dirt road for about 2 miles to the trailhead. Allow about 1 hour. On the south side of the canyon, you can find the remnants of an old copper mill and the Halfway Stage Station, a lunch stop in the late 1800s for stagecoach travelers.

Another local favorite is the **Negro Bill Canyon Trail,** named in a pre-P.C. era for William Granstaff, who lived in the area in the late 1800s. Allow 3 hours or so for this 4-mile round-trip easy to moderate hike. To get to the trailhead, go north from Moab on U.S. 191 to Utah 128, turn east (right), and go about 3 miles to a dirt parking area. About 2 miles up the trail, in a side canyon to the right, you'll find Morning Glory Bridge, a natural rock span of 243 feet. Watch out for the poison ivy (shiny leaves, serrated edges, clusters of three) that grows by a pool under the bridge.

For a more challenging hike, try the **Hidden Valley Trail.** A series of steep switchbacks will bring you to rock formations and a panorama of the Moab Valley. Allow about 4 hours for this 4-mile round-trip. To get to the trailhead, drive about 3 miles south of the Moab Information Center on US 191, turn west (right) onto Angel Rock Road, and go 2 blocks to Rimrock Road. Turn north (right) and follow Rimrock Road to the parking area. Many head back down after reaching a low pass with great views of huge sandstone fins (the 2-mile point), but you can extend the hike by continuing all the way to the Colorado River on a four-wheel-drive road.

(For another good hike, see the Corona Arch Trail, below.)

ALSO RECOMMENDED . . . DIY ROCK ART TOURING

A regular passenger vehicle is good enough to reach the local petroglyph sites. The earliest work you'll see is called "Archaic," with both abstract geometric designs and representational forms. The representational forms are often called Barrier Canyon–style, after the canyon that holds some stunning examples of them. (Barrier Canyon is now called Horseshoe Canyon, and as the old name suggests, it's not particularly accessible, especially from this part of Utah.) Archaic (5000 B.C. to A.D. 1) gave way to Anasazi, Fremont, and Formative styles, which overlap and last until the middle of the 13th century. The Utes took over from there. If you see a horse, you know the image is post-Spanish (1540 and later).

The **Kane Creek** trail can be picked up from Kane Creek Drive (it intersects Main near the McDonalds). Take the drive to the evocatively named Moonflower Canyon. A fenced-off panel there features geometric shapes, animal figures, and a dramatic Barrier Canyon–style figure in a stylized headdress. Another mile down the road you'll pass a panel with more animals and a trail design that might be a map of the way up Kane Springs Canyon. Keep on Kane Creek Drive, going over a cattle guard as the road turns to gravel. Keep your eye out for a couple of parking pull-outs 1.7 miles from the last panel. About 75 feet west of the road you'll see a big boulder covered in rock art. Facing the road is a trippy image called the "birthing scene." There are also snake, centipede, horse, and bear print images.

The **Courthouse Wash** rock art site is in Arches, and is a convenient stop on the way to or from the park entrance. The site is accessed from a large parking lot on 191 just north of the intersections of 128 and the river (and just south of the main Arches entrance). A half-mile hike takes you to the cliffs that overlook 191. The panel is almost 20 feet high and 50 feet long, with Archaic Barrier Canyon-style images. Bighorn sheep, shields, and a beaked bird join ghostlike humanoid forms.

Potash Road (aka Utah Scenic Byway 279) has rock art scattered across several miles. Pick up 279 from 191 south of the main Arches entrance. About 5 miles down you'll see a parking pull-out with an "Indian Writing" interpretive sign. Formative-era petroglyphs can be seen up the rock wall on the cliff side of the road.

Warriors with shields mingle among geo-metrics and a line of "paper doll cutouts." Another 200 yards down the road is another signed panel, this one of a bear hunt. Less than a mile away, a pullout will direct you to allosaurus tracks preserved in the sandstone. For a great side hike off 279, hit the nearby **Corona Arch Trail.** The 3-mile round-trip will take you a couple of hours, with mostly walking broken up by steep stretches (there are handrails and a short ladder to help you out). There are two other arches besides Corona, plus a colorful slickrock canyon and the Colorado River. You'll find a registration box and trailhead near the railroad; after crossing the tracks, follow an old roadbed onto the trail, which is marked with cairns (piles of stones).

If you keep going on 279, in a few miles you'll see signs for Jug Handle Arch. Above the parking lot to the north you'll find more rock art. The canyon widens from this point, and the road turns uphill. If you're in a suitable vehicle, you can get to Canyonlands this way, although the rough road and sheer cliff edges make it a precarious ride.

On the Road to Flagstaff, AZ

Moab, UT to Flagstaff, AZ 323 miles

On the Road **Nuts & Bolts**

....

Where to Fill Up   Moab has tons of stations, and you shouldn't have too much problem on most of this drive. Just remember to check the gas gauge before detouring too far from the main road. Natural Bridges, for example, doesn't have a station within 40 miles.

The Tolls   There are none.

The Fastest Way   191 south across the Arizona State Line to 160 west to 89 south. This should take about 7 hours, depending on how much you allow yourself to digress.

The Long Way Round There's an almost unlimited number of distractions on this route, which is one of the country's most scenic. A 64-mile detour north and west will take you to Page, AZ, and Lake Powell. A 94-mile trip south of the 160 interchange brings you to Canyon de Chelly, AZ. A 66-mile trip south and east of Bluff, UT, will bring you to the Four Corners National Monument. If you want to push even further south into Arizona, 90 miles east of Flagstaff is Holbrook, AZ, near the edge of the Petrified Forest.

Rules of the Road According to dumblaws.com, birds have the right of way on all Utah highways.

Four Corners Highlights

Maybe my will is weak, but it's hard for me to drive around this part of the country without being tempted to turn down every single side road and see where it leads. Most time budgets don't afford that kind of freedom, but if there's any one leg of the roadtrip to ignore the straight line between Point A and Point B, this is it.

We've given you some excellent options to take (and take your time) on the way to Flagstaff. In some, like Page/Lake Powell, you could certainly break your trip for a few days if you were so inclined.

Meandering along, the first potential stop is only 40 miles south of Moab on 191, where you can pick up 211 headed west. Some 35 miles down a canyon road is the Needles District of Canyonlands National Park. If you're not interested in the park, this is still a worthy turnoff for checking out **Newspaper Rock** ★★ (☎ 435/587-1500; www.blm.gov/utah/monticello), 12 miles down 211. This sandstone panel is so inscribed with petroglyphs it seems to function as a newspaper, albeit one that spans 1,300 years. Everyone from the Fremont to the Ancestral Puebloans to the Utes and Navajo put their hand to this rock, as did one J. P. Gonzales of Monticello, UT, who herded sheep in the canyon in the early 1900s. Among the widely varying images are two horned, shamanistic figures towards the center, which I find incredibly mysterious and compelling.

If you do make it to the **Needles District** ★★★ of Canyonlands, you'll find an incredible selection of hikes and four-wheel-drive roads good for both jeeps and bikes. For a spectacular view of the Colorado River, the 14-mile round-trip **Colorado River Overlook Road** is popular with all three constituencies (four-wheelers, backpackers, and mountain bikers.) Considered among the park's easiest 4×4 roads, the first part is accessible by high-clearance two-wheel-drives, although things get rougher and rockier from there. Starting at the Needles Visitor Center (open daily 9am–4:30pm, extended hours from spring to fall), the road takes you past numerous panoramic vistas to a spectacular 360-degree view of the park and the Colorado River, some 1,000 feet below.

For a glimpse of the ancients, an easy, short (.3-mile) hike will take you to the **Roadside Ruin.** There, you'll see a prehistoric granary, used by the people some 700 to 1,000 years ago to store foods like corn and nuts. If you only have time for a quick jaunt, the 2.4-mile **Slickrock Foot Trail** loop leads to colorful canyon, cliff, mesa, and striped needle viewpoints. Those with time to really explore can take the 11-mile round-trip **Elephant Hill–Druid Arch** hike. This is a 4 to 6 hour trip and is moderately difficult, with some steep drop-offs. You'll hike through narrow rock canyons, past colorful spires and pinnacles, and on to the huge Druid Arch, a dark rock

With a little stretching, you can be in four states at once.

with a resemblance to the structures at Stonehenge.

The **Confluence Overlook Trail,** an 11-mile round-trip day or overnight hike, leads to a spectacular bird's-eye view of the confluence of the Green and Colorado rivers and the 1,000-foot-deep gorges they've carved. The hike is moderately difficult, with steep drop-offs and little shade. Allow 4 to 6 hours. For those staying at Squaw Flat Campground (p. 497), the **Big Spring–Squaw Canyon Loop** is a convenient, moderately difficult 7.5-mile loop (3–4 hr.) over steep slickrock. The trail winds through cliffs and mesas, and woodlands of piñon and juniper.

If you do side-trip down 211, you can pick up a beautiful back road to the next major town (Blanding, UT). About 8 miles west of 191 (and 4 miles east of Newspaper Rock), turn south onto Jackson Spring. This paved, two-lane road winds through the **Manti-La Sal National Forest** (☎ 435/637-2817; www.fs.fed.us/r4/mantilasal), an alpine

island made all the more stunning by its contrast to the red rocks below. You'll drive past evergreen forests, aspen, cattle, alpine lakes, and distant vistas of sandstone canyons.

This leg of the trip features some of the most amazing (and trippy) road scenes in the country. Let surreal life unfold beyond your windshield while enjoying these dragged-out, desert-friendly tunes.

STAYING OVER IN BLANDING

The town of **Blanding** (☎ 435/678-3662; www.blandingutah.org) is tiny, but it has everything you'd need for an overnight. Blanding is 74 miles from Moab; the drive takes about an hour and 15 minutes.

In the middle of town there's a **Comfort Inn** (711 South Main St.; ☎ 800/622-3250 or 435/678-3271) with rooms for around $63 a night. (Don't be put off by the rusting cars and tractors circling the building like some sort of *Dawn of the Vehicular Dead* scene—the rooms are clean.) On 755 South

Playlist: Desert Drives

→ *Maria B,* **Bobby Conn,** "Llovessonngs," 1999

→ *Chameleon,* **Herbie Hancock,** Head Hunters," 1973

→ *Pink Moon,* **Nick Drake,** "Pink Moon," 1972

→ *Dr. Bernice,* **Cracker,** "Cracker," 1992

→ *Night Comes In,* **Richard & Linda Thompson,** "Pour Down Like Silver," 1975

→ *A Sailor's Life,* **Fairport Convention,** "Unhalfbricking," 1969

→ *In the Light,* **Led Zeppelin,** "Physical Graffiti," 1975

→ *Deep Red Bells,* **Neko Case,** "Blacklisted," 2002

→ *Life's Greatest Fool,* **Gene Clark,** "No Other," 1974

→ *Sleeping Pill,* **Yo La Tengo,** "May I Sing with Me," 1992

→ *Let's Dance,* **M. Ward,** "Transfiguration of Vincent," 2003

→ *Mr. E's Beautiful Blues,* **Eels,** "Daisies of the Galaxy," 2000

→ *Blonde on Blonde,* **Nada Surf,** "Let Go," 2002

→ *One More Cup of Coffee (Valley Below),* **Bob Dylan,** "Desire," 1976

Main St. you'll find a **Super 8** (☎ 435/678-3880) where rooms start at around $53.

Dining here doesn't really rise above the takeout treats level. Inside the Gofer gas station on the south end of town is a **Taco Time** (861 S. Main St.; ☎ 435/678-2306), which is a slightly fresher version of Taco Bell. Tacos are $2 to $3 each. The **Patio Drive-In** (95 N. Highway 191, on the north edge of town; ☎ 435/678-2177) has classic diner molded plastic seats and black and white tiles. Fries, a sandwich, and a drink cost $6; double cheeseburgers are a good choice here. The Patio claims to have the best shakes in the Four Corners (they're so thick a straw barely suffices), and you'll get no argument from this correspondent.

The **Blanding Visitor Center** (12 North Grayson Pkwy.; ☎ 435/678-3662) gives out a free Outdoor Adventure Gift Pack, with trail bars and the like. An on-site Pioneer Museum probably won't hold your attention for long, even if you're writing a dissertation on the early Mormon settlers of Blanding, UT. Much more interesting is:

MTV **Best ✔** →**Edge of the Cedars State Park** ★★★ This museum has a premier collection of Indian artifacts. Displays include pottery, tools, turkey-down blankets, a willow-stick loom carrying case, insect-leg and shell jewelry, and an incredible red and blue macaw-feather sash that looks fresh from the sales rack, even though it's 850 years old. You can easily fill an afternoon here, avoiding the heat. Behind the building is the ruin of a small Indian village, with a restored kiva you can climb down into. *660 West 400 North.* ☎ *435/678-2238. www.stateparks.utah. gov. Admission $3. Daily 9am–5pm; 8am–6pm in summer.*

At the south end of Blanding you can pick up route 95, which runs west through scenic and desolate terrain. This area is dotted with Indian ruins, some of which aren't much to look at. One site I love is the **Butler Wash Ruin** (follow the sign from 95), which is not exactly overrun with tourists. My signature in the visitors' log was the first for over two months, and the previous people had been a cleaning crew.

Weren't You Carrying the Extra Water?

It can be a fine line between Paradise and Hell in the desert Southwest. Pretty landscapes can take on a sinister cast very quickly if you don't make basic preparations. In Natural Bridges, I found the scenery so gorgeous I couldn't bring myself to turn around, even though I had only planned on a quick ramble. I ended up hiking right through lunch, and right through my water supply. Somehow I managed to forget that the steep downhill that began the trail would be even steeper when it was time to climb back up. By then, it was the hottest part of the day, and with each step on rebelling legs, I was increasingly parched. Stupid? *Imbecilic.* And it's not like it would have taken some amazing effort to be properly outfitted: I had trail bars and Gatorade sitting in the car, and there was free water at the visitor center. When in doubt, make the minor effort it takes to be properly prepared. You'll feel more free to enjoy the scenery if you're not stressing about how much time you have, or whether you can afford to chance the next overlook. And the downside of not having it together out here is just too extreme.

A short hike will take you to a narrow canyon with dwellings snuggled into cave walls, like a miniature Mesa Verde. If you hike up to your right along the canyon rim you'll find a small natural bridge that's a perfect spot for tranquil contemplation.

If you continue west on 95, a turnoff onto 275 (40 miles from Blanding) brings you to:

📺 ⓜⓣⓥ (Best 😊) → **Natural Bridges National Monument** ★★ There are three bridges here: one old, one young, and one mature. All three are spectacular, and easily accessed via the loop road. You can get a lot out of this park just by driving to the viewpoints, but as always, a short walk opens up even more impressive vistas. A short, steep hike down to Sipapu Bridge will take you past the ruins of an ancient granary. My favorite hike is from Kachina Bridge to another ruin, Horse Collar, a well-preserved cliff dwelling near Sipapu (5.6 miles from Kachina). The trail wends past canyon walls, with cottonwoods providing shade breaks, and the terrain seemingly constructed to an ideal human scale. Sharp eyes will find petroglyphs, and a tower in the cliff wall with its peach-colored stucco

still in showroom condition. Stock up on drinking water at the visitor center, as there is no water elsewhere in the park. *Highway 275.* ☎ *435/692-1234. www.nps.gov/ nabr. Admission $6 per car, free with National Parks Pass. Visitor center open daily 8am– 5pm.*

FROM BLANDING TO BLUFF (AND SOME GREAT PARKS)

If you don't want to backtrack to 191, you can turn south onto 261 when 275 dead ends coming out of Natural Bridges. About 92 miles down the road you'll reach 316, where a right turn brings you to **Goosenecks State Park** (☎ **435/678-2238;** www.stateparks.utah.gov). This small park is set on a rim high above the San Juan, with spectacular views of the river some 1,000 feet below. The meanders are so sharp, it takes the river more than 5 miles to progress a single linear mile. When you take in the view, you're taking in 300 million years of geologic history. The park is open round-the-clock; primitive camping is permitted at no charge.

From here, you can save a lot of miles by heading straight down toward Monument Valley (p. 511) and Arizona. If you're tempted to backtrack a little, however, there's lots to see. Either way, you'll get an adventure, as the pavement ends before 261 does. This last stretch, connecting to 163, is an old mining road called the **Moki Dugway**. It's insanely steep, with a gravel surface instead of pavement and tight turns, and distracting views of the Valley of the Gods and Monument Valley. Driving the dugway isn't hard—a regular old passenger car will take it just fine—but it is a little harrowing.

Basing Yourself in Bluff

A 24-mile ride east will take you to the dusty crossroads town of **Bluff**. About 2¹/₄ miles west of town is a camping and picnicking area called the **Sand Island Recreation Site** (☎ 435/587-1500; www.blm.gov/utah/monticello), which has an impressive petroglyph panel, with hundreds of figures spanning Archaic to cowboy times. Between the San Juan River and a high rock bluff are picnic tables, vault toilets, and graveled campsites; camping is $10 per night.

A second camping option in Bluff is the **Cadillac Ranch RV Park**, U.S. 191 (P.O. Box 157), Bluff, UT 84512 (☎ **800/538-6195** or 435/672-2262; www.bluffutah.org/cadillac ranch), a down-home place on the east side of town with sites around a small fishing lake (no license needed and no extra charge for fishing). There are 10 tent sites plus restrooms with showers. The campground is open year-round, but water is turned off in winter. Cost per site is $16 for tents and $18 to $19 for RVs; paddle boats can be rented at $4 per half-hour.

For a night's rest with a roof, I recommend the 28-unit **Recapture Lodge** ★, US 191 (P.O. Box 309), Bluff, UT 84512-0309 (☎ **435/672-2281**; www.recapturelodge.com). On the main street near the town center, the lodge has attractive Western fixings and a nature trail that follows the

San Juan River along the back of the property. Rates for two range from $46 to $56 in summer and $38 to $44 the rest of the year.

For food, the **Cottonwood Steakhouse** ★★, on US 191 on the west side of town (☎ 435/672-2282), is an Old West–style restaurant specializing in beef and buffalo. In warm weather, diners can sit at picnic tables outside under cottonwood trees. Dinners are $11 to $22; the restaurant is open daily from 5:30pm, March through October. Lighter fare is served at the **Twin Rocks Cafe** ★, on US 191 on the east end of town (☎ **435/672-2341**; www.twinrocks.com). The most popular items are the regional dishes—the sheepherder's sandwich, Navajo taco, and beef stew with Navajo fry bread. Lunch and dinner entrees are $6.50 to $17. The cafe is open daily from 7am to 9pm in summer, with slightly reduced hours in winter. Indian arts and crafts are sold next door at Twin Rocks Trading Post.

A 35-mile ride from Bluff (north on 191 and east on 262) will get you to **Hovenweep National Monument** ★★ (☎ **970/562-4282**; www.nps.gov/hove), near the Colorado–Utah border. Although small (dwarfed by Mesa Verde, for example), this canyon rim settlement is still very striking. A 2-mile loop trail winds past 20-foot-tall sandstone towers, in a mix of square, oval, circular, and D-shaped constructions. The buildings are something of a mystery, with archaeologists theorizing uses as diverse as guard towers, celestial observatories, ceremonial structures, water towers, or granaries. In addition to the towers, there are the remains of cliff dwellings and a kiva, petroglyphs, and a reconstructed dam. Entry is $6 per vehicle, free with National Parks Pass. The visitor center has exhibits, restrooms, and drinking water, and is open daily from 8am to 5pm. Trails are open sunrise to sunset.

A 30-site campground is $10 per night. Reservations are not accepted, but this is a remote monument, and even during the peak times you shouldn't have a problem getting a space.

Another 40 miles on the odometer will take you to the **Four Corners Monument** (☎ 928/871-6647; www.navajonation parks.org), the only place in the U.S. where four states meet. The vibe here is of a shopping mall in the center of a post-apocalyptic gravel quarry. Indian crafts are arrayed along the perimeter, with badlands stretching off in the distance in every direction. In the middle of the site is a two-person-at-a-time platform, where you can photograph companions performing the Twister game of touching New Mexico, Utah, Arizona, and Colorado at one moment. Concession stands sell Navajo fry bread ($3), Navajo tacos ($5), and Navajo burgers ($6). There really isn't much here beyond the one photo op, but it's a pretty great photo op. The monument is off 597, which can be picked up from 160. From Hovenweep, take 162 until it turns into 41, and then head west on 160. Open daily from 7am to 8pm from March through August, 8am to 5pm the rest of the year. Admission is $3 per person.

MOVING ON TO CANYON DE CHELLY & MONUMENT VALLEY

If you get back on 160 headed west, 34 miles of driving will take you to the exit for 191. A drive of 65 miles south will bring you to **Canyon de Chelly National Monument** (☎ 928/674-5500; www.nps.gov/cach). Twin rim roads take you past stunning vistas of a canyon that's been lived in for almost 5,000 years. Unlike most of the other parks in the region, this one is very much still active, with Navajo homes spread across the terrain. The 15-mile North Rim Drive overlooks Canyon del Muerto, while the 16-mile South Rim Drive overlooks Canyon de Chelly. With stops, the drive along either rim road can easily take 2 to 3 hours. If you have time for only one, make it the South Rim Drive, which accesses the **White House Ruins Trail** ★★, the only way to descend into the canyon without an Indian guide or a ranger. From the White House Overlook you can see the 80-room White House Ruins (inhabited from 1040–1275), which are among the largest in the canyon. The trail descends 600 feet to the canyon floor and crosses Chinle Wash to provide an up-close viewing. The 2.5-mile round-trip hike takes about 2 hours; be sure to carry water. At the very end of the South Rim Drive is the monument's most spectacular view, the Spider Rock Overlook, which has a clear sightline to a slender 800-foot tall twin-tower pinnacle.

Another way to see Canyon de Chelly and nearby Canyon del Muerto is on what locals call shake-and-bake tours ★, via six-wheel-drive truck. The trucks operate out of **Thunderbird Lodge** (☎ 800/679-2473 or 928/674-5841; www.tbirdlodge.com), making stops for photographs, ruins, Navajo farms, and rock art. Half-day trips cost around $40 per person, $65 for full day.

The Canyon de Chelly visitor center is open daily, May through September from 8am to 6pm (MST) and October through April from 8am to 5pm. The monument itself is open daily from sunrise to sunset.

From here, you can go back up 191 and take 160 west to 163 north. This iconic stretch of land is officially known as the:

➜ **Monument Valley Navajo Tribal Park** ★★ Even if this is your first time here, you're probably already well acquainted with the landscape. Starting with John Ford and John Wayne's *Stagecoach* and continuing to any modern advertisement that calls for the epic West,

Monument Valley has long imprinted itself on pop culture and the national imagination. In real life, the spacing of the towers, arches, buttes, cliffs, and mesas is, if anything, even more dramatic. The area is easy to see by car, with a 17-mile self-guided dirt road looping you past The Mittens, Elephant and Camel Buttes, Totem Pole, and The Thumb. The road is rough, but not as bad as that first half-mile. Allow about 2 hours.

To get out on the land, you'll need an official tour guide. **Goulding's** (☎ 435/727-3231; www.gouldings.com) charges $35 for a 2¹/₂-hour tour; $45 for a 3¹/₂-hour tour; and $70 for a full-day tour that includes lunch. Prices include the park admission fee. If you want a real up-close experience of the park, this is the way to go. Ruins, petroglyphs, arches, and movie set locations are among the highlights.

The visitor center/museum is located about 4 miles east of U.S. 163 on the Monument Valley access road. It contains a viewing deck, exhibits, and a restaurant that serves Navajo and American dishes all day. ☎ 435/727-5870. www.navajonation parks.org. Admission $5 per person. Daily Apr–Sept 7am–7pm; Oct–Mar 8am–5pm.

Welcome to Lake Powell & Glen Canyon, AZ

Back south on 163, you'll reach 160 at Kayenta, AZ. Thirty-two miles southwest on 160 will bring you to the exit for 98, which runs 64 miles northwest on the way to **Page,** AZ. Page is at the south end of Glen Canyon, which began filling up with Colorado River water after the completion of the Glen Canyon Dam in 1963. The man-made lake it created, Lake Powell, is the country's second largest, with more shoreline than the entire west coast of the U.S. The town of Page is only a couple of years older than Lake Powell. The place is small and friendly, with an economy heavily

structured around the two million visitors who come to play on the lake each year.

There's a lot to do here; we go into a fair amount of detail below. There's also a good selection of places to stay and eat if you're inclined to hang around for a few days.

SLEEPING
Campgrounds
There are campgrounds at **Wahweap** (☎ 928/645-2433) and **Lees Ferry** (☎ 928/355-2319) in Arizona (p. 516), and at Bullfrog, Hite, and Halls Crossing in Utah. Some scrubby trees provide a bit of shade at the Wahweap site, but the wind and sun make this a rather bleak spot in summer. Nevertheless, because of the lake's popularity, these campgrounds stay packed for much of the year. Wahweap charges $18 per night and Lees Ferry charges $10; reservations are not accepted.

Hotels & Motels
➔ **Best Western Arizonainn** Perched right at the edge of the mesa on which Page is built, this modern motel has a fine view across miles of desert, as do half of the guest rooms. The hotel's pool has a 100-mile view. 716 Rimview Dr. (P.O. Box 250), Page, AZ 86040. ☎ 800/826-2718 or 928/645-2466. Fax 928/645-2053. www.bestwestern.com. 103 units. Apr–June $49–$89 double; July to mid-Oct $79–$109 double; mid-Oct to Mar $44–$54 double. Rates include continental breakfast. Amenities: Small outdoor pool; exercise room; Jacuzzi; coin-op laundry. In room: A/C, TV, dataport, coffeemaker, hair dryer, iron.

➔ **Days Inn and Suites Lake Powell** ★ One of the newer hotels in town, the Days Inn is close to the lake, with nice views of the Vermillion Cliffs. The regular spaces are roomy enough, and the suites are very nice-sized. Prices fluctuate, with winter rates being almost 50% of the June through October peak prices. 961 N. Highway 89

(P.O. Box 3910), Page, AZ 86040. ☎ 877/525-3769 or 928/645-2800. Fax 928/645-2604. www.daysinn.net. 82 units. Apr–May $79–$89 double; June–Oct $89–$99 double; Nov–Dec $59–$69 double; Jan–Mar $49–$59 double. Rates include continental breakfast. Amenities: Outdoor pool. In room: A/C, TV, dataport, coffeemaker, hair dryer, iron.

EATING

➜ **The Dam Bar & Grille** ★ AMERICANA Warehouse-size space holds this dam-themed restaurant. Cement walls, hard hats, and a big bolt-shooting transformer add to the atmosphere. The menu covers sandwich, pasta, and steak standards, with an excellent rotisserie chicken. The lounge area is a popular local hang out, and next door is the affiliated Gunsmoke Saloon, a barbecue joint slash nightclub. 644 N. Navajo Dr. ☎ 928/645-2161. www.damplaza.com. Reservations recommended in summer. Main courses $7–$22. Mid-May to Oct Mon–Sat 11:30am–10pm, Sun 4–10pm; Nov to mid-May Sun–Thurs 4–9pm, Fri–Sat 4–10pm.

➜ **Fiesta Mexicana** ★ MEXICAN This outpost of a regional chain is a big-time local favorite. The decor is garish in a festive way, with Mexican blankets serving as curtains. The kitchen does well with straight-ahead items like burritos and enchiladas. Margaritas are the best in town. Watch out, however, as they're served in absurdly oversize glasses. 125 South Lake Powell Blvd. ☎ 928/645-4082. Main courses $8–$12. Daily 11am–9pm.

THE TOP ATTRACTIONS

➜ **Glen Canyon National Recreation Area** ★★ Before the canyon was flooded, Glen Canyon was one of the most remote places in America. It was also one of the most scenic. A bitter battle was fought to forestall the dam, but in the end the needs of recreation, water supply, and hydroelectric power won out. Although some spectacular places were submerged, this is still an almost unimaginably beautiful spot. Think of Canyonlands or the Grand Canyon, only with a ginormous lake tying everything together. There are 96 major side canyons, which get so narrow in some places you can't even turn a motorboat around. Hiking the ridges provides great lake views, but the best way to tour here is by water. Houseboats are a very popular option. Equipped like floating hotel suites, they come with showers and kitchens, and can sleep from 8 to 12 people.

Antelope Point Marina (☎ 928/608-4499; www.antelopepointlakepowell.com) rents big, new boats for around $6,000 to $7,000 a week (which isn't as pricey as it sounds; if you've got 10 people, it works out to $85–$100 a day, which is not out of line for a hotel room with an amazing water view, although it doesn't count your gas costs). Antelope Point is the lake's newest marina, with a brand-new restaurant and lounge built on the largest slab of floating concrete in the U.S.

The **Wahweap Marina** (☎ 888/486-4665 or 928/645-2433; www.lakepowell.com) also rents houseboats, as well as accompanying motorboats and water skis. Rates in summer range from about $138 to $611 per day, depending on the type of craft. Weekly rates are also available.

If you're looking for more self-propelled touring and less internal combustion, sea kayaks are a good option. Afternoon winds can make paddling difficult, but mornings are often calm. A kayak will also allow you to explore canyons too narrow for powerboats. Rentals are available at **Twin Finn Diving/Lake Powell Kayak Tours,** 811 Vista Ave. (☎ 928/645-3114), $45 to $55 per day for sea kayaks, with sit-on-top kayaks $35 to $45 per day. All-day tours are $95 to $105. Multiday kayak tours are operated by **Hidden Canyon Kayak** (☎ 800/343-3121 or 928/645-8866; www.diamondriver.

By The Time I Get to Arizona . . .

Timekeeping gets a little screwy in the Four Corners area. The culprit is Arizona, which doesn't switch to Daylight Saving Time. During daylight saving (Mid-Mar to late Nov), the time in Arizona and California is the same, and New Mexico and Utah are 1 hour ahead. The rest of the year, Arizona follows Mountain Standard Time, making it 1 hour ahead of California and the same as Utah and New Mexico. But wait, there's more!

Within the state of Arizona, the Navajo Reservation *does* switch to daylight saving time. So on the rez, everything synchs with Utah and New Mexico. However, the Hopi Reservation, which is completely surrounded by the Navajo Reservation, does *not* switch to daylight saving, meaning they're in synch with Arizona time year-round. And although Utah follows Daylight Saving Time, Dangling Rope Marina on Lake Powell, in Utah, runs on Arizona time and does not recognize daylight saving. I was told the basic reason for all this mess is that Arizonians love their drive-in movies, and daylight saving makes them wait too long for the flicks to start. (A more plausible explanation is that transferring an extra hour of daylight to the more active part of the day puts more strain on cooling systems, which already have plenty to do during the sweltering desert summers.)

com/kayak), which charges $600 to $850 for 4- to 6-day trips.

Wahweap Marina also offers tours of the lake on larger boats. The **Antelope Canyon Cruise** ($29) is an hour and a half jaunt to the red walls of the lake's southeast corner.

To see more of the lake, you might consider the full-day tour to **Rainbow Bridge National Monument** ★★★ (☎ 928/608-6404; www.nps.gov/rabr). About 40 miles from Wahweap Marina and Glen Canyon Dam, in a narrow side canyon, Rainbow Bridge is the world's largest natural bridge—the U.S. Capitol dome would fit under the 290-foot high span. When you see the bridge's unlikely symmetry (the shape really is a little like a rainbow turned to stone), you may get a glimpse of why the Navajo consider it sacred. A short trail from the boat dock leads to gorgeous views, although out of respect for Indian beliefs, you're asked not to get too close to the bridge. (Don't miss the big three-toed dinosaur tracks just on your right at the trail's end.)

Lake Powell Resorts and Marinas (☎ 888/486-4665 or 928/645-2433; www.lakepowell.com) offers full-day tours ($100) that include a box lunch and many hours of glorious lake vistas. Unfortunately, to see the bridge without the help of a boat, you'll have to walk 14 miles (each way) through Navajo land. *Wahweap south entrance, 3 miles north of Page on 89. Antelope Point Marina, 3 miles east of Page on 98, turn north on BIA Hwy N22B. Glen Canyon National Recreation Area. ☎ 928/608-6404. www.nps.gov/glca. Admission $15 per vehicle, free with National Parks Pass. Park open daily.*

What Else to See & Do in Page

FREE →**Glen Canyon Dam, Carl Hayden Visitor Center** ★ This impressive engineering feat involved the pouring of almost 5 million cubic yards of concrete. The dam generates hydroelectric power and stores essential water for the region. The visitor center has an amazingly intricate diorama of the canyon and dramatic views of the dam. To see more, catch a 45-minute tour (13 a day are given during the summer season, fewer at other times of the year).

Note that security precautions require that you pass through a metal detector in order to visit. And pretty much any bag is prohibited (purses, backpacks, camera cases, binocular cases all have to be left in your car). Wallets, cameras, and binoculars are allowed. *Beside the dam on US 89 just north of Page.* ☎ *928/608-6404. www.usbr.gov. Visitor center open daily from 8am to 6pm between Memorial Day weekend and Labor Day weekend, and from 8am to 5pm other months.*

→ **Antelope Canyon** ★★ Photo surveys of Arizona almost always include a shot of eroded sandstone corkscrewing up narrow walls and spotlighted by dramatic shafts of light. These are called "slot canyons," and one of the most prominent is right outside of Page. Antelope Canyon has an upper and a lower part. At both spots you'll find Navajo guides collecting park entry permits ($6 per person) and fees for guide services ($15). At Upper Antelope Canyon, the guide will drive you from the highway to the canyon and then pick you up again after your hike. At Lower Antelope Canyon, the guide will probably just show you the entrance. A more detailed 1½-hour tour is available from **Antelope Canyon Adventures** (☎ 866/ 645-5501 or 928/645-5501; www.jeeptour. com), or **Antelope Canyon Tours** (☎ 866/645-9102 or 928/645-9102; www. antelopecanyon.com), both of which charge $20 (plus Navajo permit fee) for a basic tour. Photographic tours cost between $35 and $62. *2½ miles outside Page off Ariz. 98 at milepost 299.* ☎ *928/698-3384. www. navajotours.com. May–Oct upper canyon open daily 8am–5pm, lower canyon 8am–4pm; Nov–Apr hours vary and closures are common.*

If you want to enjoy a slot canyon that isn't packed ass to gills with shutterbugs, consider taking a backcountry tour with **Slot Canyon Hummer Adventures** (☎ 928/645-2266; www.slotcanyon hummeradventures.com). Their big yellow Hummer four-wheels it through reservation land to a scenic, private canyon. A 3-hour tour with ample shooting time costs $69 per person.

MORE PLAYING OUTSIDE
Watersports
Besides the Lake Powell boating options listed above, you can also check out a small section of the Colorado River not tamed by the dam. Float trips from Glen Canyon Dam to historic Lees Ferry are operated by **Wilderness River Adventures** (☎ 800/ 528-6154 or 928/645-3279; www.lake powell.com) between March and October. Half-day trips cost $62; try to reserve at least 2 weeks in advance.

If you're just looking for a good place for a **swim** near Lake Powell Resort, take the Coves Loop just west of the marina. Of the three coves, the third one, which has a sandy beach, is the best. The Chains area, another good place to jump off the rocks and otherwise lounge by the lake, is outside Page down a rough dirt road just before you reach Glen Canyon Dam.

The view beneath Lake Powell is as scenic as the view above; to explore underwater, contact **Twin Finn Diving Center,** 811 Vista Ave. (☎ 928/645-3114; www.twin finn.com), which charges $45 a day for scuba gear.

Hiking
Page's **Rimview Trail** runs along the edge of Manson Mesa, which holds Page, and has views of Lake Powell and the entire red-rock country. The loop trail is 8 miles long, but if you want to do a shorter hike, try the stretch heading east (clockwise) from the trailhead. This trail is also great for mountain biking. Head north on North Navajo Drive from downtown Page and you'll find the trailhead at the end.

More good hiking can be found 40 miles away at Lees Ferry. Lees Ferry is named for John D. Lee, who started a service here in 1871. It was the only crossing for many miles, and travelers relied on it until the Navajo Bridge (highway 89A) was constructed in 1928. Of the day hikes in the area, the 2-mile **Cathedral Wash Trail** is the most interesting, following a dry wash through a narrow canyon with unusual rock formations. The trailhead is at the second turnout after turning off US 89A. Be aware that this wash is subject to flash floods.

Lees Ferry is also the southern trailhead for famed **Paria Canyon** ★, a favorite of canyoneering backpackers. Forty-five miles long, the trail follows the meandering route of a narrow slot canyon for much of its length. Most hikers start from the northern trailhead, which is in Utah on US 89. For more information on hiking in Paria Canyon, contact the **Arizona Strip Interpretive Association/Interagency Visitor Center,** 345 E. Riverside Dr., St. George, UT 84770 (☎ **435/688-3246;** www.az.blm.gov/asfo/asia.htm).

Closer to town, you can enjoy an amazing viewpoint with only minimal effort. **Horseshoe Bend** is a huge loop of the meandering Colorado River. The trailhead (5 miles south of the Carl Hayden Visitor Center on U.S. 89, just south of milepost 545) leads three-quarters of a mile to the edge of a cliff, where you look down at a dramatic scene hundreds of feet below. This is another of Page's great photo ops.

Welcome to Flagstaff

The mental image I had of Flagstaff was of a small desert town, caked in dust, with a main street ripe for gunfights. Maybe I was thinking of Tombstone. Turns out, Flagstaff is a sophisticated place, with well-preserved historic blocks, the continent's largest ponderosa pine forest, and enough wherewithal

to support two separate sushi restaurants. It's also one of those cities where the residents feel like they're really onto something. At 7,000 feet, they have four real seasons (unlike the rest of the state), easy access to skiing and hiking, and Northern Arizona University, whose students help keep things lively.

The Grand Canyon, Wupatki, and Sunset Crater are all on the way to Flagstaff. If you want to stop off at one of those parks next, see p. 521. Otherwise, Flagstaff makes an excellent base camp for touring Northern Arizona.

GETTING AROUND

Flagstaff's small population (60,000 within city limits) makes the town easy to get around. Downtown Flagstaff is just north of I-40. Milton Road, which at its southern end becomes I-17 to Phoenix, leads past Northern Arizona University on its way into downtown and becomes Route 66, which runs parallel to the railroad tracks. San Francisco Street is downtown's main street. Humphreys Street leads north out of town toward the San Francisco Peaks and the South Rim of the Grand Canyon.

On Foot

The historic district downtown is compact and easily walkable. It's bounded by Route 66, San Francisco Street, Aspen Avenue, and Birch Avenue. Hotels, shops, restaurants, and bars are all clustered here.

By Bus & Taxi

Call **A Friendly Cab** (☎ **928/774-4444;** www.afriendlycab.com) if you need a taxi. A pickup is $3, each mile an additional $1.30. **Mountain Line Transit** (☎ **928/779-6624;** www.mountainline.az.gov) provides public bus transit around the city 7 days a week; the fare is $1, $3 for an all-day pass.

Flagstaff Highlights

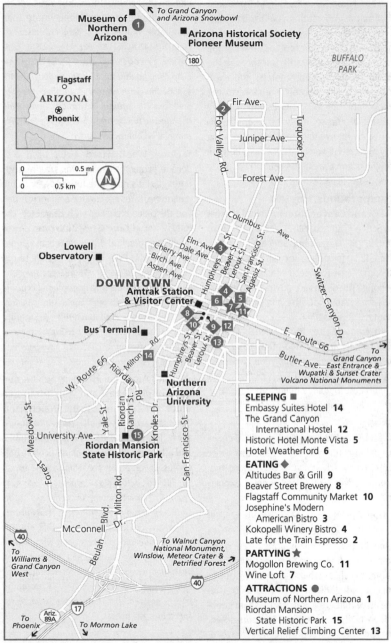

Museum of Northern Arizona

↖ To Grand Canyon and Arizona Snowbowl

■ Arizona Historical Society Pioneer Museum

BUFFALO PARK

180

Flagstaff
ARIZONA
⊛ Phoenix

0   0.5 mi
0   0.5 km
N

Fir Ave.

Juniper Ave.

Turquoise Dr.

Fort Valley Rd.

Forest Ave.

Columbus Ave.

Lowell Observatory ■

Elm Ave.
Dale Ave.
Cherry Ave.
Birch Ave.
Aspen Ave.

Humphreys St.
Beaver St.
Leroux St.
San Francisco St.
Agassiz St.

Switzer Canyon Dr.

DOWNTOWN
Amtrak Station & Visitor Center

Bus Terminal ■

Humphreys St.
Beaver St.
Leroux St.

E. Route 66

To Grand Canyon East Entrance & Wupatki & Sunset Crater Volcano National Monuments

Butler Ave.

W. Route 66

Riordan Rd.

Milton Rd.

Northern Arizona University

Meadows St.

Forest

Yale St.

Riordan Ranch St.

Riordan Rd.

Knoles Dr.

San Francisco St.

University Ave.

Riordan Mansion State Historic Park

McConnell

Beulah Blvd.

Milton Rd.

To Walnut Canyon National Monument, Winslow, Meteor Crater & Petrified Forest →

40

17

Ariz. 89A

To Phoenix

To Mormon Lake

40

To Williams & Grand Canyon West

SLEEPING ■
Embassy Suites Hotel **14**
The Grand Canyon
    International Hostel **12**
Historic Hotel Monte Vista **5**
Hotel Weatherford **6**

EATING ◆
Altitudes Bar & Grill **9**
Beaver Street Brewery **8**
Flagstaff Community Market **10**
Josephine's Modern
    American Bistro **3**
Kokopelli Winery Bistro **4**
Late for the Train Espresso **2**

PARTYING ★
Mogollon Brewing Co. **11**
Wine Loft **7**

ATTRACTIONS ●
Museum of Northern Arizona **1**
Riordan Mansion
    State Historic Park **15**
Vertical Relief Climbing Center **13**

SLEEPING

Like Moab and Santa Fe, Flagstaff is tourist destination enough that you'll spend a little more for accommodations. Flagstaff made its fortune as a railroad town. Some 80 to 100 trains a day still pass through the center of town. Many motels, and even some of the nicer hotels, are close to the tracks, and the racket does affect some guests. Of course, if you've been conditioned by many years of sleeping in a big city apartment, you may consider clanging freight trains a welcome relief from more serious noise issues.

Campgrounds/Hostels

The **Grand Canyon International Hostel** (19 S. San Francisco St.; ☎ **888/442-2696** or 928/779-9421; www.grandcanyonhostel. com) is a friendly spot with dormitory sleeping (4 people per room) and private doubles. The dorms are $16 to $18 and doubles are $32 to $39; both come with complimentary breakfast.

Mormon Lake RV Park & Campground (Main St., Mormon Lake, AZ; ☎ **928/354-2227;** www.mormonlakelodge. com) has plenty of Old West charm about half an hour outside of Flagstaff. Tent sites are $10 and pine cabins start at $45.

Cheap

Flagstaff has the normal allotment of chain hotels, including three Super 8s, three Motel 6s (which adds up to 42!), and two Econo Lodges. For a less generic experience, consider:

➔ **Historic Hotel Monte Vista** ★★ Originally opened in 1927, the Monte Vista is packed with enough unrestored retro flair you'll find it easy to believe Clark Gable, Carole Lombard, and Gary Cooper once bedded down here. Some of the guests of that era are still around, in spectral form. The place is a little run-down, but low rates attract a fun, young crowd.

An excellent Thai restaurant and a nightclub on the ground floor allow you to party it up without worrying about more than a stumble home. *100 N. San Francisco St., Flagstaff, AZ 86001.* ☎ *800/545-3068 or 928/ 779-6971. Fax 928/779-2904. www.hotelmonte vista.com. 50 units, 4 with shared bathrooms. $65 double with shared bathroom; $78–$95 double with private bathroom. Amenities: Restaurant; lounge; massage; coin-op laundry. In room: TV, hair dryer.*

➔ **Hotel Weatherford** ★ It's been a 2-decade project restoring this striking 1897 hotel, and it's not quite finished yet. In the meantime, rates are low for a historic hotel, and the place is packed with character. The fully restored **Zane Grey Ballroom** is now an elegant bar, and downstairs is the popular **Charly's Pub & Grill.** *23 N. Leroux St., Flagstaff, AZ 86001.* ☎ *928/779-1919. Fax 928/773-8951. www.weatherfordhotel.com. 10 units, 3 with shared bathrooms. $60–$65 double; $95–$105 suite. Amenities: Restaurant (American/Southwestern); 2 lounges. In room: No phone.*

Doable

➔ **Little America Hotel** ★ Set on 500 acres of pine forest and with a trail that winds for 2 miles through the property, this hotel is a great, quiet alternative to downtown. The decor is dated but comfortable, and all rooms come with small private balconies. *2515 E. Butler Ave., Flagstaff, AZ 86004.* ☎ *800/865-1410 or 928/779-7900. Fax 928/ 779-7983. www.littleamerica.com. 247 units. $89–$129 double. Amenities: 3 restaurants (American, Continental, deli); lounge; outdoor pool; croquet court; exercise room; Jacuzzi; children's playground; concierge; car-rental desk; business center; room service; massage; coin-op laundry. In room: A/C, TV, dataport, fridge, coffeemaker, hair dryer, iron, high-speed Internet access.*

Splurge

➔ **Arizona Sled Dog Inn** ★★ Nestled into a forest south of Flagstaff, don't be surprised if you wake to elk grazing right outside your window. Guest rooms are modern lodge rustic, comfortable and uncluttered. The hot tub out back is always welcome, especially at the end of an active day. If you're wondering about the name, there's an adjacent kennel full of Siberian huskies. *10155 Mountainaire Rd., Flagstaff, AZ 86001.* ☎ *800/754-0664 or 928/525-6212. www.sleddoginn.com. 10 units. $105–$149 double; $170–$225 suite. Rates include full breakfast. Amenities: Jacuzzi; sauna; bike rentals. In room: A/C, no phone.*

➔ **Embassy Suites Hotel** ★ A little on the corporate side, this hotel does offer big, elegant suites. Separate living rooms afford plenty of space to spread out. Although in hearing range of the trains, this is a comfortable place to stay. Friendly touches include a complimentary cocktail hour and full made-to-order breakfast. *706 South Milton Rd., Flagstaff, AZ 86001.* ☎ *800/ 362-2779 or 928/774-4333. www.flagstaff. embassysuites.com. 119 units. $99–$159 double. Rates include full breakfast. Amenities: Seasonal pool; spa; exercise room; laundry. In room: A/C, Wi-Fi, microwave, fridge, coffeemaker.*

EATING

As a college town, it's not hard to find cheap food in Flagstaff. It's also surprisingly easy to find sophisticated food, with Asian restaurants and a couple of high-end fine dining options. For simpler meals, the local brewpubs are a good alternative. In addition to Arizona-made beer, you'll also find wine and vodka, in keeping with that independent, DIY streak that runs through Westerners.

Takeout Treats

Late for the Train Espresso, 1800 N. Fort Valley Rd. (☎ **928/773-0308;** www. lateforthetrain.com), on US 180 as you drive north out of town, will get you fueled up for a run to the Grand Canyon. In addition to coffees from around the world, you can get good, fresh sandwiches here ($4.75–$5.75). A second location is at 107 N. San Francisco St. (☎ **928/779-5975**).

From mid-June to early October, you can get fresh fruits, vegetables, and baked goods from local farmers at the **Flagstaff Community Market** (in a lot off West Phoenix Ave., just east of Milton Rd./Route 66, just west of South Beaver St.; ☎ 928/ 774-7781; www.flagstaffmarket.com). The market is open Sunday mornings only, from 8am to noon.

Cheap

➔ **Beaver Street Brewery** ★ BURGERS/ PIZZA This large microbrewery does great pizzas and salads, in addition to the stellar homemade brews. The Beaver Street pizza is packed with flavor courtesy of sun-dried tomatoes, basil, pesto, and goat cheese. It is often packed with college students, and a woodstove provides plenty of atmosphere if you have to wait. The brewery also operates the adjacent **Beaver Street Brews and Cues,** 3 S. Beaver St., which has pool tables and a 120-year-old mahogany bar. *11 S. Beaver St.* ☎ *928/779-0079. www.beaverstreetbrewery.com. Main courses $8–$11. Daily 11:30am–10pm (limited bar menu until midnight).*

Doable

➔ **Altitudes Bar & Grill** ★★ A ski lodge theme (there's a special "Shot Ski" for group slammers) reinforces the laid-back vibe at this Flagstaff newcomer. The menu focuses on bar food, with tasty 1/2-lb. burgers, chilies, and wraps. Hummus and fresh salads cover the healthier end of the spectrum. The bar makes a virtue of its proximity to the railroad, offering $2 shot specials whenever a train rolls through (which, as noted above, is 80 to 100 times per day). Live entertainment and a big front porch make this a good space to linger. *2 S. Beaver St.* ☎ *928/214-8218. Main courses $12–$15. Daily 11am–11:30pm.*

→ **Kokopelli Winery Bistro** ★ ITALIAN Arizona winery Kokopelli produces an admirable range of vintages, with reds, whites, and champagnes. You can sample them with bistro fare at this casual Heritage Square spot. Lunch is the main event, with good panini and excellent French onion soup. The soup reappears at dinner, along with pasta and some French-inflected entrees. *6 E. Aspen St., Suite 110.* ☎ *928/226-WINE. www.kokopelliwinery.com. Main dishes $6.50–$7.50 lunch, $11–$14 dinner. Mon–Wed 11:30am–6pm; Thurs–Sat 11:30am–10pm; Sun 11:30am–5pm.*

Splurge

→ **Josephine's Modern American Bistro** ★★★ SOUTHWESTERN The Craftsman Bungalow that holds Josephine's is on the National Register of Historic Places, making a refined backdrop for innovative cuisine. Southwestern flavors abound, with green chile on a massive pork *osso buco* and mole adorning veal chops. Vegetarians can opt for roasted spaghetti squash with chipotle cider. Lunch has a slew of elaborate sandwiches for under $10. *503 N. Humphrey's St.* ☎ *928/779-3400. www.josephinesrestaurant. com. Reservations recommended. Main courses $7.50–$9.75 lunch, $19–$30 dinner. Mon–Fri 11am–2:30pm and 5–9pm; Sat 5–9pm; Sat lunch and Sun dinner in the summer.*

PARTYING

Flagstaff Live, a free weekly, will get you up to speed on the cultural calendar. Close proximity of college students encourages

national touring acts to stop in. The major venue is **The Orpheum Theater,** 15 W. Aspen St. (☎ **928/556-1580;** www.orpheum presents.com), in downtown Flagstaff.

Bars, Pubs & Live Music

→ **Mogollon Brewing Co.** ★★ If it smells a little like a brewery in here, it's totally understandable. Big vats in back produce fresh beer for the taps. There's also a towering copper still, which is the first contraption in Arizona to legally make vodka. Although the High Spirits label isn't sold here, the super-smooth liquor is available in stores throughout the state. Behind the production room is a stage that hosts live music, mostly on the weekends. *15 N. Agassiz St.* ☎ *928/773-8950. www.mogbrew.com. Daily 2:30–11pm.*

→ **Museum Club** ★★ This club on the outskirts of town began life as a 1931 museum for a hunter's taxidermy collection, which helps explain why it's also referred to as "The Zoo." The classic roadhouse interior includes a fireplace with ancient grinding stones incorporated into it. This place is pretty authentically Western, so if you can't deal with country music or line dancing, this might not be the place for you. *3404 E. Rte. 66.* ☎ *928/526-9434. www.museum club.com. Daily 11am–2am.*

→ **Wine Loft** ★ The idea of a brick-walled wine bar in downtown Flagstaff might have some old ranchers spinning in their graves, but this is an exceedingly pleasant spot to spend some time. Fruits of the vine are available in a large by-the-glass selection. There's a short appetizer menu and some nights feature live jazz. *17 N. San Francisco St., above the Artists Gallery.* ☎ *928/773-9463. Mon–Thurs 3pm–midnight; Fri–Sat, 2pm–2am; Sun 4pm–midnight.*

WHAT TO SEE & DO IN FLAGSTAFF

→ **The Arboretum at Flagstaff** This arboretum is the highest-elevation research

Flagstaff makes an excellent base for exploring Northern Arizona.

garden in the U.S. Plants of the high desert, coniferous forest, and alpine tundra (all environments found around Flagstaff) are the focus. There isn't a ton to see, but the grounds are tranquil, with lovely mountain views. *4001 S. Woody Mountain Rd.* ☎ *928/774-1442. www.thearb.org. Admission $5. Daily 9am–5pm. Guided tours 11am and 1pm. Closed Dec 16–Mar 31.*

[MTV] **Best** ❂ → **Museum of Northern Arizona** ★★★ For a 3-D history lesson, this engaging museum is a great stop. The Colorado Plateau, which the Four Corners region rests on, is illuminated with objects like a marsupial molar (it's theorized that the area is the original birthplace of marsupials). As for the people, the museum's impressive collections of katsinas and ancient pottery are helpfully grouped by tribe. Also on display is a fragment of a kiva wall mural, which has been likened to an American Sistine Chapel. *3101 N. Fort Valley Rd. (3 miles north of downtown Flagstaff*

on US 180). ☎ *928/774-5213. www.musnaz. org. Admission $5. Daily 9am–5pm.*

→ **Riordan Mansion State Historic Park** ★ A family that never threw anything away and some design ambition make this old house worthy of a visit. Timber baron brothers Michael and Timothy Riordan had twin mansions built in 1904, connected in the center by a game room fixed up with Western stylings. Mission-style and Art Nouveau furnishings are surprisingly sophisticated given how out of the fashion loop Flagstaff must have been. *409 W. Riordan Rd. (off Milton Rd./Ariz. 89A, just north of the junction of I-40 and I-17).* ☎ *928/779-4395. www.azstateparks.com. Admission $6. May–Oct daily 8:30am–5pm; Nov–Apr daily 10:30am–5pm. Guided tours on the hour.*

OUTTA TOWN: FLAGSTAFF AREA

→ **Sunset Crater Volcano National Monument** ★ Volcanoes seem more the stuff of Hawaiian or Krakatoan landscapes, but northeast of Flagstaff you can find some 400 volcanic craters. Sunset Crater is the youngest, born around A.D. 1064. It erupted repeatedly for a century, creating the sunset-colored red and yellow cone, and covering 800 square miles with ash, lava, and cinders. You can explore the area by car, foot, or bike. Aspen trees grow from the lava beds in places, creating a colorful contrast. Near the informative visitor center is the small Bonito Campground, which is open from late May to mid-October. *14 miles north of Flagstaff off US 89. ☎ 928/ 526-0502. www.nps.gov/sucr. Admission $5 (also valid for Wupatki National Monument), free with National Parks Pass. Daily sunrise to sunset. Visitor center June–Aug daily 8am– 6pm; Sept–Nov and Mar–May 8am–5pm; Dec–Feb 9am–5pm.*

→**Wupatki National Monument** ★★ Taking advantage of a new ash layer, which absorbed moisture, the Sinagua people successfully farmed this desolate area from around A.D. 1100 until shortly after 1200. The largest of the pueblos is the three-story Wupatki Ruin, in the southeastern part of the monument. Nearby ruins, including Nalakihu, Citadel, and Lomaki, are easily accessed by car. Wukoki Ruin, built on a sandstone island in the middle of the desert, is particularly picturesque. The ruins of this monument have a more hands-on feel than most. *36 miles north of Flagstaff off US 89. ☎ 928/679- 2365. www.nps.gov/wupa. Admission $5 (also valid for Sunset Crater Volcano National Monument), free with National Parks Pass. Daily sunrise to sunset. Visitor center June– Aug daily 8am–6pm; Mar–May and Sept–Nov daily 8am–5pm; Dec–Feb daily 9am–5pm.*

→**Petrified Forest National Park** The Petrified Forest can be a bit of a letdown. Maybe if the name were the Heavily Looted Stone Log District instead, visitors wouldn't come with a subconscious expectation of thousands of leafy branches

turned overnight to stone. It's not that the wood here isn't beautiful, with iron, manganese, and carbon creating vivid colors. And it's not that the science isn't incredible—a dinosaur-era swamp where recrystallized silica from volcanic ash replaced the cells of fallen trees. Maybe a person just gets a little jaded before they've looked at very much petrified wood. One of the more interesting applications of the stone here is **Agate House,** at the end of a ³/₄-mile trail near the south entrance. This is a restoration of an ancient dwelling that was made up of chunks of petrified wood. A second ruin (of boring old regular rocks), **Puerco Pueblo,** can be found further up the 27-mile drive, near a petroglyph panel called Newspaper Rock. The park's north end offers views of the Painted Desert. *North entrance 25 miles east of Holbrook on I-40, south entrance 20 miles east of Holbrook on US 180. ☎ 928/524-6228. www.nps.gov/ pefo. Admission $10 per vehicle, free with National Parks Pass. Open daily 8am–5pm (7am–7pm in summer).*

Holbrook, the town nearest to Petrified Forest National Park, has lots of cheap chain hotels if you're not basing yourself in Flagstaff. It also has the legendary **Wigwam Motel** (811 W. Hopi Dr.; ☎ **928/ 524-3048;** www.galerie-kokopelli.com/ wigwam), a surviving Route 66 relic. Fifteen concrete wigwams (okay, tepees) were built here in the 1940s, and for about $45 you can spend the night in one. The parking lot is a time warp itself, filled with classic cars.

→**Meteor Crater** ★ Ever wonder what it would look like if a chunk of rock traveling at 40,000 mph smashed into the side of the Earth? The Barringer Meteorite Crater, 550 feet deep and 2¹/₂ miles in circumference, will give you a pretty good idea. At the rim of the canyon you'll have a view of what 20 million tons of TNT do to the scenery. A small museum holds exhibits on

Sleep in a tepee at Holbrook's Wigwam Motel.

astrogeology and an Apollo space capsule (the crater so resembles those on the moon, NASA sent its astronauts to train here). *20 miles west of Winslow at Exit 233 off I-40.* ☎ *800/289-5898 or 928/289-5898. www.meteorcrater.com. Admission $15. Open daily Memorial Day to Labor Day 7am–7pm; Labor Day to Memorial Day daily 8am–5pm.*

The town of **Sedona** is 30 miles south of Flagstaff (via 89 or 17), and is worthy of a trip of its own. Sedona is more or less Arizona's answer to New Mexico's Santa Fe, with a fair amount of New Agey types and stunning natural landscapes. The red rocks that surround town make for incredible hiking.

PLAYING OUTSIDE

Mountains dominate Flagstaff views, and the **Arizona Snowbowl** (☎ **928/779-1951;** www.arizonasnowbowl.com) is a key component of the local economy. From the slopes of Mount Agassiz you can see all the way to the North Rim of the Grand Canyon on a clear day. There are four chairlifts and 32 runs. A recent ruling allowing the use of snowmaking equipment should make this a more reliable destination. All-day lift tickets are $46. Summer visitors can enjoy the views by riding the chairlift. There are restaurants near the summit, as well as cabins ($79 double weekday, $105 weekend, including breakfast, dinner vouchers, and lift tickets) if you want to get some stargazing in. Round-trip lift-tickets are $10. Take US 180 north from Flagstaff for 7 miles and turn right onto Snow Bowl Road.

Also on Snow Bowl Road is the trailhead for one of the area's best hikes. The **Humphreys Peak Trail** climbs 3,000 feet in 4.5 miles. The peak's 12,633-foot summit is the highest point in Arizona and views are as spectacular as you'd expect.

A shorter hike is to **Red Mountain** in the Coconino National Forest, 2.5 miles round-trip. The payoff there is a red-walled cinder cone with rare exposed interior walls. Take 180 north and around

Northern Arizona Festivals

These festivals aren't the most elaborate, but they're good opportunities to see the community out in force:

→ **Flagstaff Winterfest:** Flagstaff livens up February with a month's worth of activities. Skiing leads the way, with both Nordic and alpine competitions. There's also sled-dog races, snowboard and snowshoe events, and snowmobile drag races; **flagstaffarizona.org.**

→ **Hopi Festival of Arts and Culture:** Coming up on its 75th anniversary, this arts fest brings together dozens of booths selling carvings, paintings, jewelry, pottery, and textiles. Cultural attractions include music, dancing, and storytelling. Early July at the Museum of Northern Arizona; **www. musnaz.org.**

→ **Navajo Festival of Arts and Culture:** This late-July event covers a lot of cultural ground. Music, dancing, and fashion shows join beading and pottery demonstrations. Also look for Navajo rug weavers, working on traditional upright looms. At the Museum of Northern Arizona; **www.musnaz.org.**

→ **Grand Canyon Music Festival:** Although there can be a few blues or pop performances, the focus of this festival is classical. Concerts are held in the intimate, acoustically superb Shrine of the Ages Auditorium, on the canyon's South Rim. Mid-September; **grandcanyonmusicfest.org.**

→ **Route 66 Days:** Route 66 passes through Flagstaff, and the road's lore is celebrated at this annual mid-September event. Look for lots of vintage rides and portly guys in Elvis drag. If you're behind the wheel of an antique, classic, muscle car, street rod, or custom pickup, you can even join the parade; **www.flagstaffroute66days.com.**

milepost 24; take a forest road leading west to the trailhead parking area. For information on other hikes in the forest, contact the **Peaks Ranger District,** 5075 N. Hwy. 89, Flagstaff (☎ **928/526-0866;** www.fs.fed.us/r3/coconino).

Rock climbers can join the locals at **Canyon Vista,** about 15 minutes from downtown. Limestone cliffs in the midst of a ponderosa forest make for a scenic setting. Head south on Milton Road and follow the signs to Lake Mary Road just before I-17.

Six miles down Lake Mary Road, after the second cattleguard, take a left up a dirt road. Park at the gate, or further down by the campground. Vertical Relief Climbing Center (205 S. San Francisco St.; ☎ **928/ 556-9909;** www.verticalrelief.com) rents out equipment for $10 a day. Their downtown facility has 6,500 square feet of indoor climbing terrain. If the weather's bad, this is a great way to stay active. You can get a day pass for $15; pass, rental equipment, and lessons combined are $29.

On the Road to the Grand Canyon, AZ

Flagstaff, AZ to the Grand Canyon, AZ 80 miles

If you take the eastern route to the Grand Canyon from Flagstaff you'll be on route 89, the paved version of a trading route that dates back millennia. The crossroads of 64 and 89 at Cameron, AZ, make for a good stop off. The **Cameron Trading Post** (☎ 800/338-7385 or 928/679-2231; www.camerontradingpost.com) has been around since 1916, and the original stone building just above the banks of the Little Colorado still remains. The gallery there now sells museum-quality artifacts, clothing, and jewelry, and is definitely worth a look around.

A big, kitschy main building has cheap gifts and rug-making demonstrations. In the back is a high-ceiling Old West–style restaurant, open daily from 6am to 10pm (lunch $8–$10, dinner $8–$19). The Navajo tacos, made with fried bread, are the popular choice here. (Don't bother with regular-size: The mini is more than enough food.) The 62-unit motel out back is very comfortable, with rates ranging from $49 to $119, depending on how close you are to peak season.

To enter the Grand Canyon from the west, from Flagstaff take 180 north and west through the San Francisco Mountains, a trip of 80 miles. This is the more popular route, and hence more crowded, so I recommend coming from the east.

Some 90% of park visitors go to the South Rim of the canyon, but the North Rim is equally stunning. It's open only in the warmer months and the road loops almost 100 miles from 89, so there're reasons why it's less trafficked.

Welcome to the Grand Canyon

🎬 Best ● It's not impossible to be underwhelmed by the Grand Canyon, but you really have to work on it. Some 4 million visitors come through the park every year. The resulting congestion can make communing with nature seem easier at your local shopping mall. If you try a drive-by tour here, limiting yourself to quick photo ops at the overlooks, you may leave wondering what all the fuss is about. With a little effort, however, the Grand Canyon will reveal itself as one of the most extraordinary places on the planet.

The Earth's history can be read in the canyon's layers. The story begins with vast, ancient seas, which deposited sediment across Northern Arizona. Over millions of years, the sediments turned into limestone and sandstone. Twenty-one distinct sedimentary layers can be seen in the park, the oldest more than a billion years old. (The rock at the very bottom, Vishnu schist, dates from 2 billion years ago.)

It took the Colorado River (with help from the wind and the rain) some 3 to 6 million years to reveal these layers. Only in the last 4,000 of those years have humans called this place home. If you hike down to the canyon floor, you'll pass an Ancestral Puebloan ruin right on the banks of the Colorado. The Hualapai and Havasupai tribes still live here, concentrated on the south side of the Colorado River.

Grand Canyon **Nuts & Bolts**

Area Code   The telephone area code at the Grand Canyon is 928.

Banks & ATMs   There's an ATM at the **Bank One** (☎ 928/638-2437) at Market Plaza, which is near Yavapai Lodge. The bank is open Monday through Thursday from 9am to 5pm and Friday from 9am to 6pm.

Contact   The park website is www.nps.gov/grca; the visitor information number is ☎ 928/638-7888.

Fees for Entry   Admission is $25 per vehicle, free with National Parks Pass.

Garages   A public garage with 24-hour emergency towing service (☎ 928/638-2631) operates inside the park on the South Rim. The garage itself is open from 8am to noon and 1 to 5pm daily.

Hospitals/Clinics   If you have a medical emergency on either rim, dial ☎ **911** to obtain assistance from Park Rangers. The **South Rim Walk-In Clinic** (☎ 928/638-2551) is on Clinic Drive, off Center Road (the road that runs past the National Park Service ranger office). The clinic is open Monday through Friday from 9am to 6pm and Saturday from 10am to 2pm (may be open later in summer). It provides 24-hour emergency service as well. The nearest pharmacies are in Williams, AZ. Health services are nonexistent on the **North Rim.** In non-emergency situations, you'll need to drive all the way to the hospital in Kanab, UT. North Rim emergency medical services are provided by rangers on duty.

Hours   The park is open 24 hours a day, 7 days a week.

Laundry   Laundromats can be found inside the park on both rims. Open 6am to 11pm daily in summer (shorter hours in winter), the **South Rim laundromat** is in the Camper Services building near Mather Campground. Open 7am to 9pm daily, the **North Rim laundromat** is near the North Rim Campground.

Outfitters   On the South Rim, **Canyon Village Marketplace** (☎ 928/638-2262, open daily 7am to 8pm in summer, 8am to 7pm in winter) in Grand Canyon Village rents and sells camping and backpacking equipment. There is no equipment for rent on the North Rim, but the **North Rim General Store** (☎ 928/638-2611, ext. 270), usually open from 7am to 9pm, sells a very limited supply of camping equipment.

Police   For police emergencies, phone ☎ **911.**

Post Office   On the **South Rim,** the post office (☎ 928/638-2512) in Market Plaza has window hours from 9am to 4:30pm on weekdays and from 11am to 3pm Saturdays. On the **North Rim,** a tiny post office at Grand Canyon Lodge is open Monday to Friday 8am to 4pm and Saturday 10am to 2pm.

Radio   KSGC, 92.1 FM, provides news, music, the latest weather forecasts, and travel-related information for the Grand Canyon area.

Time Zone   Arizona is on Mountain Standard Time, but it doesn't follow daylight saving time. See box, p. 514.

Transit Info   ]Information on road conditions in the Grand Canyon area is available by calling ☎ 888/411-7623 or 928/638-7888.

Weather   Recorded weather information, updated every morning, is available at ☎ 928/638-7888. Forecasts are also posted at the main visitor centers.

Where to Fill Up   There is only one gas station inside the park on the South Rim. **Desert View Chevron,** on Highway 64, 25 miles east of Grand Canyon Village, is open 24 hours daily (Apr 1–Sept 8am–6pm). If you're entering the park from the

Grand Canyon Highlights

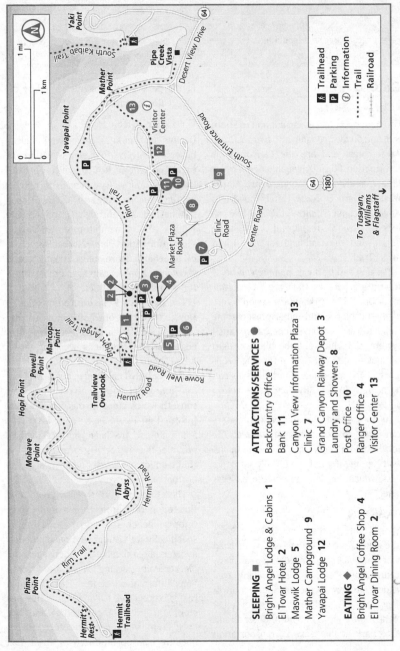

Legend

🄺 Trailhead
🄿 Parking
ⓘ Information
· · · · · Trail
+++++ Railroad

ATTRACTIONS/SERVICES ●
Backcountry Office **6**
Bank **11**
Canyon View Information Plaza **13**
Clinic **7**
Grand Canyon Railway Depot **3**
Laundry and Showers **8**
Post Office **10**
Ranger Office **4**
Visitor Center **13**

SLEEPING ■
Bright Angel Lodge & Cabins **1**
El Tovar Hotel **2**
Maswik Lodge **5**
Mather Campground **9**
Yavapai Lodge **12**

EATING ◆
Bright Angel Coffee Shop **4**
El Tovar Dining Room **2**

south and are running low on fuel, make sure to gas up in **Tusayan,** 1 mile south of the park's south entrance. On the North Rim, the **Chevron Service Station** is open daily 8am to 5pm (7am–7pm in summer), also seasonally. You can also get gas at the general store across from Kaibab Lodge, 18 miles north of the North Rim on Highway 67. Prices will be higher here, so gas up well before you approach the park if you can.

Getting Around

ORIENTATION

Grand Canyon Village is built on the South Rim and divided roughly into two sections. At the east end are the Canyon View Information Plaza, Yavapai Lodge, Trailer Village, and Mather Campground. At the west end are El Tovar Hotel, the Bright Angel, Kachina, Thunderbird, and Maswik lodges, several restaurants, the train depot, and the trailhead for the Bright Angel Trail.

Parking and traffic in summer can be as frustrating here as they are in a major metropolis. The Park Service is well aware of the problems, and they've taken some steps toward a convenient mass-transit system. Unfortunately, the planned light rail has stalled out due to funding problems. In the meantime, shuttle busses can be a big help (see "By Park Bus" section below).

As for getting into the park, summers can bring 20- to 30-minute waits at the South Rim entrance gate. You can cut the waiting time if you have a National Parks Pass, which will let you use the express lane.

PARKING

At peak times, try the lot at the Market Plaza (the general store), which is up a side road near Yavapai Lodge and the Canyon View Information Plaza. A paved hiking trail leads from here to the historic section of the village in less than 1.5 miles, and most of the route is along the rim. Another option is to park at the Maswik Transportation Center parking lot, which is served by the Village Route shuttle bus.

BY PARK BUS

During peak months (Mar–Nov), shuttle buses operate on four routes within the park. The **Village Route** (which operates from one hour before sunrise to 9pm in winter, 10pm in spring and fall, and 11pm in summer) circles through Grand Canyon Village with frequent stops at the Canyon View Information Plaza, Market Plaza (site of a general store, bank, laundry, and showers), hotels, campgrounds, restaurants, and other facilities.

The **Hermit's Rest Route** bus (Mar 1–Nov 30 only, runs one hour before sunrise to one hour after sunset) takes visitors to eight canyon overlooks west of Bright Angel Lodge.

The **Kaibab Trail Route** bus (runs from one hour before sunrise to one hour after sunset), which stops at the Canyon View Information Plaza, Pipe Creek Vista, the South Kaibab trailhead, and Yaki Point, provides the only access to Yaki Point, the trailhead for the South Kaibab Trail to the bottom of the canyon.

The **Canyon View/Mather Point Route** (operates from 7:30am until 5:30 or 6:30pm, depending on the season) is specifically for visitors who need mobility assistance and shuttles between the Mather Point parking lot and the Canyon View Information Center. There's also a Hiker Express bus to Yaki Point. This bus stops at Bright Angel Lodge and the Back Country Information Office. Hikers needing transportation to or from Yaki

Point when the bus is not running can use a **taxi** (☎ 928/638-2822).

BY TRAIN

In the early 20th century, most visitors to the Grand Canyon came by train. You can arrive in retro style by taking the **Grand Canyon Railway** (☎ 800/843-8724 or 928/773-1976; www.thetrain.com), which runs from Williams to Grand Canyon Village. There are two daily trains in summer and one daily train in winter, spring, and fall.

The railway is like a moving museum, with cars of different eras showing off the evolution of passenger interiors. A mix of early-20th-century steam engines (Memorial Day to Labor Day) and 1950s-vintage diesel engines (during other months) do the pulling. The scene through the windows is of endless grasslands, broken up only by the occasional ranch or raven on a fencepost. Actors in cowboy and bandit drag provide entertainment, which is definitely on the hokey side. The round-trip takes 8 hours, including 3¼ hours at the canyon. There are five classes of service, with coach round-trip fares starting at $60 (slightly higher during peak months). Train travel allows you to avoid the traffic congestion and parking problems in Grand Canyon Village, and you can sip $3.50 cocktails as you watch the scenery roll slowly past.

BY HELICOPTER

If you've never ridden in a helicopter, the experience is much smoother and quieter than you probably imagine. Several tour companies operate out of Grand Canyon Airport in Tusayan, and a helicopter ride is one of the most memorable ways to experience the canyon. It's an incredible thrill to be hurtling over the tips of a ponderosa forest and suddenly having the ground drop away, a whole mile away, with the red canyon walls rising up around you. For your own peace of mind, I recommend going with a reputable firm that flies new aircraft. **Maverick Helicopters** (☎ 800/962-3869 or 928/638-2622; www.maverickhelicopter.com) has state-of-the-art choppers with wraparound glass for better panoramic viewing. Trips start at $133 per person for a 25- to 30-minute ride. If you think the views from the overlooks are breathtaking, wait until you see the formations from the sky.

It Gets Cold Up There (and Hot Down There)

The South Rim is 7,000 feet high, and unlike most of Arizona gets *very* cold in winter. Snow is not uncommon between November and May. Winter temperatures can get below 0°F at night, with daytime highs in the 20s or 30s. Summer temperatures at the rim range from highs in the 80s to lows in the 50s. The North Rim, which is slightly higher and therefore slightly cooler, is open to visitors only from May to October because the access road isn't cleared of snow in winter.

As you hike down, you'll notice the mercury going up. On the canyon floor, summer temps can reach 120°F, with lows in the 70s. Winters are temperate 50s for highs and 30s for lows. July, August, and September are the wettest months because of frequent afternoon thunderstorms. April, May, and June are the driest months, but you still might encounter rain, or even snow.

▲▲ Precautions at the Edge
UH-OH

Okay, I know it's totally obvious, but be careful near the edge of the canyon. This place is distractingly beautiful. If you're framing a photograph, or posing for someone else, be especially mindful of the edge. If you do go hiking, remember that you're starting out at 7,000 ft. in the sky—if you're not acclimated to the altitude, take things slow. Make sure you have enough water, too (1 gallon per person per day is recommended). Don't try to hike down to the river and back in 1 day. There's a disturbing poster at the top of the South Kaibab Trail that inquires if you can run a marathon. The sign goes on to detail the tragic death of Margaret Bradley, a top Boston Marathon finisher, who died from dehydration in the canyon in 2004 (she had only fruit, 3 protein bars, and 1.5 liters of water with her). If you're not sufficiently prepared, you can easily get into trouble in the canyon. Even if you're used to running 90 miles a week.

Sleeping

The Grand Canyon is as popular as national parks get, and there are only so many hotel rooms to go around. High demand means you should make reservations way in advance if you can—if you show up in mid-summer without anything set up, you'll probably get shut out. That said, Williams (p. 533) has tons of hotel rooms, as does Flagstaff, so in a pinch you should be able to come up with something.

INSIDE THE PARK
Campgrounds/Hostels

On the South Rim, there are two campgrounds and an RV park. **Mather Campground,** in Grand Canyon Village, has more than 300 campsites. Reservations can be made up to 5 months in advance and are highly recommended for stays between April and November (reservations not accepted for other months). Contact the **National Park Reservation Service** (☎ **800/365-2267** or 301/722-1257; reservations.nps.gov). Between late spring and early fall expect the place to be booked solid. Campsites are $18 per night ($12 per night Dec–Mar; reservations not accepted).

Desert View Campground, with 50 sites, is 26 miles east of Grand Canyon Village and open from mid-May to mid-October only. No reservations are accepted. Campsites are $10 per night.

Cheap

➔**Bright Angel Lodge & Cabins** ★ What began in 1896 as a collection of tents and cabins is now the park's most affordable lodge. The best and most popular units are the rim cabins, which should be booked a year in advance for summer. Outside the winter months, other rooms should be booked at least 6 months in advance. A tour desk, fireplace, museum, and restrooms bring constant crowds into the lobby. *West Rim Dr., Grand Canyon Village.* ☎ *888/297-2757 for reservations, 928/638-2631 for on-site service. www.grandcanyonlodges.com. 89 units, 20 with shared bathrooms. $56 double with sink only; $68 double with sink and toilet; cabins start at $89. Amenities: 2 restaurants (American, steakhouse/Southwestern); lounge; ice-cream parlor; tour desk. In room: No phone.*

➔**Phantom Ranch** ★★ Phantom Ranch is the only lodge at the bottom of the Grand Canyon. Built in 1922, it retains a classic ranch atmosphere. Rustic stone-walled cabins and 10-bed gender-segregated dormitories are your sleeping options. Make reservations as early as possible, and don't forget to reconfirm. It's also sometimes possible to get a room the day you arrive if there are any last-minute cancellations. Start calling for cancellations a day or two before you arrive. Put your name on the waiting list at the Bright Angel Lodge transportation desk the day before you want to stay at Phantom Ranch. Family-style meals must be reserved in advance. The menu consists of beef-and-vegetable stew ($21), a vegetarian dinner ($21), and steak ($31). Breakfasts ($18) are hearty, and sack lunches ($10) are available as well. Between meals, the dining hall becomes a canteen selling snacks, drinks, gifts, and necessities. After dinner, it serves as a beer hall, which is a nice amenity for refreshment-seekers at the nearby campground. Mule-back baggage service between Grand Canyon Village and Phantom Ranch is available ($55 each way). ☎ 928/638-3283 for reconfirmations. 11 cabins, 40 dorm beds. $81 double in cabin; $30 dormitory bed. Amenities: Restaurant (American); lounge. In room: No phone.

Doable

→ **Maswik Lodge** ★ A little way from the rim, this lodge has been modernized without sacrificing too much of its character. If you don't mind roughing it a bit, the 28 old cabins, which are available only in summer, have lots of rustic charm. The second-floor Maswik North rooms have high ceilings, balconies, and more modern comforts. *Grand Canyon National Park Lodges/Xanterra Parks & Resorts.* ☎ 888/297-2757 or 303/297-2757. *www.grandcanyonlodges.com.* 278 units. $76–$124 double (winter discounts available); $76 cabin. Amenities: Cafeteria; lounge; tour desk. In room: TV.

→ **Yavapai Lodge** At the east end of Grand Canyon Village, this sprawling complex is the largest lodge in the park.

Although you stand a better shot of getting a reservation here, the place is short on charm and lacking in canyon views. The Yavapai East wing is the nice side, set under shady pines. *Grand Canyon National Park Lodges/Xanterra Parks & Resorts.* ☎ 888/297-2757 or 303/297-2757. *ww.grandcanyonlodges.com.* 358 units. $96–$113 double; discounts available in winter. Amenities: Cafeteria; tour desk. In room: TV.

Splurge

→ **El Tovar Hotel** ★★ El Tovar Hotel opened in 1905 and celebrated its centennial with a total overhaul. Built of local rock and Oregon pine by Hopi craftsmen, it's the park's premier lodge. The vibe is classic Western, with rustic furniture and animal heads on the lobby walls. The hotel is just off the rim, although a limited number of rooms have canyon views. *Grand Canyon National Park Lodges/Xanterra Parks & Resorts.* ☎ 888/297-2757 or 303/297-2757. *www.grandcanyonlodges.com.* 78 units. $134–$194 double; $244–$304 suite. Amenities: Restaurant (Continental/Southwestern); lounge; concierge; tour desk; room service. In room: TV.

IN TUSAYAN (OUTSIDE THE SOUTH ENTRANCE)

If you can't get a reservation for a room in the park, this is the next closest place to stay. Unfortunately, airport proximity can make this area noisy. Popular with tour groups, it can also be booked up during summer months. The hotels listed here are lined up along US 180/Ariz. 64.

Camping

Two miles south of Tusayan is the U.S. Forest Service's **Ten-X Campground.** This campground has 70 campsites, is open mid-April through September, and charges $10. It's usually your best bet for finding a site late in the day.

You can also camp just about anywhere within the **Kaibab National Forest,** which borders Grand Canyon National Park, as long as you are more than a quarter mile away from Ariz. 64/US 180. Several dirt roads lead out from the highway, although flush toilets are not on the forest's list of amenities. For more information, contact the **Tusayan Ranger District,** Kaibab National Forest, P.O. Box 3088, Grand Canyon, AZ 86023 (☎ **928/ 638-2443;** www.fs.fed.us/r3/kai).

Cheap

➔**Rodeway Inn Red Feather Lodge** With more than 200 units, this motel is often one of the last places to fill up. Rooms aren't exactly stylish, but they're comfortable. A pool and hot tub are nice amenities. *Ariz. 64 (P.O. Box 1460), Grand Canyon, AZ 86023.* ☎ *800/424-6423 or 928/ 638-2414. Fax 928/638-2707. www.redfeather lodge.com. 215 units. $75–$149 double. Amenities: Restaurant (American); seasonal outdoor pool; exercise room; hot tub. In room: A/C, TV, dataport, coffeemaker, hair dryer.*

Doable

➔**Grand Hotel** ★★ This place actually does a decent job of living up to its name. The mountain lodge–style lobby reminds you you're way out west, as do the flagstone fireplace, log-beam ceiling, and fake ponderosa trunks holding up the roof. Just off the lobby are a dining room (with evening entertainment ranging from Native American dancers to country-music bands) and a small bar with saddles for bar stools. Guest rooms are spacious, some with small balconies. *Ariz. 64 (P.O. Box 3319), Grand Canyon, AZ 86023.* ☎ *888/634-7263 or 928/638-3333. Fax 928/638-3131. www. visitgrandcanyon.com. 120 units. $79–$159 double; $198 suite. Amenities: Restaurant; lounge; indoor pool; Jacuzzi. In room: A/C, TV, dataport, coffeemaker, hair dryer.*

Splurge

➔**Holiday Inn Express–Grand Canyon** ★ One of the area's newest hotels, this place is modern and well-designed, if not exactly long on character. Although these suites are fairly pricey, they're among the nicest accommodations around. *Ariz. 64 (P.O. Box 3245), Grand Canyon, AZ 86023.* ☎ *888/ 473-2269 or 928/638-3000. Fax 928/638-0123. www.gcanyon.com/HI. 194 units. $112–$159 double; $152–$250 suite. Rates include continental breakfast. Children under 18 stay free in parent's room. Amenities: Indoor pool; Jacuzzi. In room: A/C, TV, dataport, hair dryer, iron, high-speed Internet access.*

Eating

INSIDE THE PARK

There are cafeterias all through Grand Canyon Village, making quick, cheap meals easy to find. The Yavapai and Maswik lodges both have cafeteria service, and there's a **delicatessen** at Canyon Village Marketplace on Market Plaza.

The **Bright Angel Fountain,** at the back of the Bright Angel Lodge, serves hot dogs, sandwiches, and ice cream, and is always crowded on hot days. At Desert View (near the east entrance to the park), there's the **Desert View Trading Snack Bar.** All of these places are open daily for all three meals, and all serve meals for $8 and under.

SUPPLIES

There are three grocery stores inside the park. The largest, **The Canyon Village Marketplace** (☎ **928/638-2262**), is in Market Plaza in Grand Canyon Village. Its hours are usually 7am to 8pm in summer, 8am to 7pm the rest of the year. **Desert View General Store** (☎ **928/638-2393**), at Desert View (25 miles east of Grand Canyon Village on Hwy. 64), is open daily 8am to 6pm in summer, 9am to 5pm the rest of the year. On the North Rim, the only provisions are at the **North Rim General Store** (☎ 928/638-2611, ext. 270), adjacent to North Rim Campground. It's usually open daily 7am to 9pm.

➜ **Bright Angel Coffee Shop** AMERICAN As the least expensive of the three restaurants on the rim of the canyon, this casual Southwestern-themed coffeehouse in the historic Bright Angel Lodge is constantly packed. Meals are simple and not especially memorable, although some tables have something of a view. Hiker-friendly fare, like tacos, fajitas, and spaghetti, is available. *At the Bright Angel Lodge.* ☎ *928/ 638-2631. Reservations not accepted. Main courses $7–$16. Daily 6:30–10:45am and 11:15am–10pm.*

➜ **El Tovar Dining Room** ★★ CONTINENTAL/SOUTHWESTERN If you want to experience the historic El Tovar, a lunch here is a good way to do it. Although definitely a splurge at dinner, sandwiches and stellar burgers hover around $10 at lunchtime. Italian and Asian touches make for a sophisticated menu. The atmosphere is excellent, with dark, rough-hewn wood screaming Old West. *At the El Tovar Hotel.* ☎ *928/638-2631, ext. 6432. Reservations required for dinner. Main courses $11–$16 lunch, $18–$30 dinner. Daily 6:30–11am, 11:30am–2pm, and 5–10pm.*

IN TUSAYAN (OUTSIDE THE SOUTH ENTRANCE)

Tusayan boasts a steakhouse and a pizza place, as well as chains such as McDonald's, Pizza Hut, and Wendy's. For a more formal experience, you might consider the:

➜ **Canyon Star** ★ SOUTHWESTERN Creative touches liven up a Southwest menu at this good-size restaurant. Elk tenderloin, barbecued buffalo brisket, and buffalo burgers are among the exotic

meats on offer. Live music, including Native American songs and dances, can be heard in the evenings. *At the Grand Hotel, Ariz. 64.* ☎ *928/638-3333. Main courses $8–$11 lunch, $13–$25 dinner. Daily 7–10am and 11am–10pm.*

EATING & SLEEPING IN WILLIAMS

Best ● If you can't find a place to stay in the park, Williams, AZ, is your best nearby alternative. Though small, Williams is long on charm, with a tight cluster of historical streets. The last Route 66 town to be bypassed by I-40 (in 1984), it holds an impressive collection of retro motels, restaurants, and bars. Informative plaques give the background on many of the buildings if you want to take a self-guided walking tour. Williams is particularly convenient if you're riding on the Grand Canyon Railway (p. 529), which has its depot just on the outskirts of town.

Sleeping

There are several campgrounds near Williams in the Kaibab National Forest. They include **Cataract Lake,** 2 miles northwest of Williams on Cataract Lake Road, with 18 sites; **Dogtown Lake,** 8 miles south of Williams off Fourth Street/ County Road 73, with 51 sites; **Kaibab Lake,** 4 miles northeast of Williams off Ariz. 64, with 72 sites; and **Whitehorse Lake,** 19 miles southeast of Williams off Fourth Street/County Road 73, with 105 sites. All campgrounds are first-come, first-served, and charge $10 to $12 per night.

The town's main strip is packed with old hotels, many preserving their retro signage. **The Canyon Motel** (1900 E. Rodeo Rd.; ☎ **800/482-3955** or 928/635-9371; www.thecanyonmotel.com) is an updated 1940s motor lodge. While the new rooms in duplex flagstone cottages are nice enough, the real attractions are the railroad cars parked in the front yard. You have your choice of a caboose or a Pullman car (rates start at $50, higher for the caboose). Further up the road, **The Lodge** (200 E. Route 66; ☎ **877/563-4366** or 928/635-4534; www.thelodgeonroute 66.com) is another newly renovated Route 66 survivor. Interiors have a lodge feel, but with nicer appointments, and lots of space. King suites start at around $99.

Retro dining experiences come easily in Williams. **Cruiser's Café 66** (233 W. Rte. 66; ☎ **928/635-2445**) is housed in a 1930s gas station packed with Mother Road memorabilia. The menu (main courses $7–$20) sticks to American bar food terrain, highlighted by smoked baby back ribs and fajitas. **The World Famous Sultana Saloon** (301 W. Route 66; ☎ **928/635-2021;** www.famoussultana.com) holds Arizona's longest-standing liquor license. The adjacent steakhouse has a mead hall feel, filling a former movie theater. Mounted deer heads keep watch over diners enjoying basic steaks, ribs, and chicken (entrees $11–$29). Peppery, bacon-laden cowboy beans are an excellent side. For dessert, **Twisters 50's Soda Fountain** (417 E. Route 66; ☎ **928/635-0266;** www. route66place.com) is a friendly, old-time place, with classic black-and-white tile floors and lots of Coca-Cola memorabilia. Banana splits and root beer floats are good options here.

In the morning, **Pine Country Restaurant** (107 N Grand Canyon Blvd.; ☎ **928/635-9718**) has the best breakfast around. Huevos rancheros are the way to go, enjoyed in a pleasant lace and pine setting. After dinner (entrees $8–$13), save room for amazing pie—there are 46 different varieties that rotate through the big glass display case.

Hiking the Canyon

The first time I really ventured below the rim of the Grand Canyon I felt a sense of amazement (and maybe a little bit of shame) that I had managed to live my life this long and never seen this place. To really have a feel for the land, you need to experience the shifts of scale you get from going up and down it. The textures and colors of the sandstone, limestone, shale, and schist will also change with the rise and set of the sun.

Like most national parks, a short walk away from the main gathering points will get you a lot of space to yourself. The Grand Canyon's two main trails, Bright Angel and South Kaibab, get a lot of use (both by foot and by mule), but once you get a couple of miles down the crowds really thin out.

DAY HIKES

The Grand Canyon inverts normal hiking procedure: The early part is all downhill, with the serious climb saved for the return trip. If you're not up for a loss and gain in elevation, the **Rim Trail** is the path to take. You can travel as far as Pipe Creek Vista (east of Grand Canyon Village) to Hermit's Rest, which is 8 miles west of the village. The part that passes through Grand Canyon Village is the most crowded stretch of trail in the park.

To the west of the village, after the pavement ends, the Rim Trail leads another 6.7 miles out to Hermit's Rest. For most of this distance, the trail follows Hermit Road, which means you'll have to deal with traffic noise (mostly from shuttle buses). Try to beat the crowds by heading out here first thing in the morning. If you get off at The Abyss shuttle stop, it's a 4-mile hike to Hermit's Rest, which is, as the name suggests, a great place to rest. From here you can catch a shuttle bus back to the village.

Hiking the Grand Canyon may be one of the most memorable things you do.

The canyon's most well-known route is **Bright Angel Trail,** which starts just west of Bright Angel Lodge in Grand Canyon Village, where the majority of park visitors tend to be. This is also the preferred mule route, meaning you'll be tiptoeing around manure and yielding right of way to the lumbering beasts. The trail runs down a side canyon, limiting the views. Longer day hikes include Indian Garden (9 miles round-trip) and Plateau Point (12 miles round-trip), which are both just over 3,000 feet below the rim. There is year-round water at Indian Garden. If you go down Bright Angel, right after you cut through the hole in the rock near the trail's beginning, look up at the overhanging rock to your left. You'll see some interesting petroglyphs up there.

The **South Kaibab Trail** ★★★ begins near Yaki Point east of Grand Canyon Village and is the preferred route down to Phantom Ranch. This trail follows a ridge-line, so the views are much better than Bright Angel—the best of the day hikes.

Cedar Ridge is a 3-mile round-trip, and Skeleton Point is 6 miles.

Experienced hikers with good boots might be into taking on the **Hermit Trail,** which begins at Hermit's Rest, 8 miles west of Grand Canyon Village at the end of Hermit Road. The unmaintained trail loses almost all of its elevation (1,600 ft.–1,700 ft.) in the first 1½ miles. A 5-mile round-trip hike brings you to Santa Maria Spring and back. If you were to keep on going, you'd reach the Colorado River, but that's 17 miles one way from the trailhead. Alternatively, you can do a 7-mile round-trip hike to Dripping Springs. Hermit Road is closed to private vehicles from March to November, so you'll probably have to take the free shuttle bus out to the trailhead. If you take the first bus of the day, you've got a decent shot at having have the trail almost all to yourself.

BACKPACKING

Backpacking might be the best way of experiencing the canyon, although it

Walking on Air at the Grand Canyon

In March, 2007, for the first time, you could stand on air, almost a mile above the floor of the Grand Canyon, in the **Grand Canyon Skywalk** (☎ 877/716-WEST; www.grandcanyonskywalk.com). The skywalk, a cantilever-shaped glass walkway extending 70 feet from the canyon's rim is at Canyon West, a destination owned by the Hualapai Tribe at the canyon's western rim. Astronaut Buzz Aldrin and tribal elders took the ceremonial first steps, and now the Skywalk is open to the public. Access to the Skywalk will run from dawn to dusk and will cost $25 per person in addition to the cost of a Grand Canyon West entrance package. One hundred and twenty people are allowed on the bridge at a time. Admittance is first come/first serve for walk-up visitors; you can also make advance reservations via phone or on the website.

does take some advance planning. A **Backcountry Use Permit** is required for you to overnight, unless you're staying at Phantom Ranch. Reservations are taken in person, by mail, by fax (but not by phone), and online. Contact the **Backcountry Office,** Grand Canyon National Park, P.O. Box 129, Grand Canyon, AZ 86023 (☎ **928/638-7875** 1–5pm for information; fax 928/638-2125; www.nps.gov/grca). The office begins accepting reservations on the first of every month for the following 5 months. Holiday periods are the most popular—if you want to hike over the Labor Day weekend, be sure you make your reservation on May 1!

If you show up without a reservation, go to the Backcountry Information Center (open daily 8am–noon and 1–5pm), adjacent to the Maswik Lodge, and put your name on the waiting list. You must specify your exact itinerary and stick to it. Backpacking fees include a nonrefundable $10 backcountry permit fee and a $5 per person per night backcountry camping fee. American Express, Diners Club, Discover, MasterCard, and Visa are accepted for permit fees.

There are **campgrounds** at Indian Garden, Bright Angel Campground (near Phantom Ranch), and Cottonwood, but hikers are limited to 2 nights per trip at each of these campgrounds (except Nov 15–Feb 28, when 4 nights are allowed at each campground). Other nights can be spent camping at undesignated sites in certain parts of the park.

The *Backcountry Trip Planner* contains information to help you plan your itinerary. It's available through the Backcountry Office (see contact information, above). Maps are available through the **Grand Canyon Association,** P.O. Box 399, Grand Canyon, AZ 86023 (☎ **800/858-2808** or 928/638-2481; www.grandcanyon.org), and at bookstores and gift shops within the national park, including Canyon View Information Plaza, Kolb Studio, Desert View Information Center, Yavapai Observation Station, Tusayan Museum, and, on the North Rim, at Grand Canyon Lodge.

Williams marks the end of the "First Americans" tour. From here, I-40 west will take you in the direction of the "Desert to the Beach" roadtrip (p. 537). Ruined cities and haunting passages will give way to plastic and neon. In just 240 miles, you'll be smack in the middle of that ultimate modern-America-run-amok destination, Las Vegas. There's no better way to get some perspective on ancient America.

Desert to the Beach: Vegas to Baja

Text & Photos by John Vorwald

There is a natural human need for perspective. Whether it's a reaction to a life crammed into four square walls or a desire to break from urban chaos, we long for the Big Picture, for uncluttered views. This roadtrip takes us to two of America's choicest places to sand down distractions and make daily preoccupations seem a little more trivial: the desert and the sea. In both contrasting destinations, the landscape takes on a natural cohesiveness. If you're lucky, the eye may even grasp a hint of the infinite.

Our trip begins in the Nevada desert. For millennia, hermits, searchers, and prophets have satisfied a desire for solitude amid the desert's stark terrain. It's easy to see why: Stars cast shadows here, and silence can ring out like the chop of an axe. But if all you know of the desert is cactus and tumbleweeds, you're in for a surprise. Nevada's desert is alive, full of fascinating plants, brilliant colors, rare wildlife, and bizarre land formations. It's also home to the most surreal oasis on the planet: Las Vegas, baby. (Or, "Vegas, Baby!" if you're being all Rat Pack.) Believe the hype. No matter what standard of outrageousness you're expecting, and I was coming from the heart of New York City, the hyper-reality of Sin City is a hundred times more over the top. And what better antidote to an over-itinerized life than a dose of the absurd? So strap on your sense of the ridiculous; Vegas serves it up in spades.

Do you know the way to Zzyzx?

Shifting from Las Vegas's hallucinatory interiors, we'll introduce you to the calming properties of Red Rock Canyon, and help you channel your inner Fox Mulder at Area 51. We'll drive two-lane highways to the resort town of Palm Springs, California, to recuperate by the pool, and take in the desert's rough charm with a hike in Joshua Tree. In Baja, lapping waters and gentler climes await in the coastal towns of Tijuana, Rosarito, and Ensenada. If the ocean views, startling sunsets, and sunbathing aren't enough to transport you, these resort cities offer every water-related activity under the sun, from surfing to boating to horseback riding. At night,

you'll find an open sociability, with good eating and lively nightlife among a laid-back tourist crowd. You want to get away from the daily static? It's hard to be uptight on this particular plane.

Making your way from Nevada to Mexico, you may find that that the desert and the ocean are not so different, that they're really two sides of the same vista/coin. Get to where you can see the horizon—the whole horizon. Out in the stripped-down realms of the desert and at the edge of the humbling Pacific, you may regain some small part of yourself, or just enough perspective to know that things are exactly as they should be.

Superlatives: The Highs & Lows

→ **Best Use of $1 in Vegas: The Blackjack Strategy and Odds Card.** A simple credit card–size chart that, if used correctly, reduces the casino's advantage over you to less than 1%. Who wouldn't want that? (Buy one in any casino souvenir shop.)

→ **Most Original Show in Vegas: Blue Man Group.** Quirky, smart, and just plain entertaining, there's still nothing quite as original as the three bald guys in blue. See p. 562.

Desert to the Beach Highlights

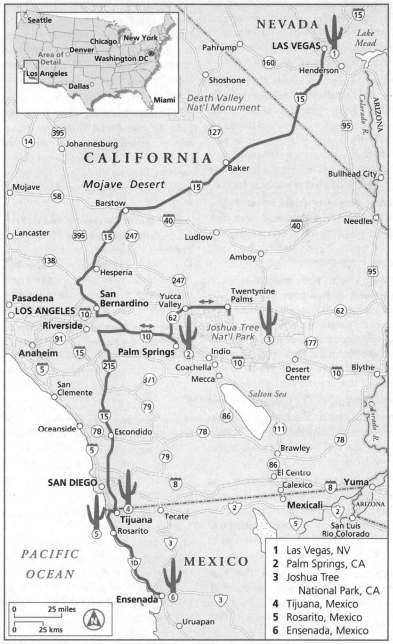

1 Las Vegas, NV
2 Palm Springs, CA
3 Joshua Tree
   National Park, CA
4 Tijuana, Mexico
5 Rosarito, Mexico
6 Ensenada, Mexico

➡ **Smartest Show in Vegas: Penn &
Teller.** Sure there's magic and juggling, but
these magicians? illusionists? truth-tellers?
BS artists? geniuses?—put on 90 minutes of
intelligent, acerbic comedy, mean stunts,
and great quiet beauty. See p. 563.

➡ **Best Vegas Strip Show that (possibly) Won't Make You Feel Sleazy: Forty
Deuce.** Maybe it's because the performers
only strip down to pasties and thongs, or
maybe it's because they're really freakin'
good dancers. Either way, the shows here
entertain without leaving you feeling like
you need a shower afterwards. See p. 558.

➡ **Best Free Attraction in Las Vegas:
MGM Grand Lion Habitat.** A large, multilevel glass structure where real live lions
frolic. Best of all, you can watch without
spending a cent. See p. 566.

➡ **Best Way to Blow $200 in a Night:
THEHotel at Mandalay Bay.** Sure, you
can splurge on hotels in Vegas, but for the
price of a standard double at many luxury
resorts, about $200 (depending on the sea-
son and day of the week) gets you a chic
suite with full living room, and three flatscreen TVs. Can you say *share?* See p. 553.

➡ **Best Hiking not in Joshua Tree: Red
Rock Canyon.** In addition to awe-inspiring natural beauty, Red Rock offers everything from boulders to big walls—and
more than 1,000 routes. See p. 568.

➡ **Best Driving Leg of this Trip: I-15
from Vegas to Palm Springs.** Big open
skies, a two-lane highway buffeted by
rugged mountains—a nice counterpoint to
anything urbane, if you've been itching to
get out of the city. See p. 575.

➡ **Joshua Tree Trail with the Best
Payoff: Fortynine Palms Oasis Trail.**
Accessible from Canyon Road in
Twentynine Palms, this trail's steep, harsh

ascent takes 3 hours but leads to a spectacular oasis of palm-shaded pools. See p. 590.

➡ **Best Place to Pretend You're in a
David Lynch Flick: Twentynine Palms.**
Just outside of Joshua Tree, this small town
boasts a working drive-in theater, dusty
roads, rusty cars, and a whole lotta eccentric desert character. See p. 587.

➡ **Most Awe-Inducing Vista: Atop the
Palm Springs Aerial Tramway.** The 14-
minute ascent to the upper slopes of
Mount San Jacinto produces jaw-dropping
views of the desert floor 5,000 feet below;
it also takes you to a different ecosystem.
See p. 584.

➡ **Most Boring Driving Leg of this Trip:
I-215—Palm Springs to the Mexico/U.S.
Border.** Open desert and two-lane highways give way to sub-suburban freeways
that make this stretch feel less like a road
odyssey and more like a trip to the mall.
See p. 593.

➡ **Best View from Sea Level: Sunset as
Seen from the Rosarito Beach Hotel.** A
room with an ocean view costs a little
more, but Baja's brilliants sunsets over the
Pacific make it worth every penny. See
p. 600.

➡ **Best Surfing in Northern Baja:
Killers.** It's not easy to get there (you need
a boat), but Killers is the location of the
winning wave in the 1997–98 K2
Challenge, a very makeable wave for confident, competent surfers. See p. 602.

➡ **Best Non-P.C. Attraction in Tijuana:
Bullfighting.** Some say it's sport, other
say it's cruel, but there's no denying that
bullfighting has a prominent place in
Mexican heritage. Many of the world's best
matadors perform at Tijuana's two stadiums, so check it out if you'd like to weigh in
on the debate. See p. 599.

Just the Facts

Trip in a Box

Total Miles From Las Vegas, NV, to Palm Springs, CA, to Ensenada, Mexico, about 500 miles.

Route I-15 toward Los Angeles to I-215 S. toward San Bernadino/Riverside; I-10 E. to Palm Springs; I-10 W. to I-215 S. to I-15 S. to I-5 S.; I-5 S to the U.S./Mexico border; Route 1 or 1D South (scenic route) to Tijuana, Rosarito, and Ensenada.

States Nevada, California, Baja (Mexico)

Trip Time 7 days or more for the whole thing, from Vegas to Ensenada.

The Short Version This trip has three major destinations—Las Vegas, Palm Springs, and Baja—all within a short distance of one another. You could make the trip in 5 days and still spend 2 days in both Vegas and Baja.

The Long Version This trip may only be about 500 miles, but you can easily stretch it out for 10 to 12 days. Spend a long weekend in Vegas, taking in the nightlife, with side trips to Hoover Dam, Red Rocks, or Area 51. Detox in Palm Springs Resorts for a couple of days before getting in touch with nature on the Joshua Tree trails. Then head down to Baja and spend 3 to 4 days touring the coastline cities of Tijuana, Rosarito, and Ensenada.

Hitting the Highlights There's no reason you can't make this trip in 4 days. If you're traveling over a long weekend, I would suggest hitting Vegas for 2 days (1 night), then heading to Palm Springs for a day before making your way down to the northern Baja coast.

When to Go At the height of summer, desert temps can be brutal, commonly hitting 115°F to 120°F. I suggest doing your trip late spring or early fall. During May/June or September, it will still feel like summer (think high 90s/low 100s), but chances are you won't encounter the stifling, can't-leave-the-hotel-room temps common in July and August. While winter temps in the desert and beach won't inspire real sunbathing, they're temperate enough (think highs in the 50s to 60s) to enjoy just about all of the outdoor activities this trip has to offer. In Palm Springs, the months from December to May are actually high season. That means that hotel rooms will be a little harder to come by (and cost a bit more), so remember to reserve all of your hotels in advance.

THE MONEY PART

The days of $1.99 buffets and $99 rates at five-star Vegas hotels are over—*way* over. Somewhere along the line, Vegas hoteliers and restaurateurs got wise and realized they didn't have to give away food or cheap rooms to bring people into town. As a result, the prices rival anything you'll find in L.A. or New York. Of course, there are inexpensive options for just about everything, from food to drinks to accommodations. In Palm Springs, prices are lower by comparison, but not by much; you can go cheap but you can also splurge. As a nice counterpoint to Vegas and Palm Springs costs, Tijuana, Rosarito, and Ensenada offer food, drink, and accommodations options that are still about 25% to 40% less expensive than anything north of the border. Even better, all three towns in Mexico accept U.S. dollars, so you don't even need to convert your cash.

ACCOMMODATIONS

Given that all of the major stops on this trip are resort towns, cheap digs aren't as easy to come by as you might expect. However, chain hotels and motels can be found around both Vegas and Palm Springs, and there are clean, comfortable nonchain options in both towns. In Tijuana, Rosarito, and Ensenada, a hotel on the beach might run you a third of what a beach hotel north of the border would cost, but you'll still be paying over $75. We've recommended one clean, comfortable option in each of the Northern Baja cities.

TRANSPORTATION

This trip only runs about 500 miles; that means you'll be spending about $60 for gas. And if you're flying in from somewhere else (which is likely if you're coming from the East Coast or Midwest), figure the

cost of a car rental. Side trips to the Hoover Dam, Red Rocks, or Joshua Tee will add to the cost, of course. Some Vegas hotels provide free parking, though many upscale ones will charge extra (up to $20 per night or more), so call ahead. Even though Vegas is small geographically, the best way to get around is with a cab, so figure around $15 per night if you want to hit the clubs and other casinos. In Palm Springs, most restaurants will be within walking or driving distance of your hotel.

FOOD

Vegas is sort of a world-themed amusement park, so it's no surprise that you can find just about any kind of cuisine here. Accordingly, every notable L.A. and New York celeb chef seems to be opening a kitchen in Vegas. It would be a shame not to try at least one upscale meal here, so we recommend budgeting $50 for at least one splurge meal. Most hotels in Las Vegas offer breakfast and brunch buffets, which run between $10 and $25, depending on where you stay. You can also get by with coffee and a muffin for about $5. Cheap options can be found in food courts in Vegas (p. 553). Both Palm Springs and Baja offer cheap fare, but you can also find moderate and expensive options, if you want to splurge. On average budget $25 a day for food.

Starting Out: Las Vegas, NV

As often as you might have seen it on TV or in a movie, there's nothing that prepares you for that first sight of Las Vegas. The skyline is a hallucination, a mélange of the Statue of Liberty, a giant lion, a pyramid, and a Sphinx, and preternaturally glittering buildings. At night, it's so bright you can actually get disoriented—and suffer from a sensory overload that can reduce you to hapless tears or fits of giggles. And

that's without setting foot inside a casino, where the shouts from the craps tables, the crash of coins from the slots, and the general roar combine into either the greatest adrenaline rush of your life or the ninth pit of hell.

Las Vegas can be whatever you want, and for a few days, *anyone* can be whatever he or she wants (or so the new marketing campaign would have you believe).

DESERT TO THE BEACH

One of the most popular shows in Las Vegas is the Cirque du Soleil.
(photo: Tomasz Rossa/Costumes: Dominique Lemieux/Cirque du Soleil Inc.)

Just be prepared to leave reality behind. Here, you'll rise at noon and gorge on endless amounts of rich food at 3am. You will watch your money grow or (far more likely) shrink. You will watch a volcano explode and pirates fight sexy showgirls. And after a while, it will all seem pretty normal. This is not a cultural vacation, okay? Save the thoughts of museums and historical sights for the real New York, Egypt, Paris, and Venice. Vegas is about fun. Go have some. Go have too much. It won't be hard.

Las Vegas Nuts & Bolts

Area Codes   The area code for Las Vegas is 702.

Banks   Banks are generally open from 9 or 10am to 5 and sometimes 6pm, and most have Saturday hours. ATMs are plentiful all around town. See also "Cash & Credit," below.

Business Hours   Banks and offices are generally open Monday to Friday 8 or 9am to 5pm. Some banks offer drive-through service on Saturday 9am to noon or 1pm. Casinos are generally open 24 hours.

Car Rentals   See "Renting a Car" under "Getting Around," later in this chapter.

Cash & Credit   It's *extremely* easy, too easy, to obtain cash in Las Vegas. Most casino cashiers will cash personal checks and can exchange foreign currency, and just about every casino has a machine that will provide cash on a wide variety of credit cards.

Emergencies Dial ☎ **911** to contact the police or fire department or to call an ambulance.

Highway Conditions For recorded information, call ☎ 702/486-3116. You can also tune in 970 AM for traffic news or 1610 AM for highway reports.

Hospitals Emergency services are available 24 hours a day at **University Medical Center,** 1800 W. Charleston Blvd., at Shadow Lane (☎ 702/383-2000); the emergency-room entrance is on the corner of Hastings and Rose streets. **Sunrise Hospital and Medical Center,** 3186 Maryland Pkwy., between Desert Inn Road and Sahara Avenue (☎ 702/731-8080), also has a 24-hour emergency room.

Liquor & Gambling Laws You must be 21 to drink or gamble; proof of age is required and often requested at bars, nightclubs, and restaurants, so it's always a good idea to bring ID when you go out, especially if you look young. There are no closing hours in Las Vegas for the sale or consumption of alcohol, even on Sunday. Don't even *think* about driving while you're under the influence, or having an open container of alcohol in your car. Beer, wine, and liquor are all sold in all kinds of stores pretty much around the clock; trust us, you won't have a hard time finding a drink. And even though people still do it with abandon, a law was passed recently forbidding open containers on the streets, so you really shouldn't be carrying that giant plastic Eiffel Tower full of strawberry margarita from Paris over to Bellagio.

Lost & Found Be sure to tell all of your credit card companies the minute you discover your wallet has been lost or stolen and file a report at the nearest police precinct. Your credit card company or insurer may require a police report number or record of the loss. Most credit card companies have an emergency toll-free number to call if your card is lost or stolen; they may be able to wire you a cash advance immediately or deliver an emergency credit card in a day or two. **Visa**'s U.S. emergency number is ☎ 800/847-2911 or 410/581-9994. **American Express** cardholders and traveler's check holders should call ☎ 800/221-7282. **MasterCard** holders should call ☎ 800/307-7309 or 636/722-7111. For other credit cards, call the toll-free number directory at ☎ 800/555-1212.

If you need emergency cash over the weekend when all banks and American Express offices are closed, you can have money wired to you via **Western Union** (☎ 800/325-6000; www.westernunion.com).

Identity theft or fraud are potential complications of losing your wallet, especially if you've lost your driver's license along with your cash and credit cards. Notify the major credit-reporting bureaus immediately; placing a fraud alert on your records may protect you against liability for criminal activity. The three major U.S. credit-reporting agencies are **Equifax** (☎ 800/766-0008; www.equifax.com), **Experian** (☎ 888/397-3742; www.experian.com), and **TransUnion** (☎ 800/680-7289; www.transunion.com). Finally, if you've lost all forms of photo ID, call your airline and explain the situation: They might allow you to board the plane if you have a copy of your passport or birth certificate and a copy of the police report you've filed.

Las Vegas Highlights

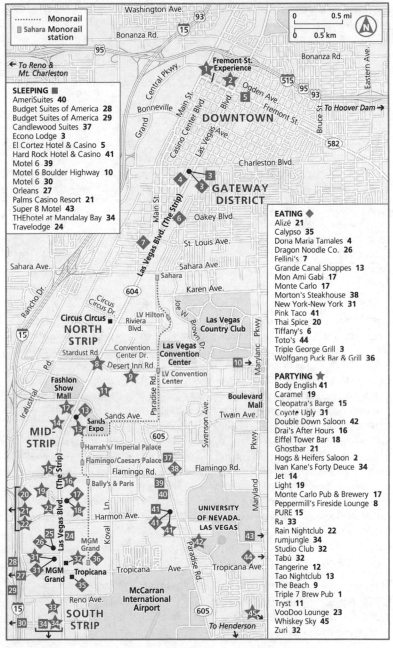

········· Monorail
▯ Sahara Monorail
station

SLEEPING ◼
AmeriSuites **40**
Budget Suites of America **28**
Budget Suites of America **29**
Candlewood Suites **37**
Econo Lodge **3**
El Cortez Hotel & Casino **5**
Hard Rock Hotel & Casino **41**
Motel 6 **39**
Motel 6 Boulder Highway **10**
Motel 6 **30**
Orleans **27**
Palms Casino Resort **21**
Super 8 Motel **43**
THEhotel at Mandalay Bay **34**
Travelodge **24**

EATING ◆
Alizé **21**
Calypso **35**
Dona Maria Tamales **4**
Dragon Noodle Co. **26**
Fellini's **7**
Grande Canal Shoppes **13**
Mon Ami Gabi **17**
Monte Carlo **17**
Morton's Steakhouse **38**
New York-New York **31**
Pink Taco **41**
Thai Spice **20**
Tiffany's **6**
Toto's **44**
Triple George Grill **3**
Wolfgang Puck Bar & Grill **36**

PARTYING ★
Body English **41**
Caramel **19**
Cleopatra's Barge **15**
Coyote Ugly **31**
Double Down Saloon **42**
Drai's After Hours **16**
Eiffel Tower Bar **18**
Ghostbar **21**
Hogs & Heifers Saloon **2**
Ivan Kane's Forty Deuce **34**
Jet **14**
Light **19**
Monte Carlo Pub & Brewery **17**
Peppermill's Fireside Lounge **8**
PURE **15**
Ra **33**
Rain Nightclub **22**
rumjungle **34**
Studio Club **32**
Tabú **32**
Tangerine **12**
Tao Nightclub **13**
The Beach **9**
Triple 7 Brew Pub **1**
Tryst **11**
VooDoo Lounge **23**
Whiskey Sky **45**
Zuri **32**

Newspapers & Magazines There are two Las Vegas dailies: the *Las Vegas Review Journal* and the *Las Vegas Sun.* The *Review Journal's* Friday edition has a helpful "Weekend" section with a comprehensive guide to shows and buffets. There are two free alternative papers, with club listings and many unbiased restaurant and bar reviews. Both *City Life* and *Las Vegas Weekly* are published weekly. And at every hotel desk, you'll find dozens of free local magazines, such as *Vegas Visitor, What's On in Las Vegas, Showbiz Weekly,* and *Where to Go in Las Vegas,* that are chock-full of helpful information—although probably of the sort that comes from paid advertising.

Parking Free valet parking is one of the great pleasures of Las Vegas and well worth the dollar tip (given when the car is returned) to save walking a city block from the far reaches of a hotel parking lot, particularly when the temperature is over 100°F. Another summer plus: The valet will turn on your air-conditioning so that you don't have to get into an "oven on wheels."

Pharmacies There's a 24-hour **Walgreens** (which also has 1-hr. photo processing) at 3763 Las Vegas Blvd. S. (☎ 702/739-9638), almost directly across from the Monte Carlo. **Sav-On** is a large 24-hour drugstore and pharmacy close to the Strip at 1360 E. Flamingo Rd., at Maryland Parkway (☎ 702/731-5373). **White Cross Drugs,** 1700 Las Vegas Blvd. S. (☎ 702/382-1733), open daily from 7am to 1am, will make pharmacy deliveries to your hotel during the day.

Police For non-emergencies, call ☎ 702/795-3111. For emergencies, call ☎ **911.**

Post Office The most convenient post office is immediately behind the Stardust hotel at 3100 Industrial Rd., between Sahara Avenue and Spring Mountain Road (☎ 800/297-5543). It's open Monday to Friday from 8:30am to 5pm. You can also mail letters and packages at your hotel, and there's a full-service U.S. Post Office in the Forum Shops in Caesars Palace.

Safety In Las Vegas, vast amounts of money are always on display, and criminals find many easy marks. Don't be one of them. At gaming tables and slot machines, men should keep wallets well concealed and out of the reach of pickpockets, and women should keep handbags in plain sight (on laps). If you win a big jackpot, ask the pit boss or slot attendant to cut you a check rather than give you cash—the cash may look nice, but flashing it can attract the wrong kind of attention. Outside casinos, popular spots for pickpockets and thieves are restaurants and outdoor shows, such as the volcano at The Mirage or the fountains at Bellagio. Stay alert. Unless your hotel room has an in-room safe, check your valuables in a safe-deposit box at the front desk.

Taxes Clark County hotel room tax is 9%, and in Henderson it's 10%; the sales tax is 7%.

Time Zone Las Vegas is in the Pacific time zone, 3 hours earlier than the East Coast, 2 hours earlier than the Midwest. For exact local time, call ☎ 702/248-4800.

Weather For local weather information, call ☎ 702/248-4800. The radio station 970 FM does weather reports.

Las Vegas Attractions

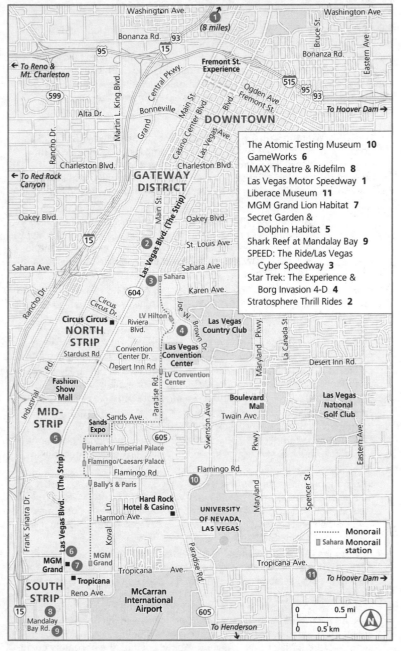

The Atomic Testing Museum **10**
GameWorks **6**
IMAX Theatre & Ridefilm **8**
Las Vegas Motor Speedway **1**
Liberace Museum **11**
MGM Grand Lion Habitat **7**
Secret Garden &
 Dolphin Habitat **5**
Shark Reef at Mandalay Bay **9**
SPEED: The Ride/Las Vegas
 Cyber Speedway **3**
Star Trek: The Experience &
 Borg Invasion 4-D **4**
Stratosphere Thrill Rides **2**

A Short List of Las Vegas Events

It may come as no surprise that Vegas doesn't offer an enormous number of annual cultural events. After all, gaming's the thing here. This town wants its visitors in the casinos spending (that is, losing) their money, not at fairs and parades. If you're looking for something off the gaming path, check the local paper and contact the **Las Vegas Convention and Visitors Authority** (☎ 877/ **VISIT-LV** or 702/892-7575; www.visitlasvegas.com) or the **Chamber of Commerce** (☎ **702/735-1616**; www.lvchamber.com) to find out about other events scheduled during your visit.

→ **NASCAR/Winston Cup** The **Las Vegas Motor Speedway, 7000** N. Las Vegas Blvd. (☎ **800/644-4444**; www.lvms.com), has become one of the premier facilities in the country, attracting races and racers of all stripes and colors. The biggest of the year are the Sam's Town 300 and the UAW-DaimlerChrysler 400 held in early March, often drawing over 150,000 race fans to town.

→ **CineVegas International Film Festival** This annual event, usually held in early June, is growing in popularity and prestige, with film debuts from both independent and major studios, plus lots of celebrities hanging around for the big parties. Call ☎ **702/992-7979** or visit their website at **www.cine vegas.com** for exact dates.

→ **World Series of Poker** Now held at **The Rio All-Suite Hotel and Casino** (3700 W. Flamingo Rd.; ☎ **800/PLAY-RIO**) in June and July instead of April and May, the event features high-stakes gamblers and showbiz personalities competing for six-figure purses. There are daily events with entry stakes ranging from $125 to $5,000. To enter the World Championship Event (purse: $1 million), players must pony up $10,000. It costs nothing to go crowd around the tables and watch the action (which, in 2003, was televised for the first time on The Travel Channel). For more information, visit the official website at **www.worldseriesofpoker.com**.

→ **Oktoberfest** This boisterous autumn holiday is celebrated from mid-September through the end of October at the Mount Charleston Lodge (☎ **800/955-1314** or 702/872-5408; www.mtcharlestonlodge.com) with music, folk dancers, singalongs around a roaring fire, special decorations, and Bavarian cookouts.

→ **International Mariachi Festival** Mandalay Bay, 3950 Las Vegas Blvd. S. (at Hacienda Ave.), started hosting this worldwide Mariachi (Mexican music) festival a few years ago, and it has become one of the city's most eagerly anticipated events. Call Mandalay Bay at ☎ **877/632-7400.** The event is usually held in early September.

→ **New Year's Eve in Las Vegas** Over the last couple of years, more and more people have been choosing Las Vegas as their party destination for New Year's Eve. In fact, some estimates indicate that by the time you read this, there will be more people ringing in the New Year in Nevada than in New York City's Times Square. A major portion of the Strip is closed down, sending the masses and their substantial quantities of alcohol into the street. Each year's celebration is a little different but usually includes a street-side performance by a major celebrity, confetti, the obligatory countdown, and fireworks.

Getting Around

It shouldn't be too hard to navigate your way around. But remember, between huge hotel acreage, increased and very slow traffic, and lots and lots of people trying to explore like you, getting around takes a lot longer than you might think. Heck, it can take 15 to 20 minutes to get from your room to another part of your hotel! Always allow for plenty of time to get from point A to point B.

BY CAR

The Strip is too spread out for walking (and Las Vegas is often too hot or too cold to make strolls pleasant). Downtown is too far away for a cheap cab ride, and public transportation is often ineffective in getting you from point A to point B. Plus, return visits call for exploration in more remote parts of the city, and a car brings freedom (especially if you want to do any side trips—bus tours are available, but a car lets you explore at your own pace rather than according to a tour schedule).

You should note that places with addresses some 60 blocks east or west from the Strip are actually less than a 10-minute drive—provided there's no traffic.

Renting a Car

If you're flying in to Las Vegas (which is fairly likely, since it's pretty far away from two-thirds of the country, and flights are plentiful and cheap), national companies with outlets in Las Vegas include **Alamo** (☎ 877/227-8367; www.goalamo.com); **Avis** (☎ 800/230 4898; www.avis.com); **Budget** (☎ 800/527-0700; https://rent.drivebudget.com/Home.jsp); **Dollar** (☎ 800/800-3665; www.dollar.com); **Enterprise** (☎ 800/736-8227; www.enterprise.com); **Hertz** (☎ 800/654-3131; www.hertz.com); **National** (☎ 800/227-7368; www.nationalcar.com); **Payless**

Las Vegas Driving Tips

Because driving on the outskirts of Las Vegas—for example, coming from California—involves desert driving, you must take certain precautions. It's a good idea to check your tires, water, and oil before leaving. Take at least 5 gallons of water in a clean container that can be used for either drinking or to fill the radiator. Pay attention to road signs that suggest when to turn off your car's air conditioner. And don't push your luck with gas—it may be 35 miles or more between stations. If your car overheats, do not remove the radiator cap until the engine has cooled, and then remove it very slowly. You might want to remove it with a towel or other cloth in case it is still too hot to touch with your bare hand. Add water to within an inch of the top of the radiator.

(☎ 800/729-5377; www.paylesscarrental.com); and **Thrifty** (☎ 800/847-4389; www.thrifty.com).

Car-rental rates vary even more than airline fares. The price you pay will depend on the size of the car, where and when you pick it up and drop it off, the length of the rental period, where and how far you drive it, whether you purchase insurance, and a host of other factors. We go into a bit more detail about car rental in chapter 2, "The Basics" (p. 15).

BY TAXI

Since cabs line up in front of all major hotels, an easy way to get around town is by taxi. Cabs charge $3.20 at the meter drop and 25¢ for each additional eighth of a mile, plus an additional $1.20 fee for being picked up at the airport. A taxi from the airport to the Strip will run you $12 to $20, from the airport to Downtown $15 to $20, and between the Strip and Downtown about $10 to $15.

If you want to call a taxi, any of the following companies can provide one: **Desert Cab Company** (☎ 702/386-9102), **Whittlesea Blue Cab** (☎ 702/384-6111), and **Yellow/Checker Cab/Star Company** (☎ 702/873-2000).

BY MONORAIL

The first leg of a high-tech monorail that will eventually become a citywide mass-transit system opened in 2004, offering riders their first and best shot of getting from one end of The Strip to the other with a minimum of frustration and expense. The 4-mile route runs from the MGM Grand at the southern end of The Strip to the Sahara at the northern end with stops at Paris/Bally's, The Flamingo, Imperial Palace/Harrah's, The Las Vegas Convention Center, and The Las Vegas Hilton along the way.

Fares are $3 (!!!) for a one-way ride (whether you ride from one end to the other or just to the next station) but discounts are available for round-trips and multi-ride/day passes.

BY PUBLIC TRANSPORTATION

The no. 301 bus operated by **Citizens Area Transit** (☎ 702/CAT-RIDE) plies a route between the Downtown Transportation Center (at Casino Center Blvd. and Stewart Ave.) and a few miles beyond the southern end of the Strip. The fare is $2 for adults, 60¢ for seniors 62 and older and children 5 to 17, and free for those under 5. CAT buses run 24 hours a day and are wheelchair-accessible. Exact change is required, but dollar bills are accepted.

Or you can hop aboard a classic street-car replica run by **Las Vegas Strip Trolley** (☎ 702/382-1404). These old-fashioned,

dark-green vehicles have interior oak paneling and are comfortably air-conditioned. Like the buses, they run northward from Hacienda Avenue, stopping at all major hotels en route to the Sahara, and then loop back from the Las Vegas Hilton. Trolleys run about every 15 minutes daily between 9:30am and 2am. The fare is $1.75 (free for children under age 5), but save your quarters because exact change is required.

Sleeping

Vegas is a town of excess, and accommodations are no exception. You'll find 9 of the 10 largest hotels in the United States—8 of the top 10 in the world—right here. And you'll find a whole lotta rooms: 140,000 rooms, give or take few hundred. Every 5 minutes, or so it seems, someone is putting up a new giant hotel or adding another 1,000 rooms to an existing one. So finding a place to stay in Vegas should be the least of your worries—even if you're on a budget.

Hotel prices in Vegas are anything but fixed, so you will notice wildly disparate price ranges. The same room can routinely go for anywhere from $60 to $250, depending on demand, and even that range is negotiable if it's a slow time. So use our price categories with a grain of salt, and don't rule out a hotel just because it's listed as "Splurge"—on any given day, you might get a great deal on a room in a pricey hotel. Just look online or call and ask.

CHEAP

➜ **El Cortez Hotel & Casino** This small hotel is popular with locals for its casual, oh, and let's just admit it, dated Downtown atmosphere. Rooms offer nothing except a place to rest your head and not get lice. And there is no room to swing a cat, dead or otherwise, in the bathrooms. But on the

Cheap Hotel Alternatives in Las Vegas

If you're determined to come to Vegas during a particularly busy season and you find yourself shut out of the prominent hotels, here's a list of inexpensive alternatives. Most offer clean, comfortable rooms for under $75.

On or Near the Strip
Budget Suites of America, 4205 W. Tropicana Ave.; ☎ **702/889-1700**

Budget Suites of America, 3655 W. Tropicana Ave.; ☎ **702/739-1000**

Travelodge, 3735 Las Vegas Blvd. S.; ☎ **800/578-7878**

Paradise Road & Vicinity
AmeriSuites, 4250 Paradise Rd.; ☎ **800/833-1516**

Candlewood Suites, 4034 Paradise Rd; ☎ **800/226-3539**

Downtown & Vicinity
Econo Lodge, 1150 Las Vegas Blvd. S.; ☎ **800/553-2666**

East Las Vegas & Vicinity
Motel 6 Boulder Highway, 4125 Boulder Hwy.; ☎ **800/466-8356**

Super 8 Motel, 5288 Boulder Hwy.; ☎ **800/825-0880**

West Las Vegas & Vicinity
Motel 6, 5085 Dean Martin Dr. (South Las Vegas); ☎ **800/466-8356**

other hand, said rooms (recently renovated) supposedly do not cost more than $40 a night, so really, whaddaya want for next to nothing (by Vegas prices)? 600 Fremont St. (between 6th and 7th sts.). ☎ 800/634-6703 or 702/385-5200. www.elcortezhotelcasino.com. 428 units. $25 and up double; $40 minisuite. Free self- and valet parking. Amenities: Casino; 2 restaurants. In room: A/C, TV.

→**Motel 6** Fronted by a big neon sign, this Motel 6 is the largest in the country, and it happens to be a great budget choice. Most Motel 6 properties are a little out-of-the-way, but this one is quite close to major Strip casino hotels (the MGM is nearby). It has a big, pleasant lobby, and the rooms, in two-story, cream-stucco buildings, are clean and attractively decorated. Some rooms have showers only; others have tub/shower bathrooms. Local calls are free. 195 E. Tropicana Ave. (at Koval Lane). ☎ 800/4-MOTEL-6 (466-8356) or 702/798-0728. www.motel6.com. 602 units. $45 and up

single. Extra person $8. Free parking at your room door. Amenities: 2 outdoor pools; Jacuzzi; tour desk; coin-op laundry. In room: A/C, TV w/pay movies.

→**Orleans** ★ If the prices hold true (as always, they can vary), this hotel is one of the best bargains in town, despite the location. The rooms are nice enough and have a definite New Orleans–French feel. Each is L-shaped, with a seating alcove by the windows, and comes complete with an old-fashioned, overstuffed chair and sofa. The beds have brass headboards, the lamps (including some funky iron floor lamps) look antique, and lace curtains flutter at the windows. The **Orleans Showroom** is an 827-seat theater featuring live entertainment, the **Orleans Arena** is a large facility for concerts and sporting events, and, of course, there's a casino. 4500 W. Tropicana Ave. (west of the Strip and I-15). ☎ 800/ORLEANS (675-3267) or 702/365-7111. www.orleanscasino.com. 1,886 units. $39 and up double; $175–$225 suite.

Free self- and valet parking. Amenities: Casino; showroom; 12 restaurants; 9,000-seat arena; 70-lane bowling center; 18 movie theaters; 2 outdoor pools; health club and spa; video-game arcade; concierge; tour desk; car-rental desk; 24-hr. room service; laundry service; dry cleaning; In room: A/C, TV w/pay movies, dataport, hair dryer, iron/ironing board, high-speed Internet access (for a fee).

➜ **Terrible's** ★★ First of all, this place isn't terrible at all (the owner is Ed "Terrible" Herbst, who operates a chain of convenience stores and gas stations). Second, it isn't a bit like the hotel it took over, the rat-trap known as the Continental. The Continental is gone, and good riddance. In its place is an unexpected bargain, a hotel frequently offering ridiculously low prices. Try this on for size: $39 a night! Near the Strip! Near a bunch of really good restaurants! Don't expect much in the way of memorable rooms; they are as basic as can be, but the pool looks like what you might find in a nice apartment complex, and there's a pennies gambling casino. *4100 Paradise Rd. (at Flamingo Rd.).* ☎ *800/640-9777 or 702/733-7000. www.terribleherbst.com. 374 units. $39 and up double. Free self- and valet parking. Amenities: 3 restaurants; outdoor pool; 24-hr. room service; laundry service. In room: A/C, TV w/pay movies, dataport, coffeemaker, hair dryer, pay-per-use Nintendo.*

DOABLE

➜ **Hard Rock Hotel & Casino** ★★ As soon as you check out the Hard Rock clientele, you'll know you are in a Vegas hotel that's like no other. The body-fat percentage plummets; the percentage of black clothing skyrockets. Yep, the hip—including Hollywood and the music industry, among others—still flock to the Hard Rock, drawn by the cool 'n' rockin' ambience. It's that Gen-X sensibility that finds tacky-chic

so very hip. Luckily, the "no-tell motel" look of the older rooms has been updated to more closely match the decor of the rooms in the newer addition.

There are several fine restaurants, including **AJ's Steakhouse, Morton's,** and **Nobu,** a branch of highly famed chef Nobu Matsuhisa's popular Japanese restaurant. If you don't want to blow all your cash, kicky and funky Mexican food can be had at lunch and dinner in the Mexican, folk-art-filled **Pink Taco** (p. 555), while three diner-type meals a day are served at the 22-seat **Counter. Mr. Lucky's 24/7** is the hotel's 'round-the-clock coffee shop. And the **Hard Rock Cafe** is adjacent to the hotel.

The Joint is a major showroom that often hosts big-name rock musicians. And if you've ever dreamed of being in a beach party movie, or on the set of one of those MTV summer beach-house shows, the reconstructed pool at the Hard Rock is for you. On Sunday afternoons, the hotel's Rehab pool party is *the* hangout scene. *4455 Paradise Rd. (at Harmon Ave.).* ☎ *800/473-ROCK (473-7625) or 702/693-5000. www.hardrockhotel.com. 657 units. $119 and up double. Free self- and valet parking. Amenities: Casino; showroom; 6 restaurants; 2 outdoor pools w/lazy river and sandy-beach bottom; small health club and spa; concierge; tour desk; salon; 24-hr. room service; laundry service; dry cleaning; executive-level rooms. In room: A/C, TV w/pay movies, dataport, hair dryer, iron/ironing board, high-speed Internet access (for a fee).*

➜ **Palms Casino Resort** ★ One of the hottest of the newer hotels, given quite the PR boost when it was Britney's base for her (first) wedding debacle. In keeping with the tropical-foliage name, it's more or less Miami-themed (but without the pastels), with a strange aversion to straight lines. Both **ghostbar** and the nightclub **Rain** have lines of people every night, offering to sell their firstborn sons for a chance to go inside. If you are a Hilton sister, or want to see if one will date you, this could be heaven.

Having said all that, the Palms has perhaps some of the most comfortable beds in Vegas, thanks to fluffy pillows and duvets that make you reluctant to rise, plus big TVs and huge bathrooms. The pool areas got party-spot makeovers, turning what were kind of bland "stand and pose" watering holes into must-visit beach areas this kind of crowd loves. Also on the property is **Alizé** (p. 556), in competition for the title Best Restaurant in Town (and owner of the title Most Gorgeous and Romantic Restaurant), the cheap and hearty **Fantasy Market Buffet,** movie theaters, a McDonald's, and other reliable chain eateries. *4321 W. Flamingo Rd. (just west of I-15).* ☎ *866/942-7777 or 702/942-7777. www. palms.com. 664 units. $99 and up double. Free self- and valet parking. Amenities: Casino; nightclub/showroom; 7 restaurants plus a food court; outdoor pool; health club and spa; concierge; business center; salon; 24-hr. room service; in-room massage; laundry service; dry cleaning; executive-level rooms. In room: A/C, TV w/pay movies, dataport, coffeemaker, hair dryer, iron/ironing board, safe, high-speed Internet access (for a fee).*

SPLURGE

➜ **THEhotel at Mandalay Bay** ★★★ If Prada were a hotel, it would look something like THEhotel. This is not a casino hotel but a world of sleek towering walls of lighting, ambiguous modern art, and both guests and employees in head-to-toe black. Like any good Vegas hotel, it wows you from the start, but in a way that coolly says, "You probably already live like this, don't you?" while handing you a nicely chilled Cosmopolitan. Sophisticated and

chic, it's all blacks, tans, woods, and mid-century (20th, that is) modern sharp lines. Best of all, every room is a genuine suite (not just separated living room and bedroom, but even includes a wet bar and second toilet).

The staff is hardly cuddly, and service reflects that. Costs at the sleek cafes are higher than even the usual elevated hotel restaurant prices. But considering what you get, you get a lot of bang for the buck. *3950 Las Vegas Blvd. S.* ☎ *877/632-7800 or 702/632-7777 www.thehotelatmandalaybay. com. 1,120 units. $189 and up suite. Free self- and valet parking. Amenities: 2 restaurants; bar; access to Mandalay Bay restaurants/pool/casino; health club and spa; tour desk; car-rental desk; business center; 24-hr. room service; laundry service. In room: A/C, 3 flatscreen TVs, CD/DVD, combo printer/fax, wet bar, hair dryer, iron/ironing board, high-speed Internet access (for a fee).*

Eating

The good news is that just about every notable chef in the world seems to be setting up shop in Vegas. The bad new is that if you dined out every meal while Vegas, you probably wouldn't have enough gas money to make it out of town. Luckily, there's plenty of cheap eats in Vegas—from food courts to small, independent eateries—so you can save your gas money and any cash left over for those coveted Clay Aiken tickets.

TAKEOUT TREATS

Food courts are a dime a dozen in Vegas, but the one in **New York–New York,** 3790 Las Vegas Blvd. S. (☎ **702/740-6969**), is the nicest one on the Strip, sitting in the Greenwich Village section of New York–New York, which means scaled replica tenement buildings, steam rising from the manhole covers, and more than a little (faux, naturally) greenery, a nice change from unrelentingly shrill plastic mall decor. The selections are the usual, but it's a better-than-average food court, with Chinese food and pizza (as befitting an ode to NYC), and excellent if expensive (for this situation) double-decker burgers, plus **Schraft's** ice cream.

The **Monte Carlo,** 3770 Las Vegas Blvd. S., between Flamingo Road and Tropicana Avenue (☎ **702/730-7777**), has some surprisingly good options, too. Sure, there's always-reliable **McDonald's,** and for sweets there is **Häagen-Dazs,** but they also have a branch of **Nathan's Hot Dogs,** New York's finest. The **Golden Bagel** offers another New York staple, big and tasty enough to satisfy even picky natives. **Sbarro** offers enticing pizza slices. If you want a good, cheap meal on the Strip and want to avoid some of those dubious night-owl specials, come here. It's open daily from 6am to 3am.

And if you head farther down the Strip, to the **Grande Canal Shoppes** at The Venetian, 3355 Las Vegas Blvd. S. (☎ **702/ 414-1000**), you can find another decent food court, with a **Panda Express,** a good pizza place (despite the confusing name of **LA Italian Kitchen**), a burrito stand, a juice joint, and, best of all, a **Krispy Kreme,** where they make the donuts on the premises. Plus, it's right by the canals of this faux Venice, one of our favorite places in Vegas.

EATING OUT
Cheap

➔ **Calypsos** ★ DINER Here's a solid, inexpensive place to fill up, which is pretty rare on the Strip. Sure, it's kind of like a Denny's, but its traditional coffee-shop choices (including a "create your own burger") are better than you might expect. There are some eccentric menu choices

like smoked-salmon plate and a rosemary-chicken sandwich on onion focaccia bread. *In Tropicana Resort & Casino, 3801 Las Vegas Blvd. S. ☎ 702/739-2222. Reservations not accepted. Main courses $6–$19. Daily 24 hr.*

➔ **Dona Maria Tamales** ★★ MEXICAN Decorated with Tijuana-style quilt work and calendars, this quintessential Mexican diner is convenient to both the north end of the Strip and Downtown. You'll start off with homemade chips and a spicy salsa served in a mortar. Meals are so large that it shouldn't be a problem getting full just ordering off the sides, which can make this even more of a budget option. The specialty is kick-ass tamales, natch; they come in red, green, cheese, or sweet. They also serve up excellent enchiladas, chiles rellenos, burritos, and fajitas. All dinners include rice, beans, tortillas, and soup or salad. *910 Las Vegas Blvd. S. (at Charleston Blvd.). ☎ 702/382-6538. www.donamaria tamales.com. Main courses $5.50–$8 at breakfast, $6–$13 at lunch or dinner. Daily 8am–11pm.*

➔ **Dragon Noodle Co.** ★★ ASIAN A good choice for a cheap meal, Dragon Noodle is one of the better Chinese restaurants in town. In addition to the usual suspects, there's some other interesting (if not radically less commonplace) choices on the menu. Food is served family-style and prepared in an open kitchen, so you know it's fresh. Be sure to try the very smooth house green tea. You might let your waiter choose your meal for you, but try the crispy Peking pork, the sweet pungent shrimp, the pot stickers, and maybe the seafood soup. *In Monte Carlo Resort & Casino, 3770 Las Vegas Blvd. S. ☎ 702/730-7965. www.dragonnoodleco.com. Main courses $5.50–$17 (many under $10). Sun–Thurs 11am–11pm; Fri–Sat 11am–midnight.*

→**Thai Spice** THAI The chill atmosphere, quick service, and good, cheap eats make this joint a local fave. The menu is extensive and offers an array of Thai dishes and even some Chinese fare. For appetizers, the *tom kah kai* soup and pork or chicken satay (served on skewers with a spicy peanut sauce) are excellent. Skip the *moo goo gai pan* in favor of terrific pad Thai and tasty lemon chicken. Lunch specials are $6.45 and include spring rolls, salad, soup, and steamed rice. **Tip:** Make sure you tell the waitress how spicy you want your food. *4433 W. Flamingo Rd. (at Arville St.).* ☎ *702/362-5308. Main courses $6.45 at lunch, $8–$15 at dinner. Daily 11:30am–10pm.*

→**Tiffany's** ★★ DINER This decidedly unflashy soda fountain/lunch counter was Las Vegas's first 24-hour restaurant, and it has been going strong for 60 years. The menu is basic comfort food: standard items (meatloaf, ground round steak, chops, and so on), fluffy cream pies, and classic breakfasts served anytime—try the biscuits and cream gravy at 3am. But the best bet is a ⅓-pound burger and "thick, creamy shake," both about as good as they get. At around $6, this is half what you would pay for a comparable meal at the Hard Rock Cafe. *1700 Las Vegas Blvd. S. (at East Oakey Blvd.).* ☎ *702/383-0196. Most items under $7. No credit cards. Daily 24 hr.*

→**Toto's** ★★ MEXICAN A family-style Mexican restaurant favored by locals, with ginormous portions and quick service, this is good value for your cash. There are no surprises on the menu, though there are quite a few seafood dishes. Everything is tasty, and they don't skimp on the cheese. The non-greasy chips come with fresh salsa, and the nachos are terrific. The operative word here is *huge;* the burritos are almost the size of your arm. The generosity

continues with dessert—a piece of flan was practically pie size. *2055 E. Tropicana Ave.* ☎ *702/895-7923. Main courses $7–$15. Mon–Thurs 11am–10pm; Fri–Sat 11am–11pm; Sun 9:30am–10pm.*

Doable

→**Fellini's** ★ ITALIAN A Vegas institution (in its original West Las Vegas location), much beloved by in-the-know locals, Fellini's is a classic Italian restaurant—you know, red gloopy sauce, garlicky cheesy bread. The menu offers a variety of options from *osso buco* to basic pizza; it might not be ambitious, but it's reliable and more than satisfying. They do a strong version of pasta (rigatoni, in this case) Amatriciana, and they are generous with the pancetta. *In Stratosphere Hotel & Casino. 2000 Las Vegas Blvd S.* ☎ *702/383-4859. Main courses $9–$24. Sun–Thurs 5–11pm; Fri–Sat 5pm–midnight.*

→**Mon Ami Gabi** ★★ BISTRO This charming bistro is one of our favorite Vegas spots. It has it all: a cool setting, better-than-average food, and, well, doable prices. Yeah, it goes overboard in trying to replicate a classic Parisian bistro, but the results are less cheesy than most Vegas attempts at atmosphere, and the patio seating on the Strip actually makes you feel like you're in a real, not a pre-fab, city. You can be budget-conscious and order just the very fine onion soup, or you can eat like a real French person and order classic steak (the filet mignon is probably the best cut, if not the cheapest) and *pommes frites* (french fries). *In Paris Las Vegas, 3655 Las Vegas Blvd. S.* ☎ *702/944-GABI. www.monamigabi.com. Main courses $16–$35. Mon–Fri 11:30am–3:30pm; Sun–Thurs 5–11pm; Fri–Sat 5pm–midnight; Sat–Sun brunch 11am–3:30pm.*

→**Pink Taco** ★ MEXICAN A mega-hip Mexican cantina, this folk-art–bedecked spot is a scene just waiting to happen, or rather, it's already happened. There are no surprises in terms of the food; you know the drill—tacos, burritos, quesadillas—but it's all tasty and filling, and some of it comes with some surprising accompaniments, like tapenade, along with the usual guacamole and sour cream. This is hip Mexican as opposed to a mom-and-pop joint, and it's a good place to eat on this side of town. *In the Hard Rock Hotel & Casino, 4455 Paradise Rd.* ☎ *702/693-5525. www. pinktaco.com. Main courses $7.50–$15. Sun–Thurs 11am–10pm; Fri–Sun 11am–midnight (bar stays open later).*

➜ **Triple George Grill** ★★ DINER We've come to expect Vegas homages to great cities and sights of the world, so maybe it was inevitable that one day there would be an homage to a restaurant. It's a virtual replica of the interior of San Francisco's 150-year-old Tadich Grill with a menu that also reflects that institution's influence. As with many faux diners, the menu is a bit all over the place—bruschetta and raw oyster appetizers; steaks, corned beef hash, blackened catfish, and veal piccata for the main courses—but all largely in the comfort food zone. *201 N. 3rd St. (at Ogden Ave.).* ☎ *702/384-2761. http://triplegeorgegrill.com. Main courses $8–$24. Sun–Thurs 11am–10pm; Fri–Sat 11am–11pm.*

➜ **Wolfgang Puck Bar & Grill** ★★ CALIFORNIAN There's nothing surprising on the menu if you've eaten in any modern cafe in the post-Puck era. Frankly, it's still a relief in Vegas, and there's enough variety that everyone in your crew should find something to satisfy, from crab cakes with basil aioli to a prime rib sandwich to homemade veal ravioli to Puck's pizzas. It's all set in an almost entirely open space, a minimalist art take on a country kitchen, and a little noisy thanks to proximity to

the casino floor and cheers from the nearby sports book. *In MGM Grand, 3799 Las Vegas Blvd. S.* ☎ *702/891-3019. www.wolfgang puck.com. Lunch $10–$24; dinner $10–$38 (most under $25). Sun–Thurs 11:30am–10:30pm; Fri–Sat 11:30am–11:30pm.*

Splurge

➜ **Alizé** ★★★ FRENCH It may not be standard roadtrip fare, but Alizé is simply one of the best restaurants in the city. Thanks to swank dining digs and stunning views in (the restaurant is situated at the top of the Palms Hotel, with three sides of full-length windows) no restaurant offers a more impressive table. Then there's the food: The executive chef is Jacques Van Staden, who trained with one of the world's greatest chefs, Jean-Louis Pallidin. The menu changes seasonally, but anything you order will be heavenly.

Fish can be a wee bit dry here, so we suggest either the stunning New York steak with summer truffle jus and potato herb pancakes, or the meltingly tender lamb chops with some shredded lamb shank wrapped in a crispy fried crepe. *In Palms Casino Resort, 4321 W. Flamingo Rd.* ☎ *702/ 951-7000. www.alizelv.com. Reservations strongly recommended. Entrees $30–$67. Sun–Thurs 5:30–10pm; Fri–Sat 5:30–11pm.*

➜ **Morton's Steakhouse** ★ STEAK/SEAFOOD A venerable steakhouse with branches throughout the U.S.—in fact, Mr. Morton is the proud papa of Peter Morton, formerly of the Hard Rock Hotel over yonder. Like **The Palm,** this place serves "guy food"—steaks, really good steaks. Anyway, this is an old-time Vegas hangout, even in its relatively new off-Strip location. In addition to your cut of beef, suggested sides include flavorfully fresh al dente asparagus served with hollandaise, or hash browns. If you just have to have a steak, this is the place. *400 E. Flamingo Rd.*

(at Paradise Rd.). ☎ *702/893-0703. www. mortons.com. Reservations recommended. Main courses $16–$48. Mon–Sat 5–11pm; Sun 5–10pm.*

Partying

This is (presumably) why you've come: Vegas's nightlife is legendary, and rest assured—it rarely disappoints. Whether you want to grab a low-key martini after dinner or indulge in an unprecedented night of debauchery, Vegas welcomes all nightlife predilections. Only problem, some of those predilections come complete with a *not* so welcome hangover, so party wisely.

BARS

→**Caramel** ★★ It's small, but worlds away from the Bellagio-business-as-usual just outside its doors. How happy the 20-somethings are that there is this hip-hop spinning, glowing, caramel-and-chocolate-coated drink glasses, glowing bar, non-threatening (and non-Euro-stodgy), scene-intensive hangout in the middle of Bellagio. How much does this prove Bellagio is trying to lure the ghostbar crowd away from the Palms? *In Bellagio, 3600 Las Vegas Blvd. S.* ☎ *702/693-7111. Daily 5pm–4am.*

→**Coyote Ugly** ★ You've seen the movie, now go have some of that prepackaged fun for yourself. Oh, come on—you don't think those bartender girls really dance on the bar and hose down the crowd just because they're so full of spontaneous rowdy high sprits, now do you? Not when the original locale built a reputation (and inspired a bad movie) on just such behavior, creating a success strong enough to start a whole chain of such frat-boy fun places? By the way, sarcastic and cynical as we are—totally fun place. Straight up. *In New York–New York, 3790 Las Vegas Blvd. S. (at*

Tropicana Ave.). ☎ *702/740-6969. www.coyote uglysaloon.com. Cover varies, usually $10 and up on weekends. Daily 6pm–4am.*

→**Double Down Saloon** ★★★ "House rule: You puke, you clean." That about sums up the Double Down. This is a big local hangout, with management quoting an old *Scope* magazine description of its clientele: "Hipsters, blue collars, the well-heeled lunatic fringe." Trippy hallucinogenic graffiti covers the walls, the ceiling, the tables, and possibly you, if you sit there long enough. *4640 Paradise Rd. (at Naples Dr)* ☎ *702/791-5775. www.doubledownsaloon. com. Daily 24 hr.*

→**Eiffel Tower Bar** ★ From this chic and elegant room, in the restaurant on the 11th floor of the Eiffel Tower, you can look down on everyone (in Vegas)—just like a real Parisian. But really, this is a date-impressing bar, and, since there's no cover or minimum, it's a cost-effective alternative to the overly inflated food prices at the restaurant. Drop by for a drink, but try to look sophisticated. And then you can cop an attitude and dismiss everything as *gauche*—or *droit*. *In Paris Las Vegas, 3655 Las Vegas Blvd. S.* ☎ *702/948-6937. Daily 11am–11:30pm.*

→**ghostbar** ★★ Probably the most interesting aspect of this desperate-to-get-into-trendy-bar-of-the-moment place (decorated with a '60s mod/futuristic silver-gleam look) is that though much is made of the fact that it's on the 55th floor, it's really on the 42nd. Something about the number 4 being bad luck in Asian cultures. Whatever. The view still is rad, which is the main reason to come here—that and to peer at those tousled-hair hotties copping an attitude on the couches. *In the Palms Resort & Casino, 4321 W. Flamingo Rd. (just west of the Strip).* ☎ *702/942-7778. Cover varies, usually $10 and up. Daily 8pm–dawn.*

DESERT TO THE BEACH

↠ **Hogs & Heifers Saloon** ★ While there is a chain of Coyote Ugly nightclubs (including one here in Vegas), the movie of the same name was actually based on the hijinks that happened at the New York version of this rowdy roadhouse saloon. New to Sin City as of 2005, the hogs here are of the motorcycle variety, and the place definitely draws a crowd that can look intimidating but is usually a friendly (and boisterous) bunch. Saucy, heckling bar maidens and outdoor barbeques on select weekends make this one of the few good options for nightlife in the Downtown area. *201 N. 3rd St. (between Ogden and Stewart aves., 1 block from the Fremont St. Experience).* ☎ *702/676-1457. Daily 10am–6am.*

MTV **Best ❢** ↠ **Ivan Kane's Forty Deuce** ★★ The brainchild of Los Angeles club impresario Ivan Kane, this is a supremely hot combo bar/nightclub/burlesque review, a modern take on the classic girlie shows, featuring *va-va-voom* clever dancers (with shows every 90 min. for at least 15 min.—longer if there are more dancers) who strip down to little pasties, short-shorts, and g-strings. Drinks are obscenely expensive, and tables are entirely bottle service. DJs spin between sets, and you can't fit a piece of paper inside on the weekends. Shows start at 11pm. *In Mandalay Bay, 2950 Las Vegas Blvd. S.* ☎ *702/632-7000. www.fortydeuce.com. Cover varies. Thurs–Mon 10:30pm–dawn.*

↠ **Peppermill's Fireside Lounge** ★ Walk through the classic Peppermill's coffee shop (not a bad place to eat, by the way) on the Strip, and you land in its dark, plush, cozy 24-hour lounge. A fabulously dated view of hip, it has low, circular banquette seats, fake floral foliage, low neon, and electric candles. It all adds up to a cozy, womblike place, perfect for unwinding a bit

after some time spent on the hectic Strip. The enormous, exotic froufrou tropical drinks (including the signature bathtub-size margaritas) will ensure that you sink into a level of comfortable stupor. *2985 Las Vegas Blvd. S.* ☎ *702/735-7635. Open daily 24 hr.*

↠ **Tangerine** ★ Taking up the space once occupied by the Battle Bar—where patrons could watch the pirate battle, back in the days before it featured girls in lingerie—now it actually features more girls in lingerie, by way of the ever-increasingly popular modern burlesque show. The show is nothing compared to what's at Forty Deuce, so your main reason for coming here will be the enormous outdoor patio lounge, where personal space is at a premium, and you know what that means . . . Shows start at 10:45pm. *In Treasure Island at The Mirage, 3300 Las Vegas Blvd. S.* ☎ *702/894-7111. Cover varies. Tues–Sat 6pm–late.*

↠ **Triple 7 Brew Pub** ★ Yet another of the many things the Main Street Station hotel has done right. Stepping into its microbrew pub feels like stepping out of Vegas. Well, except for the dueling-piano entertainment. The place has a partially modern warehouse look (exposed pipes, microbrew fixtures visible through exposed glass at the back, and a very high ceiling), but a hammered-tin ceiling continues the hotel's Victorian decor; the overall effect seems straight out of San Francisco's North Beach. It's a bit on the yuppified side but escapes being pretentious. *In Main Street Station, 200 N. Main St.* ☎ *702/387-1896. Daily from 11am–7am.*

↠ **Whiskey Sky** ★★ Probably your best bet for a trendy place that might actually have either beautiful locals or out-of-town celebs looking for a cool time but wanting a lower profile. This cool, low-key vibe is due to the bar's off-the-Strip location and also its creator, hip-bar-master Rande Gerber (Cindy Crawford's hubby). Think beds instead of couches, and you've got a sense of the gestalt. *In the Green Valley Ranch Resort, 2300 Paseo Verde Pkwy., Henderson.* ☎ *702/617-7560. Cover varies, usually $10 and up. Daily 8pm until late.*

➜**Zuri** ★ This is the best of the casino-hotel free bars (free as in no admission price), probably because of its construction, a semi-curtained enclave just off the elevators (as opposed to a space just plunked down right off or right in the middle of a casino). With swooping wood and red-velvet couches, the drinks are expensive, but at least you can hear your partner's whispered sweet nothings. That's a rare thing in a Vegas hotel. *In the MGM Grand, 3799 Las Vegas Blvd. S.* ☎ *702/891-7777. 24 hr.*

DANCE CLUBS

➜**The Beach** ★★ If you're a fan of loud, crowded, 24-hour party bars filled with tons of hotties, then bow in this direction, for you have found your mecca. This huge tropical-themed nightclub is, according to just about anyone you ask, the hottest club in the city. It's a two-story affair with five separate bars downstairs and another three up. There's free valet parking, and if you've driven here and become intoxicated, they'll drive you back home at no charge. *365 S. Convention Center Dr. (at Paradise Rd.).* ☎ *702/731-1925. www.beachlv. com. Cover free for women and $10 and up for men. Daily 24 hr.*

➜**Body English** ★★ Exactly what a Las Vegas club should be—over the top and just a little bit wrong. A clash of Anne Rice and Cher, Gothic-themed wacky decadence, with fabrics on top of wood on top of mirrors, not to mention the sort of layout that allows for intimate corners and

voyeuristic balcony viewing of the dance floor, this is just the sort of overly rich dessert of a place we crave. So do many others; it's one of the hottest spots in town, and the wait in line is so long you might well polish off a Rice novel while standing in it. *In the Hard Rock Hotel, 4455 Paradise Rd.* ☎ *702/693-5000. www.body english.com. Cover varies. Fri–Sun 10pm–late.*

➜**Cleopatra's Barge** ★ This is a small, quirky nightclub set in part on a floating barge—you can feel it rocking. The bandstand, a small dance floor, and a few (usually reserved) tables are here, while others are set around the boat on "land." It's a gimmick but one that makes this far more fun than other, more pedestrian, hotel bars. Plenty of dark makes for romance, but blaring volume levels mean you will have to scream those sweet nothings. *In Caesars Palace, 3570 Las Vegas Blvd. S.* ☎ *702/731-7110. 2-drink minimum. Nightly 10:30pm–4am.*

➜**Drai's After Hours** ★ Young Hollywood film execs and record-company types are likely to be found here, schmoozing and dancing it up to house, techno, and tribal music. *In Barbary Coast, 3595 Las Vegas Blvd S.* ☎ *702/737-0555. Cover varies, usually $20. Open Wed–Sun midnight–dawn.*

➜**Jet** ★ Done by the same folks who do Light (see below), this 2006 addition to The Mirage takes everything they did right at Bellagio and throws more money, more space, and more everything at it—with mixed results. The club is stunning, with three dance floors and four bars on multiple levels to keep you entertained and give you lots to look at. *In The Mirage, 3400 Las Vegas Blvd. S.* ☎ *702/632-7600. Cover varies, usually $20 and up. Fri–Sat and Mon 10:30pm–4am.*

➜ **Light** ★★ In contrast to the metallic high gloss that characterizes most trendy nightspots, this is a grown-up nightclub (sister to an establishment in NYC)—all wood and velvet and polite attitudes from the staff. Music leans toward both modern and old-school hip-hop and pop, with dancers (real ones) clad in pretty modest costumes. Guests are probably all tourists, but tourists of the heir-to-the-hotel-for-tune sort; yet the club doesn't feel exclusive, but more like one big open party. *In Bellagio, 3600 Las Vegas Blvd. S.* ☎ *702/693-8300. www.lightgroup.com. Cover varies, usually $25. Thurs–Sun 10:30pm–4am.*

➜ **Monte Carlo Pub & Brewery** ★ After 9pm nightly, this immense warehouselike pub and working microbrewery turns from a casual restaurant into something of a dance club. Rock videos blare forth from a large screen and 40 TV monitors around the room, while on stage, dueling pianos provide music and audience-participation entertainment. There's a full bar, and, of course, the house microbrews are featured. You can also order pizza. *In the Monte Carlo Resort & Casino, 3770 Las Vegas Blvd. S.* ☎ *702/730-7777. Open until 3am Sun–Thurs, until 4am Fri–Sat.*

MTV **Best ❶** ➜ **PURE** ★★ The biggest—and maybe the best—club on the Strip, PURE is everything a big, loud nightclub ought to be. The theme is reflected in the decor—or lack thereof, everything is as white as Ivory Soap—which is either minimalist brilliant or thematic overkill, depending on your point of view. The space is humongous with dance floors and the requisite hotties everywhere. The rooftop club is itself bigger than most regular Vegas clubs, with views of the Strip, for those who need a little fresh air. *In Caesars Palace, 3570 Las Vegas Blvd. S.* ☎ *702/731-7110. www.purenightclub.com. Cover varies. Fri–Sun and Tues 10pm–dawn.*

➜ **Ra** ★ The futuristic Egyptian-themed Ra was one of the first of the new generation of Vegas nightclubs, and while intense competition in the space has dimmed its allure, it's still one of the better all-around club experiences. It has that Vegas "we're a show and an attraction" vibe but is still not overly pretentious. The staff is friendly, which is a rare thing for a hot club. It might be worth it to go just to gawk at the heavy gilt decor. *In Luxor Las Vegas, 3900 Las Vegas Blvd. S.* ☎ *702/262-4000. www.ralv.com. Cover varies. Wed–Sat 10:30pm–4am.*

➜ **Rain Nightclub** ★★ Still one of the hottest nightclubs in Vegas. Which means you probably will spend most of your time trying to convince someone, anyone, to let you in. You and a couple of thousand of size-2 Juicy Couture jeans–clad chicks who feel they will simply cease to exist if they don't get inside. We snicker at their desperation because it makes us feel superior. But we also gotta be honest; if you can brave the wait, the crowds, and the attitude, you will be inside a club that has done everything right: multilevel layouts, DJs who play the right house and techno cuts, scaffolding that holds pyrotechnic and other mood-revvers, ubiquitous-of-late go-go girls dressed like strippers. *4321 W. Flamingo Rd.* ☎ *702/940-7246. Cover $20 and up. Thurs 11pm–dawn; Fri–Sat 10pm–dawn.*

➜ **rumjungle** ★ You may want to wince at the overkill, and we tend to write off spots like this as just trying a bit too hard. But surprisingly, rumjungle really delivers. The fire-wall entrance gives way to a wall of water; the two-story bar is full of the largest collection of rum varieties anywhere, each bottle illuminated with a laser beam of light; go-go girls dance and prance between bottles of wine to dueling congas; and the food all comes skewered on swords. What's not to like? *In Mandalay*

Bay, 3950 Las Vegas Blvd. S. ☎ 702/632-7408. Cover $10–$20. Open 'til 2am on weeknights, 'til 4am Thurs–Sat nights.

→ **Studio Club** ★ In the main rotunda of the MGM Grand, which once housed the *Wizard of Oz* walk-through diorama, this is the biggest and best of the free hotel lounges. It has an enormous and elaborate stage and band, but since it's in the middle of an area you have to cross if you are passing through from the Strip, it can be hard to navigate through on a busy weekend night. *In the MGM Grand, 3799 Las Vegas Blvd. S. ☎ 702/891-1111. Daily 4pm–4am.*

→ **Studio 54** The legendary Studio 54 has been resurrected here in Las Vegas, but with all the bad elements and none of the good ones. Forget Capote, Halston, and Liza doing illegal (or at least immoral) things in the bathroom stalls; that part of Studio 54 remains but a fond memory. The snooty, exclusive door attitude has been retained, however. Awesome. Oddly, this doesn't lead to a high-class clientele; of all the new clubs, this is the trashiest (though apparently the hot night for locals is Tues, so if you do go, go then). The large dance floor has a balcony overlooking it, the decor is industrial (exposed piping and the like), the music is hip-hop and electronic. Ho-hum. *In the MGM Grand, 3799 Las Vegas Blvd. S. ☎ 702/891-1111. www.studio54lv.com. Cover varies, but usually $10–$40. Tues–Sat 10pm–dawn.*

→ **Tabú** ★ A little by-the-numbers for a nightclub, but still, despite the name, less stripper saucy than the other new "ultra lounges" and consequently more grown up, and just as loud. With an interior of late '90s high-tech/industrial meets cheesy '80s bachelor's den, it's nothing aesthetically special, though there are some nice spots for canoodling. *At MGM Grand, 3799 Las Vegas Blvd. S. ☎ 702/891-7183. www.tabulv.com. Cover varies, but about*

$10 for men and free for women. Tues–Sun 10pm to early morning.

→ **Tao Nightclub** ★ As of this writing, this is the hottest of the Vegas hotspots. Yes, that has been mentioned in other reviews here, and yes, it changes on an almost daily basis, but welcome to the Las Vegas club scene. Done as a Buddhist temple run amok, this multilevel club is drawing the party faithful and the celebrity entourages in droves, so expect long lines and high cover charges. Wall-to-wall crowds, flashing lights, pounding music, and general chaos are overwhelming, but Tao is obviously doing something right. *At The Venetian, 3355 Las Vegas Blvd. S. ☎ 702/388-8588. Cover varies. Thurs–Sat 10pm–dawn.*

→ **Tryst** ★ Steve Wynn's first stab at a nightclub, La Bête, tanked, and mere months after it opened, they shut it down, brought in new management, revamped the place, and tried again. The result is much more subtle than the beast-themed original, but this is the Vegas nightclub scene, so it's definitely a sliding scale. The dance floor opens up onto a 90-foot waterfall, so it's all relative. Expect a slightly more refined crowd than you usually find at other dance spots, which may be a good or bad thing, depending on your viewpoint. *At Wynn Las Vegas, 3131 Las Vegas Blvd. S. ☎ 702/770-3375. Cover varies. Thurs–Sun 10pm–4am.*

→ **VooDoo Lounge** ★ Occupying two floors in the newer addition to the Rio, the Lounge combines Haitian voodoo and New Orleans Creole in decor and theme. There are two main rooms: one with a large dance floor and stage for live music, and a disco room, which is filled with large video screens and serious light action. The bartenders put on a show, a la Tom Cruise in *Cocktail*. Uh huh—they shake, jiggle, and light stuff on fire. If you make it through the show, check out the dramatic outdoor, multilevel patio, which offers some amazing views of the Strip. *In the Rio All-Suite Hotel & Casino, 3700 Las Vegas Blvd. S.* ☎ *702/252-7777. Cover $10 and up. Nightly 5pm–3am.*

BEST OF THE MAJOR SHOWS

🅼🆃🆅 ⬤ Best ⬤ ➔ **Blue Man Group** ★★★ Three hairless, nonspeaking men dipped in azure paint do decidedly odd stunts with marshmallows, art supplies, audience members, tons of paper, and an amazing array of percussion instruments made from PVC piping. If that doesn't sound very Vegas, well, it's not. It's a franchise of a New York–born performance-art troupe that seems to have slipped into town through a side door opened by Cirque du Soleil's groundbreaking successes. Might leave some scratching their heads, but it's smart and funny in the weirdest and most unexpected ways. *At The Venetian, 3355 Las Vegas Blvd. S.* ☎ *877/833-6423. www.venetian.com. Tickets $85–$110 (plus tax and service fees). Nightly at 7:30pm, with an additional 10:30pm show on Sat.*

➔ **Cirque du Soleil's KÀ** ★★★ *KÀ* subverts expectations by largely eschewing the usual Cirque format—wide-eyed innocent is taken on surreal adventure, beautiful but aimless, complete with acrobats and clowns and lots of weird floaty things—in favor of an actual plot, as a brother and sister from some mythical Asian kingdom are separated by enemy raiders and have to endure various trials and tribulations before being reunited. *In the MGM Grand, 3799 Las Vegas Blvd. S.* ☎ *866/774-7117 or 702/531-2000. www.cirquedusoleil.com. Tickets $99–$150 (plus tax). Fri–Tues at 7:30 and 10:30pm.*

➔ **Cirque du Soleil's Mystère** ★★★ Cirque du Soleil began in Montreal as a unique circus experience, not only shunning traditional animal acts in favor of gorgeous feats of human strength and agility, but also adding elements of the surreal and the absurd. The result seems like a collaboration between Salvador Dalí and Luis Buñuel, with a few touches by Magritte and choreography by Twyla Tharp. It's a world-class show—that this arty and intellectual show is playing in Vegas is astonishing. *In TI at The Mirage, 3300 Las Vegas Blvd. S.* ☎ *800/963-9634 or 702/796-9999. www.cirquedusoleil.com. Tickets $60–$95 (plus tax). Wed–Sat 7:30 and 10:30pm; Sun 4:30 and 7:30pm.*

➔ **Cirque du Soleil's O** ★★★ How to describe the seemingly indescribable wonder and artistry of Cirque du Soleil's still utterly dazzling display? An Esther Williams–Busby Berkeley spectacular on peyote? A Salvador Dalí painting come to life? A stage show by Fellini? The French troupe has topped itself with this production—and not simply because it's situated its breathtaking acrobatics in, on, around, and above a 1.5-million-gallon pool (*eau*—pronounced *O*—is French for "water"). *In Bellagio, 3600 Las Vegas Blvd. S.* ☎ *888/488-7111 or 702/693-7722. www.cirquedusoleil.com. Tickets $99–$150 (plus tax). Wed–Sun 7:30 and 10:30pm.*

➔ **Crazy Girls** *Crazy Girls,* presented in an intimate theater, is probably the raciest revue on the Strip. It features sexy showgirls with perfect bodies in erotic song-and-dance numbers enhanced by innovative lighting effects. Think of *Penthouse* poses coming to life. Perhaps it was best summed up by one older man from Kentucky: "It's okay if you like boobs and butt. But most of the girls can't even dance." *In The Riviera Hotel & Casino, 2901 Las Vegas Blvd. S.* ☎ *877/892-7469 or 702/794-9433. www.rivierahotel.com. Ages 18 and over only. Tickets $35 (plus tax); dinner and show packages available. Wed–Mon 9:30pm.*

➔ **Crazy Horse Paris** ★★ Allegedly the same show that has been running for years in a famous racy French nightclub, *Crazy Horse Paris* is just a bunch of pretty girls taking their clothes off. Except that the girls are smashingly pretty, with the kind of bodies just not found on real live human beings, and they take their clothes off in curious and, yes, artistic ways, gyrating on pointe shoes while holding on to ropes or hoops, falling over sofas while lip-syncing to French torch songs—in short, it's what striptease ought to be. Good stuff, but $60 a ticket is a lot to pay for arty striptease. *In the MGM Grand, 3799 Las Vegas Blvd. S. ☎ 877/880-0880 or 702/891-7777. www.mgmgrand.com. Ages 18 and over only. Business casual attire required. Tickets $54–$65 (includes tax and gratuity). Wed–Mon at 8 and 10:30pm.*

→ *Jubilee!* ★ A classic Vegas spectacular, crammed with singing, dancing, magic, acrobats, elaborate costumes and sets, and, of course, bare breasts. It's a basic revue, with production numbers featuring homogenized versions of standards (Gershwin, Cole Porter, some Fred Astaire numbers) sometimes sung live, sometimes lip-synced, and always accompanied by lavishly costumed and frequently topless showgirls. Humorous set pieces about Samson and Delilah, and the sinking of the *Titanic* (!) show off some pretty awesome sets. *In Bally's Las Vegas, 3645 Las Vegas Blvd. S. ☎ 800/237-7469 or 702/739-4567. www.ballys.com. Ages 18 and over only. Tickets $65–$82 (plus tax). Sat–Thurs at 7:30 and 10:30pm.*

📺 Best ☺ → **Penn & Teller** ★★★ The most intelligent show in Vegas, as these two—magicians? illusionists? truth-tellers? BS artists? geniuses?—put on 90 minutes of, yes, magic and juggling, but also acerbic comedy, mean stunts, and great quiet beauty. Looking like two characters out of Dr. Seuss, big, loud Penn and smaller, quiet Teller (to reduce them to

their basic characteristics) perform magic, reveal the secrets behind a few major magic tricks, discuss why magic is nothing but a bunch of lies, and then turn around and show why magic is as lovely an art form as any other. *In the Rio Hotel, 3700 W. Flamingo. ☎ 888/746-7784. www.riolasvegas.com. Ages 5 and over only. Tickets $60–$75 (plus tax). Wed–Mon at 9pm.*

📺 Best ☺ → **Prince at 3121** ★★★ As if we needed more evidence of his mythic cool, the artist formerly known as Weird Androgynous Sign has set up shop in his new bare-bones joint, 3121 (formerly Club Rio), where he'll play two shows a week to crowds topping out at 700. (Uh huh, let's see Michael Jackson do that.) The concept has its roots in Prince's '80s heyday, when he would play "Little Red Corvette" and "1999" at mega-arenas then sneak over to small nightclubs and kick out lesser known funk and jazz-inspired numbers with his band until dawn. Much like those impromptu concerts, the sets at 3121 have no official start time (12:30am give or take), and chances are you won't hear "Raspberry Beret" or "When Doves Cry." You will, however, be treated to a 2-plus hours of music by one of the greatest pop acts of all time—a Vegas can't-miss if there ever was one. Doors open at 8pm, and DJs keep things pumping 'til the purple magic happens. *At Rio Suites, 3700 W. Flamingo Rd. ☎ 702/777-7776. 3121.com. Tickets $125 ($350 VIP package includes dinner and bottle service). Fri–Sat; doors open at 8pm, start time varies.*

→ *Phantom of the Opera* Unavailable for review at press time, but really, what do you need to know after all this time? There's a guy in a mask, and he loves a girl who sings, and she loves him, but she also loves another boy, and there are caverns and canals and romance and tragedy and mystery and murder and light opera.

Penn & Teller's Top 10 Things One Should Never Do in a Vegas Magic Show

Penn & Teller have been exercising their acerbic wit and magical talents in numerous forums together for more than 25 years, and their show at the Rio is one of Vegas's best and most intelligent. We must confess that we couldn't get the quieter half of the duo, Teller, to cough up a few words, but the more verbose Penn Jillette was happy to share.

1. Costume yourself in gray business suits totally lacking in rhinestones, animal patterns, Mylar, capes, bell-bottoms, shoulder pads, and top hats.

2. Wear your hair in any style that could not be described as "feathered" or "spiked."

3. Use really good live jazz music instead of canned sound-alike cheesy rip-off fake pop "music."

4. Cruelly (but truthfully) make fun of your siblings in the magic brotherhood.

5. Do the dangerous tricks on each other instead of anonymous show women with aftermarket breasts and/or endangered species.

6. Toss a cute little magic bunny into a cute little chipper-shredder.

7. Open your show by explaining and demonstrating how other magicians on the Strip do their most amazing tricks, and then do that venerable classic of magic "The Cups and Balls," with transparent plastic cups.

8. Treat the audience as if they had a brain in their collective head.

9. Allow audience members to sign real bullets, load them into real guns, and fire those bullets into your face.

10. Bleed.

(You will find all 10 of these "don'ts" in the Penn & Teller show at the Rio All-Suite Hotel and Casino.)

Andrew Lloyd Webber's biggest hit will be even more high tech than the original Broadway staging, with increased special effects, and smaller, because it's been slimmed down to run the standard Vegas 90-minutes-without-intermission. *At The Venetian, 3355 Las Vegas Blvd. S. ☎ 866/641-7469 or 702/414-7469. www.venetian.com. Tickets $82–$157 (plus tax). Thurs and Sun at 7pm; Mon, Wed and Fri–Sat 7 and 10pm.*

→ **The Producers** The Vegas version of the Broadway smash (it won a record 12 Tony Awards) receives the same treatment other Great White Way refuges get when they come to Sin City: big cuts to make it run at around 90 minutes with no intermission. The story of two down-on-their-luck types who try to make a killing on Broadway by staging the worst musical ever, this is a crowd-pleaser for sure, but one that depends strongly on the skill of its headlining stars. The Hoff himself (David Hasselhoff) was featured as Roger DeBris when the show opened in Feb. 2007. *In Paris Las Vegas, 3665 Las Vegas Blvd. S. ☎ 888/266-5687. www.harrahs.com. Tickets $76–$144. Showtimes: 8pm Thurs–Tues.*

📺 Best ● → **The Second City** ★★ Second City is the Chicago-based comedy group that spawned not only *SCTV* but some of the best modern-day comics (such as Gilda Radner, John Belushi, Martin Short, and Mike Myers). This is an improv comedy show, with cast members performing stunts similar to those you might have seen on *Whose Line Is It Anyway?*— you know, taking suggestions from the audience and creating bizarre little skits and such out of them, all of it done at lightning speed with wit and a wink. Some of it can turn R-rated, so be careful bringing the kids, but do not hesitate to see it yourself. And join in—any improv group is only as good as the material fed it (so remember, there's only so much a group can do with jokes about sex and vomiting, especially if every single audience thinks that would be funny material with which to work). One of the best values and highest-quality shows in Vegas. *In The Flamingo Las Vegas, 3555 Las Vegas Blvd. S.* ☎ *800/221-7299 or 702/733-3333. www.secondcity.com. Tickets $40 (plus tax and fees). Mon–Tues and Fri at 8pm; Thurs and Sat–Sun at 8 and 10:30pm.*

What Else to See & Do

With so many glitzy hotels, casinos, off-the-hook clubs, and high-profile shows, it would be easy to ignore Vegas's lesser entertainment lights. But some of Vegas's "other" off-the-beaten path attractions offer a nice counterpoint to the over-the-top decadence of the Strip's usual suspects.

ART, GARDENS, SHARKS & THRILL RIDES

➔ **The Atomic Testing Museum** ★★★ From 1951 until 1992, the Nevada Test Site was this country's primary location for testing nuclear weapons. This well-executed museum, library, and gallery space offers visitors a fascinating glance at the test site from incipient days through modern times, with memorabilia, displays, official documents, videos, interactive displays,

motion-simulator theaters (like sitting in a bunker, watching a blast), and emotional testimony from the people who worked there. Not to be missed, even if it's only because of the Albert Einstein action figures in the gift shop. *755 E. Flamingo Rd.* ☎ *702/794-5151. www.atomictestingmuseum. org. $10 adults; $7 seniors, military, and students with ID; free for children 6 and under. Mon–Sat 9am–5pm; Sun 1–5pm.*

➔ **GameWorks** ★★ What do you get when Steven Spielberg and his DreamWorks team get in on the arcade video-game action? Grown-up, state-of-the-art fun. High-tech movie magic has taken over all sorts of traditional arcade games at GameWorks and turned them interactive, from a virtual-reality batting cage to a *Jurassic Park* game that lets you hunt dinosaurs. There are motion-simulator rides galore and actual-motion activities like rock climbing. But classic games, from Pac-Man to pool tables, are here, too, though sometimes with surprising twists, such as air hockey where multiple pucks occasionally shoot out at once.

All this doesn't exactly come cheap. There are two routes to pricing. First is the standard version, where $15 gets you $15 in game play, $20 gets you $25, $25 gets you $35, or $35 gets you $50. Alternatively, you can purchase a block of time ($20 for 1 hr., $25 for 2 hr., $30 for 3 hr., $35 for all-day play; or if you get there at opening or closing, you get 2 hr. for $20), which goes on a debit card that you then insert into the various machines to activate them. *In the Showcase Mall, 3785 Las Vegas Blvd. S.* ☎ *702/432-GAME. www.gameworks.com. See game prices listed above in the review. Sun–Thurs 10am–midnight; Fri–Sat 10am–2am. Hours may vary.*

➔ **IMAX Theatre & Ridefilm** ★ This is a state-of-the-art theater that offers both motion-simulator films and IMAX projects, some in standard two dimensions and one in 3-D. The glasses for the latter are really cool headsets (though they're a little too heavy for comfort) that include built-in speakers, bringing certain sounds right into your head. The movies change periodically but always include some extraordinary special effects. If you have a fear of heights, be sure to ask for a seat on one of the lower levels.

The IMAX Ridefilm is a motion-simulator ride with different themed "adventures" playing at different times. You may find yourself hunting for an ancient relic in a pyramid or running from the ghoulies in Dracula's castle. *In Luxor Las Vegas, 3900 Las Vegas Blvd. S. ☎ 702/262-IMAX. www.luxor. com. Admission $12 and up (prices vary depending on the movie) for IMAX Theatre; $10 for IMAX Ridefilm. Can be purchased as part of an all-attractions package for $35. Sun–Thurs 9am–11pm; Fri–Sat 9am–midnight. IMAX showtimes vary.*

➔ **Las Vegas Motor Speedway** ★★ This 176,000-seat facility was the first new super-speedway to be built in the Southwest in over 2 decades. A $200-million state-of-the-art motor-sports entertainment complex, it includes a 1¹/₂-mile super-speedway, a 2¹/₂-mile FIA-approved road course, paved and dirt short-track ovals, and a 4,000-foot drag strip. The place is so popular that they are even building condos overlooking the track for those who apparently don't want to sleep on race days. Some major hotels have shuttles to the speedway during big events, so check with the front desk or concierge. If you happen to be in town when no race is scheduled, the speedway also offers daily track tours. The $8 tours run from 9am to 4pm Monday through Saturday, and from 11am to 4pm on Sunday. *7000 Las Vegas Blvd. N., directly across from*

Nellis Air Force base (take I-15 north to Speedway Exit 54). ☎ 702/644-4443 for ticket information. www.lvms.com. Tickets $10–$75 (higher prices for major events).

➔ **Liberace Museum** ★★★ You can keep your Louvres and Vaticans and Smithsonians: *This* is a museum. Housed in a strip mall, this is a shrine to the glory and excess that was the art project known as Liberace. You've got your costumes (bejeweled), your many cars (bejeweled), your many pianos (bejeweled), and many jewels (also bejeweled). Also, the entrance itself is a giant jewel. It just shows what can be bought with lots of money and no taste. Unless you have a severely underdeveloped appreciation for camp or take your museum-going very seriously, you shouldn't miss it. The museum is 2¹/₂ miles east of the Strip, on your right. *1775 E. Tropicana Ave. (at Spencer St.). ☎ 702/798-5595. www.liberace.org. Admission $13 adults, $8.50 students. Mon–Sat 10am–5pm; Sun noon–4pm. Closed Thanksgiving, Dec 25, and Jan 1.*

FREE ➔ **MGM Grand Lion Habitat** ★★ Hit this attraction at the right time, and it's one of the best freebies in town. It's a large, multilevel glass structure in which real live lions frolic during various times of day. In addition to regular viewing spots, you can walk through a glass tunnel and get a worm's-eye view of the underside of a lion; note how very big Kitty's paws are. Multiple lions share show duties (about 6 hr. on and then 2 days off at a ranch for some free-range activity, so they're never cooped up here for long). *In MGM Grand, 3799 Las Vegas Blvd. S. ☎ 702/891-7777. Free admission. Daily 11am–10pm.*

➔ **Secret Garden & Dolphin Habitat** ★★★ White lions, Bengal tigers, an Asian elephant, a panther, and a snow leopard join the white tigers. It's really just a glorified zoo featuring only the big-ticket animals; however, it's a very pretty place, with plenty of foliage and some bits of Indian- and Asian-themed architecture.

More satisfying than the Secret Garden, the **Dolphin Habitat** was designed to provide a healthy and nurturing environment and to educate the public about marine mammals and their role in the ecosystem. The Mirage displays only dolphins already in captivity—no dolphins are taken from the wild to be exhibited. You can watch the dolphins frolic both above and below ground through viewing windows, in three different pools. *In The Mirage, 3400 Las Vegas Blvd. S. ☎ 702/791-7111. www.mirage.com. Admission $15 adults, $10 children 4–10, free for children under 4 if accompanied by an adult. Mon–Fri 11am–5:30pm; Sat–Sun and major holidays 10am–5:30pm. Hours subject to change and vary by season.*

➜ **Shark Reef at Mandalay Bay** ★ Given that watching fish can lower your blood pressure, it's practically a public service for Mandalay Bay to provide this facility in a city where craps tables and other gaming areas can bring your excitement level to dangerous heights. Watching a bunch of sharks swim is just pretty cool, but it's still just a giant aquarium which, hey, we like, but not at $16 a pop. *In Mandalay Bay, 3950 Las Vegas Blvd. S. ☎ 702/632-4555. www.mandalaybay.com. Admission $16 adults. Daily 10am–11pm.*

➜ **SPEED: The Ride/Las Vegas Cyber Speedway** ★★ Auto racing is the fastest-growing spectator sport in America, so it's no surprise that these two attractions at the Sahara are a popular stop. The first is an 8-minute virtual-reality ride, **Cyber Speedway,** featuring a three-quarter-size replica of a NASCAR racecar. Hop aboard for an animated, simulated ride—either the Las Vegas Motor Speedway or a race around the streets of Vegas. Press the gas

and you lean back and feel the rush of speed; hit a bump and you go flying. Should your car get in a crash, off you go to a pit stop.

SPEED: The Ride is a roller coaster that blasts riders out through a hole in the wall by the NASCAR Cafe, then through a loop, under the sidewalk, through the hotel's marquee, and finally straight up a 250-foot tower. At the peak, you feel a moment of weightlessness, and then you do the whole thing backward! *In the Sahara, 2535 Las Vegas Blvd. S. ☎ 702/737-2111. www.nascarcafelasvegas.com. $20 for all-day pass on both rides. Cyber Speedway (simulator) $10 (you must be at least 48 in. tall to ride), SPEED: The Ride (roller coaster) $10 for single ride. Sun–Thurs 11am–midnight; Fri–Sat 11am–1am; hours may vary.*

➜ **Star Trek: The Experience & Borg Invasion 4-D** ★ This is the undisputed champ in the Vegas motion-simulator ride category. It goes without saying that hardcore Trekkers (note use of correct term) will be delighted. On the other hand, normal, sensible fans and those who couldn't care less about *Star Trek* may find themselves saying, "I spent $39 and 2 hours in line for this?" There's a story line, but we won't spoil it for you. Suffice it to say that it involves time travel, evil doings by the Borg, something about being assimilated, and if all doesn't work out, the very history of *Star Trek* could be affected. The recently added *Borg Invasion 4-D* is a 3-D film starring several *Star Trek Voyager* cast members, and since it's "multimedia," there are more live actors, plus some surprises as the film plays. *In Las Vegas Hilton, 3000 Paradise Rd. ☎ 888/GO-BOLDLY. www.startrekexp.com. All-day pass including both attractions and museum: $39 adults, $36 seniors and children 12 and under. Dual Mission Ticket (single-use access to BORG Invasion 4-D, Klingon Encounter, plus the History of the*

Future Museum): $33.99 adults. Purchase tickets online for discounts. Daily 11:30am–7:30pm or 9:30pm, depending on the season.

→ **Stratosphere Thrill Rides** ★★ Atop the 1,149-foot Stratosphere Tower are three marvelous thrill rides. **The Big Shot** is a free-fall ride that thrusts you 160 feet in the air along a 228-foot spire at the top of the tower, then plummets back down again. Sitting in an open car, you seem to be dangling in space over Las Vegas. Amping up the terror factor is **X-Scream,** a giant teeter-totter-style device that propels you in an open car off the side of the 100-story tower and lets you dangle there weightlessly before returning you to relative safety. And now they have the aptly named **Insanity,** a spinning whirly-gig of a contraption that straps you into a seat and twirls you around 1,000 feet or so above terra firma. *Atop Stratosphere Las Vegas, 2000 Las Vegas Blvd. S.* ☎ *702/380-7777. Admission: Big Shot $8; X-Scream $8; Insanity $8; plus fee to ascend Tower: $10 for adults; $6 for locals, seniors, hotel guests, free for those dining in the buffet room or Top of the World. Multiride and all-day packages also available for varying costs. Sun–Thurs 10am–1am; Fri–Sat 10am–2am. Hours vary seasonally. Minimum height requirement for all rides is 48 in.*

PLAYING OUTSIDE

You need not be a slot-hypnotized slug when you come to Vegas. The city and surrounding areas offer plenty of opportunities for active sports. Of course, just about every hotel has a large swimming pool and health club, and tennis courts abound. In addition, all types of water sports are offered at Lake Mead National Recreation Area; there's rafting on the Colorado, horseback riding at Mount Charleston and Bonnie Springs, great hiking in the canyons, and much more.

Definitely plan to get out of those smoke-filled casinos and into the fresh air once in a while. It's good for your health *and* your budget.

Rock Climbing

📺 Best ● → **Red Rock Canyon** ★★★, just 19 miles west of Las Vegas, is one of the world's most popular rock-climbing areas. In addition to awe-inspiring natural beauty, it offers everything from boulders to big walls. If you'd like to join the bighorn sheep, Red Rock has more than 1,000 routes to inaugurate beginners and challenge accomplished climbers. Experienced climbers can contact the **visitor center** (☎ **702/515-5350;** www.redrockcanyon.blm.gov) for information.

Tennis

Tennis used to be a popular pastime in Vegas, but these days, buffs only have a couple of choices at hotels in town that have tennis courts.

Bally's ★★ (☎ **702/739-4111**) has eight night-lit hard courts. Fees per hour start at $10 for guests and $15 for nonguests. Facilities include a pro shop. Hours vary seasonally. Reservations are advised.

The Flamingo Las Vegas ★★ (☎ **702/733-3444**) has four outdoor hard courts (all lit for night play) and a pro shop. It's open to the public daily from 7am to 7pm. Rates are $12 per hour for guests, $20 per hour for nonguests. Lessons are available. Reservations are required.

Monte Carlo Resort & Casino ★ (☎ **702/730-7777**) has three night-lit courts available to the public for $15 per hour.

In addition to hotels, the **University of Nevada, Las Vegas (UNLV)** ★★, Harmon Avenue just east of Swenson Street (☎ **702/895-0844**), has a dozen courts (all lit for night play) that are open weekdays from 6am to 9:45pm, weekends 8am to 9pm. Rates are $5 per person per day.

You should call before going to find out if a court is available.

Bicycling

Escape Adventures (☎ 800/596-2953 or 702/838-6966; www.escapeadventures. com) rents bikes and biking equipment, starting at $30 per day, as well as providing guided and self-guided tours of Red Rock Canyon and Mount Charleston, which begin at $89 for a half-day self-guided tour and include the bike rental. These tours range from 7 to 23 miles and span experience and age levels, depending on your children's abilities. One that is definitely suited to children is a summer tour that's 18 miles and all downhill from the top of Mount Charleston (a shuttle takes you up the mountain).

Horseback Riding

Cowboy Trail Rides ★ (☎ 702/387-2457; www.cowboytrailrides.com) offers a variety of rides and trails in Red Rock Canyon and on Mount Charleston (at the 12-mile marker), ranging in price from $69 to $289. Falling in the middle of that price range (around $139) is a Red Rock Canyon sunset trail ride; it lasts about 90 minutes, with the canyon providing a glorious backdrop for the end of the day. Riders then return to camp for a barbecue dinner (including a 16-oz. T-bone steak), joined by the cowboys for singalongs and marshmallow roasting. They also offer other 1½-hour rides at $70. There are also riding stables at **Bonnie Springs Ranch** (☎ 702/875-4191; www.bonniesprings.com; see section earlier in this chapter) that offer guided trail rides daily through the area close to Red Rock. Rates are $35 per person per hour. Wear tennis shoes, riding boots, or hiking boots and jeans for riding.

Skiing & Snowboarding

From roughly Thanksgiving through Easter, depending on weather conditions, you can ski and snowboard at the **Las Vegas Ski & Snowboard Resort** (☎ 702/ 645-2754; www.skilasvegas.com). It rents equipment and clothing as well as provide lessons.

SPECTATOR SPORTS

Las Vegas loves the sports . . . betting. Otherwise, it isn't known for its actual sports teams. Except for minor-league baseball and hockey, the only consistent spectator sports are those at UNLV. For the pros, if watching AAA ball (in this case, a Los Angeles Dodgers farm team) in potentially triple-degree heat sounds like fun, the charmingly named and even-better merchandized **Las Vegas 51s** (as in Area 51, as in alien-themed gear!) are an option. Tickets run from $8 to $13. For the team's schedule or ticket info, go to **www.lv51. com**, or call ☎ 702/386-7200.

On sweltering days, ice hockey might be a better climate choice. The **Las Vegas Wranglers** play at the Orleans Arena. Tickets run $13 to $37, depending on how close you want to be to the action. Check for schedules and ticket availability at www.lasvegaswranglers.com or ☎ 702/ 471-7825.

The **Las Vegas Motor Speedway** (p. 566) is a main venue for car racing that draws major events to Las Vegas.

Because the city has several top-notch sporting arenas, important annual events take place in Las Vegas. The **National Finals Rodeo** is held in UNLV's Thomas and Mack Center (**www.thomasand mack.com**) each December. From time to time, you'll find NBA exhibition games, professional ice-skating competitions, or gymnastics exhibitions.

Finally, Las Vegas is well known as a major location for **boxing matches**. These are held in several Strip hotels, most often at Caesars or the MGM Grand, but

DESERT TO THE BEACH

sometimes at The Mirage. Tickets are hard to come by and quite expensive.

Tickets to sporting events at hotels are available either through **Ticketmaster** (☎ **702/893-3000;** www.ticketmaster. com) or through the hotels themselves.

Detours: Side Trips from Las Vegas

Don't let the Strip totally define your time in Vegas; this area has plenty of non-gambling attractions that are worth checking out. From Hoover Dam to Area 51, there's plenty to see on your way out of town that will add texture to your trip. Here are a few ideas.

VISITING HOOVER DAM

30 miles SE of Las Vegas

One of the most popular excursions from Las Vegas, Hoover Dam is visited by 2,000 to 3,000 people daily. But, you say, it's a dam, why should I give a damn? Because Hoover Dam is an engineering and architectural marvel, and it changed the Southwest forever. No kidding. Without it, you wouldn't even be going to Vegas.

The tour itself is a bit, um, cursory, but you do get up close and personal with the darn, I mean dam. Wear comfortable shoes; the tour involves quite a bit of walking. Try to take the tour in the morning to beat the desert heat and the really big crowds. You can have lunch out in Boulder City, and then drive back through the **Valley of Fire State Park** (a landscape of wind and water-hewn formations of red sandstone; described later in this chapter), which is about 60 magnificently scenic miles from Lake Mead (purchase gas before you start!). Or you can spend the afternoon on Lake Mead, hiking, boating, even scuba diving, or perhaps taking a rafting trip down the Colorado River.

Getting There

Drive east on Flamingo Road or Tropicana Avenue to US 515 South, which automatically turns into I-93 South and takes you right to the dam. This will involve a dramatic drive as you go through Boulder City and come over a rise, and Lake Mead suddenly appears spread out before you. It's a pretty cool sight. At about this point, the road narrows down to two lanes, and traffic can slow considerably. On normal busy tourist days, this drive would take about an hour. But because the bridge bypass won't be completed until late 2007 at the earliest, thanks to new security measures that call for most trucks and many other vehicles to be stopped and searched, during peak hours the drive is taking longer than ever. So plan accordingly.

Go past the turnoff to Lake Mead. As you near the dam, you'll see a five-story parking structure tucked into the canyon wall on your left. Park here ($5 charge) and take the elevators or stairs to the walkway leading to the new visitor center.

If you would rather go on an **organized tour,** check out **Gray Line** (☎ **800/634-6579;** www.grayline.com), which offers a Hoover Dam package that includes a buffet lunch and a side trip to the Ethel M Chocolate factory. But don't be surprised if you and that 11-year-old with daddy are the youngest ones on the bus. The 7½-hour **Deluxe Hoover Dam Tour** picks you up from your hotel at 7:30am daily; the price is $49, and admission to the dam's Discovery Tour is an additional $11.

A Brief History of Hoover Dam

There would be no Las Vegas as we know it without the Hoover Dam. Certainly, the neon and glitz that we know and love would not exist. In fact, the growth of the entire Southwest can be tied directly to the electricity created by the dam.

It's worth mentioning that until the Hoover Dam was completed in 1936, much of the southwestern United States was plagued by two natural problems: parched, sandy terrain that lacked irrigation for most of the year and extensive flooding in spring and early summer, when the Colorado River, fed by melting snow from its source in the Rocky Mountains, overflowed its banks and destroyed crops, lives, and property. On the positive side, raging unchecked over eons, the river's turbulent, rushing waters carved the Grand Canyon. So there's that.

The dam itself is a massive curved wall, 660 feet thick at the bottom, tapering to 45 feet where the road crosses it at the top. It towers 726 feet above bedrock (about the height of a 60-story skyscraper) and acts as a plug between the canyon walls to hold back up to 9.2 trillion gallons of water in Lake Mead, the reservoir created by its construction. Four concrete intake towers on the lake side drop the water down about 600 feet to drive turbines and create power, after which the water spills out into the river and continues south.

All the architecture is on a grand scale, and the design has beautiful Art Deco elements, unusual in an engineering project. Note, for instance, the monumental 30-foot bronze sculpture, *Winged Figures of the Republic,* flanking a 142-foot flagpole at the Nevada entrance. According to its creator, Oskar Hansen, the sculpture symbolizes "the immutable calm of intellectual resolution, and the enormous power of trained physical strength, equally enthroned in placid triumph of scientific achievement."

Touring the Dam

The very nice **Hoover Dam Visitor Center,** a vast three-level circular concrete structure with a rooftop overlook, opened in 1995. You'll enter the Reception Lobby (bags were not allowed inside after the Sept 11 terrorist attacks, but ask about current security measures, as they may have changed), where you can buy tickets; peruse informational exhibits, photographs, and memorabilia; and view three 12-minute video presentations about the importance of water to life, the events leading up to the construction of Hoover Dam, and the construction itself, as well as the many benefits it confers.

The center closes at 6pm, and 5:15pm is the last admission time. Admission is $11 for adults, $9 for seniors and military personnel and their dependents, $6 for children 7 to 16, and free for children under 7. There is no need to call ahead to reserve a place but for more information, call ☎ **866/730-9097** or 702/494-2517.

For more information on the dam, and sometimes discount coupons, visit **www. usbr.gov/lc/hooverdam**.

HEADING TO RED ROCK CANYON ★★★

19 miles W of Las Vegas

If you need a break from the casinos of Vegas, with their windowless, claustrophobic, noisy interiors, Red Rock Canyon is balm for your overstimulated soul. Less than 20 miles away—but a world apart—this is a magnificent unspoiled vista that should cleanse and refresh you (and if you must, a morning visit should leave you enough time for an afternoon's gambling). You can drive the 13-mile **Scenic Drive** (daily 7am–dusk) or explore it in more depth on foot, making it perfect for both athletes and armchair types.

There are a bunch of interesting sights and trail heads along the drive itself. The **National Conservation Area** (www.redrockcanyon.blm.gov) offers hiking trails and internationally acclaimed rock-climbing opportunities. Especially cool is 7,068-foot Mount Wilson, the highest sandstone peak among the bluffs; for information on climbing, contact the **Red Rock Canyon Visitor Center** at ☎ 702/363-1921. There are picnic areas along the drive and in nearby **Spring Mountain Ranch State Park** (http://parks.nv.gov/smr.htm), 5 miles south, which also offers plays in an outdoor theater during the summer.

Getting There

Just drive west on Charleston Boulevard, which becomes NV 159. As soon as you leave the city, the red rocks will begin to loom around you. The visitor center will appear on your right.

You can also go on an **organized tour. Gray Line** (☎ 800/634-6579; www.grayline.com), among other companies, runs bus tours to Red Rock Canyon. Inquire at your hotel tour desk.

Finally, you can go **by bike.** Not very far out of town (at Rainbow Blvd.), Charleston Boulevard is flanked by a bike path that continues for about 11 miles to the visitor center/scenic drive. The path is hilly but not difficult if you're in reasonable shape. But keep in mind that exploring Red Rock Canyon by bike should be attempted only by exceptionally fit and experienced bikers. So if you're hung-over, best to catch a ride out there. And it goes without saying it's not a good idea to do it in the middle of summer.

Just off NV 159, you'll see the **Red Rock Canyon Visitor Center** (☎ 702/515-5350; www.redrockcanyon.blm.gov), which marks the actual entrance to the park. There, you can pick up information on trails and view history exhibits about the canyon. The center is open daily from 8:30am to 4:30pm.

A Brief History of Red Rock Canyon

The geological history of these ancient stones goes back some 600 million years. Over eons, the forces of nature have formed Red Rock's sandstone monoliths into arches, natural bridges, and massive sculptures painted in a stunning palette of gray-white limestone and dolomite, black mineral deposits, and oxidized minerals in earth-toned sienna hues ranging from pink to crimson and burgundy. Orange and green lichens add further contrast, as do spring-fed areas of lush foliage. And formations like **Calico Hill** are brilliantly white where groundwater has leached out oxidized iron. Cliffs cut by deep canyons tower 2,000 feet above the valley floor.

Archaeological studies of Red Rock have turned up pottery fragments, stone tools, pictographs (rock drawings), and petroglyphs (rock etchings), along with other ancient artifacts. They show that humans have been in this region since about 3000 B.C. (some experts say as early as 10,000 B.C.). You can still see remains of early inhabitants on hiking expeditions in the park. (As for habitation of Red Rock, the same ancient Puebloan-to-Paiute-to-white-settlers progression related in the Valley of Fire section above occurred here.)

Seeing the Canyon

Begin with a stop at the **Visitor Center;** not only is there a $5 per-vehicle fee to pay, but you can pick up a variety of helpful literature: history, guides, hiking trail maps, and lists of local flora and fauna. You can also view exhibits that tell the history of the canyon and depict its plant and animal life. You'll see a fascinating video here about Nevada's thousands of wild horses and burros, protected by an act of Congress since 1971. You can also get permits for hiking and backpacking. Call ahead to find out about ranger-guided tours as well as guided hikes offered by groups like the Sierra Club.

BY CAR The easiest way to see the canyon is to drive the 13-mile **scenic loop** ★★. It really is a loop, and it only goes one way, so once you start, you are committed to driving the whole thing. You can stop the car to check out a bunch of fabulous views and sights along the way, or have a picnic, or take a walk or hike. As you drive, observe how dramatically the milky-white limestone alternates with iron-rich red rocks. Farther along, the mountains become solid limestone, with canyons running between them, which lead to an evergreen forest—a surprising sight in the desert.

ON FOOT If you're up for it, we can't stress enough that the way to *really* see the canyon is by hiking. Every trail is incredible—glance over your options and decide what you might be looking for. You can begin from the visitor center or drive into the loop, park your car, and start from points therein. Hiking trails range from a 0.7-mile-loop stroll to a waterfall (its flow varying seasonally) at Lost Creek to much longer and more strenuous treks. Be sure to wear good shoes; the rocks can be slippery. You must have a map—you won't get lost forever (there usually are other hikers around to help you out, eventually)—but you can get lost. Consequently, give yourself extra time for each hike (at least an additional hour), regardless of its billed length, to allow for the lack of paths, or simply to slow down and admire the scenery.

A popular 2-mile round-trip hike leads to **Pine Creek Canyon** and the creekside ruins of a historic homesite surrounded by ponderosa pine trees. Our hiking trail of choice is the **Calico Basin,** which is accessed along the loop. After an hour walk up the rocks (which is not that well-marked), you end up at an oasis surrounded by sheer walls of limestone (which makes the oasis itself inaccessible, alas). In the summer, flowers and deciduous trees grow out of the walls.

Refuelinc, at Red Rock Resort

The opening of the gleaming new luxury **Red Rock Resort,** 10973 W. Charleston Rd. (☎ **866/767-7773**), gives day trippers a new, highly desirable (and expensive) refueling point on a trip to the canyon. It's a gorgeous new facility, already a place for celeb-spotting. There's a casino, and a set of movie theaters if you realize it's really, really hot and you just don't want to take a hike after all. Best of all, the food court contains a **Capriotti's,** the economical submarine sandwich shop we highly recommend as a source for picnic munchies, and among the restaurants is a branch of the highly lauded **Salt Lick BBQ.** It doesn't quite measure up to the platonic perfection of the original in Austin, TX (p. 330), but it's here, and so are you.

As you hike, keep your eyes peeled for lizards, the occasional desert tortoise, herds of bighorn sheep, birds, and other critters. But the rocks themselves are the most fun, with cool minicaves to explore and rock formations to climb. Petroglyphs are also tucked away in various locales.

A CLOSE ENCOUNTER WITH AREA 51

150 miles N of Las Vegas

Want to feel like an extra on the *X-Files*? Just want to get an idea of the kind of spots the government picks when it needs a place in which to do secret things? Take the drive from Vegas out to the **"E. T. Highway,"** where folks were spotting aliens years before it became fashionable. This is about a 150-mile trip one-way, so it's probably not something to do on a whim, but even for non–alien buffs, it can be a long, strange—and oddly illuminating—trip indeed.

Getting There

Take I-15 north to US 93 North (paying close attention—it's an easy exit to miss; if you do, you can take NV 168 at Moapa west back to US 93), and then get off at the E. T. Highway, a 98-mile stretch of NV 375. The town of **Rachel** is approximately 43 miles away; the "black mailbox" (it's now white) road, which leads you to Area 51, actually comes first, about 17 miles down the highway. (We strongly suggest going to Rachel first, to get your bearings, chat with knowledgeable locals and other alien-spotters, and pick up some literature, including a good local map.) Turn left and keep driving; any of the dirt roads that lead off of it will get you to the Area 51 fence and gates. Veer right at the fork in the road (*not* the ranch turnoff, which you come to first) if you want to go to the most commonly talked about entrance, the one at Groom Lake (though you can't see the lake from where you are forced to stop.)

Seeing Area 51

Area 51 is a secret military facility, containing a large air base that the government will not discuss. The site was selected in the mid-1950s for the testing of the U2 spy plane and is supposedly the current testing ground for "black budget" aircraft before their public acknowledgment. But its real fame comes with the stories of aliens, whose bodies and ships were supposedly taken there when they "crashed" at Roswell. For a fairly comprehensive (and opinionated) summary of the myths and facts of Area 51, head to your friendly neighborhood Wikipedia entry: **http://en. wikipedia.org/wiki/Area_51**.

All we know for *sure* is that you turn down one of the most well-maintained dirt roads you will ever encounter, drive a few miles, and come upon a fence with a sign

that warns you against going any farther in the utmost of strict terms (though the language has been toned down from "use of deadly force authorized" to threats of fines and jail time). Along the way down that road, notice how there is absolutely no wildlife other than grasshoppers, that the Joshua trees suddenly turn to an enormous size and monstrous shape, and that the few cattle grazing around don't seem like any cattle you've seen before. Then notice those blasted-out craters in the earth, with the core sample holes in the center. When you realize you are looking at nuclear test sites, the desolation and mutations suddenly make sense. Wave hi to the guys in the military vehicles who are making damn sure you don't go through that gate, and hightail it out of there.

The other, uh, hot spot is the "town" of **Rachel** (www.rachel-nevada.com), really just a collection of trailer homes. Here's where you'll find the **Little A'Le'Inn** (☎ 866/ETHWY51; www.littlealeinn. com) diner and gift shop ("Earthlings Welcome")—where a funny *X-Files* episode was filmed. The owners don't play along as much as you might like, though they do feel they were "called there for a special purpose," but their gift shop makes up for it with humorous souvenirs (we liked the alien-head-shaped guitar pick). Plus, they serve satisfying diner food.

You can also drop in at the **Area 51 Research Center** (just look for the big yellow trailer), which was opened after its founder Glenn Campbell (no, not the singer), who is largely responsible for Area 51's recent cultural icon status, and who wrote the definitive book *Area 51 Viewer's Guide*, got kicked out of the Little A'Le'Inn. Their headquarters is now in Las Vegas, and their store may only be opening during spring and summer, so call before you visit. It stocks all manner of Area 51 logo items and a number of related books.

Area 51

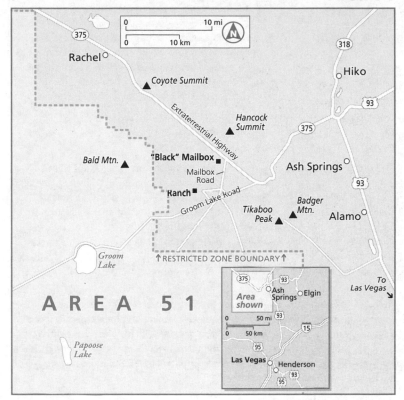

There is no place to stay out here, so plan this as a lengthy day trip. Be sure to fill your tank before you head out, as there aren't many gas stations on the way out of Vegas. If you'll be doing this drive in the heat of summer, bring water, for your car and yourself.

By the way, word is starting to spread of a *really* mysterious secret base even farther out in the desert. Just mention Area 58, and watch people go nuts.

On the Road to Palm Springs, CA

Las Vegas, NV to Palm Springs, CA 279 miles

There's nothing like driving through the desert. Maybe it's the two-lane highways that go on forever; maybe it's the sensation of smallness amid the open, arid terrain, or maybe it just feels good to get the hell outta the city. Whatever it is, the road from Vegas to Palm Springs begins with a pleasant ride on a desert highway. You'll pass the Mojave Desert Preserve, and go through areas where the sky looks like an endless blue sheet. Or you may find yourself caught in a desert thunderstorm, as we did. Either way, this is what a desert roadtrip is all about. Stock up on the water, and get your playlist in order; we're heading to Palm Springs.

On the Road **Nuts & Bolts**

Where to Fill Up We suggest you fill up before leaving Vegas. One tank of gas should get you to Palm Springs, provided you're not driving a Hummer. You can also stop off in Barstow (156 miles outside of Vegas), where you'll find plenty of gas stations.

The Tolls There are none.

The Fastest Way I-15 South toward San Bernadino/Riverside for 214 miles; I-215 South for 14 miles; I-10 East for 40 miles; CA 111 to Palm Springs for 3¹/₂ miles This should take between 3 to 4 hours, depending on traffic.

The Long Way Round This route is best for those who want to stop off in Twentynine Palms and Joshua Tree before arriving in Palm Springs. If you're feeling particularly ambitious, take I-515 South 19 miles; bear right at US 95 (Veterans Memorial Highway) and go 79 miles; I-40 West for 17 miles; National Trails Highway for 46 miles; bear left at Amboy Road for 45 miles; left at Utah Trail; take a right at US 62 (Twentynine Palms Hwy.); CA 62 to I-10 East for 4 miles; take the Indian Avenue exit; Indian Avenue less than a mile to Palm Springs. By all accounts, the back way to Palm Springs is more scenic than the I-15 route, but it will also add an hour or two to your trip.

Rules of the Road It's *way* too easy to speed on desert highways, especially when traffic is light. So, watch the speedometer. Nothing saps the momentum out of a trip faster than getting a ticket. Also, if you're in the left lane and another vehicle comes up behind you, move over to the right lane to let them pass—no matter how fast you're going. Maybe they *were* riding your back, but think of it this way: You're not the one who's going to get a ticket.

Welcome to Palm Springs

Once the Spring Break capital of the Southwest, more recently a golf course-studded retirement mecca, Palm Springs has been quietly working on changing its image and attracting a whole new crowd.

These days, no billboards are allowed in Palm Springs; all the palm trees in the center of town are backlit at night, and you won't see the word "motel" on any establishment. Sure, seniors are everywhere, dressed to the nines in leisure suits, sustaining the retro-kitsch establishments from the days when Elvis, Liberace, and Sinatra made the desert a swingin' place. But they're not alone: Hollywood's young glitterati come here looking for a respite from LA's glare.

No longer a Spring Break magnet, today the city fancies itself a European-style resort with a dash of small-town Americana—think *Jetsons* architecture and the crushed-velvet vibe of piano bars with the colors and attitude of a laid-back Aegean village. One thing hasn't changed: Swimming, sunbathing, golfing, and tennis are still the primary pastimes. And if you've just spent a weekend in Vegas, this is a good place to lay low for a day or two.

High season happens from December to May, when the mild temps—though still far from hot—offer a nice counterpoint to the

Playlist: Las Vegas to Palm Springs

→ *Viva Las Vegas*, **Dead Kennedys**, "Fresh Fruit for Rotting Vegetables," 1980

→ *Your Love is Like Las Vegas*, **The Thrills**, "So Much for The City," 2003

→ *Las Vegas*, M.I.A., "Lost Boys," 2001

→ *The Road Goes On Forever*, **The Highwaymen**, "The Road Goes On Forever," 1995

→ *Road to Nowhere*, **Talking Heads**, "Little Creatures," 1985

→ *Road to Ruin*, **The Libertines**, "The Libertines," 2004

→ *Lost Highway*, **Hank Williams**, "40 Greatest Hits," 1978

→ *Cactus*, **The Pixies**, "Surfer Rosa," 1988

→ *Desert Island*, **The Magnetic Fields**, "Holiday," 1994

→ *Highway to Hell*, **AC/DC**, "Back in Black," 1980

→ *In God's Country*, **U2**, "Joshua Tree," 1987

→ *Palm Springs*, **Claudia Medeiros**, "Palm Springs," 2005

real winter much of the country experiences at the same time. Expect hotel rates to increase by 10% to 20% during high season, with prices dropping by the same clip during low season (July–Sept).

Getting Around

The commercial downtown area of Palm Springs stretches about half a mile along North Palm Canyon Drive between Alejo and Ramon streets. The street is one-way southbound through the heart of town, but its northbound counterpart is Indian Canyon Drive, 1 block east. The mountains lie west and south, while the rest of Palm Springs is laid out in a grid to the southeast. Palm Canyon forks into South Palm Canyon (leading to the Indian Canyons) and East Palm Canyon (the continuation of Hwy. 111) traversing the towns of Cathedral City, Rancho Mirage, Palm Desert, Indian Wells, and La Quinta, before looping up to rejoin I-10 at Indio. Desert Hot Springs is north of Palm Springs, straight up Gene Autry Trail. Tahquitz Canyon Way creates North Palm Canyon's primary intersection,

tracking a straight line between the airport and the heart of town.

Hot Springs Village is a park-and-stroll kind of downtown, with restaurants, cafes and shops lining the main drag, Central Avenue. Ditch the van at the free public lot on Exchange Street at Bath Street, 1 block west of Central. You will, however, need to drive to McClard's, the California outpost of the famed barbecue joint beloved by the likes of Bill Clinton and Aerosmith. For a review of the original, see p. 344.

Sleeping

The city of Palm Springs has a wide range of accommodations, but we particularly like the inns that have opened as a result of new owners renovating the many fabulous 40- to 60-year-old cottage complexes in the wind-shielded Tennis Club area west of Palm Canyon Drive. Most are destinations in and of themselves, with activities for the whole family (including a whole lot of relaxing and pampering). If you're looking for a good base from which to shop or sightsee, Palm Springs is your best bet.

Regardless of your choice, remember that the rates below are for high season (winter, generally Nov–May). During the hotter summer months, it's common to find $300 rooms going for $99 or less, as part of off-season packages. Even in high season, discounts for midweek stays are common.

CHEAP

➔ **Casa Cody** ★ Once owned by "Wild" Bill Cody's niece, this 1920s house with a double courtyard (each with swimming pool) has been restored to fine condition. It now sports a Southwestern decor and peaceful grounds marked by large lawns and mature, blossoming fruit trees. It's in the residential, tennis-clubby part of town, a couple of easy blocks from Palm Canyon Drive, so you'll feel more like a houseguest than a hotel client. Many of the 23 units here have fireplaces and full-size kitchens. *Tip:* If you're traveling in a group, consider renting Casa Cody's **Adobe house.** A genuine Adobe home dating back to 1910, this stand-alone unit was once the weekend getaway for Charlie Chaplin and his friends. Handsomely outfitted in Indian and Mexican antique furniture, it has two full bedrooms, a working fireplace, and a stone tub in the bathroom. *175 S. Cahuilla Rd. (between Tahquitz Way and Arenas Rd.). ☎ 800/231-2639 or 760/320-9346. www.casa cody.com. 23 units. $69–$159 double. Rates include expanded continental breakfast. Amenities: 2 outdoor heated pools; Jacuzzi; in-room massage. In room: A/C, TV, fridge.*

➔ **Palm Mountain Resort and Spa** Within easy walking distance of Palm Springs's main drag, this former Holiday Inn welcomes kids under 18 free in their parent's room, making it a good choice for families. Rooms are in the two- or the three-story wing, and many have a patio or balcony, with a view of the mountains or the large Astroturf courtyard. Midweek and summer rates are as low as $99. For the best rates, book online or ask for "Great Rates." *155 S. Belardo Rd., Palm Springs, CA 92262. ☎ 800/622-9451 or 760/325-1301. Fax 760/323-8937. www.palmmountainresort.com. 119 units. Double Jan–Apr $119–$189; May–Sept $69–$139; Oct–Dec $99–$169. Rates include continental breakfast. Free parking. Amenities: Restaurant; lounge; heated pool; day spa. In room: A/C, TV, fridge, coffeemaker, hair dryer, iron.*

DOABLE

➔ **Calla Lily Inn** With a recent, extensive renovation, this nine-unit inn offers deluxe rooms with kitchens and poolside suites, all with tile floors and luxurious beds. Instead of wine at cocktail time, the Calla Lily offers a nighttime cordial or brandy. The tropical decor is enhanced by the lush landscaping with, what else, calla lilies. A 2-day minimum is required on weekends and holidays, and pets and smoking are prohibited. *350 S. Belardo Rd., Palm Springs, CA 92262. ☎ 888/888-5787 or 760/323-3654. www.callalilypalmsprings.com. 9 units. $129–$179 double. Amenities: Heated pool; Jacuzzi; on-site massage. In room: A/C, TV w/VCR and DVD, coffeemaker, iron/ironing board, robes, Wi-Fi.*

➔ **Villa Royale** ★★ This charming inn, 5 minutes from the hustle and bustle of downtown, evokes a European cluster of villas, complete with climbing bougainvillea and rooms filled with international antiques and artwork. Uniform luxuries (down comforters and other pampering touches) appear throughout. Rooms vary widely in size and ambience; larger isn't always better, as some of the inn's most appealing rooms are in the smaller, more affordable range. Many rooms have fireplaces, private patios, full kitchens, and a variety of other amenities. A full breakfast

Palm Springs Highlights

SLEEPING ■
Calla Lily Inn **6**
Casa Cody **5**
Orbit In **4**
Palm Mountain Resort
  and Spa **3**
Viceroy Palm Springs **2**
Villa Royale **11**

EATING ◆
Davey's Hideaway **9**
Europa Restaurant **10**
Murph's Gaslight **15**
Simba's **8**

PARTYING ★
Blue Guitar **7**
Citron Bar (at the Viceroy
  Palm Springs) **2**
Red 74 **13**
South Beach **12**
Zeldaz Dance Club &
  Beach Club **1**

ATTRACTIONS ●
The Living Desert Zoo &
  Gardens **14**

is served in an intimate garden setting surrounding the main pool. This is a genuine desert oasis. The hotel's romantic restaurant, **Europa** (p. 582), is a sleeper, offering some of Palm Springs's very best meals. *1620 Indian Trail (off E. Palm Canyon).* ☎ *800/245-2314 or 760/327-2314. www.villa royale.com. 31 units. $100–$250 double. Rates include full breakfast. Free parking. Amenities: Restaurant; 2 outdoor heated pools; Jacuzzi; in-room massage. In room: A/C, TV, dataport, hair dryer, iron.*

SPLURGE

➜ **Orbit In** ★★ This renovation of a classic 1950s motel gets our vote as the grooviest digs in town. With its cocktails-by-the-pool Rat Pack aesthetic, it has exceeded everyone's expectations, with an almost scholarly appreciation of the architects and designers responsible for Palm Springs's reign as a mecca of vintage modernism. Serious connoisseurs of interior design will find a museum's worth of furnishings in these rooms, each of which adheres to a theme (Martini Room, Atomic Paradise, and so on) down to customized lounge-music CDs. Contemporary comforts abound, from cushy double pillow-top mattresses to poolside misters that create an oasis of cool even during midsummer scorchers. Nearby, the eight-unit **Hideaway** is a quieter, more secluded lodging with a large saltwater pool; no Jacuzzi but access to the Orbit amenities is available. *562 W. Arenas Rd.* ☎ *877/99-ORBIT or 760/323-3585. www.orbitin.com. 10 units. $199–$299 double. Free parking. Amenities: Outdoor heated saltwater pool; spa facilities; Jacuzzi; complimentary Schwinn cruiser bikes; private patios. In room: A/C, TV/VCR, dataport, kitchenette, fridge, coffeemaker, hair dryer, iron, safe, CD player.*

➜ **Viceroy Palm Springs** ★★★ Once the choice of Hollywood celebrities, this stellar hotel, formerly the Estrella, is quiet and secluded yet close to the action. It's composed of three distinct properties from three different eras, which benefited from a chic transformation in 2002—sort of a Grecian-meets-modern Regency style popular during Palm Springs's golden era. Guest rooms vary in terms of size and amenities—some have fireplaces and/or full kitchens; others have wet bars or private balconies. The color scheme is black-and-white with lemon-yellow accents. The real deals are the studio bungalows, even though they have tiny 1930s bathrooms. Lavish landscaping is an elegant finishing touch. The restaurant, **Citron,** serves lunch and dinner (entrees $24–$34) and has a full bar. *415 S. Belardo Rd. (south of Tahquitz Way).* ☎ *800/237-3687 or 760/320-4117. www.viceroypalmsprings.com. 68 units. $209–$229 double; $325 suite. Free parking. Amenities: 3 outdoor heated pools (including children's pool); fitness room; full-service spa; 2 Jacuzzis. In room: A/C, flatscreen TV, DVD player, fridge, hair dryer.*

Eating

TAKEOUT TREATS & SUPPLIES

Palm Springs may be a small town, but there's no shortage of coffeehouses and delis to fill up on caffeine and snacks. As the name implies, **Koffi** (555 N. Palm Canyon Dr.; ☎ **760/416-2244**) offers a full array of Euro-style coffees, teas, and pastries. If you take your coffee corporate, downtown you'll find a **Starbucks** (101 S. Palm Canyon Dr.; ☎ **760/323-7412**) and **Coffee Bean & Tea Leaf** (100 N. Palm Canyon Dr.; ☎ **760/325-9402**).

To load up before hitting the road, check out **Jensen's Finest Foods** (102 S. Sunrise Way; ☎ **760/325-8282**), a gourmet grocery store and deli serving fresh baked goods, sandwiches, and salads. And if you're missing big-city life, **Manhattan in the Desert NY** (2665 E. Palm Canyon Dr.;

☎ 760/322-3354) serves up Big Apple–inspired sandwiches and baked goods.

CHEAP

➔ **Murph's Gaslight** ★ PAN-FRIED CHICKEN Join those in the know at this budget-saving lunch-and-dinner meeting place, where the chicken just keeps coming, with all the trimmings: black-eyed peas, mashed potatoes, corn bread, hot biscuits, country gravy, and fruit cobbler. Call ahead for takeout or join the family-style crowd, on a first-come, first-served basis. An early-bird special starts at 5pm for $9. If there's a wait, relax in Murph's Irish Pub. *79-860 Ave. 42, next to the airport in Bermuda Dunes near Jefferson.* ☎ *760/345-6242. $16 for full dinner. Tues–Sat 11am–3pm and 5–9pm; Sun 3–9pm.*

➔ **Sherman's Deli and Bakery** ★ KOSHER DELI Join the locals at this indoor and outdoor-patio restaurant with 2-inch-thick deli sandwiches, lox and bagels, and a bakery with rich, delicious cakes and pastries that would put any calorie-conscious dieter into trauma if it weren't for the Lite Lunch Special: chicken or matzo ball soup with half of any regular deli-variety sandwich. Iced tea is the official drink, but wine and beer are also available. *401 Tahquitz, Palm Springs.* ☎ *760/325-1199. Breakfast omelets $5.95–$8.95; deli sandwich board $7.95–$12 (includes potato salad); dinner $14–$19, early-bird dinner $11. Daily 7am–9pm.*

➔ **Simba's** BARBECUE For the best barbecued ribs in the desert, check out Simba's Ribhouse in Palm Springs. You'll also find down-home versions of chicken and dumplings, black-eyed peas, barbecued beans, corn bread, hush puppies, and sweet-potato pie. *190 N. Sunrise Way, in a former bank building.* ☎ *760/778-7630. $11–$15. Tues–Fri 11am–2pm and 5–9pm; Sat–Sun 3–10pm. Closed Mon.*

DOABLE

➔ **Davey's Hideaway** AMERICAN For a relaxed, casual, inexpensive evening, you must try Davey's Hideaway at the beginning of East Palm Canyon. This small cookshop serves salads, pasta, beef, rack of lamb, and their special fresh Atlantic salmon charbroiled or Cajun style. Nightly specials sell for $15 from 5 to 6pm. *292 E. Palm Canyon, Palm Springs (across the street from Lyon's).* ☎ *760/320-4480. Main courses $16–$29. Reservations suggested. Dinner only Sun–Thurs 5–9:30pm; Fri–Sat 5–10:30pm.*

➔ **Edgardo's Café Veracruz** ★ MEXICAN Pleasant but humble Edgardo's is a welcome change from more touristy Palm Springs restos. The expert menu features authentic Mayan, Huasteco, and Aztec cuisine. The dark interior boasts colorful masks and artwork from Central and South America, but the postage stamp–size front patio with a fountain is the best place to sample Edgardo's tangy quesadillas, desert cactus salad, poblano chiles rellenos, and oyster-tequila shooters from the oyster bar. *494 N. Palm Canyon (at W. Alejo Rd.).* ☎ *760/320-3558. Reservations recommended for weekend dinner. Main courses $8–$25 dinner, $7–$12 lunch. Daily 11am–10pm. Free parking.*

➔ **Las Casuelas Terraza** CLASSIC MEXICAN The original Las Casuelas, a tiny storefront several blocks away, is still open, but the bougainvillea-draped front patio here is a much better place to people-watch. You can order Mexican standards such as quesadillas, enchiladas, mountainous nachos, and supersized margaritas. Inside, the action heats up with live music and raucous happy-hour crowds (Mon–Fri 4:30–6:30pm). In hot weather, well-placed misters cool guests on the patio and even sidewalk passersby, making this a perfect late-afternoon or

DESERT TO THE BEACH

early-evening choice. *222 S. Palm Canyon Dr.* ☎ *760/325-2794. www.lascasuelas.com. Reservations recommended on weekends. Main courses $8–$20. Mon–Fri 11am–10pm; Sat–Sun 10am–10pm.*

SPLURGE

➔ **Europa Restaurant** ★★ CALIFORNIA/CONTINENTAL Long advertised as the "most romantic dining in the desert," Europa is a sentimental favorite of many regulars, equal parts gay and straight. This European-style hideaway exudes charm and ambience. Whether you sit under the stars on Europa's garden patio or in subdued candlelight indoors, you'll savor dinner prepared by one of Palm Springs's most dedicated kitchens and served by a discreetly attentive staff. Standout dishes include a tender *osso bucco* that falls off the bone, filet mignon on a bed of crispy onions with garlic butter, and a show-stopping salmon baked in parchment with crème fraîche and dill. And don't miss the signature chocolate mousse—smooth, grainy, and addictive. *1620 Indian Trail (at the Villa Royale).* ☎ *760/327-2314. Reservations recommended. Main courses $22–$34. Tues–Sun 6–9pm; Sun 11:30am–2pm.*

Partying

Every month a different club or disco is the hot spot in the Springs, and the best way to tap into the trend is by consulting the *Desert Guide,* or the GLBT publication, *Bottom Line.* **VillageFest** turns Palm Canyon Drive into an outdoor party every Thursday night. We've provided a few of our favorite nightspots below, but a stroll along **North Palm Canyon Drive** will introduce you to a slew of eating and drinking options for just about every budget.

BARS, PUBS & CLUBS

➔ **Blue Guitar** True to its name, this local second-story haunt serves up live blues, and lots of it. A state-of-the-art lighting and sound system back a solid roundup of weekly acts. Fridays and Saturdays bring a $10 cover, but Sunday concerts are free. The kitchen cooks up better-than-expected Southern fare, so don't be afraid to drown your sorrows in a little gumbo. *120 S. Palm Canyon Dr.* ☎ *760/327-1549. 9pm–2am Fri–Sat; other nights depending on events. $10 cover Fri–Sat; doors open 8pm. No cover Sun, doors open 7pm. Vintage Blues Video Night 6–10pm Thurs.*

➔ **Las Casuelas Terraza** In addition to serving up hearty Mexican fare (see review above), the bar at Las Casuelas draws in locals with a festive atmosphere and a long list of premium tequilas. On warm nights, grab a seat at the lively sidewalk area, where patrons sip margaritas, listen to Latin pop, and soak in the desert heat. *222 S. Palm Canyon Dr.* ☎ *760/325-2794. Mon–Sat 11am–10pm; Sun 10am–10pm. Summer hours may vary.*

➔ **Citron Bar (at the Viceroy Palm Springs)** The Citron bar offers the same sleek vibe as the hotel that houses it. Lemon yellow and white walls enliven an intimate and chic room, while hotel guests and visitors sidle up to the bar for martinis, cocktails, and specially made aperitifs. Granted, Citron closes early (10pm), but this is the perfect setting for an after-dinner dessert or a pre-dinner rendezvous. *415 S. Belardo Rd. (south of Tahquitz Way).* ☎ *800/237-3687 or 760/320-4117. www.viceroypalmsprings.com. Daily 6–10pm.*

➔ **Zeldaz Dance Club & Beach Club** If this joint had a slogan, it might be "Please everyone." Zeldaz's calendar schedules everything from comedy to show revues. The real action, though, is on dance floor, where locals and visitors bump and grind to a mix of disco, funk, soul, R&B, hip-hop, Latin, and pop. There's also gay/lesbian nights, so call ahead. *169 N. Indian Canyon*

GLBT Life in Palm Springs

The Palm Springs area is among America's top destinations for gay and lesbian travelers. Advertisements for gay-owned businesses can be found in the **Bottom Line** (www.psbottomline.com), the desert's free biweekly magazine of articles, events, and community guides for the gay reader, which is available at hotels, at newsstands, and from select merchants. The **Palm Springs Visitor and Hotel Information Center** publishes an **Official Gay Visitors Guide.** Obtain it and additional information at their office at 2781 N. Palm Canyon Dr. (☎ **888/866-2744;** www.palm-springs.org).

Palm Springs has more than two dozen gay hotels, many concentrated on Warm Sands Drive south of Ramon. Known simply as "Warm Sands," this area is home to many of the private resorts—mostly discreet, gated inns, many of them clothing-optional. Try the **East Canyon Hotel & Spa,** 288 E. Camino Monte Vista (☎ **877/324-6835** or 760/320-1928; www.eastcanyonps.com), a men's luxury resort and full-service spa; or **Casitas Laquita,** 450 E. Palm Canyon Dr. (☎ **760/416-9999;** www.casitaslaquita.com), one of two all-women resorts in town.

Dr. ☎ 760/325-2375. Open 'til 2am nightly. All-male revue 10pm Thurs–Fri; dance party with DJ Jay Rockbunk, techno/salsa/hip-hop; DJ Dynamic playing today's music, 9pm Sat.

In Palm Desert

➔ **Red 74** It's Spring Break year round at Red 74. Named after its location on Highway 74 and the owner's apparent affinity for the color red, this club goes for the pretend-like-you're-a-celeb for-a-night angle. DJs spin hip-hop, R&B, funk, old school, and reggaeton dance music, while three VIP sections offer bottle service in private red scarlet cabanas. 72-990 Hwy. 74. ☎ 760/568-6774. Tues–Sat 7pm–2am.

➔ **South Beach** Evoking that humble little beach town we all know and love, South Beach is a 12,000-sqare-foot venue that does everything it can to bring in the desert hotties: go-go dancer contests, live music, the celeb on leave from L.A., and lots and lots of dancing. Not the classiest joint in the world, but a good time if you're looking for a place to get your groove on and can't afford the ticket to Florida. 72-191

Hwy. 111 ☎ 760/773 1711. www.clubsouthbeach. com. 7pm–2am Tues–Sun.

What Else to See & Do in Palm Springs

Sure, you can lay low and just hang around the pool in Palm Springs, but for those of you who are not content to simply soak up the desert sun, this area offers some surprisingly compelling attractions to get you out of your hotel Below are three of our off-the-beaten path favorites.

ART, ANIMALS & TRAMS

➔ **The Living Desert Zoo & Gardens** ★ This 1,200-acre desert reserve, museum, zoo, and educational center is designed to acquaint visitors with the Southern California desert's unique habitats. You can walk or take a tram tour through sectors that re-create life in several distinctive desert zones. See and learn about a dizzying variety of plants, insects, and wildlife, including bighorn sheep, mountain lions, rattlesnakes, lizards, owls, golden eagles, and the ubiquitous roadrunner. 47–900 Portola Ave., Palm Desert.

Music, Movies & Other Desert Distractions: Palm Springs Events

⟶ The **Coachella Valley Music & Arts Festival** is the biggest, most cutting-edge music festival in Southern California. Bands of all stripes—from hip-hop to metal to indie—play on the same stage for two glorious days. The festival usually takes place in April. Check the website for this year's lineup, exact dates, and directions. **www.coachella.com.**

⟶ The **Palm Springs Short Film Festival** is the largest short film showcase in America. Over 300 films are presented from 29 countries on three screens for 7 days. The festival usually happens in late August. Check the website for scheduled screenings and exact dates. **www.psfilmfest.com.**

⟶ FREE **Palm Springs Pride** is an annual festival and parade celebrating the pride and diversity of the lesbian, gay, bisexual, and transgender community in the greater Palm Springs area. The festival happens in early November; check the website for exact dates. **www.pspride.org.**

⟶ FREE **Rancho Mirage Art Affaire** features fine art and select fine craft exhibits, as well as jazz, entertainment, food, and wine. The exhibit is free to the public and held at Whitewater Park in Rancho Mirage in early November. Exact dates are available on the Rancho Mirage website. **www.ranchomirage.org.**

☎ *760/346-5694. www.livingdesert.org. Admission $12 adults, $11 military. Reduced summer rates. Daily 9am–5pm (last entrance 4pm); summer (mid-June to Aug) 8am–1:30pm.*

⟶ **Palm Springs Aerial Tramway** ★★ To gain a bird's-eye perspective on the Coachella Valley, take this 14-minute ascent up nearly 5,900 feet to the upper slopes of Mount San Jacinto. While the Albert Frey–designed boarding stations retain their 1960s ski-lodge feel, newly installed Swiss funicular cars are sleekly modern and rotate during the trip to allow each passenger a panoramic view. There's a whole other world—not to mention climate—once you arrive: alpine scenery, a ski-lodge-flavored restaurant and gift shop, and temperatures typically 40° cooler than the desert floor. An upscale restaurant, Elevations, serves California-modern cuisine. Appetizers begin at $13, entrees $23. Elevations is open noon to 3pm and 4 to 8pm daily and reservations are recommended (☎ **760/327-1590**). *Tramway Rd. off Hwy. 111, Palm Springs.* ☎ *888/515-TRAM or 760/325-1391. www. pstramway.com. Tickets $22 adults. Mon–Fri 10am–8pm; Sat–Sun 8am–8pm. Tram runs every 30 min., last tram down at 9:45pm.*

⟶ **Palm Springs Desert Museum** ★ Unlikely though it may sound, this museum is well-endowed (with *art*!). Exhibits include world-class Western and Native American art collections, the natural history of the desert, and an outstanding anthropology department, primarily representing the local Cahuilla tribe. Tools, baskets, and other relics illustrate traditional Indian life, as it was lived for centuries. Check local schedules to find out about visiting exhibits (which are usually excellent). Plays, lectures, and other events are presented in the museum's **Annenberg Theater.** *101 Museum Dr. (just* west of the Palm Canyon/Tahquitz intersection), Palm Springs. ☎ 760/325-7186. www. psmuseum.org. Admission $13 adults, $5 military. Free for all each Thurs after 4pm. Tues–Wed and Fri–Sun 10am–5pm; Thurs noon–8pm. Closed Mon.

PLAYING OUTSIDE

The Coachella Valley Desert is a sunny playground, and what follows is but a sampling of outdoor activities. *Tip:* The abundant sunshine and dry air that are so appealing can also sneak up on you, in the form of sunburn and heat exhaustion. Especially during the summer, but even in milder times, always carry and drink plenty of water, and slather on that sunscreen.

All-Terrain Vehicle Tours

Desert Adventures (☎ **888/440-JEEP** or 760/324-JEEP; www.red-jeep.com), 67555 East Palm Canyon Dr. in Cathedral City, offers four-wheel-drive eco-tours led by naturalist guides. Your off-road adventure may take you to a replica of an ancient Cahuilla village, the Santa Rosa Mountain roads overlooking the Coachella Valley, or picturesque ravines on the way to the San Andreas Fault. Tours run from 2 to 4 hours and cost from $75 to $115. Advance reservations are required. The company's red Jeeps depart from the Desert Adventures Ranch on South Palm Canyon near the entrance to the Indian Canyons.

Elite Land Tours ★ (☎ **800/514-4866** or 760/318-1200; www.elitelandtours.com) offers a new way to visit the desert region: eco-exploration of the greater Palm Springs backcountry from the air-conditioned comfort of an all-terrain Hummer H2. Tours can include desert and mountain regions, exploration of ancient cultures, wildlife, and geological wonders. The Night Discovery Tour lets you view the desert wildlife after dark with special night-vision equipment. Tours run from $129 to $159 per person.

Ballooning ★★

This may be the most memorable and unconventional way to see the desert: floating above the landscape in a hot-air balloon. Choose from specialty themes like

Here's the Rub: Two Bunch Palms Desert Spa

Since the Native American Cahuilla learned how great it felt to soak in the Coachella Valley's natural hot springs, this desert has drawn stressed-out masses seeking relaxation. Our number-one choice is heavenly Two Bunch Palms. Posh yet intimate, this spiritual sanctuary in Desert Hot Springs (about 20 min. north of Palm Springs) has been drawing weary city dwellers since Chicago mobster Al Capone hid out here in the 1930s. Two Bunch Palms later became a playground for the movie community, but today it's a friendly and informal haven, with renowned spa services, bungalows on lush grounds, and lagoons of steaming mineral water. Service is famously discreet; and legions of return guests will attest that the outstanding spa treatments (nine varieties of massage, mud baths, body wraps, facials, salt rubs, and more) and therapeutic waters are what make the luxury of Two Bunch Palms irresistible. Spa treatments cost between $75 and $100 per hour. The resort is off Palm Drive (Gene Autry Trail) at 67-425 Two Bunch Palms Trail (☎ **800/472-4334** or 760/329-8791; www.twobunchpalms.com).

sunrise, sunset, or romantic champagne flights. Rides are offered by **Dream Flights** (☎ **800/933-5628** or 760/346-5330; www.dreamflights.com), and **Fantasy Balloon Flights** (☎ **800/GO-ABOVE** or 760/568-0997; www.fantasyballoonflights.com). It's not cheap though: Rates range from $110 to $170 per person for a 60- to 90-minute flight (two per day), including champagne and hors d'oeuvres. If you're looking to blow some extra cash, this is a memorable way to do it.

Bicycling

The clean, dry desert air makes for the ideal conditions for pedaling your way around town or into the desert. **Adventure Bike Tours** (☎ **760/328-0282**) will outfit you with a bike, helmet, water bottle, and certified guide. Three-hour tours, which meet at local hotels, start at about $50, and bike rentals are $10 per hour or $30 for the day. **Tri a Bike Rental,** 44841 San Pablo Ave., Palm Desert (☎ **760/340-2840**), rents road and mountain bikes by the hour ($12), the day ($30), or the week ($99), and offers children's and tandem models and helmets as well.

Hiking

The most popular spot for hiking is the nearby **Indian Canyons,** at the end of South Palm Canyon Drive (☎ **800/790-3398** or 760/325-3400; www.aguacaliente.org). The Agua Caliente tribe dwelled here centuries ago, and remnants of its culture can be seen among the streams, waterfalls, and palm groves in Andreas, Murray, and Palm canyons. The striking rock formations and herds of bighorn sheep and wild ponies are more appealing than the Trading Post in Palm Canyon, but the shop sells detailed trail maps. The Tribal Council charges admission of $8 per adult, $6 for students and military. The canyons are open 8am to 5pm, and guided hiking tours and ranger lectures are also available.

Note that the canyons are closed to visitors from late June to early September. See the website for more info, as the schedule is subject to change.

Don't miss the opportunity to explore **Tahquitz Canyon,** 500 W. Mesquite, west of Palm Canyon Drive, also in Agua Caliente territory. This scenic canyon, home of the waterfall in *Lost Horizon*, was closed to the public for nearly 30 years after careless squatters suffered injuries in the canyon, and hippies made it an all-night party zone, vandalizing land considered sacred. The tribe cleaned up decades' worth of dumping, and now that vegetation has regrown, they have begun offering $2^1/_2$-hour ranger-led hikes into their most spiritual and beautiful place. The 2-mile round-trip hike is of moderate difficulty; hikes depart daily at 8am, 10am, noon, and 2pm. The fee is $13 for adults, $6 for children ages 6 to 12; call ☎ **800/790-3398** for recorded information, or 760/416-7044 for reservations (recommended).

Ten miles east of Palm Springs is the 13,000-acre **Coachella Valley Preserve** (☎ **760/343-1234**), open daily from sunrise to sunset. It has springs, mesas, both hiking and riding trails, the Thousand Palms Oasis, a visitor center, and picnic areas.

If you're heading up to Joshua Tree National Park (see later in this chapter), consider stopping at the **Big Morongo Canyon Preserve** (☎ **760/363-7190**), which was once an Indian village and later a cattle ranch. It's open daily from 7:30am to sundown. The park's high water table makes it a magnet for birds and other wildlife; the lush springs and streams are an unexpected desert treat.

Horseback Riding

Novice and advanced equestrians alike can experience the desert's solitude and quiet on horseback, at **Smoke Tree**

Stables (☎ 760/327-1372). South of downtown, at 2500 Toleda Ave., and ideal for exploring the nearby Indian Canyon trails, Smoke Tree offers guided rides for $35 per hour, $70 for 2 hours; the 2-hour tour includes admission to an Aguacaliente Indian reservation. But don't expect your posse leader to spew facts about the natural features you'll encounter; this is strictly a do-it-yourself experience.

Tennis

Virtually all the larger hotels and resorts have tennis courts. If you're staying at a B&B, you might want to play at the **Plaza Racquet Club,** 1300 Baristo Rd. (☎ 760/323-8997). It has nine courts and runs day and evening clinics for adults, juniors, and seniors, and ball machines for solo practice. USPTA pros are on hand. The night-lit courts at **Palm Springs High School,** 2248 E. Ramon Rd., are free, open to the public on weekends, holidays, and in summer. Beautiful **Ruth Hardy Park,** at Tamarisk and Caballero streets, also has eight free night-lit courts.

Water Park

If the pool just isn't cutting it for you, **Knott's Soak City,** off I-10 south on Gene Autry Trail between Ramon Road and East Palm Canyon Drive (☎ 760/327-0499; www.knotts.com/soakcity/ps/index.shtml), is a 16-acre water playground with 12 water slides, body- and board-surfing, a wave pool, and more. Dressing rooms, lockers, and private beach cabanas (with food service) are available. Admission is $27 for adults, and rates are discounted after 3pm. The park is open daily mid-March through August, and weekends through October, from 11am to 5pm. Parking is $7 per car.

Detour: Joshua Tree N.P.

JOSHUA TREE NATIONAL PARK ★★

40 miles NE of Palm Springs

Only a short distance from Palm Springs, Joshua Tree National Park offers a desert experience like none other, making it a must see if you have a day to spare. The Joshua trees in this national park are merely a jumping-off point for exploring this seemingly barren desert. Viewed from the roadside, the dry land only hints at hidden vitality, but closer examination reveals a giant mosaic of intense beauty and complexity. From lush oases teeming with life to rusted-out relics of human attempts to tame the wilderness, from low plains of tufted cacti to mountains of exposed, twisted rock, the park is much more than a tableau of the curious tree for which it is named.

The Joshua tree is said to have received its name from early Mormon settlers traveling west, for its upraised limbs and bearded appearance reminded them of the prophet Joshua leading them to the

 Load Up on Everything

Joshua Tree National Park has *no* restaurants, lodging, gas stations, or stores. Water is available only at five park locations: Cottonwood Springs, the Black Rock Canyon Campground, the Indian Cove Ranger Station, the West Entrance (the hamlet of Joshua Tree), and the Oasis Visitor Center. Joshua Tree, Twentynine Palms, and Yucca Valley have lots of restaurants, markets, motels, and B&Bs, so you'd better bring everything you're going to need in the way of food and especially water.

DESERT TO THE BEACH

A lonely Joshua tree stands in the park named for them.

promised land. Other observers were not so kind. Explorer John C. Frémont called it "the most repulsive tree in the vegetable kingdom." That's harsh criticism for this hardy desert dweller—really not a tree but a variety of yucca and member of the lily family.

The park, which reaches the southernmost boundary of this special tree's range, straddles two desert environments. There's the mountainous, Joshua tree–studded Mojave Desert, forming the northwestern part of the park, while the Colorado Desert—hotter, drier, lower, and characterized by a wide variety of desert flora, including cacti, cottonwood, and native California fan palms—comprises the southern and eastern sections of the park. Between them runs the "transition zone," displaying characteristics of each.

In 1994, under provisions of the federal California Desert Protection Act, Joshua Tree rose to national park status and expanded to nearly 800,000 acres. The park is popular with everyone from campers to wildflower lovers and even

RVers just cruising through. It's a must-see for nature and geology lovers visiting during temperate weather, and it's more "user-friendly" than the other two hardcore desert parks.

GETTING THERE

From Palm Springs, the usual route to the **Oasis Visitor Center** in Joshua Tree National Park is to take Indian Avenue. North to the I-10 West. Then, get on Highway 62 (the Twentynine Palms Hwy.), which leads northeast for about 43 miles to the town of Twentynine Palms. Total driving time is around 2½ hours. In town, follow the signs at National Park Drive or Utah Trail to the visitor center and ranger station. Admission to the park is $10 per car (good for 7 days). Camping fees: $5 with no water, $10 with water. RVs must be under 25 feet.

VISITOR CENTERS & INFORMATION

In addition to the **Oasis Visitor Center** (☎ 760/367-5525) at the Twentynine Palms entrance, **Cottonwood Visitor Center** is at the south entrance, and the

DESERT TO THE BEACH

privately operated **Park Center** is in the town of Joshua Tree, close to the West Entrance, the unofficial portal for rock climbers.

The Oasis Visitor Center is open daily (except Dec 25) from 8am to 5pm. Check here for a detailed map of park roads, plus schedules of ranger-guided walks and interpretive programs. Ask about weekend tours of the Desert Queen Ranch, once a working homestead and now part of the park.

For information before you go, contact the **Park Superintendent's Office,** 74485 National Park Dr., Twentynine Palms, CA 92277 (☎ **760/367-5525;** www. nps.gov/jotr). The **Joshua Tree National Park Association** is another good resource; reach them at ☎ **760/367-5525** (www.joshuatree.org). Another outfit focused on the surrounding communities is **www.desertgold.com**.

CHECKING OUT THE PARK

An excellent first stop, outside the park's north entrance, is the main **Oasis Visitor Center,** alongside the Oasis of Mara, also known as the Twentynine Palms Oasis. For many generations, the native Serrano tribe lived at this "place of little springs and much grass." Get maps, books, and the latest in road, trail, and weather conditions before beginning your tour.

From the Oasis Center, drive south to **Jumbo Rocks,** which captures the essence of the park: a vast array of rock formations, a Joshua tree forest, and the yucca-dotted desert, open and wide. Check out Skull Rock (one of the many rocks in the area that appear to resemble humans, dinosaurs, monsters, cathedrals, or castles) via a 1.5-mile nature trail that provides an introduction to the park's flora, wildlife, and geology.

At Cap Rock Junction, the main park road swings north toward the **Wonderland of Rocks,** 12 square miles of massive jumbled granite. This curious maze of stone hides groves of Joshua trees, trackless washes, and several small pools of water. To the south is Keys View Road, which dead-ends at mile-high **Keys View.** From the crest of the Little San Bernardino mountains, enjoy grand desert views that encompass both the highest (Mt. San Gorgonio) and lowest (Salton Sea) points in Southern California.

Don't miss the contrasting Colorado Desert terrain found along Pinto Basin Road. To conserve time, you might plan to exit the park via this route, which ends up at I-10. You'll pass both the **Cholla Cactus Garden** and spindly **Ocotillo Patch** on your way to vast, flat **Pinto Basin,** a barren lowland surrounded by austere mountains and punctuated by trackless sand dunes. The dunes are an easy 2-mile round-trip hike from the backcountry camping board (one of the few man-made markers along this road and one of the only designated parking areas), or simply continue to **Cottonwood Springs,** near the southern park entrance. Besides a small ranger station and well-developed campground, Cottonwood has a cool, palm-shaded oasis that is the trail head for a tough hike to Lost Palms Oasis.

Hiking, Biking & Climbing

HIKING & NATURE WALKS The national park has a variety of nature trails, from strenuous challenges to interpretive walks; two of these (**Oasis of Mara** and **Cap Rock**) are paved and wheelchair-accessible. A popular route, among the 11 short interpretive trails, is **Cholla Cactus Garden,** in the park's center, where you stroll through dense clusters of the deceptively fluffy-looking "teddy bear cactus."

For the more adventurous, **Barker Dam** is an easy 1-mile loop accessible by a graded dirt road east of Hidden Valley. A

Joshua Tree National Park

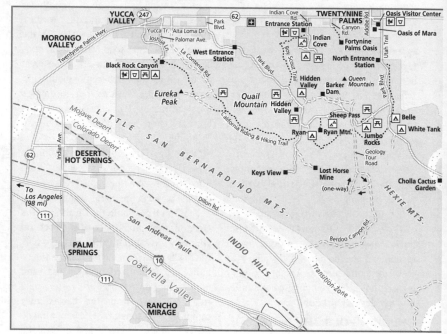

small, man-made lake is framed by the majestic Wonderland of Rocks. It's fun to scramble atop the old dam or search out Native American petroglyphs carved into the cliffs lining your return to the trail head.

The challenging **Lost Horse Mine Trail** near Keys View leads through rolling hills to the ruins of a successful gold-mining operation; from here, a short, steep hike leads uphill behind the ruins for a fine view into the heart of the park.

When you're ready for a strenuous hike, try the **Fortynine Palms Oasis Trail,** accessible from Canyon Road in Twentynine Palms. After a steep, harsh ascent to a cactus-fringed ridge, the rocky canyon trail leads to a spectacular oasis, complete with palm-shaded pools of green water and abundant birds and other wildlife. Allow 2 to 3 hours for the 3-mile round-trip hike.

Another lush oasis lies at the end of **Lost Palms Oasis Trail** at Cottonwood Springs. The first section of the 7.5-mile trail is moderately difficult, climbing slowly to the oasis overlook; from here, a treacherous path continues to the canyon bottom, a remote spot that the elusive bighorn sheep find attractive.

MOUNTAIN BIKING Much of the park is designated wilderness, meaning that bicycles are limited to roads (they'll damage the fragile ecosystem if you venture off the beaten track). None of the paved roads have bike lanes, but rugged mountain bikes are a great way to explore the park via unpaved roads, where there aren't many cars.

Try the 18-mile **Geology Tour Road,** which begins west of Jumbo Rocks. Dry lake beds contrast with towering boulders

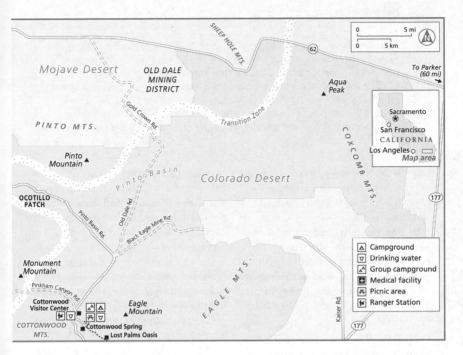

along this sandy downhill road, and you'll also encounter abandoned mines.

A shorter but still rewarding ride begins at the **Covington Flats** picnic area. A steep 4-mile road climbs through Joshua trees, junipers, and pinyon pines to Eureka Peak, where you'll be rewarded with a panoramic view. For other bike-friendly unpaved and four-wheel-drive roads, view the official park map.

ROCK CLIMBING From Hidden Valley to the Wonderland of Rocks, the park has emerged as one of the state's premier rock-climbing destinations. The park offers some 4,000 climbing routes, from the easiest bouldering to some of the sport's most difficult climbs. November through May is the prime season to watch lizardlike humans scale sheer rock faces with impossible grace.

Nomad Adventures in Joshua Tree (☎ 760/366-4684) is the local climbing store for gear sales and shoe rentals ($7.50 a day). Open weekdays from 8am to 6pm, weekends 8am to 8pm.

SLEEPING

If you're staying in the Palm Springs area, it's possible to visit the national park as a day trip. But if you'd like to stay close by or spend more time here, consider Twentynine Palms, just outside the north boundary of the national park on Highway 62, which offers budget-to-moderate lodging. For a complete listing of Twentynine Palms lodging, contact the **29 Palms Chamber of Commerce,** 6455 Mesquite Rd., Twentynine Palms, CA 92277 (☎ 760/367-3445; www.29chamber.com).

Near the visitor center, however, in the Oasis of Mara is the rustic **29 Palms**

ᴍᴛᴠ🅤 Lessons on How to Rock Out . . .

Don't go climbing the walls (or the rocks!) at Joshua Tree without any experience. And for a place to pick up the basics if you haven't clambered up any boulders before, check out the **Joshua Tree Rock Climbing School** (☎ 800/890-4745 or 760/366-4745; www.rockclimbingschool.com). In business since 1988, it offers weekend and 4-day group lessons ($110 for 1 day, $195 for 2 days, and $390–$490 for 4 days, including equipment), plus private guiding ($295 for one person; less per person for bigger groups: $125 per person in a group of five, for example).

Inn ★★ (☎ 760/367-3505; www.29palms inn.com), a cluster of adobe cottages and old cabins from the 1920s; its garden-fresh restaurant is the best in town. The 100-room **Best Western Garden Inn** (☎ 760/367-9141; www.bestwestern.com), is also a comfortable base from which to maximize your outdoor time. We also recommended the 53-room **Holiday Inn Express Hotel and Suites,** 71809 Twentynine Palms Hwy. (☎ 760/361-4009).

CAMPING Nine **campgrounds** scattered throughout the park offer pleasant though pretty spartan accommodations, with just picnic tables and pit toilets for the most part. Only two—**Black Rock Canyon** and **Cottonwood Springs**—have potable water and flush toilets, for a $10 overnight fee. Indian Cove and West Entrance have water at the ranger station, less than 2 miles from their closest campgrounds. You can make reservations online at **http://reservations.nps.gov** or by calling ☎ 800/365-2267. Hot showers are available at **Coyote Corner,** 6535 Park Blvd. in Joshua Tree (☎ 760/366-9683); they also rent climbing and camping gear.

"Sky Climbers" is the name of this sculpture outside the Twentynine Palms Historical Society.

On the Road to Northern Baja, Mexico

Palm Springs, CA to Northern Baja, Mexico 207 miles

In terms of driving, this is probably the least interesting leg of your trip. Your romantic two-lane desert highway quickly gives way to sub-suburban freeways dotted the occasional mini-malls. That makes refueling easy, but there won't be much to look at along the way.

Luckily, it's only about 3 hours from Palm Springs to Tijuana, and the range of offerings in Northern Baja—from sitting on the beach, to horseback riding, to festive nightlife—more than make up for the bland route you'll follow to get there.

On the Road Nuts & Bolts

Where to Fill Up   Again, the best option here is to fill up before leaving. One tank of gas should be enough to get you all the way to Tijuana. But if you'd rather avoid filling up south of the border, you'll see plenty of off-highway gas stations along the way. You can also stop off in San Diego (16 miles north of Tijuana, off CA 163), where there are plenty of gas stations.

The Tolls   To take the scenic route into Rosarito, you'll have to pay about US$2.75. You can pay in pesos or dollar. If you take the scenic route from Rosarito to Ensenada, you'll have to pay another US$2.75.

The Fastest Way   I-10 west for 18 miles; CA 60 West for 18 miles; I-215 South to San Diego for 31 miles; bear right at I-15 south, then go 60 miles; I-5 less than 5 miles until you cross the border; Highway 1-D (the scenic, coast-hugging toll road marked *cuota*), or the free but slower public road (Hwy. 1, marked *libre*) to Tijuana. This should take about 3 hours, depending on traffic.

The Long Way Round   The only desirable alternative to the above route is to stop off in San Diego for gas, supplies, or a bite to eat. To stop in San Diego, follow the same route above, but from the I-15, get on CA 163 11 miles into the city. Follow the signs to get you into town. If you'd like to stop off for lunch or dinner, see p. 621 for our eating recommendations in San Diego.

DESERT TO THE BEACH

Northern Baja Highlights

Northern Baja California is not only Mexico's most infamous border crossing, but it also claims to be the birthplace of the original Caesar salad and the margarita. Long notorious as a hard-partying 10-block border town, **Tijuana** has cleaned up its act a *bit* on its way to becoming a full-scale city. A growing number of sports and cultural attractions now augment the legendary shopping experience and wild nightlife.

Rosarito Beach remains a more tranquil resort town; it got a boost after the movies *Titanic* and *Master and Commander* were filmed there, and Fox Studios converted the former set into a film-themed amusement park (see below). The decidedly laid-back atmosphere makes enjoying its miles of beachfront easy. Farther south

Playlist: The Road to Baja

→ ¿Adonde Van Los Muertos?, **Kinky,** "Reina," 2006

→ My Way, **Los Lonely Boys,** "Reina," 2006

→ Que Onda Guero, **Beck,** "Guero," 2005

→ Low Rider, **Cheech and Chong,** "Up in Smoke," 2006

→ El Matador, **Los Fabulosos Cadillacs,** "Vasos Vacios," 1994

→ Maracas, **Panda,** "La revancha de principe charro," 2003

→ Labios Compartidos, **Maná,** "Amar es Combatir," 2006

→ Hotel California, **Gypsy Kings,** "Volare! The Very Best of The Gypsy Kings," 2006

→ Eres, **Café Tecuba,** "Cuatro Caminos," 2003

→ Rosarito, **Long Beach Dub All-Stars,** "Right Back," 1999

→ Oye Como Va, **Santana,** "Abraxas," 1970

on the Pacific Coast is the lovely port town of **Ensenada,** also known for its surfing and sportfishing. Tours of nearby inland vineyards (Mexico's wine country) are growing in popularity.

If you're not pressed for time, I recommend spending a night in each town, so you can experience the culture and nightlife of each. Another option is to base yourself in Tijuana or Rosarito for a few days and make day trips to the other cities. Either way, your time in these beach cities will provide a nice counterpoint to arid heat of Palm Springs and Vegas; it will also add a laid-back, Latin-inflected conclusion to your trip.

Naughty, Bawdy Tijuana, Mexico

25km (16 miles) S of San Diego

In northern Baja, 26km (16 miles) south of San Diego, the first point of entry from the West Coast of the U.S. is infamous Tijuana—a town that continues to delude travelers into thinking that a visit there means they've been to Mexico. An important border town, Tijuana is renowned for its hustling, carnival-like atmosphere and accessible decadence.

Tijuana's "sin city" image is gradually morphing into that of a shopper's mecca and a nocturnal playground. Vineyards associated with the expanding wine industry are nearby, and an increasing number of cultural offerings have joined the traditional sporting attractions of greyhound racing, jai alai, and bullfights.

You are less likely to find the Mexico you may be expecting here—no charming town squares and churches, no women in colorful embroidered skirts and blouses, no bougainvillea spilling out of every crevice. Tijuana has an urban culture, a profusion of U.S.-inspired goods and services, and relentless hawkers plying to the thousands of tourists who come for a taste of Mexico.

VISTOR CENTER & OTHER INFORMATION

A visit to Tijuana requires little in the way of formalities—people who stay less than 72 hours in the border zone do not need a passport or tourist card. That's going to change soon, however. As early as January 1, 2008, all persons, including U.S. citizens, traveling between the U.S. and Mexico, Central and South America by land or sea (including ferries), may be required to present a valid passport or other documents as

Tijuana

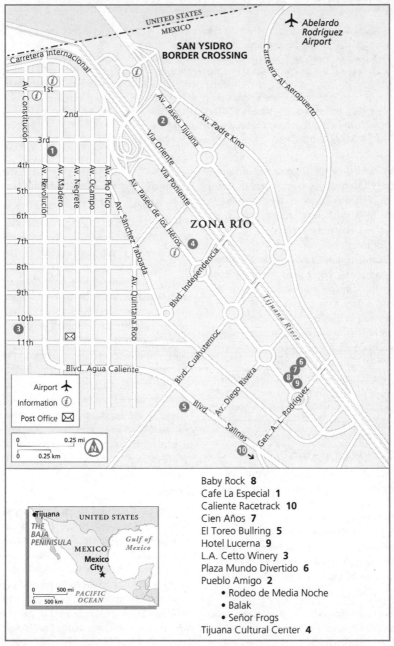

Baby Rock **8**
Cafe La Especial **1**
Caliente Racetrack **10**
Cien Años **7**
El Toreo Bullring **5**
Hotel Lucerna **9**
L.A. Cetto Winery **3**
Plaza Mundo Divertido **6**
Pueblo Amigo **2**
 • Rodeo de Media Noche
 • Balak
 • Señor Frogs
Tijuana Cultural Center **4**

Short Visit? Take the Trolley from San Diego

If you'd like to visit Baja, but would rather make it a day trip, you can also base yourself in **San Diego** (see the chapter "Rockin' the West Coast," p. 306 for our San Diego coverage) and take a trolley into Tijuana. From downtown San Diego, you can hop the **bright-red trolley** headed for San Ysidro and getting off at the last, or San Ysidro, stop (it's nicknamed the Tijuana Trolley for good reason). From here, follow the signs to walk across the border. It's simple, quick, and inexpensive; the one-way fare is $2. The last trolley leaving for San Ysidro departs downtown around midnight; the last returning trolley from San Ysidro is at 1am. On Saturday, the trolley runs 24 hours.

determined by the Department of Homeland Security. If you plan to stay longer, a tourist card is required. They're available free from the border crossing station, or from any immigration office.

For tourist information, visit the **Centro Cultural Tijuana,** Paseo de los Héroes and Mina (☎ 664/687-9600). It's in the Zona Río, the principal shopping and dining district, adjacent to the Tijuana River. For information online, visit the Tijuana Tourism board's official website, **www.see tijuana.com**. Another recommendable site is **www.tijuanaonline.org**.

The Tijuana airport is about 8km (5 miles) east of the city. To drive to Tijuana from the U.S., take I-5 south to the Mexican border at San Ysidro. The drive from downtown San Diego takes about a half-hour.

GETTING AROUND

Once you're in Tijuana, there's no reason you can't use your own car to get around. Maps are available at the border, as is Mexican car insurance (see the "Basics" chapter, p. 8). It's also easy to get around by taxi. Cab fares from the border to downtown average $5. You can also hire a taxi to Rosarito for about $20 one-way.

MONEY

There are major banks with ATMs and *casas de cambio* (money-exchange houses) all over Tijuana, but you can easily come here—or to Rosarito and Ensenada, for that matter—without changing money, because U.S. dollars are accepted everywhere.

SLEEPING

➜ **Hotel Lucerna** Once the most chic hotel in Tijuana, Lucerna now feels slightly worn, though it still has personality. The flavor is Mexican Colonial—wrought-iron railings and chandeliers, rough-hewn heavy wood furniture, brocade wallpaper, and traditional tiles. The hotel is in the Zona Río, away from the noise and congestion of downtown, so a quiet night's sleep is easily attainable. All of the rooms in the five-story hotel have balconies or patios. Hotel rates in Tijuana are subject to a 12% tax. *Av. Paseo de los Héroes, 10902 Zona Río, Tijuana.* ☎ *664/633-3900. www.hotel-lucerna. com.mx. 168 units. $85–$172 double; $90–$185 suite. Amenities: Coffee shop; outdoor pool; room service; free Internet. In room: A/C, TV, coffeemaker, hair dryer, iron.*

EATING

➜ **Cafe La Especial** MEXICAN Tucked away in a shopping *pasaje* (pedestrian boulevard) at the bottom of some stairs (turn in at the taco stand of the same name), this restaurant is a well-known purveyor of home-style Mexican cooking at reasonable prices. The gruff, efficient waitstaff carry out platter after platter of *carne asada* (grilled marinated beef served with fresh tortillas, beans, and rice). Traditional dishes like tacos, enchiladas, and burritos round out the menu, augmented by frosty cold Mexican beers. *Av. Revolución 718 (between calles 3 and 4), Zona Centro.* ☎ *664/685-6654. Main courses $5–$16. Daily 9am–10pm.*

➜ **Cien Años** MEXICAN This elegant and gracious Zona Río restaurant offers artfully blended Mexican flavors (tamarind, *poblano chile,* mango) in stylish presentations. If you're interested in haute cuisine, the buzz around Tijuana is all about this place. *José María Velazco 1407.* ☎ *664/634-3039 or -7262. Main courses $10–$20. Mon–Thurs 8am–11pm; Fri–Sat 8am–midnight; Sun 8am–10pm.*

PARTYING

Avenida Revolución is the center of the city's nightlife; many compare it with Bourbon Street in New Orleans during Mardi Gras—except here it's a regular occurrence, not a once-a-year blowout.

Tijuana has several lively dance clubs; perhaps the most popular is **Baby Rock,** 1482 Diego Rivera, Zona Río (☎ **664/634-2404**), a cousin to Acapulco's lively Baby O, which features everything from Latin rock to rap. It's near the Guadalajara Grill restaurant. It's open 9pm to 3am, with a cover charge of $12 on Saturdays.

Also popular in Tijuana are sports bars, featuring wagering on events from all over the United States as well as races from Tijuana's Caliente track. The most popular of these bars cluster in the **Pueblo Amigo** and **Vía Oriente** areas and around **Plaza Rio Tijuana** in the Zona Río, a new center designed to resemble a colonial Mexican village. Also in Zona Río is the chic club **Karma** (Paseo de los Héroes 954713; ☎ **664/900-6063**; Wed–Sat 9pm–3am). Just beyond Zona Río you'll find **Tangaloo** (Ave. Monterrey 3215; ☎ **664/681-8091**; www.tangaloo.com; Thurs–Sun 9pm–4am), a hip club featuring DJs spinning electronic dance music, with a changing theme

each Saturday night. Three of the town's hottest clubs, **Rodeo de Media Noche** (☎ **664/682-4967**; Thurs–Sun 9pm–4am), **Balak** (☎ **664/682-9222** or 607-3566; Thurs–Sat 9pm–4am; cover $15), and **Señor Frogs** (☎ **664/682-4962**; www.senorfrogs.com; daily noon–4am; no cover), are in Pueblo Amigo. Pueblo Amigo is less than 3km (2 miles) from the border, a short taxi ride or—during daylight hours—a pleasant walk.

WHAT TO DO

For many visitors, Tijuana's main event is the bustling **Avenida Revolución.** Beginning in the 1920s, American college students, servicemen, and hedonistic tourists discovered this street as a bawdy center for illicit fun. Some of the original attractions—gambling, back-alley cockfights (now illegal), and girlie shows—have fallen by the wayside, with drinking and shopping the main order of business these days. You'll find the action between calles 1 and 9; the landmark jai alai palace anchors the southern portion.

If you're looking to see a different side of Tijuana, the best place to start is the **Centro Cultural Tijuana,** Paseo de los Héroes and Mina Río Zone (☎ **664/687-9600,** ext. 9650; www.cecut.gob.mx). You'll easily spot the ultramodern Tijuana Cultural Center complex, which houses an Omnimax theater, the museum's permanent collection of Mexican artifacts, and a gallery of visiting exhibits. The center is open daily from 9am to 9pm. Admission to the permanent exhibits is free, there's a $2 charge for the special-event gallery, and tickets for Omnimax films are $4 for adults.

You'll find some classier shopping and a colorful local marketplace, plus the ultimate kid destination at **Plaza Mundo Divertido,** Vía Rápida Poniente 15035 (☎ **664/701-7133**). The park is open daily from noon to 8:30pm. Admission is free,

First Crush: The Annual Harvest Festival

If you enjoyed a visit to L.A. Cetto, Tijuana's winery (or Ensenada's Bodegas de Santo Tomás, discussed later in this chapter), then you might want to come back for the **Harvest Festival** (☎ 664/685-3031; www.lacetto.com), held each year in late August or early September. Set among the endless vineyards of the fertile Guadalupe Valley, the day's events include the traditional blessing of the grapes, wine tastings, live music and dancing, riding exhibitions, and a country-style Mexican meal. L.A. Cetto offers a group excursion from Tijuana (about an hour's drive); San Diego's **Baja California Tours** (☎ 800/336-5454 in the U.S., or 858/454-7166) also organizes a day-long trip from San Diego.

and several booths inside sell tickets for the various rides; most rides cost $1 to $11.

The fertile valleys of northern Baja produce most of Mexico's finest wines and export many high-quality vintages to Europe. For an introduction to Mexican wines, stop into **Cava de Vinos L. A. Cetto (L. A. Cetto Winery),** Av. Cañón Johnson 2108, at Av. Constitución Sur (☎ **664/685-3031,** ext. 128, or 638-5848). Shaped like a wine barrel, this building's striking facade is made from old oak aging barrels—call it inspired recycling. It's open Monday through Friday from 9am to 6pm and Saturday from 10:30am to 5pm.

If your tastes run more toward *cerveza* than wines, plan to visit the **Tijuana Brewery,** 2951 Bulevar Fundadores, Col. Juárez (☎ **664/684-2406** or 638-8662; www.tjbeer.com). Here, guided tours (by prior appointment) demonstrate the beer-making process at the brewery, where all beers are made from a select group of hops and malt. The family who owns the company has a long tradition of master brewers, who worked in breweries in the Czech Republic, bringing their knowledge back home to Tijuana. Cerveza Tijuana was founded in January 2000, and now has select distribution in the U.S. Its lager, dark, and light beers are all available to sample in the adjoining European-style pub, which features karaoke on Monday and Tuesday

nights, and live music Wednesday through Saturday. A menu of appetizers and entrees is also available. It's open Monday to Saturday from 10am to 2am.

SHOPPING

Tijuana's biggest attraction is **shopping.** People come to take advantage of low prices on a variety of merchandise (terra cotta and colorfully glazed pottery, woven blankets and serapes, embroidered dresses and sequined sombreros, onyx chess sets, beaded necklaces and bracelets, silver jewelry, leather bags and *huarache* sandals, rain sticks, Cuban cigars, and Mexican liquors). You're permitted to bring $400 worth of purchases back across the border (sorry, no Cuban cigars allowed), including 1 liter of alcohol per person. Many Americans have taken to Tijuana as a way to purchase inexpensive prescription drugs, and bring them across the border. Be aware—authorities have cracked down on this practice, and are known to arrest foreigners purchasing drugs without valid prescriptions from a Mexican doctor.

If a marketplace atmosphere and spirited bargaining are what you're looking for, head to **Mercado de Artesanías (crafts market),** Calle 2 and Avenida Negrete. Here, vendors of pottery, clayware, clothing, and other crafts fill an entire city block.

Shopping malls are as common in Tijuana as in any big American city; you shouldn't expect to find typical souvenirs there, but shopping alongside residents and other intrepid visitors is often more fun than feeling like a sitting-duck tourist. One of the biggest, and most convenient, is **Plaza Río Tijuana,** Paseo de los Héroes 96 at Avenida Independencia, Zona Río (☎ **664/684-0402),** an outdoor plaza anchored by several department stores and featuring dozens of specialty shops and casual restaurants. **Plaza Agua Caliente** (☎ **664/681-7777),** at 4558 Bulevar Agua Caliente, Col. Aviación, is a more upscale shopping center, and in addition to fine shops and restaurants, is known for its emphasis on health and beauty, with day spas, gyms, and doctors' offices found in abundance here. Other shopping malls are listed at www.seetijuana.com/tijuanasite/shopping_centers.htm.

PLAYING OUTSIDE & SPECTATOR SPORTS

Tijuana is a spectator's (and gambler's) paradise.

Bullfighting

Whatever your opinion, bullfighting has a prominent place in Mexican heritage, and is even considered an essential element of the culture. The skill and bravery of matadors is closely linked with cultural ideals regarding *machismo,* and some of the world's best perform at Tijuana's two stadiums. The season runs May through September, with events held on Sunday at 4:30pm. Ticket prices range from $25 to $50 (the premium seats are on the shaded side of the arena) and can be purchased at the bullring or in advance from San Diego's **Five Star Tours** (☎ **619/232-5049** or 664/622-2203). **El Toreo** (☎ **664/686-1510;** www.bullfights.org) is 3km (2 miles) east of downtown on Bulevar Agua Caliente at Avenida Diego Rivera. **Plaza de**

Toros Monumental, also called Bullring-by-the-Sea (☎ **664/680-1808;** www.plaza monumental.com), is 10km (6 miles) west of downtown on Highway 1-D (before the first toll station); it's perched at the edge of both the ocean and the California border.

Dog Racing

There's satellite wagering on U.S. horse races at the majestic **Caliente Racetrack,** off Bulevar Agua Caliente, 5km (3 miles) east of downtown (☎ **619/231-1910** or 664/682-3110; https://bet.caliente.com.mx), but only greyhounds actually kick up dust at the track. Races are held daily at 7:45pm, with Tuesday, Saturday, and Sunday matinees at 2pm. General admission is free, but bettors in the know congregate in the comfortable Turf Club; admission is free, and you pay $10 for your drinks, but that's refundable with a wagering voucher.

Next Stop: Rosarito Beach: Resort Town

55km (34 miles) S of San Diego; 129km (18 miles) S of Tijuana

Just 29km (18 miles) south of Tijuana and a complete departure in ambience, Rosarito Beach is a tranquil, friendly beach town. Hollywood has played a major part in Rosarito's recent renaissance—it was the location for the sound stage and filming of the Academy Award–winning *Titanic.* The former *Titanic* Museum—now called **Foxploration (www.foxploration. com)**—continues to draw the fans of this film, and moviemaking in general. The beaches between Tijuana and Rosarito are also known for excellent surf breaks.

GETTING THERE

Two roads run between Tijuana and Ensenada (the largest and third-largest cities in Baja)—the scenic, coast-hugging toll road (Hwy. 1-D, marked *cuota),* and the free but slower public road (Hwy. 1, marked *libre).*

You can eat in a castle . . . The Castle Restaurant, in Rosarito Beach.

SLEEPING & EATING

➜ **Rosarito Beach Hotel & Spa** ★
Although this once-glamorous resort has been holding steady since its heyday, it's currently defined by glaring nighttime neon and party-mania. Despite the resort's

changed personality, its unique artistic construction and lavish decoration remain. It has a wide, family-friendly stretch of beach. The stately home of the original owners has been transformed into the full-service **Casa Playa Spa,** where massages and other treatments are only slightly less costly than in the U.S. You'll pay more for a room with an ocean view, and more for the newer, air-conditioned units in the tower; the older rooms in the poolside building have only ceiling fans, but they prevail in the character department, with hand-painted trim and original tile. The mansion's dining room, **Chabert's Steakhouse** ★★, charges top dollar for excellent Continental cuisine; **Azteca** is a casual Mexican restaurant in the main building. *Note:* A renovation slated to begin in 2007 will double the number of rooms and provide a rooftop pool to a new high-rise wing of the hotel. *Bulevar Benito Juárez, Zona Centro, 22710 Rosarito.* ☎ *800/343-8582 in the U.S., or 661/612-0144. www.rosaritobeachhotel.com. 278 units. $70–$140 double; $111–$175 suites. Free*

Storming The Castle: A Rosarito Splurge

If you splurge on only one meal on this trip, I suggest storming The Castle. Built from molten rocks on a bluff overlooking the Pacific, this restaurant's fortress-like structure looks like something out of Middle Earth/*Lord of the Rings*. Spectacular ocean views are matched only by the kitchen's creations: A European-inflected menu slants towards rich, saucy dishes built around grilled chicken, steak (filet mignon served four different ways), and seafood, with flounder and salmon well represented. The are winners in every category. Among the starters, baked portobello mushrooms–filled prosciutto, Mozzarella, and tomatoes is a meaty counterpoint to lighter salmon carpaccio served with capers and red onions in olive oil and lemon juice. For entrees, the Filet Mignon served in béarnaise sauce and the flounder in pernod sauce will both satiate the heartiest appetites. Sure, prices here rival anything you'll find in L.A. or New York, but then again so does the quality. Hey, it's good to be the king. *The Castle at km. 36.6 on the free road (100 yards south of Costa Bella condos).* ☎ *661/613-2022. www.thecastlerosarito.com. Lunch $8–$15; dinner $15–$25. Sun–Thurs–Sun noon–10pm.*

On the Road to Ensenada

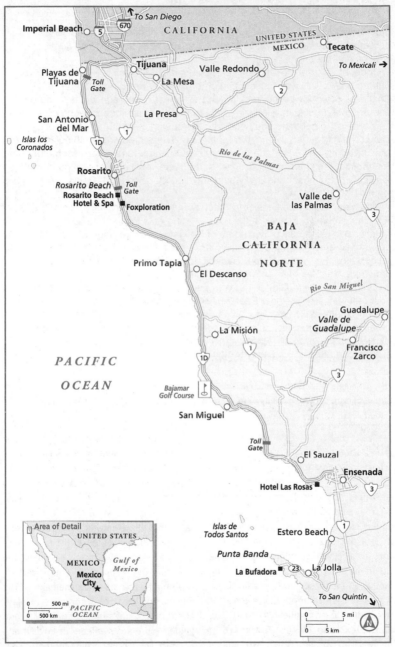

To San Diego

Imperial Beach
5
670
CALIFORNIA
UNITED STATES
MEXICO
Tecate

Playas de Tijuana
Tijuana
Valle Redondo
To Mexicali →
Toll Gate
La Mesa

San Antonio del Mar
La Presa
2

Islas los Coronados
1D
1

Río de las Palmas

Rosarito
Toll Gate

Rosarito Beach
Rosarito Beach Hotel & Spa
Foxploration

Valle de las Palmas
3

BAJA
CALIFORNIA
NORTE

Primo Tapia
El Descanso

Río San Miguel

Guadalupe
Valle de Guadalupe

La Misión
1
Francisco Zarco

PACIFIC
OCEAN

1D
3

Bajamar Golf Course

San Miguel

Toll Gate
El Sauzal

Ensenada
3

Hotel Las Rosas

Islas de Todos Santos
Estero Beach
1

Punta Banda
23
La Jolla
La Bufadora

To San Quintín

Area of Detail
UNITED STATES

MEXICO
Gulf of Mexico

Mexico City
★

0   500 mi
0   500 km
PACIFIC OCEAN

0   5 mi
0   5 km
N

Surfing, Northern Baja Style

From California and beyond, surfers come to the northern Baja coastline for perpetual right-breaking waves, cheap digs and eats, and *Endless Summer*-type camaraderie.

Undoubtedly, the most famous surf spot in all of Mexico is **Killers,** at Todos Santos Island. This was the location of the winning wave in the 1997–98 K2 Challenge (a worldwide contest to ride the largest wave each winter—and be photographed doing it). Killers is a very makeable wave for confident, competent surfers. To get there you need a boat. You can get a lift from the local *panga* (skiff) fleet, for about $100 for the day. That's pretty much the going rate, and the tightly knit Ensenada *pangueros* aren't eager to undercut each other. It's about 15km (10 miles) out to the island; there you'll anchor and paddle into the lineup. You must bring everything you'll need—food, drink, sunscreen, and so on.

Other less radical and easier-to-reach spots include Popotla, just south of Rosarito, where you'll walk to the beach through the Popotla trailer park. Calafia, also just a mile or two south of Rosarito, has a reeling right point that can get extremely heavy. San Miguel is the point break just south of the final tollbooth on the highway into Ensenada. It's an excellent wave but generally crowded.

If you're a surfer looking to get your bearings or a spectator wanting to get your feet wet, stop by Inner Reef (Km 34½; no phone). Opened in 1998 by a friendly Southern California expat named Roger, this tiny shack offers all the essentials: wax, leashes, patch kits, surfboard sales and rentals, even expert repairs at bargain prices. Roger is there from noon until sunset every day in summer, and from Wednesday to Sunday in winter.

parking. Amenities: 2 restaurants; bar; 2 outdoor pools; wading pool; spa; playground; racquetball court. In room: A/C (in some), fan (in some), TV.

PARTYING

Because the legal drinking age in Baja is 18, the under-21 crowd from Southern California tends to flock across the border on Friday and Saturday nights. The most popular spot in town is **Papas & Beer** (☎ **661/612-0444;** www.papasandbeer.com). It's a relaxed come-as-you-are-type club on the beach, just a block north of the hotel. Even for those young in spirit only, it's great fun, with outdoor tables and a bar surrounding a sand volleyball court. The **Salón Mexicano** (☎ **661/612-0144**), in the Rosarito Beach Hotel, attracts a slightly more mature evening crowd, with live music on Friday and Saturday.

WHAT TO DO

A few kilometers south of Rosarito proper lies the **seaside production site** of 1997's mega-blockbuster *Titanic,* and more recently, *Master and Commander.* On 16 otherwise dry hectares (40 acres) along the Pacific Coast, the studio has several huge tanks that fill with water to reproduce seafaring conditions. Filled with *Titanic* memorabilia, it has now become the moviemaking theme park, **Foxploration,** devoted to the art of moviemaking. The Cinemagico area has interactive displays about filmmaking and special effects, and guided tours are available in English and Spanish. There is also a play center for kids, plus a gift shop. Admission is $12 for adults, $9 for children 3 to 11. Foxploration (☎ 866/369-2252 in the U.S., or 661/614-9444; www.foxploration.com) is open Wednesday through Friday from 9am to 5:30pm, and Saturday and Sunday from 10am to 6:30pm. There's a food court with Dominos, Subway, and even Starbucks coffee.

If you have only a few hours to spend in Rosarito Beach, that's still enough time to have a swim or a horseback ride at the beach, shop for souvenirs, and dine on fish tacos or tamales from one of the family-run stands along **Bulevar Benito Juárez,** the town's main (and only) drag. The dozen or so blocks of Rosarito north of the Rosarito Beach Hotel are packed with stores typical of Mexican border towns: curio shops, cigar and *licores* (liquor) stores, and *farmacias* (where drugs like Viagra, Retin-A, Prozac, and many more are available at low cost).

Welcome to Ensenada: Port of Call

134km (83 miles) S of San Diego; 109km (68 miles) S of Tijuana

Ensenada is an attractive town on a lovely bay, surrounded by sheltering mountains. About 40 minutes from Rosarito, it's the kind of place that loves a celebration—be it for a bicycle race or a seafood festival.

GETTING THERE & INFORMATION

After passing through the final tollgate, Highway 1-D curves sharply toward downtown Ensenada.

The **Tourist and Convention Bureau booth** (☎ 646/178-2411) is at the western entrance to town, where the waterfront-hugging Bulevar Lázaro Cárdenas—also known as Bulevar Costero—curves away to the right. It's open Monday through Friday from 9am to 7pm. and Saturday and Sunday from 9am to 5pm. Taxis park along López Mateos.

SLEEPING

➔ **Hotel Las Rosas** One of the most modern hotels in the area, Hotel Las Rosas still falls short of most definitions of luxurious, yet the pink oceanfront hotel 3km (2 miles) outside Ensenada is the favorite of many Baja aficionados. It offers most of the comforts of an upscale American hotel—which doesn't leave room for much Mexican personality. The atrium lobby is awash in pale pink and sea-foam green, a color scheme that pervades throughout—including the guest rooms, sparsely furnished with quasi-tropical furniture. Some rooms have fireplaces and/or in-room whirlpools, and all have balconies overlooking the pool and ocean. One of the resort's main photo ops is the swimming pool that overlooks the Pacific and features a vanishing edge that appears to merge with the ocean beyond. If you're looking to maintain the highest comfort level possible, this would be your hotel of choice. *Hwy. 1. 3km (2 miles) north of Ensenada.* ☎ *866/337-6727 in the U.S., or 646/174-4310. www.lasrosas.com. 48 units. $152–$210 double. extra adult $25. Amenities: Restaurant; cocktail lounge; outdoor pool; tennis courts; racquetball courts; small workout room; cliff-top hot tub; business center w/Internet; tour desk; room service; massage; laundry service. In room: A/C, TV.*

EATING

➔ **La Embotelladora Vieja** ★ FRENCH/MEXICAN/MEDITERRANEAN Hidden on an industrial side street, and attached to the Bodegas de Santo Tomás winery, this looks more like a chapel than the elegant restaurant it is. Sophisticated diners will feel right at home in this stylish setting, a former aging room for the winery. It's now resplendent with red oak furniture (constructed from old wine casks), high brick

You'll be within sight of the Pacific as you drive down the coast of Baja to Ensenada.

walls, and crystal goblets and candlesticks on linen tablecloths. It goes without saying that the wine list is exemplary, featuring bottles from Santo Tomás and other Baja vintners. Look for appetizers like abalone seviche or cream of garlic soup, followed by grilled swordfish in cilantro sauce, filet mignon in port wine–Gorgonzola sauce, or quail with a tart sauvignon blanc sauce. *Av. Miramar 666 (at Calle 7).* ☎ *646/174-0807. Reservations recommended on weekends. Main courses $9–$25. MC, V. Lunch and dinner Mon–Sat; call for seasonal hours.*

PARTYING

Just like in *Casablanca,* where "everyone goes to Rick's," everyone's been going to **Hussong's Cantina,** Av. Ruiz 113, near Avenida López Mateos (☎ **646/178-3210**), since the bar opened in 1892. Nothing much has changed—the place still sports Wild West–style swinging saloon doors, a long bar to slide beers along, and strolling mariachis bellowing above the din. Be aware that hygiene and privacy are low priorities in the restrooms.

While the crowd (a pleasant mix of tourists and locals) at Hussong's can really whoop it up, they're amateurs compared to those who frequent **Papas & Beer,** Avenida Ruiz near Avenida López Mateos (☎ **646/174-0145;** www.papasandbeer. com), across the street. A tiny entrance leads to the upstairs bar and dance club. The music is loud and the hip young crowd is definitely here to party. Papas & Beer has quite a reputation with the Southern California college crowd, and has opened a branch in Rosarito Beach (see above).

WHAT TO SEE & DO

While Ensenada is technically a border town, one aspect of its appeal is its multi-layered vitality. The bustling port consumes the entire waterfront—beach access can be found only north or south of town—and the Pacific fishing trade and agriculture in the fertile valleys surrounding the city dominate the economy.

Even part-time oenophiles should pay a visit to the **Bodegas de Santo Tomás Winery** ★★, Av. Miramar 666, at Calle 7

(☎ 646/174-3601 or 178-2509; www.santo-tomas.com.), the oldest winery in Mexico, and the largest in Baja. It uses old-fashioned methods of processing grapes, first cultivated by Dominican monks in 1791 in the lush Santo Tomás Valley. Tours in English start Monday through Saturday at 10am, 11am, noon, 1pm, and 3pm. Admission is $6, including a tasting of three low-priced wines; $10 more gets you a souvenir wineglass and a tasting of 12 high-priced wines.

Ensenada's equivalent of Tijuana's Avenida Revolución is crowded **Avenida López Mateos,** roughly parallel to Bulevar Lázaro Cárdenas (Bulevar Costero); the highest concentration of shops and restaurants is between avenidas Ruiz and Castillo. Compared to Tijuana, there is more authentic Mexican art- and craftwork in Ensenada.

South of the city, 45 minutes by car along the rural Punta Banda peninsula, is one of Ensenada's major attractions: **La Bufadora,** a natural sea spout in the rocks. With each incoming wave, water is forced upward through the rock, creating a geyser whose loud grunt gave the phenomenon its name (it means "buffalo snort"). From downtown Ensenada, take Avenida Reforma (Hwy. 1) south to Highway 23 west. La Bufadora is at the end of the road. Once parked ($1 per car in crude dirt lots), you must walk downhill to the viewing platform, at the end of a 270m (986-ft.) pathway lined with souvenir stands.

La Bufadora marks the end of our "Desert to the Ocean" trip. From Highway 23, Highway 1 will take you back to the U.S., all the way to San Diego, where our "Rockin' the West Coast" roadtrip begins. Maybe you'll choose to infuse your new laid-back beach perspective with some indie rock edge as we take you through the best rock clubs the west coast has to offer. Or maybe you'll be content to go home, back to your daily life, just a little bit tired and more than a little refreshed.

DESERT TO THE BEACH

Rockin' the West Coast

Text & Photos by Maya Kroth

Y ou know you're in a rock dive if . . .

. . . the walls are painted black and covered in Jesus Lizard posters.

. . . the staff has more attitude than a teenager with PMS.

. . . there are band stickers stuck to *everything*.

. . . the bathrooms stink, and the stall doors never seem to lock right.

. . . an impenetrable row of regulars lines the bar, one of whom always seems to be talking about how epic it was when Death Cab played there for 10 people, "back in the day, before they sold out."

Every self-respecting city has at least one joint that meets some or all of these criteria, and if you love music, even the rank toilets and grouchy bouncers aren't enough to keep you away from the thrill of standing shoulder-to-shoulder in a tiny, sweltering club, watching a bitchin' live band that just might be playing arenas in a year. Even the Stones and U2 went through a club phase, and it's hard to deny that something special gets lost when you watch a band go from playing a 200-capacity club—where they might sell their own merch and hang with the common people in the smoking area after the show—to impersonal, 60,000-seat stadiums.

While a rock 'n' roll club tour can happen almost anywhere, the West Coast has a particularly awesome string of cities, each with its own killer live music scene. On

Posters, Doug Fir Lounge, Portland, OR.

this trip you'll rock the Casbah in San Diego, like Jack White and Billy Corgan once did; you might run into a hot young celeb at a club show in LA's Silver Lake. You'll learn that San Francisco's scene goes way beyond Jerry Garcia; you'll pound the same Portland pavement as Elliott Smith and the Dandy Warhols; finally, you'll see Seattle, where one of this generation's most influential songwriters played his first shows, recorded his first album, and spent his last days.

When you're not getting your eardrums shattered in the clubs, you'll be browsing eye candy on San Diego's Mission Beach Boardwalk, scarfing Dodger Dogs at Chavez Ravine, sampling the drink of choice for San Francisco hipsters, visiting the world's smallest park in Portland, and buying up some fancy-schmancy fashions at Seattle's awesomest boutiques.

With that, let's pack up the merch, make sure you're wearing the "All Access" pass (even if you bought it on eBay!), gas up the van, and hit the road. *Noooooo* sleep 'til ... Portland?

Superlatives: The Highs & Lows

➜ **Best place for impromptu skinny-dipping: Pollard Gulch Day Use Area** on the Sacramento River. See p. 660.

➜ **Best indie-rock strip club:** Portland's **Magic Gardens,** where hipster dancers take it off to the Yeah Yeah Yeahs and the clientele is anything but sleazy. See p. 673.

➜ **Most painful hangover:** Do yourself a favor: Don't mix a gin martini, sangria, and

San Francisco's scenester drink of choice, **Fernet-Branca.** See p. 656.

➜ **Best post-show cheap eats:** The perfectly crispy Belgian fries at the Neumo's-adjacent **Frites,** dunked in one of more than a dozen flavored, mayo-based dips like garlic and sun-dried tomato pesto. Yum. See p. 684.

→ **Best place to browse vinyl and rock-star graffiti: Bop Street Records** in Seattle's Ballard district, where Radiohead once spent 7 hours shopping for vinyl before Thom Yorke scrawled a personal message on the wall. See p. 681.

→ **Only major city on this trip without a bar or restaurant called Cha Cha or Cha Cha Cha:** San Diego. Everywhere else has at least one, sometimes two, or even more: There's a Tiki bar in Silver Lake called the Cha Cha (p. 639), which is descended from the original in Seattle (p. 686). LA and SF each have a pair of Cha Cha Chas; the SF ones serve tapas (p. 654) while the SoCal locations dish out Caribbean food (p. 639).

→ **Most quietly epic grunge landmark: Hall of Justice Studios** in Seattle, where Nirvana recorded "Bleach" and now a storage space for Death Cab for Cutie's gear. See p. 689.

→ **Number of places that claim to be the last place Kurt Cobain was seen alive:** At least two, including **Piecora's** and **Linda's Tavern,** both on Seattle's Capitol Hill. See p. 684 and p. 686.

→ **Best place get your music fix** *and an Entourage* **cast member's autograph:** Hollywood's **Hotel Café,** where everyone from Adrian "Vincent Chase" Grenier to Andy Dick has been spotted. See p. 631.

→ **Best rock-star tour guide: The Long Winters' John Roderick,** a songwriter by day who could easily have a second career as a rock historian. Check out his Seattle rock tour on p. 688.

→ **Best place to live out rock-star fantasies:** The **Experience Music Project** in Seattle, where interactive exhibits let you perform for virtual arena crowds and practice your scratching skills on the ones and twos. See p. 687.

→ **Best use of Morse Code: The Capitol Records building** in LA, where the red light on the roof blinks the letters H-O-L-L-Y-W-O-O-D in dots and dashes. See p. 641.

→ **Most overzealous use of black lights: Sabala's at Mt. Tabor Theatre,** in Portland, which has several wall murals that are not only done in black-light paint; they're also 3-D (ask the bartender to loan you some specs). See p. 666.

Just the Facts

Trip in a Box

Total Miles From San Diego, CA, to Seattle, WA, about 1,300 miles.

Route Mostly I-5, with alternate routes in California along Highway 101.

States California, Oregon, Washington.

Trip Time 5 days or more for the whole thing, from San Diego to Seattle.

The Short Version Conveniently, these rock centers sit on a more or less straight line up the West Coast between San Diego and Seattle. If you speed through, doing a show in each big city, you can see it all in 5 days, but you'll have a couple long hauls to consider, and you won't have enough time to soak up all the culture these five fantastic cities have to offer.

Rock 'n' Roll Roadtrip

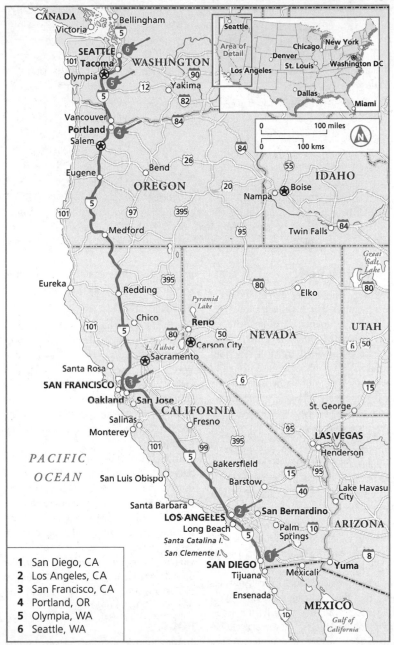

1 San Diego, CA
2 Los Angeles, CA
3 San Francisco, CA
4 Portland, OR
5 Olympia, WA
6 Seattle, WA

The Long Version   I recommend staying at least 2 nights and 2 full days in each of the five major cities to fully absorb the local flavor. There's also plenty to discover in the in-between places not fully covered here, like Orange County, Ventura/Santa Barbara, extreme Northern California, Olympia, and other places, all of which have their own pretty healthy rock scenes. If you're not in a hurry, you could even stretch this trip out for several weeks, stopping often and driving the ultra-pretty coastal routes.

Hitting the Highlights   This trip can be chopped up into more leisurely legs that make for nice long weekends: San Diego, Orange County, and Los Angeles (110 miles), LA and San Francisco (400 miles), or Portland, Olympia, and Seattle (200 miles).

When to Go   Late spring or early summer: While sun and coastal breezes make SoCal nice basically year-round, San Diego is plagued by clouds in late spring and early summer (so-called "May Gray" and "June Gloom"). San Francisco, on the other hand, is often going to be chilly at night, even in the dead of summer. The winding, high-altitude drive to Portland is treacherous enough in summer; winter conditions will only make it more dangerous. Both Seattle and Portland can be gloomy in winter.

The Money Part

A lot of the hotels, bars, diners, and other spots mentioned in this chapter were recommended by touring musicians who are well acquainted with this route. Bands (smart ones, anyway) are cash-conscious on the road, so although these five cities are some of the more expensive ones in the U.S., there are definitely ways to experience them without going broke.

ACCOMMODATIONS

Band-friendly hotels like the Jupiter in Portland and the Phoenix in San Francisco have low rates that won't break the bank, plus a funky, cool vibe not found at your average Motel 6. San Diego's got a zillion hostels and campgrounds, and LA's got no shortage of budget hotel options—just watch your back if you wind up in a seedy neighborhood. If you're gonna splurge, LA might be the place to do it: Upscale properties like the Chateau Marmont, West Hollywood Hyatt, and Beverly Hills Hotel are not only high-class, they're also chockfull of rock history—and probably rock

present, too, since you can't go 10 feet in LA without seeing a celeb.

TRANSPORTATION

The Pacific Coast has the highest regional gas prices in the country (ouch!), according to AAA. California, Oregon, and Washington rank second, ninth, and eighth, respectively, as the most expensive states to buy gas. This trip runs about 1,300 miles, which means you'll be spending about $200 for gas (more if you're side-tripping).

Though the public transit systems are decent in Portland and Seattle, they still don't come close to East Coast spots like NYC and Boston when it comes to convenience, so unless you're a big fan of riding the bus, prepare to spend some cash on cabs if you're partying. Many hotels provide free parking, but keep in mind the upscale ones usually charge extra (up to $20 per night or more), so call ahead, and don't forget to tip the valet.

FOOD

Touring musicians are usually pretty broke, but they always seem to know

ALWAYS REMEMBER TO PROTECT YOUR HEARING! (What?)

where to get the best grub at the lowest prices. This trip takes a page out of the rock-band book to keep your stomach and wallet full. You can eat for as little as $20 a day if you're scrimping. But if you prefer five-star dining to late-night burritos, all five West Coast cities have some fantastic gourmet restaurants in which to indulge.

Recommended Roadtrip Viewing & Reading

Get in the mood with these rock-related works:

→ *Almost Famous* (2000): Cameron Crowe's film, a semiautobiographical story about a teenage rock critic, was filmed at many of the sites you'll have a chance to visit on this trip.

→ *DiG!* (2004): The documentary chronicling the notorious feud between the West Coast indie favorites the Dandy Warhols and the Brian Jonestown Massacre is the perfect way to get primed for rocking out in Portland and San Francisco, the bands' respective home bases.

→ *Hype!* (1996): A documentary examining the Seattle scene as it took over the music world.

→ *We Got the Neutron Bomb: The Untold Story of L.A. Punk* (2001): Marc Spitz and Brendan Mullen's book is a compilation of oral histories of the LA punk scene, which produced such seminal bands as The Runaways, X, and The Go-Gos.

→ *Killing Yourself to Live (85% of a True Story)* (2006): Chuck Klosterman, the former *Spin* columnist, travels across the country visiting rock-star death sites and thinking about ex-girlfriends.

Starting Out: San Diego, CA

San Diego proudly calls itself America's Finest City, and with miles of picture-postcard coastline and dozens of colleges and universities in the area, it's no wonder the Southern California city is home to myriad sun-kissed, beach-body co-eds. And sure, you can find plenty of beach volleyball and beer-bong-fueled frat parties in the coastal neighborhoods, but San Diego actually has its own rock scene hiding underneath those layers of Coppertone. Once touted as "the next Seattle" in the mid-'90s, San Diego's rock renaissance never really hit the mainstream (unless you count Top 40 popsters Jewel and Jason Mraz—and most locals don't). But S.D. has spawned bands like blink-182, Switchfoot, and Rocket from the Crypt, and more recent indie-rock acts like Pinback and Louis XIV.

San Diego Nuts & Bolts

Area Codes   San Diego's main area code is 619, used primarily by downtown, uptown, Mission Valley, Point Loma, Coronado, La Mesa, El Cajon, and Chula Vista. The area code 858 is used for northern and coastal areas, including Mission Beach, Pacific Beach, La Jolla, Del Mar, Rancho Santa Fe, and Rancho Bernardo. Use 760 to reach the remainder of San Diego County, including Encinitas, Carlsbad, Oceanside, Escondido, Ramona, Julian, and Anza-Borrego.

Business Hours   Banks are open weekdays from 9am to 4pm or later, and sometimes Saturday morning. Shops in shopping malls tend to stay open until about 9pm weekdays and until 6pm weekends, and are open on secondary holidays.

Dentists   For dental referrals, contact the **San Diego County Dental Society** at ☎ 800/201-0244, or call ☎ 800/DENTIST.

Doctors   Hotel Docs (☎ 800/468-3537) is a 24-hour network of physicians, dentists, and chiropractors. They accept credit cards, and their services are covered by most insurance policies. In a life-threatening situation, dial ☎ **911.**

Drugstores   Longs, Rite Aid, and Sav-On sell pharmaceuticals and non-prescription products. Look in the phone book to find the one nearest you. If you need a pharmacy after normal business hours, the following branches are open 24 hours: **Sav-On Drugs,** 8831 Villa La Jolla Dr., La Jolla (☎ 858/457-4390), and 313 E. Washington St., Hillcrest (☎ 619/291-7170); and **Rite Aid,** 535 Robinson Ave., Hillcrest (☎ 619/291-3703). Local hospitals also sell prescription drugs.

Emergencies   Call ☎ **911** for fire, police, and ambulance. The main police station is at 1401 Broadway, at 14th Street (☎ 619/531-2000, or 619/531-2065 for the hearing impaired).

Eyeglass Repair   **Optometric Expressions,** 55 Horton Plaza (☎ 619/544-9000), is at street level near the Westin Hotel, downtown. They can fill eyeglass prescriptions, repair glasses, and replace contact lenses. The major shopping centers in Mission Valley also have eyeglass stores that can fill prescriptions and handle most repairs.

San Diego Highlights

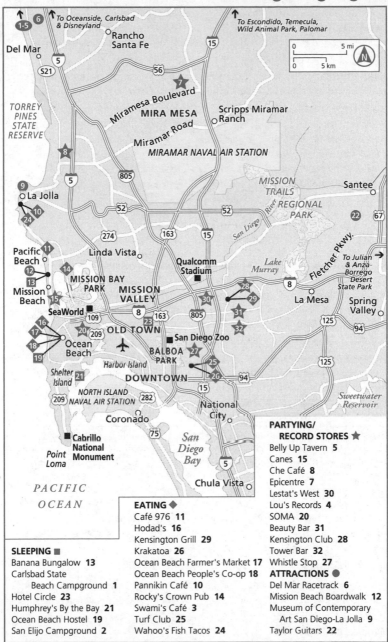

To Oceanside, Carlsbad & Disneyland

To Escondido, Temecula, Wild Animal Park, Palomar

Rancho Santa Fe

Del Mar

TORREY PINES STATE RESERVE

Miramesa Boulevard

MIRA MESA

Scripps Miramar Ranch

Miramar Road

MIRAMAR NAVAL AIR STATION

La Jolla

MISSION TRAILS REGIONAL PARK

Santee

San Diego River

Pacific Beach

Linda Vista

Qualcomm Stadium

Lake Murray

To Julian & Anza-Borrego Desert State Park

Fletcher Pkwy.

MISSION BAY PARK

MISSION VALLEY

La Mesa

Spring Valley

Mission Beach

SeaWorld

OLD TOWN

San Diego Zoo

Ocean Beach

BALBOA PARK

Shelter Island

Harbor Island

DOWNTOWN

NORTH ISLAND NAVAL AIR STATION

National City

Sweetwater Reservoir

Cabrillo National Monument

Coronado

San Diego Bay

Point Loma

PACIFIC OCEAN

Chula Vista

SLEEPING ■
Banana Bungalow **13**
Carlsbad State
  Beach Campground **1**
Hotel Circle **23**
Humphrey's By the Bay **21**
Ocean Beach Hostel **19**
San Elijo Campground **2**

EATING ◆
Café 976 **11**
Hodad's **16**
Kensington Grill **29**
Krakatoa **26**
Ocean Beach Farmer's Market **17**
Ocean Beach People's Co-op **18**
Pannikin Café **10**
Rocky's Crown Pub **14**
Swami's Café **3**
Turf Club **25**
Wahoo's Fish Tacos **24**

**PARTYING/
RECORD STORES** ★
Belly Up Tavern **5**
Canes **15**
Che Café **8**
Epicentre **7**
Lestat's West **30**
Lou's Records **4**
SOMA **20**
Beauty Bar **31**
Kensington Club **28**
Tower Bar **32**
Whistle Stop **27**

ATTRACTIONS ●
Del Mar Racetrack **6**
Mission Beach Boardwalk **12**
Museum of Contemporary
  Art San Diego-La Jolla **9**
Taylor Guitars **22**

Hospitals   Near downtown San Diego, **UCSD Medical Center-Hillcrest,** 200 W. Arbor Dr. (☎ 619/543-6400), has the most convenient emergency room. In La Jolla, **Thornton Hospital,** 9300 Campus Point Dr. (☎ 858/657-7600), has a good emergency room, and you'll find another in Coronado, at **Coronado Hospital,** 250 Prospect Place, opposite the Marriott Resort (☎ 619/435-6251).

Liquor Laws   The drinking age in California is 21. Beer, wine, and hard liquor are sold daily from 6am to 2am and are available in grocery stores.

Newspapers & Magazines   The *San Diego Union-Tribune* is published daily, and its entertainment section, "Night & Day," is in the Thursday edition (check the online edition, SignOnSanDiego.com, for more content). The free *San Diego CityBeat* is published Wednesdays and is available at many shops, restaurants, theaters, and public hot spots; it's the best source for up-to-the-week club and show listings. *San Diego* magazine is geared to the elite audience (which explains all the ads for face-lifts and tummy tucks).

Police   The downtown police station is at 1401 Broadway (☎ 619/531-2000). Call ☎ **911** in an emergency.

Post Office   San Diego's main post office is located at 2535 Midway Dr., just west of Old Town; it is open Monday through Friday from 8am to 5pm, and Saturdays from 8am to 4pm. Post offices are located downtown at 815 E St. and at 51 Horton Plaza, next to the Westin Hotel. There is a post office in the Mission Valley Shopping Center, next to Macy's. These branch offices are generally open Monday through Friday during regular business hours, plus Saturday morning; for specific branch information, call ☎ **800/ASK-USPS** or log on to **www.usps.gov.**

Restrooms   Horton Plaza and Seaport Village downtown, Balboa Park, Old Town State Historic Park in Old Town, and the Ferry Landing Marketplace in Coronado all have well-marked public restrooms. In general, you won't have a problem finding one (all restaurants, including fast-food outlets, are required to have one). Restrooms are usually clean and accessible.

Smoking   Smoking is prohibited in nearly all indoor public places, including theaters, hotel lobbies, and enclosed shopping malls. In 1998, California enacted legislation prohibiting smoking in all restaurants and bars, except those with outdoor seating.

Taxes   Sales tax in restaurants and shops is 7.75%. Hotel tax is 10.5%.

Time Zone   San Diego, like the rest of the West Coast, is in the Pacific Standard Time zone, which is 8 hours behind Greenwich Mean Time. Daylight saving time is observed. To check the time, call ☎ 619/853-1212.

Transit Information   Call ☎ **800/SD-COMMUTE.**

Useful Telephone Numbers   For the latest San Diego arts and entertainment information, call ☎ 619/238-0700; for half-price day-of-performance tickets, call ☎ 619/497-5000; for a beach and surf report, call ☎ 619/221-8824.

Weather   Call ☎ 619/289-1212.

Getting Around

San Diego's a driving city with a zillion freeways that seem to be filled with equal numbers of stoners and retirees, neither of whom are in the running for world's best driver. Watch out for speeders who'll cut you off by slicing across six lanes without even thinking about using their blinker. As a general rule, odd-numbered freeways (5, 805, 163, 15, 125) run north-south, while even-numbered ones (8, 52, 56, 78, 94) go east-west. To make matters more complicated, the 805 and 163 crisscross in the middle, so if you tend to get rattled in traffic, study your map before hitting the road.

BY CAR

Traffic is terrible in San Diego, especially during rush hour and in the North and South County. The availability and affordability of parking varies depending on neighborhood: Street parking is scarce downtown, so budget some money for that. Garages are your best bet; 6th & K Parkade (Sixth Ave. at K St); Park it On Market (Market St. between Sixth and Seventh) and the Horton Plaza Garage (entrance on Fourth Ave. at F St.) are among the more affordable lots.

BY TROLLEY

If you're staying in Mission Valley, the trolley's a reasonable way to get around; it runs through (or near) the downtown Gaslamp Quarter, the ballpark, the football stadium, and tourist attractions like Old Town, Seaport Village, and Little Italy. There's even a Midtown stop a few blocks from the city's coolest rock club, the Casbah. But if you want to see some of the other rock neighborhoods uptown, the trolley's not your best bet.

ON FOOT

Certain neighborhoods like downtown and Little Italy are walkable, but it's a long haul to get from one part of town to another.

Downtown's layout is pretty simple, with numbered streets going in one direction and lettered streets in another; in other areas the streets are named alphabetically and according to themes (like trees, birds, gemstones, and so on).

BY TAXI

Taxis aren't very easy to get outside of the Gaslamp Quarter; to call yourself one, try **Yellow Cab** (☎ 619/234-6161), **American Cab** (☎ 619/234-1111), **San Diego Cab** (☎ 619/226-8294) and **Silver Cab** (☎ 619/280-5555).

Rockin' the Casbah: The San Diego Scene

San Diego suffers from an inferiority complex, which I guess comes from living so long in the shadow of LA. Though the city's grown a lot and developed its own flavor and character, many locals are still bitter that LA gets all the good shows—a lot of touring bands skip San Diego altogether, but the new House of Blues has started to change that—and whatever stars *do* emerge seem to eventually move north.

Despite the glittery, tourist-friendly Gaslamp Quarter downtown, the scene in San Diego centers on a little 200-capacity dive near the airport called The Casbah. Of course, there are other places to see music all over town, ranging from a boozy beachside cantina to a revolutionary vegan co-op-slash-venue on the UCSD campus.

THE TOP CLUBS

MTV Best ● → **Belly Up Tavern** ★★
Known for having some of the best sound engineers in town, this 600-capacity club in San Diego's North County hosts a lot of reggae, jam bands, R&B, alt-country, and rock. *143 S. Cedros Ave. (exit Lomas Santa Fe off I-5), Solana Beach.* ☎ *858/481-8140. www. bellyuptavern.com. Shows start at 8 or 9pm nightly. Cover $5–$30. 21+ to enter.*

➜ **'Canes** ★ This beachside joint is quintessential San Diego. Just steps away from the sand (and the millions of divey beach bars in the neighborhood), 'Canes doesn't have the best sightlines in the world, but there is an upstairs smoking deck. You'll find bands like Slightly Stoopid, Badly Drawn Boy, and Dave Navarro's new band, The Panic Channel, on the bill here. *3105 Ocean Front Walk (near Mission Blvd. and Ventura Place), Mission Beach.* ☎ *858/488-1780. www.canesbarandgrill.com. Restaurant open daily 11am–2am; shows start around 8 or 9pm. Cover $6–$25+. 21+ to enter.*

MTV Best ♥ ➜ **The Casbah** ★★ This is *the* small-venue rock club in San Diego, where everyone from Nirvana to the White Stripes to Liz Phair and Pavement played to sold-out crowds (and sometimes to half-empty rooms). These days owner Tim Mays books anything from up-and-coming local bands to national indie rock and hip-hop acts, from singer-songwriters to the Suicide Girls. *2501 Kettner Blvd. (at Laurel), Midtown.* ☎ *619/232-HELL. www.casbahmusic.com. Doors open nightly at 8:30pm. Cover $0–$20. 21+ to enter.*

➜ **4th & B** ★ Recently renovated Miami-style with white walls and a VIP mezzanine, this downtown club now books mostly hip-hop and superstar DJs, with the occasional night of local bands thrown in. *345 B St. (at 4th Ave.), downtown.* ☎ *619/231-4343. www.4thandb.com. Shows at 9pm nightly. Cover $5–$50+. 21+ to enter.*

➜ **House of Blues** ★★ San Diego got its own corporate-sponsored rock venue in 2005, and it is now the place cool bands that are too big for the Casbah come to play. The 1,100-person venue has recently featured Fiona Apple, Bad Religion, Gang of Four, Nada Surf, and tons more. *1055 5th Ave. (at C St.), downtown.* ☎ *619/299-BLUE. www.hob.com/sandiego. Restaurant*

Mon–Thurs 11:30am–midnight; Fri 11:30am–2am; Sat 4pm–2am; Sun 4pm–midnight. Concert hall doors open around 8 or 9pm. Cover $5–$35+. Some all-ages shows.

ALL AGES CLUBS

➜ **Che Café** Located on the UCSD campus, the non-profit, student- run vegetarian cafe/co-op known as the Che books bands that are often as revolutionary as its name implies. Locals like Plot to Blow up the Eiffel Tower play here a lot, along with touring acts. *Gilman Rd. at Scholar's Dr. S. (on UCSD campus).* ☎ *858/534-2311. checafe.ucsd. edu. Doors open at 7 or 8pm on show nights. Cover $0–$8.*

➜ **Epicentre** It's not the best sound in town, but the 525-capacity Epicentre is one of the only places where the under-21 set can catch up-and-comers like Hard Fi and Band of Horses. *8450 Mira Mesa Blvd., Mira Mesa.* ☎ *858/271-4000. www.harmonium-inc. com/epi/concerts. Doors open at 7pm on show nights. Cover $7–$15.*

MTV Best ♥ ➜ **Lestat's** ★★ Louie Brazier, the soundman/booker for this all-ages venue next door to a 24-hour coffee shop in Normal Heights, used to be Eddie Van Halen's guitar tech; now he's known as one of the best soundmen in town, booking eclectic local and touring acts including singer/songwriters, indie-rock bands, blues shouters, and more. If you really need your booze fix, you can always hit the **Ould Sod** down the block for a pint of Guinness, as many performers often do after the gig. *3343 Adams Ave. (at Felton), Normal Heights.* ☎ *619282-0437. www.lestats. com. Shows begin nightly around 9pm. Cover $5–$15.*

➜ **SOMA** Going to shows here is like watching your favorite band in a hot, sweaty concrete barn. Too bad it's pretty much the only all-ages venue big enough for bands like Built to Spill, Modest Mouse,

Calendar of Events: 'sup in SD

→ **Street Scene:** This 22-year-old festival, held annually in August, started out as a 1-block event in the then-seedy Gaslamp Quarter. When it moved to the parking lot of Qualcomm Stadium in the 'burbs, people joked it should be called "parking lot scene," but the lineup, with recent headliners the Yeah Yeah Yeahs, Tool, Kanye West, Snoop, the Shins, and more, proves it's still cool. **www.street-scene.com.**

→ **FREE TNT,** short for "Thursday Night Thing," is a monthly hipster happening held the first Thursday of the month at the **Museum of Contemporary Art** in downtown San Diego, about a mile from the Casbah. Admission is free, the art is usually good, as are the bands and DJs. **www.mcasd.org.**

→ No Doubt once played the **Adams Avenue Street Fair** before they were famous; now the 20-year-old event—held annually in September—books mostly singer/songwriters and blues acts, filling up a 6-block stretch of uptown with food, music, crafts, and more. **www.normalheights.org/events.**

→ **FREE** The free, outdoor **PB Block Party** has been a tradition in San Diego for more than 30 years, but conservative community members put the kibosh on the event in 2006. With any luck, it'll be back in action soon, booking more eclectic acts—past performers have included Cowboy Mouth, Young Dubliners, and more. **www.pbblockparty.com.**

→ Held annually in September since 1991, the **San Diego Music Awards** honors the best in local talent with a boozy awards show that has featured live performances by San Diego stars like Jason Mraz, Unwritten Law, Switchfoot, and more. Plus, proceeds benefit music education programs. **www.sdmusicawards.com.**

ROCKIN' THE WEST COAST

and the Raconteurs, who've all played recently, although the venue more commonly hosts punk, emo, and hard-core. *3350 Sports Arena Blvd.* ☎ *619/226-SOMA. www.somasandiego.com. Doors open nightly at 6 or 7pm. Cover $8–$20+.*

RECORD STORES

MTV Best ● → **Lou's** ★★ The coolest record store in San Diego's North County, this is *the* place to go for new releases and expert opinions from the music-obsessed staffers. Frequent (and free) in-store sets bring music geeks out in droves—when Jack Johnson played the tiny parking lot one afternoon, people were spilling out onto the highway and blocking traffic just to get a glimpse. *434 N. Hwy. 101, Encinitas.* ☎ *760/753-1382. www.lousrecords.com.*

Mon–Thurs and Sat 10am–9pm; Fri 10am–10pm; Sun 11am–7pm.

→ **M-Theory** ★★ Stacks of vinyl and a giant local-band selection make this recently expanded independent record store a local favorite. Often bands like Broken Social Scene and Nada Surf will play free, all-ages in-store sets here in the afternoon before a later show at the Casbah. *Two locations: 915 W Washington St., Mission Hills.* ☎ *619/220-0485. Mon–Sat 10am–10pm; Sun 11am–7pm. 2234 30th St. (at Juniper), South Park.* ☎ *619/269-2963. Mon–Fri 11am–10pm; Sat 10am–10pm; Sun 11am–7pm. www.mtheorymusic.com.*

→ **Off the Record** ★★ Off the Record has moved since Nirvana played a legendary pre-fame in-store there, but it's still one of

More SD Events: Flowers, Art & Sandcastles

With near constant great weather, San Diego's neighborhoods are like a revolving door of celebrations, with something going on nearly every weekend, especially in the summer. Here are just a few highlights:

→ Held annually in early December, **December Nights** is Balboa Park's annual holiday festival with an international food and crafts fair, caroling, discounted museum admission, and more. ☎ 619/ 239-0512; www. balboapark.org.

→ The big boys of golf play at the PGA tour stop **Buick Invitational** held at Torrey Pines in January or February. ☎ 619/281-4653; www.buick invitational.com.

→ **Cinco de Mayo, Mardi Gras,** and **St. Patrick's Day** are all huge holidays in the Gaslamp Quarter, where dedicated revelers turn out en masse for the festivities, which often include parades and live music on outdoor stages (☎ 619/ 233-5227; www.gaslamp.org). While those holidays are big downtown, others, like **Fourth of July, Memorial Day,** and **Labor Day** are major beach days. ☎ 619/232-3101; www.sandiego.org.

→ The **Rock 'N' Roll Marathon,** held annually in June, features live bands and cheering crowds along the scenic, 26.2-mile route. ☎ 858/450-6510; www.rnrmarathon.com.

→ The **Carlsbad Flower Fields** have gorgeous ranunculuses on display in North County from March through May. ☎ 760/431-0352; www.theflower fields.com.

→ Little Italy is the place to be at least twice a year, first for **ArtWalk** (☎ 619/ 615-1090; www.artwalkinfo.com), a 2-day outdoor art stroll in April, then for **Chalk La Strada** (☎ 619/233-3898; www.littleitalysd.com), a traditional Italian celebration of food and chalk art held annually in October.

→ **Over-the-Line** is a boozy two-weekend event on Fiesta Island that has something to do with softball and a lot to do with bikinis and beer. It's held annually in July. **www.ombac.org**.

→ Competitors in the **U.S. Open Sandcastle Competition** bring ephemeral marvels of sand architecture to the shores of South County's Imperial Beach each July. ☎ 619/424-6663; www.usopensandcastle.com.

→ The **San Diego Film Festival** brings Hollywood south in September with 5 days of screenings and glitzy parties. ☎ 619/582-2368; www.sdff.org.

→ San Diego has one of the biggest **Pride Festivals** in the country, with a parade, rally, and other events livening up Balboa Park and Hillcrest every July. ☎ 619/ 297-7683; www.sandiegopride.org.

→ Tennis big shots play at the annual **Acura Classic** at La Costa Resort & Spa, held annually in late July. ☎ 760/438-5683; www.acuraclassic.com.

the major authorities on vinyl in San Diego. *2912 University Ave., North Park.* ☎ *619/ 298-4755. Mon, Wed, and Thurs 11am–9pm; Tues, Fri, and Sat 11am–10pm; Sun 11am–8pm.*

Sleeping

As one of the most popular spring break destinations, San Diego has a ton of affordable lodging options for people working on a limited budget. There are dozens of hostels and campgrounds—some even in hot neighborhoods—and plenty of hotels available in all price ranges.

CAMPGROUNDS/HOSTELS

The **Ocean Beach Hostel** ★★ (4961 Newport Ave; ☎ 800/339-7263; www.californiahostel.com) is known as a lively hangout for international travelers and students. Rates are $17 to $22 per bed, depending on the season, and the price includes free breakfast, coffee, and dinner; no extra tax is applied.

Banana Bungalow (707 Reed Ave., Pacific Beach; ☎ 858/273-3060; www.bananabungalowsandiego.com) boasts a right-on-the-beach location, no curfew, and a bunch of freebies including breakfast, Wi-Fi, and beach toys like body boards, volleyball nets, Frisbees, and more. Dorm beds are $18 to $22 per night; private rooms are $55 to $95/night, depending on season.

Hostelling International has two locations in San Diego, including one downtown (521 Market St., at 5th Ave; ☎ 888/464-4872, ext. 156; www.sandiegohostels.org), and USA Hostels has a location a few blocks away (726 5th Ave. at G St.; ☎ 800/438-8622; www.usahostels.com).

San Elijo Campground in Cardiff and **South Carlsbad State Beach** are just two of the most centralized campgrounds—dozens of other camping parks and other areas can be found in the mountains and deserts to the east as well as south in Tijuana. San Elijo (2050 N. Hwy. 101; ☎ 760/753-5091) has 171 RV and tent campsites that run $25 per day. South Carlsbad State Beach (7201 Carlsbad Blvd.; ☎ 760/438-3143) has 222 RV and tent campsites that run $35 per night. Call ☎ 800/444-7275 to reserve; reservations must be made 48 hours ahead of time and a $7.50 reservation fee is added to the prices quoted above. Find more info on San Diego County camping at **www.parks.ca.gov**.

CHEAP

There are plenty of chain hotels on the aptly named Hotel Circle in Mission Valley; they're not much to brag about, but when everything else is sold out and you just need something cheap, they'll do the trick. Try the **Super 8** (445 Hotel Circle South; ☎ 619/692-1288), **Howard Johnson** (1631 Hotel Circle South; ☎ 619/293-7792), or **Days Inn** (543 Hotel Circle South; ☎ 619/296-9615).

📺 Best ♦ → **Pensione Little Italy** ★★ Location, location, location. In the heart of Little Italy, this cute Euro-style hotel is affordable, central to both downtown and Little Italy nightlife, and a long walk or a short cab ride away from the Casbah. *606 W. Date St. (at India), Little Italy. ☎ 800/232-4683 or 619/236-8000. www.lapensionehotel.com. 75 units. $90/night. Amenities: Laundry; restaurant; parking. In room: Dataport.*

DOABLE

→ **Humphrey's Half Moon Inn & Suites** ★★ This compound on Shelter Island is a combination hotel, concert venue, restaurant, and lounge. In the summer, the outdoor theater hosts, like, a bazillion bands—some cool (Frank Black, Pink Martini), many lame (like Hootie, who somehow manages to sell it out every year). The grounds are beautifully landscaped with lush gardens and the picturesque San Diego Bay just beyond, and the rooms are comfy and well appointed. Ask about concert packages and other special rates. *2303 Shelter Island Dr. ☎ 800/542-7400. www.halfmooninn.com. $160–$190 double; $200–$400+ suite. Parking $8/night. Amenities: Bar/lounge; pool; hike/bike path;*

gym; business center; concierge; valet; room service. In room: Safe, fridge, high-speed Internet.

➜ **Lafayette Hotel & Suites** ★ This one-time Colonial mansion isn't the most pristine place in town, but it'll do. Features include a pool designed by Olympian-turned-"Tarzan" actor Johnny Weissmuller and an old-school piano bar turned hipster haven just next door called the **Red Fox Room.** The hotel has recently started hosting bands and DJs in its lobby bar, the **Spotlight Lounge.** *2223 El Cajon Blvd., North Park.* ☎ *877/DIEGO-4U or 619/296–2101. www.innsuites.com. 131 units. $100–$160. Amenities: Business center; bar; pool; laundry; pets welcome with additional $25 one-time fee per pet; sun deck; free Wi-Fi in lobby. In room: High-speed Internet, microwave.*

SPLURGE

➜ **Hotel Solamar** ★★★ One of San Diego's newer downtown hotels, and one of its only hip boutique properties, Hotel Solamar has swank guest rooms with flat-screen TVs (and an "om away from home" yoga channel), mahogany furniture, and 24-hour room service from its in-house restaurant, **Jsix.** Locals come to party at **Jbar,** the rooftop pool/bar area (complete with cabanas) that overlooks neighboring Petco Park baseball stadium. *435 6th Ave., downtown.* ☎ *877/230-0300. www.hotelsolamar.com. 219 standard rooms; 16 suites. Doubles $319–$399+; "hot date rate" is $169. Valet parking $24/day. Amenities: Restaurant; bar; pool; wine reception; business center; pets welcome with no additional fee; gym; spa services. In room: Wi-Fi, minibar.*

Eating

San Diego's about far more than just fish tacos, though you can certainly find plenty of taquerias serving up that Southland favorite. From health-conscious smoothie joints to cook-your-own steak houses,

there's a ton of rockin' (and affordable) eats to choose from.

SUPPLIES

With live music, llama rides (yes, *llama rides*), and booth after booth of fresh organic produce, baked goods, and more, the **Ocean Beach Farmers' Market** ★★ is the block party that takes over the town's main drag, Newport Street every Wednesday from 4 to 7pm (open till 8 in the summer).

Also in OB, the **People's Co-Op** (4765 Voltaire St.; ☎ **619/224-1387**; www.ob peoplesfood.com) is a member-run, vegan-friendly grocery with a full-service sit-down deli serving stuff like brown rice pudding; you don't need to be a member of the co-op to shop here.

TAKEOUT TREATS

For coffee in the beach areas, try **Pannikin** in downtown La Jolla (7467 Girard Ave.; ☎ **858/454-5453**), which also serves some tasty steamed Greek eggs with basil and feta. Students and surfers hang at **Café 976** (976 Felspar St.; ☎ **858/272-0976**), a converted 1920s beach house with deck seating and a leafy garden, not to mention an extensive menu of good eats (I love the spinach burger burrito and spicy eggplant sandwich).

Krakatoa (128 25th St.; ☎ **619/230-0272**) is another converted residence peddling caffeine out of its Golden Hill location next door to the Turf Club, while **Influx Café** (1948 Broadway; ☎ **619/255-9470**) rocks a sleek mid-century vibe and serves up tasty cupcakes and free Wi-Fi.

For more substantial grub on the run, try **Grab & Go Subs** (multiple locations including 2102 India St., Little Italy; ☎ **619/238-5353**) for sammies and **Bronx Pizza** (111 Washington St., Hillcrest; ☎ **619/291-3341**) for authentic New York–style slices. And after the bars close, you'll see a line of glassy-eyed 20-somethings queuing up at

La Posta (3980 3rd Ave., Hillcrest; ☎ 619/295-8982) for late-night carne asada burritos.

RESTAURANTS

Cheap

San Diegans love their Mexican food, but they love their waistlines too, so health-conscious south-of-the-border fare is abundant. Vegetarian dining never tasted as good as a meat-free burrito from **El Zarape** ⓜ Best❢ ★★★ (4642 Park Blvd., University Heights; ☎ 619/692-1652; tacos $1–$3.50, burritos $3–$6), which also serves beef, pork, chicken, and seafood (the scallop burrito is to die for).

Meanwhile, SoCal staple **Wahoo's** (several locations including 639 Pearl St., La Jolla; ☎ 858/459-0027; tacos $2–$3, burritos $4–$6) serves yummy blackened fish taco/enchilada combo platters with spicy Cajun white beans and sticky rice, all drenched in a creamy (and addictive) green salsa. But if you really want to go the full-fat route, try the greasy chorizo at **Las Cuatros Milpas** (it means "the four cornfields"; 1857 Logan Ave.; ☎ 619/234-4460; most items $1–$4) in Barrio Logan.

When it comes to San Diego's best burger, locals are divided between **Rocky's Crown Pub** ★★ (3786 Ingraham St.; ☎ 858/273-9140; $4–$6) in Pacific Beach and **Hodad's** ★★ (5010 Newport Ave.; ☎ 619/224-4623; $3–$9.50) in Ocean Beach. Rocky's has a dive-bar atmosphere and succulent, heavy patties (*Hint:* You'll want to eat light for the rest of the day—or week), while Hodad's is known for its beach vibe, personalized license plates mounted on the walls, and a staff that's often bitchy (in a good way).

➜**Swami's** ★★ BREAKFAST This North County breakfast spot, known for its awesome smoothies and wraps, draws a healthy crowd of locals and surfers to its cute, casual outdoor dining area just off

the 101 in Encinitas. *1163 S. Coast Hwy 101, Encinitas.* ☎ *760/944-0612. www.swamis. signonsandiego.com. Breakfast $5.50–$7.25; salads and wraps $3–$7. Mon–Fri 7am–4pm.*

➜**Turf Club** ★★ STEAK One of those cook-your-own-steak joints, the Turf Club's always packed with stylish carnivores who gather around a central grill pit, busily basting and seasoning cuts of meat, which arrive Saran-wrapped on paper plates. The veggie-friendly joint also serves portobello mushroom steaks, not to mention their signature dirty martini with blue-cheese-stuffed olives. *1116 25th St., Golden Hill.* ☎ *619/234-6363. Entrees $6–$10. Mon–Tues 5pm–midnight; Wed–Fri 5pm–2am; Sat 1pm–2am; Sun 1pm–midnight.*

Doable

Chef Isabel Cruz presides over the **Mission Cafés**, a local-favorite chain of breakfast joints with locations in Mission Beach (3795 Mission Blvd; ☎ 858/488-9060), North Park (2801 University Ave; ☎ 619/220-8992), and the East Village (1250 J St.; ☎ 619/232-7662). La Jolla's **Coffee Cup** ⓜ Best❢ ★★ (1109 Wall St.; ☎ 858/454-2819) and PB's **Cantina** (966 Felspar St.; ☎ 858/272-8400) share a similar menu, which includes healthy scrambles, crispy rosemary potatoes, and cakelike "squaw" bread. Be prepared for a lengthy-but-worth-it wait, especially on weekends. At all locations, most dishes are under $10.

➜**Buon Appetito** ★★ ITALIAN This cozy Little Italy bistro doesn't take reservations, so prepare to wait during peak hours; menu highlights include porcini mushroom risotto, Gorgonzola-topped filet mignon, and warm *burratta* (young mozzarella cheese) on a bed of spinach. *1609 India St., Little Italy.* ☎ *619/238-9880. www.buon appetito.signonsandiego.com. Starters $4.95–$12; entrees $9.95–$24. Mon–Thurs 11:30am–2:30pm and 5–10pm; Fri–Sat 11am–11pm; Sun noon–10pm.*

➔ **Red Pearl Kitchen** ★★ ASIAN Red Pearl's equation is basically traditional Chinese food + trendy fusion-style innovation + sleek design = good times. Dishes like spicy-ahi-topped tempura eggplant and cashew garlic chicken come in generous servings, but the real star here is the Jade Mistress martini, made with red-chile-infused vodka, Thai basil, apple, and simple syrup. *440 J St. (between 4th and 5th), downtown.* ☎ *619/231-1100. www.redpearl kitchen.com. Small plates $7–$12; entrees $10–$17. Dinner served Sun–Wed 5:30–10pm; Fri–Sat 5:30–11pm (lounge open until 1am). Late-night menu served in lounge until midnight.*

Splurge

➔ **Indigo Grill** ★★ SOUTHWEST This menu is a wildly eclectic mishmash of Southwestern, Mexican, and European influences, as is evident in dishes like jalapeño-maize pappardelle with fennel prawns, and salmon with squid-ink linguine. Don't miss the creamy, grits-like Indian corn pudding. *1536 India St.* ☎ *619/ 234-6802. www.cohnrestaurants.com. Starters $5–$13; entrees $18–$30. Lunch Mon–Fri 11:30am–2pm; dinner nightly 5–10pm.*

🅼🆃🆅 Best● ➔ **Kensington Grill** ★★★ CALIFORNIA CUISINE Horseradish-crusted sea bass, savory meatloaf, fresh hand-torn pasta, and beef short ribs are standouts on this seasonally varied menu. Martini Mondays, Wine Wednesdays, and Tequila Thursdays offer good deals for boozehounds, and the $20 three-course early-bird menu (offered nightly from 5–6pm) is a bargain for broke wannabe gourmands. *4055 Adams Ave., Kensington.* ☎ *619/281-4014. www.sdurbankitchen.com. Starters $6.75–$9.25; entrees $13–$29. Sun–Thurs 5–9:30pm; Fri–Sat 5–10pm.*

Partying

Downtown is tourist central and *the* place to go for mainstream-style dance clubs; The Pacific and Mission Beach areas are sorority-girl beach-bar HQ. Locals hang out in neighborhood dives in Hillcrest, South Park, and North Park, while Golden Hill, which rises above downtown to the east, is especially hipster-friendly, as is the semi-sketchy eastside nabe of City Heights.

BARS & PUBS

Thursday nights go *off* at the **Live Wire** when the tats-and-piercings set comes out for pool and a killer jukebox (2103 El Cajon Blvd.; ☎ **619/291-7450**). In the East Village, you gotta love a dive like **Landlord Jim's** 🅼🆃🆅 Best● ★★ that serves 40s in brown paper bags and has a make-out room out back (1546 Broadway at 16th; ☎ **619/233-9998**). And Hillcrest fave **Nunu's** 🅼🆃🆅 Best● ★★ is like a Denny's with booze; while it's chill for a midweek happy hour, it tends to get packed out on weekend nights (3537 5th Ave. at Ivy; ☎ **619/295-2878**).

➔ **Beauty Bar** New York, San Francisco, Vegas, and LA all have one; now San Diego's got a haven of its own where haircut hipsters can hang out and sip Stella against a kitschy beauty-parlor decor. The bar also books a pretty good slate of ultra-cool, super-under-the-radar DJs and indie rock acts; just don't expect the manicure to be as perfect as the calculatedly cool outfits of the resident scenesters. *4746 El Cajon Blvd., City Heights.* ☎ *619/516-4746. www.my space.com/thebeautybar. Mon 8pm–2am; Tues–Thurs and Sat–Sun 9pm–2am; Fri 6pm–2am. Cover $0–$5.*

➔ **Kensington Club** This half bar/half rock venue books mostly local and emerging national rock bands. *4079 Adams Ave., Kensington.* ☎ *619/284-2848. www.myspace. com/kenclub. Daily 10am–2am. Cover $0–$10.*

➔ **Tower Bar** One of SD's favorite local bands, Lady Dottie & the Diamonds—featuring 60-something line cook Dottie and her backing band of hot, young indie rockers—plays a free show at this bar, which dates back to 1932, every Monday night. Order a house-specialty Pabst-Smear (half-Guinness, half-Pabst). *4757 University Ave., City Heights.* ☎ *619/284-0158. www.the towerbar.com. Tues–Sun 2pm–2am; Mon 7pm–2am. No cover.*

MTV **Best ◑** →**Whistle Stop** ★★ A neighborhood dive in South Park, the Whistle has the occasional live band, plus indie-rock DJs, board-game nights, and a knitting club, not to mention local-celebrity bartenders (several employees moonlight in area bands). *2236 Fern St. (at Juniper), South Park.* ☎ *619/284-6784. www. whistlestopbar.com. Mon–Fri 5pm–2am; Sat–Sun 2pm–2am. Cover $0–$8.*

Piano Bars
The air is thick with irony (or is it?) at Hillcrest's **Imperial House** (505 Kalmia St.; ☎ **619/234-3525**) and the **Red Fox Room** (2223 El Cajon Blvd., North Park; ☎ **619/297-1313**), two old-school piano bars that draw equal parts blue hairs and tongue-in-check scenesters.

A British-Style Pub
One of the only places in town where you can watch rugby while eating bangers and mash, **Shakespeare's Pub** is a cozy, comfortable British pub in South Mission Hills (3701 India St.; ☎ **619/299-0230**).

CLUBS
If you're into the whole "velvet-rope, bribe-the-bouncer, $20-martini" dance club thing, **On Broadway** (615 Broadway at Sixth; ☎ **619/231-0011**) is the must-go place downtown, with superstar DJs, a sushi restaurant, and five different dance areas and lounges, including The Vault, built in the actual vault of this former bank building.

Lately the newly sprouted **Stingaree** (454 Sixth St. at J; ☎ **619/544-0867**) and

Belo (919 Fourth Ave. at E St.; ☎ **619/231-9200**) are giving the compound a run for its money.

→**Air Conditioned** ★★ This mellow, retro-chic '60s-style lounge features a sunken dance floor, 007 movie posters on the walls, and shoulder-to-shoulder crowds on weekend nights, when DJs spin hip-hop, house, and dance rock. Tuesday's Big Sonic Chill night is always a big draw. *4673 30th St., North Park.* ☎ *619/501-9831. www.airconditionedbar.com. Mon–Fri 4pm–2am; Sat–Sun 7pm–2am. Cover varies.*

→**San Diego Sports Club** ★★★ This divey joint in Hillcrest—named one of *Maxim Magazine's* Top Ten Hole-in-the-Wall Bars in America—draws a grizzled crowd of sports-loving regulars during the day to play pool and watch the game on several big-screen TVs, but later on the clientele is all asymmetrical haircuts and trendy clothes as DJs spin and pretty people dance. *1271 University Ave. (at Richmond, behind Med Grill), Hillcrest.* ☎ *619/299-7372. Mon–Fri noon–2am; Sat–Sun 9am–2am. Cover $0–$5.*

What Else to See & Do

Since you'll be spending so much time inside for shows and post-show debauchery, it's kind of essential for your sanity to do, you know, something other than rocking out . . . and maybe even outdoors. You might as well use the daytime to take advantage of San Diego's outdoor offerings and near-perfect year-round weather. From the beaches to Balboa Park, there's a ton to see and do once you sleep off that hangover.

THE TOP ATTRACTIONS
Get your art on at one of San Diego's many museums. The **San Diego Museum of Art** (1450 El Prado, Balboa Park; ☎ **619/232-7931**) has a bitchin' collection of European

An Awesome Factory Tour

FREE Everyone from Beck and blink-182 to Sonic Youth and the Killers swear by the awesomeness of the guitars produced by **Taylor Guitars,** and you can visit the factory, which is based in the San Diego suburb of El Cajon. Take a free **tour** ★★ to see how the acoustic 6- and 12-strings, basses, and electric axes are made and what makes them so special to musicians and "civilians" like Bill Clinton, Carson Daly, and, uh, Shannen Doherty. No appointment is necessary to take the tour; just show up in the lobby by 1pm and tell the receptionist you want in. The tour lasts 75 minutes. *1980 Gillespie Way, El Cajon.* ☎ *619/ 258-1207. www.taylorguitars.com. Admission is free. Factory open Mon–Fri 8am–4:30pm (closed holidays); tours given at 1pm. Reservations not required.*

and American art, while just around the corner in Balboa Park, the **Museum of Photographic Arts** (1649 El Prado; ☎ 619/238-7559) has more than 7,000 photos in its permanent collection ranging from Alfred Stieglitz to Dorothea Lange.

The **Museum of Contemporary Art** has two locations—one downtown (1001 Kettner at Broadway; ☎ 619/234-1001) and one in La Jolla (700 Prospect St. at Fay; ☎ 858/454-3541); both show edgier stuff, often with an emphasis on Tijuana artists. Small gallery **Voice 1156** (1156 Seventh St. at C, downtown; ☎ 619/235-6922) shows work in various media by local and national up-and-comers; the first Friday of the month they have free receptions with booze and a tasty cheese plate.

PLAYING OUTSIDE

Indulge in some beachfront eye candy with a stroll or bike ride down the **Mission Beach Boardwalk.** Look out for Flash, the usually-mostly-naked rollerblading dude, rumored to be alternately a UCSD professor or a local handyman, who sometimes carries a ghetto blaster and often dresses up for holidays or for no reason at all. I'll never forget the teensy red-white-and-blue sequined Speedo he donned for Fourth of July, complete with giant American flag affixed to his backpack.

Surfing is the sport of choice in San Diego, but don't try to shred the legendary breaks at **Windansea** unless you're a) really good, b) really scrappy, or c) a local—these guys are notoriously territorial. Longboard haven **Swami's** is a little mellower in North County, and if you're a beginner hit the easy breaks at Tourmaline (at the end of Tourmaline Street in Pacific Beach) or **La Jolla Shores,** where the renowned female-run **Surf Diva** gives lessons to aspiring wahines (2160 Avenida de la Playa; ☎ 858/454-8273; www.surf diva.com).

The city's two bays—the **San Diego "Big" Bay** and the smaller **Mission Bay**—offer a ton of recreational options, from kayaking to jet-skiing to sailing. Check **www.thebigbay.com** for info on the marinas and rental locations on San Diego Bay. On Mission Bay, kayaks, surfboards, bikes, and rollerblades can be rented at **Cheap Rentals** (3689 Mission Blvd., Mission Beach; ☎ 800/941-7761). **Mission Bay Sportscenter** rents powerboats, kayaks, and jet skis (1010 Santa Clara Place, Mission Beach; ☎ 858/488-1004).

If ocean kayaking is your thing, set out from **La Jolla Shores** to explore the La Jolla Caves. Rentals and guided tours are available at La Jolla Kayak (2199 Avenida de la Playa; ☎ 858/459-1114) and Hike

Bike Kayak (2246 Avenida de la Playa; ☎ 866/HB-KAYAK).

Parks

FREE → **Balboa Park** ★★ As the country's largest urban cultural park, Balboa Park is home to the **San Diego Zoo** ★★★—the town's top tourist attraction and home to 100 acres filled with most any species of plant or animal imaginable, including a pair of giant pandas on loan from the Chinese government. I dare you not to get addicted to the Zoo's online **PandaCam: www.sandiegozoo.org/zoo/ex_panda_station.html**. (The zoo admission is a hefty $33 for 1 day, $39 for 2, and it's open daily 9am–4pm; www.sdzoo.com).

The park also houses 15 major museums including the Hall of Champions sports museum, the San Diego Museum of Art, the Museum of Photographic Arts, and the Museum of Man, not to mention the Japanese Friendship Garden and a slew of international cottages built for the 1935 Exposition. The park also contains several restaurants, performing arts venues like the **Old Globe Theater,** modeled after the original, and the Spreckels Organ, one of the largest in the world. Bonus: The park has special areas for lawn bowling and Frisbee golf. Check in at the Visitors Center at 1549 El Prado for more info. *Between Sixth Ave. and Park Blvd.* ☎ *619/239-0512. Visitors Center daily 9:30am–4:30pm (longer in the summer). Park admission is free; museum admission varies from free (Timken Museum) to around $11 (Natural History Museum). Admission to select museums free on Tues.*

→ **Coronado** ★ The "island" of Coronado isn't really an island at all; it's connected to mainland San Diego by a thin strip of land called the Silver Strand, which runs from Coronado south to Imperial Beach and contains a beach and paved boardwalk great for biking or jogging. A quick trip by car over the San Diego–Coronado Bridge or a $3 one-way ride on the ferry (departing hourly from downtown S.D.; ☎ 619/234-4111) gets you to the quaint community, whose tree-lined streets are lined with cute shops and restaurants. The iconic red turrets of the nearby **Hotel del Coronado** (1500 Orange Ave., ☎ 800/HOTELDEL; www.hoteldel.com) have been attracting the cream of the crop for decades—Marilyn Monroe, Jack Lemmon, and Tony Curtis made the place legendary when they shot *Some Like It Hot* there.

→ **Torrey Pines State Beach and Reserve** This open space is a favorite among locals for its 8 miles of hike and bike trails and expansive beach area. *16500 N. Torrey Pines Rd. (between La Jolla and Del Mar).* ☎ *858/755-2063. www.torreypine.org. Free admission. Parking is $6 weekdays; $8 weekends/holidays. Park open daily 8am–sunset; visitor center opens at 9am.*

SPECTATOR SPORTS

The **San Diego Padres** got a new downtown stadium in Petco Park in 2004; five bucks gets you into the stadium's bars and the Park at the Park—a grassy area behind the stadium with a Jumbotron and partial views of the field. Reserved seats cost anywhere from $12 to $59 ($8 for bleacher seats). Call ☎ 877/FRIAR-TIX or visit www.padres.com for info. There's not a lot of cheap parking available downtown, but on the upside, the trolley's cheap and runs directly to the stadium.

The **San Diego Chargers,** the city's NFL team, plays from August to December at Qualcomm Stadium in Mission Valley (about 7 miles east of the coast on I-8). Tickets run from $54 to $92 and are available via Ticketmaster or at the Chargers ticket office at Gate C at Qualcomm

Stadium (open Mon–Fri 8am–5pm; select Sat 10am–4pm). Call ☎ **877-CHARGERS** or visit www.chargers.com for info.

Bet the ponies at the **Del Mar Racetrack,** 20 miles north of downtown in the seaside community of Del Mar (☎ **858/755-1141;** www.dmtc.com). Built by Bing Crosby in 1937, the track is open for live racing Wednesday to Monday from mid-July to early September (general admission tickets start at $6; parking is $6 or $20 for valet).

On the Road to Los Angeles, CA

San Diego to Los Angeles, 110 miles

If you don't time your trip correctly, this could be the longest 100 miles you've ever driven. Traffic in San Diego and LA is notoriously bad, and only getting worse on the main arteries—I-5 and I-405—running through Orange County between the two metro areas. I-5 will take you past South Coast Plaza, a major shopping mecca in OC, as well as Disneyland and Angels Stadium in Anaheim. I-405 runs west of the 5 and might be a better bet if you're headed to LA beach areas like Venice or Santa Monica. You can generally make it from point A to point B in about 2 hours if you leave before 2pm on weekdays; during rush hour it can take up to 4 hours.

You'll go faster if you're a carpool (two or more passengers); carpool lanes on I-5 are closed to single drivers at all times. If traffic's really screwed, consider taking Toll Road 73—a pay road that connects the I-5 at San Juan Capistrano to the I-405 in Long Beach and costs around $4 each way (call ☎ **800/378-TRAK** or visit www.thetollroads.com for info).

SoCal Playlist: Heading to LA

On the radio:
→ **FM 94/9** (94.9 FM), San Diego
→ **91X** (91.1 FM), San Diego
→ **Indie 103** (103.1 FM), Los Angeles
→ **KROQ** (106.7 FM), Los Angeles
→ **KCRW** (89.9 FM), Los Angeles

On the iPod/CD player:
→ *Hotel California,* **Eagles,** "Hotel California," 1976
→ *Walking in L.A.,* **Missing Persons,** "Spring Session M," 1982
→ *California,* **Phantom Planet,** "The Guest," 2002
→ *Dani California,* **Red Hot Chili Peppers,** "Stadium Arcadium," 2006
→ *Hella Good,* **No Doubt,** "Rock Steady," 2001
→ *Los Angeles,* **X,** "Los Angeles," 1980
→ *Los Angeles, I'm Yours,* **The Decemberists,** "Her Majesty," 2003
→ *Smoke Two Joints,* **Sublime,** "40 Oz to Freedom," 1992
→ *California Girls,* **Beach Boys,** "Summer Days (and Summer Nights!)," 1965
→ *What's My Age Again?* **Blink-182,** "Enema of the State," 1999

Detour: Behind the Orange Curtain

If you want to take your time soaking up the Low-Cal rock scene, add a stop at Gwen Stefani's former stomping grounds in Orange County. Not just the backdrop for teenage catfights on *Laguna Beach*, OC is also a haven for beach rock, punk, emo, and all-ages clubs. Some notable places to check out: the all-ages **Chain Reaction** in Anaheim (1652 W Lincoln Ave.; ☎ 714/ 635-6067; www. allages.com), the hipster-chic **Detroit Bar** in Costa Mesa (843 W. 19th St.; ☎ 949/642-0600; www.detroitbar.com), and the **Coach House,** a historic songwriter's stop in San Juan Capistrano (33157 Camino Capistrano; ☎ 949/496-8930; www.thecoachhouse.com). There's also a couple of big-deal concerts in Orange County, including **Inland Invasion,** a concert thrown by LA radio station KROQ in September, and **the Hootenanny,** a rockabilly/punk fest and custom car show held every July.

Welcome to Los Angeles, CA

From Janis Joplin to the Doors to the Red Hot Chili Peppers, there's so much rock history in LA that you could write a whole book (or 12) about Hollywood alone.

Well, I don't have that kind of time, and neither do you most likely, so let's be selective, shall we? We're going to keep our focus mostly on the smaller, newer venues in Hollywood and the eastside neighborhood of Silver Lake, home to Beck, a handful of awesome little rock clubs, and more than a few scenesters in skinny jeans.

Los Angeles Nuts & Bolts

Area Codes West of La Cienega, including Beverly Hills and the beach communities, use the 310 area code. Portions of Los Angeles County east and south of the city, including Long Beach, are in the 562 area. The San Fernando Valley has the 818 area code, while points east—including parts of Burbank, Glendale, and Pasadena—use 626. What happened to 213, you ask? The Downtown business area still uses 213. All other numbers, including Griffith Park, Hollywood, and parts of West Hollywood (east of La Cienega Blvd.) now use 323.

Business Hours Offices are usually open weekdays from 9am to 5pm. Banks are open weekdays from 9am to 3pm or later and sometimes Saturday mornings. Stores typically open between 9 and 10am and close between 5 and 6pm from Monday through Saturday. Stores in shopping complexes or malls tend to stay open late: until about 9pm on weekdays and weekends, and many malls and larger department stores are open on Sundays.

Drinking Laws Drinking age is 21; bring ID when you go out. Supermarkets and convenience stores in California sell beer, wine, and liquor. Most restaurants serve alcohol, but some only serve beer and wine—it depends on the type of liquor license they own. By law all bars, clubs, restaurants, and stores cannot sell or serve alcohol after 2am, and "last call" tends to start at 1:30pm.

Emergencies   Call ☎ **911** to report a fire, call the police, or get an ambulance anywhere in the United States. This is a toll-free call (no coins are required at public telephones).

Hospital   The centrally located (and world-famous) **Cedars-Sinai Medical Center,** 8700 Beverly Blvd., Los Angeles (☎ 310/423-3277), has a 24-hour emergency room staffed by some of the country's finest MDs.

Newspapers & Magazines   The *Los Angeles Times* (www.latimes.com) is a high-quality daily with strong local and national coverage. Its Sunday "Calendar" section (www.calendarlive.com) is an excellent guide to entertainment in and around LA, and includes listings of what's doing and where to do it. The *LA Weekly* (www.laweekly.com), a free weekly listings magazine, is packed with information on current events around town. *Los Angeles* magazine (www.lamag.com) is a city-based monthly full of news, information, and previews of LA's art, music, and food scenes.

Police   In an emergency, dial ☎ **911.** For nonemergency police matters, call ☎ 213/485-2121; in Beverly Hills, dial ☎ 310/550-4951.

Smoking   Heavy smokers are in for a tough time in Los Angeles. There is no smoking in public buildings, sports arenas, elevators, theaters, banks, lobbies, restaurants, offices, stores, bed-and-breakfasts, most small hotels, and bars. The only exception is a bar where drinks are served solely by the owner. Some neighborhood bars turn a blind eye and pass you an ashtray anyway.

Taxes   Sales tax in Los Angeles is 8%. Hotel tax is charged on the room tariff only (which is not subject to sales tax) and is set by the city, ranging from 12% to 17% around Southern California.

Time   Los Angeles is in the Pacific Standard Time zone, which is 3 hours behind Eastern Standard Time. For the correct time, call ☎ 853-1212 (in any LA area code).

Weather   Call **Los Angeles Weather Information** (☎ 213/554-1212) for the daily forecast. For beach conditions, call the **Zuma Beach Lifeguard** recorded information (☎ 310/457-9701).

Getting Around

BY CAR

Even 25 years after the Missing Persons song, with the ozone layer becoming a rapidly fading memory, it's still true: *Nobody* walks in LA. Angelenos love their cars, so prepare to spend a lot of time in yours.

Traffic is a constant, so you're probably best off finding one neighborhood that you like and bouncing around there. If you do need to get across town, allow about 20 minutes to get from Silver Lake to West Hollywood, and another 20 to the beaches beyond, though traffic can be so unpredictable it's kind of futile to estimate times. There's no hard-and-fast rule for parking either; sometimes you get lucky with lots or street parking, sometimes—especially in high-traffic areas of Hollywood—you're stuck having to fork over cash to valet.

Hollywood Highlights

In Praise of In-N-Out Burger

Yeah, we know: fast food is *so* over. We saw *Supersize Me* and we, too, were grossed out. Still, there's one roadside attraction in the far west that should not be missed, *Fast Food Nation* notwithstanding, and that's 📺 Best❂ **In-N-Out Burger.** With retro signage and a supersimple menu (burgers, cheeseburgers, shakes, fries, sodas), what sets In-N-Out apart from its generic megachain counterparts is twofold. First, it's a family-run joint with employee-friendly business practices like way-higher-than-minimum-wage wages (which, among other things, makes it the only fast-food place somewhat endorsed by *Nation* author Eric Schlosser). Second, the food is really freakin' good. The fries are cooked in vegetable oil, not beef fat, and everything's made to order, so don't be surprised if you're idling in the drive-thru longer than you might at DQ. Plus, the ethic is definitely more "have it your way" than at those other greasy spoons. Longtime loyalists know the In-N-Out "secret menu" by heart, with its zillion different ways of customizing your burger: **animal style** (extra spread and grilled onions), **protein style** (no bun, wrapped in lettuce), and so on. Check **in-n-out.com/secretmenu.asp** for a partial list.

After opening its first location in Baldwin Park, Calif., in 1948, In-N-Out now has more than 120 restaurants in California, Nevada and Arizona and has served its burgers to many a celebrity, notably at *Vanity Fair*'s post-Oscar parties. Oh, another bonus? It's open late, till 1am weekdays and 1:30 on weekends—perfect for fueling up before an all-nighter on the road.

BY METRORAIL

I've met longtime residents who have absolutely no idea that a subway even exists in Los Angeles—or maybe they've just blocked out the painful memories of the congestion caused when the city tore up streets to build the under- and above-ground rail lines. But, alas, a rail system does exist, and people actually do ride it sometimes. It costs $1.35 per trip and there are four main lines: the Red Line subway connects downtown's Union Station with stations in North Hollywood; the above-ground Blue Line runs from downtown to Long Beach. The Green Line goes from LAX to East LA, while the Gold Line serves Pasadena from downtown. Call ☎ 213/922-2000 or visit www.mta.net for info.

BY TAXI

Try **Checker Cab** (☎ 323/654-8400), **LA Taxi** (☎ 213/627-7000), or **United Taxi**

(☎ 213/483-7604). The charge is $1.90 to start, then $1.60 per mile.

Beyond the Sunset Strip: the LA Rock Scene

The good news about LA is that a night doesn't go by in this town without a decent rock show. The bad news? There's, like, a bazillion venues to choose from. This section focuses on the smaller clubs that book mostly indie rock, hip-hop, and singer/songwriter stuff.

Since this is LA, don't be surprised if you encounter some of this town's trademark 'tude, especially among the clubs' indier-than-thou patrons (and sometimes the staff, too). And if you happen to run into some young Hollywood actor types, just follow local custom—pretend to ignore them (then snap their picture with your cellphone and post it on a gossip blog. Just kidding!)

ROCK VENUES

➜ **The Echo** This one-time Latin disco retains a bit of the seediness of its former tenant in the lame decor, but with eclectic DJ and band bookings, it's become known as one of the more cutting-edge venues in town. *1822 Sunset Blvd.* ☎ *213/413-8200. www.attheecho.com. Daily 9pm–2am. Cover $0–$15. 21+ to enter.*

MTV **Best ♥** ➜ **Hotel Café** ★★★ Neither a hotel nor really a cafe anymore (though it used to be BYOB-only before obtaining a liquor license), this increasingly buzzworthy singer/songwriter venue in Hollywood has birthed stars like Gary Jules (remember that killer "Mad World" cover?) and Cary Brothers (you know him from the *Garden State* soundtrack). Celebrities—the ones with good taste, anyway—love the cozy, candlelit club, which is booked and co-owned by former Buddyhead sex columnist Marco Shafer. The club recently got a face-lift but still books some of the best unsigned and emerging talent on the circuit. Do yourself a favor and see a show here—but don't forget to turn your cell to vibrate: This room is known for its attentive audiences. *1623 ½ N. Cahuenga Blvd. (at Hollywood)* ☎ *323/461-2040. www.hotelcafe. com. Daily 7pm–2am. Cover range usually between $7–$15. 21+ to enter.*

MTV **Best ♥** ➜ **Largo** ★★ Largo's probably most famous for being the regular Friday-night hang for multi-instrumentalist Jon Brion, who's probably most famous for being Paul Thomas Anderson's favorite composer and the production guru behind people like Aimee Mann and Fiona Apple, who've been known to make surprise cameos at Brion's Largo nights. *432 N. Fairfax Ave.* ☎ *323/852-1273; www.largo-la. com. Cover $5–$20. 21+ except with dinner reservation (then all ages).*

➜ **Silverlake Lounge** Though the name's spelled wrong ("It's two words!" insists

one resident friend), the booking at this Sunset Boulevard club is right on, with a steady stream of local and touring indie rock bands performing 5 nights a week (alums include Rufus Wainwright and Bright Eyes). Friday through Sunday, though, the club becomes a Latino drag/trans hangout—which can be fun if that's how you roll, but if you're set on catching live music on weekends, you'll have to cruise elsewhere. *2906 Sunset Blvd., Silver Lake.* ☎ *323/663-9636. www.foldsilver lake.com. Daily 3pm–2am. Cover $0–$10. 21+ to enter.*

➜ **Spaceland** ★★★ This comfortable neighborhood hangout takes the outer-space gimmick all the way, so you'll see weird saucer-looking things hanging from the smoking area toward the back of the club and martini-swilling aliens painted on the bathroom doors. The first bands to grace the intimate stage (decorated high-school-dance-style with blue and gold metallic streamers) were Beck and Foo Fighters, in case that tells you anything about the club's pedigree. *1717 Silver Lake Blvd.* ☎ *323/661-4380. www.clubspaceland. com. Daily 8pm–2am. Cover $5–$15. 21+ to enter.*

➜ **Viper Room** ★ Founded by Johnny Depp in 1993, this live-music hot spot rose to infamy when River Phoenix OD'd on the sidewalk in front of the club. Still a popular spot with celebs and mere mortals, the club remains a spot for live music, and also hosts **Atmosphere** every Tuesday night, featuring the sounds of trance, drum and bass, garage, techno, and hip-hop spun by an eclectic assemblage of DJs, MCs, and mix masters. On Mondays, a head-banging tribute to '80s metal/hard rock shakes the walls. *8852 Sunset Blvd., West Hollywood.* ☎ *310/358-1881. www.viperroom.com. Cover $10. 21+ to enter.*

Elliott Smith Mural.

ALL-AGES ROCK CLUBS

→ **Troubadour** This West Hollywood mainstay radiates rock history—from the 1960s to the 1990s, the Troub really has seen 'em all. Audiences are consistently treated to memorable shows from the already-established or young-and-promising acts that take the Troubadour's stage. But bring your earplugs—this beer- and sweat-soaked club likes it loud. All ages are accepted. *9081 Santa Monica Blvd., West Hollywood.* ☎ *310/276-6168. www.troubadour. com. Cover varies $0–$20.*

→ **The Roxy** ★ Veteran record producer/executive Lou Adler opened this Sunset Strip club in the mid-1970s with concerts by Neil Young and a lengthy run of the pre-movie *Rocky Horror Show.* Since then, it's remained among the top showcase venues in Hollywood. *9009 W. Sunset Blvd.* ☎ *310/276-2222. www.theroxyonsunset.com. All ages. Cover varies $10–$30.*

A Tribute to Elliott Smith

Before October 21, 2003, the swaths of red and blue painted on the exterior of Solutions! Speaker Repair on Sunset Boulevard near Malo were just a visually interesting piece of public art that Elliott Smith used as the album cover to what would become the last record released while he was alive, "Figure 8." After his death that day, the mural became a makeshift memorial to the songwriter, with notes, candles, photos, empty bottles of Johnny Walker, and countless fan messages—"Elliott, your music made a difference to us," "Thank You Elliott"—scrawled right on the wall. *(Between 4334 and 4326 Sunset Blvd., between Fountain and Bates.)*

The Big LA (and beyond) Music Festivals

→ **Coachella:** It's not technically LA, more like Palm Springs, but this annual 2-day music festival held at the Empire Polo Fields in Indio is a must-attend event for many Southland music fans, causing a mass migration to the desert every spring in April or May. **www.coachella.com.**

→ **International Pop Overthrow:** This festival was started in LA but recently franchised to other cities like Chicago, New York, Nashville—even Liverpool, England. The fest books between 100 and 200 international pop bands at venues throughout the city every year in late July/early August. **www. internationalpopoverthrow.com.**

→ **Sunset Junction:** Held annually in August, this three-stage music festival in Silver Lake has featured entertainment from belly dancers, DJs, and a slew of bands like Fels, Black Rebel Motorcycle club, Hank III (Williams, that is!), and more. ☎ **323/661-7771** or visit **www.sunsetjunction.org** for info.

→ **Arthur Fest:** A 2-day music festival put on by the folks at *Arthur* magazine, this Silver Lake event began in 2005 with a full slate of up-and-coming rock acts. **www.arthurmag.com.**

→ LA radio station **KROQ** puts on two massive concerts each year: **Weenie Roast** in the summer and **Acoustic Christmas** in the winter. Look for the usual lineup of the day's trendiest rock, hip-hop, and reggae bands. **www. kroq.com.**

→ **Whisky A Go-Go** ★ This legendary bi-level venue personifies LA rock 'n' roll, from Jim Morrison and X to Guns N' Roses and Beck. Every trend has passed through this club, even though it's not what it was in its heyday. With the hiring of an in-house booker a few years ago, the Whisky began showcasing local talent on free-admission Monday nights. All ages are welcome. *8901 Sunset Blvd., West Hollywood.* ☎ *310/652-4202, ext. 15. www.whiskyagogo. com. Cover varies $10–$30.*

RECORD STORES

→ **Amoeba** Don't even walk in here if you're on any kind of timetable, 'cause this massive music emporium, imported from the Bay Area, is some kind of wormhole that sucks you in and doesn't spit you out until you've spent your whole paycheck on Radiohead rarities and obscure Death Cab 7-inches. With more than a half million CDs, records, and tapes, both new and used, it's easy for any rock fan to lose an afternoon at this two-story spot, which also hosts in-stores. *6400 W Sunset Blvd., near the Arclight.* ☎ *323/245-6400. www. amoebamusic.com. Mon–Sat 10:30am–11pm; Sun 11am–9pm.*

For more indie goods and in-stores, try **Fingerprints** in Long Beach (4612-B E. 2nd St.; ☎ 562/433-4996), **Rockaway Records** in Silver Lake (2395 Glendale Blvd.; ☎ 323/664-3232), and **Rhino Records** in Westwood (2028 Westwood Blvd.; ☎ 310/474-8685).

Sleeping

In sprawling Los Angeles, location is everything—don't book a hotel in Encino or El Segundo just because you found a good rate online. Stay close to the action with a centrally located hotel in Hollywood or West Hollywood, where there are plenty of

ROCKIN' THE WEST COAST

options in all price ranges, from ritzy Sunset Strip properties to the cheapie motel Jim Morrison once called home.

HOSTELS

➜ **Orbit Hotel** ★★ This place calls itself the "sexiest hostel in the world." I'm not so sure about that, but with a retro design scheme they describe as "Austin Powers meets the Jetsons," it definitely looks hipper than your average hostel. In the heart of the Melrose District, the two-story, 32-room Orbit is close to Melrose's abundant shopping. Private rooms have queen-size beds and TVs, while the dorms pack four to six beds in each room, each with a private bath and shower. Perks include free TV show tickets, free Wi-Fi, an upstairs lounge with big-screen TV and jukebox, regular BBQs and soccer games, an on-site cafe, and deals on car rental. *7950 Melrose Ave. (at Fairfax).* ☎ *800/4-HOSTEL or 323/655-1510. www.orbithotel.com. Dorms $20–$23; private rooms $59–69 single/$69–79 double, plus $20 key/linen deposit. Prices include tax. 30 rooms, 6 dorms with 4–6 beds each. Amenities: Free parking; cafe; shuttle; 24-hr. check-in (no curfew); Internet; bike rental; laundry; coffee/tea; lockers; luggage storage. In room: Private bathrooms, Wi-Fi.*

➜ **USA Hostels Hollywood** ★ Located just off the Walk of Fame in the center of Hollywood, this hostel's open to international travelers and out-of-state students only (non-California college ID required at check-in). With private bathrooms in every room, the hostel also has free Wi-Fi, a common area with TV and DVD player and foosball, plus a garden patio that hosts a thrice-weekly barbecue and free, all-you-can-make pancake breakfasts. There's also walking tours, a weekly pub crawl, and—this is key—no curfew. *1624 Schrader Blvd. (at Selma).* ☎ *800/524-6783. www.usahostels.*

com. Dorms $22–$25; private/semi-private rooms $54–$64 (online discounts available). Amenities: No curfew; shuttles/tours; Internet; Wi-Fi; games; laundry; common room w/TV/ DVD In room: Wi-Fi, private bath.

CHEAP

In addition to the listings below, there's a **Best Western** in Hollywood (6141 Franklin Ave. between Vine and Gower; ☎ **800/ 287-1700;** $129–$169 double), which as a great little cafe in the lobby, **101 Hills Coffee Shop,** and a centrally located **Days Inn** (7023 Sunset Blvd. between Highland and La Brea; ☎ **800/329-7466;** $120–$170 double; $135–$210 Jacuzzi suite), which is just east of the Sunset Strip.

➜ **Alta Cienega Motel** ★ Don't ask for room no. 32 unless you're a hard-core Doors fan and you don't mind other hard-core Doors fans knocking on your door asking to take a look around the room where Jim Morrison lived from 1968 to 1970 . . . in which case, have at it: The room's still decorated with the man's personal effects. Mr. Mojo Risin, indeed! *1005 N. La Cienega Blvd. (at Santa Monica).* ☎ *310/652-5797. www.altacienegamotel.com. $56–$60 single; $64–$69 double. Amenities: Continental breakfast; free parking. In room: High-speed Internet.*

➜ **Magic Castle Hotel** ★ Named for the illusionist club just uphill, this apartment building turned garden-style motel at the base of the Hollywood Hills offers LA's best cheap sleeps, but you won't see the Magic Castle Hotel in *Travel + Leisure* anytime soon—the rooms are done in high Levitz style. *7025 Franklin Ave. (between La Brea and Highland aves.).* ☎ *800/741-4915 or 323/851-0800. www.magiccastlehotel.com. 49 units. $129 double; $149–$239 suite. Parking $8. Amenities: Continental breakfast; pool; laundry. In room: Dataport, free Wi-Fi.*

DOABLE

Ⓜ️ ⬤ Best ⬤ ➔**Beverly Laurel Motor Hotel** ★★ With more style than your average motel, the budget-basic Beverly Laurel has well-kept rooms with diamond-print spreads and eye-catching artwork, plus a tiny pool that's a little public for carefree sunbathing, but it does the job on hot summer days. Nobody serves better burgers than the motel's own coffee shop, **Swingers** (p. 638), where it's not uncommon to find your fave alt-rocker tucking into a 3pm breakfast in the vinyl booth next to yours. *8018 Beverly Blvd. (between La Cienega Blvd. and Fairfax Ave.).* ☎ *800/ 962-3824 or 323/651–2441. 52 units. $89–$94 double. Free parking. Amenities: Heated outdoor pool; access to nearby health club; car-rental desk; laundry service. In room: Dataport, minifridge, microwave.*

➔ **Farmer's Daughter** ★★ Once a dumpy old motor lodge that housed contestants on *The Price Is Right* (CBS studios are right across the street), the Farmer's Daughter has since been renovated into a stylish boutique hotel. The hotel, whose former tenants include a pre-fame Charlize Theron, features a country-kitsch design scheme and its own French-country restaurant, **TART.** *115 S. Fairfax Ave. (between Beverly Dr. and 3rd St.).* ☎ *800/334-1658 or 323/937-3930. www.farmersdaughter hotel.com. 66 units. $129–$159 double; from $179 suite. Valet parking $12. Amenities: Restaurant/bar; coffee/tea; pool; concierge; laundry/dry cleaning. In room: CD player, complimentary DVD library, free high-speed Internet access, minifridge, personal safe.*

➔ **Roosevelt Hotel** ★★ This 12-story Hollywood landmark across from Grauman's Chinese was built in 1927 but enjoyed a renaissance recently thanks to a $15-million renovation and tabloid coverage of more than a few starlet spats that went down at the hotel's exclusive **Teddy's** and **Tropicana Bar,** located just off the Olympic-size pool, whose mural was originally painted by David Hockney. Rooms feature colorful extra-large bathrooms and dark-wood platform beds with luxurious Frette linens. The property's also home to an über-hip steakhouse called **Dakota** and a late-night burger bar called **25 Degrees.** *7000 Hollywood Blvd.* ☎ *800/950-7667 or 323/466-7000. www. hollywoodroosevelt.com. 302 units. $275–$340 double; from $405 suite. Valet parking $18. Amenities: 2 restaurants; 3 bars; pool/Jacuzzi; spa/gym; concierge; activities desk; 24-hr. room service; laundry/dry cleaning. In room: Video games, high-speed dataport, minibar.*

SPLURGE

➔**Beverly Hills Hotel** ★★★ Immortalized on the cover art for the Eagles' *Hotel California*, this star-studded haven (aka "the Pink Palace") was, and still is, center stage for Hollywood dealmakers, who can still be found lounging by the Olympic-size pool (into which Katharine Hepburn once dove fully clothed) and digging into Dutch apple pancakes in the iconic **Polo Lounge,** where Hunter S. Thompson kicked off his adventure to Las Vegas, and where Ozzy Osbourne has been known to sip his afternoon "tea." *9641 Sunset Blvd. (at Rodeo Dr.), Beverly Hills.* ☎ *800/283-8885 or 310/276-2251. www.beverlyhillshotel.com. 203 units. $440–$545 double; from $900 suite or bungalow. Parking $23. Amenities: 3 restaurants; bar; 2 lounges; pool; tennis courts; gym; spa; whirlpool; concierge; car-rental desk; courtesy limo; business center; 24-hr. room service; in-room or poolside massage; laundry/dry cleaning; video rentals. In room: CD player, fax/copier/scanner, DSL dataport, minibar.*

➔**Chateau Marmont** ★★★ Perched secretively in a curve above the Sunset Strip, the 1920s-era landmark has been the temporary residence for everyone from Jim Morrison and Maroon5's Adam Levine

ROCKIN' THE WEST COAST

I Love LA: More Festivals & Events

In such a huge city with so much diversity, LA's got a celebration for virtually every group of people or things your imagination can dream up:

→ **Tournament of Roses,** Pasadena: *You* know . . . the New Year's Day parade with lavish floats and music is followed by the Rose Bowl football game and a night-long party along Colorado Boulevard. ☎ 626/449-4100; www.tournamentofroses.com.

→ **Chinese New Year:** Dragon dancers and martial arts masters parade through the streets of Downtown's Chinatown in late January. ☎ 213/617-0396; www.lachinesechamber.org.

→ **Mardi Gras,** West Hollywood: The festivities—including live jazz and lots of food—take place along Santa Monica Boulevard in late February or early March. ☎ 800/368-6020.

→ **American Indian Festival and Market:** Traditional dances, storytelling, arts and crafts, and food come to the Los Angeles Natural History Museum in late March. ☎ 213/744-DINO.

→ **Toyota Grand Prix:** In mid-April, Long Beach hosts a weekend of Indy-class auto racing and entertainment, which draws world-class drivers, celebrity contestants, and spectators. ☎ 888/82-SPEED or www.long beachgp.com.

→ **Cinco de Mayo:** A carnival atmosphere with large crowds, live music, dancing, and food takes place throughout the city but mainly at El Pueblo de Los Angeles State Historic Park, Downtown; ☎ 213/628-1274. May 5.

to Lindsay Lohan and John Belushi, who overdosed in Bungalow no. 2. Even if you can't afford to stay in one of the quirky antiques-filled rooms, suites, cottages, or bungalows—many of which have fireplaces and kitchenettes—drop in for a drink and some sly celebrity-spotting in the hotel's newly renovated lobby and garden adjunct, **Bar Marmont.** *8221 Sunset Blvd. (between La Cienega and Crescent Heights).* ☎ *800/242-8328 or 323/656-1010. www.chateaumarmont.com. 63 units. From $335 double; from $425 suite; from $450 cottage; from $1,700 bungalow. Valet parking $21. Amenities: Restaurant; bar; pool w/sun deck; exercise room; 24-hr. concierge; business center; 24-hr. room service; in-room massage; laundry/dry cleaning; CD library; free Wi-Fi. In room: Dataport, minibar, fridge, laptop-size safe.*

→ **Hyatt West Hollywood** ★★ The debauched history of this legendary 13-story Sunset Strip hotel—formerly called the "Riot House" or the "Riot Hyatt" back when members of Led Zeppelin rode motorcycles through the lobby—was all but erased by a $7-million renovation in 1997. Back in the day, Little Richard lived in the penthouse and the place looked like something out of *Almost Famous* (which was filmed on the premises). These days, rooms have smart decor and generic but just-fine comforts; suites have wet bars and groovy tropical aquariums built into the wall. The rooftop pool is a killer perch for peeping into the nearby hillside luxury homes, and the hotel's chic dim sum restaurant, **CHI,** is co-owned by Justin

→ **Venice Art Walk:** This nearly 30-year-old festival takes place in Venice's galleries and studios every year in late May. ☎ **310/392-WALK;** www.venicefamilyclinic.org.

→ **Long Beach Lesbian & Gay Pride Parade:** Shoreline Park in Long Beach hosts this annual May event, which features music, dancing, food, and more than 100 decorated floats. ☎ **562/987-9191.**

→ **Playboy Jazz Festival:** Traditionally emceed by Bill Cosby, this mid-June event draws top jazz musicians to the Hollywood Bowl. ☎ **213/480-3232.**

→ **Beach Festival,** Huntington Beach: This 2-week-long event at the end of July features two surfing competitions—the U.S. Open of Surfing and the world-class Pro of Surfing—plus extreme sports like BMX biking, skateboarding, and more. ☎ **714/969-3492;** www.surfcityusa.com.

→ **Festival of Arts & Pageant of the Masters:** A 60-plus-year tradition in artsy Laguna Beach, this summer festival centers on a performance-art re-creation of famous old masters paintings (as seen on *Arrested Development!*). ☎ **800/487-FEST;** www.foaporn.com.

→ **Hollywood Film Festival:** Fifty-plus international films screen while celebs and up-and-coming filmmakers attend workshops, parties, and markets in October. ☎ **310/288-1882;** www.hollywoodawards.com.

Timberlake. *8401 Sunset Blvd. (at Kings Rd., 2 blocks east of La Cienega).* ☎ *800/633-7313 or 323/656-1234. www.westhollywood.hyatt.com. 262 units. $170–$290 double; from $325 suite. Valet parking $25; self-parking $18. Amenities: Indoor/outdoor restaurant; bar; rooftop pool; exercise room; concierge; business center; room service; laundry/dry cleaning. In room: Dataport; Wi-Fi, safe.*

Eating

SUPPLIES

→ **Bristol Farms** This gourmet grocer, a Southland minichain, is the place to go when you need to pick up rare imported cheeses and mango chutney on your way to a chichi party in the Hollywood Hills. Or just gawk at celebrities doing the same thing. *7880 Sunset Blvd.* ☎ *323/874-6301. www.bristolfarms.com. Daily 8am–11pm.*

→ **Farmers Market** ★★ Lettering that reads "Meet me at Third and Fairfax" indicates your arrival at the 70-year-old farmers market near The Grove mall. The huge market features vendors selling fresh flowers and produce, meats, poultry, and seafood plus ready-made treats—everything from BBQ and crepes to gumbo and ice cream. *6333 W. 3rd (at Fairfax).* ☎ *323/933-9211. www.farmersmarketla.com. Mon–Fri 9am–9pm; Sat 9am–8pm; Sun 10am–7pm.*

→ **Rock 'n' roll Ralph's** Okay, so officially it's just "Ralph's," but this Sunset Strip grocery store is widely referred to as Rock 'n' roll Ralph's for its proximity to Guitar Center and various other music shops in the area, as well as its black-clad, dyed-hair, guitar-case-toting clientele. The supermarket in the movie *Go* was supposedly based on this grocery store. *7257*

ROCKIN' THE WEST COAST

Sunset Blvd. (at Poinsettia). ☎ 323/512-8382. Open 24 hr.

TAKEOUT TREATS

➔ **Joan's on Third** This awesome deli, a one-time Kirsten Dunst/Jake Gyllenhaal fave, has tempting cupcakes, build-your-own sandwiches, and a deli with new gourmet offerings every day: You'll find dishes like Korean short ribs, mac & cheese, curried chicken salad, exotic mushrooms, couscous, and more. *Tip:* There's parking out back, and you can call ahead to place your order if you already know what you want. 8350 W. 3rd St. (between La Cienega and Fairfax). ☎ 323/655-2285; www.joansonthird. com. Mon–Sat 10am–8pm; Sun 11am–6pm.

➔ **Pink's Hot Dogs** ★★ This crusty, iconic corner shop has lines down the block (even at midnight) and its own valet, who deftly parks the luxury cars driven by patrons craving one of Pink's 24 varieties of politically incorrect hot dogs, many of which are named after celebrities (the "Martha Stewart" is a 10-incher with mustard, relish, onions, chopped tomatoes, sauerkraut, bacon, and sour cream). Bruce Willis reportedly proposed to Demi Moore in the parking lot. 709 N. La Brea Ave. (at Melrose Ave.). ☎ 323/931-4223. www.pinks hollywood.com. Chili dog $2.65. No credit cards. Sun–Thurs 9:30am–2am; Fri–Sat 9:30am–3am.

RESTAURANTS
Cheap

➔ **El Coyote Café** ★ MEXICAN The bar scene alone is a great reason to hang out at this popular (yet cheap) family-run Mexican joint. The fare is traditional Mexican and well prepared; recommended plates include the enchilada Howard smothered with chile con carne, ostrich tacos (yes, ostrich), and sizzling fajita platters washed down with (duh) a margarita—or six. 7312 Beverly Blvd. (at N. Poinsettia Place).

☎ 323/939-2255. www.elcoyotecafe.com. Entrees $8–$10. Mon–Thurs and Sun 11am–10pm; Fri–Sat 11am–11pm.

📺 Best 🏆 ➔ **King's Road** ★★ AMERICAN My favorite of LA's many great, affordable breakfast cafes, King's Road is a mellow, celeb-friendly hangout with a few sidewalk tables and a menu packed with the usual breakfast fare, plus healthy stuff like an egg-white scramble with garden burger crumbles, a savory chicken-sausage omelet, and a huge vegetarian burrito. 8361 Beverly Blvd. (at Kings). ☎ 323/655-9044. Breakfast $4.25–$11; entrees $11–$14. Mon–Sat 7:30am–10pm; Sun 7:30am–7pm.

➔ **Swingers** ★★ DINER The Beverly Laurel Motor Hotel's adjacent coffee shop serves typical greasy-spoon fare alongside signature offerings like the high-octane Rocket Shake (complete with espresso-bean crunchies) and tofu-enhanced vegetarian dishes. I once spotted one of the Madden twins from Good Charlotte—I'm not sure which—browsing the jukebox, which kicks out jams ranging from punk rock to *Schoolhouse Rock.* 8020 Beverly Blvd. (west of Fairfax Ave.). ☎ 323/653-5858. www.swingersdiner.com. Most items less than $8. Daily 6am–4am.

➔ **Toi on Sunset** ★★ THAI Because it's open *really* late, Toi has become a fave of Hollywood hipsters who make post-clubbing excursions to this rock 'n' roll eatery a few blocks from the Sunset Strip. Menu highlights include hot-and-sour chicken, coconut soup, and the house specialty: chicken curry *somen,* a spicy dish with green curry and mint sauce spooned over thin Japanese rice noodles. 7505½ Sunset Blvd. (at Gardner St.). ☎ 323/874-8062. www. toirockinthaifood.com. Main courses $6–$11. Daily 11am–4am.

Doable

➔ **Michelangelo's** ★★ ITALIAN This place serves average Italian fare with nice ambience and sidewalk seating on Silver Lake Boulevard down the block from Spaceland. *1637 Silver Lake Blvd.* ☎ *901/272-7111. Reservations recommended. Main courses $14–$24. Mon–Fri 11am–3pm; brunch Sat 10am–2pm, Sun 10am–3pm; dinner Mon–Thurs 5–10pm; Fri–Sat 5–11pm.*

➜ **Rainbow Bar & Grill** ★ AMERICAN A former hair-band hangout in the '80s, this Sunset Strip joint is decorated with all kinds of rock memorabilia, from gold records to autographed photos of metal greats. Slash has his own corner table here, and Motorhead's Lemmy Killmeister still hangs out. The menu is standard fare: chicken, steaks, fish, and spaghetti, plus everyone's favorite: pizza. *9015 Sunset Blvd.* ☎ *310/278-4232. www.rainbowbarandgrill.com. Salads $6–$11; entrees $14–$35. Mon–Fri 11am–2am; Sat–Sun 5pm–2am. 21+ to enter.*

Splurge

➜ **Cha Cha Cha** ★★ CARIBBEAN/CUBAN Housed in fun and funky space on the seedy fringe of downtown, Cha Cha Cha is an eclectic hodgepodge of pulsating Caribbean music, wild decor, and kaleidoscopic clutter. Try the spicy black-pepper jumbo shrimp, saffron paella, or breakfast offerings like plantain, yucca, onion, and herb omelets or scrambled eggs with fresh tomatillos served on hot grilled tortillas. *656 N. Virgil Ave. (at Melrose Ave.), Silver Lake.* ☎ *323/664-7723. Main courses $12–$22. Sun–Thurs 8am–10pm; Fri–Sat 8am–11pm. Valet parking $3.50.*

🎬 **Best ◉** ➜ **Il Sole** ★★★ ITALIAN I'll admit it: I first started coming here in hopes of eating carpaccio in Jennifer Aniston's immediate vicinity, since it's well known the actress and Brad used to chow down at this cozy Italian joint, which is partially owned by Bowie/Rolling Stones booking agent Andrew Hewitt. But the stellar penne *arrabiatta* and non-pretentious atmosphere—plus super-low, super-flattering

lighting—keep me coming back. *8741 Sunset Blvd. (at Sherbourne).* ☎ *310/657-1182. Starters $11–$26; entrees $19–$44. Mon–Fri noon–3pm and 6–11pm; Sat 6–11pm; Sun 5:30–10pm.*

Partying

Where to party in LA all depends on the kind of experience you're going for. If you want to do it up Lohan-style, there's no shortage of velvet-rope nightclubs where tipsy starlets dance on banquettes while packs of paparazzi stalk the exits hoping for the money shot. But if you're only in town for a night or two and don't want to waste hours waiting in line for a club like that, I've included some slightly less scene-y places too, many of which are in easy stumbling distance of the live venues listed above.

BARS & PUBS

L.A. bars generally close at 2am, the legal limit for booze sales in California. Most regular bars won't charge a cover unless there's some kind of entertainment being offered—bands, DJs, strippers—in which case you might pay anywhere from $3 to $20. But even then you can sometimes avoid paying the cover if you arrive early—before 9 or 10 p.m.

➜ **Burgundy Room** ★★ Of the three bars nearest the Hotel Café, this is my favorite. The loud, narrow DJ/jukebox bar has a ridiculously tiny "dance floor" (anywhere else such limited square footage would hardly qualify as a bathroom stall) but that doesn't stop some liquored up patrons from trying. *1621 ½ N. Cahuenga Blvd. (at Selma).* ☎ *323/465-7530. Daily 8pm–2am. 21+ to enter.*

➜ **Cha Cha** ★★ This one-time Silver Lake gay bar hosts more hipsters than queens these days; descended from Seattle's original kitsch-mad Tiki hut, the Cha Cha's a chill place to see, be seen, and sip fruity drinks worthy of a tiny umbrella. *2375*

Glendale Blvd. (at Silver Lake). ☎ *323/660-7595. www.chachalounge.com. Daily 5pm–2am. 21+ to enter.*

➔ **El Carmen** ★★ Opened by LA restaurant-and-bar impresario Sean Macpherson, the man with the mescal touch, El Carmen conjures the feel of a back-alley Mexican cantina of a bygone era. Vintage Mexican movie posters, vibrant Latin American colors, and oil paintings of masked Mexican wrestlers decorate the Quonset-hut interior, while an eclectic jukebox offers an array of tunes from Tito Puente to the Foo Fighters. The busy bar boasts a gargantuan list of more than 100 tequilas and a small menu of tacos and light fare. *8138 W. 3rd St., Los Angeles.* ☎ *323/852-1552. Mon–Fri 5pm–2am; Sat–Sun 7pm–2am; no to minimal cover charge.*

➔ **Forty Deuce** Owner Ivan Kane reopened this suave nightclub, formerly known as Kane. Designed as "back-alley, striptease lounge," the low bar, lounge chair seating, vintage brass registers, and cocktail tables with chic lamps all chip in to create a sexy, burlesque-esque vibe. Dancers use the bar as a runway, so watch your cocktail. *5574 Melrose Ave., Hollywood.* ☎ *323/465-4242. www.fortydeuce.com. Wed–Sat 9pm–2am; cover varies $10–$20.*

➔ **Red Lion Tavern** ★★ A hidden veteran of the Silver Lake circuit, this kitschy, over-the-top German tavern—complete with dirndl-clad waitresses—is where neighborhood hipsters mingle with cranky, working-class German expats. The place serves hearty half-liters of Warsteiner, Becks, and Bitburger, but braver souls—with bottomless bladders—can take on a 1.5-liter boot. The astonishingly good food offerings include schnitzel, bratwurst, and potato pancakes. *2366 Glendale Blvd., Silver Lake.* ☎ *323/662-5337. Daily 11am–2am; no cover.*

➔ **Tropicana** ★★ You'll recognize the Hotel Roosevelt's poolside bar from its innumerable mentions in *Us Weekly* as the backdrop to catfights between this or that Hollywood starlet du jour—that is, *if* you can get past the velvet rope. *7000 Hollywood Blvd.* ☎ *323/769-7260. www.hollywoodroosevelt.com. Daily 7am–6pm and 9pm–2am.*

➔ **Velvet Margarita** ★ This funky, late-night Mexican cantina has a fondness for Elvis and a bevy of quality margaritas on the menu, along with fresh Latin dishes like seviche. *1612 N Cahuenga Blvd.* ☎ *323/469-2000. Sun–Wed 11am–2am; Thurs–Sat 11am–4am.*

DANCE CLUBS

LA goes through hot spots like Kleenex; by the time you read this half these places might have new names or just be "so over." The cover charge can be anywhere from $10 to $30 and, once inside, drink prices are steep as well, around $10 or more for cocktails, less for beer.

Open up the nearest celeb tabloid to figure out where the Olsen twins and Jessica Simpson are partying this week; some recent "it" joints include **LAX** (1714 Las Palmas Ave; ☎ **323/464-0171**), **Guy's** (8713 Beverly Blvd; ☎ **818/766-8311**), **Mood** (6623 Hollywood Blvd; ☎ **323/465-3336**), and **Hyde** (8029 W Sunset Blvd; ☎ **323/655-8000**).

➔ **The Conga Room** Attracting such Latin-music luminaries as Pucho & The Latin Soul Brothers, this one-time health club on the Miracle Mile has quickly become *the* nightspot for live salsa and merengue. In the dining room a chef serves up savory Cuban fare in a setting that conjures the romance of pre-Castro Cuba; there's also a stylish cigar lounge. *5364 Wilshire Blvd., Los Angeles.* ☎ *323/938-1696. www.congaroom.com.*

→ **Nacional** ★ Co-owned by a guy who grew up in the Playboy mansion, Nacional is one of Hollywood's most desirable dance floors. The Cuba-inspired club hosts a hip and gorgeous crowd in its modernist, marble-and-wrought-iron-bedecked interior. *1645 Wilcox Ave., Hollywood.* ☎ *323/962-7712.*

→ **Star Shoes** ★ From the same club gurus who run Beauty Bar around the corner, Star Shoes is a combo shoe store and dance club that's usually packed with a trendy young crowd who bump around the narrow dance floor, and the DJs are among the best in town. *6364 Hollywood Blvd., Hollywood.* ☎ *323/462-7827. www.starshoes. org.*

What Else to See & Do

As much as everybody who lives in LA might talk about how much they hate it, there's so much to do here, there's really no reason to leave. And, again, we urge you to break up even the most rockin' roadtrip by getting out and about in the cities you pass through.

There's a ton of culture in the city—not to mention great shopping, sports, and that whole outdoor thing (with the waves and the mountains and the surfing, the, you know, California stuff . . .) and, of course, (Hollywood) star-gazing.

THE TOP ATTRACTIONS

The heart of LA rock history can be found along the **Sunset Strip,** a 1³/₄-mile stretch of Sunset Boulevard from Crescent Heights Boulevard to Doheny Drive. It includes sites like the **Comedy Store;** the **Argyle Hotel,** where Clark Gable, Marilyn Monroe, and John Wayne once lived; and, of course, clubs like the **Viper Room,** the **Whiskey,** and **House of Blues.** Farther east on Sunset is the **Hollywood Rock Walk** near

Guitar Center (7425 Sunset Blvd.; ☎ **323/874-1060**), where superstars like Chuck Berry, Little Richard, Santana, and the Van Halen brothers left handprints or signatures.

Visiting a celebrity gravesite can either be a morbid or moving experience. Roy Orbison and Dean Martin are just two of the musicians buried at **Westwood Memorial Park** (1218 Glendon Ave., Westwood; ☎ **310/474-1579**), whose other famous residents include Rodney Dangerfield, Don Knotts, Natalie Wood, and Marilyn Monroe. Johnny and Dee Dee Ramone are laid to rest at **Hollywood Forever** (6000 Santa Monica Blvd.; ☎ **323/243-2366**), which is also the backdrop for one of LA's weirder social events, **Cinespia.** The outdoor cemetery movie screenings draw more than 1,000 people every Saturday in the summertime. See www.cinespia.org for info.

FREE → **Capitol Records Building** Opened in 1956, this 13-story tower, just north of the legendary intersection of Hollywood and Vine, is one of the city's most recognizable buildings. The world's first circular office building is often, but incorrectly, said to have been made to resemble a stack of 45s under a turntable stylus (it kinda does, though). Nat "King" Cole, songwriter Johnny Mercer, and other 1950s Capitol artists populate a giant exterior mural. Look down and you'll see the sidewalk stars of Capitol's recording artists (including John Lennon). In the lobby, numerous gold albums are on display. *1750 Vine St.* ☎ *323/462-6252.*

FREE → **The Getty Center Los Angeles** ★★ Since opening in 1997, the Richard Meier—designed Getty Center has become LA's cultural acropolis and international mecca. Perched on a hillside in the Santa Monica mountains, the post-modernist complex is most frequently visited for the museum galleries displaying collector J. Paul Getty's enormous collection of art: antiquities, Impressionist paintings (including van Gogh's *Irises*), glimmering French furniture, contemporary photography, and more. Visitors to the center can park at the base of the hill and ascend via a cable-driven electric tram; once inside, grab a GettyGuide at the information desk. It's a handheld multimedia system that looks like an orange iPod and comes loaded with various ready-to-go tours—use of it, and admission, are free. Cameras and video cams are permitted, but only if you use existing light (no flash). *1200 Getty Center Dr., Los Angeles.* ☎ *310/440-7300. www.getty.edu. Free admission. Tues–Thurs and Sun 10am–6pm; Fri–Sat 10am–9pm. Closed major holidays. Parking $7.*

PLAYING OUTSIDE

For the LA coastal experience, head west toward the beach towns of Santa Monica and Venice. Ride the Ferris wheel at the **Santa Monica Pier,** then walk, bike, or skate down to **Venice Beach** via a paved pedestrian Promenade, which becomes Ocean Front Walk and gets progressively weirder until it reaches an apex at Washington Boulevard and the Venice fishing pier. Some people swim and sunbathe in Venice, but the area's character is really defined by the characters on the Ocean Front Walk. To get there, take the 10 West to the Fourth Avenue exit. Or stay central and get your exercise with a hike up **Runyon Canyon,** a 130-acre park just off Hollywood Boulevard with hiking trails offering views of the Hollywood sign, the Sunset Strip, and the Capitol Records building, to name a few landmarks. Access the park via the Vista Street entrance just beyond Franklin Avenue.

SPECTATOR SPORTS
Baseball

Five-time World Series champs the **Los Angeles Dodgers** (☎ 323/224-1448; http://losangeles.dodgers.mlb.com) play at the old-school Dodger Stadium (1000 Elysian Park near Sunset Blvd.), which is known for its ginormous Dodger dogs.

The newly renamed **Los Angeles Angels of Anaheim** (☎ 888/796-HALO; http://losangeles.angels.mlb.com) play American League ball at Anaheim Stadium (2000 S. State College Blvd. near Katella Ave.), in Anaheim, about 30 minutes from Downtown LA. The regular Major League baseball season runs from April to October.

Basketball

Los Angeles has two NBA franchises: the upstart **LA Clippers** (www.clippers.com), who've never won a championship, and the LA Lakers, who've won 14. Both teams play in the **STAPLES Center** in Downtown LA (1111 S. Figueroa St.) for celebrity fans like Jack Nicholson, Leonardo DiCaprio, Heather Locklear, and Dyan Cannon. For tickets to see either team, call ☎ **213/742-7340** or log on to www.staplescenter.com.

The WNBA also plays in LA, with perennial contenders the **LA Sparks** (led by All-Star and Olympic gold medalist Lisa Leslie) also resident in the Staples Center from May to September (**www.wnba.com/sparks**).

Horse Racing

Located just down the road from LAX, the scenic **Hollywood Park Racetrack** (1050 S. Prairie Ave., in Inglewood (☎ **310/419-1500**; www.hollywoodpark.com), features thoroughbred racing from mid-April to July, as well as from mid-November through mid-December.

Ice Hockey

The **LA Kings** (☎ 888/546-4752; www.lakings.com) hold court at the STAPLES

Center home; down the road in Orange County, the **Anaheim Ducks** (☎ 714/940-2900; www.anaheimducks.com) play at the Arrowhead Pond in Anaheim. The hockey season typically runs from October through mid-April, with playoffs following.

On the Road to San Francisco, CA

Los Angeles to San Francisco, 390 miles

Tell people you're driving from LA to San Francisco and you'll automatically get the question: "101 or 5?"—a reference to the two main routes connecting NorCal and SoCal. Though I like Highway 101, some will tell you the coastal freeway takes "like a thousand years longer" than the more direct but also hotter, smellier, and more treacherous Interstate 5, whose winding, 18-wheeler filled, ulcer-inducing pass known as the Grapevine is notorious for its high accident rate (admittedly, conditions have improved since the road was widened). In my experience, it's only about 30 to 60 minutes longer on the 101, but it's *so* worth it.

Leaving Hollywood, the 101, like any LA freeway, can get congested, but it clears up as you head north and it stays manageable until Santa Barbara, when it can get bunched up again (watch for speed traps). On this mostly 70-mph route, you'll see great ocean vistas in Ventura and Pismo Beach, which is a good place for a pit stop—try **Old West Cinnamon Rolls** on Pacific Coast Highway for warm, gooey cinnamon treats (861 Dolliver St.; ☎ 800/959-6133).

On the Road Nuts & Bolts

Where to Fill Up   Anywhere but Santa Barbara—gas is pricey there! There are lots of gas stations off the 101 near Highway 156 in Prunedale, by which point you may be reaching the bottom of the tank if you filled up in LA.

The Fastest Way   I-5 all the way to San Francisco. This route is hotter, less scenic, and more stressful through the Grapevine. It'll take you about 5 hours, depending on how heavy your foot is and how many stops you make.

The Long Way Round   Taking Highway 101 along the coast is much more scenic and only a little bit longer than I-5; if you have an extra hour to spare, go this way. If you have a few extra hours to spare, try taking Highway 1, which literally hugs the coast the entire way (p. 647). This could take anywhere from 8 to 10 hours or more depending on traffic.

Rules of the Road   Know your carpool lane rules; some areas always require two people in the HOV (High Occupancy Vehicle) lane, others only during rush hour. Watch those signs.

Watch out for steep grades just north of Santa Barbara, and shut your windows and car vents approaching Gilroy, the self-proclaimed garlic capital of the world.

Gridlock hits again getting in to San Jose and is generally pretty hellish throughout the Bay Area. Staying on 101 will take you all the way into the heart of San Francisco, but you can sometimes avoid traffic by taking 85 North to 280 North into the city—it's a greener, more scenic way to go.

Recharge with an iced latte from **Coffee Society** (21265 Stevens Creek Blvd.; ☎ **408/725-8091**) in Cupertino: Just exit 85 at Stevens Creek before the ramp to 280.

Welcome to San Francisco

San Francisco's one of the best cities in the world, even with all that annoying fog. Don't get me wrong, the city has its share of gorgeous, sunny summer days; but it's no surprise to find yourself considering a scarf and mittens on your way out on an August evening while people in San Jose, just 50 miles south, are flirting with heat stroke. What I like best about SF is the number and variety of neighborhoods packed into 46 square miles on the tip of the Peninsula—from bustling ethnic nabes like Chinatown and North Beach to the vibrant, gay-friendly Castro to the increasingly yuppified Mission and South of Market (SOMA) districts. Watch your back in the Tenderloin, which in addition to being home to some great music venues, bars, and hotels, is also a favorite hang for some of the city's sassiest hookers.

San Francisco Nuts & Bolts

Area Code The area code for San Francisco is 415; for Oakland, Berkeley, and much of the East Bay, 510; for the peninsula, generally 650. Napa and Sonoma are 707. Most phone numbers in this book are in San Francisco's 415 area code, but there's no need to dial it if you're within city limits.

Business Hours Most banks are open Monday through Friday from 9am to 5pm. Most stores are open Monday through Saturday from 10 or 11am to at least 6pm, with shorter hours on Sunday. But there are exceptions: Stores in Chinatown, Ghirardelli Square, and PIER 39 stay open much later during the tourist season, and large department stores, including Macy's and Nordstrom, keep late hours.

Doctors **Saint Francis Memorial Hospital,** 900 Hyde St., between Bush and Pine streets on Nob Hill (☎ 415/353-6000), provides emergency service 24 hours a day; no appointment is necessary. The hospital also operates a **physician-referral service** (☎ 800/333-1355 or 415/353-6566).

Drugstores **Walgreens** pharmacies are all over town, including one at 135 Powell St. (☎ 415/391-4433). The store is open Monday through Friday from 7am to midnight and Saturday and Sunday from 8am to midnight; the pharmacy is open Monday through Friday from 8am to 9pm, Saturday from 9am to 5pm; it's closed on Sunday. The branch on Divisadero Street at Lombard (☎ 415/931-6415) has a 24-hour pharmacy.

Earthquakes There will always be earthquakes in California, most of which you'll never notice. However, in case of a significant shaker, there are a few basic precautionary measures you should know. When you are inside a building, seek cover; do not run outside. Stand under a doorway or against a wall, and stay away from windows. If you exit a building after a substantial quake, use stairwells, not elevators. If you are in your car, pull over to the side of the road and stop—but not until you are away from bridges, overpasses, telephone poles, and power lines. Stay in your car. If you're out walking, stay outside and away from trees, power lines, and the sides of buildings. If you're in an area with tall buildings, find a doorway in which to stand.

Emergencies   Dial ☎ **911** for police, an ambulance, or the fire department; no coins are needed from a public phone.

Internet Access   Surprisingly, San Francisco has very few Internet cafes. However, there are locations around town where you can get online access, perhaps with a sandwich and a cup o' joe. You can do your laundry, listen to music, dine, and check your stocks online at SoMa's **Brainwash,** 1122 Folsom St., between Seventh and Eighth streets (☎ 415/861-FOOD). It's open Monday through Friday from 7am to 11pm and Saturday and Sunday from 7:30am to noon; rates are $3 for 20 minutes. For access without the ambience, try **Copy Central,** 110 Sutter St., at Montgomery Street (☎ 415/392-6470), which provides access cards costing 20¢ per minute. It's open Monday through Thursday from 8am to 8pm and Friday from 8am to 7pm. Ditto **Kinko's,** 1967 Market St., near Gough Street (☎ 415/252-0864), which charges 25¢ per minute. Both of these companies have numerous locations around town. If you've got wireless access, you're in luck. Most major hotels have wireless access in their lobbies as well as their rooms, so if you stroll into a hotel lobby and pull up a sofa, you can almost always get instantly connected.

Laundry   Most hotels offer laundry service. But if you want to save money you can easily tote your gear to a local laundromat or dry cleaner. Ask your hotel for the nearest location—they're all over town. Or for a scene with your suds, go to SoMa's **Brainwash,** 1122 Folsom St., between Seventh and Eighth streets (☎ 415/861-FOOD). It's open Monday through Friday from 7am to 11pm and Saturday and Sunday from 7:30am to noon and also offers music, food, and online access.

Liquor Laws   Liquor stores and grocery stores, as well as some drugstores, can sell packaged alcoholic beverages between 6am and 2am daily. Most restaurants, night-clubs, and bars are licensed to serve alcoholic beverages during the same hours. The legal age for purchase and consumption of alcohol is 21; proof of age is required.

Newspapers & Magazines   The city's main daily is the *San Francisco Chronicle,* which is distributed throughout the city. Check out the Chronicle's massive Sunday edition that includes a pink "Datebook" section—an excellent preview of the week's upcoming events. The free weekly *San Francisco Bay Guardian* and *San Francisco Weekly,* tabloids of news and listings, are indispensable for nightlife information; they're widely distributed through street-corner kiosks and at city cafes and restaurants.

Police   For emergencies, dial ☎ **911** from any phone; no coins are needed. For other matters, call ☎ 415/553-0123.

Safety   San Francisco, like any other large city, has its fair share of crime, but most folks luckily don't have firsthand horror stories. In some areas, you need to exercise extra caution, particularly at night—notably the Tenderloin, the Western Addition (south of Japantown), the Mission District (especially around 16th and Mission sts.), the lower Fillmore area (also south of Japantown), around lower Haight Street, and around the Civic Center. In addition, there are a substantial number of homeless people throughout the city, with concentrations in and around Union Square, the Theater District (3 blocks west of Union Square), the Tenderloin, and Haight Street, so don't be alarmed if you're approached for spare change. Just use common sense. For additional crime-prevention information, phone **San Francisco SAFE** (☎ 415/553-1984).

Smoking   Since 1998, smoking has been prohibited in restaurants and bars. Hotels are also offering more nonsmoking rooms, which often leaves those who like to puff out in the cold—sometimes literally.

Taxes   An 8.5% sales tax is added at the register for all goods and services purchased in San Francisco. The city hotel tax is a whopping 14%. There is no airport tax.

Time Zone   San Francisco is in the Pacific Standard Time zone, which is 8 hours behind Greenwich Mean Time and 3 hours behind Eastern Standard Time. To find out what time it is, call ☎ 415/767-8900.

Transit Information   The San Francisco Municipal Railway, better known as **MUNI,** operates the city's cable cars, buses, and streetcars. For customer service, call ☎ 415/673-6864 weekdays from 6am to 8pm, weekends from 8am to 6pm. At other times, you can call this number to get recorded information.

Getting Around

BY CAR

With steep hills, scarce parking, and some of the world's crookedest streets, San Francisco is not a drivin' town. Park the car, and get around by other means when you are here. You can try your hand at public transit, but this city's best seen on foot and, especially in sketchy neighborhoods and at night, from the backseat of a cab.

BY MUNI

This is how the locals get around if they don't drive. MUNI, short for San Francisco Municipal Railway, refers to SF's system of streetcars, buses, and cable cars. Fares are $1.50 for buses, which can get you most anywhere in the city but tend to get pretty crowded during rush hour and on weekends. The Metro Streetcars run underground along Market Street downtown, serving the Mission, the Castro, Golden Gate Park, SFSU, and outlying areas. Many locals wouldn't be caught dead on the cable car, but if you want to do it just for the experience you'll have to shell out $5 and be prepared to wait. The cable car's three lines include the tourist-filled Powell-Hyde and Powell-Mason cars, which basically run from Union Square to Fisherman's Wharf, and the more commuter-oriented California, which runs through the financial district and Chinatown. Call ☎ **415/673-MUNI** or visit www.sfmuni.com for schedules and route information.

BY TAXI

Taxis are the transport of choice in SF if you're out on the town. Flagging one down is generally pretty easy in touristy areas like Fisherman's Wharf and North Beach; to call your own, try **Veteran's Cab** (☎ 415/552-1300), **Yellow Cab** (☎ 415/626-2345), **DeSoto Cab** (☎ 415/970-1300), or **Luxor Cab** (☎ 415/282-4141). Rates are $2.85 for the first mile; 45¢ each $1/5$ of a mile after (verify).

Detour: Coastal Highway 1

If you have some serious time to spare, one of the most beautiful coastal drives *ever* exists along the Central Coast on Highway 1, which splits from the 101 at San Luis Obispo and runs all the way to San Francisco. This route takes you past **Hearst Castle** ★★★, the 115-room mansion of newspaper magnate William Randolph Hearst that hosted luminaries like Charles Lindbergh, Harpo Marx, Douglas Fairbanks Jr., Jean Harlow, Clark Gable, and others. A few miles up the road is scenic **Big Sur,** whose picturesque craggy cliffs have inspired everyone from Jack Kerouac, who wrote a novel about the place, to the Red Hot Chili Peppers, who name-checked the town in their 1999 single "Road Trippin'."

If you're making a night of it in Big Sur, splurge on dinner at **Nepenthe** (48510 Hwy 1; ☎ 831/667-2345; www.nepenthebigsur.com) and a stay at the ultra-upscale **Post Ranch Inn** (☎ 831/667-2200; www.postranchinn.com), a favorite among celebrities and well-heeled adventure travelers, or consider a meditative yoga retreat at **Esalen Institute** (55000 Hwy 1; ☎ 831/ 667-3000; www.esalen. org). North of Big Sur is posh **Carmel,** whose village-like downtown is the very definition of "quaint"—quirky, too: The town actually enacted a law that requires people to obtain a permit to wear high heels (no word on how strictly that one's enforced, though).

Next up: foggy **Monterey**—best known for its aquarium and for being the backdrop to many a John Steinbeck novel—which eventually gives way to hippy **Santa Cruz,** a fantastic place to spend an afternoon sipping organic green tea, thrift-store shopping, or riding the wooden Giant Dipper roller coaster, a National Historic Landmark that's been featured in movies like *The Lost Boys.* In Santa Cruz, Highway 1 changes its name to Cabrillo Highway and winds through **Half Moon Bay** and **Pacifica** before merging with Interstate 280 just south of San Francisco. Traveling this route takes a lot longer and the road's a lot more winding than the average freeway, so make sure you're alert and well-caffeinated before your tackle these curves.

Punks, Hippies & Hipsters: The SF Rock Scene

The Bay Area's rock history is long and colorful, going back to the golden days of Haight-Ashbury, the Dead, and thousands of epic '60s-era shows at the Fillmore. In the '80s, bands like Journey and Faith No More put the Bay Area on the map, and more recently, the city's been a haven for punk (NOFX's Fat Wreck Chords is headquartered here, while Green Day's Billie Joe Armstrong cut his teeth across the bay in Berkeley's legendary 924 Gilman Street), pop (Third Eye Blind was spawned in the city), hip-hop (rapper E-40 brought hyphy to the mainstream in 2006), and indie rock (SF's Deerhoof opened the Radiohead tour, and Rogue Wave's been making its own waves from its Oakland home base).

The hipsters here know their music, but don't let that intimidate you—somehow the crowds in SF are still more laid-back than in Southern California.

THE CLUBS

🅼 Best ● → **Bottom of the Hill** ★★★
Voted one of the best places to hear live rock in the city by the *San Francisco Bay Guardian,* this popular neighborhood club attracts an eclectic crowd ranging from rockers to real-estate salespeople.

San Francisco Highlights

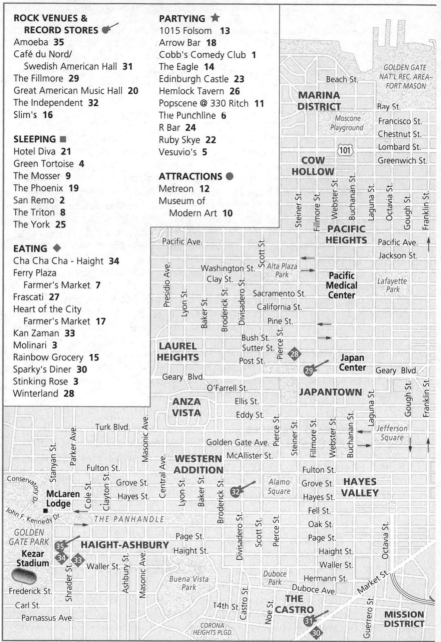

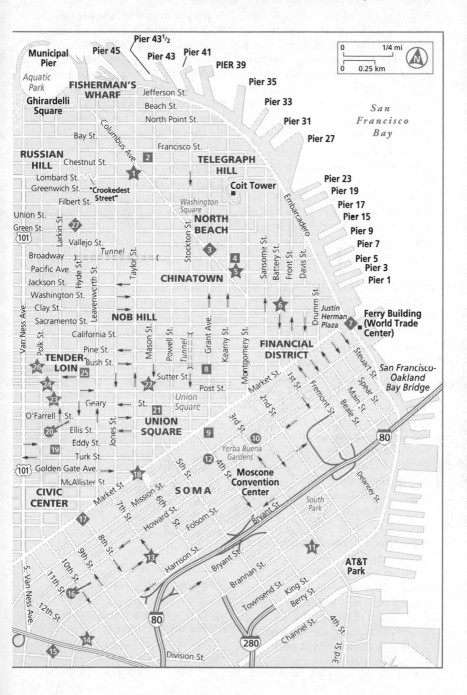

Municipal Pier

Aquatic Park

FISHERMAN'S WHARF

Ghirardelli Square

Pier 45
Pier 43½
Pier 43
Pier 41
PIER 39
Pier 35
Pier 33
Pier 31
Pier 27

Jefferson St.
Beach St.
North Point St.

San Francisco Bay

Bay St.

Columbus Ave.

Francisco St.

RUSSIAN HILL

Chestnut St.

②

TELEGRAPH HILL

Lombard St.
Greenwich St.
Filbert St.

"Crookedest Street"

Washington Square

Coit Tower ■

Pier 23
Pier 19
Pier 17
Pier 15
Pier 9
Pier 7
Pier 5
Pier 3
Pier 1

Union St.
Green St.
(101)

㉗

Larkin St.

Vallejo St.

NORTH BEACH

Stockton St.

③

Embarcadero

Broadway
Pacific Ave.
Jackson St.
Washington St.
Clay St.
Sacramento St.

Tunnel

Hyde St.
Leavenworth St.
Taylor St.

Sansome St.
Battery St.
Front St.
Davis St.

④
⑤

CHINATOWN

NOB HILL

⑥

Drumm St.

Justin Herman Plaza

⑦ ■ **Ferry Building (World Trade Center)**

Van Ness Ave.
Polk St.

California St.
Pine St.
Bush St.

Mason St.
Powell St.

Grant Ave.
Kearny St.
Montgomery St.

FINANCIAL DISTRICT

Steuart St.

San Francisco–Oakland Bay Bridge

TENDERLOIN

㉖
㉕
㉔
㉓
⑳

Geary St.

O'Farrell St.
Ellis St.
Eddy St.
Turk St.

Jones St.

Sutter St.
Tunnel
⑧
Post St.

Union Square

㉒

㉑

UNION SQUARE

⑨

Market St.
1st St.
2nd St.
Fremont St.
Beale St.
Main St.
Spear St.

⑩

3rd St.

(80)

⑲

(101) Golden Gate Ave.
McAllister St.

4th St.
5th St.

⑫
Yerba Buena Gardens

Moscone Convention Center

⑱

CIVIC CENTER

⑰

Market St.
Mission St.
7th St.
8th St.
9th St.
10th St.
11th St.
S-Van Ness Ave.
12th St.

Howard St.
6th St.
Folsom St.

SOMA

⑬

Harrison St.

South Park

Bryant St.

⑪

AT&T Park

Bryant St.
Brannan St.
Townsend St.
King St.
Berry St.
Channel St.
3rd St.
4th St.

⑯

(80)

⑭
⑮

(280)

Division St.

0   1/4 mi
0   0.25 km
Ⓝ

The main attraction is live music every night, but the club also offers pretty good burgers and a bar menu, outdoor seating on the back patio, and an awesome barbecue on Sundays from April through August from 4 to 7pm. Happy hour runs Wednesdays to Fridays from 4 to 7pm. *1233 17th St. (at Missouri St.).* ☎ *415/621-4455. www.bottomof thehill.com. Cover $6–$12.*

MTV **Best ●** → **Café du Nord** ★★★ Although it's been around since 1907, this basement supper club is rightfully self-proclaimed as the place for a "slightly lurid indie pop scene set in a beautiful old speakeasy." An eclectic crowd hangs at the front room's 40-foot mahogany bar and noshes on things like phylo-wrapped prawns with romesco sauce. The upstairs **Swedish American Hall** (see below) sometimes opens up for all-ages shows. *2170 Market St. (at Sanchez St.).* ☎ *415/861-5016. www.cafedunord.com. Cover $5–$15.*

→**Great American Music Hall** ★★ SF's oldest nightclub and sister to Slim's, the 600-capacity GAMH is on a nudie-bar-filled block in the seedy Tenderloin district. But the turn-of-the-20th-century venue's historic character (think: marble columns, balcony seating, and an oak dance floor) and stellar booking (anything from post-rock to indie to hip-hop, but all quality stuff) has a way of making you not care so much about the sketchy neighborhood. *859 O'Farrell St.* ☎ *415/885-0750. www.musichallsf. com. Cover $10–$25+. 21+ to enter.*

More Clubs Worth Checking Out

12 Galaxies (2565 Mission St.; ☎ **415/ 970-9777**; www.12galaxies.com) is a huge 6,000-square-foot space in the Mission that still manages to keep an intimate feel with a bunch of different hangout areas and candlelit tables lending a cabaret vibe. Twinkling Christmas lights and a roomy back patio complete with free Ping-Pong make **Thee Parkside** ★★ (1600 17th St.;

☎ **415/503-0393**; www.theeparkside.com) SF's homiest dive; the Portero Hill hangout books rock, country, and Americana.

The 500-capacity **Independent** (628 Divisadero St.; ☎ **415/771-1421**; www. independentsf.com), formerly known as the Justice League, has cycled through a variety of names but has remained one of the city's go-to rock and hip-hop venues for 3 decades.

ALL AGES

→**The Fillmore** ★★ Made famous by promoter Bill Graham in the '60s, the Fillmore showcases big names in a moderately sized standing-room-only space. Check listings in papers, call the theater, or visit their website for information on upcoming events. And if you make it to a show, check out the fabulous collection of vintage concert posters chronicling the hall's history. *1805 Geary Blvd. (at Fillmore St.).* ☎ *415/346-6000. www.thefillmore.com. Tickets $17–$45.*

→**Slim's** Co-owned by Boz Scaggs, this glitzy restaurant and bar serves California cuisine and seats 200, but it's usually standing room only during almost nightly shows ranging from performers of home-grown rock, jazz, blues, and alternative music. Bonus: Shows are always open to all ages. *333 11th St. (at Folsom St.).* ☎ *415/522-0333. www.slims-sf.com. Cover $0–$30.*

→**Swedish American Hall** The space upstairs from Café du Nord hosts occasional all-ages shows. *2170 Market St. (at Sanchez St.).* ☎ *415/861-5016. www.cafedunord. com. Cover $5–$15.*

RECORD STORES

→**Amoeba** *Rolling Stone* theorized that this place just might be the best record store in the world; before it expanded to a giant warehouse smack in the center of Hollywood, Amoeba was just a really cool shop on Berkeley's Telegraph Avenue. The SF location used to be a bowling alley and

If You're Going to San Francisco: Music Fests

→ **Noise Pop:** Started in 1993, this is *the* indie rock event in the city, with 7 days packed with performances from 100+ bands, plus art, movies, and lots of booze. ☎ 415/375-3370; www.noisepop.com.

→ **International Pop Overthrow:** An outgrowth of the LA festival, SF's version happens annually in August at Thee Parkside and the Red Devil Lounge. **www.internationalpopoverthrow.com.**

→ **BFD:** Held at Shoreline Park in Mountain View, BFD is radio station Live 105's annual summer blowout. ☎ 800/696-1053; www.live105.com.

→ **Mission Creek Music & Arts Festival:** Held in May, this festival features more discovery acts than trendier Noise Pop, with an emphasis on local talent. This same group also produces the Winter Ball and the San Francisco Folk Explosion Tour. **www.mcmf.org.**

is now home to more than 100,000 CDs and records. Both locations host in-store appearances. *1855 Haight St.* ☎ *415/831-1200 and 2455 Telegraph Ave., Berkeley.* ☎ *510/549-1125. www.amoebamusic.com. Both locations Mon–Sat 10:30am–10pm; Sun 11am–9pm.*

→ **Aquarius** ★★★ Founded in 1970, Aquarius calls itself the store that's "old enough to know better." The tiny Mission District shop stocks a wide selection of music from a lot of bands you may have never heard of in genres ranging from indie and hip-hop to sludge-metal and underground techno from Eastern Europe. It's like the anti-Virgin, and I, for one, like that. *1055 Valencia between 21st and 22nd.* ☎ *415/647-2272. www.aquariusrecords.com. Mon–Wed 10am–9pm; Thurs–Sun 10am–10pm.*

→ **Force of Habit Records** This is the place to go in the Mission for punk rarities, vinyl, and DJ gear, plus nerdy Star Wars and Simpsons memorabilia. *3565 20th St. at Lexington.* ☎ *415/255-PUNK. www.forceof habit.com. Wed–Sun noon–7pm.*

Sleeping

SF is expensive across the board, but especially when it comes to lodging. Still, with several modestly priced hotels and motels, it's not impossible to stay on budget.

CAMPGROUNDS/HOSTELS

Like San Diego, San Fran has a bunch of decent hostels. **The Green Tortoise** (494 Broadway; ☎ **800/867-8647;** www.green tortoise.com; $23–$25 dorm, $56–$65 private) has a pretty bitchin' location in the heart of North Beach, around the corner from one of Kerouac's favorite bars, Vesuvio's.

Elements Hotel in the Mission (2524 Mission St.; ☎ **866/327-8407;** www. elementshotel.com; $25/person dorm, $60 private) is right across the street from 12 Galaxies and has a tanning deck, in-house restaurant and cafe, and lounges on each floor with free internet. As with most hostels, these both require proof of international or out-of-state residency at check-in.

There's not much camping in San Francisco proper, but you *can* pitch a tent at **Angel Island State Park** (☎ **415/435-5390;** www.angelisland.org), a forest-covered island in the San Francisco Bay that's accessible by ferry (call ☎ **415/705-5555** for ferry info). Campsites are $15 to $20 per night, and you should come prepared to haul your gear up to 2 miles to the sites.

CHEAP

➜ **The Mosser** ★★ "Hip on the Cheap" is a good way to describe this place, which includes an on-site restaurant/bar and recording studio, Studio Paradiso. The least expensive rooms share a bathroom but are an incredible deal with rates starting at $69; as with any off-Union-Square hotel, be watchful at night in this slightly sketchy 'hood. *54 Fourth St. (at Market).* ☎ *800/227-3804. www.themosser.com. 166 units, 112 with private bathroom. $69–$89 (shared bathroom); $159–$249 (private bathroom). Parking $29. Amenities: Restaurant; bar; concierge; laundry/dry cleaning. In room: Dataport, hispeed Internet for $9.95/day.*

➜ **The San Remo Hotel** ★★ This small, European-style *pensione* in a quiet North Beach nabe is one of the best budget hotels in the city, though rooms are small and bathrooms are shared. The decor is cozy country, so you might have to ignore the wicker in favor of giving your credit card a break. *2237 Mason (at Chestnut).* ☎ *800/352-REMO. www.sanremohotel.com. 62 units. $55–$95 double; $155–$175 penthouse (private bath). Amenities: Gym access; massage; laundry; TV lounge. In room: Fan.*

DOABLE

🅜 Best ☺ ➜ **Phoenix Hotel** ★★ Known as a rock 'n' roll motel, this funky, retro, band-friendly motor lodge on the edge of the Tenderloin feels like a '70s-style party place like something out of *Almost Famous.* The groovy **Bambuddha Lounge,** just off the lobby, serves Southeast Asian cuisine in a hip setting, and there are even oh-so-trendy cabanas surrounding the pool, which offer a great perch for gawking at the hotel's hot rocker residents. *601 Eddy (at Larkin).* ☎ *800/248-9466. www.thephoenixhotel.com. 44 units. $149–$169 double. Free parking. Amenities:*

Bar; pool; concierge; massage; laundry/dry cleaning. In room: Dataport, fridge and microwave (in some rooms), Wi-Fi.

➜ **York Hotel** ★★ Even locals hang out at the York, since it houses the **Empire Plush Room,** one of the city's best jazz clubs. The hotel, which was featured in Hitchcock's *Vertigo,* offers gym access and continental breakfast with its rates, plus cheery rooms with all the standard amenities, including flatscreens in some rooms. *940 Sutter St. (between Leavenworth and Hyde).* ☎ *800/808-9675. www.yorkhotel.com. Breakfast included. Parking $25 ($35 valet). $119–$149 double. Amenities: Jazz club; bar; gym; laundry. In room: Wi-Fi (Superior King rooms).*

SPLURGE

➜ **Hotel Diva** ★★ This Union Square boutique aims for a chic, sexy vibe by way of blue carpeting and modern decor with an industrial flair (let's just say it took me 5 min. to figure out how the light switches worked). Little touches like Internet lounges on most floors and a DVD rental kiosk in the "diva's boudoir" set this small spot apart from its more opulent neighbors, but be prepared to pay Union Square prices for parking ($35 per night, plus tax!). While awaiting the valet, you can browse the autographs carved into the concrete "sidewalk of fame": everyone from "Dany" (yes, he spelled his own name wrong) Glover to Chita Rivera to Devo has left their mark. *440 Geary (between Mason and Taylor).* ☎ *800/553-1900. www.hoteldiva.com. $119–$179 double; $212–$492 suite. Valet parking $35/day+tax. Amenities: Cafe; gym; meeting rooms; Internet lounges; DVD/iPod rental; laundry/dry cleaning; Wi-Fi. In room: Wi-Fi, CD player, dataport.*

➜ **Hotel Triton** ★★ With environmentally friendly rooms and a handful of suites designed by rock stars, this hip boutique

More Fabulous SF Festivals

- **Chinese New Year:** This weeklong celebration starts with the crowning of "Miss Chinatown USA" and culminates with a parade through Chinatown. ☎ 415/982-3000; www.chineseparade.com.

- **San Francisco International Film Festival:** Headquartered at the Kabuki each year starting in late April and running through early May, this is America's oldest film festival. ☎ 415/561-5000; www.sffs.org.

- **Bay to Breakers:** This 12km (7.5 mile) citywide run, held in May, snakes through Golden Gate Park and features more than 60,000 participants dressed up in wacky (sometimes naughty) costumes. ☎ 415/359-2800; www.baytobreakers.com.

- **Carnaval:** This is the Mission's largest annual event, which includes a parade route down Mission lined with more than half a million spectators. ☎ 415/920-0125; www.carnavalsf.com.

- **North Beach Festival:** For more than 50 years this neighborhood event has livened up historic North Beach with food, drink, arts, poetry, dancing, chalk art, and people-watching (close to 75,000 people attend every Father's Day weekend). ☎ 415/989-2220; www.sfnorthbeach.org.

- **Stern Grove Midsummer Music Festival:** Pack a picnic and head out early to enjoy classical, jazz, and ethnic music and dance at this annual summer festival. ☎ 415/252-6252; www.sterngrove.org.

- **LGBT Pride Parade:** Up to half a million people descend on SF at the end of June each year for this huge event, which includes a parade and festival with hundreds of food, crafts, and information booths, plus music. ☎ 415/864-3733; www.sfpride.org.

- **Fillmore Street Jazz Festival:** Held in Pacific Heights in July, this several-block-long festival features live jazz, great food, vendors, and more. ☎ 510/970-3217; www.fillmorejazzfestival.com.

- **Folsom Street Fair:** This SOMA leather fest is a neighborhood favorite. ☎ 415/861-3247; www.folsomstreetfair.org.

- **Halloween in the Castro:** This is a huge night in the Castro, when streets shut down so a mixed gay/straight crowd can strut their stuff in exotic costumes.

ROCKIN' THE WEST COAST

hotel has personality *and* a conscience. The "Eco Rooms" are stocked with planet-friendly soaps and linens (there are even some room packages with parking discounts for hybrid cars). Celebrity suites have been personalized by musicians Anthony Kiedis (of Red Hot Chili Peppers), Carlos Santana, and Jerry Garcia, not to mention comedian Kathy Griffin and muralist Wyland. The lobby hosts nightly wine receptions with chair massages and tarot card readings; live DJs spin on Friday nights. *342 Grant (at Sutter).* ☎ *800/21-HOTEL. www.hoteltriton.com. $149–$219 double; $239–$399 suite. Parking $37/day. Amenities: Cafe; gym; fresh-baked cookies twice a day; wine reception; business center; room service; laundry/dry cleaning; Wi-Fi. In room: flat-screen TV, dataport, minibar.*

Eating

SUPPLIES

Get your tempeh/tofu/organic produce fix at **Rainbow Grocery Cooperative** (1745 Folsom at Division St.; ☎ 415/863-0621), a crunchier, co-op version of Whole Foods for the pierced-and-tatted set.

North Beach, meanwhile, has several Italian delis to choose from, including the century-old **Molinari's** (373 Columbus at Vallejo; ☎ 415/421-2337)—try the Luciano Special, with prosciutto, coppa, mozzarella, and sun-dried tomatoes on grilled focaccia.

You can also pick up fresh produce at the **Heart of the City Farmer's Market** (held Wed and Sun from 7am–3pm at the United Nations Plaza, 1182 Market at Eighth; ☎ 415/558-9455) and the huge **Ferry Plaza Farmer's Market** (held Sun and Tues 10am–2pm, Thurs 4–8pm, and Sat 8am–2pm; ☎ 415/291-3276).

TAKEOUT TREATS

You don't even have to be a vegetarian to dig the seitan cheesesteaks at **Jay's** in the Mission (3285 21st St. at Valencia; ☎ 415/285-5200). Sure, you can get the full-fat, Niman Ranch beef-filled traditional cheesesteak here too, complete with onions, mushrooms, and peppers, but the meatless versions are *soo* good. **Hazel's Kitchen** serves standing-room-only sandwiches in Potrero Hill (1331 18th St. between Missouri and Texas; ☎ 415/647-7941). Or grab late-night giant burritos at **El Farolito** (2779 Mission St.; ☎ 415/824-7877).

RESTAURANTS

Cheap

➔**Cha Cha Cha** TAPAS With two hugely popular locations, Cha Cha Cha serves up spicy Cuban/Cajun small plates that are just tasty and affordable enough to make people wait up to 2 hours for a table. *1801 Haight at Shrader. ☎ 415/386-7670 and 2327.*

Mission St. ☎ 415/648-0504. www.cha3.com. Dinner Sun–Thurs 5–11pm; Fri–Sat 5–11:30 (open until 1am in the Mission). Lunch daily 11am–4pm (Haight St. location only). Dinners $10–$15; tapas $5–$10.

➔**La Taqueria** TACOS A friend of mine was raving about La Taqueria's chorizo tacos from 1,000 miles away. Try it with a cup of yummy, creamy horchata. *2889 Mission St. (at 25th). ☎ 415/285-7117. Mon–Sat 11am–9pm; Sun 11am–8pm. $3–$8. Cash only.*

➔**Sparky's** DINER There's an after-hours club in San Francisco called the End Up, but the real post-show end-up is this 24-hour diner in the Castro, which can fill up with glassy-eyed rock kids craving the 3am chow-down. The menu's got the usual breakfast fare—omelets, pancakes—plus vegan-friendly soy stuff. *242 Church St. at Market, Castro. ☎ 415/626-8666. $5–$15. Open 24 hr.*

Doable

➔**Andalu** ★★★ TAPAS This stylish Mission tapas joint serves small, flavorful plates crafted from exotic ingredients, like ahi tartar tacos, polenta french fries, portobello mushroom with bone marrow, and, for dessert, banana lumpia split topped with dulce de leche ice cream. *3198 16th St. at Guerrero. ☎ 415/621.2211. www.andalusf. com. Sun–Tues 5:30–10pm; Wed–Thurs 5:30–11pm; Fri–Sat 5:30pm–12:30am. Most dishes $5–$10.*

➔**Kan Zeman** MIDDLE EASTERN Low tables, belly dancers, and hookahs set the stage at this funky Haight Street spot, which serves classic Middle Eastern dishes like kabobs, Jordanian lamb shank, falafels, and more. *1793 Haight St. at Shrader. ☎ 415/751-9656. www.kanzeman.com. Mon–Thurs 5pm–midnight; Fri 5pm–2am; Sat noon–2am; Sun noon–midnight.*

➔**Stinking Rose** ★★ ITALIAN This North Beach institution worships at the altar of that most fragrant of bulbs, garlic. The parsley pesto has an awesome kick, but you might want to pop a Trident after indulging in the 40-clove chicken. *420 Columbus Ave., North Beach.* ☎ *415/781-7673. www.thestinkingrose.com. Salads/starters $6–$13; entrees $14–$28. Daily 11am–11pm.*

Recently tons of sleek new eateries have popped up along Mission and Valencia streets, including **Ramblas Tapas Bar** (557 Valencia at 17th; ☎ **415/565-0207;** $5–$15), two **We Be Sushi** locations (538 Valencia St.; ☎ **415/565-0749** and 1071 Valencia; ☎ **415/826-0607;** $8–$12), popular creperie **Ti Couz** (3108 16t St. at Valencia; ☎ **415/252-7373;** $2–$11), and **Foreign Cinema** (2534 Mission St.; ☎ **415/648-7600,** $14–$25), where foreign films screened on the patio provide the backdrop to an oyster bar and a menu packed with fresh seafood. If you're feeling indecisive, just cruise around the area browsing menus until you find something you like.

Splurge

➜ **Frascati** ★★★ CALIFORNIA SF's got its share of trendy hot spots, so this small, casually upscale Mediterannean place in Russian Hill is refreshingly different. The atmosphere is cozy and the food's awesome and interestingly combined, like the mussels with chorizo, lamb carpaccio with eggplant caponata, and swordfish with polenta and olive salsa verde. Get the house-specialty black-and-white bread pudding for dessert. *1901 Hyde St. (at Green), Russian Hill.* ☎ *415/928-1406. www.frascatisf. com. Starters $7–$15; entrees $22–$25. Mon–Sat 5:30–10pm; Sun 5–9pm.*

➜ **Winterland Restaurant** ★ This restaurant stands on the site of the former Winterland Ballroom, the skating rink turned concert venue that hosted everyone from the Dead, the Stones, and Jimi Hendrix to Led Zeppelin, Jefferson Airplane, and Elvis Costello. The Band and the Sex Pistols played their last shows

here, but now instead of dishing out heaping piles of rock, the Winterland has stuff like clam seviche with lychee fruit and roasted sweetbreads with quail eggs served sunny side up. *2101 Sutter St.* ☎ *415/563-5025. www.winterlandrestaurant.com. Starters $6–$10; entrees $18–$29. Mon–Thurs 5:30–10:30pm; Fri–Sat 5:30–11pm (bar menu Thurs–Sat until 12:30am). Closed Sun.*

Partying

With the exception of the financial district, which is kind of a ghost town after dark, almost all of San Francisco's neighborhoods go *off*. To make your party plan, just pick your destination: the Castro is a well-known gay enclave; the Mission is a total hipster haven; the quaint Marina District is pegged as a yuppie hangout; North Beach is crowded with restaurants, bars, strip clubs, and tons of people; the Haight is fun, eclectic, and still hippie-ish decades after Jerry Garcia; and gentrifying warehouse district SOMA is still home to some worthwhile spots.

BARS & PUBS

➜ **Arrow Bar** ★ This cramped scenester spot features DJs and a comfy, candlelit chill-out lounge, plus dollar drinks and Pabsts on Sundays. The bar's myspace page might sum it up best when it states: "We are famous throughout the planet for throwing the most retarded, intense, and wasted parties in all the Bay Area. If you like rock stars, strippers and nuns come down, and take one home." *10 Sixth (at Market).* ☎ *415/255-7920. www.myspace.com/ arrowbar. Mon 9pm–2am; Tues–Fri 5pm–2am; Sat–Sun 7pm–2am. No cover. 21+.*

➜ **Doc's Clock** ★ The interior of this mellow Mission district dive is lit up by candles and pink neon, while its patrons, a mix of locals and hipsters, get lit up thanks to the bartenders' strong pours. *2575 Mission (at 21st).* ☎ *415/824-3627. www.docsclock.*

Hangover for Hipsters

Fernet-Branca is a bitter Italian liqueur that's caught on with San Francisco hipsters in a big way. The flavor clocks in somewhere between paint thinner and shoe polish, and though I've indulged on several occasions, I can't stand the taste, and have my doubts that anyone else does either (despite several folks I know who like to brag that they've "developed a taste for it"). For some reason, San Francisco consumes more Fernet than anywhere else in the States—more per capita, even, than any place on the planet, according to a recent *SF Weekly* story. Maybe it's the saffron—one of about 40 ingredients that comprise the secret recipe—an herb from which Ecstasy can be derived.

You take it as a shot with a ginger back (or small glass of ginger ale to chase away the aftertaste). It's not any more expensive than your average top-shelf booze, about $5 a shot. Fernet's known as a hangover cure, and bartenders claim it leaves you clearer the next morning than other spirits—provided you don't mix it with anything else. Problem with that logic, though, is that I, for one, generally only think a shot of the syrupy black liquid is a good idea when I'm already three sheets to the wind on whiskey and red wine. Still, when it comes to alcohol-induced pains, the mark left by Fernet is a meaningful one, because once the taste trauma is gone, the high and inevitable camaraderie that comes from sharing something so terribly transcendent make it totally worthwhile.

Though you can find it most anywhere in the city, the Tenderloin's **R Bar** is particularly dedicated to worshiping at the altar of Fernet. Find it at 1176 Sutter (at Polk); ☎ **415/567-7441.**

com. *Mon–Sat 6pm–2am; Sun 8pm–midnight. No cover. 21+ to enter.*

➜ **Edinburgh Castle** ★★ Soak up the friendly atmosphere along with British Isles ale at this snug Civic Center/Tenderloin bar, which is known for its crazy-popular trivia night. *950 Geary Blvd. (at Polk).* ☎ *415/885–4074. www.castlenews. com. Daily 5pm–2am. No cover.*

➜ **The Eagle Tavern** ★ Creative facial hair seems to be a staff requirement. This SoMa biker bar with a gigantic outdoor patio draws an upbeat gay and indie rock crowd with attractions like live music, pool, and mud wrestling. *398 12th St. (at Harrison).* ☎ *415/626-0880. www.sfeagle.com. Daily noon–2am. 21+ to enter.*

➜ **Hemlock Tavern** ★★ This Tenderloin bar, walking distance from the Great American, books rock bands in the small back room (follow the big red arrow) while hipsters sip Fernet-Branca in the front bar as metallic fish and mounted deer heads look on. Bonus for smokers: a glass-encased smoking area like the ones you see at the airport. *1131 Polk St.* ☎ *415/923-0923. www.hemlocktavern.com. Cover $0–$8. 21+ to enter.*

➜ **Vesuvio** ★★ This legendary, laid-back beatnik hangout is packed to the second-floor rafters with neighborhood writers, artists, songsters, wannabes, and everyone else ranging from longshoremen and cab drivers to businesspeople. *255 Columbus Ave. (at Broadway).* ☎ *415/362-3370. www.vesuvio. com. Daily 6am–2am. No cover. 21+ to enter.*

DANCE CLUBS

MTV Best ⚫ ➜ **"popscene" @ 330 Ritch** ★★★ Who says indie kids don't dance? Run by Live 105 music director Aaron Axelson, this weekly club spins the underground alt-rock jams every Thursday night, often with live sets by up-and-coming bands and guest DJs (past turntablists have included members of Franz Ferdinand, Death Cab, and the Yeah Yeah Yeahs). *330 Ritch St. (off Townsend between 3rd and 4th).* ☎ *415/541-9530. www. popscene-sf.com. Thurs 10pm–2am. $5 for 21+, $8 18–21. 18+ to enter.*

More Clubs Worth Checking Out

A former 1890s Victorian playhouse, **Ruby Skye** (420 Mason between Geary and Post; ☎ **415/693-0777;** www.rubyskye.com) is downtown's most glamorous and gigantic club where hundreds of partyers boogie on the ballroom floor. Meanwhile, **1015 Folsom** in the SOMA district (1015 Folsom St. at Sixth; ☎ **415/431-1200;** www.1015. com) has a giant dance floor and house, disco, and acid-jazz DJs that attract 20- and 30-somethings en masse.

COMEDY CLUBS

San Francisco's stand-up comedy scene gave the world Margaret Cho, Patton Oswald, and Greg "He's Just Not That Into You" Behrendt, among many talented others. Catch a rising star at Cobb's Comedy Club in North Beach (915 Columbus St.; ☎ **415/928-4320;** www.cobbscomedyclub. com) and the Punchline in the financial district (444 Battery St.; ☎ **415/397-4337;** www.punchlinecomedyclub.com).

What Else to See & Do

You could spend weeks getting lost in San Francisco—discovering still more great bars and restaurants, cute neighborhoods, and outdoor activities, from playing in the park to watching Barry Bonds hit his zillionth home run. Being bored in San Francisco is more than just unlikely; it's almost criminal.

THE TOP ATTRACTIONS

Since you'll be driving anyway, consider the self-guided, **49-mile scenic drive** ★; it's one easy way to orient yourself with the city as it follows a rough circle around the bay and passes all the best-known sights, from Chinatown to the Golden Gate Bridge, Ocean Beach, Seal Rocks, Golden Gate Park, and Twin Peaks. Although it makes an excellent half-day tour, this mini-excursion can easily take longer if you decide, for example, to stop to walk across the Golden Gate Bridge or to have tea in Golden Gate Park's Japanese Tea Garden. The San Francisco **Visitor Information Center** (☎ **415/391-2000;** www.onlyinsanfrancisco.com), at Powell and Market streets, distributes free route maps. Try to avoid the downtown area during the weekday rush hours from 7 to 9am and 4 to 6pm.

Consider hitting SoMA for some SF culture; the neighborhood that runs from Market and Townsend between The Embarcadero and Division Street has become the city's newest cultural center since clubs took over the area's old warehouses. Today, the gentrified nabe is home to **Yerba Buena Center for the Arts** and **Yerba Buena Gardens,** the **San Francisco Museum of Modern Art,** and the **Metreon Entertainment Center.**

And for a glimpse into the city's hippie past, try the **Haight-Ashbury Flower Power Walking Tour** (☎ **415/863-1621**), in which Pam and Bruce Brennan ("the Hippy Gourmet"—see www.hippygourmet. com) lead an exploration of hippie haunts like the Grateful Dead's crash pad, Janis Joplin's house, and other reminders of the Summer of Love. Tours begin at 9:30am on Tuesdays and Saturdays. The cost is $15 per person (cash only). Reservations are required and the tour starts at the corner of Stanyan and Waller streets.

PLAYING OUTSIDE

📺 Best ✪ FREE → **Golden Gate Park** ★★★ Spend 1 sunny day stretched out on the grass along JFK Drive, reading in the Shakespeare Garden, or strolling around Stow Lake, and you, too, will understand the allure of this 1,017-acre landmark park, which consists of hundreds of attractions and gardens—notably **Rhododendron Dell, The Rose Garden, Strybing Arboretum,** and the tulips and daffodils around the **Dutch windmill**— connected by wooded paths and paved roads.

Start with a visit to **McLaren Lodge and Park Headquarters** (at Stanyan St. and Fell St.; ☎ **415/831-2700**) for a park map ($3) and info on how to find the park's hidden spots. The park contains lots of recreational facilities from tennis courts and polo fields to a golf course and fly-casting pools. The Strawberry Hill boathouse handles boat rentals. The park is also home to the Planetarium, the Conservatory of Flowers, the Japanese Tea Garden, and the newly renovated **de Young Museum.** The park can be accessed at several different points, including off 19th Avenue at Lincoln and at the end of Fell Street

BIKING

SF Parks & Rec maintains two city bike trails: one goes from Golden Gate Park to Lake Merced (about 8 miles), and the other traverses the city, starting in the south, and continues over the Golden Gate Bridge. A bike map is available for about $5 at many bike shops and from the San Francisco Visitor Information Center, at Powell and Mason streets, for $3.

Ocean Beach has a public walk- and bikeway that stretches along 5 waterfront blocks of the Great Highway between Noriega and Santiago streets. It's an easy ride from Cliff House or Golden Gate Park. **Avenue Cyclery,** 756 Stanyan St., at Waller Street, in the Haight (☎ **415/387-3155**), rents bikes for $7 per hour or $28 per day.

Walking & Hiking

The **Golden Gate National Recreation Area** offers incredible walks, including the

3.5-mile paved trail along the Golden Gate Promenade, from Aquatic Park to the Golden Gate Bridge. You can also hike the **Coastal Trail** all the way from the Fort Point area to Cliff House. For more information or to pick up a map of the Golden Gate National Recreation Area, stop by the park service headquarters at Fort Mason at the north end of Laguna Street (☎ **415/ 561-4700**). Find more info at the Parks and Rec Web site, www.sfgov.org/site/recpark_index.asp.

SPECTATOR SPORTS
Baseball

The National League **San Francisco Giants** ★ play at **AT&T Park** (Third and King sts. in SOMA; ☎ **415/972-2000**; www.sfgiants.com) from April to October. Tickets are hard to come by, but you can try to track them down through **Tickets. com** (☎ **510/762-2277**; www.tickets.com). The American League's **Oakland Athletics** play across the bay at the McAfee Coliseum (Hegenberger Rd. exit from I-880, Oakland; ☎ **510/430-8020**), accessible through BART's Coliseum station.

Basketball

The NBA'S **Golden State Warriors** (☎ **510/ 986-2200**; www.nba.com/warriors) play in The Arena in Oakland, a 19,200-seat facility, from November through April. Tickets are available at the arena and by phone through **Tickets.com** (☎ **510/762-2277**).

Football

The **San Francisco 49ers** (www.sf49ers. com) play at Monster Park/Candlestick Park (Giants Drive and Gilman Avenue) on Sundays August through December. Tickets sell out early in the season but are available at higher prices through ticket agents beforehand and from scalpers. The 49ers' archenemies, the **Oakland Raiders** (www. ofma.com), play at McAfee Stadium; call ☎ **800/949-2626** for ticket information.

On the Road to Portland, OR

San Francisco, CA to Portland, OR 635 miles

on the Road Nuts & Bolts

Where to Fill Up There's a gas station on Mission and 14th near the Duboce on-ramp in SF, but you'll find cheaper gas as you get farther outside the city. *Don't* stop at the Exxon on Pollard Flat Road near Shasta Lake—gas is up to 50¢ more per gallon than at stations just over the Oregon border.

The Tolls There's one $3 toll just for the Carquinez Bridge (eastbound only) at the Contra Costa-Salano County Line.

The Fastest Way I-80 E to I-5 N via 505, which lets you bypass Sacramento; I-5 goes all the way up to Portland and beyond.

The Long Way Round If you have more time, consider taking 101 up the coast; you'll see the quaint small towns of Marin, Sonoma, and Mendocino counties, as well as the surprisingly rockin' college town of Arcata (see "*Detour:* The Coastal Route: Highway 101," above, for more attractions on this route).

Rules of the Road Speed limits drop as the road gets curvier entering Oregon, which also charges a $97 fine for drivers caught not wearing a seatbelt.

Once again you've got two choices when heading from SF to Portland: the fast way (intense, direct I-5) or the scenic way (coastal US 101), only this time, the interstate represents a significantly shorter route—about 3 hours. Whatever route you choose, *don't* attempt this drive in 1 day, especially if you're the only driver; because it's not only long, it also becomes winding and complicated toward the end, requiring

North Coast Playlist: SF to Portland

On the radio:
- → **Live 105** (105.3 FM), San Francisco
- → **KSCU** (103.3 FM), Santa Clara
- → **94/7 FM,** Portland

On the iPod/CD player:
- → *Journey to the End of the East Bay*, **Rancid,** ". . . And Out Come the Wolves," 1995
- → *86,* **Green Day,** "Insomniac," 1995
- → *Truckin',* **Grateful Dead,** "American Beauty," 1970
- → *California,* **Rogue Wave,** "Descended Like Vultures," 2005
- → *East Bay,* **NOFX,** "I Heard They Suck Live," 1995
- → *Cool Scene,* **Dandy Warhols,** "Thirteen Tales from Urban Bohemia," 2000
- → *Portland Rain,* **Everclear,** "Welcome to the Drama Club," 2006

ROCKIN' THE WEST COAST

Detour: The Coastal Route: Highway 101

If you're taking the coastal route from San Francisco toward Portland, you'll exit the city via the Golden Gate Bridge (take Divisadero toward the water and follow the signs). This route takes you past the quaint houseboats of Sausalito and through Marin County and Petaluma (where Winona Ryder grew up).

You'll pass the adorable village of Healdsburg and Lake Mendocino on your way toward the **Hopland Brewery,** whose signature brew is a damn fine micro called Red Tail Ale ★ (13351 S Hwy. 101; ☎ **707/744-1361;** www.mendobrew.com). The road then winds through the massive **Humboldt Redwoods State Park** (☎ **707/946-2263;** www.humboldtredwoods.org) and out toward the coast near Eureka and the college town of **Arcata,** where Humboldt State kids party at clubs like the **Alibi** (744 9th; ☎ **707/822-3731;** www.thealibi.com) and **Humboldt Brews** (856 10th St.; ☎ **707/826-BREW;** www.humboldtbrews.com) as demonstrated in the documentary *Rural Rock & Roll.*

After Arcata, you'll pass through **Redwood National Park,** where there's great camping if you've a mind to stay overnight (☎ **707/464-6101;** www.nps.gov/redw), and stay along the coast, until you catch US 199 North to link back up with I-5 just south of Ashland. It's about 6 hours from San Francisco to Arcata, and about another 4 from Arcata to Ashland.

Scenery lovers won't mind taking the long route because of the spectacular vistas of the Oregon Coast. If you stick with Highway 101 all the way up to Lincoln City, you can experience part of the 300-odd miles of Coast

the kind of alertness and concentration that tends to be lacking after 10 hours on the road. You can get as far as Ashland, OR, in about 5 hours, at which point consider treating yourself to a meal and a stroll through the quaint Shakespeare-crazed town before crashing out in some cheapie motel (see "Detour: In Fair Ashland . . ." below).

If you're taking I-5, get on Highway 101 to I-80 east from San Francisco (there's an on-ramp to 101 at Van Ness where Duboce turns into 13th St.) to go over the Bay Bridge; you'll have a chance to stop in Sacramento if you want to see the state capital and pay your respects to the home of Tower Records. As we went to press, the company was in the final stages of shutting its doors, as time marched on and "record stores" continued to recede into the past.

In the 1940s, chain founder Ross Solomon used to sell vinyl platters out of the old Tower Pharmacy; the space is now called the **Tower Café** (take the 15th St. exit off I-80 to 1518 Broadway; ☎ **916/441-0222;** www.towercafe.com), with a good, recommendable, not-too-expensive menu of breakfast/lunch/dinner.

The more direct route to Portland, however, bypasses Sacramento completely, so if you're in a hurry just take the I-505 connector from I-80 to I-5. Once on the 5, fire up the A/C through Redding, CA, then prepare for some bitchin' scenery heading through **Shasta Lake.** You might even stop for a dip in the **Sacramento River;** one way to access it is via the 🆁🆅 Best🌙 **Pollard Gulch Day Use Area.**

To get there, exit I-5 at Pollard Flat, turn left on Eagle's Roost Road, and turn right

Range–backed shoreline that alternates sandy beaches with rocky capes and headlands.

Between Reedsport and Florence, check out the giant dunes, some as tall as 500 feet, at the **Oregon Dunes National Recreation Area** (855 US 101; ☎ 541/271-3611; www.fs.fed.us/r6/siuslaw). There's also a bunch of cute little artsy fishing towns along these icy Pacific waters, and their quaintness hasn't been lost on tourists, who crowd the streets in summer months, especially in northern cities like Newport and Lincoln City. Check out the historic Old Town area in **Florence,** whose brick and wood buildings capture the flavor of a 19th-century fishing village, or spend some time in counterculture-friendly **Yachats** (pronounced *Yah*-hots, which is a Chinook Indian word for "dark waters at the foot of the mountains"). Tidepooling and storm-watching are some of the natural attractions in Yachats; if you're staying over, rent a rustic cabin nestled among the fir trees at the **Shamrock Lodgettes** (105 US 101; ☎ 800/845-5028; www.shamrocklodgettes.com) and grab a bite at **La Serre,** which has a seafood-heavy menu and excellent desserts (Second Ave. at Beach St.; ☎ 541/547-3420).

To get back to the big cities, catch OR 18 in Lincoln City to OR 22 toward Salem, then jump on the 5 to head into Portland. This route takes about 16 hours—14 along the coast from SF to Lincoln City, then another 2 heading inland to Portland. It's a worthy detour and maybe a nice break if you're heading from city to city to hear that rock 'n' roll.

on the narrow, winding driveway marked Pollard Gulch. The little road leads to a small parking lot with a picnic area, hiking trails, and a path down to the river. Be careful, though; the water can get moving pretty fast, so when in doubt, opt for wading over swimming.

Welcome to Portland

PDX, P-town, the Rose City, call it what you will—Portland is a shining example of why people like the Pacific Northwest so much. There's gorgeous scenery, liberal politics, and tons of character, not to mention really good beer. Geographically, Portland is bisected by the Willamette River, which runs north-south and is crossed by eight downtown bridges: Fremont, Broadway, Steel, Morrison, Hawthorne, Marquam, and Ross Island and the main one at Burnside Street, which separates north and south Portland, creating four quadrants. Northeast houses the Irvington neighborhood (good for cheap eats); Northwest is where the money is (good for shopping and trendy restaurants). Southwest contains downtown, Old Town, and Chinatown; and Southeast is home to tons of bars, clubs, cafes, and cute neighborhoods. There's also the North Portland area, which has historically been a little sketchy but is sprouting a pretty cool scene, particularly along Mississippi Avenue.

Getting Around

Portland is progressive not just politically but also when it comes to public transit—in order to control congestion downtown, the city created a bus/light rail/streetcar

Detour: In Fair Ashland, Where We Lay Our Scene . . .

Just after you cross the California/Oregon border (about 286 miles south of Portland), you might want to take a detour to Ashland, OR, which really *is* all about the Bard, with a world-famous Shakespeare Festival and tons of Shakespeare-related activities going on year-round. But Ashland actually has a 21st-century scene, too. It orbits around the **Mobius** (281 4th St. between A and B; ☎ 541/488-8894; www.themobius.com), a small art venue/performance space/recording studio/cafe that books everything from little-known Afro-Cuban electro bands and burlesque troupes to DJs, poetry slams, and the Kabbalah Dream Orchestra. If you're making an evening of your stop in Ashland, drop in on the Mobius but fill up on a fantastic spicy tempeh MaHarissa wrap at **Pangea** (272 E Main St.; ☎ 541/ 552-1630; www.pangea ashland.com), a cheap, crunchy joint on the main drag, or splurge on one of the fancier places that offer creekside seating.

Throw back a few at the **Beau Club** (347 E Main St.; ☎ 541/482-4185), and, if you're crashing here, the **Columbia** (262½ E Main; ☎ 800/718-2530; www. columbiahotel.com) is smack in the middle of town and has decent rates ($49–$69 in the winter; $60–$125 in summer). Cheaper chains can be found about 10 miles north in Medford; try the **Travelodge** at 954 Alba Dr. off Exit 27 (☎ 541/773-1579).

And if you're into that Shakespeare guy, you're in luck. The **Oregon Shakespeare Festival** (15 S. Pioneer St., box office: ☎ 541/482-4331; www.osfashland.org) is one of the best regional theaters in the West, and it offers a long, varied season of both classic and new work played in repertory in three performance spaces, in a season that runs from February to October. Tickets range from $29 to $72, with discounts for previews, and during the early and late part of the season. There's also a backstage tour available.

system that's totally free within an area known as the **Fareless Square,** a 300-block chunk of downtown in the area between I-405 on the south and west, Hoyt Street on the north, and the Willamette River on the east. Outside that area, fares on the bus, the light-rail (called the MAX) and the streetcar are $1.30 to $1.60, depending how far you go, or you can get an all-day ticket for $4, which is good in all zones. The $10 **Adventure Pass** is good for 3 days of unlimited bus and MAX rides.

ON THE MAX

Basically a modern trolley, **The Metropolitan Area Express (MAX)** is Portland's aboveground light-rail system that connects downtown Portland with the airport, the eastern suburb of Gresham, the western suburbs of Beaverton and Hillsboro, and North Portland. Pioneer Courthouse Square is a convenient place to catch the MAX, but if you're going outside of the Fareless Square, buy your ticket and stamp it in the time-punch machine on the platform before getting on the MAX.

ON THE STREETCAR

The **Portland Streetcar** (☎ 503/238-RIDE; www.portlandstreetcar.org) runs from Portland State at the south end of downtown, through the Pearl District (home to tons of restaurants and shops) to Nob Hill in Northwest. Vintage streetcars run for free on weekends.

Portland Highlights

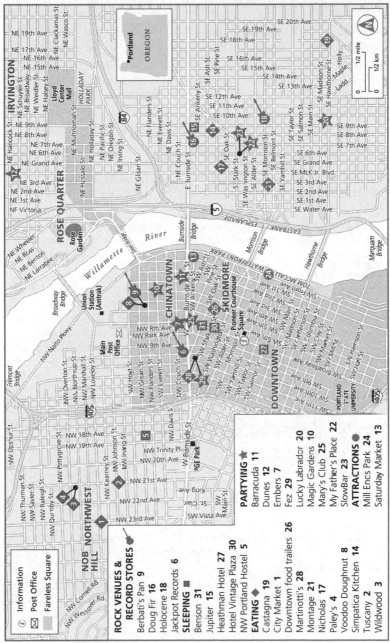

Portland Nuts & Bolts

Area Codes   The Portland metro area has two area codes—503 and 971—and it is necessary to dial all 10 digits of a telephone number, even when making local calls.

Doctor   If you need a physician referral while in Portland, contact the **Medical Society of Metropolitan Portland** (☎ 503/222-0156). The **Oregon Health Sciences University Hospital,** 3181 SW Sam Jackson Park Rd. (☎ 503/494-8311), has a drop-in clinic.

Emergencies   For police, fire, or medical emergencies, phone ☎ **911.**

Hospitals   Three conveniently located area hospitals are **Legacy Good Samaritan,** 1015 NW 22nd Ave. (☎ 503/413-7711); **Providence Portland Medical Center,** 4805 NE Glisan St. (☎ 503/215-1111); and the **Oregon Health Sciences University Hospital,** 3181 SW Sam Jackson Park Rd. (☎ 503/494-8311), which is just southwest of the city center and has a drop-in clinic.

Hot Lines   The *Oregonian's* **Inside Line** (☎ 503/225-5555), operated by Portland's daily newspaper, provides information on everything from concerts and festivals to sports and the weather.

Internet Access   If you need to check e-mail while you're in Portland, first check with your hotel. Otherwise, visit a **Kinko's.** There's one downtown at 221 SW Alder St. (☎ 503/224-6550) and in Northwest at 950 NW 23rd Ave. ☎ 503/222-4133). You can also try the **Multnomah County Library,** 801 SW 10th Ave. (☎ 503/988-5123), which is Portland's main library and offers online services. And if you're traveling with a wireless-enabled laptop, you can find free Wi-fi throughout Portland's downtown area as of December 2006; other parts of the city will get it in 2007.

Liquor Laws   The legal minimum drinking age in Oregon is 21. Aside from on-premise sales of cocktails in bars and restaurants, hard liquor can only be purchased in liquor stores. Beer and wine are available in convenience stores and grocery stores. Brewpubs tend to sell only beer and wine, but some also have licenses to sell hard liquor.

Newspapers & Magazines   Portland's morning daily newspaper is the *Oregonian.* For arts and entertainment information and listings, consult the "A&E" section of the Friday *Oregonian* or pick up a free copy of the ***Portland Mercury*** or ***Willamette Week*** at Powell's Books or other bookstores, convenience stores, or cafes.

Pharmacies   Convenient to most downtown hotels, **Central Drug,** 538 SW Fourth Ave. (☎ 503/226-2222), is open Monday through Friday from 9am to 6pm, Saturday from 10am to 4pm.

Police   The downtown police station is at 1111 SW Fourth Ave. (☎ 503/823-3333). Call ☎ **911** in an emergency.

Post Offices   The most convenient downtown post office is University Station, 1505 SW Sixth Ave. (☎ 503/274-1362), open Monday through Friday from 7am to 6pm, Saturday from 10am to 3pm. For more information, call ☎ 800/275-8777.

Restrooms   There are public restrooms underneath Starbucks coffee shop in Pioneer Courthouse Square, in downtown shopping malls, and in hotel lobbies.

Safety   Because of its small size and progressive emphasis on keeping downtown alive and growing, Portland is still a relatively safe city; in fact, strolling the downtown streets at night is a popular pastime. Take extra precautions, however, if you venture into the entertainment district along West Burnside Street and in Chinatown at night. Certain neighborhoods in north and northeast Portland are the centers for much of the city's gang activity, so before visiting any place in this area, be sure to get very detailed directions so you don't get lost. If you plan to go hiking in Forest Park, don't leave anything valuable in your car. This holds true in the Skidmore Historic District (Old Town) as well.

Smoking   At most high-end restaurants, the smoking area is usually in the bar/lounge, and although many restaurants have separate bar menus, most will serve you off the regular menu even if you are eating in the bar. You can still smoke in bars in Portland, but a lot of bars are nonsmoking by choice. To see a list of non-smoking bars, go to www.barflymag.com/features/NS.html.

Taxes   Portland is a shopper's paradise—there's no sales tax. However, there is an 11.5% tax on hotel rooms within the city and a 12.5% tax on car rentals (plus an additional airport-use fee if you pick up your rental car at the airport; this additional fee is anywhere from around 11% to around 16%). Outside the city, the room tax varies.

Time Zone   Portland is on Pacific Time, 3 hours behind the East Coast. In the summer, daylight saving time is observed and clocks are set forward 1 hour.

Transit Info   For bus, MAX, and Portland Streetcar information, call the **TriMet Customer Assistance Office** (☎ 503/238-7433).

Weather   If it's summer, it's sunny; otherwise, there's a chance of rain. This almost always suffices, but for specifics, call the Portland Oregon Visitor Association's **weather information hot line** (☎ 503/275-9792). If you want to know how to pack before you arrive, check **www.cnn.com/weather** or **www.weather.com**.

BY BUS

Buses run throughout the city and in the Fareless Square are free. For all the deets on bus routes and times, pick up a *TriMet Guide* or stop by the **TriMet Customer Assistance Office** at Pioneer Courthouse Square (☎ **503/238-7433;** www.trimet. org; open during regular business hours).

ON FOOT

Like San Francisco, Portland is a walking town—in fact, it was voted one of America's best walking towns. I found this out the hard way when I realized my Portland friends' idea of "a quick walk" from the hotel to the restaurant was actually a 20-block trek—not so fun in 3-inch heels. So bring good shoes, because walking is a great (and calorie-burning) way to see this place.

BY TAXI

Taxis are easy to find at major hotels, but harder to flag down in the streets—you'll have to call for one. **Broadway Cab** (☎ 503/227-1234) and **Radio Cab** (☎ 503/227-1212) both offer 24-hour radio-dispatched service and accept American Express, Discover, MasterCard, and Visa. Fares are $2.50 for the first mile, $1.80 for each additional mile, and $1 for each additional passenger.

The Portland Rock Scene

Though Portland had one of the more notable hard-core punk scenes back in the '80s, these days it's better known for churning out pretty, rain-soaked alternative and indie sad-boy rock. Elliott Smith was from Portland, and Everclear, the Decemberists, the Shins, and Modest Mouse's Isaac Brock all call PDX home. (If you haven't already, make sure to watch the documentary *Dig!*, which chronicled the notorious feud between the Brian Jonestown Massacre and Portland's Dandy Warhols.) In addition to the bevy of quality local bands, Portland's also a major stop for touring acts. The best can be found at the following venues.

➜ **Berbati's Pan** ★★★ Next to Voodoo Doughnut in Old Town, Berbati's books the best of the local rock scene and bands on the verge of breaking national. Be sure to check out the back bar, which is 150 years old. *10 S.W. Third Ave.* ☎ *503/248-4579. www.berbati.com. Cover $5–$15.*

➜ **Doug Fir** ★★★ This fairly new venue adjacent to the band-friendly Jupiter Hotel is designed to look like a ski lodge/log cabin, with a diner/coffee shop atmosphere upstairs and the rock venue in the basement. Because it's so new, the club lacks the entrenched character that comes from years of rock debauchery, but shows all the signs of becoming a well-worn favorite within a few years. *830 E. Burnside St.* ☎ *503/231-9663. www.dougfirlounge.com. Daily 7am–4am. Cover $5–$15.*

➜ **Holocene** ★★ Lots of different hangout areas define this giant warehouse space near the Doug Fir. There's a living room–like dining area, a smoking room, and a dance floor that attracts a mix of hipsters, club kids, and the LGBT crowd. A yummy apps-and-cocktail menu complements a solid slate of rock bands and DJs. *1001 S.E. Morrison St.* ☎ *503/239-7639. www.holocene.org. Cover $0–$15.*

🎵 **Best** ● ➜ **Mississippi Studios** ★★★ If you love some lyrics with your music, this is the place to go to see quality singer/songwriters in a cozy, intimate setting among a respectful crowd that actually (whoa) *listens* to the performers onstage. The North Portland venue is also a recording studio. *3939 N. Mississippi.* ☎ *503/288-3895. www.mississippistudios. com. Shows start between 7 and 10pm. Cover $7–$20. 21+ to enter (usually).*

➜ **Sabala's at Mt. Tabor Theatre** ★★ Named after current owner Jason Sabala, who used to run the legendary Austin venue Emo's, Sabala's is housed in a former movie theater and books a weird array of hard-core, goth, hip-hop, and rock acts in the main room, while the hallway leading into the bar and the bar itself are covered in comic-book style neon murals lit up by black lights. As if that wasn't enough, all the murals are in 3-D (ask the bartender to borrow some 3-D shades to prove it). *4811 S.E. Hawthorne.* ☎ *503/238-1646; www. sabalasmttabor.com. Shows start at 9:30pm. Cover varies, around $5. 21+ to enter.*

RECORD STORES

➔ **Music Millennium** ★★ Rumor has it this record store, the oldest in the Pacific Northwest, is where U2's The Edge shops when he comes to town. They also book some bitchin' in-store appearances from singer/songwriters like Pete Yorn (past in-stores have featured Matthew Sweet, Soundgarden, Sheryl Crow, Randy Newman, and Cheap Trick). *3158 E Burnside.* ☎ *503/ 231-8926 and 801 NW 23rd;* ☎ *503/248-0163. www.musicmillenium.com. Mon–Sat 10am– 10pm; Sun 11am–9pm.*

➔ **Jackpot Records** ★ Sonic Youth's Thurston Moore is a fan of this place, owned by local music geek Isaac Slusarenko. The shop specializes in collectible vinyl and Portland bands, and even puts on its own annual film festival. *203 S.W. 9th Ave.* ☎ *503/222-0990. Mon–Sat 10am–8pm; Sun 11am–6pm. Also: 3736 SE Hawthorne Blvd.* ☎ *503/239-7561. Mon–Thurs 10–7; Fri–Sat 10am–8pm; Sun 11am–6pm. www.jackpotrecords.com.*

Sleeping

Portland has a wide variety of lodging options in all price ranges, including some unique places the likes of which you won't find anywhere else. This isn't a city to waste on generic chains when for the same price, you can stay somewhere with a lot more local flavor. Since most of the music venues and other joints mentioned in this chapter are in Southeast, many of the following lodging recommendations are in that neighborhood.

Just over the river from Portland is Vancouver, Washington, which has a bunch of cheap, generic lodging options to choose from if you don't mind driving in and out of town each day. Try the **Ramada Inn** (9107 NE Vancouver Mall Dr.; ☎ **360/ 253-2205**) or the **Best Western** (11506 NE 3rd St.; ☎ **360/254-4000**).

HOSTELS

In the Hawthorne District in Southeast, the 36-bed **Portland Hostel** (3031 SE Hawthorne Blvd.; ☎ **866/447-3031** or 503/ 236-3380; www.portlandhostel.org; $17–$20 dorm, $40–$46 private) is housed in an old converted house complete with cozy front porch. The **Northwest Portland International Hostel** (425 NW 18th Ave. at Glisan St.; ☎ **888/777-0067** or 503/241-2783; nwportlandhostel.com; $17–$20 dorm, $36–$69 private) has two to four beds per dorm plus private rooms, and it's just 2 blocks away from a brewery (bonus!).

CHEAP

➔ **White Eagle** ★★ In industrial North Portland, this century-old "rock 'n' roll" hotel, saloon, and rock dive has booked live music nightly for decades. Performers like Robert Cray held residencies here in the '70s, and Isley Brothers and ZZ Top have been known to drop in. Accommodations are basic—clean and furnished with antiques—you stay at this place for the overall experience (and the easy access to the downstairs bar). *836 N. Russell St.* ☎ *866/271-3377 or 503/335-8900. www. mcmenamins.com, 11 units. $30 bunk rooms; $40 $60 full/queen Amenities: Restaurant; bar. In room: Wi-Fi.*

DOABLE

Portland's home to a bunch of swank boutique hotels, among them the historic, wine-themed **Hotel Vintage Plaza** ★★ (422 SW Broadway; ☎ **800/243-0555** or 503/228-1212; www.vintageplaza.com; $109–$259 double), which was built in 1894 and is *the* place to stay in Portland if you know your chardonnay from your carignane.

The hotel hosts wine tastings every night, while upstairs in the starlight rooms, greenhouse-style wall-to-ceiling windows make for a romantic vibe at night and sunny, breezy ambience in the day.

ROCKIN' THE WEST COAST

Detour: That's so Cheesy!

If you're a cheese fan by any stretch of the imagination, make time for a stop at the **Rogue Creamery** just north of Medford. The place got my attention when I saw a tiny truck on the interstate that boasted "World's Best Blue Cheese," so when I saw signs for the creamery farther down the road I had to investigate. Inside an unassuming storefront on a dusty stretch of road off the historic main drag is a whole cheese factory and retail shop selling everything from imported Italian olives to housemade "Oregonzola." The best part, though, is the free samples of fresh curds (rubbery bits of cheese before it goes through the process that officially turns it into cheese). The curds are subtly flavored with garlic, pesto, artichoke, or even chocolate. Serve some of their Crater Lake Blue Cheese with fig preserves on toast points and you'll be the envy of your next cocktail party. *311 N. Front St. (Hwy. 99), Central Point, OR 97502;* ☎ *866/ 665-1155; www.roguegoldcheese.com; Mon–Fri 9am–5pm, Sat 9am–6pm, Sun 11am–5pm.*

📺 **Best** ❂ → **Jupiter Hotel** ★★ Like the Phoenix in San Francisco, the Jupiter is a funky, band-friendly motel, in this case adjacent to one of the city's best clubs, the Doug Fir. With a simple, boutique hotel style but without the over-the-top sheen that comes with those more expensive places, the Jupiter is the best pick for savvy travelers with an eye for design and money-saving deals. Plus there're condoms on the bed stand and special-rate packages ranging from the naughty-and-nice leather "LUV" deal to a spa package. *800 E Burnside St.* ☎ *877/800–0004 or 503/230–9200. www.jupiterhotel.com. $99– $109 single; $109–$129 double. Amenities: Restaurant; lounge; business center; laundry. In room: Wi-Fi.*

SPLURGE

→ **The Benson** ★★★ With a marble fireplace and Austrian crystal chandeliers, you can see why this is the lodging of choice for presidents and celebrities, who are often spotted in the Lobby Bar, which has live jazz at night. In the vaults below the lobby, you'll find the **London Grill,** well known for its Sunday brunch. *309 SW Broadway.* ☎ *888/523-6766 or 503/228–2000. www.bensonhotel.com. 287 units. $119–$229 double; $209–$299 junior suite; $500–$900 suite. Valet parking $22. Amenities: 2 restaurants; lounge; gym; concierge; business center; 24-hr. room service; dry cleaning. In room: Dataport, minibar.*

→ **The Heathman Hotel** ★★★ With its understated luxury, The Heathman is one of the finest hotels in the city. A favorite for business travelers and culture hounds alike, The Heathman's rooms are basic and tend to be quite small, but are nicely furnished—basically what you get here is luxury in a small space. The corner rooms are lighter and more spacious. *1001 SW Broadway, Portland, OR 97205.* ☎ *800/551- 0011 or 503/241–4100. www.heathmanhotel. com. 150 units. $150–$239 double; $199–$775 suite. Parking $22. Amenities: Restaurant; lounge; gym; concierge; 24-hr. room service; laundry/dry cleaning. In room: Dataport, minibar, French-press coffeemaker.*

Rock & Roots Fests in PDX

→ **FREE** **PDX Pop Now!:** This free, all-ages celebration of Portland talent takes place over one weekend every July. ☎ 971/244-8760; www.pdxpop now.com.

→ **Halleluwah:** The 2006 edition of this rock fest featured indies like Deerhoof and resurrected idol Vashti Bunyan and took place over 2 days at Disjecta Interdisciplinary Arts Center in Southeast. **www.halleluwah.org.**

→ **Pickathon:** Roots music is highlighted in this 2-day summer festival of music, crafts, workshops, food, and beer held about 20 minutes outside of Portland at Pendarvis Farm. Hiking and camping, too. **www.pickathon. com.**

Eating

SUPPLIES

Marinotti's Café & Deli (404 SW 10th Ave.; ☎ 503/224-9028) downtown has a variety of interesting gourmet offerings, like imported wines and cheeses and thick salami sandwiches. If you still haven't mastered the art of al dente, cruise by Hawthorne's **Pastaworks** (3731 SE Hawthorne Blvd.; ☎ 503/232-1010), a specialty grocer and deli that also offers cooking classes. Across town at **City Market** (735 NW 21st Ave.; ☎ 503/221-3004) in Nob Hill you can choose from among 10 different kinds of sausage and other prepared foods.

TAKEOUT TREATS

Downtown Portland, especially around SW 5th at Stark, is also home to dozens of small **fast-food trailers** peddling all kinds of ethnic fare—everything from vegan burritos to barbecue and Indian curries to Czech Schnitzelwitches, which you can get for about five bucks.

MTV **Best ♦** → **Voodoo Doughnut** ★★ Rock towns always have to put their rock 'n' roll spin on everything. In Austin it's Death Metal Pizza; in Portland it's Voodoo Doughnut, the tiny shop next door to Berbati's Pan whose menu would make John Waters blush. They do naughty things with fried bread here (a big, black, triple

cream-filled Cock 'n' Balls, anyone?). Or maybe a Triple Chocolate Penetration, or a candy-bar-topped Butter Fingering? Elvis would dig the giant chocolate-banana-peanut-butter Memphis Mafia, and believe it or not they actually have a variety of vegan doughnuts, too. They also give Swahili lessons and can legally preside over marriages; too bad they're only open 22 hours a day. *22 SW 3rd Ave.* ☎ *503/241-4704. www.voodoodoughnut.com. $1–$5. Closed Mon–Fri 11am–1pm and Sat 4–6am.*

RESTAURANTS

Cheap

→ **Esparza's Tex-Mex Café** ★ TEX-MEX With red-eyed cow skulls on the walls and marionettes, model planes, and stuffed iguanas and armadillos hanging from the ceiling, the decor here—and the menu for that matter—can only be described as Tex-eclectic. Enchiladas, tamales, and tacos sound standard until you realize they're filled with ostrich, buffalo meat, or smoked salmon (don't trip; there's chicken and beef, too). The *nopalitos* (fried cactus) are worth a try, and the margaritas are some of the best in Portland. While you're waiting for a seat (there's almost always a wait), check out the vintage tunes on the jukebox. *2725 SE Ankeny St.* ☎ *503/234-7909. Main courses $7.50–$18. Tues–Sat 11:30am–10pm (in summer Fri–Sat until 10:30pm).*

Time to make the doughnuts . . .

[MTV] (Best ☻) →**Montage** ★★ This lively late-night place is tough to find under the Morrison Bridge in Southeast, but once you do it's so worth it. With a waiting list even at 1am, Montage specializes in traditional and weird variations on mac & cheese (with spam, with pesto, and so on), plus Cajun standards like red beans and rice and jambalaya—all at very wallet-friendly prices. Portions are hefty, but fear not; they'll pack up your leftovers for you in way more creative aluminum foil shapes than your average takeout joint (I saw one guy walk out with a four-foot-tall foil giraffe, while my friend had to take his garlic mac 'n' cheese home in a silvery, sperm-shaped package). Don't forget to slurp down an oyster shooter with your Mt. Gay rum "Homojito." *301 SE Morrison St. (at SE 3rd).* ☎ *503/234-1324. www.montageportland. com. Starters/salads $5–$15; entrees $8–$16. Mon–Sat 11:30am–2pm; Sun–Thurs 6pm–2am; Fri–Sat 6pm–4am; bar open earlier.*

→**Nicholas Restaurant** MIDDLE EASTERN This little hole in the wall on an unattractive stretch of Grand Avenue gets packed, no thanks to the decor or ambience. The big draw is the great food and cheap prices. In spite of the heat from the pizza oven and the crowded conditions, the customers and waitstaff still manage to be friendly. Try the *Manakish,* Mediterranean pizza with thyme, oregano, sesame seeds, olive oil, and lemony-flavored sumac; other standards like creamy hummus, baba ghanouj, kabobs, falafel, and gyros are also served. *318 SE Grand Ave. (between Pine and Oak sts.).* ☎ *503/235-5123. www.nicholasrestaurant. com. Main courses $4.75–$11. No credit cards. Mon–Sat 11am–9pm; Sun noon–9pm.*

Doable

→**Assaggio** ★★ RUSTIC ITALIAN This trattoria in the Sellwood neighborhood focuses on pastas and wines; the menu lists a dozen or more pastas, and the wine list includes more than 100 wines, almost

The Fests of Wine & Roses (and Film)

→ **Portland International Film Festival:** Foreign films and documentaries screen at theaters throughout the city at this February fest. ☎ **503/221-1156;** www.nwfilm.org.

→ **Portland Indie Wine Festival:** This 2-day festival is held in the Pearl District in May to showcase Oregon's smallest independent vintners. ☎ **503/595-0891;** www.indiewinefestival.com.

→ **Portland Rose Festival:** Spanning almost a month, P-town's biggest celebration dates back to 1888 and features a parade, music festival, arts festival, and dragon-boat races. ☎ **503/227-2681;** www.rosefestival.org.

→ **Portland Arts Festival:** This juried arts and crafts show also features music and microbrews. ☎ **503/227-2681;** www.rosefestival.org.

→ **Oregon Brewers Festival:** Held in July in Waterfront Park, this is one of the country's largest independent craft brewers' festivals. ☎ **503/778-5917;** www.oregonbrewfest.com.

→ **The Bite of Oregon:** Sample some of Portland's finest restaurants at this annual mid-August event in Waterfront Park. ☎ **503/248-0600;** www.bite oforegon.com.

→ **Oktoberfest:** Polka and brews, on Oaks Park amusement Center. ☎ **503/233-5777;** www.oakspark.com.

all Italian. The atmosphere in this tiny place is theatrical, with indirect lighting, dark walls, and the likes of Mario Lanza playing in the background. Don't be surprised if after taking your first bite, you suddenly hear a Verdi aria. The pastas, with surprisingly robust flavors, are the main attraction. *Assaggio* means a sampling or a taste, and that is exactly what you get if you order salad, bruschetta, or pasta Assaggio-style—a sampling of several dishes, all served family-style. This is especially fun if you're here with a group. *7742 SE 13th Ave. ☎ 503/232-6151. www. assaggiorestaurant.com. Main courses $11–$17; 3-course prix-fixe dinner $26. Tues–Thurs 5–9:30pm; Fri–Sat 5–10pm.*

→**Simpatica Kitchen** ★★★ BRUNCH You can tell a restaurant is really good when it's stashed away in a basement with hardly any signage directing you where to go. That's the situation with this catering company, which has been packing 'em in during Sunday brunch, served from 9am to 2pm; one taste of the veggie strata or Belgian waffles with orange maple syrup and you'll understand why. *Mmmmm . . . . 828 SE Ash. ☎ 503/235-1600. www.simpatica catering.com. Most dishes $8–$10. Sun 9am–2pm.*

→**Equinox** ★★★ ORGANIC/ECLECTIC This place just off Mississippi is all about local organic produce and hormone-free meat and poultry, and the menu's full of fancy-sounding dishes and upscale ingredients like mesclun and "balsamique citrus crema." Good thing the prices aren't quite as fancy, with most entrees hovering around the $15 mark. On sunny weekend mornings the outdoor patio is an awesome complement to Equinox's excellent food. *830 N Shaver St. ☎ 503/460-3333. www. equinoxrestaurantpdx.com. Starters $4.50–$9; entrees $8.50–$18.50. Wed–Thurs and Sun 5–10pm; Fri–Sat 5pm–12am. Brunch Sat–Sun 9am–2pm.*

For even more doable choices, wander down to Restaurant Row on NW 21st Avenue, where standouts include **Tuscany Grill** (811 NW 21st Ave.; ☎ **503/243-2757**; www.tuscanygrill.com), **Wildwood** (1221 NW 21st Ave.; ☎ **503/248-9663**; www.wild woodrestaurant.com), which specializes in Pacific Northwest cuisine, and the French-influenced bistro **Paley's Place** (1204 NW 21st Ave; ☎ **503/243-2403**; paleysplace. citysearch.com).

Splurge

➜**Castagna** ★★ FRENCH/ITALIAN Castagna is a magnet for Portland foodies despite its less than stylish location and minimalist (though thoroughly designed) interior. Try the stellar New York steak, served with a heaping mound of shoe-string potatoes, or go for more adventurous offerings like duck breast with dried cherry and chervil sauce or halibut with artichoke, cardoon, salsify, and clams in a white wine–thyme sauce. A cheaper cafe abuts the main dining room and serves much simpler fare. *1752 SE Hawthorne Blvd.* ☎ *503/231-7373. Main dishes $22–$27; cafe main courses $9–$16. Main restaurant Wed–Thurs 5:30–9:30pm; Fri–Sat 5:30–10:30pm. Cafe Mon–Thurs 5–10pm; Fri–Sat 5–11pm; Sun 5–9:30pm.*

Partying

This is a town that is waiting to be painted red. Things that other cities have long since outlawed—like smoking indoors and gambling—are still legal here. Oddly, a lot of the cooler bars here feel like glorified Denny's, only with slot machines, so if you prefer comfortable, low-key joints to trendy dress-code hot-spots, you'll feel right at home at these joints.

BARS & PUBS

➜ **Dunes** ★ There's no sign indicating your arrival at Dunes, but the Northeast club still manages to pull crowds with live bands and DJ nights. *1909 NE M.L. King Blvd., next to Dirty Little Secret.* ☎ *503/493-8637. www.dunes.cc.*

➜ **McMenamins Kennedy School** ★★ Never thought they'd ever start serving beer in elementary school, did you? However, in the hands of the local McMenamins brewpub empire, an old northeast Portland school has been transformed into a sprawling complex complete with brewpub, beer garden, movie theater pub, a cigar-and-cocktails room, and even a bed-and-breakfast inn. *5736 NE 33rd Ave.* ☎ *503/288-2192. www.mcmenamins.com. Daily, 7am–1am*

➜ **The Lucky Labrador Brew Pub** ★★ With its warehouse-size room, industrial feel, and picnic tables on the loading dock out back, this is a classic (and dog-friendly) local in Southeast. *915 SE Hawthorne Blvd.* ☎ *503/236-3555. www.luckylab.com. Mon–Sat 11am–12am; Sun 12pm–10pm.*

➜ **My Father's Place** ★★ Next door to Slow Bar, My Father's Place is a comfy diner and hipster lounge with cheap bloody marys and an arcade room in back. *523 SE Grand Ave.* ☎ *503/235-5494. Daily 6am–2:30am.*

➜ **Slow Bar** ★★ The drinks and the people watching are better than the bar food at this scenestery little spot in Southeast. *533 SE Grand Ave.* ☎ *503/230-7767. www. slowbar.net. Mon–Fri 11am–2:30am; Sat–Sun 5:30pm–2:30am.*

DANCE CLUBS

➜ **Barracuda** ★ See-and-be-scene at one of four bars at this tropics-themed hot spot while sipping one of their huge tropical drinks with a friend (they won't even serve the 60-ouncers to singles). *9 NW Second Ave.* ☎ *503/228-6900. Tues 7pm–2:30am; Wed–Thurs 10pm–2:30am; Fri–Sat 7pm–4am; cover $10 (free before 10pm).*

➔ **Embers Avenue** ★★ Though primarily a gay disco, this spot is also popular with straights. There are always lots of flashing lights and sweaty bodies until the early morning. Look for drag shows 5 nights a week. *110 NW Broadway.* ☎ *503/222-3082. Mon–Fri 11:30am–2:30am; Sat–Sun 1pm–2:30am Cover free–$5.*

➔ **Fez Ballroom** ★ The flattering lighting and fluffy pillows thrown around set a sexy vibe as DJs spin everything from techno to funk and bartenders pour 'em strong to help you get up your liquid courage. *316 SW 11th Ave. at Stark.* ☎ *503/221-7262. Cover free–$15.*

STRIP CLUBS

I'm not really a strip-club kinda girl, but I mention these two PDX nudie bars for a reason. First, **Mary's Club** (129 SW Broadway; ☎ **503/227-3023;** www.marysclub.com) was Portland's first topless bar, where Courtney Love danced under the name "Michelle" in the '80s, back before she got famous and cleaned up—or just got famous.

Meanwhile ⓜ Best⚫ **Magic Gardens** (217 NW 4th Ave.; ☎ **503/224-8472**) in Chinatown can only be described as an indie-rock strip club. Non-silicone enhanced hipster chicks dance to—gasp!—*good* music like the Yeah Yeah Yeahs, which isn't spun by some cheesy DJ but comes from the jukebox. The clientele is all cute guys with designer jeans and bedhead and their girlfriends, whose (clothed) presence makes the vibe decidedly less sleazy than your average topless bar.

What Else to See & Do

Portland's really proud of its plant life, so you should, you know, spend some time outdoors. It seems there's an upside to having all that rain dumped on you all year, and the reward comes in the form of lush forests, gardens, and green spaces. In addition to the natural stuff, there's also a lot of ways to spend money at various shopping neighborhoods and public markets.

SHOPPING

Remember those blister-causing heels from my 20-block walk (p. 665)? Bought those on **NW 23rd** (between Burnside and Thurman), the tony shopping district sometimes called "trendy third," which is home to boutique after boutique hawking everything from jeans to bath products to, yes, the cutest pumps *ever*. In Southeast, **SE Hawthorne** between 35th and 50th is home to decent thrift and vintage shops like Buffalo Exchange and Red Light, plus Imelda's shoe store and a few bath shops and bookstores, including the famous Powell's.

ⓜ Best⚫ ꜰʀᴇᴇ ➔ **Portland Saturday Market** ★★ This downtown market is actually held on both Saturday and Sunday, and with ethnic food, free entertainment, and around 300 artists and craftspeople hawking their stuff, it's arguably the city's single-most important and best-loved event. Don't miss it. *Underneath the west end of the Burnside Bridge between SW First Ave. and SW Naito Pkwy.* ☎ *503/222-6072. www.saturdaymarket. org. Free admission. 1st weekend in Mar to Christmas Eve Sat 10am–5pm; Sun 11am–4:30pm.*

PLAYING OUTSIDE

Above downtown Portland in Washington Park, the 5-acre **International Rose Test Garden** (400 SW Kingston Ave., Washington Park; ☎ **503/823-3636;** free admission) is among the biggest in the country and features one garden devoted to miniature roses and another to buds mentioned in Shakespearean plays. Hey, they don't call it the City of Roses for nothing. Also in **Washington Park:** the Japanese Garden, the Oregon Zoo, the

ROCKIN' THE WEST COAST

Vietnam Veterans Living Memorial, and the 175-acre Hoyt Arboretum (☎ 503/228-8733; www.hoytarboretum.org), which has 10 miles of hiking trails and free guided tours on weekends at 2pm. Get maps and stuff at the Arboretum Visitor Center, 4000 SW Fairview Blvd. (open Mon–Sat 9am–4pm).

Five thousand acres of forest and 65 miles of trails for hiking, biking, and jogging make **Forest Park** (☎ 503/823-PLAY) the largest forested city park in the country. On the flip side, Portland also lays claim to the world's smallest park. Hogging 452.16 square inches of land on the median strip of Naito Parkway at the corner of SW Taylor St., **Mill Ends Park** came into being when a hole for a telephone pole was dug in the middle of Naito Parkway. Dick Fagan, a columnist whose office overlooked the hole, planted flowers in it, because weeds started growing before the new pole arrived. He dubbed it Mill Ends Park, after his column, and it was officially designated a Portland city park in 1976.

Spectator Sports

The NBA's **Portland Trail Blazers** (☎ 503/231-8000 or 503/234-9291; www.nba.com/blazers) pound the boards at the Rose Garden arena. Call for current schedule and ticket information. Tickets are $10 to $127. If the Blazers are doing well, you can bet that tickets will be hard to come by.

The **Portland Beavers Baseball Club** (☎ 503/553-5555; www.portlandbeavers.com), the AAA affiliate of the San Diego Padres, plays minor-league ball at PGE Park, SW 20th Avenue and Morrison Street. Tickets are $6 to $10.

On the Road to Seattle, WA

Portland, OR to Seattle, WA 173 miles

The Portland-to-Seattle leg of this trip is a straight shot up I-5 that takes about 3 hours, depending on traffic. Just outside the city you'll cross over the Columbia River and the Washington state line. In Washington, you'll start seeing lovely little signs that say, SAFETY BREAK: FREE COFFEE as you approach rest areas, so take advantage if you're feeling sleepy on the roads.

You'll drive past **Mount St. Helens** volcanic monument and **Lewis & Clark State Park** heading toward **Olympia,** which is worth a stop if you're interested in visiting the stomping grounds of grunge and riot grrrl pioneers like Kurt Cobain and the ladies of Sleater-Kinney, who named their band after a street here in Olympia. The city's also home to indie labels K Records, one-time home to Modest Mouse and Built to Spill, and Kill Rock Stars, which has put out releases by Bikini Kill and Elliott Smith, among others.

If you do stop in Olympia, check out the **Capitol Theater** (206 5th Ave. SE; ☎ 360/754-5378), where Nirvana got its start. And if you happen to be driving through on a Tuesday between 6 and 8pm, tune into 89.3 FM to hear **Radio8Ball,** a quirky advice show that works just like a regular Magic 8 Ball, only with music: Callers ask the 8 Ball a question, and the show's hosts put their music library on shuffle and analyze the lyrics to come up with the answer.

Watch your speed entering cities: While I-5 has long 70-mph stretches, outside of Olympia the speed limit drops back down to 60, and in Washington the fine for not wearing a seatbelt goes up to $101. Pretty soon you'll pass Tacoma, the SEA-TAC Airport, and into Seattle, the next stop on our trip.

The road to indie legend; or: how to pick a band name.

Welcome to Seattle

Any self-respecting rock roadtrip has to include a stop in Seattle. It's the birthplace of grunge, yes, but the Seattle rock scene has remained active and relevant even a dozen years after Kurt Cobain's death. Besides its legendary clubs, bitchin' bar scene, and quality restaurants, the ultra-caffeinated Emerald City is also home to the corporate headquarters of evil empires like Starbucks and Microsoft (sort of . . . Bill Gates's HQ is about 15 mins. outside of town in Redmond). Take some time to get to know this city, from the tourist- and character-filled waterfront and trendy Belltown, to the funky U district and gay- and hipster-friendly Capitol Hill.

Seattle Nuts & Bolts

Area Code The area code is 206 in Seattle, 425 for the Eastside (including Kirkland and Bellevue), and 253 for south King County (near the airport).

Business Hours Banks are generally open Monday through Friday from 9am to 5pm (some also on Sat 9am–noon). Bars generally open around 11am but are legally allowed to be open Monday through Saturday from 6am to 1am and Sunday from 10am to 1am.

Doctor To find a physician, check at your hotel for a referral, contact **Swedish Medical Center** (☎ 800/SWEDISH; www.swedish.org), or call the referral line of the **Virginia Mason Medical Center** (☎ 888/862-2737).

ROCKIN' THE WEST COAST

Emergencies   For police, fire, or medical emergencies, phone ☎ **911.**

Hospitals   Hospitals convenient to downtown include **Swedish Medical Center,** 747 Broadway (☎ 206/386-6000; www.Swedish.org), and **Virginia Mason Medical Center,** 1100 Ninth Ave. (☎ 206/583-6433 for emergencies or 206/624-1144 for information).

Internet Access   First, ask at your hotel to see if it provides Internet access. Alternatively, you can head to the **Seattle Central Library,** 1000 Fourth Ave. (☎ 206/386-4636), which has hundreds of online computer terminals. Visitors can obtain a free 1-day visitors pass to the library, which includes 1 hour of Internet access.

Liquor Laws   The legal minimum drinking age in Washington State is 21. Besides on-premises sales of cocktails in bars and restaurants, hard liquor can only be purchased in liquor stores. Beer and wine are available in convenience stores and grocery stores. Brewpubs tend to sell only beer and wine, but some also have licenses to sell hard liquor.

Newspapers & Magazines   The *Seattle Post-Intelligencer* and *Seattle Times* are Seattle's two daily newspapers. *Seattle Stranger* is the city's great (and free) arts-and-entertainment weekly.

Pharmacies   Conveniently located downtown pharmacies include **Rite Aid,** with branches at 319 Pike St. (☎ 206/223-0512) and 2603 Third Ave. (☎ 206/441-8790). You can also call Rite Aid (☎ 800/748-3243) for the location nearest you. For 24-hour service, try **Bartell Drug Store,** 600 First Ave. N. (☎ 206/284-1353), in the Lower Queen Anne neighborhood.

Police   For police emergencies, phone ☎ **911.**

Restrooms   There are public restrooms in Pike Place Market, Westlake Center, Pacific Place, Seattle Center, and the Washington State Convention and Trade Center. You'll also find restrooms in most hotel lobbies and coffee bars in downtown Seattle.

Safety   Although Seattle is a relatively safe city, it has its share of crime. The most questionable neighborhood you're likely to visit is the Pioneer Square area, which is home to more than a dozen bars and nightclubs, and is safe by day but sketchy by night. Watch your purse or wallet at Pike Place Market, too.

Smoking   Seattle's bars and restaurants became smoke-free as of November 2005, and not only that, you can't smoke within 25 feet of the entrance.

Taxes   Seattle has an 8.8% sales tax. In restaurants, there's an additional .5% food-and-beverage tax. The hotel-room tax in the metro area ranges from around 10% to 16%. On rental cars, you pay an 18.5% tax, plus, if you rent at the airport, a 10% to 12% airport concession fee (for a whopping total of around 30%!).

Time Zone   Seattle is on Pacific Standard Time (PST), making it 3 hours behind the East Coast.

Transit Info For 24-hour information on Seattle's Metro bus system, call ☎ 206/553-3000. For information on the Washington State Ferries, call ☎ 800/84-FERRY or 888/808-7977 in Washington or 206/464-6400.

Weather Check the *Seattle Times* or *Seattle Post-Intelligencer* newspapers for forecasts. If you want to know what to pack before you depart, go to **www.wrh.noaa.gov/seattle**, **www.cnn.com/weather**, or **www.wunderground.com/US/WA**.

Getting Around

Free public transit within downtown and a compact city layout means you can ditch the car in Seattle if you want to. Walking is a fantastic way to get to learn the city (and firm up the glutes—the hills on the Pike/Pine have a way of making the booty burn). If you're considering public transit, know about these discount pass deals: On Saturday, Sunday, and holidays, you can purchase an **All-Day Pass** on any bus or streetcar for $2.50; it's good anywhere outside the downtown Ride Free Area. On other days of the week, you can purchase a **Visitor Pass**, for $5, which can be used on buses, the water taxi, and the Waterfront Streetcar. For more information, contact **Metro** (☎ 206/624-7277; http://transit.metrokc.gov). Exact change is required on buses and streetcars.

BY METRO

Seattle's **Metro** (☎ 800/542-7876 in Washington or 206/553-3000; http://transit.metrokc.gov) **bus system** is free between 6am and 7pm in the downtown Ride Free Area; outside that area, fares $1.25 to $2.

Seattle Playlist: Grunge and Grunger

On the radio:
- → **KEXP** (90.3 FM), Seattle
- → **The End** (107.7 FM), Seattle
- → **Radio8Ball** on KAOS (89.3 FM), Olympia (Tues 6–8pm)

On the iPod/CD player:
- → *Frances Farmer Will Have Her Revenge on Seattle*, **Nirvana**, "In Utero," 1993
- → *Exit Does Not Exist*, **Modest Mouse**, "This is a Long Drive for Someone With Nothing to Think About," 1996
- → *The Journey*, **Alice in Chains**, "Music Bank," 1999
- → *Beyond the Wheel*, **Soundgarden**, "Ultramega OK," 1988
- → *Rearviewmirror*, **Pearl Jam**, "Vs," 1993
- → *Tonight I Think I'm Gonna Go Downtown*, **Mudhoney** with Jimmy Dale Gilmore, "Buckskin Stallion Blues," 1994
- → *Carparts*, **Long Winters**, "The Worst You Can Do Is Harm," 2002
- → *It's Cold*, **Smoosh**, "She Like Electric," 2004
- → *Title and Registration*, **Death Cab**, "Transatlanticism," 1977
- → *Pike St./Park Slope*, **Harvey Danger**, "King James Version," 2000

Seattle Highlights

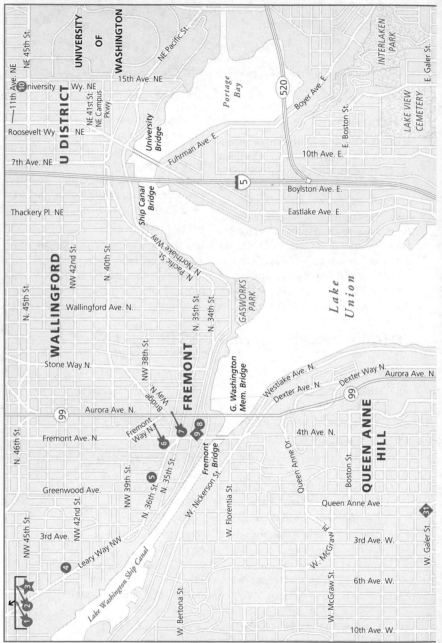

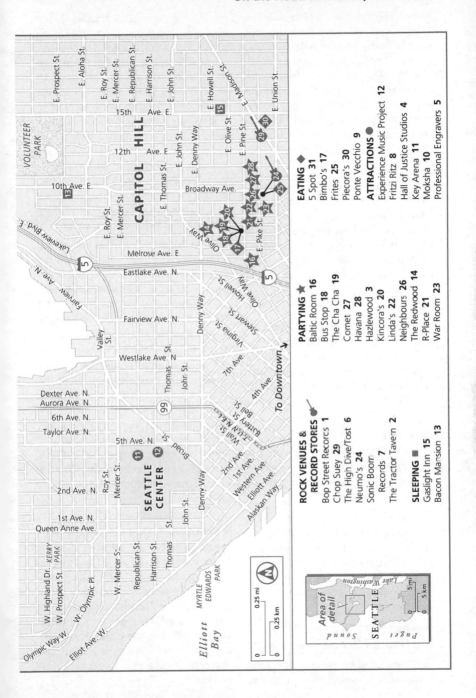

PARTYING ★
Baltic Room **16**
Bus Stop **18**
The Cha Cha **19**
Comet **27**
Havana **28**
Hazlewood **3**
Kincora's **20**
Linda's **22**
Neighbours **26**
The Redwood **14**
R-Place **21**
War Room **23**

ROCK VENUES & RECORD STORES ●
Bop Street Records **1**
Chop Suey **29**
The High Dive/Tost **6**
Neumo's **24**
Sonic Boom Records **7**
The Tractor Tavern **2**

SLEEPING ■
Gaslight Inn **15**
Bacon Mansion **13**

EATING ◆
5 Spot **31**
Bimbo's **17**
Frites **25**
Piecora's **30**
Ponte Vecchio **9**

ATTRACTIONS ●
Experience Music Project **12**
Fritzi Ritz **8**
Hall of Justice Studios **4**
Key Arena **11**
Moksha **10**
Professional Engravers **5**

Note: When traveling out of the Ride Free Area, you pay when you get off the bus; when traveling into the Ride Free Area, you pay when you get on the bus.

Metro also operates old-fashioned **streetcars** along a waterfront route that hits tourist attractions like Pioneer Square, the Seattle Aquarium, IMAX Dome Theater, and Pike Place Market. One-way fares run $1.25 to $1.50.

BY MONORAIL

The **Seattle Monorail** (☎ 206/905-2620; www.seattlemonorail.com) runs from downtown to Seattle Center and passes right through the middle of the Experience Music Project, with departures every 10 minutes (pending any schedule changes caused by monorail repairs). The one-way fare is $1.50.

BY WATER TAXI

Water taxis run between the downtown Seattle waterfront (Pier 55) and Seacrest Park in West Seattle, near Alki Beach. For a service schedule, check with Metro (☎ 206/205-3866; http://transit.metrokc. gov). The one-way fare is $3 or free with a valid bus transfer or all-day pass.

ON FOOT

Seattle is surprisingly compact but also very hilly going from downtown to, say, Capitol Hill. Watch the jaywalking, though—it's a ticketable offense.

BY TAXI

Taxis can be hard to hail on the street, so if you decide not to use public transit system, call **Yellow Cab** (☎ 206/622-6500) or **Farwest Taxi** (☎ 206/622-1717). The flag-drop charge is $2.50; after that, it's $2 per mile.

Moving Past Grunge: The Seattle Scene

The birthplace of grunge and the current headquarters to some of the most relevant

music being made in the U.S., Seattle is a *serious* music city. One glance at the calendar section of the *Stranger*, Seattle's kick-ass local alt-weekly, is enough to make any rock fan from the flyover states green with envy. On any given night—well, except Sundays and Mondays, which seem to be kinda slow—an impressive array of bands perform here, from hipster rock acts at Neumo's to garage-punk at the Sunset Tavern to hip-hop and electronic at Chop Suey. Then there are the town's many bars, which provide a whole other outlet for bands to bring the rawk. Here's an overview of the major players in the club scene.

➜ **Chop Suey** ★★ One of the busier clubs on the Hill, Chop Suey's booking runs the gamut from hip-hop to DJs to rock, while the red-lit interior is done up, as the name might suggest, with Chinese lanterns and Bruce Lee pictures. *1325 E. Madison St.* ☎ *206/324-8000. www.chopsuey.com. Cover $0–$15. Occasional all-ages shows.*

➜ **The Crocodile Café** ★★★ Giant papier-mache snakes hanging from the ceiling decorate this Belltown staple, a combination nightclub, bar, and restaurant. Most famous for being *the* place to play in the grunge era, the Crocodile is owned by Stephanie Dorgan, wife of REM's Peter Buck, and books mainly alt-rock bands Tuesday through Saturday nights. *2200 Second Ave.* ☎ *206/441-5611. www. thecrocodile.com. Cover $6–$20.*

➜ **High Dive** ★★ Just one of many small venues popping up all over Seattle, Fremont's High Dive is a good spot to grub on some barbecue and check out up-and-coming indie bands for cheap (cover's usually free or less than $10). Don't forget to stop in on adjacent martini bar **Toast Lounge** (☎ 206/547-0240; www.toast lounge.com). *513 N. 36th St.* ☎ *206/632-0212. www.highdiveseattle.com. Daily 4pm–2am. 21+ to enter.*

Seattle: Music Festival Nirvana

➜ **Bumbershoot Music and Arts Festival:** Though it's been scaled back to just a 3-day festival, this nearly 40-year-old event (held in Sept at Seattle Center) is still one of the most important of Seattle's music scene, where headliners like Kanye West and Blondie mix with indies like Spoon and the New Pornographers. There are also film, dance, comedy, theater, and arts programs. **www.bumbershoot.org.**

➜ **Sasquatch!:** This massive music fest is promoted by House of Blues at the Gorge amphitheater in George, WA (about 3 hr. outside of Seattle) every Memorial Day weekend. **www.hob.com/sasquatch.**

➜ **Seattle Music Fest:** This cheap, all-ages festival at Alki Beach in early August books mostly emerging bands that you might not have heard of unless you're a super music nerd, plus slightly more famous acts like Soul Coughing's M. Doughty and They Might Be Giants. ☎ **866/208-6293;** www. northwestarts.org/seattlemusicfest.

Best ➜ Neumo's ★★★ This Capitol Hill venue boasts great booking (think: indie rock, hip-hop, electronica, and anything else you can read about on Pitchfork), balcony seating, and an adjacent hangout room called the Bad Juju Lounge, a separate space whose calendar is split between live bands and DJs. The only downside: When Neumo's is packed, it's *packed.* Sold-out shows are not for agoraphobes. *925 E. Pike St. (at 10th).* ☎ *206/ 709-9467. www.neumos.com. Cover $5–$20+. Occasional all-ages shows.*

➜ **Showbox** Though it was dark for much of the grunge era, this 1,000-seat venue is still a major player when it comes to larger venues in Seattle. Across from Pike Place Market, the Showbox has green walls, a green leather-trimmed bar, and sunken seating area and an adjacent lounge, appropriately named the **Green Room.** *1426 First Ave.* ☎ *206/628-3151. www.show boxonline.com. Cover $5–$25.*

➜ **Tractor Tavern** If your music taste ranges beyond whatever the hipster blog du jour tells you to listen to, the Tractor is the place to be. The club is tight with the folks that publish alt-country bible *No*

Depression—Wilco played here back in the day. You'll find tractor-tire chandeliers hanging from the ceiling, while onstage bands play anything from rockabilly to Hawaiian slack-key guitar to singer-song-writers to banjo music to Celtic to folk to zydeco. *5213 Ballard Ave. NW.* ☎ *206/789-3599. www.tractortavern.citysearch.com. Cover $5–$20.*

RECORD STORES

Best ➜ Bop Street Records ★★★ The frazzled and utterly devoted music geek that runs Bop Street says that this Ballard store houses tens of thousands of vinyl records, and I believe him. Musicians leave their scrawl on the walls here—ask someone to show you where Thom Yorke wrote "My credit card got very ill after being in here" after a 7-hour shopping spree (which ended with the band giving everyone in the store a guest-list-plus-one for the Radiohead show that night). *5219 Ballard Ave. NW.* ☎ *206/297-2232. Mon–Thurs noon–6pm; Fri–Sat noon–midnight; Sun 1–6pm.*

➜ **Sonic Boom** ★★ This notable record store/label has three locations, not count-ing in the basement underneath the original

Fremont shop, which is entirely devoted to vinyl. Since 2000 the mini-chain has hosted in-stores from the Shins, way before *Garden State,* and a pre-"O.C." Death Cab for Cutie. *Three locations: 2209 NW Market St., Ballard.* ☎ *206/297-BOOM. 514 15th Ave. E., Capitol Hill.* ☎ *206/568-BOOM. 3414 Fremont Ave. N., Fremont.* ☎ *206/547-BOOM. www.sonicboomrecords.com. Mon–Sat 10am–10pm; Sun 10am–7pm.*

Sleeping

From hip budget hotels to quaint, centrally located B&Bs to waterfront palaces where The Beatles used to stay, Seattle has options.

CAMPGROUNDS/HOSTELS

A block away from Pike Place Market and the Waterfront Aquarium downtown, **Hostelling International-Seattle** (84 Union St.; ☎ **888/622-5443;** dorms $25–$35, private $63–$81) offers free breakfast, Wi-Fi, laundry, and a game area. And the views from some of the rooms look right over the harbor (at a fraction of what you'd be paying in some of the fancier places nearby). Of course, you'll be sharing that view with the other folks in your multi-bedded room.

Also downtown, the **Green Tortoise** (1525 Second Ave; ☎ **888/424-6783;** www. greentortoise.com; dorms $23–$36, private room $48–$68), which has a sister hostel in San Francisco, treats its travelers to free food and Internet, too, and is conveniently close to the Crocodile, Showbox, and more area venues.

There's also a **KOA** just south of town in Kent (5801 S. 212th, Kent; ☎ **800/562-1892;** tent sites $29–$36/night) and another 50 tent and RV sites at **Saltwater State Park** between Seattle and Tacoma (Exit 149 from I-5, then S. on US 99, right on 240th and left on Marine View Dr; ☎ **206/764-4128;** $15/night), but it's in the flight path of the Sea-Tac airport, so keep that in mind.

CHEAP

➜ **Ace Hotel** ★★ One of Seattle's hippest economy hotels in one of the city's trendiest nabes (Belltown), Ace is like a scenester B&B, only minus the second B. The hotel's minimalist decor means pretty much everything is painted white or made of steel and it's basically a step above a hostel, aside from the eight large rooms with private bathrooms (ask about the room with the shower behind the bed). Don't plan on going to sleep early. *2423 First Ave.* ☎ *206/448-4721. Fax 206/374-0745. www.acehotel.com. 28 units, 14 with shared bathroom. $65–$99 double with shared bathroom; $130–$199 double with private bathroom. Parking $17. In room: TV, dataport, Wi-Fi.*

➜ **Moore Hotel** ★★ "I went out of my way to work here," said the guy manning the check-in counter at this Belltown hotel adjacent to the Moore Theater. He likes mom-and-pop-places, and thought this one was "special." The recently renovated mom-and-pop-owned inn is basic, clean, Euro-style budget lodging. The rooms on the sides of the hotel are larger and have claw-foot tubs but can be a little dark and dreary, while the street-facing rooms are smaller, brighter, noisier, and some only have a shared bathroom. The quarters don't really lend themselves to luxurious lounging, but you didn't want to spend a ton of time in your room anyway, right? *1926 Second Ave.* ☎ *800/421-5508 or 206/448-4851. www.moorehotel.com. 140 units (45 with shared bathroom). $55 double with shared bathroom; $69–$79 double with private bathroom; $95–$130 suite. Parking $15. Amenities: Restaurant; lounge.*

DOABLE

Seattle's got a ton of B&Bs that are often cheaper than the downtown hotels. If you don't' mind feeling like you're sleeping over at grandma's, try the **Gaslight Inn** (1727 15th Ave.; ☎ **206/325-3654;** www.

Folk, Film & Food: More Seattle Festivals

➔ **Seattle International Film Festival:** This festival showcases new foreign and indie films over several weeks from mid-May to mid-June. ☎ 206/324-9996; www.seattlefilm.com.

➔ **Northwest Folklife Festival:** Held at Seattle Center, this is the largest folk festival in the country, with dozens of national and regional folk musicians performing on numerous stages, held Memorial Day weekend. ☎ 206/684-7300; www.nwfolklife.org.

➔ **Summer Brewfest:** St. Edward State Park in Kenmore hosts this celebration of seasonal microbrews, kicking off the summer beer-drinking season on Father's Day weekend. ☎ 206/633-0422; www.washingtonbrewfest.com.

➔ **U District Street Fair:** This is the first big street fair of the season with crafts booths, food vendors, and live music, held annually in mid-May. ☎ 206/547-4417; www.udistrictstreetfair.org.

➔ **Fremont Fair:** Seattle's favorite 'hood hosts a celebration of the summer solstice with a wacky parade, naked bicyclists, food, and arts and crafts during the third weekend in June. ☎ 206/694-6706; www.fremontfair.com.

➔ **Seattle Pride:** Capitol Hill comes alive with 2 days of revelry over the last weekend in June, making this is the largest LGBT march and festival in the Northwest. ☎ 877/722-9561 or 206/322-9561; www.seattlepride.org.

➔ **Seafair:** This is the biggest event of the year, with parades, boat races, an air show, ethnic festivals, and sporting events taking place all over Seattle from early July to early August. ☎ 206/728-0123; www.seafair.com.

➔ **Bite of Seattle:** Held the third weekend in July at Seattle Center, this event features sample bites from Seattle restaurants plus wine tasting. ☎ 425/283-5050; www.biteofseattle.com.

gaslight-inn.com; $78–$98 double with shared bathroom, $98–$148 double with private bathroom; $128 studio; $148–$178 suite), a Craftsman bungalow furnished with original Stickley pieces and a pool in the backyard.

The **Bacon Mansion Bed & Breakfast** ★ (959 Broadway E.; ☎ 800/240-1864 or 206/329-1864; www.baconmansion.com; $84–$109 double with shared bathroom, $104–$189 double with private bathroom) is a turn-of-the-20th-century Tudor that comes complete with crystal chandelier, grand piano and huge dining-room table, library. Both locations are convenient to the Capitol Hill action.

➔**Inn at El Gaucho** ★★ This plush little second-story Belltown inn is for folks who can afford a little better than the Ace. Located above the retro-swanky **El Gaucho** steak house and **Pampas Room** jazz club, this place feels like a real find thanks to the nondescript front door hiding a luxurious little second-floor lobby and nicely appointed rooms, which feature plush feather beds, leather furniture, plasma TVs, and more. *2502 First Ave.* ☎ *866/354-2824 or 206/728-1133. inn.elgaucho.com. 18 units. $155–$345 suite. Valet parking $20. Amenities: Restaurant; lounge; concierge; room service; laundry/dry cleaning. In room: Dataport, high–speed Internet access, Wi–Fi.*

SPLURGE

➔ **The Edgewater** ★★ The only Seattle hotel built right on the bay, The Edgewater has some of the city's most amazing views and a lodge-themed design scheme, complete with cozy fireplaces in the rooms. Beatles fans can even stay in the same suite the Fab Four had when they visited back in 1964. *Pier 67, 2411 Alaskan Way, Seattle, WA 98121.* ☎ *800/624-0670 or 206/728-7000. www.edgewaterhotel.com. 223 units. $169–$539 double; $575–$2,500 suite. Valet parking $22. Amenities: Restaurant; lounge; gym; bikes; concierge; business center; room service; massage; laundry/dry cleaning. In room: Dataport, minibar, coffeemaker, high-speed Internet access, Wi-Fi.*

SUPPLIES

➔ **Pike Place Market** ★★ Sure it's touristy, but it's also fun to munch your way through this landmark Seattle market, which has dozens of fast food vendors serving quick bites ranging from pâté and picnic stuff (**DeLaurenti** ★★, 1435 First Ave.; ☎ **206/622-0141**) to the Eastern European treats that've been around way longer than Hot Pockets (**Piroshky, Piroshky,** 1908 Pike Place; ☎ **206/441-6068**). For more substantial picnic fare, perhaps some wild salmon with ginger-orange salsa or wild-mushroom risotto, head to **Dish D'Lish** (☎ **206/223-1848**), just a few steps away from the flying fish at Pike Place Fish. Get the Lebanese Breeze at the **Garlic Garden** (☎ **877/207-5166** or 206/405-4022; www.garlicgarden.com), just around the corner from *Rachel* (the pig statue) to spread on some bread from **Le Panier,** a good French bakery (☎ **206/441-3669**) or watch 'em hand-make the cheese they use in the stellar mac and cheese at **Beecher's,** 1600 Pike Place (☎ **206/956-1964;** www.beecherscheese.com).

TAKEOUT TREATS

For some of the best baked goodies in the city, head to **Macrina** ★★, 2408 First Ave. (☎ **206/448-4032;** www.macrinabakery.com), a neighborhood bakery/cafe that's a cozy place for a quick, cheap breakfast or lunch. In the morning, the smell of baking bread wafts down First Avenue and draws in many a passerby.

And when the post-show salt craving strikes, hit up **Piecora's** (1401 E. Madison St.; ☎ **206/322-9411**), which is across the street from Chop Suey and seems like your average slices joint, except it might well be the last place Kurt Cobain was seen alive. Even better, try 🄼 Best● **Frites** (925 E. Pike St.), next door to Neumo's on Capitol Hill. Serving Belgian-style fries with about a thousand different mayo-based dipping sauces to choose from, Frites provides a deliriously good way to soak up a belly full of booze, especially considering it's open until 2:30am.

➔ **Bimbo's Bitchin' Burrito Kitchen** The Cha Cha Lounge's next-door taco shop continues the Cha Cha's kitschy design scheme, with Mexican wrestling masks serving as decoration. Bimbo's serves up "almost mostly organic" burritos, quesadillas, and so on. Faves include the super-hot Burrito Inferno, garlic-roasted potato tacos, and the uniquely flavored cumin-lime sour cream. *506 E. Pine St.* ☎ *206/329-9978. Most dishes under $8. Mon–Thurs noon–10pm; Fri–Sat noon–midnight; Sun 2–10pm.*

RESTAURANTS
Cheap

CJ's (2619 1st Ave.; ☎ **206/728-1648**) is good to know as one of the few places to get breakfast on a weekday in Seattle's downtown and Belltown neighborhoods— I guess this is more of a coffee-and-cigarette town than a bacon-and-eggs one. If you're downtown and you need a middle-of-the-night burger, the 24-hour **Hurricane Café** (2230 7th Ave.; ☎ **206/682-5858**) is the place to nosh on burgers and waffles with the punks and club kids of Seattle.

➜ **The 5 Spot** ★ LATE-NIGHT/DINER Every 3 months or so, this diner changes its menu to reflect a different regional U.S. cuisine, so you might find Brooklyn comfort food one season, Cuban-influenced Miami-style meals the next. Kitschy atmosphere follows the cuisine theme. Look for the sign at the top of Queen Anne Hill showing neon coffee pouring into a giant coffee cup. *1502 Queen Anne Ave. N. ☎ 206/285-7768. www.chowfoods.com. Main courses $8.75–$18. Mon–Fri 8:30am–midnight; Sat–Sun 8:30am–3pm and 5pm–midnight.*

➜ **Noodle Ranch** ★ PAN-ASIAN This Belltown hole in the wall serves Pan-Asian cuisine for the hip but financially challenged crowd. It's a lively scene, and flavor-packed dishes like fish grilled in grape leaves or the Mekong grill—rice noodles with a rice-wine/vinegar-and-herb dressing topped with grilled pork, chicken, beef, or tofu, plus lots of vegetarian options. *2228 Second Ave. ☎ 206/728-0463. Main courses $8–$12. Mon–Thurs 11am–10pm; Fri 11am–11pm; Sat noon–10pm.*

Doable

➜ **Palace Kitchen** ★★ LATE-NIGHT/MEDITERRANEAN Palace Kitchen's bar attracts almost as many customers as its restaurant. The atmosphere is urban chic, with cement pillars and simple wood booths, while the short menu features a nightly selection of unusual cheeses (try the goat-cheese fondue) and different preparations from the apple-wood grill, like the Palace burger royale. For dessert, the coconut cream pie is an absolute must. *2030 Fifth Ave. ☎ 206/448-2001. www.tomdouglas.com. Main courses $12–$30. Daily 5pm–1am.*

➜ **Pontevecchio** ★★ ITALIAN For a nice but not-too-expensive dinner before a show at the Tractor or Sunset, try this cozy Fremont spot. White linen tablecloths and candlelight set a date-night vibe, while the menu includes southern Italian faves like bruschetta, eggplant with portobello mushrooms, delicately al dente pasta, and tender chicken. There's also live music and dancing Wednesday through Saturday nights. *710 N 34th St. ☎ 206/633-3989. Entrees $10–$24. Mon–Sat 11am–3pm; 6–11pm.*

➜ **Wild Ginger Asian Restaurant & Satay Bar** ★★ PAN-ASIAN A longtime Seattle favorite, this restaurant shares space with the Triple Door and has a large satay bar where you can watch the cooks grill little skewers of everything from chicken to scallops to prawns to lamb. Try the Panang beef curry, savory ginger salmon, and refreshing (and *strong*) ginger martini. *1401 Third Ave. ☎ 206/623-4450. Satay sticks $2.95–$5.65; main courses $7.25–$14 at lunch, $9–$24 at dinner. Mon–Sat 11:30am–2am; Sun 4:30pm–2am.*

Splurge

➜ **Campagne** ★★ FRENCH Overlooking Elliott Bay, elegant Campagne relies heavily on the wide variety of fresh ingredients provided by adjacent Pike Place Market, so the menu changes with the seasons but always includes several interesting salads and the sort of French dishes that might not be familiar to American diners: lamb shoulder marinated in anchovies and garlic, rib-eye steak with roasted marrow bone, salt cod and curry fritters with aioli. *In the Inn at the Market, 86 Pine St. ☎ 206/728-2800. www.campagnerestaurant.com. Main courses $20–$33. Daily 5:30–10pm (late-night menu Fri–Sat until midnight).*

Partying

Seattle's got a superb nightlife scattered in several neighborhoods around town. The center for gay and hipster nightlife is still around Capitol Hill and the burgeoning Pike/Pine Corridor. The traditional arts and culture stuff can be found around Seattle Center and Pioneer Square, while nearby Belltown's becoming less seedy, more trendy. Fremont and Ballard, to the north, are mellower and a little more suburban but still have their share of chill hangouts.

BARS & PUBS

I highly recommend a bar crawl along the Pike/Pine, where a bunch of excellent little places are all within easy stumbling distance of each other. I asked an acquaintance of mine where to go to meet greasy rock boys in Seattle, and without hesitation she said **"The Cha Cha"** ★★★ (504 E. Pine St.; ☎ 206/329-9978). Indeed, this place pulls hipsters thanks to cute, Viva Mexico! decor (the bar looks like a *palapa* and sombreros of all sizes cover the walls) and a happy hour that lasts for 2 whole days (specials are in effect all day Sun and Mon and 4–8pm on other nights).

Then grab a seat on one of the comfy couches at **Kincora's** ★★ (518 E. Pine St.; ☎ 206/325-0436) to sip a pint, play some pool or a board game, and maybe catch a band or two. Over on Pike is a newish Cuban-inspired place called **Havana** (1010 E. Pike St.; ☎ 206/323-CUBA), then **the Comet Tavern** ★★ (922 E. Pike St.; ☎ 206/323-9853), a chill locals joint with a lofted area housing video games and pinball, and **Linda's Tavern** ★★ (707 E. Pine St.; ☎ 206/325-1220), another popular local hang with a lively patio and a buffalo head mounted above the bar.

Also in the 'hood is **Redwood** ★★★ (514 E. Howell St.; ☎ 206/329-1952), which has an old-style saloon vibe and is owned by some of the guys in local breakout act Band of Horses. If you're into the bars-owned-by-musicians thing and you happen to be in Ballard, stop in at the tiny, cozy **Hazlewood** ★★ (2311 NW Market St.; ☎ 206/783-0478), which is co-owned by Ben Sheperd of Soundgarden. The low-ceilinged upstairs area is the preferred place to post up.

In Belltown, **the Black Bottle** ★★ (2600 First Ave.; ☎ 206/441-1500) is a classy but inviting place to sip a glass of wine (or six) and indulge in their rockin' chocolate cake before hitting up the upscale **Belltown Billiards** nearby (90 Blanchard St.; ☎ 206/448-6779).

DANCE CLUBS

➜ **Neighbours** This has been the favorite dance club of Capitol Hill's gay community for years. As at other clubs, different nights of the week feature different styles of music. You'll find this club's entrance down the alley. *1509 Broadway. ☎ 206/324-5358. www.neighboursonline.com. Cover $0–$12.*

➜ **Baltic Room** This swanky Capitol Hill hangout for the beautiful people stages a wide range of music (mostly DJs) encompassing everything from dance-hall reggae to hip-hop and *bhangra* (contemporary Indian disco). *1207 Pine St. ☎ 206/625-4444. www.balticroom.com. Cover $3–$10.*

Other places to get your dance on include **the War Room** ★★★ (722 E. Pike St.; ☎ 206/328-7666), which has a popular rooftop patio and an even more popular hip-hop night called "Yo, Son!," the three-level **R-Place** (619 E. Pine St.; ☎ 206/322-8828) for its Thursday night amateur strip show; and the gay-friendly **Bus Stop** (508 E. Pine St.; ☎ 206/322-9123), which uses the tag line "I got off at the Bus Stop!"

Reciprocal Recordings: Grunge history was made here.

What Else to See & Do

From perfecting your air guitar skills to trolling the boutiques for vintage finds, the Emerald City definitely isn't hurting for stuff to do.

THE TOP ATTRACTIONS

MTV **Best ☺** ➜ **Experience Music Project** ★★ Seattle's humongous lump-o'-color rock museum is the brainchild of Microsoft cofounder Paul Allen and was designed by avant-garde architect Frank Gehry, who is

MTV🆄 Seattle Music History 101:

With the Long Winters' John Roderick

The notion of a guided tour automatically makes me want to take a nap. They're usually just so *boring*. But when the tour guide's in a band and all the stops are the stuff of alt-rock legend, it has a way of keeping my interest.

Asking around about must-see rock sites in Seattle somehow led me to **John Roderick,** the smarty-pants songwriter behind the fantastic indie band the Long Winters. Something of a history buff, Roderick offered to take me on an abbreviated version of his rock history tour of Seattle one recent afternoon.

Our trip began at the Terminal Sales Building, one-time headquarters for **Sub Pop** (1932 First Ave. at Virginia), which started out in a space the size of an elevator shaft before expanding to two floors, according to Roderick. The label that launched Nirvana has since moved, but it's still fun to drive by and imagine what it must've been like to party at those legendary suites, with their sweeping views of Puget Sound and a rooftop garden that hosted "more than a few over the top episodes," according to another local.

Farther down First is **Vain** (2018 First Ave.) on the site of the legendary Vogue nightclub, where Soundgarden, Mudhoney, and Nirvana played a million times; rock stars still go there, only now it's for a cut and color, since the space was converted into a salon-slash-art-gallery. Up on Second Ave. is the **Rendezvous,** an old-school movie screening room turned dive bar where bands not big enough to land gigs at the Crocodile would play (Death Cab and Modest Mouse are alums).

known for pushing the envelope of architectural design. Originally planned as a memorial to Seattle native Jimi Hendrix, the museum grew to encompass not only Hendrix but all of the Northwest rock scene (from "Louie Louie" to grunge) and the general history of American popular music. In one interactive room you can play guitars, drums, keyboards, or even DJ turntables. In another, you can experience what it's like to be onstage performing in front of adoring fans. EMP's **Liquid Lounge,** a small club with no cover and a wide range of musical sensibilities, is a good place to catch anything from a reggae dance party to a hip-hop or acoustic show. *325 Fifth Ave. N. ☎ 206/770-2702. www.emp live.com. Admission $19.95. Memorial Day to Labor Day daily 10am–8pm; Labor Day to Memorial Day Tues–Thurs and Sun 10am–6pm, Fri–Sat 10am–8pm.*

→ **Seattle Art Museum** ★★ You can't miss this downtown art museum. Just look for Jonathon Borofsky's *Hammering Man,* an animated three-story steel sculpture that pounds out a silent beat in front of the museum. Inside, you'll find one of the country's best collections of Northwest Coast Indian artifacts, a large collection of African art, and exhibits covering European and American works from several periods. Free guided tours of the different collections are offered. *Note:* Due to a major expansion project, the Seattle Art Museum will be closed the first week of January 2006 until sometime in spring 2007. *100 University St. ☎ 206/654-3100. www.seattleartmuseum. org. Admission $7. Tues–Wed and Fri–Sun 10am–5pm; Thurs 10am–9pm. Closed Thanksgiving and Christmas (open some holiday Mon).*

Over in Fremont, which calls itself "The Center of the Universe" (apparently because no other place had claimed the title), you can rifle through stacks of vinyl at **Bop Street** or the original **Sonic Boom Records** (p. 681) before driving by the nearby studios where some of those very albums were recorded. The nondescript concrete building marked **Professional Engravers** (417 N. 36th St.) is actually a recording studio that Stone Gossard bought with his Pearl Jam money, where Soundgarden laid down tracks for "Down on the Upside." Less than a mile away, a dilapidated, oddly shaped little shack with no sign just might be the most quietly epic landmark in the city, 'cause it's where Nirvana recorded "Bleach" with producer Jack Endino for $600. Mudhoney and Sleater-Kinney also recorded here, and the studio's sort of been handed down to Seattle's alt-rock royalty through the years—in the Nirvana days it was called Reciprocal Recordings, then Word of Mouth Productions, then John'n'Stu's Recording, and now that it's owned by Death Cab for Cutie's Chris Walla (and used mostly as a space to store Death Cab's gear), it's called the ▦ Best● **Hall of Justice** (4230 Leary Ave. NW, at 6th St.).

My tour only lasted 2 hours, but something tells me it could've gone on for days—this town is dripping in grunge-era history. And you don't even need a guy in a rock band to point it out for you: Just ask around. Everybody's got a story.

For more Seattle music sites, visit the city's **Music Map** at **www.seattle.gov/ music/map.** For more on the Long Winters and their latest record, "Putting the Days to Bed," visit www.thelongwinters.com.

→ **Space Needle** ★★ From a distance it looks like a flying saucer on top of a tripod, and when it was built for the 1962 World's Fair, the 605-foot-tall Space Needle was meant to be a glimpse at the future of architecture. Today it's the quintessential symbol of Seattle, with a 520-foot-high observation deck and a pricey restaurant, **SkyCity,** atop the tower. If you don't mind standing in line and paying quite a bit for an elevator ride, make this your first stop in Seattle so that you can orient yourself. *Seattle Center. 400 Broad St. ☎ 206/905-2100. www.spaceneedle.com. Admission $13 (free if dining at SkyCity). Sun–Thurs 9am–11pm; Fri–Sat 9am–midnight. Valet parking $13 all day.*

If you don't want to deal with the crowds, try the 943-foot **Bank of America Tower** (☎ 206/386-5151), at the corner of

Fifth Avenue and Columbia Street, whose 73rd floor has an observation deck with even more awesome views. Admission is $5 and it's open weekdays from 8:30am to 4:30pm. The **Smith Tower** (506 Second Ave.; ☎ 206/622-4004; www.smithtower. com) also offers excellent views from its 35th-floor observation deck. Deck hours vary; check in advance to be sure it will be open when you want to visit. Admission is $6.

SHOPPING

Belltown's got some seriously cute boutiques, including three adorable shops on the same block called **Nancy** ★★ (1930 2nd Ave.; ☎ 206/441-7131), **Schmancy** ★★ (1932 2nd Ave.; ☎ 206/728-8008) and **Fancy Pants** ★★★ (1914 2nd Ave.; ☎ 206/ 956-2945) aka "Trilogy of Awesome" (the

If You Believe in Forever . . .
Rock 'n' Roll Graves

If the rock-star gravesite thing doesn't creep you out, there are two stops to consider in the Seattle area. One is **Jimi Hendrix's grave** (350 Monroe Ave. Northeast; ☎ 425/255-1511; www.jimihendrixmemorial.com) at Greenwood Memorial Park in Renton, about 15 miles outside of Seattle. The grave marker is simple, with a guitar and the words "Forever in our hearts" engraved in the stone. To get there, take Exit 4 off the 405 South, turn left at the first light (Third St.) and proceed for about a mile until you see the cemetery parking lot on your left, near the corner of Fourth and Monroe. Meanwhile, **Viretta Park** is the closest thing Seattle has to a memorial site for **Kurt Cobain** (some of whose ashes were also scattered in the Wishkah River), whose body was discovered in the greenhouse of his nearby Lake Washington home on April 8, 1994. These days there are fences around the home itself, which Courtney sold in 1997, but fans and pilgrims leave offerings and memorabilia on a bench in the park, located at 151 Lake Washington Blvd. E (☎ **206/684-4075**).

shopkeepers' term, not mine—though I wouldn't disagree). Fancy Pants owner Sally Brock started explaining to me how Fancy Pants used to just be Pants and Nancy used to be Fancy, but I was too distracted by the cute T-shirts and panties to get the rest of the story. And since we're rhyming, why not check out **Fritzi Ritz** (750 N. 34th St.; ☎ **206/633-0929**) in Fremont, where all the vintage clothes are carefully labeled with the decade from whence they came. **Moksha** (4542 University Way NE; ☎ **206/632-1190**) in the U District has a great little collection of trendy stuff inspired by Indian fashions, and Capitol Hill is packed with retro treasure-troves.

PLAYING OUTSIDE

FREE MTV Best❂ ➔ **Gas   Works Park** ★★★ At the north end of Lake Union in North Seattle is a vast space of green lawns surrounding the rusting hulk of an old industrial plant. Locals love flying kites at the park's Kite Hill. *2101 N. Northlake Way at Meridian Ave. North.* ☎ *206/684-4075.*

SPECTATOR SPORTS
Baseball

Seattle's most popular pro team is the American League **Mariners** (☎ **206/346-4000** or 206/346-4001; www.seattle mariners.com), who play to consistently large crowds at their new home, the retro-style **Safeco Field,** which features a retractable roof and real grass. Tickets are $7 to $55, and it's hard to find two seats together on game day. Order in advance at **Mariners Team Stores** (Fourth and Stewart sts. downtown and in the Bellevue Sq. shopping mall) or through **Ticketmaster** (☎ 206/622-HITS; www.ticket master.com). Oh, and parking at Safeco sucks, so plan to leave your car behind.

Basketball

The NBA's **Seattle SuperSonics** (☎ **800/4NBA-TIX,** 800/743-7021, or 206/283-3865; www.supersonics.com), who play in the Key Arena at Seattle Center, seem to do alright every season, even though they usually trail behind the Portland Trail Blazers as a regional favorite. You can usually get tickets ($10–$129 at the arena box

Detour: Olympic National Park

When you've finished exploring Seattle, travel west about 2 hours to **Olympic National Park** ★★★. This huge chunk of land, the Olympic Peninsula—upwards of 900,000 acres—groups beaches, glaciers, mountains, lakes, and rainforests all in one place. The park is home to the 7,965-foot-tall Mount Olympus, 63 miles of driftwood-strewn shoreline, soothing hot springs, and many a muggy, moss-covered rainforest, which are soaked by 12 to 14 feet of precipitation each year. You'll need a car to get around the park, which doesn't have a public transit system; admission is $15 per vehicle for up to a week. Though you can get a sample of a few of the park's offerings with a several-hours-long day trip, serious outdoorsy types will want to consider an overnight trip, either camping in the park or staying in one of the nearby towns; either way, if staying over, start your trip planning far in advance, as lodging can book up quickly. Camping on one of the beautiful beaches (Ruby, Rialto, First, Second, and so on) is an experience not to be forgotten. If you don't have a tent, you can make a shelter with huge pieces of driftwood that have washed up onshore. If you're lucky, someone might have left theirs for you to use. There are several ways to get there depending on which side of the park you're visiting. The most often-used method is to take a ferry from Seattle to Bainbridge Island, then take 101 toward Port Angeles; there are several park entrances along 101, and remember to watch out for logging trucks on the two-lane roads. Get more park info from the **Olympic National Park Visitor Center** (☎ **360/565-3130**) or visit www.nps.gov/olym.

office or through Ticketmaster; ☎ **206/628-0888**) on short notice, except for games against the Lakers and the Trail Blazers, which are packed. The Sonics' WNBA counterpart, playing from May to September is the **Seattle Storm (www.wnba.com/storm)**, which won the league championship in 2004, led by All-Star and Olympians Sue Bird and Lauren Jackson. In October 2006, the team was sold, and locals were lobbying to keep the new owners from moving the franchise(s) to . . . Oklahoma City. The new owners have until July 2007 to come to terms with Seattle officials on plans to build a new arena and keep the teams in town.

Football

The NFL's **Seattle Seahawks** (☎ **888/635-4295** or 206/381-7816; www.seahawks.com) play at the newish **Qwest Field** (800 Occidental Ave. S.; ☎ **206/381-7582**; www.qwestfield.com), built on the site of the old Kingdome next to Safeco Field. Tickets are $33 to $315 via **Ticket-master** (☎ **206/622-HAWK;** www.ticketmaster.com) and pretty easy to come by except for games against Oakland and Denver.

Other Sports

From mid-April to mid-October you can bet the ponies at **Emerald Downs** (2300 Emerald Downs Dr.; ☎ **888/931-8400** or 253/288-7000; www.emeralddowns.com), in Auburn, which is south of Seattle off WA 167 (reached from I-405 at the south end of Lake Washington). And if you're a soccer fan, catch the United Soccer League's **Seattle Sounders** (☎ **206/622-3415;** www.seattlesounders.net) at Qwest Field. Tickets are $12 to $17 via Ticketmaster (☎ **206/628-0888**).

The end . . . that's all she wrote!!

American Highways

By *Kelsy Chauvin*. Photos by *Kelsy Chauvin & Kim Musler*

From the mists tangled in the Great Smoky Mountains' peaks, to the dusty open road of Route 66, to the natural wonders of the New Mexican plains—there are flavors, sights, and sounds through which only first-hand experience will do. If you've only seen the pictures, then you know the United States has mighty incredible scenery, but there's nothing to drive it home (and away from home) and perhaps nothing more innately American than taking it in on a cross-country roadtrip.

We're leaving from Charlotte, the hub of the burgeoning New South, built squarely on the foundations of the Old South. Charlotte is the prelude to a strand of classic southern cities singular in their microcosms of history, culture, and, oh boy, such good food. We'll be passing through Nashville, St. Louis, and Branson, Missouri (aka the Midwest's answer to Las Vegas . . . or possibly Atlantic City). Each city's air is filled with galloping live music, while their menus are filled with plenty of chicken-fried steak, smothered green beans, and cold American beer.

Gas up the car and keep on westward, where the Central time zone gives way to American deserts. In Tulsa, the tumbleweeds sprout among old oil-barons' estates, rolling across Oklahoma, and through Amarillo in the Texas panhandle. With leather boots on your feet and a suddenly familiar ear for country accents, we'll head on through Albuquerque, then wind south through New Mexico, where Mother Nature seems to have tried out nearly every recipe in her book over the past few million years.

Getting your kicks on . . .

Weathered and reliable, the roads between these heartland cities are the bloodline of the U.S. economy, with thousands of miles of interstates peppered with 18-wheelers who set the standard for speed limits (figure out their rhythms and they just might spare you a ticket). And it's okay to pray a little that their mud flaps are in good shape when a sudden afternoon downpour douses the highway and you're stuck behind yet another daunting tractor-trailer.

If a cross-country roadtrip is on your radar already, pack the car! And if you're not quite convinced, don't let the thought of your car's odometer clicking beyond 2,500 miles scare you. The adventure lies in pleasant, subtle surprises like dirt-cheap (and spotless!) motels and the endless warm welcomes behind the counters of local diners—not to mention the joy of how clear your head gets when life's essentials boil down to gas stops, bathroom breaks, and cruise control.

Superlatives: The Highs & Lows

➜ **Best Onion Rings:** The first step to angioplasty begins with Charlotte's **South 21 Drive-In,** where all your deep-fried fantasies come true. See p. 705.

➜ **Best Giant Peach:** The prize for juiciest peach in the country goes to the **Gaffney Peach Water Tower** on I-85 in northern South Carolina, which stands 13 stories tall and holds a million gallons of water. See p. 710.

➜**Worst Sandwiching of Semis:** The confluence of three interstates into Nashville means unless you're driving an 18-wheeler, you might get an inferiority complex. See p. 717.

➜ **Biggest Statue in the Universe:** Okay, really it's just the tallest indoor statue in the country. But at 42 feet, Goddess **Athena Parthenos** is Nashville's biggest diva. See p. 721.

American Highways Roadtrip

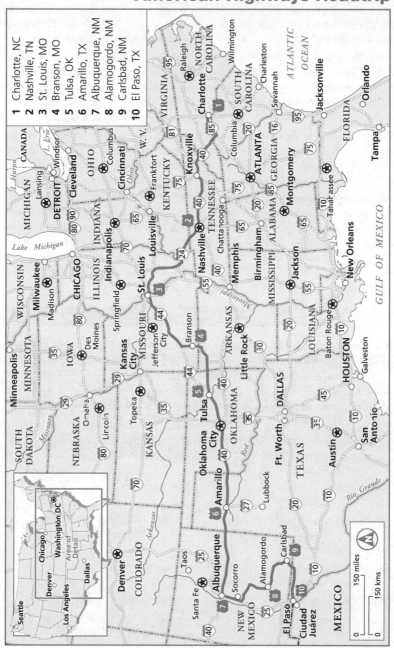

1	Charlotte, NC
2	Nashville, TN
3	St. Louis, MO
4	Branson, MO
5	Tulsa, OK
6	Amarillo, TX
7	Albuquerque, NM
8	Alamogordo, NM
9	Carlsbad, NM
10	El Paso, TX

➜ **Best Recycling Program:** St. Louis's **City Museum** has turned a few of its city's junkyard gems into the Midwest's quirkiest gallery/pavilion/playland. See p. 741.

➜ **Best Exterior-Only Attraction:** Time-sucking, pricey, and painfully claustrophobic, beware of the lure to travel to the top of St. Louis's **Gateway Arch.** It's *way* better from outside. See p. 747.

➜ **Best Landlocked Aquarium:** A living oxymoron: In the desert plains, there are a million gallons of water filling the **Oklahoma Aquarium.** See p. 766.

➜ **Best Chicken-Fried Breakfast:** Somewhat daunting from outside, it's worth mustering the courage to enter Amarillo's **Stockyard Café** for hearty—*cowboy* hearty—chicken-fried steak and eggs. See p. 777.

➜ **Longest History Tour:** How does 12 billion years of history fit into one museum? Find out at the **New Mexico Museum of Natural History and Science.** See p. 793.

➜ **Strangest Roadblock:** On occasion, traffic on **White Sands Boulevard** in Alamogordo will be halted while the nearby Air Force base tests missiles. See p. 798.

➜ **Freakiest Natural Forms:** Lion's tails, draperies, drinking straws, and, well, a few more freaky and obscene sort of shapes ought to slacken your jaw as you behold the natural formations inside **Carlsbad Caverns.** See p. 812.

➜ **Biggest Burrito West of the Pecos. And East of It:** If you can find it anywhere, you'll find it in El Paso: **Rafa's Burritos** creates incredibly good ones that are literally as big as your arm. See p. 825.

Just the Facts

Trip in a Box

Total Miles   From Charlotte to El Paso, 2,387 miles—but you'll probably end up doing closer to 3,000 (or beyond) depending on side trips and driving within each city.

Segment Miles   Charlotte to Nashville is 420; Nashville to St. Louis is 310; St. Louis to Branson is 255; Branson to Tulsa is 220; Tulsa to Amarillo is 367; Amarillo to Albuquerque is 290; Albuquerque to Alamogordo is 210; Alamogordo to Carlsbad is 150; Carlsbad to El Paso is 165.

Basic Routes   I-77 and I-40 Charlotte to Nashville; I-24 and I-57 to St. Louis; I-44 and US 65 to Branson; US 65 and US 412 to Tulsa; I-40 to Amarillo; I-40 to Albuquerque; I-25, US 380, and US 54 to Alamogordo; US 82 and US 285 to Carlsbad; US 62/180 to El Paso.

States   North Carolina, South Carolina, Tennessee, Kentucky, Illinois, Missouri, Arkansas, Oklahoma, Texas, New Mexico.

Trip Time   10 to 14 days for the whole thing, from Charlotte to El Paso.

The Short Version   A shorter trip, while possible, might make the whole thing feel more rushed than relaxing. Still, it is possible as long as you stick to the interstates, breeze through each city, and skip many of the detours and smaller sights—and potentially all of Branson and NW Arkansas. A better option may be to break the trip into two or three trips.

The Long Version   If you can afford the time, a longer trip is the best way to catch many more sights and recreation areas found on smaller highways, and avoid speeding in state trooper–heavy states like Oklahoma. Not to mention, you'll be getting the most from visits to the dozen-plus cities you'll experience.

Hitting the Highlights   The Charlotte-Nashville-St. Louis triple-play can be done in an extended weekend, and maybe add a day if you're really into the Great Smoky Mountains (all told, 730 miles). Branson to Amarillo (via Tulsa) will synopsize the Ozarks, Route 66, and the middle-American plains in less than 4 days (587 miles). But if nature and serenity are calling you, spend at least half a week exploring New Mexico's parks, lakes, trails, and mountain ranges, ending with a visit to old El Paso (525 miles).

When to Go   Any time except mid-summer and mid-winter are best, in order to avoid extreme weather (especially big storms). Spring or fall lets you catch scenery at its most vivid. Just remember, since it's a long adventure, you'll be driving in assorted climates that will vary no matter the time of year.

The Money Part

The good news is that each town on this journey is relatively cheap in nearly every department, from food to gas to lodging—well, not that gas is ever really "cheap" any more, but it is a good 10% less expensive in middle America than in many major cities. And it pays to take advantage of even cheaper gas stations, hotels, and restaurants offered by businesses just outside the downtown areas and/or the city limits. Besides, you can't put a price tag on the local flair that comes with skipping ubiquitous national chains.

ACCOMMODATIONS

No matter where you go or what the season, there's almost always a $30-a-night single-room motel in this trip's cities, especially in less-traveled states where you can find some great bargains. Even better deals are available for campers, for whom campsites can be cheaper than the price of a meal. Then, after a few nights of skimping, you might afford a $100-a-night (or upwards) hotel in the heart of town where you can rest in luxury, or a B&B that feeds you the best breakfast of the whole trip. Lodging is an especially good deal when you're traveling with one or more friends, since many motels and campsites appeal to families by setting a single price per room/campsite regardless of how many in your party.

One side note is that you won't find too many hostels, either of the Hostelling International or private backpacker variety in many of these smaller cities—which is okay since you can stay at a motel for about the same or not much more.

TRANSPORTATION

If gas is running $3 or less per gallon, and you're driving a fuel-efficient car, expect to spend around $300 on fuel for this trek. In general, gas is cheapest right outside cities, with the cheapest of all around southern Missouri. A good rule of thumb is to gas up no later than when you get down to about a quarter-tank, especially on long

Full-Tank Playlist

→ *Zero Point,* **The Rogers Sisters,** "Purely Evil," 2002
→ *Body Movin',* **Beastie Boys,** "Hello Nasty," 1998
→ *Here Comes Your Man,* **Pixies,** "Here Comes Your Man," 1989
→ *Buena Vista,* **The Starlight Mints,** "Built on Squares," 2003
→ *Going, Going, Gone,* **Stars,** "Nightsongs," 2003
→ *My Baby Just Cares for Me,* **Nina Simone,** "Let It Be Me," 1987
→ *Straight, No Chaser,* **Thelonious Monk,** "The Composer," 1988
→ *Title and Registration,* **Death Cab for Cutie,** "Transatlanticism," 2003
→ *I've Got the World on a String,* **Louis Prima,** "Capitol Collectors Series,"
  1991

stretches in Oklahoma, Texas, and New Mexico.

Tolls crop up only in Oklahoma on this trip. But don't worry; they're cheap. Another minimal expense is parking, which is really only a concern in the busier downtown areas of cities like Charlotte, Nashville, St. Louis, and Albuquerque—and even there you probably won't pay more than about $8 or $10 a day, most likely at your hotel.

As for inner-city travel, while pretty much every city on this itinerary offers buses (and a train in St. Louis), they may not make much sense for visitors like us, with limited time in town. Driving is not ideal if the idea is to save both dollars and fuel emissions, but it is the best way to get the lay of the land in just a day or two.

FOOD

Food, glorious, regional food: The cream of the crop in this department is likely whatever the locals advise—provided you're talking to locals who know their towns well.

From Charlotte to Amarillo, you'll find yourself with endless options for steak 'n potatoes, along with many, many fried foodstuffs without having to resort to the big fast-food chains. Such options continue westward, where the new staple of Tex-Mex or "new Mexican" emerges. While such Mexican food is consistently simple and cheesy, be wary of quality in any super-cheap Mexican joints. And, logically, Mexican food gets more traditional and reliably tasty as you head south.

Everywhere you go, there's always a diner with a filling $4-or-less breakfast deal, and a similarly cheap afternoon/evening menu. Though their coffee quality, sadly, varies greatly.

To maintain a little more health, be willing to splurge occasionally for more expensive restaurants that offer fresh vegetables and salads with substance ($8 and up). And in nearly every city there are sushi/Asian food choices for getting a nice fill of fresh ingredients, and/or cleansing soup and tea.

Another way to be kind to your system is by shopping at any farmers markets you run across, and picking up the local bounty at roadside fruit and vegetable stands, where it's okay to rely on freshness, as well as local and seasonal flavor. Such places are also a great place to pick up snacks for the car.

One note about keeping hydrated: You'll save money and *lots* of plastic bottles by reusing a 20-ounce (or so) bottle and refilling it with gallons of spring-water purchased at local grocery stores. Of all of them, superstores are cheapest, with a gallon selling for less than a dollar. (Remember, water is one of the long road-tripper's best friends, since it helps your body flush out new and unusual germs, and aids in both digestion and circulation.)

OTHER EXPENSES

Depending on your interests, you may also find additional, and pretty minimal, expenses to get into national parks. For example, White Sands National Monument (which should not be missed) is only $3 per car, and Carlsbad Caverns is $6 per adult for the amazing self-guided tour.

Cover charges for live music and entertainment venues, museums, and landmarks may also add to the expense sheet—but if such things are even remotely in your budget, it's probably worth the money to get the full experience of a place you may never visit again. We've also marked with the "Free" icon those places that don't charge for admission.

Starting Out: Charlotte, NC

The "Queen City" of the Carolinas is both understated and charming. Centrally located on the Eastern seaboard, it's a happenin' convention town, is sporty with its Carolina Panthers and NASCAR scene (as well as two pro hoops franchises), and its booming financial hub. Constantly reinventing itself, behold the skyscrapers cropping up all over Center City (and the increasingly fancy restaurants among them) as testament to it being the biggest city in the Carolinas. But don't be fooled by Charlotte's big-city towers—there is still plenty of southern charm to back it up.

Charlotte Nuts & Bolts

Area Code The telephone area code in Charlotte (in Mecklenburg County) is **704.**

Business Hours Banks generally are open Monday to Friday from 9am to 3pm (some are also open Sat 9am–noon); ATMs, of course, are available 24/7. Offices are open Monday to Friday 9am to 5pm. Bars and clubs tend to stay open until midnight during the week, 2am on weekends.

Doctor Carolinas HealthCare System has a physician referral service (☎ 704/355-7500) and a general number for Carolinas Medical Center (☎ 704/355-2000).

Drugstores Eckerd, CVS/Pharmacy, and Rite Aid are the popular chains in the area. Eckerd stores are most likely to be open late, usually until midnight.

Emergencies Call ☎ **911** if you need the police, the fire department, or an ambulance.

Hospitals There are six major hospitals in the Charlotte area representing two healthcare systems: Carolinas HealthCare System, 1000 Blythe Blvd. (☎ 704/355-2000), and Presbyterian Healthcare, 200 Hawthorne Lane (☎ 704/384-4000).

Internet "Noda" is the cool neighborhood around the University of North Carolina–Charlotte, and there you will find many a cafe and bar with Internet access, free and for small fees. Start with **SK NetCafe,** 1425 Elizabeth Ave. (☎ 704/334-1523),

Jackson's Java, 8544 University City Blvd. (☎ 704/548-1133), or **Panera Bread** (multiple locations). The **Public Library of Charlotte & Mecklenburg County** also offers free Internet via computer stations and Wi-Fi in some branches.

Libraries   The main **Public Library of Charlotte & Mecklenburg County** branch is at 310 N. Tryon St. (☎ 704/336-2725) in the Fourth Ward. To find the closest local branch, visit www.plcmc.org. You can also access the Internet for free at many of the branches (see "Internet" above).

Liquor Laws   You have to be 21 to drink in North Carolina, and liquor cannot be served before noon on Sunday.

Newspapers & Magazines   The city's large-circulation, mainstream newspaper is the *Charlotte Observer* (www.charlotte.com). Pick up the free alternative weekly *Creative Loafing* (www.creativeloafing.com) to get the scoop on arts, politics, and entertainment while you're in town.

Police   The non-emergency number for the Charlotte-Mecklenburg Police Department is ☎ **704/353-1000.**

Post Office   The city's main post office is at 201 N. McDowell St. (☎ 704/333-5135); other locations can be found using the city name or a local zip code at www.usps.com.

Radio   On the FM dial, turn to public-radio WFAE (90.7) for NPR, WSOC (103.7) for country, WNKS (95.1) for popular rock, and WPEG (97.9) for hip-hop and R&B. On AM stations you'll find mostly talk, sports, and Christian music and talk.

Taxes   North Carolina has a 7.5% sales tax and tacks on a 6% hotel tax.

Television   You'll find CBS (WBTV) on Channel 3, ABC (WSOC) on Channel 9, NBC (WCNC) on Channel 6, Fox (WCCB) on Channel 18, and PBS (WTVI) on Channel 42.

Time Zone   Charlotte is on Eastern Standard Time and observes daylight saving time.

Transit Information   The Charlotte Area Transit System (CATS) can be reached at 704/336-RIDE and online at www.charmeck.org/Departments/CATS.

Visitors Bureau   Call ☎ 800/722-1994 or check out www.charlottecvb.org to get more information about Charlotte (and see box below).

Weather   Check the local weather at http://weather.charlotte.com.

Getting Around

There are three main areas to focus on during a brief visit to Charlotte: Center City, Noda, and the South End. As the central area for the city's thriving convention scene, **Center City** (aka "Uptown") is where you'll find loads of "name" hotels and standard-fare and chain restaurants, but not too much personality. Much more interesting is **Noda,** near the University of North Carolina–Charlotte (UNCC) in the northeast part of town. Nearby you'll find cheap hotels up and down highway-like North Tryon Street and adjacent streets, and niches of nice local establishments. Meanwhile, across town in the "historic" **South End,** shops and restaurants are cropping up all over as the city rehabilitates its trolley line (which is out of service through spring 2007).

Charlotte Highlights

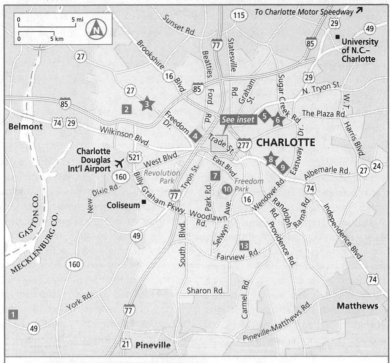

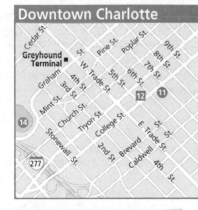

Downtown Charlotte

SLEEPING ■
Best Value Inn **2**
Holiday Inn Center City **12**
McDowell Nature Preserve **1**
The Morehead Inn **7**
The Park Hotel **13**

EATING ◆
Boudreaux's Louisiana Kitchen **5**
The Coffee Cup **4**
South 21 Drive In **9**

PARTYING ★
The Evening Muse **6**
Mac's Speed Shop **8**
Scorpio **3**

ATTRACTIONS ●
Bank of America Stadium **14**
Freedom Park **10**
Levine Museum of
   the New South **11**

For More Information...

→ Charlotte Convention & Visitors Bureau: ☎ 800/722-1994 or 704/331-2700; www.charlottecvb.org

→ Charlotte Transit: ☎ 704/366-RIDE; www.charmeck.org/Departments/CATS

→ Charlotte Parks & Recreation: ☎ 704/704/336-3854; www.parkandrec.com

→ Charlotte Visitor Information Center: ☎ 704/334-2282

→ *Charlotte Observer* daily newspaper: www.charlotte.com

→ *Creative Loafing* weekly newspaper: charlotte.creativeloafing.com

BY CAR

The car in Charlotte is, as in most smaller American cities, the fastest way to get around. The Center City area is encircled by fast-flowing I-277, with other highways linking to it in all directions. And speaking of directions, asking a local how to get around will most surely involve hopping on an interstate, for at least a little bit. The good news is that such highway-hopping makes Charlotte's outer neighborhoods pretty fast to get to, and once there, it's pretty easy to navigate along a select few main streets.

PUBLIC TRANSIT

Once the Charlotte trolley is back in service in South End in '07, it will travel through the perfect snapshot strip of Charlotte—from South End to Center City, along the main thoroughfare that is Tryon Street—and set you back only $1. But in the meantime, if mass transit is your preference, you can catch a local **Charlotte Area Transportation System (CATS)** bus. It's a good deal at $1.20 a ride (local within Charlotte), and if you are staying for several days, consider an unlimited-ride, weekly pass for $12. Call 704/366-RIDE or visit www.charmeck.org/Departments/CATS for route and schedule information.

ON FOOT

There are a handful of neighborhoods in Charlotte that are good for strolling, but the best is the South End. It has plenty of shops, cafes, and people-watching. Noda, while likely to become the next walkabout locale, is compact enough that you can see everything on foot in less than 15 minutes. It is near enough to UNCC, however, that you may stumble across more places to roam. Center City, too, is a good walking district, though the people-watching consists of men and women in businesswear by day, and conventiongoers by night. Outside of these areas, you're probably best off traveling with wheels.

BY TAXI

Charlotte has a few cab companies waiting to give you a lift: **Crown Cab** (☎ 704/334-6666), **Diamond Cab** (☎ 704/333-3030), and **Charlotte Checker Cab** (☎ 704/333-1111). The initial ("drop") charge is $2, and $2 for each mile. A flat rate from the airport to Center City is $20.

Sleeping

Hotels pepper Charlotte's Center City, which accommodates visitors to the city's convention centers, sports arenas, and corporate towers. As a result, it's the best place to nab a deal on a chain hotel—just remember to book ahead, in case some huge convention has descended and monopolized the good deals. For last-minute accommodations, you might be better off heading for the outskirts of town, especially north around UNCC; this

Charlotte Festivals: Art, Food & Beer!

Along with the three pro sports teams and crazy Carolina NASCAR scenes, Charlotte's got music, food, art, and lots more that it likes to show off to the tourists (okay, and locals) via assorted festivals.

→ One of Charlotte's biggest annual events is **Festival in the Park,** which draws about 75,000 people over its 4 days. Held the third weekend after Labor Day annually, the free festival transforms Charlotte's Freedom Park (near South End) into an artist's haven, complete with juried art contests. Several stages of live music, plenty of food choices, and other impromptu entertainment are also on the menu (☎ **704/338-1060;** www.festivalinthe park.org).

→ Start your hangover early with the **Charlotte Oktoberfest.** The all-day-Saturday festival draws up to 5,000 attendees to Memorial Stadium in late September, where more than 250 kinds of beer are available for unlimited samples, all for $35 to $25 if you buy tickets in advance (**www.charlotte oktoberfest.com**).

→ Fall is a big time for festivals, because also in September is the **Charlotte Shout,** a month-long art, culture, and entertainment festival. Taking place in venues and open spaces all over Charlotte, Shout hosts 1-night and signature events, some of which take place in a series—like the Sunset Jazz Festival, and "Blues, Brews & BBQ" weekend (**www.charlotteshout.com**).

→ Come spring, partake in the NASCAR culture for the huge, free late May **Food Lion Speed Street 600 Festival.** For one weekend every late May, 8 city blocks (around Tryon and W. 3rd St.) become the land of concerts, racing displays, demos, games, and—surprise!—beer drinking (☎ **704/455-6814;** www.600festival.com).

→ Hear your belly rumble in anticipation of the **Taste of Charlotte.** Held the first weekend in June on Tryon Street between 1st and 6th, this free food-fest puts together 3 days of restaurant sampling, wine and beer tastings, open-air shopping, and live music. And do come hungry, because for $20 you get a cup full of festival coins to redeem at dozens of food booths (☎ **704/947-6590;** www.tasteofcharlotte.com).

is also the area of town that offers plenty of "mom-and-pop" motels, in addition to chains. (For more places to stay in Charlotte, see the Southern BBQ Roadtrip, p. 320.)

CAMPGROUNDS

→**Copperhead Island** If McDowell (see below) is too big for you, just north of it in the middle of Lake Wylie is this small island, home to eight campsites, a boat launch, fishing piers, and nature trails. And if that weren't enough, you can even rent the place—literally, the entire island—for a few hundred bucks a day. *15200 Soldier Rd.* ☎ *704/583-1284. www.charmeck. org/Departments/Park+and+Rec/Inside+The+ Department/Divisions/Natural+Resources/Ca mping.htm. Rent-a-tent campsites ($45/night); entire island rental (weekday $355, weekend/ holiday $435). Reservations should be made 5 days in advance.*

→**McDowell Nature Preserve** You've died and gone to outdoor heaven: McDowell is home to camping, trails, picnic areas, nature preserve, biking, fishing, and a waterfront area on Lake Wylie. Its 1,108 acres pretty much have it all, including $4 bundles of firewood and $1 bags of ice. It's easy to find, just a few miles south of Charlotte proper (just north of the South Carolina border). Entry is daily from 7am to sunset. *15222 York Rd. (Hwy. 49 South).* ☎ *704/583-1284. www.charmeck. org/Departments/Park+and+Rec/Inside+The+ Department/Divisions/Natural+Resources/ Nature+Preserves/McDowell.htm. Drive-to campsites ($18/night), rent-a-tent campsites ($38/night), and other options, including RV site. Reservations should be made 5 days in advance.*

CHEAP

The best place for bargain-style motels is on the northeast edge of town, near UNCC. Try a drive along the long, winding **N. Tryon Street** (take the I-277 loop there) to find motels in the $35 to $50 range, like the **Holiday Motel** (6001 N. Tryon St.; ☎ **704/596-7185**) and the **Relax Inn** (6426 N. Tryon St.; ☎ **704/921-9123**). To frame your expectations: Around these parts, you'll quickly find that the reason for low prices might be because instead of having Wi-Fi, these motels are still bragging about having cable TV. Oh well, you can check your e-mail at an Internet cafe!

➜**Best Value Inn** ★ It's right by the airport, but the airport ain't far from central Charlotte and Noda. This smaller-chain location is clean, simple, and easy on the wallet. The usual amenities (cable, A/C, laundry) are available, and it's hard to beat its easy-access off I-85, a few minutes from all the Charlotte action. *3200 S. I-85 Service Rd.* ☎ *704/398-3144. www.bestvalueinn.com. 100 units. $35–$60 single; $55–$90 double, including continental breakfast. Free parking. $10 fee for pets. Amenities: Outdoor pool.*

DOABLE

Center City lodging will likely offer the most hotel options in a concentrated, central area. Web surfing may even lead to nightly deals of $100 or less on familiar chain hotels like the **Best Western** (201 S. McDowell St.; ☎ **800/WESTERN;** www.bestwestern.com), and **Hampton Inn** (530 East 2nd St.; ☎ **704/373-0917;** www. hamptoninn.com).

📺 Best ❷ ➜ **Holiday Inn Center City** ★★★ Recently renovated and smack in the middle of Charlotte's uptown, this 15-story, 296-unit hotel is a friendly place to hang your hat for a night or two. And while rates vary depending on the day of the week, the place could be worth every penny you spend on it for the amazing rooftop pool. *230 N. College St.* ☎ *888/890-0245 or 704/ 335-5400. www.ichotelsgroup.com. Singles or doubles $99–$179; suites $200–$250. Self-parking $10/night. Dogs accepted for $75 per day. Amenities: Bar/lounge; cafe/restaurant; rooftop jogging track and fitness room; Wi-Fi throughout.*

➜**The Park Hotel** ★★ Now part of the Marriott chain, the "boutique"-feeling Park is in the heart of Charlotte's South Park neighborhood (to the east of South End). Rooms are reliably clean, staff is obliging, and it's a quick jaunt to Center City, stadiums, and everything else you might need. *2200 Rexford Rd.* ☎ *800/334-0331 or 704/ 364-8220. www.theparkhotel.com. 192 units. Singles or doubles $99–$220. Free parking. $75 fee for pets. Amenities: Cable TV; Internet; weekend breakfast; outdoor pool; fitness room.*

SPLURGE

➜**The Morehead Inn** ★★ This southern estate lies in one of Charlotte's oldest neighborhoods, a few minutes from uptown. Quiet, elegant, and historic, it is considered one of the finer inns in western North

Carolina. Think fireplaces, cozy nooks, and cushy furniture. And if this is your kind of place, be sure to splurge on a corner room like "The Romany," with its queen-size four-poster bed and a separate office den. *1122 E. Morehead St., Charlotte, NC 28204. ☎ 888/MOREHEAD or 704/376-3357. www. moreheadinn.com. 12 units. $120–$190 double. Rates include breakfast. MC, V. Amenities: Nonsmoking rooms; dataport.*

Eating

It's easy to do as the Southerners do when in the South—that is, to indulge in mighty fine and plentiful deep-fried delicacies. You will find many an establishment for well-made (as well as mediocre) fries, rings, and burgers; there's plenty to choose from in Charlotte. (For more places to eat in Charlotte, see the Southern BBQ Roadtrip, p. 320.)

SUPPLIES
Farmers Markets

The year-round **Charlotte Regional Farmers Market** ✶ takes place at 1801 Yorkmont Rd. from March to December, Tuesday through Saturday, 8am to 6pm, and with limited hours on Sunday (May–Aug) and October through February (☎ 704/357-1269; www.ncdamarkets.org). Not far from the airport on the city's west side, it is owned and run by the state specifically to serve North Carolina farmers, giving buyers a chance to interact directly with the folks who grow the produce, make the various jams, and bake the bread (and more).

More limited options are the **North End Green Market,** held June to October, Wednesday and Saturday from 8am to 2pm at 128 S. Tryon St. (☎ 704/332-2227); and the open-air **North Mecklenburg Farmers Market,** taking place June through September Wednesday and Saturday from 8am to 2pm at Cornelius Elementary School, 700 N. Tryon St. (☎ 704/336-2561).

There's also the well-situated **Center City Green Market,** held on Saturdays from May to September on Seventh Street between College and Brevard (☎ 704/332-2227; www.centercitygreenmarket.com).

TAKE-OUT TREATS

Ease into the misty Carolina morning at mellow **SK Netcafe and Bar** ★★, where you can catch up on e-mail over a cafe au lait and a fresh pastry. Located on the east side of the Center City I-277 loop, SK offers free Wi-Fi with purchase and cafe computers at $4/hour with purchase. (1425 Elizabeth Ave., ☎ 704/334-1523).

The South End's ice-cream detour *du jour* is **Mr K's** (2107 South Blvd.; ☎ 704/375-4318), which is both easy to find and where it's easy to indulge, though its week-day-only hours (Mon–Fri 10am–9pm) make it more of a workday scene. If evening treats are what you're after, grab a shake at nearby **Pike's Soda Shop** (1930 Camden Rd.; ☎ 704/372-0092).

Well-rested Charlotte offers few late-night restaurants to the after-party partiers. But there is a good ol' Carolina chain **Brixx Pizza,** with three Charlotte locations, open Monday through Saturday until 1am (☎ 704/347-4729; www.brixxpizza.com). Another solid local pizza-and-burger chain is **Fuel,** whose five locations are open until 11pm on weekends and 10pm on weekdays (☎ 877/992-PIZZA; www.therestaurant group.com).

EATING OUT
Cheap

📺 Best 😊 → **South 21 Drive In** ★★★ AMERICAN How can you argue with a 1955 classic drive-in that's still got the best burgers and onion rings in town? Maybe the glory days of car culture have passed, but South 21 is still satisfying, and one-of-a-kind. And unlike national competitors, its original car-to-kitchen radio system is still going strong—let's hear it for old-school

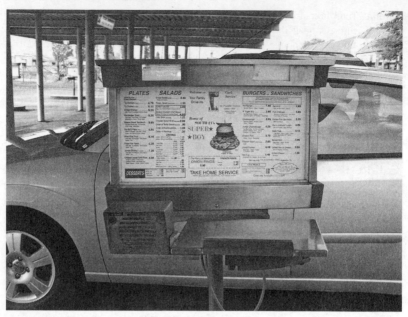

South 21 Drive In menu.

technology! *3101 E. Independence Blvd.* ☎ *704/377-4509. www.south21drivein.com. Big burgers under $5; shakes, rings, and fries under $3. Cash only. Tues 11am–3pm; Wed–Thurs 11am–9pm; Fri–Sat 11am–10pm (closed Sun–Mon).*

→**The Coffee Cup Grill** AMERICAN *The* place for your authentic Charlotte breakfast staples of eggs, biscuits and grits, and afternoon delights like country-style steak with real mashed potatoes, stewed okra, and mac-and-cheese. It's best not to show up with any expectations since this diner's not decorated to impress, but it is friendly and filling. *914 S. Clarkson St.* ☎ *704/375-8855. Breakfast $4–$10; entrees $5–$11. Mon–Fri 7:30am–3 pm; Sat–Sun 7:30am–noon.*

→**Phat Burritos** MEXICAN Minimalist decor, hearty fare. This is Charlotte's answer to mission-style burritos, both in size and price. Tacos, sandwiches, and other Mexican standards are also on the menu, and a nice outdoor patio is a good place to take your time and people-watch on the weekend. *1537 Camden Rd.* ☎ *704/332-7428. Burritos $7 and under. Mon–Sat 11am–9pm; Sun 11am–7pm.*

Doable

→**Nikko** ★ JAPANESE Voted best sushi in town by local weekly *Creative Loafing,* Nikko is reasonably priced, fresh, and friendly. Tucked into a sort of business center building, be careful not to drive right past it the first time—it's worth keeping an eye out for. One warning, though: The atmosphere varies, running the gamut from business lunches to dates to birthday dinners. *1300 South Blvd.* ☎ *704/370-0100. www.nikkosushibar.net. Lunch $7–$20; dinner $20–$30. Mon–Thurs lunch 11:30am–2:30pm; Sun–Thurs 5–10pm; Fri–Sat 5–11pm.*

Ⓜ Best ☺ →**Boudreaux's Louisiana Kitchen** ★★★ CAJUN Jambalaya, etoufee, and gumbo, oh my! It's hard to find such a comprehensive Cajun/Creole menu outside of the French Quarter—not to mention such a well-done one. All the traditional numbers are here (oysters, crawfish, catfish), along with some delicious vegetarian and Yankee variations. Plus desserts . . . try the Bourbon Street Pecan Pie. *501 E. 36th St.* ☎ *704/331-9898. www. boudreauxs.com. Reservations recommended. Salads, soups, and starters $3–$9; main courses $6–$18. Sun–Thurs 11:30am–10pm; Fri–Sat 11:30am–11pm.*

Splurge

➔ **LaVecchia's Seafood Grille** ★★ SEAFOOD This family-owned and operated business is a locally celebrated best all-around restaurant and best seafood dining room in greater Charlotte. It's on the fancy side, and decorated with art and sculpture by the South Carolina artist Mike Williams. This is *the* place in town to partake of Maine lobster, aged beef, and both fresh- and saltwater fish. There's an outdoor patio for the warmer months, where diners dine on "she-crab" soup, mussels, calamari, and stuffed shrimp with crabmeat. *325 E 6th St.* ☎ *704/370-6776. www. lavecchias.com. Reservations required. Main courses $24–$41. Mon–Thurs 5:30–10pm; Fri–Sat 5:30–11pm.*

Partying

Where there are college students, there are bars, which means that Noda and east towards UNCC are great places to partake in cheap beer ($3 is fairly standard for a brew, maybe $4 or $5 for a mixed drink, and even less during Happy Hour) and friendly conversation. The small enclave of bars and restaurants on N. Davidson Street at E. 36th Street is a friendly little strip. Center City and South End also hold their own, though, with bars spanning the sports, dives, and biker scenes.

BARS, PUBS & CLUBS
Noda/University City

➔ **The Dog Bar** BAR Definitely a neighborhood joint, the Dog Bar is self-proclaimed to be "Charlotte's only dog-friendly bar." Great drinks, friendly atmosphere, outdoor patio (fenced in, naturally), and live music draw many a dog and master, and many pet-free folks, too. If you are traveling with Fido, you must purchase a membership for each dog at the cost of $10, and your dog must wear his/her membership tag on their collar while at the dog bar. *3307 N. Davidson St.* ☎ *704/370-3595. www.dogbarnoda.com. Wed–Thurs 5pm–midnight; Fri–Sat 5pm–2am; Sun noon–10pm (during NFL season). No cover.*

➔ **Solstice Tavern** ★ BAR Beer specials and hearty pub grub are on the menu daily at the friendly and new-ish Solstice, which feels more upscale, but still has drafts at dive-bar prices ($2.50 for most domestics). *3221 N. Davidson St.* ☎ *704/342-2556. Daily 11:30am–2am. No cover.*

Center City/Uptown

➔ **Dixie's Tavern** BAR If you're looking for the place with the Jager shot specials and hot-wing deals, you've found it. Brassy and casual, Dixie's Cajun theme doesn't necessarily jive with the gung-ho Pittsburgh Steelers craziness, but after a half rack of Coors Light longnecks, who cares? *301 E. 7th St.* ☎ *704/374-1700. www.dixiescharlotte.com. Mon–Sat 11am–2am.*

➔ **Menage Ultra Lounge** CLUB For those who want to see and be seen in Charlotte, this three-level "upscale" nightclub has a 40-foot indoor slide, nightly music and drink specials, and solid DJs. Dirty jeans are discouraged. *118 W. 5th St.,* ☎ *704/377-8000. www.menageultralounge. com. Tues–Wed and Fri–Sat 10pm–2am. Cover $5–$10 (except special events).*

South End

➜ **Mac's Speed Shop** The tag-line pretty much captures it: "Beer, Bikes & BBQ." With its huge picnic bench–filled front patio and regular bike nights, Mac's is the place to go for a huge beer selection and grill menu among folks who will treat you like family by night's end—especially if you praise their Harleys. *2511 South Blvd.* ☎ *704/522-MACS.* *www.macspeedshop.com. Daily 11:30am–2am. No cover.*

Ashley Park

➜ **Scorpio** CLUB This popular lesbian and gay nightclub has been going strong for years, with gays (and straights) flocking from as far as Tennessee to partake in the heat and hustle. Located on the west side of Center City, it's actually several clubs within a club, including a large dance bar, and the "Queen City Saloon" country bar. And sometimes the weekend crowd is so vast you'll think everybody in Charlotte has gone gay for the night. *2301 Freedom Dr.* ☎ *704/373-9124. Wed–Thurs 8pm–3am; Fri–Sun 9pm–4am. Cover $2–$6.*

LIVE MUSIC

Rock/Folk

🅜 Best 💿 ➜ **The Evening Muse** ★★★ Intimate and charming, this is the kind of place where you could a) see a future music legend perform, b) meet a new friend for life, c) fall in love with Charlotte, or d) all of the above. Though it welcomes all kinds, the Muse tends toward the folksy, making it warm and mellow, and serves good beer. Live music in one or two shows a night draws a pretty steady crowd, which also means it's a great place to chat up cool Charlotteans and catch some local talent. *3227 N. Davidson St.* ☎ *704/376-3737. www.theeveningmuse.com. Sun–Thurs 6pm–midnight (sometimes closed Mon); Fri–Sat 6pm 'til whenever. No cover most nights.*

Jazz/Blues/Rock/Zydeco

➜ **Double Door Inn** ★★ Blues greats like Stevie Ray Vaughn, Willie Dixon, and Buddy Guy have rocked the stage of this classic Charlotte venue since it opened in 1973. Housed in a renovated 1920s house on the border of downtown Charlotte and the Elizabeth district, it has a likable, battered, absolutely unpretentious ambience. You might catch a zydeco band if you're lucky. *218 E. Independence Blvd.* ☎ *704/376-1446. www.doubledoorinn.com. Mon–Fri 11am–2am; Sat–Sun 8:30pm–2am. Cover $6–$15.*

What Else to See & Do

Charlotte is an easygoing city, but don't let that fool you. It is, after all, home of umpteen sports teams (and stadiums) and host of NASCAR races thrice yearly, as well as year-round blow-out events and festivals. And it's artsy too.

HANGING OUT

FREE ➜ **Freedom Park** ★ Though it's south of Center City, the 98-acre Freedom Park is sort of the Central Park of Charlotte. You'll be hard-pressed to find that anything vaguely city-park-like is missing. Check out the multiple walking and biking trails, 7-acre lake, amphitheater, outdoor shelters (with grills), nature center, batting cages, and all manner of sports courts. It's also home to events and festivals throughout the year (see "Charlotte Festivals: Art, Food & Beer," p. 703). *1900 East Blvd.* ☎ *704/432-4280. www.charmeck.org/Departments/Park+and+Rec/Home.htm. Open daily, dusk to dawn.*

PLAYING (INDOORS)

Bowling

Lace up the rentals and grab a ball for a night at the **University Lanes** (☎ **704/596-4736;** 5900 N. Tryon St.; www.amf.com/universitylanesnc). Closed Sundays

charlotte Culture Vulture

A Museum & Performing Arts Center

Roam through the corridors of the **Levine Museum of the New South** (☎ 704/333-1887; 200 E. Seventh St; www.museumofthenewsouth.org; closed Mon) for a sampling of southern history. The museum leads you through social history via interactive galleries, as well as the multisensory "Cotton Fields to Skyscrapers" permanent exhibit—which goes so far as to address lunch-counter sit-ins via personal accounts.

Meanwhile, take in a show at the happenin' **Blumenthal Performing Arts Center** (130 N. Tryon St.; ☎ 704/372-1000; www.blumenthalcenter.org). Opened in 1992, it's home to three theaters for productions ranging from rock concerts to Broadway shows to intimate stage events.

---

but open late all other nights, this is one of those bowling alleys that's big enough that you'll always get a lane, and cheap enough that your wallet won't ache the next morning.

PLAYING OUTDOORS
Horseback Riding & Fishing

The 2,500-acre **Latta Plantation Park** is the largest nature preserve in the county, at 6211 Sample Rd. in Huntersville (☎ 704/875-1391; www.charmeck.org/Departments/Park+and+Rec/Home.htm), 12 miles northeast of the city center. It's a quiet place to take in local flora and fauna; relax among the butterflies, birds, and waterfowl; and sign up at the equestrian center (fancy, eh?) to rent a horse for $23 and take a guided 7-mile trail. A nature center and picnic areas round out the program. Oh, and fishing is permitted, swimming isn't. You will need a permit if you decide to cast a line. It costs county residents $1/day, but non-county residents have to fork out $15 for a season permit, which can be purchased at Wal-Mart and other local sporting goods retailers. Call ☎ 888-2HUNTFISH or visit www.ncwildlife.org for more info.

Swimming

Charlotte's two outdoor city pools help relieve the heat between Memorial and Labor Days: **Cordelia** at 2100 N. Davidson St. (☎ 704/336-2096) and **Double Oaks** at 1200 Newland Rd. (☎ 704/336-2653). If you're more into the call of the wild, you can also dive into **Wylie Lake** at McDowell Nature Preserve (p. 703).

SPECTATOR SPORTS
Football

You may recall the **Carolina Panthers** from their near-upset of the New England Patriots in the 2004 Super Bowl. They're still going strong, filling Bank of America Stadium all season long with fans from all over the region. Grab seats while you're in town at the ticket office (☎ 704/358-7800; 800 S. Mint St., southeast side of the stadium; Mon–Fri 8:30am–5:30pm); or order through Ticketmaster (☎ 704/522-6500; www.cpanthers.com or www.ticketmaster.com).

NASCAR

If the smell of burning rubber turns your crank, **Lowe's Motor Speedway** is the place for you (☎ 800/455-FANS for tickets; ☎ 704/455-3204 for tours; 5555 Concord Pkwy. S., Concord, NC; www.lowesmotorspeedway.com). Called the "Mecca of Motorsports," this track hosts three NASCAR NEXTEL cup events each year, with other events and tours available year-round (with a few exceptions).

Basketball

The **Charlotte Bobcats** are the local NBA heroes, though they're still building momentum since they joined the league for the 2004–2005 season (replacing the Charlotte Hornets, who headed to New Orleans in 2003) (☎ **704/262-2287;** www.nba.com/bobcats).

Baseball

Playing in a stadium 12 miles south of Charlotte (okay, fine—it's actually in South Carolina), the **Charlotte Knights** are the AAA-league affiliate of the Chicago White Sox. Which means, of course, that if you hit a Knights game, you could be seeing the next great MLB slugger. Plus, at $12 for box seats, minor-league games are so much fun (☎ **704/357-8071;** 2280 Deerfield Dr.; www.charlotteknights.com).

On the Road to Nashville, TN

Charlotte, NC to Nashville, TN 420 miles

Yes, it's 420 miles between Charlotte and Nashville, but it's completely worth the drive if you have the time (and the gas money) just for the incredibly scenic state highways, like the Blue Ridge Parkway and US 412, heading up through the Great Smoky Mountains. Lush, green hills absorbed via winding, two-lane roads will kickstart the first leg of the roadtrip, and give you a snapshot of beautiful Carolina scenery.

Great Smokies tunnel.

And once through the mountain drive, gas up in Pigeon Forge, Tennessee—home of Dollywood and the launching of your crash course into the proud hillbilly culture that crops up again and again across our country's "Bible Belt."

Northern Carolina Highlights

There's a short way and a long way to leave Charlotte for Nashville. Here's why you should take the long way: You get to swing through South Carolina, adding another state to your "done" list and getting a gander of the world's fruitiest water tower from I-85: The Gaffney, South Carolina, hyper-realistic giant peach 📺 **Best ●** (don't let the peach seam make you think it's a giant ass). And while you're 'round those parts, why not pick up a little peach salsa or peach relish or something nice for mom? Mmmm . . . peaches!

Connect to I-26 north around Spartanburg, SC, and visit the lovely and relaxing town of **Asheville, NC,** where you can grab lunch and chat with the hippies. A word of warning about "Ashe-vegas," though: It is awfully cute and friendly, and stopping for too long there could very well distract you from the long drive ahead. Keep your focus!

On the Road Nuts & Bolts

Where to Fill Up Gas up before entering the Great Smoky Mountains since there's no place to get gas inside the park, and it's a bit of a drive with many a potential diversion. But other than that, there are plenty of stations along the highways. Gas prices don't vary much between North Carolina, South Carolina, and Tennessee, with one exception: Pigeon Forge, and just north of it, where gas prices drop a bit.

The Fastest Way I-77 north to I-40, west through Asheville, and straight over to Nashville in about 7 hours.

The Long Way Round If you're okay adding at least an hour or two to the drive, hop on I-85 west through Spartanburg, South Carolina, to I-26 north to arrive in Asheville in about 75 minutes. Take I-40 west to Waynesville, onto Rt. 19 to Cherokee In 50 minutes, then north through the Great Smoky Mountains (Rt. 441) for about an hour. Emerge in Tennessee, head north via highway 66 up to I-40 west to Nashville for the last 3½ hours.

Rules of the Road Try not to be alarmed by the sign that says "Warning: Steep, winding mountain road ahead" upon entering the Smokies Parkway—it's really not that bad. Meanwhile, back on the interstate, beware the conflux of 18-wheelers on the way to Nashville.

Coffee to Go In Tennessee, driving is not to be done while asleep, says dumblaws.com.

Picnic Point Grab lunch to go in Asheville so you can soak up some fresh Smoky Mountain air with a picnic at any number of great lookout points.

Press on westward toward the **Blue Ridge Parkway,** where you can get your last tank of gas in the small, souvenir-shop of a town called Cherokee before turning north through the Great Smoky Mountains. A stop at the **Oconaluftee Visitors Center** (☎ 865/436-1200; www.nps.gov/grsm) will yield a stack of brochures on things to do and see during your time in the country's most-visited national park.

If you're soaking up the Smokies on the move, the awestrikingly beautiful 35-mile drive ★ should take you about an hour (depending on traffic—try a weekday for less of it). But if you can afford more time, you can do a picnic, hike a section of the **Appalachian Trail,** or detour west 2 miles from the heart of the park to its highest peak, **Clingmans Dome** (6,642 ft.).

Because all good things must end, you will eventually reach Gatlinburg, the Smokies' northern entry/exit, and soon arrive in **Pigeon Forge,** population 5,083. Welcome to Tennessee, friend! This 12-square-mile town is famous the world over for one amazing attraction: **Dollywood** (☎ 865/428-9488; www.dollywood.com). And in case you can afford the time to hit some rides, prices vary by season, and are cheapest during the winter off season at $42.40/day for adults and $24.55/day for children 4 to 11, including tax (summer is $47.95 for adults, $36.80 for kids).

However, there's more to Pigeon Forge than Dolly Parton's roller coasters, if you'll pardon the expression. You'll see it all on the Pigeon Forge Parkway (the giant strip you drive through on): Mini-NASCAR

Nashville Highlights

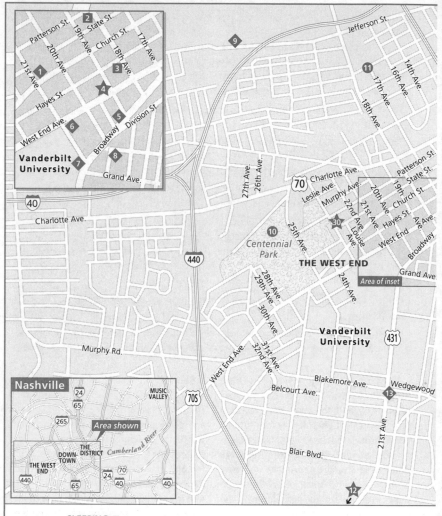

SLEEPING ■
Best Western Music Row **15**
Days Inn Vanderbilt/Music Row **3**
Music City Hostel **2**
Wyndham Union Station **21**
EATING ◆
Elliston Place Soda Shop **1**
Goten **6**
Harper's **9**

EATING (continued)
Jack's Bar-B-Que **26**
Mafiaoza's **16**
Nashville Public
Market **18**
Nick & Rudy's **7**
Noshville **5**
Pancake Pantry **13**
South Street **8**

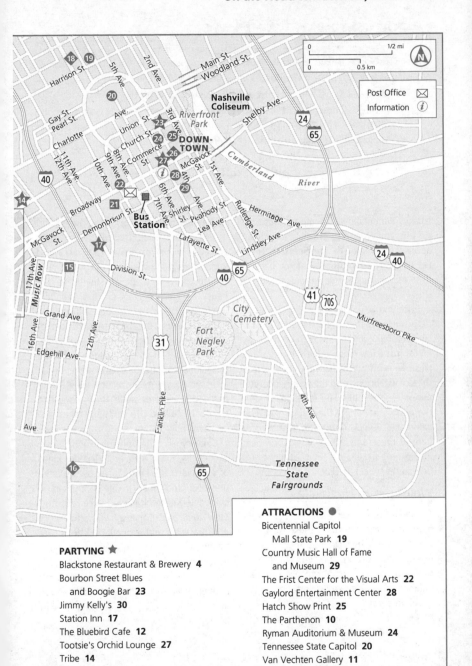

PARTYING ★

Blackstone Restaurant & Brewery **4**

Bourbon Street Blues
  and Boogie Bar **23**

Jimmy Kelly's **30**

Station Inn **17**

The Bluebird Cafe **12**

Tootsie's Orchid Lounge **27**

Tribe **14**

ATTRACTIONS ●

Bicentennial Capitol
  Mall State Park **19**

Country Music Hall of Fame
  and Museum **29**

The Frist Center for the Visual Arts **22**

Gaylord Entertainment Center **28**

Hatch Show Print **25**

The Parthenon **10**

Ryman Auditorium & Museum **24**

Tennessee State Capitol **20**

Van Vechten Gallery **11**

Giddy'up to Nashville Playlist

→ *Hey, Good Lookin'*, **Hank Williams,** 1951
→ *Nashville Blues,* **Doc Watson,** "Doc Watson," 1964
→ *Be-Bop-A-Lula,* **Gene Vincent and His Blue Caps,** 1956
→ *Blue Suede Shoes,* **Carl Perkins,** 1956 (recorded performance on display at the Country Music Hall of Fame)
→ *Expectations,* **Belle & Sebastian,** "Tigermilk," 1999
→ *Take You on a Cruise,* **Interpol,** "Antics," 2004
→ *Get Rhythm,* **Johnny Cash,** "Original Sun Albums: Johnny Cash," 2005
→ *Little Sister,* **Elvis Presley,** 1961

tracks! Water slides! Theme restaurants! And, if you've got to crash, crazy-cheap accommodations like the **Scenic Motel** (☎ 865/453-6330), that'll set you back as little as $25 for a single room ($30 during the summer rush).

Once you've gotten your fill of the alternate universe that is Pigeon Forge, grab some caffeine and keep north on highway 66 for just a few more miles to hop on I-40 west. In a bit more than a 3-hour cruise, the sky will brighten in the distance as you approach Nashville. You can almost hear the musicians tuning their guitars as you get close. (Quick note: You'll enter the Central time zone in Knoxville, TN, which means you'll relive 1 hour of your life behind the wheel. Trippy.)

Welcome to Nashville

Though it is the state capital, Nashville may be better known as Music City, the country music mecca. But there's a lot more going on in this city of nearly 600,000, not the least of which is a perfect balance of small-town warmth and urban sophistication.

Nashville is an increasingly popular tourist draw for its world-class museums,

major-league sports, booming dining and after-hours scenes, and distinct skyline ringed by rolling hills, rivers and lakes, and wide-open green spaces.

Ultimately, though, Nashville is the heart of country music, that uniquely American blend of gospel, blues, and mountain music that has evolved into a $2-billion-a-year industry. At its epicenter, Nashville is still the city where unknown musicians can become overnight sensations, where the major record deals are cut and fortunes are made (and lost), and where the **Grand Ole Opry** still takes center stage.

Country isn't the only music you'll hear in this city. Rock, R&B, and all other kinds of musicians are being lured by the city's one-of-a-kind vibe. (If this is any sort of evidence, Kid Rock moved here recently.) They come here for inspiration, to record new material, and for collaborations with Nashville's music pros. No matter the genre, the city seems to attract more musicians each year, which means there's enough live music in Nashville to keep you humming long after you hit the highway home.

Nashville Nuts & Bolts

Area Code   The telephone area code in Nashville, in Davidson County, is 615.

Business Hours   Banks are generally open Monday to Thursday 9am to 4pm, Friday 9am to 5 or 6pm, and Saturday morning. Office hours in Nashville are usually Monday to Friday 8:30am to 5pm. In general, stores in downtown Nashville are open Monday to Saturday 10am to 6pm. Shops in suburban Nashville malls are generally open Monday to Saturday 10am to 9pm and Sunday 1 to 6pm. Bars in Nashville are frequently open all day long and are allowed to stay open daily until 3am, but sometimes close earlier.

Doctor   If you need a doctor, call **Medline** (☎ 615/342-1919), available Monday to Friday 8am to 5pm; or contact the **Vanderbilt Medical Group Physician Referral Service** (☎ 615/322-3000) or **Columbia Medline** (☎ 800/265-8624).

Drugstores   The following **Walgreens** pharmacies are open 24 hours a day: 518 Donelson Pike (☎ 615/883-5108); 5600 Charlotte Pike (☎ 615/356-5161); and 627 Gallatin Rd. (☎ 615/865-0010); or call ☎ 800/925-4733 for the nearest Walgreens.

Emergencies   Phone ☎ 911 for fire, police, emergency, or ambulance. If you get into dire straits, call **Travelers' Aid** of the Nashville Union Mission, 639 Lafayette St. (☎ 615/780-9471). It's primarily a mission that helps destitute people, but if you need help in making phone calls or getting home, they might be able to help.

Hospitals   The following hospitals offer emergency medical treatment: **St. Thomas Hospital,** 4220 Harding Rd. (☎ 615/222-2111), and **Vanderbilt University Medical Center,** 1211 22nd Ave. S., in the downtown/Vanderbilt area (☎ 615/322-5000).

Internet   Nashville's **Centennial Park** offers Wi-Fi, as do many a cafe in neighborhoods all over town, such as **Bongo Java,** 2007 Belmont Blvd. (☎ 615/385-5282) and **Caffeine Café,** 156 Demonbreun St. (☎ 615/259-4993). The **Nashville Public Library** also has free Wi-Fi in the main building and some branches; just get the access code from a service desk inside. As always, you can visit www.wififreespot.com for a list of free wireless access locations.

Libraries   The new Main Library of Nashville and Davidson County is at 615 Church St. (☎ 615/862-5800). It's open Monday to Thursday 9am to 8pm, Friday 9am to 6pm, Saturday 9am to 5pm, and Sunday 2 to 5pm. There are also branch libraries scattered around town, but they are closed city-wide on Friday.

Liquor Laws   The legal drinking age in Tennessee is 21. Bars are allowed to stay open until 3am every day. Beer can be purchased at drug, grocery, or package stores, but wine and liquor are sold through package stores only.

Newspapers & Magazines   The *Tennessean* (www.tennessean.com) is Nashville's morning daily and Sunday newspaper. The alternative weekly is the *Nashville Scene* (www.nashvillescene.com), and the *All the Rage* (www.nashvillerage.com) is a good weekly source for music and entertainment while you're in town. There's also the LGBT paper *Out & About* (www.outandaboutnewspaper.com) distributed monthly all over the city and state.

Police   The non-emergency number for the Nashville Police Department is ☎ 615/862-8600. Call ☎ 911 for emergencies.

Post Office   The main post office at 901 Broadway (☎ 800/275-8777), convenient to downtown and the West End, and will accept mail addressed to General Delivery. It's open Monday to Friday 8am to 5pm and on Saturday 8am to 2pm. There's also a post office in the downtown arcade at 16 Arcade (☎ 615/248-2287), which is open Monday to Friday 8:30am to 5pm; other locations can be found using the city name or a local zip code at www.usps.com.

Radio   Nashville has more than 30 AM and FM radio stations. Some specialize in a particular style of music, including gospel, soul, big band, and jazz. Of course, there are several country music stations, including WSM (650 AM and 95.5 FM), the station that first broadcast the Grand Ole Opry, and the popular WSIX (97.9 FM). WPLN (90.3 FM) is Nashville's National Public Radio station, and WRLT (100.1 FM) plays "adult alternative" music. For college radio, tune to Vanderbilt University's WRVU (91.1 FM).

Taxes   The Tennessee state sales tax is 9.25%. The Nashville hotel and motel room tax is 5%, which when added to the 9.25% makes for a total hotel-room tax of 14.25%. There is a 2% car-rental tax plus an additional car-rental surcharge.

Television   Local television channels include 2 (ABC), 4 (NBC), 5 (CBS), 8 (PBS), 17 (FOX), 30 (UPN), 39 (independent), and 58 (WB).

Time Zone   Tennessee is on Central Standard Time.

Transit Information   Call ☎ 615/862-5950 or visit www.nashvillemta.org for information on the MTA bus system or trolleys.

Visitors Bureau   Call ☎ **800/657-6910** or check out www.visitmusiccity.com to get more information about Nashville.

Weather   For the local forecast, call the **National Weather Service** (☎ 615/754-4633) or visit www.tennessean.com.

The Plant That Ate the South

Sometimes called "the plant that ate the south," **kudzu** (*pueraria montana*) is the big-leafed ivy that literally blankets trees, telephone poles, and anything else in its reach. Kudzu originated in Japan, and was introduced into the United States as an ornamental vine at the Philadelphia Centennial Exposition of 1876. For a few decades following, farmers planted it as livestock feed and to prevent soil erosion—and then noticed that its rapid growth was taking over, well, everything. By 1953, kudzu was reclassified as weed and no longer acceptable as a ground-cover plant. Kudzu sprouts up to a foot a day in the summer months, and the southeastern U.S. is now the land of the leafy vine, with acres upon acres of kudzu covering, and eventually smothering, other vegetation from Florida to as far away as Pennsylvania and Texas. Herbicides that kill the root system, combined with serious mowing, are part of long-term methods for controlling the plant, with more extensive biological control being investigated.

Getting Around

Nashville was built on a bend in the Cumberland River, which generally defined the city's shape. The **downtown** area is a grid of streets located on the Cumberland's west side. Numbered avenues run parallel to the river on a northwest-southeast axis, while streets perpendicular to the river have names. Though the grid pattern is interrupted by I-40, it basically continues until you get to Vanderbilt University in the **West End** area.

For the most part, Nashville is a sprawling modern city. Downtown has the most foot traffic, while the rest of the city's neighborhoods are mostly geared toward vehicles—at least to get there.

Among them **The District** (www.thedistrictnashville.org), on the edge of downtown, is its own historic district along Second Avenue, Lower Broadway, and Printer's Alley. It's loaded with shops, restaurants, nightclubs, and bars and encompasses "Honky Tonk Highway"—a particularly rowdy little block of neon and live music all day and all night. The term "hootenanny" may be overheard or applied here.

Then there's the **West End,** where the moneymakers and musicians of the Nashville scene gather (the area also encompasses **Hillsboro Village**). Located near the Vanderbilt University campus, this is a bit of an upscale neighborhood and is home to many small shops, lots of excellent (and often expensive) restaurants, and several hotels. **Music Row** is a few blocks over from the West End, located around the corner of 16th Avenue South and Demonbreun Street (pronounced "De-*mon*-brein"). Here, recording studios and record companies make this neighborhood the center of the country music recording industry.

Farther out and different scenes entirely are **Belle Meade** (7 miles southwest of downtown Nashville, via West End Ave.) and **Music Valley** (around 15 miles northeast of downtown, via highway 41A). The former is home to Nashville's mansions and upper-crust; the latter, home to all things Grand Ole Opry.

BY CAR

Because the city and its many attractions are quite spread out, I'm afraid the car is yet again the best way to get around town. It's surprisingly easy to find your way around, at least, and to find parking, even downtown. But bring plenty of cash. Parking can cost a few coins in the meter or upwards of $10 in lots during special events. (For a good roundup on Nashville

 Attack of the 18-Wheelers

Three interstates, one convergence. That's Nashville—and it means that if you're heading in from any direction on I-40, I-65, or I-24, you're subject to a highway chock-full of semi tractor-trailers. In an SUV or larger car, this may not be quite as daunting. But being behind the wheel of a compact hatchback may make you feel like a mouse among elephants. The good news is that professional truckers tend to be cautious and considerate. *Tend* to be. Sometimes, either they can't see or just don't care enough not to cut you off or suddenly sandwich you between three or four like-size behemoths. And God help you if it's dark and stormy on top of it. So, before you hop onto the interstate, be sure to have your music pre-queued and keep your eyes on the road and your hands upon the wheel (to quote the Doors)!

parking details, check out www.parkit
downtown.com.) Oh, and the only time
driving is much of a problem is during
morning and evening rush hours. At these
times, streets leading south and west out
of downtown can get darn congested.

A key issue to watch out for when driving around Nashville is the numerous divi-
sions of the interstates that encircle the
city. If you don't pay close attention to
which lane you're supposed to be in, you
can easily wind up heading in the wrong
direction at 55 mph.

BY PUBLIC TRANSIT

Although Nashville is served by the extensive and efficient **Metropolitan Transit
Authority (MTA)** bus system, it's designed
for locals and commuters, and not terribly
practical for tourists. But it is cheap, so if
you're up for tackling it, call the Customer
Service Center (☎ **615/862-5950**), Monday
through Friday, 6:30am until 6pm for
insight. There's also the MTA information
center and ticket booth located on
Deaderick Street at Fifth Avenue, and open
Monday to Friday 6:30am to 8pm; Saturday
8am to 1pm.

MTA bus stops are marked with blue-
and-white signs; in the downtown area,
signs include names and numbers of all the
routes using that stop. All express buses
are marked with an X following the route

number. **Adult fares** are $1.10 ($1.50 for
express buses) and exact change is
required. You can purchase a weekly pass
good for unlimited local rides from Sunday
to Saturday for $15 per adult or $9 per
youth age 19 and under; a picture ID is
required.

For a quick way to get around downtown
on weekdays, look for the **LunchLINE** shuttles. As a convenience to downtown workers, the Central Business Improvement
District and Nashville Downtown
Partnership offers a free trolley that loops
through the heart of downtown weekdays
from 11am to 1:30pm. Riders may hop on or
off at any of the 15 stops. No tickets are
required.

The downtown route passes by many
points of interest in downtown Nashville
and is a good way to get acquainted with
the city. For more information, call ☎ **615/
743-3090** or check out www.nashville
downtown.com.

ON FOOT

Downtown Nashville is the only area
where you're likely to do much walking.
But hey, there's tons to do there. The
Country Music Hall of Fame, Ryman
Auditorium, Honky Tonk Highway, Frist
Center for the Visual Arts, and Riverfront
Park—all within walking distance.

For More Information...

➔ Nashville Convention & Visitors Bureau: ☎ 800/657-6910; www.visitmusic
   city.com

➔ Tennessee Department of Tourism: ☎ 800/836-6200 or 615/741-2158;
   www.tnvacation.com

➔ Nashville Transit: ☎ 615/862-5950; www.nashvillemta.org

➔ *Tennesseean* daily newspaper: www.tennesseean.com

➔ *Nashville Scene* weekly newspaper: www.nashvillescene.com

➔ Tennessee State Parks: www.tnstateparks.com

➔ Tennessee Backroads: www.tennesseebackroads.org

Nashville Events: Lots of Music Festivals!

As if the year-round music, history, and honkytonks weren't enough, there are a crazy lot of yearly fairs and festivals in Nashville. In addition to this list, **www.musiccityusa.com** has a calendar that'll tip you off to more events while you're in town.

➙ Nashville Songwriters Association International puts on **Tin Pan South** every March/April at venues all over the city (**www.tinpansouth.com**).

➙ Great indie musicians like Ben Folds and My Morning Jacket have taken the stage at Vanderbilt University's **Rites of Spring** festival, held every late April on its Alumni Lawn (**www.ritesofspring.com**).

➙ The **CMA Music Festival/Fan Fair** is the big Nashville to-do, packing the Coliseum every mid-June. Tickets don't come cheap (they start at $125 for the 4-day package), but for your money you get to revel among thousands of country-music fans to the tunes of 100+ big-name bands and singers (☎ **800/CMA-FEST**; www.cmafest.com).

➙ Laid back and a little bizarre, check out the **Tomato Art Festival** and its exhibits, tastings, and contests. It takes place around the cool East End throughout July and August (**www.tomatoartfest.com**).

➙ Labor Day weekend summons jazz and blues greats from around the world for the **Music City Jazz, Blues & Heritage Festival.** For $15/day, you get to see Riverfront Park turn into a symphony of jazz, blues, reggae, funk, gospel, soul, and R&B. Bring your blanket and picnic basket (☎ **615/255-9600**; www.nbl4u.com).

➙ The **Tennessee State Fair** crops up in Nashville every mid-September, drawing more than 200,000 visitors to check out its rides, exhibits, games, music, and livestock shows. This 10-day extravaganza is one of the city's biggest annual events. Plus there are racing pigs! (☎ **615/862-8980**; www.tennesseestatefair.org).

➙ The third weekend in October heralds the **Music & Molasses Festival,** bringing traditional southern bluegrass music, storytellers, crafts, and food to the Historic Ellington Agricultural Center (**www.tnagmuseum.org**).

Of course, there are a few walking strips beyond downtown, especially if you care to pick up some local, neighborhood vibes. Try a stroll up and down **Music Row** (which lives on both 16th and 17th aves. between Demonbreun St. and Grand Ave.) and a cool little strip called 12th **Avenue South.** There's also a growing restaurant scene in **East Nashville,** over on the other side of the river, generally around Main Street and S. 10th Street.

BY TAXI

For a quick ride, call **American Music City Taxi** (☎ 615/262-0451), **Checker Cab** (☎ 615/256-7000), or **Allied Taxi** (☎ 615/244-7433). The flag-drop rate is $3; after that it's $2 per mile, plus $1 for each additional passenger.

Sleeping

Nashville caters to tens of thousands of country music fans yearly, so it's awash in inexpensive and moderately priced hotels.

Many of them are downtown, and there you can usually find a reasonable deal on a nice place—especially because they're competing with a cluster of newer, moderately priced hotels in the airport area along Elm Hill Pike, just a quick jaunt east of the city on I-40.

The majority of the hotel and motel rooms in the city are in the $75 to $120 range (and on most weekends $100 might buy you a room at one of the downtown high-rise hotels). If you want to be close to the city's best restaurants and wealthiest neighborhoods, book a room in a West End hotel. If you want to splurge, there are several good luxury hotels in downtown Nashville, including two in historic buildings.

But for sheer visual impact, you can't beat the massive **Opryland Hotel**, 2800 Opryland Drive (☎ **866/972-6779**; www.gaylordhotels.com), where Southern opulence and Disney-esque tropical fantasies merge to create a hotel that is as much a destination as it is a place to stay. A night here will run you $200 on average (varies by season), and you may feel like you're in some kind of Vegas-Disney-country livin' wonderland.

CAMPGROUNDS/HOSTEL

➔ **Bledsoe Creek State Park** About 30 miles northeast of Nashville off Hwy. 25 (near Gallatin) is 164 acres of beautiful Tennessee State Park land. Complete with water and electric hookups, bathhouses, and grills, this is a great place to relax in the wilderness on the quiet bank of Bledsoe Creek. Boating, hiking, and other sports are all part of the package, as well as fishing in Old Hickory Lake. It's open year-round, and reservations are not taken for the park's 26 campsites. *400 Zieglers Fort Rd. ☎ 615/452-3706. http://state.tn.us/environment/parks/BledsoeCreek. Campsites $18/night. Cash only.*

➔ **Music City Hostel** ★★ A few minutes from downtown on the West End is this new hostel that's drawing plenty of U.S. and international travelers. It has options for dorm-style beds or private rooms available nightly or even by the month (three apartments are also available), plus it's super clean and a great bargain. There's no fitness center (as you might expect), but there is free Wi-Fi, and they rent bikes and helmets for $7/day. Oh, and to keep costs low, the hotel only checks voicemail once a day, so send a reservation e-mail, too! (info@musiccityhostel.com). *1809 Patterson St. ☎ 614/692-1277. www.musiccityhostel.com. 15 bunk beds, 2 private rooms. $25 dorm bunk bed; $55 for private room (for 1 or 2 people); $774 for private room for a month. Free parking. No pets, nonsmoking. Reservations recommended.*

➔ **Nashville KOA** Out yonder in Music Valley is one full-package KOA, with its free Wi-Fi, showers, on-site laundry, shuttles to the Grand Ole Opry, and entertainment planning. Both cabins and tent camping are available, and the whole place is about a 15-minute drive to downtown. And it's wise to make reservations since summer months stay pretty booked, and it'll save you a few bucks. *2626 Music Valley Dr. ☎ 615/889-0286 or 800-562-7789. www.nashvillekoa.com. Tent campsites $30/night no hookups; $40/night with water and electric, cabins $51/night for 1 room, $61/night for 2 rooms, and RV sites. Reservations save $5 and are recommended by phone or online.*

CHEAP

The **West End** and **Music Row** are the best places for hotel deals near downtown, and there you will find many a cheap hotel chain. There are also bargains to be found out in **Music Valley,** like the **Red Roof Inn,** 2460 Music Valley Dr. (☎ **615/889-0090**), charging $60 to $90 double (with an outdoor pool and an adjacent miniature-golf course).

I said "Greece," not "Grease"

The centerpiece of Nashville's **Centennial Park** is not a fountain or a simple monument. No, in Nashville, they think outside the box—and the testament to that global mindset comes in the form of the **Parthenon** (p. 732). A full-scale replica of Greece's 483 B.C. temple, Nashville's Parthenon, originally built of wood and brick, opened in 1897 for the Tennessee Centennial Exhibition. It out-lasted other structures built for the exhibition, and served for decades as a city museum, before being rebuilt as a permanent, concrete structure in 1931, com-plete with reproduced Parthenon Marbles. But the story doesn't end there, because in 1982 Nashvillians decided to up the ante for this museum and fill in the interior with some Ancient Greece–style decor—that is, they commissioned sculptor Alan LeQuire to replicate the 42-foot-tall, gilded statue of Goddess **Athena Parthenos** [MTV] [Best] that stood in the original Greek temple. It is, quite possibly, the most striking, bizarre, and cool tribute to classicism in the country.

Near the **airport,** check out the **Best Western Airport,** 701 Stewart's Ferry Pike (☎ **615/889-9199**), which charges $50 to $70 for a double (adjacent to Uncle Bud's restaurant) and the **Super 8 Motel– Nashville/Airport/Music City,** 720 Royal Pkwy. (☎ **615/889-8887**), charging $54 to $65 for a double.

➔ **Best Western Music Row** ★ It's hard to beat this location, just a click away from all the good downtown sights and venues. Remodeled in 2005, bargain-priced rooms are standard, although the suites offer sig-nificantly more space for just a few extra dollars. The lounge hosts live music nightly, but it won't disturb your sleep. *1407 Division St.* ☎ *800/228-5151 or 615/242-1631. www.bestwestern.com. 102 units. $59–$159 single or double. Rates include continental breakfast. Free local calls. Free parking. Pets up to 20 pounds $5 per day. Amenities: Lounge; outdoor pool; dataport and Wi-Fi; fridge and microwave in 20 units.*

DOABLE

➔ **Days Inn Vanderbilt/Music Row** This refurbished motel dates back to the 1960s, and though it's not a palace, it is a smart choice if you're on a budget for its central location and standard amenities, includ-ing breakfast. Music Row, Vanderbilt University, and Centennial Park are all within walking distance. *1800 West End Ave.* ☎ *800/329-7466 or 615/327-0922. www.days inn.com. 151 units. $72–$109 single or double, including continental breakfast. Free parking. Amenities: Outdoor pool; exercise room; com-plimentary shuttle to nearby medical center; dataport and Wi-Fi.*

➔ **The Millennium Maxwell House Hotel** ★ And why is a hotel named for a brand of coffee? The original Maxwell House, where President Theodore Roosevelt once stayed, was in downtown Nashville. This modern-day successor is a 10-story hotel that sits just off I-65, about 1½ miles north of downtown. The rooms are rather basic but relaxing and pleasant. South-side rooms on the upper floors of the hotel have a great view of the Nashville skyline and are worth requesting. Glass elevators on the outside of the building also take full advantage of the unob-structed views. *2025 Metro Center Blvd.* ☎ *800/457-4460 or 615/259-4343. www. millennium-hotels.com. 289 units. $80–$140 double; $175–$400 suite. Free parking.*

AMERICAN HIGHWAYS

Style & Substance at the Hall of Fame

The extent to which the **Country Music Hall of Fame** (p. 731) pays tribute to the genre, as well as to music in general, is so thought-out it's downright fanatical. In fact, the homage runs so deep it's in the foundation of the building. For example, a bird's-eye view of the $37-million museum shows that it's built in the form of a bass clef, and the upward-arching roof resembles the fin of a 1950s Cadillac. And if you're as fanatical as the architects, you might also notice that the facade windows look like piano keys, the spire conjures a radio tower, and the tiered rotunda is proportioned like vinyl 78s and 45s and CDs.

Amenities: Restaurant; outdoor pool; nearby golf course; 2 lighted tennis courts; exercise room; concierge; tour desk; business center; coin-op laundry; dataport in all rooms.

SPLURGE

➔**Wyndham Union Station** ★★ How can you beat a grandly restored hotel inside a National Historic Landmark? This Wyndham occupies the Romanesque Gothic former Union Station railway terminal (ca. 1900), with the former main hall of the station—complete with vaulted ceiling and Tiffany stained glass installations—serving as the lobby. The hotel's best accommodations are the gallery deluxe rooms, which have 22-foot-high ceilings and huge arched walls of glass that overlook the lobby. A few other rooms also have high ceilings and large windows and, though unique, can get quite hot in the afternoon. Be sure to check out the vault-like McKinley Room, with its arched windows, stone walls, and Spanish floor tiles, which has been converted to a conference room. *1001 Broadway.* ☎ *800/996-3426 or 615/726-1001. www.wyndham.com. 125 units. $129–$189 single or double; $215–$250 suites. Valet parking $14. Pets less than 20 pounds accepted for $45 nonrefundable deposit per visit. Amenities: Restaurant and lounge; access to adjacent fitness center; limited room service; same-day dry cleaning; dataport and Wi-Fi; video games.*

Eating

Southern cooking, with its fatback and chitlins, collard greens, and fried everything, is ubiquitous in Nashville, often appearing in the form of "meat-and-three" restaurants, where you get your choice of three sides with your entree. But this doesn't mean that the city hasn't branched out as far as international cuisine. There are plenty of good Italian, French, German, Japanese, Chinese, and even Thai restaurants around.

It's just that, well, as long as you're below the Mason-Dixon line, you owe it to yourself to try some real country cookin'. Barbecue and fried catfish are two inexpensive staples you shouldn't miss, as are a few restaurants serving "New Southern" cuisine that works in traditional and not-so-traditional ingredients.

SUPPLIES

In Nashville, the market to beat all markets is the year-round **Nashville Public Market.** Across the street from the Bicentennial Mall at 900 8th Ave., this huge indoor farmers market has 100+ farm stalls and 100 flea-market stalls. There are also more than a dozen prepared food vendors and gourmet- and imported-food stalls, selling everything from Jamaican meat patties to hundreds of different hot sauces. The market is open daily 8am to 7pm in summer, 9am to 6pm the rest of the year (☎ 615/880-2001; www.nashville farmersmarket.com).

In summer months (and sometimes though early fall), there's also the **Nashville Food Fair** (☎ 615/444-6104), for which five churches around town host farmers from around the region. The Food Fairs take place usually 1 or 2 days a week; call for details or check www.ams.usda. gov/farmersmarkets/States/Tennessee. htm.

There's also the **Peanut Shop** ★, a true Nashville institution. This tiny shop in the Arcade (connecting Fourth Ave. N. and Fifth Ave. N.) has been in business since 1927 and still roasts its own peanuts. In fact, there are more styles of peanuts sold here than you've probably ever seen in one place (☎ 615/256-3394; www. nashvillenut.com).

HANG OUT/TAKEOUT

An African word for "village" was the inspiration for the name of the **Kijiji Coffee House,** 1207 Jefferson St. (☎ 615/321-0403), a popular day-long hangout near Fisk University in north Nashville. It opens at 8am daily, and stays open late for live jazz and poetry readings both at this location and at a newly opened second location downtown, at 121 Second St. N. (☎ 615/734-3400).

Another good cafe over in hip Hillsboro Village is **Fido,** 1812 21st Ave. S. (☎ 615/385-7959), a big place with an artsy, urban feel. The space used to be a pet shop, but now it's the friendliest coffeehouse in Nashville.

One insider treat among Nashvillians is "hot chicken," and no place does it better than **Prince's Hot Chicken Shack** (☎ 615/226-9442). Located northeast of downtown at 123 Ewing Dr., anything hotter than medium spice might make you spontaneously combust. P.S., avoid carbonated beverages here—the combination hot 'n spicy and fizzy water could be lethal.

A good chaser to Prince's is **Noshville,** 1918 Broadway (☎ 615/329-NOSH; www. noshville.com), where you can douse your taste buds with a cold shake or coat them with a huge slice of cheesecake. You can also relax with an appetizer and a beer, likely while taking in great live music, at **Radio Café** in the East End, 1313 Woodland St. (☎ 615/228-6045).

To fill up after a night at the bar, or wherever, try the West End's 24-hour hot spot, **Café Coco,** 210 Louise Ave. Desserts, coffee, salads, sandwiches, and vegetarian options help keep Coco jumpin' day and night. (☎ 615/321-2626; www.cafecoco.com).

EATING OUT
Cheap
➔**Elliston Place Soda Shop** ★ AMERICAN   Open since 1939, this is one of the oldest restaurants in Nashville, and it looks it. The lunch counter, black-topped stools, and signs advertising malted milks and banana splits all seem to have been here since the late '30s. The time-capsule sort of soda shop serves plate lunches of an entree and veggies, with four different specials of the day. Of course, you can also get club sandwiches, steaks, and hamburgers, and the best chocolate shakes in town.

2111 Elliston Place (West End). ☎ *615/327-1090. Main courses $2–$6. Mon–Fri 7am–7pm; Sat 7am–5pm.*

➔**Harper's** ★★ AMERICAN/SOUTHERN   If the thought of slow-simmered turnip greens, crispy fried chicken, tender sweet potatoes, and fluffy yeast rolls makes your mouth water, wipe off your chin and immediately head to the Jefferson Street district for Nashville's best soul food. Be sure to save room for a slice of pie or a heaping bowl of banana pudding. Popular with white-collar professionals and blue-collar laborers alike, Harper's attracts a friendly, diverse clientele. Plus this immaculate soul-food cafeteria accepts credit cards, and does not allow smoking. *2610 Jefferson St. ☎ 615/329-1909. Main courses $4–$7. Mon–Fri 6am–8pm; Sat–Sun 11am–6pm.*

→**Jack's Bar-B-Que** ★★ BARBECUE When the barbecue urge strikes in The District, don't settle for cheap imitations; head to Jack's, where you can get pork shoulder, Texas beef brisket, St. Louis ribs, and smoked turkey, sausage, and chicken. It ain't fancy, but it's *goooood*. There's another Jack's at 334 W. Trinity Lane (☎ **615/228-9888**), in north Nashville. *416 Broadway. ☎ 615/254-5715. www.jacks barbque.com. Main courses $3–$9.50. Summer Mon–Sat 10:30am–10pm; winter Mon–Wed 10:30am–3pm, Thurs–Sat 10:30am–10pm. Open Sun only for Tennessee Titans home games.*

→**Loveless Café** ★★ SOUTHERN If you can spare the time, take a trip out past the city's western suburbs for some of the best country cooking in the Nashville area. The famous, old-fashioned Loveless roadhouse is a Nashville institution. People rave about the cooking with good reason: The country ham with red-eye gravy, Southern fried chicken, and homemade biscuits with homemade fruit jams are made just the way Granny used to make them back when the Loveless family opened their place nearly 40 years ago. And come prepared to endure a long wait to get one of the few available tables inside. *8400 Tenn. 100, about 7½ miles south of Belle Meade and the turnoff from US 70 S. ☎ 615/646-9700. www. lovelesscafe.com. Reservations recommended. Daily 7am–9pm.*

→**Mafiaoza's** PIZZA With a toasty fire crackling in the pizza ovens and the dim roar of a lively cocktail crowd, this pizzeria in the trendy 12th Avenue South district has built a loyal following. An outdoor patio gives patrons a great place to hang

while throwing back a few beers or bottles of vino. Skip the soggy, tomato-laden bruschetta and go with the meaty pasta dishes and thin-crust pizzas, sold by the slice or whole pie. *2400 12th Ave. S. ☎ 615/ 269-4646. www.mafiaozas.com. Main courses $6.75–$25. Tues–Fri 4pm–3am; Sat–Sun 11am–3pm.*

→**Pancake Pantry** ★★ AMERICAN The *New York Times, Bon Appetit,* and long lines in all kinds of foul weather attest to hearty eats of this West End breakfast/ brunch/lunch joint. College students, country-music stars, NFL players, tourists, and locals alike queue up outside the red-brick building, waiting patiently for their coffee and syrupy stacks. Lunch items are also available in addition to the extensive breakfast menu. *1796 21st Ave. S. ☎ 615/383-9333. Main courses $5–$15. Mon–Fri 6am–3pm; Sat–Sun 6am–4pm.*

Doable

→**Goten** ★ JAPANESE Glass-brick walls and a high-tech Zen-like elegance set the mood at this West End Japanese restaurant, across the street from Vanderbilt University. The valet parking is a clue that this restaurant is slightly more formal than other Japanese restaurants in Nashville (making the food an even bigger bargain). Don't come here expecting watery bowls of miso soup and a few noodles. Hibachi dinners are the specialty, with the menu leaning heavily toward steaks, which are just about as popular in Japan as they are in Texas. However, if you're into fish, the sushi bar here is Nashville's best, and you can get slices of the freshest sashimi in town. A sister restaurant, **Goten 2,** is at 209 10th Ave. S. (☎ **615/251-4855**). *110 21st Ave. S. ☎ 615/321-4537. www.nashvillecity. com. Reservations recommended. Main courses $10–$20. Mon–Fri 11am–2pm; Sun–Thurs 5–10pm; Fri–Sat 5–11pm.*

Nashville's Parthenon, with Athena.

Best ● ➜**Martha's at the Plantation** ★★★ NEW SOUTHERN Fried green tomatoes with horseradish sauce, salmon and artichoke quiche, and herbed chicken-breast salad are indicative of the lunch menu at this delightful restaurant on the grounds of Belle Meade Plantation. It's a little, um, "elegant," but it hits all the right notes for a classic southern meal. Regional favorites include buttermilk-battered fried chicken with milk gravy, baked cheese grits, and savory cheddar olive spread. Wash it down with a crisp sauvignon blanc or tea-flavored punch, and save room for either sugar cookies with minty lemon sorbet, or the wicked fudge pie with vanilla-bean ice cream. *5025 Harding Rd.* ☎ *615/353-2828. www.marthasat theplantation.com. Main courses $8–$12. Daily 11am–2pm.*

➜**Monell's** ★★ AMERICAN Dining out doesn't usually involve sitting at the same table with total strangers, but be prepared for just such a family-style experience here. Housed in a restored Victorian brick home, this homey lunch and weekend dinner spot feels as if it has been around for ages, which is just what the proprietors want you to think. A meal at Monell's is meant to conjure up family dinners at Grandma's house, so remember to say "please" when you ask for the mashed potatoes or peas. The food is good, "meat-and three" home cookin' most of the year, and everything is all-you-can-eat. In December (the 1st–23rd), Monell's gets fancy and offers reservation-only Victorian dinners ($40). *1235 Sixth Ave. N. (12th Ave. S. area).* ☎ *615/248-4747. Main courses $9–$16. Mon–Fri 10:30am–2pm; Fri 5–8:30pm; Sat 8:30am–1pm and 5–8:30pm; Sun 8am–4pm.*

➜**South Street** ★ SOUTHERN The flashing neon sign proclaiming "authentic dive bar," a blue-spotted pink cement pig, and an old tire swing out front should clue you

Nashville's Honky Tonk Highway.

in that this place doesn't take itself too seriously. In fact, this little wedge-shaped eatery in the West End is as country as an episode of *Hee Haw*, and with Harleys often parked out front to boot. On the menu, you'll find everything from fried pickles to handmade nutty buddies. However, the mainstays are crispy catfish, pulled pork barbecue, smoked chicken, ribs, and steaks with biscuits. If you're feeling flush, you can opt for the $43 crab-and-slab dinner for two (two kinds of crab and a "slab" of ribs). *907 20th Ave. S.* ☎ *615/320-5555. www.pansouth.net. Main courses $9–$13. AE. Mon–Sat 11am–3am; Sun 11am–midnight.*

Splurge

➜**Aquarium** SEAFOOD The novelty alone of dining amid 20,000 gallons of water teeming with tropical fish has ensured that the family crowd has been swamping this new Opry Mills eatery-as-entertainment venue. But it's still worth checking out if you're into kitsch, and fish. Seafood platters come broiled, grilled, blackened, or fried, and the menu includes burgers, sandwich wraps, soups, and salads. *516 Opry Mills Dr.* ☎ *615/514-3474. www. nashvilleaquarium.com. Main courses $16– $28. Mon–Thurs 11am–10pm; Fri 11am–11pm; Sat 10:30am–11pm; Sun 10:30am–9pm.*

➜**Nick & Rudy's** ★ STEAK One of Nashville's newest locally owned steakhouses, this upscale restaurant has the look and feel of a comfy country club, minus the pretentiousness. Oysters and French onion soup are the favorites, along with generous steaks, chops, seafood, chicken, and pork dishes. There's no extra charge for the Old World charm, and tableside preparations of Caesar salads and bananas Foster set the place apart. *204 21st Ave. S.* ☎ *615/329-8994. www.nickandrudys. com. Reservations recommended. Main courses $16–$28. Mon–Fri 11am–2pm; Mon– Sat 5–10pm.*

Partying

Be prepared for both staying up and sleeping late while in Nashville, because there is an endless stream of evening diversions.

BARS, PUBS & CLUBS

Nashville nightlife happens all over town but predominates in two main areas: The District and Music Valley. **The District,** an area of renovated warehouses and old bars, is the livelier and more central of the two. Here you'll find the **Wildhorse Saloon** and two dozen other clubs showcasing band after band after band on any given weekend night (and sometimes weeknights, too). On the sidewalks, people are shoulder to shoulder as they parade from one club to the next, and in the streets, stretch limos vie for space with tricked out pickup trucks. Within The District, Second Avenue is currently the main drag, but nightclubs in the alley between Church and Union streets have regularly hosted top-name performances (though today the alley has lost most of its luster).

Music Valley, on the other hand, offers a more family-oriented, suburban nightlife scene. This area on the east side of Nashville is where you'll find the Grand Ole Opry, the Nashville Palace, the Texas Troubadour Theatre, and Ernest Tubb Record Shop's *Midnite Jamboree,* as well as the Opryland Hotel, which has several bars and features plenty of live music.

Downtown/The District

➜**Tootsie's Orchid Lounge** ★ This rowdy country dive has been a Nashville tradition since the days when the Grand Ole Opry was still performing in the Ryman Auditorium around the corner. Back then, Opry stars like Patsy Cline and Loretta Lynn used to duck into Tootsie's for a drink. Today, you can see signed photos of the many stars who have downed a few here—from Willie Nelson to Waylon Jennings to Neil Young. Free live country music spills out onto the sidewalks daily 10am to 3am, and celebrities still occasionally make the scene. *422 Broadway.* ☎ *615/ 726-0463. www.tootsies.net. No cover.*

➜**Market Street Brewery & Public House** This dark, oaky pub is in a renovated warehouse in the heart of The District and has by far the most character of any microbrewery in Nashville. Most of the wide variety of brews served here are fairly light, with wheat beer a specialty. *134 Second Ave. N.* ☎ *615/259-9611. Sun–Thurs 11:30am–11pm; Fri–Sat 11:30am–1am.*

→**Wildhorse Saloon** Run by the same company that gave Nashville the Opryland Hotel and stages the Grand Ole Opry, this massive dance hall is home sweet home for boot-scooters. Attracting everyone from country music stars to line-dancing senior citizen groups, the Wildhorse is the scene to make these days in Nashville. There's live music most nights by both new bands and the big names in contemporary country. If you sashay up an appetite, the place serves barbecue 11am to midnight. The saloon is open until 1am Mondays through Thursdays, and until 3am on Fridays and Saturdays. *120 Second Ave. N.* ☎ *615/251-1000. www.wildhorsesaloon.com. Cover $4–$6 ($10–$15 for special events).*

West End/Music Row

→**Blackstone Restaurant & Brewery** Nashville's most upscale brewpub draws a lot of business travelers who are staying in nearby hotels. Elegantly inviting are the cushioned chairs, fireplace, and a long, marbled bar. The food, including wood-fired pizzas and pretzels, is consistently good. But the beer is the main focus. Choose from a variety of brews including several that change with the seasons. There's also a six-pack sampler. *1918 West End Ave.* ☎ *615/327-9969. Mon–Thurs 11am–11pm; Fri–Sat 11am–midnight; Sun 11am–10pm. No cover.*

→**Jimmy Kelly's** This place is straight out of the Old South and might have you thinking you've stepped onto the set of a Tennessee Williams play. Jimmy Kelly's is primarily a restaurant and the bar isn't very large, but you'll feel as though you're part of a Nashville tradition when you have a drink here. It's always lively, and the clientele tends to be older and well-to-do. *217 Louise Ave.* ☎ *615/329-4349. www.jimmykellys.com. 5pm–midnight. No cover.*

Music Valley

→**Nashville Palace** Open nightly from 5pm to 1:30am for live country and Western music, a dance floor, and a full restaurant, this venue features acts familiar to fans of the Grand Ole Opry. Tuesday and Wednesday are Talent Nights (winners from both nights compete on Thurs nights), so be on the lookout for the next Randy Travis, the country music star who got his start here. The Palace is easy to find, located directly opposite the Opryland Hotel entrance. *2400 Music Valley Dr.* ☎ *615-889-1540. Cover $5.*

Gay/Lesbian

There is a slow-growing gay nightlife district in Nashville, south of Broadway (and The District) along Fourth Avenue South, where you'll find no fewer than three gay bars. There's also one more neighborhood-y, lesbian-geared joint across town that shouldn't be missed.

🅼 Best ● →**Lipstick Lounge** ★★★ It's hard to beat a bar/club/live-music venue as loud and proud as this place. Lesbian owned-and-operated, the place draws plenty of girls—and plenty of everyone else for that matter—to its unassuming East End locale. The place is known for the high-quality karaoke Monday through Thursday at 9pm, and on Friday nights owners (and twin sisters, and retired professional backup singers) Ronda and Jonda take the stage with their house band to rock the joint 'til . . . whenever. *1400 Woodland St.* ☎ *615/226-6343. www.thelipsticklounge.com. Opens daily at 4pm. Cover $2–$10.*

→**Tribe** ★ An energized crowd of Nashville's most beautiful dancing queens/kings congregates nightly at this SoHo-slick club. Straight or gay, it doesn't matter—as long as you're confidently hip and ready for a good time. Martinis, a full menu of munchies, music videos, and silver and granite decor cast a shimmering spell on partygoers until the wee hours of the morning. *1517A Church St.* ☎ *615/329-2912. www.tribenashville.com. No cover.*

LIVE MUSIC

Live music surrounds you in Nashville. There are dozens of clubs featuring live country and bluegrass music, and pretty cool rock, jazz, and folk-music scenes, too. Like Memphis, Nashville overflows with talented musicians who play where they can, much to the benefit of anyone with open ears.

Every Thursday, the city's arts-and-entertainment weekly, the **Nashville Scene,** is distributed to restaurants, clubs, convenience stores, and other places. There's also the **Jazz & Blues News,** a free monthly newsletter with news and event listings that's found at local bookstores and cafes. Between these and the Friday issue of the **Tennessean,** Nashville's morning daily, you'll get all the wheres and whens for the coming week's music highlights.

Country

→ **Legends Corner** Today's starving artists are tomorrow's country music superstars (or at least they hope so!), and this beloved dive in The District sets the stage for such happily-ever-after scenarios. Diehard barhoppers insist that Legends Corner has downtown's best live local music and one of the friendliest staffs in Music City. Nostalgic memorabilia on the walls adds a quaint, down-home charm. And you can't beat the price: The tip jar gets passed around the room like a collection plate, enabling the rowdy crowds to help support the struggling pickers and grinners who've put Nashville on the map. *428 Broadway.* ☎ *615/248-6334. No cover. Ages 21 and older only after 6pm.*

MTV **Best ●** → **Ryman Auditorium** ★★★ Once the home of the Grand Ole Opry, this historic theater was renovated a few years back and is once again hosting performances with a country and bluegrass music slant. The Ryman was showcased in the documentary *Down From the Mountain,* a film version of the all-star bluegrass concert performed there featuring music from the movie soundtrack *O Brother, Where Art Thou?* In 2003, the venue was the site of a star-studded memorial concert for the late Johnny Cash. Today, musicians of all genres revere the intimate auditorium, where the acoustics are said to be better than Carnegie Hall's. In recent years, acts as diverse as Beck, Yo-Yo Ma, Coldplay, Al Green, and India.Arie have played to packed houses at this National Historic Landmark. *116 Fifth Ave. N.* ☎ *615/254-1445 or 615/889-6611. www.ryman.com. Tickets $18–$43.*

Jazz/Blues/Bluegrass/Rock

→ **The Bluebird Cafe** ★★ For a quintessential Nashville experience, visit this unassuming 100-seat club that remains one of the nation's premier venues for up-and-coming and established songwriters. Surprisingly, you'll find the Bluebird not in The District or on Music Row but in a suburban shopping plaza across the road from the Mall at Green Hills. There are usually two shows a night. Between 6 and 7pm, there is frequently music in the round, during which four singer-songwriters play some of their latest works. After 9pm, when more established acts take the stage, a cover charge sets in. This is the place in Nashville to catch the music of people you'll be hearing from in coming years. Because the club is so small, reservations (taken noon–5pm) are recommended, and sometimes required. *4104 Hillsboro Rd.* ☎ *615/383-1461. www.bluebirdcafe.com. No*

ᴍᴛᴠ🅤 Nashville's African-American Heritage

African Americans constitute one-quarter of Nashville's population and for more than 200 years have played important roles in shaping this city. For example, **Fisk University,** founded 1866, is one of the oldest historically black universities in the country, and its campus houses the **Carl Van Vechten Gallery,** one of the country's major collections of African-American art. Pick up a copy of the *African American Guide to Cultural & Historic Sites* brochure at the visitor center downtown in the Gaylord Entertainment Center, among other places, or visit **www.nashvillecvb.com/diversity** to learn more about Nashville's African-American heritage,. There are also tours such as the **Nashville Black Heritage Tour** (☎ 615/890-8173) that show you the churches, schools, and other sites that helped shape the city's diverse cultural landscape.

cover for early shows, but a minimum $7 order per person at tables. Cover fees vary ($8–$20) for late shows after 9pm.

➔**Bourbon Street Blues and Boogie Bar** If you're wandering around in The District wishing you could hear some wailing blues guitar, head over to Printer's Alley and check out the action at this smoky club. *220 Printers Alley.* ☎ *615/242-5837. www.bourbonstreetblues.com. Mon–Fri 4pm–whenever; Sat–Sun 4pm–3am. Cover $5–$10.*

➔**F. Scott's Restaurant** Live jazz is presented nightly at this suburban outpost of chic. An extensive wine list and upscale dinner menu enhance its appeal for culture vultures. Free valet parking is an added perk at this classy and smoke-free establishment, located a stone's throw from the Mall at Green Hills. *2210 Crestmoor Rd.* ☎ *615/269-5861. www.fscotts.com. Mon–Thurs 5:30–10pm; Fri–Sat 5:30–11pm; Sun 5:30–9pm. No cover.*

➔**Station Inn** ★ Widely regarded as one of the best bluegrass venues around, this club lies in the warehouse district south of Broadway in downtown. The large stone building is nondescript, but keep looking and you'll find it. *402 12th Ave. S.* ☎ *615/2553307. www.stationinn.com. Mon–Sat*

7pm–2am; Sun 7pm–midnight. Shows start nightly at 9pm. Cover $7 Tues–Sat, free Sun.

➔**3rd & Lindsley Bar & Grill** Eight blocks south of Broadway, in a new office complex surrounded by old warehouses, you'll find Nashville's premier blues club. The atmosphere may lack the rough edges and smoke you'd expect of a real blues club, but the music is true blues, with some rock and Top 40. *818 3rd Ave. S.* ☎ *615/259-9891. Mon–Fri 11am–2am; Sat–Sun 5pm–2am. Cover free–$10.*

What Else to See & Do

It doesn't take much time in Nashville to discover its big draw, what with the whole "Music City" nickname, Opry-dominated tourist culture, and legendary **Country Music Hall of Fame** framing the downtown landscape. But there are many opportunities to let this sort of simple, rather eccentric city sweep you off your feet. The **Cheekwood Botanical Garden, Frist Center for the Visual Art,** and **Hatch Show Print** letterpress will prove to you that its cultural clout extends well beyond music. And a single visit to the bewildering full-size reproduction of the **Parthenon**—with its 42-foot-tall gilded sculpture of Athena—will at least alert you to its stately-yet-quirky side. Don't be surprised if you find yourself out of time in Nashville much too soon.

And hey, you might do well to invest $35 in a 🎵 Best ❂ **Total Access** pass through the Nashville Convention & Visitors Bureau (501 Broadway and 150 Fourth Ave. N.; ☎ **800/657-6910** or **615/259-4747;** www.visitmusiccity.com), which allows entrance to four attractions around town (out of 12 available choices).

MUSICAL HISTORY

🎵 Best ❂ → **Country Music Hall of Fame and Museum** ★★★ Country music fan or not, this is a great museum. And if you're not a fan, you may leave as one. Here's a sample of some of what you'll find: Elvis's gold-leafed Cadillac (a gift from Priscilla); Emmylou Harris's petite, bejeweled cowboy boots; Bob Dylan's barely legible inscription scrawled across a lyric sheet. But there's a lot going on in this giant museum, like the multimedia exhibits where you can explore bluegrass, cowboy music (a la Roy Rogers), country swing, rockabilly, Cajun, honky-tonk, and contemporary country music through personalized CD listening posts, interactive jukeboxes, and computer stations. The Grand Ole Opry gets its due, too, with a mind-boggling array of memorabilia, enhanced by vintage Opry recordings. The museum also showcases such down-home *objects d'art* as Naomi Judd's rusted wringer-and-tub-style washing machine, and the kitschy cornfield from TV's *Hee Haw*—complete with Junior Samples' denim overalls and Lulu Roman's plus-size gingham dress.

If you want to arrange a visit to the old RCA recording studio, where Elvis laid down a few hits, you'll need to sign up here at the Hall of Fame. The studio is located in the Music Row area of Nashville. Allow 2 to 3 hours. *222 Fifth Ave. S. (at Demonbreun).*

☎ *800/852-6437 or 615/416-2001. www.country musichalloffame.com. Admission $17 adults, $8.95 children 6–17. Daily 9am–5pm.*

🎵 Best ❂ → **Ryman Auditorium & Museum** ★★★ If you're enamored with music history, you could devote several hours to a self-guided tour of this National Historic Landmark where you're free to stand onstage—even belt out a few bars if the spirit moves you—or sit in the hardwood "pews," and wander the halls upstairs and down, looking at memorabilia in glass showcases. However, the typical tourist may be satisfied with a quick walk through the stately red-brick building. In either case, the best way to experience the Ryman is to attend a performance here. The site of the Grand Ole Opry from 1943 to 1974, the Ryman Auditorium is known as the "Mother Church of Country Music," the single most historic site in the world of country music. Originally built in 1892 as the Union Gospel Tabernacle by riverboat captain Tom Ryman, this building served as an evangelical hall for many years. By the early 1900s, the building's name had been changed to honor its builder and a stage had been added. That stage, over the years, saw the likes of Enrico Caruso, Katharine Hepburn, Will Rogers, and Elvis Presley. The Grand Ole Opry began broadcasting from here in 1943. For the next 31 years, the Ryman Auditorium was host to the most famous country music radio show in the world. However, in 1974, the Opry moved to the then-new Grand Ole Opry House in the Music Valley area. Since its meticulous renovation in 1994, the Ryman has regained its prominence as a temple of bluegrass, country, and other music. Its peerless acoustics make it a favored venue of rock's best singer/songwriters and classical musicians, as well. *116 Fifth Ave. N. (between Commerce and Broadway).* ☎ *615/254-1445 or 615/889-3060. www.ryman.com.*

Admission $8 adults, $4 children 4–11, free for children under 4. Daily 9am–4pm. Closed Thanksgiving, Dec 25, and Jan 1.

➜ **Hatch Show Print** This is the oldest letterpress poster print shop in the country and not only does it still design and print posters for shows, but it also sells posters to the public. Reprints of old circus, vaudeville, and Grand Ole Opry posters are the most popular. *316 Broadway.* ☎ *615/256-2805. www.hatchshowprint.com. Free Admission.*

ORGANIZED TOURS

The Opryland Hotel, 2800 Opryland Dr. (☎ **615/883-2211;** www.oprylandhotel. com), operates the paddle-wheel boat—the ***General Jackson*** (☎ **615/458-3900**)—on the Cumberland River. Tours depart from a dock near the Opryland Hotel. At 300 feet long, the *General Jackson* showboat hearkens back to the days when riverboats were the most sophisticated way to travel. You go on this cruise for the paddle-wheeler experience, not necessarily for the food (not so great) and entertainment that go along with it. During the summer, the Southern Nights Cruise offers a three-course dinner and dancing under the stars to live bands. Fares for this trip cost $71 to $82. Midday cruises are also available April to October and cost $43 (includes a lunch and entertainment). Special-event cruises with such themes as Valentine's Day, Mardi Gras, tailgating, and the holidays are offered year-round. Prices vary. Call for details.

Grand Ole Opry Tours (☎ **615/883-2211;** www.gaylordhotels.com) is the official tour company of the Opryland Hotel; it offers tours similar to those of Gray Line. One of this company's more popular offerings is the Grand Old Nashville City Tour, a 3-hour excursion that takes you past the homes of country legends and also includes a self-guided tour of the Ryman

Auditorium and several other points of interest throughout the city. The cost is $29.

Gray Line of Nashville, 2416 Music Valley Dr. (☎ **800/251-1864** or 615/883-5555; www.graylinenashville.com), offers more than half a dozen different tours ranging in length from 3½ hours to a full day. On the popular 3-hour tour of the stars' homes, you'll ride past the current or former houses and mansions of Hank Williams, Sr., Dolly Parton, Kix Brooks, and Ronnie Dunn (separate homes), Trisha Yearwood, Martina McBride, and Alan Jackson. Other themed tours focus exclusively on historical sites, honky-tonks and nightlife, and other specialty areas. Tour prices range from $10 to $69 for adults.

OTHER TOP ATTRACTIONS

➜ **The Parthenon** ★★ Centennial Park, as the name implies, was built for the Tennessee Centennial Exposition of 1897, and featured this full-size replica of the Athens Parthenon. The original structure was meant to be temporary, however, and by 1921 the building, which had become a Nashville landmark, was in an advanced state of deterioration. In that year, the city undertook reconstruction of its Parthenon and by 1931 a new, permanent building stood in Centennial Park. The building now duplicates the floor plan of the original Parthenon in Greece. Inside stands the 42-foot-tall statue of Athena Parthenos, the goddess of wisdom, prudent warfare, and the arts. Newly gilded with 8 pounds of gold leaf, she is the tallest indoor sculpture in the country. (See "I said 'Greece,' not 'Grease'" p. 721.)

In addition to this impressive statue, there are original plaster casts of the famous Elgin marbles—bas-reliefs that once decorated the pediment of the Parthenon. Down in the basement galleries, you'll find an excellent collection of 19th- and 20th-century American art. The

Parthenon's two pairs of bronze doors, which weigh in at 7¹/₂ tons per door, are considered the largest matching bronze doors in the world. A recent renovation of the building included air-conditioning, which should make for pleasant viewing on muggy summer days. Allow about 30 minutes. *Centennial Park, West End Ave. (at West End and 25th aves.).* ☎ *615/862-8431. www.parthenon.org. Admission $4 adults, $2.50 seniors and children. Oct–Mar Tues–Sat 9am–4:30pm; Apr–Sept Tues–Sat 9am–4:30pm, Sun 12:30–4:30pm. (Closed Sun after Labor Day.)*

📺 Best ☺ ➔ **The Frist Center for the Visual Arts** ★★★ Opened in April 2001, the Frist Center for the Visual Arts brings world-class art exhibits to the historic downtown post office building. The nonprofit center does not maintain a permanent collection but rather presents exhibitions from around the globe. Upstairs, the **ArtQuest Gallery** ★ encourages visitors to explore a range of art experiences through more than 30 interactive multimedia stations. Creative kids and likeminded adults could spend hours here.

In addition to its stellar exhibitions, the Frist is free to visitors 18 and under. *919 Broadway.* ☎ *615/244-3340. www.fristcenter. org. Admission $8.50 adults, $7.50 seniors, $6.50 college students (with ID), free for visitors 18 and under. (Admission prices may be charged for special exhibitions.) Mon and Fri 10:30am–9pm; Tues–Thurs and Sat 10:30am–5pm; Sun 1–5pm. Closed Thanksgiving, Dec 25, and Jan 1. Between 9th and 10th aves. next to the Union Station Hotel.*

➔ **Cheekwood Botanical Garden & Museum of Art** ★★ Once a private estate, Cheekwood today has much to offer both art lovers and garden enthusiasts. The museum and gardens are situated in a 55-acre park that's divided into several formal gardens and naturally landscaped areas. The museum itself is housed in the original Cheek family mansion, which was built in the Georgian style with many architectural details brought over from Europe. Among the mansion's most outstanding features is a lapis lazuli fireplace mantel. Within the building are collections of 19th- and 20th-century American art, Worcester porcelains, antique silver serving pieces, Asian snuff bottles, and a good deal of period furniture.

The grounds are designed for strolling, and there are numerous gardens, including Japanese, herb, perennial, dogwood, magnolia, iris, peony, rose, and azalea—and there are greenhouses full of orchids. Don't miss the glass bridge that awards hikers along the wooded sculpture trail. You'll also find a gift shop and good restaurant, The Pineapple Room, on the grounds. Allow a couple of hours to tour the museum, or up to a full day if you plan to explore the grounds and garden as well. *1200 Forrest Park Dr. (8 miles southwest of downtown).* ☎ *615/356-8000. www.cheekwood.org. Admission $30 per household, $10 adults, $8 seniors, $5 college students and children 6–17, free for children under 6. (Half-price after 3pm.) Tues–Sat 9am–5pm; Sun 11am–4:30pm. Closed Thanksgiving, Dec 25, Jan 1, and 3rd Sat in Apr. Take West End Ave. and continue on Tenn. 100 almost to Percy Warner Park.*

HANGING OUT

To celebrate the 200th anniversary of Tennessee statehood, Nashville constructed the impressive **Bicentennial Capitol Mall State Park** (☎ **615/741-5280**), north of the state capitol. The mall, which begins just north of James Robertson Parkway and extends (again, north) to Jefferson Street between Sixth and Seventh avenues, is a beautifully landscaped open space that conjures up the countryside with its limestone rockeries and plantings of native plants. As such, it is a great place for a leisurely stroll. The western edge of the park offers fantastic views of the capitol.

However, this mall is far more than just a park. It is also a 19-acre open-air exhibition of Tennessee history and geography and a frame for the capitol, which sits atop the hill at the south end of the mall. Also at the south end of the mall is a 200-foot-long granite map of the state, and behind this are a gift shop/visitor center, a Tennessee rivers fountain, and an amphitheater used for summer concerts. Along Sixth Avenue, you'll find a walkway of Tennessee counties, with information on each county (beneath the plaques, believe it or not, are time capsules). Along Seventh Avenue is the Pathway of History, a wall outlining the state's 200-year history. Within the mall, there are also several memorials.

Out in the Belle Meade area, **Percy Warner Park,** 2500 Old Hickory Blvd. (☎ **615/370-8051;** www.nashville.org/parks/warner.htm), is the crown jewel of Nashville green spaces. Named for Percy Warner, a local businessman and avid outdoorsman, the wooded hills and rolling meadows extend for more than 2,000 acres. Hiking and equestrian trails draw nature enthusiasts. Though popular with bicyclists, be aware that they must share the winding, paved roads with vehicular traffic. Perfect for picnics and other outdoor pursuits, the park offers clean shelters, restrooms, and even a 27-hole golf course.

After visiting this park, it seems appropriate to take a stroll around **Centennial Park,** on West End Avenue at 25th Avenue. This park, built for the 1896 centennial celebration, is best known as the site of the Parthenon, but also has many acres of lawns, 100-year-old shade trees, and a small lake.

PLAYING OUTSIDE
Boating/Fishing

In the summer, a wide variety of boats, from canoes and paddle boats to personal watercraft and pontoon boats, can be rented at **Four Corners Marina** on Percy Priest Lake, 4027 Lavergne Couchville Pike, Antioch (☎ **615/641-9523**). This grocery store sells bait, tackle, and fishing licenses year-round. The gorgeous lake, only a few miles east of downtown, is surrounded by a series of parks, trees, and natural beauty rather than commercial and residential development.

At Kingston Springs, about 20 miles west of Nashville off I-40, you can rent canoes from **Tip-a-Canoe,** 1279 US 70, at Harpeth River Bridge (☎ **800/550-5810** or 615/254-0836; www.tip-a-canoe.com), or bring your own. The Harpeth River, a designated State Scenic River, includes a 7-mile loop that allows canoers the freedom of going it alone without having to be picked up. This section, called "The Narrows of the Harpeth," begins and ends in roughly the same area. Canoe trips of varying lengths, from a couple of hours up to 5 days, can be arranged. Rates start at $18 per canoe, which includes the shuttle upriver to your chosen put-in point. Trips lasting 2 days cost $50, while 5-day trips cost $125. The river is mostly Class I water with some Class II and a few spots where you'll have to carry the canoe.

Horseback Riding & More

If you want to go for a ride through the Tennessee hills, there are a couple of nearby places where you can rent a horse. The **Ramblin' Breeze Ranch,** 3665 Knight Rd., Whites Creek (☎ 615/876-1029), 7 miles north of downtown Nashville, rents horses for $20 an hour ($15 for children ages 7–12). **Ju-Ro Stables,** 735 Carver Lane, Mt. Juliet (☎ 615/773-7433), is located about 15 minutes from Nashville on I-40 east, at the Mt. Juliet exit, and charges $15 an hour for rides around Old Hickory Lake ($30 for moonlight rides).

Golf

Three area resort courses consistently get praised by Nashville golfers. The

Hermitage Golf Course, 3939 Old Hickory Blvd. (☎ 615/847-4001; www.hermitage golf.com), is a challenging course on the bank of the Cumberland River. Greens fees are $33 to $59 and can be booked in advance online. The Vanderbilt **Legend's Club of Tennessee,** 1500 Legends Club Lane, Franklin (☎ 615/791-8100; www.legends club.com), is a bit farther out of town but offers a 36-hole course designed by Tom Kite and Bob Cupp. Greens fees for the Legend's Club are $33 to $79. For many golfing visitors, however, the **Opryland's Gaylord Springs Golf Links,** 18 Springhouse Lane (☎ 615/458-1730; www. gaylordsprings.com), is most convenient. This par-72, 18-hole course is set on the bank of the Cumberland River. The course boasts not only challenging links, but also an antebellum-style clubhouse that would have made Rhett Butler feel right at home. Greens fees are $75 to $90.

Swimming

Most of the hotels and motels listed above have pools, but if you'd rather jump in a lake, head for **Percy Priest Lake.** You'll find this large man-made reservoir just east of downtown Nashville at Exit 219 off I-40. Stop by the information center to get a map showing the three designated swimming areas, which are all free, though parking costs $4 per car.

SPECTATOR SPORTS

Football

Ever since moving to Nashville (from Houston, where they were the Oilers) in 1999, the **Tennessee Titans** have drawn loyal crowds to the 68,000-seat Nashville Coliseum on the banks of the Cumberland River. The stadium is at 1 Titans Way, Nashville, TN 37213 (☎ 615/565-4200; www.titansonline.com).

NASCAR/Auto Racing

NASCAR racing is a Southern institution, and every Saturday, aspiring stock-car drivers race their cars at the **Nashville Speedway USA** (☎ 615/726-1818; www. nashvillespeedway.com) on the Tennessee State Fairgrounds. The race season, which runs from April through November, also includes several pro series races, as well as a celebrity charity race. Saturday admission is $15, while tickets to the pro races run $35 to $45.

The **Music City Raceway,** 3302 Ivy Point Rd., Goodlettsville (☎ 615/876-0981; www. musiccityraceway.com), is the place to catch National Hot Rod Association (NHRA) drag-racing action. The drag strip, known as Nashville's "Playground of Power," has races on Tuesdays, Fridays, Saturdays, and some Sundays between March and October. Admission is $10.

Hockey

Nashville's own NHL hockey team, the **Nashville Predators** (☎ 615/770-PUCK; www.nashvillepredators.com), plays at the Gaylord Entertainment Center on lower Broadway in downtown Nashville. Ticket prices range from $10 to $95.

Baseball

The **Nashville Sounds** (☎ 615/242-4371; www.nashvillesounds.com), a AAA affiliate of the Milwaukee Brewers, play from April to September at Greer Stadium, 534 Chestnut St., off Eighth Avenue South. Admission ranges from $6 general to $10 for reserved box seats ($5–$9 for children).

Horse Shows

Horse shows are important events on the Nashville area's calendar. The biggest and most important horse show of the year is the **Annual Tennessee Walking-Horse National Celebration** (☎ 931/684-5915). This show takes place 40 miles southeast of Nashville in the town of Shelbyville and is held each year in late August. Advance reserved ticket prices range from $7 to $15, while general-admission tickets are $5 to $10.

The city's other big horse event is the annual running of the **Iroquois Steeplechase** (☎ 615/322-7284) on the second Saturday in May. This is one of the oldest steeplechase races in the country and is held in Percy Warner Park in the Belle Meade area. Proceeds from the race benefit the Vanderbilt Children's Hospital. Tickets are $12 at the gate or $10 in advance.

On the Road to St. Louis, MO

Nashville, TN to St. Louis, MO 310 miles

When the time comes to say farewell to Nashville, hop on I-24 west, which is really sort of north, and head for St. Louis. (*Note:* Tennessee State Troopers are looking for you lead-footed folks, so mind the speed limit for a while.) It's not a short drive, at a bit over 5 hours, but it is incredibly green and scenic, especially if you're willing to take advantage of a few smaller highways.

The main detour begins near Hopkinsville, Kentucky, where you can hop on 68 west and through **Land Between the Lakes National Recreation Area** (☎ 270/924-2000; www.lbl.org). You'll likely be one of few cars on the road, and be dazzled by glimpses of serene Lake Barkley on the east and Kenlake on the west. If you can't resist stopping in the park, you'll have options like hiking, mountain biking, fishing, hunting, horseback riding, and wildlife viewing. But if you wish to press on, there's still plenty to appreciate on a mellow cruise through this fecund corner of Kentucky.

Exit the park and continue north on 68 through Fairdealing and Draffenville, where you're sure to see the classic farm items lingering on front lawns, dilapidated barns, horse-drawn carts, and an abandoned truck or two. You'll eventually return to I-24, pass through Paducah (whose name is cooler than anything within the town), and into Illinois. Queue Sufjan Stevens' brilliant song "Metropolis" as you pass through this border town and catch sight of the "Home of Superman" water tower.

I-24 runs out where it meets I-57, which you'll take north for about 45 minutes then connect with I-64 west (near Mt. Vernon). You're just an hour away from St. Louis now, so soak up this last bit of Illinois before crossing the border into Missouri in the form of the Mississippi River.

Meet Me in St. Louis, Louie!

→ **Sufjan Stevens,** "Come on Feel the Illinoise!," 2005 (the whole, excellent album)

→ *St. Louis Blues,* **Chuck Berry,** "Blues," 2003

→ *Blueberry Hill,* **Fats Domino,** 1956

→ *Stars and Sons,* **Broken Social Scene,** "You Forgot It in People," 2002

→ *If She Wants Me,* **Belle & Sebastian,** "Dear Castastrophe Waitress," 2003

→ *I'm the Man Who Loves You,* **Wilco,** "Yankee Hotel Foxtrot," 2002

→ *Live at P.J.'s,* **Beastie Boys,** "Check Your Head," 1992

→ *Portland, Oregon,* **Loretta Lynn (with Jack White),** "Van Lear Rose," 2004

→ *Blue Moon of Kentucky,* **Patsy Cline,** 1963

On the Road Nuts & Bolts

Where to Fill Up   This is a particularly easy segment of the journey for finding gas, since there are small towns all along the interstates. In fact the only place you should really fill up is around Hopkinsville, before heading to the Land Between the Lakes.

The Fastest Way   I-24 west for about 180 miles, to I-57 north. Then about 60 miles up to I-64 west, then 80 miles into St. Louis. It's that simple, and a little more than 5 hours total without many stops.

The Long Way Round   Head west on I-24 to Rt. 68 west, near Hopkinsville, KY. That takes you through Land Between the Lakes National Recreation Area, back up to I-24 around Reidland, KY. Keep on west to I-57 north, then continue to I-64, where you cruise right into St. Louis. The diversion makes the total more like 6 hours, barring extended time in the Land Between the Lakes.

Rules of the Road   Keep an eye out for state troopers looking for speeders outside of Nashville, and keep it slow through the two-lane Rt. 68.

Picnic Point   It will be hard not to stop and take in the quiet times in the Land Between the Lakes, so you might as well pick up lunch upon leaving Nashville.

Welcome to St. Louis

St. Louis is one of those cities that opens up the more you get to know it. Landmarked by the shining steel **Gateway Arch,** built in 1966 to commemorate westward pioneers, St. Louis is equal parts historic, touristy, and lived-in.

The city was established in 1764 as a French trading post, and its economy boomed after the Louisiana Purchase and as a major port for steamboats traveling the Mississippi. Today, visitors from within the Midwest and well beyond come to catch a Cardinals game, tour the home of Budweiser beer, take in some jazz and art, and celebrate Mardi Gras with the biggest festival this country offers outside of New Orleans.

St. Louis Nuts & Bolts

Area Code   The telephone area code in St. Louis is 314.

Business Hours   Banks are open Monday to Friday 8:30am to 4:30pm, and some banks have extended drive-up and Saturday hours. Stores vary widely around town, as do bars and clubs—though typically establishments that host live music and serve alcohol stay open until anywhere from 1am to 3am.

Doctors   The city has compiled a comprehensive listing of doctors at www.thecity ofstlouis.org.

Drugstores   Walgreens, Shop 'n Save, and Rinderer's, are available all over St. Louis, and a few Walgreens stay open 24 hours including one in the Central West End, 4218 Lindell Blvd.

Emergencies   For police, fire, or medical emergencies, phone ☎ **911.**

Hospitals   **Barnes Hospital** is at 1 Barnes Jewish Hospital (☎ 314/362-5000), and St. Louis University Hospital is at 3635 Vista Ave. (☎ 314/577-8000).

Hot Lines   **Time & Temperature by KMOX** is available at ☎ 314/321-2222, and the city's **Special Events Fun Phone Recording** is at ☎ 314/421-2100.

Libraries   The **St. Louis Public Library** main branch is located at 1301 Olive St. (☎ 314/241-2288), and is open every day but Sunday. Check out www.slpl.org to pinpoint the systems 16 other branches.

Liquor Laws   The legal drinking age in Missouri is 21. In St. Louis, bars with special licenses are allowed to stay open until 3am, though stores must close by 1:30am. Liquor, beer, and wine can be purchased at any type of grocery or convenience store.

Newspapers & Magazines   The *St. Louis Post-Dispatch* is the local daily (www. stltoday.com) and the *Riverfront Times* (www.riverfronttimes.com) is the city's arts-and-entertainment weekly.

Police   For police emergencies, phone ☎ **911.** You can also call the St. Louis Police at ☎ 314/615-4000.

Post Office   The main downtown post office is at 1720 Market St. ☎ 314/436-4073.

Radio   Plenty of music means plenty of radio stations in St. Louis. Among them are KWMU at 90.7 broadcasting NPR, KSHE 94.7 and KYKY 98.1 for rock/pop, KSD 93.7 and WIL 92.3 for country, and KLOU 103.3 for oldies.

Taxes   Sales tax in St. Louis is 7.616%, with an additional 7.5% tax for lodging.

Television   In St. Louis, NBC (KSDK) is channel 5, CBS (KMOV) is channel 4, PBS (KETC) is channel 9, and FOX (KTVI) is channel 2.

Time Zone   St. Louis is on Central Standard Time.

Transit Info   Call ☎ 314/231-2345 for MetroLink route and schedule information, or visit www.metrostlouis.org.

Visitors Bureau   Call ☎ 800/916-0092 or ☎ 314/421-1023 or check out www. explorestlouis.com to get more information about St. Louis, and locations of nearby visitor centers.

Weather   For weather information, call ☎ 314/321-2222, or visit www.weather.com.

Getting Around

One thing you'll find out about St. Louis pretty quickly: It's pretty spread out. Sure, you could fill a good day or two just in the **Downtown** area, where you'll find the Gateway Arch, Busch Memorial Stadium, Union Station, Laclede's Landing, and plenty of shopping and stuff. But beyond that you're probably in for a drive or a train ride to **The Loop,** the **Central West End,** or **Forest Park,** all of which are a ways away from each other, and worth checking out.

By the way, when you arrive, it might be wise to pick up a copy of *Explore St. Louis,* the city's official visitors guide, from your hotel or one of many attractions. It's a great resource with several detailed maps, and has coupons for restaurants and attractions.

St. Louis Highlights

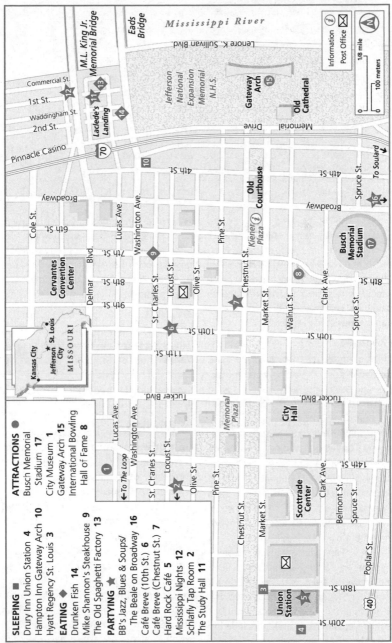

Mississippi River

Lenore K. Sullivan Blvd

Eads Bridge

M.L. King Jr. Memorial Bridge

Information ℹ
Post Office ✉

1/8 mile

100 meters

Commercial St.

1st St.

Waddingham St.

2nd St.

Jefferson National Expansion Memorial N.H.S.

Gateway Arch ⑮

Old Cathedral

Pinnacle Casino

70

Memorial Drive

Lacede's Landing

⑫ ⑬ ⑭

4th St.

⑩

Broadway

Cole St.

6th St.

Lucas Ave.

Washington Ave.

Pine St.

Old Courthouse

Kiener Plaza ℹ

4th St.

Broadway

Spruce St.

To Soulard

⑯

7th St.

Delmar Blvd.

8th St.

9th St.

St. Charles St.

Locust St.

Olive St.

⑨

Cervantes Convention Center

Chestnut St.

Market St.

Walnut St.

Clark Ave.

Spruce St.

8th St.

⑧

⑦

Busch Memorial Stadium ⑰

10th St.

10th St.

St. Louis City

Jefferson City

Kansas City

MISSOURI

6

11th St.

Tucker Blvd.

Lucas Ave.

Washington Ave.

St. Charles St.

Locust St.

Olive St.

Pine St.

Chestnut St.

Market St.

Tucker Blvd.

Memorial Plaza

City Hall

Scottrade Center

Clark Ave.

14th St.

Belmont St.

Spruce St.

14th St.

To The Loop

1

2

Union Station

3

4

5

18th St.

20th St.

Poplar St.

40

SLEEPING ■
Drury Inn Union Station **4**
Hampton Inn Gateway Arch **10**
Hyatt Regency St. Louis **3**

EATING ◆
Drunken Fish **14**
Mike Shannon's Steakhouse **9**
The Old Spaghetti Factory **13**

PARTYING ★
BB's Jazz, Blues & Soups/
The Beale on Broadway **16**
Café Breve (10th St.) **6**
Café Breve (Chestnut St.) **7**
Hard Rock Café **5**
Mississippi Nights **12**
Schlafly Tap Room **2**
The Study Hall **11**

ATTRACTIONS ●
Busch Memorial
Stadium **17**
City Museum **1**
Gateway Arch **15**
International Bowling
Hall of Fame **8**

For More Information...

→ St. Louis Convention & Visitors Commission: ☎ 800/916-0092 or 314/421-1023; www.explorestlouis.com
→ St. Louis Special Events "Fun Phone": ☎ 314/421-2100
→ MetroLink Transit: ☎ 314/231-2345; www.metrostlouis.org
→ St. Louis Community Information Network: stlouis.missouri.org
→ St. Louis Parks & Recreation Department: stlouis.missouri.org/citygov/parks/
→ Gateway Arch: ☎ 877/982-1410; www.gatewayarch.com
→ *Riverfront Times* weekly newspaper: www.riverfronttimes.com
→ *St. Louis Post-Dispatch* daily newspaper: www.stltoday.com

BY CAR

If you're driving, be aware of long red lights and costly parking, especially downtown and near the big attractions. Most hotels and high-end restaurants offer valet parking. Hotels almost always charge a fee for this service and restaurants sometimes charge as well, though occasionally only a tip is expected.

BY TRAIN

The **MetroLink** (☎ 314/231-2345; www.metrostlouis.org) travels between the airport and east St. Louis, with stops at Delmar Loop, Forest Park, Central West End, Union Station, Busch Stadium, downtown (at 8th and Pine and Convention Center), Laclede's Landing, and other neighborhoods. A one-way ticket costs $1.50 for the entire zone minus the airport (tickets to and from the airport are $3); a day pass costs $4. Travel is free on weekdays from 11:30am to 1:30pm between Union Station and Laclede's Landing.

In Forest Park, where many of St. Louis's top sights are located, a shuttle bus called Zip2 travels from the Forest Park MetroLink Station to 14 attractions. The service runs daily beginning Memorial Day weekend to Labor Day and is included in the $4 MetroLink day pass.

ON FOOT

Downtown St. Louis is not only where many things to do are, it's also where a lot of hotels are—making it a pretty walkable area. Likewise, once you arrive in The Loop or Forest Park, you can ditch the car and lace up your walking shoes.

BY TAXI

It's tough to hail a cab in St. Louis, so try calling **Laclede Cab** (☎ 615/652-3456) or **Yellow Cab of St. Louis** (☎ 314/993-TAXI). The first mile is $3; after that, it's $1.50 per mile. Each additional passenger is $1 extra.

SLEEPING

Downtown is where the Cervantes Convention Center is, which also means there are lot of hotels downtown. You might also have some luck finding a decent room with smaller motels around **Grand Center,** the neighborhood of St. Louis University, and around **Forest Park.**

One cool thing about St. Louis is that it has an impressive number of hotels in renovated historic buildings. In addition to the choices below, consider the **Westin St. Louis,** downtown next to Busch Stadium at 811 Spruce St. (☎ 314/621-2000; www.westin.com/stlouis), which gave new life to a group of former 19th-century railroad warehouses and boasts a gorgeous, contemporary interior.

CAMPGROUNDS/HOSTELS

There's not much for tent camping around St. Louis since most suburban campgrounds are made for RVs. But there is the full-service **KOA Granite City** just north and east across the Mississippi River in Illinois, 3157 W. Chain of Rocks Rd. (☎ 618/931-5160). It'll run you as little as $20 to pitch a tent there, with options for water and electric hookups.

Within St. Louis there's also the **Huckleberry Finn Youth Hostel** (1904 S. 12 St. (☎ 314/241-0076), which is actually open to guests of all ages. It's just south of downtown in Soulard, the French historic neighborhood. At $20/night ($5 key deposit) for a clean bunk, this is hard to beat if you're traveling on the cheap.

CHEAP

Speaking of cheap, chain motels come standard in St. Louis, and the cheapest of them are around Lambert Airport, just 20 or so minutes northwest of downtown and reachable by MetroLink. Among them are the **Ramada Airport North,** 9079 Dunn Rd. (☎ 314/731-7700), **Red Roof Inn–**

Bridgeton, 3470 Hollenburg (☎ 314/291-3350), and **Days Inn North Airport,** 7350 N. Hanley Rd. (☎ 314-524-2500). Each of their rooms starts at around $45.

Other moderate St. Louis hotel zones are a bit west of Lambert Airport in **Westport Plaza,** and south around **Sunset Hills** and **Fenton,** not far from Six Flags St. Louis.

DOABLE

➜**Best Western Inn at the Park** If you're drawn to the 1,371 acres that make up Forest Park, look no further than this hotel, sitting on its northeast corner. It's clean, friendly, covers all the standard amenities, and has free parking (somewhat rare in good St. Louis locations). *4630 Lindell Blvd.* ☎ *800/373-7501 or 314/367-7500. www.bestwestern. com. 128 units. $79–$129 single or double. Amenities: Free parking; outdoor pool; fitness center; sauna/steam room; dataport.*

➜**Hampton Inn–Gateway Arch** Its great location is this hotel's biggest selling point, at just a hop-skip away from the Arch, Laclede's Landing, and all the other downtown sights. Rooms are clean and have super-comfy beds, plus there's a great indoor pool with a view of the Arch, and in-and-out parking is only $10/day (pretty good for downtown). *333 Washington Ave.*

Junkyard Heaven

📺 Best❂ **City Museum** may be the only place in the country where a full-size yellow school bus is parked—okay, "parked" is a loose term—precariously on the roof of a five-story building. Opened in 1997 in the 600,000 square foot former International Shoe Company, it is the brainchild of "sculptor and serial entrepreneur" Bob Cassilly. Within its fence and red-brick walls are old chimneys, salvaged bridges, construction cranes, miles of tile, and two abandoned airplanes, all collected from within St. Lou's municipal borders. Ingeniously harmonized, today the museum draws playful people of all ages to partake in its mélange of playground, funhouse, surrealistic pavilion, and architectural marvel of unique, found objects (☎ 314/231-CITY; www.citymuseum.org). See p. 747 for more details.

☎ *314/621-7900. www.hamptoninnstlouis. com. 190 units. $89–$199 single or double. No pets. MetroLink: Convention Center. Amenities: Free breakfast; indoor pool; exercise room; game room; free Internet via dataport or Wi-Fi.*

SPLURGE

➧ **Drury Inn Union Station** ★ Part of a St. Louis–based chain, this beautifully restored former YMCA, built in 1907, is across from Union Station and offers rooms with refrigerators, microwaves, and free popcorn and soda; free evening beverages and snacks (Mon–Thurs); free local calls; and many other perks (including laundry facilities), making this a great place for families. Note that some rooms face inward, meaning no views. *201 S. 20th St.* ☎ *800/378-7946 or 314/231-3900. www. druryinn.com. 176 units. $114–$124 double. Breakfast buffet included. Free covered parking. MetroLink: Union Station. Pets permitted. Amenities: Restaurant; indoor pool; exercise room.*

➧ **Hyatt Regency St. Louis** ★★ Located in restored Union Station, with its many shops and restaurants, this hotel boasts Missouri's most spectacular lobby—the station's former Grand Hall, with a six-story vaulted ceiling and gold-leaf frescoes. Most of the spacious (and quiet) rooms are in a modern addition beneath the trusses of the former train shed and feature such luxuries as bathroom TVs. For more pampering, stay in the Regency Club in the historic part of the station, which has the added perks of its own lounge, complimentary breakfast, and bathrobes. Everyone from business travelers to families stay here. *One St. Louis Union Station (18th and Market sts.).* ☎ *800/233-1234 or 314/231-1234. www.stlouis.hyatt.com. 539 units. $189–$259 doubleValet parking $18; self-parking $12. MetroLink: Union Station. Amenities: 2 restaurants; outdoor pool; health club.*

Eating

Dining in one of St. Louis's distinctive neighborhoods ranks high on a shortlist of must-dos. Clustered around Forest Park is the trendy **Central West End,** with its grand residences, antiques stores, and fashionable eateries (many with sidewalk seating). **The Loop** is named after an old streetcar turnaround and home to funky shops, art galleries, ethnic restaurants, and the St. Louis Walk of Fame. There's also **The Hill,** an Italian district famous for its many Italian restaurants (a perennial favorite is **Charlie Gitto's Pasta House,** 5226 Shaw Ave.; ☎ **314/772-8898;** www. charliegittos.com).

Laclede's Landing, down by the Gateway Arch, is more touristy, and it's where you'll find **The Old Spaghetti Factory,** housed in an old warehouse at 727 N. 1st St. (☎ **314/621-0276;** www.osf.com). Nearby in Union Station is the **Hard Rock Cafe** (☎ **314/621-7625;** www.hardrockcafe. com) and a food court.

SUPPLIES

Stock up on local fresh fruit, vegetables, spices, baked goods, and other delights at the year-round **Soulard Farmers Market.** Open 7:30am to 5pm Wednesday through Saturday, this market draws hundreds of shoppers to its indoor/outdoor mall on Carroll Street between 7th and 9th streets (☎ **314/622-4180;** www.soulard market.com). Besides being a great place to stock up on roadtrip treats that skip the preservatives, it's a great reason to spend a day roaming around Soulard and back up the Mississippi Riverfront to downtown.

TAKEOUT TREATS

For a reliably strong cup o' joe and a fresh pastry, head to one of two downtown locations for **Café Breve,** 909 Chestnut and

St. Louis Events: Music, Balloons & Blues

St. Louis is a pretty busy hub of a city, with a diverse bunch of annual happenings, including some of these fun festivals:

→ Every Fat Tuesday weekend, St. Louis's historic Soulard district transforms into **Mardi Gras** wonderland—the biggest of its kind outside New Orleans. With parades, drinking, art shows, drinking, cooking demos, and more drinking, it's best to show up thirsty and let the celebratory atmosphere do the rest (☎ 314/771-5110; www.mardigrasinc.com).

→ Bring $14, your letterman's jacket, and a load of energy to the rousing **Greater St. Louis Marching Band Festival.** Now in its 4th decade, more than 14,000 people a year come out every late October to hear dozens of high school marching bands try to out-do each other inside the Edward Jones Dome (☎ **314/469-9082;** www.gslmbf.com).

→ If hot-air balloons are totally alien to you, **the Great Forest Park Balloon Race** is a great way to discover your appreciation for them. Founded in 1973, this mid-September festival sends dozens of colorful and sometimes themed balloons floating over the city (**http://promos.stltoday.com/balloonrace/index.html**).

→ Early September brings the **Budweiser Big Muddy Blues Festival** to Laclede's Landing. It's free and brings big-name blues bands to five stages over a 3-day weekend. BYO picnic and chairs (**www.bigmuddyblues.com**).

→ Music, food, art, politics, and a big parade arrive in Tower Grove Park every late June for **St. Louis Pridefest,** one of the region's biggest LGBT events (**www.pridestl.org**).

→ The ever-growing community **Earth Day Festival** energizes environmentalism via exhibitions, performances, and demonstrations to Forest Park's Muni Theater every late April (**www.stlouisearthday.org**).

417 N. 10th St. (☎ **314/231-BEAN;** www.brevecoffee.com), where you can also check your e-mail with their free Wi-Fi. **Kayak's Coffee,** 276 N. Skinker Blvd. (☎ **314/862-4447;** www.kayakscoffee.com), over by Washington University, is another friendly wake-up zone, with free Wi-Fi, and good coffee and treats. It's also a good wind-down zone, and stays open 'til midnight daily.

It's a St. Louis tradition to drop by **Ted Drewes Frozen Custard,** 6726 Chippewa (☎ **314/481-2652),** after a night on the town. Founded more than 75 years ago, this roadside parlor and Route 66 attraction specializes in frozen custards, including a thick dip called a "Concrete," available in flavors ranging from chocolate chip to Heath Bar and so thick that it's served upside down. It's southwest of downtown in Shrewsbury, and open daily March through December. An additional location is open summers only at 4224 S. Grand (☎ 314/352-7376; www.teddrewes.com).

RESTAURANTS
Cheap
→**Blueberry Hill** ★ SANDWICHES/BURGERS In the lively Loop district, this St. Louis institution is a treasure-trove of pop-culture memorabilia, including vintage posters, lunchboxes, and more Chuck

AMERICAN HIGHWAYS

Berry memorabilia than you can shake a stick at. The CD jukebox, with 3,000 selections, is awesome, and the hamburgers are among the best in town. Live music is staged in the Elvis Room and Duck Room several nights a week (Chuck Berry still performs here on occasion), and outside on the sidewalk is the St. Louis Walk of Fame honoring famous St. Louisans, including Josephine Baker, Tennessee Williams, Ulysses S. Grant, Kevin Kline, and Tina Turner. *6504 Delmar.* ☎ *314/727-0880. www.blueberryhill.com. Main courses $4.50–$9. AE, DC, MC, V. Mon–Sat 11am–1am; Sun 11am–midnight.*

→ **City Diner** ★★ AMERICAN Breakfast, lunch, or late-night pancakes are on the menu at this retro-American diner, formerly the *South* City Diner. Located near St. Louis University, the place will serve up fresh-cut fries with a side of Elvis on the 1950s-style jukebox 24 hours a day on weekends (and 'til 11pm weekdays). If you're there for breakfast, try the biscuits and gravy. *3139 S. Grand.* ☎ *314/772-6100. www.citydiner.us. Main courses $4–$11. Mon–Thurs 7am–11pm; Fri–Sat 24 hr.*

→ **Lagniappe's** CAJUN/ITALIAN A friendly place with a huge outdoor patio in the Soulard district, Lagniappe's (pronounced LAN-yap, meaning "a little something extra") is a great place to relax with a nice, filling menu of classic Cajun dishes, as well as pasta and fish. The lunch menu is, of course, cheaper, but there are nightly specials and deals on everything from catfish to fettuccine to be had from its mainly Italian dinner menu. *2501 S. 9th St.* ☎ *314/771-2090. Lunch $5–$8; dinner $7–$25. Tues–Thurs 11am–2pm and 5–10pm; Fri 11am–2pm and 5–11pm; Sat noon–2pm and 5–11pm.*

Doable

→ **Meriwether's** NEW AMERICAN On the second floor of the Missouri History Museum, this light and airy casual restaurant overlooking Forest Park offers soups, salads (such as a Mediterranean chicken salad with olives, artichoke hearts, feta, and red onion), sandwiches (a grilled salmon BLT), quiche, and main dishes (blue-corn-encrusted catfish), as well as a children's menu. This is a good place for lunch if you're visiting the many sights in Forest Park, but other recommendations include the casual **Boathouse** with its sandwiches, pizzas, and rental paddleboats (☎ **314/367-2224;** www.boathouse forestpark.com); and **Puck's,** in the Saint Louis Art Museum (☎ **314/655-5490;** www.wolfgangpuck.com), with its innovative American cuisine and popular Sunday brunch. *Missouri History Museum, Forest Park.* ☎ *314/361-7313. Main courses $7–$11. Mon–Sat 11am–2pm; Sun 10am–2pm.*

→ **The Schlafly Tap Room** ★★ AMERICAN A few blocks north of Union Station, in a 1904 brick building that used to house a printing company, this microbrewery brews more than 30 kinds of Schlafly brand beer on the premises (eight or so are usually on draught) and serves a variety of sandwiches and entrees, many of which include beer in their recipes, including beer-battered shrimp, Oatmeal Stout meatloaf, and beer-and-cheddar soup. An upstairs bar offers live music every Friday, Saturday, and Sunday evening. *2100 Locust St.* ☎ *314/241-2337. www.schlafly.com. Main courses $5.95–$12. Mon–Thurs 11am–10pm; Fri–Sat 11am–midnight; Sun noon–9pm.*

Splurge

→ **The Drunken Fish** JAPANESE/SUSHI Delicious sushi by day, lounge scene by night. Despite a bit of kitsch, this three-location chain is a great place for people-watching over large cuts of sushi and warm sake. The romantic dinner setting turns into a nightclub in the later hours, with kung-fu movies showing in the background. *639 West Port Plaza* ☎ *314/275-8300; #1 Maryland Plaza Dr.* ☎ *314/367-4222.; 612 North 2nd St.* ☎ *314/241-9595. Lunch $9–$15; dinner $14–$24. Mon–Fri 11am–2pm and 5–10:30pm; Sat 5pm–1am; Sun 5pm–midnight.*

➜ **Mike Shannon's Steaks and Seafood** STEAKS/SEAFOOD Owned by a former Cardinals baseball great (and current sportscaster—whose radio show is broadcast live from a booth in the restaurant after Fri–Sat home games), this downtown fine-dining venue is formal yet relaxed, with white tablecloths in wood-paneled rooms and displays of sports memorabilia. It caters mainly to a business crowd with a menu that concentrates on aged steaks and seafood, plus sandwiches for lunch. With Busch Stadium just a couple minutes' walk away, it's a popular stop for a meal before or after a Cardinals game. *100 N. 7th St.* ☎ *314/421-1540. www.shannonsteak.com. Main courses $16–$42. Mon–Fri 11am–11pm; Sat 5–11pm; Sun 5–10pm.*

Partying

The Loop and **Laclede's Landing** are the best bar and club zones in St. Louis, each serving as strips for cruising around for whatever scene suits your fancy for the night—be it live music, dancing, or just friendly conversation at the bar among the locals. More music of the blues and jazz varieties tends to be around **Soulard,** with its New Orleans–like atmosphere.

BARS, PUBS & CLUBS

Perhaps St. Lou's most reliable can't-miss spot is the Loop's block-long **Blueberry Hill,** 6504 Delmar (☎ **314/727-0880;** www.blueberryhill.com), which pretty much has it all between its themed barrooms, hearty burgers, sidewalk tables, ever-rockin' jukebox, and stages.

There are also a handful of gay and lesbian bars/clubs sprinkled throughout the city, and the most-talked-about one is **Absolutli Goosed,** 3196 S. Grand Blvd. (☎ **314/772-0400;** www.absolutligoosed. com), a martini-happy bar that's just plain happy. The Central West End's **Novak's Bar,** 4146 Manchester Rd. (☎ **314/531-3699;** www.novaksbar.com), is also a popular stop with a great atmosphere, drag shows, DJs, and drink specials.

➜ **Pin-Up Bowl** ★★ Martinis in the front, bowling in the back—that's the theme of this Art Deco bar/restaurant/bowling alley. Well-situated between Blueberry Hill and The Pageant, grab one of eight lanes ($4/game without reservations, $30–$40/hr. with), one of several signature martinis, and let the good times roll. *6191 Delmar in The Loop.* ☎ *314/727-5555. www.pinupbowl.com. Mon–Thurs 3pm–3am; Fri–Sun noon–3am.*

➜ **The Study Hall** This bar/club/venue draws a good weekend crowd down to its Laclede's Landing location. It's a big place where lots of groups come to soak up drink specials, hear live music (Fri–Sat), play games, and don Mardi Gras beads for the full party effect. Its motto says it all, "Expanding minds one drink at a time." *118 Morgan St.* ☎ *314/241-4646. www.studyhallbar.com. Wed–Sat 8pm–3am. Cover varies.*

LIVE MUSIC

Rock, etc.

📺 **Best ◐** ➜ **The Pageant** ★★★ A 1,500-seat venue backed by the cool Halo Bar, this place is the full package, and likely to be recommended by a St. Louis local when asked where to find good music. Located in the heart of the Loop, it's the place to see all kinds of musicians—from Death Cab for Cutie to Alice Cooper to Ani DiFranco—as well as comedians big and small. *6161 Delmar.* ☎ *314/726-6161. www.thepageant.com. Halo Bar open daily 7pm–3am (opens at 5pm show nights). Ticket prices for shows vary; no cover in the bar.*

Jazz/Blues

Good bets for live music virtually every night of the week include **BB's Jazz, Blues & Soups,** 2 blocks south of Busch Stadium at 700 S. Broadway (☎ **314/436-5222;** www.bbsjazzbluessoups.com), and, across the street, **The Beale on Broadway,** 701 S. Broadway (☎ **314/621-7880;** www.beale onbroadway.com), home to live blues, soul, and R&B. **Mississippi Nights** brings top-rated touring bands to Laclede's Landing at 914 S. 1st St. (☎ **314/421-3853**); while in Soulard, the **1860 Hard Shell Cafe & Bar,** 1860 S. 9th St. (☎ **314/231-1860**), offers blues, R&B, rock, and more nightly.

➜ **Broadway Oyster Bar** ★ It's been called one of the best blues bars in the country, but this unassuming venue is the best place to hear great live music over big plates of Cajun-Creole seafood and delicacies. Bands take the stage on the patio 7 nights a week in this favorite Soulard haunt. *736 S. Broadway.* ☎ *314/621-8811. www. broadwayoysterbar.com. Sun–Thurs 11am–1:30am; Fri–Sat 11am–3am. Cover $4–$5.*

➜ **King's Palace Café** ★ With its battered wood floor, this bar has the most authentic, old-time feel of any club on Beale Street. Though this is primarily a restaurant serving good Cajun food, including a knock-out gumbo, there's live jazz and blues nightly. *162 Beale St.* ☎ *901/521-1851. www.kingspalacecafe.com. Sun–Thurs 11am–10:30pm; Fri–Sat 11am–close. No cover.*

What Else to See & Do

There's shopping, sports, and tourist attractions—all part of the reason why St. Louis is a great city for roaming with no particular place to go (to quote Chuck Berry). If you've got the time, that is. If your days are numbered in River City, it might be wise to devise an itinerary to be sure to catch the coolest sights.

The good news is that many of St. Louis's top attractions are clustered in or around expansive **Forest Park,** site of the 1904 World's Fair and one of the nation's largest parks (it beats New York's Central Park by 500 acres).

THE TOP ATTRACTIONS

A surprisingly interesting attraction is one you might stumble on, quite literally, when visiting University City's Delmar in the Loop. It's the **St. Louis Walk of Fame** ★, comprised of 113 bronze stars embedded in the sidewalk—and you'll probably be surprised how many artists, athletes, musicians, actors, and politicians were born here, including Josephine Baker, Miles Davis, Chuck Berry, Tina Turner, John Goodman, Maya Angelou, T. S. Eliot, Charles Lindbergh, Kevin Kline, Yogi Berra, and the list (or sidewalk, rather) goes on.

For another piece of low-cost, as in "free," fun, check out the top-rated **St. Louis Zoo** ★, Forest Park (☎ **314/781-0900;** www.stlzoo.org), with its Big Cat Country, Jungle of the Apes, River's Edge with elephants and hippos, Penguin and Puffin Coast, the 904 Flight Cage aviary, insectarium with everything from giant cockroaches to a butterfly house, and animal-contact area called Children's Zoo. (**Note:** Some of the zoo attractions charge modest fees: Zooline Railroad, the 3-D Movie, and the Children's Zoo cost

$4/person children under 2 are free; the Children's Zoo offers free entrance for the first hour of each day).

FREE → **Anheuser-Busch Brewery** ★ Anheuser-Busch, one of the world's largest beer brewers, was established at this site in the 1860s, and many architectural gems from that time period remain. Tours of the brewing process take in the 1885 Clydesdale stable, the historic 1892 Brew House, and the packaging plant, ending with free beer (which is the real reason people go, of course). Allow 1¹/₂ hours. Tours begin at 12th and Lynch streets (I-55 at Arsenal). *12th and Lynch sts. ☎ 314/577-2626. www.budweisertours.com. Free admission. June–Aug Mon–Sat 9am–5pm, Sun 11:30am–5pm; Sept–May Mon–Sat 9am–4pm (Nov–Feb from 10am), Sun 11:30am–4pm. Tours are several times an hour on first-come, first-served basis. Frequency depends on demand (as often as every 10 min. in summer and about every 30 min. in winter).*

MTV **Best ●** → **City Museum** ★★ Don't freak out when you see it—it's totally safe, despite the large metal objects and vehicles suspended overhead. This found-object museum makes the most of junk, and I do mean junk, repurposed as living, interactive sculpture. Its tag-line is "Explore the unexpected," and by the time you leave this wonderland of salvage, you may never look at abandoned sheet metal the same way. (See also "Junkyard Heaven," p. 741) *701 N. 15th St. ☎ 314/231-CITY. www.citymuseum.org. $12 adults, $8 after 5pm Fri–Sat. Mon–Thurs 9am–5pm (closed Mon–Tues, Labor Day through Memorial Day); Fri 9am–1am; Sat 10am–1am; Sun 11am–5am.*

MTV **Best ●** → **Gateway Arch/Jefferson National Expansion Memorial** America's tallest monument (and note that the "MTV Best" designation applies to the outside,

not the inside of this attraction), this graceful rainbow of shining steel rises 630 feet above downtown and the Mississippi River, commemorating westward expansion in the 1800s. Tram rides to the top can involve lengthy waits in the summer and on weekends; come first thing in the morning to purchase tickets (or order tickets in advance online), then take in the **Museum of Westward Expansion,** which traces the journey of Lewis and Clark and those who followed. Extra fees are charged for both the Arch Odyssey Theatre, which features changing 45-minute movies on a giant IMAX screen, and the Monument to the Dream film documenting the Arch's construction. Plan on spending at least 2 hours here—could be way more, depending on the season. *707 N. 1st St. (between Memorial Dr. and Lenore K. Sullivan Blvd., on the riverfront). ☎ 877/982-1410. www.gatewayarch.com. Admission for tram and 1 movie $12 adults, $9 children 13–16, $5.50 children 3–12. Memorial Day to Labor Day daily 8am–10pm (tram until 9:10pm); rest of year daily 9am–6pm (tram until 5:10pm).*

→ **International Bowling Hall of Fame** Also known as the Big Lebowski's heaven on earth, you may find yourself both endeared and bewildered at the space and energy devoted to a sport that's arguably built around booze (and rented shoes). Easy to find right outside Busch Stadium, this is a 50,000-square-foot homage to a game they say was first played by ancient Egyptians in 3200 B.C. And if you're a genuine bowling fan, you're likely to flip out at the interactive games and features within, a sampling of which is available on the museum website. *111 Stadium Plaza. ☎ 314/231-6340. $7.50 adults. Sun–Mon 11am–4pm (Oct–Mar); daily 9am–5pm (Apr–Sept).*

→**Missouri Botanical Garden** ★★ Opened in 1859, this is the country's oldest and one of its best botanical gardens: a 79-acre delight featuring the nation's largest Japanese strolling garden, a Chinese garden, a geodesic-domed rainforest greenhouse, an 1882 brick conservatory housing camellias, a scented garden for the visually impaired, a sculpture garden with works by Carl Milles, a hedge maze, a home-gardening resource center, and themed gardens ranging from a Victorian garden to an English woodland garden. A must-see for gardeners, who can easily spend 2 or 3 hours of bliss here. *4344 Shaw Blvd. (Vandeventer exit off I-44).* ☎ *314/577-9400. www.mobot.org. Admission $7 adults, $5 seniors, free for children 12 and under. Daily 9am–5pm (Memorial Day to Labor Day grounds close Wed 9pm and are open Wed and Sat 7–9am for walkers).*

FREE →**Saint Louis Art Museum** Housed in a Beaux Arts–style building constructed for the 1904 World's Fair, this great museum is a buffet of the arts, where visitors can sample as much as they like of the displays from around the globe and from virtually all time periods. It contains works ranging from ancient and medieval art to European old masters, French Impressionists, American art from 1800 to 1945, and contemporary art. Its pre-Columbian and German Expressionist collections are ranked among the best in the world (it owns more paintings by Max Beckmann than any museum in the world). Other galleries feature Islamic and ancient art; an Asian collection; an Egyptian collection (including three mummies); arms and armor; and art from Africa, Oceania, and the Americas. There are also displays of Chinese, European, and American decorative arts. You should spend at least 2 hours here. *Fine Arts Dr., Forest Park.* ☎ *314/721-0072. www.slam.org. Free admission;*

special exhibitions cost extra (but are free on Fri). Tues–Sun 10am–5pm (Fri to 9pm).

FREE →**St. Louis Union Station** Once the nation's busiest passenger-rail terminal, this restored 100-year-old terminal is one of St. Louis's biggest attractions and now contains more than 80 specialty shops, restaurants, and even a small lake with paddleboats. Be sure to take a peek at the Grand Hall, now the lobby of the Hyatt Regency. *1820 Market St.* ☎ *314/421-6655. Free admission. Shops Mon–Sat 10am–9pm; Sun 10am–6pm.*

PLAYING OUTSIDE

Forest Park is the Central Park of the entire Midwest (only bigger), with tennis courts, skating rinks, boathouses, walking trails, and golf courses (yes, plural). The **Riverfront, Tower Grove Park,** and other smaller municipal parks provide plenty of chances to stretch your legs while in town.

Perhaps the biggest amusement-attraction for kids young and old, however, is **Six Flags St. Louis,** 30 miles west of downtown on I-44 (☎ **636/938-4800;** www.sixflags.com), with thrill rides like the 5,000-foot-long Boss roller coaster, plus Looney Tunes Town, live entertainment, and even a water park with a wave pool, slides, and more. Admission is $40 adults, $25 kids under 48 inches tall; discount tickets are often available on the park's website.

RIVER TOURS

Gateway Arch Riverboat Cruises (☎ **877/982-1410** or 314/923-3048; www.gatewayarchriverboats.com), departing throughout the year from the levee below the Arch, offers 1-hour narrated sightseeing trips aboard replica 19th-century paddle-wheelers called the *Tom Sawyer* and *Becky Thatcher.* One-hour cruises are $10 adults and $4 children.

HISTORIC HOMES

The **Campbell House Museum**, 1508 Locust St. (☎ 314/421-0325; www.campbell housemuseum.org), is an 1851 Victorian mansion with most of its original furnishings intact. The Romanesque Revival–style 1889 **Samuel Cupples House**, 3673 W. Pine Blvd. (☎ 314/977-3025), is a gem of the Gilded Age on the campus of Saint Louis University, containing 42 rooms, a glass collection, and other fine and decorative arts. Tours of the house cost $4. The **Chatillon-DeMenil Mansion**, 3352 DeMenil Place (☎ 314/771-5828; www.demenil.org), was a four-room farmhouse in 1848, later expanded to 14 rooms in the Greek Revival style. It contains period furnishings, a collection of 1904 World's Fair memorabilia, and two paintings by Missouri artist George Caleb Bingham. Admission to each house costs $4.

From 1900 to 1903, the **Scott Joplin House State Historic Site**, 2658 Delmar Blvd. (☎ 314/340-5790; www.mostate parks.com/scottjoplin.htm), was the modest four-family antebellum home of the musician and composer known as the "King of Ragtime." Now a National Historic Landmark, it offers 25-minute guided tours that include Joplin's second-floor apartment with furnishings representative of the times and a player-piano that rags out renditions of Joplin's best-known tunes, including "The Entertainer."

PERFORMING ARTS

Grand Center is the top performing arts district of St. Louis, with the 1920s-era **Powell Symphony Hall**, 718 N. Grand Blvd. (☎ 314/534-1700), home of the **St. Louis Symphony Orchestra** (www.slso.org), founded in 1880 and America's second-oldest symphony orchestra. The **Fabulous Fox Theatre**, 527 N. Grand Blvd. (☎ 314/534-1111; www.fabulousfox.com),

is a lavish, 1929 Byzantine venue for musicals, dance, and concerts. The **Grandel Theater**, 3610 Grandel Sq., is the home of the **St. Louis Black Repertory Company** (☎ 314/534-3810; www.theblackrep.org), which stages contemporary works by African-American playwrights. The **UMB Bank Pavilion**, 14141 Riverport Dr. (☎ 314/298-9944; www.umbbankpavilion. com), presents big-name concerts; while **The Muny**, in Forest Park (☎ 314/361-1900; www.muny.com), which opened in 1916 and is the nation's oldest and largest outdoor musical theater, features Broadway musicals in summer.

SPECTATOR SPORTS

Baseball

Watch the 2006 World Champion **St. Louis Cardinals** knock a few out of Busch Stadium, 7th Street downtown (☎ 314/421-2400; www.stlcardinals.com). Tickets will cost you anywhere from $13 to $240. Stadium tours are also available four times daily on non-game days for $10 (☎ 314/421-3263).

The Frontier League **Gateway Grizzlies** are a less-expensive but still-exciting minor-league option, playing at 2301 Grizzlie Bear Blvd. across the river in Sauget, Illinois (☎ 618-337-3000; www. gatewaygrizzlies.com). Tickets range from just $5 to $8.

Football

Edward Jones Dome is the home of the 2000 Super Bowl Champs **St. Louis Rams**. Pick up tickets for $44 to $91 at the Dome ticket office, 901 N. Broadway, by phone, or online (☎ 314/425-8830 or 800/246-7267; www.stlouisrams.com).

NASCAR

Across the river in Madison, Illinois, is the **Gateway International Raceway**, 700 Raceway Blvd. (☎ 618/482-2400 or 866-35-SPEED; www.gatewayraceway.com), host of NASCAR, drag, motorcycle, and all other kinds of races.

Hockey

The NHL is alive and well in St. Louis by way of the **St. Louis Blues,** who play at the Scottrade Center (formerly the Savvis Center), 15th Street at Clark Avenue (☎ 314/ 622-BLUE; www.stlouisblues.com). Ticket prices range from $15 to $135.

On the Road to Branson, MO

St. Louis, MO to Branson, MO 255 miles

Sure, there are diversions leaving St. Louis like **Six Flags** (☎ 636/938-4800; www. sixflags.com) and **Meramec Caverns** (☎ 800/676-6105; www.americascave. com), but this leg of the trip is a chance to hop on the highway with a stack of CDs (or your favorite long playlist) and cruise. You'll have a few chances to drive segments of the original two-lane **Route 66** alongside the interstate, where you can absorb some of the "Mother Road" in all its dilapidated glory—though you'll have many more chances to drive on Route 66 through Oklahoma, Texas, and New Mexico.

The faster, perhaps more practical option is sticking to I-44 west (speed limit 70 mph), where you'll enter the **Ozark Plateau** and encounter waves of rolling hills over miles and miles of mountains. You may also want to stop into **Mark Twain National Forest** on the west side of Rolla (☎ 573/364-4621; www.recreation.gov) for some fresh air and scenery on the banks of the Big Piney River. If you're on a leisurely schedule, you can also hike, bike, camp, and more here.

If you press on through southern Missouri, after about 3½ hours on I-44 you'll arrive at east **Springfield,** where you connect with Rt. 65 South, and behold the onslaught of billboards for Branson's countless theaters, hotels, resorts, and theme parks. Prepare yourself, friend, for the bizarro world you are about to enter.

On the Road Nuts & Bolts

Where to Fill Up   There are plenty of filling stations along I-44 on your way out of St. Louis, but be sure to take advantage of what might be cheaper gas outside of Springfield, before heading south to Branson.

The Fastest Way   I-44 west (which is actually southwest) is the bulk of the trip at 3½ hours (220 miles), heading right into Springfield. There you'll hop on Highway 65 South for about 45 miles into Branson.

The Long Way Round   Upon leaving St. Louis on I-44 you'll see the first of many turnoffs for "Historic Route 66" around Eureka. You can take this or any of these recurring exits to catch some of the flavor of the "Mother Road," Missouri-style. Rolla, about 100 miles outside of St. Louis, has a small sampling of Route 66 nostalgia, including vintage cars and old-school roadside motels, making it a good place to take a break from the road.

Rules of the Road   Summer in Missouri means more crowded highways, and drivers around these parts are on the rude side, so beware of tailgaters and speeding trucks who don't mind cutting you off.

Picnic Point   One of several Mark Twain National Forest parks in Missouri goes on for miles just past Rolla, and you can turn in around Doolittle or Devil's Elbow for some scenic picnicking on a Big Piney River bluff.

Welcome to Branson

In the home stretch into Branson you may try out a few local radio stations. A scan of the dial will introduce you, one after another, to a plethora of Christian rock, talk, and gospel stations. If this genre is not your bag, don't let it scare you—rather, let it begin to season you for a taste of what the geographical center of this country is up to, if you're from the big city.

It is here in Branson, which calls itself the "Live Entertainment Capital of the World," that families, good Midwestern kids, RV-happy retirees, and hillbilly musicians and their fans flock for wholesome, old-fashioned fun (see "'Hillbilly': Before Country Became Country," p. 756). And its merchants do a mean business catering to more than 7 million visitors every year (see "The Little Resort Town That Could. And Did.," below)

And when you arrive, if you're feeling overwhelmed, swing by one of the two **Branson/Lakes Area Welcome Centers** in town at Highways 65 and 248, and Highways 65 and 160 (☎ **800/296-0463**). They'll sort you out.

Getting Around

There are really two sides to Branson: the compact historic side to the east of US 65, and the sprawling resort side to the west of it. On the historic end of town, you'll find a small "downtown" area where you can park your car, walk around, and talk to some of the locals and friendly shop owners. East of this area, on Lake Taneycomo (which is shaped like a river), there's also Branson Landing, a more trendy outdoor mall that opened in spring 2006.

On the resort side, you have the big 76 Country Boulevard loop—aka "The Strip"— which connects to both Shepherd of the Hills Expressway (the long way) and Roark Valley Road (the short way). Vacationers generally stay at motels on this slow and winding strip, and repeatedly drive around it to check out Branson's neon-lit theaters, shopping centers, and assorted activities. While there's tons of eye candy here, it may get old if traffic slows to a crawl (as it sometimes does), making a drive around the entire loop take as much as an hour.

There's also Gretna Road, running right through the middle of the 76 loop, and

Playlist: Goin' Hillbilly (with a little Rock)

→ *Travelin' Blues*, **Jimmie Rogers**, 1928

→ *Jambalaya (On the Bayou)*, **Hank Williams**, 1952

→ *Honey Don't*, **Elvis Presley**, 1955

→ *Rocky Top*, **Dolly Parton**, "Live and Well," 2004

→ *You're Lookin' at Country*, **Loretta Lynn**, "You're Lookin' at Country," 1971

→ *I'm the One Mama Warned You About*, **Mickey Gilley**, "Live at Branson," 2006

→ *Rehumanize Yourself*, **The Police**, "Ghost in the Machine," 1981

Welcome to Branson.

offshoots that will take you northwest to Silver Dollar City, west to Table Rock Lake, and south to Table Rock Dam, Welk Resort, and Showboat Branson Belle.

Take note: Branson is a car town, with no mass transit. On the bright side, that means free parking almost everywhere.

Sleeping

Branson offers countless resorts, bed-and-breakfasts, luxury hotels, and bargain motels—some going for as little as $20/night, no reservations required. Accommodations with a bit more character are found around the little downtown

Every Day's a Festival in Branson!

It's kind of like a festival every day in Branson, only in free-standing theme parks, theater and show spaces, and the outdoor mall that is Branson Landing. Still, a few annual events make for seasonal attractions and guaranteed good people-watching.

→ The 3-decade-old **Plumb Nellie Days Hillbilly Festival** (☎ 417/334-1548) kicks off the summer in downtown Branson, turning Main Street into an arts, crafts, music, and games street fair. By the way, "Plumb Nellie" ain't the mayor of Branson—it's an expression that basically means "darn nearly," as in, "That festival sells plumb nellie everything!"

→ For 5 days in early April, **Branson Fest** comes to the Welk Resort in south Branson. The $30 daily admission ($130 for the 5-day package; **www. explorebranson.org**) gets you access to plenty of live music, the business expo, and the arts and heritage area, where you can learn about Ozark Mountain culture and history.

→ Silver Dollar City hosts the monthlong **Festival of American Music and Crafts.** Bluegrass and country-Western musicians, trick riders and ropers, barn dancers, cowboy craftsmen, and thousands of their fans flood the park every mid-September to late October (the ticket price is the regular $48 daily adult admission; **www.bransonsilverdollarcity.com**).

area, such as the **Landmark Inn,** 313 Commercial St. (☎ **417/334-1304**). There are plenty of camping facilities around town, too, including **Cooper Creek Resort** (☎ **800/261-8398** or 417/334-4871; www.coopercreekresort.com) on Lake Taneycomo, where a campsite with hookups goes for just $18/night. You can also try something different by staying in a houseboat; contact **Gage's Long Creek Marina** (☎ **800/255-5561** or 417/334-1413; www.tablerocklakeresort.com) or **Tri-Lakes Houseboat Rentals** (☎ **800/982-2628** or 417/739-2370; www.tri-lakes houseboat.com).

Here are a few lodging highlights in the Cheap/Doable range:

→**Branson Hotel Bed and Breakfast** Established as an inn in 1903 and located 2 blocks from historic downtown Branson, this nonsmoking B&B offers well-appointed, comfortable rooms, each decorated differently in Victorian style with antique furniture and ceiling fans but also featuring cable TV and air-conditioning. Innkeepers Cynthia and Randy Parker, who live on the premises, serve breakfast in a bright, glass-enclosed room and, in the afternoon, offer homemade snacks, iced tea, and coffee in the parlor. Guests can relax on the old-fashioned front porch, seated in Adirondack chairs. *214 W. Main St.* ☎ *800/933-0651 or 417/335-6104. www.branson hotelbb.com. 7 units. $79–$109 single or double. Rates include breakfast. Smoking not permitted.*

→**Grand Country Inn** ★ Families who want to be in the thick of 76 Country Boulevard with its never-ending string of theaters, go-cart tracks, restaurants, shops, and motels will find this property to their liking. It includes **Splash Country Indoors,** a large indoor/outdoor water park free to hotel guests, as well as two buffet restaurants, a theater with a variety of music shows throughout the day, and

AMERICAN HIGHWAYS

The Little Resort Town That Could–And Did

Branson the resort town really was never anything but that. Incorporated in 1912, this small town on the White River had a few thousand visitors coming every year to check out Marvel Cave—featured in Harold Bell Wright's 1907 novel *Shepherd of the Hills*—and Lake Taneycomo. Tourism grew over the next few decades, and by 1960, Silver Dollar City amusement park opened and an outdoor theater was built at Shepherd of the Hills Farm. The enterprising Mabes family got in on the action by playing homemade instruments as "The Baldknobbers" in the Ozarks Jubilee music show. Table Rock Lake drew fishermen, new theaters drew in more musical talent, and a rebuilt US 65 allowed them all fast, easy access into town. Today, Branson is home to about 6,000 residents, and the vacation site for more than 7 million visitors a year.

indoor minigolf. There's so much to do, most guests don't care that rooms are rather basic and ordinary. Local telephone calls are free. To find it, just look for the world's largest banjo. *Grand Country Sq. 1945 W. Hwy. 76.* ☎*800/828-9068 or 417/335-3535. www.grandcountry.com. 319 units. $60–$100 double. Off-season rates and packages available. Amenities: 3 restaurants; indoor/outdoor waterpark; 3 pools (1 indoor).*

➔**Indian Point Resorts** On a wooded point on Table Rock Lake 2½ miles from Silver Dollar City and 6 miles from Branson, this casual, low-key lakefront resort appeals mainly to families with its recreational facilities (playgrounds; volleyball and badminton; game room; free paddleboats; and marina with rentals for fishing and ski boats, pontoons, and WaveRunners) and a wide range of accommodations, all equipped with stocked kitchens and barbecue grills. These include comfortable if rather standard motel-like units, ranging from one-room efficiencies for two people to four-bedroom units that sleep 10, free-standing cottages, and log cabins of various sizes with fireplaces and decks. Slightly more upscale condos offer the additional luxuries of laundry facilities, dishwashers, fireplaces, and decks overlooking the lake.

There's even an RV park here, along with rental RVs and mobile homes. *Indian Point Rd.* ☎ *800/888-1891 or 417/338-2250. www.indianpoint.com. 92 units, 32 cottages and cabins. $65–$98 double; $55–$95 cottages for 2 people; $92–$135 cabins for 2 people; $99–$155 condo double. Off-season rates and packages available. Amenities: 3 outdoor pools, in-room kitchens.*

Eating

Food ain't hard to come by in Branson, but you might have to invest a little time in finding a place beyond run-of-the-mill fast and/or fried foods. In addition to these choices, one place that stands out is **Happy Banana,** located in the Shoppes at Branson Meadows shopping arcade at 4580 Gretna Rd. (☎ **417/339-5577**), with its Caribbean theme, menu items like Jamaican jerked pork sandwiches and Cancún coconut shrimp, and live music Tuesday through Saturday nights, improv comedy Sunday evenings, and karaoke on Mondays.

CHEAP

➔**Branson Café** ★ AMERICAN This casual, busy, friendly diner in downtown Branson—a real regulars' hangout—has been the place to go since 1910 for down-home country cooking, including fried chicken, catfish, and sandwiches. Leave room for one of the famous pies. (In case it's closed or crowded, the **Farmhouse,** a similar local-diner scene, is right across the street.) *120 W. Main St.* ☎*417/334-3021. Reservations accepted. Main courses $4.50–$9.25. Mon–Sat 6am–8pm.*

DOABLE

➜**BT Bones Steakhouse** AMERICAN/ STEAKS Popular with an older crowd, this dimly lit restaurant/bar is one of the few places offering free live country music nightly from 6pm. Take in the tunes as you chow down on your choice of sandwiches, buffalo burgers, steaks, prime rib, chicken, and barbecue ribs. *2280 Shepherd of the Hills Expwy. (at Roark Valley Rd.).* ☎*417/335-2002. Reservations not accepted. Main courses $6.95–$23. Sun–Thurs 11am–10pm; Fri–Sat 11am–11pm.*

SPLURGE

➜**Candlestick Inn** ★★ STEAKS/ SEAFOOD On the other side of Lake Taneycomo, on a bluff with fine views over downtown Branson, this upscale restaurant with an outdoor deck is the place for romantic dining or a special occasion. In business since 1962, it specializes in fresh seafood like lobster tail and aged Black Angus beef, but the trout amandine and beef Wellington are stand-outs. Lunch serves up sandwiches, salads, quiche, and daily specials. *E. Hwy. 76.* ☎ *417/334-3633. www.candlestickinn.com. Reservations recommended. Main courses $19–$44. Wed–Fri 11am–3pm; Sun–Thurs 5–9pm; Fri–Sat 5–10pm (closed Mon in winter).*

➜**Top of the Rock** CALIFORNIA CUISINE Perched atop a mountain with one of the Ozarks' best views, this casual, relaxed lodge overlooks a golf course and Table Rock Lake. Sunsets are spectacular from the outdoor patio. Owned by Big Cedar Lodge and decorated in rustic woods and

If You Like Branson That Much . . .

If you're drawn to stay awhile in Branson, you might be a little strange, but you're certainly wise in terms of job hunting—because there are a lot of places hiring pretty much year-round and especially in the summer. If you can spare a season, you might inquire directly with a few of your favorite resorts and attractions to fill in during the vacation high season. It could make for your most memorable summer job ever. Plus you probably won't be spotted there by anyone you know.

stone, it's the best place in town (or perhaps the only) to get wood-fired pizzas, homemade pasta creations, and rotisserie half chicken. The grilled salmon, Kansas City strip steak, hamburgers, and sandwiches are also worth a try. *150 Top of the Rock Rd. (at MO 65 and 86).* ☎ *417/339-5320. Reservations recommended (request a window seat). Main courses $7.95–$28. Summer daily 11am–9:30pm; off season Sun and Wed–Thurs 11am–8pm, Fri–Sat 11am–9:30pm.*

Partying

There is a modicum of partying to be done in Branson, though not in freestanding bars, since most are folded into restaurants. One such friendly place to grab a beer is **Garfield's** on the south end of Branson's Landing (☎ **417/335-3701;** www. garfields.net), where you can grab a table on the patio around dusk and watch the evening mist rise up from Lake Taneycomo.

Rocky's Lounge, 120 N. Sycamore St. (☎ **417/335-4765**), is a downtown bar where younger folks occasionally congregate. Across Lake Taneycomo at 136 Carter Rd. is a more local sort of haunt called **Dillon's Pub** (☎ **417/334-9651**).

"Hillbilly": Before Country Became Country

For a lot of people, the term "hillbilly" isn't one you'd likely use in a complimentary way. But out here in Branson (and Kentucky, and Missouri, and Arkansas), "hillbilly" is the self-proscribed nomenclature of proud, God-fearin' country folk. Coined way back (and across the pond) in the 17th century, it was originally used by southern Irish Catholics toward northern, hill-dwelling Irish followers of Protestant King William III. It carried into the New World, commonly used by Confederate plantation owners in reference to rural types who lived mostly in the mountains of Appalachia and the Ozarks (and who remained neutral during the Civil War). By the 1950s, the term stuck to what is now known as country and Western music, and still generally refers to old-school country music by artists like Jimmie Rodgers and Hank Williams. It also, perhaps more commonly, is a term used to disparage small-town Americans and their culture—at least when it's not being embraced by the very same people in celebration of their heritage.

There are also many places to catch some live music over drinks, such as the **Club Vegas Supper Club,** 3431 W 76 Country Blvd. (☎ **417/337-5886**) and the ranch-styled steakhouse **B.T. Bones,** 2280 Shepherd of the Hills Expwy. (☎ **417/335-2002**). Loosen up with some country dancing at **Planet Branson** 'til 1:30am for a $5 cover (440 State Hwy. 248; ☎ **417/335-7881**).

What Else to See & Do

Surrounded by three pristine lakes, Branson has fishing, swimming, boating, and golfing (not in the lakes) for the outdoorsy types. It also has expansive nightlife from entertainers who present everything from country music to comedy and magic acts in more than 100 live shows daily. There are also many large and small theme parks and a handful of museums, including **Ripley's Believe It or Not!,** 3325 W. Hwy. 76 (☎ **417/337-5300**; www.ripleysbranson.com), showcasing oddities and records from around the world.

SHOWTIME

It all started in 1959 with the **Baldknobbers Jamboree** (☎ **417/334-4528**; www.baldknobbers.com), when four brothers began performing twice a week in a converted building by Lake Taneycomo (see "The Little Resort Town That Could—And Did," p. 754). In 1968, the **Presleys' Country Jubilee** (☎ **417/334-4874**; www.presleys.com) opened the first theater on West Highway 76, after years of performing to sellout crowds in cool underground venues—Ozark caves. Both are still going strong, offering family-oriented country music, dancing, and comedy.

They're joined by more than 45 other theaters, most with performances from mid-March or April to December and with two shows a day in peak season. Ticket prices average $22 to $32 for adults (more for dinner shows) and half price or free for kids. It's a Branson tradition for many performers to sign autographs after the show.

Branson was once known as *the* place for live country music. And though **Roy Clark, Mel Tillis,** the **Oak Ridge Boys,** and other country greats still return for engagements at Branson theaters, the past decade has brought an explosion of Las Vegas–style productions. Andy Williams was the first major non-country star to build a venue here in 1994 at his **Moon River Theatre** (☎ **800/666-6094** or 417/334-4500; www.andywilliams.com). Lately, entertainment includes everything from magic shows like the **Kirby VanBurch Show** (☎ 417/337-9333; www.starlite-entertainment.com) to throwbacks like **Lost in the '50s** and **Stuck in the '70s** (☎ 417/337-9333; www.starlite-entertainment.com for both). For comedy, Russian **Yakov Smirnoff** (☎ 800/336-6542 or 417/332-1234; www.yakov.com) is the big name with his own venue, and generally centers his acts on the quirks of everyday life and male-female relationships.

A strange, yet wildly popular show is by **Shoji Tabuchi** (☎ 417/334-7469; www.shoji.com), whose repertoire ranges from country and jazz to classical and Broadway, in shows glammed up with elaborate production numbers; lasers and visual effects; an 18-piece orchestra; and lots of sequins.

Physical feats come by way of **Incredible Acrobats of China** (☎ 417/335-2000; www.acrobatsofchina.com), and **Cirque** (☎ 800/884-4536 or 417/336-1220; www.remingtontheatre.com), with its fantastical sets, costumes, and athleticism onstage and in the air.

The **Dixie Stampede Dinner & Show** (☎ 800/520-5544 or 417/336-3000; www.dixiestampede.com), owned by Dolly Parton and billed as "Branson's Most Fun Place To Eat," is the big dinner show in town, featuring dishes served without silverware so as to eat with your fingers, like country folk. There you'll take in a buffalo stampede, horses, trick riders, races, singing, and dancing. Beware here of audience participation in friendly competition between Confederate and Yankee rivals.

Branson's oldest and most widely beloved theater is the **Shepherd of the Hills Homestead and Outdoor Theater** (☎ 800/653-6288 or 417/334-4191; www.theshepherdofthehills.com), an outdoor amphitheater that for more than 45 years has presented evening reenactments of Harold Bell Wright's 1907 novel, *The Shepherd of the Hills* (see "The Little Resort Town That Could—And Did," p. 754). The mystery/love drama unfolds on a football-field-size dirt stage with 80 performers, 30 horses, a fire, a shootout, a hoedown, comedy, and, essentially, entertainment for the whole family. During the day, the grounds are open for homestead tours of Old Matt's Cabin (the original home of the characters in the book), a trip up Inspiration Tower for fine views of the Ozarks, and horseback trail rides.

THEME PARKS

➔**Celebration City** Branson's newest theme park centers on the top events and eras of 20th-century America, with areas based on such themes as Route 66 and a boardwalk harking back to the days of arcades and amusement rides. Mostly, however, it's a place for evening family fun, with more than 30 rides and attractions (including three roller coasters) and a nightly outdoor laser and fireworks display that takes viewers on a visual tour of important events of the 20th century. *Hwy. 376.* ☎ *800/831-4FUN or 417/336-7100. www. silverdollarcity.com. Admission $27 adults. June–Aug Mon–Fri 2–10pm, Sat–Sun noon–10pm.*

➔**Silver Dollar City** About 5 miles west of Branson, this is the biggest and best of the area's theme parks, featuring more than a dozen thrill rides (such as the Wildfire roller coaster with its 15-story vertical drop and speeds up to 66 mph), imaginative playgrounds, live entertainment at a dozen arenas (from gospel to country and bluegrass), restaurants featuring tradi-tional cuisine, about 60 specialty shops, and nearly 100 resident craftspeople practicing their trades, all in a wooded, 1880s mountain-town setting. **Marvel Cave,** the site's original attraction, has 32 miles of passages, which you can explore with a guide on a 1-hour tour (included in the admission price to Silver Dollar City). Plan on arriving first thing in the morning to avoid traffic jams, and spend all day here. Kids of all ages love this place. *W. Hwy. 76.* ☎ *800/831-4FUN or 417/336-7100. www.silver dollarcity.com. Admission $39 adults. End of May to mid-Aug daily 9:30am–7pm; Sept–Dec Wed–Sun varying hours.*

➜ **White Water Park** This 12-acre water-park features a half-dozen rides and slides, a float down Lazy River, a wave pool, lots of water blasters, geysers, and shower shooters at Raintree Island. For little ones, there's Little Squirts Water Works slides, nozzles, and sprays. *3501 W. Hwy. 76.* ☎ *800/ 831-4FUN or 417/336-7100. www.silverdollarcity. com. Admission $32 adults. End of May to mid-June and end of Aug daily 10am–6pm; mid-June to mid-Aug daily 9am–8pm.*

TRAIN & BOAT TRIPS

Departing from downtown Branson's century-old depot from March to December, the **Branson Scenic Railway,** 206 E. Main (☎ **417/334-6110;** www.bransontrain.com), revives the romance of classic rail travel with 40-mile round-trips through the wooded Ozark hills aboard restored vintage 1940s and 1950s dome and passenger cars. (FYI: These trips appeal to a largely older crowd.)

For a lunch or dinner cruise on Table Rock Lake, board the showboat ***Branson Belle,*** 4800 Mo. 165 (☎ **800/831-4FUN** or 417/336-7100; www.silverdollarcity.com), a luxury paddle-wheel boat offering 2-hour cruises with dining, music, comedy, and entertainment April through December. For a land and water tour, **Ride the Ducks,** 2320 W. Hwy. 76 (☎ **417/334-DUCK;** www.bransonducks.com), is an 80-minute tour aboard World War II amphibious military vehicles, stocked with corny jokes and a cruise of Table Rock Lake (Mar–Dec).

PLAYING OUTSIDE

Those who fish favor Table Rock Lake for bass and Lake Taneycomo for trout.

State Park Marina, on Highway 165 inside Table Rock State Park (☎ **417/334-BOAT;** www.stateparkmarina.com), is Branson's closest marina. It's open from March to October, starting daily at 8am (at 7am June–Aug) until about dusk. It's free to get in, has several public swimming areas, and you can rent equipment 'n stuff while you're there: a rod and reel for half a day goes for just $5; a canoe is $19 for two hours; a ski boat is $199 for four hours; and a WaveRunner costs $119 for two hours.

Outdoor enthusiasts should head to **Dogwood Canyon Nature Park** (☎ **417/ 779-5983;** www.dogwoodcanyon.com), a beautiful 10,000-acre private wilderness refuge for elk, bison, Texas longhorns, deer, and other wildlife. For $34.95 you can get an all-day "Adventure Pass" to Dogwood that gives access to hiking, biking, tram tours, and self-guided trout fishing. It will cost an additional $15 for each add-on activity, be it a horseback ride or kayak or bike rental, and $25 per paddle-boat rental (seasonal). It's best to come early in the day, because the park is open at 8:30am in the winter months and at 8am the rest of the year, but closes as early as 4:30 in the winter, and at 6pm in the summer.

Some of the Branson area's seven 18-hole golf courses, open to the public year-round, are described in the brochure "Branson Golf," available at local Welcome Centers (☎ **800/296-0463**). A favorite is the 9-hole par 3 **Top of the Rock,** 150 Top of the Rock Rd. (☎ **417/339-5312**). It's owned by Big Cedar Lodge (which does everything to perfection), was designed by Jack Nicklaus, has great views of Table Rock Lake, includes a practice facility and a good restaurant, and is one of the few courses in the nation to be recognized as an Audubon Signature Cooperative.

Eighteen-hole **Branson Creek Golf Club** (☎ **417/339-4653;** www.branson creekgolf.com) is one of Missouri's top public courses. Open year-round, 18 holes (cart and pre-game range balls included) will set you back as little as $48 in January and February with fees rising as the summer comes: March, November, December $60; April $76; May through October $90 (Sun–Thurs) or $94 (Fri–Sat).

On the Road to Tulsa, OK

Branson, MO to Tulsa, OK via Eureka Springs, AR 220 miles

Say farewell to the semi-surreal world of Branson and ease back into reality with a nice country drive through northwestern Arkansas. You'll travel down some very quiet, curvy roads, and potentially miss some not-very-well-marked turns—just keep an eye on your odometer to gauge if you've gone too far. The main reason to take the chance on missed turns, however, is that this is a segment of incredibly lush Arkansas scenery that allows a glimpse into rural life in this corner of the country.

Once you're through this wedge of Arkansas, and the Ozark Mountains run out, you enter Oklahoma and can see the topography change from forest land to desert plains in a matter of miles. It's a mystical experience that essentially marks the halfway point of the trip, as well as the transition into the new lay of the land you'll be exploring over the next few days.

On the Road **Nuts & Bolts**

Where to Fill Up   Hopefully, you have enough gas when you leave Branson that you don't have to fill up there, because prices are higher in town. If you hang on for about 20 miles into Arkansas, gas should be noticeably cheaper. By the way, you might find a real dip in gas prices around Siloam Springs on the Oklahoma border.

The Tolls   A stretch of Rt. 412 in eastern Oklahoma, which is being converted into the Cherokee Turnpike (interstate), has a $2.25 toll.

The Fastest Way   Rt. 65 south for about 30 miles to Bear Creek Springs, AR, then west on Rt. 412 for about 175 miles straight into Tulsa. The whole trip should take around 3¹/₂ hours.

The Long Way Round   The super-scenic route is via 65 south for just 10 miles to 86, then west to the border town of Blue Eye. There you'll connect to 13 south for just a couple of miles, and onto 21 west for about 10 miles to Berryville. Then hop on 62 west and you'll arrive in Eureka Springs in less than 10 miles. Upon leaving Eureka Springs, head south on 23 for 8 miles and west on 12 (through Clifty) for 5 miles, to 45 south for 2 miles to Hindsville. There you'll connect to Rt. 412, where you head west

AMERICAN HIGHWAYS

and arrive in Tulsa in about 125 miles. Without stops and slow highway traffic, this drive should take you around 4 hours.

Rules of the Road   Yes, this is the most intricate, small-road segment of the whole cross-country trip, so do soak up the scenery *while* watching for road signs. It's also a great place to slow down and enjoy the rural pace, and don't be surprised if you're the only car on the road for some segments. However, once you reach Oklahoma on 412, stick to the speed limit because this highway's crawling with troopers.

Light Reading   Dumblaws.com reports that in Oklahoma, it's illegal to read a comic book while operating a motor vehicle. Glad that's cleared up. You can, however, talk on your cellphone, as Oklahoma has no ban on hand-held phoning while driving.

Lunch Stop   The small hillside village of Eureka Springs, AR, is the can't-miss lunch stop on this leg of the trip, so take a break, grab an iced tea, and watch the world go by.

Welcome to Tulsa

Wide open spaces—the song could've been written for Tulsa, a spacious little city built on boom times from the railroad, ranch, oil, and aviation industries. Through the past century its square mileage has compounded as the city line absorbed its suburbs, and today, "T-town" is considered a highly livable city with a sturdy economy. It is, however, still a low-key kind of town, where people stick to their cars (okay, trucks) rather than wearing out their shoes. Fortunately, a handful of quirky sights, music venues, museums, restaurants, and pro sports teams help mix it up.

Getting Around

It's a city that draws many a Midwestern visitor, thanks to its central location in the American plains. But mostly Tulsa is a driving town by and for locals, with just a couple of neighborhoods serving as good hubs for dinner, drinks, or an evening stroll.

One of them is the **Brady District,** on the northwest edge of downtown on and around East Brady St. This little enclave, sometimes called the "Blue Dome District"

for one its distinctive old buildings, is home to friendly bars with good pub grub.

Because Oklahoma was one of the first states where African Americans became landowners, Tulsa also has some genuine Southern culture, brought in by immigrants from the Southland. Most of the action is centralized north of Brady in the **Greenwood Cultural District,** where you'll find heritage sites and the Oklahoma Jazz Hall of Fame.

Over by the bend in the Arkansas River is **Brookside,** a larger shopping-and-dining main drag situated on South Peoria Avenue between 33rd and 52nd streets. A few blocks north of it is **Cherry Street** (technically 15th St.), where a few nice dinner spots line the strip between Peoria and Harvard.

Tulsa doesn't offer much for mass transit—just the infrequent **Tulsa Transit** buses (☎ 918/582-2100; www.tulsatransit.org)—and because it is quite spread out you might find yourself behind the wheel during the bulk of your visit. Still, once you find the restaurant, gallery, or other spot that's calling your name, you're sure to be greeted by a Tulsan who's overjoyed to have you there.

Tulsa Highlights

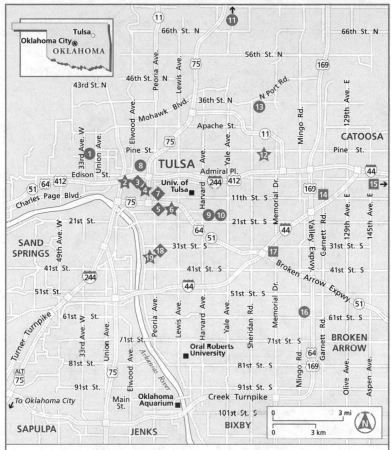

SLEEPING ■
Embassy Suites **17**
KOA Campground Tulsa **15**
Super 8 Motel **14**

ATTRACTIONS ●
All Star Sports Complex **16**
Bell's Amusement Park **9**
Golden Driller **10**
Gilcrease Museum **1**
Greenwood Cultural Center and
    Oklahoma Jazz Hall of Fame **8**
Tulsa Air & Space Museum **13**
Tulsa Speedway **11**

EATING ◆
Brookside Lao Thai **18**
Caz's Chowhouse **3**
Corner Café on
    old Route 66 **7**
Doe's Eat Place **5**

PARTYING ★
Bamboo Lounge **12**
Cain's Ballroom **2**
The Continental **4**
Crow Creek
    Tavern **19**
Kilkenny's Irish Pub **6**

Tulsa's Golden Driller.

Sleeping

Funny thing about Tulsa—there's a little strip of hotels that have their own little subdivision just off **I-44** near Memorial Drive. That's because this spot is just a quick hop from both the Tulsa Airport and the Expo Center, where much of the economical action is centered. You'll find all the usual suspects here, and mostly at around $99 to $149/night for luxury spaces: **Best Western Tulsa Inn** (3212 S. 79th E. Ave.; ☎ **918/858-2100**), **Embassy Suites** (3332 S. 79th E. Ave.; ☎ **918/622-4000**), **Hampton Inn** (3209 S. 79th E. Ave.; ☎ **918/663-1000**), and many more.

Detour: Eureka Springs, AR

Another big reason to take the long route to Tulsa is to stop for a spell in **Eureka Springs,** Arkansas. Named one of America's "Dozen Distinctive Destinations" by the National Trust for Historic Preservation, Eureka Springs first drew interest because of its natural springs with purported healing powers. It was settled in the late 1800s as a spa destination (it celebrated its 125th anniversary in 2004) and today its entire downtown district is on the National Register of Historic Places. While baths and spa treatments are still available, the city is nationally renowned for its art and well-preserved Victorian-era architecture. It's a charming, cozy village with historic homes, winding roads, and quaint (and I don't use that word flippantly) antiques and crafts shops.

You could spend hours, if not days, wandering around Eureka Springs' little hilly streets and ducking into small restaurants and shops with their handmade wares. One place you should go is the 19th-century **Basin Park Hotel,** 12 Spring St. (☎ **800/643-4972** or 479/253-7837; www.basinpark.com), where you can sit on the balcony and relax in peace over lunch or a midday coffee or iced tea.

The town also has attractions, including the **Eureka Springs and North Arkansas Railway,** 299 N. Main St. (☎ **479/253-9623;** www.esnarailway.com), a restored 1906 steam passenger train that takes a scenic route through the Ozark Hills. Architecture buffs shouldn't miss **Thorncrown Chapel,** off US 62 West (☎ **479/253-7401;** www.thorncrown.com), a church whose design, incorporating wood beams and glass in a woodland setting, was chosen in 2001 as one of the "Top 10 Designs of the 20th Century" by The American Institute of Architecture.

There are also tons of hotel chains large and small, and a few independents, all along I-44 making them easy to find and often a good bargain. Less expensive options, like in the $40 to $50 range, are nearer to the airport on the eastern side of Tulsa, like the **Super 8 Motel–Tulsa East** (11525 E. Skelly Dr.; ☎ 918/438-7700) and **Garnett Inn** (1036 S. Garnett Rd.; ☎ 918/438-4500).

If you're feeling the call to splurge, try the **Cedar Rock Inn** ★★ B&B, 4501 W. 41st St. (☎ 918/447-4493; www.cedarrock inn.com; suites $195–$295, but call for discounted rates), to relax in one of its five luxurious suites, each with a carved-wood fireplace. On the flipside, if you're trying to save a buck, there's camping at the **KOA Campground Tulsa,** 193rd East Ave. and I-44, Cartoosa, OK (☎ 918/266-4227; tent space for two $21–$25), which is actually the nearest camping to the city since tent camping is illegal within the city limits.

Eating

You may be surprised to find that steak and potatoes are not always on every menu in Tulsa. There are even a few Thai and sushi joints around if you need some actual non-red-meat and/or fiber in your supper.

Then again, this is cow country. And if steak is your thing, the first place to check out is **Doe's Eat Place** ★ on Cherry Street. Doe's specializes in T-bone, porterhouse, and sirloin cuts, and grills each one exactly—*exactly*—as you want it (1350 E. 15th St.; ☎ 918/585-DOES; www.does tulsa.com; steak entrees $17–$40+; daily 5–10pm).

AMERICAN HIGHWAYS

Tulsa, Oklahoma! The Playlist

→ *American Idiot*, **Green Day**, "American Idiot," 2004
→ *T-U-L-S-A*, **Asleep at the Wheel**, "Hang Up My Spurs," 2002
→ *Tulsa Time*, **Eric Clapton**, "Timepieces, Vol. I," 1988
→ *Take Me Back to Tulsa*, **Merle Haggard**, "Tribute to the Best Damn Fiddle Player," 1970
→ *Walkin' After Midnight*, **Patsy Cline**, 1961
→ *Wide Open Spaces*, **Dixie Chicks**, "Wide Open Spaces," 1998
→ *Hotwax*, **Beck**, "Odelay," 1996
→ *One Way or Another*, **Blondie**, "Parallel Lines," 1978
→ *Just Can't Get Enough*, **Nouvelle Vague**, "Nouvelle Vague," 2004

For more eclectic, homestyle burgers and such, grab a seat on the patio at **Caz's Chowhouse** ★★ (18 E. Brady St.; ☎ 918/588-CHOW; entrees $6–$12; Mon–Sat 2pm–2am; Sun 5pm–2am). If you're feeling the call of cheap and delicious Southeast Asian food, head to **Brookside Lao Thai** (3316 S. Peoria Ave.; ☎ 918/747-8812; lunch $6–$8; dinner $9–$14, and free Wi-Fi; lunch Mon–Fri 11am–2pm; dinner Sun–Thurs 5–10pm, Fri–Sat 5–11pm).

Before you hit the road again, grab a pancake sandwich, French toast, or standard bacon 'n eggs at the Western-U.S. chain **Village Inn** (2745 S. Harvard Ave. and other locations; ☎ 918/742-3515; breakfast $4–$8; Sun and Mon 6am–midnight; Tues–Sat 24 hr.), or go real local with the **Corner Café** on old Route 66 (1103 S. Peoria Ave.; ☎ 918/587-0081; breakfast served all day, $3.50–$7; daily 6am–9pm).

Partying

A good starting point is dinner at **Crow Creek Tavern** (3534 S. Peoria Ave.; ☎ 918/749-9100; Mon–Sat 11am–1am), or you can just pull up a chair for its great happy hour and hear a few local musicians, who take the stage nightly.

A great time and music galore await you at historic **Cain's Ballroom** ★★ (423 N. Main St.; ☎ 918/584-2306; www.cainsballroom.com), where the stage has been graced by the likes of Bob Dylan, Eric Clapton, Loretta Lynn, and Modest Mouse. It's also on the National Register of Historic Places. Call for nightly show times, special DJ nights, and prices.

The Continental (1st St. at Elgin; ☎ 918/592-7844; Tues–Fri 4pm–2am, Sat 8pm–2am) is a swell downtown drinks, apps, and live music haunt with $1.50 bottled beer during its 4 to 7pm weekday happy hour. You can also grab a Guinness and jaw with the locals at warm 'n friendly **Kilkenny's Irish Pub** (1413 E. 15th St.; ☎ 918/582-8282; Mon–Fri 11am–2am, Sat–Sun 10am–2am), where you can also fill up on great shepherd's pie.

Tulsa's got a couple of gay bars, and its oldest and friendliest one (though pretty guy-centric) is the **Bamboo Lounge**, 7204 E. Pine St. (☎ 918/836-8700; www.bambooloungetulsa.com; daily noon–2am).

Beyond these recommended joints, to find out what's on, get hold of a copy of the local entertainment paper *Urban Tulsa Weekly* (www.urbantulsa.com) to check out its surprisingly long lists of shows and venues.

Tulsa's Homage to Oil: the Golden Driller

He's 76 feet tall, weighs 43,500 pounds, and wears a size 112 hard hat. He's the **Golden Driller,** aka the "Giant Oil Man Statue," or "Tulsa Oil Man," or "Larry" (so I hear). No matter what you call him, he's T-town's biggest, proudest tribute to the oil industry. Located at 4145 E. 21st St. South, he stands guard outside the International Petroleum Exhibition (IPE) Building at the Tulsa State Fairground with his right hand resting on a genuine former oil derrick. "Golden Boy"—yet another nickname—was built in 1953 and was only a temporary addition to the IPE, but he was so popular that the city strengthened him and fixed him permanently to the site in 1966 (he got another makeover in 1979 that turned him to gold). The Driller, with his size 393DDD shoes (who measures this stuff?), can withstand 200-mph winds and has survived tornadoes, shotgun blasts, and even an arrow in the back. Good thing his ego is as big as his . . . feet.

What Else to See & Do

Like the city itself, things to do in Tulsa are sort of spread out, both by date and by geography. In light of this, when planning your trip, do some homework to make sure you'll be around to catch a cool festival, art expo, or rodeo while you're there.

But then again, there are some everyday places to go to get a little Dust Bowl flavor— apart from some of the cool bars and clubs. One place to start is an evening in the **Greenwood Cultural District,** known as "Black Wall Street" during the early-1900s heyday. Here, the **Greenwood Cultural Center and Mabel B. Little Heritage House,** 322 N. Greenwood Ave. (☎ 918/596-1020; www.greenwoodculturalcenter.com; Mon–Fri 9am–5pm, Sat 11am–1pm; free admission), will educate you on the city's rich African-American history— including in 1921 one of the country's worst race riots. Nearby, the Oklahoma Jazz Hall of Fame, 111 E. First St. (☎ 918/596-1001; www.okjazz.org; Tues–Sat 9am–6pm, Sat 9am–6pm), offers up listening kiosks, preserved photos, and other tributes to the state's jazz, blues, and gospel musicians. It also hosts special events and music nights.

OK: Here's some Tulsa Fairs & Festivals!

→ The **Oklahoma Blues Festival** takes over the Brady District every first weekend of May, turning the streets into a concert zone with food, drinks, and general carousing (☎ **918/583-6919;** www.okblues.com).

→ If jazz is more your bag, there's also the free Oklahoma **JazzFest** at downtown's Barlett Square in mid-June (☎ **918/596-1001;** www.okjazz.org).

→ The Expo Center gets crafty—and artsy—each mid-July thanks to the **Heart of Tulsa Arts and Crafts Show,** which hosts local and regional artists and craftsmen selling their wares (tickets $6 for all 3 days). Be on doily alert (**www.aaoth.com**).

→ September is time to check out blue-ribbon farm animals on parade at the **Tulsa State Fair.** The 2-week mix of rides, games, food, and exhibitions comes to the Expo Center every late September/early October ($8 tickets, ride prices vary; ☎ **918/744-1113;** www.tulsastatefair.com).

AMERICAN HIGHWAYS

Ride 'Em Cowboy! (or at least watch them from the bleachers)

So you'd love to see some rodeo while you're in Tulsa, eh? Good thing there's a barnyard full of tours and festivals to catch some action. Just remember to call and check websites for schedules and ticket information before you plan any trips—these bull-rider types sometimes need a little prodding.

→ The **Longhorn Championships Rodeo** arrives every late January at the Expo Square Pavillion (☎ **800-357-6336;** www.longhornrodeo.com).

→ There's also the **PRCA Xtreme Bulls Tour and Pace Pro Rodeo Chute-Out** at the Tulsa Convention Center (☎ **918/596-7111**—call for current schedule).

→ Tulsa also hosts the **Professional Women's Rodeo Association** tour at least once a year, sometimes as part of the PRCA, sometimes on its own (☎ **719/576-0900;** www.wpra.com—call for current schedule).

→ The **International Gay Rodeo Association** includes Tulsa with the help of its local partner, the Sooner State Rodeo Association. The 2007 rodeo takes place March 31st and April 1st (**www.soonerstaterodeo.com**—check site for location and details).

There are also many art galleries in **Brookside** and on **Cherry Street,** and pretty cool public art around town, especially along **Riverside Drive** through downtown as part of the NatureWorks program, which puts up new artists' sculptures about nature yearly.

MUSEUMS, ETC.

There's a good number of museums in Tulsa, particularly ones devoted to certain niche interests, like dolls and toys (**Willis Museum of Miniatures,** 627 N. Country Club Rd.; ☎ **918/584-6654**), linens (**International Linen Registry Museum,** 4107 S. Yale Ave.; ☎ **918/622-5223**), and fish, 📺 Best● **Oklahoma Aquarium** (300 Aquarium Dr.; **www.okaquarium.org**)—okay, I guess that last one's not so unusual, even for a land-locked state.

FREE → **Gilcrease Museum** ★ Tulsa's main museum is quite an impressive outfit, housing the world's largest collection of art of the America West—who knew it was all so interesting, and beautiful? It also features extensive anthropological collections from throughout the 20th century. *1400 N. Gilcrease Museum Rd.* ☎ *918/596-2700. www. gilcrease.org. Free admission. Daily 10am–5pm except Dec 25; public tours daily at 2pm.*

→ **Tulsa Air & Space Museum** ★ This former airplane hangar out by the Tulsa Airport—once the busiest in the world thanks to the oil industry—has been remade into an aeronautical, Air Force, and NASA–junkie's heaven. Pretend you're in *Top Gun* and have a seat in an F-14 Tomcat, take a ride in a flight simulator, or operate the same robotic arms that the Space Shuttle astronauts do. Then catch up on your constellations at the neighboring planetarium building. *3624 N. 74th E. Ave.* ☎ *918/834-9900. www.tulsaairandspace museum.com. Admission $10. Tues–Sat 10am–5pm; Sun 1–5pm.*

Cain's Ballroom.

PLAYING OUTSIDE

Whatever you do while in Tulsa, don't miss at least a quick glimpse of the **Golden Driller** outside the International Petroleum Exposition building (see "Tulsa's Homage to Oil: the Golden Driller," p. 765), and around the corner at **Bell's Amusement Park** (3901 E. 21st St.; ☎ 918/744-1991; open limited summer times only), see the **Zingo**—a classic wooden roller coaster. There's also the **All Star Sports Complex** (10309 E. 61st St.; ☎ 918/459-0399) for a little batting cage, video arcade, or minigolf action.

If you're more in the mood for some quiet, quality outdoors time, in north Tulsa (near the airport) there's the 1,665-acre **Mohawk Park,** where you can bring a picnic or grill your own, hike or bike one of nine trails, get in on a game at one of the fields, or just relax under the trees. If you want to ramp up the action, drive about 10 miles northwest of Tulsa to **Walnut Creek State Park** (☎ 918/865-2066; www. oklahomaparks.com) on Lake Keystone just outside of Prue, OK. There you can get in on swimming, boating, fishing, hiking, horseback riding, and even spend the night in one of 172 (wow!) campsites.

SPECTATOR SPORTS

There are four pro sports teams in Tulsa (two of which pay tribute to the oil industry, which says a little about the city, no?).

You can catch some **Tulsa Drillers** AA baseball at Drillers Stadium, 4802 E. 15th St. (☎ 918/744-5901; www.tulsadrillers. com), or head over to Expo Square, 21st Street South and Yale, to catch the **Tulsa 66ers** play basketball for the NBA Development League (☎ 918/585-8444; www.tulsa66ers.com). The downtown Tulsa Convention Center, 100 Civic Center, is home away from home for fans of the **Tulsa Oilers** hockey team (☎ 918/584-2000; www.tulsaoilers.com), and the local arena football team, the **Tulsa Talons** (☎ 918/664-4453; www.tulsatalons.com).

If the smell of motor oil is more your speed, there's also the **Tulsa Speedway,** up by Mohawk Park at 4424 E. 66th St. N. (☎ 918/425-7551).

On the Road to Amarillo, TX

Tulsa, OK to Amarillo, TX, 367 miles

You're in for a long, straight drive today, pardner. Sure, there are a few bends in the road on the way to Oklahoma City, but for the most part be ready for expanses of you and the open road—a terrific time to do some major pondering about virtually everything in the world. Believe me, you have time.

Detour: Oklahoma City

Start with a quick swing through Oklahoma City, where you can follow signs straight into downtown and visit the **Oklahoma City National Memorial and Museum** (☎ 888/542-HOPE). I had heard that this outdoor memorial of the 1995 bombing of the Murrah Federal Building was extremely well done, and remarkably powerful. It's true, and this is a stop worth making. (To get there coming in from Tulsa, connect from I-44 to I-235 south and exit at 6th Street. Follow the brown signs to the Memorial to 620 N. Harvey, at 6th Street. It's about 106 miles southwest of Tulsa.)

When you're ready to hit the road again, fill up your tank and head west on I-40. In less than an hour you can visit the **Oklahoma Route 66 Museum** in Clinton (see "Five Minutes with Pat Smith," p. 771), which is about 84 miles west of Oklahoma City, and then resume the long drive across the prairie to the center of the Texas panhandle. Don't be surprised if on this leg of the journey you sometimes see dark, strangely beautiful squalls looming on the horizon. Such afternoon storms are common, and you can usually drive right through them in just a few minutes (just not at 75 mph). If it's really bad, though, you can follow the lead of your fellow drivers who have pulled onto the shoulder while it passes.

Oklahoma City Memorial.

On the Road Nuts & Bolts

Where to Fill Up   This is the leg of the trip where gas stations are on the sparse side, so don't be shy about filling up when you still have half a tank—especially between Clinton and Amarillo.

The Tolls   There's a $3.50 toll on the Turner Turnpike (I-44) between Tulsa and Oklahoma City.

The Fastest Way   The speed limit is mostly 75 mph on the Oklahoma interstates, so it'll take you about 90 minutes (or so) on I-44 to cover the 109 miles west to Oklahoma City. Hop onto I-40 west, and if you stick with only gas stops from there, you'll get to Amarillo in about 4 hours (260 miles).

The Long Way Round   The side-road diversions are few and far between around these parts, but there are, once again, repeated turnoffs from the interstates to drive on "Historic Route 66" for a few dozen miles at a time. Upon leaving Oklahoma City on I-40, it's about an hour (85 miles) to Clinton, home of the Route 66 Museum. After Clinton, you're in for a good 175 miles of wide-open flat lands. Beware of sudden and intimidating thunderstorms—at least you can drive right through them.

Rules of the Road   75 miles per hour, baby! Listen, they're giving you the chance to *legally* drive really fast, so there's no need to push your luck by going faster . . . especially because troopers like to stake out on overpasses and behind bushes with their radar guns. They're pretty crafty, and their motto is "No tolerance."

Picnic Point   Halfway between Oklahoma City and Clinton, you can stop by Red Rock Canyon State Park near Hinton for a little picnicking, followed by a little rappelling down the canyon walls.

AMERICAN HIGHWAYS

Welcome to Amarillo

You made it! And your welcome wagon in Amarillo consists of a big neon cowboy waving "howdy!" to you as you drive across the city line. He is the herald of the city, and the **Big Texan Steak Ranch and Motel,** home of the free 72-ounce steak—so long as you finish it in an hour (p. 775).

Amarillo is right in the middle of the Texas Panhandle Plains. This region is distinguished by a high mesa—3,000 feet above sea level—that tapers downhill to the south and east, bordered by spectacular canyons and unique geological formations. Nomadic tribes inhabited the area for much of the last 12,000 years, and in 1541, Vásquez de Coronado claimed the land for Spain.

By 1845, Texas was the 28th American state, and significant change was on the way by the late 19th century. Ranchers began to graze cattle here, railroads crisscrossed the mesa, and agriculture took hold as the predominant industry. Million-acre ranches became the norm. During the fall and winter of 1874 and 1875, the indigenous tribes battled the U.S. Army in the Red River War, culminating with the dispersal of Comanches, Kiowas, and Southern Cheyennes to reservations in Oklahoma.

The landscape took another turn in the 1920s when oil was discovered, and ranchers found themselves sitting on "black gold" mines. (Check out the James Dean/Liz Taylor/Rock Hudson epic *Giant* for a great portrayal of life during this period.)

The Dust Bowl days devastated development in the 1930s, but the area eventually recovered and boom times were on again following World War II.

The Panhandle Plains might strike passersby as drab and monotonous, but the region is worth a closer look if you can afford the time. The magnificent palette of Palo Duro Canyon, the wild artistic injection brought on by Amarillo's Stanley Marsh 3, and the region's ranching heritage all are cool surprises worth some time on a cross-country trip.

As for Amarillo, whose name means "yellow" literally and "wild horse" figuratively, any visitor will find it to be charming, warm, and eclectic—so long as you can get beyond the strip malls and chain stores. The town is well-known as a cattle-shipping capital that "smells like money" when the Amarillo Livestock Auction is in full swing.

Take the highway that's the best . . . to Amarillo

→ *(Get Your Kicks On) Route 66,* **Bobby Troupe,** 1946 (other versions by Asleep at the Wheel, Rolling Stones, Brian Setzer Orchestra, Depeche Mode, Chuck Berry, John Mayer, and more)

→ *The Power Is On,* **The Go! Team,** "Thunder, Lightning, Strike," 2004

→ *Amarillo Fair,* **Aaron Watson,** "A Texas Café," 2006

→ *Amarillo Bound,* **Louis Homen,** "Never Too Late," 2002

→ *The Nashville Jump,* **Chet Atkins & Colorado Mountain Boys,** "High Rockin' Swing," 2004

→ *Steady, as She Goes,* **The Raconteurs,** "Broken Boy Soldiers," 2006

→ *Behind the Wheel,* **Depeche Mode,** "Music for the Masses," 1987

→ *Police & Thieves,* **The Clash,** "The Clash," 1977

Five Minutes with Pat Smith

Seein' as Oklahoma is the state with the most original Route 66 highway still in place, it's only right that the **Oklahoma Route 66 Museum** is the best place to learn the whole darn history. And there's no better way to take it in than with a tour from Pat Smith, the director who's been with the museum since its founding in 1995.

Pat makes you feel right at home, showing you through the 6 decades of the "Mother Road." Let her introduce you to authentic "filling station" pumps, old road signs, parking meters (invented in Oklahoma City), and whole cars—including a 1928 International Harvester with an engine held together by bailing wire.

The museum makes the most of its modest size. In less than an hour, you can tour through the history of the highway in rooms broken out by decade—each with accompanying music, relics, and photos. The 1950s room is like standing in a diner, complete with jukebox and 1951 Ford. The 1960s room is broken out into half family vacation/half psychedelic hippie roadtrip.

The last room is the 1970s and beyond, where you can also sit for a spell and take in the short film, "Route 66: An American Odyssey," and learn about how the highway was officially decommissioned in 1985.

"It took five interstates to replace Route 66," Pat says, adding that the museum sees more than 35,000 visitors a year, including many international Route 66 enthusiasts.

She will also tell you that there's no more appropriate place for the Route 66 Museum than Clinton, since this small town 85 miles west of Oklahoma City was the national headquarters for Route 66's construction in the 1920s. So check out the '55 Thunderbird in the front room, pick yourself up a key chain, and hit the road again (☎ 580/323-7866; www.route66.org).

It also has its agricultural roots intact, and is a popular stopover for tourists, with a plethora of motels and restaurants catering to the cross-country crowd.

Getting Around

Amarillo's location on a major east-west highway—Route 66 until 1970 and I-40 thereafter—has made it a bona fide strip town. The city's primary north-south artery is US 87, which splits into four one-way, north-south streets in the downtown area. (From the west, these streets are Taylor, Fillmore, Pierce, and Buchanan.) South of I-40, US 87 becomes I-27, which leads to Canyon and Lubbock. The northern boundary of downtown is 1st Avenue, the southern boundary I-40.

Sixth Avenue is Route 66 in town, and the Route 66 Historic District begins at 6th Avenue and Georgia Street and continues west along 6th Avenue for a mile to Western Street Amarillo Boulevard is a major east-west route through the northern stretch of the city. Along with Georgia Street, Ross-Mirror and Washington streets are among the busiest north-south roads in Amarillo. Loop 335 is comprised of four roads (Soncy Rd., FM 1719, Lakeside Dr., and Hollywood Rd.) that circumnavigate the city.

Aside from some one-way streets downtown, Amarillo is a snap to navigate by car, with relatively little traffic. (Instead of a rush hour, locals like to say they have a "rush minute.")

Amarillo City Transit (☎ 806/378-3095) is the bus system that runs Monday

AMERICAN HIGHWAYS

The "Dust Bowl" in a Nutshell

Welcome to the Great Plains, known in the 1930s as the "Dust Bowl" following decades of farming techniques that stripped the grass and exposed the soil. The 5-year drought that followed led to winds that blew away the region's topsoil—all of it—and led to an ecological disaster that left a half million Oklahomans, Arkansans, Kansans, and Texans homeless. Recovery began in 1935 under F.D.R. with the simple measure of planting trees. A lot of trees: 200 million trees, actually, planted as a belt from Abilene, Texas, to Canada. The government also started teaching farmers about soil conservation, crop rotation, and other measures to improve the land and prevent erosion. And when the rain finally returned in 1939, the Dust Bowl was washed away and fields of wheat returned.

through Saturday from 6:15am to 7pm, and accommodates shoppers heading to the big shopping centers, and visitors to Harrington Regional Medical Center. Adult rides cost 75¢.

Taxi service is provided by **AA Royal Cab** (☎ 806/379-5454), **Yellow Cab** (☎ 806/374-8444), and **Bob & Son Taxi Service** (☎ 806/373-1171).

Get added insight about things to do from the **Amarillo Convention & Visitor Council's** information center at 401 S. Buchanan St. (☎ 800/692-1338 or 806/374-8474; www.visitamarillotx.com), open 7 days a week. There's also the **Texas Travel Information Center** on the city's east side on Frontage Rd. just west of I-40.

Sleeping

Amarillo's location on I-40 makes it an ideal stopping point on cross-country trips. Several inexpensive mom-and-pop motels line Amarillo Boulevard (Loop 335) in northern Amarillo, but finding a good room in that area is a hit-or-miss proposition. A better bet is the I-40 corridor: You'll find dozens of cheap chain motels located just off the interstate, including **Best Western Amarillo Inn,** 1610 Coulter Dr. (☎ 800/528-1234 or 806/358-7861); **Courtyard by Marriott,** 8006 I-40 W.

(☎ 800/321-2211 or 806/467-8954); **Holiday Inn,** 1911 I-40 E. at Exit 71 (☎ 800/HOLIDAY or 806/372-8741); **Motel 6,** 6030 I-40 E. at Exit 66 (☎ 800/466-8356 or 806/359-7651); **La Quinta Inn,** 1708 I-40 E. at Exit 71 (☎ 800/531-5900 or 806/373-7486); and **Quality Inn and Suites,** 1803 Lakeside Dr. (☎ 800/847-6556 or 806/335-1561). Room taxes in Amarillo add about 15% to lodging bills.

CAMPING

Several camping options exist in and around Amarillo, with numerous RV campgrounds in the city as well as primitive tent-camping options at **Lake Meredith National Recreation Area** (see "What Else to See & Do," p. 779).

➜**Amarillo KOA** Located in a secluded spot near the airport on Amarillo's eastern fringe, this campground is in good shape. There's a heated outdoor pool, playground, game room, and gift shop with sundries and supplies. Plus, a chuck wagon dinner is served nightly during the summer. *1100 Folsom Rd.* ☎ *800/562-3431 (reservations only) or 806/335-1792. 123 sites, including RV spaces, 23 tent sites, and 5 cabins. $20–$30 campsites; $38–$50 cabins. Located east of Lakeside Dr. (I-40 Exit 75) via US 60.*

Amarillo Highlights

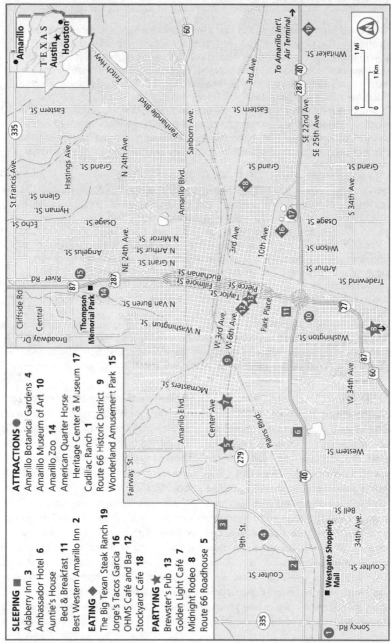

SLEEPING ■

Adaberry Inn **3**
Ambassador Hotel **6**
Auntie's House
 Bed & Breakfast **11**
Best Western Amarillo Inn **2**

EATING ◆

The Big Texan Steak Ranch **19**
Jorge's Tacos Garcia **16**
OHMS Cafe and Bar **12**
Stockyard Cafe **18**

PARTYING ★

Brewster's Pub **13**
Golden Light Café **7**
Midnight Rodeo **8**
Route 66 Roadhouse **5**

ATTRACTIONS ●

Amarillo Botanica Gardens **4**
Amarillo Museum of Art **10**
Amarillo Zoo **14**
American Quarter Horse
 Heritage Center & Museum **17**
Cadillac Ranch **1**
Route 66 Historic District **9**
Wonderland Amusement Park **15**

Abstract Artistic Expression

When you roam around Amarillo and see colorful municipal-style signs that say things like, "Road does not end" or "What is a village without village idiots?" you're looking at the work of one artistically inclined philanthropist. The man in question is Stanley Marsh 3, the grandson of an early Texas oilman. And by the way, he prefers the Arabic "3" over the Roman "III," as he finds it less pretentious. Whatever you say, Stan!

Marsh is the man behind 200 irreverent and random slogan-bearing signs on display outside Amarillo homes and businesses. The ever-enigmatic Marsh says of the signs, "They are to be looked at. The signs are just there, like the Rock of Gibraltar or the Statue of Liberty. They are a system of unanticipated rewards."

In the 1970s, Marsh collaborated with an art group called Ant Farm to create the quintessential roadside-kitsch attraction, the famous **Cadillac Ranch** (p. 778) on the west side of Amarillo. The ranch consists of 10 Cadillacs (years 1949 to 1963) half buried nose down in the earth, each with a few decades' worth of graffiti spraypainted on.

Marsh's eccentric public art vision extends south, too, to the junction of I-27 and Sundown Lane, where a sculpture of a pair of disembodied legs greets passersby. There's also "Floating Mesa"—hundreds of sheets of plywood painted the color of a blue sky on the side of a mountain. Unless it's overcast, the resulting impression is that the summit is floating. It is located about 8 miles northwest of Amarillo via Tascosa Road.

A lot of Marsh's neighbors are amused by his creations, but not all of them. Those Amarillians repelled by their presence have decried them as eyesores with little or no artistic value. In response, Marsh was once quoted as saying, "Art is a legalized form of insanity, and I do it very well."

DOABLE

→ **Ambassador Hotel** ★★ The 10-story Ambassador is Amarillo's tallest hotel. It's also the cowboy city's touch o' class. The rooms are spacious and many of the upper-floor rooms have great views. The lobby is a five-story atrium with a sloping glass enclosure over an excellent cafe and a small pool, and the service and amenities are the best in town. *3100 I-40 W. (Exit 68B on Georgia St.).* ☎ *800/817-0521 or 806/385-9869. www.ambassadoramarillo.com. 265 units, including 2 suites. $99–$129 double; $399 suite. Amenities: 2 restaurants; bar; indoor heated pool; exercise room; indoor Jacuzzi; courtesy car; business center; dataport in room.*

→ **Auntie's House Bed & Breakfast** ★ This 1912 Prairie Craftsman home, now on the National Register of Historic Places, is one of the panhandle's top urban B&Bs. Each room is themed with everything from sports to antiques to the frilly floral look. There's also the 800-square-foot "Enchanted Cottage" out back for you romantic types. It has a cozy bed, a large shower with two heads, a two-person Jacuzzi, and a bidet. Also in the backyard: a big hot tub and a barbecue for everyone. Breakfast at Auntie's includes innkeeper Corliss Burroughs's gourmet biscuits—butterscotch, strawberry cream cheese, and peach are just a few of the possibilities.

Cadillac Ranch.

1712 S. Polk St. ☎ *888/661-8054 or 806/371-8054. www.auntieshouse.com. 4 units, including 1 suite and 1 guest cottage. $89 double; $129 suite; $225 cottage. Amenities: Breakfast; outdoor Jacuzzi. No phone in room.*

SPLURGE

→**Adaberry Inn** ★★ The Adaberry Inn rose to national prominence when it served as Oprah Winfrey's home for 2 months in 1999 while she fought a defamation lawsuit brought on by Amarillo-area cattle ranchers (but that's another story). The thoroughly modern Adaberry B&B speaks for itself as to why she'd pick this place. The rooms are each themed after a particular city: Missoula features a Western motif; and Key West offers a more tropical setting with aquatic artwork, a latticed ceiling, and yellow walls. The best, though, is the Aspen suite (Oprah's room), which features a rock fireplace, a Jacuzzi for two, and ski-themed decor.

Seven of the rooms have private balconies or patios. There's also a game room with a putting green and a pool table downstairs, adjacent to a state-of-the-art home theater. You can watch sunsets over the Lost Canyon from the inn's main balcony, or wander on the trails in the Adaberry's backyard. *6818 Plum Creek Dr.* ☎ *806/352-0022. www.adaberryinn.com. 9 units. $109 double; $195 suite. Smoking and pets are not permitted inside the inn. Amenities: Breakfast; exercise room; game room; dataport.*

Eating

▼ Best ● →**The Big Texan Steak Ranch** ★★★ STEAK You'll see the first billboards touting the Big Texan's legendary deal—"Eat a 72-ounce steak dinner in an hour and get it for free!" (Homer Simpson did it!)—hours before it appears on the north side of I-40 upon entering town. Beyond the hype, the Big Texan is a unique attraction in itself, with a gift shop, motel, old-fashioned shooting gallery, and extensive collection of taxidermy and kitsch. Costumed cowboy musicians perform every night, and a full-blown Opry-style revue showcases local talent every Tuesday.

AMERICAN HIGHWAYS

The Big Texan serves 72-oz. steaks!

With so much going on, you might forget that the Big Texan is a restaurant, but its legendary steaks are what put the place on the map, and they're darn good. Beyond the 72-ouncer (which sports a $72 price tag if you don't finish it), the restaurant also serves juicy prime rib, rib-eye, and other steaks in a dinner that includes salad, bread, and two side dishes. A smattering of seafood and barbecue dishes help mix it up. Breakfast and lunch are comparable: all-American and ultra-hearty.

For the record, some 40,000 people have tried to eat the 72-ounce steak since its introduction in 1959, and nearly 7,000 have succeeded. One—a wrestler named Klondike Bill—inhaled two of the dinners in the 1-hour time limit. *7701 I-40 E. ☎ 800/657-7177 or 806/372-6000. www.bigtexan.com. Reservations accepted for large parties only. Main courses $5–$16 breakfast, $7.50–$30 lunch and dinner. Daily 7:30am–10:30pm.*

→ **Jorge's Tacos Garcia** TEX-MEX Jorge's proprietor, George Veloz II, dreamed of opening a Tex-Mex restaurant since he was in middle school. Fittingly, Jorge's Tacos Garcia is the spitting image of his childhood vision, right down to the stained-glass windows, century-old wrought-iron chandeliers, and the fountain out front. The "West Texas Tex-Mex" recipes are time-tested at Jorge's from a family that has been in the restaurant business for half of a century. Try the batter-free *rellenos,* the *enchiladas de chile verde,* and the *taquitos de barbacoa,* grilled tacos loaded with "Mexican barbecue." *1100 S. Ross St. ☎ 806/371-0411. Reservations not accepted. Main courses $6–$14. Mon 10:30am–9:30pm; Tues–Sat 10:30am–10pm; Sun 10:30am–3:30pm.*

→ **OHMS Café and Bar** ★ ECLECTIC My pick for a lunch spot, the chalkboard menu changes daily at this pleasant downtown eatery, which doubles as a gallery for local artists. (By the way, OHMS stands for "On Her Majesty's Service." It was named by the former owner, a native of the United Kingdom.) Lunch is served cafeteria-style, with regular offerings that include shepherd's pie, linguine with fresh basil and Brie, and herbed baked chicken, all with soup or salad (with tasty homemade dressings) and fresh bread. Dinner is a bit pricier and healthier than the Amarillo norm, and includes pan-seared salmon, rosemary-mustard pork loin, and ahi tuna. The art on display changes monthly, and live acoustic music is fairly regular. *619 S. Tyler St.* ☎ *806/373-3233. Main courses $7.50 lunch, $10–$20 dinner. Mon–Fri 11:30am–1:30pm; Thurs–Sat 6–10pm (bar open later).*

📺 **Best** 🎵 ➜ **Stockyard Cafe** AMERICAN   Where the Big Texan is kitschy and Disney-esque, the Stockyard Cafe is the real deal: Diners just don't get any more cowboy than this. Tucked away at the site of one of the largest livestock auctions in the world, this restaurant is smoky, old-fashioned, and furnished plainly with a few cowhides, burlap, and the requisite taxidermy thrown in. But it's the food that keeps those cattlemen coming—styled by a chef/owner from Texas who trained in New York. The chicken-fried steak and gravy is incredible, and so hearty it'll keep you full all day. But everything on the menu is fresh and Texas-size. By the way, don't be intimidated when you drive up and smell the livestock—it's clean and friendly inside. *100 S. Manhattan St., in the Amarillo Livestock Auction Building.* ☎ *806/374-6024. Reservations not accepted. Main courses $4.50–$10 lunch, $6–$10 dinner. Mon–Sat 6:30am–2:30pm; Fri–Sat 5–9:30pm.*

Partying

While there's not a wide variety of party places to pick from, there are two main nightlife districts to check out: the **Historic Route 66 District** and **South Polk Street** downtown, between 7th and 8th avenues. **Brewster's Pub,** 715 S. Polk St. (☎ **806/342-0782**), is what you might expect in a Texas town—it's a big sports bar with a game room and live music four nights a week.

Rough and raw, the **Golden Light Cafe,** 2908 W. 6th Ave. (☎ **806/374-9237**), is a Route 66 landmark, open since 1946 with a grill and heaps of nostalgia. For country and Western fans, there's **Midnight Rodeo,** 4400 S. Georgia St. (☎ **806/358-7083**), featuring a gargantuan dance floor centered about an oval bar. Another good venue for live music—primarily country—is the hubcap-laden **Route 66 Roadhouse,** 609 S. Independence St. (☎ **806/355-7399**), where you'll also find pool tables and dartboards.

What Else to See & Do

Just when you thought you'd be in and out of Amarillo in no time, they go and offer up a barnyard full of museums, shopping, parks, and sporty stuff to do. And you may find that the Texas mood begins with the right duds.

Head over to **Cavender's Boot City,** 7920 I-40 W. at Coulter Drive (☎ **806/358-1400**), for a huge selection of boots, along with hats, belt buckles, jeans, jewelry, and practically every other Western wearable on the market. There's also Amarillo's biggest enclosed shopping center, the **Westgate Shopping Mall,** 7701 I-40 W., between the Coulter Drive and Soncy Road exits (☎ **806/358-7221;** www.westgatemalltx.com), where you'll find the usual chain stores and a few local proprietors. You can go vintage shopping in the **Historic Route 66 District** (W. 6th Ave. between Georgia and Western sts.), where more than 100 stores add some old-school flair to local shopping, eating, and the occasional street festival.

ATTRACTIONS

➜ **American Quarter Horse Heritage Center & Museum** Dedicated to the history of the equine breed named for its

Amarillo Events: How About Some Rodeo?

Fairs and festivals in Amarillo are limited to a few big ones, and a few niche celebrations. And of course, plenty of rodeo action.

→ Get your kicks at the **Tri-State Fair & Rodeo** every mid-September. This weeklong festival at the Tri-State Fairgrounds will cost to $8, but in return you get live music, PRCA rodeo events, and some funky random entertainment, like a hot-wing eating contest, and ventriloquist and "master" hypnotist shows (☎ 806/376-7767; www.tristatefair.com).

→ Don your 10-gallon Stetson for the annual **Old West Days & Ranch Riders Rodeo,** with its parade, costume contests, and rodeo out at Bell Avenue at Amarillo Boulevard (though there's a rumor the location may change soon). It's put on annually by the Will Rogers Range Riders for July 4th (☎ 806/355-2212).

→ Who knew there was so much Celtic pride in the Panhandle Plains? Nevertheless, the history and heritage of people who helped build the region is celebrated at **Celtic Festival and Craft Faire,** happening in mid-October at the Tri-State Fairgrounds (**www.celticamarillo.org**).

→ The Working Ranch Cowboys Association (WRCA) holds its annual **World Championship Ranch Rodeo** in Amarillo in mid-November. Real working cowboys compete in wild cow milking, bronco riding, and team penning at the Amarillo Civic Center (☎ 806/378-3096; www.wrca.org).

→ In early June, there's the **Cowboy Roundup USA,** with a ranch rodeo and a chuck wagon cook-off over at the Tri-State Fairgrounds (☎ 806/372-4777; www.cowboyroundupusa.org).

speed when racing a quarter-mile, this museum explains and explores all things horses and the culture surrounding them. If you dig the equine, expect to spend an hour or so here, starting with the welcome show in the modern Theater of America's Horse. Galleries and exhibits follow, there are also live demonstrations at an on-site stable. *2601 I-40 E. at Quarter Horse Dr.* ☎ *806/376-5181. www.aqha.org. Adults $4. Daily Mon–Sat 9am–5pm; June–Oct Sun noon–5pm.*

FREE →**Cadillac Ranch** ★ One of the country's more recognizable and bizarre roadside attractions, Cadillac Ranch is where you'll find 10 vintage Cadillacs (dating 1949–64) buried up to their backseat in a wheat field west of Amarillo, rising out of the earth at the same angle as Cheops Pyramid in Egypt. Conceived and funded by Amarillo's Stanley Marsh 3, the eccentric grandson of one of the Panhandle's most successful oilmen, Cadillac Ranch was constructed in 1974 in cahoots with the Ant Farm, a San Francisco–based art collective. It was relocated west in 1997 to its present site to escape the shadow of Amarillo's growth. Cadillac Ranch is also interactive, seein' as Marsh encourages visitors to add their creative touches with spray paint, markers, or keys (see "Abstract Artistic Expression," p. 774). *I-40 W., South Frontage Rd. between exits 60 (Arnot Rd.) and 62 (Hope and Holiday roads). Free admission. Daily 24 hr.*

MORE ATTRACTIONS

→**Amarillo Botanical Gardens** Horticulture is on parade at these outdoor gardens, with displays of flora indigenous to the high plains region. It's also a pleasant, if low-key, spot to take a 30-minute break from the road. There's also a special "scent garden" designed for visitors with sight impairments. Temporary exhibits on regional horticultural subjects are housed indoors here, too, as is a new tropical greenhouse. *1400 Streit Dr., at Harrington Regional Medical Center.* ☎ *806/352-6513. www.amarillobotanicalgardens.org. Adults $4. Tues–Fri 9am–5pm; Sat–Sun 1–5pm.*

FREE → **Amarillo Museum of Art** The only accredited art museum for miles around, this institution houses quite a collection of paintings, photographs, and sculptures in its galleries, and a smaller permanent collection with many a piece of regional 20th-century art, as well as a nice Asian exhibit. The museum hosts nearly 20 changing exhibits annually in its six galleries; recent programs included works by Georgia O'Keeffe, a former area resident. *2200 S. Van Buren St., on the campus of Amarillo College.* ☎ *806/371-5050. www.amarilloart.org. Free admission. Tues–Fri 10am–5pm (until 9pm on Thurs); Sat–Sun 1–5pm. Closed major holidays.*

FREE → **Amarillo Zoo** It's a small and generally unspectacular zoo, though it excels at preserving and displaying the High Plains indigenous, or "Texotic," animals. The highlight is a 20-acre range populated by grazing bison. There's also the mustang, the wild horse of the American West, and mountain lions, Texas longhorns, and spider monkeys. *Thompson Memorial Park, about 1 mile north of downtown on US 287.* ☎ *806/381-7911. Free admission (donations accepted). Tues–Sun 9:30am–5pm. Closed major holidays.*

→ **Wonderland Amusement Park** An Amarillo landmark since the glory days of Route 66, Wonderland is the Panhandle's top amusement park, with two dozen nostalgic rides on a 15-acre chunk of Thompson Park. Summon your inner child to ride the three roller coasters, six water rides, and carousel. There's also a minigolf course and an arcade. *2601 Dumas Dr., at Thompson Memorial Park.* ☎ *800/383-4712 or 806/383-3344. www.wonderlandpark.com. Individual rides $1.50 each plus a $4 gate admission fee. Unlimited rides $11–$13 weeknights, $15–$19 weekends. Apr to Labor Day Sat–Sun 1–10pm; May Tues and Thurs–Fri 6:30–9:30pm; June to mid-Aug Mon–Fri 7–10:30pm; Sept–Oct Fri–Sun 7–10pm. Closed Nov–Mar.*

HANGING OUT/PARKS

There's plenty of outdoor recreation in Amarillo, from golf courses to pools and parks, as well as several lakes, reservoirs, and state parks in the area. The best recreation spot is **Palo Duro Canyon State Park** (☎ 806/488-2227; www.paloduro canyon.com) about 27 miles southeast of the city.

The 60-mile Palo Duro Canyon is home to colorful cliffs, groves of juniper and cottonwood trees, and other awe-inspiring geology and natural attractions. Of the 200 species of animals that venture into the canyon, you're most likely to see mule deer and wild turkeys. There's also the famed Pioneer Amphitheatre, the venue for the musical drama *Texas Legacies;* several hiking, biking, and horseback riding trails; and a visitor center/museum/bookstore with interpretive exhibits on the canyon's formation, history, and wildlife.

The park's admission fees for day use are $3 adults, $2 seniors, free for children ages 12 and under. There are additional fees for campsites (see "Camping," below). The gates are open daily 8am–10pm.

The **Lake Meredith National Recreation Area** (☎ 806/857-3151; www.nps.gov/lamr), 38 miles northeast of Amarillo via Tex. 136, is another outdoor hot spot, with boating, fishing, hunting, horseback riding, camping, hiking, swimming, scuba diving, wildlife and bird-watching, and four-wheeling. The site is also home to **Alibates Flint Quarries National Monument** (www.nps.gov/alfl), the point of origin for a significant percentage of arrowhead points found throughout the Great Plains. While the monument is closed to most recreational activity, there are guided tours during the summer at 10am and 2pm and at other times of the year by reservation. Aside from boat-launching fees, access to Lake Meredith is free to the public.

Wildcat Bluff Nature Center, 2301 N. Soncy Rd. (☎ **806/352-6007;** www.wildcatbluff.org; adults $3), is the best spot for hiking and wildlife viewing in the city itself, offering about 2 miles of moderate trails on its 600 acres of cottonwood-shaded hills. The center's wildlife population includes mule deer, horned toads, coyotes, and turkey vultures.

The major city parks in Amarillo include: **Thompson Memorial Park,** at Dumas Drive and 24th Avenue, home to Wonderland Amusement Park and the Amarillo Zoo, as well as a 36-hole golf course, 1 mile of jogging/walking trails, a heated outdoor pool (open seasonally), ball fields, picnic sites with grills, and fishing ponds; **John S. Stiff Memorial Park,** at SW 48th Avenue and Bell Street, with ball fields, three indoor and eight outdoor tennis courts, an outdoor heated pool, and picnic sites; and **Southeast Regional Park,** at SE 46th Avenue and Osage Street, with an outdoor heated pool, ball fields, fishing ponds, and picnic areas. You can call the Parks and Recreation Department at ☎ **806/378-3036** for more details on local parks.

FISHING

Catfish and bass are the top choices for anglers in the Panhandle. For no fee (outside of the cost of a Texas state fishing license), you can hit several ponds in Amarillo's city park system, including **Thompson Memorial Park** at Dumas Drive and 24th Avenue, **Martin Road Park** at NE 15th Avenue and Mirror Street, **Southeast Regional Park** at SE 46th Avenue and Osage Street, and **Harrington Regional Medical Center Park** at SW 9th Avenue and Wallace Street. **Lake Meredith National Recreation Area** is another popular regional fishing spot. At the lake's marina (☎ **806/865-3391**) you can pick up basic fishing supplies, concessions, and a fishing hut ($4 for 12 hr.).

HIKING & BIKING

Aside from the hiking opportunities at **Wildcat Bluff Nature Center,** there are two hiking trails at **Lake Meredith National Recreation Area.** The Devil's Canyon Trail is a moderate one-way trail that leaves from Plum Creek on the north side of the lake and continues into the canyon for 1.5 miles. Numerous foot trails also traverse **Palo Duro Canyon State Park.**

The closest mountain biking trails to Amarillo are 27 miles away in **Palo Duro Canyon State Park.** The 3-mile Devil's Canyon Trail at **Lake Meredith National Recreation Area** is also accessible to mountain bikers.

HORSEBACK RIDING

There are several horse-friendly trails in **Lake Meredith National Recreation Area,** in McBride Canyon and alongside Plum Creek on the lake's north side. The National Park Service provides corrals at the Plum Creek and Mullinaw campgrounds, but riders need to bring their own horses. **Palo Duro Canyon State Park** also has 1-hour guided horse tours for $20.

SPECTATOR SPORTS

The **Amarillo Gorillas** play in the Central Hockey League at the Amarillo Civic Center (the "Jungle"), 401 S. Buchanan St. in downtown Amarillo (☎ **806/242-7825** for ticket information; www.amarillogorillas.com). The schedule runs from mid-October to late March with ticket prices ranging from $10 to $20.

Motor-sports fans can get a racing fix at **Route 66 Motor Speedway,** about 10 miles east of downtown Amarillo at 3601 E. Amarillo Blvd. (☎ **806/383-7223**). The oval dirt track is ¹/₂ mile long. Races are held on Saturday nights from mid-April to October; admission is $6 to $20.

On the Road to Albuquerque, NM

Amarillo, TX to Albuquerque, NM 290 miles

Let's be honest: There's not a whole lot to the 4-hour drive between Amarillo and Albuquerque, I-40 is a pretty straight road due west, with what has by now become the common turn-offs to cruise on Route 66 for short and/or long segments. This is not a complaint, though—it's actually a cool tour, with deserts and mountains in the distance, and a chance to let the serenity of the Southwest wash over you. (But still beware of state troopers ready to catch you exceeding the 75-mph speed limit.)

There is a good midway point in Tucumcari, New Mexico, where you can stop for lunch or an ice cream at one of a few classic diners in this small desert town. And while you're there, snap a photo of yourself at the **Blue Swallow Motor Court,** since it's one of the real-deal Route 66 relics.

Welcome to Albuquerque

It's a pretty organized town, that Albuquerque, NM ("There's a NEW Mexico?" C. Montgomery Burns). And mighty warm and friendly, too—the kind of charming city you fantasize about living in after just an hour or so of basking in the nice weather and easygoing pace. Fortunately, that means it's a nice place to visit, too, and there are lots of great restaurants and attractions.

Albuquerque is on the Rio Grande River, a waterway that's allowed a city to spring up in this vast desert, and it continues to be at the heart of the area's growth.

New Mexico-Style Mellow Musica Playlist

→ *Buddy,* **De La Soul,** "3 Feet High and Rising," 1989

→ *New Mexico,* **Johnny Cash,** "Original Sun Sound of Johnny Cash," 1958

→ *Callin' in Twisted,* **Reverend Horton Heat,** "Revival," 2004

→ *Ocean Breathes Salty,* **Modest Mouse,** "Good News for People Who Love Bad News," 2004

→ *Poster of a Girl,* **Metric,** "Live It Out," 2005

→ *The Sporting Life,* **The Decemberists,** "Picaresque," 2005

→ *Scarlet Begonias,* **Sublime,** "40 Oz. to Freedom," 1992

→ *Chan Chan,* **Buena Vista Social Club,** "Buena Vista Social Club," 1997

AMERICAN HIGHWAYS

Combined with the railroad, which set up a major stop here in 1880, Albuquerque has had an economic explosion in the past century. It was a major national center for military research and production since WWII, and became a trading center for the state, whose populace is widely spread across the land.

Albuquerque Nuts & Bolts

Area Code   The telephone area code for New Mexico is 505, and the state cell-phone area code is 575.

Business Hours   **Offices** and **stores** are generally open Monday to Friday, 9am to 5pm, with many stores also open Friday night, Saturday, and Sunday in the summer season. Most **banks** are also open Monday to Friday, 9am to 5pm. Some may be open Saturday morning. Most branches have ATMs available 24 hours. Call for specific hours.

Dentists   Call the Albuquerque District Dental Society (☎ 505/237-1412) for emergency service.

Doctors   Call the Greater Albuquerque Medical Association (☎ 505/821-4583) for information.

Emergencies   For police, fire, or ambulance, dial ☎ **911.**

Hospitals   The major hospital facilities are **Presbyterian Hospital,** 1100 Central Ave. SE (☎ 505/841-1234, or 505/841-1111 for emergency services); and **University of New Mexico Hospital,** 2211 Lomas Blvd. NE (☎ 505/272-2111, or 505/272-2411 for emergency services).

Internet Access   For $3 you can use a public library computer for a 3-hour period. Several branches of the library also offer free Wi-Fi. The city provides free Wi-Fi at many public locales, including the **Civic Plaza, Aquarium & Botanic Garden,** and several different **transit centers.** It's a well-wired town, so you'll find hotspots in lots of cafes, restaurants, and bars, too.

Library   The Albuquerque/Bernalillo County Public Library's **main branch** is at 501 Copper Ave. NW, between Fifth and Sixth streets (☎ 505/768-5140). You can find the locations of the 17 branch libraries at **www.cabq.gov/library**.

Liquor Laws   The legal drinking age is 21 throughout New Mexico. Bars may remain open until 2am Monday to Saturday and until midnight on Sunday. Wine, beer, and spirits are sold at licensed supermarkets and liquor stores. It is illegal to transport liquor through most Native American reservations.

Lost Property   Contact the city police at ☎ 505/242-COPS.

Newspapers & Magazines   The two daily newspapers are the *Albuquerque Tribune* (☎ 505/823-7777; www.abqtrib.com) and the *Albuquerque Journal* (☎ 505/823-7777; www.abqjournal.com). You can pick up the *Alibi* (☎ 505/346-0660; www.alibi.com), Albuquerque's free alternative and entertainment weekly, at newsstands all over town, especially around the University of New Mexico.

Pharmacies   **Walgreens** has many locations in Albuquerque (☎ 800-WALGREENS). Two centrally located ones that are open 24 hours are 8011 Harper Dr. NE at Wyoming (☎ 505/858-3134) and 5001 Montgomery Blvd. NE at San Mateo (☎ 505/881-5210).

Police   For emergencies, call ☎ **911.** For other business, contact the **Albuquerque City Police** (☎ 505/242-COPS) or the **New Mexico State Police** (☎ 505/841-9256).

Post Offices   To find the nearest U.S. Post Office, dial ☎ 800/275-8777. The service will ask for your zip code and give you the closest post office address and hours.

Radio   The local AM station KKOB (770) broadcasts news and events. FM band stations include KUNM (89.9), the University of New Mexico station, which broadcasts Public Radio programming and a variety of music; KPEK (100.3), which plays alternative rock music; and KHFM (95.5), which broadcasts classical music.

Taxes   In Albuquerque, the sales tax is 5.8125%. An additional hotel tax of 5% will be added to your bill.

Taxis   Yellow Cab (☎ 505/247-8888) serves the city and surrounding area 24 hours a day; fare is $5.36 for the first mile, $2.50 for each additional mile, and $1.07 for each extra passenger.

Television   There are five Albuquerque network affiliates: KOB-TV (Channel 4, NBC), KOAT-TV (Channel 7, ABC), KQRE-TV (Channel 13, CBS), KASA TV (Channel 2, FOX), and KNME-TV (Channel 5, PBS).

Time   All of New Mexico is on Mountain Standard Time. It's 2 hours earlier than New York, 1 hour earlier than Chicago, and 1 hour later than Los Angeles.

Transit Information   **ABQ Ride** is the public bus system. Call ☎ 505/243-7433 for schedules and information.

Weather   For time and temperature, call ☎ 505/247-1611. To get weather forecasts on the Internet, check www.accuweather.com and use the Albuquerque zip code 87104.

Getting Around

BY CAR

The city's sprawl takes a little bit of getting used to, because at first it seems like Albuquerque is just a grid of big roads lined with malls and fast-food joints fronting the residential areas tucked behind them.

The city is essentially split into quadrants created by the north–south I-25 and the east–west I-40. A lot of the city's main attractions are in the southwest quadrant, including **downtown** and **Old Town.** Downtown is pretty much all suits and heels by day, but at night it turns into quite

the nightlife scene. **Old Town** is the most touristy part, and makes you feel like you're walking in a Southwestern village with adobes and a town square. Albuquerque's aquarium and botanical gardens are here, as well as its zoo.

The area you might be drawn to is in the southeast **University of New Mexico district,** or **Nob Hill,** where Central Avenue is the "new" name of **Route 66.** This strip is still home to old court motels with their funky '50s signs, and it's also where you'll find many cool little cafes and shops. Nearby Lomas Street has a similar scene.

AMERICAN HIGHWAYS

Detour: All Around Albuquerque

There are plenty of things to see and do outside of the Albuquerque city limits. You can drive up the **Turquoise Trail** (NM 14) to Madrid ("MAH-drid") in under 30 minutes to hang out with hippie artist types, and/or take a little jaunt to Santa Fe (p. 468) for some genuine New Mexico tourist culture.

There are also 10 Native American pueblos located within an hour's drive. Two of them, the Coronado and Jemez state monuments, preserve ancient pueblo ruins. If you'd like to combine a tour of the archaeological sites and inhabited pueblos, consider driving the **Jemez Mountain Trail** ★. Head north on I-25 to Bernalillo, where you can visit the **Coronado State Monument.** Continue west on US 550 to Zia Pueblo. Six miles farther on US 550 takes you to NM 4, where you'll turn north and drive through orchards and along narrow cornfields of **Jemez Pueblo.** Farther north on NM 4, you'll find another archaeological site, the **Jemez State Monument.** You'll also find Jemez Springs, where you can stop for a hot soak. The road continues to the **Los Alamos** area, where you can see the spectacular ruins at **Bandelier National Monument.** From there you have the option of returning the way you came or via Santa Fe.

And speaking of pueblos, remember that non–Native Americans are welcome to visit pueblos and reservations, so long as the tribal laws and guidelines are followed.

Generally, stay out of cemeteries and ceremonial rooms as these are sacred grounds—not museums or tourist attractions. Don't peek into doors and windows, and don't climb on top of buildings. Also, most pueblos require a permit to carry a camera or to sketch or paint on location, and many prohibit photography at any time.

Don't wander around on your own, and don't go into private buildings without being escorted by someone who lives there or who has the authority to take you inside. Be respectful of ceremonial dances, and don't speak during or applaud after them—they aren't dancing for your amusement; they are dancing as part of their ceremony.

Roughly paralleling I-40 to the north is **Menaul Boulevard,** the focus of midtown and uptown shopping, as well as the hotel districts.

And if you're looking for an address, remember to note the directional of NE, NW, SE, or SW, because Central Avenue divides the city into north and south, and the railroad tracks (running just east of First Street downtown) divide it east from west.

Parking

Since you're most likely going to be driving through this spread-out town, you'll be glad to know that parking is generally not tough here. There are meters on most main streets, but they're only in effect weekdays 8am to 6pm. As for hotels, really only the large downtown hotels charge for parking.

By the way, traffic is really only a problem at certain hours. Avoid I-25 and I-40 at the center of town around 5pm.

BY BUS & TROLLEY

Albuquerque is easy to navigate, and has a pretty efficient mass-transit system in **ABQ Ride** (☎ 505/243-7433; www.cabq. gov), which is everywhere in town. Adult fares are $1, and you can get all the routes

Albuquerque Highlights

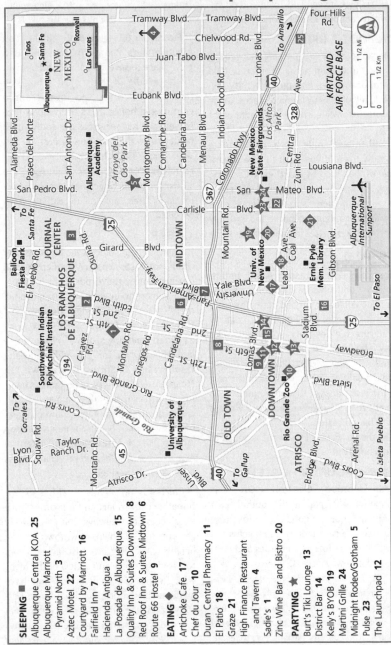

SLEEPING ■
Albuquerque Central KOA **25**
Albuquerque Marriott
Pyramid North **3**
Aztec Motel **22**
Courtyard by Marriott **16**
Fairfield Inn **7**
Hacienda Antigua **2**
La Posada de Albuquerque **15**
Quality Inn & Suites Downtown **8**
Red Roof Inn & Suites Midtown **6**
Route 66 Hostel **9**

EATING ◆
Artichoke Cafe **17**
Chef du Jour **10**
Duran Central Pharmacy **11**
El Patio **18**
Graze **21**
High Finance Restaurant
and Tavern **4**
Sadie's **1**
Zinc Wine Bar and Bistro **20**

PARTYING ★
Burt's Tiki Lounge **13**
District Bar **14**
Kelly's BYOB **19**
Martini Grille **24**
Midnight Rodeo/Gotham **5**
Pulse **23**
The Launchpad **12**

and schedules on its website. There's also a $1 trolley between Old Town and downtown attractions; it runs every 35 minutes.

ON FOOT & BIKE

You can get away with parking and walking in the three main areas of interest (Old Town, downtown, and the university district). All of them are nice places to be outside for a while with no particular place to go.

And Albuquerque is a really bike-friendly town. If you want to take advantage of that, stop by **Northeast Cyclery,** 8305 Menual Ave. NE (☎ **505/299-1210**), for a rental. There, a 24-hour rental runs $25/day for mountain bikes and $30/day for road bikes; prices include a helmet.

Sleeping

Albuquerque has many, many hotels, which is good news for those of us looking for nice rooms at a good rate. The only time this bargain-hotel deal doesn't apply is during big festivals—specifically, the New Mexico Arts and Crafts Fair (late June), the New Mexico State Fair (Sept), and the Balloon Fiesta (early Oct). The rest of the year, most of the city's hotels have vacant rooms so guests can usually score some bargain rates.

By the way, a tax of nearly 11% is added to every hotel bill.

CAMPGROUNDS/HOSTELS

➔**Albuquerque Central KOA** This campground/RV park in the foothills east of Albuquerque is a good choice for those who want to save money and be close to town. It offers lots of amenities and convenient freeway access. *12400 Skyline Rd. NE.* ☎ *800/562-7781 or 505/296-2729. www. albuquerquekoa.com. $19–$36 tent site; $38–$55 1-room cabin; $48–$65 2-room cabin. All prices valid for up to 2 people. Additional adult $5, child $3. Free parking. Pets welcome. Amenities: Outdoor pool (summer only);* *Jacuzzi; bike rentals; store; coin-op laundry; bathhouse; miniature golf; playground; wheelchair-accessible restroom; free Wi-Fi.*

➔**Route 66 Hostel** Right on Albuquerque's Route 66 strip, this is a great place to save a buck and still be right in the middle of things, just a hop-skip from downtown and Old Town. It's in a century-old house that's been nicely preserved, and has served as a friendly youth hostel since the '70s. *1012 Central Ave. SW.* ☎ *505/247-1813. http://members.aol.com/ route66hos/htmlRT66/. $15 dorm-style, $20 single, $25 double. Amenities: Kitchen access including free snacks; no curfew; linen rental $1.*

CHEAP

It's hard to beat some of the bargains that chain motels serve up in Albuquerque, and not just out by the airport (which, in any case, is close to downtown). For example, there's the **Econo Lodge Downtown/ University,** 817 Central Ave. NE (☎ **505/ 243-1321**), charging $39 to $69 for a single and $69 to $99 for a double; and the **Quality Inn & Suites Downtown,** 411 McKnight NW (☎ **505/242-5228**), charging $53 for a single or double. You can also cruise down Central Avenue and pick any of many Route 66–kitsch, mom-and-pop motels, like the **Aztec Motel,** 3821 Central Ave. NE (☎ **505/254-1742**), charging as little as $20 for a single.

➔**Fairfield Inn** ★ This hotel has exceptionally clean rooms and a location with easy access to freeways that can quickly get you to Old Town, downtown, or the heights. Ask for an east-facing room to avoid the noise and a view of the highway. Rooms are medium-size and have medium-size bathrooms. Each has a balcony or terrace. You probably couldn't get more for your money in a chain hotel anywhere else. *1760 Menaul Blvd. NE.* ☎ *800/ 228-2800 or 505/889-4000. www.fairfieldinn.*

com. 188 units. $69 double. Additional person $10. Rates include continental breakfast. Free parking. Amenities: Indoor/outdoor pool; health club; Jacuzzi; sauna; dataport.

→ **Red Roof Inn & Suites Midtown** It's not too fancy, but it is clean and in a great central location, right off of I-25. Plus there's an indoor pool, free breakfast, and the option of Nintendo and kitchenettes. *1635 Candelaria NE.* ☎ *800/733-7663 or 505/ 344-5311. www.redroof.com. 75 units. $45–$55 single or double. Free parking. Amenities: Indoor pool; breakfast, dataport.*

DOABLE

→ **Courtyard by Marriott** If you don't like high-rises, this is the best choice for airport-area hotels. Opened in 1990, this four-story Marriott is, as advertised, built around a landscaped courtyard. It accommodates mostly business travelers, but some families, too. The units are roomy and comfortable, with nice wood furniture and firm beds. Ask for a balcony room on the courtyard. *1920 Yale Blvd. SE.* ☎ *800/321-2211 or 505/843-6600. www.marriott.com. 150 units. $71–$107 double. Weekend rates available. Free parking. Amenities: Restaurant; lounge; indoor pool; exercise room; Jacuzzi; valet; coin-op laundry; dataport.*

→ **La Posada de Albuquerque** ★ Built in 1939 by Conrad Hilton as the famed hotelier's first inn in his home state of New Mexico, this hotel is on the National Register of Historic Places and feels like old Spain. It was remodeled in 1996, but still has its historic vibe. An elaborate Moorish brass-and-mosaic fountain is at the center of the tiled lobby, which is surrounded on all sides by high archways, creating the feel of a 19th-century hacienda courtyard. The furniture throughout is handcrafted, and the more spacious rooms have big windows looking out across the city and toward the mountains. Plus if you want easy access to

downtown, Old Town, and the Civic Plaza, this hotel is a great choice. **Conrad's Downtown,** La Posada's elegant restaurant, features Southwestern cuisine from Jane Butel, who has a cooking school on the premises. There's also the popular **Lobby Bar,** with live entertainment Wednesday through Saturday nights. *125 Second St. NW (at Copper Ave.).* ☎ *800/777-5732 or 505/242-9090. www.laposada-abq. com. 114 units. $89–$115 single or double; $195–$275 suite. Free parking. Amenities: Restaurant; bar; access to nearby health club; dataport.*

SPLURGE

→ **Albuquerque Marriott Pyramid North** ★ About a 15-minute drive from Old Town and downtown, this Aztec pyramid–shaped structure provides decent rooms in an interesting environment. The 10 guest floors are grouped around a hollow skylit atrium. Vines drape from planter boxes on the balconies, and water falls five stories to a pool between the two glass elevators. The rooms, remodeled in 2003, are spacious, though not extraordinary, all with picture windows and great views. With lots of convention space at the hotel, you're likely to encounter name-tagged conventioneers here. *5151 San Francisco Rd. NE.* ☎ *800/228-9290 or 505/821-3333. www. marriott.com. 310 units. $139–$184 double; $140–$275 suite. (Ask about special weekend and package rates.) Free parking. Amenities: Restaurant; lounge; indoor/outdoor pool; health club; Jacuzzi; sauna; business center; room service; dataport.*

→ **Hacienda Antigua** ★★ This 200-year-old adobe home was once the first stagecoach stop out of Old Town in Albuquerque. Now, it's one of Albuquerque's most elegant inns. The very green, artistically landscaped courtyard is a great respite for tired travelers. The rooms are comfortable and decorated

AMERICAN HIGHWAYS

Albuquerque Events: Balloon on Over!

There is an impressive number of arts and crafts festivals and juried shows in Albuquerque, mostly in spring and fall, as well as a few big nationally known events.

→ The **National Fiery Foods/Barbecue Show** is your chance to taste the hottest of the hot and plenty of milder flavors, too. A good 10,000 attendees show up at this early March fest to taste sauces, salsas, candies, and more. There are cooking demonstrations, too. It all happens at the Albuquerque Convention Center (☎ **505/873-8680;** www.fiery-foods.com).

→ Late April brings the **Gathering of Nations Powwow** to Albuquerque's University Arena. Here you can see dance competitions, arts-and-crafts exhibitions, and the Miss Indian World contest (☎ **505/836-2810;** www.gatheringofnations.com).

→ Every late June for 4 decades now, the **New Mexico Arts and Crafts Fair** has brought out more than 200 New Mexico artisans for a juried show. It's held at the State Fairgrounds, and has nonstop entertainment and a range of Hispanic arts and crafts (☎ **505/884-9043;** www.nmartsandcraftsfair.org).

→ Labor Day weekend's **New Mexico Wine Festival at Bernalillo** (near Albuquerque) is a great place to try excellent New Mexico wines, and to take in the art show and live entertainment, all for $10 (☎ **505/867-3311;** www.newmexicowinefestival.com).

→ The **New Mexico State Fair and Rodeo** is one of America's top state fairs, and there's a lot going on here: horse racing, a nationally acclaimed rodeo, entertainment by big country artists, Native American and Spanish villages, livestock shows, and arts and crafts. It takes over the Albuquerque State Fairgrounds for 17 days in September, and adult tickets are only $5 (☎ **505/265-1791;** www.exponm.com).

→ The world's largest balloon rally is the 9-day **Albuquerque International Balloon Fiesta** ★★ where you see more than 750 colorful balloons take flight for races and contests. There are mass ascensions at sunrise, "balloon glows" in the evening, and balloon rides for those looking for a lift. The launch area is Balloon Fiesta Park in north Albuquerque, and the action happens in mid-October for $6/person (☎ **800/733-9918;** www.balloonfiesta.com).

→ Nearly 300 artists and craftspeople working in all sorts of media come to the State Fairgrounds for the **Weems Artfest.** It takes place for 3 days every early November, and is one of the top 100 arts-and-crafts fairs in the country (☎ **505/293-6133;** www.weemsgallery.com).

with antiques. "La Capilla," the home's former chapel, is now a room with a queen-size bed, a fireplace, and a carving of St. Francis (the patron saint of the garden). "La Sala" has a king-size bed and a large Jacuzzi, with a view of the Sandia Mountains. All the rooms are equipped with fireplaces and signature soaps. A gourmet breakfast is served in the garden during warm weather and by the fire in winter. But light sleepers beware—the Santa Fe Railroad runs by this inn, with one to three trains passing by each night. *6708 Tierra Dr. NW.* ☎ *800/201-2986 or 505/345-5399. www.haciendantigua.com. 8 units. $129–$209 double. Additional person $25. Free parking. Pets welcome with $30 fee. Amenities: Outdoor pool; Jacuzzi; gourmet breakfast.*

Eating

TAKE-OUT TREATS/SUPPLIES

Albuquerque offers an endless number of cafes, New Mexican, and continental places on every big street. But if you're looking for something quick, you can stop by any of the local **Satellite Café** sites (a central one is at 3513 Central Ave. NE (☎ **505/256-0345**) for coffee, pastry, or a sandwich—oh, and free Wi-Fi. There's also an understated '60s-style diner on the eastern edge of Nob Hill called **Milton's Restaurant,** 725 Central Ave. NE (☎ **505/842-5291**), where you can pick up cheap standard fare with a few New Mexican options to boot.

There's also the **Flying Star Café** chain that has a huge, delicious selection of food for takeout or to stay, all made with organic and hormone-free ingredients. Its five locations around town are open for breakfast, lunch, and dinner; central locations are at 3416 Central Ave. SE (☎ **505/255-6633**); 8001 Menaul Blvd. NE (☎ **505/293-6911**); and 4026 Rio Grande Blvd. NW (☎ **505/344-6714**).

You can also stock up on fruit, veggies, baked goods, and more at one of several **Albuquerque Growers' Markets** around town (www.abqgrowersmkts.org). Try the **Downtown Market** at Robinson Park (8 and Central Ave.; ☎ **505/243-2230**) on Saturday afternoons, mid-June through mid-October, or the **Central Market** at 7605 Central Ave. NE (☎ **505/869-5203**) Saturdays and Tuesdays, July through October.

RESTAURANTS
Cheap

➜ **Chef du Jour** ★ ECLECTIC This small, quiet, and informal one-room cafe (with a few outdoor tables) serves elegant food at really good prices. There's an open kitchen along one side and oddly matched tables. The menu changes every week, and includes items like smoked chicken quesadilla with barbecue drizzle and a garden burger with smoked Gouda cheese. And this is cool: All of the condiments, from the ketchup to the salsa, are homemade. The restaurant is a little difficult to find, by the way; travel south from the plaza, cross Lomas, and find San Pasquale. *119 San Pasquale SW.* ☎ *505/247-8998. Reservations recommended. Lunch $3–$9, dinner $6–$20. Mon–Fri 11am–2pm; Fri–Sat 5:30–10pm. Closed Christmas Eve through New Year's Day.*

➜ **Duran Central Pharmacy** ★ NEW MEXICAN You could go to one of the touristy New Mexican restaurants in the middle of Old Town and have lots of atmosphere and mediocre food, or you could come here instead, where locals eat, and feast on better, more authentic fare. It's a few blocks up Central, east of Old Town, and there's really a pharmacy here. You walk through it to get to the restaurant, which is a little plain, with a red tile floor and small tables, as well as a counter. A bowl of green chile stew and a homemade tortilla is an excellent choice, as is the blue-corn enchilada plate and the *huevos rancheros* (eggs over corn tortillas, smothered with chile). The menu is short, but you can count on authentic northern New Mexican food. *1815 Central Ave. NW.* ☎ *505/247-4141. Menu items $4.20–$8.10. No credit cards. Mon–Fri 9am–6:30pm; Sat 9am–2pm.*

➜ **El Patio** ★★ MEXICAN Cute, cheap, and tasty, Nob Hill's El Patio is where the locals come for a reliably good plate of

Mexican favorites. The menu is short and simple, with great enchiladas, tacos, and special *platos*. Don't forget to try a margarita (or a pitcher) and chips 'n guacamole. It is a small restaurant, but with the nice New Mexican weather, you'll likely have the option of sitting outside on the patio—where a lone acoustic guitarist sometimes sits playing tunes. *142 Harvard Dr. SE.* ☎ *505/268-4245. Dinner $7–$15. Mon–Thurs 11am–9pm; Fri–Sat 11am–9:30pm; Sun noon–9pm.*

➜ **Sadie's** ★ NEW MEXICAN It used to be in a bowling alley, but even in its big "new" location something is still drawing crowds: It's the food—simply some of the best in New Mexico, with tasty sauces and large portions. Try the enchilada, or signature stuffed *sopaipilla* dinner. All meals come with chips and salsa, beans, and *sopaipillas*. There's a full bar, with excellent margaritas (and TV screens for you sports lovers). A casual atmosphere where kids can be themselves makes this a nice spot for families. *6230 4th St. NW.* ☎ *505/345-5339. Main courses $7–$14. Mon–Sat 11am–10pm; Sun 11am–9pm.*

Doable

➜ **Artichoke Cafe** ★★ CONTINENTAL An art gallery as well as a restaurant, this hot spot makes for an innovative dining experience. Set in three rooms with dim lighting, it's a nice romantic place. The staff is friendly and efficient, serving up special bevs like ginger beer, Jamaican iced coffee, microbrews, and an excellent assortment of California and French wines. You might start with an artichoke, steamed with three dipping sauces, or have roasted garlic with Montrachet goat cheese. Fresh fish specials are reliably good, and from the regular menu try the pumpkin ravioli with butternut squash, spinach, and ricotta filling with hazelnut-sage butter sauce. And there are nice

salads and gourmet sandwiches for lunch, as well as fancier dishes. *424 Central Ave. SE.* ☎ *505/243-0200. Reservations recommended for dinner. Main courses $7–$12 lunch, $13–$24 dinner. Mon–Fri 11am–2:30pm; Mon 5:30–9pm; Tues–Sat 5:30–10pm; Sun 5–9pm.*

➜ **Graze** ★★ NEW AMERICAN This relatively new restaurant offers a chance to sample the divine creations of chef Jennifer James without the higher costs of her namesake restaurant in the Northeast Heights. It's not exactly a chicken-fried steak kind of place, though you might very well see some refined version of that on this inventive menu. The place is set in a minimalist room with hardwood floors and sunny colored walls, accentuated by excellent service. The portions are intentionally small, with the notion that diners will order many and share. You might try the "piccolo frito" (flash-fried calamari), with baby tomatoes, garbanzo beans, and basil, or the grilled tuna, with sweet ponzu sauce. *3128 Central Ave. SE.* ☎ *505/268-4729. Reservations recommended on weekend nights. Individual plates $6–$20. Tues–Sat 11am–11pm.*

Splurge

➜ **High Finance Restaurant and Tavern** ★ CONTINENTAL This restaurant is less about the food, and more about the experience of eating here. Set high above Albuquerque, at the top of the Sandia Peak Tramway, it's a fun and romantic dinner adventure. There's comfy furniture, decent service, and nice seafood, steaks, and a full bar. The restaurant recommends that you arrive at the Tramway base 45 minutes before your reservation. *40 Tramway Rd. NE (atop Sandia Peak).* ☎ *505/243-9742. www.highfinancerestaurant.com. Reservations requested. Main courses $8–$13 lunch, $15–$45 dinner. Tramway $10 with dinner reservations ($15 without). Summer daily 11am–9pm; winter daily 11am–8pm.*

➜ **Zinc Wine Bar and Bistro** ★★ NEW AMERICAN Welcome to the newest "in" place, serving up imaginative food meticulously prepared. It gets a little crowded and noisy at peak hours, but congenial service alleviates that some. Plenty of businesspeople fill the seats, dining on such treats as blackened flank steak, Greek salad at lunch, or portobello-crusted Alaskan halibut with chorizo sausage polenta. There are also "wine flights" that let diners sample a variety of wines from a particular region for a set price. Or you may opt for an excellent martini. In the lower level, a lounge serves less formally in a wine cellar atmosphere with live music playing 2 to 3 nights a week (open Mon–Sat 4pm–1am; food served to midnight). *3009 Central Ave. NE.* ☎ *505/254-ZINC. Reservations recommended. Main courses $7.50–$12 lunch, $14–$25 dinner. Sun–Fri 11am–2:30pm; Mon–Thurs 5–10pm; Fri–Sat 5–11pm.*

Partying

Albuquerque has a pretty happenin' nightlife scene, as befits a city of 700,000 people. There are plenty of cheap, cool bars, and nightclubs that run the gamut of music, with rock, jazz, and country predominant.

Pick up a copy of the free entertainment weekly *Alibi* (www.alibi.com) when you get into town for current listings. You can also check out the free state-wide LGBT newspaper the *New Mexico Voice* (commonly found in cafes and shops around UNM) for more things to do.

BARS, PUBS & CLUBS

➜ **District Bar** With cheap drinks that are even cheaper at Happy Hour and during special brand nights, this is a busy downtown bar with a decent kitchen to help soak up the alcohol. It's got a great big patio where dogs are welcome, too. The white-collar types enjoy karaoke here on Monday and Tuesday—you've been warned. *4th and Copper Ave.* ☎ *505/243-003. www.districtbar.com. Daily 5pm–2am. Cover varies (not more than $5).*

➜ **Kelly's BYOB** Near the university, Kelly's is a local brewpub set in a renovated auto body shop. And don't let the "BYOB" fool you—that actually stands for "Brew Your Own Beer," since you can actually devote two weeks to concocting your very own flavor of ale in Kelly's on-premises brewworks. The place has tasty pub fare, excellent brew specials, and cover-free live music Thursday to Saturday. *3222 Central SE.* ☎ *505/262-2739. www.kellysbrewpub.com. Mon–Sat 11am–2am; Sun noon–11:30pm. No cover.*

➜ **Martini Grille** ★ On the eastern side of Nob Hill, this is a friendly gay and "young professional" spot, for folks happy to lush out on more than 30 flavors of martinis within a seductive bat-cave atmosphere. There's music always, and live entertainment on most weekends. *4200 Central SE.* ☎ *505/255-4111. Mon–Fri 4pm–2am; Sat 5pm–2am; Sun 5pm–midnight. Cover varies.*

➜ **O'Niell's Pub** A favorite club in the University of New Mexico area, this Irish bar serves up good pub grub, friendly conversation, as well as live local music on Saturday nights and Celtic and bluegrass on Sunday evenings. *4310 Central Ave. SE.* ☎ *505/255-OPUB. www.oniells.com. Mon–Sat 11:30am–2am; Sun 11:30am–midnight. No cover.*

➜ **Pulse** If you're ready to get sweaty on the dance floor, head to Pulse for high-energy thumping. It's predominantly gay, but friendly and open to all (like every place in Albuquerque). Blu is the low-key spin off on the south side of the building, often hosting live music. *4100 Central Ave. SE.* ☎ *505/255-3334. www.pulseandblu.com. Wed–Sat 9pm–2am; Sun 8pm–midnight. No cover.*

AMERICAN HIGHWAYS

You Say Chili, We Say Chile

You'll never see "chili" on a menu in New Mexico. New Mexicans are adamant that *chile*, the Spanish spelling of the word, is the only way to spell it—no matter what your dictionary may say.

Virtually anything you order in a restaurant is likely to be topped with a chile sauce. If you're not accustomed to spicy foods, certain varieties will make your eyes water, your sinuses drain, and your palate feel as if it's on fire. (*Warning:* No amount of water or beer will alleviate the sting. Drink milk, or scarf a *sopaipilla* drizzled with honey.) But don't be scared away from genuine New Mexico chiles, because the pleasure of eating them far outweighs potential pain. Start slowly, with salsas and sauces first, and some *rellenos* (stuffed peppers) next. Before long, you'll be buying *chile ristras* (chiles strung on rope) to bring home for cooking a la Southwest.

LIVE MUSIC

Country

➔**Midnight Rodeo/Gotham** The Southwest's largest nightclub (capacity 2,500), this place has bars in all corners; it even has its own shopping arcade, including a boutique and gift shop. A DJ spins records nightly until closing; the hardwood dance floor is so big (5,500 sq. ft.) that it resembles an indoor horse track. There's also a hip-hop and techno dance bar called Gotham here. *4901 McLeod Rd. NE (near San Mateo Blvd.).* ☎ *505/888-0100. Closed Mon–Tues. $4 cover Fri–Sat.*

Rock & Jazz

➔**Burt's Tiki Lounge** This club won the weekly paper *Alibi's* award for the best variety of drinks. But more importantly, it has tons of live music just about every day of the week, as well as drink specials, and charges no cover, "ever." *313 Gold Ave.* ☎ *505/243-BURT. www.burtstikilounge.com. Mon–Sat 8pm–2am. No cover.*

➔**The Launchpad** Find yourself at a lively music venue with lots of booze to share at this downtown favorite haunt. It's perhaps the best place in town to catch national indie bands on the rise. *618 Central Ave. SW.* ☎ *505/764-8887. www.launch* *padrocks.com. Mon–Fri 4pm–2am; Sat 8pm–2am; Sun hours vary. Cover $3–$12.*

What Else to See & Do

Albuquerque's original town site is **Old Town** ★★, and it's where you'll find an authentic, preserved New Mexican neighborhood. Old Town is centered around the plaza, next to the venerable **Church of San Felipe de Neri,** and the portal to numerous restaurants, art galleries, and crafts shops. Major museums are also within a few blocks, as are the 25,000-square-foot **Albuquerque Aquarium** and the 50-acre **Rio Grande Botanic Garden** (near Central Ave. and Tingley Dr. NW), both worth a visit.

But don't get stuck in Old Town. Elsewhere you'll find the **Sandia Peak Tramway;** the **University of New Mexico,** with its museums; and a bunch of other attractions of the historical and natural variety. And if you can afford the time for day trips, there are also several pueblos and monuments on the outskirts of town (see the section "Native American Traces South of Santa Fe" on p. 476, in the roadtrip "On the Trail of the First Americans.").

ᴹᵀᵛ🆄 Visiting the home of the Lobos

The state's largest institution of higher learning, the University of New Mexico, stretches across a 70-acre campus about 2 miles east of downtown Albuquerque. There are five campus museums, all free, and all constructed (like other UNM buildings) in a modified pueblo style. Look for performances at **Popejoy Hall,** varied public events at nearby **Keller and Woodward Halls,** and **Jonson Gallery** on the north-central campus.

A self-guided walking tour is a good way to see the campus and hit the museums. Start on the west side (parking meters and/or permits are your options—get permits inside the museums), and head for the **Maxwell Museum of Anthropology,** Redondo Drive, south of Las Lomas Road (☎ 505/277-4404; www.unm.edu/~maxwell; Tues–Fri 9am–4pm; Sat 10am–4pm). Here you'll find amazing Southwestern anthropological finds dating back 10,000 years, and along with artifacts, you'll also get to visit a re-created archaeological site, complete with string markers, brushes, and field notes.

From the Maxwell, walk east into the campus to the Duck Pond, pass Mitchell Hall, then turn south (right) and walk over to the **Geology Museum** (☎ 505/277-4204) and **Meteorite Museum** (☎ 505/277-1644). As museums go, it's tough to beat ones that *cover the gamut of recorded time*—from dinosaur bones to moon rocks. But these do, and it's fairly awe-striking to see a sink-size chunk of meteorite that weighs as much as a car. Both of these museums are open Monday to Friday 9am to 4pm.

You can walk east from here and over to the Fine Arts Center, where the **University of New Mexico Art Museum** (☎ 505/277-4001; http://unmart museum.unm.edu) is located. You'll find changing exhibits, and a permanent collection of Old Masters', New Mexican, and Spanish-colonial works. There's also the Tamarind Lithography Archives, and one of the largest university-owned photography collections in the U.S. It's open Tuesday to Friday 9am to 4pm, Tuesday evening 5 to 8pm, and Sunday 1 to 4pm. **1 University Hill NE** (north of Central Ave.) ☎ 505/277-0111. www.unm.edu.

TOP ATTRACTIONS

→ **National Atomic Museum** The museum itself offers the next-best introduction to the nuclear age after the Bradbury Science Museum in Los Alamos, NM, making for an interesting 1- to 2-hour stroll. It traces the history of nuclear-weapons development, beginning with the top-secret Manhattan Project of the 1940s, including a copy of the letter Albert Einstein wrote to President Franklin D. Roosevelt suggesting the possible need to beat the Germans at creating an atomic bomb—a letter that surprisingly went ignored for nearly 2 years. You'll find a permanent Marie Curie exhibit in the lobby and full-scale models of the "Fat Man" and "Little Boy" bombs, as well as displays and films on the peaceful application of nuclear technology, including nuclear medicine and alternative-energy sources. *1905 Mountain Rd. NW (P.O. Box 5800, MS1490).* ☎ *505/245-2137. www.atomicmuseum.com. Adults $4. Daily 9am–5pm. Closed New Year's Day, Easter, Thanksgiving, and Christmas.*

ᴹᵀᵛ **Best💲** → **New Mexico Museum of Natural History and Science** ★★ This museum will take you through 12 billion years of natural history, from the formation of the universe to the present day. You'll start by seeing stones and gems, then dinosaur skeletons cast from real bones, then the progression of flooding in the southwestern United States, beginning 100 million years ago and continuing until 66 million years ago, when New Mexico became dry. You'll also get to check out the tropical oasis exhibit with aquariums of alligators and a simulated time-travel ride taking you through 38 million years of history. Interactive volcanic displays, fossil discovery and examination, and the LodeStar Astronomy Center and planetarium follow. And by the time you leave, you many need a moment to reacclimate to this millennium. *1801 Mountain Rd.* ☎ *505/841-2800. http://museums.state.nm. us/nmmnh/nmmnh.html. Adults $5. (Dyna-Theater, Planetarium, and Virtual Voyages cost up to $6 extra.) Daily 9am–5pm. Closed on major holidays, Thanksgiving, and Christmas.*

➜**Sandia Peak Tramway** ★★ Climb aboard for a half-day trip on this "jigback," which will take you up to the city's best outlook, Sandia Peak. You'll be able to hike on a few different trails—La Luz Trail takes you on a steep and rigorous trek from the base to the summit—see some wildlife, and absorb extraordinary views in all directions. There's also a popular and expensive eatery, **High Finance Restaurant and Tavern,** at Sandia's summit (p. 790). Oh, and the tram does not operate on very windy days. Not that you would want it to. *10 Tramway Loop NE.* ☎ *505/856-7325. www.sandiapeak.com. Adults $15. Memorial Day to Labor Day daily 9am–9pm; spring and fall Thurs–Tues 9am–8pm, Wed 5–8pm; ski season Thurs–Tues 9am–8pm, Wed noon–8pm. Closed 2 weeks each spring and fall for maintenance; check website for details. Parking $1 daily. AE, DISC, MC, V. To reach the base of the tram, take I-25 north to Tramway Rd. (exit 234), then proceed east about 5 miles on Tramway Rd. (NM 556); or take Tramway*

Blvd., exit 167 (NM 556), north of I-40 approximately 8½ miles.

ARTS & CULTURE

➜**Albuquerque Museum of Art and History** Drawing on the largest U.S. collection of Spanish colonial artifacts, displays here include Don Quixote–style helmets, swords, and horse armor. You can wander through an 18th-century compound with adobe floor and walls, and see gear used by *vaqueros,* the original cowboys who came to the area in the 16th century. There are also interactive exhibits, an old-style theater screening historical films, and the chance to take an Old Town walking tour (daily at 11am all-year, except during winter). *2000 Mountain Rd. NW.* ☎ *505/243-7255. www.albuquerquemuseum.com. Adults $4. Tues–Sun 9am–5pm. Closed major holidays.*

➜**Indian Pueblo Cultural Center** Owned and operated as a nonprofit organization by the 19 pueblos of New Mexico, this is the place to begin an exploration of Native American culture. You'll get to see the **evolution of the various pueblos** from prehistory to present, films of Native American artists making their wares, and **Native American dancers** performing in an outdoor arena (twice daily on weekends). You can also try some Indian fry bread and a bowl of *posol* in the small restaurant here. *2401 12th St. N.* ☎ *800/766-4405 or 505/843-7270. www.indianpueblo.org. Adults $4. AE, DISC, MC, V. Daily 9am–4:30pm; restaurant 8am–3pm. Closed major holidays.*

➜**Musical Theatre Southwest** Formerly known as the Albuquerque Civic Light Opera Association, this maturing company has now condensed its name and expanded its season. From February to January, six major Broadway musicals, in addition to several smaller productions, are presented each year at either Popejoy Hall or the MTS's own 890-seat Hiland Theater. Most productions are staged for three consecutive weekends, including some Sunday matinees. *4804 Central Ave. SE.* ☎ *505/262-9301. www.musicaltheatresw.com. Tickets $15–$30 adults; students and seniors receive a $2 discount.*

→ **National Hispanic Cultural Center** ★ Located in the historic Barelas neighborhood on the Camino Real, this museum explores Hispanic arts and life through visual arts, drama, music, dance, and other programs. Look for photographs by Miguel Gandert, and exhibits in the 11,000-square-foot gallery space. Plans are under way to incorporate a cultural cooking component into the center, which would allow visitors to sample Hispanic foods from all over the world. *701 4th St. SW (corner of 4th St. and Avenida Cesar Chavez).* ☎ *505/246-2261. www.nhccnm.org. Adults $3. Tues–Sun 10am–5pm; restaurant 8am–3pm. Closed major holidays.*

PLAYING OUTSIDE

Holy mackerel is there a lot of outdoor stuff to do in this neck of the woods! However, if you want to be outside and *not* be in constant motion, just head for the **Rio Grande Nature Center,** 2901 Candelaria Rd. (☎ **505/344-7240;** www.rgnc.org). For $1 admission, that's where you'll find 270 acres of riverside forest, 100-year-old cottonwoods, and great native flowers and smaller wildlife.

Ballooning ★

Your pick-me-up awaits, with the help of several hot-air balloon operators; rates start at about $135 per person per hour. Call **Rainbow Ryders,** 11520 San Bernardino NE (☎ **505/823-1111**), or **World Balloon Corporation,** 1103 La Poblana NW (☎ **505/293-6800**). If you have your heart set on a flight, reserve a time early in your stay, because flights are sometimes canceled due to bad weather. That way, if you have to reschedule, you'll have enough time to do so.

If you like to watch, go to the annual **Albuquerque International Balloon Fiesta** ★★, which is held the first through second weekends of October (see "Albuquerque Events," p. 788).

Biking

Albuquerque is a major bicycling hub in the summer, for both road racers and mountain bikers. For an excellent map of Albuquerque bicycle routes, call the **Albuquerque Parks & Recreation Department** at ☎ **505/768-3550** or visit **www.cabq.gov** for one of its comprehensive "Bike Path" maps. A great place to bike is **Sandia Peak** (☎ **505/242-9133;** www.sandiapeak.com) in Cíbola National Forest. You can't take your bike on the tram, but a chairlift is available for uphill or downhill transportation with a bike. Bike rentals are available at the top and bottom of the chairlift ($38 for adult bikes and $28 for junior ones). The lift costs $14 and runs on weekends, with Friday added in July and August, and the trails range from easy to very difficult.

Down in the valley, the Paseo del Bosque trail ("bosque" is a Spanish word for "wooded area") that runs along the Rio Grande is accessed through the Rio Grande Nature Center (p. 794).

To the east, the **Foothills Trail** runs along the base of the mountains. It's a fun 7-mile-long trail with excellent views. Get there by driving east from downtown on Montgomery Boulevard, past the intersection with Tramway Boulevard. Go left on Glenwood Hills Drive and head north about a half-mile before turning right onto a short road that leads to the Embudito trail head.

Northeast Cyclery, 8305 Menaul Blvd. NE (☎ **505/299-1210**), rents bikes at the rate of $25 to $35 per day. Multiday discounts are available, and all rentals come with helmets.

Hiking

- The 1.5-million-acre **Cíbola National Forest** has many hiking opportunities. Within town, the best hike is the **Embudito Trail**, which heads up into the foothills, with spectacular views down across Albuquerque. The 5.5-mile one-way hike is moderate to difficult. Allow 1 to 8 hours, depending on how far you want to go. You get to it by driving east from downtown on Montgomery Boulevard past the intersection with Tramway Boulevard. Go left on Glenwood Hills Drive and head north about a half-mile before turning right onto a short road that leads to the trail head.

The premier Sandia Mountain hike is **La Luz Trail,** a very strenuous journey from the Sandia foothills to the top of the Crest. It's a 15-mile round-trip jaunt, and it's half that if you take the Sandia Peak Tramway (see "Top Attractions" earlier in this chapter) either up or down. Allow a full day for this hike. Access is off Tramway Boulevard and Forest Service Road 333. For more details contact the **Sandia Ranger Station,** Highway 337 south toward Tijeras (☎ 505/281-3304).

Fishing

There are no real fishing opportunities in Albuquerque, but there is a nearby fishing area known as **Shady Lakes** (☎ 505/898-2568), open early March through late October. The most common catches are rainbow trout, black bass, bluegill, and channel catfish; permits are required, but pretty cheap (for the season $5.50 per adult and $3.25 for kids for all-you-can-catch trout; $8 for catch-and-release of any type of fish). To reach Shady Lakes, take I-25 north to the Tramway exit. Follow Tramway Road west for a mile and then go right on NM 313 for a half-mile.

Sandia Lakes Recreational Area (☎ 505/897-3971), also located on NM 313, is another popular fishing spot, and has a bait and tackle shop. It too requires a fishing permit, which runs $10 for adults ($8 for kids) and comes with an eight-fish limit.

Golf

There are a bunch of public courses in the Albuquerque area. The **Championship Golf Course at the University of New Mexico,** 3601 University Blvd. SE (☎ 505/277-4546), is one of the best in the Southwest and was rated one of the country's top 25 public courses by *Golf Digest.* **Paradise Hills Golf Course,** 10035 Country Club Lane NW (☎ 505/898-7001), is a popular 18-hole golf course on the west side of town. Other Albuquerque courses are **Ladera,** 3401 Ladera Dr. NW (☎ 505/836-4449); **Los Altos,** 9717 Copper Ave. NE (☎ 505/298-1897); **Puerto del Sol,** 1800 Girard Blvd. SE (☎ 505/265-5636); and **Arroyo del Oso,** 7001 Osuna Rd. NE (☎ 505/884-7505).

If you're willing to drive a short distance just outside Albuquerque, you can play at the **Santa Ana Golf Club at Santa Ana Pueblo,** 288 Prairie Star Rd., Bernalillo, 87004 (☎ 505/867-9464), which was rated by the *New York Times* as one of the best public golf courses in the country. Club rentals are available (call for information). There's also **Isleta Pueblo,** 4001 Hwy. 47 (☎ 505/869-0950), south of Albuquerque, which has an 18-hole course.

Horseback Riding

If you want to get in a saddle and eat some trail dust, call the **Hyatt Regency Tamaya Resort and Spa,** 1300 Tuyuna Trail, Santa Ana Pueblo (☎ 505/771-6037). The resort offers 2½-hour-long rides near the Rio Grande for $60 per person. The resort is located about 15 miles north of Albuquerque. From I-25 take exit 242, following US 550 west to Tamaya Boulevard, and drive 1½ miles to the resort.

En el vino la verdad

On top of everything else New Mexico has to offer, wineries are springing up all over the state. Wineries in Albuquerque or within a short driving distance of the city include **Anderson Valley Vineyards,** 4920 Rio Grande Blvd. NW (☎ **505/ 344-7266**); **Sandia Shadows Vineyard and Winery,** 11704 Coronado NE (☎ **505/856-1006;** www.nmwine.com/wineries/sandiashadows.htm); and **Gruet Winery,** 8400 Pan-American Hwy. NE (☎ **505/821-0055;** www.gruet winery.com). Call for tours and wine-tasting hours.

River Rafting

River rafting is found farther north, in the area surrounding Santa Fe and Taos; however, Albuquerque is the home of **Wolf Whitewater,** 4626 Palo Alto SE (☎ **505/ 262-1099;** www.wolfwhitewater.com), one of the best rafting companies in the region.

Skiing

Sandia Peak Ski Area is a good place for skiing if you're passing through during the winter. There are plenty of beginner and intermediate runs. (More challenging ones are up near Santa Fe and Taos.) The ski area has twin base-to-summit chairlifts to its upper slopes at 10,360 feet and a 1,700-foot vertical drop, and 30 runs above the day lodge and ski-rental shop. All-day lift tickets are $38 for adults and $33 for skiers 13 to 20. The season runs mid-December to mid-March. Contact the ski area, 10 Tramway Loop NE (☎ **505/242-9133**), for more information, or call ☎ **505/857-8977** for ski conditions.

Cross-country skiers should check out the trails of the Sandia Wilderness from Sandia Peak Ski Area, or venture an hour north to the remote Jemez Wilderness and its hot springs.

Tennis

Albuquerque has 29 public parks with tennis courts. Because of the city's size, your best bet is to call the **Albuquerque Convention and Visitors Bureau** (☎ **800/284-2282**) to find out which park is closest to your hotel.

SHOPPING

→ **Flea Market** ★ Every Saturday and Sunday of the year the fairgrounds host this market from 8am to 5pm. It's a great place to pick up some locally made turquoise and silver jewelry and crafts, as well as cheap manufactured stuff like socks and T-shirts. The place has a fair atmosphere, and it's free. *New Mexico State Fairgrounds. For information call the Albuquerque Convention and Visitors Bureau.* ☎ *800/284-2282.*

→ **Jackalope International** Wandering through this vast shopping area is like an adventure to another land—to many lands, actually. You'll find Mexican *trasteros* (armoires) next to Balinese puppets. The store sells sculpture, pottery, and Christmas ornaments, too. *834 US 550. Bernalillo.* ☎ *505/867-9813.*

→ **Western Warehouse** Pick up a little Western wear here, and get to pick from an enormous collection of boots (8,000 pairs of boots altogether). It claims to have the largest selection of work wear and work boots in New Mexico. *6210 San Mateo Blvd. NE.* ☎ *505/883-7161.*

SPECTATOR SPORTS

Baseball

The **Albuquerque Isotopes** (stolen from Springfield . . . just ask Homer Simpson!) play 72 home games at Isotopes Park, as part of the Pacific Coast League. Tickets range from $5 to $10. For information, contact ☎ 505/924-2255 or see **www. albuquerquebaseball.com**. Isotopes Park is located at 1601 Avenida Cesar Chavez SE. Take I-25 south to Avenida Cesar Chavez and go east, to the intersection with University Boulevard.

Basketball

The **University of New Mexico Lobos** play an average of 16 home games from late November to early March. Capacity crowds cheer the team at the 17,121-seat University Arena (fondly called "The Pit"). For tickets and information call ☎ 505/925-LOBO (www.golobos.com).

Football

The **University of New Mexico Lobos** Division I football team plays a September-to-November season, usually with five home games, at the 30,000-seat University of New Mexico Stadium. For tickets and information call ☎ **505/925-LOBO** (www.golobos.com).

Hockey

The **New Mexico Scorpions** play in the Western Professional Hockey League. Their home is at Tingley Coliseum, New Mexico State Fairgrounds (☎ **505/881-7825;** www.scorpionshockey.com).

Horseracing/Slots

The **Downs at Albuquerque Racetrack and Casino,** New Mexico State Fairgrounds (☎ 505/266-5555; www.abqdowns.com), is the place to catch thoroughbred and quarterhorse racing on weekends from April to July, and during the State Fair in September. General admission is free. There's also a 300-slot casino there open daily noon to midnight.

On the Road to Alamogordo, NM

Albuquerque, NM to Alamogordo, NM 210 miles

Break out the sunscreen for this leg of the trip. It's just under 4 hours to drive to Alamogordo, but there are a couple of natural New Mexico–style roadside attractions worth stopping for, and that requires some protection from the bold Southwestern sun. You'll be heading out of Albuquerque on I-25 south, and can likely stay on cruise control (75 mph) all 87 miles to Highway 380 west, just south of **Socorro**. This is when you really feel like you're entering the scenery you've been seeing from the interstate.

You'll first pass by the **White Sands Missile Range** (☎ 505/678-1134; www.wsmr.army.mil) where the first nuclear bomb was detonated in a 1945 test. Ground zero is known as the "Trinity Site," and the nearly half-mile-wide, 8-foot-deep crater it left is now marked with a modest lavastone monument inside the range. They say the site has only trace amounts of radiation remaining. The whole area is strictly off limits to civilians—except twice a year, on the first Saturday of April and October.

After a little less than an hour on Highway 380, you'll find yourself at the **Valley of Fires Recreation Area** (☎ 505/648-2241). (Entrance to the Valley of Fires, by the way, is $5 per vehicle two or more people, paid on the honor system at the trail-head; "quiet hours" are from 10pm–7am.) It sounds like the title of a melodramatic soap opera (wait, is that redundant?), but it's the country's best preserved natural lava field. Park the car and take a walk on a well-maintained (and wheelchair-accessible) loop path through the fields in under 40 minutes. Behold the wild concept that lava doesn't just flow from volcanoes, but also from cracks in the earth's crust. Here in the Tularosa Valley, the lava covers more than 125 square miles and is more than 160 feet deep in the

Music & Missiles Playlist

→ *Seven Nation Army,* **The White Stripes,** "Elephant," 2003
→ *Sunrise on Cicero,* **DeVotchKa,** "SuperMelodrama," 2002
→ *Step Aside,* **Sleater-Kinney,** "One Beat," 2002
→ *Deep Shag,* **Luscious Jackson,** "Natural Ingredients," 1994
→ *Runaway Lover,* **Madonna,** "Music," 2000
→ *China Girl,* **David Bowie,** "Let's Dance," 1983
→ *Where Is My Mind,* **Pixies,** "Surfer Rosa," 1998
→ *Monkey Wrench,* **Foo Fighters,** "The Color and the Shape," 1997
→ *Mambo Sinuendo,* **Ry Cooder & Manuel Galban,** "Mambo Sinuendo," 2003

center. It also has led to plants and wildlife adapting to the landscape and climate by changing color and growing in new ways.

After the Valley of Fires, you'll quickly arrive in **Carrizozo,** home of the legendary green chile cheeseburger at the **Outpost.** Just turn right at the stop sign (US 54) and the restaurant will be on your left in a few blocks—it's windowless and plain, but it's a main local hang out. And the burger is darn good, but the onion rings might be better.

Press on south, and in less than 30 minutes you'll reach the east-bound turn-off for the **Three Rivers Petroglyph Site and Picnic Area** (☎ 505/525-4300; www.recreation.gov). This is an excellent glimpse of central New Mexico's natural beauty, decorated by 21,000+ petroglyphs (prehistoric rock carvings). In less than an hour, you can stretch your legs on a rocky half-mile hike and discover some of the millennium-old rock etchings left by the *Jornada Mogollon* tradition, which defined much of the Southwest region's culture beginning in 400 A.D. (For more information on petroglyphs and the people who made them, see the roadtrip "On the Trail of the First Americans," which also spends significant time in New Mexico.)

On the Road Nuts & Bolts

Where to Fill Up   You should be able to do this leg on one full tank leaving Albuquerque, but if you want to play it safe, stop for a tank refill in Carrizozo.

The Fastest Way   South on I-25 out of Albuquerque for about 90 miles (just over an hour's time, at the 75-mph speed limit). Hop on US 380 west at San Antonio, right after Socorro. In an hour (65 miles) you'll hit Carrizozo, where you can turn south onto US 54. Then it's just an hour or so into Alamogordo. The whole trip, minus stops, is under 4 hours.

The Long Way Round   My recommended long way is the same as the fast route, only with stops at Valley of Fires, Carrizozo's Outpost, and Three Rivers Petroglyphs thrown in (see above). If you include them, you'll add 2 to 4 hours to the trip total, but few extra miles.

AMERICAN HIGHWAYS

Rules of the Road You may find yourself a bit lonely on this leg, since it's mostly locally traveled, smaller highways. That's actually the best part. So relax and cruise on through while soaking up the expansive scenery—you'll miss it when the trip's over.

Welcome to Alamogordo

In another half-hour, you'll be making your way into lovely, low-key Alamogordo, also known as the-city-nearest-to-White-Sands. But the town itself has some cool things to see and do—just not a lot of them, seein' as the population is a scant 36,000, and much of it is related to the neighboring Holloman Air Force Base.

Getting Around

Alamogordo is on the eastern edge of the Tularosa Valley, at the foot of the Sacramento Mountains. US 54 (White Sands Blvd.) is the main street, extending many miles north and south. The downtown district, such as it is, is just 3 blocks east of White Sands Boulevard at 10th Street.

Sleeping

Hotels in Alamogordo are pretty exclusively along White Sands Boulevard, the north–south highway through town. There

you'll find the usual chains at small-town rates.

➔ **Best Western Desert Aire** This recently renovated brick-and-stucco hotel is the place to stay in Alamogordo. The medium-size rooms are cozy and have decent furnishings and minifridges. You'll find firm beds and average-size, functional bathrooms. You can also request a room with a kitchenette. The suites are cheap and have 3-foot-deep Jacuzzi tubs. *1021 S. White Sands Blvd. ☎ 800/565-1988 or 505/ 437-2110. www.bestwestern.com. 99 units. $52–$75 single or double; $65–$79 suite. Includes breakfast. Rates change seasonally. Pets welcome with $50 deposit. Amenities: Outdoor pool; Jacuzzi; sauna; game room; coin-op laundry; dataport.*

➔ **Days Inn Alamogordo** Clean, comfortable rooms with standard furnishings are what you'll find at this two-story motel built in 1987. Remodeling is ongoing, so ask for the most up-to-date room. Each is

When the Sand Turned Green . . .

The world changed at precisely 5:29am on July 16, 1945, when the first atomic bomb fell from a 100-foot-tall steel tower in the White Sands Missile Range's Trinity Site. That short fall set off an explosion equivalent to 18,000 tons of TNT. It vaporized the tower and sent shock waves that broke windows 120 miles away. In the huge, shallow crater it left and on the surrounding desert land, a new substance was discovered—or created. **Trinitite,** also called "atomite" and "Alamogordo glass," is the result of melted sand and, some theorized, sand that was drawn into the fireball and rained down in liquid form. Green-tinted and glassy, the trinitite blanketed the site until the U.S. government collected samples, then bulldozed over and buried the remainder in 1952. Today, trinitite samples remain mildly radioactive, as does the site, which in 1 hour emits a comparable amount of radiation to watching television for 1 year (on average). It also is a National Historic Landmark (p. 803).

medium-size, with decent beds and a small bathroom; all have the usual amenities. *907 S. White Sands Blvd., Alamogordo, NM 88310.* ☎ *800/DAYS-INN or 505/437-5090. Fax 505/434-5667. www.daysinn.com. 40 units. $49–$55 double. Amenities: Outdoor pool; coin-op laundry; dataport; microwave.*

→ **Holiday Inn Express** This hotel is fairly new, and on the south end of town so you can make a quick getaway to White Sands. It's immaculately clean, has suite-size rooms, nice cozy beds, and a big airy dining/common area where you can lounge with your free breakfast and good coffee. *1401 S. White Sands Blvd.* ☎ *888/HOLI-DAY or 505/434-9773. www.ichotelsgroup.com. 107 units. $50–$100 single or double. No pets. Amenities: Outdoor pool; coin-op laundry; Wi-Fi; microwave.*

CAMPGROUNDS & HOSTELS

A pleasant, rural, and cheap alternative to the hotel scene is the **Cloudcroft Hostel,** 20 miles west in the mountain town of Cloudcroft, 1049 Hwy. 82, between mile marker 10 and 11 (☎ **505/682-0555;** www.cloudcrofthostel.com). Bunk beds go for $17/night and private rooms are $30/night.

If you've got even a minor inclination, don't miss the chance to camp at **White Sands National Monument.** It's not an easy prospect; only tents are allowed, you have to walk quite a distance to the campground, and there are no toilets or running water, and no fires allowed. But more importantly, seeing the sunrise over the dunes or catching them under a full moon is an experience you will forever retreat to in the corners of your mind. (See "Camping," under "White Sands National Monument," p. 804.)

If you'd rather have amenities with your camping, try **Alamogordo Roadrunner** (☎ **877/437-3003** or 505/437-3003; www. roadrunnercampground.com). It has laundry and grocery facilities, as well as a

recreation room/area, swimming pool, playground, shuffleboard, and planned group activities in winter. It's on 24th Street in Alamogordo, just east of the US 54/70/82 junction. If you're looking for something in between, **Oliver Lee State Park,** 15 miles southeast of Alamogordo via US 54 and Dog Canyon Road (☎ **505/437-8284**), is a good choice, with 44 sites, 10 full hookups, picnic tables, grills, tenting availability, a playground, and hiking trails.

Eating

Apart from legions of fast-food joints, there's not a whole lot to choose from in Alamogordo. In addition to the following recommended places, there are a few local hang outs, all reasonable, like **Gigi's Pizza,** 3111 Thunder Rd. (☎ **505/434-5811;** Mon–Fri 11am–9pm), and **Ramona's Restaurant,** 2913 N. White Sands Blvd. (☎ **505/437-7616;** daily 6am–10pm).

By the way, if you're just looking for a good cup of coffee—also with Wi-Fi—try **Plateau Espresso,** 2724 N. Scenic Dr. (☎ **505/434-4466**).

→ **Margo's** ★ MEXICAN For 28 years, the Sandoval family has been feeding New Mexicans and travelers hearty, flavorful food at a decent price. The tradition continues here, with a traditional Mexican-restaurant menu. The windowless building it's in isn't much for atmosphere, but the food is reliable—especially the Margo's Special, a combo plate with guacamole salad, beef taco, enchilada, chile relleno, Spanish rice, and refried beans. Lunch specials provide smaller portions at a great price. (And try sopaipillas or flan for dessert.) *504 E. 1st St. (1 block east of White Sands Blvd.).* ☎ *505/434-0689. Main courses $4.25–$11 lunch and dinner. Daily 10:30am–9pm.*

→**Memories Restaurant** ★ AMERICAN
This restaurant is set in a 1907 Victorian
home in a residential neighborhood right
on the edge of historic downtown. And it's
busy all day, with people flocking for crab
salad over avocado, grilled shrimp, croissant sandwiches, and specials like prime
rib. It's a comfortable place, especially
considering that you're eating in rooms
that were once the living room and den.
1223 New York Ave. (corner of 13th St.). ☎ 505/
437-0077. Reservations recommended. Main
courses $5–$10 lunch, $11–$17 dinner. Mon–
Sat 11am–9pm.

NEARBY PLACES
TO EAT & SLEEP

→**Casa de Sueños** ★ NEW MEXICAN
A fun, south-of-the-border stop, this newish restaurant about 15 miles north of
Alamogordo, outside Tularosa, serves
tasty New Mexican fare, with a good dose
of the whimsy of Mexico. Decorated with
Mexican folk paintings and a country
home mural, it exudes a fiesta atmosphere.
Outside, the broad patio is lit with little
Christmas lights and has chili peppers on
the tablecloths. Breakfast, lunch, and dinner—they're all great, but at least try a
little something with the green chile sauce,
made with fresh chiles and perfectly seasoned. *35 St. Francis Dr., Tularosa, NM.*
☎ 505/585-3494. Reservations recommended
on weekends. Main courses $4–$8 breakfast,
$7–$13 lunch and dinner. Mon–Fri 11am–9pm;
Sat 9am–9pm; Sun 9am–8pm.

→**The Lodge at Cloudcroft** ★★ In
nearby Cloudcroft (20 miles west of
Alamogordo), this lodge is a well-preserved relic of another era. From the grand
fireplace in the lobby to the homey
Victorian decor in the guest rooms, it
exudes gentility and class. There's a 9-hole
golf course, one of the country's highest at
9,000 feet above sea level, and the site
of numerous regional tournaments. All

rooms in The Lodge are mid-size, have
views, and are filled with antiques in every
corner. Some even have jet tubs. Guests
are greeted by a stuffed bear sitting
on their bed and a sampler of homemade
fudge from The Lodge Mercantile. In 1991,
more rooms were added in separate buildings; they are most often rented out in
blocks.

Rebecca's (☎ 505/682-2566), The
Lodge's restaurant, is named for the resident ghost, believed to have been a cham-
bermaid in the 1930s who was killed by her
lumberjack lover. But despite the legend,
the restaurant is just a nice place to sit for
a friendly meal. You can choose from many
"American" choices, like hearty salads,
steak, and some seafood options. Lots of
windows mean bright, sunny mornings
for breakfast that turns into romantic
evening dining. *1 Corona Place (P.O. Box 497),*
Cloudcroft, NM. ☎ 800/395-6343 or 505/682-
2566. www.thelodgeresort.com. 61 units. $109–
$159 double; $169–$329 suite. Free parking.
Pets welcome with limitations and fee.
Amenities: Restaurant; bar; outdoor heated
pool; golf course; access to nearby tennis
courts; exercise room; spa; Jacuzzi; sauna;
bike and snowmobile rentals.

Partying

Military personnel must hang out inside
the confines of nearby Holloman Air Force
Base, because there just aren't a lot of
bars in Alamogordo. But you can try the
fun local joint **Shooters Bar & Night
Club,** 5201 Highway 70 West (☎ 505/443-
6000; Mon–Sat 4pm–2am), which also
has karaoke and free pool on some weeknights. Another friendly spot to get a beer
and a burger is **Plaza Bar,** 1004 N. White
Sands Blvd. (☎ 505/437-9495; Mon–Fri
11am–10pm).

There's also the option to head to
Tularosa, which is just 12 miles north, and
make a night of it playing pool or poker,

where's the car?

UH-OH

If you're not camping, you can choose to roam around for a long while—just be really conscious of where you parked the car. Seriously. When in doubt, stick with the posted trails.

dancing, or just hanging on the patio at **Tulie's Cantina,** 313 Granado St. (☎ 505/585-3055; Mon–Thurs 4–10:30pm; Fri–Sat 4pm–2am).

White Sands National Monument

Arguably the most memorable natural area in this part of the Southwest, **White Sands National Monument** preserves the best part of the world's largest gypsum dune field—an area of 275 square miles of pure white gypsum sand reaching out over the floor of the Tularosa Basin in wavelike dunes. Plants and animals have evolved in special ways to adapt to the bright white environment here. Some creatures have a bleached coloration to match the whiteness all around them, and some plants have evolved ways to survive the smothering pressures of the blowing sands.

The surrounding mountains—the **Sacramentos** to the east, with their forested slopes, and the serene **San Andres** to the west—are composed of sandstone, limestone, sedimentary rocks, and pockets of gypsum. Over millions of years, rains and melting snows dissolved the gypsum and carried it down into Lake Lucero. Here the hot sun and dry winds evaporate the water, leaving the pure white gypsum to crystallize. Then the persistent winds blow these crystals, in the form of minuscule bits of sand, in a northeastern direction, adding them to growing dunes. As each dune grows and

moves farther from the lake, new ones form, rank after rank, in what seems an endless procession.

The dunes are especially enchanting at sunrise and under the light of a full moon, but you'll have to camp here to experience this extraordinary sight (see "Camping," below).

ESSENTIALS

Getting There & Visitor Info

The visitor center is 15 miles southwest of Alamogordo on US 70/82.

Note: Due to missile testing—you heard me right—on the adjacent White Sands Missile Range, this road is sometimes closed for up to 2 hours at a time. When driving near or in the monument, tune your radio to 1610 AM for information on what's happening, or call **White Sands National Monument** at ☎ 505/479-6124 (www.nps.gov/whsa).

Admission is $3 for adults (free for children 16 and under). Memorial Day to Labor Day, the visitor center is open daily from 8am to 7pm, and Dunes Drive is open daily from 7am to 9pm. Ranger talks and sunset strolls are given nightly at 7 and 8:30pm during summer. During the rest of the year, the visitor center is open daily from 8am to 5pm, and Dunes Drive is open daily from 7am to sunset.

Highlights

The 16-mile **Dunes Drive** loops through the "heart of sands" from the visitor center. Information available at the center tells you what to look for on your drive. Sometimes the winds blow the dunes over the road, which must then be rerouted. All the dunes are in fact moving slowly to the northeast, pushed by prevailing southwest winds, some at the rate of as much as 20 feet per year.

In the center of the monument, the road itself is made of hard-packed gypsum.

AMERICAN HIGHWAYS

(***Note:*** It can be especially slick after a storm, and big ponds can form, so drive cautiously.)

Visitors can park their cars in designated areas and explore a bit. You can climb a dune for a better view of the endless sea of sand, which is pretty phenomenal, and also sled down them. (Advice from a hardcore New Mexico adventurer is to test yourself in a high-dune long jump—just make sure the receiving end's sand is loose enough that you'll sink into it, not smack the surface.)

It's also great to hike around. The Big Dune Trail is a good one near the entrance, and you can probably do it in under 45 minutes depending on your tendency to wander. Just be sure to take advantage of the vast and unparalleled serenity White Sands offers, because you'll think about it a lot once you've left.

In summer, ranger-guided nature walks and evening programs also take place in the dunes—they're a nice way to learn about all the crazy nature going on out there.

Camping

To see the dunes at sunrise or under a full moon is extraordinary, and camping is the only way to do it, since the park closes at dusk and reopens after dawn. In that time, it's just primitive camping with tents only, and no water, facilities, or campfires. You'll hike ³/₄ mile to the campsite where you can pitch a tent—but get there in the morning if there's a full moon, because the campsites go quickly. (Availability shouldn't be a problem at other times. And there's no camping fee, just the regular $3 entrance fee to the park.) You must register at the visitor center, get clearance, and pay a small fee. Call ☎ **505/479-6124** for information.

If backcountry camping isn't your speed, try one of the other campgrounds in nearby Alamogordo and Las Cruces

 Safety Tips in the Sands

The National Park Service emphasizes that (1) tunneling in this sand can be dangerous because it collapses easily and could suffocate a person; (2) sand-surfing down the dune slopes, although permitted, can also be hazardous, so it should be undertaken with care, and never near a road; and (3) hikers can get lost in a sudden sandstorm if they stray from marked trails or areas. It's best to bring a compass and a bottle of water.

(see the "Sleeping" section earlier in this chapter).

What Else to See & Do

White Sands is amazing, and you may find yourself spending a disproportionate amount of time there. But there are other attractions about town. One of them is the small, historic village of **La Luz,** just 3 miles north of Alamogordo. It has attracted a number of resident artists and craftspeople who live, work, and display some of their products for sale. Worth seeing are the old adobe corral and the small Our Lady of Light Church.

→ **New Mexico Museum of Space History** ★ The New Mexico Museum of Space History comes in two parts: the International Space Hall of Fame and the Clyde W. Tombaugh IMAX Dome Theater. Both are located on the lower slopes of the Sacramento Mountains, 2 miles east of US 54, and just above New Mexico State University's Alamogordo branch campus.

The Space Hall of Fame occupies the "Golden Cube," a five-story building with walls of golden glass. Visitors start on the

Alamogordo Events: Balloons & Jazz!

→ Alamogordo's big to-do is the annual **White Sands Balloon Invitational.** For 2 days every mid-September, more than 80 balloons launch over the park at 7am. I'm sure I don't have to tell you to bring a camera (☎ 505/437-3500; www.alamogordo.com/activites/balloon.html).

→ The U.S. military opens up the White Sands Missile Range only twice a year for the **Trinity Ground Zero Tour,** so if you're into it, call for a reservation and plan your trip for the designated first Saturday in April or October (☎ 505/678-1134; www.wsmr.army.mil).

→ Every late February, Alamogordo's Flickinger Center for the Performing Arts (and a few other venues) hosts the **White Sands Film Festival.** Documentaries, shorts, and features compete for top honors (☎ 505/434-5882; www.whitesandsfilmfestival.com).

→ The annual **Cottonwood Arts & Crafts Festival** arrives in Alameda Park every early September, bringing in handmade arts and crafts to the fine citizens (and guests) of Alamogordo (☎ 505/437-6120).

→ Relax with live music under the summer moon at the **Tailgate Summer Jazz Series.** It's held every second and fourth Saturday night in June, July, and August at the New Mexico Museum of Space & History's upper parking lot. Walk up for $7, or drive (space permitting) for $30 (☎ 505/437-2202; www.flickingercenter.com).

→ See the region from two wheels instead of four with the **SunShine Spin 25 & 50.** A benefit for the Lance Armstrong Foundation, this road cycling event will tour you across either 25 or 50 gorgeous (and challenging) New Mexico routes every mid-July ($35 entry) (☎ 505/237-9700; www.swcp.com).

---

top floor and work their way down. En route, you'll relive the accomplishments of the first astronauts and cosmonauts, including America's Mercury, Gemini, and Apollo programs, and the early Soviet orbital flights. There's also spacecraft and a lunar exploration module exhibited. Displays tell the history and purposes of rocketry, missiles, and satellites and provide an orientation to astronomy and other planets.

At Tombaugh Theater, IMAX projection and Spitz 512 Planetarium Systems create earthly and cosmic experiences on a 2,700-square-foot dome screen. *Located at the top of NM 2001.* ☎ 877/333-6589 or 505/437-2840. *www.spacefame.org. Admission to International Space Hall of Fame $2.50 adults.*

IMAX Theater $6 adults (additional charge for double feature). Prices subject to change without notice. Daily 9am–5pm.

→ **Toy Train Depot** The brainchild of John Koval (whom you're likely to meet at the door), this museum will blow train fanatics away. Koval started the nonprofit museum, housed in a genuine 1898 railroad depot, 10 years ago as a means of celebrating it. The museum meanders back through three rooms, each filled with tracks laid along colorful miniature cityscapes and countryside—1,200 feet of track altogether. The highlight is the last room, a re-creation of Alamogordo, Carrizozo, and Cloudcroft, where six trains swirl over bridges, through tunnels, and

A rocket presides over the New Mexico Museum of Space History.

along flats. The trains date from the 1800s, and there are also numerous examples from the 1930s to the 1950s. Rides through the grounds on 12-inch and 16-inch gauge trains are offered. *1991 N. White Sands Blvd.* ☎ *888/207-3564 or 505/437-2855. www.toy traindepot.homestead.com. Admission $3. Train rides $4. Wed–Sun noon–4pm.*

SOMETHING NUTTY

FREE →**Eagle Ranch Pistachio Groves** This is a nutty little step into the world of pistachio farming. New Mexico's first and largest pistachio groves, Eagle Ranch offers free 45-minute tours weekdays at 10am and 1:30pm in summer and at 1:30pm in winter. You'll get a brief history

Detour: Visiting Dog Canyon

Fifteen miles southeast of Alamogordo via US 54 and Dog Canyon Road, you'll find **Oliver Lee Memorial State Park**. It's nestled at the mouth of Dog Canyon, and is a stunning break in the steep escarpment of the Sacramento Mountains. The site has drawn visitors for thousands of years, and springs and seeps support many rare and endangered plant species, as well as a rich animal life. Hiking trails into the foothills are well marked, and you can pick up lots of local history in the visitor center. There also are picnic and camping grounds, with showers, electricity, and a dump station.

A little on the history: **Dog Canyon** was one of the last strongholds of the Mescalero Apache, and it was the site of battles between Native Americans and the U.S. Cavalry in the 19th century. Around the turn of the 20th century, rancher Oliver Lee built a home near here and raised cattle. Guided tours from the visitor center to Lee's restored house give a taste of early ranch life in southern New Mexico.

The park is open 24 hours a day; admission is $5 per car. The visitor center is open daily from 9am to 4pm. Guided tours are offered Saturday and Sunday at 3pm, weather permitting. For more information, call ☎ **505/437-8284.**

of the farm and tour the facility, salting and roasting departments, and groves. And then, of course, you'll eat some pistachios. *7288 US 54/70 (5 miles north of Alamogordo).*

☎ *800/432-0999 or 505/434-0035. www.eagle ranchpistachios.com. Free admission. Gift shop and gallery Mon–Sat 8am–6pm; Sun 9am–6pm.*

On the Road to Carlsbad, NM

Alamogordo, NM to Carlsbad, NM 150 miles

Relatively speaking, it's a short drive to Carlsbad from Alamogordo at only 3¼ hours. That gives you a few hours to be leisurely in **Cloudcroft** ★, a picturesque mountain village of 750 people high in the Sacramento Mountains. It's just 20 or 30 minutes from Alamogordo on US 82 in the surrounding Lincoln National Forest. Winding your way up the mountain highway you may feel your ears pop—that's a result of climbing twice as high as the Tularosa Valley to a dizzying elevation of almost 9,000 feet.

Cloudcroft was founded in 1899 when railroad surveyors reached the mountain summit and built a lodge for Southern Pacific Railroad workers.

Today, The Lodge is Cloudcroft's biggest attraction and biggest employer (see "Nearby Places to Eat & Sleep," p. 802). Other accommodations are also available in town, including the new **Cloudcroft Hostel** (see "Sleeping" p. 809). There's also many a recreational opportunity. And check with the **Cloudcroft Chamber of Commerce** to learn of any mini-festivals coming up. It's located in a log cabin in the center of town, on the south side of US 82 (☎ 505/682-2733; www.cloudcroft.net).

The **Sacramento Mountains Historical Museum and Pioneer Village**, US 82 east of downtown Cloudcroft (☎ **505/682-2932**), encapsulates the community's early days through preserved pioneer

Playlist: Cruising to Carlsbad

→ *Doo Wap (That Thing)*, **Lauryn Hill**, "The Miseducation of Lauryn Hill," 1998
→ *Race for the Prize*, **The Flaming Lips**, "The Soft Bulletin," 1999
→ *Can't Find My Way Home*, **Eric Clapton (Blind Faith)**, "Crossroads," 1969
→ *Under Pressure*, **David Bowie with Queen**, 1981
→ *Such Great Heights*, **The Postal Service**, "Give Up," 2003
→ *Paranoid Android*, **Radiohead**, "OK Computer," 1997
→ *Mas*, **Kinky**, "Kinky," 2002

buildings, historic photos, and exhibits of turn-of-the-20th-century railroad memorabilia, clothing, and other artifacts. Call for hours since they vary.

Nearby, **Lincoln National Forest** (☎ 505/682-2551) maintains the unique **La Pasada Encantada Nature Trail,** a short footpath from Sleepygrass Campground, off NM 130 south of town, with signs in Braille inviting walkers to touch the various plants, leaves, and trees. (If you have the chance, smell the bark of a Ponderosa Pine—it smells like vanilla.)

A new trail is a several-mile moderate hike to the historic **Mexican Canyon Railroad Trestle.** The trail head is in a U.S. Forest Service picnic area, west of the junction of US 82 and NM 130, where you'll also find a short walk to an observation point offering spectacular views across White Sands Missile Range and the Tularosa Basin. The picnic area also has tables, grills, drinking water, and restrooms.

National Solar Observatory— Sacramento Peak (☎ 505/434-7000; http://nsosp.nso.edu), 18 miles south of Cloudcroft via NM 6563, a National Scenic Byway, attracts astronomers from around the world to study the sun and its effects on our planet. There are three observatories here, with two open to the public for free self-guided tours (allow at least an hour), open daily from 8am to 6pm. Free guided tours are offered Saturday at 2pm from May to October. The visitor center, which is open daily from 10am to 6pm, has a gift shop and scientific exhibits geared toward children.

On the Road **Nuts & Bolts**

Where to Fill Up   Fill up in Alamogordo and you should be good, then again in Artesia to play it safe.

The Fastest Way   West on US 82 through Cloudcroft to Artesia (2½ hr.), where you turn right on US 285 for 37 miles and right into Carlsbad. Barring stops, you'll be there in a little over 3 hours.

The Long Way Round   A half-hour west of Alamogordo puts you in the small mountain town of Cloudcroft, where you can stop for a walk in the forest or sit for lunch at The Lodge. It's worth making the most of your time there, because beyond it you'll drive back into the desert without much to see but straight desert roads.

Rules of the Road US 82 starts out winding up the mountain, so take your time on those sharp curves. But once you're through, hit the cruise control for a 70-mph drive almost the whole rest of the way—there aren't many cops around to pull you over, but you never know (especially around Artesia).

Welcome to Carlsbad

Carlsbad is a city of 27,800 on the Pecos River. It was founded in the late 1800s, and the whole area was controlled by Apaches and Comanches until just a little over a century ago. Besides getting a good tourist business from Carlsbad Caverns, the town thrives on farming, with irrigated crops of cotton, hay, and pecans. And here are your Carlsbad factoids: The area is the largest producer of potash in the United States. (Potash, or carbonate of potash, is an impure form of potassium carbonate mixed with other potassium salts. Potash has been used since antiquity in the manufacture of glass and soap and as a fertilizer. Thank you Wikipedia!) The town was named for the spa in Bohemia of the same name.

The **caverns** (see "Carlsbad Caverns National Park," later in this chapter) are the big attraction, having drawn more than 33 million visitors since opening in 1923. A satellite community, **White's City** (www. whitescity.com), was created 20 miles south of Carlsbad at the park entrance junction. The family of Jack White, Jr., owns all its motels, restaurants, gift shops, and other attractions.

Getting Around

Carlsbad is a simply laid-out town. You'll arrive from Artesia on US 285 south, which is the main drag through town. Most fast-food and big grocery stores line it as you enter the city limits. A mile or two in, you cross the Pecos River, and the main road bends to the right to become US 180/62 south (also called National Parks Highway). That's the western continuation of

the main drag, while US 285 is the eastern continuation (it takes the name South Canal Street there). On the south half, you'll find the older, more residential part of town, followed by a few hotels.

For maps and added info, stop by the **Carlsbad Chamber of Commerce** and the **Carlsbad Convention and Visitors Bureau,** both at 302 S. Canal St. (US 285), (☎ **800/221-1224** or 505/887-6516; www. carlsbad.org). They're open Monday from 9am to 5pm, and Tuesday through Friday from 8am to 5pm.

Sleeping

Hotels in Carlsbad are mostly on the south end of town, along South Canal St. and highway 180/62 on the way to Carlsbad Caverns National Park. The Best Western Cavern Inn (see below) is the closest to the National Park, but the downside to staying there is that your restaurant and activity options are limited.

➜ **Best Western Cavern Inn** If you're all about the caverns, this is the place to stay. The lobby is within an Old West storefront, and the accommodations are across the street. The staff here seems a bit overworked, so you may not get the service you would in Carlsbad. It has two main sections; the best is the **Guadalupe Inn,** which is built around a courtyard, and has nicer rooms. In back is a big pool surrounded by greenery. Next door, the two-story **Cavern Inn** provides 1970s rooms that are large and recently remodeled, though the small bathrooms with jetted tubs could use a little sprucing up.

In the White's City arcade you'll find a post office, grocery store, gift shop, the

Million Dollar Museum of various antiques and paraphernalia, and Granny's Opera House, a theater for weekend melodramas scheduled intermittently. *17 Carlsbad Cavern Hwy. at NM 7, White's City, NM. ☎ 800/CAVERNS or 505/785-2291. www.bestwestern.com. 63 units. May 15–Sept 15 $65–$115 double; Sept 16–May 14 $50–$80 double. Rates include breakfast. Pets welcome with $10 fee. Amenities: 2 restaurants; 2 outdoor pools; tennis court; volleyball; basketball; Jacuzzi; game room; shopping arcade, dataport.*

➔ **Best Western Stevens Inn** This is a comfortable and welcoming enough place after the rigor of traveling. The grounds are decently landscaped, and the inn is comprised of numerous buildings built in different eras. Some rooms need to be upgraded, so be sure to request a remodeled one or, better yet, request one of the brand-new rooms at the south end of the property, which are large and have large bathrooms; each has a fridge and microwave, and some have full kitchens. All the rest of the rooms are medium-size, decorated in a Southwestern print, and have firm beds. Bathrooms are small but have outer double-sink/vanities. The Inn's **Flume restaurant** is one of the better spots to eat in town. *1829 S. Canal St. ☎ 800/730-2851, 800/528-1234, or 505/887-2851. www.bestwestern.com. 221 units. $59–$69 double; $69–$99 suite. Rates include breakfast buffet. Small pets allowed, with $25 deposit. Amenities: 2 restaurants; bar; large outdoor pool; exercise room; playground; business center; coin-op laundry; same-day dry cleaning; dataport; microwave.*

➔ **Day's Inn** This pale stucco, two-story motel on the south end of town offers reliable rooms with good amenities. The rooms are pretty standard, with firm beds and medium-size bathrooms. To avoid the street noise, request a room at the back of the property. *3910 National Parks Hwy.*

Catch a Flick in the Desert Air . . .

Depending on your timeframe in Carlsbad, you may find yourself at a loss for something different to do—which is a perfect time to see what's showing at the **Fiesta Drive-In**. It's the big weekend draw in town, with three screens playing current movies Friday through Monday at 7:45pm each night. *401 Fiesta Dr. ☎ 505/885-4126. www.fiestadrivein.com. $4 per person or $10 a car load; $2 per person on Mon. Gates open at 7:15pm.*

☎ 800/DAYS-INN or 505/887-7800. www.daysinn.com. 50 units. $60–$80 double. Rates include continental breakfast. Amenities: Large indoor pool; Jacuzzi; dataport; microwave.

➔ **Holiday Inn** ★ Housed in a Territorial-style building, this is the first-rate full-service hotel in downtown Carlsbad. It was built in 1960 but has regular renovations. Rooms aren't as large as those at the Best Western Stevens Inn, but they're more refined with white wooden furniture and Southwestern prints. Large executive rooms have comfortable chairs and ottomans as well as jetted tubs. The **Phenix Bar and Grill** has sandwiches, burgers, soups, and salads. *601 S. Canal St. ☎ 800/HOLIDAY or 505/885-8500. www.holiday-inn.com. 100 units. $86–$115 double. Rates include full breakfast. Pets allowed with $25 fee. Amenities: Restaurant; outdoor pool; exercise room; Jacuzzi; sauna; playground.*

CAMPING

Brantley Lake State Park (☎ 505/457-2384) in Carlsbad has tent and RV camping, with hookups. Picnic tables, grills, and recreational facilities are available, and boating and lake fishing are big here. **Carlsbad RV Park and Campground,** on the south end of town at 4301 National Parks Hwy. (☎ **888/878-7275** or **505/885-6333;** www.carlsbadrvpark.com), is a large, full-service campground with a swimming pool and playground.

Eating

→ **Bamboo Garden** ★ CHINESE & AMERICAN This family-owned spot offers a good alternative to all that New Mexican food. It's a casual and friendly place, with comfy booths and elaborate Chinese chandeliers. Service is good and the food (both Chinese and American) is cheap—in fact, you can go pretty crazy on the $7.55 all-you-can-eat buffet, which dangerously includes self-serve, soft-serve ice cream. Locals flock for both lunch and dinner. *1511 S. Canal St.* ☎ *505/887-5145. Main courses $5–$11 lunch and dinner. Tues–Sun 11am–2pm and 5–9pm.*

→ **Blue House** ★ CAFE/BAKERY On a quiet residential street just north of historic downtown is this gem. Set in a Queen Anne–style blue house with morning-glory vines adorning the front fence, this cafe serves up great coffee and simple, fresh, and imaginative fare. Excellent baked goods top the breakfast menu. For lunch, try the feta spinach croissant, a deli sandwich on French country bread, or something sweeter, like the cream cheese raspberry coffee cake. Espresso, lattes, and Italian sodas are also big draws. *609 N. Canyon Rd.* ☎ *505/628-0555. All menu items under $8. No credit cards. Mon–Sat 7:30am–3:30pm. Call to confirm hours. Take Canal Street to Church Street east, then south on Canyon Rd.*

MTV (Best ◕) → **Lucy's** ★★★ MEXICAN When you walk in the door of this busy restaurant, Lucy is likely to wave you toward the dining room and tell you to find a seat. That sums up the nature of the place—and a sign of the good home-style food to come. Since 1974, Lucy and Justo Yanez's restaurant has been dedicated to the words of a Mexican proverb printed on the menu: *El hambre es un fuego, y la comida es fresca* (Hunger is a burning, and eating is a coolness). Start with a margarita or Mexican beer, and fill up on Lucy's personal adaptations of old favorites—often invented by requests from regulars. Everything is made by hand, and all is pretty great. *701 S. Canal St.* ☎ *505/887-7714. Reservations recommended on weekends. Main courses $3.75–$12 lunch and dinner. Mon–Sat 11am–9:30pm.*

→ **Pasta Café Italian Bistro** ITALIAN This new restaurant in the center of town works toward an Italian bistro feel but doesn't quite succeed. The main dining room has a hallway feel, and the noise carries. A better bet is the little houselike replica within the dining room, which is cozier. Or, opt for the wraparound porch. The service is good, and the food is surprisingly diverse with some seafood options. Most people, though, opt for pasta dishes. Try the lasagna or fettuccini Alfredo, or pizza. Come early and check out the bar, where you'll hear live music on weekend nights. *710 Canal St.* ☎ *505/887-7211. Reservations recommended in summer. Main courses $6–$15 lunch, $7–$22 dinner. Sun–Thurs 11am–9pm; Fri–Sat 11am–10pm.*

→ **Velvet Garter Saloon and Restaurant** AMERICAN This is the only restaurant in the immediate caverns area. It's a simple place that does well with its menu. The steaks are good quality and come with a trip to the salad bar, baked potato, vegetable, and bread. You can get reliably good pasta dishes, too. In the same building, **Fat Jack's** serves breakfast and lunch in a setting heavy with linoleum.

Standards such as eggs and bacon, sandwiches, and burgers are some of the only offerings near the caverns, so the place fills up depending on the season. The saloon is unmistakable, with long-horns mounted over the door. *26 Carlsbad Cavern Hwy., White's City.* ☎ *505/785-2291. Reservations recommended in summer. Main courses $10–$20 (Velvet Garter); $5.50–$10 breakfast or lunch (Fat Jack's). Velvet Garter daily 4–10pm (last seating at 9:30pm); Fat Jack's winter daily 7am–4pm; summer daily 6:15am–4pm. Saloon daily 4–10pm.*

Partying

Fairly recently, Carlsbad has developed a nighttime scene. You have a few in-town options. The **Silver Spur,** 1829 S. Canal St. (☎ **505/887-2851**), has live country and Western music most nights and free hors d'oeuvres during happy hour, as well as a big-screen TV.

The **Firehouse Fire Escape,** 222 W. Fox St. (☎ **505/234-1546**), has DJ-style dancing in the upstairs of an old firehouse. The **Post Time Saloon,** 313 W. Fox St. (☎ **505/628-1977**), is a huge place with pool tables, three bars, and a dance floor. The club offers a range of DJ mixes, including country, *Tejano,* and karaoke.

Carlsbad Caverns National Park

One of the largest and most spectacular cave systems in the world is 📺 Best ♦ **Carlsbad Caverns,** which comprises some 100 known caves that snake through the porous limestone reef of the Guadalupe Mountains. Fantastic and grotesque formations wow visitors, who find every shape imaginable (and unimaginable) naturally sculpted in the underground world—from frozen waterfalls to strands of pearls, from soda straws to lion's tails, from draperies to ice-cream cones.

Although Native Americans had known of the caverns for centuries, they were not discovered by white settlers until about a century ago, when they saw daily sunset flights of bats from the cave. Jim White, a guano miner, began to explore the main cave in the early 1900s and to share its wonders with tourists. By 1923, the caverns had become a national monument, upgraded to national park status in 1930.

ESSENTIALS
Getting There & Visitor Info

Take US 62/180 from Carlsbad, which is 23 miles to the northeast. The scenic entrance road to the park is 7 miles long and originates at the park gate at White's City. Van service to Carlsbad Caverns National Park from White's City, south of Carlsbad, is provided by **Sun Country Tours/White's City Services** (☎ **505/785-2291**).

Information about the park is available through the **Carlsbad Caverns National Park,** 3225 National Parks Hwy. (☎ **800/ 967-CAVE** for tour reservations, 505/785-2232 for information about guided tours, and 505/785-3012 for bat flight information; www.nps.gov/cave).

General admission to the park is $6 for adults, $3 for children ages 6 to 15, and free for children under age 6. It's good for 3 days and includes entry to the two self-guided walking tours. Ranger-guided tours range from $7 to $20, depending on the type of tour, and **reservations are required.** The visitor center and park are open daily from Memorial Day to mid-August from 8am to 7pm; the rest of the year they're open from 8am to 5pm. They're closed Christmas.

TOURING THE CAVERNS

Two caves, **Carlsbad Cavern** and **Slaughter Canyon Cave,** are open to the public. The National Park Service has installed facilities, including elevators, to

Carlsbad Caverns

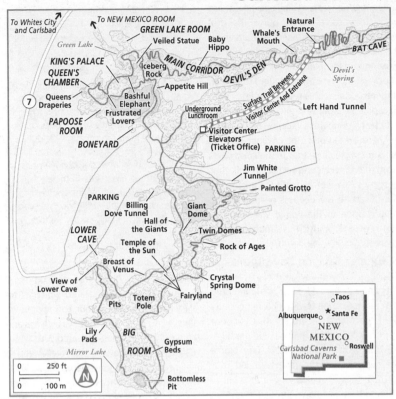

To Whites City and Carlsbad

To NEW MEXICO ROOM

GREEN LAKE ROOM

Green Lake

Veiled Statue

Baby Hippo

Whale's Mouth

Natural Entrance

BAT CAVE

KING'S PALACE QUEEN'S CHAMBER

Iceberg Rock

MAIN CORRIDOR

DEVIL'S DEN

Devil's Spring

(7) Queens Draperies

Appetite Hill

PAPOOSE ROOM

Bashful Elephant

Frustrated Lovers

Underground Lunchroom

Surface Trail Between Visitor Center And Entrance

Left Hand Tunnel

BONEYARD

☐ Visitor Center

Elevators (Ticket Office)

PARKING

Jim White Tunnel

Painted Grotto

PARKING

Billing Dove Tunnel

Giant Dome

LOWER CAVE

Hall of the Giants

Twin Domes

Temple of the Sun

Rock of Ages

Breast of Venus

View of Lower Cave

Crystal Spring Dome

Fairyland

Pits

Totem Pole

Lily Pads

BIG

Mirror Lake

ROOM

Gypsum Beds

0   250 ft
0   100 m

N

Bottomless Pit

Taos

Albuquerque ○ ★ Santa Fe

NEW MEXICO

Carlsbad Caverns National Park ■ ○ Roswell

---

make it easy for everyone to descend 750 feet (75 stories!) and visit the lower cavern—visitors in wheelchairs are common, since there's a paved path with guard rails throughout the main caves. Oh, and a kennel for pets is available, too.

In addition to the main tours described here, ask the visitor center info desk folks about other ranger-guided tours, including climbing and crawling "wild" cave tours (which are BYO kneepads). Be sure to call days in advance because some tours are offered only 1 day a week. Spelunkers who seek access to the park's undeveloped caves need special permission from the park superintendent.

Carlsbad Cavern Tours

You can tour Carlsbad Cavern in one of three ways. The first and least difficult is to take the elevator from the visitor center 750 feet down to the start of the self-guided tour of the Big Room.

More difficult and time-consuming, but vastly more rewarding, is the 1-mile self-guided tour along the Natural Entrance route (which is actually safe and paved, but slippery). It follows the traditional explorer's route, entering the cavern through the large historic natural entrance. The walkway winds into the depths of the cavern and leads through a series of underground rooms; it should take you about an hour, and will give your thighs a good workout since parts of it are very steep. At its lowest point, the trail reaches the Big Room where you can go on a short or long tour of its 14 acres. By the way, this is the place where you may be shocked (and/or a bit saddened) to find an underground rest area, complete with cheapo snack bar and gift shop, and kids practicing obnoxious vacation behavior.

The third option is the 1½-hour ranger-guided Kings Palace tour that also departs from the underground rest area. This tour descends 830 feet beneath the surface of the desert to the deepest portion of the cavern open to the public. Reservations are required, and an additional fee is charged.

Slaughter Canyon Cave Tours

Slaughter Canyon Cave was discovered in 1937 and was mined for bat guano (manure that makes a great fertilizer) commercially until the 1950s. It consists of a corridor 1,140 feet long, with many a side passageway. The lowest point is 250 feet below the surface, and the ranger-guided tour through it is 1¾ miles long—but is more strenuous than hiking through the main cavern. There is also a serious 500-foot-rise hike from the parking lot to the cave mouth. The tour lasts about 2½ hours, and no more than 25 people can go at a time, and then only by reservation. Everyone needs a flashlight (bring fresh batteries), hiking boots or shoes, and a container of drinking water. Kneepads are also recommended.

Slaughter Canyon Cave is reached via US 180, south 5 miles from White's City, to a marked turnoff that leads 11 miles into a parking lot.

Other Guided Tours

Be sure to ask at the visitor center about the Left Hand Tunnel, Lower Cave, Hall of the White Giant, and Spider Cave tours.

carlsbad cavern Tour Tips

Slippery paths abound in the Caverns, so wear flat shoes with rubber soles, and *no* high heels. A light sweater or jacket feels good in the constant temperature of 56°F, especially when it's 100°F outside in the sun. The cavern is well lit, but you can bring a flashlight for backup (though shining it just anywhere may disturb creatures in their nooks). Also, it's a whisper-only zone, despite the noisy visitors who shortcut to the Big Room via the elevators. Rangers stroll through the cave to answer questions.

These vary in degree of difficulty and adventure, from Left Hand, which is an easy half-mile lantern tour, to Spider Cave, where you can expect tight crawlways and canyonlike passages, to Hall of the White Giant, a strenuous tour where you're required to crawl long distances, squeeze through tight crevices, and climb up slippery flow-stone—lined passages. But what a way to experience some of the earth's great depths!

Call in advance for times of each tour. All these tours depart from the visitor center.

Bat Flights ★

Every sunset from May to October, a crowd gathers in a small amphitheater outside the Natural Entrance of the cave to watch a quarter-million bats take flight for a night of insect feasting. (The bats winter in Mexico.) All day long, the Mexican free-tailed bats sleep in the cavern; at night, they all strike out on an insect hunt. A ranger program is offered around 7:30pm (verify the time at the visitor center) at the outdoor Bat Flight Amphitheater.

Carlsbad Events: Going Bats!

→ It's worth rising early for the Carlsbad Caverns' **Bat Flight Breakfast** every year on the second Thursday of August. An early-morning buffet breakfast is served while participants watch a quarter-million bats return to the cave from their nightly insect hunt. Call ☎ **505/785-3012** for details and exact date.

→ From Thanksgiving to New Year's Eve (except Christmas Eve), take a pontoon-boat ride during **Christmas on the Pecos.** It's Carlsbad's seasonal tour of Christmas light displays on riverside homes and businesses (☎ **800/221-1224** or 505/887-6516; www.christmasonthepecos.com).

On the second Thursday in August (usually), the park sponsors a **Bat Flight Breakfast** from 5 to 7am, during which visitors watch the bats return to the cavern. The cost is $6 for adults. For information, call ☎ 505/785-2232, ext. 0.

Other Park Activities

Aside from the caves, the park offers a 10-mile one-way **scenic loop drive** through the Chihuahuan Desert to view Rattlesnake and Upper Walnut canyons. So pack a lunch and head for Rattlesnake Springs Picnic Area, on County Road 418 near Slaughter Canyon Cave—a water source for hundreds of years for the Native Americans, and a primo birding spot. Backcountry hikers must register at the visitor center before going out on any of the trails in the park's 46,766 acres.

What Else to See & Do

Carlsbad's pride and joy is the broad Pecos River. There's a 3½-mile **riverwalk** along the idyllic shady banks, beginning around the north end of Riverside Drive. This is a lovely place for a picnic, and a municipal beach at the north end has changing rooms and showers if you'd like to cool off.

Then there's the **Carlsbad Museum and Art Center,** 418 W. Fox St., 1 block west of Canal Street (☎ 505/887-0276). It's home to Apache relics, pioneer artifacts, and a solid art collection. The museum's store has a small but fine selection of jewelry at reasonable prices. The museum is open Monday through Saturday from 10am to 5pm; admission is free, though they won't refuse a donation.

MORE OUTDOOR FUN

They take care of outdoorsy types in Carlsbad, with plenty of recreational facilities around. Hit up the **City of Carlsbad Recreation Department** (☎ 505/887-1191) to check in on seasonal hours for the two dozen parks, golf courses and tennis courts, swimming pools, municipal beach, and shooting and archery ranges.

→ **Living Desert Zoo & Gardens State Park** ★ Set within 1,200 acres of authentic Chihuahuan Desert, this park contains more than 50 species of desert mammals, birds, and reptiles, and almost 500 varieties of plants. Even for someone not into zoos, this is a pleasant 1⅓-mile walk. You pass through displays that point out vegetation and geologic formations. You're likely to see lizards and other wild creatures, as well as captive ones, and you can duck into the new nocturnal exhibit. You'll also get to see golden eagles and great horned owls among the birds of prey in the aviary, and large animals such as deer and elk in outdoor pastures.

Inside the park there's also a rehabilitation program to take care of sick or injured animals that can no longer survive in the wild. Plus there's a killer view from the park, high atop the Ocotillo Hills on Carlsbad's northwest side. *1504 Miehls Dr.* ☎ *505/887-5516. www.livingdesert.org. Adults $5; group rates available. Memorial*

Day weekend to Labor Day 8am–8pm, last park entry by 6:30pm. Rest of year 9am–5pm, last park entry by 3:30pm. Closed Christmas. Take Miehls Dr. off US 285 west of town and proceed just over a mile.

On the Road to El Paso, TX

Carlsbad, NM to El Paso, TX 165 miles

It's you and the highway for 165 miles from Carlsbad to El Paso. Of course, the **Caverns** are on the way 23 miles outside of town. Then in another 25 miles you'll be at the entrance to the **Guadalupe Mountains.** If you have time, and/or want to get in some last-minute hiking, camping, or amazingly scenic roaming in nature, consider a visit.

DETOUR: GUADALUPE MOUNTAINS NATIONAL PARK

Get this: About 250 million years ago, the Guadalupe Mountains were an immense reef poking up through a tropical ocean. Marine organisms fossilized this 400-mile-long Capitan Reef as limestone; later, as the sea evaporated, a blanket of sediments and mineral salts buried the reef. Then, just 10 to 12 million years ago, a mountain-building uplift exposed a part of the fossil reef. This has given modern scientists a unique opportunity to explore earth's geologic history, and outdoor lovers a playground in the wilderness.

The steep southern end of the range makes up **Guadalupe Mountains National Park** and includes Guadalupe Peak—the highest in Texas at 8,749 feet—while the northern part lies within Lincoln National Forest and Carlsbad Caverns National Park. Wildly different than in the surrounding desert, deer, elk, mountain lions, and bears are found in these forests, while isolated basins and protected valleys are home to rampant vegetation rare elsewhere in the Southwest.

Essentials

Enter the park from US 62/180, 55 miles southwest of Carlsbad. Admission is $3, and the visitor center is open June through August daily from 8am to 6pm September through May from 8am to 4:30pm. You can reach the **Park Ranger** at ☎ 915/828-3251; www.nps.gov/gumo). The park has more than 80 miles of trails; most are steep, rugged, and rocky. No lodging, restaurants, stores, or gas exist within 35 miles of the park. Leashed pets are permitted only in the campground parking area.

Highlights

The visitor center has exhibits and slide programs that tell the story of the Guadalupe Mountains, as well as ranger-guided walks and lectures. You can get maps, backcountry permits, and other information at **McKittrick Canyon Visitor Center** (10 miles northeast via US 62/180 and a side road; ☎ 915/828-3381) and the **Dog Canyon Ranger Station** (reached through Carlsbad via NM 137 and County Rd. 414, about 70 miles; ☎ 505/981-2418).

Most of the park's 86,416 acres are reached only by 80 miles of foot or horse trails through desert, canyon, and high forest. The visitor center can provide you with a brief trail guide. A longer guide, titled *Trails of the Guadalupe,* is available for purchase at the visitor center as well.

One of the most scenic hikes in Texas is to the top of **Guadalupe Peak,** an 8.5-mile round-trip trek accessed from the Pine Springs Campground. Super scenic **McKittrick Canyon** is protected by its

Adios, Amigos Playlist

→ *The Ballad of John and Yoko,* **Beatles,** 1969
→ *He's a Rebel,* **Vicki Carr,** 1962 (she's from El Paso)
→ *It Happened in El Paso,* **Bobby Fuller,** "Breakin Rocks," 2003 (she's from El Paso)
→ *Old el Paso,* **Riders in the Sky,** "Prairie Serenade," 1992
→ *Coquette,* **Biréli Lagrène,** "Gypsy Project," 2001
→ *Melodia del Rio,* **Ruben Gonzalez,** "Introducing . . . Ruben Gonzalez," 1997
→ *I've Been Everywhere,* **Johnny Cash,** "Unchained," 1956

high sheer walls, with a green swath of trees growing along the banks of its spring-fed stream. It is a great spot for hiking and wildlife voyeurism, and it's an especially lovely sight during fall foliage season (late Oct to mid-Nov). The **McKittrick Canyon Trail** travels more than 10 miles into the canyon and up onto a ridge. If you're interested in day-hiking it, be aware that you'll walk a mile before it becomes scenic. If you're going backcountry, you need permits and your own water, and camping must be in designated areas.

Camping
Pine Springs and Dog Canyon both have developed camping areas, with restrooms and water, but no hookups or showers. Fires, including charcoal, are not permitted.

On the Road Nuts & Bolts

Where to Fill Up Gas is priciest right outside the Caverns, so to save a few cents per gallon either fill up in Carlsbad, or right across the Texas border around Nickel Creek.

The Fastest Way If you've hit Carlsbad Caverns and are heading to El Paso in the same day, it's easy to hop on US 180/62 and haul straight into El Paso. Sticking to the 75 mph speed limit will get you there in 3 hours or less.

The Long Way Round This is the roadtrip's final stretch, which means you're probably worn out and ready to just get to El Paso already. If that's the case, see above. But if you can scrape together some energy and time, you'll enjoy a visit to **Guadalupe Mountains National Park,** just 25 miles southwest of Carlsbad Caverns (p. 812). Afterwards, resume the US 180/62 line and cruise to your final destination.

Rules of the Road 75 mph on a two-lane road—that's when you know you're in a rural corner of Texas. It's also another time when going super fast is totally legal.

Welcome to El Paso

Here, in the sunswept, mountainous desert of Texas's westernmost corner (next stop: Mexico!) is El Paso, the state's fourth-largest city. It's built between two mountain ranges on the shores of the Rio Grande, and it's a kind of urban history book, with chapters on Spanish

AMERICAN HIGHWAYS

conquistadors, ancient highways, gunfighters, border disputes, and modern sprawl.

The Franklin Mountains that contain downtown El Paso are the reason for its storied history. They served as natural defense for the American Indians who inhabited the area for more than 10 millennia, while the Rio Grande brought water. The canyon formed by the mountains made the Spanish explorers who first crossed the Rio Grande in the 16th century see an ideal north-south route—soon earning the area the name "Camino Real" (or "King's Highway").

Spain's flag over El Paso was eventually replaced by a Mexican one when independence was established in 1821. But it was a short-lived era, as Mexico ceded the land north of the Rio Grande to the United States at the end of the Mexican-American War (1846–48). The railroad brought commerce to El Paso in 1881, along with the nickname "Sin City" thanks to the saloons, brothels, and casinos that lined every major street. This is when notorious gunfighters like Billy the Kid and John Wesley Hardin called the city home.

In the 20th century, agriculture, manufacturing, and international trade brought boom times. The city's symbiotic relationship with Ciudad Juárez just across the border has gone on for centuries, even more so since the century-old border dispute was resolved in the 1960s and the North American Free Trade Agreement was signed in 1994.

Compared with Santa Fe or Tucson, El Paso is in many ways the "real" Southwest—unpolished, undiluted, and honest. Separated by the Rio Grande, El Paso and Ciudad Juárez each represent their country's largest border city, and El Paso's local culture is now a fusion of Mexican and American traditions, pretty distinct from the way of life in eastern Texas.

A day or two to explore El Paso is worth it—take the time to check out downtown, enjoy some Tex-Mex food, and learn what a border town is all about.

El Paso **Nuts & Bolts**

Area Code The telephone area code in El Paso, in El Paso County, is 915.

Doctors Call El Paso County Medical Society (☎ 915/533-0981).

Drugstores Walgreens Drug Stores has a 24-hour prescription service at 1831 N. Lee Trevino Dr. (☎ 915/594-1129).

Emergencies For police, fire, and medical emergencies, call ☎ 911. To reach the Poison Center, dial ☎ 800/764-7661 or 915/544-1200.

Hospitals Full-service hospitals, with 24-hour emergency rooms, include Sierra Medical Center, 1625 Medical Center Dr. (☎ 915/747-4000), just northwest of downtown, and Del Sol Medical Center, 10301 Gateway W. (☎ 915/595-9000), on the east side of the city.

Internet The main **El Paso Library** is downtown at 501 N. Oregon St., and you can get on a computer there for free for 1-hour intervals. There are also Wi-Fi cafes and restaurants all over town, including **Kristoph's Coffees**, 1506 N. Lee Trevino Dr. (☎ 915/5925136), and **Jamocha Coffee**, 2231 N. Mesa St. (☎ 915/838-7177).

Newspapers & Magazines The *El Paso Times* (www.elpasotimes.com) is the city's only daily English language newspaper, and an El Paso edition of *El Diario de Juárez* (www.eldiario.com.mx) is published in Spanish daily. *El Paso Scene* (www.epscene.com) is the city's free monthly arts-and-entertainment paper.

Post Office The main post office, located downtown at 219 E. Mills Ave., is open Monday through Friday from 8:30am to 5pm, Saturday from 8:30am to noon.

Safety El Paso has among the lowest crime rates of any major U.S. city, but it's far from crime-free, and drugs and auto theft are the two major problems. It's important to keep aware of your surroundings at all times and ask at your hotel or a visitor center about the safety of a given neighborhood, especially after dark. *Note:* When visiting Mexico, remember that Ciudad Juárez is one of the world's most active drug-smuggling centers. Gangs have also grown in numbers in Juárez in recent years.

Taxes In the city of El Paso, the total sales tax is 8.25% and 14% for lodging.

Time Zone El Paso is in the Mountain Standard Time zone, like nearby New Mexico but unlike the rest of Texas, which is in the Central Standard Time zone. Set your clock back 1 hour if you enter El Paso from the east.

Transit Information The local bus system is **Sun Metro** (☎ 915/533-3333; www.sunmetro.org), which runs from 4:30am to 8:15pm on weekdays, with slightly shorter hours on weekends and holidays. The fare is $1 for adults.

Visitors Bureau The **El Paso Convention & Visitors Bureau** is located at One Civic Center Plaza, in the El Paso Convention and Performing Arts Center (☎ 800/351-6024 or 915/534-0601; www.visitelpaso.com). The CVB's biannual *El Paso: The Official Visitor's Guide* is a good publication to pick up while you're there. For information on Ciudad Juárez across the border, contact **Fiprotur Chihuahua,** Av. de las Americas #2551, Ciudad Juárez, Mexico (☎ 888/654-0394; www.juarez.info).

Getting Around

The Rio Grande and the Franklin Mountains have guided the urban development of El Paso for more than 400 years. It's created a sort of U-shaped city, with the Franklin Mountains in the center and the downtown area at the bottom.

While El Paso has a public bus system, cars are—surprise!—the norm. Parking is rarely an issue, even downtown.

When you are preparing to fly home, the **El Paso International Airport** is only 20 minutes away, just a mile north of I-10 via Airway Boulevard on the city's east side (☎ **915/77780-4749;** www.elpasointernationalairport.com). Beware

of traffic congestion that could double the trip time.

BY CAR

The main artery to the east and west is I-10, bisecting El Paso between downtown and the Franklin Mountains. And because of those mountains and the interstate, you can pretty much gauge where you're at and which direction is which, and navigate pretty instinctively.

Street parking is free almost everywhere except downtown, where the meters must be fed at 25¢/hour. The covered garages downtown charge $3 to $6 per day. There are also many outdoor lots that are geared toward tourists on day trips to Ciudad

El Paso

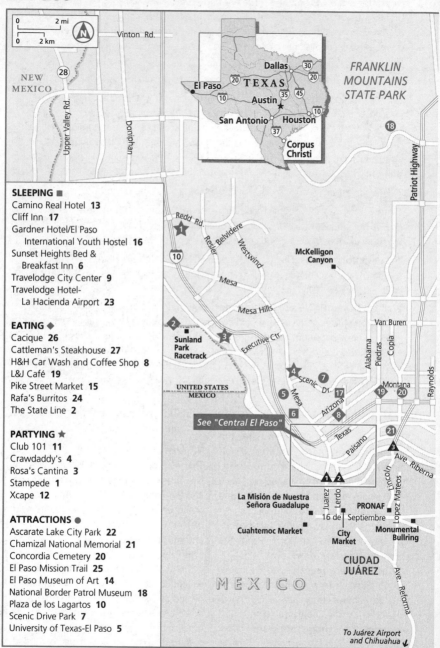

SLEEPING ■
Camino Real Hotel **13**
Cliff Inn **17**
Gardner Hotel/El Paso
   International Youth Hostel **16**
Sunset Heights Bed &
   Breakfast Inn **6**
Travelodge City Center **9**
Travelodge Hotel-
   La Hacienda Airport **23**

EATING ◆
Cacique **26**
Cattleman's Steakhouse **27**
H&H Car Wash and Coffee Shop **8**
L&J Café **19**
Pike Street Market **15**
Rafa's Burritos **24**
The State Line **2**

PARTYING ★
Club 101 **11**
Crawdaddy's **4**
Rosa's Cantina **3**
Stampede **1**
Xcape **12**

ATTRACTIONS ●
Ascarate Lake City Park **22**
Chamizal National Memorial **21**
Concordia Cemetery **20**
El Paso Mission Trail **25**
El Paso Museum of Art **14**
National Border Patrol Museum **18**
Plaza de los Lagartos **10**
Scenic Drive Park **7**
University of Texas-El Paso **5**

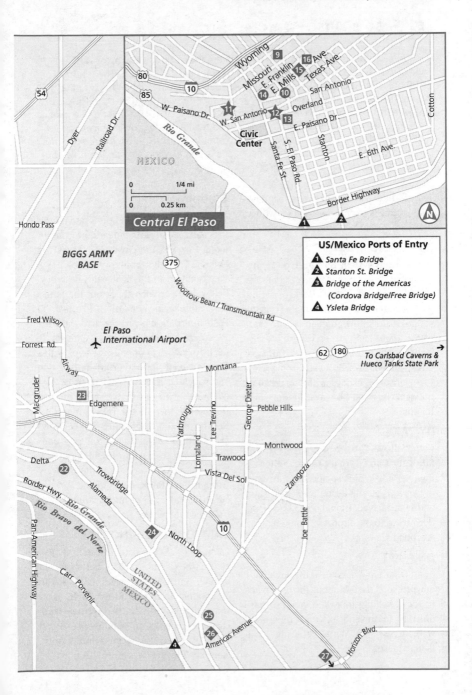

Central El Paso

US/Mexico Ports of Entry

1 Santa Fe Bridge
2 Stanton St. Bridge
3 Bridge of the Americas
   (Cordova Bridge/Free Bridge)
4 Ysleta Bridge

El Paso's Artsy 'Gators

In El Paso's downtown San Jacinto Plaza, the **Plaza de los Lagartos,** a fiberglass fountain comprised of snarling alligators, basks in the sun. The toothy 1993 piece by pop artist (and El Paso native) Luis Jimenez harks back to the gators that called the plaza home for nearly a century. In the 1880s, El Paso's mayor first deposited the reptiles in the plaza's fountain as something of a joke; surprisingly, they thrived amid the hustle and bustle of the growing city until they were deemed a potential hazard and removed in the 1960s. *(In San Jacinto Plaza, bordered on the east and west by Mesa and Oregon sts., and north and south by Main and Mills sts.)*

Juárez. These usually run $2 to $5 per day—local advice is to only park in a lot with an attendant.

BY PUBLIC TRANSIT

El Paso's bus system, **Sun Metro** (☎ 915/533-3333; www.sunmetro.org), operates one of the world's largest fleets of natural gas–powered buses. The main transfer station is downtown on San Jacinto Plaza at Mesa and Main streets. There are also trolleys that run between the UTEP campus and downtown. Buses run from 4:30am to 8:15pm on weekdays, with shorter hours on weekends and holidays; the fare is $1 for adults.

BY TAXIS

Both **Yellow Cab** (☎ 915/533-3433) and **Sun City Cab** (☎ 915/544-2211) offer 24-hour service in El Paso and the surrounding area. Typically a ride is $1.65 to start, and $2.25 each additional mile (a ride from downtown to the airport, at about 9 miles, is around $22–$25).

ON FOOT

Apart from a few strips near the university, downtown El Paso is about the only place fit for a walking tour. You can also park on the south end of downtown and walk across the Santa Fe Bridge into Ciudad Juárez.

Sleeping

There are tons of chain hotels and motels in El Paso, mostly either near the airport or along I-10. FYI, the city's room taxes add about 14% to lodging bills.

In addition to the properties described below, you can also check out the hotels and motels located off I-10 near El Paso International Airport, like the **Best Western Airport Inn,** 7144 Gateway E. (☎ 800/528-1234 or 915/779-7700), with a double rate of $64, and **Comfort Inn,** 900 Yarbrough Dr. (☎ 800/228-5150 or 915/594-9111), with a double rate of $85. Downtown, there is the **Travelodge City Center** at 409 E. Missouri St. (☎ 800/578-7878 or 915/544-3333), offering doubles for $50 to $60. In the Sunland Park area, the pick of the litter is the **Holiday Inn Sunland Park,** 900 Sunland Park Dr. (☎ 800/658-2744 or 915/833-2900), with a double rate of $105.

CAMPGROUNDS/HOSTEL

Camping in El Paso is almost entirely RV-centric (hello, snowbirds!), but there are a few tent-camping sites at Franklin Mountains. At **Hueco State Park,** 6900 Hueco Tanks Rd. #1 (☎ 915/857-1135), camping depends on volunteers—so call ahead to see if the campground is open. (see also "Playing Outside," p. 829).

El Paso Events: Cinco de Mayo & More!

It seems the fine people of El Paso love their celebrations, because year-round you can find festivals in El Paso. Many of them are managed by the **El Paso Festival Association,** which keeps an up-to-date website of goings-on about town (☎ 915/351-1191; www.elpasofestivals.com).

→ If you love salsa—the sauce or the dance—do not miss the annual **Salsa Festival** every late September. It's held at Cohen Stadium, and for 2 days you can eat very well, hear live music, try samples from the salsa competition, get in on some dancing (or watch the pros), and witness the burn of the jalapeño-pepper eating contest. Tickets go for $12/day (☎ 915/351-1191; www.elpasofestivals.com).

→ Each early May brings the **Cinco de Mayo Festival** to the banks of Ascarate Lake. Between the margaritas, mole, and mariachis, you may think you're south of the border. There are also slow- and fast-pitch softball tournaments. Tickets will run you $5 to $10, depending on when you buy them (☎ 915/351-1191; www.elpasofestivals.com).

→ Hear the roar of Harleys at the **Custom Car & Chopper Festival,** held every early June on Texas Avenue; $10 tickets ($12 at the door) will let you mingle with motorcycle pros and their custom bikes, with live music and lots of beer to boot (☎ 915/351-1191; www.elpasofestivals.com).

→ FREE Head to the University of Texas at El Paso campus for the rockin' **Border Music Festival,** held every mid-March. Rock, punk, country— it's all there (☎ 915/747-5481; www.bordermusicfestival.com).

→ FREE One of the most significant rituals of Mexican culture is celebrated on October 29 each year, with the **Dia de los Muertos Festival.** A parade, contests, and illuminated altars honor and celebrate the dead, and just in time for Halloween (☎ 915/351-1191; www. elpasofestivals.com).

→**Franklin Mountains State Park**
About 20 minutes from downtown, the park has a few developed tent campsites with grills (but no water or electricity) set in one of the most scenic and recreation-happy parks around (p. 829). The park is open daily 8am to 5pm year-round, but campers get a combination to the gate so they can come and go after day-use hours. *1331 McKelligon Canyon Rd. (I-10 west to Canutillo/Trans-Mountain exit; park is 3¾ miles east).* ☎ *915/566-6441 or 800/792-1112. www.tpwd.state.tx.us/spdest/findadest/parks/franklin/fee.phtml. 5 sites, reservations recommended. $8 nightly (daily admission fees may apply). Cash only. Pets allowed with strict regulations. No hookups, no campfires.*

→ **Gardner Hotel/El Paso International Youth Hostel** ★★ A downtown mainstay since 1922, the Gardner Hotel is locally known as the place gangster John Dillinger stayed while on the run in the 1930s. The public areas are well kept, especially the lobby, which has been restored to its original condition with a marble staircase, mauve carpeting, and historical photographs. There are two shared hostel rooms—one for males and one for females—each with two bunk beds and desks. There are also private accommodations—some with no frills, some with the original antique furnishings, all with private bathrooms. Shared-room guests also share bathrooms and kitchen, and also have access to a television, pool table, and a pay Internet kiosk. *311 E. Franklin St., El Paso, TX 79901.* ☎ *915/532-3661. www.gardner hotel.com. 50 units. $18 dormitory bunk; $20–$64 private rooms.*

CHEAP

➜ **Travelodge Hotel—La Hacienda Airport** ★ Some roadside motels surprise you with their attention to detail—this is one of them. Situated northeast of downtown off busy Montana Avenue, the grounds here are worlds apart, centered about a shady courtyard surrounding a heated pool. The rooms are housed in 10 different brick buildings; some are on the small side, albeit well maintained and comfortable, while the newer, larger rooms are a notch above the norm. There are eight Jacuzzi rooms, each with a picture window that separates the tub from the bedroom. *6400 Montana Ave.* ☎ *800/772-4231 or 915/772-4231. www.the.travelodge. com/elpaso05473. 91 units. $49–$75 double; $85 suite; $95 Jacuzzi room. Rates include continental breakfast. Pets accepted with $10 per night fee. Amenities: Restaurant; bar; outdoor heated pool; exercise room; Jacuzzi; business center; dataport; fridge.*

DOABLE

➜ **Cliff Inn** ★ Located on the slope of the Franklin Mountains above downtown El Paso, the Cliff Inn is an unusual mid-priced hotel with a distinct personality. Palm trees, Art Deco interior, tiled lobby, with a touch of kitsch—all make for a comfortable vibe, leading to comfortable and well-maintained rooms (though maybe a bit dated). Some of the rooms have kitchenettes and great city views. *1600 Cliff Dr. (adjacent to the El Paso Medical Center).* ☎ *866/254-3346 or 915/533-6700. 80 units, including 1 suite. $60 double; $80–$90 suite. Rates include continental breakfast. Amenities: Restaurant; bar; concierge; courtesy car; kitchenette (in some units); fridge.*

➜ **Sunset Heights Bed & Breakfast Inn** Named for the historic district in which it resides, Sunset Heights is El Paso's only B&B. It's a stately three-story Victorian inn shaded by palm trees and guarded by wrought-iron fencing. The rooms are comfortable and romantic, with natural wood and period furnishings. The Oriental Room, with a private balcony, claw-foot tub, and city view, is my pick. The crowning touches are the backyard, with a nice pool surrounded by gardens, and breakfast. *717 W. Yandell Ave.* ☎ *915/544-1743. 4 units, including 1 suite. $85–$95 double; $125 suite. Rates include full breakfast. Amenities: Outdoor pool; Jacuzzi; no phone in rooms.*

SPLURGE

➜ **Camino Real Hotel** ★★ El Paso's finest hotel is the only Camino Real hotel or resort outside of Mexico. It's just 6 blocks north of the border, adjacent to the El Paso Convention and Performing Arts Center and within easy walking distance of all the downtown attractions. It's also listed on the National Register of Historic Places, and is formerly known as the Hotel Paso del Norte, first opened in 1912. The lavish marble-and-cherrywood lobby is under a stunning glass dome from Tiffany's. In 1986, a modern 17-story tower was built next to the old Paso del Norte, expanding the lobby and more than doubling the hotel's capacity.

The oversize rooms have great beds and decor punctuated by massive mirrored armoires and downtown great views. The selection is rounded out by a wide variety of elegant suites with Victorian and Southwestern motifs. *101 S. El Paso St.* ☎ *800/769-4300 or 915/534-3000. www.camino real.com. 359 units. $99–$150 double; $160–$990 suite. Underground parking $5 daily. Amenities: 3 restaurants; bar; outdoor heated pool; exercise room; sauna; courtesy car; business center; 24-hr. room service; dataport.*

Eating

This may come as a shock, but Mexican food is pretty common in El Paso. Much of it is outstanding, too. There are, however, other options—but it's still better if you like the traditional tortillas, rice, and beans.

TAKEOUT TREATS

Beyond the options listed below, you can't go wrong grabbing a quick breakfast or lunch at **Cacique,** 305 Ya Ya Lane (☎ 915/859-5287), at the Tigua Cultural Center on the El Paso Mission Trail (p. 828). For coffee or a plump sandwich, hit the Seattle-themed **Pike Street Market,** 207 Mills St. (☎ 915/545-1010), a downtown hangout popular with suits and slackers alike.

If you want an amazingly good burrito in an authentic Mexican takeout place right near the border (east of downtown), go to ▥ Best❶ **Rafa's Burritos,** 408 Dodge St. (☎ 915/779-6221). The menu is in Spanish, but the staff will translate for you. There's also the cheap local fave **Chico's Tacos,** 5303 Montana Ave. (☎ 915/772-7777), with three more locations around town.

EATING OUT

Cheap

➔ **H&H Car Wash and Coffee Shop** ★ TEX-MEX/COFFEE SHOP A dinky coffee shop straight out of the 1960s, the H&H is a bit weathered, noisy, and not much to look at. It doesn't matter—the place is home to some of the best inexpensive Tex-Mex in town. It's packed with locals from open to close, scarfing down specialties like *carne picada* (diced sirloin with jalapeños, tomatoes, and onions), huevos rancheros, and chiles rellenos. For hungry road-trippers with dirty cars and tight budgets, you can't get any more convenient than the H&H: Gas up, get your car washed, and have a bite to eat, all in one fell swoop. The car wash operates from 9am to 5pm during the week and from 9am to 3pm on Saturdays,

charging $10 to $15 for a complete hand cleaning, inside and out. *701 E. Yandell Dr. at Ochoa St. ☎ 915/533-1144. Reservations not accepted. Main courses $5–$7. Mon–Sat 7am–3pm.*

➔ **L&J Café** ★★ TEX-MEX Nicknamed "The Old Place by the Graveyard" because of its proximity to the Concordia Cemetery (p. 828), the L&J has been an El Paso landmark since it first opened its doors in 1927, and the rowdy bar and the checkerboard-floored dining room are both now legendary. For Tex-Mex fanatics, the chicken enchiladas, overflowing with fluffy meat and buried under chunky green chile and Jack cheese, approach perfection. Fiery and addictive, the chile con queso and *caldillo* (beef and potato stew with a green chile and garlic kick) are as good as you'll find anywhere. There are also healthy versions of many entrees, prepared with less cheese and tortillas that aren't fried. The service is quick and friendly, even when the place is filled to capacity—as it is most of the time. *3622 E. Missouri St. ☎ 915/566-8418. Reservations not accepted. Main courses $5–$10. Mon–Fri 10am–8pm; Sat 10am–6pm (bar open later).*

Doable

➔ **The State Line** BARBECUE So named because it straddles the Texas–New Mexico border, the State Line is where El Paso heads for barbecue, and with good reason. The platters of slow-cooked barbecue—ribs, beef, pork, chicken, sausage, and turkey, all served with potato salad, coleslaw, and baked beans—make for a sure cure for hunger. Expect a heavy dose of nostalgia with your meal, in the form of an antique "love tester" and weathered wooden walls plastered with collages of RC Cola ads, cigar box covers, and apple-crate labels. There are also "Blue Plate Specials" with steak or seafood, a couple of all-you-can-eat options, and sandwiches

AMERICAN HIGHWAYS

at lunch. *1222 Sunland Park Dr.* ☎ *915/581-3371. Reservations accepted for large parties only. Main courses $5–$21 lunch, $10–$21 dinner. Summer daily 11:30am–10pm; winter daily 11:30am–9:30pm.*

Splurge

➔ **Cattleman's Steakhouse at Indian Cliffs Ranch** ★ STEAKS Established in 1969, this steakhouse feels like a city unto itself, as a desert outpost dedicated to the consumption of enormous cuts of beef. In the main building, there are seven themed dining rooms—ranging from tropical to the kitschy to the authentically Western—as well as a patio with a spectacular view of nearby Sand Cliff Lake. Also on the property: a mini-zoo with goats, ostrich, buffalo, and a rattlesnake pit; and a movie set used by several Hollywood productions. With all of the activity, it's a surprise the food ever gets any notice, but the thick steaks here are tough to top (and tender to taste). Perpetually voted the best in the El Paso area, they range in size from the 6-ounce "Lady's Filet" to the hearty-beyond-belief "Cowboy," a 2-pound porterhouse. There are also barbecue and seafood dishes, but if you're a vegetarian, you're out of luck. *Fabens Rd., 5 miles north of I-10, Exit 49 (29 miles east of El Paso via I-10 and Fabens Rd.).* ☎ *915/544-3200. Reservations not accepted. Main courses $9–$29. Mon–Fri 4:30–10pm; Sat 12:30–10pm; Sun 12:30–9pm.*

Partying

El Paso's entertainment scene is spread throughout the city, and remarkably diverse, with bars and clubs hosting plenty of live rock, country, *Tejano,* and jazz.

The free, monthly *El Paso Scene* and its online counterpart, **www.epscene.com**, are the best places to start for exploring arts-and-entertainment. The Friday *El Paso Times* (www.elpasotimes.com) also lists performance and shows, as does *The Prospector,* UTEP's student newspaper.

Scenic Drive Park

Located high above downtown atop the cliffs of the Franklin Mountains, this municipal park (Scenic Dr. between Rim Rd. and Alabama Ave.) offers amazing views of El Paso and surrounding area. With the naked eye or coin-op telescopes, you can see from the University of Texas at El Paso to downtown, across the Rio Grande to Juárez, and even parts of New Mexico.

For bar/restaurant action, head to **Crawdaddy's,** 212 Cincinnati St. (☎ **915/533-9332**), a cozy-but-rowdy haunt favored by the UTEP crowd. There you can get daily $1 beer specials and cayenne-spiced Cajun dishes. It's located amid a strip of bars and restaurants out on Cincinnati Street, one of the city's livelier blocks at midnight.

One of the most regal places in the Southwest to sip a cocktail, **Dome Bar,** 101 S. El Paso St. in the Camino Real Hotel (☎ **915/534-3000**), is light-years beyond a typical hotel bar. **Rosa's Cantina,** 3454 Doniphan Dr. (☎ **915/833-0402**), was made famous by country legend Marty Robbins in his 1959 hit "El Paso."

LIVE MUSIC

Going strong for more than a decade, **Club 101,** 500 San Francisco St. (☎ **915/544-2101**), is a downtown alternative hot spot featuring DJs and local and national rock acts. **Stampede,** 5500 Doniphan Rd. (☎ **915/833-6397**), is an El Paso country-and-western institution that has recorded and live music Thursday through Saturday. **Xcape,** 209 S. El Paso St. (☎ **915/542-3800**), caters to the young and hip with shows ranging from Latin to techno. Located in a century-old theater renovated for the new millennium, it's open Friday and Saturday.

What Else to See & Do

El Paso's main shopping district is downtown and targets both Mexican and American shoppers. There are also several enclosed malls scattered around the city, and you're likely to find tons of places to buy Western wear, Southwestern art, and Mexican imports.

You can start at **Cowtown Boots,** 11401 Gateway W. (☎ **915/593-2929;** www.cowtownboots.com), which claims to be the world's largest Western wear store at 40,000 square feet filled with boots (alligator to ostrich), jeans, clothing, and accessories.

For tongue-searing delicacies to bring home, hit the **El Paso Chile Company,** 909 Texas Ave. (☎ **888/4-SALSAS** or 915/544-3434; www.elpasochile.com) for its sauces with names like "Hellfire & Damnation."

El Paso's sister city, **Ciudad Juárez,** is also worth a visit if you've got the time. It's the fourth-largest city in Mexico with approximately two million residents. (Together, the cities form the largest binational population in the world.) Juárez is seedy in the same way as other border cities like Nogales and Tijuana, but it is more of a real Mexican city, not one built on tourism alone. It's got more history and industry, and makes for an interesting stop for an afternoon, or even a whole day for its outdoor markets, historic missions, and hap'nin' nightlife.

You can drive or walk across one of the five border bridges, which, aside from the "Free Bridge" (or Cordova Bridge) south of I-10 via US 54, all charge nominal tolls, even to pedestrians, of 25¢ to $2. The most convenient points of entry are the two downtown bridges, at Stanton Street and Santa Fe Street. U.S. currency is welcome practically everywhere in Juárez.

Remember: The U.S. now "may" (says the State Department website) require travelers to Mexico to present a passport—so maybe skip Mexico if you didn't bring it with you, or you don't have one.

ARTS, CULTURE & SOME HISTORY & PARKS

FREE ➔ **Ascarate Lake City Park** Centered on a 44-acre artificial lake, this municipal park consists of 400 acres of undeveloped terrain crisscrossed by trails. Swimming in the lake is prohibited, but fishing is allowed (the lake is stocked with channel catfish and rainbow trout). Plus there's golfing at the park's 27-hole golf course. There's also an aquatics center with an indoor Olympic-size pool and ball fields. *6900 Delta Dr., between Alameda Ave. and Border Hwy.* ☎ *915/772-3941. Free admission to park, although some attractions have fees, including the golf course and Western Playland Amusement Park. Daily dawn–dusk.*

FREE ➔ **Chamizal National Memorial** ★ When the Mexican-American War ended in 1848, the two countries agreed upon a border: the center of the deepest channel of the Rio Grande. However, as historian Leon C. Metz once wrote, "Rivers are never *absolutely* permanent. They evaporate, flood, change channels, shrink, expand and even disappear. Rivers are, by nature, capricious." After the war, the Rio Grande gradually shifted southward, resulting in a diplomatic stalemate between Mexico and the United States over the boundary's location. This impasse lasted until 1967, finally ending when presidents Lyndon B. Johnson and Adolfo López Mateos signed the Chamizal Treaty. Parcels of land were exchanged, residents and businesses uprooted, and a permanent, concrete channel was constructed to signify a more predictable boundary.

The 55-acre park at the Chamizal National Memorial commemorates the dispute's settlement with a bevy of facilities: 2 miles of foot trails, an outdoor amphitheater that hosts many free concerts, and a visitor center/museum (expect to spend 30 min. touring the museum). It's a nice open space that's more accessible and greener than the Franklin Mountains, and larger than the other municipal parks. There is also a walkway to the adjacent Bridge of the Americas leading to the memorial's Mexican counterpart, **Parque Chamizal,** with an anthropology museum and an amusement park in Ciudad Juárez. *800 S. San Marcial Dr., at Paisano Dr. and US 54 (Patriot Fwy.).* ☎ *915/532-7273. www.nps. gov/cham. Free admission, with fees for some events in the amphitheater. Park daily 5am–10pm. Visitor center daily 8am–5pm.*

FREE → **Concordia Cemetery** On El Paso's "Boot Hill," Concordia is the final resting place of numerous infamous outlaws who met their maker in the city's wilder days. The gravestones here, which mostly date to the second half of the 19th century, remain haunting reminders of El Paso's storied past. Near the northern gate, the most notable grave is that of notorious John Wesley Hardin, known as "The Fastest Gun in the West." After his 1895 assassination in downtown El Paso, Hardin was put to rest here alongside other gunslingers (including Hardin's killer) and a generation of law-abiding citizens. Hardin's grave is said to be El Paso's most-visited attraction. *Copia St. and I-10.* ☎ *915/562-7062. Free admission. Daily 24 hr. Immediately north of I-10 via Copia St. (Exit 22A).*

FREE → **El Paso Mission Trail** ★ First established in the 17th and 18th centuries, three historic Spanish missions provide a link to El Paso's colonial past. All three are among the oldest continually active missions in the country, with great architecture and rich history. But if you only have time to hit only one, drive out to San Elceario; unlike Ysleta and Socorro, it's removed from the modern urban development and still feels like it's from a different era and culture.

From I-10, exit Zaragosa Road (Exit 32) and head south 3 miles to **Mission Ysleta,** 9501 Socorro Rd. at Zaragosa Road, established in 1682 in what was then Mexico. The silver-domed chapel here was built in 1851 after floods shifted the Rio Grande and washed away all of the previous structure, save the foundation.

Heading southeast on Socorro Road for 3 miles takes you to **Mission Socorro** (☎ **915/859-7718**), established in 1682, 1 day after Mission Ysleta. The original adobe chapel (1692) was washed away by a flood in the 1740s, rebuilt, destroyed again in 1829, and finally replaced in 1843 by the current, recently restored structure.

Presidio Chapel San Elceario (☎ **915/851-2333**), established at its present location in 1789 as a Spanish military outpost, sits 6 miles south of Mission Socorro on Socorro Road. Parishioners built the present-day church in 1877 as the centerpiece of the village plaza, which retains its historic charm to this day. This structure is the largest of the three missions, and an example of the blending of American Indian and Spanish architectural styles, with majestic arches and a pressed-tin ceiling. The surrounding village has been gaining fame in recent years as the site of "The First Thanksgiving," said to have taken place in 1598, 23 years before the Plymouth Thanksgiving.

Visitors are welcome to tour the missions on their own; expect to spend at least 3 hours if you visit all three. Bus tours are offered on occasion by the **El Paso-Juárez Trolley Company** (☎ **915/544-0062**). *An 8-mile stretch of Zaragosa and Socorro roads, southeast of downtown El Paso via I-10.* ☎ *915/534-0630. Free admission.*

FREE → **El Paso Museum of Art** ★★
Though some used to say the museum
lacked a regional focus, it now is home to
amazing landscapes and personal portraits
that evoke the region's look and feel. Of the
five permanent galleries, three are dedicated to the cultures that have commingled
in El Paso for the last 400 years: One is dedicated to Mexican art of the 17th to 19th
centuries, one to European art from the
13th to 18th centuries, and one to American
works dating from 1800 to the mid-1900s.
There are also seasonal exhibits that usually feature edgier contemporary works.
The museum begs for an unhurried hour of
your time. *1 Arts Festival Plaza.* ☎ *915/532-
1707. www.elpasoartmuseum.org. Free admission. Tues–Sat 9am–5pm; Sun noon–5pm.*

FREE → **National Border Patrol
Museum** The only museum dedicated to
the U.S. Border Patrol, this facility does a
good job presenting displays on all aspects
of the federal agency, founded in El Paso
in 1924. Give yourself about a half-hour
to peruse such highlights as the "Lady
Liberty" exhibit, a Statue of Liberty replica
and text and diaries about the immigrant
experience; and two former Border Patrol
aircraft: a Piper Super Cub plane and a
Hughes OH-6A helicopter. There are also
exhibits on Border Patrol dogs, electronics,
and ground vehicles. *4315 Transmountain Dr.*
☎ *915/759-6060. Free admission (donations
accepted). Tues–Sun 9am–5pm. Closed Mon
and major holidays.*

TOURS

The **El Paso–Juárez Trolley Company** ★
(☎ **915/544-0062**) has trolley tours that
venture into Mexico, New Mexico, and historic El Paso for $10 to $20, depending on
the package. Juárez tours depart hourly
from One Civic Center Plaza from 10am to
4pm year-round. Call for information on
other, seasonal tours.

Stop by the **El Paso CVB** (☎ **915/
534-0601**; www.elpasocvb.com) to pick up
brochures on self-guided historic walking
tours of both El Paso and Ciudad Juárez.

PLAYING OUTSIDE

At nearly 24,300 acres, **Franklin Mountains State Park** is the largest urban
wilderness park in the United States and a
favorite destination of El Pasoans looking
to hike, bike, or climb. The mountains are
covered by cacti and ocotillo, and populated by small mammals, birds, reptiles,
deer, and the occasional mountain lion. At
7,192 feet, the summit of North Franklin
Mountain is about 3,000 feet higher than
the city below.

The mountains, the final southern ridge
of the geological phenomenon that created the Rockies, are home to about 40
miles of developed hiking and mountain
biking trails. The hikes are mostly moderate to difficult; try the 1.2-mile round-trip
to the Aztec Caves or the more difficult 9.2-
mile round-trip to the peak of North
Franklin Mountain.

If you don't want to break a sweat,
take the **Wyler Aerial Tramway** (☎ **915/
566-6622**) to the summit of Ranger Peak
($7 adults). Beyond the trails and the tram,
the park is also a renowned rock-climbing
spot and home to an outdoor amphitheater.

There's also **Hueco Tanks State
Historic Site,** located 30 miles northeast
of El Paso via US 62/180 and Ranch Road
2775. It's another popular rock-climbing
destination and world-class bouldering
site. Centered about three small, rocky
outcroppings that loom above the surrounding desert, the park gets its name
from the *huecos* (depressions) that catch
rainwater and attract life. Many of the
rocks are marked by pictographs left by
native tribes over the last 10,000 years.
Tours of these fragile sites are offered

AMERICAN HIGHWAYS

at 9am and 11am in the summer and 10am and 2pm in the winter; reservations are recommended.

There are 6.5 miles of trails at Hueco and some campsites, though availability depends on volunteers.

The park charges $4 for day use and $10 to $12 for campsites. Bikes are not permitted. For more information, contact Hueco Tanks State Historic Site, 6900 Hueco Tanks Rd., #1 (☎ 915/857-1135).

Golf

The 27-hole **Painted Dunes Desert Golf Course,** located 9 miles northeast of I-10 via US 54 at 12000 McCombs St. (☎ 915/821-2122; www.painteddunes.com), is one of the top municipal courses in the country. Nonresident greens fees range from $36 to $46, cart included. El Paso native Lee Trevino began his illustrious professional golf career at **Emerald Springs Golf and Conference Center,** 20 miles east of town at 16000 Ashford St. (☎ 915/852-9110). Greens fees are $29 to $34, cart included. There are also **Ascarate Golf Course** in Ascarate Lake City Park (☎ 915/772-7381), with greens fees of $13 to $16 (carts: $10) and **Cielo Vista Golf Course,** 1510 Hawkins Blvd. (☎ 915/591-4927), with greens fees of $19 to $24 (carts: $10).

Horseback Riding

Rio Grande Valley Ranch, 300 Farm Rd. 259 (☎ 915/877-4447), is a full-service equestrian facility, offering trail rides (about $20 for an hour), stabling, and riding lessons.

Mountain Biking

Franklin Mountains State Park (see above) is by far the most popular mountain-biking destination in the El Paso area. About 70 miles of trails are open to bikers now, 50 of them added during a 2005 extension project.

SPECTATOR SPORTS

A little fact about El Paso: It's the most populous American city that is not home to a major-league sports franchise (MLB, NHL, NFL, or NBA). Good thing there's the University of Texas at El Paso (UTEP) Miners and the minor leagues to help sports fans get out some energy.

Baseball

The **El Paso Diablos,** the AA Texas League affiliate of the Arizona Diamondbacks, play an April-to-August schedule at 10,000-seat Cohen Stadium, 9700 Gateway Blvd. N. The stadium is one of the country's more colorful ballparks—sluggers hold out their batting helmets to the crowd for donations after home runs. Single-game tickets are $5 to $7. Call ☎ 915/755-2000 or visit www.diablos.com for schedules.

Basketball

The UTEP fields a Western Athletic Conference (WAC) team, the **Miners,** that plays from December to March at the Don Haskins Center, 2801 N. Mesa St. Tickets range from $5 to $15 for single games. Call ☎ 915/747-5234 or visit www.utepathletics.com to purchase tickets or for more information.

Football

The **UTEP Miners** football squad plays a WAC schedule from September to December on campus at the Sun Bowl. Single-game tickets are $6 to $15. Also, the stadium hosts the second-oldest New Year's bowl game in the nation. Call ☎ 915/747-5234 or visit www.utepathletics.com for schedules or to purchase tickets.

Horseracing/Slots

There is live horse racing just outside of western El Paso (actually in New Mexico) at **Sunland Park Racetrack and Casino,** 1200 Futurity Dr. (☎ 505/874-5200; www.

sunland-park.com). The racing season runs from November to April (simulcast racing from around the country is featured year-round). There are also three restaurants, five lounges, and a casino with 700 slot machines.

Rodeo

The **PRCA Southwestern International Livestock Show and Rodeo** is held every September at the Cohen Stadium, 9700 Gateway Blvd. N. Call ☎ **915/755-2000** (www.elprodeo.com) for schedules and ticket information.

End of the Road

It's pretty likely that by now you've seen your odometer click past the 3,000-mile mark. Congratulations! It's no easy feat to weather the long haul of a cross-country road trip, surviving repeat appearances of state troopers, overbearing 18-wheelers, sudden afternoon thunderstorms, and emergency bathroom stops. If you played your cards right, you should be winding down in El Paso with a nice, post-trip margarita and maybe a *plato* of delicious local Mexican food, where you can breathe easy and reflect on the past many hundred miles.

Don't be surprised if on your last night of the trip, before heading home with your overstuffed luggage and weary eyes, images from your favorite parts of trip flash in your head—and you don't even remember which thing happened in which city. (You'll sort it all out once you're home.) But whether it's the fried chicken in Branson, that great band in Nashville, or the sexy cowboy boots you bought in Amarillo, the best part of the trip might just be having the whole thing with you wherever you go from now on.

BEFORE MUSIC GOES ANYWHERE ELSE, IT GRADUATES FROM mtvU.

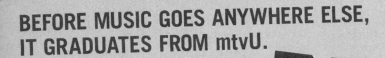

NEW ARTISTS, VIDEOS AND CONCERT TOURS - IF IT'S MUSIC, WE'VE GOT IT. BUT THAT'S NOT ALL: STUDENT FILMS, KILLER INTERNSHIPS, JOB OPPORTUNITIES, CONTESTS THAT JUMPSTART CAREERS, CAMPUS EVENTS AND MUCH MORE! mtvU ENHANCES YOUR ENTIRE COLLEGE EXPERIENCE.

TUNE IN ALL SEMESTER LONG.

NOW YOU CAN WATCH mtvU 24/7 AT mtvU.COM